ABOUT NICOLÁS KANELLOS

Nicolás Kanellos is the Brown Foundation Professor of Hispanic Studies and director of Recovering the U.S. Hispanic Heritage of the United States, the premier center for research on Latino documentary history in the United States. He is founding publisher of both the noted Hispanic literary journal *The Americas Review* and the nation's oldest and most esteemed Hispanic publishing house, Arte Público Press. Dr. Kanellos has received numerous awards and recognition for his work, including the Anderson Imbert Lifetime Achievement Award by the North American Academy of the Spanish Language. He has authored or contributed to numerous books on Hispanic history, culture, and literature, including *Hispanic Literature of the United States: A Comprehensive Reference*, the *Hispanic-American Almanac*, and the *Handbook of Hispanic Cultures in the United States*. His books have won numerous awards, including the American Library Association's Best Reference Work and selection by *Choice* to the top fifty outstanding academic books. He resides in Houston, Texas.

CONTRIBUTORS

Roberto Alvarez
Department of Anthropology, Arizona State University

Ramiro Burr
San Antonio Express-News and *Billboard*

Gilbert Paul Carrasco
School of Law, Villanova University

José Fernández
Department of Foreign Languages, University of Central Florida

Gary Keller
Bilingual Review Press, Arizona State University

Thomas M. Leonard
Department of History, Philosophy, and Religious Studies, University of North Florida

Manuel Peña
Foreign Languages, California State University, Fresno

Jacinto Quirarte
College of Fine and Applied Arts, University of Texas, San Antonio

Arturo Rosales
Department of History, Arizona State University

Guadalupe San Miguel
History Department, University of Houston

Federico Subervi
Department of Radio-Television-Film, University of Texas, Austin

Dennis Valdez
Chicano Studies Program, University of Minnesota

Jude Valdez
College of Business, University of Texas, San Antonio

ALSO FROM VISIBLE INK PRESS

African American Almanac: 400 Years of Triumph, Courage and Excellence
by Lean'tin Bracks, Ph.D.
ISBN 978-1-57859-323-1

The American Women's Almanac: 500 Years of Making History
by Deborah G. Felder
ISBN 978-1-57859-636-2

Black Firsts: 500 Years of Trailblazing Achievements and Ground-Breaking Events
by Jessie Carney Smith, Ph.D.
ISBN 978-1-57859-688-1

Black Heroes
by Jessie Carney Smith, Ph.D.
ISBN 978-1-57859-136-7

Freedom Facts and Firsts: 400 Years of the African American Civil Rights Experience
by Jessie Carney Smith and Linda T. Wynn
ISBN 978-1-57859-192-3

The Handy African American History Answer Book
by Jessie Carney Smith, Ph.D.
ISBN 978-1-57859-452-8

The Handy American History Answer Book
by David L. Hudson Jr.
ISBN 978-1-57859-471-9

The Handy Christianity Answer Book
by Stephen A. Werner, Ph.D.
ISBN 978-1-57859-686-7

The Handy Islam Answer Book
by John Renard, Ph.D.
ISBN 978-1-57859-510-5

Native American Almanac: More Than 50,000 Years of the Cultures and Histories of Indigenous Peoples
by Yvonne Wakim Dennis, Arlene Hirschfelder, and Shannon Rothenberger Flynn
ISBN 978-1-57859-507-5

iv

Native American Landmarks and Festivals: A Traveler's Guide to Indigenous United States and Canada
by Yvonne Wakim Dennis and Arlene Hirschfelder
ISBN 978-1-57859-641-6

Originals! Black Women Breaking Barriers
by Jessie Carney Smith, Ph.D.
ISBN 978-1-57859-759-8

Trailblazing Women: Amazing Americans Who Made History
by Deborah G. Felder
ISBN 978-1-57859-729-1

Please visit us at VisibleInkPress.com

LATINO ALMANAC

FROM EARLY EXPLORERS TO CORPORATE LEADERS

ALSO FROM VISIBLE INK PRESS

Latino Almanac: From Early Explorers to Corporate Leaders

Visible Ink Press®
43311 Joy Rd., #414
Canton, MI 48187-2075

Visible Ink Press is a registered trademark of Visible Ink Press LLC.

Most Visible Ink Press books are available at special quantity discounts when purchased in bulk by corporations, organizations, or groups. Customized printings, special imprints, messages, and excerpts can be produced to meet your needs. For more information, contact Special Markets Director, Visible Ink Press, www.visibleink.com, or 734-667-3211.

Managing Editor: Christa Gainor
Art Director: Alessandro Cinelli, Cinelli Design
Cover Design: John Gouin, Graphikitchen, LLC
Typesetting: Marco Divita
Proofreader: Larry Baker
Indexer: Shoshana Hurwitz

Paperback ISBN: 978-1-57859-611-9
Hardcover ISBN: 978-1-57859-778-9
eBook ISBN: 978-1-57859-753-6

Cataloging-in-Publication Data is on file at the Library of Congress.

10 9 8 7 6 5 4 3 2 1

LATINO
ALMANAC

FROM EARLY EXPLORERS TO CORPORATE LEADERS

Nicolás Kanellos, Ph.D.

For the love of my life, Cristelia Pérez, and my dear loved son, Miguel José.

Para el amor de mi vida, Cristelia Pérez, y mi adorado hijo, Miguel José.

CONTENTS

INTRODUCTION

The twenty-first century has seen the fruition of the seeds that were planted some four centuries ago, when the Western Hemisphere was colonized predominantly by Spain, and as a consequence, the peoples of Europe and Africa were brought together with the natives of the hemisphere. The United States, originating from Dutch and British colonies and expanding to include territories and peoples originally governed by Spain, in many ways developed in conflict with the Spanish Empire, its colonies, and later the independent states in the Caribbean, in North America, and on the Central American isthmus. From the earliest colonial times, the people whom today we identify as Latinos or Hispanics—and who inhabited the hemisphere before the landing of the British at Plymouth or Jamestown—have always lived within the United States and have participated in all cultural developments, industries, education, and even wars of the American republic. Hispanics or Latinos shed their blood in domestic wars, including the Revolutionary War and the Civil War, and in wars on foreign soil right up to the twenty-first-century conflicts in the Middle East and elsewhere. Latinos have just as much birthright as any other ethnic constituents of the nation, and as overwhelmingly *mestizo* (mixed) peoples, Latinos share DNA and history with the Native Americans and thus once again can claim precedence over the Euro-Americans. Because of their mixed ancestry and their presence among the oldest and newest of immigrants, Latinos share a rich culture marked by diversity. In all its multiplicity, this culture continues to profoundly influence the collective American experience.

Latinos now constitute the largest minority group in the United States, and based on their fertility rate and the young median age of their population, Latinos may grow to form as much as 40 percent of the population in the latter half of this century. It is important to know who they are, where they came from, what they contribute to the nation, and how they are influencing the development of the nation's culture and identity. With this in mind, I embarked on *Latino Almanac: From Early Explorers to Corporate Leaders* as a means to provide accurate and insightful information on Latinos so that we as Americans can shed the prejudices and misinformation that have developed since the days of competition between the English and Spanish Empires, since the days of U.S. expansion southward and westward and into the Caribbean at the expense of the Hispanic peoples and their governments, and since the days when—despite treaties and laws—Hispanic lands and rights were expropriated. Out of conflict and competition, many stereotypes and falsehoods were fostered, both consciously and subconsciously, as racial and xenophobic rationales for exploiting and despoiling Latinos.

In the face of the racism and xenophobia, however, and despite the attendant lack of access to greater educational, economic, and political opportunities, Latinos have nevertheless contributed greatly both to the nation and to their own development and prosperity in many fields. *Latino Almanac* highlights many of these achievements and contributions, as well as some of the barriers that have existed to their achievement. Although this volume could easily double in size, Visible Ink Press and I have elected to offer fifteen chapters on subjects that will be of interest to the general reader and to students in various levels of schooling: Overview; History; Business; Labor; Politics and Law; Religion; The Military; Science, Technology, and Medicine; Media; Art; Literature; Theater; Film; Music; and Sports.

Each of the fifteen chapters in the *Latino Almanac* tells part of the story and reveals the impact of Cubans, Central Americans, Dominicans, Mexican Americans, and other Latinos. Biographical profiles highlight Latinos who have excelled in their fields of endeavor. Information throughout the book on individuals can be found through the index, and a bibliography points the reader to further research. Nearly three hundred illustrations—including photographs, drawings, and tables—reinforce the discussion in each chapter.

The majority of Latinos are working-class citizens. Even many of those Latinos in the professional class share working-class backgrounds. Most are *mestizos*—the product of mixed races or cultures—for the Spanish, American Indian, and African heritages have blended in every aspect of life to produce today's Latino peoples. The Spanish culture, which introduced and reinforced a common language and religion for these peoples for centuries, still serves as a unifying factor for Latinos, regardless of whether an individual speaks Spanish in daily life. While the Spanish spoken by Cubans, Dominicans, Mexican Americans, Puerto Ricans, and U.S. Central Americans may have minor lexical and pronunciation differences—similar to the differences between U.S. and British English—they have little difficulty in conversing with each other, and they all read and write the exact same texts without difficulty. In addition, they share the experience in the United States of being bilingual. These central factors—social class, ethnicity, linguistic-cultural background, and minority status—unify the people. Similar factors unify the information presented in the *Latino Almanac*, which also strives to respect the tremendous diversity in racial, ethnic, geographic, and historical backgrounds among Latinos today.

A word about nomenclature is necessary at this juncture. Aside from the unfriendly names Latinos have been subjected to, over time as a group they have been referred to in English as Spanish Americans, Hispanic Americans, Latins, and Hispanics. In Spanish, first of all they identify themselves either by their ethnicity or place of origin: *cubanos, dominicanos, españoles, guatemaltecos, mexicanos, puertorriqueños, salvadoreños, venezolanos*, and so on. Beginning in the mid-nineteenth century when people from various Latin American countries found themselves living in the same U.S. cities and needed to come together as an identifiable group—and it should be noted that these countries were just then forming their own national cultures and political states—they called themselves either *hispanoamericanos* (from the Spanish-speaking Americas) or *latinoamericanos* (from the French-, Spanish-, and Portuguese-speaking Americas). They were very specific in their nomenclature to mark the difference between the former inhabitants of the Spanish colonies and those of the French and Portuguese ones. Obviously, those polysyllabic terms were cumbersome, and so they shortened them to *hispanos* and *latinos* (both used as nouns and adjectives). These made their way into English as Hispanic(s) and Latin(s). Today, these terms have lost much of their original specificity and have almost become synonymous, although the Spanish-speaking communities overwhelmingly still prefer *hispano*. But in common everyday usage *in English*, "Latino" is popular today, while "Hispanic" in the late twentieth century was more current. In order to make the *Latino Almanac* more accessible, therefore, Visible Ink Press and I have opted to use the slightly more popular "Latino," precisely because our book is published in English for a broad audience.

Latino Almanac: From Early Explorers to Corporate Leaders began as a paperback abridgement of a massive library reference, *The Hispanic Almanac*, when the term "Hispanic" was more current in the late twentieth century. It was the product of a national team of outstanding scholars who invested their time, energy, and genius to create the first comprehensive treatment of Latinos. In their labors for that volume, as well as in their day-to-day work, these scholars were actively engaged in the difficult task of working with original documentary sources, oral interviews, and fieldwork to create a written record of Latino life where none before existed. The original contributors and those who updated this new edition thirty years later are dedicated to filling an informational void that has existed for too long relating to the history and culture of Latinos. I am gratified that this fine work now finds a wider readership through the *Latino Almanac*.

Nicolás Kanellos

OVERVIEW

Since the second half of the twentieth century, Latinos in the United States have received a great deal of attention and have become part of the national consciousness. There are several reasons for this, the foremost being the rapid increase in the size of the Latino population. As can be seen from the statistics presented in this chapter, Latinos are increasing at a much higher rate than the total population and have already become the nation's largest minority group. This is not only because Latinos have a slightly higher birth rate than other Americans but because from 1980 to the present, Latin Americans from throughout the Western Hemisphere have migrated to the United States in far greater numbers than any other group. The reasons for this mass migration are varied. The historical trend of the United States encouraging migration from south of the border and the Caribbean when labor is needed for an expanding economy holds true today for Mexicans, Central Americans, Cubans, and Dominicans, as well as for Puerto Ricans, who are already U.S. citizens. However, in the 1980s the Central American republics became the place in this hemisphere where the Cold War became very hot, with the United States directly involved in opposing Cuban-Russian influence in liberation movements in El Salvador, Honduras, Guatemala, and Nicaragua. Then, too, military dictatorships in South America were often supported by U.S. government administrations. The political and material involvement of the United States in these conflicts and right-wing regimes had the effect of pointing political exiles toward the U.S. Thus, in addition to the thousands of political refugees from Central America who streamed across the southern U.S. border, from the 1980s onward a great number of political exiles from Argentina, Chile, Colombia, and Venezuela have arrived as well.

The size of the immigrant population and its effects on society have been intensely debated. What is undeniable, however, is that today we are witnessing the Latinization of the United States. In every sphere, from entertainment to the sciences, Latinos are making their mark, changing the monolithic, monocultural image of the United States, swerving the axis of history and identity away from European origins to that of the Americas, which in themselves combine and mix the heritages of Amerindians, Africans, Asians, and Europeans.

Accompanying this Latinization is the growing realization that the United States is, of course, multicultural, but most definitely trending toward an English-Spanish bilingualism in many spheres: the arts, education, business, communications, sports, and more. The bilingual, bicultural movement has also focused attention on Latino demands that society's institutions, especially those devoted to education, develop programs in Spanish as well as in English to meet their needs and reflect their culture.

A fourth reason for the expanded impact of Latinos is the economic and political power that Latinos have gained as their numbers have grown. The sheer size of the Latino population makes it an important economic group in areas where Latinos are concentrated, which is in all of the major cities and media markets. Latinos are also an important voting bloc and now elect members of their own to political positions in states such as Arizona, California, Colorado, Florida, Illinois, Nevada, New Jersey, New Mexico, New York, and Texas. In the 2019 Democratic primary for president, for the first time a Latino, Julián Castro, was a serious contender. In other states, Latinos play an important role in electing non-Latinos to office. For decades now, all presidential cabinets included Latinos as the secretaries of various departments. With this growing political power, not only nationally but in states, cities, and counties throughout the country, Latinos now occupy important leadership positions.

These issues, among others, are pushing many Latino concerns to the forefront, and for many observers of American society they portend a national minority group whose economic, political, and social influence can only continue to increase.

LATINO IDENTITY IN THE UNITED STATES TODAY

For many Euro-Americans, these trends have caused great concern. As the United States becomes a nation in which Anglo-Americans become the mi-

Latinos constitute an important voting bloc. Here potential voters gather for a Latinos for Obama Picnic in September 2008.

nority, much of the traditional thinking about American identity and citizen rights has been challenged. Some people resent the use of Spanish in businesses and the media; others fear the effects of unlimited immigration at the southern U.S. border. The competition from low-wage labor, according to some, depresses the pay and benefits for all workers. The fact is that many U.S. industries actively recruit immigrant workers, despite laws or the protests of politicians, and the work in those industries, such as agriculture, represents the type of arduous labor in poor working conditions that few other "Americans" would do. That Latino immigrants have been charged with benefiting from welfare has been disproven time and again; Latinos, including immigrants, contribute far more to the national and state economies than they ever derive from them, often missing out on social security benefits, insurance, and other resources the government offers to people in lower economic conditions.

Today an uneasy ethnic solidarity exists among Latinos. At the political level there is much rhetoric that attempts to bring them all under one rubric, and, indeed, the terms "Hispanic," "Latino," and "Latinx" have been fostered as agents of this process. While Cubans are conservative on issues dealing with Cuba and Communism, they share the same ideology with Central Americans, Dominicans, Mexican Americans, and Puerto Ricans when it comes to cultural maintenance and resistance to what many consider debasing American values. Another bond is language, an issue that has been forced into the political arena by the "English only" movement. All Latinos resent the onus placed on them because they speak Spanish, a language that is despised in many quarters of the Anglo-American community.

Language

Spanish-speaking communities in the United States are, in approximate descending order of size, of the following origins: Mexican, Central American, Puerto Rican, and Cuban. Of the Central Americans, Salvadorans are the most numerous. The Dominican population of New York City is rapidly growing; Dominican Spanish is quite similar to Puerto Rican Spanish, although members of each group are aware of differences. Large numbers of Colombians and Venezuelans are found in Houston, Miami, New York City, and elsewhere, but they come from many dialectic zones and do not exercise a strong centralizing influence on any variety of U.S. Spanish. Finally, several small but close-knit Spanish-speaking groups' use of Spanish does not fall under the four large categories previously mentioned. These include Sephardic (Judeo) Spanish-speakers in New York, Miami, and other urban areas, the Isleños of southeastern Louisiana, descendants of Canary Island settlers who arrived at the end of the eighteenth century, and the pre-Castro Cuban Spanish communities of Key West and Tampa, which have been overshadowed by more recent Cuban immigration.

Cubans, Puerto Ricans, and Dominicans can instantly identify their own forms of Spanish, but outsiders note more similarities than differences among the varieties of Spanish that originate in the Caribbean. Pronunciation is the single most important unifying factor, since Caribbeans are known for "swallowing" the final consonants, which are clearly heard, for example, in the Spanish of Mexico and parts of Central America. This slurring over final sounds also contributes to the impression that Caribbean Spanish is spoken faster than other varieties.

Even during the colonial period, striking differences in the Spanish spoken in different regions of Central America could be observed, in fashions that do not always correspond to what might be supposed by looking at a map. For instance, Costa Rica, between Nicaragua and Panama, shares more similarities with Guatemala, to the far north, than with neighboring Nicaragua. Honduran and Salvadoran Spanish blend together smoothly, but the contrast with Guatemalan Spanish is striking, and Nicaraguan Spanish is also rather different. Costa Rican Spanish bears no resemblance to neighboring Panamanian Spanish to the south, which is not surprising in view of the fact that Panama was formerly a province of Colombia, administered from Bogotá and largely populated from Colombia's coastal provinces, where even today speech is very similar to that of Panama. Guatemalan Spanish, by contrast, is similar to the Spanish of Mexico's Yucatán region, largely due to the common Mayan heritage.

The pronunciation of Nicaraguan Spanish is in many ways similar to Cuban and Puerto Rican Spanish. To the casual listener, Salvadoran Spanish is closer to Mexican Spanish than to any of the Caribbean varieties, an impression that is confirmed by history. Salvadoran and Mexican Spanish share a large quantity of vocabulary items derived from Native American languages, principally Nahuatl and, to a much lesser extent, Mayan.

Mexican varieties of Spanish share more similarities with Central American speech, particularly Salvadoran, than with any Caribbean dialects. The same Native American language families had a strong influence on Mexican Spanish, and the patterns of colonial administration resulted in similar profiles in central Mexico and the highland capitals of Central America. "Mexican" Spanish existed in what is now U.S. terri-

tory several centuries before the nations of Mexico or the United States came into being. More Mexican Spanish was incorporated through U.S. territorial expansion (the Texas revolution and the Mexican-American War), and still more Mexican varieties are the result of twentieth-century immigration. Each stage of Mexican Spanish presence in the United States has its own peculiarities, although the similarities outweigh the differences.

The majority of Latinos born or raised in the United States speak English, whether as a home language or a strong second language; the majority are bilingual to some degree. Arrivals from Spanish-speaking countries also learn English, to a greater or lesser extent depending on such factors as age upon arrival, previous study of English, urgency of using English in the workplace or in the home environment, children

Fresco y Más grocery store in Miami, Florida, features signs in English and Spanish. Most U.S. Latinos are bilingual to some degree.

in school who bring English into the home, and economic conditions that provide opportunities for acquiring English. As happens with speakers of other languages, Spanish-speakers who learn English during adolescence or later frequently retain an "accent," regardless of the level of fluency eventually attained. Even in bilingual communities where most residents learned English in childhood, a slight "Latino" or "Hispanic" flavor is often found in English.

Traditionally, Latino English has been seen in a negative light, as a way of speaking that needs to be corrected. More recently, linguists have studied Latino English as it is actually used, without preconceived notions, and have discovered that it has a role in maintaining community solidarity. The shift from Spanish to English affects all Latin American groups in the United States, and maintaining an ethnically marked form of English is sometimes a semiconscious way of resisting total assimilation to the American "melting pot." Research has demonstrated that some speakers deliberately switch varieties of English depending on whether they are inside the ethnic neighborhood or in an Anglo-American setting. Community activists and grassroots political campaigners often find it more effective to use ethnic varieties of English, which arouse a more favorable response from their audience. Among educators and community leaders, debate is ongoing as to the desirability of Latino English. Some feel that it is an impediment to economic and social advancement, while others insist that it is the attitudes of society that must be changed first. This controversy shows no signs of being resolved in the near future.

Except for recent arrivals or in a few isolated rural areas, the majority of Latinos in the United States speak English. A gradual but definite shift from Spanish to English occurs in most Latino communities, the same course followed by every other immigrant language brought to the United States, and the speed with which this language shift takes place is increasing.

It is frequently asked whether a uniquely "U.S." variety of Spanish exists. It seems, after considering the full panorama of Spanish-language usage in the United States, that the answer in general is no. Spanish in the United States continues to be divided mainly according to the country of ancestral origin: Mexican, Puerto Rican, Cuban, and so forth. Even in cities where more than one large Latino group is found, a single language variety usually prevails. Despite dictionaries that claim to describe such dialects, it is almost impossible to justify the existence of "American" varieties of Spanish: "Mexican American," "Puerto Rican American," "Cuban American," and so forth. What is found in the United States is greater use of English, and shifting of some Spanish words to match equivalent English terms. This does not make for separate dialects of Spanish, especially since the use of English elements is not consistent from speaker to speaker. In fact, the claim of a special U.S. Spanish is often a by-product of negative attitudes toward Spanish-speakers in the United States, as held by Spanish-speakers from other nations as well as by many Americans.

The nonexistence of a unique U.S. Spanish dialect is not a negative result. Spanish use in the United States is expanding rather than shrinking, and this expansion involves styles and ranges of language in addition to the number of speakers. U.S. Spanish is, more than ever, closely tied both to the international Spanish-speaking community and to American society and culture. What is uniquely U.S. Spanish is the complex pattern of bilingual language usage, which finds its highest form of expression in bilingual literature. By being able to communicate bilingually, U.S. Spanish-speakers command an extraordinarily rich language repertoire, which is at once part of Latin American and U.S. society and also uniquely Latino.

Religion

Latinos are an eminently religious people. Throughout the centuries, regardless of the accessibility of priests or places of worship or the availability of religious instruction, they have maintained their faith through the nurturing of their families and villages. Often misunderstood and chastised as ignorant, retrograde, or pagan, they have clung to the symbols of a deep spirituality received from their elders. Religious expression is apparent in the exchanges of everyday life—in the readiness with which Latinos add the expressions *gracias a Dios* (thanks be to God) or *Si Dios quiere* (God willing) and the ever-present invocations to God, the Virgin, and the saints. The manner of religious expression for U.S. Latinos is fundamentally Christian (77 percent). However, while Catholicism is the dominant religion of Spanish-speaking peoples throughout the world, Latinos in the United States present more diverse religious choices. Recent surveys show that now only 48 percent are Catholic, while 25 percent are Protestant of varied denominations. For the first time in history, 20 percent of Latinos report no religious affiliation. The rest are divided among the other world religions, including Judaism, Jehovah's Witnesses, Latter-day Saints, and others.

An instrument of evangelization, most widely utilized in the Spanish territories in the Americas, including what became the United States, was the mission, a temporary institution established and run by priests who resided among or in proximity to native populations. The missionary usually came right on

the heels of the conquistador and built his rudimentary chapel and living quarters at a reasonable distance from the military garrison, once the area was somewhat pacified. Instead of force, it was the missionary's works of mercy and his teachings that often brought about the evangelization of the native people. The vulnerability of the unarmed, nonthreatening padre was often his greatest strength. Missionaries could succeed where the conquistadors failed. Such was the case in the Sonora region of northern Mexico (southern Arizona today) and in the peninsula of Baja California, where the hostility of the natives prevented soldiers from making inroads. After several failed attempts, the Mexican viceroy entrusted the Jesuits with this conquest, which they performed successfully with no other weapon than the cross.

The assertion that missions and missionaries served the purposes of the empire cannot be denied. The missions contributed to the pacification of Amer-

While Catholicism is the dominant religion of Spanish-speaking peoples throughout the world, only 48 percent of U.S. Latinos are Catholic, and 25 percent are Protestant. The rest are divided among the other world religions, including Judaism, Jehovah's Witnesses, and Latter-day Saints.

ican Indians, and in so doing facilitated the process of colonization. They fostered the development of townships in their immediate vicinity. Furthermore, by Christianizing and Latinoizing the Amerindians, the missionaries transformed entire populations into loyal subjects of the Spanish kings and obedient followers of the Roman Church.

The missions were secularized during the first part of the nineteenth century, either for political reasons or because their original aims had been achieved. By this time and because in most cases their residents had fused with the people of the surrounding townships and farms, missions became the nuclei for modern-day parishes. It is not uncommon for the descendants of the first Amerindian neophytes baptized within mission walls to still flock to the same old church buildings generation after generation.

One of the services offered by the church, which served to both Christianize and Latinoize the native and mestizo populations, was formal education. In townships and missions, the clergy was expected to establish schools, both for boys and girls, to teach the children to read and write and learn the catechism. The curriculum sometimes included Amerindian languages. They also taught the skills—such as cattle and sheep ranching, European techniques of farming and irrigation, carpentry and other crafts—that would produce wealth for the mission, the church, and the Crown.

Evolving Pan-Latinism

Variety entertainment programs, soap operas, and talk shows that air nationally on Spanish-language television networks and radio stations are many times crafted to bring a balanced appeal to the variegated Spanish-speaking peoples taking their turn at the American opportunity structure. A plethora of slick-cover magazines have appeared since about the 1980s aimed at all the Latino groups. Some use English, others Spanish, or they contain bilingual renditions. Added to that is the online world of internet sites, blogs, and social media dedicated to myriad Latino topics, including numerous opportunities for Latinos to publish their literary and nonfiction writing, upload their videos and music, and chat. These expanded opportunities for self-

and community expression help to consolidate Latinos of the United States into a national community. In other words, they find they have more in common than what separates them. This is pan-Latinism in formation, and it is a totally U.S. phenomenon.

In large cities such as Los Angeles, Chicago, Houston, Miami, and New York, Latinos of all kinds are thrown together, and many times common ties result in an affinity and some mingling, including intermarriage. In Chicago, Mexicans and Puerto Ricans, who have lived together since the 1940s, have merged into political coalitions, and interethnic marriages have produced thousands of Mexican–Puerto Rican offspring. The melding of Salvadorans, Nicaraguans, Puerto Ricans, Mexicans, and Spaniards in San Francisco has also been transpiring at least since the mid-nineteenth century, and there, during the heady 1960s movements, a strong Latino consciousness emerged in such barrios as the Mission District. In Houston (as in other areas), entrepreneurs have tapped the Latino market, creating a chain of enormous supermarkets called Fiesta that cater to the tastes of every imaginable Latino group.

Another possible scenario is that differences will make for a separate evolution in the respective communities. As each Latino group evolves in the United States, with separate identities, they may become ensconced and comfortable in their own elaborated ethnicity. Indeed, this is true of the older and larger Latino groupings, who see themselves as Mexican Americans, Cuban Americans, and mainland Puerto Ricans. Hispanos in northern New Mexico, who are for all intents and purposes Mexican Americans, at times even remain insular from this group. So what can be expected from them when it comes to identifying with a larger national denomination?

Furthermore, interethnic prejudices still persist at the community level among some Latinos. For example, at times Latin American and Spanish immigrants living in the United States distance themselves from Mexican Americans or Puerto Ricans so that they will not be mistaken for them by non-Latinos who hold prejudices against those groups. They may buy into Anglo-American prejudices and unwarranted stereotypes against certain groups in an unconscious effort to ingratiate themselves with the mainstream population. This tendency, however, is more pronounced among the middle- and upper-class immigrants rather than among the working classes that make up the vast majority of Latinos in the United States. This is true even if back home they might never have dreamed of having these misgivings toward fellow Latin Americans.

As implied, another common source of inter-Latino antipathy is based on class origin. If the majority of one group is working class, as is the case with Mexicans, Puerto Ricans, and Central Americans, middle-class immigrants who come from South America often find it difficult to relate to what they consider a lower-class culture. They also demonstrate this orientation, of course, toward the working class back in their homelands. That phenomenon is also borne out among some upper-class Mexicans in the United States who look with disdain at compatriots who come from the *clases populares*.

There is even opposition to amalgamation among some Latino intellectuals who see the whole trend toward Latinization as a tool of consumerism. Obviously, it would be easier to aim at a large market rather than at disparate groups. There is also a residue of resentment within some in the Latino community toward Cuban exiles because of that group's persistent support of a conservative domestic political agenda and foreign policy toward Latin America. But the ultimate fear is that a bland, malleable ethnic group will emerge from pan-Hispanism.

The process is going to find its own level. Despite the destructive prejudices that exist between Latino groups or the well-intended admonitions of intellectuals, common roots exist for Latinos regardless of national or class origin. These will eventually make crucial links that no one can foresee. Rather than resist, Latinos would be better off trying to shape this irresistible force into a positive ideal of kinship and humanity so that they can take their rightful place in the American mosaic, and even become a remarkably potent political power. It is the society as a whole and decision-makers at every level that need to avail themselves of the particular benefits Latinos bring to the United States, such as a bilingualism and biculturalism that can be essential in communications, business, and diplomacy, for example, in relations with Latin America and the world.

LATINO DIVERSITY

According to the 2010 U.S. Census, Latinos numbered approximately 50.5 million people and composed approximately 16 percent of the total U.S. population of 308 million. As such, Latinos make up the largest ethnic minority group in the United States. If the number of undocumented Latino immigrants could be accurately counted, the growth rate and size of the Latino population would be much greater. At the current rate of growth (which exceeds that of non-Latinos), the Latino population by 2050 may represent half of the total population of the United States. More than half of the population growth between 2000 and 2010 is attributable to Latinos. Yet the Latino population is not a homogeneous group. It shares a common culture, but beyond this, the groups that make up the Latino population differ significantly in many important ways. The four major groups are Mexican Americans, Puerto Ricans, Cubans, and Salvadorans. Three quarters (31.8 million) of Latinos in 2010 claimed Mexican origin, while Puerto Ricans accounted for 4.6 million, Cubans 1.8 million, and Salvadorans 1.8 million. Other Latino peoples, from the Dominican Republic and Central and South America, accounted for 12.3 million. There are major historical, cultural, and demographic differences between these groups.

To understand the problems facing many Latinos, how the problems arose, and why they still exist today, we must examine the Latino American experience in history. Unique milestones have shaped the collective experience of Latinos and have influenced American attitudes and decisions throughout the past. Unlike any other ethnic group in the United States, Latinos are the only people to become citizens by conquest, with the exception of certain Native Americans.

> Latinos make up the largest ethnic minority group in the United States.

The histories of Mexicans, Puerto Ricans, Cubans, and Salvadorans are radically different. The Spaniards conquered the Amerindians of Mexico and, by mating with them, produced the mestizo or Mexican people. Mexicans, therefore, have a strong Amerindian as well as Spanish heritage.

The islands of Cuba and Puerto Rico and the countries of Central America were also conquered by the Spaniards. Both islands were originally populated with the Arawak and Carib Indians, while Central America was populated by Maya and other groups. The first areas of contact were the Caribbean islands, where the Spaniards forced the native populations into slavery to work in mines and fields. The Spaniards began importing enslaved people from Africa to Cuba, Santo Domingo, and Puerto Rico, then later to various countries of Central America. In the Caribbean islands, enslaved Africans eventually outnumbered and began to marry into the Amerindian population. Thus, Cubans, Dominicans, and Puerto Ricans not only have an Amerindian and Spanish heritage but a strong African ancestry as well—this is also true for the residents of many coastal areas of Central and South America, while the mountainous regions of Bolivia, Colombia, Ecuador, Peru, and Venezuela are densely populated by Indigenous groups.

From the landing of Christopher Columbus in the Western Hemisphere in 1492 until the early nineteenth century, the entire Spanish-speaking world was controlled by Spain. The Spanish settled in North America long before the American Revolution, with the earliest settlement established at Saint Augustine, Florida, in 1563. Spanish settlers then began immigrating to the Southwest and founded El Paso, Texas, in 1598 and Santa Fe, New Mexico, in 1609. By 1760 there were an estimated twenty thousand settlers in New Mexico and twenty-five hundred in Texas. In 1769 the mission at San Diego, California, was established, and the colonization of California began.

Painted tiles commemorate the founding of the Mission San Diego de Alcalá, California, by Junípero Serra in 1769.

Mexican Americans

In 1810 in Mexico, Father Miguel Hidalgo y Costilla led the revolt against Spain, and Mexico gained its independence in 1821. Soon after Mexico became independent, Anglo-American settlers began to move into the Mexican territories of the present-day U.S. Southwest, especially Texas. In 1836 Anglo settlers and some *Tejanos* (Mexicans residing in Texas) declared the Republic of Texas independent of Mexico. In 1846 the United States invaded Mexico under the banner of Manifest Destiny. The Treaty of Guadalupe Hidalgo ended the Mexican War that same year. Under the treaty, half the land area of Mexico, including Texas, California, most of Arizona and New Mexico, and parts of Colorado, Utah, and Nevada, was ceded to the United States. The treaty gave Mexican nationals one year to choose U.S. or Mexican citizenship. Seventy-five thousand Latino people chose to remain in the United States and become citizens by conquest. James Gadsden was later sent to Mexico to complete the U.S. acquisition of the Southwest and negotiated the purchase of an additional 45,532 square miles, which became parts of Arizona and New Mexico. As more Anglos settled in the newly acquired lands, the new Latino citizens gradually became a minority population in the Southwest. Many lost or were cheated out of their lands and became a resident working class, when once they had been farmers and ranchers. The 1848 gold rush lured a flood of Anglo settlers to California, which became a state in 1850. Settlement in Arizona and New Mexico occurred at a slower pace, and they both became states in 1912.

The Treaty of Guadalupe Hidalgo guaranteed the property rights of the Latino landowners by reaffirming land grants that had been made by Spain and Mexico prior to 1846. However, the treaty did not explicitly protect the language or cultural rights of these new U.S. citizens. Over the next fifty years, most southwestern states enacted language laws inhibiting Latino participation in voting, judicial processes, and education. More devastating, the Reclamation Act of 1902 dispossessed many of these same Latino Americans of their land, thus protecting a process that had been unfolding informally since the end of the war. Only in New Mexico were the civil rights of the descendants of the original Spanish-speaking settlers protected to some extent.

Such conditions of discrimination discouraged immigration to the United States for most of the late nineteenth century, even though the United States had no immigration statutes relating to the admission of foreign nationals until 1875. In fact, entering the country without a visa was not a punishable offense until 1929. However, in the 1890s there was a demand for low-wage laborers to construct American railroads, and Mexican immigration was encouraged, especially after 1882, when Congress passed the Chinese Exclusion Act of 1882, which virtually ended immigration from China to the United States.

Twentieth-Century Population Movements

By 1910 conditions in Mexico deteriorated under the considerable political repression of the dictatorship of President Porfirio Díaz, who ruled Mexico for most of a thirty-five-year span, from 1876 to 1911. Dispossession of property, widespread poverty, and runaway inflation forced many Mexicans to join forces in revolt. After the Mexican Revolution began in 1910, hundreds of thousands of people fled north from Mexico and settled in the Southwest at a time when the United States needed manpower for the expanding economy at the same time that many of its young men were fighting a war in Europe. Between 1910 and 1930 about 10 percent of the entire population of Mexico immigrated to the United States, including 685,000 legal immigrants. They were welcomed during this period, and special rules were developed in 1917, during World War I, to permit "temporary" Mexican farm workers, railroad laborers, and miners to enter the United States to work. By the late 1920s as much as 80 percent of the farm workers in Southern California were of Mexican descent.

The Great Depression of the 1930s brought rapid change to Mexican immigration. From 1929 to 1934, more than four hundred thousand persons were "repatriated" to Mexico without any formal deportation proceedings. Thousands of U.S. citizens were illegally deported because they were of Mexican descent.

The first Braceros arrive in Los Angeles by train in 1942, photographed by Dorothea Lange.

During World War II, the United States again needed workers, and immigration was encouraged. In 1942 an arrangement was made with the Mexican government to supply temporary workers, known as *braceros*, for American agriculture. Formalized by legislation in 1951, the Bracero Program brought an annual average of 350,000 Mexican workers to the United States until its end in 1964.

Mexican Americans again faced economic difficulties and discrimination because of competition for jobs during the late 1950s. This led to Operation Wetback, in which 3.8 million people of Mexican descent were deported between 1954 and 1958. Only a small fraction of that amount were allowed deportation hearings prior to being deported. Thousands more legitimate U.S. citizens of Mexican descent were also arrested and detained.

In 1965 the United States enacted a law placing a cap on immigration from the Western Hemisphere for the first time, which became effective in 1968. Immediate family members of U.S. citizens were not subject to the cap and could legally immigrate. Legal immigration from Mexico averaged about 60,000 persons per year from 1971 to 1980. A substantial number of undocumented persons entered the United States from Mexico during those years, and that number has increased dramatically since. Estimates of the number of undocumented immigrants in the United States often range from three to five million people. In the early 1980s, programs to apprehend undocumented immigrants were again implemented, and once more there were reports of violations of civil rights of U.S. citizens and lawful permanent residents of Mexican descent.

Deportations of Mexicans and other foreign nationals peaked under President Barack Obama, reaching three million during his eight years in office; it hit its peak in 2012 with 432,281 removals. President Donald Trump, however, after calling Mexicans rapists and criminals during his presidential campaign, once in office employed other strategies to curtail or limit immigration from south of the border, such as building walls along the border, ending America's admission of political refugees, ending certain types of visas, launching mass detainments at the border and in Mexico itself with cooperation from Mexican president Andrés Manuel López Obrador, and deploying the terrorist tactic of separating children from their families when they attempted to cross the border. Under Trump, Immigration and Customs Enforcement (ICE) apprehended some 851,508 people in just 2019, the highest number in twelve years.

During the Trump administration, the majority of people apprehended or stopped from entering the United States were family groups seeking asylum from the so-called Northern Triangle countries of El Salvador, Guatemala, and Honduras, not Mexico. Throughout his presidency, Trump raised the specter of caravans of hundreds of thousands of criminals heading for the United States and inflamed anti-Latino sentiments in the United States while encouraging American nativism and racism such that the level of hate crimes against Latinos skyrocketed. Federal Bureau of Investigation (FBI) data show that there was a 24 percent increase in hate crime incidents against Latinos in 2017—that is, at the beginning of the Trump administration—compared to 2016.

Caribbean Experiences

Mexican Americans are only a part of the entire Latino population. Many other Spanish-speaking peoples became U.S. citizens under different circumstances. For example, Florida (originally covering an area from the Atlantic coast almost to the border of Texas) and the Louisiana Territory, Puerto Rico, and Cuba were possessions of Spain until the nineteenth century.

Florida was claimed for Spain after its discovery by Juan Ponce de León in 1513. Saint Augustine in Florida was the earliest settlement established in North America, founded in 1563. It remained a possession of Spain until 1819. After Andrew Jackson led a U.S. military force into Florida, capturing two Spanish forts, Spain sold Florida to the United States for $5 million under the Onís Treaty.

Puerto Ricans, like the first Mexican Americans, became U.S. citizens through conquest. In 1898, following the brief Spanish-American War, Puerto Rico became a possession of the United States through the Treaty of Paris. Many Puerto Ricans assumed that annexation meant that all Puerto Ricans were U.S. citizens, thus entitling them to all the rights and privileges of citizenship. However, that was not the case. Many Puerto Ricans were denied the right to vote, and many were prevented from moving to the U.S. mainland. To this day, Puerto Rico remains a colony of the United States, without the benefits enjoyed by states of the Union, such as representation in Congress or the right to vote for the president.

Nearly twenty years later, the Jones Act of 1917 finally resolved this problem, making all Puerto Ricans U.S. citizens. Since then, Puerto Ricans have had the

This street painting in the Little Havana neighborhood in Miami, Florida, portrays famous Cuban and Puerto Rican musicians and cultural icons. About one million Cuban Americans live in the United States, the majority in Florida.

unrestricted right to travel between the island and the mainland. By the early 1920s, there were significant Puerto Rican communities in U.S. cities, most notably New York.

Cuba also became a U.S. possession in 1898 through the Treaty of Paris, which ended 387 years of Spanish rule. However, Cuba was a possession only for a brief time and became independent in 1902; but the United States insisted on an amendment to Cuba's constitution that effectively made the nation's government dependent on the United States. In the late nineteenth century, a small number of Cubans migrated to the United States, mainly to Florida and New York. By 1930 only about twenty thousand Cubans lived in the United States, and by 1950 only about thirty-five thousand.

The vast majority of Cuban Americans immigrated to the United States after 1959, when Fidel Castro took power in Cuba. Between 1959 and 1962, twenty-five thousand Cubans were "paroled" to the United States using a special immigration rule. The immigration laws did not provide for special refugee status without proof of physical persecution until 1965. In 1966 a program was initiated to airlift Cubans to the United States, but it was halted by Castro in 1973. Over 250,000 Cubans were airlifted to the United States during that period.

Throughout the remainder of the 1970s, many Cubans immigrated to the United States by routes through other Latin American countries. In 1980 a "boatlift" of Cubans from Mariel Harbor was permitted by Castro, and about 130,000 refugees arrived in the United States. Controversy surrounded this boatlift because a small percentage of the refugees were from Cuban prisons and institutions for the mentally ill.

Today 1.8 million Cuban Americans live in the United States, with the majority residing in Florida, although there are increasing numbers in California, Illinois, Massachusetts, New York, and New Jersey. While many early Cuban refugees expected to return to Cuba, the continuation of the Communist regime under Castro led many to conclude that they would not be able to go back. They have become naturalized citizens at a much higher rate than any other Latin American immigrant group.

IMMIGRATION PATTERNS

At different times in U.S. history, waves of immigrants have arrived from other Latin American countries, such as Nicaragua, Colombia, the Dominican Republic, Guatemala, Honduras, and El Salvador, as well as many others. More than half of these immigrants have come to the United States since 1970. Often they have entered the United States through Mexico; others, such as Dominicans, have entered through Puerto Rico. Some have entered legally under established immigration quotas; others have come as students or tourists and stayed in the United States after their temporary legal status expired. Many immigrants from the Caribbean and Central and South America have come through circuitous and difficult routes to escape civil war, poverty, and repression.

More recent Central American immigration can be traced largely to economic and political conditions in the source countries. During the 1960s, the establishment of the Central American Common Market led to economic growth and improved conditions in the region. In 1969, however, the border war between Honduras and El Salvador led to the collapse of the common market and the rapid decline of economic conditions in Central America.

Since 1979, political upheaval and civil wars in Nicaragua, El Salvador, and Guatemala have contributed to large migrations of refugees to the United States. The United States has been the primary destination because of the centuries of economic ties of those countries with the United States and because of U.S. involvement in the civil wars that produced the refugees. The number of Central and South Americans in the United States in 1950 was about fifty-seven thousand. Estimates in 1985 ranged from 1.4 million to 1.7 million, but these figures are low because of difficulties in accurately counting large numbers of undocumented emigrants from Central and South America and because of recent surges in outmigration. Central American immigration, however, has overtaken South American immigration, with as many as 3.5 million residing in the United States today—half that figure arriving before the year 2000. Between

1980 and 2017, the Central American immigrant population in the United States multiplied tenfold. Of the Central Americans, Salvadorans comprise the largest group and represent approximately the same number of residents in the United States as Cuban-origin people, thus tying Cubans for their portion of the Latino population at 1.8 million. Because of several devastating earthquakes and hurricanes in Central America, the United States designated Hondurans, Nicaraguans, and Salvadorans as eligible for Temporary Protected Status (TPS), which granted immigrants from those countries work authorization and provisional relief from deportation, which was still in effect in the early 2020s for those residing in the United States during those natural disasters.

Immigration patterns to the United States are different for Mexican Americans, Cubans, Puerto Ricans, and Salvadorans. The primary factor that continues to pull Mexican immigrants to the United States today is the demand for cheap labor. Constant migration from Mexico means that within the Mexican American community there is always a large number of Mexican immigrants.

As a result of the two immigration movements, the number of Cubans in the United States increased rapidly. In 1959 there were only thirty thousand Cubans in the United States, and in 2010 there were 1.8 million. Cubans have become a major economic, political, and cultural force in Florida, especially in Miami, which has the largest concentration of Cubans in the United States.

The pattern of migration from Puerto Rico to the United States is different from that of either Mexico or Cuba. Puerto Rico became a possession of the United States in 1898, and Puerto Ricans were granted U.S. citizenship in 1917. Thus, Puerto Ricans who migrate to the United States are not considered immigrants in the same sense as Mexicans and Cubans. In 2018 there were approximately 5.8 million Puerto Ricans living in the United States and a little over three million living on the island of Puerto Rico. By 2021, the island population had decreased to 2.8 million due to devastation from hurricanes and the economic collapse they left in their path. The primary destination of these recent migrants has been Florida, especially the Orlando area. Florida and New York have the largest Puerto Rican populations, each with 20 percent of the total stateside population. The Puerto Rican population in the states, rather than the island, grew 65 percent between 2000 and 2020.

The Development of U.S. Immigration Law

Americans have always taken pride in their immigrant heritage but ironically have feared new immigration at the same time. Since the United States declared its independence from Great Britain in 1776, protectionism has had its place in the population's subconscious. In later years it was often used as justification for restricting immigration.

In 1965 a major revision of immigration law resulted when Congress amended the Immigration and Nationality Act of 1952, which maintained a restrictive limit on immigration from particular countries. The national origin quota system was abolished. A complex seven-category preference system for granting visas was created in its place. The 1965 amendments gave preference to family reunification. Spouses, parents, and children of U.S. citizens were given preference in awarding visas and were not bound by a quota. The amendments maintained limits on immigration through the seven-category preference system, providing for immigration from each country of no more than twenty thousand immigrants per year. Race or national origin was no longer a consideration. More important, the 1965 amendments imposed a quota ceiling on immigration from countries in the Western Hemisphere as well. This marked the first time in U.S. history that such a numerical restriction was placed on immigration from these countries.

Amendments to the law passed in 1978 removed the ceilings for each hemisphere and established a worldwide competition for 290,000 visas granted each year. Every country in the world was subject to the seven-category preference system and to the 20,000-per-year limit. The 1965 and 1978 amendments led to a dramatic shift in immigration. No longer were Europeans, formerly favored by law, the largest group of immigrants. They now represented only 13 percent of the total. Asians benefited most, representing 21 percent of the total number of immigrants entering the United States per year. Im-

Amendments in 1965 to the Immigration and Nationality Act gave preference to family reunification but imposed a quota ceiling on immigration from countries in the Western Hemisphere—the first time in U.S. history that such a numerical restriction was placed on immigration from these countries.

migration from Latin American countries and the Caribbean remained at about 40 percent of the total.

The Immigration Act of 1990 continued to permit immigration of immediate relatives of U.S. citizens without numerical limitation but set a "pierceable" overall cap on worldwide immigration of 700,000 for fiscal years 1992 through 1994, and of 675,000 for fiscal year 1995. The seven-category preference system has been replaced by one based on family relationships, employment, and diversity. The per-country limit is 25,000.

The 1970s and early 1980s brought a different kind of immigration problem to the attention of the American public. The rise in politically motivated violence in Central America spurred a massive increase in undocumented immigration to the United States. The flight of "boat people" from Indochina following the Vietnam War created an enormous refugee settlement challenge for the United States. In a six-month period alone in 1980, some 125,000 Cubans arrived in Florida in an uncontrolled sea migration to the United States. At about the same time, more than 10,000 Haitians fled the repressive regime of dictator Jean Claude Duvalier and sailed to the United States in overcrowded fishing boats.

These immigrants—or more appropriately, refugees—created a problem for U.S. immigration authorities. They were not eligible to enter the United States as immigrants under established quotas without visas, nor could many of them meet the requirements to enter the United States under an exemption to the quota system as refugees. Previous U.S. law provided for the admission of persons fleeing persecution or having a well-founded fear of persecution from Middle Eastern or Communist-dominated countries. This was advantageous to the Cubans fleeing Fidel Castro and the Vietnamese fleeing the Communist regime in Vietnam but was no help to the thousands of Central

Americans who were fleeing political violence. The Refugee Act of 1980 removed the ideological definition of "refugee" as one who flees from a Communist regime, thus allowing thousands to enter the United States as refugees who otherwise would have been excluded.

Geographic Concentration

The majority of Latinos are concentrated in four border states and make up a large segment of the population of these states: New Mexico (49.1 percent), Texas (39.6 percent), California (39.3 percent), and Arizona (31.6 percent). Fully one-half of the U.S. Latino population resides in these border states. In fact, two of these states account for 45 percent of the total U.S. Latino population: California (15.6 million) and Texas (11.5 million). The other states with large Latino populations are Florida (5.5 million), New York (3.7 million), Illinois (2.2 million), and New Jersey (1.8 million). In twenty-one states, Hispanics account for more than 50 percent of statewide population increases from 2010 to 2019. In six of these states—New York, New Jersey, Pennsylvania, New Mexico, Rhode Island, and Mississippi—Latino population growth exceeded that of the overall population during this time. Puerto Ricans are the largest group in New York and New Jersey, and Cubans are the largest in Florida. Puerto Ricans and Mexican Americans are the largest groups in Illinois. Salvadorans have concentrated in California, the Washington, D.C., area, and Texas. Approximately one-third of Latinos are immigrants, and nearly 80 percent of them are U.S. citizens.

The ten states with the largest increase in the number of Latinos are California, Texas, New York, Florida, Illinois, New Jersey, Arizona, New Mexico, Colorado, and Massachusetts, in that order. The following thirteen states have a population exceeding 10 percent (largest Latino population to smallest): Connecticut (16.5 percent), Rhode Island (15.9 percent), Utah (14.2 percent), Oregon (13.3 percent), Washington (12.9 percent), Idaho (12.7 percent), Massachusetts (12.3 percent), Kansas (12.1 percent), Nebraska (11.2 percent), Oklahoma (10.9 percent), Hawaii (10.7 percent), Maryland (10.4 percent), and Wyoming (10.1 percent). The three most populous

Latino states had the biggest increases of this population from 2010 to 2019: Texas (2.0 million increase), California (1.5 million), and Florida (1.4 million). The size of California's Latino population is larger than the total population of all but nine states. The southern region of the United States experienced the fastest growth in Latino population, increasing by 26 percent from 2010 to 2019, followed by the Northeast (18 percent), Midwest (18 percent), and West (14 percent). Nearly half (48 percent) of Latino population growth since 2010 has taken place in the South.

Birth Rates

Latinos once had the second-highest birthrates of Americans, just lower than that of Hawaiian/Pacific Islanders. But the birthrate for Latinas fell by 31 percent from 2007 to 2017, attributable mostly to generational differences between Latino immigrants and their American-born daughters and granddaughters. Thus, they are following the general trends of American fertility rates; two-thirds of Latinos are born in the United States and have higher levels of education and employment security.

All Latinas in the United States have roughly the same fertility rate: seven to eight babies per thousand, slightly higher than the average for all Americans. At one time Mexican Americans had the highest birthrate among Latinos at 14.8 babies per thousand mothers, but with an increase in educational attainment, their rates, along with those of other highly fertile populations, has descended to approach the U.S. norm.

When reviewing the statistics of this diverse culture, it helps to understand the new phase of the labor history of Latinos that began around the turn of the twentieth century, when employers in the Southwest, and soon afterward in the Midwest, began to recruit workers from the Mexican border. Their efforts set in motion a movement that shaped migration patterns from Mexico throughout the twentieth century. Using labor contractors and other recruiters, they brought in workers from Mexico to perform largely unskilled, low-paying tasks. This planned labor migration quickly stimulated another pattern of individual migration that took on an independent character and outpaced the rate of migration by labor recruitment. During the early twentieth century, a majority of Latino workers in the United States were Mexican immigrants and their children. In sheer numbers, the new arrivals soon overwhelmed the older Mexican-descent residents in most parts of the Southwest and Midwest, except New Mexico.

Occupation and Education

Historically, Mexico offered U.S. employers a reservoir of workers because of its high level of unemployment and very low incomes. The wage differential between Mexico and the United States throughout the century has always been very sharp. At present, an unskilled wage worker in the United States can earn approximately ten times as much as in Mexico, although the differences are largely offset by much higher prices for food, rent, and other living expenses in the United States.

> An unskilled wage worker in the United States can earn approximately ten times as much as in Mexico.

In the early twentieth century, Mexicans were recruited largely for agricultural work, railroad construction and maintenance, and heavy industry and mining enterprises. Smaller numbers found employment in domestic and other service occupations and in manufacturing. Mexican immigrant families often worked as a single unit in cotton, sugar beet, and fruit and vegetable planting, cultivation, and harvesting operations, especially in the Southwest. In other occupations, including mining, manufacturing, and most service occupations, adult workers were the rule, as child labor laws were harder to evade, restricting the employment of children.

As a result of the patterns of labor recruitment that evolved in the early twentieth century, cities and towns on and near the Mexican border, and eventually throughout the Southwest and in many Midwestern settings, developed large labor pools of Mexican workers who were available to perform unskilled, low-paying jobs throughout the year. Characteristically, the Mexican workers found employment largely in seasonal tasks and experienced high rates of unemployment and frequent changes in employers. Although many of them brought skills from Mexico,

few of the tasks they performed in the United States required high levels of training or English-language proficiency to perform.

Education and Skill Levels

A major feature of recent labor migration has been the inclusion of people from a much wider range of countries in Latin America and with a greater diversity of working and educational backgrounds. Whereas Mexicans and Puerto Ricans continue to migrate for the most part as unskilled, semiskilled, or skilled workers, immigrants from other parts of the Caribbean and Central and South America have a wide range of backgrounds, including business and professional. The largest immigrant groups originating in Spanish-speaking South America are the Colombians (790,000), the Peruvians (467,000) and the Ecuadorians (443,000), all of diverse class backgrounds and levels of education. In the twenty-first century, Venezuela experienced hyperinflation and great social upheaval due to the leadership of President Hugo Chávez and his successor Nicolás Maduro, who imposed a Castro-Cuban economic model on the country. This has led to a great outmigration to the countries of South America and the United States. Since 2015, Venezuelan immigration to the United States has risen by 54 percent, going from 256,000 to 394,000. Venezuelan immigrants tend to have a higher level of education than other South American immigrants and are mostly of middle-class backgrounds.

In recent times due to economic instability and drug cartel violence in northern Mexico, an entrepreneurial class of Mexicans has migrated to the border states, with the San Antonio–Houston region benefitting the most. Entrepreneurial and skilled immigrants were characteristic of the first generation of Cuban refugees beginning in the 1960s, when the Fidel Castro–led revolution brought about great social and political change in their country. Later waves of Cuban immigrants were not as prosperous. The Mariel boatlift included many individuals from very poor, unskilled backgrounds, and with a lack of adequate job training. Many of them had great difficulty becoming incorporated into the work regimen of the United States.

Cuban Americans are primarily a middle-class population with relatively high levels of education, occupational status, and income. Mexican Americans and Central Americans are primarily a working-class population holding blue-collar occupations and have low levels of education and income. Generally, Puerto Ricans rank in between Cubans and Mexican Americans/Central Americans, but are closer to the latter than Cubans in terms of their educational attainment, occupational status, and income.

The high level of education among Cubans reflects the middle-class status of the Cubans who migrated to the United States in the early 1960s.

Overall, less than 23 percent of Latinos have a two-year college degree or higher. Cubans enjoy the highest levels of educational attainment, with 40 percent having a college degree as compared to 16 percent among Latinos in general. Cuban Americans born in the United States have a higher college graduation rate, at 38 percent, than their island-born parents at 23 percent. Only 6.2 percent of immigrants from Mexico have a bachelor's degree or higher; however, some 25 percent of these immigrants have graduated high school. Moreover, the percentage of Mexican Americans graduating college is 17.4 percent; among this group, high school graduation rates have decreased even within the third generation. Some 30 percent of Puerto Ricans have a college degree; this includes both populations on the island and the continent. Only 8 percent of Salvadorans have obtained a college degree.

The high level of education among Cubans reflects the middle-class status of the Cubans who migrated to the United States in the early 1960s. Later generations of Cubans are continuing to achieve high levels of education as well.

The number of Latinos either working or looking for work as a percent of the civilian non-institutional population is 66.1 percent. That is higher than the rate for non-Hispanics, at 62.2 percent. The groups with the highest labor force participation rates among Latinos were Salvadorans (72.2 percent), other Central Americans (70.8 percent), and South Americans (70 percent). Mexican Americans, Puerto Ricans, and Cubans each have around 61 percent participation rate. Mexican immigrants make up less than 4 percent of the national labor force. However, Mexican Americans make up 61 percent of the national Latino labor force. What Mexican Americans, Puerto Ricans, Cubans, and Salvadorans have in common is being concentrated in the skilled and semiskilled occupations. The Latino male employment rate is at 87 percent, which is lower than the 92 percent rate for U.S.-born Whites and greater than the rate of 77 percent for U.S.-born African Americans. Mexican/Mexican American and Cuban men are employed at the same rate regardless of whether they were born in the United States, but Puerto Ricans have an overall lower rate at 80 percent (84 percent for U.S.-born and 77 percent for island-born). Approximately 50 percent of all Mexican American males and 43 percent of all Cuban and Puerto Rican males hold skilled and semi-skilled occupations. Where the groups differ is in managerial and professional and technical sales and administrative support occupations. Cubans hold more of these types of occupations than either Puerto Ricans or Mexican Americans.

Approximately 55 percent of all Cuban females over age sixteen are in the civilian labor force, compared with 42 percent of Puerto Rican females and 51 percent of Mexican American females. The female occupational distribution resembles that of the males in that Cuban females have a higher occupational status than Puerto Rican and Mexican American females. One significant difference is the higher proportion of Mexican American females in service occupations. Approximately 27 percent of the Mexican American females hold service occupations, compared with 16 percent of Puerto Rican and Cubans females. However, studies show that after education attainment, employment gaps narrow for all groups.

Latinos are self-employed at rates between African American and White rates. Cuban men and women are self-employed at relatively high rates: foreign-born Cuban males at 17 percent, which is higher than the rates for U.S.-born White males (14 percent). Puerto Ricans, on the other hand, have low self-employment rates similar to those of African Americans, whether they are island-born or U.S.-born: 6 percent for men and 4 percent for women. Mexican self-employment rates are in between those of Cubans and Puerto Ricans. But women born in Mexico have a relatively high rate at 8 percent, as do women from El Salvador and Guatemala (11 percent) and other Central Americans (8 percent). Much of this self-employed work by Spanish American immigrant women is in domestic service.

The distribution of Latinos in employment sectors depends more on whether they were foreign born or native born. In general, 18 percent of Latino immigrant men work in construction and 11 percent in agriculture. Latina immigrants are overrepresented in manufacturing at 19 percent. Foreign-born Latinos of both genders have very low representation among manager, professional, technical, and sales personnel. They are most likely to be employed in the service

and labor sectors. This is principally because of low educational attainment and diminished English-language skills. The employment distribution for U.S.-born Latinos, however, approaches that of Whites, with Latinos employed in the same industries at similar rates. But the actual rank in those industries is lower for Latinos. For instance, 24.3 percent of Latino males are employed as managers or professionals, while 35.8 percent of Whites have those careers. Latinos in service professions are at 13.4 percent, while Whites are at 7.9 percent in service jobs. There are fewer Latinas in managerial and professional positons (37.7 percent) than White women (44.9 percent); more Latinas in technical and sales positions (39.2 percent) than White women (35.6 percent); and more in service (14 percent) than White women (11 percent).

Central and South Americans and Other Latinos

In addition to Mexican Americans, Puerto Ricans, and Cubans, the Latino population consists of Dominican Americans, Central and South Americans, and people who are classified by the U.S. Census Bureau as having "other Latino origins." This latter category includes those whose origins are in Spain and those identifying themselves generally as Latino, Spanish, Spanish American, Hispanic, Latino, and so on. Central and South Americans make up 25 percent of the total Latino population. There are 3.5 million Central Americans and nearly 3 million South Americans living in the United States today.

Generally, Central and South Americans tend to have characteristics that resemble the Cubans rather than the Mexican American or Puerto Rican populations. The median age of Central and South Americans is 27.9 years. Both groups tend to be highly educated. Approximately 15.1 percent of Central and South Americans have four or more years of college.

Both groups also have a relatively high occupational status, with 12.7 percent of males and 14.5 percent of females of the Central and South American groups holding managerial and professional occupations. At the lower end of the occupational hierarchy, Central and South Americans and "other" Latinos tend to mirror the situation of Cubans, Mexican Americans, and Puerto Ricans in that there is a relatively large number of males concentrated in the operators, fabricators, and laborers category and a large number of females concentrated in the service occupations.

THE FAMILY

The family is considered the single most important institution in the social organization of Latinos. It is through the family and its activities that all people relate to significant others in their lives, and it is through the family that people communicate with the larger society. The family incorporates the idea of *la familia* (the extended family), which includes—in addition to the immediate nuclear household—relatives who are traced on both the female and male sides. These include parents, grandparents, brothers and sisters, cousins, and to a certain extent any blood relatives that can be identified through the hierarchy of family surnames. This broad-ranging concept has important consequences for actual social and cultural behavior. It places individuals as well as nuclear families into a recognizable network of social relations within which mutual support and reciprocity occur.

Important supportive institutions of *la familia* include the extended family, *parentesco* (the concept of familism), *compadrazgo* (godparenthood), *confianza* (trust), and family ideology. Among Latinos, family ideology sets the ideal and standards to which individuals aim; it is the guiding light to which all look and attempt to shape their behavior for themselves as well as for the perception others have of them. It holds all individuals together, and all individuals should put family before their own concerns. It is the means of social and cultural existence. Family ideology also defines the ideal roles and behaviors of family members. The ideal family is a patriarchy that revolves around a strong male figure who is ultimately responsible for the well-being of all individuals "under his roof." The concept of "machismo" is embedded in this ideal, in which men are viewed as virile, aggressive,

The family is considered the single most important institution in the social organization of Latinos.

and answerable only to themselves. In real life, however, this is rarely realized. Degrees of male authoritarianism vary both within and across groups, but for the most part women are strong contributors to decision making and are often the internal authority figures in the family. In both subtle and direct ways, women not only contribute to decision making but often have the authority in the family. This is contrary to the stereotype in which the woman is viewed as subservient and deferent to "her man" and that child rearing and household chores should be her main concern. In fact, one of the greatest of changes in the Latino family in the United States is in the woman's role. A very high percentage of households are headed by women, especially among Puerto Ricans in New York. However, family ideology continues to be verbally expressed as a value and cultural norm, often in contradiction to actual family behavior.

Children should be subservient and show respect to all elders, *respeto* (respect) being a concept held by all individuals. In a variety of studies in education, Latino children, especially those of new migrants, do behave in a "culturally prescribed manner" that is congruent with family ideology. However, as in all other aspects of family ideology among Latinos, children's roles have experienced drastic changes. Education in the American system and exposure to people outside the immediate family and network of relatives has affected children in many ways. Children often become the social brokers between their parents and the outside world. They are the best speakers of English and know society's cultural nuances more thoroughly than parents.

Latino groups in the United States do not generally live in an extended family household. The reality is that Latinos tend to favor the nuclear family and a separate household. The extended family living in single households is generally a transitory stage in family and household development. It is seen primarily during the migrant stages of first arrival when newcomers need support and help in adjusting and finding their way in a new environment. The reality of the extended Latino family is that it transcends geographical barriers and has functioning units in both the country of origin and in the United States. It is in this sense that the institution of the family has taken on a hybrid form through the strategic expression of migrants adapting to a new environment.

Latinos have used the extended family in conjunction with other kinship institutions that form part of the extended *familia* and family ideology. As in the family in general, the Catholic religion has had a very strong influence in *familia* institutions. Religious rites of baptism and marriage take on special meanings that have evolved into sociocultural expressions important among Latinos in the United States. *Compadrazgo* (godparenthood), marriage, and *parentesco* (kinship sentiment) are primary institutions that need to be understood in relation to the family. These are multidimensional elements that together help maintain *la familia*. *Compadrazgo* is formed usually through the baptism of a child, with parents choosing *padrinos* (godparents) from close friends or relatives. *Compadrazgo* is the extension of kinship to nonrelatives and the strengthening of responsibilities between kin. *Padrinos* sponsor the child in baptism and confirmation ceremonies. They are also chosen to be groomsmen and bridesmaids at weddings. *Compadres* (co-parents) ideally have special responsibilities toward the godchild and in the past have been expected to take the parental role if parents were to pass away, except in the case of marriage sponsorship. This special parental relationship is maintained throughout life. In addition, although not recognized in much of the literature, the *ahijado/a* (godchild) has a special responsibility toward the *padrino/a*. This is manifested in varying degrees, but can be seen when the *padrino* is elderly; *ahijados* may pay special attention almost as if the *padrino* were a grandparent.

Confianza (trust) is of particular importance to both the institutions of *compadrazgo* and *parentesco* among Latinos in the United States, and is the basis of the relationships between individuals in many spheres of social activity. It is evident in business relations among entrepreneurs who work on the basis of trust, and among friendships in which trust is fundamental. But *confianza* goes beyond relationships between individuals and forms the underlying base of reciprocity of all types. *Confianza* is the primary factor that builds relationships and forms the basis for trust in the institutions of *parentesco* and *compadrazgo*. In a sense, the combined expression and practice of *com-

padrazgo and *parentesco* produce the continued trust that is expressed as *confianza*. To have *confianza* with an individual is not just to regard that person with trust, but to regard the relationship with special sentiment, respect, and intimacy. *Confianza* developed in friendship can, for example, lead to a relationship of *compadrazgo* and to expressing *parentesco* to individuals who are not kin, as for example an individual who is from a home region and is a friend or compadre of kin.

The institution of marriage varies tremendously among Latinos in the United States and, like the family in general, has been adapted to a number of different socioeconomic conditions. The value of a religious wedding is not, nor has it ever been, the sole means for recognizing unions between men and women. Among Dominicans, for example, marital unions consist of *matrimonio por la iglesia* (church wedding), *matrimonio por ley* (civil marriage), and *unión libre* (free union). Church weddings carry higher prestige and are more prevalent among persons of higher socioeconomic status, but free unions allow for early cohabitation in the migrant settlement. Marriage, however, has been an institution that strengthens extended family ties and incorporates individuals and their kin into network alliances under *parentesco*. Marriage, in addition to its important function of uniting conjugal pairs in critical household formation and procreation of children, is an institution used in the primary adaptive processes to the United States. Marriage among Latinos continues to be within their own group (endogamous)—that is, Mexicans marrying Mexicans, Puerto Ricans marrying Puerto Ricans, and so on. Some intermarriage happens between groups, but this is infrequent, and there is a growing rate of intermarriage with Anglo-Americans, especially among second-generation Latinos. This is especially true of Mexican Americans.

THE ISSUES OF LATINAS

Traditional Attitudes Regarding the Roles of Latinas

The traditional cultural stereotype of the Latino female is based on a dualistic perspective of the sexes and a strong belief in appropriate roles for each gender. Traditional attitudes regarding female roles are also informed by the assumption that "natural" gender roles exist, and any deviation is deemed inappropriate. Hence, females and males are strongly encouraged to accept the prescribed gender roles. These include submissive behavior for females and aggressive behavior for males. The wife is expected to accept the husband's role as absolute authority. The woman is characterized as self-sacrificing to the needs of others and confined to the home. She is to be nurturing to husband and children. A woman's primary function is to bear and raise her husband's children. Training for these roles begins early. In childhood, girls are expected to help with the housework and care for the other children. Boys are given more freedom than girls and expected to learn what roles each will assume as adults.

The most traditional role of the female is to be wife and mother. Her domain becomes the home—the private realm and not the public realm. The male is expected to take on the responsibilities for providing for the family and engaging in the public realm. He is the ultimate authority in the family. Among the roles of children, a daughter must always be responsive to the males in the family. A female is the responsibility first of her father and then her husband. Self-autonomy and independence are considered inappropriate for a female and are labeled selfish. The quality of selflessness is the highest, most treasured quality in a female. It is the female who is traditionally allowed to be emotional. The male is expected to remain a stoic individual and is commonly discouraged from expressing his emotions. Traditionally, it is the female who is expected to uphold and defend the moral code of the community. She is expected to follow the strictly defined code more vehemently than the male. This is also true for religion. Religious rituals and beliefs are the responsibility of the female. She is the spiritual and moral leader of the family.

Traditionally, Latino communities are patriarchal, and yet slowly women have gained power in the public realm, subverting traditional gender roles. For example, Puerto Rico is considered a male-centered society, yet San Juan has had female mayors and governors. During the Mexican Revolution of 1910, women played an important role and became national heroes. There have been female predidents of Spanish American countries. The first acknowledged Mexican poet was Sor Juana Inés de la Cruz, a woman. Traditional gender attitudes, which informed women of the importance of passive, nurturing behavior, did not stop women from seeking power in and outside the family. Historically, many women were leaders in the Cuban and Puerto Rican movements for independence from Spain. Latinas have also been leaders in labor movements in the United States since the early twentieth century.

> Traditionally, Latino communities are patriarchal, and yet slowly women have gained power in the public realm, subverting traditional gender roles.

The American women's movement and heightened consciousness about forms of oppression have politicized some Latinas, who have become active in women's organizations. Nevertheless, the contact between Latinas and feminists has been limited. The reasons for the limited participation include racism within those organizations and the sense by Latinas that an underlying assumption of feminism is an attempt to destroy the concept of family.

Latinas and Women's Liberation

The women's movement has been seen by the Latino community as destructive to the common good of the family. The movement also has carried assumptions about the importance of independence and self-autonomy, a direct challenge to traditional Latino attitudes concerning the importance of relationships to family and community. As critics of the women's movement, some Latinas, such as Marta Cotera and Gloria Anzaldúa, argue in their writing that the feminist movement has alienated Latinas because of its devaluation of traditional values. What has emerged from Latinas' experience with feminism is an acknowledgment by Latino feminists of pride in their traditional heritage but with a realistic attitude toward its limitations, as well as an acknowledgment of the limitations of feminism. For example, African American women first discussed feminism's ignorance of cultural differences, creating the space for development of Latino feminism. Currently, Latino feminists take into consideration all aspects of society that intersect to define women and their progress; this "intersectionality" encourages consideration of race, gender, social class, historical determinants, and other issues. Thus, Latino feminism is different from mainstream feminism because it tries to accommodate cultural traditions and spiritual issues as well as race, gender, class, and other intersecting determinants. Concerns that Latino feminism attempts to address include economic and educational needs and child care, as well as how those issues are affected in the context of Latino cultural traditions. While the women's movement has focused attention on issues concerning gender inequality, traditional gender roles were already in the process of being challenged and questioned by Latinas. To some extent, the women's movement provided the example and the language with which Latinas could challenge traditional attitudes toward women's roles. But it should be emphasized that Latinas have had their own feminist and suffrage movements since the mid-nineteenth century.

One of the realities that comes with change, such as immigration, is the accompanying high level of stress. Tension and discomfort within families increase with change. Marital strife seems to be a product of the renegotiation of gender roles. Conflicting attitudes from one society to another as to gender roles increases confusion and stress in the family, especially when children and grandchildren are raised by immigrants who have not completely embraced the attitudes of mainstream American life. The children's socialization in a more permissive and liberal society may lead to conflict with their parents and grandparents.

While economic necessity sent Latinas into the workforce originally, women now have more options as to their roles in society. They may opt for a traditional role, a nontraditional one, or a combination of the two, spending a certain period of their time in traditional roles and then moving on to the workforce.

One of the most important attributes of Latinas is their diversity. To consider them all alike is to take away from their identity and simplify their complex world. So when we discuss Latinas, we must also keep in mind what diversity means within that group. Latina diversity is manifested by several subgroupings, including Mexican Americans, Puerto Ricans, Cubans, Dominicans, and natives of the specific regions of Central and South America. Each subgroup can trace specific cultural traditions to their region of origin. For example, the Caribbean influence on Puerto Rican and Cuban women in the United States is different from the Mexican influence on Mexican American women.

Class status levels among Latinas are as varied as in the mainstream society: working class, middle class, upper class, white collar, blue collar. Depending on the individual, her values may represent her class more than her culture.

Education

Another important difference among Latinas is educational level. A large proportion have had no formal education. Then there are those who have had formal education but have not completed high school; this is a large segment of the population, reflecting the less than 50 percent high school graduation rate among Latinos. The attitudes and values expressed by these women are influenced by their education.

Fewer than half of Latinos graduate from high school. Also, most Latino parents of adolescents do not possess a college degree. Overall, less than 23 percent of Latinos have a two-year college degree or higher. Cubans enjoy the highest levels of educational attainment, with 40 percent having a college degree as compared to 16 percent among Latinos in general. There are very few educated role models for adolescent girls. The pattern these girls see consistently is that of a woman who has quit school. Among Latinas, who are becoming single heads of household in ever-increasing numbers, few even have high school degrees. In addition, of those who do graduate from high school, fewer than half enroll in college, and the majority of those who do attempt higher education enter two-year colleges. For Latina girls, low aspirations are the norm conveyed to them. The pattern that emerges is that of an undereducated, underskilled population

of women who are fast becoming single parents. However, as mentioned earlier, Latinas are recognizing the necessity for education to find employment opportunities and are beginning to return to school; in fact, more Latinas are enrolled in and graduating from college in the early 2020s than Latino men.

Employment

Employment has become one of the most important issues Latinas face. Now that many of the traditional roles for women have been challenged, they face the stresses of seeking and keeping employment. In 1981, among Latinas over age twenty, approximately 50 percent were employed. That number has consistently grown, such that the employment rates for Latinas born in the United States are 76 percent for Mexican and Puerto Rican women (close to the corresponding rate of 78 percent for African Americans) and 80 percent for Whites, and 83 percent for Cubans—the highest of all. For those women born in the home country, however, employment rates in the United States are at least 10 percentage points lower than for U.S. natives, with this immigrant–native gap reaching 20 percentage points for Mexicans. Latinas are more likely to be employed in manufacturing and service industries than in other areas. Latinas are also more likely to earn some 12 percent less than the national norm for women in their job categories, while men earn some 31 percent less than most of the population. In addition, Latinas are consistently underemployed and somewhat underpaid. Among all these statistics, it is noteworthy that Cuban American women earn 20 percent more than their White counterparts.

Single Heads of Household and Child Care

Latinas are becoming single heads of household in ever-increasing numbers. As women assume the roles of traditional heads of household, child care becomes a necessary issue. Faced with the limited availability of affordable child care, Latinas may find themselves unable to afford to work. They stay at home to care for their children and find themselves unable to meet monetary needs. Unable to find affordable child care, they turn to the state for assistance.

One response of many Latinos to the shortage of affordable child care is to turn to the extended family.

One response of many Latinos to the shortage of affordable child care is to turn to the extended family. Many Latino children are cared for by their grandmothers or aunts. The ability to turn to members of the family is one of the strengths of Latino culture. The closeness of Latino families allows a woman to turn to her mother or sister or some family member in times of need. For many Latinas, this closeness is a double-edged sword. Along with the closeness comes a sense of not having any privacy, as well as feeling suffocated by the abundance of nurturing. Common among Latinas is an inability to acknowledge individuality. These women only know themselves in relation to their parents, their children, their husband. Once they decide to assert their individuality, they find themselves faced with emotional stress.

For many Latinas, issues of survival for themselves and their children continue to be the most immediate concern. Undereducated and underemployed, these women face the harsh issue of day-to-day survival.

Health Issues

Health issues of Latinas have only recently begun to be explored by the medical establishment. Already documented, however, are several common ailments. For example, evidence indicates that Latinas (and Latino males), because of their traditional cultural diet, are at high risk for diabetes.

Another issue is the ability to pay for health services. Many Latinas are underinsured or have no health insurance. Many hold jobs like housekeeping and farm work that provide very limited or no health benefits. As with the rest of the population, the inability to receive affordable health care is at a crisis level.

Undocumented Immigrants

There exists a truly invisible Latina: the undocumented worker. Without immigration papers, usually with no formal education and no skills in English, the Latina who is not a citizen or authorized resident in the United States is silenced and invisible. Estimates vary as to the number of undocumented immigrants. They continue to be the most exploited members of the Latino community.

Many of these women work in the fields as migrant workers. Farmers are able to pay substandard wages and not fear government reprisal because these workers hold no legal rights in the United States and hence will not report them. These women also work in service industries as unskilled laborers and as housekeepers. Because of their undocumented status and limited English, an underground community exists in the midst of U.S. society. Recently, such unions as the Service Workers International Union have organized protections for such workers as the cleaning staffs of office buildings, among many other services workers with large Latina representation.

Religion

A cultural and personal concern for Latinas is religion. While most Latinas are Roman Catholic, many are beginning to question some of the traditional attitudes the church has about women. As Catholic dogma is very clear as to the status of female subservience to man and God, women are beginning to test the limits of dogma. Admittedly, few Latinas actively voice their opposition to the dictates of the Catholic Church; a more quiet revolution is actually occurring. For example, the Catholic Church does not condone artificial forms of birth control, yet more and more Latinas are seeking birth control. And more and more Latinas, especially of the second and third generations, are leaving the church for other, more liberal religions.

Traditionally, the woman's position in the Catholic Church has been to serve the needs of the community. Women have not been allowed to participate in the Mass except as members of the congregation. If a woman wanted a more active role in the church, she became a nun and lived in a world separate from all males and laypersons. The leadership and power within

While most Latinas are Roman Catholic, many are beginning to question some of the traditional attitudes the church has about women and are even leaving the church for other, more liberal religions.

the church was reserved only for priests. However, in the past fifty years the church has encouraged a more active role for women. Clearly, a change has occurred in the status of women within the traditional ceremony, allowing both male and female laypersons to participate in the Mass. In its own ranks, the church still continues the practice of limiting and designating certain duties to either the priest or the nun. The most exalted positions within the Catholic Church are all restricted to males: priest, bishop, cardinal, and pope. The leadership of the church continues to remain the domain of men.

> Latino children constitute the majority of the school enrollment in the nation's most populous states: California, Illinois, New York, Texas, and Florida.

Politics

In the political realm, Latinas continue to be underrepresented, if not ignored. No research has been done on the voting patterns of Latinas. What is now becoming more readily available are the voting patterns for Latino communities. Whether or not Latinas differ from Latino men in their political participation is unclear.

Politically, Latinas are making an impact. Today there are Latina governors, mayors, representatives, and senators, and Latinas are active at the city and county levels throughout the nation. Latinas have many diverse political concerns, as do all women. They are particularly concerned about health, welfare, and children's and family issues, but they do not hesitate to organize and vote on a wide range of subjects, from foreign affairs to the environment. The tradition of subservience, silence, and passivity, if it ever really existed as stereotypes suggested, are changing rapidly, and Latinas are making a greater impact on the general society.

LATINO CHILDREN AND YOUTH

In the twenty-first century, Latino children constitute the majority of the school enrollment in the nation's most populous states: California, Illinois, New York, Texas, and Florida. They are already approaching or have surpassed those figures in such urban centers as Chicago, Houston, Los Angeles, Miami, and New York City. With "White flight" to the suburbs and the rapid growth of private schools in the United States, more racial segregation in the nation's schools exists today than before the momentous *Brown v. Board of Education* decision in 1954. Latino and African American youths are not only racially isolated in schools; they are the segment of society most adversely directly affected by social policy and trends that have raised the levels of unemployment, drug culture, and crime in inner cities. With dropout rates over 50 percent in some urban school districts and the parents of school dropouts already making up the ranks of the working poor, many Latino youth are destined to an underclass life of unemployment, marginalization, and internment by the criminal justice system.

An underperforming economy at the close of the twentieth century, coupled with increased immigration from Latin America, created considerable anti-immigrant sentiment in the states traditionally most welcoming of entrants to the lower end of the labor pool: California, Florida, Illinois, New York, and Texas. Politicians and nativists have created a bandwagon of complaints and protests decrying the high costs of absorbing immigrants, supposedly with welfare, education, and the criminal justice system ranking highest. And high among proposals by politicians is the withholding of public education to children of undocumented immigrants. During the Trump administration, the party in power also threatened to abolish birthright citizenship, so that the children of immigrants could be deported. This followed upon years of onslaught against the use of the Spanish language by the "English only" movement.

The microcosm of Latino at-risk youth is a segment of the society with among the highest rates of school drop out, health problems, and teen pregnancy. Unless youths in general in the United States are attended to in a better and more humane manner, Latino youth in particular will continue to be endangered and also represent a danger to society as a whole.

THE FUTURE OF LATINOS

Clearly, Latinos represent one of the fastest-growing populations in the United States. They have always constituted an important, although unrecognized, resource for the country, providing from the early days of the republic the human and technological resources that would eventually make the Southwest, in particular, a richly endowed contributor to the national economy and the national identity. Whereas Latinos were political expatriates and welcomed immigrants in the early states of the republic, by the turn of the twentieth century they were Americans by purchase of what became the southern states and by conquest of the northern half of Mexico and of Puerto Rico and Cuba. During the twentieth century they have been economic and political refugees to the United States in direct proportion to the growth of this country's political and economic imperialism. The cumulative effect of this three-centuries-long relationship has resulted in Latinos becoming, in the twenty-first century, omnipresent in every sector of U.S. society. This diverse group is now the largest minority in the United States and is ascending to economic and political power.

But the group has to bear the brunt of developing solutions to its internal organization—particularly the limits placed upon the role of women in its families and in the workplace, and the racism and tension faced by Latinos in a society that is not always willing to see them as Americans. External issues require creative answers: prejudice against and segregation of Latinos in education, unemployment and underemployment, crime and drug use, poor health services, and levels of diabetes that are among the highest in the United States.

Economic, Political, and Cultural Integration

What is sure to attend the Latinoization of the United States in the twenty-first century is a new definition of political and economic borders and of linguistic and cultural borders. The approval of the North American Free Trade Agreement in the twentieth century and its successor, the United States–Mexico–Canada Agreement (USMCA), in the twenty-first century place the United States well on the road to an integration of the three largest economies of the hemisphere, leading to a unified workforce, a common currency, and tricultural, trilingual (English, Spanish, and French) commerce.

The growth of Spanish-language print and electronic media, not only in the United States but throughout the hemisphere, is reinforcing and preserving the language and cultural identity of Latinos and Spanish Americans from Tierra del Fuego to Alaska. Currently three Spanish-language television networks broadcast the same programs and sentiments by satellite the length of the hemisphere, far outstripping the reach of English-language television—and those three networks are headquartered in the United States. Where the satellites and cables go, so does print culture, as well as other forms of material and expressive culture. Latinos have a high degree of internet and cell phone usage, and their access to information and communications is unprecedented, creating greater opportunities for solidarity among all Hispanic-origin peoples. That means greater solidarity and further integration not only of Latinos in the United States but among the Spanish American republics, as well, who are also ready to integrate their economies with an eye toward total hemispheric economic integration in the future. From this hemispheric perspective, the role of Latinos and Latino culture in the United States becomes central to developing the potential for becoming the hub for negotiations in all spheres of life of the Hispanophone and Anglophone Americas. That is, Latinos can use their bilingual skills and bicultural understanding to become a broker between cultures and across borders. Because of these advantages, they are also predisposed to learning other languages and cultures and to becoming brokers across multiple types of borders.

> Latinos can use their bilingual skills and bicultural understanding to become a broker between cultures and across borders.

With the end of the Cold War and the attendant resolution of regional conflicts, particularly in Central America, and the return of governments to democratic rather than autocratic rule in the Southern Cone, some of the traditional barriers to isolationism and discord among the Spanish American republics may have met sufficient terminus to prepare the Southern Hemisphere for economic integration. But both Mexico and the countries of the Southern Hemisphere have to share the benefits of economic advancement more equitably in their societies—as does the United States—with particular attention to the long-marginalized and exploited Indigenous populations, just as the United States needs to attend to fairer income distribution and decreasing racism in the treatment of its minorities. The United States' interpretation of stability in Latin America can no longer be the support of dictators and oligarchies, nor can U.S. industry continue to encourage degradation of the environment and undermine the organization of labor by relocating to Latin America industries that inordinately exploit human and natural resources. These larger issues all determine the destiny of Latinos in the United States, which has always been conditioned by the dynamics of international trade and politics.

It is not surprising, then, that the future of Latinos depends on many factors that are regional, national, and international in scope. Hispanism is an international identity. It is bilingual, bicultural, multinational, multiracial. How Latinos interact on national and international levels will help to define the prosperity or bankruptcy of hemispheric life in the next century.

HISTORY

This chapter presents a historical overview of the major Latino groups that have made their home in the United States, focusing on peoples from Mexico, Puerto Rico, Cuba, and Central America. While each group is unique unto itself, several factors deeply rooted in the formation of their national and cultural identity bind them together. Foremost among these are their link to Spain and the geographical proximity the nations share within the Caribbean and the Gulf of Mexico.

SPANISH LEGACY

Mexicans, Cubans, Puerto Ricans, and Central Americans share many commonalities. The main language spoken by the groups is Spanish, most are Roman Catholic, and much of their folklore is similar.

The presence of Paleolithic humans (game hunters and cave dwellers) in the Iberian Peninsula is known because of archaeological evidence left by the culture, the most famous being cave drawings of the animals on which the dwellers depended for food. More advanced cultures are known as Iberian, but not much is known about these early agricultural and village people except that they migrated to the peninsula from Africa several thousand years before the birth of Christ.

A few centuries later, about 1000 BCE, a wave of Celtic warriors, hunters, and part-time keepers of livestock converged on the peninsula from somewhere in present-day Hungary near the Danube River. They mixed with the Iberians and established a unique Iberian-Celtic culture. These Gaelic-speaking nomads eventually settled in almost every part of Europe. The strongest cultural vestiges with which most Americans are familiar are those of Scotland, Wales, and Ireland. In Spain and France, cultural manifestations from the Celtic period are also evident, although not as salient as in the British Isles. There is, for example, in northwestern Spain a province known as Galicia where Gaelic characteristics have lingered to the present time. There, such Gaelic modes as the bagpipe and the kilt are used in ceremonies.

Gaelic culture in the rest of Spain, however, was overwhelmed by a series of invasions and colonization efforts, which shortly before the birth of Christ greatly transformed the linguistic, racial, and economic systems of the peninsula. The first interlopers having significant influence in the evolution of the peninsula were the Greeks and the Phoenicians, who arrived about the same time as the Celts. Both groups went to Iberia to mine tin and establish a series of trading outposts. They were not prodigious colonizers, and Iberian-Celtic culture remained strong, although over time the more advanced cultural expression of the Greeks and Phoenicians became diffused among the earlier settlers. The Iberian-Celts developed sculpture and other artistic motifs that significantly took on the characteristics of Greek classical realism, and they borrowed technological innovations, such as transportation vehicles and mining techniques.

Later in the second century BCE, Carthage challenged the expansion of the Roman Empire in Europe and Africa. Carthage was a civilization centered along a large portion of the North African coast and was greatly influenced by Greek achievements. The Carthaginians were not successful in the Iberian Peninsula, however. They were able to wrest authority over the region away from the Greeks, but in 133 BCE the Romans defeated the Carthaginian army at Numantia. This was just one of the many Roman victories that ensured the expansion of Rome into most of Europe, including the Iberian Peninsula.

The Roman colonization of Iberia was classic in every sense of the word. Unlike previous invaders, such as the Greeks, Phoenicians, and Carthaginians, they settled in, families and all, subordinated and enslaved the natives, and set up a plantation system based on slave labor. They remained in the peninsula until their empire began to crumble about 400 CE.

Castilian, the language we now call Spanish, became the dominant language everywhere in the Iberian Peninsula except Portugal. The kingdom of Castile managed to conquer and dominate every other region of Iberia except Portugal. It was the Romans who distinguished between the western and eastern parts of the peninsula, giving the name "Hispania" to the east and "Lusitania" to the west. The word "Spain" came from "Hispania," and although Portugal did not retain "Lusitania" as a place-name, any term associated with that country or its language is still prefixed by "Luso-." In the United States, the term "Hispanic" developed in the nineteenth century as a translation of *Hispanoamericano*, which refers to the Spanish-speaking people of the Western Hemisphere, including Spa-

nish speakers of Indigenous ancestry. The term "Latino" also has roots in the nineteenth century, as short for *Latinoamericano*, which back then and during most of the twentieth century referred to speakers of Spanish, French, and Portuguese in the Americas, including people of Indigenous ancestry. Today "Latino" in English has come to mean Spanish-speaking people of the Americas but not Portuguese or French speakers. Therefore, the language of Spain is still a strong identifier of Latinos today.

The political system introduced by the Romans had a profound effect on the evolution of government structures at all levels in Spain and, by extension, in its colonies in Spanish America. Perhaps the most enduring feature of this legacy is the careful attention given to the formation of city political culture. The Romans called this process *civitas*. Anyone who travels in almost any town in Latin America can see a faithful replication of the town square, or plaza, with its main Catholic church engulfed in a carefully drawn complex of government buildings dominated by the municipal or state center. The Romans also thought that it was the responsibility of government to build a bathhouse, an amphitheater, and a coliseum near the town center, regardless of the size of the town. This tradition, of course, was followed in Latin America, where one can find similar institutions even in small villages, if only in modest proportions. In the United States, such a civic impulse is certainly present, but not to the same degree as in Latin America and the American Southwest. Many U.S. towns and cities took their shape in response to purely economic exigencies, and then either some planning or virtually none at all followed.

The legal and judicial system in Latin America is quite different from the common law tradition familiar to people living in England and its former colonies. The Latin American judicial system, drawn from the Napoleonic Code, does not have juries. Rather, judges make the final decisions on all cases brought before the courts. However, today's legal system in the United States has benefitted from laws that were introduced by Latinos in Florida, Louisiana, and the Southwest, such as the ability of women to inherit property, the right of adopted children to be treated like biological children and inherit property, common-law marriage, and community property. Some of these

The large farms and ranches found in Latin America, typical of the landholding system in Spain (pictured here) and Portugal, came from the Roman plantation system known as latifundia.

laws were generated in medieval Spain and came to the United States through Mexico and the Southwest and have enriched the national legal system.

Apart from their language and governmental legacies, the Romans were influential in other areas as well. For example, the large farms and ranches found in Latin America, typical of the landholding system in Spain and Portugal, came from the Roman plantation system known as *latifundia*. Finally, Christianity, especially Catholicism, was one of Rome's most enduring legacies. In Iberia, the religion became Rome's greatest cultural and historical hallmark, to be spread even further one thousand years later when Spain embarked on its own powerful empire.

Other ethnic groups followed the Romans into Spain, leaving a continuing heritage that also is part of the Latino tradition throughout Latin America and in the United States. The most aggressive of these

were Germanic tribes that had been migrating from Asia Minor, slowly penetrating every region where Rome held sway. Some Germanic tribes had been within the empire long enough to serve in Roman legions as mercenaries, and many others were Romanized by them. When the Roman Empire fell, some of these Germanic tribes began to carve out their own fiefdoms along with other groups in the empire. But outside tribes, more barbaric and less inclined to Roman ways, poured into the former Roman realms, pillaging and carving out their own regional baronies. Vandals, Celts, and Visigoths moved into the Iberian Peninsula but were eventually Romanized. As Roman political influence declined, the Germanic clans, already having relinquished many aspects of their language, began to speak one of the variations of Latin evolving in the peninsula, and they embraced Christianity. The latter process was of such intensity that, as the Germanic tribes mixed with the inhabitants of

Spain, who by then were an admixture of all the groups that had previously lived in Iberia, they all came to call themselves Christians as a means of identifying themselves ethnically.

Iberia was now lapsing into the Dark Ages. This was the beginning of feudalism, an era in which hundreds of small baronies, carved out of the vastness of the Roman Empire, resorted to raiding each other for territorial aggrandizement. The economic system that had held the empire together evaporated, leaving in its place a factional economic and political system. Technologically, the Germanic tribes were underdeveloped, and they depended a great deal on raising livestock. From the empire of Rome they managed to salvage some rudimentary metallurgical and other techniques of production. Because a great part of their lives were spent raiding and pillaging, the tribes introduced to Iberia a warrior cult, which was perhaps the most important cultural ingredient of their society. Along with this came the rigid code of conduct that usually accompanied such societies. Adherence to Christianity, once they entered into former Roman realms, added a religious fervor to the military code. This impulse found its expression throughout Christian Europe in the Crusades against the Muslim peoples and in Iberia in a phenomenon known as the Reconquest.

Perhaps Iberia would have remained under the solid sway of feudalism, as did the rest of Europe, if it had not been for the invasion of Arabic-speaking Muslims from North Africa in the beginning of the eighth century. More commonly known as the Moors, these latest newcomers to the peninsula remained for eight hundred years and, next to the Romans, had the greatest influence on the culture of the Iberians. The invasion was spurred by the rise of an Islamic expansion impulse in North Africa that quickly engulfed the Persian Gulf all the way to India and north into southern Europe. This expansion was inspired by a religious fervor left after the life of Mohammed, the founder of Islam, who was born in Mecca in the seventh century CE.

The first Moors crossed the Strait of Gilbraltar in 711 CE, and they brought to the peninsula such an advanced culture that its merits could not help but influence the moribund feudal structure left in the wake of Rome's decline. The Muslims left few stones unturned in their quest for technological and philosophical knowledge, borrowing and improving on much of what was known to the world at the time. From the Far East they acquired advanced metallurgical skills, including the making of steel, and medicinal knowledge. In the civilizations of the West, Muslims stemmed the decline of Greek and Roman philosophical, agricultural, and architectural systems.

The Moors pushed the Christians all the way to the northern reaches of Iberia, but many Christians remained behind Moorish lines, where they were tolerated and allowed to maintain and evolve their Christian and Castilian cultures. Along with the Moors came thousands of Jews, who were also tolerated in Islamic domains, and many of whom served as merchants, teachers, and medical practitioners in such great Muslim cities as Sevilla, Granada, and Cordoba.

The surge that pushed the Christians north lasted until the eleventh century, when the Moorish caliphate of Córdoba began to disintegrate into smaller, less-effective kingdoms. The Christian Castilians then embarked on a protracted effort to regain the lands they had lost to the Moors in the previous three hundred years. This Reconquest was attempted piecemeal fashion, since Castilians could not mount unified efforts, because both their economic and political systems were feudal.

The Reconquest lasted until 1492, when King Boabdil was ousted from Granada, the last Moorish stronghold, by the forces of the Castilian Queen Isabella and her Aragonese husband, Ferdinand. The marriage of these two monarchs from neighboring Iberian kingdoms in 1469 unified the two largest kingdoms on the peninsula and eventually led to the entire unification of Spain. However, the whole peninsula was not to be consolidated in this fashion because the Portuguese, in the western portion of Iberia, had managed by themselves to defeat and eject the Arab caliphs at the beginning of the fifteenth century, before Castile did.

Before the Catholic Kings, as Ferdinand and Isabella came to be known, could effectively accomplish this unity, however, the power of the feudal lords acquired by the partition of former Moorish caliphates had to be curbed. Ferdinand and Isabella

Christopher Columbus Arrives in America, *painting by Gergio Deluci, 1893.*

accomplished this by several means. First they embarked on establishing political institutions that challenged the local rule of the nobility. Then they linked the long struggle of the Reconquest to their own process of consolidation, thus appropriating the nascent nationalism evoked by that struggle to unify the disparate baronies of the peninsula.

In 1492 the Catholic Kings expelled the Moors and the Jews from Spain. In 1493 they acquired from Pope Alexander VI, who himself had been born in Spain, the papal patronage. This was a concession of major proportions, because it gave the Spanish monarchs complete dominion over the operations of the Catholic Church in Spain. As one can imagine, this was a vehicle of great advantage for the consolidation efforts envisioned by the two monarchs.

The long initial struggle to fend off and finally push out the Moors engendered in the Germanic Castilians an even more resilient warrior culture that by 1492 was, no doubt, the most salient expression of their society. Values such as valor, honor, audacity, and tenacity were highly prized. But the Castilians inherited many other positive characteristics from the many groups that had invaded and inhabited Iberia. Little was lost from such exposure, so when Columbus sailed and encountered the New World in 1492, Spain was truly a compendium of its multiethnic past. This complexity of cultures became the Latino stamp imprinted on its colonies in the New World.

Columbus's fateful voyage certainly changed the course of history. It opened a vast new region for exploration and exploitation for the Europeans.

THE INDIGENOUS CARIBBEAN POPULATIONS

In Mexico and parts of Central America, some twenty-five million Amerindians had developed an advanced civilization. In spite of major efforts by the Spaniards to eradicate Indigenous culture, much has remained to this day. But in the Caribbean, the Amerindians were fewer in number, and their societies were not as developed as those on the Mexican, Central, and South American mainland. Tragically, cultural and racial genocide took a greater toll in the Caribbean. The Indigenous populations there were greatly reduced almost from the outset of the colonization process from being enslaved and overworked and because of the diseases brought over by Spaniards, to which the native people had no immunities. Nonetheless, the inhabitants of Cuba, Puerto Rico, and Hispaniola (the original name given by the Spaniards to what is today Haiti and the Dominican Republic) have retained many vestiges of Indigenous society. However, the largest non-Hispanic influence in the Caribbean came from Africa. Thousands of enslaved Africans were brought over first to work the mines, then to work the large sugar plantations that served the Spaniards as the mainstay of the islands' economies. Today the vestiges of this important heritage are seen in much of Caribbean culture and, of course, in the racial makeup of Caribbean peoples.

The Indigenous groups in the Caribbean were mainly Carib and Arawak, who lived in seminomadic villages throughout the Greater (the larger islands of Cuba, Puerto Rico, and Hispaniola) and Lesser Antilles (the many smaller islands such as Jamaica, Trinidad and Tobago, etc.), and as far south as the coasts of what are today Venezuela and the Guineas. The Carib were considered by the Spaniards to be fiercer than the Arawak, but both groups hunted, fished, and gathered wild plants such as the manioc root for food.

Their way of life had evolved very little in thousands of years. Since the traditional methods of ob-

Reconstruction of a Taíno village in Cuba.

taining food had always yielded results, few incentives existed for innovation. Their lives revolved around villages that they were prone to abandon when economic need dictated. Politically, they depended on a council of elders for guidance. Religious beliefs were linked to the hunting-gathering economy, and they relied primarily on shamans for observance of rituals. Village homes required very little to build. Those using palm leaves and wood ribbing were among the most sophisticated. Some lived in dugouts that were called *barbacoas*.

Before the Spanish Conquest, the Taíno, an Arawakan group that dominated the islands of Cuba, Puerto Rico, and Santo Domingo, had a highly developed social and political system. In the twelfth century, they had displaced, throughout the Antilles, the less-developed Ciboney, who lived in cave-like dwellings and who foraged and fished to survive. Taíno-Arawak settlement was based on fishing and extensive planting of corn, squash, beans, and chile peppers, the same foodstuffs cultivated on the Mexican mainland. Because of extensive dependence on fishing, the Taíno had an extraordinary maritime ability and moved from island to island setting up villages whose populations numbered in the hundreds. But shortly before the Spanish occupation of the Greater Antilles, warlike Carib Indians swept into the Caribbean and drove many of the Arawak out and captured Arawak women. As a result, to the Spaniards, Arawak became known as a language of females. Like the Arawak, the Carib were excellent sailors who crossed much of the Caribbean in huge canoes that were fitted with woven cloth sails and carried as many as fifty people.

The lifestyle of these island people was drastically altered after the arrival of Columbus and the Spaniards. The first island settled by the Europeans was Hispaniola, which is the present-day Dominican Republic and Haiti. Columbus naively ordered his translator to enter into negotiations with the Great Mogul of India, insisting, as he did until his death in 1506, that he had found a direct route to India by sailing west from Spain. As quickly deduced by everyone else, what the great discoverer had encountered was a gigantic landmass that blocked direct passage to the real India; even so, the name "Indies" stuck. The name "America" was adopted in northern Europe because of the writings of Amerigo Vespucci, the Italian cartographer who explored the newly found lands. The Spaniards, however, always referred to the New World as Las Indias.

The fate of the "Indians," so called because of the colossal miscalculation made by Columbus, was tragic beyond almost any other experience of Indigenous peoples in the Americas. From their rude conquest, Columbus and his settlers envisioned rewards that the natives were ill prepared to deliver. Columbus, a Genoese from a seafaring merchant tradition, insisting that he was in Asia, expected to trade with the simple Carib and Arawak. The trouble was that the Caribbean natives had no surplus after they took care of their needs, and even if they had, their fare was of little use to Columbus in setting up trading posts.

Most of the Spanish settlers accompanying Columbus were steeped in the tradition of the Reconquest, and they counted on a subjugated population to do their bidding. They expected to establish feudal baronies. Columbus opposed such a tradition, but he capitulated nonetheless and gave his men *encomiendas*. Developed in feudal Spain, the encomienda was booty given to a Spanish conqueror of a Moorish caliphate. The award was usually the land that had belonged to the caliph, and according to Christian standards of the time, the prize was befitting a hero who had defeated the despised "infidels," as the Moorish Muslims were called. But just as the natives were unable to fit into Columbus's trade scheme, they were just as unsuited to provide labor or tribute.

The Spanish attempt to establish feudal baronies resulted in a debacle for all parties involved. But it was worse for the Amerindians, who were either worked to death in gold mines that yielded little gold or were forced to feed the demanding Spaniards. The result was mass starvation. The final blow in this endless chain of mistreatment was the introduction of European diseases, such as smallpox and measles, against which the natives had no immunities. This inadvertent intrusion was the most tragic of the European offerings. Numbering over one million in the Caribbean islands before Columbus's voyage, the Amerindians were eventually decimated. Their lineage, however, was not extinguished altogether. Numerous offspring resulted from the Spanish rape of native women, creating a small but formidable mestizo population, which continued the Amerindian genes in the islands.

The Conquest of Cuba

When Columbus and his Spanish sailors first arrived on the island that was named Cuba on October 27, 1492, they disregarded the native peoples who lived by subsistence agriculture and fishing. Columbus's attention was fixed on Hispaniola, where he established the first permanent Spanish colony. It was not until 1508 that the island was systematically charted by Sebastián de Ocampo, who circumnavigated the island gathering information about the coastlines and harbors that would prove useful for the eventual occupation.

The first Spanish political system was not established in Cuba until many years after Columbus's encounter with the natives of the Caribbean. Diego Velásquez de Cuéllar was commissioned governor of Cuba in 1511 after he had led an expedition that defeated the Arawak-Taíno nations. Velásquez, who first arrived in the New World at Hispaniola with Columbus's second voyage in 1493, was by then a veteran colonist with many years of experience in dealing with Caribbean natives. In the conquest, which was conducted in typical Spanish fashion, hundreds of men, women, and children were slaughtered. Many fled to the mountains or to other islands, such as Puerto Rico, only to be caught up with again in later expeditions.

Spared the encomienda for some nineteen years after the first arrival of Europeans in the Caribbean, Cuba's natives were finally subjected to the abhorrent institution after 1511. Columbus, who had expected trade, not feudal conquest, gave this prerogative to his men in Hispaniola, setting the precedent for the next sixty years of Spanish conquest. Giving this grant was against Columbus's better judgment, but he found that he had no choice because it seemed like the only way to reward the Spaniards, who demanded some kind of prize for their participation in the momentous expedition.

Velásquez had no such scruples, and the parceling out of human beings proceeded in hasty fashion. Velásquez himself became a virtual feudal lord of Cuba, and by 1515 he founded what became Cuba's two largest cities, Santiago and Havana. His power was such that he directed the explorations of the Mexican Gulf Coast by Francisco Hernández de Córdoba and his nephew Juan de Grijalva. These expeditions betrayed the existence of civilizations in the interior of Mexico, prodding Velásquez to put his brother-in-law, Hernán Cortés, in charge of the expedition that resulted in the conquest of Mexico. Velásquez remained governor of Cuba until the 1520s, and, like that of other Spanish conquerors, his rule left an indelible stamp on the formation of Cuban society.

The initial Cuban economy, based on raising livestock and placer mining of gold, was propped up with labor provided by the ubiquitous encomienda. Because of the demand for pork, cattle hides, and gold in the other Spanish colonies, especially after the conquest of Mexico, Cuba provided tremendous opportunity for the first settlers.

Unfortunately, European disease and the forced labor in the mines took a grim toll, and many natives became ill and died or were virtually worked to death. The amount of gold on the island was limited. Soon the supply was exhausted, frustrating the Spaniards to such a point that they made the Taínos work harder so that decreasing sources could yield the same previous results. Indiscriminate livestock raising was also destructive to the Amerindian way of life. Huge, untended herds trampled the fragile crops, reducing the harvest on which the natives depended for their main source of food. Ironically, the Spanish-based economy in Cuba declined very quickly because of competition from livestock raisers in Mexico and in other new colonies.

Then, when silver was discovered in the Zacatecas province of Mexico and Potosí in Peru, a rush to these areas depopulated Cuba when many Spanish adventurers left to find riches elsewhere. They clamored to leave for newly conquered Mexico and Peru, even though the Crown futilely imposed harsh sanctions to those who deserted their encomiendas. The near-abandonment of the initial economy was so disastrous for the natives that it made their unwilling sacrifice even more tragic. The surviving Indigenous groups must have wished that more of the exploitative Spaniards had left and never returned. But the Cuban economy revived. Because of the ideal position of the island, it became an entrepôt for silver coming from New Spain (roughly the area of present-day Mexico) and Peru and for European goods destined for the rich colonial markets.

Havana's fine harbor allowed the city to achieve dominance by the mid-sixteenth century, even though it did not become the capital of Cuba until 1607. The British and French, anxious to capture the booty offered by incoming ships, subjected the city to numerous attacks. Fortifications made the city safer, and it soon became the most important naval and commercial center for the Spanish colonies in the Caribbean. Ships with gold and silver from Mexico and South America were formed into fleets at Havana in the 1550s so that the Spanish navy could protect them from pirates during the journey back to Spain. By the eighteenth century, Havana was the New World's greatest port.

> Havana's fine harbor allowed the city to achieve dominance by the mid-sixteenth century, even though it did not become the capital of Cuba until 1607.

The Conquest of Puerto Rico

Unlike Cuba, the island of Puerto Rico was not seen by Europeans until Columbus's second voyage to the New World in 1493. The Taíno Indians living on the island called it Borinquen, but Columbus renamed it San Juan Bautista, even though he did not attempt to settle the island, concentrating instead on Hispaniola. As in Cuba, the Taíno received a few years of respite from the Spanish mistreatment. But sixteen years later, Ponce de León and a crew of fifty followers subdued the thirty thousand or so inhabitants of the island, and it was renamed Puerto Rico. The Spaniards overwhelmed the large population of Taínos by using terror tactics as they approached each village. Reducing the natives' ability to resist Spanish incursions throughout the Caribbean was a lack of cohesion and the poor communication among the scattered villages. If they had offered organized resistance, even in the face of superior weapons, horses, and other advantages held by the Spaniards, it would have been impossible for the Spaniards to succeed.

Following the pattern established in Hispaniola and Cuba, in Puerto Rico the Spaniards immediately set out to raise livestock and other foodstuffs for the expanding colonial market. But sugarcane was also planted after the conquest, and the natives were pressed into the encomienda system to tend to the cane. Harsh treatment and lack of experience with systematic labor rendered the natives almost useless for work on sugar plantations, however. Besides, by the 1580s, diseases had all but wiped out the Taínos of Puerto Rico. The flourishing of sugar production would have to await the coming of large numbers of enslaved Africans.

THE INDIGENOUS MEXICAN POPULATION

In Mexico the greatest cultural influence, along with the Spanish language, was its momentous Indigenous history. In 1518 Hernán Cortés set out from Cuba to explore the mainland of Mexico in order to confirm reports of the existence of large civilizations in the interior. As the Spaniards were to discover, the reports were indeed true beyond their wildest dreams. It is theorized that civilization in southern Mexico and most of Central America, or Mesoamerica as the area is known archaeologically, was developed by people who migrated across the Bering Strait more than fifty thousand years ago. The first humans to cross into the North American continent entered in waves before the strait was inundated by the melting polar caps in 10,000 BCE. Their livelihood depended on hunting the giant mastodons and other big game and gathering wild plants.

Social organization was limited, since they were mobile and traveled in small bands following the trail of animals. At best, they had a leader who ruled by consent of the other hunters and who had proved his worth in both hunting and defending his group from marauders. They lived in caves and rude shelters as they traversed the countryside in their pursuits. Like other Paleolithic big-game hunters from Europe, Africa, and Asia, they worshiped the very game on which they depended for food. Hence, drawings of mastodons and tapirs have been found on the bone artifacts they used as tools, leaving archaeologists to surmise that this was a form of worship.

Hunting and gathering, which provided a healthy, plentiful diet (Paleolithic man was bigger than present-day descendants), might have continued, but a significant climatic change about 7200 BCE forever altered the course of human history. Mesoamerica became more arid, creating the desert conditions we know today. The lush green land on which large animals depended for food disappeared. Humans had to turn to other sources of food and entered a stage designated as the Archaic Period. The former hunters became scroungers, depending on wild plants for their sustenance and to a lesser degree on smaller animals

Early inhabitants of Mesoamerica planted and irrigated the seeds of wild plants, such as maize, squash, beans, and amaranth (pictured here in flower), a type of gluten-free grain.

for protein. During this long period, which lasted until 2500 BCE, the gatherers became more and more adept at food acquisition and storage, but they also discovered that they could cultivate some of the plants for which they had previously scrounged.

This discovery was the first major step toward civilization. Slowly, the inhabitants of Mesoamerica began to plant and irrigate the seeds of wild plants, such as maize, squash, beans, and amaranth. In the process, they also domesticated some of the wild animals they hunted. Unlike in the rest of the world, wild cattle and horses had not survived the decline of big game. Only the bison in the northern part of the continent lived on. Domestic animals included only turkeys and small dogs. Not surprisingly, the course of development for the native peoples of the Americas did not include beasts of burden except for the people themselves.

Still, once domestication of both plants and animals pervaded Mesoamerica in an era called the Formative Period, 2500 BCE to 250 CE, material progress proceeded at an astonishing rate. First, villages appeared throughout the region as new techniques of cultivation resulted in flourishing plots of crops. Terracing (the plowing of platforms on hills) and *chinampas* (man-made islands on bodies of water) greatly increased the ability to produce. The resulting surpluses released many workers from agricultural work and made possible the emergence of specialists, such as potters, toolmakers, and even entertainers, such as musicians, acrobats, and dancers.

In addition, the simple metaphysical exigencies related to hunting and gathering gave way to a dramatic sophistication in religious practices, a process hastened by the ability to specialize. Farmers increasingly needed more precise prediction of the weather so that planting and harvesting could be planned accordingly. Shaman priests provided this valuable knowledge as they studied the heavens and acquired the astronomical skills necessary to forecast weather changes. Farmers looked to their religious leaders more and more for guidance, leading to a dependence that put the priests, with their metaphysical teachings, in leadership roles. Such control gave priests political power, which they exercised to their advantage. They demanded tribute and labor from the commoners and leaders alike, until the priesthood and the leadership converged into a theocracy.

About 250 CE, throughout the Americas, pre-Columbian civilization reached its apogee, and human development entered into the era known as the Classical Period. Large urban centers with specialized production techniques entered into trade arrangements with other cities. During the Formative Period, between 1200 BCE and 400 BCE, a high civilization (which in most of Mesoamerica did not appear until the Classical Period) had emerged in selected regions of Mesoamerica. A society known today as the Olmec built large cities with ceremonial centers and advanced architecture, pottery, and art. But most important, the Olmec developed a knowledge of astronomy and math that allowed them to invent a calendar system almost as accurate as ours today. Such development was limited to La Venta and San Lorenzo on the Gulf of Mexico, while the rest of Mesoamerica continued in the village mode even after the decline of these great centers.

In the Classical era, many communities, especially those of the Maya and Zapotec, whose centers were close to the old Olmec centers, probably were influenced by the older, declined civilization. The Zapotec, in fact, occupied Monte Albán, a city with marked Olmecan characteristics, while the Maya built centers like Chichén Itza in Yucatán and El Tajín in Vera Cruz. The Maya excelled in math and astronomy, a definite inheritance from the Olmec, and they produced the most delicate pieces of art in all the Americas.

The newer methods (terracing and *chinampas*) of cultivation were more beneficial to the societies of the hilly and lake-filled Valley of Mexico. There Teotihuacán, the most impressive center in the Classical Period, was built twenty-five miles northeast of the what is now Mexico City. The city had over 200,000 inhabitants, huge pyramids, and a large market where the most advanced pottery and obsidian wares were traded.

Throughout Mesoamerica, thriving agricultural communities existed, dedicated to cultivating maize, the ears of which were about ten times larger than during its initial planting in the Archaic Period. Maize was indispensable, but an array of other crops were also important in the diet of Mesoamericans. Unfortunately, in the tenth century CE, one by one the

Classical centers in both the highlands and the tropical lowlands declined. Archaeological evidence points to several causes. In the Mayan lowlands, reliance on slash-and-burn agriculture probably led to the exhaustion of the soil. The method works as long as there is plentiful new land to be brought under cultivation. Also, another climate change (bringing even drier weather) prompted nomadic outsiders from the north, known as Chichimecas, to migrate to Mesoamerica looking for water. It is believed that these newcomers pillaged and sacked the cities of Mesoamerica one by one. The Classical Period thus came to an end, and although the barbaric newcomers replaced and imitated the old civilizations, they never surpassed them in philosophical or technical achievement. Because of the warlike orientation of the new cities, the era has been called the Militaristic Period. This was the

At the Toltec city of Tula, about sixty miles northwest of present-day Mexico City, these giant monoliths once supported the roof of a temple on top of the pyramid where they stand.

state of society when the Spaniards arrived in the early sixteenth century.

The Toltec were the first of the former Chichimeca group of tribes to have approached the degree of development of their predecessors. Their most impressive city was Tula, about sixty miles northwest of the present-day Mexican capital. The center, known for its giant monoliths that resemble sentries on guard, remained the most important city in the Valley of Mexico until it too fell to other marauding Chichimeca. The Toltec also occupied the city of Monte Albán, which had served the Zapotec before them. According to myth, it is to there that Quetzalcoatl, the god known as the plumed serpent, was banished and expected to return in the future. As with Tula, the Toltec also abandoned Monte Albán, probably for the same reasons.

One of the last Chichimeca tribes to enter the central valley was the Aztec, who just a few years prior had left their mythical homeland of Aztlán in search of a new home as Huitzilopochtli, their god of the sun, had mandated. According to legend, they would know where to settle once they encountered an eagle devouring a serpent on top of *nopal* (prickly pear cactus) in the middle of a lake. They wandered south looking for the sign and finally saw it in the middle of Lake Texcoco, where they built Tenochtitlán.

This legend has a basis in truth. The Aztec arrived in the Valley of Mexico about the thirteenth century and were such a nuisance, since they continued the Chichimeca lifestyle of pillaging, that they were banished by Atzcapotzalco leaders to an island in the center of the lake, which they fortified and used as a base of operation. From there they imitated other city-states and built their own magnificent city, which surpassed all the others in size and beauty, while they defeated and dominated the other communities in the lake region. They went through several stages and emperors until the Spaniards conquered them in 1521.

The Conquest of Mexico

If there were any doubts among the Spaniards about the existence of an advanced civilization in the interior of Mexico, they were put to rest almost as soon as Cortés landed on the Gulf Coast at a bay he named Veracruz. The reports received from the natives first encountered on the Mexican mainland were too compelling for any misgivings. After scuttling some of his ships so that the four hundred Spaniards that accompanied him could not return, Cortés set out to find the source of this civilization. Cortés, an audacious conquistador from Estremadura in southern Spain, had inherited the warrior mentality so deeply ingrained in that part of the Iberian Peninsula. In the time-honored tradition of the Reconquest, Cortés wanted to subjugate the civilization of Mexico and establish himself as its feudal lord.

After declaring the landing site a town (Veracruz), the conquistadores set out for the city of Tenochtitlán, which was considered a populous center of great wealth and power. Along the way he and his men encountered resistance in Cholula, but through the intelligence and language-interpreting services offered him by an Amerindian maiden given to him by natives in Tabasco, he was able to defeat the Cholulans and continue on to Tenochtitlán. On the way he picked up native allies from the city of Tlaxcala. This group became a ready ally because the Aztec were their hated enemy. Various Aztec leaders had attempted to dominate them and force them to pay tribute, as they had done with other cities in the valley for years. But the Tlaxcalans resisted fiercely. Moctezuma, the Aztec emperor who ruled the great city of Tenochtitlán, had spies who had kept him informed of the progress of the approaching Spaniards ever since they had landed on the coast. But he did not know what to make of them. Paradoxically, he was at a loss as to how to deal with the intruders. The Aztec emperor actually thought that Cortés was the long-lost god Quetzalcoatl and that the rest of the Spaniards were immortal. By the time the Europeans arrived at the city, Moctezuma was paralyzed with indecision, and Cortés seized the opportunity to sequester the vacillating king in his palace. The Spaniards set up house inside the walls of the city, as did the thousands of Tlaxcalan allies. On July 1, 1520, the Spaniards were forced out, just a year after they had come into the city. The Spaniards called this *La Noche Triste* (The Sad Night). Moctezuma was stoned to death by his own people during this debacle.

Cortés was not a man to give up very easily, so he retreated to the town of Coyoacán, where he set up headquarters to plan the defeat of the city. He quickly built brigantines and armed them with cannons. Cortés laid siege to the city, not allowing supplies to go in. In time he attacked the starving Aztecs and the neighboring Tlatelolcans, who were also decimated by European diseases.

The siege finally forced a surrender, and Cortés had the city of Tenochtitlán razed. The beginning of Spanish Mexico commenced with the building of a European city on top of the old Aztec capital. However, the old conqueror was eventually stripped of his power, banished back to Spain, and replaced by professional viceroys who ostensibly represented the needs of the Crown. The Spaniards then ruled Mexico until 1821, a full three hundred years after the conquest, indelibly stamping their Hispanic mark on Mexican society. Still, what is considered Indigenous has remained in many ways.

THE SPANIARDS IN THE VALLEY OF MEXICO

After Cortés razed Tenochtitlán, he set out to build a Spanish city, ironically rescuing from the rubble the very same building materials used by the Aztec. His conquistadors then continued to explore and bring under Spanish rule other Indigenous communities. Pedro de Alvarado ventured south to the Yucatán Peninsula and Guatemala, while Cortés's enemy and rival, Nuño de Guzmán, brutally subjugated the vast realm of the Tarascans to the west. Cortés dispensed encomiendas left and right as a way of rewarding his men, but he reserved for himself the largest encomienda of all, practically all of Oaxaca. In 1529 he was authorized to use the title El Marqués del Valle de Oaxaca.

In the initial years of the conquest in the Valley of Mexico, as in the Caribbean, the encomienda remained the main prize sought by conquistadors. Many of the onerous aspects of the institution had been somewhat mitigated with the Laws of Burgos. Promulgated by the Crown in 1512, the regulations were in response to the extremely harsh treatment that desperate colonists in the Caribbean imposed on natives through the deplorable encomienda. Now Spaniards had to abide by regulations that forbade overworking the natives and that required the *encomendero* (the recipient of an encomienda) to provide for the spiritual welfare of the Amerindians. This usually consisted of supporting a prelate and building a church within the jurisdiction of the encomienda grant. In New Spain, as the vast territory claimed by Spain on the North American continent came to be called, the encomienda became for the natives an acculturation vehicle to Spanish ways.

The most important Spanish acquisition for the Amerindians, usually through the encomienda, was Catholicism. Spanish friars in the beginning of the colonization process exhibited a great amount of zeal, imbued as they were with an inordinate amount of idealism, which characterized the Catholic Church during this period of internal reform. They traveled far and wide, proselytizing and winning over hundreds of thousands to the Christian faith. The converts were so numerous, however, that they could not really assimilate Catholicism completely, and the tendency was to combine, syncretically, pre-Columbian beliefs with the new teachings.

By 1540 another major phenomenon began to drastically change the social and racial character of central Mexico. From the moment they set foot on Mexican soil, the conquistadors violated the women of the conquered tribes and took them as concubines, with only a few marrying the native women. The consequence was a large progeny of children who were half Spaniard and half Amerindian. This new racial ensemble came to be known as mestizo, and after a few generations, the possible variations of mixture became so profuse that over one hundred categories of *mestizaje* existed by the end of colonial rule in 1821.

> The conquistadors violated the women of the conquered tribes and took them as concubines. The consequence was a large progeny of children, half Spaniard and half Amerindian, who came to be known as mestizo.

In 1504 Queen Isabella died, and twelve years later King Ferdinand succumbed as well. Succeeding them was their heir Charles V, who was born to their daughter Juana la Loca and her Hapsburg husband, Prince Phillip of Austria. It fell to the young king to wrest that realm away from Cortés and his *encomenderos*, a process begun almost as soon as the value of the conquest was realized. In 1524 Charles established the Council of the Indies, designed to oversee the administration of the colonies of the New World. An *audiencia* (a court of judges and administrators) was appointed in 1527 as a major step in asserting royal control. It was presided over by Nuño de Guzmán, who set out to destroy the power of Cortés, his old rival. But the rapacious Guzmán seemed to be a worse threat than the feudalistic Cortés, and the whole *audiencia* slate was replaced a year later by a president and judges more loyal to the Crown. To supervise and establish the Catholic faith, Juan de Zumárraga was named archbishop of New Spain in 1527.

The most ambitious move in the effort to consolidate royal power in New Spain was the appointment of Antonio de Mendoza, an extremely capable administrator who served the Crown well as viceroy for many years. In 1542 the New Laws were promulgated, a stroke designed to end the feudal encomienda, ensuring the predominance of Hapsburg control over the area. Mendoza found that he could not effectively implement the restrictive measures without provoking insurrection from the armed *encomenderos*, so he opted for allowing the controversial institution to die out on its own. Encomiendas were only good as long as there were natives to parcel out, but because of the horrible epidemics caused by European diseases, the Indigenous population was decimated within a century.

In the meantime, the Spanish zeal for exploration and conquest led to incursions north of the Caribbean islands and Mexico into many regions of what is today the United States. Juan Ponce de León had sailed and landed on the shores of Florida in 1513, exploring most of the coastal regions and some of the interior. Continuing their maritime adventures, the Spanish explorers in the 1520s cruised along the northern shore of the Gulf of Mexico, seeing Alabama, Mississippi, and Texas, and also sailed up the Atlantic coast to the Carolinas. Between 1539 and 1541 a large, well-equipped group of explorers led by Hernando de Soto journeyed into the interior of North America looking for mineral wealth through present-day Florida, Georgia, South Carolina, Alabama, Mississippi, Arkansas, Louisiana, and Texas.

At the same time that de Soto was in the midst of his exploration, Francisco Vásquez de Coronado prepared for a momentous trek that took him and another large group of Spaniards north to present-day Arizona, New Mexico, Texas, and Oklahoma. In 1541 he set out from Mexico City in search of the Seven Cities of Cíbola, a mythical region rumored to rival Tenochtitlán in wealth and splendor. To supply Coronado's party, Hernando de Alarcón sailed up the Gulf of California and took his three ships against the current of the Colorado River, reaching present-day Yuma, Arizona.

MOVEMENT TO THE NORTH

In transcendental terms, Coronado's feat has great historical significance. But at the time, his explorations were considered a disappointment because of the failure to find the fabled cities of Cíbola and Quivera, another fabled city of gold. Dispelling the myths of greater glory and riches in the far north dampened enthusiasm for any further forays so far away from the viceroyalty of Mexico City. In addition, the discovery of silver in the immediate north, soon after Coronado returned empty-handed, ensured that the Spaniards would concentrate all their efforts closer to their home base, and the expansion and real settlement northward commenced in earnest.

In 1546 Captain Juan de Tolosa, leading a small expedition of soldiers and missionaries into El Gran Chichimeca, as the wild region north of Querétaro was known, discovered a rich vein of silver in a mountain known as La Bufa. The strike was located in what is now the city of Zacatecas, some three hundred miles north of Mexico City. It was the first of a series of finds in a fanlike pattern spreading from Zacatecas into Guanajuato, Querétaro, and San Luis Potosí. In the last half of the sixteenth century, Spanish officials in Madrid, far from central Mexico, concentrated all their efforts on spurring mining activity both in New Spain and in Peru, where even greater silver deposits were uncovered.

But before the rich minerals could be adequately exploited, the Central Corridor had to be made safe from hostile Amerindian residents. Although sparsely settled by the nomadic Chichimecas, the natives resisted the unwelcome intrusion of large numbers of Spaniards and mestizo workers, precipitating fifty years of warfare. By the end of the sixteenth century, the nomads were brought under control through a combination of extensive military and religious proselytizing campaigns. As the mining regions were carved out from Chichimeca territory, thousands of mestizos, sedentary Indians from the former Aztec Empire, and Spaniards migrated to the *reales* (mining camps) and settled there permanently. The mining economy and the arid desert environment of El Gran Chichimeca engendered unique social conditions where a new Mexican ethnic identity was forged. Here the population was not as linked to either the large, sedentary Indian civilization and culture of the central highlands or the cities that were large centers of administration, commerce, and Spanish culture, such as Mexico City and Puebla.

While the inhabitants of the mining frontier drew on Spain and the more settled Amerindian areas for cultural continuity, the exigencies of the new environment generated an even more vibrant source of identity and culture. The process was carried north as the mining frontier moved in that direction in the seventeenth and eighteenth centuries. By 1800 the Spaniards had reaped $2.25 billion worth of silver from the vast array of rich mines. In the Spanish system, all wealth belonged to the Crown, and the miner was granted a *real* (a royal concession giving him or her the right to exploit the mine). The Crown received one-fifth of all the take, or the royal fifth; however, these concessions would remain in the miner's family, ensuring a continuation of *patria potestad* (the original authorization) usually under a patriarch.

Within a few years the grantees of the *reales* turned to wage labor, and hundreds of thousands of mestizos, who were born in the decades immediately after the conquest in the highlands, poor Whites, and acculturated natives poured into the Central Corridor to work not only in mining but also on the haciendas, which specialized in raising livestock and agriculture for consumption in the *reales*. Thus, the hacienda became an indispensable corollary to mining, and within a few decades both of these activities determined the social arrangements of the region. The economy, based on wage labor, created a proletariat that was able to work in a more diverse opportunity structure than in the central highlands.

Smaller mining operators followed missionaries north to the frontier. A persistent pattern emerged in which the missionaries "tamed" the natives so that the miners could follow, once they were "softened" to European ways. The missionaries provided the service unwittingly, but they served that purpose nonetheless. Parral, at the northern end of the corridor in Chihuahua, and Alamos, in Sonora, were thus settled by Spanish-Mexicans. By the mid-1600s the mines had played out, so then miners in the frontier were forced to settle down and turn to agriculture and the operation of smaller-scale mining known as *gambusino*.

For today's Mexican Americans, the social and cultural transformation of the Central Corridor is particularly important, because the culture that emerged in northern New Spain (today's American Southwest) during the colonial period is an extension and reflection of the mining society in this region. In addition, Mexican immigrants who in the early twentieth century swelled existing Latino communities throughout the United States came from this region as well, reinforcing the unique Mexicanness that had already been established in the Southwest.

The reasons for settling the extreme northern frontier of New Spain were not as related to mining as they were in the case of the Central Corridor. Nonetheless, the process of colonization was a slow but sustained extension of the northward movement that started with the founding of the Zacatecas mines. By the time Mexico acquired its independence from Spain in 1821, permanent colonies existed in coastal California, southern Arizona, South Texas, and most of New Mexico and southern Colorado. The imprint of evolving Mexican culture so evident in the Central Corridor was also stamped on today's Southwest. It contained a mestizo-*criollo* (pure-blooded Spanish descendant) racial mixture with a strong reliance on raising livestock, subsistence agriculture, and mining. Leaders of most colonizing expeditions were persons born in Spain, but the rank-and-file soldiers, artisans, and workers in general were of mixed blood (mestizos) or *criollos* born in New Spain.

The first foray out of the Central Corridor after Coronado's unsuccessful trek was in the 1590s into Pueblo Indian territory in northern New Mexico. Fifty years earlier, Coronado had written of these sedentary peoples who lived in large agricultural settlements containing multistory houses with well-ordered political and religious systems. His attempts to buffet them into encomiendas provoked fierce resistance, and as a result he and his party were forced to abandon New Mexico. This failure contributed to the overall disillusionment with exploration. Nonetheless, the possibility of exploiting the labor of the Pueblos and saving their souls, modest as this potential might have been, remained a lure after Coronado. The attraction glowed even more forty years later when Antonio de Espejo reported in 1583 the possibility of silver deposits in New Mexico.

Spurred by Espejo's report, Juan de Oñate, the grandson of a Zacatecas mining pioneer from Spain, was granted a charter to explore into present-day New Mexico as early as 1595. In 1598 he and his group set out along the Central Corridor from the more civilized Zacatecas to the uncertainty of the north. Oñate's party, made up of Spaniards, *criollos*, and mestizos, also contained Tlaxcalan Indians, who had remained loyal to the Spaniards after helping Hernán Cortés defeat the Aztec in 1521. They served in menial positions as carriers, servants, and laborers. After reaching the Rio Grande, the explorers and missionaries then traveled along the river valley, established a minor post in present-day El Paso, and continued on up through upper Rio Grande valley into Pueblo Indian territory.

Oñate was ordered to return in 1608, but Franciscan missionaries and settlers remained attracted to the communities of sedentary natives. Santa Fe was founded in 1610, followed by other settlements. The clerics wanted to convert the natives, and the civilians hoped to put them into encomiendas and demand gold as tribute. The efforts to enslave the natives backfired, however. In 1680 a Pueblo Indian named Popé led a rebellion that forced the Spaniards and Christianized

Amerindians out of northern New Mexico southward toward El Paso, and they founded Ysleta just north of El Paso. The latter community is said to have housed the *genízaros* (acculturated Comanche captive-slaves), Christianized Pueblos, and the faithful Tlaxcalans. Sixteen years later, many of those settlers who had fled returned to northern New Mexico and reestablished a presence, but with a new respect for the Pueblos.

The Pueblo uprising also turned the interest of Spaniards toward Texas. But the story of the exploration of Texas has to be told within the context of the colonization of the large province of Coahuila, of which Texas was an extension. The first newcomers were prospectors searching for precious metals, and indeed some silver mines were opened in Monclova, Coahuila, such as the Santa Rosa. But the diggings were sparse, and most of the attention was soon turned to agriculture and livestock. Motivated by the need to provide foodstuffs and livestock to the rich mining regions to the south, in 1689 the first royal *mercedes* (land grants) were granted to Spaniards in the fertile valleys of Monclova, just south of the present border.

Like Oñate, the Spaniards in the northeast also brought Tlaxcalans to provide labor for their haciendas. Many of these enterprising natives established themselves as artisans in Saltillo and acquired a reputation as excellent weavers and silversmiths. Many of the modern inhabitants of Coahuila and immigrants to Texas from this area are descendants of the Tlaxcalans. Saltillo acquired great importance because it served as an entrepôt between the livestock-raising areas to the north and the silver and mercantile communities to the south. In the eighteenth century, a new dynasty of Spanish kings, the Bourbons, initiated reforms that led to a revitalization of the silver industry. As a consequence, by 1767 Saltillo had become a prosperous commercial hub with a population of over two thousand, and as new settlers arrived to colonize the northeast, they filtered through this beautiful colonial city. Saltillo and the northern regions represented the frontier of the Spanish Empire. Spanish Jews, known as Sephardics, having been persecuted and expelled from the Iberian Peninsula starting in 1492, took refuge in the border areas of the empire, far from the centralized government and the Inquisition. Close to Saltillo, they founded the important city of Monterrey and imparted a special industrious character to the whole region. Because of the pervasiveness of Jewish refugees in the north, many northern Mexicans and Mexican Americans share Jewish genes and may maintain Jewish cultural practices unknowingly.

Large, sprawling haciendas with huge herds of cattle and sheep characterized the economy and societal life of the northeast by 1800. The biggest landholding belonged to the Sánchez-Navarro family. It was sixteen million acres in size. This latifundia was so immense that it took in almost half of the province, and its mainstay was sheep raising. Peonage was the lot of many of the lower classes, as that was the only method by which *hacendados* (landowners) could deter their workers from going off to work in the mines. But hindering the effectiveness of the haciendas were constant depredations by the Comanche, who had learned that raiding hacienda livestock was more prosperous than hunting the buffalo. This provoked the Spanish government to establish buffer zones across the Rio Grande, or the Rio Bravo, as it is known in Mexico.

At the turn of the eighteenth century, a persistent priest named Francisco Hidalgo, from his base of San Juan Bautista, a settlement on the Rio Grande about 150 miles west of Laredo, zealously set out to work among the native inhabitants north of the river. Initially his requests for support were ignored by Spanish officials, so he sought help from the French, which prompted the Spaniards to act because they recognized the threat France would pose if its colonists made inroads with the natives. Domingo Ramón in 1717 was sent to colonize along the Nueces River and to build missions. In 1718 the San Antonio de Béjar and de Valero mission churches were built where the city of San Antonio is located today. The chapel in the de Béjar mission was called El Alamo. The efforts to colonize Texas remained very difficult because of the nomadic, warlike character of the tribes. Therefore, instead of spreading the gospel, the Spaniards spent most of their time pacifying the resistant natives.

The French remained a threat, however. To thwart Spanish efforts to colonize and settle Texas, the French supplied the natives with firearms and gunpowder. Nonetheless, colonization remained a priority on the Spanish colonial agenda. In 1760 after the Seven Years' War (also known as the French and Indian War), which united France and Spain against Britain, France ceded claims to all lands west of the Mississippi to avoid giving them to the victorious British. Overnight, New Spain's territory expanded dramatically. Then, in the American Revolution of 1776, the Spaniards, because of their alliance with France, were able to obtain lands all the way to Florida. Virtually all of that territory lacked Hispanic settlers, however. In Texas, most of the settlers lived in clusters of villages along the lower Rio Grande valley. By 1749, 8,993 settlers and 3,413 Amerindians lived in what came to be known as Nuevo Santander. Laredo was on the north bank of the river, and Meier, Camargo, and Reynosa were on the south bank.

> Large, sprawling haciendas with huge herds of cattle and sheep characterized the economy and societal life of the northeast by 1800.

Also during this same period, colonists were pushing north and establishing ranches in the Nueces River valley. The Crown encouraged the settlement of this region to create a buffer zone against all intruders, such as the Comanche and the French. By 1835, three million head of livestock, cattle, and sheep roamed the region between the Nueces River and the Rio Grande, and about five thousand persons inhabited the region. Most border people did not inhabit the towns, however. Instead, they lived on ranches as tight-knit family groups and clans on land granted by the Spanish Crown. Having to withstand the depredations of the Comanche promoted even tighter cohesion and class cooperation than was true on the larger haciendas farther south in the interior of Mexico.

Arizona was the next area of the northernmost frontier to be explored and settled. The region was part of the province of Sonora, but it acquired a distinct geographical name, Pimería Alta, because of the numerous Pima Indians that inhabited southern Arizona and northern Sonora. Its settlement, then, was simply an extension of the colonization of Sonora. The first Europeans in Sonora were Jesuit missionaries who in 1591 introduced a new religion, European crops, and livestock to Yaqui and Mayo in southern Sonora. The natives were more receptive to the latter offerings than to the former, but they were receptive, nonetheless. When the first colonists arrived from New Spain some fifty years later, they found wheat and other European crops abundantly planted by natives on mission lands.

Pedro de Perea, a miner from Zacatecas, was allowed the first *entrada* (Spanish Crown colonization sanction) into Sonora in 1640, and he arrived with forty soldiers in 1641. Because of problems with local leaders in Sinaloa and Jesuit missionaries in Sonora, he went to New Mexico, where he recruited twelve families and five Franciscan priests. The local Jesuits objected to the viceroy in Mexico City, and eventually the Franciscans went back, but the families stayed.

Then a series of silver discoveries led to more settlement along the Sonoran River valleys by colonists who came directly from Zacatecas, Durango, and Sinaloa.

By the 1680s most settlers dedicated their efforts to mining, but many others raised crops and livestock to supply the mines. Farmers and miners lived in the same towns, which usually contained a store for goods not available locally. The settlers introduced tools, livestock, and crops never before seen in Sonora.

Intense dependence on mining made the Sonoran communities very unstable, because when production of the local mine played out, the community dispersed. Also, mercury, which was indispensable to the amalgamation of silver, was a monopoly of the Spanish Crown. In the seventeenth century, prices

In 1691 Father Eusebio Kino made the first inroads into Arizona. He established a mission in 1700 at San Xavier del Bac, near present-day Tucson, and in 1702 he founded another mission some thirty miles south in Tumacácori, the site of this statue.

were hiked up so high that it was impossible to operate the mines profitably. As happened elsewhere in New Spain when mining opportunity waned at the end of the century, more and more Mexican settlers engaged in subsistence agriculture rather than mining. But also, as elsewhere in New Spain, the eighteenth-century Bourbon reforms precipitated in Sonora a growing and booming economy. More settlers came in from the other provinces of New Spain and from Spain itself. Consequently, the Indigenous population declined in proportion. In 1765, only 30 percent of the population was made up of settlers from New Spain, while by 1800 that figure had changed to 66 percent.

In the Santa Cruz Valley, Pimas and Tohono O'odham (known as Pápagos by Spaniards) predominated in the northern half near Tucson, and settlers occupied the southern part. The missionaries, however, preceded the settlers, pacifying the natives and making the area safer for colonization. This impetus surged the line of settlement even farther north in Sonora to Pimería Alta (northern Sonora and southern Arizona), theretofore the domain of Jesuit missions. In 1691 Father Eusebio Kino, an untiring Jesuit missionary, made the first inroads into Arizona and established a mission in 1700 at San Xavier del Bac, near present-day Tucson, and in 1702 he founded another mission some thirty miles south in Tumacácori. In 1706, a presidio was established next to that complex, in Tubac, complementing the mission in much the same way as the haciendas did the *reales*.

By the 1730s, settlers were in what is now the Santa Cruz Valley of the Sonoran Desert, mining silver at Arizonac just south of the present-day border. The name "Arizonac" was Pima for "land of few springs" and is how the state of Arizona derived its name. To deal with disturbances like the uprisings instigated by the Pima in the 1750s or the incursion by the Apache in the 1730s, the settlers built presidios and manned the military garrisons, extending their influence even farther north. Basically, the same pattern of missions and presidio life as in the earlier settlements was established along the Altar and Santa Cruz valley of Pimería Alta in the eighteenth century. Ironically, the farther north settlers moved, the more they relied on wheat rather than maize as a staple. This was even true among the natives. The Tohono O'odham, for

example, had taken to making what we know today as "Indian fried bread" and wheat flour tortillas.

Because Jesuit influence in the Spanish Empire had become so pervasive, in 1767 the Bourbons expelled them from the realm, and the communities throughout Sonora were forced to undergo significant alterations. After the expulsion, the mission system declined despite the Franciscans replacing the Jesuit order. Former mission farms were put to livestock raising, and because foodstuffs from the missions were scarce, the settlers had to engage in more extended agricultural activity. As a result, Mexican settlements proliferated in the river valleys of the Sonoran Desert. Small villages existed everywhere, and the new arrivals assumed the way of life forged by the earlier settlers. Between the 1790s and 1820s, the Apache threat subsided because of successful military tactics and negotiations on the part of local leaders, and the settlements began to thrive in Pimería Alta. At one point as many as one thousand settlers lived in the Santa Cruz Valley. But with the independence of Mexico, the Spanish Crown abandoned its fortifications, and the Apache lost no time in taking advantage of the opportunity. Overrunning Pimería Alta, they forced the settlers to the southern part of the desert.

As in Arizona, the establishment of colonies in California was an extension of the Spanish drive into northwestern New Spain. In 1769 José de Gálvez, an aggressive representative of the Bourbons in New Spain, gave orders to settle Alta California from Baja California, and the same year a tired expedition led by the Franciscan Fray Junípero Serra founded the San Diego mission. A year later another mission was built in Monterey. During this period of flux, Juan Bautista de Anza, the Sonoran-born son of a Spanish official who himself became an officer, and Pedro de Garcés, a Spanish Franciscan missionary, founded the first overland route to California in 1774.

For the Franciscans, converting numerous California natives became the main incentive in the drive northward. The first exploration of Juan Bautista de Anza resulted in the reinforcement of a mission along the beautiful Pacific coast in Monterey and the additional building of a presidio. Two years later, de Anza lead another expedition and founded San Francisco, where the presidio is still a landmark.

In a few years, familiar religious and military institutions—the mission and the presidio—dotted the California coastline all the way from San Diego to San Francisco. Soldiers of various racial mixtures, missionaries, and Amerindians made up the demographic profile of the coast. The soldiers were encouraged to go as settlers and to take their families, as was the tradition in other frontier regions of New Spain. Those who did not have mates found suitable partners among the native women, to the chagrin of the missionaries, who considered the mestizo soldiers a bad influence on the native communities. As time went by, many of the soldiers became landowners, especially after 1831, when mission property was confiscated by the now-independent Mexican government. Some of these former soldiers acquired thousands of acres, laying the foundation for some of the old California families.

ANGLO ENCROACHMENT INTO THE MEXICAN NORTH

While Spain attempted to hold off encroachment into the northern regions of New Spain by other European imperialists, a series of events took place that changed the relationship between the Hispanic and Anglo areas of North America. In 1776 Anglo-Americans declared their independence from England, and thirty-four years later Mexicans proclaimed their independence from Spain. In both areas new nations were formed. The thirteen former British colonies came to be known as the United States of America in 1781, and the newly independent people of New Spain named their nation the Republic of Mexico.

Both areas had immense problems as they experimented with new forms of government and attempted to get their economies afloat. Mexico, however, had the more difficult time. Anglo-Americans had a preexisting political structure and economy, which allowed them to make a relatively smoother transition into independent status. Spain had ruled and controlled its domains with an iron hand and had imposed a rigid economic and social caste system on its colonial subjects, which allowed the Catholic Church to have inordinate influence on their everyday lives. As a consequence, the Mexicans were not as well prepared for the democratic ideals to which they aspired in the 1824 constitution. The result was years of confusion and interminable internal strife, which greatly weakened the economy and made the new nation vulnerable to outside powers.

The area of greatest weakness was in the far northern frontier. As has been indicated, Spain had difficulty in peopling its vast territory in New Spain. This condition made the area even more vulnerable to outside powers. To augment its forces in the interior of New Spain, which were busy squelching the independence movement that had started on September 16, 1810, with the insurrection of Father Miguel Hidalgo y Costilla, the Spaniards withdrew their troops from the frontier presidios. This further weakened the lines of defense in the north, inviting incursions from the newly independent but aggressive North Americans.

The danger of Yankee encroachment was apparent to the Spaniards much earlier. In 1803 a powerful France under Napoleon Bonaparte acquired from Spain the Louisiana Territory, which France had ceded during the Seven Years' War in the previous century. Napoleon, who was vying for dominance in Europe and needed revenue quickly, sold the vast territory to the United States, whereupon the borders of the expanding infant nation connected directly with New Spain.

Anglo-Americans lost no time in determining what the new acquisition meant for the fledgling country. To the consternation of Spain, President Thomas Jefferson funded the historical expedition of Meriwether Lewis and William Clark in 1804. Spain was obviously worried that the exploration was a prelude to the settlement of the territory by Anglos. Then in 1806, Zebulon Pike, an army officer searching for the headwaters of the Red River in Arkansas, entered Spanish territory in Colorado, built a fort, and raised the colors of the United States. Spanish officials found and destroyed the fortification and arrested Pike and his men. Taken to Santa Fe and then to Chihuahua City farther south, Pike saw more of New Spain than most anybody else who was not a Spanish subject. In the memoirs of his adventure, Pike recognized the potential for trade with Mexico. This piqued the interest of many of his fellow Anglo-Americans.

A series of other events demonstrated that Anglo-Americans were anxious to fulfill what they considered their Manifest Destiny to settle areas even beyond their sovereign realm. In 1820 U.S. Army surgeon James Long led a revolt in Spanish Texas, ostensibly as part of the independence movement against the Spanish but obviously acting as a filibuster for his countrymen. Spain finally entered into deliberations with Moses Austin, a Catholic from Missouri, to settle Anglo-Catholic families in Texas. The rationale for this seemingly paradoxical policy was to people the region between the more populated portions of New Spain and the United States with persons who owed a loyalty to Spain, even if they were not Hispanic. Initially, the Austin colony was made up of three hundred families in East Texas who were given generous *empresario* land grants. The stipulation was that they had to be Catholic, become subjects of the Crown, and abide by Spanish law. Moses died during the process, so the contract was concluded with Stephen, his son. These negotiations were concluded in 1821, right before Mexico acquired its independence under the leadership of Augustine Iturbide, a former Spanish officer who wanted to lead the newly independent nation down the path of monarchy. But Mexico honored the agreements that were established by Spain.

Iturbide was overthrown in 1823, and a more liberal constitutional government was established in 1824. The new constitution called for a president, a congress, nineteen states with their own legislatures, and four territories. That same year, Erasmo Seguín, a delegate to the national congress from Texas, persuaded a willing congress to pass a colonization act designed to bring even more Anglo settlers to Texas. Between 1824 and 1830 thousands of Anglo families entered East Texas, acquiring hundreds of thousands of free acres and also buying land much cheaper than they could have in the United States. By 1830 Texas had eighteen thousand Anglo inhabitants and more than two thousand enslaved Africans.

Anglo-Americans found it difficult to live under Mexican rule from the outset. They had an aversion to the Spanish language and the Mexican laws and legal system (in particular, the nonexistence of juries). In 1824 Texas was joined with Coahuila into a gigantic state, with most of the population residing in the Coa-

huila portion of the entity. Anglo-Texans rankled at the remoteness of the seat of government in faraway Saltillo in Coahuila, and exacerbating this sentiment was the inability of the Mexican government to provide adequate protection from the marauding Comanche. Anglos also feared the threat to the institution of slavery. Indeed, in 1829 the Mexican government abolished slavery during the liberal administration of Vicente Guerrero, the second president under the constitution. The uproar in Texas was so intense that Guerrero decided not to enforce the law. Nonetheless, slaveholders in Texas knew that their days were numbered.

Perhaps the most vexing development for Texans was the Immigration Law of 1830. In 1827 Manuel Mier y Terán, a military officer charged with assessing the general conditions in Texas, concluded that Anglos posed a threat to the sovereignty of Mexico. Then in 1830, a coup d'état by Guerrero's vice president, Anastasio Bustamante, installed a conservative government that was intent on closing off the borders of Mexico

General Antonio López de Santa Anna championed the cause of independence from Spain and became president of Mexico in 1833.

to outsiders. The result was the law that forbade any new immigration into Texas, an act that greatly concerned Anglos, who wanted to expand the economy and their culture by emigration from the United States.

All in all, the sentiment for independence from Mexico was on the increase in Texas. In 1832 General Antonio López de Santa Anna ousted Bustamante, and he was elected president the following year. But he allowed his liberal vice president, Valentín Gómez Farías, to institute some anticlerical reforms against the Catholic Church. This provoked powerful Mexican conservatives to act decisively. Somehow, General Santa Anna was persuaded in 1835 to oust his own vice president and to dissolve congress and institute a more closed system than even Bustamante had attempted a few years earlier. One of the first steps taken by Santa Anna under his centralized conservative constitution of Las Siete Leyes (The Seven Laws) was to dismantle the state legislatures and dismiss the governors and replace them with military officials. In Texas, Mexican troops were sent to enforce restrictive customs along the Gulf Coast, leading to a skirmish with Anglos, who did not want their trade with the United States disrupted.

To the disgruntled Texans, all seemed lost. The rumblings for independence increased. Late in 1835, Santa Anna sent General Martín Perfecto de Cos to San Antonio to administer the new federal laws, but he was repelled by Anglo-Texans and Mexican Texans who were determined to resist. The Anglos fortified themselves in the mission of El Alamo and awaited the inevitable retribution. Santa Anna decided then to take matters into his own hands and, mustering a large force, descended on San Antonio. Mexican Texan scouts warned of the impending attack, but Anglo defenders under Colonel Travis did not believe the first messages. When it was obvious that the threat was real, the Anglos prepared for battle. Instead of attacking immediately, the Mexican army laid siege to the fortified mission, which lasted two weeks. Santa Anna ordered a *degüello* attack, which means taking no prisoners, and all the vastly outnumbered defenders were killed even after they surrendered.

After the massive defeat at the Alamo, the Texas army, led by General Sam Houston, fled eastward with Santa Anna's troops in hot pursuit. At Goliad, a town east of San Antonio, the Mexicans decisively defeated the Texans, and, as at the Alamo, they took no prisoners. These defeats served to galvanize Texan resistance, and eventually Santa Anna committed a military blunder that led to the defeat of his army and his capture at San Jacinto, located near present-day Houston. The Texans declared their independence and wrested from a reluctant Santa Anna terms of surrender that included Texas's independence. Mexican officials never accepted the agreement reached with Santa Anna, but Texas remained independent, nonetheless, until 1845, when it was annexed to the United States.

The Texas rebellion caused hard feelings between Mexico and the United States, and the rift eventually grew to proportions of war in 1846. In 1836 Mexico had charged the United States with backing the rebels, an allegation denied vehemently by U.S. officials. That the United States immediately recognized the Texas Republic was proof enough for the Mexicans, however, and they warned that annexation of Texas by the United States would mean war. Another cause of discord between the two uneasy neighbors was two million dollars in damage done to Anglo-American properties in Mexico as a consequence of revolutionary violence in Mexico.

Then in February 1845, the United States voted for the annexation of Texas, and Mexico broke off relations but stopped short of declaring war. Apparently, Mexico at this point was about to recognize Texas's independence and did not want any border problems. Still, the issue that eventually brought the two nations into warfare was the matter of the boundary. When Texans declared their independence in 1836, they claimed the lower Rio Grande as their southern border. The Mexicans insisted that the Nueces River, a few hundred miles to the north, was the border. With the annexation, the United States accepted the Texas version of the boundary dispute.

It was no secret that many Anglo-Americans wanted to fulfill their Manifest Destiny of expanding their country all the way to the Pacific coast. At the very moment of annexation, U.S. officials under President James K. Polk continued trying to buy vast areas of Mexico's northernmost territories, including California. In the fall of 1845, the American president sent John Slidell to Mexico with an offer of 25 million dollars for California, but Mexican officials refused even to see him. General Zachary Taylor was then sent across the Nueces River to set up a blockade of the Rio Grande at its mouth on Port Isabel, and Mexicans retaliated by attacking the U.S. troops on April 25, 1845. Casualties ensued. President Polk immediately went to Congress and obtained a declaration of war against Mexico.

Two years of war followed. That it took so long was somewhat surprising, considering Mexico's weak political situation. From the time that Texas was annexed until the war ended in 1847, six different presidents attempted to make foreign policy, quite often at odds with each other. Nonetheless, the Mexican will to resist was underestimated, and it was difficult for an inexperienced U.S. Army to fight on foreign soil. The U.S. invasion took place from four different directions. Troops under General Taylor crossed from the north across the Rio Grande, while General Stephen Watts Kearny took an army overland to New Mexico and then to California. There he encountered considerable resistance from the Californios (Mexican Californians) at the Battle of San Pascual before reaching Los Angeles. California was also assaulted by sea by Commodore John C. Fremont. But the most decisive drive was by General Winfield Scott, who bombarded Vera Cruz and then proceeded with the most sizable force all the way to Mexico City, with the Mexicans offering the greatest resistance at Churubusco (part of present-day Mexico City).

Not all Americans supported the war. Newspapers carried reports that General Scott admitted that his men had committed horrible atrocities. By September, his troops occupied Mexico City. General Santa Anna had been president since December of 1846, but his attempts to fend off the American invasion were hopeless, and in November he resigned in disgrace. The Mexicans refused to come to the bargaining table until they were thoroughly routed. Finally, in February 1848 they signed the Treaty of Guadalupe Hidalgo, which brought the war officially to an end.

The treaty provided fifteen million dollars for the vast territories of New Mexico, Arizona, and California and parts of Nevada, Utah, and Colorado. The provisions of the treaty most important to an understanding of the history of Mexican Americans had to do with the Mexicans who remained in the territory acquired by the United States. They had a year to retreat into Mexico's shrunken border or they automatically would become citizens of the United States. They would then acquire all the rights of citizens. In addition, the treaty assured southwest Mexicans that their property would be protected and they would have the right to maintain religious and cultural integrity. These provisions, which the Mexican negotiators at the town of Guadalupe Hidalgo had insisted on, seemed protective of the former Mexican citizens, but these stipulations were only as good as the ability and desire to uphold the promises.

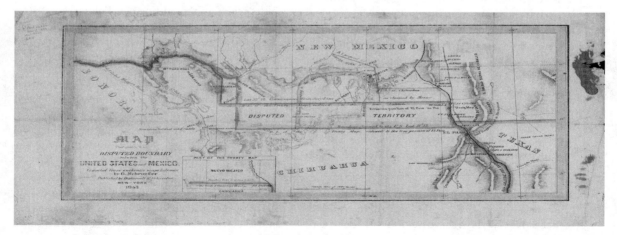

After errors were found on the 1847 map that had been used to negotiate the Treaty of Guadalupe Hidalgo, the map's publisher, John Disturnell, issued this corrected map in 1953, illustrating the resultant disputed boundary lines.

Mexicans under U.S. Rule

The territorial acquisition delineated in the Treaty of Guadalupe Hidalgo did not include southern Arizona and southern New Mexico. That region, which included the area from present-day Yuma along the Gila River (twenty-five miles south of Phoenix) all the way to the Mesilla Valley, where Las Cruces, New Mexico, is located, was sold to the United States by General Santa Anna the year that he returned to power in 1853. Ironically, hundreds of Mexicans who in 1848 had moved south into the Mesilla Valley or the Santa Cruz Valley in southern Arizona found themselves in the United States again. The provisions in the Gadsden Treaty regarding Mexicans in the newly annexed territory were similar to those in the Treaty of Guadalupe Hidalgo. Few Mexicans had any faith that any of the provisions protecting Mexicans would be honored, and many were embittered because they felt betrayed by Mexico. But the Mexican government did attempt to attract Mexicans from the southwestern United States into what became the northernmost Mexican region in the present-day border states. Of the 80,000 or so Mexicans living in the ceded territories, only a few thousand took up the offer.

The promise that the remaining Mexicans would receive all the rights accrued to U.S. citizens did not really materialize. New Mexico, with the largest number of Mexicans, perhaps 60,000, was able to achieve some political self-determination for its citizens. But there and everywhere else in what was now the southwestern United States, the newly minted U.S. citizens were systematically discriminated against. Except in New Mexico, Anglo immigration overwhelmed Mexicans in the newly acquired territories almost from the beginning. In Texas, for example, the population increased from 30,000 in 1836 to 140,000 in 1846. While there was migration from Mexico, this rapid increase in population was mainly due to the influx of Anglos from the United States. Mexicans were outnumbered six to one.

The 1836 Texas constitution stipulated that all residents living in Texas at the time of the rebellion would acquire all the rights of citizens of the new republic, but if they had been disloyal, these rights were forfeited. Numerically superior Anglos, embittered with Mexicans during the rebellion, retaliated by mistreating or forcing Mexicans off their property. Many Mexicans simply crossed the border and went to Mexico; others became a resident proletariat, working the land they once owned or joining the migrant worker stream. In 1857 Anglo businessmen attempted to run off Mexican teamsters, who had dominated the transport of goods in South Texas since the colonial period, by hiring thugs to strong-arm the carters off the trails. The attempt was not wholly successful, but it demonstrated the increasing antipathy toward Mexicans and a continuing violation of the guarantees offered by the Treaty of Guadalupe Hidalgo.

When Texas joined the union in 1845, only one Mexican Texan was a delegate to the convention that framed the new state constitution. And in the convention itself, there were many who felt that Mexicans should not be allowed to vote. But in the end, they were not denied suffrage. In spite of this victory, Mexican Texans were intimidated into not voting, and the result was that few politicians were Mexicans. After Texas became a state, few Mexicans participated in politics. In 1850, of the sixty-four members in the state legislature, none had been born in Texas or Mexico. Whenever Mexicans did vote, their power was diminished because they were dominated by political bosses who were able to buy in mass the votes of Mexicans. In addition, there were White-only primaries from which Mexicans were barred, and since the Democratic Party dominated in Texas, the elections were really decided in these primaries. Poll taxes—that is, taxes levied for voting—also served to deter from voting those with few economic resources; this included most Mexicans and African Americans.

In California, while Mexicans and Anglos did not have the same legacy of conflict that characterized race relations in Texas, many of the newcomers were from the U.S. South, where prejudice against racial minorities was the rule. Slavery still reigned in the South, but in a California that had been part of Mexico it had been abolished, and many Mexican Californians had African heritage. The irony was that because of the Treaty of Guadalupe Hidalgo, Afro-Mexicans became full U.S. citizens in the newly incorporated states of the Southwest while freed Blacks and, of course, enslaved Blacks could not be citizens in the rest of

Gold diggers on the Sacramento River. The gold rush of 1849 attracted thousands of Anglos to California, greatly reducing the ratio of Mexicans to Anglos. Mexicans were 15 percent of the population in 1850 but only 4 percent in 1870.

the United States. Political participation of Californios was also minimal in the state, although in the beginning their integration was more evident than in Texas. For example, out of forty-eight delegates, eight Mexican Californians were selected to participate in the state constitutional convention of 1849 when California joined the Union.

The constitutional convention was the last major political event in which Mexicans participated. The gold rush of 1849 attracted thousands of Anglos, which resulted in an even more imbalanced ratio of Mexicans to Anglos. In 1850 Mexicans were 15 percent of the population, but twenty years later that figure dropped to only 4 percent. Political and economic influence declined first in the north, the area that attracted the majority of Anglos, because of the gold-fields. The lack of political influence led to legislation contrary to Californio interests. For example, in 1851 the six southern counties where most Mexicans resided were taxed five times the rate of other local entities.

In 1855 so-called greaser laws were passed that prohibited bearbaiting, bullfights, and cockfights, clearly aimed at prohibiting the customs of the Californios. Vagrancy laws were passed, also aimed at Mexicans, because when a community wanted to force Mexicans out, these laws were applied selectively.

In New Mexico, Mexicans participated more fully in both the economy and in politics than in any other region. A major reason for this was that Latino New Mexicans remained a numerical majority until the turn of the century. Anglos came to quickly dominate the southeastern part of the state, but New Mexican *hispanos*, which was their preferred name, maintained control in the north around Santa Fe and Albuquerque. From 1850 to 1911 the Hispanos dominated most key political slots and controlled the territorial legislature until the 1890s. Ironically, one reason it took so long for the New Mexican territory to become a state was a reluctance among Anglo politicians in Washington, D.C., to allow a new state dominated by Mexicans.

In Arizona, which was part of the New Mexican territory until 1863, Mexicans maintained some political power in the area that was purchased under the Gadsden Treaty in 1853. This was especially true in and around Tucson, which became the territorial capital after Arizona separated from New Mexico. Political and economic cooperation was more evident between Anglos and Mexicans in this area because economic activity depended greatly on trade through the state of Sonora. With the coming of the railroads in the 1880s, however, the relationship between both groups became more strained as a new influx of Anglos who did not need to cooperate with Mexicans overwhelmed the older Anglo population. Politically, this demographic shift translated into lack of political power. The territorial seat was removed to Prescott, away from Mexicans, and eventually to Phoenix when Arizona became a state. Mexicans in southern Arizona retained a modicum of political power, and the few Mexican legislators in Arizona until the 1950s all came from that section.

Lack of protection for Mexicans in the Southwest was most obvious in the violation of property rights. While the Treaty of Guadalupe Hidalgo was vague regarding property, it did constitute the most definite commitment in the document. As more Anglos entered the Southwest and the area became more economically developed, land values rose and the thirst for land became more apparent. The system of keeping records of property claims differed between Mexico and the United States. As a consequence, proof of title became an immediate burden for Mexicans throughout the newly acquired territories.

To address the issue of property ownership, Congress passed the California Land Act of 1851 to facilitate legalization of land belonging to Californios prior to the takeover. Instead of helping the Californios resolve their property problems quickly, however, official procedures sometimes took years, forcing the ranchers to turn over huge tracts of land to the very lawyers who were adjudicating their cases. Then in 1862, the Homestead Act was passed in Congress, allowing squatters in the West to settle and claim vacant lands. In California, thousands converged on lands claimed by Mexicans, creating legal entanglements that were many times settled in favor of the squatters.

Many of the homesteaders were front men for speculators who took these free lands and held them for future use or sale.

In the New Mexico territory an even slower system, the surveyor of general claims office, was established in 1854. It took that office fifty years to settle just a few claims, and in the meantime many Mexicans in New Mexico were also defrauded of their land in grabs similar to those in California. During the 1890s, for example, as the Santa Fe Railroad was built from Kansas through the northern part of the territory, land speculators known as the Santa Fe Ring concocted ruses that divested hundreds of Latino landowners of their farms and ranches.

All in all, New Mexicans did not suffer the same degree of land usurpation as in other parts of the Southwest, but the acreage held by Latinos prior to the Mexican-American War declined considerably. In the final analysis, while the Treaty of Guadalupe Hidalgo did not precisely define the rights of Mexicans, it is clear that most of the guarantees were not upheld, and Mexicans in the Southwest declined considerably, economically and politically, during their experience with Anglo domination. But by the 1890s, considerable immigration from Mexico resulted in the swelling of Mexican communities throughout the Southwest, changing the character of Mexican life in the United States.

AFRICA AND THE MAKING OF SOCIETY IN CUBA AND PUERTO RICO

While New Spain evolved a society made up primarily of an Amerindian-Spanish race mixture, in the islands Africans and Europeans commingled with the few Amerindian survivors to form the Spanish Caribbean community. Sugarcane transformed the Caribbean region into a lucrative source of wealth for the Spaniards. But because the natives were too few for the Spaniards' purposes, the Europeans found another adequate source of labor in Africa. The slave trade had been started by the Portuguese in the fifteenth century, but it did not become profitable until the great plantation system developed in such American regions as Brazil, the British colonies in North America, and, of course, the Caribbean islands.

The source of enslaved captives in Africa was the western coast between the Senegal River to the north and Angola to the south. Africans were captured and sold to European traders, usually Portuguese, by slave hunters who many times were also Africans. Varying forms of slavery already existed among these ethnic groups where workers toiled in large-scale agricultural systems. Slaves were sought in this area, rather than in other African areas, because the people there already had some experience with systematic work demands.

The slaving expeditions in West Africa brought untold anguish to the Black Africans who were affected by the raids. Families were broken up as the young males (the most sought after) were torn from their homes. That was only the beginning of the suffering, however. In preparation for the odious voyage, captured Africans were first housed in overcrowded slave castles called *barranconas*, where thousands perished. In the trip across the Atlantic, thousands more died in the crowded hulls of the slave ships making their way either to the Caribbean islands or to Brazil, where these human beings were auctioned off and sold like cattle in huge markets.

In the Caribbean islands, this human chattel was sent to work the hundreds of plantations developed by colonists from the major European imperial powers. Not all slaves wound up on the plantation fields, however, as they were also sold to artisans as helpers or to the huge households of rich merchants within the plantations themselves. Although males were preferred as slaves, hundreds of thousands of females were also entered into the market. Women worked just as hard, and it was not lost on enslavers that by allowing their enslaved workers to bear children, even by promoting a family structure based on the new conditions encountered in the Caribbean, they could ensure that the offspring would be born into slavery—even if some of those offspring were the children of the White plantation owners and overseers. This perpetuated a valuable human commodity within their own domain.

In Cuba and Puerto Rico, under Spanish rule, slavery was legal until late into the nineteenth century.

But the growth of slavery everywhere in the Caribbean New World was intimately linked to the fortunes of sugarcane production. However, a large-scale sugar plantation system did not emerge in either Cuba or Puerto Rico until the end of the eighteenth century. Up to that point, independent peasant farmers, squatters who relied little on enslaved Africans, and peons on large haciendas predominated. Consequently, the development of slavery was slow. Between 1550 and 1650, the enslaved population only increased from 1,000 to 5,000.

But that does not mean that life was in any way promising for enslaved workers. Whenever they could, *cimarrones* (runaway slaves) ran away to Cuba's Orient province, creating scores of fortified communities called *palenques*. Indicative of the discontent of the Africans in Cuba was the persistence of the feared slave rebellions. For example, 300 rebelled on one plantation in 1727, killing practically all of the Whites, and one year later all the copper mines were closed off in Santiago because of uprisings in that province.

In the late eighteenth century, the African population began to rise rapidly. Following thirty years of warfare between the European imperial powers, the British occupied Cuba in 1763, ushering in an intensive period of economic development; thus, sugarcane production expanded dramatically. From the time the first enslaved African stepped foot on Cuba to 1770, 60,000 were introduced to the island. Then between 1770 and 1790 there was a striking increase in human traffic. At least 50,000 Africans arrived in those years alone. At the end of the century, a unique opportunity arose for investors in Cuban sugar production. The collapse of the Haitian sugar industry after rebels had ravaged that country in the 1790s led to an even larger number of enslaved people on the island. During this time, 30,000 French émigrés and their enslaved workers entered Cuba from Santo Domingo during a time of rising prosperity in sugar and coffee. An untold number also entered Puerto Rico's coastal areas.

The enslaved population continued to grow into the early nineteenth century, and by 1827 enslaved Africans accounted for about 40 percent of the Cuban population, which was over 700,000. By midcentury, the percentage of African-born slaves expanded to about 70 percent of the enslaved population, and for

Sugarcane production in Cuba in the late nineteenth century.

the first time, Blacks outnumbered Whites. In the 1850s the combination of free and enslaved Afro-Cubans made the Black population over 56 percent. According to one study, 550,000 enslaved humans were imported into Cuba between 1812 and 1865 in spite of the worldwide ban on the slave trade that was instituted by the British in the 1820s.

A remarkable expansion in Cuban sugar production accounted for the growth of human traffic in the nineteenth century. While many of the enslaved toiled on coffee *fincas* or haciendas or tobacco *vegas*, most worked on sugar *ingenios*. The percentage of Blacks, which throughout the colonial period had been among the smallest in the Caribbean, was now larger than anywhere else. Quite predictably, during the nineteenth century, slave rebellions became more common. In these, Whites were often killed, and retribution was quick and brutal. Suppression of the uprisings was often consummated by the indiscriminate execution of the enslaved, regardless of their involvement. Rebellions increased because of the larger number of newly arrived enslaved Africans with immediate memories of their lost freedom; they were resentful and less accepting of their lot.

Independence sentiment was delayed in Cuba because of this reliance on slavery by Whites. Lacking

was the diversity of dissatisfied classes that characterized other colonies in New Spain whose independence struggles started early in the nineteenth century. Island society reflected the dichotomy of the Black and White races more than ever. The Haitian example, where the independence movement was unleashed by the pent-up emotions of the enslaved, struck a familiar chord of fear among the White planter class.

The thirst for sugar in the United States also came to play in Cuba before the U.S. Civil War, as congressmen and senators, and eventually presidents, lobbied for the United States to purchase or otherwise take Cuba and admit it as a slave state. Spain rebuffed offers by two separate presidents to purchase Cuba, and the issue became moot after the Civil War when slavery was abolished. It is also noteworthy that a number of Cuban officers fought on the side of the Confederacy during the war.

The world was changing as industrialization and technological innovation required new markets and the use of more diverse amounts of raw materials. Cuba could not remain out of step for long in its use of outmoded methods in the production of sugar. In the second half of the nineteenth century, some Cuban and Spanish capitalists realized that Cuba's success in the impending order required diversified production and the use of wage labor, which was cheaper and more efficient than slavery. As a consequence, the sugar industry was modernized, made more competitive, and expanded. Foreign capital from the United States was largely responsible for the innovations, and the colonial economy passed increasingly into the hands of North Americans.

To meet the wage-labor demands, 125,000 Chinese were brought to Cuba between 1840 and 1870 to work as cane cutters, to build railroads in rural areas, and to serve as domestics in the cities. Also, the influx of European immigrants, primarily from Spain, increased during that period. Newly arrived Spaniards became concentrated in the retail trades and operated small general stores called *bodegas*. In the 1880s slavery was abolished by Spain in a gradual program that took eight years. The influx of new people in this period made Cuba more heterogeneous, leading to the social diversity that is so apparent today. Immigration to the United States before the revolution of 1959 was more reflective of this racial variety. But as Cuban flight from Communism increased, the outflow came more from the descendants of European emigrants.

In the nineteenth century the sale of humans did increase, but it was not as important in establishing a rural culture as was the case in Cuba. In many regions of Puerto Rico, a large class of rural poor Whites and persons with a mixed European, African, and Amerindian heritage dominated. Their way of life was strictly preindustrial. Country folk eked out a living as peasants, tenants on subsistence farms, or craftsmen in the towns and villages. This group came to be known as *jíbaros* (a South American word for "highlander" or "rustic") and remain to this day an identifiable group in both Puerto Rico and on the continentel United States.

As happened in Cuba in the first half of the 1800s, the importation of enslaved humans increased because of an expansion in sugar plantations. At the same time, however, foreign investment and immigration grew, and the mixed classes who comprised the rural peasants and working people were marginalized by an empowered planter class and a large-scale export agricultural system. But the influx of enslaved workers during the nineteenth century was larger than ever,

and African culture achieved a greater voice at the folk level, albeit mixing with a still-strong *jíbaro* expression.

In Puerto Rico there has not been an upheaval such as the Mexican Revolution of 1910 or the Cuban Revolution of 1959 that would have provoked large-scale immigration of the middle and upper classes to the United States. As a consequence, the character of Puerto Rican society in the United States is more reflective of Puerto Rico's diversity. Unlike the case of Cubans in Florida, in cities where Puerto Ricans have gone in large numbers, such as New York and Orlando, the fine blend of *jíbaro*/mestizo, African, and European cultures is evenly dispersed. In Mexican American society, on the other hand, the impact of the upper classes has been greatly mitigated by their wholesale return to Mexico after the revolution in the 1920s and during the Great Depression. Moreover, since the 1940s, the amplified immigrant stream that continues to arrive to this day is largely working class.

INDEPENDENCE OF CUBA AND PUERTO RICO

As is the case with Mexico, independence from Spain and the eventual subordination of the island economies to U.S. interests provide the foundation for understanding migration from Cuba and Puerto Rico. Along with the Philippines, Cuba and Puerto Rico remained the only major Spanish colonies that did not win their independence during the massive struggles that wracked the entire Spanish Empire in the early nineteenth century. In the second half of the century, both of these Caribbean holdings experienced conspiracies and rebellions, although efforts to finally obtain independence were not successful until 1898. In Cuba, a nationalist movement was vitalized in the latter part of the century as Spain's treatment of the colony became increasingly arbitrary. A crosscut of the Cuban classes became more and more resentful as the inept and corrupt colonial government imposed heavier taxes and, through censorship, restricted their freedom.

But much of the sentiment for liberty came from the sizable class of middle-class farmers and merchants who opposed slavery and desired to be free of the Spanish colonial tie. On the first issue, Madrid waffled, and although total freedom was eventually granted to the enslaved people, it came very slowly and much later than even in the United States. In October 1868 a group of Cuban rebels led by Carlos Manuel de Céspedes, a plantation owner who freed his slaves, took advantage of revolutionary fomentation in Spain itself and declared independence at Yara in the eastern portion of the island. This region had few slaves and was a hotbed of emancipation activity.

A provincial government headed by de Céspedes was established in Orient province, where Yara is located, and from there the movement obtained widespread support. The bloody Ten Years' War (1868–78) ensued, in which Spanish attempts to evict the rebels from the eastern half of Cuba were unsuccess-

ful. Guerrilla tactics used by the rebels stymied the efforts of Spanish troops, but neither side could really win a clear victory. The war came to an end when both rebels and Spaniards signed the Pact of El Zajón in 1878. The document promised amnesty for the insurgents and home rule; it also provided freedom for the slaves that fought on the side of the rebels.

Eventually, slavery was abolished, but Spain's failure to provide political reform provoked the Cubans to reconsider independence. In 1895 the poet and patriot José Martí opened the final battle for independence. Much of the planning for this insurrection was done in New York, where Martí had obtained Yankee support. But looming darkly behind the whole liberation cause were North American economic and political interests. Because of its proximity, Cuba had strategic value for the United States, but as long as it was

Carlos Manuel de Céspedes declared Cuban independence from Spain in 1868, beginning the Ten Years' War between Cuba and Spain, and became the first president of Cuba.

under Spain, many Americans thought that it would fall into the wrong hands. In the nineteenth century Americans tried to buy the island from Spain on several occasions. In 1869, taking advantage of the chaos of the Ten Years' War, the United States offered $100 million for the island but was rejected. So it was not surprising, when independence seemed more likely at the end of the nineteenth century, that U.S. officials pressed to influence the unfolding process.

The trajectory toward independence in Puerto Rico was not as conspicuous as in Cuba, but a strong sentiment for freedom emerged nonetheless. Puerto Rican nationalism was influenced by the same conditions that provoked the feeling in Cuba. While the planter classes expressed a wish for political autonomy from the mother country, they also wanted to maintain an economy based on slavery and peonage. Equivocal and confused about their desires, the *criollo* elites vacillated and were reluctant to assume the lead toward acquiring independence.

The nationalist movement was directed more by activists from the urban middle class and small farmers. This was especially true after 1850, when the Madrid government assumed a more mercantilistic stance. But in spite of high-tariff barriers that were designed to force Puerto Ricans to pay more for American-made goods so that Spanish merchandise would be cheaper, Spain's hold over the Spanish Caribbean steadily declined as it lost control over the sugar trade to the Americans. By 1870, 68 percent of Puerto Rican sugar products were marketed in the United States, and only 1 percent were sent to Spain. Exerting its imperial power, Madrid, by the time of independence, managed to regain 35 percent of the market and continued to provide the Caribbean colonies with some finished products. Still, U.S. merchants were buying 61 percent of all Puerto Rican exports while providing the lion's share of all industrial machinery necessary for processing sugarcane. Eventually, it became evident to the Puerto Ricans, as it did to the Cubans, that the link to the mother country was both intrusive and unnecessary.

The earliest indication of a strong united Puerto Rican nationalism goes back to 1867. On April 27, a mutiny among Spanish troops stationed on the island provoked the colonial governor, who was uneasy over

the possibility of freedom movements, to not only execute the mutineers but also round up and exile known sympathizers of independence. Among these was Ramón Emeterio Betances, who fled to New York, where he joined other like-minded Puerto Ricans and Cubans. On September 23, 1868, this group declared an abortive insurrection known as El Grito de Lares. Members of the *criollo* middle class, *jíbaros* and free Afro–Puerto Ricans who lived in the coffee-growing region of Lares were the main supporters of the effort. The poorly planned attempt was doomed from the outset, and Spain easily defeated the insurrectionists.

But the movement did not die with the failure of the Lares revolt. As in Cuba, Puerto Ricans remained dissatisfied with the mother country's feeble attempts to redress their accumulating grievances. Later in the century, such patriots as the intellectual José Julián Acosta and the young and untiring newspaper editor Luis Muñoz-Rivera were responsible for forcing major concessions from Spain. A covenant was signed in 1897 that granted to both Cuba and Puerto Rico autonomy and home rule.

But much of the movement for complete independence was already set in motion, and these gestures from Spain were too little, too late. Increasingly, a vital core of Puerto Rican conspirators joined their Cuban co-colonialists in a movement for freedom. But every leap toward freedom from Spain threw the revolutionaries into the American sphere of influence. When José Martí initiated the final battles for independence in 1895 in Cuba, much of his preparation was done in the United States. Martí had started his pro-independence party, the Cuban Revolutionary Party (PRC), in Tampa, Florida. Many of the patriots, such as Tomás Estrada Palma, the first president of independent Cuba, acquired U.S. citizenship while in exile and then returned to the island to join the insurgency. Tragically, the valiant efforts of these patriots involved them with the United States to such a degree that the final price was costly. In the end, Cuba and Puerto Rico traded one master for another.

American support quickly turned into outright confiscation of the Cuban and Puerto Rican rebel cause. President William McKinley, reflecting an American longing for a maritime empire, seized the opportunity given him by the explosion in Havana

Harbor of an American naval ship, the *Maine*, and declared war against Spain on April 28. Five months later Spain capitulated and signed the Treaty of Paris, transferring Cuba, Puerto Rico, and the Philippines to the United States. President McKinley quickly achieved the overseas realm that he wanted.

Cuba, unlike Puerto Rico, was allowed to become independent and promulgate a constitution, but hopes for true Cuban sovereignty were quickly dashed when Cuban politicians were pressured into including the Platt Amendment in their founding document. The provision allowed the United States to intervene militarily in Cuban affairs. The two neighboring Caribbean islands had much in common but had evolved separate cultural and ethnic identities. Overnight, both began an intimate, albeit antagonistic, relationship with the United States. Out of such closeness, migration to the mainland ensued.

EARLY MEXICAN IMMIGRATION TO THE UNITED STATES

Mexican immigration to the U.S. by the beginning of the twentieth century can be placed roughly in three categories. The first is migrants who were left outside the borders of a shrinking Mexico after 1836, 1848, and 1853 and the natives who, although not really migrants, were considered foreigners in their native land. The second category consists of migrants who continued entering and leaving the U.S. Southwest in a pre-established pattern that preceded the takeover. The third and most important group, in terms of the bigger picture of immigration, are Mexicans who arrived in response to the dramatically expanding need for laborers after the 1880s.

Three significant events occurred in Anglo-Mexican relations that set the stage for this immigration pattern. The Texas Rebellion (1836), the Mexican War (1848), and the Gadsden Purchase (1853) severed immense territorial lands—and the eighty thousand or so Mexicans who were living on them—from Mexico. These Spanish-speaking settlers were dispersed in sparsely settled areas throughout the lost territories.

In less than forty years, they had been subjects of Spain and citizens of Mexico and were now entering a new phase. The inhabitants were descendants of the Spanish-Mexican settlers who had migrated from the interior of Mexico and in many areas had pushed aside or conquered the Indigenous groups that occupied the land before them. Now they found themselves conquered and colonized, separated from their political and cultural roots by an invisible and, for a time, unpatrolled boundary line.

When the United States took over these territories, it acquired a Mexican population that was for all intents and purposes a continuation of Mexico's northern frontier. The inhabitants during the Mexican period had migrated freely back and forth across what was later to become a border. Movement made by parents, grandparents, brothers, uncles, and kin of all types meant that an extensive network of family ties existed in a region that was now politically divided. In southern Arizona, for example, thousands of Mexicans had abandoned their lands for Sonora during the independence period in the early nineteenth century, mostly because of a menacing increase in Amerindian depredations.

In spite of the changed political status, migration within the border region continued during the early occupation period, and immigrants were, for the most part, oblivious to the geopolitical distinctions that national governments made so carefully. Various factors stimulated this migration. In some cases economic inducements, such as the discovery of gold in California, provoked a massive outpouring of miners from Sonora and other parts of Mexico. They arrived before the influx of the Anglo forty-niners, and mining techniques introduced by these northern Mexican miners prevailed in the numerous mining centers of California during the heyday of the gold rush. After 1836 thousands of peons fled the large haciendas of northeast Mexico, seeking their freedom in South Texas; the border was much closer now.

In general, before 1870 there were only minimal economic inducements to Mexican immigration to the United States. Anglos who came after 1836 and 1848 interacted within the native Mexican economy through raising stock and some mining. Markets for southwestern products did expand during the early years of the Anglo takeover as as population growth throughout the territories demanded more foodstuffs. Mexicans in Texas, New Mexico, and California, however, had been trading with American interests in the East before the Texas rebellion and the Mexican border campaign. With the changeover to American rule, trade patterns were little changed, except that markets in the East for cattle hides, tallow, wool, and other stock-raising products widened and diversified. Furthermore, in New Mexico and Arizona a flourishing trade developed as the U.S. Army increased its efforts to subdue and destroy the nomadic Indian tribes. Provisions for troops and Indian reservations were channeled through private merchant houses in Santa Fe, Albuquerque, and Tucson.

Trade with Mexico, which before the nineteenth century had been the main source of external activity in all of the Southwest, continued after 1848, and many Mexicans entered the Southwest as transport workers or to act as agents for merchant houses in Monterrey, Mexico. During the American Civil War, when southern ports were blocked off by the Union Navy, cotton was transported through Texas to such Mexican ports as Tampico in order to ship the product to European markets. Moreover, Arizona ports of entry to Mexico served California exporters and importers as a gateway to the Mexican ports of Guaymas and Mazatlan for shipping to the United States east around the Cape of Good Hope and over the Isthmus of Panama.

First Through Train from HOUSTON, TEXAS, to NEW ORLEANS, LOUISIANA, upon the opening of MORGAN'S LOUISIANA AND TEXAS RAILROAD.
—Photographed by—
McCLURE & GORMLEY, of 131 Poydras Street, N. O.

After 1880, the railroad brought dramatic changes in the southwestern economy and stimulated Mexican immigration tremendously. Shown here is the first through train from Houston, Texas, to New Orleans, Louisiana, in 1880.

Initially, the labor needs of this slowly expanding economy were met by the resident population. Some immigration from Mexico, Europe, and the eastern United States provided the rest. Except for some cotton in Texas and gold and silver mining in other southwestern areas, there was little requirement for intensive labor use. After 1880, because of the railroad, dramatic changes in the southwestern economy stimulated Mexican immigration tremendously. Radical economic transformations that occurred not only in the Southwest but in Mexico as well dictated this later trend. By 1900 a railroad network integrated Texas, New Mexico, Arizona, and California with northern Mexico and parts of central and southern Mexico. The economic impact of the railroads soon drew Mexicans into the United States in a movement that dwarfed the influx of previous years. After the 1880s, then, the strong ties that previous *norteño* (northern) immigrants had to the Southwest and its native peoples diminished as railroads induced the migration of Mexicans whose roots were farther and farther from the border.

In northern Mexico, similar railroad building took place during the same years. The new railroads were financed by American interests, and, as in the American Southwest, the northern Mexican economy became linked to the crucial markets of the U.S. industrial basin in the Midwest and the Northeast. In northern Mexico an economic transformation resulted, and adjacent areas along both sides of the U.S.-Mexican border supported similar agriculture and mining interests that depended completely on the same railroad network to market their products.

The Southwest was still sparsely populated during this period of rapid economic growth. Thousands of Anglos and Europeans had come in before the railroad era, and even more came after trains revolutionized transportation. Initially, many were induced by the discovery of gold and silver, but more consistently they came as farmers, small-scale merchants, and clerks, and to work in other middle-sector positions. Many of them were squatters who slowly drew away the lands of the old Mexican elites. But a great many were middle-class entrepreneurs and agents of eastern companies who during the railroad era forcibly acquired millions of acres that had once belonged to wealthy Mexicans. It was these entrepreneurs who were responsible for the huge agribusiness and mining development in the Southwest. In the process it was discovered that the resident Mexican population was not sufficient to meet the growing labor needs. The poorer classes of Anglos did not compete with Mexicans because of the low wages offered in agriculture or because of the menial type of labor involved. Besides, many of the poorer Anglos were involved in their own endeavors on small farms and ranches.

In California, Chinese labor continued to be used after the building of the transcontinental railways from Northern California during the 1860s and the development of Southern California after the 1870s. In the 1880s the first Chinese exclusion acts were passed by Congress in response to nativist pressures, but surreptitious entry continued into the twentieth century. In other parts of the Southwest, a dependence on Mexican labor remained the only alternative. Since railroad building in most of Mexico had resulted from the same thrust that built the lines in the Southwest, workers from Mexico were used in the construction, and the same reserves were utilized within both political zones. European laborers were also used in the West, but only a small number filtered southwest of industrialized cities like Chicago and Kansas City.

Once Mexican immigrants were in the United States, they could, in many ways, identify with the Southwest, which at the turn of the century was still very Mexican. Nevertheless, the Mexican was an immigrant in every sense of the word. Unable to speak or understand English, the dominant language, they were subject to immigration laws and regulations and forced to adapt to a foreign pattern of racism and discrimination. The native Mexican American, while faced with similar problems, could benefit from lengthy exposure to the gringo to make the adaptations necessary for survival and to participate more within the system.

Among the immigrants themselves, adaptation and the difficulty of life in the United States varied. Much depended on their economic conditions when crossing the border, the ability to transport families, the type of labor they performed, the distance between origins in Mexico and ultimate destination in the United States, and the type of community they lived in once in the United States. Before the Mexican Revolution of 1910, because practically all immigrants came from the lower classes, poverty was an endemic problem. The only commodity that such immigrants could trade was their labor.

These newer immigrants tended to cluster around existing Mexican communities, and their cultures competed with and then mingled with the older *norteño*-Southwest societies. Distinctions were made among the Mexicans themselves, whenever the three groups were thrown together, and often a social order existed, with the central Mexican at the bottom.

Rapid economic expansion in the Southwest also meant that the settlement of Mexicans shifted beyond the original native Latino centers. Anglos and Mexicans were attracted to the numerous new communities that sprang up along the length of the railway lines in new agricultural sections and in the emerging mining districts. Here the Mexican *colonias* (colonies) were all new, made up of displaced Southwest natives and Mexican immigrants. Such communities were formed in cotton-based towns in Texas during the early 1900s, and the same was true of the countless communities in the sugarbeet-growing regions of Colorado and California and in the mines of Arizona and New Mexico.

By 1915 Mexicans could be found as far north as Chicago and Kansas City. Most were from west-central Mexico. Thus, when the United States demanded a greater amount of labor during World War I, it was the inhabitants of the cities and villages along the railroad lines in Mexico who already had exposure to the American North, particularly those from the Bajío region of Mexico, who were recruited. During the fifteen years or so following the start of the Mexican Revolution in 1910, a massive outpouring from Mexico greatly changed the demographic profile of Mexicans in the United States.

THE MEXICAN REVOLUTION AND IMMIGRATION TO THE UNITED STATES

The Mexican Revolution entailed a tremendous exodus of human beings fleeing political persecution, military impressment, depressed economic conditions, and simply the crossfire of violent events. The hard-fought struggles and their aftermath bred new social and economic conditions that drastically altered and disrupted Mexican society to the point that many people who would not have emigrated under their previous circumstances flocked to the United States in large numbers.

After Francisco I. Madero issued the Plan de San Luis Potosí in 1910, eventually hardly any region of Mexico was left untouched by the struggle that followed; almost every citizen and foreigner in the republic was affected. All in all, Mexicans endured twenty years of bloodshed. Many were caught up in the struggle because they believed the revolution was for the best. Others did not want the revolution because it was not in their interest. The majority simply did not understand it or could not relate to its limited goals. Many of the disaffected, finding their Mexico torn asunder, left.

Most refugees were from the lower and middle classes, but families like the Creels, the Terrazas of Chihuahua, and other wealthy *norteños* lived comfortably while in the United States, accompanied by their liquid assets, which were deposited in American banks along the border. It was not until 1915 that the flight of large numbers of refugees assumed massive proportions in the Bajío (west-central Mexico) and its environs during a time when not only the direct destruction of the battles, but also the economic side effects of war, served to expel people from Mexico. During the struggles in Mexico, World War I spurred growth in every sector of the U.S. economy, owing primarily to the nation's position as a supplier to warring factions in Europe. Labor requirements had never been so great, yet disruption in trans-Atlantic transportation during the war and utilization of potential European emigrants in opposing armies were beginning to hinder the influx of workers from traditional European sources. When the United States became directly involved, American laborers were drafted, and a vacuum was created in industry, agriculture, mining, and transportation. These sectors looked south of the border to meet demands for expanding labor requirements during a time when Mexico was experiencing one of its worst economic crises.

Obtaining easy access to Mexican labor during this time of duress in Mexico and labor scarcity in the Southwest proved to be more difficult than had been the case in previous years, however. In February, Congress, in response to nativist pressures, enacted the Immigration Act of 1917, imposing a literacy requirement and an eight-dollar head tax on all individual immigrants. The act was passed before the United States entered the war, apparently without considering the manpower shortages that the wartime economy could create. The bill was designed to curb an "undesirable" influx from southern and eastern Europe, an immigrant group characterized by immigration officials as being two-thirds illiterate. Nevertheless, the act ultimately inhibited immigration to the United States from Mexico. Some of the Mexican states, such as Michoacán, a source of large numbers of emigrants, had illiteracy rates as high as 85 percent. In addition, the eight-dollar head tax was prohibitive for most migrants, many of whom arrived at the border destitute. Legal immigration of Mexicans suffered a temporary setback that year.

Surreptitious entry continued, but initially the interests that needed Mexican labor wanted legal, free, and easy access to this valuable reserve to the south. As the summer harvests approached, agriculturists and related interest groups became desperate, and they pressured Congress to waive implementation of immigration laws in the case of Mexicans. During June, Congress complied, but the waiver was applicable only to agricultural workers, and there was so much red tape involved in meeting waiver requirements that eventually both the employers and Mexican workers preferred illegal entry. In essence, the general requirement of the 1917 act stimulated clandestine immigration. Unauthorized immigration intensified in later years after another act, in 1924, required that Mexicans add a ten-dollar visa fee to the already existing head tax, thus increasing the total that every immigrant paid to eighteen dollars. A lucrative trade emerged after 1917 in smuggling undocumented immigrants across the Rio Grande. It consisted mainly of ferrying large groups of Mexican laborers on rafts to the U.S. side.

If the 1917 act proved to be an obstacle to legal entry, agriculturalists and other interest groups were more frustrated by what seemed a worse threat to their steady supply of labor. In May 1917 the Selective Service Act became law. While Mexican citizens were not eligible for the draft in the United States unless they applied for their first naturalization papers, they were obliged to register with the local draft board, a requirement that Mexicans were loath to comply with for fear of being drafted. Besides, during this era, first-generation Mexican Americans were indistinguishable from many Mexican-born citizens. Consequently, nationals from Mexico were mistakenly drafted anyway.

The conscription problem was eventually resolved, and Mexican immigration resumed a normal flow. Mexicans by 1915 were also beginning to enter California in larger numbers. Asian labor had been heavily relied on in the past, but the Southern California agricultural sector had expanded tremendously since 1915, and Chinese workers no longer sufficed. Secretary of Labor William Wilson suggested in June 1917 that the waiver be extended to nonagricultural sectors, such as transportation. The years of rapid economic expansion brought about by U.S. involvement in World War I resulted in Mexican migration to geographic regions where they had previously never worked, in such sectors as oil fields, munitions factories, meat-packing plants, and steel mills. Hundreds of *colonias* expanded or were established anew in cities such as Los Angeles, Kansas City, Chicago, Phoenix, and Houston.

A lamentable side effect of the struggle was an increase in anti-Mexican prejudice. Americans resented and feared the revolution, which many times was brought to their doorstep at the border. The revolutionary Pancho Villa and his followers, for example, raided into American territory to obtain supplies, and on some occasions Americans were killed in these incursions. In 1914 President Woodrow Wilson ordered the invasion of Vera Cruz in an effort to depose Victoriano Huerta, a general who assassinated President Francisco Madero, the founder of the revolutionary movement, and took over Mexico. To get support from the American people for the invasion, however, Mexicans were cast as undisciplined and violent. By the 1920s Anglo-American opinion of Mexicans was lower than before the revolution, and these emotions were taken out on Mexicans living in the United States. Americans failed to see that brutality is part of any war, not just a trait manifested by Mexicans during this era. Indeed, strong parallels exist between the behavior of soldiers, both Union and Confederate, during the American Civil War.

THE "MEXICO LINDO" GENERATION

In the 1920s economic expansion continued, owing to commercial agriculture and large-scale mining activity. But in addition, the United States was experiencing an all-time-high economic expansion in manufacturing. Increasingly, Mexican labor was used in cities. At the same time, immigration increased to floodtide proportions, coming from farther south in central Mexico, including Jalisco, Guanajuato, Michoacán, and San Luis Potosí. With the new infusion of immigrants from areas so remote from the Southwest, Mexicans found few familiar surroundings in agricultural or mining towns and in cities like Houston, Dallas, and Chicago. Also in this period, the vast majority of persons living in the United States who were considered of Mexican origin were either born in Mexico or the children of immigrants; the original Mexican residents of the United States were considered "Americans."

During the Mexican Revolution, a sizable portion of the Mexican urban middle classes and elites, who were the critical core in Mexico imbued with nationalistic feelings, immigrated to the United States. They were the most important source of nationalism, expressed by the phrase "México Lindo," in addition to being the carriers of indigenismo (pride in the Amerindian heritage of Mexico) and other forms of patriotism.

Obviously, the maintenance of Mexican culture and the Spanish language was seen as the most necessary nationalist statement. The names given to their mutual aid societies, such as La Sociedad Benito Juárez, México Bello, and Sociedad Cuauhtemoc, to name a few, demonstrate the close allegiance to Mexico. During this time the self-identifier was "Mexicano/a" in Spanish and "Mexican" in English.

Finding work, setting up homes, building churches, and coping with a hostile reception from Anglos dominated the lives of Mexicans in the *colonias*. Segregation, police brutality, and general rejection drove home the need to coalesce and embrace unity. The badge of inferiority imposed by the Anglo provoked the immigrants to dispel negative stigma by forcefully demonstrating that Mexicans engaged in positive cultural activities. They believed that Mexican artistic and cultural contributions were as good as or better than those in Anglo America.

Another strong component of immigrant identity was a form of indigenismo, or the proud recognition of Mexico's pre-Columbian Indian ancestry. This ideology was deeply rooted in Mexican history and given profound expression by Mexican intellectuals and writers in the colonial period and throughout most of the nineteenth century. Understandably, the sentiment was carried to the *colonias* in the United States by immigrant leaders who deliberately maintained and projected this image. In this respect, reverence to Our Lady of Guadalupe, the Virgin Mother, who is considered to be an Indian, and the homage paid to Benito Juárez, also an Indian, are part of this tradition. Every major *colonia* in the United States had an organization named after Juárez and a Catholic church named Our Lady of Guadalupe. Religion served to provide more than a spiritual focus. It served to give a sense of purpose to the community, because it was the immigrants themselves who built and maintained the churches.

But in this early era the immigrants had to contend with intense police brutality, segregation, abuse in the workplace, and general rejection from the mainstream community. In the early part of the century El Congreso Mexicanista (the Mexican Congress) was held in Texas to implement a strategic plan to stem the tide of legal abuses and violence against Mexicans. The meeting was attended by representatives from Mexican communities across Texas, and although the lack of political power limited its success, the effort demonstrated that Mexicans were willing to defend themselves. It also served as model

> Finding work, setting up homes, building churches, and coping with a hostile reception from Anglos dominated the lives of Mexicans in the *colonias*.

By the early twentieth century, every major colonia in the United States had a Catholic church named Our Lady of Guada-lupe. The Shrine of Our Lady of Guadalupe pictured here is in Santa Fe, New Mexico.

for later political mobilization. In later years, many other organizations also strived to end abuses against Mexicans in the justice system, such as the Asamblea Mexicana, organized in Houston in 1925. Perhaps the most distressing abuse was the disproportionate execution of Mexicans in prisons throughout the United States; Mexicans spent much of their collective energy attempting to save condemned men. In many parts of the United States, Mexicans formed organizations, usually called La Liga Protectora Mexicana (the Mexican Protective League), that served to protect the legal rights of Mexicans. On several occasions, Mexican consuls met with the state governor or the board of pardons and paroles, usually accompanied by members of Mexican organiza-tions that had collected petitions with thousands of signatures pressing for clemency.

In 1921 a depression caused severe destitution among Mexicans who suddenly found themselves unemployed. The Mexican government, working through its consulate service, formed *comisiones honoríficas* (honorary commissions) to protect the rights of hundreds of thousands of Mexicans who found themselves stranded in many communities and unable to return home after prices for mining and agricultural products had collapsed. Thousands were repatriated with money provided by the Mexican government, but those who remained found themselves destitute until the economy recovered.

Recovery from the 1921 crisis was quick, and economic expansion throughout the 1920s went beyond the boom conditions precipitated by World War I. Mexicans were again in demand, and during this decade their influx dwarfed previous entries. Resistance to Mexican immigration was intense, however. The larger their numbers became in the United States, the more nativists thought Mexicans were a threat to cultural and racial integrity. But employers would not countenance any restriction of a valuable labor supply. Indeed, when the National Origins Quota Act passed in 1924 to curtail immigration, lobbyists representing agricultural and mining interests managed to persuade Congress not to include the Western Hemisphere. This ensured that the Mexican labor source would be protected. Nativists, such as Representative John C. Box of Texas, wanted to stop immigration from Mexico completely, but in the spirit of the prosperous decade, the desires of the powerful employers who needed Mexican labor were not overcome.

> By the mid-1930s it was apparent that a fusion of cultures was evolving.

During this period, a product of the heavy inflow was the appearance of many new *colonias* with familiar México Lindo institutions. The leadership promoted cohesion and unity more successfully when practically everyone was newly arrived, was segregated from the rest of the society, and was working and bringing in some money. They expected their stay in the United States to be temporary, although most stayed until their death. As the American-born children of those who remained grew older, slowly the elders' influence waned as younger family members began to adopt American ways and identify with the United States as their permanent home.

DEPRESSION, REPATRIATION, AND ACCULTURATION

The Great Depression altered the lives of everyone, and it also dramatically changed the evolution of the Mexican *colonias*. Mexicans who had been so desirable as workers in the previous decade became unwanted throughout the United States in the 1930s. From throughout the United States, thousands of Mexicans left, many times pressured by community authorities. But those who resisted repatriation were more rooted and, in most cases, had families with growing children. Indeed, during the decade, a generation grew up that had no memories of Mexico. Their only home had been the barrios in their immigrant communities.

A cultural shift became apparent in the early 1930s. The dominant immigrant posture of the 1920s gave way to "Mexican American" adaptation, which was characterized by assimilation of U.S. values and a less-faithful adherence to Mexican culture. By the mid-1930s it was apparent that a fusion of cultures was evolving. Cultural expression of Mexican Americans in this period was obviously influenced by Anglo society. Immigrant symbolism did not disappear in the 1930s, but the reinforcing influence from Mexico declined with the Depression-related hiatus in immigration. Ostensibly pure Mexican traditions were barely kept alive by the aging immigrants, who also were losing their influence over younger Mexican Americans born in the United States.

The México Lindo source of identity, then, however virulent it seemed in the initial *colonia*-building stage, did not survive the massive repatriation of Mexicans that had been provoked by the Great Depression. Repatriation, especially from the large cities, was massive and highly organized. This was especially true in Los Angeles and industrial cities in the Midwest, but thousands left from more rural communities as well. For those remaining in the United States, Americanization was seized upon by the new leadership through organizations such as the Latin American Club in cities like Phoenix and Houston and the Mexican American Political Club in East Chicago. These groups, of course, were intent on achieving political clout. Even the word "Mexican" seemed to be abandoned in this period, as the term "Latin American" attests. Besides, the leaders of these organizations were no longer immigrants who intended to return to Mexico. They consisted of a new and younger generation that was either born in the United States or very young upon arriving. Overall in the decade, significant alterations took place for the second-generation Mexican Americans who had been born or raised in the United States. Increasingly more graduated from high school, and their expectations from the larger society were more extensive. The depression of the 1930s subsided because of wartime spending, and by the end of the decade, thousands of young Mexican Americans had grown up in the United States exposed to the greater Anglo society through such New Deal agencies as the Civilian Conservation Corps and National Youth Administration, both designed to enroll young people and keep them off the streets during this era of massive unemployment.

WORLD WAR II AND THE MEXICAN AMERICAN GENERATION

When the United States entered World War II in 1941, Mexican Americans responded to the war effort enthusiastically. In spite of continuing discrimination, patriotism among Mexican Americans was intense as they felt like part of the United States. Unlike their parents, they had no direct ties to Mexico. Thousands joined their White and Black counterparts in all branches of the armed forces. Most Mexican women stayed behind, but many moved to California and other industrial areas in the boom years of the war and worked in places where Mexicans had never been allowed. The League of United Latin American Citizens (LULAC) spread throughout the United States in the 1940s, and thousands of Mexicans not serving in the military engaged in many "homefront" efforts, such as bond drives. After the war, Mexican Americans strove to achieve political power by making good use of their war record. Many Mexican American war veterans were motivated by the continued discrimination that greeted them after the war. In 1947 the American G.I. Forum was organized by Mexican American veterans in response to the denial of a funeral home in Three Rivers, Texas, to bury a Mexican American killed in the Pacific. The organization went on to become a leading advocate for civil rights. In

addition, many American Legion posts for Mexican Americans were founded by these same veterans.

Immigration to the United States had greatly decreased during the Great Depression, during which time a generation of Mexican Americans was greatly influenced by Anglo culture. Because few new immigrants came, much cultural reinforcement from Mexico was lost. When World War II ended, Mexican American G.I.s came back by the thousands to their barrios in cities and small towns alike. Many young people who had postponed wedding plans during the years of strife now married and had babies. These Mexican American soldiers came back more assertive, ready to take their place in a society that, by any reckoning, they had fought to preserve. After the war, hundreds of young, married Mexican American couples moved to the growing suburbs and were further acculturated.

In spite of acculturation, however, Mexican culture in the United States did not subside. The Bracero Program began in 1942 and was instrumental in reviving immigration to the United States during the war years, reinstating the crucial link to Mexico. The program, in which U.S. labor agents actually went to Mexico and recruited thousands of workers, was prompted by the wartime need for labor. The experienced braceros (manual laborers) inspired many others to immigrate on their own. Many of these contract laborers worked primarily in agricultural communities and in railroad camps until the program ended in 1965; however, some of them stayed, or they returned after having been delivered back to Mexico. Ever since then, the renewal of immigration has continued unabated.

But in spite of the resurgence of Mexican immigration and the persistence of Mexican cultural modes, Mexican Americans could not help but become Americanized in the milieu of the 1950s and 1960s, when more and more acquired educations in Anglo systems, lived in integrated suburbs, and were subjected to Anglo-American mass media, especially when television came into its own. It is difficult to measure just how pervasive Americanization was at that time. Certainly, the culture of Mexican Americans, fused as it was with the general society in the United States, had become more acceptable to the mainstream, although prejudice and rejection persisted. Nonetheless, Mexican Americans, more integrated into society, were more effective than ever in their efforts to break down obstacles to economic and social mobility. For example, in the 1950s and early 1960s segregation was abolished in Texas, Arizona, and many other communities, largely through the efforts of LULAC and the Alianza Hispano Americana (Latino American Alliance), another civil rights organization in the Southwest.

FROM CHICANOS TO LATINOS

The late 1960s and early 1970s was a time of intellectual foment and rebellion in the United States. Caught up in the mood, young Mexican Americans throughout the country sought a new identity while struggling for the same civil rights objectives of previous generations. This struggle became known as the Chicano movement. The word "Chicano" was elevated from its pejorative usage in the 1920s to denote lower-class Mexican immigrants and from its slang usage of the 1940s and 1950s to substitute for "Mexicano." It now symbolized the realization of a newfound and unique identity. Proudly, Chicanos proclaimed an Indo-Latino heritage, and they accused older Mexican Americans of pathologically denying their racial and ethnic reality because of an inferiority complex.

In the movement, an attempt was made to use some of the same symbols of their immigrant grandfathers, but with a few added touches. Tapping several intellectual traditions, movement leaders attempted

A "Chicano Power!" sign at California State University, Los Angeles, in 2006, created by M.E.Ch.A. (Movimiento Estudiantil Chicano de Aztlán), a political action organization created in California in the 1960s.

to define true ethnic character. Allusions were made to factual and mythical pasts used so often by *indigenistas* (indigenists). In addition, participants in the movement differed from the previous Mexican American generation in that they did not care whether they were accepted, and they rejected assimilation. Many of the images they construed reflected their alienation as they blended pachuco cultural modes, pinto (ex-convict) savvy, pre-Columbian motifs, and myth with a burning conviction that Chicanos were deliberately subordinated by a racist American society. Chicano student organizations sprang up throughout the nation, as did barrio groups such as the Brown Berets. Thousands of young Chicanos pledged their loyalty and time to such groups as the United Farm Workers Organizing Committee, which, under César Chávez, had been a great inspiration for Chicanos throughout the nation. An offshoot of both impulses, the farm worker and the student movement, was La Raza Unida party in Texas, an organization formed in 1968 to obtain control of community governments where Chicanos were in the majority.

In the 1990s the term "Latino," which has considerable longevity, took a special generic meaning referring to any person living in the United States who is of Hispanic ancestry. During the 1970s and 1980s the term "Hispanic" competed with "Latino" to be adopted across the country. Still today, many communities, especially in Texas, for instance, freely employ the terms "Hispanic" and *hispano* to signify peoples of Spanish-speaking heritage. But when individuals and families refer to themselves, their national origin always comes to the fore: Mexican, Puerto Rican, Cuban, Dominican, Salvadoran, Guatemalan, and so on. Furthermore, second- and third-generation Latinos often specify their U.S. breeding as Chicano, Mexican American, Nuyorican, Cuban American, and so on. The nomenclature game is complex, leading to endless debates that are often not based on history or accurate etymology. What is indisputable is that *hispano* is a short term for *hispanoamericano* and reflects a Western Hemispheric identity, or *mestizaje*, not an exclusively Spanish one. The nineteenth-century term *latinoamericano*, shortened to *latino*, originally signified anyone with a background in the Hispanophone, Lusophone, or Francophone Americas. However, during the last few decades it has come to signify membership in the broad and diverse group of Mexican-origin, Cuban-origin, Puerto Rican–origin … all the way down the list to Venezuelan-origin peoples residing in the United States today.

Today, immigration from Mexico, the Caribbean, and Central and South America continues unabated. Since the 1960s, a massive influx of Latino immigrants has reinforced Latino culture in the United States. All in all, the culture and identity of the individual groups change once they reside in the United States and have children, reflecting both inevitable generational fusion with Anglo society and the continuing influence of immigrants from throughout the Spanish-speaking world.

MIGRATION TO THE UNITED STATES FROM PUERTO RICO

Most of the two million Puerto Ricans who have trekked to the U.S. mainland in the twentieth century were entrants from the World War II or postwar era. And unlike the immigrant experience of Mexicans, or of Cubans before 1959, the vast majority of Puerto Ricans entered with little or no red tape. After 1917, the passage of the Jones Act granted Puerto Ricans citizenship, even if they were born on the island. Migration out of Puerto Rico was a defined trend quite a few years before the Spanish-American War, however, establishing a pattern that would be repeated and accelerated in the twentieth century.

The first migrant wave was stimulated by escalating economic relations between Puerto Rico and the United States. Exchange between both areas actually began in the eighteenth century but did not achieve large proportions until the second half of the nineteenth century. Still a colony of Spain, however, the island was subjected to the mother country's mercantilistic hold, thus trade was clandestine. For Puerto Rican planters and Yankee merchants, the exchange of sugar and molasses produced on the island for American goods that were cheaper than those from Spain was mutually satisfying. The chain of smuggling activity that led to the first Anglo incursions into Texas and California was, significantly, part of this very same process. The economic contact with North Americans eventually resulted in the divestment of Texas, New Mexico, and California from Mexico. A similar fate was in store for Puerto Rico and Cuba.

In the early nineteenth century the economic relationship was sufficiently mature for Cuban and Puerto Rican traders to found a benevolent society in New York to serve merchants and their families from both island colonies. But economic ties were not the only attraction in the United States for Puerto Ricans and Cubans. Many also found in the northern colossus a haven for plotting against Spain. From the time of El Grito de Lares, an insurrection in 1868, to the time Puerto Rican exiles formed part of the Cuban Rev-

olutionary Party's governing board at the end of the century, hundreds traveled to the mainland. Staying for years, some sent for families and found employment to sustain themselves. While most of the first exiles were from the *criollo* middle classes, eventually skilled artisans and laborers, all dissatisfied with Spain's rule, joined their compatriots in New York.

Large-scale immigration, however, is linked more to structural changes in the Puerto Rican economy during the course of the latter nineteenth century than any other condition. The freeing of slaves in the 1870s and the rise of coffee as a significant competitor of sugar created new land-tenure systems and more fluid labor conditions. As in Mexico during the regime of Porfirio Díaz, such radical changes disrupted the

A coffee and banana farm in Adjuntas, Puerto Rico. The freeing of slaves in the 1870s and the rise of coffee as a significant competitor of sugar created new land-tenure systems and more fluid labor conditions on the island.

fabric of rural life, forcing Puerto Ricans into day agricultural labor or into the urban centers like San Juan. The population also increased dramatically in the course of the nineteenth century, from 583,000 in 1860 to one million in 1900. Meanwhile the labor market was not developing at the same rate. As a consequence, many of the unemployed decided to cast their lot with contractors who sought agricultural workers in other regions of the Caribbean. Eventually others found their way to the United States.

Hastening the process of migration to the United States was the acquisition of Puerto Rico after the Spanish-American War. In May 1898, Spanish fortifications in San Juan were bombarded by the U.S. Navy while U.S. Army troops invaded the rest of the island to ferret out the Spaniards. Cheering crowds, longing for their independence, enthusiastically welcomed the U.S. forces entering Ponce under General Nelson Miles. Little did they know that soon they would trade the sovereignty of Spain for the tutelage of the United States. Quickly, a military government was established for Puerto Rico under General Guy V. Henry. But the transition was negotiated not with Spain but with Puerto Ricans, led by Luis Muñoz-Rivera. Muñoz had assumed the leadership of the home-rule government granted by the Spanish Crown just before the occupation by the United States, and now he had to deal with another foreign interloper.

A quasi republic under U.S. dominance was established by the Foraker Act in 1900. It created a lower house with thirty-five members, but the highest-ranking officials had to be appointed by the president of the United States. In essence, there would have been more self-direction under the autonomy agreement reached with Spain right before the American takeover. Muñoz-Rivera continued to serve his people as a politician, however, as an organizer of the Federalist Party and as commissioner to the United States Congress from the protectorate. To the dismay of Puerto Ricans, this position did not carry very much power.

In spite of the victory of the Jones Act, Puerto Rico was quickly deluged by American economic interests. Absentee landlords built large, modern sugar plantations that wiped out even more preindustrial subsistence farming than was the case during the last years of the Spanish period. Even coffee production, in which thousands of workers had been employed, declined as the capital-intensive sugar plantations and refineries covered much of the island. In the towns and cities, artisans such as independent shoemakers, carpenters, and other craftsmen found their livelihoods abolished by manufactured commodities produced in the United States.

To be sure, as a result of the American intervention, schools, hospitals, and public projects were built. This development, designed to improve life on the island, also paved the way for the new American investors and hastened the end of a way of life on which most Puerto Ricans depended for survival. Additionally, jobs that employed many women in tobacco factories and domestic service all declined. As the twentieth century progressed, island workers were marginalized and reduced to part-time miscellaneous work, which in Puerto Rico is known as *chiripeo*. Unemployment and underemployment created even greater pressure to leave Puerto Rico.

In the early part of the century, Hawaii's sugar industry was in need of experienced workers, and a few thousand Puerto Ricans were recruited. First they traveled to New Orleans by ship, then by train to San Francisco, and then by water again for the last leg of the journey. Small *colonias* emerged in both San Francisco and New Orleans because some workers decided not to make the full trip and remained at these debarkation points. Most of the island people migrated to the eastern seaboard of the United States, however. In 1910, according to census figures, 1,513 Puerto Ricans were living on the mainland, two-thirds in New York. Like Mexicans, their fellow Latinos in the Southwest, Puerto Ricans continued to arrive during World War I and the prosperous 1920s when jobs were plentiful.

U.S. immigration policy also influenced the pattern of migration from Puerto Rico. Two national origin quota acts designed to curtail immigration from eastern and southern Europe and Asia were passed in 1921 and 1924. With fewer workers coming in from these areas, a labor shortage ensued. The Western Hemisphere was not included in the quota policy, however, so employers turned there for labor. Mexico became a major source of workers, as did Puerto

Rico. It was easier for recruiters to target Puerto Ricans because they could travel freely to the continent as citizens. By 1930 there were approximately fifty-three thousand living in various North American communities, although most were in New York City. There, they concentrated in Brooklyn, the Bronx, and East Harlem. As their numbers increased in later years, these barrios remained the core areas of first arrival.

Early Settlement of Puerto Ricans in the United States

The establishment of Puerto Rican *colonias* was similar to that of the Mexican immigrant *colonias*, characterized earlier as the México Lindo phase of the Mexican American experience. As Puerto Ricans first arrived on the mainland, they looked back to their island origins for identity. Although Puerto Rico, unlike Mexico, was not an independent nation, the vital nationalism pervading the island during the rise of independent sentiment was tapped by newcomers to the United States looking for a source of ethnic consciousness. In the quest for roots during the Puerto Rican struggle for independence from Spain, the Indigenous name of the island, Borinquen, was revived. Immigrants, in their new environment, used *Borinquen querido* (beloved Borinquen) to refer to a homeland to which they felt closer once they had left it. When the United States took over the island, love and identification with their roots increased even more, and many Puerto Ricans felt the U.S. occupation was as a continuation of the colonial experience. In fact, a strong movement for independence from the United States developed in the early twentieth century and eventually erupted into acts of violence in the 1950s; however, activists throughout the century were often repressed by Puerto Rican and even U.S. authorities such as the Federal Bureau of Investigation.

The Spanish language, perpetuated through a barrage of newspapers, music, radio, and theater, also solidified Borinquen kindredness and allowed Puerto Ricans to identify with other Latinos in New York, such as Cubans, Dominicans, Venzuelans, and Spaniards.

The Catholic religion also served as a cohesive ingredient. As it did for Mexicans in Mexico, Catholi-cism in Puerto Rico took a unique shape according to the exigencies of local island society. On the mainland, the particular features of Puerto Rican worship served as an additional focus, bringing the islanders together in a common ceremony. Still, it was mainly in New York where Catholic churches existed that catered primarily to Puerto Ricans, although other Spanish-speakers also attended. Significantly, language affinity was perpetuated in these religious institutions as well. Also, there were Catholic lay groups, such as the Caballeros de San Juan (Knights of St. John), that played many socio-religious functions in the community similar to the Knights of Columbus. What distinguished some Puerto Rican religious practices from those of Mexicans and others, however, was the cult of the Siete Potencias Africanas (Seven African Powers), a sychretic of popular African beliefs and Catholicism.

Formal multipurpose organizations and clubs were probably the most important vehicle for cohesion, and they also served to make Puerto Rican settlement more visible in the city. The most common associations were the *hermandades* (brotherhoods). These societies, which could be traced to emancipation groups in the nineteenth century, provided mutual aid and intensified ethnic nationalism. Attending to primordial needs of the community, the brotherhoods appeared very quickly after the arrival of Puerto Ricans on the mainland. Additionally, merchant organizations and groups associated with labor unions also proliferated.

Political activity was also apparent during the initial building stages of the *colonias*. Associated with the desire for independence back home, such groups as the Club Borinquen, through such periodical organs as *Alma Boricua* (Puerto Rican Soul) and *El Machete Criollo* (The Criollo Machete), had as their main agenda freedom from colonial rule. But because throughout most of the twentieth century Puerto Ricans were citizens before they set out from their homeland, they were able to participate much more than Mexican immigrants in American electoral politics. Usually associating with the Democratic Party, but not always, they organized political groups and joined the ethnic machines prevalent in eastern cities as early as 1918. This of course was one year after the Jones Act granted Puerto Ricans citizenship. In the 1920s, La Liga Puertorriquena (the Puerto Rican League), an

A monument dedicated to Puerto Rican composer Rafael Hernández, in the city of Puebla, Mexico.

organization made up primarily of community associations, became an unabashed supporter of the Democratic Party.

As was the case in the Mexican *colonias* in the United States, Puerto Rican businessmen perpetuated ethnic bonds by providing Caribbean food, barbershops, religious relics, and—very important—Latin records and the phonographs to play them. Music and theater were two of the most important exponents of Puerto Rican solidarity, and by the 1930s such theaters as El Teatro Hispano in New York featured not only Spanish-language drama but also musical groups. Puerto Ricans pursued their penchant for music at the family level as well. Practically every gathering, whether it was a baptism, wedding, or coming-out party, had the obligatory singing trio of two guitar players and a maraca player. The music itself intensified the link with the homeland and defined Puerto Ricans' experience as immigrants. Rafael Hernández, a trained composer and owner of a music store in New York, wrote numerous songs that embodied the spirit of this genre. Hernández's most famous piece is "Lamento Borincano" (Borinquen Lament), which narrates the plight of the poor migrant who has to leave his homeland during economic crisis. The song, like the Mexican "Canción Mixteca" (Mixteca Song), was a poignant but romantic reminder of the beauty and rural simplicity of the homeland.

As happened with Mexican immigrants during the Great Depression, there was a reverse migration. Between 1930 and 1934, probably 20 percent of the Puerto Ricans living in the United States went back to the island, although they were not coerced to the same degree as Mexicans to return home. Those who could hold on to their jobs, primarily in service sectors of New York and other eastern cities, became acculturated more to life in the United States. Moreover, the U.S. cities in which Puerto Ricans lived had a vital urban life that exerted a strong influence on growing families.

Post–World War II Puerto Ricans in the United States

The most massive migration of Puerto Ricans, almost two million, occurred after World War II. While the wartime Bracero Program brought over 100,000 Mexicans to work in the labor-scarce economy of the war period, Puerto Ricans did not start immigrating in large numbers until the postwar boom era. They came in response to a classical push-pull phenomenon. Simply put, wages were higher and employment was more plentiful than on the island. Operation Boot Strap, a strategy designed to develop Puerto Rico economically, resulted in altering the employment structure, as had the modernization of the sugar industry earlier in the century. The project was the brainchild of the popular governor Luis Muñoz Marín, the son of nationalist patriot Luis Muñoz-Rivera. The plan emphasized investment, primarily American, in light industry and manufacturing. To a large degree, the process did provide more technical employment for some Puerto Ricans. But as investors turned away from sugar production, agricultural employment declined, and Operation Boot Strap did not adequately provide replacement jobs. Then in the 1960s, petrochemical plants and refineries, activities that required even less labor than light industry, pervaded much of the economy. The net result was inevitable: more migration.

As their numbers increased on the mainland, Puerto Ricans transcended their New York home, moving to textile mill towns in Rhode Island and Connecticut, factories in Chicago, and the steel mills of Pennsylvania, Ohio, and Indiana. The most remarkable feature of the new immigration was that it was airbound. The large volume of passengers leaving Puerto Rico soon drove the price of fares down and gave opportunity to new airlines, which pressed sur-

plus World War II cargo planes into service. By 1947 more than twenty airlines provided service between San Juan and Miami and San Juan and New York. In the 1950s Puerto Ricans were also landing in New Jersey cities and paid, on average, forty dollars for a one-way ticket.

The newer arrivals, like their Mexican counterparts in Los Angeles and Chicago, crowded into large barrios in New York and other eastern cities. The cold weather in the Northeast was inhospitable and almost unbearable for the hundreds of thousands who had left their tropical island. Adaptation in this environment was very difficult, indeed. What is abundantly clear, and here there are some very close parallels to the Mexican American experience during the

This metal Puerto Rican flag stands at Humboldt Park in Chicago, Illinois. Chicago holds the third-largest concentration of Puerto Ricans in the United States, after New York City and Philadelphia.

postwar period, is that early Puerto Rican immigrants built a foundation of organizations and institutions that made life more bearable for later arrivals.

Many second-generation Puerto Ricans acquired some social mobility within the society to which their parents had migrated before the war, and in some cases these first-generation parents were already professionals upon arriving. For the most part, however, prewar communities that cushioned the shock for the immigrants were strongly working-class in structure, very much like those of Mexican Americans. Unlike Mexican Americans, second-generation Puerto Ricans in the 1930s did not coalesce into organizations like the League of United Latin American Citizens, which was started in Texas in 1929 by frustrated Mexican Americans who found practically every avenue to opportunity in the United States blocked. Perhaps for Puerto Ricans in the United States before the 1950s, segregation was not as intense as it was for Mexicans in the Southwest, a problem that was particularly acute in Texas.

The third-largest concentration of Puerto Ricans, after New York City and Philadelphia, sprang up in the Chicago area. The birth of the Chicago *colonias* dates to World War II. Today, approximately 200,000 live in the city proper, and many thousands more in Gary and East Chicago, Indiana, and Milwaukee. One of the most important organizations in the early formation of the *colonias* was the Caballeros de San Juan (Knights of St. John). Its main function was to provide leadership and religious values in the Puerto Rican community. Other groups known as *hermandades* emerged in the 1950s and 1960s and were similar to the ones formed in New York in the early 1900s. Religion continued to serve as a focal point of the community, and Puerto Ricans identified strongly with the folk level of worship, as did Mexican immigrants. In fact, they shared, in an amicable arrangement, Our Lady of Guadalupe churches in both South Chicago and in East Chicago with Mexicans. As more and more Puerto Ricans committed to remaining on the mainland during the 1950s and 1960s, they encountered a great amount of rejection, but at the same time they demonstrated a growing concern for social and economic mobility. Their early employment pattern consisted of menial jobs in the service sector of the Chicago economy and in light factory work—in essence, low-paying work. And because of housing discrimination, Puerto Ricans were relegated to low-rent but overcrowded housing. Exacerbating these grievances were inequities in the courts and a persistent pattern of police brutality in the barrio.

To face that challenge they resorted, as did Mexican Americans during this same period, to self-help and civil rights organizations. Like Mexican Americans, thousands of Puerto Ricans served in World War II and the Korean conflict. Because many of these soldiers left directly from the island, before they could speak English, the military became an educational experience. Upon being discharged, many opted to remain on the continent, where economic opportunity seemed to beckon. But even for former soldiers, there were still many obstacles that had to be overcome to achieve any kind of equality.

The emergence of the Puerto Rican Forum in New York in the mid-1950s demonstrated a clear departure from the *Borinquen querido* organizations of the 1930s and 1940s that defined their identity in terms of political and cultural links to the island. The forum proposed an agenda to eliminate problems associated with urban poverty. In 1961 Aspira (Aspire) was founded to promote the education of youth by raising public and private sector funds. Clearly, both of these organizations were similar to the Mexican American organizations in the Southwest during the same period. Aspira, more than the Puerto Rican Forum, acquired a national following, serving Puerto Ricans wherever they lived in large numbers.

But when these organizations did not seem to alleviate the frustrations and despair that were common in many barrios, the politics of passion broke out. During this time, the rise of militant organizations that rejected the orientation of earlier groups emerged. As the Chicano and Black pride movements pervaded the consciousness of their respective communities, a similar voice was heard in the Puerto Rican barrios throughout the country. Foremost among the new militants were the Young Lords, a grassroots youth group that was similar to the Black Panthers in the Black community and the Brown Berets in the Chicano. They promoted Borinquen pride and put forth an agenda to change poverty-stricken neighborhoods. In both New York and Chicago, the Young Lords promoted neighborhood improvements using tactics such as sit-ins in service agencies and churches.

Damage is evident in the community of El Maní in Mayagüez, Puerto Rico, immediately after Hurricane Maria in September 2017.

In the twenty-first century, Puerto Rican immigration has intensified again principally because of acts of nature and imperfect human response to them. Puerto Rico had the misfortune to receive direct hits from two category 5 hurricanes, Irma and María, in 2017. The devastation to life and property was immense, virtually leveling thousands of buildings and even the forestry in Puerto Rico, leaving people without electricity, communications, water, and services for months. The effects of the devastation and interruption to life were so great that they will be felt for decades to come, especially because the hurricanes hit when the Puerto Rican government was on the verge of bankruptcy. What made the situation worse was the failure to respond in a timely fashion by U.S. departments, especially the Federal Emergency Management Agency (FEMA), and President Donald Trump's lack of concern for the Puerto Rican people; even today many Americans do not know that Puerto Rico is a colony of the United States and that Puerto Ricans are Americans. The disruption of the economy and the plunging conditions of life on the island con-

sequently led to a massive outmigration of Puerto Ricans to the continent. The island lost 4.3 percent of its population from 2017 to the end of 2018, thus losing about 143,000 residents. The state receiving the greatest influx of Puerto Ricans was Florida, whose Boricua (Puerto Rican) population grew to 1,187,437 in 2018. However, considerable numbers of Puerto Ricans also built up communities in Texas and Arizona, far from their largest concentrations in New York, New Jersey, Pennsylvania, and Chicago.

Despite hurricanes and economic woes, Puerto Ricans continue their movement back and forth, and such proximity keeps the fervor of their identity alive. Puerto Rico's status vis-à-vis the United States is still uncertain. In 1953 the island's capacity was upgraded from its protectorate status to commonwealth, a change that had the support of many Puerto Ricans. Today, given the disastrous hurricanes and their aftermath, many Puerto Ricans feel they were treated unfairly because they do not have the benefits and rights of statehood. Whereas in the past they were undecided between maintaining the commonwealth status quo and becoming a state—and meanwhile various groups militated for independence—there is a general feeling that eventually, Puerto Ricans will pursue statehood. While independence has been an idealistic cause and the subject of much song, literature, and conflict, it would eliminate the ability of Puerto Ricans to enter and leave the continent freely. Probably for that reason alone, many who have families scattered on both the island and the mainland oppose such a status.

Puerto Ricans are, next to Mexican Americans, the largest Latino group in the United States and will continue to play an important role in the evolution of the rubric Latino ethnicity that emerged in the 1980s and is pervading the United States at the present time. Whatever the future brings in terms of the continent-island political link, the millions of Puerto Ricans who came to the mainland in the course of the last two centuries have already left their mark.

EARLY CUBAN IMMIGRATION TO THE UNITED STATES

Large-scale Cuban immigration to the United States occurred much more recently than that from either Puerto Rico or Mexico. In fact, over one million Cubans have entered the country since the Cuban Revolution of 1959. But like those of Puerto Ricans, Cuban communities in the United States can be traced back to the nineteenth century. From the outset, Florida, because of its proximity to the island and its Latino past, has been the destination of practically all Cubans. Each wave, starting with the first one in the 1860s, has many similar characteristics. A feature that distinguishes Cuban immigration from Mexican and Puerto Rican immigration is that Cubans have come in similar proportions from the middle class and the working class. As has been indicated, most immigrants from Mexico and Puerto Rico have been from the working class.

As early as the first major independence attempt in 1868, Cubans left for Europe and the United States in sizable numbers. At least 100,000 had left by 1869,

both as political refugees and in search of better economic conditions. The wealthier émigrés fled to Europe to live in relative luxury, and middle-class merchants and professionals went to cities on the U.S. East Coast, such as New York. But the majority were workers who crossed the ninety miles or so to Florida. Cuban cigar manufacturers in Florida that had been operating in Key West since the 1830s eagerly welcomed the new arrivals for their factories. Key West was ideal for cigar making because of its access to the tobacco plantations of Cuba. But more important, Cuban cigar makers, such as the Spaniard Vicente Martínez Ybor, abandoned their Cuban operations and relocated to Florida, where they would not be as affected by Spanish mercantilistic policies. By the 1870s Key West had become practically a Cuban town.

The Cuban community in the Florida town soon manifested strong ethnic solidarity, made even stronger by the affinity they felt for the Cubans fighting for independence back in their island home. Revolutionary clubs were formed to raise funds for the cause and to help such exiles as Carlos Manuel de Céspedes, who were organizing support in New York in the 1860s. A few years before he launched the 1895 independence bid, Jose Martí often visited Key West and Tampa, which became an even larger cigar-making center, and considered the Florida towns' Cuban communities a key source of support for the cause of independence.

Once they established a base, Cubans became involved in local American politics. By 1875 there were over one thousand Cubans registered to vote in Monroe County, where Key West is located. The city's first mayor, who had the same given name as his father, was the son of Carlos Manuel de Céspedes, the hero of the Ten Years' War. In 1885, following labor problems in Key West, the manufacturer Martínez Ybor moved his operations to an area east of Tampa. The new development was named Ybor City, and soon other cigar manufactures operated in the new complex. By 1900 there were approximately 100 cigar-making factories in Tampa. Tampa became the center of cigar making in Florida. As in Key West, ethnic solidarity was bonded by the commitment to Cuban independence. Consequently, class differences were blurred as both wealthy owners and workers saw themselves supporting the same sacred cause. Other

Cuban communities in Florida, smaller than the Key West and Tampa enclaves, also supported the independence movement, providing the exile aggregation with strong intra-ethnic links throughout the state. Racial differences between the White and Black Cubans tested the ability to bond, however. The tension became worse in Florida when Jim Crow laws separated the races, and Cuban Blacks were forced to form their own institutions.

When Cuba was free of Spain, many exiles went back, but for many who had set roots in their respective émigré communities and who had children growing up in the United States, returning was difficult. Significantly, the Cuban presence in Florida during the last half of the nineteenth century was marked by many accomplishments. The first labor movements were Cuban, many businesses were operated and owned by Cubans, bilingual education received an impetus in the state, and, in cities like Key West and Tampa, Cubans were responsible for many improvements in city services and civic culture.

As Cuban political and economic influence increased in the nineteenth century, the Cubans played an increasingly more important role in U.S. policy toward the Spanish colonies in the Caribbean. But while helping the cause of independence, U.S. politicians also wanted to control a Cuba that one day would be free of Spanish dominance. Just as the struggle for Cuban independence had resulted in chaotic conditions leading to emigration, domination by Americans in the twentieth century fostered economic and political tensions that also provoked exile and emigration.

The Florida enclaves established by earlier immigrants served the Cubans who continued to arrive in Florida during the first fifty years of the twentieth century. Many left Cuba because of continued political turmoil on the island. In the 1920s, for example, a small number of young intellectuals moved to Miami to escape the repressive policies of Gerardo Machado and to plot against him. A dictator who ruled Cuba with the blessing of the United States, Machado was finally overthrown by a worker and student coalition in 1933. His demise was precipitated by the collapse of the U.S. economy, on which Cuba was completely dependent. He and his cronies, then, like countless others before them, also sought asylum in Florida.

Since Cuba did not really achieve political peace after Machado's ouster, Miami, as well as other Florida communities, continued to be a refuge for Cubans who were not welcome in Cuba by the politicians in power.

THE REVOLUTION OF FIDEL CASTRO AND CUBAN IMMIGRATION

It was for political reasons as well that the most dramatic exodus out of Cuba began after 1959. That year, Fidel Castro made his triumphant entry into Havana after he and his revolutionaries had defeated the brutal and repressive regime of Fulgencio Batista, a dictator who had been deeply involved in Cuban politics since the 1930s. Batista had become perhaps the most astute opportunist in the history of Cuba, and he returned Cuba to levels of corruption not seen since the Machado years. But at least in this period, he seemed content to allow democracy to take its course by allowing elections. Two irresolute and corrupt administrations followed Batista's in 1944 and 1948, dashing any hopes that these new leaders would bring political stability and honesty to the troubled island republic. Consequently, many Cubans became disillusioned with the promises of democracy. Then in 1952 Batista seized power again, this time as an arrogant dictator. Batista then took Cuba to new heights of repression and corruption.

For much of this time, Batista had the support of the United States. Ever since Cuba's independence, Americans had remained vigilant about political events on the island. While policy toward Cuba followed the distinct requirements of the various U.S. administrations, both Republican and Democrat, the main course of foreign policy was to protect the extensive investments held by Americans in Cuba. The Platt Amendment allowed for intervention in Cuba whenever it seemed necessary to an American president. Indeed, before the 1920s, U.S. troops were sent three times to Cuba to intervene in internal affairs.

In the opinion of many Cubans, the United States had blatantly held Cuba as an economic and political colony. Even though the hated Platt Amend-

In an image from Cuban currency, Fidel Castro and rebel soldiers enter Havana on January 8, 1959. Castro's ascent ousted the dictator Fulgencio Batista, but his own administration prompted waves of emigration from Cuba to the United States.

ment was abrogated in 1934, it was apparent that Americans, during Batista's last rule in the 1950s, controlled most of the economy and much of the political process. By the time a young lawyer named Fidel Castro initiated guerrilla warfare against Batista, the former sergeant's feral methods of running his country began to alienate even the most cynical of American supporters. Thus, when Castro came to power in February 1959, his 26th of July Movement did not meet too much resistance from the United States, and at home he acquired a wide and popular following.

To Washington officials during the presidency of Dwight D. Eisenhower, Castro turned out to be more than what they bargained for, however. The young revolutionary exhibited an eclectic ideology, but it was clear that the new government was no longer going to permit American dominance, a stance that quickly alienated the Eisenhower administration. Another position soon embraced by Castro involved extensive land reform and radical restructuring of the economy. Very quickly, many of those affected, such as landowners and other members of the upper classes, turned against the revolution. Castro, to protect his fledgling movement, repressed those who re-

sisted, and soon thousands of the disaffected left for the United States in a time-honored tradition established during the many previous shake-ups.

Increasingly, Castro adopted socialistic ideas and turned to the Cuban Communist Party for support, but not before the Eisenhower administration broke off relations with his revolutionary government. Eventually, the Soviet Union pledged its support to Castro, while the American government initiated a plan to welcome refugees. Eisenhower's motives to allow disaffected Cubans to enter the United States unencumbered were largely political. The 1950s were characterized by a Cold War mentality in which the Soviet Union and the United States waged an intense propaganda campaign for world prominence and acceptance. The flight of refugees was correctly anticipated by American officials to be middle class and essential to Cuba's economic well-being. Thus, their escape would deprive Cuba of technical and professional skills, serve as a propaganda victory against Communism, and, by extension, deliver a blow to the Soviet Union's world prestige. But the Eisenhower administration projected another role for the exiles. Considering the history of discontented Cubans using the United States as a mustering point for insurgency against governments on the island, American officials foresaw the potential for a repetition with the latest wave of arrivals.

With the election of John F. Kennedy to the U.S. presidency, relations between the two countries did not improve. President Eisenhower had encouraged Cuban refugees to prepare an invasion of Cuba to topple Castro, and in the Cold War atmosphere of the early 1960s, Kennedy subsumed this policy. In April 1961, Cuban exiles who were trained and armed by the United States but who did not receive direct military support in their invasion attempted a foray into Cuba that was doomed from the beginning. The failure of the infamous Bay of Pigs invasion embittered the thousands of Cubans who were in exile, but Castro's position at home was strengthened. To many observers throughout the world, especially in the Third World, the United States was clearly taking the side of the usurpers, who were attempting to overthrow a legitimately based government.

With the Bay of Pigs fiasco behind him, Kennedy continued to welcome Cuban refugees and to provide more structured military training for Cubans, most of whom still desired another attempt at overthrowing Cuba's Communist government. But in 1962 Kennedy redeemed himself from the Bay of Pigs disgrace by backing down the Soviet Union on a Russian plan to establish missile bases in Cuba. After this, the more viable of the two courses inherited from the Eisenhower years was to expand the refugee program.

Increasingly, welcoming refugees became more important to the U.S. policy of destabilizing the Cuban revolutionary government than armed insurrection or outright invasion. Such a course deprived Cuba of the merchants, technicians, and professionals so necessary to the island's struggling economy. In the ten years after the disastrous Bay of Pigs invasion, almost 500,000 Cubans left the island. Because of the heavy influx, a special program was initiated to settle the refugees outside of Florida. Although the majority of the fleeing Cubans stayed in Florida, thousands more went to other regions of the United States, especially to California, New York, and Chicago, areas that already had large populations of Latinos. An elaborate project ensued that included numerous prerogatives for incoming Cubans. Refugee emergency housing, English-language training, federal educational funds for Cuban children, and medical care became part of a package that facilitated the immigration process.

When Lyndon B. Johnson became president after Kennedy's assassination, he also vowed to embrace Cubans who wished to leave the island. Cubans then qualified for immigration status under special immigration provisions for refugees fleeing repressive governments. But Fidel Castro himself announced as early as 1965 that Cubans could leave Cuba if they had relatives in the United States. Castro stipulated, however, that Cubans already in Florida had to come and get them at Camarioca Bay. Nautical crafts of all types systematically left Miami to Camarioca, returning laden with anxious Cubans eager to rejoin their families on the mainland. The spectacle of the motley fleet of boats converging on Miami docks was dramatic, but the trip was also dangerous for the thousands of fleeing Cubans. Many of the boats were not seaworthy and capsized. An airlift was then organized with a great deal of publicity and fanfare. Thousands more arrived in the United States before the flights ended in 1973.

Castro also tapped the refugee issue so that he could gain moral backing from the rest of Latin America and from the millions of Cubans living on the island who still supported him. He charged those who wanted to leave the island with betrayal, branding the emigrants with the epithet *gusano* (worm), which rhymes with *cubano* and is a derogatory name. In addition, he constantly reminded the world that although Americans welcomed Cubans as displaced persons fleeing political persecution, they would not allow the same considerations to Argentines, Chileans, Guatemalans, Haitians, and other Latin Americans escaping repressive governments—basically because the United States supported those regimes.

The final and most dramatic influx of Cubans came in the early 1980s. By that time much of the hard antipathy that Cubans felt toward Castro had become as much ritualistic as real. A generation had grown up in the United States that did not have the same sentiments as their parents. In addition, President Jimmy Carter, determined to depart from the Cold War policies of his predecessors, made advances toward Castro, urging his reconciliation with the Cubans in the United States. Remarkably, moderate elements within that community responded and advocated harmonizing relations with the aging Castro. In 1977 a group of young Cuban exiles called the Antonio Maceo Brigade traveled to Cuba to participate in service work and to achieve a degree of rapprochement with the Cuban government. Back in Florida, many of the exiles branded these young envoys as traitors, and a clear message was sent out to rest of the Cuban community that any sympathizers would have to face their wrath.

Nonetheless, Castro's overtures to the exiled Cubans escalated, and they were met with some positive response. His offer was the more attractive because he promised to release political prisoners as well, most of whom had relatives in the United States. Cuban American adherence to reconciliation with Castro and his government continued to provoke intense opposition from conservative members of the exile community, however. Indeed, some of the advocates of a dialogue with the Communist leader were assassinated by armed paramilitary Cubans, but in spite of the opposition, relations between the exile community and Castro improved during the Carter years. They improved so much, in fact, that the earlier tact of using the refugee issue for propaganda purposes was lost as the tension abated between Castro and Cubans in the United States.

In April 1980, however, a dramatic incident received worldwide attention: a bus carrying a load of discontented Cubans crashed through the gates of the Peruvian embassy in Havana, and the passengers received political asylum from Peru. When it became apparent that what the gate-crashers really wanted was to leave Cuba, Castro began to revise his policy of gradually allowing Cubans to leave. In a calculated move, the Castro government announced that whoever wanted to leave Cuba should go to the Peruvian embassy. Immediately, ten thousand people crowded in. The Cuban government then processed and gave exit documents to those who came forth. Cuban exiles who happened to be on the island at the time of the embassy gate-crashing, upon their return to Miami, organized a flotilla of forty-two boats. With Castro's blessing, they began the round-the-clock evacuation of the "Havana Ten Thousand," and Carter,

as did presidents before him, decided to welcome the new influx of Cuban exiles.

Since the flotilla converged at Mariel Harbor to pick up passengers, which totaled over 125,000 by the time the boatlifts ended at the end of 1980, the refugees became known as the Marielitos. The explanation given by Castro for this whole phenomenon was rather simplistic. He charged that his policy of allowing exiles to visit the island had contaminated many erstwhile revolutionaries with the glitter of consumerism. It is probably true that travelers from the United States to the island did tempt Cubans with their abundance of consumer products, convincing many that life in a capitalist society was easier than life in Cuba. Nonetheless, Castro had to accept that socialism was at this point experiencing many difficulties and not delivering on many of the promises made some twenty years earlier.

The new refugees differed significantly from the earlier waves of displaced Cubans. Few were from the middle and upper classes of pre-Castro Cuba, as were most exiles then living in the United States, and there were also some racial differences. The new arrivals were more reflective of the general racial composition of Cuba; many Blacks and mulattoes were in the Marielito ranks. Furthermore, in a crafty move, Castro deliberately cast out many political and social misfits during the boatlift, an act that unfairly stigmatized the majority of 1980 émigrés, who were in the main normal, hardworking Cubans.

During the Marielito exit, Fidel Castro and President Carter became entangled in a now familiar struggle over which country would get more political capital from the refugee issue. Thousands of new arrivals crowded into processing centers, living in tent cities and even a football stadium in Miami. Many of the refugees became frustrated over the delay in being able to leave the camps. For many, the stay in these "temporary camps" stretched out into months, even years. The Castro government was quick to imply that the United States was not really that anxious to provide refuge to Cubans who were poor, uneducated, and racially not as White as the previous influx.

While these charges probably had some validity, the truth was more complex. Unlike previous émigrés,

A boat crowded with Cuban refugees arrives in Key West, Florida, during the 1980 Mariel boatlift.

most of the Marielitos did not have families in Florida or elsewhere in the United States, and receiving a discharge from a camp required having an American sponsor. At first Cuban Americans and other Americans were anxious to provide this service, but as the excitement and newness of the boatlift wore off, sponsors became harder to come by. The stigma suffered by Marielitos also led to difficulties once they were released. To be sure, a hard-core criminal element was dispersed among the new arrivals, but Marielitos were no different from the millions of immigrants who had preceded them to American shores in previous years. They sought to work and to find opportunities in their new environment. After all, that was the reason they had come.

The last large wave of Cuban immigration to the United States was the direct consequence of a world event of dramatic proportions: the dissolution of the Soviet Union in 1991, which effectively ended the Cold War between capitalism and communism. Since the days of the Cuban missile crisis, the Soviet Union had propped up the Cuban economy as a showcase for communism in the Western Hemisphere. With the loss of Soviet subsidy to the economy, Castro announced a "special period in peacetime" of belt-tightening that that instituted food rationing, energy conservation, and reduced public services. Shortages of food, medical supplies, raw materials, and fuel were immediately experienced and led to years of deprivation for many Cubans as well as a surge in unemployment. Over the next decades, Fidel Castro and his successor, his brother Raúl Castro, introduced more flexibility in the controlled economy, including the development of private businesses. But the new liberalization has not been enough to make the economy fully independent, and economic refugees continue to abandon the island and head for the United States as a steady stream, although not in the massive numbers that were experienced after the success of the Revolution in 1959.

As did Mexicans and Puerto Ricans, Cubans before the Castro era immigrated to the United States to work, to flee violence and repression, and, in general, to make a new life for themselves. Consequently, to survive, they forged fraternal organizations and looked to their homeland and culture to provide them with the necessary identity to build strong ethnic solidarity. In this respect Cuban Americans differ little from Mexican Americans and Puerto Ricans.

The vast, overwhelming majority, however, arrived in the United States since 1959. To be sure, fewer Cubans than Mexicans and Central Americans have immigrated to the United States in this same period, but the influx of the Cubans is part of a very long history of massive working-class immigration across the border. Cubans, because of the political conditions that provoked them to leave, were primarily from the more privileged classes. As a consequence, advantages of education, wealth, and racial acceptance allowed them to succeed in the United States at a faster pace than Mexicans and Puerto Ricans. In addition, because it was politically convenient, Cubans received an inordinate amount of assistance from U.S. administrations, from Eisenhower to Reagan, which helped their effort to settle and adapt. This has provoked invidious comparisons and charges that the cards were stacked in their favor. Much of this sentiment has some foundation in fact, but it also has to be recognized that Cuban Americans have demonstrated a great amount of their own native initiative and drive, a fact that accounts for a large part of their success.

F. Arturo Rosales

> As did Mexicans and Puerto Ricans, Cubans immigrated to the United States to work, to flee violence and repression, and, in general, to make a new life for themselves.

BUSINESS

On January 1, 1994, the North American Free Trade Agreement (NAFTA) between the United States, Mexico, and Canada went into effect. It had long been anticipated in the Latino community that NAFTA would greatly benefit many Latino-owned businesses for various reasons, including Latinos' advantage in knowing the Mexican culture, having the ability to conduct business in Spanish, and having a history of serving as cultural mediators for international business. NAFTA would also be beneficial for the concentration of Latino companies in states that border geographically on Mexico and in the possibility of rendering services to larger U.S. corporations desiring to do business in Mexico. In the larger sphere, it was anticipated that Latinos working in U.S. corporations would become invaluable in helping these companies set up to do business in Mexico and with Mexican clients. Whether in operating their own businesses or serving as mediators for other firms, Latinos in business had the opportunity, as never before, to be the planners, facilitators, and entrepreneurs of international trade. This trade would include not just Mexico but all of Spanish America as other countries in the hemisphere pursued integrating their economies with that of North America. It is true that Latino businesses have benefitted from both NAFTA and the renegotiated United States–Mexico–Canada agreement. But in the years since NAFTA was signed, Latino business grew for far more varied reasons and opportunities than those offered by the treaty, foremost of which was the demographic growth of Latinos in the United States.

There is another important side to the business relationship between the United States and Mexico. It is the largely untold story of Mexico-based corporations contributing to the U.S. economy and operating some of the largest businesses in the United States. For instance, Mexico's Grupo Bimbo, the largest bread producer in the world, owns and operates such beloved brands in the United States as Sara Lee, Oroweat, Boboli Pizza Crust, and Thomas' English Muffins, among many others. Borden Milk dairy products is owned by Mexico's Lala, the second-largest producer of dairy products in the United States. Mexico's Cemex is the second-largest cement manufacturer in the United States. Mexican automobile components companies have plants in various U.S. states.

FACTS AND FIGURES ABOUT LATINO BUSINESSES

Latino-owned businesses form a dynamic and complex sector of commerce in the United States. At

Mexico's Grupo Bimbo, the largest bread producer in the world, owns and operates such beloved brands in the United States as Sara Lee, Orowheat, Boboli Pizza Crust, and Thomas' English Muffins.

the same time that the Latino population was increasing dramatically, Latino businesses also multiplied and solidified their role in the national economy. During the 1980s Latino-owned businesses made impressive and important advances. In 1977 there were approximately 219,000 Latino-owned businesses, according to the U.S. Census Bureau. By 1982 slightly more than 248,000 Latino-owned businesses were thriving, a 13 percent increase. By 1987, 422,000 Latino-owned businesses were performing, an increase of 70 percent. By comparison, the number of nonminority businesses grew 18 percent from 1977 to 1982 and 14 percent from 1982 to 1987. And the growth just kept increasing since then. Latino businesses grew 40.2 percent from 2012 to 2018—more than twice the 18.8 percent growth rate of other U.S. firms. As of 2019, approximately one out of every seven businesses in the United States was Latino-owned.

According to the U.S. Small Business Administration, as of January 2018 U.S.-born Latinos owned roughly six hundred thousand of the 12.2 million businesses in the United States. The industry distribution of U.S.-born Latino business owners is roughly similar to the industry distribution of Whites. U.S.-born Latino men are relatively concentrated in construction, and U.S.-born Latina women are relatively concentrated in health care and social assistance. U.S.-born Latino entrepreneurs make important contributions to the economy, generating $26 billion in business income. On the other hand, approximately 1.2 million business owners in the United States are immigrant Latinos. Business ownership is higher among immigrant Latinos than U.S.-born Latinos and, in fact, is comparable to business ownership rates among non-Latino Whites. Business income, however, is substantially lower for immigrant Latino business owners than both U.S.-born Latino business owners and non-Latino White business owners. Immigrant Latino male business owners are highly concentrated in construction, and immigrant Latina female business owners are highly concentrated in other services (a category that includes beauty, laundry, and cleaning services). Latino immigrant entrepreneurs make important contributions to the economy, generating $36.5 billion in business income. (Statistics reporting and calculations are inconsistent for many reasons; in 2018 *Small Business Daily* reported that Latino businesses contributed $700 billion to the national economy.) Both U.S.-born and immigrant Latino entrepreneurs generate less income than Whites, in part because of the industries they pursue as well as because they are young, less educated, and have lower levels of wealth than the average White entrepreneurs. Latinos generate this amount of business despite discrimination in lending and other forms of discrimination that they face. According to the 2017 Small Business Credit Study by the Federal Reserve Banks, 45 percent of Latino business loan applicants were turned down for insufficient credit history and 37 percent for having too low a credit score. In comparison, White applicants were turned away at rates of 33 percent and 26 percent, respectively. Nevertheless, a Stanford University study concluded that as of February 2020, Latino business ownership had grown a whopping 34 percent over the previous ten years, while general business ownership had grown by only 1 percent. Latino businesses in that period accounted

for 4 percent of U.S. business revenues and 5.5 percent of U.S. employment, some three million workers. There is no telling at this writing how Latino businesses will fare throughout the COVID-19 pandemic and its recession that began in March of 2020; what is certain is that small business owners have suffered greatly.

Caution needs to be exercised in interpreting Latino business growth over the years. The data collected in each census period are not entirely compatible. Changes in survey methodology, for example, account for some of these inconsistencies. However, there is no doubt that significant growth of Latino-owned businesses has occurred.

Tables 1 and 2 show estimates of business ownership among U.S.-born and immigrant Latino men and women in the years leading up to 2015. Table 3 estimates Latino business ownership and income in the same time period.

Although 49.1 percent of all Latino businesses are owned by Mexican-origin entrepreneurs, other ethnic groups within the U.S. Latino community have significant business interests. For example, 11.1 percent of all Latino businesses are owned by Cuban Americans; however, Cuban American businesses are

Table 1: Male: Industry Distribution of Business Owners among U.S.-Born and Immigrant Latinos: American Community Survey Five-Year Estimate (2015)

Group	U.S.-Born Latinos	Immigrant Latinos	Non-Latino Whites	Total
Number of Businesses	349,155	740,701	5,500,308	7,447,639
Agriculture/Extraction	1.7%	1.6%	7.5%	5.9%
Construction	27.3%	38.6%	24.9%	25.1%
Manufacturing	2.9%	2.3%	4.4%	3.9%
Wholesale	2.5%	2.2%	2.9%	2.8%
Retail	6.8%	6.0%	7.1%	7.4%
Transportation	6.9%	7.8%	4.6%	6.0%
Information/Finance	8.6%	2.9%	9.6%	8.7%
Professional Services	21.4%	22.5%	20.9%	20.8%
Educational Services	1.1%	0.4%	1.0%	1.0%
Health Care and Social Assistance	3.7%	1.5%	4.8%	4.6%
Accommodation, Recreation, and Entertainment	6.7%	4.4%	5.5%	6.0%
Other Services	10.6%	9.8%	6.8%	7.8%

Table 2: Female: Industry Distribution of Business Owners among
U.S.-Born and Immigrant Latinos: American Community Survey Five-Year Estimate (2015)

Group	U.S.-Born Latinos	Immigrant Latinos	Non-Latino Whites	Total
Number of Businesses	191,917	409,728	2,773,079	3,935,844
Agriculture/Extraction	0.8%	0.5%	2.7%	2.1%
Construction	3.4%	1.9%	3.5%	3.0%
Manufacturing	2.3%	1.5%	2.9%	2.7%
Wholesale	1.6%	1.2%	1.6%	1.6%
Retail	8.6%	7.4%	8.9%	8.8%
Transportation	1.4%	1.2%	1.3%	1.3%
Information/Finance	9.7%	3.0%	10.7%	9.3%
Professional Services	18.8%	18.3%	23.3%	21.4%
Educational Services	2.4%	0.5%	3.2%	2.7%
Health Care and Social Assistance	19.6%	17.0%	15.6%	17.1%
Accommodation, Recreation, and Entertainment	7.3%	5.1%	7.7%	7.7%
Other Services	24.0%	42.5%	18.6%	22.4%

Table 3: Total: Business Ownership and Income among
U.S.-Born and Immigrant Latinos: American Community Survey Five-Year Estimate (2015)

Group	U.S.-Born Latinos	Immigrant Latinos	Non-Latino Whites	Total
Number of Business Owners	584,516	1,232,720	8,820,771	12,159,527
Percent of Population	3.8%	7.8%	7.3%	6.4%
Number (15+ hours/week worked)	541,425	1,150,582	8,277,854	11,388,697
Percent of Population	3.5%	7.3%	6.8%	6.0%
Percent of Workforce (15+ hours)	5.2%	10.5%	9.6%	8.7%
Average Business Income	$44,777	$29,590	$63,329	$57,357
Average Business Income (15+ hours)	$47,385	$31,005	$66,618	$60,375

proportionately the most profitable, making up 14.8 percent of sales receipts and 14.8 percent or $8.1 billion of the annual payroll of all Hispanic-owned firms. The remaining 39.8 percent of Latino business ownership is made up of Puerto Ricans and the other diverse Latino groups.

Some 26 percent of Latino businesses have no employees and are staffed by a single individual who is typically the owner. More than half (51 percent) have between two and five employees, and 14 percent have six to ten employees. As stated earlier, nationally,

these businesses employ some three million individuals and generate $36.5 billion. The geographic distribution of Latino-owned businesses follows the residence patterns of U.S. Latino populations as a whole. Most Mexican-owned businesses were in the U.S. Southwest, though their number has grown in other areas as well, like the U.S. South, New York, and Illinois. According to the U.S. Census, these states had the greatest number of Latino firms: California, Florida, Texas, New York, and Illinois. Seventy percent of Cuban-owned businesses were located in Florida, and most Puerto Rican–owned businesses were in Florida, New York, and Illinois. Most businesses owned by individuals from the Dominican Republic were located in New York. After California, Florida, Texas, New York, and Illinois, most other Latino-owned businesses were located in New Jersey, Arizona, New Mexico, Colorado, and Virginia. Most of the Latino businesses in these states are located in large urban areas.

Table 4 shows the ten metropolitan statistical areas (MSAs) with the largest number of Latino population and Latino companies and the percentage of Latino companies in the respective MSA, as of 2012. These ten MSAs account for close to 50 percent of the total number of Latino businesses in the United States and 50 percent of the gross sales. The greatest concentration of the one hundred fastest-growing Latino companies are located in California and Florida.

Latino-owned businesses for the most part are small businesses. In fact, according to a Small Business

Table 4: Top Ten Metro Areas by Total Latino Population and Number of Latino-Owned Businesses (LOBs)

Metropolitan Area	Latino Population	Latino Share	Number LOBs	LOB Share
Los Angeles, Long Beach, Anaheim	5,979,000	45.1	393,051	26.5
New York, Newark, Jersey City	4,780,000	23.9	339,415	15.4
Miami, Ft. Lauderdale, W. Palm Beach	2,554,000	43.3	423,163	47.0
Houston, The Woodlands, Sugar Land	2,335,000	36.4	164,923	27.2
Riverside, San Bernardino, Ontario	2,197,000	49.4	122,233	36.5
Chicago, Naperville, Elgin	2,070,000	21.8	89,523	9.9
Dallas, Fort Worth, Arlington	1,943,000	28.4	117,582	18.3
Phoenix, Mesa, Scottsdale	1,347,000	30.1	54,393	16.0
San Antonio, New Braunfels	1,259,000	55.7	81,126	43.3
San Diego, Carlsbad	1,084,000	33.3	62,753	21.4

Population and Origin in Select U.S. Metropolitan Areas, 2014. Source: U.S. Census Survey of Business Owners, 2012 and Pew Research Center, Hispanic.

Daily survey in 2018, 49 percent of Latino firms had no employees other than the business owner, and 51 percent had between two and five employees; 14 percent had 6 to 10 employees. According to the survey, 81 percent of Latino business owners reported their businesses as profitable, compared to 68 percent of all survey respondents. The three MSAs with the largest number of Latino-owned business that do have employees are Chicago (59 percent), New York (73 percent), and Phoenix (97 percent). According to *Forbes*, the average revenue of Latino-owned businesses improved 46.5 percent in 2019, increasing to $479,413 from $327,189 in 2018. That growth brought Latino revenues almost to the level of non-Latino business, which averaged $25,067 more in 2019. Prior to that level, revenues from sales by Latino-owned businesses grew from $258,702 in 2016–17 to $327,189 in 2017–18, an increase of 26.5 percent. As

of 2019, it was more expensive to run a Latino business: the average operating expense was 45 percent ($215,846) of the average annual revenue ($479,413), while for non-Latinos it was 40.6 percent. However, taking aggregated figures for the high number of Latino businesses in the United States and the low levels of revenue for so many of them, it is likely that there is a large proportion of Latino business owners with part-time operations.

Independently owned businesses are the foundation of economic activity in the United States. They embody the American dream of financial independence and self-determination. Even in the relatively mediocre economies of recessions past and present, Latino businesses have continued to grow and prosper. The impressive gains made by Latino-owned businesses in the past decades will most assuredly continue into the future as younger and better-educated Latinos are attracted to self-employment. Business ownership will become an increasingly attractive career option for growing numbers of Latinos. In addition, more and more corporations are removing barriers to the advancement of minorities, and the following decades will see Latino leadership shine, often based on the solid record of some of the prominent Latinos in business highlighted below.

Jude Valdez and Nicolás Kanellos

PROMINENT LATINOS IN BUSINESS

Deborah Aguiar-Vélez (1955–2016)

Computers

Born on December 18, 1955, in New York City, Deborah Aguiar-Vélez received a B.S. degree in chemical engineering from the University of Puerto Rico in 1977 and a certificate from the University of Virginia Entrepreneurial Executive Institute in 1989. In her early career, she was a systems analyst for Exxon and then worked in the small business division of the New Jersey Department of Commerce. After that, she founded and was president of her own business, Sistemas Corporation. Her honors include selection in 1990 as an Outstanding Woman Entrepreneur Advocate by American Women in Economic Development and selection for Coca-Cola commercials as a Hispanic woman entrepreneurial role model. Aguiar-Vélez served on the boards of the Latino Women's Task Force, the Latino Leadership Opportunity Program, and the New Jersey Women's Business Advisory Council, which she chaired from 1987 to 1988. Aguiar-Vélez passed away from lung cancer on October 19, 2016.

Gabriel Eloy Aguirre (1935–2017)

Born on January 12, 1935, in Akron, Ohio, Gabriel Eloy Aguirre worked for SaniServ in Indianapolis as a refrigeration repairman and later in the sales division, from 1957 to 1977; in 1977, he became the owner of the company, which manufactured ice cream and frozen

beverage machines. SaniServ machines are found in restaurants, hotels, universities, and military institutions. Equipment made by the company is used by Wendy's restaurants to make its "Frosty" frozen treat. He ran SaniServ until 1995, when the company became part of Affinis Co. For his outstanding success with the company, he was named the 1988 Minority Entrepreneur of the Year by U.S. president Ronald Reagan. Aguirre was heavily involved in the U.S. Hispanic Chamber of Commerce and numerous community activities promoting minority businesses and interests, prompting then-Mayor William Hudnut to declare Christmas Eve 1987 "Gabe Aguirre Day" in Indianapolis. In addition, he served in the community on numerous boards and as president of school boards and police commissions. In 1988, he was appointed to the board of the U.S. Senate Task Force on Latino Affairs. Aguirre died on October 30, 2017, in Brownsburg, Indiana.

Carlos José Arboleya (1929–2020)

Banking

Born on February 1, 1929, in Havana, Cuba, Carlos José Arboleya was a graduate of the University of Havana who developed his early career in banking as the Havana manager of the First National City Bank of New York. After the Cuban Revolution of 1959, he immigrated to the United States, where as a bank executive, he offered loans and financial guidance to Cuban exiles fleeing the island and starting anew in the United States. In the course of his career, he worked at a number of banks in Miami, moving up the ranks from clerk to bank administrator. By 1966, he was executive vice president of the Fidelity National Bank of South Miami; by 1973, the co-owner, president, and director of the Flagler Bank; and by 1977, president and CEO of the Barnett Banks of Miami. In 1983, he became vice chairman of the Barnett Bank of South Florida. He rose to the position of vice chairman in 1981 for the Southern Region while simultaneously serving as president of Barnett Leasing Company and Barnett Visa and MasterCard operations for the Southern Region, positions he held until his retirement in 1994. He served on the boards of such organizations as the American Institute of Banking, the Inter-American Affairs Action Committee, the National Advisory Council for Economic Opportunity, the American Arbitration Association, and the Cuban American Foundation. Among his many honors are the American Academy of Achievement Gold Plate Award in 1974, the Horatio Alger Award of the American Schools and Colleges Association in 1976, and the American Red Cross Man of the Year Award in 1988. Arboleya died on March 29, 2020.

Humberto Cabañas (1947–)

Hotel Management

Born on September 3, 1947, in Havana, Cuba, Humberto Cabañas received a B.S. degree in hotel and restaurant management from Florida International University in 1974 and went on to rise through the ranks at Sheraton, Doral, and Stouffer hotels until becoming the founding president and CEO of the Benchmark Hospitality Group in the Woodlands, Texas, in 1979. Benchmark is a leading U.S.-based hospitality management company and recognized global leader in the management and marketing of resorts, hotels, and conference centers. Benchmark properties include the Woodlands Executive Conference Center and resort, the Woodlands Country Club, the Exxon Conference Center, the Tournament Players Golf Course, and the San Luis Resort Hotel on Galveston Island. He has been a president of the International Association of Conference Centers, from which he received a Distinguished Service Award in 1988. Cabañas serves on the industry advisory committee for the Conrad Hilton School of Hotel and Restaurant Management of the University of Houston. Cabañas received both the Florida International University Torch Award by the Alumni Association and the Medallion Award from FIU.

Marcelo Claure (1970–)

Telecommunications Executive

(Raúl) Marcelo Claure, the son of a Bolivian diplomat, was born in Guatemala on December 9, 1970. Claure spent most of his childhood in La Paz, Bolivia, where he received his primary education. In 1989, Claure came to the United States for his college education and graduated from Bentley College in Waltham, Massachusetts with a bachelor of science degree in economics and finance in 1993. In 1995 he bought USA Wireless, a cellular retailer, and expanded the company before selling it one year later. In 1996 Claure became president of Small World Communications, a communications and distribution company. In 1997 he founded Brightstar as a small, Miami-based wireless distributor and transformed it into the world's largest global wireless distribution and services company; its revenues exceeded $10 billion, and it had achieved a presence in more than fifty countries when Claure sold the company to Sprint. Brightstar was recognized as the largest Hispanic-owned business in U.S. history. Claure then served as executive chair of the board of Sprint Corporation. He also served as chief operating officer of SoftBank Group Corp. and chief executive officer of SoftBank International, a Japanese multinational conglomerate, and was a member of the SoftBank board of directors. He additionally served on the board of Arm, a leading chip technology developer.

Claure most recently was Sprint CEO. Sprint is one of the world's largest telecommunications companies, providing service to 54.6 million customers in nearly two hundred countries around the world. Claure joined the company in August 2014 and took it through a significant transformation, growing revenue, reducing expenses by more than $6 billion, while massively improving the quality of its products and services. During Claure's four years as CEO, Sprint revitalized its brand and went from losing millions of customers to gaining more than 2.1 million. The company achieved its best financial results in company history. The company also increased its adjusted EBITDA from $6 billion to $11 billion and reversed a trend of cash flow losses into generating $945 million in free cash flow in fiscal year 2017. For the first time in eleven years, the company was net income positive. As a successful entrepreneur and having accrued a fortune, Claure became chair of Inter Miami, Miami's newest major league soccer franchise, which played its first season in 2020. Claure was named a Young Global Leader of the World Economic Forum and is a member of Ernst & Young's Entrepreneur of the Year Hall of Fame. In 2008 Claure and Nicholas Negroponte founded One Laptop Per Child, an organization that provides laptops to impoverished grade-school students. By 2019 One Laptop Per Child had delivered 2.5 million computers to students in sixty countries. Claure in 2016 created the 1Million Project Foundation through the Sprint Corporation. The foundation aims to provide free computer and internet access to one million disadvantaged students in the United States.

María Contreras-Sweet (1955–)
Banking and Public Administration

Born as one of six children in Guadalajara, Mexico, María Contreras-Sweet immigrated to the United States when she was five years old. Her single mother struggled to support her children in the types of jobs open to working-class immigrants, including working at a poultry plant. Contreras-Sweet earned a bachelor's degree in political science and public administration from California State University, Los Angeles, and at the age of twenty-four served as a district manager for the U.S. Census Bureau. In 1995, Contreras-Sweet started her own research consulting company specializing in Latino marketing. In 1999 she became the state's first Latina cabinet official, serving five years as secretary of the Business, Transportation, and Housing Agency, managing 44,000 employees and a $14 billion budget. She led the creation of the state's Department of Managed Health Care and its Office of the Patient Advocate. Subsequently, she served as vice president of public affairs for the 7 Up/RC Bottling Company, where she was a leading corporate negotiator for the creation of the Beverage Container Recycling and Litter Reduction Act expanding California's recycling system. In 2006 she founded the Latino-owned ProAmérica Bank to serve small and midsize businesses. She left the bank to serve on President Barack Obama's cabinet, the first Latina to lead the U.S. Small Business Administration. At the SBA, from 2014 to 2017 she oversaw the world's largest business counseling network, the federal small-business contracting program, and a $120 billion loan program. Contreras-Sweet has been a director since March 2017 of Contreras-Sweet Enterprises and Rockway Equity Partners. She has garnered numerous awards and recognitions, including honorary doctorates from California State University (2016) and Tufts University (2017). In recognition of her international leadership, the Global Entrepreneurship Congress established the María Contreras-Sweet Award for Global Impact.

Gilbert Cuéllar Sr. (1911–1986)
Restaurant Chain Executive

Gilbert Cuéllar Sr. was the chairman and CEO of the famous Tex-Mex restaurant chain founded by his family in 1928, when Mexican food was not all that familiar to American diners; the family started the practice of featuring photos of the plates on their menu to help the diners select their orders. Originally started as an outlet for the food grown on their family farm in Kaufman, Texas, the parents and twelve siblings grew the operation into one of the largest Mexican restaurant chains in the nation. The Cuéllars also owned El Chico Commissary, a successful business that produced canned and frozen El Chico products for distribution in grocery stores in twenty-two states. In 1968, the company went public with a 172,000-share offering of its common stock. By 1970, El Chico was operating forty-four restaurants. Formerly known as El Chico Corporation, the Dallas-based chain later became Southwest Cafés and, under Cuéllar's direction, expanded to various states under such local names as Cantina Laredo, Cuéllar's Café, Casa Rosa, and El Chico Restaurants. First becoming associated with the corporation in 1970, Cuéllar served in various capacities, including manager of quality control, product research and development, and director of marketing research. In 1977, Campbell Taggart acquired the restaurant chain, and Cuéllar and his son were able to repurchase El Chico Corporation in 1982. In 1986, Cuéllar was named chairman of the corporation.

Martha de la Torre
(1957–)

Media Executive

Born on July 13, 1957, in East Los Angeles to Ecuadorean immigrant parents, Martha de la Torre is the co-founder and president of El Clasificado and EC Hispanic Media. De la Torre is a graduate of Loyola Marymount University, where she earned a B.S. in accounting. She joined Arthur Young & Company in 1978 and became a certified public accountant and audit manager specializing in banks and businesses targeting the U.S. Hispanic market. In 1986, she served two years as chief financial officer of *La Opinión*, the largest Spanish language daily in the United States. In 1998, to start El Clasificado, she and her husband/cofounder sold their house and moved in with her parents to raise the cash when other financing was not available. De la Torre has grown El Clasificado into the largest Hispanic classified ad platform, ranked among the top 115 classified marketplaces in the world according to Similarweb.com. Today, yearly revenues are approximately $20 million. Besides El Clasificado, included in her conglomerate EC Hispanic Media are Quinceanera.com, Su Socio de Negocios, EmpleosLatino.com, Al Borde, Pantera Digital, and Twyzle, which specializes in the Latino market and offers print, digital, social media, and event advertising and marketing solutions to its clients. In 2010, CNBC named de la Torre one of the top ten Hispanic entrepreneurs. El Clasificado was recognized as "Best Classified Website" by *Editor and Publisher* in 2014. De la Torre was awarded the Marcia Lamb Inner City Innovation Award at the ICIC 2016 Inner City 100 Awards for growing job opportunities in the inner cities. She formerly served on the board of regents for Loyola Marymount University and was chair of the International Classified Media Association (ICMA) headquartered in Amsterdam.

Roberto C. Goizueta (1931–1997)

Beverage Company Executive

Born on November 18, 1931, in Havana, Cuba, Roberto C. Goizueta received a B.S. degree in chemical engineering in 1953 from Yale University. He began at the Coca-Cola Company as an assistant vice president of research in 1964; by 1981, he had become the chairman of the board and CEO of Coca-Cola, one of the world's largest corporations. It was the first time the Coke board had ever not chosen a native Georgian. The *New York Times* credited him with "strengthening [Coca-Cola's] global dominance in soft drinks and building one of the greatest generators of shareholder wealth in corporate history." While he was CEO, the total value of Coke stock grew from $4.3 billion in 1981 to more than $152 billion by the time he left the company. In 1991, Goizueta earned a bonus of nearly $83 million in stock, one of the largest ever. Goizueta was active in service nationally and internationally. He was the founding director of the Points of Light Initiative and sat on the boards of the Ford Motor Company and Eastman Kodak, among others. He was a trustee of Emory University. Among his many honors were being chosen a Gordon Grand Fellow of Yale University in 1984, the 1984 Herbert Hoover Humanitarian Award of the Boys Clubs of America, and the 1986 Ellis Island Medal of Honor. Goizueta died on October 18, 1997.

Frederick J. González (1949–2004)

Design Engineering Executive

Born on June 28, 1949, in Detroit, Michigan, Frederick J. González received a B.S. degree in engineering and an M.S. degree in architecture and urban planning from Princeton University in 1971 and 1972, respectively. After working for three years as an architect for Smith, Hinchman & Grylls Associates, in 1975 he and his father founded their own firm, González Design Engineering, in Madison Heights, Michigan, for which he served as CEO from 1977, when his father died, until 2004. In 1979, he also became the president of Semi-Kinetics, a printed circuit board assembly line in Laguna Hills, California. In the 1990s, Gonzalez Design Group expanded into the manufacture of steel shipping containers (Gonzalez Manufacturing Technologies) and finally full-system integration for body shop and assembly systems (Gonzalez Production Systems). Gonzalez Design Group is a leading full-service integrator of tooling and assembly systems, from transportation to aerospace and defense.

Today, Gonzalez Group is comprised of three companies located in Oak Park, Troy, and Pontiac, Michigan, as well as in Querétaro, Mexico. Following a 1968 automobile accident, González, who had been a high school football star, was paralyzed from the waist down. Despite this and business barriers, González became an outstanding businessman. In 1995, González helped develop the Hispanic Manufacturing Center on Clark Street in southwest Detroit. Among his and his company's honors were being named by the White House as the National Minority Service Firm of the Year in 1975, selection as the 1989 Minority Businessman of the Year, and selection as the 1989 Minority Supplier of the Year by the National Minority Business Development Council. González participated on many boards, including the board of directors of the U.S. Latino Chamber of Commerce. González and his brother/partner, Gary, were featured in full-page ads by General Motors as successful suppliers to the car company. González died on February 22, 2004. In 2004, the Ric González Memorial Foundation was founded to award scholarships to deserving Latino students.

Carlos Miguel Gutiérrez (1953–)

Corporate Executive

Born on November 4, 1953, in Havana, Cuba, Carlos Miguel Gutiérrez was the son of a pineapple plantation owner. He immigrated to the United States with his family in 1960 and then to Mexico, where his father accepted a position with the J. Heinz Company. Gutiérrez was a student at the Technological Institute of Monterrey's Querétaro campus but never obtained a degree. In 1975, Gutiérrez became a sales representative for Kellogg Corporation in Mexico. From that humble position, he worked his way up to top management and in January 1990 was named corporate vice president of product development at Kellogg headquarters in Battle Creek, Michigan; in July of that year, he became executive vice president of Kellogg USA. In January 1999, he became a member of the Kellogg board of directors. In April 1999, he was appointed president and CEO, becoming the only Latino CEO of a Fortune 500 company. Gu-

tiérrez was also the youngest CEO in the company's nearly one-hundred-year history. Gutiérrez is credited with bringing Kellogg out of a long slump, and in its September 2004 issue, *Fortune* called Gutiérrez "The Man Who Fixed Kellogg," stating it was "the slick salesmanship, financial discipline, and marketing savvy that he learned in his youth and blend[ed] with disarming charisma, steely resolve, and an utter lack of pretension" that helped bring the company back. In 2004, President George W. Bush nominated Gutiérrez as secretary of commerce. After the U.S. Senate confirmed him for secretary, the board of Kellogg accepted his resignation as CEO. Notable during his service as secretary was his leadership in the passage of CAFTA-DR, an important trade agreement that expanded opportunities for U.S. exports throughout Latin America. Gutiérrez also led the way in promoting the Colombia Free Trade Agreement. After serving in the Bush administration, Gutiérrez established and served as chairman of Global Political Strategies (GPS), an international strategic consulting service. From December 2010 to February 2013, Gutiérrez served as vice chairman of Citigroup in the Institutional Clients Group and was a member of the Senior Strategic Advisory Group. He is currently a co-chair of Albright Stonebridge Group, a strategic advisory firm. Gutiérrez has served on the board of directors of Occidental Petroleum, GLW Corning, and Intelligent Global Pooling Systems. Despite being a lifelong Republican, Gutiérrez voted for Hillary Clinton in the 2016 presidential election.

Anthony R. Jiménez (1961–)

Information Systems Technology Executive

Born in the Portsmouth Naval Hospital in Virginia, Anthony "Tony" R. Jiménez was the middle child of a Puerto Rican father and a Cuban American mother. His father's twenty-year career in the Navy took the family to several states as well as to Spain. Shortly after graduating from high school, Jiménez enlisted in the Army, serving for twenty-four years, retiring in 2003. While serving, he received an Army active-duty ROTC scholarship and earned a bachelor's degree in business management from St. Mary's University in San Antonio, Texas. Jiménez later earned a master of arts degree in computers and information systems from Missouri's Webster University (1993) and a master of science degree in acquisition management from Florida Institute of Technology (1999). Jiménez literally founded MicroTech on his kitchen table in 2004 as a one-man operation. Today, he is the award-winning chairman and chief executive officer of the company, one of the largest Hispanic-owned IT integrators in the nation. Under his leadership MicroTech is focused on technology services, cloud computing, product solutions, network systems integration, cybersecurity, telecommunications, mobility, and managed services and solutions. Today, MicroTech is a profitable half-billion-dollar company with skilled professionals in more than forty states supporting more than one hundred prime contracts throughout the federal government and providing IT, network, and telecom support to numerous Fortune 500 companies around the globe. Throughout the years MicroTech has been consistently recognized for its achievements. Several national organizations have honored MicroTech, adding it to their fastest-growing company lists, including *Inc., Washington Business Journal, CRN,* and *Digital Software Magazine.* According to *Hispanic Business Magazine,* MicroTech was the No. 1 Fastest-Growing Hispanic-Owned Business in the Nation for three consecutive years (2009–2011). Additionally, Jiménez has been recognized as one of the "Most Powerful Minority Men in Business" by the Minority Enterprise Executive Council, and one of the "100 Most Innovative Entrepreneurs in the Nation" by Goldman Sachs. An important part of Jiménez's commitment to this nation's youth are his efforts to advance science, technology, engineering, and math (STEM) initiatives. In April 2016, Jiménez was named to the STEMconnector List of 100 CEO Leaders in Science, Technology, Engineering, and Math (STEM).

Frank A. Lorenzo (1940–)

Former Airline Company Executive

Born on May 19, 1940, in New York City, Frank A. Lorenzo received a B.S. degree from Columbia University in 1961 and an M.B.A. degree from Harvard University in 1963. He began his career in air transportation as a financial analyst for Trans World Airlines from 1963 to 1965 and by 1966 had founded and become chairman of his own company, Lorenzo, Carney and Company. From 1972 to 1980 he served as president and chairman of Texas International Airlines, which eventually became a major national and international holding company for Continental Airlines (today merged under the umbrella of United Airlines), for which he served as president from 1980 to 1985 and then as chairman and CEO from 1986 to 1990. During his eighteen-year tenure, his airline empire grew from fifteen jet aircraft (at Texas International) with revenues of $73 million, to Continental's combined fleet of 350 jet aircraft and revenues of over $5 billion. After developing the company into the world's largest carrier through the purchase of various other carriers, Lorenzo was embattled by strikes, rising costs, competition, and the problems of deregulation, and he was eventually forced to resign. Since 1990, Lorenzo has been chairman of Savoy Capital, Inc., professionally devoted to asset management, private investments, and venture capital. Lorenzo is a trustee and vice chairman of the Hispanic Society of America, the national museum of Spanish art, culture, and history located in New York City. In 1986, Lorenzo established the Olegario Lorenzo Memorial and Lorenzo Family Scholarship Funds at Columbia College.

Arturo "Arte" Moreno (1946–)

Advertising Executive and Professional Sports Team Owner

Born on August 14, 1946, Arturo Moreno is the oldest of eleven children born to Mexican immigrant parents. Raised and educated through high school in Tucson, he served in Vietnam while in the Army and returned to study marketing, graduating from the University of Arizona in 1973. After college, he worked for outdoor advertising firms (billboards) around the country and returned to Tucson to work in Outdoor Systems, where he ascended to the role of CEO and took the company public in 1996. In 1998 Moreno sold the company to Infiniti Broadcasting for $8 billion; this became the basis for his fortune, which he used in 2003 to purchase the Anaheim Angels baseball team from the Disney Company for $180 million. Moreno immediately invested heavily in upgrading the team; as a result, in his first year the team attracted 750,000 more spectators than when it had won the World Series in 2002. The team had six straight winning seasons from 2004 to 2009, the first time the team had three or more consecutive winning seasons in its history. Moreno spearheaded changing the name of the team to the Los Angeles Angels, which caused quite a bit of backlash from Anaheim and Orange County fans, but the success of the team has quelled the negative sentiments. The Angels won the American League Western Division championship in 2004, 2005, 2007, 2008, 2009, and 2014. In April 2016, *Forbes* estimated the Angels' value at $368 million. The cap to Moreno's success with the Angels was his purchase in 2019 of Angels Stadium and its parking lots from the City of Anaheim for $325 million.

Oscar Muñoz (1959–)

Airline Company Executive

Born the oldest of nine children on January 5, 1959, in Southern California to Mexican American parents, Oscar Muñoz was the first in his family to obtain a college education, earning a BS in business from the University of Southern California in 1982 and an M.B.A. from Pepperdine University. Muñoz worked his way up to the administrative ranks of Qwest, AT&T, Coca-Cola, and PepsiCo until he became the president and chief operating officer at CSX Corporation in 2012. During his tenure, CSX transformed itself into an industry leader in customer focus, reliability, and financial performance. CSX was named one of Institutional Investor's Most Honored Companies for a decade of excellent financial performance, including increasing its operating income by nearly 600 percent. On September 8, 2016, he became the CEO of United Airlines, one of the largest airline companies in the world. Muñoz had one of the greatest personal comebacks in the corporate world after suffering a heart attack shortly after becoming the CEO; on January 5, 2016, he received a heart transplant and bounced back on March 16 in time to work out several contentious labor-management issues that kept the airline on firm footing. Muñoz's tenure as CEO ended in 2020, when he transitioned to the role of executive chairman of the board. Muñoz has served on the University of North Florida's board of trustees.

Antonio Neri (1967–)

Technology Company Executive

Born May 10, 1967, in Argentina, Antonio Neri is an immigrant who worked himself up the organizational ladder to become the president and CEO of Hewlett Packard Enterprise (HPE), one of the largest IT firms in the world. After studying engineering at the National Technological University in Buenos Aires, he went to Italy to work in a small tech firm and then joined Hewlett Packard in Amsterdam in 1995 as a call center agent who could speak to clients in Spanish and Italian. At the time, he failed the company's English test, but his supervisors believed in him and that he could learn the language, which he did. He later was transferred to Boise, Idaho. He moved to Houston in 2004 to work for the company's PC services business, then became head of the technology services business in 2011 in San Jose, California. In 2015 he became the senior vice president and general manager for the company's server and networking units; and in 2018 he became the CEO. At this writing, he is in charge of setting up the new U.S. headquarters for the firm in Houston, Texas. Neri became a U.S. citizen in 2012.

Robert Ortega Jr. (1947–)

Construction Company Executive

Born on February 1, 1947, in El Paso, Texas, Robert Ortega Jr. received B.S. and M.S. degrees in civil engineering from the University of Texas at El Paso in 1970 and 1980, respectively. He worked as an engineer in the U.S. Public Health Service, the U.S. Bureau of Reclamation, and the El Paso Housing Department before founding Construction Management Associates in 1983. In 1988, his company was rated the fifth-fastest-growing Latino company in the United States by *Hispanic Business* magazine. In 1989, the company was named the Outstanding Small Business for the City of El Paso by the Small Business Administration. In 1980, Ortega was named Young Engineer of the Year and, in 1989, Engineer of the Year by the Texas Society of Professional Engineers. He is a past president of the Texas Society of Civil Engineers and of the Associated Builders and Contractors.

Jorge M. Pérez
(1949–)
Real Estate Executive

Jorge M. Pérez was born on October 17, 1949, in Buenos Aires, Argentina, to Cuban parents. His father had been the head of a pharmaceutical company in Havana before it was nationalized by the Cuban revolutionary regime. Pérez grew up in Bogota, Colombia, and came to the United States to attend college; he graduated summa cum laude from C.W. Post College in Long Island and earned his master's in urban planning from the University of Michigan. He moved to Miami in 1968, and in the 1970s he provided public housing in neighborhoods like Miami's Little Havana and Homestead. In 1979, he founded Related Group with New York builder Stephen M. Ross. Pérez built his fortune by building and operating low-income multifamily apartments across Miami. The firm became the largest affordable housing builder in Florida by the middle of the decade. He then branched off into rental apartments before becoming one of the most prolific high-rise condo builders in the southern United States. Pérez has owned numerous condo towers around the country and has built apartments and condos in Atlanta, South Florida, Fort Myers, Tampa, Dallas, Denver, Phoenix, and Las Vegas. In 2020, Pérez retired as president and CEO of Related

Group and passed the titles on to his son, Jon Paul Pérez. During his career, Pérez developed or managed more than ninety thousand residences. In addition, he built projects in Argentina, Brazil, Panama, Uruguay, and Mexico. Pérez is a famed philanthropist; among his gifts was $40 million to the Herzog & de Meuron–designed Pérez Art Museum Miami (PAMM). *Time Magazine* named Pérez one of the top twenty-five most influential Hispanics in the United States, and he has appeared on the cover of *Forbes* twice. Pérez is an Ellis Island Medal of Honor recipient. He was ranked 316th on the *Forbes* 400 list with a net worth of $2.6 billion in October 2018.

María Ríos (?)

Waste Management Executive

Maria Ríos immigrated with her family from El Salvador to the United States as a thirteen-year-old who did not speak English. She received a two-year degree from Houston Community College and a business degree from the University of Houston in 1997. Ríos is the president and CEO of Nation Waste, Inc. (NWI), the first multimillion-dollar female Hispanic–owned waste removal company in U.S. history and one of the largest minority-owned companies in the state of Texas. NWI is a waste disposal company specializing in construction, demolition, commercial/industrial nonhazardous waste removal, portable toilets, and recycling services. In 2018, Ríos delved into artificial intelligence (AI) and began revolutionizing the worker safety industry when she launched a new division, Nation Safety Net, in partnership with IBM to improve worker safety in large industries. In the United States nearly five thousand people die and approximately twenty-seven million work days are lost each year because of injuries in the workplace. To keep workers safe and reduce workplace injuries, Nation Safety Net created a program that uses environmental sensors and wearable devices to identify potential dangers and to help employees avoid injury. In 2019, Ríos's success in AI was recognized when she served as featured speaker on global technology innovation in Russia, Colombia, Switzerland, Israel, India, and Tunisia. Currently, Ríos serves as the global ambassador for the International Women's Entrepreneurial Challenge (IWEC), which recognized her as one of the top twenty-seven women entrepreneurs in the world. *Fortune* named Ríos as one of the 2013 *Fortune* Most Powerful Women Entrepreneurs in the United States, and Goldman Sachs honored her as one of its 100 Most Intriguing Entrepreneurs. In 2006, Ríos received the Gold Medal Award for Entrepreneur of the Year given by the National White House Congressional Committee in Washington, D.C. In 2019 she was featured on the front cover of *Forbes Central America*.

John Rodríguez (1958–)

Advertising and Public Relations

Born on August 9, 1958, in New York City, John Rodríguez is cofounder and president of AD One, an advertising and public relations firm in Rochester, New York. Rodríguez completed his bachelor's degree at the Rochester Institute of Technology, where he majored in advertising and photography. He continued his education by attending classes at local universities, working toward a master's degree in communications. As a young entrepreneur, he built AD One into a successful firm that specializes in international sales promotion, recruitment, and the Latino market. AD One has successfully completed projects for many clients across the region, including Eastman Kodak Company, Bausch and Lomb, Preferred Care, the University of Rochester, the Girl Scouts, Rochester City School District, and Mobil Chemical. Rodríguez has a strong sense of responsibility toward the community in which he lives and works. His commitment to his community and to Latino people is expressed in many ways. Rodríguez has also ventured into politics. He served as campaign director for his sister-in-law, Nancy Padilla, the first Latino elected to the Rochester City Council. For Rodríguez, having individuals sensitive to the Latino community in key policy-making positions is critical.

Edgardo G. Santiago (1949–)

Controller

Born on September 26, 1949, in Ponce, Puerto Rico, Edgardo G. Santiago received a B.S. degree in accounting from Baruch College in 1975 and an M.B.A. degree in finance from Pace University in 1979. He began his career as an accounting clerk for Guy Carpenter & Co. in 1969. He worked for American International Marine and for MacMillan until 1975, when he became the controller of Philip Morris International, where he held various financial management positions. After twenty-two years at Philip Morris, he took positions in Florida in finance and business development with various remittance companies, including Western Union, Orlandi Valuta, Vigo Remittance, and Sigue Remittance Corp. After retirement, he became involved with two nonprofits: he was executive vice president and founding member of HAAPE (Helping Adults with Autism Perform and Excel) and an executive board member of YAWA (Young Adults with Autism). He also is a board member of CASE (Caribbean Autism Support Education) foundation, helping educators and parents understand and educate children with autism.

Rea Ann Silva (1961–)

Cosmetics Executive

Born to a Mexican mother and a Portuguese father in Los Angeles, Rea Ann Silva was brought up in Los Angeles by her single mother and became a single mother herself. She became a makeup artist for the entertainment business, including doing the makeup for music, film, and television stars. Silva studied at the Fashion Institute of Design & Merchandising but really found her vocation at the makeup counter at the department store where she was employed. Eventually she became department head for the TV show *Girlfriends*, which featured four female lead actresses; it was one of the first shows shot in high definition, so Silva had to develop new techniques on their makeup. Her real-life experience included making up a vast array of women of color. In 2002 she developed a tool that would apply makeup seamlessly, and that is how she invented the egg-shaped Beautyblender sponge that has made her a fortune. In 2019 retail sales were projected to hit $215 million. Silva went on to develop other products, such as Bounce, a long-wear matte foundation that's full coverage, that are found at major retailers around the country. With forty shades of foundation, Silva aims at a diverse audience for her product.

Lionel Sosa (1939–)

Advertising Executive

Born on May 27, 1939, in San Antonio, Texas, Lionel Sosa became a graphic artist who developed a career in advertising, founding his own company, Sosart, in 1966. In 1974, he became a partner with Ed Yardang and Associates. In 1984, he founded Sosa and Associates, for which he serves as chairman and CEO. Sosa and Associates is the leading firm in handling national accounts targeted at Latino consumers. Beginning in the 1960s, Sosa became a leading agency for Republican political campaigns, including the Reagan and both Bush campaigns. He has served as the Hispanic media consultant in a total of eight Republican presidential campaigns and in 2015 was inducted into the American Association of Political Consultants Hall of Fame. His Republican affiliation was terminated, however, during the campaign of Donald Trump, who openly attacked Mexicans and Latinos. Thus, in 2016, he openly supported Hillary Clinton's presidential campaign. In 1990, *Adweek* magazine named Sosa and Associates the Agency of the Year and the Hottest Agency in the Southwest, with 1989 billings of $54.8 million. Sosa's clients include American Airlines, Anheuser-Busch, Burger King, Coca-Cola USA, Montgomery Ward, and Western Union. Among his many awards are the 1990 Entrepreneur of the Year, the 1989 Marketing Person of the Year Award, the 1989 Silver Award from the Public Relations Society of America, and the Gold ADDY from the American Advertising Foundation in 1988.

Matías de Tezanos (1979–)

Entrepreneur of Diverse Businesses

Matías Rodrigo de Tezanos Posse was born on November 11, 1979, in San Jose, Costa Rica. While in high school in Guatemala, de Tezanos began selling web services to local businesses in Guatemala City. Forced by his parents, de Tezanos went to college to study dentistry but dropped out after two years because what he really loved was the internet, and that was before the course of study in IT was available in Guatemala. The day after dropping out, de Tezanos cofounded a web design company. After that initial

foray, he started an online advertising company, ClickDiario Network, with a partner on many of his ventures: Julio González. The companies they launched from Central America and Mexico were LoPeor.com, S.A. (2000); Tarjetas Internet Corporation (2000–2002); and ClickDiario Network, Mexico (since 2002). In the United States, he established eleven different companies, including Autoweb.com, Inc.; ClickDiario Network; and HealthCare.com, Inc. Currently he is chairman of Kaptyn, Inc.; chief executive officer and co-managing director at PF Holdings LLC (which he founded); secretary, managing director, and director at Auto Holdings Ltd.; chief executive officer and director at People F, Inc. (which he founded in 2011); president and director at PF Auto, Inc. (a subsidiary of People F, Inc.); chief executive officer of Autoweb.com, Inc. (which he founded in 1995); and founder of Hotels.com at Hotels.com LP. As of 2005, ClickDiario had grown into a massive network that reached an estimated 50 percent of Spanish-speaking internet users worldwide, with sales offices in Miami, Mexico City, Buenos Aires, and Guatemala City. The network welcomed four million visitors a day, delivered one billion ad impressions each month, and had over ten million opt-in subscribers before he sold it to Livedoor. De Tezanos is on the board of seventeen other companies. He was honored as a Young Global Leader by the World Economic Forum in 2009 and named one of the top ten Hispanic entrepreneurs by *Inc.* magazine during 2011 and 2012.

Solomon Dennis Trujillo (1951–)

Media and Technology Executive

Born on November 17, 1951, in Cheyenne, Wyoming, Solomon "Sol" Trujillo attended high school and the University of Wyoming in his hometown. He earned both a B.S. in business and an M.B.A. at Wyoming, and he began his career in 1974 with the Mountain Bell division of AT&T. By age thirty-two he had ascended to vice president of Mountain Bell in New Mexico. In 1996, Trujillo became president of US West, then president and CEO in 1998. In 2000, he became CEO of Graviton and in 2003 of Orange S.A., a Paris-based multinational wireless giant with fifty million customers in nineteen countries. After this series of short tenures, in 2005 Trujillo became CEO of Telstra Communications, Australia's largest communications and media company, which was transforming itself from government ownership to private corporation—and Trujillo was to lead the company in the makeover. Trujillo cut down expenses and staffing while upgrading the networks and systems and introduced 3G to the entire Australian continent; Telstra's network became the largest and fastest in the world. So great was Trujillo's success that in 2008 he was named CEO of the Year by a leading tele-communications magazine. Over his career, Trujillo became known as a digital pioneer and champion of high-speed broadband to stimulate productivity and advance innovation across all sectors of the economy. In 2009, Trujillo retired from Telstra and returned to the United States. However, he once again entered the fray and became a director in Australia of a start-up company, Unlocked, a system for display advertising on consumer devices, in 2016.

Nina Vaca (1971–)
IT Consulting Executive

Nina Vaca was born in 1971 in Quito, Ecuador, and immigrated as a child to Los Angeles with her family, who established a series of small businesses there. The family moved to Texas in 1990, where Vaca graduated with a bachelor of arts degree in speech and communication and a minor in business administration from Texas State University in 1994. During the growth of her business, Vaca studied in executive education programs at Harvard Business School's Corporate Governance Executive Program, the Tuck School of Business, and the Kellogg School of Management at Northwestern. Nina founded Pinnacle Group in 1996 and has served as its chairman and CEO for over two decades. During that time Pinnacle grew rapidly. What started as a one-woman IT staffing firm has grown into a workforce solutions powerhouse providing multiple service lines to industry leaders in the telecommunications, financial services, transportation, and technology industries. In 2007, Pinnacle began providing services nationwide and in 2009 entered the Canada market. Pinnacle has since expanded internationally to serve clients in Europe, Latin America, the Asia Pacific region, and beyond. Pinnacle has been included in the *Inc.* 500/5000 list of fastest-growing companies thirteen times, and in 2015 and 2018 it was named the fastest-growing women-owned/led company by the Women Presidents Organization. In 2019 she joined the Forbes Technology Council to provide insight into the technology industry along with other world-class technology executives. Among her many awards are the Hispanic Women's Network of Texas Trailblazer of the Year (2019), Minority Business Hall of Fame and Museum Inductee (2016), Enterprising Woman of the Year Award (2016), Women Presidents Organization Fastest Growing Women-Owned Business Award (2015), and the Goldman Sachs Most Intriguing Entrepreneurs (2013).

LABOR

Latinos are the fastest-growing major group in the labor force of the United States. The Latino labor force has grown more than six times larger over the past forty years, from 4.3 million people in 1976 to 26.8 million in 2016. (In contrast, the overall labor force, comprising all other groups combined, grew by less than half—from about ninety-two million in 1976 to 132 million in 2016.) The Hispanic share of the labor force is projected to increase more than that of any race or ethnic group by 2026. From 2018 to 2028, the Latino share of the labor force is projected to increase more than that of any other race or ethnic group, increasing from 17.5 percent in 2018 to 20.9 percent in 2028. Their youth relative to other groups in the workforce and continued high rates of immigration indicate that Latinos will continue to increase their representation. From 2018 to 2028, the share for Latino men is projected to increase from 9.9 percent to 11.7 percent, while the share for Latina women is projected to increase from 7.5 percent to 9.2 percent. The groups with the highest labor force participation rates among Latinos were Salvadorans (72.2 percent); other Central Americans, excluding Salvadorans (70.8 percent); and South Americans (70.0 percent). Puerto Ricans and Cubans (each at 61.7 percent) had the lowest labor force participation rates.

Although the numbers have increased rapidly, conditions of employment for Latinos have deteriorated over the years. Many worker protections and benefits have been lost, incomes have declined in absolute terms, and the gap between Latinos and Anglos has widened.

As of 2020, the U.S. Bureau of Labor Statistics calculated that the median weekly earnings of Latino men, ages twenty-five to fifty-four, were $886 compared with $1,154 for White men. Latina women's weekly earnings for the same age group were $748, compared with $968 for White women.

LATINOS IN ORGANIZED LABOR

As a predominantly working people, Latinos have long been involved in efforts to organize as workers. One of their earliest groups, the Caballeros de Labor (Knights of Labor), was active in the Southwest in the late nineteenth century. Modeled after the American organization by the same name, Knights of Labor, its major stronghold was in New Mexico. It was never formally chartered, and it was more interested in land loss to recently arriving Anglos than labor issues.

During the late nineteenth and early twentieth centuries, a much greater number of Latino workers organized their own *mutualistas*, or mutual aid societies. These organizations engaged in social activities and provided for basic needs of workers, including insurance and death benefits for members. *Mutualistas* functioned largely as self-help organizations and did not threaten employers, which helps explain their greater success than unions.

Apart from the *mutualistas*, labor organizing among Latinos in the late nineteenth and early twentieth centuries was hindered by several factors. Latinos were concentrated geographically in largely anti-union settings in the South and Southwest. They also faced hostility and discrimination because of societal atti-

tudes, which often portrayed them as taking jobs away from Anglo workers. The major labor organization in the nation, the American Federation of Labor (AFL), tended to be craft-exclusive and structurally not interested in the participation of largely unskilled Latino workers. More important, the AFL itself could not resolve internally the nativism and racism pervasive in American society that often led it and its local unions to adopt exclusionary policies. These problems severely reduced Latino participation in organized labor and resulted in significant organizing efforts outside the mainstream labor federation.

In the early twentieth century, union organizing among Latino workers increased in many areas. The most notable efforts took place in agriculture, which was still the most significant single occupation for Latinos. Most organizing took place under the auspices

The child of a migratory farm laborer sits in a cabbage field during the harvest at a Farm Security Administration (FSA) labor camp in Texas, 1942.

of independent Mexican unions, while in some cases independent interethnic unions or multiethnic organizations existed, often with support from the radical Industrial Workers of the World. Railroad and other urban workers joined together for brief periods under the leadership of independent or socialist organizations and, occasionally, the AFL. Many miners formed union organizations with the support and encouragement of the Western Federation of Miners in the early years of the twentieth century.

Following a low point during the 1920s, labor organizing among Latino workers reached new peaks during the Great Depression. Independent organizations not affiliated with mainstream organized labor were most active and more typically composed of independent Mexican groups, socialists, and members of the Communist Party. In the later 1930s, leaders in the newly formed Congress of Industrial Organizations (CIO) also exhibited interest in organizing unskilled workers, and the CIO participated in the famous pecan shellers' strike in San Antonio in 1938, involving mostly young Mexican and Mexican American women. Organizers Emma Tenayuca and Manuela Solís Sager gained attention in Texas at that time and remained active in labor for many years afterward.

Organizing and strikes also occurred in the 1930s among mining, industrial, and agricultural workers throughout the country. Mexican farm workers in California were particularly active throughout the decade. Their efforts were highlighted by the Central Valley cotton strike of 1933, in which several groups of independent Mexican union organizers and radicals offered support. The AFL considered these activities a serious challenge to its dominance, and in many occupations it permitted the formation of local unions for the first time to attract Mexican workers into its fold.

The turbulence of the 1930s reflected a sharp increase in expressions of sympathy toward unionism and unions among Latino workers. Much of the support had been latent but untapped until that time. Immigrants from Mexico frequently had strong union sympathies because of their earlier experiences before they arrived in the United States. Nonetheless, traditional unions made only partial inroads into the Latino working population during the decade, hindered by continued employment discrimination, the success of employer efforts to pit workers against each other, and divisions within organized labor.

World War II served as a partial brake to direct labor organizing among Latino workers. But progressive elements within organized labor remained active, particularly in the struggle to eliminate many of the statutory forms of employment discrimination that Latinos and other workers continually faced. Their efforts contributed to the formation of the Fair Employment Practices Committee (FEPC) in 1941. The FEPC investigated discrimination throughout the country by private companies with government contracts. Over a third of its cases in the Southwest involved Mexicans. Despite the efforts of U.S. president Harry Truman, the FEPC was terminated at the end of World War II.

Unionization among Latino workers increased rapidly in the 1940s and 1950s, as Latino workers and sympathizers within both the AFL and CIO struggled for reforms that permitted them equal access and fair treatment. In many local unions they formed their own caucuses to demand representation and changes in discriminatory procedures by the union hierarchy and to encourage the union to challenge discriminatory practices by employers. They demonstrated union loyalty, sympathy, and a class-consciousness reinforced by their work experiences and treatment in the workplace. During this period they participated in many notable strikes, including the "Salt of the Earth" strike by miners in Silver City, New Mexico, which was led by the International Union of Mine, Mill, and Smelter Workers between 1950 and 1953. The efforts of the National Farm Labor Union, later called the National Agricultural Workers Union, to organize in California during the 1940s and 1950s were also noteworthy. Ernesto Galarza demonstrated keen insight as a union leader, scholar, and role model for a later generation of Chicano activists.

Among Latinos, a number of independent unions again began to form in both Puerto Rico and in the continental United States. The most notable was the National Farm Workers Association in California, led by César Chávez. It began as an independent organization in 1962 and became part of the AFL-CIO in 1966. It is now known as the United Farm Workers of America. During its numerous strikes and boycotts of table grapes, wines, and lettuce, it popularized many tactics, involving ethnic alliances, community organizing, and a focus on protecting the environment, organizing strategies for organized labor that have become more popular since then. Another creative venture, The East Los Angeles Community Union (TELACU) was formed in 1971 as the result of cooperative efforts between the United Auto Workers and community organizers in East Los Angeles to build a "community" union.

Union organizing activity in the United States peaked in the 1950s. From the early 1960s through the 1970s, the number of union members in the nation increased, though at a much slower rate than overall employment. The decrease in the rate of unionization during this period resulted from the reduction of jobs in highly unionized sectors, the growth of employment in traditionally nonunion occupations, the lack of vigilance of union leadership, increasingly sophisticated antiunion activities among employers, and unfriendly government policy that did not enforce protective labor legislation. Unfortunately, many of these policies persist, and union membership has declined steadily, as the concentration in wealth in the top 10 percent of society is at its greatest level and the middle class has shrunk to its lowest level since the post–World War II decades.

From the beginning of the Reagan presidency in 1981 until 1985, union membership fell rapidly

Picketers from International Ladies' Garment Workers' Union (ILGWU) Local 148-102 hold placards in English and Spanish to announce their strike against Sears Roebuck for unfair labor practices, February 1965.

while total employment rose. Between 1985 and 1990 union membership declined more slowly, while total employment continued to rise. The decline in the 1980s was due to factors unfavorable to unions during the past generation, coupled with the most hostile federal government policy toward labor organizing and unions since the 1920s. Today, union membership is at a historic low since the 1950s; in 2019, the percent of wage and salary workers who were members of unions—the union membership rate—was 10.3 percent. There were 14.6 million workers belonging to unions that year.

Unionization levels vary according to geography and occupation. Rates are highest in the Northeast and Midwest and lowest in the South and Southwest, where Latino workers are most concentrated. In 2019 the union membership rate of public-sector workers (33.6 percent) was more than five times higher than the rate of private-sector workers (6.2 percent). It seems that private employers had a greater ability than the government to thwart worker organization despite the more rigid laws restricting labor organizing in the public sector. The highest unionization rates were among workers in protective service occupations (33.8 percent) and in education, training, and library occupations (33.1 percent). Men continued to have a higher union membership rate (10.8 percent) than women (9.7 percent). African American workers remained more likely to be union members than White, Asian, or Latino workers. Nonunion workers had median weekly earnings that were 81 percent of earnings for workers who were union members ($892 versus $1,095). Among states, Hawaii and New York had the highest union membership rates (23.5 percent and 21.0 percent, respectively), while South Carolina and North Carolina had the lowest (2.2 percent and 2.3 percent, respectively).

Within the public sector, the union membership rate was highest in local government (39.4 percent), which employs many workers in heavily unionized occupations, such as police officers, firefighters, and teachers. Private-sector industries with high unionization rates included utilities (23.4 percent), transportation and warehousing (16.1 percent), and telecommunications (14.1 percent). Low unionization rates occurred in finance (1.1 percent), insurance (1.4 percent), professional and technical services (1.4 percent), and food services and drinking places (1.4 percent).

Total Latino union membership was almost eighteen million in 2019. Nationally, 10.6 percent of union membership was made up of Latino men and 9.7 percent of Latina women. Today, many Latinos serve as union officers, vice presidents, directors, and presidents.

IMMIGRATION AND MIGRATION

Immigration remains an important factor accounting for the expansion of the labor force in the United States. The rates of immigration from the 1980s to 2020, as shown earlier in this almanac, have increased dramatically. Legal immigration during the first decade of the twentieth century reached 8.8 million, while during the 1980s, 7.3 million immigrants were granted permanent residence. The immigrants are overwhelmingly young and in search of employment, and Latino immigrants continue to account for more than 40 percent of the total.

Several formal and informal programs have been established to encourage immigration of workers to the United States. The best-known forms of organized labor recruitment have involved agricultural workers from Mexico and Puerto Rico. These include the mechanisms in the Bracero Program and Operation Bootstrap. Labor recruitment by the U.S. Farm Placement Service to encourage labor migration for temporary seasonal employment has also influenced permanent settlement patterns. The H-2 Program within the Immigration and Nationality Act of 1952, as amended by the Immigration Reform and Control Act of 1986 (IRCA), has until recently (except under the Trump administration) continued to guide immigration patterns to the United States.

Internal migration has also affected the population patterns of Latinos within the United States. The most general patterns of migration include the dispersal of Mexicans from their historic concentrations in the Southwest to the Midwest, the Pacific Northwest, and recently to Florida, the East Coast,

A series of programs called Operation Bootstrap led to the industrialization of Puerto Rico after World War II. Here, a woman works in a garment shop in Puerto Rico, c. 1950.

and the Deep South; the spread of Puerto Ricans beyond New York to other areas of the country; and the relocation of Cubans to places other than Miami. Most of this migration has been through informal mechanisms, established at the level of individuals and families, and by word of mouth.

The major net flows of Latinos within the United States are from the Northeast and Midwest to Florida, Texas, and California; from New York to neighboring states in the Northeast; from California to neighboring states in the West; and from Puerto Rico to the Northeast and Florida. Cuban Americans are becoming increasingly concentrated at somewhat higher levels in Florida, while Central and South Americans are becoming more concentrated in California, Texas, and New York. People of Mexican origin are tending to disperse from the Southwest, while Puerto Ricans are moving

away from their center of concentration in New York City and, of course, the island of Puerto Rico.

The total impact of migration and immigration from the 1970s to the present has been twofold. In absolute numbers, Latinos have dispersed to a greater number of states and in wider areas within those states. In proportionate terms, they have concentrated at somewhat higher rates in the states already having large Latino populations. In 1970, 82 percent of the Latino population of the nation lived in nine states, with the proportion rising to 86 percent in 1990. The major recipients of Latino immigrants are California, Texas, and New York, and to a lesser degree Florida, Illinois, and New Jersey.

The Bracero Program

The Bracero Program, also referred to as the Mexican Farm Labor Program or the Mexican Labor Agreement, began as a bilateral agreement between the governments of Mexico and the United States. It was given congressional sanction in 1943 as Public Law 45. Both governments considered it an important part of the Mexican contribution to the World War II effort.

The program was very popular among agricultural employers, who quickly organized and lobbied Congress to ensure its continuation beyond the end of the war. They were able to extend it temporarily several times, claiming a shortage of able and willing workers in the United States. At the peak of the program in the late 1950s, the United States admitted more than 400,000 contract workers each season, almost twice as many as the number entering the country during the entire wartime emergency from 1942 to 1947.

The program was anathema to Mexican Americans and labor groups, who eventually gathered convincing evidence that, despite contract guarantees, braceros were not protected against abuses by employers and labor contractors, their working conditions were not adequate, and they frequently were not paid the wages guaranteed them by contract. The opposition also demonstrated the program had an adverse effect on wages and working conditions of domestic workers and stifled unionization efforts not only in agriculture but also in southwestern industry. The

An official examines a bracero's teeth and mouth while others wait for examination at the Monterrey Processing Center, Mexico, 1956. Despite contract guarantees, braceros were not protected against abuses by employers and labor contractors, their working conditions were not adequate, and they frequently were not paid contracted wages.

struggle against the program in the 1950s focused largely on its adverse effects, seeking reforms requiring employer compliance with contract guarantees and permitting braceros to join unions. This effort, nevertheless, failed, convincing opposition later in the decade to conduct an all-out attack on the program. Ultimately, a combined group of labor union representatives, Mexican American groups, religious and civic organizations, and their allies gained the support of a more pro-labor Democratic administration and obtained Congressional termination of the "temporary" program in 1964. The Bracero Program had brought approximately 4.5 million legal Mexican workers into the United States during its lifespan.

Since 1964, employer groups in agriculture have initiated several efforts in Congress to pass new and modified versions of the Bracero Program by hiring temporary seasonal contract workers from Mexico. Their efforts did not succeed for many years. However, the United States reinitiated temporary foreign worker programs, sometimes referred to as guest worker programs, which have more than doubled in size in recent decades: more than nine hundred thousand visas were granted in 2019, up from some four hundred thousand in 1994. Among the various fields targeted for these visas, agricultural work is the most represented. The H1B, H2A, H2B, and H4 visas, the largest of these programs, have been the subject of some of the most heated debate. The Donald J. Trump administration promised to reform these programs in line with its Buy American and Hire American agenda, but its proposals to overhaul the country's immigration system faced strong opposition in Congress. Meanwhile, amid the 2020 pandemic of a new coronavirus disease, COVID-19, Trump halted most foreign worker visa programs.

The termination of Public Law 78 in 1964 was an important victory for Mexican American and labor groups and helped pave the way for a flurry of labor-organizing efforts in agriculture in the late 1960s.

The *Maquiladoras*

The abolition of the Bracero Program also demanded greater efforts by the Mexican government to relieve its own unemployment via industrialization. The most important element of its border industrialization program is the *maquiladora* (assembly plant) program, initiated in 1965. Mexico found industrialists and politicians in the United States very interested in the industrialization program. Mexico hoped that it could raise the standard of living in the northern border region, while both the U.S. and Mexican governments were concerned about the possible negative political and economic consequences of leaving hundreds of thousands of Mexican workers stranded on the border without employment when the Bracero Program was ended. Industrialists were eager to reap the benefits offered by tax and tariff breaks and by the availability of unemployed and underemployed workers in Mexico.

The central feature of the plan established "twin plants" on both sides of the Mexico-U.S. border. It also set up a duty-free zone, which permits industrialists in the United States to ship unfinished goods to Mexico under bond for partial assembly or completion. The goods are then returned duty free to the "twin plant" on the U.S. side, to complete the manufacturing process. In the early years of the program, about two-thirds of the products involved in the program were electric and electronic goods. As the program expanded in the 1970s and 1980s, the range of products expanded rapidly. By the end of the 1980s, electric and electronic goods represented only about 35 percent of the total; textiles, clothing, and shoes, 18 percent; furniture, 10 percent; transportation equipment (including car motors), 9 percent; and a range of other goods, 28 percent.

The scale of production in the *maquiladora* industry also grew impressively. In 1966 it comprised fifty-seven plants with about four thousand workers. By 1979 it had about 540 plants hiring 120,000 workers, and by 1986 there were 844 plants employing 242,000 workers. By 1990 more than one thousand plants were employing about 450,000 workers. By 2020, there were 2,812 *maquiladoras* employing 1.2 million people.

Workers at a textile maquiladora *(assembly plant) in Tlaxcala, Mexico.*

The *maquiladora* program in its actual operation is not at all as it was initially conceived. Its original intent was to alleviate the unemployment of male workers stranded at the end of the Bracero Program. Yet, the workforce in the *maquiladoras* from the beginning has been approximately 85 percent female, mostly teenage women with very high rates of turnover. The program does not offer steady employment to unemployed men.

Another flaw in the original plan is that the "twin plant" concept never became operational. While the production phase was conducted in the Mexican plants, the "plants" on the U.S. side were essentially warehouses. Like their counterparts in Mexico, the operations in the United States offered low-wage, unskilled employment. The *maquiladora* program in effect became a runaway shop taking advantage of cheap Mexican labor and exemption from tariffs.

U.S. companies involved in *maquiladora* operations assert that the program enables them to produce in Mexico rather than transfer their operations to Asia. Yet, during the 1980s Japanese industrialists took advantage of the *maquiladoras* by sending greater amounts of raw materials to Mexico to have them finished, then shipped duty free into the United States. This led to a storm of protest in the United States, because, as U.S. representative Duncan Hunter of California complained, "The Japanese can essentially use the program simply as a conduit into American markets without conferring benefits on American businessmen." In their discussion of the *maquiladora* program, very few politicians have considered the adverse impact on the much larger group of workers in the United States continuously displaced by the program.

The North American Free Trade Agreement between Mexico and the United States expanded even further the *maquiladora* concept in scale offering potentially greater tax abatements for U.S. businesses. It increased the number of runaway shops already relocated from the South and Southwest across the border, where labor costs are lower, and worker and environmental protection is very weak. Furthermore, in Mexico it is difficult for organized labor and environmental and public interest groups from the United States to challenge corporations that are rooted in the United States and produce almost exclusively for the domestic market. Although advocates of the Free Trade Agreement maintain that it would expand the size of markets in both Mexico and the United States, the sharp wage differential between Mexico and the United States made it very difficult for Mexicans to afford to purchase the goods produced for export to the United States. In terms of worker protection, environmental damage, and the threat to the unity of Latino and Latin American workers on both sides of the border, the *maquiladora* program and the North American Free Trade Agreement posed even greater threats than the Bracero Program. The United States-Mexico-Canada Agreement, which replaced NAFTA in 2019, did not address any of these problems.

Migrant Farm Labor

A migrant worker is a person employed at a job temporarily or seasonally and who may or may not have a permanent residence in another community, state, or nation. It is a misconception to portray farm workers solely as migrants or Latinos, or to portray all migrant workers as farm workers. Migrants comprise only a small portion of the total of the ethnically diverse farm labor force of the United States. Seasonal migrant workers are employed in a wide range of occupations, including mining, forestry, and fishing, in addition to agriculture, which is the best-known form of migrant labor in the United States.

Most people who work on farms are either families who own or rent them or residents of nearby farms and communities who travel to work and return home at the end of the workday. Migrant farm workers are concentrated in the harvest operations of fruit and vegetable crops in several locations throughout the United States. At other times of the year, they seek employment in agricultural or other occupations, often where they are permanently settled.

The number of migrant agricultural laborers has declined sharply since the late 1930s when about four million people worked each season. Because of the problems of keeping track of them, it is very difficult to make an accurate estimate of their numbers. It is likely that about one million people were employed as migrant farm workers in the United States annually during the 1980s.

Agricultural migrants at the dawn of the twentieth century frequently were foreign immigrants who worked on farms temporarily while saving money to buy farms or seeking more permanent employment in nearby cities. On the West Coast, a large portion of the migrant farm workers in the late nineteenth and early twentieth centuries were Asians, while in other parts of the country most were Europeans and their children. With the expansion of the sugar beet, vegetable, and cotton industries in the early twentieth century, Mexican migrant workers increasingly took over seasonal farm labor, frequently returning to the Mexican border or nearby cities at the end of work in a crop or at the end of the season.

With the onset of the Great Depression, many Mexican migrant workers were displaced by southern laborers, who dominated the migrant agricultural labor force in the 1930s and 1940s. In the 1950s and 1960s Afro-American workers continued as the most numerous migrants along the eastern seaboard states, while Mexican and Mexican American workers soon dominated the migrant paths between Texas and the Great Lakes, the Rocky Mountain region, and the area from California to the Pacific Northwest. Some observers noted very rough patterns of movement referred to as "migrant streams" that went northward from Florida, Texas, and Southern California each season in the 1940s and 1950s; but these became increasingly blurred over time.

In spite of more sophisticated government programs on behalf of farm workers and governmental efforts to coordinate the needs of workers with the demands of employers since the 1950s, the movement of migrant workers between jobs remains very haphazard. Migrant and seasonal farm workers continue to experience long periods of unemployment, and they are among the worst-paid and least-protected workers in the nation. They suffer high rates of illness, retain low levels of education, and find few advocates within political circles. As outsiders to local communities, often separated by language and ethnic barriers, they seldom participate in decisions affecting the communities where they are employed.

In the 1960s and 1970s the migrant agricultural workforce changed rapidly. With the rise of the Black Power and Chicano movements, the appearance of modest protective legislation, and the increasingly successful unionization efforts of farm workers, employers increasingly sought to recruit and hire foreign workers to replace the citizens. Along the East Coast, they recruited increasingly from the Caribbean and supplemented with workers from Mexico and Central America. In other parts of the country, they recruited mostly from Mexico and Central America. In the 1980s and 1990s the vast majority of migrant farm workers in the United States have been foreign born. Many of them migrate seasonally from Mexico and the Caribbean to the United States through the H-2 Program, which became an important mechanism of labor recruitment following the termination of the Bracero Program. In recent decades, undocumented workers from Latin America have become the most important part of this labor force in many locations. Today, Mexicans are the most represented immigrants in the agricultural guest worker programs.

HISPANIC EMPLOYMENT IN INDUSTRY
Service Industries

The employment profile of workers in the United States has changed sharply in recent decades. The major category of service is increasing, while that of manufacturing is declining. The service industries include a wide range of activities, including private household work; restaurant, hotel, and food services; and health and personal service occupations. Employment in service industries, which nearly doubled between 1970 and 1990, is high among females in most areas. The rate of Latino employment in service occupations is about double that of the non-Latino population for males and about 40 percent higher for females.

In general, the distribution of Latinos in employment sectors depends more on if they were foreign born or native born. In general, today 18 percent of Latino immigrant men work in construction and 11 percent in agriculture. Latina immigrants are overrepresented in manufacturing at 19 percent. Foreign-born Latinos of both genders have very low representation

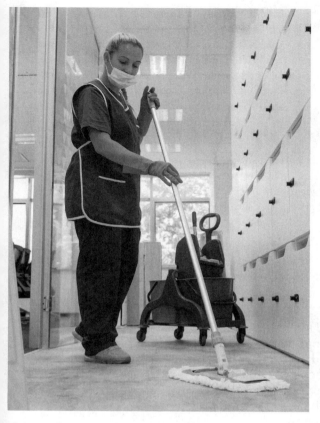

The rate of Latino employment in service occupations is about double that of the non-Latino population for males, and about 40 percent higher for females.

among manager, professional, and technical and sales personnel. They are most likely to be employed in the service and labor sectors. This is principally because of low educational attainment and diminished English-language skills. The employment distribution U.S.-born Latinos, however, approaches that of Whites, with Latinos employed in the same industries at similar rates. But the actual rank in those industries is lower for Latinos. For instance, 24.3 percent of Latino males are employed as managers or professionals, while 35.8 percent of Whites have those careers. Latinos in service professions are at 13.4 percent, while Whites are at 7.9 percent in service jobs. There are fewer Latinas in managerial and professional positons (37.7 percent) than White women (44.9 percent); more Latinas in technical and sales positions (39.2 percent) than White

women (35.6 percent); and more (14 percent) in service than White women (11 percent).

Manufacturing and Basic Industries

Manufacturing and basic industries, traditionally the mainstay of the U.S. economy and historically the indicator of the leading economic nations in the world, are declining rapidly. Manufacturing occupations include precision production workers, craft and repair people, as well as operators, fabricators, and laborers. Both Latino males and females are highly overrepresented in this category, double those of non-Latino females.

◆◆◆

FEDERAL EMPLOYMENT PROGRAMS AND LAWS

Title VII and the Equal Opportunity Commission

The Economic Opportunity Act (EOA) of 1964 was the centerpiece of President Lyndon B. Johnson's War on Poverty. The philosophy behind the War on Poverty espoused private initiative, and local efforts had not resolved longstanding problems of discrimination and poverty during the postwar boom in the United States. Furthermore, the government believed efforts to improve conditions were consistently thwarted by private interests, often in conjunction with local and state governmental authorities, where low-income or poverty-stricken families, African Americans, and Latinos were seldom represented. The federal government thus decided to initiate a program to provide training for workers to encourage recruitment and to monitor hiring practices of public and private employers across the nation.

The EOA also created the Office of Economic Opportunity (OEO) to administer a number of programs on behalf of the nation's poor. These included the Job Corps, the Community Action Program (CAP), and the Volunteers in Service to America (VISTA).

The Job Corps is a job-training program whose goal seeks to help disadvantaged youths ages sixteen to twenty-one find employment. In 1990 the typical Job Corps enrollee was eighteen years old, 83.5 percent were high school dropouts, 75 percent were minorities, 75 percent had never had a prior full-time job, 67 percent were male, and almost 40 percent came from families on public assistance.

VISTA, conceived as a domestic equivalent to the Peace Corps, worked with the poor in urban and rural locations. CAP was the primary OEO program, in which local groups combined the efforts of local government, business, labor, civic, and religious organizations and the poor to mobilize local resources to alleviate poverty.

Title VII of the Civil Rights Act of 1964 comprised the most important statute of the War on Poverty addressing employment discrimination. It prohibits discrimination on the basis of gender, creed, race, or ethnic background, "to achieve equality of employment opportunities and remove barriers that have operated in the past." Discrimination is prohibited in advertising, recruitment, hiring, job classification, promotion, discharge, wages and salaries, and other terms and conditions of employment.

> Title VII of the Civil Rights Act of 1964 prohibits discrimination on the basis of gender, creed, race, or ethnic background, "to achieve equality of employment opportunities and remove barriers that have operated in the past."

Title VII also established the Equal Employment Opportunity Commission (EEOC) as a monitoring device to prevent job discrimination. In effect, it renewed and expanded the Fair Employment Practices Committee, which had been dismantled at the end of World War II. The EEOC works in conjunction with state agencies in investigating charges of discrimination.

The issue of employment discrimination led to a great deal of litigation, and several of the important employment lawsuits directly involved Latinos. *Espinoza v. Farah Manufacturing Co.* (1973) held that Title VII does not protect discrimination against aliens. The Supreme Court also held, however, that Title VII prohibits practices that have "the purpose or effect of discriminating on the basis of national origin." In *Carino v. University of Oklahoma Board of Regents* (1984), the Court held that an employer cannot refuse to hire an individual "because the individual has the physical, cultural or linguistic characteristics of a particular national origin group," or discriminate "because of the individual's accent or manner of speaking."

In reaction to equal employment legislation and the increasing presence of Latinos and other non-English-speaking people in the workplace, some states in the 1980s and 1990s enacted so-called English-only amendments to their constitutions. Collectively they imposed English as the official language of their state.

Following the spirit of this legislation, many employers attempted to restrict the use of foreign languages by imposing English-only rules in the workplace. Such actions are prohibited under Title VII, which prohibits discrimination on the basis of national origin. EEOC policy provides that rules that "require employees to speak English only at all times are presumptively unlawful because they unduly burden individuals whose primary language is one other than English, and tends to create a hostile or discriminatory environment based on national origin."

Language rights thus became an important employment issue challenging Latino workers in the 1990s, particularly where their numbers were high. Public and private employers commonly engaged in hiring Latino employees because of their special skills as translators but seldom granted them compensation or considered such skills as important factors in job promotion. In *Pérez et al. v. Federal Bureau of Investigation* (1988), Latino FBI agents offered their special skills to the FBI more than Anglo Spanish-speakers and non-Spanish-speakers did but did not receive compensation. The federal district court held that by being concentrated in interpreting tasks, the Latino agents were treated differently from and denied promotional opportunities offered to Euro-American agents. Eventually, all of these laws and practices were challenged in the courts as discriminatory and were forced to be wiped from the books and from employment conditions.

As a result of positive legislation and court interpretations, conditions of employment for Latinos registered significant improvements in several areas during the 1960s and much of the 1970s.

The EEOC and CETA under Presidents Nixon and Carter

During Richard Nixon's presidency, the first efforts to dismantle President Lyndon B. Johnson's War on Poverty began. The Nixon administration did not overtly attack the concept of equal opportunity, nor did it challenge the theories or actual programs already established to deal with the chronically unemployed. Rather, its desire for changes focused on attempts to realign political relationships involving federal, state, and local governments and community organizations.

> During the Carter administration, the federal government expressed an increased commitment to equal opportunity, and the Comprehensive Employment and Training Administration (CETA) was strengthened.

Its remedies were part of its New Federalism program. The Great Society programs in the OEO were centralized, with training programs and a strong oversight mechanism headed by the federal government. Local involvement was conceived largely through participation in the organizations where citizens were directly involved, especially through CAP. The New Federalism sought to reduce federal involvement and place the programs in the hands of state and local governments.

While in theory local control should be superior in meeting local needs, the creators of the New Federalism conceived the change in political terms. The political problem they perceived was that under the War on Poverty programs, a modest shift in local power occurred away from the old elites—particularly Anglo politicians—in the direction of the poor, particularly Latinos and African Americans. They believed they could return power to the old elites by removing

the presence of the federal government and eliminating the community organizations.

The poor were justifiably dubious of Nixon's argument that local officials were most responsive to those most in need, having recent memories of breaking down local barriers to education and employment, with the assistance of federal government intervention.

The Nixon administration placed all employment and training programs, previously in the OEO, into the new Comprehensive Employment and Training Administration (CETA), created in 1973. The major difference between the old and the new poverty efforts was that the earlier employment and training programs were clearly targeted to specific population groups and allocated as "categorical" grants, on the basis of national and local considerations. Under CETA, allocations were granted directly to local politicians in the form of "bloc" grants to state and local governments, which could then make decisions on the kinds of programs to establish. Another change was that the CETA plan reduced the power of the federal government's regulations, standards, and other monitoring mechanisms created to ensure the efficacy of the local programs. Furthermore, although the new plan intended to allow local people to determine needs locally, no affirmative action guidelines were established to ensure that the poor and, especially, women, African Americans, and Latinos, the people for whom the programs were intended, would be represented in the decision-making process. This was particularly evident as CAP was severely weakened. The success of CETA rested on the goodwill of federal and local authorities. During the Nixon administration, many of the community leaders were removed, and CETA programs were made increasingly the province of local politicians.

During Jimmy Carter's administration, the federal government expressed an increased commitment to equal opportunity, and CETA was strengthened. It is no coincidence that at this time the economic well-being of Latinos and other nonwhites peaked and the gap with the White population narrowed.

Furthermore, CETA was considered a success by most of its Latino participants. In fiscal year 1978, 142,000 youths, or slightly more than one-tenth of those enrolled in CETA programs, were Latinos. Overall, approximately 5 percent of the country's Anglo youth, 19 percent of African Americans, and 13 percent of Latino youth participated in CETA programs that year. Latino participation ranged from 23 percent of Puerto Ricans, 13 percent of Mexican Americans, and 7 percent of Cubans. Interviews conducted that year indicated that more than 87 percent were satisfied with the program, and more than 70 percent believed that it improved their job chances. Nevertheless, CETA and government training programs for the unemployed were being more strongly criticized than ever before by their nonparticipant detractors, who found their own opportunity when Ronald Reagan was elected president.

The Job Training Partnership Act

The Reagan administration philosophy led to a profound change in government policy on job training programs based on both political and economic thought. Politically, the Reagan administration adopted the position that although it must still provide a "safety net" to assist the needy, such assistance should be distinguished from support, and it did not view support as a federal government responsibility. It also carried the New Federalism concept much further politically and economically than President Nixon by reducing the amount of federal assistance for job creation and other social service programs.

The federal government also reduced its direct involvement by operating more in "partnership" with private business as well as state and local government bodies. The impact of government philosophy and policy is clearly evident in the Job Training Partnership Act (JTPA) of 1983, the central employment training program of the Reagan and George H. W. Bush years. The JTPA, like its predecessor, CETA, delivers employment and training services to the economically disadvantaged in need. Compared with CETA, the JTPA depends much more on the private sector to deliver these services.

The new program departs sharply from earlier direct job creation strategies that were central to projects of the 1960s and the 1970s. Federally funded jobs created by the Public Service Employment, offering employment to both the cyclically and structurally unemployed, were eliminated under the JTPA. Part of the concept of less government support for the poor, it represented a 60 percent reduction in subsidies for youth employment. It severely reduced employment prospects for many disadvantaged youth whose first full-time employment had come from CETA and its predecessors.

Several structural problems in the JTPA specifically hinder Latino participation. A high proportion of Latinos are needy, in part because of a nearly 50 percent high school dropout rate and because over one-fourth are not fully proficient in English. The JTPA penalizes these people more than any other among the poor by not including precisely those who are most disadvantaged and harder to place. In addition, the JTPA has income-based eligibility stipulations requiring that people must either be receiving food stamps or not have more than a specific level of income. Many Latinos who are eligible for JTPA, however, are imbued with a work ethic that makes them unwilling to accept food stamps. Still others are not eligible because they are willing to accept jobs that place them in an income level slightly above the sharply increased level of eligibility requirements. Another problem is that the JTPA has increased requirements for documentation of eligibility beyond those of CETA—a policy that has been criticized as unduly burdensome. Furthermore, Mexican Americans, in particular, lack familiarity with government programs, and the means of informing them about JTPA programs are woefully lacking. Finally, Latinos lack a presence in most JTPA policy-making forums, and thus lack consistent advocates to set policies.

The impact of Reagan job training policy, continued under the Bush administration, is further evident in the case of the Job Corps, created under the EEOC, and presently part of the JTPA. The Job Corps has residential and nonresidential centers where enrollees take intensive programs in education, vocational training, work experience, and counseling. It is popular in both parties of Congress, and the U.S.

Department of Labor (USDL) has acknowledged its success. A 1985 USDL study determined that the Job Corps returns $1.38 to the U.S. Treasury in only three years for each $1.00 invested by the federal government. The funds come from continuing taxes paid by former Job Corps trainees once they begin employment and from reduced welfare payments. The Job Corps, serving the most disadvantaged, nonetheless, was among the programs cut most sharply by the JTPA.

The structural design of the incentives process created by the JTPA reveals severe difficulties in the program. Local JTPA offices are motivated by incentives based on the actual number of people hired by private employers. This has led to the process of "creaming" in client selection. Creaming selects the least-disadvantaged individuals because they are the easiest to place. The programs have targeted services primarily to in-school youth or high school graduates; thus, service to high school dropouts has declined sharply.

Furthermore, local employers are paid by JTPA funds to hire employees. This leads to widespread abuse, for it allows employers to receive government funds to "hire" individuals they would have otherwise hired without JTPA "incentives" of several weeks' or months' pay. The JTPA has become a major government subsidy for private employers, not a training program for those most in need.

Originally New Federalism was designed to transfer power from the federal government to local agencies and employers. In effect, it has taken away power from the poor and from community organizations, which have remained largely outside the decision-making process. In the past, community organizations worked in conjunction with federal government administrators. Under the JTPA, however, funding is granted directly to governmental agencies and private proprietors as rewards for their support. Because the monitoring system is so lax and community participation dismantled, efforts to expose the JTPA have been long delayed. As a result, the JTPA has shortchanged the needs of Latinos, African Americans, and others most in need of training, as well as society at large, while serving the narrow interests of employers in the private sector and their allies.

Employment Rights

During the 1980s the Reagan and Bush administrations also launched an attack on civil rights legislation as it extended to the workplace. The new Supreme Court justices appointed by Presidents Reagan and Bush helped change the direction of court protection of employees. In effect, its rulings have relaxed the duties of employers and have made it much more difficult for women and non-Whites to convince the courts that violations of civil rights laws have taken place. The attack peaked in a series of 1989 Supreme Court decisions relating to employment law. In *Patterson v. McLean Credit Union*, the Supreme Court ruled that an individual could no longer sue for racial harassment at work under a 1966 civil rights statute: "A practice of racial harassment adopted after an employee was hired does not by itself violate that employee's rights under the statute." In effect, it permitted the employer to hound petitioner Brenda Patterson out of her job because of race.

In *Wards Cove Packing Co. v. Atonio*, the Court ruled that a group of employees who were able to demonstrate that an Alaska cannery that hired Whites for well-paid and skilled jobs and minorities for low-paid, unskilled jobs, and even segregated employees by race in mess halls and dormitories, did not offer sufficient evidence of employment discrimination. It reversed twenty-eight years of well-established law in its holding by imposing a heavier burden on employees in proving its employer did not have legitimate business reasons for engaging in such practices.

During the same period, other Supreme Court cases severely limited the filing of discrimination charges, and the Court further ruled that a civil rights statute could not be used to sue local governments for damages for acts of discrimination. These and other cases successfully narrowed the coverage of civil rights statutes, making it extremely difficult for women and minorities to prove discrimination.

The erosion of past civil rights legislation by the Supreme Court during the Reagan and Bush administrations resulted in efforts by representatives of civil rights, African American, and Latino organizations to initiate a push for a new Civil Rights Act in

1990 to return to previous standards. The legislation sought to redress the discriminatory impact of recent Supreme Court decisions that in sum eliminated much of the thrust of equal employment opportunity law established in the previous generation. Although the 1990 bill had overwhelming support in both houses of Congress, the Bush administration vetoed the legislation on the grounds that it promoted quotas. A series of compromises produced a watered-down Civil Rights Act in 1991.

But even during the Barack Obama administration, with Reagan- and Bush-era conservative judges still on the Court, civil rights were further eroded with the *Shelby County v. Holder* (2013) landmark decision regarding the constitutionality of two provisions of the Voting Rights Act of 1965: Section 5, which requires certain states and local governments to obtain federal preclearance before implementing any changes to their voting laws or practices; and Section 4(b), which contains the coverage formula that determines which jurisdictions are subjected to preclearance based on their histories of discrimination in voting. The Supreme Court mandated an end to the preclearance of states, such as Texas and the Carolinas, that had engaged in patterns of voter discrimination to have the states apply for clearance from the Justice Department any time they attempt to change voting districts and voting procedures; this decision enabled states that had systematically worked to disenfranchise minority voters to continue to do so under a whole new slew of strategies, such as limiting absentee voting, limiting the number of polling places in minority districts, purging voter rolls, and, of course, intense gerrymandering.

Along the same lines of limiting the voting power of everyday citizens, the Supreme Court addressed campaign finance in its landmark decision of *Citizens United v. Federal Election Commission* (2010). Basically, the Court decided that corporations have the same right to free speech as citizens and therefore, the government must not restrict their expenditures on political communications. The effect of the decision is to allow corporations to use their considerable financial power to support their political candidates, a power that has the potential to overwhelm the financial support given by real people and real citizens to their candidates. This has solidified the role of

money in arriving at political decisions at all levels of government. And of course, Latinos and other minorities who have more meager means than even White middle-class citizens have thus seen their electoral power diminished in comparison.

Affirmative Action

Affirmative action, centering on the Civil Rights Act of 1964, was a central concept of the Great Society programs of the Johnson administration. It accepted the premise that the high levels of unemployment and ongoing discrimination that women and many non-White groups encountered were impediments to the vision of the Great Society. The federal government accepted the responsibility to devise "affirmative action" programs to remedy such discriminatory practices and their consequences.

The federal mandate was to encourage employers to voluntarily increase the presence of underrepresented minorities in the workforce to levels commensurate with their presence in the local community. Compliance officers in the Equal Employment Opportunity Commission (EEOC) and the Department of Labor set goals, targets, and timetables for employers.

Affirmative action programs were immediately criticized by some conservative elements who argued that affirmative action favored minorities over more "qualified" Anglos. The struggle over affirmative action continued into the 1970s, 1980s, and 1990s, when opponents coined the term "reverse discrimination," by which they suggested that White males were victims of discrimination as a result of affirmative action on behalf of women, African Americans, Latinos, and other underrepresented groups.

The attacks on affirmative action have had a profound impact on hiring policies in many sectors of private and public employment. They have contributed to the overall decline of the economic position of Latinos and other ethnic minorities from the 1980s to the present, both in absolute levels and in comparison with Anglo-Americans. It is most telling in top management positions in large corporations, where most surveys indicate that at least 95 percent of positions are still held by White males.

The federal government has failed not only to abide by its responsibility to serve as watchdog over affirmative action policies in the private sector but also to take affirmative steps itself. Although the Reagan administration could point to an increase in Latino representation in the federal workforce from 4.3 percent to 4.8 percent between 1980 and 1988, the Latino population during that period increased from 6.4 percent to 8.1 percent. Thus, Latino underrepresentation in federal employment during the Reagan administration increased sharply, from 50 percent to 69 percent. The underrepresentation was most stark in the highest levels. At the top scale of government, senior executive service, Latinos accounted for only 1 percent of the employees.

Despite Reagan's retrenchment on affirmative action and quotas, the Supreme Court reaffirmed affirmative action policies, holding that courts could order race-based quotas to fight discrimination in worker unions in *Sheet Metal Workers' International Association v. EEOC* (1986). In 1987, in *Johnson v. Transportation Agency, Santa Clara County, California*, the Supreme Court ruled that sex or race was a factor that could be considered in a pool of qualified candidates by employers. The impact of such decisions today is not clear. So far in the twenty-first century, debates on affirmative action have focused more on higher education than on employment.

Immigration and Naturalization Service

The U.S. Immigration and Naturalization Service (INS) existed from 1933 to 2003, at which point its functions were divided among three organizations: U.S. Citizenship and Immigration Services (USCIS), U.S. Immigration and Customs Enforcement (ICE), and U.S. Customs and Border Protection (CBP), all overseen by the new Department of Homeland Security (DHS). The number of undocumented aliens cannot be precisely determined, and it is the subject of intense debate. In the 1970s INS commissioner

Leonard Chapman, seeking to increase funding and expand the power of his organization, claimed that the United States harbored as many as twelve million undocumented workers. Other observers most commonly place the number in the range of 3.5 million to five million people.

Popular perceptions and the press portray almost all undocumented workers as Mexicans. This is further bolstered by the policies of the DHS, whose enforcement efforts are concentrated along the land border between Mexico and the United States, rather than at seaports and airports, or along the United States' northern border. About 95 percent of INS apprehensions at the dawn of the twenty-first century were Mexicans, yet it is likely that only about half of all undocumented workers in the United States are Latinos, the remainder being mostly natives of Europe and Asia.

> About 95 percent of INS apprehensions at the dawn of the twenty-first century were Mexicans, yet it is likely that only about half of all undocumented workers in the United States are Latinos.

In addition to their numerical importance, undocumented workers have been at the center of several political battles. On several occasions in recent decades, a national hysteria among citizens developed over their presence, typically during periods of economic recession and depression. Debates intensified during those periods over whether the undocumented take jobs away from U.S. citizens.

Operation Wetback, which occurred during a time of recession in 1954, involved a concerted campaign by the federal government that successfully apprehended more than one million undocumented Mexican workers. The frenzy subsided when the government and private employers expanded the scale of the Bracero Program, reducing the demand of agricultural employers for undocumented workers.

Following abolition of the Bracero Program in the mid-1960s, the number of undocumented workers again began to increase, and a new hysteria appeared in public circles, accompanied by increased activity by the border patrol. By 1977 the INS was again apprehending more than one million undocumented workers each year.

The effect of undocumented workers on the economy has stirred a wide-ranging debate in the nation. One side of the argument is that they are a major drain on public services and that they displace U.S. citizens by accepting low-paying jobs. These arguments frequently are based on stereotypes and ethnic biases, and they seldom address the related issue of why employers are permitted to disregard protective labor statutes and immigration law.

An opposing position is that the undocumented pay taxes, and because they seldom use available social services, they make a very positive contribution to the nation's economy. Further, the jobs in which they are employed typically are those that others are unwilling to perform.

Undocumented workers retain most employment rights of citizens, including those of minimum wage, joining and participating in union activities, the right to sue over contracts, and other protection under federal labor law. They are also deemed "employees" within the meaning of the National Labor Relations Act and are protected under its provisions. Legal cases have also recognized the right to worker's compensation and protection under the Fair Labor Standards Act. Nonetheless, employers frequently use the INS to escape their responsibilities under these laws and report for deportation workers who attempt to organize unions or assert other employment rights.

> Undocumented workers retain most employment rights of citizens, including those of minimum wage, joining and participating in union activities, the right to sue over contracts, and other protection under federal labor law.

The Immigration Reform and Control Act of 1986

Sensitive to the increased immigration that began in the 1960s and the economic uncertainty of the 1970s, the Gerald Ford administration appointed several task forces to address the issue of undocumented entry into the United States. It encouraged several congressional representatives to introduce new legislation to control immigration to the United States. After more than a decade of debate, Congress enacted the Immigration Reform and Control Act of 1986, popularly referred to as IRCA.

IRCA contains three major provisions. First, it establishes civil and criminal penalties, referred to as employer sanctions, on employers who fail to verify the documentation of employees hired since 1986 regarding whether they are eligible to work. This marks the first time in U.S. history that employers have been prohibited by law from hiring undocumented workers. Second, IRCA provided a one-time provision to legalize undocumented workers in the United States. The legalization process included a separate program to legalize seasonal agricultural workers (SAWs) in the United States. Third, the law specifically prohibits several forms of employment discrimination. In response to the concerns of Latino and civil rights groups that the employer sanctions would result in discrimination, the law mandated that the General Accounting Office (GAO) conduct an ongoing investigation of the impact of IRCA for three years. IRCA specifically provides Congress with the statutory authority to repeal employer sanctions if the GAO's final report were to conclude that widespread discrimination existed. To facilitate the provisions of the law, Congress also strengthened the power and personnel of the INS.

The GAO made its final report on IRCA to Congress on March 29, 1990. It observed that the implementation and enforcement of employer verification and sanctions provisions were not carried out satisfactorily, that they had caused a widespread pattern of discrimination against members of minority groups, and that they caused unnecessary regulatory burdens on employers. Many employers were confused about the law and its application and initiated illegal discriminatory hiring practices against Latinos, Asians, and other people who appeared "foreign." Even Anglo workers experienced discriminatory practices. The GAO concluded that a "widespread pattern" of discrimination existed based on national origin, practiced by 19 percent of the employers surveyed, that included not hiring foreign-appearing or foreign-sounding job applicants for fear of noncompliance with the law. A "sting" operation involving pairs of Latino and Anglo "testers" revealed that "Anglo testers received 52 percent more job offers than the Latino testers with whom they were paired."

The GAO investigation was narrow in its view of what constituted "widespread discrimination" and did not support repealing employer sanctions. Other agencies and civil rights activists documented cases of discrimination, such as employers firing both undocumented workers and those who were applying for legalization, depriving them of seniority and other benefits, imposing English-only rules, withholding paychecks, failing to pay overtime, harassing them sexually, assaulting them physically, and violating other civil and constitutional rights. In effect, IRCA pushed undocumented workers into even less regulated and more exploitative jobs.

> The Latino workforce is younger than other major workforce groups, and in the future it will represent an even greater portion of the workforce.

Employers have also suffered the impact of employer sanctions. Estimates of total costs to businesses to perform record-keeping required by employer sanctions vary from $182 million to $675 million per year. Furthermore, businesses are paying millions of additional dollars in fines and otherwise suffering financially because of loss of workers and INS intrusions into the workplace.

In meeting one of its original goals, preventing the entry of undocumented workers into the United States, IRCA appears to have been successful in its first two years. Since that time, the entry of undocumented workers has increased sharply. By the early 1990s it appeared that the prohibitions of IRCA had not had a long-term impact on rates of undocumented entry into the country. They have proved to be a nuisance to employers and an additional burden to all workers—undocumented, legal residents, and citizens alike.

Thus, the GAO report and other evidence confirmed the fears of Latino groups before its enactment—that the law would intensify discrimination against Latinos. On the basis of the GAO report and other evidence, employer sanctions are causing widespread discrimination. Latino activists are trying to convince Congress to comply with its own mandate and repeal employer sanctions.

YOUTH EMPLOYMENT

The Latino workforce is younger than other major labor groups, and in the future it will represent an even greater portion of the workforce. Latinos have lower levels of schooling than other groups. Among youths ages sixteen to twenty-one not attending college, more than two-fifths of employed Afro-Americans and Anglo-Americans are high school graduates, compared with less than one-third of Latinos. Latino youths are more likely to work full time and year round than either Anglo- or Afro-American youths. As with other groups, Latino male youths are more likely to be employed than females.

Youths of all backgrounds tend to have much higher unemployment rates than older workers, and their rate of unemployment is more sensitive to business cycles. Anglo youths have the lowest unemployment level, while African Americans have the highest rate of unemployment, which tends to be less sensitive to changes in the economy than either the Anglo or Latino rates. Unemployment rates for Latinos fluctuate between the two others. During upturns in the economy, the rate of unemployment declines more sharply for Latino youths, while during downturns, it rises much more rapidly than for either Anglo- or Afro-Americans.

Dennis Valdez

PROMINENT LATINO LABOR ORGANIZERS

César Chávez (1927–1993)

Born on March 31, 1927, near Yuma, Arizona, to a family of migrant farm workers, César Chávez attended nearly thirty schools, eventually achieving a seventh-grade education. During World War II he served in the navy, after which he returned to migrant farm labor. He eventually settled down in 1948 in the barrio of Sal Si Puedes ("Get Out If You Can") in San Jose, California. It was in San Jose that he began working for the Community Service Organization (CSO) as a community organizer. By 1958 he had become general director of the CSO in California and Arizona. In 1962, wishing to organize farm workers, he resigned the CSO directorship and moved to Delano, California, where he became head of the United Farm Workers Organizing Committee, which is today known as the United Farm Workers, AFL-CIO. From 1965 on, Chávez and his fledgling union embarked on a number of history-making strikes and national boycotts of agricultural products that became the most successful in the history of farm labor in the United States. Principally because of Chávez and his organization's efforts, the California legislature passed the California Labor Relations Act in 1975, which provides secret ballot union elections for farm workers. Owing to his efforts, as well, there have been many improvements in wage, health, and housing conditions for farm workers in California and Arizona. Chávez is remembered as a tireless and spiritual leader of farm workers everywhere, bringing to national attention their plight through media appearances and interviews, hunger strikes, and well-organized boycotts. Chávez died on April 23, 1993, and is memorialized today by streets, schools, and other institutions named in his honor, and in 1993 a newly discovered asteroid, 6982 Cesarchavez, was named for him. Other awards include the Jefferson Award for Greatest Public Service Benefiting the Disadvantaged

(1973), the *Pacem in Terris* Award (1992), a Catholic award meant to honor "achievements in peace and justice," and the Presidential Medal of Freedom (1994), the country's highest honor for nonmilitary personnel, conferred by President Bill Clinton. In 2006, California governor Arnold Schwarzenegger inducted Chávez into the California Hall of Fame.

Linda Chávez-Thompson (1944–)

Born on August 3, 1944, possibly somewhere in West Texas, to a sharecropping family, Linda Chávez-Thompson began working outside her home farm as a cotton picker at age ten, and at age sixteen she dropped out of school to help support her family. In 1967, Chávez-Thompson became a secretary on the staff of the Construction Laborers' Local 1253 in Lubbock, Texas, and she began moving up in labor organizing, joining the staff of the North Texas Laborers District Council. In 1971 she became an international representative on the staff of the American Federation of State, County, and Municipal Employees. She kept moving up in the union structures and in 1993 was the first Hispanic woman elected to the Labor Council of the AFL-CIO; in 1995 she was elected executive vice president of the AFL-CIO and in 1996 was elected a vice president of the Labor Council for Latin American Advancement. She served as vice president until 2007. She was the first woman, person of color, and Latina elected to an officer position within the union. She is credited with having radically changed the union's stance on immigration reform. The Texas native was the Democratic nominee for lieutenant governor of Texas in 2010 but was defeated by her Republican opponent. In 1997 she was elected vice chair of the Democratic National Committee and was reelected in 2007 for another four-year term.

Bert Corona (1918–2001)

Bert Corona was born on May 29, 1918, in El Paso, Texas, where his parents had immigrated in 1914 or 1915 from Mexico as refugees from the Mexican Revolution. He attended public schools in El Paso and in 1936 accepted an athletic scholarship to attend the University of Southern California; during his college days, he organized tenants for better housing and in 1937 began a relationship with the Congress of Industrial Organizations (CIO) in developing unions in the Southwest. He worked with the CIO in organizing cannery and warehouse workers. As a college student he also assisted in organizing a strike of the International Longshore and Warehouse Union (ILWU) and was subsequently elected secretary of the union local; in 1941 he was elected president of the local. Continuing with the CIO, Corona went on to organize workers in various industries in the Los Angeles area, often working with Mexican and other ethnic groups. In the 1940s he sought an alliance of all Latino workers in the United States under the banner of the Spanish-Speaking Peoples' Congress led by Luisa Moreno. The Congress and the CIO did not limit their organizing to labor but expanded to work for the civil rights of Latinos. When World War II broke out, Corona enlisted, but he was detained within the Army various times for his prior union activities, being labeled a Communist and agitator, and thus was kept out of combat service. After the war, Corona and his wife moved into public housing and soon organized the Mexican-American Committee for Justice in Housing. He also became part of a group's failed attempt to organize a third political party, the Independent Progressive Party, in the San Francisco Bay area. In the 1950s he became affiliated with the Asociación Nacional México-Americana (Mexican American National Association), which supported independent progressive unions, and he became the association's chief organizer in Northern California. In 1960 Corona and his associates cofounded the Mexican American Political Association, which they formed out of their disaffection for the Democratic Party; Corona served as president from 1966 to 1971. Corona was also a pioneer in education for Mexican Americans, contributing to the development of the Mexican American Youth Conference and even serving as president of the Association of California School Administrators. Throughout his later life, Corona maintained his activism and during the last decades taught Chicano Studies at the University of California, Northridge and California State University. Corona died on January 15, 2001.

Héctor Figueroa (1962–2019)

Héctor José Figueroa was born on April 3, 1962, in Ponce, Puerto Rico, to parents who were teachers. Figueroa attended the University of Puerto Rico but dropped out. He moved to New York City where he obtained a degree in economics from New York University. After doing some graduate work at the New School for Social Research, he dedicated the rest of his life to union work. He started as a researcher for the Amalgamated Clothing and Textile Workers Union in New York and then joined the Service Employees International Union (SEIU) in Washington. He did a stint in Puerto Rico managing a successful campaign to organize public employees there. Figueroa returned to New York in 2000 and became the secretary-treasurer of 32BJ. He was elected president in 2012 and reelected in 2018. The SEIU is one of the most powerful unions on the East Coast. The 32BJ chapter of the SEIU represents more than 170,000 building cleaners, security guards, doormen, and airport workers. In his seven years of leadership, the union local added about fifty thousand members. One of his greatest successes came in 2018: the Port Authority of New York and New Jersey's agreement to raise the minimum wage to $19 an hour for about forty thousand workers at the three main airports serving New York City. He also had success in increasing minimum hours and protecting immigrants from targeting by the U.S. Immigration and Customs Enforcement (ICE). Figueroa died July 11, 2019.

Ernesto Galarza (1905–1984)

Born on August 15, 1905, in Tepic, Nayarit, Mexico, Ernesto Galarza immigrated to the United States as a refugee with his family during the Mexican Revolution. Galarza attended schools in Sacramento, California, where he was orphaned while in high school and thus had to support himself. Galarza went on to Occidental College and then received a master's degree from Stanford University in 1929. He later received a Ph.D. degree in education from Columbia

University. Galarza then worked as a research assistant in education for the Pan American Union from 1936 to 1947, when he was promoted to chief of the Division of Labor and Social Information. In 1947 he became research director for the AFL's National Farm Labor Union and moved to San Jose, California. In 1947 Galarza organized a strike against the DiGiorgio Corporation in Arvin, California, that lasted thirty months. During the next fifteen years he dedicated his life to agricultural workers, serving as secretary-treasurer and vice president of the union, which held more than twenty strikes during that time. During the 1960s Galarza worked as a professor, researcher, and writer of various books on farm labor topics. His most famous book, *Merchants of Labor* (1964), documented the abuses within the Bracero Program and helped to bring about the end of the program. Without competition and strike breaking from guest workers, the union cause was advanced and prepared the field for the advent of César Chávez and the United Farm Workers in 1965. In the 1970s Galarza developed materials for bilingual education, including original books for children. Other books of his are still read in university classrooms today: *Spiders in the House and Workers in the Field* (1970) and *Barrio Boy* (1971). Galarza died on June 22, 1984.

Gilberto Gerena Valentín (1918–2016)

Gilberto Gerena Valentín is a key figure in Puerto Rican labor organizing on mainland United States and had a central role in the 1964 boycott of New York City schools. According to *Centro Voces*, he had a part in the founding and development of "all the major Puerto Rican organizations in the postwar period, including the Congreso de Pueblos, the Puerto Rican Day Parade, the National Association for Puerto Rican Civil Rights, the Puerto Rican Folklore Festival and the Puerto Rican Community Development Project." Gerena Valentín was also a pioneer in the creation of coalitions with the principal African American civil rights organizations, playing a central role in the mobilization of Puerto Ricans for the famed marches on Washington in 1963 and 1968. In 2013, Gerena Valentín published his memoir, *My Life as a Community Activist, Labor Organizer, and Progressive Politician in New York City.*

Dolores Fernández Huerta (1930–)

Dolores Clara Fernández was born on April 10, 1930, in Dawson, a small mining town in the mountains of northern New Mexico. Her father, a farm worker, was a union activist who was elected to the New Mexico legislature in 1938. But the dominant influence in her life was her mother, Alicia Chávez, who ran a restaurant and a hotel that catered to and cared for farm workers. After her parents' divorce when Huerta was three years old, she spent most of her childhood and early adult life in Stockton, California. She studied education at the University of the Pacific's Delta College and became an elementary school teacher. In 1955 she began work with Fred Ross and César Chávez, pioneer organizers of the Mexican American chapter of the Community Service Organization, which worked for the economic progress of Latinos. In 1960, Huerta cofounded the Agricultural Workers Association, which set up voter registration drives and pressed local governments to improve living conditions in Mexican American neighborhoods. In 1962, she cofounded with Chávez the National Farm Workers Association, which would later become the United Agricultural Workers Organizing Committee and later the United Farm Workers (UFW). One of her first victories as a lobbyist for the farm workers union was obtaining Aid for Dependent Families (AFDC) and disability insurance for farm workers in California in 1963. She worked with Chávez in administering the union, and in 1965 Huerta directed the famed national boycott of grapes that resulted in the entire California table grape industry signing a three-year collective bargaining contract with the UFW in 1970. As part of the strike and boycott, in 1966 Huerta negotiated a contract between the union and Schenley Wine Company; it was the first time that farm workers had ever brought an agricultural business or corporation to the bargaining table. Huerta eventually became the lobbyist for the UFW in Sacramento, California, and was instrumental in the enactment of the Agricultural Labor Relations Act of 1975, which was the first law of its kind in the

United States to grant farm workers in California the right to collectively organize and bargain for better wages and working conditions. Among her many awards are the Eugene V. Debs Foundation Outstanding American Award, the Eleanor Roosevelt Award for Human Rights, and the Presidential Medal of Freedom. In 1993, she was the first Latina inducted into the National Women's Hall of Fame.

Luisa Moreno (1906–1992)

Known as Luisa Moreno, Blanca Rosa López Rodrigues was born into a wealthy family in Guatemala City on August 30, 1906, but received her elementary education in San Francisco. After graduating from high school in Guatemala, she returned to the United States to pursue a college education because women were not allowed to attend university in her home country; she went on to graduate from Holy Name University in Oakland, California. She worked for a time as a reporter in Mexico City and, later, as a seamstress in New York City, where she experienced firsthand labor exploitation and racial discrimination, especially in the garment industry. She thus became active in labor organizing and was even beaten by police during a strike. When Moreno joined the Communist Party in 1930, she changed her name to Luisa Moreno. She first became a professional labor organizer in 1935 as part of the American Federation of Labor (AFL), and after that she worked with the Unified Cannery, Agricultural, Packing, and Allied Workers of America (UCAPAWA), part of the Congress of Industrial Organizations (CIO). While in the UCAPAWA, she helped organize workers at pecan-shelling plants in San Antonio, Texas, and cannery workers in Los Angeles, industries that employed hundreds of women, many of whom were Latinas. In 1938 she sought to unite all Latino workers of the United States, regardless of their nationalities or ethnicities, into the National Congress of Spanish-Speaking Peoples. While working in California in 1941, she was named the international vice president of the UCAPAWA. In 1943 she cofounded the Citrus Workers Organizing Committee in Riverside and Redlands, California. During World War II she founded various organizations to support Mexican immigrant workers. In 1947 Moreno retired from her activism and was deported

to Guatemala in 1950 after being hounded and persecuted because of her organizing activities and her Communist Party affiliation. Moreno died on November 3, 1992, in Guatemala.

Emma Tenayuca (1916–1999)

Born on December 21, 1916, in San Antonio, Texas, Emma Tenayuca received her primary and secondary education there. Before even graduating from Brackenridge High School in 1934, Tenayuca was organizing workers and protests, which at times led to her arrest. Tenayuca was instrumental in the establishment of two international ladies' garment workers unions and was active in a more politically oriented organization, the Woman's League for Peace and Freedom. Out of her idealism and concern for exploited workers, Tenayuca joined the Communist Party in 1936. She became known as *La Pasionaria* (The Impassioned) in remembrance of an earlier women's activist in Spain, when she became the major organizer and leader of one of the largest Latino worker strikes in history: the 1938 Pecan-Sheller's Strike in San Antonio on behalf of the National Workers' Alliance. The strike involved the walkout of thousands of pecan shellers from the approximately 130 factories that made up one of San Antonio's major industries. The strike was successful after thirty-seven days, when arbitration was started and ultimately led to a substantial raise for the workers, imposed by the National Labor Relations Board. After the success of the strike, Tenayuca was targeted by authorities and mobs as a Communist and had to leave San Antonio. She took refuge first in Houston, then in California, where she continued her labor-organizing activities. While there, she also went on to pursue advanced education. She obtained her B.A. in education at San Francisco State College in 1952 and, after moving back to Texas, her M.A. in education at Our Lady of the Lake University in San Antonio in 1968. She taught in the Harlandale School District in San Antonio until her retirement in 1982. Tenayuca died on July 23, 1999.

POLITICS AND LAW

Since the late 1900s, Latino Americans have become one of the largest and fastest-growing groups of elected officials in the United States. Former New Mexico governor Bill Richardson has stated, "National candidates and both major political parties are undertaking major campaigns to woo Latino American support. We are recognized as the nation's fastest growing minority group and are being courted as such. This attention will only increase our political strength."

LATINOS IN THE POLITICAL PROCESS

Widespread political activity at the national level by Latinos has been intermittent since the first Latino was elected to Congress. Joseph Marion Hernández was elected to the House of Representatives as a delegate from the Florida Territory in 1822 as a member of the Whig Party. No other Latino held national office for thirty years. A total of eleven Latinos were elected to the U.S. Congress in the entire nineteenth century, all from New Mexico except for one from California and Representative Hernández from the Florida Territory. From the turn of the century until the 1950s, a total of fifteen Latinos served in Congress—five from New Mexico, two from Louisiana, and eight resident commissioners from Puerto Rico, which became a U.S. possession in 1898. Since the 1960s the number of Latino Americans elected to Congress has been steadily increasing. In 2020, there were 128 Latinos serving in the U.S. Congress.

For a century the majority of Latinos holding political office at the local level was limited to southwestern states, southern Florida, and New York City. Since the 1960s growth in the population of Latinos and favorable civil rights legislation have combined to create opportunity for Latino candidates to win public office in other areas of the country and at all levels of elected government. Latinos have made the greatest inroads at the municipal level, where they are now the majority population of the largest cities in the United States.

The National Association of Latino Elected and Appointed Officials (NALEO) directory lists 6,832 Latino elected officials in office throughout the nation in 2019. The directory lists the names and addresses of Latino members of every elected body, from school board members to senators.

LATINO VOTING AND THE VOTING RIGHTS ACT OF 1965

The primary aim of the Voting Rights Act of 1965 was African American enfranchisement in the South. Specifically, obstacles to registration and voting faced by African Americans were the major concern of those who framed the statute in the 1960s. Its potential as a tool for Latinos was not fully realized until the act was extended and amended in 1970.

The 1970 amendments to this landmark legislation added a provision that was designed to guard against inventive new barriers to political participation by requiring federal approval of all changes in voting procedure in certain jurisdictions, primarily southern

states. Disgruntled officials in Mississippi and other southern states embarked on schemes to dilute African American voter impact in elections by eliminating single-member districts and creating at-large voting.

The U.S. Supreme Court responded, in *Allen v. State Board of Elections* (1969), by extending federal authority to object to proposed discriminatory alterations in voting districts, the introduction of at-large voting, and other such changes, in addition to reaffirming the original power to object to discriminatory innovations involving registration and voting.

Until 1980 (with the single exception of the 1930 census), the U.S. Census Bureau classified Latinos as "White," and many people argued that to extend coverage of the Voting Rights Act to a group who considered themselves White was unjustifiable. The Fifteenth Amendment rights secured by the statute

Representative Barbara Jordan of Texas speaks to President Gerald R. Ford (seated) in 1975 at the signing ceremony for H.R. 6219, Extending the Voting Rights Act of 1965, which amended the act to include "language minorities," specifically including Spanish-speakers.

protected against denial of the right to vote only on account of "race, color or previous condition of servitude." If Latinos were White, they were ineligible for the special protection of the Voting Rights Act.

During congressional hearings to extend the Voting Rights Act in 1975, J. Stanley Pottinger, assistant attorney general of the U.S. Justice Department's Civil Rights Division, saw the labeling problem as inconsequential and told Congress that the Justice Department's practice "has been to treat Indians, Puerto Ricans, and Mexican Americans as racial groups." His argument hardly settled the matter for everyone, but Congress agreed to amend the act to include "language minorities," which specifically included Spanish speakers.

In addition, the Voting Rights Act Amendments of 1975 made permanent the national ban on literacy tests. The amendments condemned any action by states, which was no longer limited to southern states, to realign voting districts to dilute the impact of minority voters who resided within the district. Any redistricting plan would have to be approved by the federal government.

In 1980 the U.S. Supreme Court, in *City of Mobile v. Bolden*, rejected a challenge to at-large elections in Mobile, Alabama, because the Court was not convinced that the city had acted with the purpose of discriminating against minority voters. The Court, in its sharply divided decision, found that the city had not violated the Voting Rights Act. Congress reacted to the Supreme Court decision with the important Voting Rights Act Amendments of 1982. The amendments, under Section 2, prohibit any voting law or practice created by a state or political subdivision that "results" in denial of the right of any citizen of the United States to vote on account of race, color, or language-minority status. The amendments eliminated the need to prove that the state or political subdivision created a voting law with the "intention" of discriminating against minority voters.

In one of the first cases to be tried under Section 2 of the 1982 amendments, *Velásquez v. City of Abilene*, prominent judge Reynaldo G. Garza delivered the opinion of the U.S. Court of Appeals for the Fifth Circuit. Garza stated for the court that the in-

tention of Congress was clear in cases of vote dilution, referring to the 1982 amendments. Garza stated that the city of Abilene's use of at-large voting, bloc voting, and other voting mechanisms resulted in vote dilution and had a discriminatory effect on Latino American voters in the city.

A year later the Fifth Circuit Court made a similar ruling in *Jones v. City of Lubbock*. Lubbock, a medium-sized city in Texas with a diverse population, had a clear White majority. Under an at-large voting scheme, the majority uniformly elected an all-White city council. The court found that the voting method used by the city polarized voting between the White majority and minority voters, and the result was discrimination against minority voters.

Holdouts of racially discriminatory electoral patterns have continued to come under intense pressure from the courts to end discrimination against minority voters. Over the last few decades the success in the courts was contributing to the growing numbers of Latinos holding elected offices across the United States. In 1991, for the first time in history, the city of Abilene had two Latinos on its city council; the city of Lubbock had one Latino on its city council, as well as a Latino county commissioner.

However, after the 2010 census and the sweeping into power of conservative Republicans, partisan gerrymandering increased steeply, with the purpose of disenfranchising minorities. As of 2020 very few of the 435 congressional districts in the United States have a competitive partisan balance between parties. A conservative Supreme Court upheld partisan gerrymandering in *Rucho v. Common Cause* (2019), thus giving state legislatures a free hand in disguising their intent to discriminate by drawing district maps to dilute minority votes. Many states where Latinos and other minorities are a sizeable part of the citizenry have also devised numerous ways to dilute or discourage their voting, including shortening absentee and mail-in voting periods, reducing the number of polling places in minority neighborhoods, and changing the addresses and dates for voting. Another Supreme Court decision abolished the Voting Rights Act requisite that states that had a record of discrimination against voters had to apply and be precleared any time they sought to

Members of the Congressional Hispanic Caucus travel to the U.S.-Mexico border in January 2020 to investigate the Trump administration's "remain in Mexico" policy and the "tent courts" in Matamoros, Mexico, being used to process asylum claims.

change election rules and practices. Under *Shelby County v. Holder* (2013), the court held that the preclearance of changes was outdated and no longer responded to current electoral conditions; basically it affirmed the idea that so much progress against discriminatory practices had been made that preclearance was obsolete and a burden on the states in question. To the present, but especially during the 2016 elections, all manner of strategies to discourage and limit minority voting have been employed.

CONGRESSIONAL HISPANIC CAUCUS

While great strides have been made in Latino electoral empowerment and representation in gov-

ernment, the growing Latino population remains significantly underrepresented at all levels of government—despite the 7,087 Latinos in office in 2021, according to the National Association of Latino Elected and Appointed Officials (NALEO). The Latino population is young and made up of many noncitizens, and Latino voting levels have traditionally fallen well below the national average. In spite of favorable legislation, advocates actively seeking to increase Latino voter registration still cite poverty, inadequate education, language barriers, and alienage as critical obstacles that have discouraged voting. Despite these problems, Latinos have been going to the polls in increasing numbers.

The Congressional Hispanic Caucus, organized in December 1976, is a bipartisan group of members of Congress of Latino descent. The caucus is dedicated to voicing and advancing, through the legislative process, issues affecting Latinos in the United States and its territories.

Organized as a legislative service organization under the rules of Congress, the caucus is composed solely of members of the U.S. Congress. Under these rules, associate membership is offered to dues-paying members of Congress who are not of Latino descent. With its associate members, caucus membership represents the states, Puerto Rico, Guam, and the U.S. Virgin Islands.

Although every issue that affects the quality of life of all U.S. citizens is a Congressional Hispanic Caucus concern, national and international issues that have a particular impact on the Latino community are the focus. The caucus monitors legislative action as well as policies and practices of the executive and judicial branches of government that affect these issues.

LATINO MEMBERS OF CONGRESS (2020)

House of Representatives

Pete Aguilar (1979–)

Pete Aguilar was born on June 19, 1979, in Fontana, California, part of a fourth-generation California family. He put himself through college, studying government and business administration at University of the Redlands. Aguilar's political career began in 2001 when California governor Gray Davis appointed him deputy director of the Inland Empire Regional Office of the Governor; he eventually became interim director. Aguilar served on the Redlands City Council beginning in 2006 and in 2010 became mayor. He served as mayor from 2010 to 2014, during which time he was also the president of the Inland Empire Division of the League of California Cities. He was elected to Congress in 2016 and now serves as chief deputy whip in the House Democratic Caucus and whip of the Congressional Hispanic Caucus. The issues Aguilar has fought for in Congress include immigration, job creation, trade practices, gun control, national security, LGBT issues, veteran affairs, drug prevention, student loan debt, and environmental protection.

Nanette Díaz Barragán (1976–)

Born in Harbor City, California, on September 15, 1976, Barragán is the youngest of eleven children raised by immigrant parents from Mexico. Barragán was elected to the U.S. House of Representatives in November 2016, becoming the first Latina ever to represent California's 44th Congressional district. She has an undergraduate degree from UCLA and a law degree from the University of Southern California. Prior to becoming a congresswoman she steered outreach efforts for African Americans in the Office of Public Liaison for the Clinton White House and worked for the National Association for the Advancement of Colored People (NAACP) focusing on racial health disparities and discrimination. Barragán was the first woman in twelve years to be elected to the Hermosa Beach City Council and then the first-ever Latina to serve as mayor of the city. She is the second–vice chair of the Congressional Hispanic Caucus and a member of the Progressive Caucus. She serves on the House Committee on Homeland Security and was appointed to the exclusive House Committee on Energy and Commerce.

Salud Carbajal (1964–)

Salud Carbajal was born in Moroleón, Mexico, on November 18, 1964, and later immigrated with his family as farm workers to Arizona, eventually settling in Oxnard, California. Carbajal served eight years in the U.S. Marine Corps Reserve, including active duty service during the Gulf

War in 1992. Carbajal earned a bachelor's degree from the University of California at Santa Barbara and a master's degree in organizational management from Fielding Graduate University. Prior to representing the Central Coast in Congress beginning in 2016, Salud served as Santa Barbara County's First District supervisor for twelve years, beginning in 2004. In Congress, Carbajal has demonstrated a strong commitment to protecting the natural environment and resources, enhancing public safety, creating economic opportunities, and working regionally to address transportation, housing, and workforce challenges. Carbajal sits on the House Committee on Armed Services, the House Committee on Agriculture, and the House Committee on Transportation and Infrastructure, where he was elected to serve as a vice chair. The congressman has used his role as a vice chair on the House Committee on Transportation and Infrastructure to create jobs by securing investments in the nation's crumbling infrastructure and rebuilding areas damaged by natural disasters.

Tony Cárdenas
(1963–)

Tony Cárdenas was born on March 31, 1963, in Pacoima, California, one of eleven children to immigrant parents. As the son of a farm worker, Cárdenas worked his way through college and earned his engineering degree from the University of California, Santa Barbara. Before representing California's 29th district in Congress, Cárdenas was first elected to the California State Assembly in 1996. He went on to serve three terms in the assembly and in 2003 was elected to the Los Angeles City Council. An engineering degree and a business background prepared him for the day-to-day duties of an elected official, while his experience allowed him to find practical and realistic solutions to difficult problems. Cárdenas was first elected to Congress in 2013, becoming the first Latino to represent the San Fernando Valley. Now in the 117th Congress (2021–2023), Cárdenas sits on the House Committee on Energy and Commerce. He has worked on and authored legislation to lower prescription drug prices, protect American consumers, combat climate change, and ensure that everyone has access to affordable, quality health care. The Committee on Energy and Commerce is the oldest of the "authorizing" committees in the House.

Joaquín Castro
(1974–)

Joaquín Castro was born in San Antonio, Texas, on September 16, 1974. A second-generation Mexican American, he attended public schools and went to and graduated from Stanford University (1996) and Harvard Law School (2000). He returned to San Antonio at twenty-eight years old, joined a private law practice, and was elected to the Texas Legislature. He served five terms as state representative for District 125. In 2012, Castro was elected to serve in the U.S. House of Representatives as representative of Texas's 20th Congressional District, which covers a large portion of San Antonio and Bexar County. Castro serves on the House Permanent Select Committee on Intelligence, the House Foreign Affairs Committee, and the House Education and Labor Committee. He was the 2013 copresident for the House freshman Democrats and currently serves as chair of the Texas Democratic Caucus and the Hispanic Congressional Caucus.

Gil Cisneros
(1971–)

Born on February 12, 1971, Gilbert R. Cisneros Jr. was raised in Southern California and attended college on a Naval Reserve Officer Training Corps (ROTC) scholarship, becoming the first in his family to graduate from college. He earned a bachelor's degree in political science from the George Washington University, an M.B.A. from Regis University, and a master's degree in urban education policy from Brown University. Cisneros served as a supply corps officer in the U.S. Navy, completing both a Western Pacific and Mediterranean deployment. He was awarded the Navy Commendation Medal, the Navy Achievement Medal, the National Defense Medal, and the Armed Forces Expeditionary Medal. He worked as a shipping and manufacturing manager for Frito-Lay until he was laid off in 2010. Cisneros won California's Mega Millions lottery for $266 million and became a philanthropist. He and his wife Jacki founded the Gilbert and Jacki Cisneros Foundation, which invests in college access and affordability programs for students and veterans. Cisneros was sworn in as representative of California's 39th Congressional District on January 3, 2019, which includes portions of Orange, Los Angeles, and San Bernardino counties. In his one term in the House, Cisneros served on the Armed Services Committee and the Veterans' Affairs Committee. He was also a member of the Congressional Hispanic Caucus and the Congressional Asian Pacific American Caucus. He was defeated in his reelection bid in 2020. In April 2021, President Joe Biden nominated him as undersecretary of defense for personnel and readiness, and the U.S. Senate confirmed him four months later. He is a staunch advocate for national defense, service members, and veterans.

Lou Correa (1958–)

Lou Correa was born on January 24, 1958, in Anaheim, California. His mother was a hotel housekeeper and his father a worker at a paper mill. A product of the Anaheim public schools, Correa graduated from California State University, Fullerton with a degree in economics. He earned his J.D. and M.B.A. degrees from the University of California, Los Angeles (UCLA). Correa has supported public health and safety services, mental health care, and health and safety programs for children. He has championed affordable higher education and taxpayer equity. Since entering office, Correa has introduced legislation to protect the legal rights of immigrants, care for veterans, and fight against the wasteful spending of taxpayer money.

Jim Costa (1952–)

Born on April 13, 1952, in Fresno, California, James Manuel Costa was raised on a dairy farm; he is a third-generation family farmer. A product of Fresno County schools, Costa is a graduate of San Joaquin Memorial High School and has a bachelor's degree in political science from California State University, Fresno. Before being elected to the U.S. House of Representatives, Costa served for twenty-four years in the California State Legislature. He has served the San Joaquin Valley in the U.S. House of Representatives since January of 2005. Costa uses his position on the Natural Resources Committee to fight for the Valley's fair share of water. This includes securing funding for dams, working to overturn unfair federal water regulations, and increasing Valley water allocations. On the Agriculture Committee, Costa has worked to increase federal support for Valley agriculture through the Farm Bill and other programs.

Henry Cuéllar (1955–)

Born on September 19, 1955, in Laredo, Texas, as one of eight children to migrant farm workers, Henry Cuéllar has a passion for education that accounts for his being the most degreed member of Congress. After earning his associate's degree summa cum laude from Laredo Community College, he enrolled in Georgetown University in Washington, D.C. While working part-time jobs, he managed to graduate cum laude. When he returned to Texas, Cuéllar completed a master's degree in international trade at Texas A&M International University and then earned both a J.D. and Ph.D. in government from the University of Texas at Austin. Recently, Cuéllar received a professional certificate in budget and finance from Georgetown University. Beginning in 1981, Cuéllar started practicing law. From 1984 he served as a Texas state representative; in 2001 he was appointed secretary of state of Texas by Governor Rick Perry, a Republican. In 2004 he was elected to Congress, where he serves as the only Texas Democrat on the powerful U.S. House Appropriations Committee. He is the vice chair of the House Appropriations Subcommittee on Homeland Security and also serves on the Defense Subcommittee and the Subcommittee on Agriculture, Rural Development, Food and Drug Administration, and Related Agencies. Cuéllar was named chief deputy whip for the 116th Congress.

Cuéllar considers himself a conservative Democrat and in the 115th Congress voted with Donald Trump nearly 70 percent of the time.

Antonio Delgado (1977–)

Born on January 28, 1977, in Schenectady, New York, to African American and Puerto Rican parents, Antonio Delgado graduated from Colgate University in 1999. He earned a Rhodes Scholarship and received an M.A. from Oxford University in 2001. He went on to attend Harvard Law School. Delgado's professional experiences include a career in the music industry focused on empowering young people through hip-hop culture and working as an attorney, and he has dedicated significant time to pro bono work in connection with criminal justice reform. Delgado won election to Congress in 2018 to represent New York's 19th district. He serves on the committees for agriculture, small business, and transportation infrastructure.

Mario Díaz-Balart (1961–)

Born on September 25, 1961, in Ft. Lauderdale, Florida, to Rafael and Hilda Díaz-Balart, Mario Díaz-Balart is the youngest of four brothers. He studied political science at the University of South Florida in Tampa. He was elected to the Florida House in 1988 and moved to the Florida Senate in 1992. He returned to the Florida House in 2000. Díaz-Balart was elected to the U.S. House of Representatives in 2002 to represent Florida's 25th Congressional district. He chaired a number of different committees, including the Combined Appropriations/Ways and Means/Finance and Tax Committee. Now in his tenth term, Díaz-Balart is a senior member of the House Committee on Appropriations; is the ranking member of the Subcommittee on Transportation, Housing and Urban Development; and serves on the Defense Subcommittee. He passionately serves his constituents, acting tirelessly in defense of individual rights and liberties, promoting economic prosperity, and supporting a strong national defense. He is well known for his advocacy of human rights and democracy around the world, as well as for his staunch support of the United States' global allies.

Veronica Escobar (1969–)

Born on September 15, 1969, Veronica Escobar was educated in El Paso schools and obtained a B.A. from the University of Texas at El Paso and an M.A. from New York University. A third-generation El Pasoan, she represents Texas's 16th Congressional District. She was the first woman elected to this seat and the first of two Latinas from Texas to serve in Congress. Escobar serves on the prestigious House Judiciary Committee and House Armed Services Committee. She was elected by her colleagues to serve as cofreshman representative to leadership in the 116th Congress and in that capacity serves as a member of the House Democratic Leadership Team. She holds leadership positions on the Congressional Hispanic Caucus (CHC) and the Congressional Progressive Caucus (CPC) as the freshman representative and vice chair, respectively. She is also vice chair of the Democratic Women's Caucus. She is a member of the New Democrat Coalition and the Women's Working Group on Immigration, where she serves as co-chair. Before serving in Congress, Escobar was an English teacher at the University of Texas at El Paso and El Paso Community College.

Adriano Espaillat (1954–)

Born on September 27, 1954, in Santiago, Dominican Republic, Adriano Espaillat has represented New York's Thirteenth Congressional District since being first elected to Congress in 2016. Espaillat serves as a member of the influential U.S. House Foreign Affairs Committee, the House Committee on Transportation and Infrastructure, and the House Small Business Committee. He is a member of the Congressional Hispanic Caucus (CHC) and serves in a leadership role as CHC whip. He is also chairman of the CHC Task Force for Transportation, Infrastructure and Housing. Espaillat is a senior whip of the Democratic Caucus and deputy whip of the Congressional Progressive Caucus. A steadfast champion for working- and middle-class New Yorkers, Espaillat is a staunch advocate of a fair living wage, immediate and effective investments in affordable housing, meaningful criminal justice reform, infrastructure improvements, expanded youth programs, and better educational opportunities. In 1996 he became the first Dominican American elected to a state legislature. In 2002, Espaillat was elected chair of the New York State Black, Puerto Rican, Hispanic and Asian Legislative Caucus.

Bill Flores (1954–)

Born in and raised in Stratford, a small town in the Texas Panhandle, Flores is a ninth-generation Texan. While growing up in this agricultural community, he learned the value of hard work, starting at age nine by working cattle with his father. He became an entrepreneur early in life by starting a small cattle herd at age twelve; it ultimately grew into the Rafter O Cattle Company, a partnership with his three brothers, which at its peak owned over five hundred head of cattle. He paid his own way through college, graduating with honors from Texas A&M University in 1976 with a B.B.A. in accounting. He then earned the Texas Certified Public Accountancy (C.P.A.) license in 1978. Flores graduated from Houston Baptist University with an M.B.A. degree in 1985. He went on to work for a "Big 8" accounting firm for a few years, followed by thirty years in the oil and gas business. In 2009, frustrated by what he viewed as destructive legislation coming out of Washington, he retired from the private sector to run for Congress. In November 2010, he beat an incumbent congressman by the largest margin of victory that election cycle. He served from 2011 to 2021. In Congress, he served on the powerful House Energy and Commerce Committee and the Committee on the Budget; and for the 114th Congress, his House colleagues elected him to serve as chairman of the Republican Study Committee, the largest and most influential caucus in the U.S. Congress.

Rubén Gallego (1979–)

Born on November 20, 1979, in Chicago, Illinois, to a Colombian mother and a Mexican father, Rubén Gallego represents the 7th District of Arizona, including parts of Phoenix, Glendale, and Tolleson, in the U.S. House of Representatives. He was first elected in 2014. Gallego is a Marine Corps combat veteran, a lifelong community leader, and the son of Hispanic immigrants. He was the first in his family to attend college, graduating from Harvard University with a degree in international relations. Gallego has largely focused on U.S. national security in his time in Washington. As a member of the House Armed Services Committee, he has led the response to Russia's attack on NATO, maintaining the European Deterrence Initiative. Gallego was elected to the Arizona House of Representatives in 2010 and served until 2014. He is also a member of the House Natural Resources Committee, where he serves as chair of the Natural Resources Subcommittee for Indigenous Peoples of the United States, fighting to uphold tribal sovereignty and federal trust responsibility to Native Americans and Alaska Natives. Gallego is the first vice chair of the Congressional Hispanic Caucus.

Jesús "Chuy" García (1956–)

Born the youngest of four children on April 12, 1956, in Los Pinos, Durango, Mexico, Jesús García was raised by his mother while his father worked in the United States, first under the World War II–era Bracero Program and later at a cold-storage plant in Chicago. In 1965, García and his family immigrated to the United States with permanent resident status. Prior to his election to Congress in November of 2018, García was a member of the Cook County Board of Commissioners. As commissioner, he opposed housing discrimination against disadvantaged communities, raised the minimum wage, and mandated that county employees have access to paid sick leave. He also passed an ordinance ending Cook County's cooperation with the Immigration and Customs Enforcement Agency (ICE). The measure was the first of its kind in the nation and set an example followed by more than 250 other localities. García began organizing for workers' rights and more inclusive city services during his college years at the University of Illinois in Chicago. He entered political life in 1984, when he was elected committeeman of the Cook County Democratic Party. García was next elected to represent Chicago's 22nd Ward on the City Council. García went on to serve in the state legislature. In 1993, he passed the Language Assistance Services Act, which requires hospitals and long-term care facilities to provide resources for effective communication with limited-English-speaking and deaf patients. In 2015, García became the first Chicago mayoral candidate to push a sitting mayor into a runoff. Since assuming office as a congressman in 2019, García has been a progressive voice fighting to improve the lives of his working-class neighbors, many of whom are immigrants like him. He serves on the Financial Services Committee, Natural Resources Committee, and the Transportation and Infrastructure Committee. He is the founder of the Future of Transportation Caucus.

Mike García (1976–)

Born on April 24, 1976, in Santa Clarita, California, to Mexican immigrant parents, Mike García is a graduate of the U.S. Naval Academy. In 1998, he earned a master of arts in national security policy studies from Georgetown University, after which he served as an F/A-18 pilot, flying more than thirty combat missions in Afghanistan. From 2009 to 2018, García worked at Raytheon Intelligence & Space. In May 2020 he was elected to represent California's 25th congressional district in a special election to fill a suddenly open seat. García is a member of the Committee on Transportation and Infrastructure and the Committee on Science, Space, and Technology. As a Republican, Garcia believes in strengthening the military and cutting taxes and funding to the Department of Education.

Sylvia García (1950–)

Born on September 6, 1950, in San Diego, Texas, Sylvia Rodríguez García attended public schools in South Texas, went on to study social work at Texas Women's University, and worked as a social worker before getting into politics. Throughout her political career, she has been concerned with the issues of welfare, women's protection and rights, immigration, and all of the other themes that are important to Latinos and poor people. During her political career, she also obtained a law degree from Texas Southern University to add heft to her political positions. In the 1980s she served as a judge and in 1998 became the City of Houston's controller. In 2002 García was elected to the Harris County Commissioner's Court and served in that position until 2010. In 2013 she was elected to the Texas state legislature, and in 2018 García was elected to Congress. She and Veronica Escobar became the first Latina congresswomen from Texas. Of great distinction was her selection to serve on the team of seven House members to manage the first impeachment proceedings against President Donald Trump in 2020. García serves on the Judiciary and the Financial Services Committees. She is also the vice chair of the Majority Leader's Taskforce on Poverty and Opportunity.

Jimmy Gómez (1974–)

Born on November 25, 1974, in Fullerton, California, Jimmy Gómez is the son of Mexican immigrants. Gómez attended Riverside Community College before receiving a B.A. in political science from the University of California, Los Angeles (UCLA), and an M.A. in public policy from Harvard University's John F. Kennedy School of Government. Prior to his election to Congress in June of 2017, Gómez served four and a half years in the California State Assembly, where he served as chair of the Assembly Appropriations Committee. In the Assembly, Gómez distinguished himself as a proven national champion of paid family leave and combatting climate change. He became a key figure in authoring landmark legislation to address public health, environmental justice, water conservation, access to education, civic engagement, campaign finance disclosure, LGBT rights, and affordable housing. He is an assistant whip in the 117th Congress and a member of the House Committee on Oversight and Reform and the House Committee on Ways and Means. He is a member of the Congressional Progressive Caucus (CPC) and a vice chair of the Future Forum.

Vicente González (1967–)

Born on September 4, 1967, in Corpus Christi, Texas, into a working-class family, Vicente González dropped out of high school in the eleventh grade. He earned his GED in 1985 and then attended Del Mar College, where he received an associate's degree in banking and finance in 1990. He worked his way through college at Embry-Riddle Aeronautical University, earning a bachelor's degree in business aviation in 1992; he later earned a law degree from Texas Wesleyan University School of Law (now Texas A&M School of Law) in 1996. While attending law school, González worked as an intern in the office of then-congressman Solomon P. Ortiz. In 1997, González opened his law practice, V. Gonzalez & Associates. In Congress, he is fighting to protect Social Security and Medicare and to ensure that veterans, military members, and their families have the care and compensation they earned through their service. He is working across party lines and with local, state, and federal government to expand economic opportunity for all. He serves on the Subcommittees on Investor Protection, Entrepreneurship, and Capital Markets; Housing, Community Development, and Insurance; and Diversity and Inclusion. In his second term, González was appointed to the House Foreign Affairs Committee. González has advocated for revamping American foreign policy in Central America.

Jenniffer Aydin González Colón (1976–)

Born August 5, 1976, in San Juan, Puerto Rico, Jenniffer Aydin González Colón obtained a bachelor's degree from the University of Puerto Rico. During her studies she served as the executive director of the Young Republican Federation of Puerto Rico. She obtained her J.D. from the Interamerican Universty of Puerto Rico Law School. When González was elected to the Puerto Rican House of Representatives on February 24, 2002, she became the first female elected representative of San Juan's Fourth District, the youngest member of the 14th Legislative Assembly, and the youngest woman ever to be elected to the Puerto Rico Legislative Assembly. Then, at age thirty-two, she was elected speaker of the House. In November 2015, she was elected chairwoman of the Republican Party of Puerto Rico. On November 8, 2016, González was elected resident commissioner of Puerto Rico, a nonvoting member of the U.S. House of Representatives; she was the first woman to occupy that office.

Raúl Grijalva (1948–)

Born on February 19, 1948, on Canoa Ranch, Arizona, the son of a migrant farm worker who came to the United States under the Bracero Program, Grijalva earned a bachelor's degree in sociology from the University of Arizona. He participated in the Chicano Movement and was a leader of the Raza Unida Party. Grijalva began his career in public service as a community organizer in Tucson. More than four decades later, he continues to be an advocate for those in need and a voice for the constituents of his home community. From 1974 to 1986, Grijalva served on the Tucson Unified School District Governing Board, including six years as chairman. In 1988, he was elected to the Pima County Board of Supervisors, where he served for the next fifteen years, chairing the board for two of those years. Grijalva resigned his seat on the Board of Supervisors in 2002 to seek office in Arizona's newly created Seventh Congressional District. Despite a nine-candidate primary and the challenge of being outspent three to one by his closest competitor, Grijalva was elected with a twenty-point victory, thanks to a diverse coalition of supporters who led the largest volunteer-driven election effort in Arizona. Grijalva advocates Medicare for all, debt-free college, raising the federal minimum wage, expanding Social Security, moving to 100 percent renewable energy, comprehensive immigration reform, and paid leave and child care. In 2018, Grijalva became chair of the House Natural Resources Committee. He also serves on the Committee on Education and the Workforce, is the chairman emeritus of the Congressional Progressive Caucus, and a long-standing member of the Congressional Hispanic Caucus.

Jaime Herrera Beutler (1978–)

Born on November 3, 1978, in Glendale, California, Jaime Herrera Beutler was raised in Ridgefield, Washington. She earned her bachelor of arts degree in communications from the University of Washington.

Beutler served as an intern in both the Washington State Senate and the White House. She worked on the congressional staff of U.S. representative Cathy McMorris Rodgers (R-Spokane), and then served as state representative from Washington State's 18th Legislative District from 2007 until being elected to Congress in 2010. Herrera Beutler was first elected to Congress at the age of thirty-one to represent Southwest Washington's 3rd District. She was ranked the fifteenth most bipartisan member of the U.S. House by Georgetown University and the Lugar Center. As a senior member of the House Appropriations Committee, Herrera Beutler has successfully secured federal support for vital priorities in the Columbia Gorge and coastal communities, including maintenance of the Columbia River, dredging for small ports along the coast, and resources for salmon recovery.

Mike Levin (1978–)

Born on October 20, 1978, in Inglewood, California, to a Mexican American mother and a Jewish father, Mike Levin was raised a Catholic in Lake Forest, California, in South Orange County. He attended Loyola High School in Los Angeles before attending Stanford University. While at Stanford, Levin served as president of the student body. He attended law school at the Duke University School of Law in Durham, North Carolina, before returning to his native Orange County. Before being elected to Congress in 2018, Levin cofounded CleanTech OC, a clean energy trade association, and he was the director of government affairs at FuelCell Energy from 2014 to 2017. He also served as the vice president of Better Energy Systems, a consumer-facing clean tech startup in Berkeley, California, and was on the board of directors of the Center for Sustainable Energy. Throughout his career, Levin has been a passionate leader on environmental protection, clean energy, and combating climate change. Levin has also championed efforts to expand access to affordable health care, lower the cost of higher education, preserve Social Security and Medicare, prevent gun violence, enact comprehensive immigration reform, and protect a woman's right to choose. He is a member of the Congressional Progressive Caucus.

Ben Ray Luján (1972–)

Born on June 7, 1972, in Nambé, New Mexico, the son of a New Mexico legislator, Ben Ray Luján worked as a blackjack dealer after graduating from high school. He later earned a bachelor's degree from New Mexico Highlands University in business. In 2004, Luján was elected to the New Mexico Public Regulation Commission and later served as its chairman. He then went on to serve as the New Mexico Cultural Affairs Department's director of administrative services and chief financial officer. During his time as a U.S. representative (2009–2021), Luján championed efforts to create good-paying, green jobs in New Mexico, expand quality health care and protect patients with preexisting conditions, preserve natural resources and sacred sites, build a clean-energy economy, and uplift the middle class. He was a member of the House Energy and Commerce Committee, sitting on the Health Subcommittee, Consumer Protection and Commerce Subcommittee, and Communications and Technology Subcommittee. In 2013, Luján was appointed to the House Democratic Leadership as a Chief Deputy Whip. In the 114th Congress, Luján served as chair of the Democratic Congressional Campaign Committee and was elected by his colleagues to again serve in this role for the 115th Congress. He served as the assistant speaker in the 116th Congress and was the highest-ranking Hispanic in Congress. In 2020, he was elected to the U.S. Senate.

Brian Mast (1980–)

Born July 10, 1980, in Grand Rapids, Michigan, Brian Mast's maternal grandparents were immigrants from Mexico. Mast graduated from South Christian High School in 1999 and then enlisted in the Army as a combat engineer. He served in Afghanistan, where he lost both legs to an IED explosion; he was highly decorated. In 2016, he obtained a bachelor's degree from Harvard University, where he studied economics, with minors in government and environmental studies. That same year, Mast won the election to represent

Florida's 18th congressional district. Mast sits on the Veteran Affairs Committee, the Foreign Affairs Committee, and the Transportation Infrastructure Committee. He voted 94 percent of the time in line with President Donald Trump's positions. Mast is a staunch conservative on all issues important to Latinos, such as immigration, health care, taxes, and abortion.

Alex Mooney (1971–)

Born on June 7, 1971, in Washington, D.C., Mooney was raised in Frederick, Maryland. Mooney's mother, Lala (Suárez) Mooney, was born and raised in Fidel Castro's Cuba, where she was thrown into jail for seven weeks for opposing Castro's Communist regime. When she was twenty, she escaped Cuba and fled to the United States to restart her life. Mooney's father, Vincent, was sent to Vietnam when Lala was expecting their first child. Mooney graduated from Dartmouth College in 1993 with a major in philosophy. While attending Dartmouth, he ran for the New Hampshire House of Representatives in Grafton County's 10th District. He finished in last place with 8 percent of the vote. He was elected to the Maryland State Senate, representing District 3 from 1999 to 2011, and was a chairman of the Maryland Republican Party. When Mooney was elected in 2014 to represent West Virginia's 2nd congressional district, he became the first Latino to represent the state; he was reelected in 2016, 2018, and 2020. He is a principled conservative fighting for lower taxes and less government regulations on businesses to create more jobs in America. Mooney serves on the House Financial Services Committee, which oversees some of the most important economic issues facing West Virginia, such as banking, insurance, housing, and investment policies.

Debbie Mucarsel-Powell (1971–)

Born on January 18, 1971, in Guayaquil, Ecuador, Debbie Mucarsel-Powell immigrated to the United States from Ecuador as a young girl with her mother and sisters. She learned the struggles immigrants face at an early age when her mother worked double shifts while attending night school to learn English. At age fifteen, Mucarsel-Powell started helping her mother by working at a doughnut shop before school. She worked her way through high school and college, and she earned her bachelor's degree in political science from Pitzer College. She then gained her master's degree in international political economy from Claremont Graduate University. She returned to Miami and, from 2003 to 2007, served as the director of development at Florida International University. From 2007 to 2011, she was the associate vice president for advancement at FIU's Herbert Wertheim College of Medicine and the associate dean at the College of Medicine, where she worked to grow programs that improve health care access for Floridians. In 2019 she became the first Ecuadorian American and first South American immigrant member of Congress. In her one term in the U.S. House, she served on the House Judiciary Committee, where she sat on the Immigration and Citizenship Subcommittee and Crime, Terrorism, and Homeland Security Subcommittee. She worked on the Judiciary Committee fighting for immigration reform and commonsense gun safety. She also served on the Transportation and Infrastructure Committee, where she advocated for South Florida on the Water Resources and Environment Subcommittee and Economic Development, Public Buildings, and Emergency Management Subcommittee. She was defeated in 2020 in her bid for reelection.

Grace Napolitano (1936–)

Born on December 4, 1936, in Brownsville, Texas, Grace Flores Napolitano got married after high school and moved with her husband to California, where they raised five children. She began her political career in 1986 as a member of the Norwalk City Council, and in 1989 Napolitano's fellow council members selected her to serve as mayor. Napolitano was elected in 1992 to the California Assembly, where she quickly earned a reputation as a hard worker and champion for international trade/economic expansion, environmental protection, transportation, immigration, small business, and women's issues. She was first elected to Congress in 1998 and currently serves on the House Committee on Transportation and Infrastructure and is the chairwoman on the Subcommittee on Water Resources and Environment. She continues to advance projects and policies that relieve congestion, improve transit, and reduce the negative impacts on the Ports of Long Beach and Los Angeles. Napolitano also serves on the House Committee on Natural Resources and is a longtime promoter of conservation, water recycling, desalination, and groundwater management as solutions to Southern California's water needs. Napolitano is the founder and cochair of the Congressional Mental Health Caucus, where she has been active in securing mental health parity in the Affordable Care Act, promoting mental health legislation, and working with prominent figures to increase funding and access to mental health services in Congress. She is also the founder and cochair of the Congressional Youth Challenge Caucus, which supports Youth Challenge, a program run by the National Guard cadre using military discipline and education to help at-risk youth complete high school to emerge better armed with knowledge and training for success. Napolitano is the former chairwoman of the Congressional Hispanic Caucus.

Alexandria Ocasio-Cortez (1989–)

Born on October 13, 1989, in the Bronx borough of New York City to Puerto Rican parents, after high school Alexandria Ocasio-Cortez attended and graduated *cum laude* from Boston University (2011) with degrees in economics and international relations. During this period she also had the opportunity to work in the office of the late senator Ted Kennedy. Her role in Senator Kennedy's office provided a firsthand view of the heartbreak families endured after being separated by Immigration and Customs Enforcement (ICE). These experiences led her to organize Latino youth in the Bronx and across the United States and eventually work as an educational director with the National Hispanic Institute, a role in which she helped Americans, DREAMers, and undocumented youth in community leadership and college readiness. During the 2016 presidential election, she worked as a volunteer organizer for Bernie Sanders in the South Bronx, expanding her skills in electoral organizing and activism that has taken her across the country and to Standing Rock,

South Dakota, to stand with Indigenous communities, then back to New York's 14th Congressional District to launch her people-funded, grassroots campaign for Congress. When she was sworn in to Congress in January of 2019, Ocasio-Cortez became the youngest woman to ever serve in that institution. Ocasio-Cortez is a member of the Democratic Socialists of America and is committed to serving working-class people over corporate interests and advocating for social, racial, economic, and environmental justice. She advocates a progressive platform that includes Medicare for All, a federal jobs guarantee, the Green New Deal, and abolishing the U.S. Immigration and Customs Enforcement. Ocasio-Cortez supports progressive policies such as single-payer Medicare for All, tuition-free public college and trade school, a federal job guarantee, the cancellation of all $1.6 trillion of outstanding student debt, guaranteed family leave, ending the privatization of prisons, enacting gun-control policies, and energy policy relying on 100 percent renewables.

Lucille Roybal-Allard (1941–)

Born on June 12, 1941, in Boyle Heights, California, Lucille Roybal-Allard is the eldest daughter of former congressman Edward R. Roybal of California and the first Latina to directly follow her father into Congress. She received her B.A. degree from California State University in 1965. In 1987, she was elected to the California State Assembly, where she served until 1992. She was elected to the U.S. House of Representatives in 1992, representing the newly created 33rd District; she was the first Mexican American woman elected to Congress. The congresswoman is the first Latina to serve as one of the twelve "cardinals," or chairs, of a House Appropriations subcommittee as well as the first Latina to serve on the House Appropriations Committee. She is also the first woman to chair the Congressional Hispanic Caucus; the first woman to chair the California Democratic congressional delegation; and the founder of the Women's Working Group on Immigration Reform. Roybal-Allard is deeply committed to environmental and women's issues. She is an original coauthor of the Development, Relief, and Education for Alien Minors (DREAM) Act, which would allow certain U.S.-raised immigrant youth to earn lawful permanent residence and eventual American citizenship. In 2019, she introduced the newest version of this bill—HR 6, the Dream and Promise Act—which passed in 2021. Her Newborn Screening Saves Lives Reauthorization Act, which tests newborns for treatable genetic disorders, has helped to save the lives of thousands of babies. Her Sober Truth on Preventing (STOP) Underage Drinking Act has been instrumental in reducing underage drinking and its consequences. Roybal-Allard has won numerous awards in recognition of her work in these areas, including the 1992 Feminist of the Year Award from the Feminist Majority Foundation, the 1991 Legislator of the Year Award from the National Organization for Women, and the 1990 and 1991 Highest Legislative Rating from the League of Conservation Voters.

Raúl Ruiz (1972–)

Born on August 25, 1972, in Zacatecas, Mexico, Raúl Ruiz immigrated with his farm worker parents as a child to the United States and was raised in Coachella, California. He graduated from the University of California, Los Angeles *magna cum laude* in 1994 and went to Harvard University to become a physician; after graduation and two more degrees from Harvard he returned to his home state, where he worked in the emergency room at Eisenhower Medical Center in Rancho Mirage. He founded the Coachella Valley Healthcare Initiative in 2010. In 2011, he became senior associate dean at the School of Medicine at the University of California, Riverside. Ruiz was first elected to Congress in 2012 and reelected repeatedly thereafter. He serves on the House Energy and Commerce Subcommittee on Environment, the House Energy and Commerce Subcommittee on Communications and Technology, and the House Energy and Commerce Subcommittee on Oversight and Investigations.

Gregorio Kilili Camacho Sablan (1955–)

Born on January 19, 1955, on Saipan, the largest of the U.S. Mariana Islands, Gregorio Kilili Camacho

Sablan is the first and only person to represent the people of the Northern Mariana Islands in the U.S. House of Representatives. He graduated from Marianas High School on Saipan, then attended the University of Guam before continuing college in Berkeley, California. A family crisis brought him home before his studies were complete, but it was during his college days that Sablan decided to go into public office. He began service in the administration of the Commonwealth of the Northern Mariana Islands' first governor, Carlos S. Camacho, and then was elected to the Third Northern Mariana Islands Legislature in 1981. Sablan began service as a delegate (nonvoting member) to the U.S. House of Representatives on January 6, 2009, and has been reelected to that office six times. He is the chair of the Subcommittee on Early Childhood, Elementary and Secondary Education of the House Committee on Education and Labor, and he is a member of the Subcommittee on Higher Education and Workforce Investment. He also serves as vice chair for insular affairs on the House Committee on Natural Resources. Because of the large number of veterans in the Marianas and the need to improve services to them, Sablan was selected for the House Veterans' Affairs Committee. He also serves on the Disability Assistance and Memorial Affairs Subcommittee.

Michael San Nicolás (1981–)

Born on January 30, 1981, Michael San Nicolás graduated with a bachelor of arts degree from the University of Guam in 2004. San Nicolás served as Guam's delegate (nonvoting member) to the U.S. House of Representatives beginning in 2013. He has worked to secure funding for the payment of war claims pursuant to the Guam World War II Loyalty Recognition Act, to extend coverage for Social Security Supplemental Security Income to the Territory of Guam, to secure reimbursement of the Earned Income Tax Credit for Freely Associated States (FAS) migrants residing in Guam, and to address herbicide exposure for veterans who served in Guam, among other issues. San Nicolás currently serves as vice chair of the House Financial Services Committee and is serving on that committee and its subcommittees on Investor Protection, Entrepreneurship, and Capital Markets and on National Security, International Development, and Monetary Policy, respectively, and the Committee on Natural Resources and its subcommittees on Indigenous Peoples of the United States and on Oversight and Investigations.

Linda T. Sánchez (1969–)

Linda T. Sánchez was born on January 28, 1969, in Orange, California, the sixth of seven children, to immigrant parents from Mexico. Her father, Ignacio, worked as an industrial machinist and mechanic at a plastics and rubber plant, and her mother, María, was an elementary school teacher who decided to further her education by attending school at night. Sánchez attended the University of California, Berkeley, where she earned a B.A. in Spanish literature with an emphasis in bilingual education in 1991. After working her way through school as a bilingual aide and an ESL instructor, she went on to earn a law degree from the University of California, Los Angeles, in 1995. Elected to the U.S. House of Representatives in 2002, Sánchez is the first Latina to serve on the powerful House Committee on Ways and Means and the House Judiciary Committee. A lifelong progressive, Sánchez has devoted her career to helping working people get ahead: advocating for families, improving America's education system, and bringing jobs to Southern California. Throughout her time in Congress, Sánchez has been a steadfast advocate for working people, including improving school safety; enabling more women, minorities, and veterans to establish small businesses; reforming the tax code to provide relief for long-term caregivers; bringing scrutiny to the misuse of arbitration that unfairly harms workers; and keeping families in their homes through changes to bankruptcy law. In the 114th Congress, Sánchez served as chair of the Congressional Hispanic Caucus (CHC). In 2009, Sánchez introduced the Gender Equity in Health Premiums Act to bar health insurance companies from charging women more for health care premiums than men. The Gender Equity in Health Premiums Act became part of the Affordable Care Act, which President Barack Obama signed into law in 2010.

José E. Serrano (1943–)

José Serrano was born in Mayagüez, Puerto Rico, on October 24, 1943. In 1950, when he was seven years old, his family moved to public housing in the South Bronx. Serrano attended public schools and went to Lehman College of the City University of New York. He served in the U.S. Army medical corps from 1964 to 1966. Serrano was employed by Manufacturers Hanover Bank from 1961 to 1969, except for his military service, and served on New York City's District 7 School Board from 1969 to 1974. He was a New York state assemblyman from 1974 until he was elected to Congress in 1990. Serrano served from 1991 to 2021. He was a senior member of the House Appropriations Committee and was chairman of the Subcommittee on Commerce, Justice, and Science. His positon as the top Democrat on the subcommittee allowed Serrano to help oversee the budgets of multiple agencies, including the Department of Justice and FBI, the Department of Commerce, the National Science Foundation, NASA, the Legal Services Corporation, and other agencies. He was considered the dean of the Congressional Hispanic Caucus and served as chair of the caucus from 1993 to 1994. He was the longest-serving Puerto Rican in Congress.

Albio Sires (1951–)

Born on January 26, 1951, in the Cuban town of Bejucal, Albio Sires grew up in the waning years of pre-Communist Cuba. His family fled in January 1962 with the help of relatives in America. Sires became a star basketball player at Memorial High School in West New York, New Jersey, and received a four-year basketball scholarship from St. Peter's College. He graduated from St. Peter's in 1974; he later went on to receive a master's degree from Middlebury College in Vermont in 1985. Sires was a teacher and business owner before entering public service. He served as mayor of West New York from 1995 to 2006. Sires also served in the New Jersey State Assembly, where he was Speaker of the Assembly for two terms; he was the first Latino to serve as acting governor of New Jersey. In Congress since 2006, Sires serves on three committees: Foreign Affairs, Transportation and Infrastructure, and Budget. On the Foreign Affairs Committee, Sires is the chairman of the Western Hemisphere, Civilian Security, and Trade Subcommittee and is a member of the Europe, Eurasia, Energy, and the Environment Subcommittee. He is focused on bolstering U.S. relations around the world and working with allies to promote peace, security, and prosperity.

Darren Soto (1978–)

Born on February 25, 1978, in Ringwood, New Jersey, to a Puerto Rican father and an Italian mother, Darren Soto is the first Floridian of Puerto Rican descent to serve in Congress. He graduated with a B.S. degree in economics from Rutgers University (2000) and a law degree from George Washington University School of Law (2004). Initially joining his local Orlando Young Democrats club to make friends, he was soon encouraged to run for the Florida House. At the age of twenty-nine, he ran, won, and served for a decade in the Florida Legislature, fighting to create high paying jobs, increase access to higher education, and ensure clean water, land, and air for his constituents. Soto passed landmark legislation protecting families of fallen firefighters, giving victims of sexual assault more time to report their attackers, and allowing DREAMers to be admitted to the Florida Bar. In the U.S. House of Representatives since 2017, Soto serves on the Energy Committee and the National Resources Committee; he is also on the Democratic Steering and Policy Committee. Soto is a staunch advocate for DREAMers and has worked with fellow members of the Hispanic Caucus to pass the Development, Relief, and Education for Alien Minors (DREAM) Act. In 2018 during the House Committee on Natural Resources meetings, Soto helped lead opposition to the Trump administration proposals to permit oil drilling off Florida's Gulf and Atlantic coasts.

Norma J. Torres (1965–)

Born on April 4, 1965, in Guatemala, Norma J. Torres immigrated to the United States with family members when she was five years old. She became a citizen in 1992. She was a labor union activist and served as the shop steward for local 3090 of the municipal employees union. She served as a state senator, assembly member (elected in 2008), and mayor (elected in 2006) and council member in Pomona, California. Torres earned her bachelor's degree in labor studies from the National Labor College in Maryland in 2012. Torres was elected to the House of Representatives in 2014. Now in her fourth term in Congress, Torres currently serves on the powerful House Appropriations and Rules Committees. The Appropriations Committee is responsible for appropriating all federal spending, domestic and abroad. As a member of the Rules Committee, she helps determine the consideration of all legislation on the House floor. Previously, she served on the Foreign Affairs, Homeland Security, and Natural Resources Committees. As a member of the Foreign Affairs Committee, Torres worked to address the root causes of migration from Central America and has fought to ensure accountability and transparency for U.S. funds spent abroad. Notably, her amendment to require the secretary of state to send Congress a list of corrupt officials in Honduras, El Salvador, and Guatemala was adopted in the National Defense Authorization Act for fiscal year 2019 and signed into law.

Xochitl Torres Small (1964–)

Born on November 15, 1964, in Portland, Oregon, and raised in Las Cruces, New Mexico, Xochitl Torres Small is the daughter of a school teacher and a social worker who later became a bus driver. She graduated from Georgetown University in just three years to minimize her student debt. In 2009 she began her political career in the office of U.S. senator Tom Udall as his first field representative in southern New Mexico. She worked on such issues as rural broadband and health care access to economic development and border security. One issue that she was particularly drawn to was water, the lifeblood of southern New Mexico. Inspired by her work on water, Torres Small went to law school at the University of New Mexico, where she concentrated on water and natural resources law. After graduating, she worked from 2015 to 2016 for U.S. District Court judge Robert C. Brack, who hears thousands of cases per year related to the southern border. She saw firsthand the need to address immigration, border security, and economic development in tandem. Most recently, she was an attorney focused on water and natural resources issues. In addition to her legal work, she served on the board of a local co-op and provided pro bono counsel at a homeless shelter. In her one term in Congress (2019–2021), she was committed to tackling the unique issues facing rural communities like those in southern New Mexico including health care accessibility, infrastructure development, and job growth. She served on the Armed Services Committee, the Agricultural Committee, and the Homeland Security Committee. She was defeated in her bid for reelection in 2020. In 2021 she was nominated and confirmed as undersecretary of agriculture for rural development.

Juan Vargas (1961–)

Juan Vargas was raised on a chicken ranch in National City, in California's 51st District. He is one of ten children, born to his parents, Tomás and Celina Vargas, on March 7, 1961. His father immigrated to the United States from Mexico in the late 1940s as part of the Bracero Program that brought millions of Mexican guest workers to the United States on short-term visas. Through the Bracero Program, Vargas's father became a legal resident and his mother went on to earn her U.S. citizenship. Vargas attended the University of San Diego on scholarship, graduated magna cum laude with a B.A. in political science in 1983. In 1987, he earned a master of humanities from Fordham University in New York City and in 1991 earned his law degree from Harvard Law School. As a young adult, Vargas entered the Jesuits, a Catholic religious order, where he worked with disadvantaged communities, including orphaned children and internally displaced people in the jungles of El Salvador. Vargas was elected to the San Diego City Council in 1993 and in 2000 to the California State Assembly. Following the end of his term in the State Assembly in 2006, Vargas went on to serve as vice president of external affairs for Safeco Insurance and vice president of corporate legal for Liberty Mutual Group. In 2010, Vargas returned to public service and was elected to the California State Senate. Vargas was first elected to the U.S. Congress in 2012. Currently, he is in his fifth term in Congress, serving on the Committee on Financial Services and the Committee on Foreign Affairs.

Filemón Vela Jr. (1963–)

Born on February 13, 1963, in Harlingen, Texas, and raised in Brownsville, Filemón Vela has deep roots in South Texas. His ancestors purchased land from the McAllen family to establish the Laguna Seca Ranch, where the first citrus orchard in Hidalgo County was planted. Vela's father, Filemón Vela Sr., was appointed by President Jimmy Carter as a federal judge in the Southern District of Texas. His mother, Blanca Sánchez Vela, served as the first female mayor of Brownsville. Vela attended Saint Joseph Academy in Brownsville. After graduating in 1985 from Georgetown University in Washington, D.C., he attended and received his law degree from the University of Texas School of Law in 1987. His interest in public service grew from his work helping individuals seek justice in state and federal courts as an attorney for over twenty years in South Texas. He was elected to Congress in 2012. Vela is a member of the House Agriculture Committee, where he serves as the chairman of the General Farm Commodities and Risk Management Subcommittee. Vela has been a strong advocate for immigrant rights, education programs including Head Start and Pell Grants for college students, and federal health care centers.

Nydia Velázquez (1953–)

Nydia Velazquez was born in Yabucoa, Puerto Rico, on March 23, 1953. In 1992, Velázquez, the daughter of a sugarcane worker and a professor, became the first Puerto Rican woman ever elected to serve in the U.S. House of Representatives. She defeated long-term incumbent Stephen Solarz in a hotly contested race. Velázquez received a B.A. in political science from the University of Puerto Rico in 1974 and a master's degree from New York University in 1976. She then worked as a professor of Puerto Rican studies at CUNY's Hunter College and in 1984 became the first Puerto Rican woman to serve on the City Council of New York City. In

1989 she was appointed director of the Department of Puerto Rican Community Affairs in the United States. In 1992, she was elected to Congress. Velázquez is currently serving her fifteenth term as the representative for New York's 7th Congressional District. She is the chairwoman of the House Small Business Committee (the first Latina to chair a full committee), a senior member of the Financial Services Committee, and a member of the House Committee on Natural Resources.

Senate

Catherine Cortez Masto (1964–)

Born on March 29, 1964, in Las Vegas, Catherine Cortez Masto earned a bachelor of science in business administration in finance from the University of Nevada, Reno in 1986, and a J.D. from Gonzaga University School of Law in 1990. Cortez Masto has spent her career fighting for Nevada's working families. She served two terms as attorney general of Nevada, and in November 2016 she made history by becoming the first woman from Nevada and the first Latina ever elected to the U.S. Senate. During her time as Nevada's top prosecutor, Cortez Masto became well known as an advocate for seniors, women, and children. She led the push to break up sex trafficking rings throughout the state. Cortez Masto currently serves as the ranking member of the Economic Policy Subcommittee of the U.S. Senate Committee on Banking, Housing, and Urban Affairs; and the ranking member of the Water and Power Subcommittee of the Energy and Natural Resources Committee. In Congress, Cortez Masto remains a strong advocate for women and children and is working to pass legislation to strengthen women's health care. On being the first Latina in the Senate, she told *Latina Style* magazine in 2017, "It's my turn to leave behind an open door for women who want to follow in my footsteps. We must ensure that those that work hard and play by the rules can succeed at becoming whoever they want—that the tools and resources

are there to help them get ahead. And that's exactly what I'm going to work for ever day."

Ted Cruz (1970–)

Born on December 22, 1970, in Calgary, Alberta, Canada, Rafael Edward Cruz settled in Houston with his parents when he was a child. Cruz's mother was born in Delaware to Irish and Italian parents; his Cuban refugee father is a pastor in Dallas. Cruz received his B.A. from Princeton University in 1992 and his law degree from Harvard in 1995. Before being elected to the Senate, Cruz served as solicitor general in Texas. During the George W. Bush administration, Cruz served as an associate deputy attorney general in the U.S. Justice Department and as the director of policy planning at the U.S. Federal Trade Commission. Cruz was elected to the U.S. Senate to represent Texas in 2012. In 2016, Cruz ran unsuccessfully for the Republican nomination for the presidency. He returned to the Senate to resume his fight to require the Library of Congress to use the term "illegal aliens." At the 2016 Republican Convention, he defied the GOP, denying Donald Trump his endorsement, urging the audience to "vote their own conscience"; he has since been a staunch supporter of Trump and was one of the few senators in 2021 to vote to decertify the election of Joseph Biden to the presidency.

Bob Menéndez (1954–)

Robert Menéndez was born in New York City on January 1, 1954. He grew up the son of Cuban immigrants in a tenement building in Union City, New Jersey. He received his B.A. degree from St. Peter's College in 1976 and his law degree from Rutgers Law School in 1979. He first entered public service as a nineteen-year-old college student when his high school would not provide books to students who could not afford them. Menéndez launched a successful petition drive to reform the local school board and a year later won a seat on that very board, becoming the youngest school board member in

New Jersey. He went on to become mayor of Union City, then a state legislator, and was elected to Congress in 1992. He was the first Latino New Jersey has ever sent to Congress and the first Democratic Cuban American to serve in the House. Elected to the U.S. Senate in 2006, he has served as chairman of one of the most powerful committees in the Senate, the Foreign Relations Committee, where he established himself as a new foreign policy leader, where he advocates for women and children struggling with oppressive poverty in Central America and Africa, and stands by democracy activists struggling to reform governments from Cuba to China to Russia. He served as chairman of the Banking Subcommittee on Housing, Transportation, and Community Development, where he fought for smart growth, jobs for the twenty-first century, and updating the nation's aging transportation system.

Latinos in Congress since 1822

House of Representatives

Name	Party and State	Years Served
Joseph Marion Hernández	W-Florida	1822–1823
Jose Manuel Gallegos	D-New Mexico	1871–1873
Miguel Antonio Otero Sr.	D-New Mexico	1856–1861
Francisco Perea	R-New Mexico	1863–1865
Jose Francisco Chaves	R-New Mexico	1865–1867
Trinidad Romero	R-New Mexico	1877–1879
Mariano Sabino Otero	R-New Mexico	1879–1881
Romualdo Pacheco	R-California	1879–1883
Tranquillino Luna	R-New Mexico	1881–1884
Francisco Manzanares	D-New Mexico	1884–1885
Pedro Perea	R-New Mexico	1899–1901
Julio Larringa	U-Puerto Rico*	1905–1911
Luis Muñoz Rivera	U-Puerto Rico*	1911–1916
Ládislas Lázaro	D-Louisiana	1913–1927
Benigno Cárdenas Hernández	R-New Mexico	1919–1921
Félix Córdova Dávila	U-Puerto Rico*	1917–1932
Nestor Montoya	R-New Mexico	1921–1923
Dennis Chávez	D-New Mexico	1931–1935
Joachim Octave Fernández	D-Louisiana	1931–1941
José Lorenzo Pesquera	NP-Puerto Rico*	1932–1933
Santiago Iglesias	C-Puerto Rico*	1933–1939
Bolívar Pagán	C-Puerto Rico*	1939–1945
Antonio Manuel Fernández	D-New Mexico	1943–1956
Jesús T. Piñero	PD-Puerto Rico*	1945–1948
Antonio Fernós-Isern	PD-Puerto Rico*	1949–1965
Joseph Manuel Montoya	D-New Mexico	1957–1964
Henry B. González	D-Texas	1961–1999
Edward R. Roybal	D-California	1962–1992
E. (Kika) de la Garza	D-Texas	1965–1997
Santiago Polanco-Abreu	PD-Puerto Rico*	1965–1969
Manuel Luján Jr.	R-New Mexico	1969–1988
Jorge Luis Córdova	NP-Puerto Rico*	1969–1973

House of Representatives (contd.)

Name	Party and State	Years Served
Herman Badillo	D-New York	1971–1977
Jaime Benítez	PD-Puerto Rico*	1973–1977
Baltasar Corrada	NP-Puerto Rico*	1977–1984
Ben Blaz	R-Guam*	1985–1992
Jaime B. Fuster	D-Puerto Rico*	1985–1992
José E. Serrano	D-New York	1991–2021
Robert A. Underwood	D-Guam*	1993–2003
Charles Rangel	D-New York	1971–2017
Robert García	D-New York	1978–1990
Matthew Martínez	D-California	1982–2001
Solomon P. Ortiz	D-Texas	1983–2011
Bill Richardson	D-New Mexico	1983–1997
Esteban Torres	D-California	1983–1999
Barbara Vucanovich	R-Nevada	1983–1997
Albert Bustamante	D-Texas	1985–1993
Ileana Ros-Lehtinen	R-Florida	1989–2019
Ed Pastor	D-Arizona	1991–2015
Xavier Becerra	D-California	1993–2017
Henry Bonilla	D-Texas	1993–2007
Lincoln Díaz-Balart	R-Florida	1993–2011
Luis Gutiérrez	D-Illinois	1993–2019
Bob Menéndez	D-New Jersey	1993–2006
Frank Tejeda	D-Texas	1993–1997
Rubén Hinojosa	D-Texas	1997–2017
Silvestre Reyes	D-Texas	1997–2013
Loretta Sánchez	D-California	1997–2017
John E. Sununu	R-New Hampshire	1997–2003
Ciro Rodríguez	D-Texas	1997–2005
Charlie González	D-Texas	1999–2013
Joe Baca	D-California	1999–2013
Hilda Solís	D-California	2001–2009
John Salazar	D-Colorado	2005–2011
Ben Ray Luján	D-New Mexico	2009–2021
Quico Canseco	R-Texas	2011–2013
Raúl Labrador	R-Idaho	2011–2019
David Rivera	R-Florida	2011–2013
Bill Flores	R-Texas	2011–2021
Pete Gallego	D-Texas	2013–2015
Joe García	D-Florida	2013–2015
Michelle Luján Grisham	D-New Mexico	2014–2018
Gloria Negrete McLeod	D-California	2013–2015
Carlos Curbelo	R-Florida	2015–2019
Rubén Kihuen	D-Nevada	2017–2019
Gil Cisneros	D-California	2019–2021

House of Representatives (contd.)

Name	Party and State	Years Served
Debbie Mucarsel-Powell	D-Florida	2019–2021
Xochitl Torres Small	D-New Mexico	2019–2021
Lucille Roybal-Alard	D-California	1993–present
Nydia M. Velázquez	D-New York	1993–present
Grace Napolitano	D-California	1999–present
Mario Díaz-Balart	R-Florida	2003–present
Raúl Grijalva	D-Arizona	2003–present
Linda Sánchez	D-California	2003–present
Henry Cuéllar	D-California	2005–present
Albio Sires	D-New Jersey	2006–present
Jaime Herrera Beutler	R-Washington	2011–present
Tony Cárdenas	D-California	2013–present
Joaquín Castro	D-Texas	2013–present
Raúl Ruiz	D-California	2013–present
Juan Vargas	D-California	2013–present
Filemón Vela	D-Texas	2013–present
Pete Aguilar	D-California	2015–present
Rubén Gallego	D-Arizona	2015–present
Alex Mooney	R-West Virginia	2015–present
Norma Torres	D-California	2015–present
Nanette Barragán	D-California	2017–present
Salud Carbajal	D-California	2017–present
Lou Correa	D-California	2017–present
Adriano Espaillat	D-New York	2017–present
Vicente González	D-Texas	2017–present
Brian Mast	R-Florida	2017–present
Darren Soto	D-Florida	2017–present
Jimmy Gómez	D-California	2017–present
Antonio Delgado	D-New York	2019–present
Veronica Escobar	D-Texas	2019–present
Chuy García	D-Illinois	2019–present
Sylvia García	D-Texas	2019–present
Anthony González	R-Ohio	2019–present
Mike Levin	D-California	2019–present
Alexandria Ocasio-Cortez	D-New York	2019–present
Mike García	R-California	2020–present

Senate

Name	Party and State	Years Served
Dennis Chávez	D-New Mexico	1935–1962
Joseph Montoya	D-New Mexico	1964–1977
Bob Menéndez	D-New Jersey	2006–present
Ted Cruz	R-Texas	2012–present
Catherine Cortez Masto	D-Nevada	2016–present

*Source: Congressional Latino Caucus. *Nonvoting member of Congress. Party Affiliation: D = Democrat; R = Republican; C = Congress; PD = Popular Democrático; NP = Nuevo Progresista; U = Unida; W = Whig.*

SELECT ELECTED AND APPOINTED OFFICIALS, PAST AND PRESENT

Alexander Acosta (1969–)

Born on January 16, 1969, in Miami, Florida, the son of Cuban refugees, Acosta received his bachelor's degree from Harvard University in 1990 and his law degree from Harvard Law School in 1994. On his road to conservatism, Acosta clerked for future Supreme Court justice Samuel Alito and then joined a private law firm. He also taught employment law at George Mason University Law School. In 2013 he became chairman of the U.S. Century Bank, the largest domestically owned Hispanic community bank in Florida and one of the fifteen largest Hispanic community banks in the nation. In the George W. Bush administration, Acosta held various positions in the Justice Department's Civil Rights Division, rising to assistant attorney general for that division in 2003; it is the highest rank in the Justice Department ever attained by a Latino. In 2005 Acosta became U.S. attorney for the southern district of Florida. In 2009 he moved across town to serve as dean of the Florida International University College of Law. In 2017 Acosta became the secretary of labor, the only Latino in President Donald Trump's cabinet. In July 2019, Acosta resigned from the positon amid a scandal regarding actions he took while U.S. attorney in southern Florida.

Eduardo Aguirre (1964–)

Born on July 30, 1946, in Cuba, Eduardo Aguirre came to the United States in 1961 as an unaccompanied youth via Operation Pedro Pan. Aguirre earned his bachelor's degree from Louisiana State University and also graduated from the American Bankers Association's National Commercial Lending Graduate School. From 2003 to 2005, Aguirre served as the first director of the U.S. Citizenship and Immigration Services and as an undersecretary in the Department of Homeland Security. He was also the acting chairman of the U.S. Export-Import Bank, where he was responsible for leading the financing

of complex transactions in transportation, technology, and energy projects, among others. President George W. Bush appointed Aguirre as U.S. ambassador to Spain and Andorra; he served from 2005 to 2009. Aguirre is chairman and CEO of Atlantic Partners Group L.L.C., a consulting group offering strategic, geopolitical, and business advice to clients. He also serves on several corporate boards, including the U.S. subsidiaries of Spanish multinationals BBVA and Iberdrola Renewables. He is a recipient of the Ellis Island Medal of Honor and the Americanism Award by the Daughters of the American Revolution.

Toney Anaya (1941–)

One of ten children born to New Mexican parents on April 29, 1941, in Moriarty, New Mexico, Toney Anaya spent his childhood in an adobe house with a dirt floor and no electricity or plumbing. Although his parents had no more than a couple of years of schooling, they encouraged their children to get a good education. Anaya attended New Mexico Highlands University on a Sears Foundation scholarship. Anaya moved to Washington, D.C., where he graduated from Georgetown University. In 1967, he received his law degree from American University. During this time, he worked for two New Mexico senators: while at American University, he worked for Dennis Chávez, and following graduation he worked for Joseph Montoya. In 1970, Anaya returned to New Mexico. He ran for attorney general of New Mexico in 1974 and won, serving until 1978. In 1982, Anaya was elected governor of New Mexico, where he served until 1986.

Jerry Apodaca (1934–)

Former New Mexico governor Jerry Apodaca was born on October 3, 1934, in Las Cruces, New Mexico, where his family had lived for over one hundred years. He graduated from the University of New Mexico in 1957 and worked as a teacher and businessman. In 1966, Apodaca entered politics and was elected to the New Mexico state senate as a Democrat. After eight years in the state legislature, Apodaca, at age forty, was elected in 1974 as the first Latino governor of New Mexico in over fifty years (Governor

Octaviano Larrazolo had served from 1918 to 1920). After Apodaca's term as governor ended, President Jimmy Carter appointed him as chairman of the President's Council on Physical Fitness and Sports. Following this appointment, Apodaca resumed his business interests and served on the board of directors of the Philip Morris Company.

Polly Baca-Barragán (1941–)

The first Latina woman to be elected state senator to the Colorado legislature, Polly Baca-Barragán was born on February 13, 1941, in La Salle, Colorado. In 1963 she graduated from Colorado State University. During the 1960s, she was active in the Democratic Party and worked on the presidential campaigns of John F. Kennedy, Lyndon B. Johnson, and Robert F. Kennedy. From 1971 to 1972 she was director of Spanish-speaking affairs for the Democratic National Committee. In 1974 Baca-Barragán made a successful bid for state representative to the Colorado legislature. In 1978 she became the first Latina to be elected to the Colorado State Senate and was reelected in 1982.

Herman Badillo (1929–2014)

The first Puerto Rican ever elected as a voting member of Congress, Herman Badillo was born on August 21, 1929, in Caguas, Puerto Rico. Orphaned at age five, he was sent to live with relatives in New York City in 1940. He attended the City College of New York, where he graduated with honors, then attended the Brooklyn Law School at night. In 1961, Badillo entered politics, narrowly losing a race for the state assembly. After serving in several local appointed positions, he ran unsuccessfully for mayor of New York. Badillo gained popularity as a result of his strong showing in the mayoral election and later won election to Congress in 1970. He served as a U.S. congressman from New York for four terms, representing the 21st District. After serving in Congress for seven years, Badillo resigned in 1978 to accept an appointment as

deputy mayor of New York City under Mayor Edward Koch. Badillo went into the practice of law in New York after leaving the deputy mayor's office. In 1986, he ran for the post of New York state comptroller. He lost the statewide race but carried 61 percent of the New York City vote.

Romana Bañuelos (1925–2018)

Born on March 25, 1925, in the mining town of Miami, Arizona, to poor, undocumented Mexican immigrants, Romana Bañuelos became the first Mexican American and the sixth woman to hold the post of treasurer of the United States. During the Great Depression, she was forced at age six to accompany her parents when they were deported to Mexico in 1931. She grew up in Mexico and at age nineteen moved back to the United States and settled in Los Angeles. In 1949, she started a small tortilla factory with $400. Over the following twenty years, she developed Romana's Mexican Food Products into a $12 million per year business, employing hundreds of workers and producing dozens of food items. She also helped to establish the Pan American National Bank in Los Angeles, of which she was a director and chairwoman. In 1971, President Richard Nixon appointed Bañuelos treasurer of the United States. She served as treasurer from December 1971 until February 1974.

Casimiro Barela (1847–1920)

Born in Embudo, New Mexico, on March 4, 1847, and educated in Mora by Archbishop Jean-Baptiste Salpointe, Casimoro Barela moved with his family to Colorado in 1867, where they raised cattle. In 1869, Barela was elected justice of the peace and over the next six years held several elected posts, including county assessor and sheriff. In 1875, Barela was elected as a delegate to the state constitutional convention, in which he took a leadership role. He secured a provision in the constitution protecting the civil rights of Spanish-speaking citizens as well as publication of laws in both Spanish and English, but this provision was limited to twenty-five years. Barela was elected to the first Colorado senate in 1876 and served until 1916. He was twice elected president of the Colorado senate. Barela died on December 18, 1920.

Xavier Becerra
(1958–)

Born on January 26, 1958, in Sacramento, California, to Mexican parents, Xavier Becerra graduated with a B.A. in economics from Stanford University in 1980 and a law degree from Stanford Law School in 1984. He began his work as a legal aid lawyer in Massachusetts and then started his career in politics as an administrative assistant to California state senator Art Torres in 1986. From 1987 to 1990 Becerra was deputy attorney general in California and was elected and served as a California state senator from 1990 to 1992. He was elected to Congress in 1992 and served until 2001, when he ran unsuccessfully for mayor of Los Angeles. In 2017, Becerra became attorney general of California, where he was at the forefront of legal efforts on health care, leading twenty states and the District of Columbia in a campaign to protect the Affordable Care Act from being dismantled by Republicans and the Trump administration. In 2021, newly elected president Joe Biden named him secretary of health and human services, the first Latino to fill that cabinet position.

Jovita Carranza
(1949–)

Born June 29, 1949, in Chicago, Illinois, to working-class immigrant parents from Mexico, Carranza has B.A. and M.B.A. degrees from the University of Miami, with additional postgraduate training in management and finance from the University of Michigan and the University of Chicago. She started at the United Parcel Service in the 1970s as a box handler and eventually ascended to vice president of domestic operations and president of international operations for Latin America and the Caribbean—she was the highest ranking Latina in the company's history. From 2006 to 2009 Carranza served in President George W. Bush's administration as deputy administrator of the Small Business Administration. After leaving her government position, she founded and served as president of the JCR Group, a consulting firm for business development for corporations and NGOs. During the 2016 presidential election, Carranza was a member of the Trump campaign's National Hispanic Advisory Council, and after Trump was elected, he nominted her and the U.S. Senate confirmed her appointment as treasurer of the United States. In 2019, President Trump nominated Carranza to be administrator of the Small Business Administration; once again, the Senate confirmed her appointment.

Arturo Carrión (1913–1989)

Former deputy assistant secretary of state under President John F. Kennedy, and the first Puerto Rican to be appointed to such a high State Department position, Arturo Carrión was born in Havana, Cuba, on November 16, 1913. He earned a B.A. degree from the University of Puerto Rico in 1935, an M.A. degree from the University of Texas in 1936, and a Ph.D. degree from Columbia University in 1950. Carrión taught at the University of Puerto Rico and became chairman of the history department. He then went into politics and served as undersecretary of Puerto Rico's State Department, in charge of external affairs. He joined the Kennedy administration in 1961 as deputy assistant secretary of state for inter-American affairs, serving until the assassination of President Kennedy in 1963. After leaving the State Department, Carrión became special assistant to the secretary general of the Organization of American States. He later returned to Puerto Rico to become president of the University of Puerto Rico.

Leonel Castillo (1939–2013)

Leonel Castillo was born on June 9, 1939, in Victoria, Texas. He graduated from St. Mary's University in San Antonio, Texas, in 1961. Castillo joined the Peace Corps after graduation and served in the Philippines from 1961 to 1965. Upon his return to the United States, he attended the University of Pittsburgh, where he received his master's degree in social work in 1967. Castillo then returned to Texas and lived in Houston, where he took an active role in local politics. In 1970, he won a surprise victory in his election as Houston city comptroller against a twenty-five-year incumbent. In 1974, he was named treasurer of the Texas Democratic Party. When President Jimmy Carter appointed Castillo to head the Immigration and Naturalization Service (INS) in 1977, Castillo became the first Latino in history to head that government unit.

Lauro Cavazos (1927–)

Born on January 4, 1927, on the King Ranch in Kingsville, Texas, the son of a foreman, Lauro Cavazos earned B.A. and M.A. degrees in zoology from Texas Tech University and a Ph.D. in physiology in 1954 from Iowa State University. Cavazos left a distinguished career as the president of Texas Tech University in Lubbock, Texas, to join President Ronald Reagan's cabinet in 1988 as secretary of education. Previously, Cavazos had been the dean of Tufts University School of Medicine. He was reappointed secretary of education by President George H. W. Bush in 1989. Cavazos was instrumental in persuading Bush to sign the executive order creating the President's Council on Educational Excellence for Latino Americans.

Dennis Chávez (1888–1962)

Born on April 18, 1888, Dennis Chávez was a member of the U.S. House of Representatives and the first Latino U.S. senator. Chávez was born as the third of eight children in a village west of Albuquerque, New Mexico, to a poor family. Chávez attended school in Albuquerque, but family poverty forced him to drop out in the eighth grade to work delivering groceries. He continued to educate himself in the evenings at the public library. From 1906 to 1915, he worked for the Albuquerque city engineering department. In 1912, Chávez worked as a Spanish interpreter for the successful Democratic candidate for U.S. Senate, Andrieus Jones. Jones obtained a clerkship in the Senate for Chávez, who entered law school at Georgetown University in Washington, D.C. In 1920, Chávez was

awarded a law degree. Chávez then returned to New Mexico, where he began a successful law practice and ran for public office. In 1930, Chávez defeated the incumbent Republican and won a seat in the U.S. House of Representatives. He was reelected to the House in 1932. In the 1934 elections, Chávez ran for the U.S. Senate seat held by the powerful Republican Bronson Cutting and was defeated by a narrow margin. Chávez challenged the validity of Cutting's reelection, charging vote fraud, and took the challenge to the floor of the U.S. Senate. While the challenge was pending, Cutting was killed in an airplane crash. Chávez was appointed by the governor of New Mexico to succeed Cutting. Chávez was reelected easily in the 1936 elections. As a Democratic senator, Chávez was a staunch supporter of President Franklin D. Roosevelt's New Deal. As chairman of the Public Works Committee, Chávez obtained federal funding for irrigation and flood control projects in New Mexico. As a Western isolationist, he opposed U.S. entry into World War II and argued that the country should follow a policy of strict neutrality. During the years after the war, Chávez did some of his best work in the Senate. Perhaps his greatest contribution to Latinos, and to the nation, was his support of education and civil rights. Chávez drafted a bill to create the federal Fair Employment Practices Commission and fought tirelessly for its enactment. In all, Chávez was elected to the Senate five times. A champion of civil rights and full equality for all Americans to the last, the long and distinguished national career of this son of New Mexico was ended by a heart attack in mid-November 1962.

Henry Cisneros (1947–)

Born on June 11, 1947, in a west-side Mexican barrio of San Antonio to a civil servant, Henry Cisneros was educated in the city's parochial schools and attended Texas A&M University, where he received a B.A. degree and a master's degree in urban planning in 1970. In 1971 Cisneros moved to Washington, D.C., where he worked for the National League of Cities and began full-time graduate studies in public administration at George Washington University. During 1971, at age twenty-four, Cisneros became the youngest White House fellow in U.S. history. When his fellowship ended, he earned a second master's degree, in public administration, at Harvard University. He then went on to complete his work at George Washington University and received a Ph.D. degree in public administration. He returned to San Antonio and taught government at the University of Texas. Cisneros ran for the city council on the Good Government League ticket in 1975 and won. He gained a reputation as a bright, young politician, and in 1977 he was reelected in a landslide. In 1981, Cisneros ran for mayor of San Antonio, the ninth-largest city in the United States, and won with 62 percent of the vote. In 1983, he was reelected with 94 percent of the vote, again reelected in 1985 with 72 percent, and reelected in 1987 with twice as many votes as his closest opponent. After he left office as mayor, Cisneros founded Cisneros Asset Management, which manages hundreds of millions of dollars of pension funds. Cisneros was named secretary of the Department of Housing and Urban Development (HUD) by President Bill Clinton in 1992. Cisneros was widely viewed as a coalition builder in working to reform HUD regulations and programs to make the department's services more accessible to the poor. In many professional opinions, Cisneros was the best secretary of HUD in history. Among his many accomplishments was the implementation of HOPE VI, a program that tore down the worst dilapidated public housing projects and replaced them with new homes in mixed-income developments. Under Cisneros HUD also significantly expanded home ownership throughout the country to its highest level since 1981. After leaving HUD in 1997, Cisneros became an executive at media companies and sat on various corporate boards. Back in San Antonio he founded CityView, a company that invests in low-income and medium-income homes.

Fernando E. Cabeza de Baca (1937–)

Fernando E. Cabeza de Baca was born in 1937 in Albuquerque, New Mexico. He received his early education in New Mexico, and at the end of the 1950s he received a degree in public administration from the University of New Mexico in Albuquerque. He also studied at the University of New Mexico School of Law. During the Vietnam War, he served in the U.S. Army and returned from the war disabled and decorated. In the late 1960s and early 1970s de Baca held high-ranking positions with the New Mexico Department of Transportation, the Civil Service Commission, and the Department of Health, Education and Welfare. He then became chairman of the Federal Regional Council for the Western United States. In 1974 President Gerald Ford appointed de Baca as special assistant to the president for Hispanic affairs. In this role, at age thiry-seven, he became both the youngest and the highest-ranking federal executive of Latino descent.

Cari Domínguez (1949–)

Cari Domínguez was born on March 8, 1949, in Havana, Cuba. Her family immigrated to the United States, and she was raised in Takoma Park, Maryland. She holds a bachelor's degree (1971) and a master's degree (1997) from American University in Washington, D.C. She was also a fellow of the MIT Advanced Study Program in Public Management. In 1974, Domínguez joined the Office of Federal Contract Compliance Programs, where she held a variety of positions until 1983. She was the architect of the Labor Department's Glass Ceiling Initiative. In 1984, she left the Department of Labor and began working for the Bank of America in San Francisco, where she served as corporate manager of equal opportunity programs. In 1986, she was promoted to vice president and director of executive programs, in charge of executive compensation and benefits programs, succession planning, development, and staffing services. President George W. Bush appointed Domínguez to director of the Equal Employment Opportunity Commission, in which she served from 2001 to 2006.

Alberto R. González (1955–)

Born on August 4, 1955, in San Antonio, Texas, to a Mexican migrant worker father and a homemaker mother, Alberto González was raised and schooled in Humble, Texas. He began his college education at the U.S. Air Force Academy but left to finish his bachelor's degree in 1979 at Rice University in Houston.

He earned a law degree from Harvard Law School in 1979. González was an attorney at one of Houston's leading firms, Vinson and Elkins, from 1982 to 1994, when he left the firm to become legal counsel to Governor George W. Bush. In 1999, Bush appointed González to the Supreme Court of Texas, and González won election on his own in 2000. When Bush became president, González served as White House counsel from 2001 to 2005, and then attorney general of the United States from 2005 to 2007. On August 26, 2007, under pressure from Congress for his enabling controversial policies of the Bush administration, González tendered his resignation. In the following years, González taught at Texas Tech University and in 2011 became the Doyle Rogers Distinguished Chair of Law at Belmont University College of Law.

Jimmy Gurulé (1951–)

Jimmy Gurulé was born June 14, 1951, in Salt Lake City, Utah. He received both his bachelor's degree (1974) and his law degree (1980) from the University of Utah. Prior to joining the Department of Justice, Gurulé was an associate professor of law at the University of Notre Dame Law School. He is a former president of the Latino National Bar Association. Gurulé was appointed assistant attorney general by President George H. W. Bush and was sworn in on August 3, 1990. He was the highest-ranking Latino in the history of the Department of Justice. As assistant attorney general for the Office of Justice Programs, Gurulé was responsible for coordinating policy, management, and priorities within the Office of Justice Programs in Washington, D.C., and its five program bureaus and field offices. He worked to form partnerships among federal, state, and local government officials to improve administration of justice, combat violent crime and drug abuse, meet the needs of crime victims, and find innovative ways to address problems such as narcotics trafficking, gang-related crime, white-collar crime, and corruption. Gurulé was awarded the Attorney General's Distinguished Service Award in 1990 for his excellence as an assistant U.S. attorney in prosecuting the killers of Drug Enforcement Administration special agent Enrique Camarena, who had been working in Guadalajara, Mexico. From 2001 to 2003 Gurulé

served in the Department of the Treasury as the undersecretary for enforcement.

Isabel Guzmán (1970– or 1971–)

Born in Burbank, California, to a Mexican American family, who is also of Jewish, German, and Chinese descent, Isabel Casillas Guzmán moved with her family from Texas to Los Angeles in the 1960s. She has a B.S. in science from the Wharton School of the University of Pennsylvania. She served as the deputy chief of staff and senior advisor to the administrator of the Small Business Administration under President Barack Obama from 2014 to 2017. From 2017 to 2019, Guzmán served as the director of strategic initiatives at ProAmerica Bank in Los Angeles. From 2019 to 2021, she served as the director of California's Office of the Small Business Advocate. In January 2021 President Joe Biden appointed Guzmán to be head of the Small Business Administration. She is the first Latino to hold that cabinet position.

Edward Hidalgo (1912–1995)

Former Secretary of the Navy Edward Hidalgo was born on October 12, 1912, in Mexico City. His family immigrated to the United States in 1918, and he was naturalized in 1936. He holds law degrees from both countries, a J.D. degree from Columbia University, which he received in 1936, and a similar degree from the University of Mexico, which was conferred in 1959. During World War II, Hidalgo was special assistant to Secretary of the Navy James Forrestal in 1945–46 and was a member of the Eberstadt Commission on the Unification of the Military Services in 1945. After the war, he returned to private practice as an attorney. In 1965, Hidalgo was named special assistant to Secretary of the Navy Paul Nitze. From 1977 to 1979 he served as assistant secretary of the Navy and then was appointed secretary of the Navy by President Jimmy Carter in 1979; he served until 1981.

Manuel Luján Jr. (1928–2019)

Born on May 12, 1928, in San Ildefonsoe Pueblo, New Mexico, Manuel Luján Jr. grew up in Santa

Fe, New Mexico, and earned his B.A. degree from the College of Santa Fe. His father had been the mayor of Santa Fe and had also run unsuccessfully for higher offices. After college, Luján was a partner in a family insurance and real estate business. In 1976, he helped found the Republican National Hispanic Assembly. Luján served as a Republican congressman and represented the 1st District of New Mexico in the U.S. House of Representatives from 1969 to 1989. In Congress, Luján was the ranking minority member of the House Interior Committee. In 1989, President George H. W. Bush appointed Luján as the forty-sixth secretary of the interior. After leaving office at the end of the Bush term, Luján worked as a consultant and lobbyist. In 2004, he founded the Hispanic Alliance for Progress Institute, a conservative think tank focusing on political issues from a Hispanic perspective. He died on April 25, 2019.

Michelle Luján Grisham (1959–)

Born October 24, 1959, in Los Alamos, New Mexico, to a family whose roots date back to colonial times, Michelle Luján earned a B.A. in university studies from the University of New Mexico in 1981 and her law degree from the University of New Mexico School of Law in 1987. She served as secretary of health of New Mexico from 2004 to 2007 and as Bernalillo County commissioner from 2010 to 2012. Luján Grisham was elected and served in Congress as a Democrat from 2013 to 2019. In 2016, Luján Grisham was elected chair of the Congressional Hispanic Caucus. On November 6, 2018, she became the first Democratic woman elected governor in New Mexico and the first Democratic Hispanic woman elected governor in U.S. history.

Robert Martínez (1934–)

Born in Tampa, Florida, on December 25, 1934, Robert Martínez received his bachelor's degree in education from the University of Tampa in 1957 and a master's degree in labor and industrial relations from the University of Illinois in 1964. Martínez went into business following college and owned and operated a restaurant in Tampa until 1983. He became involved in local politics in the late 1970s and was elected to

two terms as a Republican mayor of Tampa from 1979 to 1986. In 1986, Martínez was elected governor of Florida and served one term; he was the first Latino to hold that office. During his tenure as governor, President Ronald Reagan named Martínez to the White House Conference on a Drug-Free America. Martínez was appointed by President George H. W. Bush as director of the Office of National Drug Control Policy; he served in that position from 1991 to 1993.

Susana Martínez (1959–)

Born on July 14, 1959, in El Paso, Texas, to Mexican American parents, Susana Martínez earned a B.A. in criminal justice from the University of Texas at El Paso in 1981 and a law degree from the University of Oklahoma College of Law in 1986. After passing the bar, she was an assistant district attorney in Doña Ana County, New Mexico, from 1986 to 1992 and thereafter was elected district attorney; she served until running for governor of New Mexico in 2010. She was elected and reelected, and served as governor until 2019. Martínez was a Democrat until 1995, when she switched to the Republican Party and advocated many of its conservative positions. When she ran for governor, a key issue was closing the border with Mexico.

Alejandro Mayorkas (1959–)

Born on November 24, 1959, in Havana, Cuba, to Jewish parents, Alejandro Mayorkas immgrated to Miami with his refugee parents in 1960 but was raised in Beverly Hills, California. He received his B.A. from the University of California, Berkeley, in 1981 and his law degree from Loyola Law School in 1985. He has spent the major part of his career in government service, beginning in 1989 as an assistant U.S. attorney and in 1998 the youngest U.S. attorney in history. In 2001, he went into private practice and by 2008 was named one of the "50 Most Influential Minority Lawyers in America" by the *National Law Journal*. By 2009 he was back in government service, having been appointed the director of U.S. Citizenship and Immigration Services by President Barack Obama, thus becoming the highest-ranking Cuban American in the Obama administration. Under Mayorkas the agency developed the Deferred Action for Childhood Arrivals (DACA) program to shield from deportation people who entered the United States as minors without documents. From 2013 to 2016, he served as deputy secretary of homeland security. In 2021, Mayorkas was one of the first appointments made by President Joe Biden: to serve as secretary of homeland security. He thus became the first Latino to head that department.

Gloria Molina (1948–)

A longtime member of the Los Angeles County Board of Supervisors, Gloria Molina was born in Los Angeles on May 13, 1948, to Mexican parents who had immigrated to the United States the year before. She grew up and received her early education in the small town of Pico Rivera, California, and then attended East Los Angeles College. In 1967, an accident suffered by her father forced her to become the full-time provider for the family at age nineteen. Her job as a legal assistant did not prevent her from continuing her education, and she received a bachelor's degree from California State University in Los Angeles. In 1973, she was the founding president of the Comisión Femenil de Los Angeles (Women's Commission) and served as national president from 1974 to 1976. Molina was first elected to office in 1982 as state assemblywoman for the 56th District of California. In 1987, she was elected to the Los Angeles City Council, on which she served as councilwoman of the 1st District until 1991. In 1991, she was elected to the Los Angeles County Board of Supervisors. Molina is the first Latino American in history elected to the California state legislature, the Los Angeles City Council, and the Los Angeles County Board of Supervisors. Prior to being elected to public office, Molina served in the Jimmy Carter administration as a deputy for presidential personnel. After leaving the White House, she served as deputy director for the U.S. Department of Health and Human Services in San Francisco.

Joseph Montoya (1915–1978)

Joseph Montoya was born on September 24, 1915, in the small village of Pena Blanca, New Mexico, where his father was county sheriff. Montoya's parents were descendants of eighteenth-century Spanish immigrants to New Mexico. After graduating from high school in 1931, he attended Regis College in Denver, Colorado. In 1934, he entered Georgetown University Law School in Washington, D.C. In 1936, during his second year of law school, Montoya was elected as a Democrat to the New Mexico House of Representatives at age twenty-one, the youngest representative in the state's history. Two years later, he received his LL.B. degree from Georgetown University and was reelected to the state legislature. In 1940, Montoya was elected to the state senate; at age twenty-five, he was the youngest senator in the state's history. He served a total of twelve years in the state legislature. He then was elected to four terms as lieutenant governor of New Mexico, serving from 1947 to 1951 and from 1955 to 1957. In 1957, at age forty-two, Montoya was elected as a Democrat to the first of four consecutive terms in the U.S. House of Representatives. He established a reputation as a hardworking legislator and loyal party man. He followed a moderate political course and was regularly returned to Congress with well over 60 percent of the vote. When Senator Dennis Chávez died in 1962, his seat was temporarily filled by Evan Mechem, who had just lost his bid for reelection as governor but who was legally allowed to name himself to the vacant Senate seat. But Mechem lost the seat to his former lieutenant governor, Montoya, in a special election in November 1964. Montoya also won a second term to the Senate in 1970. One of the most influential senators in Washington, he was a member of the Appropriations Committee and the Public Works Committee. However, in the early 1970s Montoya's popularity at home waned, and he was defeated in his bid for reelection in 1976 by former astronaut Harrison Schmitt.

Julián Nava (1927–)

Born on June 19, 1927, in Los Angeles, California, to a family that had fled Mexico during the Mexican Revolution, Julián Nava grew up in East Los Angeles. He served in the Navy Air Corps during World War II and, upon return, obtained an education through the G.I. Bill. Nava graduated from Pomona College with an A.B. degree in 1951 and from Harvard

University with a Ph.D. degree in 1955. After graduation he has served as a lecturer and professor of history at various universities in Colombia, Venezuela, Puerto Rico, Spain, and California. From 1957 to 2000, Nava was a professor of history at California State University, Northridge. In 1967, Nava was elected to the Los Angeles school board and later served as president of the board. Nava served as ambassador to Mexico from 1979 to 1981; he was the first Mexican American to ever hold that post. After his service as ambassador and teaching, Nava became a filmmaker, writing and producing various documentaries. The Los Angeles Unified school District has named two schools in his honor.

Antonia Novello (1944–)

The first woman and first Latino surgeon general of the United States, Antonia Novello was born in Fajardo, Puerto Rico, on August 23, 1944. She received a B.A. degree in 1965 and an M.D. degree in 1970 from the University of Puerto Rico. Novello was awarded her master's degree in public health from Johns Hopkins University in 1982. Novello joined the U.S. Public Health Service in 1978 after working in the private practice of pediatrics and nephrology. She served in various capacities at the National Institutes of Health (NIH) beginning in 1978, including serving as deputy director of the National Institute of Child Health and Human Development. In 1990, President George H. W. Bush appointed Novello as the fourteenth surgeon general. She was the first Latino to ever hold that post. As surgeon general, Novello promoted the health of women, children, and minorities, and she created policy to curb underage drinking, smoking, and AIDS. She led in the creation of the Healthy Children Ready to Learn initiative. From 1999 to 2006 Novello served as the commissioner of health of New York. From 2008 to 2014, Novello served as vice president of Women and Children Health and Policy Affairs at Disney Children's Hospital in Orlando, Florida.

Katherine Ortega (1934–)

Born on July 16, 1934, in rural south-central New Mexico, Katherine Ortega received her early education in Tularosa, New Mexico. From her early years, she excelled in mathematics and accounting. After high school, Ortega worked at the Otero County Bank for two years until she saved enough money to go to college. She graduated from Eastern New Mexico State University at Portales in 1957 and began her own accounting firm. In 1969, she moved to Los Angeles to work as a tax supervisor and later became a vice president of the Pan American National Bank. She became the first woman president of a California bank when she was named president of the Santa Ana State Bank in 1975. In 1978, she returned to New Mexico with her family and became active in the Republican Party. In April 1982, President Ronald Reagan appointed Ortega to a Presidential Advisory Committee on Small and Minority Business Ownership. In December of that year, she was appointed one of five members and chair of the Copyright Royal Commission. In 1983, President Reagan appointed Ortega as U.S. treasurer. She remained at that post throughout the Reagan presidency. In 1984, she was chosen to be the keynote speaker at that year's Republican National Convention, the first Latina to deliver the lead speech at a national convention. As treasurer she spearheaded the effort to design new U.S. currency. She remained treasurer during George H. W. Bush's first six months as president and later served as an alternative representative to the United Nations General Assembly.

Francis Ortiz (1926–2005)

Born in Santa Fe, New Mexico, on March 14, 1926, Francis "Frank" Ortiz received his B.S. degree from the School of Foreign Service at Georgetown University in 1950 and went on to pursue a career in diplomacy. He attained an M.S. degree in 1967 from George Washington University and also studied at the National War College and the University of Madrid. His career in the foreign service took him to posts in Ethiopia, Mexico, Peru, Uruguay, Argentina, Barbados, and Grenada from 1953 to 1979. His ambassador stints were Grenada and Barbados (1977–

79), Guatemala (1979–80), Peru (1981–83), and Argentina (1983–86). His honors include the 1952 Honor Award from the State Department, the 1964 and 1973 Superior Award, the 1980 Gran Cruz de Mérito Civil from Spain, and the 1964 U.S./Mexican Presidential Chamizal Commemorative Medal. From 1944 to 1946, Ortiz served in the U.S. Air Force; he received the Air Medal for his service. He died on February 27, 2005.

Miguel Otero
(1829–1882)

Born in Valencia, Nuevo México, on June 21, 1829, Miguel Otero was the son of Vicente Otero, an important local leader during both the Spanish and Mexican eras. After completing his early education in Valencia, Otero was sent to Missouri in 1841 to attend Saint Louis University. Six years later, he went to Pingree's College in New York. He later taught there and then began the study of law. In 1851, he returned to Saint Louis, where he continued his legal studies and was admitted to the bar. He returned to New Mexico (now a U.S. territory) and in 1852 was elected to the territorial legislature. Two years later, he was appointed New Mexico attorney general. In 1855 was elected territorial delegate to Congress. In Congress, Otero's efforts ensured that the transcontinental railroad would cross through New Mexico, giving great promise to the territory's future.

Romualdo Pacheco
(1831–1899)

Romualdo Pacheco was born in Santa Barbara, California, on October 31, 1831. He was the son of an aide to the Mexican governor of Alta California, Manuel Victoria. Pacheco's father was killed in battle shortly after his birth. His mother remarried, and Pacheco's stepfather sent him to Honolulu to be educated at an English missionary school. After the U.S. takeover of California, Pacheco left the sea to manage the family's large estate and began to show an interest in politics. During the 1850s, Pacheco was successively elected county judge and state senator as a Democrat. Having switched from the Democratic Party to the Union Party (and later to the Republican Party) at the

outbreak of the Civil War, Pacheco was reelected to the state senate, and from 1863 to 1867 he served as state treasurer. In 1871 he was elected lieutenant governor and became governor of California in 1875 when then-Governor Newton Booth was appointed to the U.S. Senate. In the next election Pacheco failed to secure the Republican nomination for governor. Pacheco served in the U.S. House of Representatives in 1877–78 and 1879–83, after which he returned to his family business interests in California. In 1890, he was named minister plenipotentiary to Central America by President Benjamin Harrison. He remained in that post until early in President Grover Cleveland's term in 1893.

Federico Peña
(1947–)

Born in Laredo, Texas, on March 15, 1947, Federico Peña was raised in Brownsville, Texas. He received his early education there and attended the University of Texas at Austin, where he received both an undergraduate degree (1969) and a law degree (1972). Peña follows in a tradition of public service in his family. One of his great grandfathers served as mayor of Laredo during the Civil War and another was a member of that city's first school board. Peña's grandfather held the office of alderman in Laredo for almost a quarter of a century. In 1983, at age thirty-six, Peña was elected Denver's thirty-seventh mayor. He was reelected to a second term in 1987. At the time he entered office, he was among the youngest chief executives in Denver history. Mayor Peña's efforts to strengthen Denver's economy placed the city in the national spotlight; in fact, the U.S. Conference of Mayors selected Denver over one hundred other cities as the winner of its prestigious City Liveability Award. Peña did not seek a third term in 1991. Peña is viewed as a visionary for his leading role in the building of a multibillion-dollar airport on the outskirts of Denver. Peña was named secretary of the Department of Transportation by President Bill Clinton in 1992. In this position, he managed a budget of $36 billion a year, with which he oversaw the growth and maintenance of the national infrastructure, including the nation's ailing airline and maritime industries. He worked to upgrade the U.S. highway system to facilitate trade between Mexico and Canada under the North American Free Trade Agreement. In 1997 Peña was named secretary of energy in the Clinton cabinet. For the next eighteen months he developed the Clinton administration's Comprehensive National Energy Strategy and oversaw the largest privatization in the history of the U.S. government. In 1998 he returned to Denver and joined Vestar Capital Partners. In 2008, Peña became presidential candidate Barack Obama's national campaign cochair and after the victory became a member of the advisory board to the transition committee.

Thomas Pérez (1961–)

Born on October 7, 1961, in Buffalo, New York, to Dominican immigrant parents, Thomas Pérez received a bachelor's degree from Brown University in 1983. In 1987 he received both a master's of public policy from Harvard University's John F. Kennedy School of Government and a juris doctorate from Harvard Law School. He went on to serve as the secretary of Maryland's Department of Labor, Licensing and Regulation. From 2002 until 2006, he was a member of the Montgomery County Council. He was the first Latino ever elected to the council and served as council president in 2005. Pérez was a law professor for six years at the University of Maryland School of Law and was a part-time professor at the George Washington School of Public Health. He later served as deputy assistant attorney general for civil rights under Attorney General Janet Reno. In 2013, President Barack Obama swore in Pérez as secretary of labor. Among his accomplishments in the office were implementing the Matthew Shepard and James Byrd Jr. Hate Crimes Prevention Act; expanding equal housing opportunity by bringing and settling the largest fair-lending cases in history; protecting schoolchildren from discrimination, bullying, and harassment; expanding access to employment, housing, and educational opportunities for people with disabilities; protecting the right to vote for all eligible voters free from discrimination; and safeguarding the employment, housing, fair lending, and voting rights of service members. Pérez was chair of the Democratic National Committee from 2017 to 2021.

Bill Richardson (1947–)

Born on November 15, 1947, in Pasadena, California, Bill Richardson spent his boyhood in Mexico City. He graduated from Tufts University in 1970 and received a master's degree from the Fletcher School of Law and Diplomacy in 1971. Richardson served as governor of New Mexico from 2003 to 2011, was a U.S. ambassador to the United Nations and secretary of energy in the Clinton administration, and a U.S. congressman representing New Mexico. He was chairman of the 2004 Democratic National Convention; while governor he served as chair of the Democratic Governors Association. Richardson was first elected to Congress in 1982 to represent New Mexico's newly created Third District, one of the largest in square miles and one of the most ethnically diverse in the country: 40 percent Anglo, 40 percent Latino, and 20 percent Native American. Richardson rose relatively quickly to become a member of the House leadership and served as chief deputy majority whip. Richardson served as chair of the Congressional Hispanic Caucus in the 98th Congress (1983–85) and as chair of the House Natural Resources Subcommittee on Native American Affairs in the 103rd Congress (1993–94). As a ranking Democrat with ties to Mexico, Richardson helped facilitate the NAFTA agreement in 1993. Richardson was also enlisted as a troubleshooter for the United States, sent to various hotspots and crisis areas, such as Nicaragua, Guatemala, Cuba, Peru, India, North Korea, Bangladesh, Nigeria, Sudan, and North Korea. For his peacekeeping efforts in these crises, he was nominated three times for the Nobel Prize.

Ileana Ros-Lehtinen (1952–)

Born on July 15, 1952, in Havana, Cuba, Ileana Carmen Ros y Adato Ros-Lehtinen attended Florida International University, where she received both a bachelor's and a master's degree. After graduating from college, Ros-Lehtinen taught at a private school in Miami that she owned and operated. In 1982 Ros-

Lehtinen was elected to the Florida legislature. In 1986 she was elected to the Florida state senate, where she served until 1989. When she was elected to the U.S. Congress in 1989, she became the first Cuban American and the first Latina elected to Congress. Ros-Lehtinen served as a U.S. congresswoman from Florida from 1989 to 2013 for the 18th District and from 2013 to 2019 for the 27th District. By the time of her retirement in 2019, she had accomplished much as the only Latina senator, including serving as the chair of the House Foreign Affairs Committee from 2011 to 2013. In 1989, she gave the first Republican response to the State of the Union address in Spanish; she repeated that in 2011 and in 2014. In September 2011, Ros-Lehtinen became the first Republican member of Congress to co-sponsor the Respect for Marriage Act, which would repeal the Defense of Marriage Act. In July 2012, Ros-Lehtinen became the first Republican in the House to support same-sex marriage.

Edward Roybal (1916–2005)

Edward Roybal was born on February 10, 1916, in Albuquerque, New Mexico, into a middle-class Mexican American family. When he was four, his family moved to the Boyle Heights area of Los Angeles. After graduating from high school, he began working for the Civilian Conservation Corps. Later he continued his education at the University of California and Southwestern University. Roybal took a position as a health care educator beginning in the late 1930s. He served in World War II during 1944–45 and returned to Los Angeles to continue to work in health care. Following World War II, a group of concerned Mexican Americans formed a group to elect a Mexican American to the Los Angeles City Council, and Roybal was their choice for candidate. In 1947, he ran and was defeated. Instead of giving up, Roybal and the group intensified their efforts to get out the vote in East Los Angeles, and in his second bid for city council in 1949 Roybal was elected. He was the first Mexican American on the council since 1881. Roybal was reelected several times and served on the council for thirteen years. Roybal was first elected to Congress in 1962 as a Democrat from the 25th District of California. During his three decades in Congress, Roybal worked for social and economic reforms. In 1967, he introduced legislation that became the first federal bilingual education act. In 1982 as chairman of the Congressional Latino Caucus, he led the opposition to employer sanctions for hiring the undocumented, which ultimately was enacted as the Immigration Reform and Control Act of 1986. Throughout his tenure, Roybal consistently advocated greater citizen participation in party politics and in federal and local governments.

Marco Rubio (1971–)

Born on May 28, 1971, in Miami, Florida, to Cuban immigrant parents, Marco Rubio earned a B.A. in political science from the University of Florida in 1993 and a law degree from the University of Miami School of Law in 1996. Shortly after becoming a lawyer, Rubio launched his political career and was elected in 1998 as city commissioner for West Miami; in 2000 he was elected to the Florida House of Representatives and served nearly nine years. He served as speaker of the house from 2006 to 2008. In 2010, Rubio was elected to the U.S. Senate and was reelected in 2016. He ran unsuccessfully for president in 2015, but his conservatism was outdone by Donald Trump. He subsequently became a great supporter of Trump.

Brian Sandoval (1963–)

Born on August 5, 1963, in Redding, California, Brian Sandoval received his schooling in Nevada. He earned his B.A. degree in English and economics in 1986 and a law degree from the Ohio State University Moritz College of Law in 1989. In 1994 he was elected to the Nevada assembly and served until 1998, when he was appointed to the Nevada Gaming Commission. He was elected attorney general in 2002 and in 2004 was appointed by President George W. Bush as a federal district judge. He served as a judge until 2009, when he resigned to run for governor of Nevada. The Republican candidate was elected in 2010, was reelected in 2014, and served until 2019. In 2020, he became president of the University of Nevada, Reno.

Xavier Suárez (1949–)

Born on May 21, 1949, in Las Villas, Cuba, the son of an engineering professor, Xavier Suárez attended Villanova University, studying engineering, and graduated first in his class in 1971. Suárez went on to Harvard Law School and the John F. Kennedy School of Government at Harvard, where he obtained the joint degrees of J.D. and master of public policy in 1975. After graduation, Suárez moved to Miami and began to practice law with the firm of Shutts & Bowen. In 1985, Suárez was elected as Miami's first Cuban-born mayor of Miami, and he was reelected to second and third terms in 1987 and 1989. He sat out the 1993 election but ran again in 1997 and won his fourth term. President George W. Bush appointed Suárez to the board of directors of the Legal Services Corporation. Suárez's son, Francis, has been Miami's mayor since 2017.

Esteban Torres (1930–)

Esteban Edward Torres was born on January 27, 1930, in Miami, Arizona, where his Mexican-born father was a miner. When his father was deported in 1936 as a result of his union-organizing activities, the family moved to East Los Angeles, where Torres received his early education. After graduating from high school in 1949, Torres joined the Army and served during the Korean War. After being discharged in 1954, Torres took a job on an assembly line at Chrysler and attended California State University at night, receiving his B.A. degree in 1963. Torres was introduced to politics by way of his activism in the local branch of the United Auto Workers (UAW) union. In 1958 his coworkers elected him chief steward of the Local 230. He was later appointed the UAW organizer for the western region of the United States. In 1963 he was tapped by Walter Reuther as a UAW international representative in Washington, D.C., and from 1964 to 1968 he served as the union's director of the Inter-American Bureau for Caribbean and Latin American Affairs. In 1968 Torres returned to Los Angeles, founding The East Los Angeles Community Union (TELACU), a community action organization that grew under his stewardship into one of the nation's largest antipoverty agencies. In 1974, Torres narrowly lost his first bid for the Democratic nomination for the U.S. House of Representatives. In 1977, President Jimmy Carter appointed Torres as the U.S. representative to UNESCO, with diplomatic rank. President Carter also appointed Torres as his special assistant for programs and policies concerning Mexican Americans. After President Ronald Reagan took office in 1981, Torres returned to California. The next year, he was elected to Congress as a Democrat representing the 34th District in California and served until 1999. He was a member of the House Banking, Finance and Urban Affairs Committee and was chairman of its Consumer Affairs Subcommittee. Torres was also a member of the House Small Business Committee and a member of the Congressional Latino Caucus. In his congressional career, Torres supported labor, the environment, and NAFTA.

Catalina Vásquez Villalpando (1940–)

Villalpando was born April 1, 1940, in San Marcos, Texas, and is a graduate of Southwest Texas State University. Villalpando joined Communications International, a multinational telecommunications systems integrator, and became a senior vice president. From 1985 until her executive appointment, Villalpando directed all public relations and marketing for the company's northeast region, based in Washington, D.C. Villalpando served as White House special assistant for public liaison to President Ronald Reagan from 1983 to 1985. Prior to assuming her duties at the White House, she served as liaison director for the Republican Party of Texas. In 1989, President George H. W. Bush appointed Villalpando as the thirty-ninth treasurer of the United States.

LATINO JUDGES IN FEDERAL COURTS

As of the end of 2019, 80 percent of all sitting federal judges in the United States were White, while the U.S. population was only 60 percent White. And 73 percent of all sitting judges were male, while men made up slightly less than half of the population. Latinos comprised just 6.6 percent of sitting judges and 9 percent of active judges on the federal bench. There were only twenty-seven Latinas sitting on the federal courts, comprising approximately 2 percent of all sitting federal judges. Among active judges, only about 3 percent were Latinas. There were only sixteen Latina judges sitting on U.S. courts of appeals, comprising just 5.5 percent of all sitting U.S. circuit judges. Among active federal judges, this number decreases to thirteen, amounting to just 7.4 percent of all active judges serving on U.S. courts of appeals. There are only seventy-three sitting Latino judges serving on federal district courts, comprising just 6.9 percent of all sitting district court judges. Among active district court judges, this number decreases to fifty-six, amounting to just 9.6 percent of all active judges serving on U.S. district courts. The one and only judge of Latino extraction to sit on the Supreme Court is Sonia Sotomayor, nominated by President Barack Obama in 2009. There is only one sitting Latino judge on the 5th Circuit—which covers Louisiana, Mississippi, and Texas—accounting for just 4 percent of that court's composition, despite the fact that Hispanics comprise more than 32 percent of the jurisdiction's population. There are no active Latino judges serving on the 5th Circuit. Latino judges comprise just 4 percent of all Donald Trump's judicial appointees. In comparison, 9.5 percent of former president Obama's appointees were Latino. Trump did not appoint a single Latino judge to a U.S. courts of appeal.

According to the Federal Judicial Center of the United States, in 2020 there were 132 Latino members of federal tribunals, but this included judges in the District of Columbia and Puerto Rico as well as U.S. magistrates and administrative law judges.

Courts of Appeal

The ninety-four U.S. judicial districts are organized into twelve regional circuits, each of which has a U.S. Court of Appeals. These courts hear appeals from the district courts located within its circuit and appeals from decisions of federal administrative agencies. In addition, the Court of Appeals for the Federal Circuit has nationwide jurisdiction to hear appeals in specialized cases, such as those involving patent laws and cases decided by the Court of International Trade and the Court of Federal Claims.

Today, the following Latino judges sit on the courts of appeals: José Alberto Cabranes, Second Circuit; Julio M. Fuentes, Third Circuit; Luis Felipe Restrepo, Third Circuit; Albert Díaz, Fourth Circuit; Fortunato Pedro Benavides, Fifth Circuit; Carlos T. Bea, Ninth Circuit; Consuelo María Callahan, Ninth Circuit; Ferdinand Francis Fernández, Ninth Circuit; Mary Helen Murguía, Ninth Circuit; Richard A. Paez, Ninth Circuit; Kim McLane Wardlaw, Ninth Circuit; Carlos F. Lucero, Tenth Circuit; Adalberto José Jordan, Eleventh Circuit; Jimmie V. Reyna, Federal Circuit; and Kara Farnández Stoll, Federal Circuit.

U.S. District Courts

The U.S. district courts are the trial courts of the federal court system. The district courts try nearly all categories of federal cases, both civil and criminal. There are ninety-four federal district courts, including at least one district court in each state, the District of Columbia, Puerto Rico, the Virgin Islands, Guam, and the Northern Mariana Islands. The Latino judges in these courts are:

Rosemary Márquez, Arizona; Frank R. Zapata, Arizona; James A. Soto, Arizona; Edward J. García, California; Edward John Dávila, California; Fernando M. Olguín, California; Gonzalo P. Curiel, California; Jesús G. Bernal, California; John A. Méndez, California; Philip S. Gutiérrez, California; Roger T. Benítez, California; Yvonne González Rogers, California; Christine M. Argüello, Colorado; William Joseph Martínez, Colorado; Rudolph Contreras, District of Columbia; Carlos Eduardo Mendoza, Florida; Cecilia M. Altonaga, Florida; Federico A. Moreno, Florida; José Alejandro González Jr., Florida; José E. Martínez, Florida; Marcia Morales Howard, Florida; Rodolfo A. Ruiz II, Florida; Roy Kalman Altman, Florida; Virginia M. Hernández Covington, Florida; Steven D. Grimberg, Georgia; Jorge Luis Alonso, Illinois; Ronald A. Guzmán, Illinois; Louis Guirola Jr., Mississippi; Gloria Maria Navarro, Nevada; Esther Salas, New Jersey; John Michael Vásquez, New Jersey; Joseph H. Rodríguez, New Jersey; Judith C. Herrera, New Mexico; Kenneth J. Gonzales, New Mexico; M. Christina Armijo, New Mexico; Martha Alicia Vázquez, New Mexico; Analisa Torres, New York; Dora L. Irizarry, New York; Edgardo Ramos, New York;

Nelson S. Román, New York; Vernon S. Broderick, New York; Victor Marrero, New York; Marco Antonio Hernández, Oregon; Cathy Bissoon, Pennsylvania; Eduardo C. Robreño, Pennsylvania; Juan Ramón Sánchez, Pennsylvania; Nitza I. Quiñones Alejandro, Pennsylvania; Aída M. Delgado-Colón, Puerto Rico; Daniel R. Domínguez, Puerto Rico; Francisco Augusto Besosa, Puerto Rico; Jay A. García-Gregory, Puerto Rico; Pedro A. Delgado Hernández, Puerto Rico; Raúl Manuel Arias-Marxauch, Puerto Rico; Alia Moses, Texas; David Briones, Texas; David Campos Guaderrama, Texas; David Steven Morales, Texas; Diana Saldaña, Texas; Fernando Rodríguez Jr., Texas; Frank Montalvo, Texas; Hilda G. Tagle, Texas; José Rolando Olvera Jr., Texas; Kathleen Cardone, Texas; Marina García Marmolejo, Texas; Micaela Alvarez, Texas; Nelva Gonzales Ramos, Texas; Orlando Luis García, Texas; Philip Ray Martínez, Texas; Randy Crane, Texas; Ricardo H. Hinojosa, Texas; Xavier Rodríguez, Texas; Ricardo S. Martínez, Washington; and Salvador Mendoza Jr., Washington.

> Latinos have made the greatest inroads at the state, county, and municipal court levels, where hundreds have been appointed or elected to these courts.

State, County, and Municipal Courts

Latinos have made the greatest inroads at the state, county, and municipal court levels, where hundreds have been appointed or elected to these courts. Latino judges have served on state courts throughout the history of the United States but almost always at the lowest levels. In recent years this trend has changed, as large numbers of Latinos have been both appointed and elected to all levels of state courts.

Today, Latinos serve on some of the highest state courts in the nation as state supreme court justices and as state appeals court judges. Most dramatic are the large numbers of Latinos serving in lower state courts. More than one thousand Latinos serve on various state trial courts.

Critics of the process of selecting judges charge that the system is subject to a wide range of problems and abuses, including discrimination against minorities. The appointment process, critics charge, is also subject to political interference from special interest groups, influence peddling, and highly inflammatory campaigning by opposition groups. The nominee's qualifications are rarely the test of whether he or she should be a judge. For example, a 1988 analysis of U.S. Supreme Court appointments published in *Texas Lawyer* found that of twenty-seven failed nominations to the Court, only five were denied because of qualifications or ethical concerns. Political concerns were the primary reasons the other nominees were not confirmed.

Discrimination is a serious problem in the appointive system. The Mexican American Legal Defense and Educational Fund (MALDEF) recently concluded that the appointive system is discriminatory. According to MALDEF, approximately 97 percent of all individuals making judicial appointments are White, which consequently tends to limit the opportunities for minority nominees. (MALDEF states that the elective system is of the greatest benefit to Latinos and other minorities.) Instead of taking politics out of the system, the appointive process takes the voter out of the system. According to the Center for American Progress, more than 80 percent of judges are White.

Fortunately, today the majority of states select judges through the election process. Eight states choose all their judges in partisan elections; twelve use nonpartisan elections. One state, Virginia, uses legislative election exclusively to select its judges. Another thirteen states have variable procedures, appointing judges to certain courts and electing them to others.

SELECT LATINO JUDGES

Raymond Acosta (1925–2014)

Raymond Acosta was born on May 31, 1925, in New York City and grew up in Teaneck, New Jersey. After graduating from high school in 1943, Acosta joined the U.S. Navy during World War II and took part in the Normandy invasion. He returned to New Jersey after the war and graduated from Princeton University in 1948. Acosta received his law degree in 1951 from Rutgers University Law School in Newark, New Jersey. From 1951 to 1954, he was in private practice in Hackensack, New Jersey, and worked for the Federal Bureau of Investigation in Washington, D.C., from 1954 to 1958. In 1958, he moved to Puerto Rico to serve as assistant U.S. attorney there. From 1962 to 1980, he was in the private sector, practicing law in San Juan, Puerto Rico, with the firm of Igaravídez & Acosta, and held posts with various real estate and banking interests. From 1980 to 1982, Acosta was the U.S. attorney for Puerto Rico. In 1982, President Ronald Reagan appointed Acosta to the U.S. District Court for the District of Puerto Rico. He became a senior judge in 1994. In 2008 the Puerto Rican Bar Association was renamed in his honor. He died on December 23, 2014.

Robert Aguilar (1931–2020)

Born on April 15, 1931, in Madera, California, Robert Aguilar attended the University of California, Berkeley, where he received his B.A. degree in 1954. He then went on to receive his law degree from the University of California Hastings College of Law. He practiced law with the firms of Mezzetti & Aguilar, Aguilar & Aguilar, and Aguilar & Edwards from 1960 to 1979. In 1979 to 1980, Aguilar served as a California Superior Court judge for Santa Clara County. He was later appointed to the U.S. District Court for the Northern District of California by President Jimmy Carter in 1980. In 1991 he withdrew from hearing cases while he appealed his November 1990 conviction on two charges: illegally disclosing a wiretap to its subject and lying to the FBI to obstruct a grand jury probe. His conviction was overturned in 1996, and he returned to the bench before retiring that same year. He returned to private practice and retired from that in 2015.

Arthur Alarcón (1925–2015)

Born on April 14, 1925, in Los Angeles, California, Arthur Alarcón served in the Army before studying for his B.A. degree and graduated from the University of Southern California in 1949. He received his law degree from USC in 1951. Alarcón served as a deputy district attorney in Los Angeles County, California, from 1952 to 1961. He was an executive assistant to the governor of California from 1962 to 1964 and chaired the California parole board in 1964. He served as a judge of the Superior Court of California for the County of Los Angeles from 1964 to 1978. He was an associate justice of the California Court of Appeal Second Appellate District from 1978 to 1979. President Jimmy Carter appointed him to the U.S. Court of Appeals for the Ninth Circuit in 1979. He served as a senior judge from 1992 until his death on January 28, 2015.

Cecilia M. Altonaga (1962–)

Born on December 26, 1962, in Baltimore, Maryland, Cecilia Altonaga received her B.A. from Florida International University in 1983 and her J.D. from Yale Law School in 1986. She served in the Dade County (Florida) Attorney's Office from 1986 to 1987 and was assistant county attorney for Dade County, Florida, from 1988 to 1996. She became a judge for the Miami-Dade County Court, Eleventh Judicial Circuit, and served from 1996 to 1999. Then she served as a judge for the Circuit Court of Florida, Eleventh Judicial Circuit, from 1999 to 2003. President George W. Bush appointed her judge of the U.S. District Court for the Southern District of Florida in 2003. She is the first Cuban American woman to be appointed as a federal judge in the United States.

Micaela Alvarez (1958–)

Born in 1958 in Donna, Texas, Micaela Alvarez received her bachelor's degree from the University of Texas in 1980 and her law degree from the University of Texas Law School in 1989. She worked in private practice in McAllen, Texas, from 1989 to 1995 and from 1997 to 2004. She served as a presiding judge in Hidalgo County's 139th District Court from 1995 to 1996. President George W. Bush appointed her judge for the U.S. District Court for the Southern District of Texas in 2004.

John Argüelles (1927–)

Former California Supreme Court justice John Argüelles was born on August 22, 1927, in Los Angeles, California, to Arturo Argüelles, a Mexican American who graduated from Columbia University with an accounting degree, and Eva Powers, the daughter of an Oklahoma judge. Argüelles was educated in public schools in Los Angeles and served in the Navy during World War II. He went on to UCLA, where he received a degree in economics in 1950. He continued his education at the UCLA Law School and received his degree in 1954. Argüelles practiced law in East Los Angeles and Montebello, California, from 1955 to 1963. During that time he was president of the local bar association and was elected to the Montebello City Council with the largest vote in that city's history. In 1963 Governor Edmund G. Brown Sr. appointed Argüelles municipal court judge for the East Los Angeles Municipal Court. He was then elevated to the Los Angeles Superior Court by Governor Ronald Reagan in 1969. Argüelles was appointed to the California Court of Appeal for the Second District in 1984 by Governor George Deukmejian. Three years later, Deukmejian named Argüelles to the California Supreme Court, where he served until his retirement in 1989. At the end of 1989, Argüelles joined the law firm of Gibson, Dunn & Crutcher.

M. Christina Armijo (1951–)

Born in January 1951, in Las Vegas, New Mexico, Armijo received her bachelor's degree from the University of New Mexico in 1972 and her law degree from the University of New Mexico School of Law in 1975. She served as staff attorney for Sandoval County Legal Services from 1976 to 1978 and then went into private practice until 1996. She served as a judge in the New Mexico Court of Appeals from 1996 to 2001. President George W. Bush appointed her judge for the U.S. District Court for the District of New Mexico in 2001, and she served as chief judge from 2012 to 2018. She became a senior judge on February 7, 2018. She retired in 2018.

Joseph Francis Baca (1936–)

New Mexico Supreme Court justice Joseph Baca was born in Albuquerque, New Mexico, in 1936 to Mexican American parents. He graduated from the University of New Mexico in 1960 with a degree in education. He studied law at George Washington University in Washington, D.C., and received his degree in 1964. Baca served as assistant district attorney in Santa Fe from 1965 to 1966, then as special assistant to the attorney general of New Mexico from 1966 to 1972. He also established a private law practice in Albuquerque during this time. In 1972 Baca was appointed by Governor Bruce King to fill a vacancy in the New Mexico District Court for the Second District in Albuquerque. Baca was elected to six-year terms in 1972, 1978, and 1984. In 1988, Baca was elected to an eight-year term as justice of the New Mexico Supreme Court and served until 2010. Baca is the recipient of numerous awards, including the J. William Fulbright Award for Distinguished Public Service from George Washington University Law School and the Outstanding Judicial Service Award from the New Mexico Bar Association.

Fortunato B. Benavides (1947–)

Born on February 3, 1947, in Mission, Texas, Fortunato Benavides received his B.B.A. from the University of Houston in 1968 and his law degree from the University of Houston Law Center in 1972. He worked in private practice in McAllen, Texas (1972–77, 1980–81, 1993–94) and served as a judge in the Hidalgo County Court (1977–79 and 1981–84). He was a justice in the Thirteenth Court of Appeals of Texas from 1984 to 1991 and a judge for the Texas Court of Criminal Appeals from 1991 to 1992. He served as a visiting supreme court judge of Texas in 1993. In 1994 President Bill Clinton nominated him and he was confirmed by the Senate to become a judge for the U.S. Court of Appeals for the Fifth Circuit. He became a senior judge on February 3, 2012.

Francisco Augusto Besosa (1949–)

Born on October 26, 1949, in San Juan, Puerto Rico, Francisco Besosa received his A.B. from Brown University in 1971 and his law degree from Georgetown University Law Center in 1979. He served in the U.S. Army from 1971 to 1977 in Intelligence and then went into private practice in Puerto Rico (1979–83 and 1986–2006). While Besosa was in private practice, he was appointed to the U.S. Magistrate Judge Merit Selection Panel in 1993. He served as assistant U.S. attorney for the District of Puerto Rico from 1983 to 1986. President George W. Bush nominated him and he was confirmed by the Senate as judge for the U.S. District Court for the District of Puerto Rico in 2006.

José A. Cabranés (1940–)

Born on December 22, 1940, in Mayagüez, Puerto Rico, José Cabranés is the first native Puerto Rican appointed to the federal court within the continental United States. Cabranés moved with his family to New York from Puerto Rico when he was only five. After attending public schools in the Bronx and Flushing, Queens, he graduated from Columbia College in 1961. He received his law degree from Yale University Law School in 1965 and an LL.M. degree in international law from the University of Cambridge in Cambridge, England, in 1967. Cabranés served as general counsel of Yale University from 1975 to 1979. Previously he had practiced law at the firm of Casey, Lane & Mittendorf in New York City from 1967 to 1971; taught law at Rutgers University School of Law in New Jersey from 1971 to 1973; and served as special counsel to the governor of Puerto Rico and as administrator, Office of the Commonwealth of Puerto Rico, Washington, D.C. He also served in the administration of President Jimmy Carter as a member of the President's Commission on Mental Health from 1977 to 1978; as a member of the U.S. delegation to the Belgrade Conference on Security and Cooperation in Europe from 1977 to 1978; and as consultant to U.S. secretary of state Cyrus Vance in 1978. In 1979, Carter appointed Cabranés to the U.S. District Court for the District of Connecticut, where he subsequently served as its chief judge. In December 1988 U.S. Supreme Court chief justice William H. Rehnquist named Cabranés as one of five federal judges for the

fifteen-member Federal Courts Study Committee, created by an act of Congress "to examine problems facing the federal courts and develop a long-range plan for the future of the federal judiciary." Cabranés was seriously considered as a possible nominee for appointment to the U.S. Supreme Court when Justice Harry Blackmun retired in 1994. That same year, President Bill Clinton appointed Cabranés to the U.S. Court of Appeals for the Second Circuit. Cabranés was elected to the American Law Institute in 1980 and became a life member of the institute in 2005. Among his many awards, in 2000 he received the Federal Bar Council's Learned Hand Medal for Excellence in Federal Jurisprudence.

Santiago E. Campos (1926–2001)

Born on December 25, 1926, in Santa Rosa, New Mexico, Santiago Campos served in the U.S. Navy during World War II. He attended Central College in Fayette, Missouri, and received his law degree from the University of New Mexico in 1953. Campos was assistant attorney general for the state of New Mexico from 1955 to 1957. He was a New Mexico district judge from 1971 to 1978. President Jimmy Carter appointed Campos to the U.S. District Court for the District of New Mexico in 1978. He served as chief judge from 1987 to 1989 and senior judge from December 26, 1992, until his death on January 20, 2001.

Silvia Luisa Carreño-Coll (1963–)

Born in 1963 in Santo Domingo, the Dominican Republic, Silvia Carreño-Coll received her B.A. from Emerson College in 1983 and her law degree from the University of Puerto Rico School of Law in 1986. She then worked as an attorney in the Federal Litigation Division of the Puerto Rico Department of Justice from 1986 to 1989 and assistant U.S. attorney for the District of Puerto Rico from 1989 to 1995. She was associate regional counsel for the Caribbean Environmental Protection Division, U.S. Environmental Protection Agency, from 1995 to 2011. President Donald Trump nominated her and she was approved by the Senate as a judge for the U.S. District Court for the District of Puerto Rico in 2020.

Rubén Castillo (1954–)

Born on August 12, 1954, in Chicago, Illinois, to a Mexican father and a Puerto Rican mother, Rubén Castillo received his B.A. from Loyola University Chicago in 1976 and his law degree from Northwestern University School of Law in 1979. He was in private practice in Chicago from 1979 to 1984 and 1991 to 1994. He served as assistant U.S. attorney for the Northern District of Illinois from 1984 to 1988 and regional counsel for the Mexican American Legal Defense Fund from 1988 to 1991. He was vice chair of the U.S. Sentencing Commission from 1999 to 2010. President Bill Clinton nominated him and he was confirmed by the Senate in 1994 to the position of judge for the U.S. District Court for the Northern District of Illinois. He served as chief judge from 2013 to 2019, when he retired.

Carmen Consuelo Cerezo (1940–)

Born in San Juan, Puerto Rico, in 1940, Carmen Cerezo attended the University of Puerto Rico, where she received her B.A. degree in 1963 and her LL.B. degree in 1966. In 1967 she was appointed chief law clerk for the chief justice of the Supreme Court of Puerto Rico. Cerezo also received a master of laws degree from University of Virginia School of Law in 1988. She was a judge on the Puerto Rico Court of Inter Appeals from 1976 to 1980, and she was on the Superior Court of Puerto Rico from 1972 to 1976. President Jimmy Carter appointed Cerezo to the U.S. District Court for the District of Puerto Rico in 1980, where she served until her retirement in 2021. She served as chief judge from 1993 to 1999. Cerezo is the first Latina to serve on a federal bench and the first female federal judge in Puerto Rico.

Rudolph Contreras (1962–)

Born on December 6, 1962, in Miami, Florida, to Cuban refugee parents, Rudolph Contreras received a B.S. from Florida State University in 1984 and a J.D. from the University of Pennsylvania Law School in 1991. He was in private practice in Washington, D.C., from 1991 to 1994. He served as assistant U.S. attorney for the District of Columbia from 1994 to 2003 and from 2006 to 2012; he served as chief of the Civil Division from 2006 to 2012. He became judge of the U.S. District Court for the District of Columbia through President Barack Obama's nomination and the Senate's confirmation in 2012 and continues to serve in the position. In 2016 he began serving as judge for the Foreign Intelligence Surveillance Court.

Edward John Dávila (1952–)

Born on June 21, 1952, in Palo Alto, California, Edward Dávila received his B.A. from California State University, San Diego, in 1976 and his law degree from the Hastings College of Law, University of California, in 1979. Dávila served as a deputy public defender in Santa Clara County, California, from 1981 to 1988. He was in private practice in San Jose, California, from 1988 to 2001 and served as a judge of the Superior Court of California, County of Santa Clara, from 2001 to 2011. President Barack Obama nominated him and the Senate confirmed him as judge for the U.S. District Court for the Northern District of California in 2011.

James DeAnda (1925–2006)

Born on August 21, 1925, in Houston, Texas, to Mexican immigrant parents, James DeAnda received his B.A. degree from Texas A&M University and his J.D. degree from the University of Texas in 1950. He was in private practice from 1951 until 1979. In 1979, DeAnda was appointed to the U.S. District Court for the Southern District of Texas, where he subsequently became chief judge. He served until he retired on October 1, 1992, and went into private practice with Solar & Fernandez until 2005. He died on September 7, 2006. DeAnda is remembered as being a lead lawyer for the plaintiffs in the famous case to desegregate juries argued before the Supreme Court: *Hernandez v. Texas* (1954). He was also one of the founders of the Mexican American Legal Defense and Education Fund, which has gone on to win many discrimination cases in favor of Latino plaintiffs.

Albert Díaz (1960–)

Born in 1960 in Brooklyn, New York, to Puerto Rican parents, Albert Díaz received his B.S. from the University of Pennsylvania's Wharton School in 1983 and his J.D. from the New York University School of Law in 1988. He also obtained an M.S. from Boston University in 1993. He served as prosecutor, defense counsel, and chief review officer in the Legal Services Support Section of the U.S. Marine Corps at Camp Lejeune in North Carolina from 1988 to 1991 and in the U.S. Navy's Office of the Judge Advocate General in Washington, D.C., from 1991 to 2000. He was in private practice in Charlotte, North Carolina, from 1995 to 2001 and then served as a judge in the North Carolina Superior Court from 2001 to 2005. He became a special judge for the North Carolina Business Court in 2005 and served until 2010, when President Barack Obama's nomination as judge for the U.S. Court of Appeals for the Fourth Circuit was confirmed by the Senate.

Ferdinand Francis Fernández (1937–)

Born on May 29, 1937, in Pasadena, California, Ferdinand Fernández attended the University of Southern California and was awarded his B.A. in 1958 and his J.D. in 1962. In 1963 he also obtained a master of law degree from Harvard Law School. He was in private practice from 1964 to 1980 with the law firm of Allard, Shelton & O'Connor in Pomona, California. He was a judge for the Superior Court of California, County of San Bernardino, from 1980 to 1985. Fernández was on the U.S. District Court for the Central District of California from 1985 to 1989. In 1989, he was appointed to the U.S. Court of Appeals for the Ninth Circuit by President George H. W. Bush. He became a senior judge on June 1, 2002. Fernández was reportedly considered as a potential replacement for retiring U.S. Supreme Court justice Thurgood Marshall. On February 28, 2020, Fernández dissented when the Ninth Circuit ruled 2–1 that the Trump administration could not force refugees pursuing asylum in the United States to wait in Mexico while their applications were being processed, even extending into months. On March 11, 2020, the Supreme Court agreed with Fernández and permitted Trump's "Remain-in-Mexico" policy to continue.

José Antonio Fusté (1943–)

Born in 1943 in San Juan, Puerto Rico, José Fusté attended the University of Puerto Rico, where he received his B.A. degree in 1965 and his LL.B. degree in 1968. He was in private practice from 1968 to 1985 with the law firm of Jiménez and Fusté. He was appointed to the U.S. District Court for the District of Puerto Rico by President Ronald Reagan in 1985. He served as chief judge from 2004 to 2011 and retired on June 1, 2016. Since 1972 he has taught admiralty law at the University of Puerto Rico.

Fernando J. Gaitán Jr. (1970–)

Born in 1948 in Kansas City, Kansas, Fernando Gaitán received his bachelor's degree from Pittsburg State University, Kansas, in 1970, and his J.D. from the University of Missouri–Kansas City School of Law in 1974. He started as an attorney for Southwestern Bell Telephone Company from 1974 to 1980. He served as a judge of the Circuit Court of Missouri, Sixteenth Judicial Circuit from 1980 to 1986, and as a judge of the Missouri Court of Appeals, Western District, from 1986 to 1991. President George H. W. Bush appointed Gaitán to the U.S. District Court for the Western District of Missouri in 1991. He served as chief judge from 2007 to 2014 and became a senior judge on January 3, 2014.

Edward J. García (1928–)

Born in 1928 in Sacramento, California, Edward García attended the Sacramento City College and graduated in 1951. He received his law degree from the McGeorge School of Law in 1958. He served in the U.S. Army, Air Corps from 1946 to 1949. He was deputy district attorney of Sacramento County, California, from 1959 to 1972; supervising deputy from 1964 to 1969; and chief deputy from 1969 to 1972. From 1972 to 1984, he was a judge for the Sacramento Municipal Court. García was deputy district attorney for Sacramento County from 1959 to 1964, supervising deputy district attorney from 1964 to 1969, and chief deputy district attorney from 1969 to 1972. He was a Sacramento Municipal Court judge from 1972 until 1984. President Ronald Reagan appointed García to the U.S. District Court for the Eastern District of California in 1984. He became a senior judge on November 24, 1996, and retired into inactive senior status on November 30, 2012.

Hipólito Frank García (1925–2002)

Born on December 4, 1925, in San Antonio, Texas, Hipólito García served in the U.S. Army during World War II. He then attended St. Mary's University, where he received his B.A. degree in 1949 and his LL.B. degree in 1951. He served as the deputy district clerk of Bexar County, Texas, from 1950 to 1952 and was an assistant criminal attorney for Bexar County from 1952 to 1963. He was in private practice from 1963 to 1964, a judge for the Bexar County Court at Law Number Two (1964–74), and a judge for the Bexar County 144th District Court (1975–80). He was a Texas county court judge from 1964 to 1980. In 1980 President Jimmy Carter appointed García to the U.S. District Court for the Western District of Texas. He died on January 16, 2002. In 2004, the Hipólito F. Garcia Federal Building and United States Courthouse in downtown San Antonio was named in his honor.

Orlando Luis García (1952–)

Born on November 18, 1952, in Jim Wells County, Texas, Orlando García graduated from the University of Texas with a B.A. in 1975 and from the University of Texas School of Law in 1978. He was in private practice in San Antonio, Texas, from 1978 to 1990 and served as a Texas state representative from 1983 to 1991. He served as a justice for the Fourth Court of Appeals of Texas from 1991 to 1992. He became a judge for the U.S. District Court for the Western District of Texas, pursuant to President Bill Clinton's nomination and senate confirmation in 1994. He has served as chief judge since 2016.

Marina García Marmolejo (1971–)

Born in Nuevo Laredo, Mexico, Marina García Marmolejo received her B.A. from the University of the Incarnate Word in 1992, an M.A. from St. Mary's

The Hipólito F. García Federal Building and United States Courthouse in San Antonio, Texas, was named after U.S. District Court Judge García in 2004.

University, Texas, in 1996, and her J.D. from St. Mary's University School of Law in 1996. She was an assistant federal public defender in the Western District of Texas from 1996 to 1998 and an assistant federal public defender in the Southern District of Texas. She served as an assistant U.S. attorney for the Southern District of Texas from 1999 to 2007. From 2007 to 2011 she was in private practice in San Antonio and Austin. She became a judge for the U.S. District Court for the Southern District of Texas in 2011 pursuant to President Barack Obama's nomination and Senate confirmation.

Emilio M. Garza (1947–)

Born on August 1, 1947, in San Antonio, Texas, Emilio Garza attended the University of Notre Dame and was awarded his B.A. degree in 1969 and M.A. degree in 1970. He served in the U.S. Marine Corps as a captain from 1970 to 1973. He received his law degree from the University of Texas in 1976. He was in private practice from 1976 to 1987 with the law firm of Clemens, Spencer, Welmaker & Finck. Garza was a judge for the U.S. District Court for the Western District of Texas from 1988 to 1991. President George H. W. Bush appointed Garza to the U.S. Court of Appeals for the Fifth Circuit in 1991.

Reynaldo Guerra Garza (1915–2004)

Reynaldo Garza was born on July 7, 1915, in Brownsville, Texas, to parents who were both born in Mexico and had immigrated to the United States in 1901. Garza attended the University of Texas, where he received his law degree in 1939. He practiced law in Brownsville as a solo practitioner until he joined the air force during World War II. After the war, he resumed his private practice until 1950, when he joined the firm of Sharpe, Cunningham & Garza. President John F. Kennedy appointed Garza to the U.S. District Court for the Southern District of Texas in 1961; in 1974 he became chief judge of that court. In 1979, Garza was appointed to the U.S. Court of Appeals for the Fifth Circuit by President Jimmy Carter. In 1987, U.S. Supreme Court chief justice William H. Rehnquist appointed Garza to the Temporary Emergency Court of Appeals of the United States. He was

later named by Rehnquist as chief judge of that court. President Carter offered the position of attorney general of the United States to Garza, who declined the cabinet post because he would have had to resign from his position as a federal judge, which is a lifetime appointment. He served as a senior judge from 1982 until his death on September 14, 2004.

Gilberto Gierbolini-Ortiz (1926–2009)

Born on December 22, 1926, in Coamo, Puerto Rico, Gilberto Gierbolini attended the University of Puerto Rico, where he received his B.A. degree in 1951 and his LL.B. degree in 1961. He was a captain in the U.S. Army and served during the Korean War from 1951 to 1957. Gierbolini served as assistant U.S. attorney for Puerto Rico from 1961 to 1966, as a superior court judge from 1966 to 1969, as assistant secretary of justice for Puerto Rico from 1969 to 1972, and as solicitor general of Puerto Rico from 1970 to 1972. Gierbolini was in the private practice of law between 1972 and 1980. In 1980, President Jimmy Carter appointed Gierbolini to the U.S. District Court for the District of Puerto Rico. He served from 1991 to 2004, becoming a senior judge in 1993. He died on December 29, 2009.

Kenneth John Gonzales (1964–)

Born on October 26, 1964 in Espanola, New Mexico, Kenneth Gonzales graduated from the University of New Mexico with a B.A. in 1988 and from the University of New Mexico School of Law in 1994. He served as assistant U.S. attorney for the District of New Mexico from 1999 to 2010 and U.S. attorney for the District of New Mexico from 2010 to 2013. President Barack Obama nominated him and the Senate confirmed him for the position of judge of the U.S. District Court for the District of New Mexico in 2013.

David Campos Guaderrama (1954–)

Born on May 23, 1954, in Las Cruces, New Mexico, David Guaderrama graduated from New Mexico State University with a B.A. in 1975 and from the Notre Dame Law School in 1979. He was in private practice in El Paso, Texas, from 1979 to 1986 and then chief public defender in El Paso County from 1987 to 1994. He served as a judge in El Paso County 243rd District Court from 1995 to 2010. He was a U.S. magistrate judge for the U.S. District Court for the Western District of Texas from 2010 to 2012. He became a judge for the U.S. District Court for the Western District of Texas pursuant to President Barack Obama's nomination and confirmation by the Senate in 2012.

Philip S. Gutiérrez (1959–)

Born on October 13, 1959, in Los Angeles, California, Philip Gutiérrez graduated from the University of Notre Dame with a B.A. in 1981 and from the University of California, Los Angeles, School of Law in 1984. He was in private practice in California from 1986 to 1997 and then served as judge of the Superior Court of California, County of Los Angeles, from 1997 to 2007. He became judge of the U.S. District Court for the Central District of California pursuant to President George W. Bush's nomination and Senate confirmation in 2007. He has served as chief judge since 2020.

Ronald A. Guzmán (1948–)

Born on November 18, 1948, in Rio Piedras, Puerto Rico, Ronald Guzmán graduated from Lehigh University with a B.A. in 1970 and the New York University School of Law with his J.D. in 1973. He was in private practice from 1973 to 1974 and an assistant state's attorney for Cook County, Illinois, from 1975 to 1980. He served as a staff attorney (part-time) for the Association House of Chicago from 1980 to 1984 and then returned to private practice until 1990. He served as a U.S. magistrate judge for the U.S. District Court for the Northern District of Illinois from 1990 to 1999. He became a judge for the U.S. District Court for the Northern District of Illinois pursuant to President William J. Clinton's nomination and Senate confirmation in 1999. He became a senior judge on November 16, 2014.

Marco Antonio Hernández (1957–)

Born in 1957 in Nogales, Arizona, Marco Hernández moved to Oregon when he was seventeen and worked his way through college as a dishwasher, janitor, and teacher's aide. He graduated from Western Oregon State College with a B.A. in 1983 and from the University of Washington School of Law with a J.D. in 1986. He was a staff attorney for Oregon Legal Services in Hillsboro, Oregon, from 1986 to 1989 and a deputy district attorney for Washington County, Oregon, from 1989 to 1994. He served as a judge in the Oregon District Court, Washington County, from 1995 to 1998 and a judge for the Oregon Circuit Court, Washington County, from 1998 to 2011; he became the presiding judge in 2002 and served in that capacity until 2005. He became a judge of the U.S. District Court for the District of Oregon pursuant to President Barack Obama's nomination and Senate confirmation in 2011. He has served as chief judge since 2019.

Judith C. Herrera (1954–)

Born on April 28, 1954, in Chicago, Illinois, Judith Herrera graduated from the University of New Mexico with a B.A. in 1976 and Georgetown University Law Center with her J.D. in 1979. She worked as an assistant district attorney in Santa Fe, New Mexico, from 1979 to 1980, after which she was in private practice in Santa Fe from 1980 to 2004. She was elected to the Santa Fe city council and served from 1981 to 1986. She was nominated by President George W. Bush and confirmed by the Senate as judge for the U.S. District Court for the District of New Mexico in 2004 and became a senior judge in 2019.

Ricardo Hinojosa (1950–)

Born on January 24, 1950, in Rio Grande City, Texas, Ricardo Hinojosa attended the University of Texas, where he received his B.A. degree in 1972. He received his law degree from Harvard University Law School in 1975. He was in private practice as a partner in the law firm of Ewers & Toothaker in McAllen, Texas, from 1976 until 1983. In 1983, Hinojosa was appointed by President Ronald Reagan to the U.S. District Court for the Southern District of Texas. He served on the U.S. Sentencing Commission from 2003 to 2014 and as chair of the commission from 2004 to 2009.

Dora L. Irizarry (1955–)

Born on January 26, 1955, in San Sebastian, Puerto Rico, and raised in the Bronx, New York, Dora Irizarry graduated from Yale University with a B.A. in 1976 and from Columbia Law School with a J.D. in 1979. She worked as an assistant district attorney for Bronx County, New York, from 1979 to 1987, and in the Office of the Special Narcotics Prosecutor from 1981 to 1987. She then served as an assistant district attorney in the Office of the Special Narcotics Prosecutor for New York County, New York, from 1987 to 1995. She served as a judge in the Criminal Court of the City of New York from 1995 to 1997 and was an acting justice in the New York State Court of Claims from 1997 to 2002, in Kings County from 1997 to 1998, and in New York County from 1998 to 2002. In 2002, Irizarry resigned from her judgeship to become the Republican nominee for attorney general of New York, challenging Democratic incumbent Eliot Spitzer. She was the first Latina to seek statewide office in New York State, but she was defeated. She was in private practice in New York City from 2002 to 2004. President George W. Bush nominated and the Senate confirmed her for the position of judge of the U.S. District Court for the Eastern District of New York in 2004. She served as chief judge from 2016 to 2020, when she became a senior judge.

George La Plata (1924–2010)

Born on October 17, 1924, in Detroit to Mexican American parents, George La Plata attended Wayne State University, where he received his B.A. degree in 1951. He received his law degree from the Detroit College of Law in 1956. La Plata also served in the U.S. Marine Corps during World War II (1943–1946) and again from 1952 to 1954, reaching the rank of colonel. La Plata, in conjunction with George Menéndez, advisor to the Republic of Mexico, helped pioneer the representation of migrant workers in Michigan, Ohio, and Indiana during the 1950s. From 1956 to 1979, La Plata was in private practice. He

served as a Michigan county judge from 1979 to 1985. When appointed to that position in 1979, he became the first Latino judge in Michigan history. President Ronald Reagan appointed La Plata to the U.S. District Court for the Eastern District of Michigan in 1985, while he was teaching at the Detroit College of Law. After his retirement in 1996, La Plata remained active in providing pro bono services to Latinos in his community. He died on November 14, 2010.

Héctor Manuel Laffitte (1934–)

Born on April 13, 1934, in Ponce, Puerto Rico, Héctor Laffitte received his B.A. from the Interamerican University of Puerto Rico in 1955, his law degree from the University of Puerto Rico in 1958, and his LL.M. degree from Georgetown University in 1960. Laffitte was the civil rights commissioner for the commonwealth of Puerto Rico from 1969 to 1972. He was in private practice from 1972 to 1983 with the firm of Laffitte, Domínguez & Totti. President Ronald Reagan appointed Laffitte to the U.S. District Court for the District of Puerto Rico in 1983. He served as chief judge from 1999 to 2004 and became a senior judge in 2005. He retired on February 16, 2007.

Barbara Lagoa (1967–)

Born on November 2, 1967 in Miami, Florida to Cuban parents, Barbara Lagoa was raised in Hialeah. She graduated from Florida International University with a B.A. in 1989 and the Columbia Law School with a J.D. in 1992 and was in private practice in Miami from 1992 to 2002. She served as an assistant U.S. attorney for the Southern District of Florida from 2003 to 2006. She became a judge for the Florida District Court of Appeal, Third District in 2006 and served until 2019, when she became a justice in the Florida Supreme Court. President Donald Trump nominated and the Senate confirmed her to the position of judge in the U.S. Court of Appeals for the Eleventh Circuit in 2019.

Carlos F. Lucero (1940–)

Born on November 23, 1940, in Antonito, Colorado, Carlos Lucero graduated from Adams State

College with a B.A. in 1961 and George Washington University Law School with a J.D. in 1964. He clerked for two years and then was in private practice from 1966 to 1995, when President Bill Clinton nominated and the Senate confirmed him for judge in the U.S. Court of Appeals for the Tenth Circuit in 1995.

Alfredo Márquez (1922–2014)

Born on June 30, 1922, in Winkelman, Arizona, Alfredo Márquez served in World War II as an ensign in the U.S. Navy. After the war, he attended the University of Arizona, where he received his B.S. degree in 1948 and his law degree in 1950. Márquez served as assistant attorney general in Arizona from 1951 to 1952, as prosecutor for the city of Tucson, as assistant county attorney for Pima County from 1953 to 1954, and as an aide to Representative Stewart Udall (D-Arizona) in 1955. Márquez was in private practice with the firm of Mesch, Márquez & Rothschild from 1957 until 1980, when he was appointed by President Jimmy Carter to the U.S. District Court for the District of Arizona, where he served until his death on August 27, 2014.

Rosemary Márquez (1968–)

Born on February 28, 1968 in Los Angeles, California, to Mexican immigrants, Rosemary Márquez received her bachelor's degree from the University of Arizona in 1990 and her law degree from the same institution in 1993. She served in the Pima County (Arizona) Attorney's Office from 1993 to 1994 and became deputy county attorney in 1994. She then served as an assistant legal defender in Pima County from 1994 to 1996 and assistant federal public defender for the District of Arizona 1996 to 2000, when she went into private practice until 2014. That year, President Barack Obama nominated her for judge of the U.S. District Court for the District of Arizona; she received her commission on May 19, 2014.

Víctor Marrero (1941–)

Born on September 1, 1941, in Santurce, Puerto Rico, Víctor Marrero graduated from New York University with a B.A. in 1964 and from the Yale Law School with an LL.B. in 1968. He worked as an assistant

to New York City mayor John V. Lindsay from 1968 to 1970 and then became the assistant administrator and neighborhood director for Model Cities Administration in New York City until 1973. He worked as the executive director of the Department of City Planning from 1973 to 1974 and subsequently the special counsel to the comptroller of New York City from 1974 to 1975, when he became the first assistant counsel to Governor Hugh Carey of New York from 1975 to 1976. He served as chairman of the City Planning Commission from 1976 to 1977 and commissioner and vice chairman of the New York State Housing Finance Agency from 1978 to 1979. He served as undersecretary of housing and urban development from 1979 to 1981 and then moved to private practice from 1981 to 1993. He was appointed U.S. ambassador on the Economic and Social Council of the United Nations, for which he served from 1993 to 1997. He then served as U.S. ambassador and permanent representative of the United States to the Organization of American States from 1998 to 1999. President Bill Clinton nominated and the Senate confirmed him as judge for the U.S. District Court for the Southern District of New York in 1999. He achieved senior judge status in 2010. Among his notable decisions were his twice striking down parts of the USA Patriot Act, and on October 7, 2019, dismissing an attempt by President Donald Trump to prevent his accountants from complying with a New York prosecutor's subpoena for Trump's tax returns.

Ricardo F. Martínez (1951–)

Born on June 23, 1951, in Mercedes, Texas, and raised in Whatcom County, Washington, Ricardo Martínez graduated from the University of Washington with a B.S. in 1975 and the University of Washington School of Law with a J.D. in 1980. He served as an assistant prosecutor for King County, Washington, from 1980 to 1990. He served as a judge in the Superior Court of the State of Washington, King County, from 1990 to 1998. He was a U.S. magistrate judge for the U.S. District Court for the Western District of Washington from 1998 to 2004. President George W. Bush nominated and the Senate confirmed him as judge for the U.S. District Court for the Western District of Washington in 2004. He has served as chief judge from 2016 to the present.

William Joseph Martínez (1954–)

Born in 1954 in Mexico City, Mexico, José Guillermo Martínez Escalante immigrated to Chicago with his family when he was a boy and changed his name to William Joseph Martínez in 1974. He graduated from the University of Illinois with both a B.A. and a B.Sc. in 1977 and from the University of Chicago Law School with a J.D. in 1980. He worked as a staff attorney for the Legal Assistance Foundation of Chicago from 1980 to 1987 and was in private practice in Denver, Colorado, from 1988 to 1992 and 1997 to 2010. He served as a regional attorney for the U.S. Equal Employment Opportunity Commission in Denver from 1992 to 1996. President Barack Obama nominated and the Senate confirmed him as a judge for the U.S. District Court for the District of Colorado in 2010.

John A. Méndez (1955–)

Born on September 4, 1955, in Oakland and raised in San Leandro, California, John Méndez graduated from Stanford University with a B.A. in 1977 and from Harvard Law School with a J.D. in 1980. He was in private practice in California from 1980 to 1984, 1986 to 1992, and 1993 to 2001. He served as an assistant U.S. attorney for the Northern District of California from 1984 to 1986 and from 1992 to 1993. He was a judge in the Superior Court of California, County of Sacramento, from 2001 to 2008. President George W. Bush nominated and the Senate confirmed him for the position of judge of the U.S. District Court for the Eastern District of California in 2008.

Carlos Eduardo Mendoza (1970–)

Born on February 18, 1970, in Hialeah, Florida, Carlos Mendoza graduated from Central Florida Community College with an A.A. in 1991, from West Virginia University with a B.A. in 1993, and from the West Virginia University College of Law with a J.D. in 1997. He was a U.S. Marine Corps Reserve corporal from 1989 to 1995 and a U.S. Navy lieutenant in the JAG Corps from 1997 to 2005. He served as a special

assistant U.S. attorney for the Eastern District of Virginia from 2004 to 2005 and an assistant state attorney and division chief for the State of Florida from 2005 to 2008. He was assistant city attorney for St. Augustine, Florida, from 2008 to 2011 and a judge for the Circuit Court of Florida, Seventh Judicial Circuit, from 2011 to 2014. President Barack Obama nominated and the Senate confirmed him for the position of judge for the U.S. District Court for the Middle District of Florida in 2014.

Salvador Mendoza Jr. (1971–)

Born on November 20, 1971, in Pacoima, California, to parents who immigrated to the United States from Mexico, Salvador Mendoza was raised in Washington State and graduated from the University of Washington with a B.A. in 1994 and the University of California, Los Angeles, School of Law, with a J.D. in 1997. He worked as an assistant attorney general in Washington State from 1997 to 1998. He was a deputy prosecutor for Franklin County, Washington, from 1998 to 1999 and then went into private practice from 1999 to 2013. He was judge pro tem in various Washington counties from the Pasco Municipal Court from 2002 to 2013. He served as a judge of the Superior Court of the State of Washington, Benton and Franklin Counties, from 2013 to 2014. President Barack Obama nominated him and the Senate confirmed him for the position of judge for the U.S. District Court for the Eastern District of Washington in 2014.

Frank Montalvo (1956–)

Born on May 6, 1956, in Bayamón, Puerto Rico, Frank Montalvo graduated from the University of Puerto Rico with a B.S. in 1976, the University of Michigan with an M.S. in 1977, and the Wayne State University Law School with a J.D. in 1985. He worked as an engineer for General Motors from 1983 to 1988 while he studied for the bar and went into private practice in San Antonio, Texas, from 1988 to 1994. He was a judge for Bexar County's 288th District Court from 1995 to 2003. President George W. Bush nominated and the Senate confirmed him as judge for the U.S. District Court for the Western District of Texas in 2003.

David Steven Morales (1968–)

Born in 1968 in Edinburg, Texas, David Morales graduated from St. Edward's University with a B.B.A. in 1990 and the St. Mary's University School of Law with his J.D. in 1994. He served in various positions within the Office of the Attorney General in Texas from 1994 to 2011, including deputy first assistant attorney general from 2010 to 2011. He was general counsel for the Texas governor from 2011 to 2014 and then deputy general counsel for the University of Texas System Board of Regents from 2014 to 2016. He was in private practice in Austin from 2016 to 2019. President Donald J. Trump nominated and the Senate confirmed him for the position of judge of the U.S. District Court for the Southern District of Texas in 2019.

Carlos Moreno (1948–)

Born on November 4, 1948, in Los Angeles, California, to Mexican immigrant parents, Carlos Moreno graduated from Yale College with a B.A. in 1970 and Stanford Law School with a J.D. in 1975. He served as a deputy city attorney in Los Angeles, California, from 1975 to 1979 and then was in private practice in Los Angeles from 1979 to 1986. He was a judge in the Compton Municipal Court from 1986 to 1993 and a judge in the Superior Court of California, County of Los Angeles, from 1993 to 1998. President Bill Clinton nominated and the Senate confirmed him for the position of judge of the U.S. District Court for the Central District of California in 1998. He served until 2001, when he resigned to become an associate justice of the Supreme Court of California, on which he served until his retirement in 2011. He came out of retirement to serve as U.S. ambassador to Belize, which he left at the end of Barack Obama's presidency.

Federico Moreno (1952–)

Born on April 10, 1952 in Caracas, Venezuela, Federico Moreno immigrated to the United States with his family in 1963. In 1974, Moreno graduated from the University of Notre Dame, where he received his B.A. degree in government. He worked as a janitor and in restaurants to pay his way through college. After graduating, he taught at the Atlantic Community College in Mays Landing, New Jersey, and at Stockton State College in Pomona, New Jersey, in 1975 and 1976. In 1978, Moreno received his law degree from the University of Miami School of Law. Moreno was an associate with the law firm of Rollins, Peeples & Meadows in 1978 and 1979 and served as an assistant federal public defender from 1979 to 1981. He was a partner in the law firm of Thornton, Rothman & Moreno from 1982 to 1986. He served as Dade County judge in 1986 and 1987. Moreno was a Florida circuit court judge from 1987 until 1990. President George H. W. Bush appointed Moreno to the U.S. District Court for the Southern District of Florida in 1990. He became a senior judge in 2020.

Carlos Murguía (1957–)

Born in 1957 in Kansas City, Kansas, to Mexican immigrant parents, Carlos Murguía graduated from the University of Kansas with a B.S. degree in 1979 and the University of Kansas School of Law with his J.D. degree in 1982. He was in private practice in Kansas City, Kansas, from 1982 to 1987. He worked as a hearing officer in the Kansas District Court, Twenty-Ninth Judicial District, from 1984 to 1990. He served as the coordinator of the Immigration Amnesty Program, El Centro, Inc., from 1985 to 1990 and served as a judge for the Kansas District Court, Twenty-Ninth Judicial District, from 1990 to 1999. President Bill Clinton nominated and the Senate confirmed him to the position of judge for the U.S. District Court for the District of Kansas in 1999, when he became the first Latino to serve as a federal judge in Kansas. He resigned in 2020.

Mary Helen Murguía (1960–)

Born on September 6, 1960, in Kansas City, Kansas, to Mexican immigrant parents, Mary Helen Murguía graduated from the University of Kansas with a B.A. and a B.S. in 1982 and from the University of Kansas School of Law with a J.D. in 1985. She served as an assistant district attorney for Wyandotte County, Kansas, from 1985 to 1990 and then an assistant U.S. attorney for the District of Arizona from 1990 to 2000. She worked in the Executive Office for U.S. Attorneys, U.S. Department of Justice, from 1998 to 2000. President Bill Clinton nominated and the Senate confirmed her to the position of judge for the U.S. District Court for the District of Arizona in 2000. She served in that position until President Barack Obama nominated her and the Senate confirmed her position as judge for the U.S. Court of Appeals for the Ninth Circuit in 2011.

Gloria María Navarro (1967–)

Born on May 2, 1967, in Las Vegas, Nevada, Gloria Navarro graduated from the University of Nevada, Las Vegas, with a B.A. in 1989 and the Arizona State University College of Law with a J.D. in 1992. She was in private practice in Las Vegas from 1993 to 2001 and a deputy special public defender for Clark County, Nevada, from 2001 to 2004. She served as chief deputy district attorney, Civil Division, for Clark County from 2005 to 2010. President Barack Obama nominated and the Senate confirmed her for the position of judge of the U.S. District Court for the District of Nevada in 2010. She served as chief judge from 2014 to 2019.

Philip Newman
(1916–2002)

The first Mexican-born U.S. judge, Philip Newman was born on July 25, 1916, in Mexico City to a German American father and a Mexican mother. His family fled Mexico when he was ten years old during the Mexican Revolution and settled in California. Arriving destitute in the United States, Newman's father put himself through law school at night and became an attorney. Newman also became an attorney in 1941. He won landmark cases protecting the rights of individuals against unwarranted searches and seizures and leading to changes in immigration law. In 1964, Newman was appointed by Governor Edmund G. Brown to a Los Angeles municipal judgeship, where he remained until his retirement in 1982. Interested in promoting legal services for the poor and

relations with Mexico, Newman served as president of the Immigration and Naturalization Lawyers Association and as president of the Mexican-American Scholarship Foundation for Careers in Law. In 1966, Newman was named by President Lyndon B. Johnson to the National Advisory Committee of the Neighborhood Legal Services program in the Office of Economic Opportunity and served for six years. He was a founding member and legal counsel of the Community Service Organization and vice president, secretary, and director of the Youth Opportunities Foundation. In 1981, after nearly eighteen years on the bench, Newman announced that he would not seek reelection because of what he called the "politicizing and demeaning of the judiciary by pressure groups, politicians and some of the media." He thus went into private legal practice and maintained his social activism.

José Rolando Olvera Jr.
(1963–)

Born in 1963 in Houston, Texas, José Olvera graduated from Harvard University with a B.A. in 1985 and from the University of Texas School of Law with a J.D. in 1989. He was in private practice in McAllen, Texas, from 1990 to 1993 and then in Brownsville from 1994 to 2000, 2003 to 2004, and 2007 to 2008. He was a judge for the Texas District Court, 357th Judicial District, from 2001 to 2002 and then the 138th Judicial District from 2005 to 2006, followed by serving as a judge in the Brownsville Municipal Court from 2007 to 2008. He served as a judge in the Texas District Court, 445th Judicial District, from 2009 to 2015. He was also the presiding judge for the Fifth Administrative Judicial Region of Texas from 2011 to 2015. President Barack Obama nominated and the Senate confirmed him to the position of judge, U.S. District Court for the Southern District of Texas in 2015.

Richard A. Paez (1947–)

Born on May 5, 1947, in Salt Lake City, Utah, Richard Paez graduated from Brigham Young University with a B.A. in 1969 and the University of California, Berkeley, School of Law with a J.D. in 1972.

He worked as a staff attorney for California Rural Legal Assistance from 1972 to 1974, for the Western Center on Law and Poverty from 1974 to 1976, and for the Legal Aid Foundation of Los Angeles from 1976 to 1981, becoming the director of litigation in 1980. He served as a judge in the Los Angeles Municipal Court from 1981 to 1994. President Bill Clinton nominated and the Senate confirmed him for the position of judge, U.S. District Court for the Central District of California in 1994. He served until 2000 when President Clinton nominated him and the Senate confirmed him for the position of judge for the U.S. Court of Appeals for the Ninth Circuit.

Juan Manuel Pérez-Giménez (1941–2020)

Born on March 28, 1941, in San Juan, Puerto Rico, Juan Pérez-Giménez received his B.A. degree in 1963 and his LL.B. degree in 1968 from the University of Puerto Rico; his M.B.A. degree was conferred by George Washington University in 1965. He was an assistant U.S. attorney for Puerto Rico from 1971 to 1975. He was in private practice in San Juan from 1968 to 1971 and was then an assistant U.S. attorney for the District of Puerto Rico from 1971 to 1975. He served as a U.S. magistrate judge for the District of Puerto Rico from 1975 to 1979. President Jimmy Carter appointed Pérez-Giménez to the U.S. District Court for the District of Puerto Rico in 1979. He served as chief judge from 1984 to 1991 and was senior judge from March 28, 2006, until his death on December 10, 2020.

Jaime Pieras Jr. (1924–2011)

Born on May 19, 1924, in San Juan, Puerto Rico, Jaime Pieras served in the U.S. Army during World War II. He received his B.A. degree from Catholic University in 1945 and his J.D. degree from Georgetown. He served in the U.S. Army as a second lieutenant from 1946 to 1947. He was in private practice in Hato Rey, Puerto Rico, from 1949 to 1953 and again from 1954 to 1982, when he was appointed to the U.S. District Court for the District of Puerto Rico by President Ronald Reagan. He died on June 11, 2011, in San Juan, Puerto Rico.

Edward Charles Prado (1947–)

Born on June 7, 1947, in San Antonio, Texas, Edward Prado attended the University of Texas, where he received his B.A. degree in 1969 and his J.D. degree in 1972. He was a member of the U.S. Army Reserve from 1972 to 1987. He served as assistant district attorney for Bexar County, Texas, from 1972 to 1976, and assistant federal public defender for the Western District of Texas from 1976 to 1981. Prado served as a judge for Bexar County's 187th District Court in 1980 and U.S. attorney for the Western District of Texas from 1981 to 1984, when President Ronald Reagan appointed Prado to the U.S. District Court for the Western District of Texas. Prado was appointed by U.S. Supreme Court chief justice William Rehnquist to serve as the chairman of the Criminal Justice Act Review Committee from 1991 to 1993. He left the district court on May 13, 2003, to accept another nomination, this time by President George W. Bush to a seat vacated by Robert M. Parker on the Court of Appeals for the Fifth Circuit. He served on that bench until becoming ambassador to Argentina in 2018, a position he served until 2021.

Nitza Ileana Quiñones Alejandro (1951–)

Born in January 1951 in Hato Rey, Puerto Rico, Nitza Quiñonez Alejandro graduated from the University of Puerto Rico, School of Business Administration, with a B.B.A. in 1972 and the University of Puerto Rico School of Law with a J.D. in 1975. She worked as a staff attorney for the Community Legal Services of Philadelphia from 1975 to 1977 and then was an attorney advisor for the U.S. Department of Health and Human Services in Philadelphia from 1977 to 1979. She was a staff attorney for the U.S. Department of Veterans Affairs in Philadelphia from 1979 to 1991 and judge in the Court of Common Pleas of Philadelphia County from 1991 to 2013. President Barack Obama nominated and the Senate confirmed her to the position of judge for the U.S.

District Court for the Eastern District of Pennsylvania in 2013.

Raúl Anthony Ramírez (1944–)

Born on March 8, 1944, in Los Angeles, California, Raúl Ramírez received an associate of arts degree from Glendale Junior College in 1965 and a bachelor of arts degree from Los Angeles State College in 1967. After receiving his law degree in 1970 from the University of the Pacific, McGeorge School of Law, Ramírez went into private practice. He served as a municipal court judge in Sacramento from 1977 until 1980. In 1980, he was appointed by President Jimmy Carter to the U.S. District Court for the Eastern District of California. He resigned on December 31, 1989. Since then he has been in private practice. In 1996, he opened his own firm, Ramírez Arbitration and Mediation Services.

Edgardo Ramos (1960–)

Born in 1960 in Ponce, Puerto Rico, Edgardo Ramos moved with his mother and six brothers and sisters to Newark, New Jersey, when he was a boy. He graduated from Yale College with a B.A. in 1982 and Harvard Law School with a J.D. in 1987. He was in private practice in New York City from 1987 to 1992 and 2002 to 2011. He served as an assistant U.S. attorney for the Eastern District of New York from 1992 to 2002. President Barack Obama nominated and the Senate confirmed him to the position of judge of the U.S. District Court for the Southern District of New York in 2011.

Nelva Gonzales Ramos (1965–)

Born on August 22, 1965, in Port Lavaca, Texas, Nelva Gonzales Ramos graduated from Southwest Texas State University with a B.S. in 1987 and from the University of Texas School of Law with a J.D. in 1991. She was in private practice in Corpus Christi, Texas, from 1991 to 1997 and 1999 to 2000. She served as a judge in the Corpus Christi Municipal Court from 1997 to 1999 and in the Nueces County 347th District Court from 2001 to 2011. President Barack Obama nominated and the Senate confirmed

her for the position of judge in the U.S. District Court for the Southern District of Texas in 2011.

Luis Felipe Restrepo (1959–)

Born in 1959 in Medellín, Colombia, Luis Restrepo was raised in Virginia and became a U.S. citizen in 1993. He graduated from the University of Pennsylvania with a B.A. in 1981 and Tulane University Law School with a J.D. in 1986. Restrepo served as a law clerk for the ACLU National Prison Project in Washington, D.C., from 1986 to 1987 and then was an assistant defender for the Defender Association of Philadelphia from 1987 to 1990. He was assistant federal public defender for the Eastern District of Pennsylvania from 1990 to 1993 and then went into private practice until 2006. He served as a U.S. magistrate judge for the U.S. District Court for the Eastern District of Pennsylvania from 2006 to 2013. President Barack Obama nominated and the Senate confirmed him for the position of judge for the U.S. District Court for the Eastern District of Pennsylvania in 2013. He served until 2016, when he was again nominated and confirmed for the position of judge on the U.S. Court of Appeals for the Third Circuit, where he continues to serve.

Jimmie V. Reyna (1952–)

Born on November 11, 1952, in Tucumcari, New Mexico, Jimmie Reyna graduated from the University of Rochester with a B.A. in 1975 and the University of New Mexico School of Law with a J.D. in 1978. He was in private practice in Albuquerque, New Mexico, from 1979 to 1986 and in Washington, D.C., from 1986 to 2011. President Barack Obama nominated and the Senate confirmed him for the position of judge on the U.S. Court of Appeals for the Federal Circuit in 2011. Reyna is the author of two books dealing with his specialty, international trade: *Passport to North American Trade: Rules of Origin and Customs Procedures under NAFTA* and *The GATT Uruguay Round: A Negotiating History (1986–1992): Services.* In private practice he represented clients before the Court of International Trade and before foreign governmental, administrative, and judicial bodies.

Cruz Reynoso (1931–2021)

Cruz Reynoso was born on May 2, 1931, to farm worker parents in the small town of Brea, California, where he was raised and received his early education. He attended Fullerton Junior College and Pomona College, where he earned his B.A. degree in 1953. From 1953 to 1955, he served in the U.S. Army. After his discharge, Reynoso entered the study of law at the University of California, Berkeley, and was awarded his degree in 1958. That same year he began the private practice of law in El Centro, California. During the 1960s, Reynoso acted as assistant chief of the Division of Fair Employment Practices for California. From 1967 to 1968, he was associate general counsel to the Equal Employment Opportunity Commission in Washington, D.C., returning to California to become the first deputy director and then director of California Rural Legal Assistance, which was a free legal service that challenged segregation and other discriminatory practices in the agricultural belts of California. In 1972, he accepted a position at the University of New Mexico Law School, where he served for four years. In 1976, Reynoso was appointed to the California Court of Appeal in Sacramento as an associate justice. Governor Jerry Brown then appointed him to the California Supreme Court in 1982. Reynoso became the first Latino on the court and served until 1986. In 1987, he entered private practice with the firm of O'Donnell & Gordon in Los Angeles and subsequently was of counsel to Kaye, Scholer, Fierman, Hays & Handler in Sacramento. Reynoso was honored by appointment to four presidential commissions, including the Select Commission on Immigration and Refugee Policy and the UN Commission on Human Rights. He was appointed to the law faculty of the University of California, Los Angeles, in 1990. In 2000, President Bill Clinton presented Reynoso with the Presidential Medal of Freedom, the United States' highest civilian honor.

Dorothy Comstock Riley (1924–2004)

Dorothy Comstock Riley was born on December 6, 1924, in Detroit, Michigan, to Latino parents. She attended Wayne State University, where she received both her B.A. degree in politics and her law degree. She went into private practice in 1950 and established the firm of Riley and Roumell in 1968. Riley sat on the Michigan Court of Appeals from 1976 until 1982, when she was appointed to fill a vacancy on the Michigan Supreme Court as an associate justice. She was elected to that position in 1984 and was named chief justice in 1987. She was reelected in 1992 but retired in 1997 due to illness. She died on October 23, 2004. In 1991 she was inducted into the Michigan Women's Hall of Fame, and the State Bar of Michigan presented Riley with its Distinguished Public Servant Award in 2000.

Fernando Rodríguez Jr. (1969–)

Born in 1969 in Harlingen, Texas, Fernando Rodríguez graduated from Yale University with a B.A. in 1991 and the University of Texas School of Law with a J.D. in 1997. He worked as a teacher for Teach for America in Houston, Texas, from 1991 to 1994. He served as a briefing attorney for Justice Nathan L. Hecht of the Supreme Court of Texas from 1997 to 1998, when he went into private practice in Dallas until 2009. He served as a field office director for the International Justice Mission in Bolivia and the Dominican Republic from 2010 to 2018. President Donald J. Trump nominated and the Senate confirmed him for the position of judge on the U.S. District Court for the Southern District of Texas in 2018.

Joseph H. Rodríguez (1930–)

Born on December 12, 1930, in Camden, New Jersey, to a Puerto Rican mother and a Cuban father, Joseph Rodríguez received his B.A. degree from LaSalle University in 1955 and his J.D. degree from Rutgers University in 1958. He was in private practice from 1959 to 1982 with the firm of Brown, Connery, Kulp, Wille, Purcell & Greene and was also an instructor at Rutgers University School of Law from 1972 to 1982. In 1982, Rodríguez was appointed New Jersey public advocate, a state cabinet position, and served until 1985. Rodríguez was the first Latino president of the New Jersey State Bar Association. He litigated landmark cases in the areas of education and housing. President Ronald Reagan appointed Rodríguez to the U.S. District Court for the District of New Jersey in

1985. In 1998 he became a senior judge in the district court. Rodriguez has always been involved in community affairs and continues to be active today.

Xavier Rodríguez (1961–)

Born on September 20, 1961, in San Antonio, Texas, Xavier Rodríguez graduated from Harvard University with a B.A. in 1983 and the University of Texas School of Law with a J.D. in 1987. He also received an M.P.A. degree from the University of Texas LBJ School of Public Affairs in 1987. He was in private practice in San Antonio from 1987 to 2001 and 2002 to 2003. He served as a justice on the Supreme Court of Texas from 2001 to 2002. President George W. Bush nominated and the Senate confirmed him to the position of judge on the U.S. District Court for the Western District of Texas in 2003.

Luis D. Rovirá (1923–2011)

Born on September 8, 1923, in San Juan, Puerto Rico, Luis Rovirá received his early education in Pennsylvania when his parents divorced. He later moved to Colorado for his postsecondary education but decided to enlist in the U.S. Army during World War II. After the war Rovirá attended the University of Colorado on the G.I. Bill and received both B.A. and law degrees. He was in private practice with the firm of Rovirá, DeMuth & Eiberger until 1976. In 1976, Rovirá was appointed to the Colorado District Court for the second district. In 1979, he was elevated to the Colorado Supreme Court as an associate justice and became chief justice in 1990, becoming the first Latino chief justice of any state supreme court. Rovirá retired in 1995 from the Colorado Supreme Court; he was seventy-two, the mandatory retirement age in Colorado. Rovirá died on October 30, 2011.

Esther Salas (1968–)

Born on December 29, 1968, in Los Angeles, California, to a Cuban mother and a Mexican father. When Esther Salas was five, she and her siblings moved with their mother to Union City, New Jersey. She graduated from Rutgers University with a B.A. in 1991 and the Rutgers School of Law–Newark with a J.D. in 1994. She was in private practice in Plainfield, New Jersey,

from 1995 to 1997 and served as an assistant federal public defender for the District of New Jersey from 1997 to 2006. She served as a U.S. magistrate judge for the U.S. District Court for the District of New Jersey from 2006 to 2011. President Barack Obama nominated and the Senate confirmed her as judge on the U.S. District Court for the District of New Jersey in 2011. Salas has always been active in Latino and minority concerns and was recognized as a leader, which included serving as president of the Hispanic Bar Association of New Jersey from 2001 to 2002 and president of the Hispanic Bar Foundation of New Jersey. She was a member of the Governor's Hispanic Advisory Committee for Policy Development, the Supreme Court Committee on Minority Concerns, and the Supreme Court Committee on Women in the Courts.

Diana Saldaña (1971–)

Born on April 30, 1971, in Carrizo Springs, Texas, Diana Saldaña spent summers as a migrant farm worker in the Midwest from the age of ten through law school. Saldaña graduated from the University of Texas with a B.A. in 1994 and the University of Texas School of Law with a J.D. in 1997. She served as a staff attorney in the Office of the General Counsel, U.S. Department of Agriculture, in 1998 and as a trial attorney for the Civil Rights Division, U.S. Department of Justice, from 1998 to 1999. She was in private practice in Houston from 2000 to 2001 and then served as an assistant U.S. attorney for the Southern District of Texas from 2001 to 2006. She served as a U.S. magistrate judge for the U.S. District Court for the Southern District of Texas from 2006 to 2011. President Barack Obama nominated and the Senate confirmed her to the position of judge on the U.S. District Court for the Southern District of Texas in 2011.

Juan Ramón Sánchez (1955–)

Esther Salas was born on December 22, 1955, in Vega Baja, Puerto Rico, Juan Sánchez graduated from the City College of New York with a B.A. in 1978 and the University of Pennsylvania Law School with a J.D. in 1981. He served as a staff attorney for Legal Aid of Chester County, Pennsylvania, from 1981 to 1983, after which he went into private practice until 1997. He served as a public defender in Chester County from 1983 to 1997. He was a judge on the Court of Common Pleas of Chester County from 1998 to 2004. President George W. Bush nominated and the Senate confirmed him for the position of judge on the U.S. District Court for the Eastern District of Pennsylvania in 2004. He has served as chief judge from 2018 to the present.

James Alan Soto (1950–)

Born on July 1, 1950, in Nogales, Arizona, James Soto graduated from Arizona State University with a B.S. in 1971 and the Arizona State University College of Law with a J.D. in 1975. He was deputy city attorney (part-time) for Nogales from 1975 to 1983 and town attorney (part-time) for Patagonia, Arizona, from 1975 to 1992. He was in private practice in Nogales from 1975 to 2001. Soto served as deputy county attorney (part-time) for Santa Cruz County, Arizona, in 1979 and then served as the presiding judge on the Arizona Superior Court, Santa Cruz County, from 2001 to 2014. President Barack Obama nominated and the Senate confirmed him for the position of judge on the U.S. District Court for the District of Arizona in 2014.

Sonia Sotomayor (1954–)

Born to Puerto Rican working-class parents on June 25, 1954, in Bronx, New York, Sonia Sotomayor was raised by her mother at times in public housing after her father died when she was nine years old. She graduated *summa cum laude* from Princeton University with a B.A. in 1976 and the Yale Law School with a J.D. in 1979. She started her distinguished career as an assistant district attorney for New York County, New York, from 1979 to 1984. She was in private practice in New York from 1984 to 1992. She spent the rest of her career as a federal court judge. President George H. W. Bush nominated her and the Senate confirmed her for the position of judge on the U.S. District Court for the Southern District of New York in 1992, where she served until 1998, when President Bill Clinton nomi-

nated her and the Senate confirmed her for the position of judge on the U.S. Court of Appeals for the Second Circuit. She served in that position until 2009, when President Barack Obama nominated and the Senate confirmed her for the positon of U.S. Supreme Court justice. She became the first person of Latino heritage to serve as a Supreme Court justice. The Bronxville housing project and cultural center where she partially grew up, a complex of twenty-eight buildings, was named in her honor in 2010. Sotomayor is one of the most celebrated women in the United States and has received numerous honorary degrees and awards for her achievements and for what she has expressed in her speeches, writings, and judicial decisions about equal rights for minorities and women as well as the protection of civil rights in general.

Analisa Nadine Torres (1959–)

Born on November 19, 1959, in New York, New York, Analisa Torres graduated from Harvard University with an A.B. in 1981 and the Columbia Law School with a J.D. in 1984. She was in private practice in New York City from 1984 to 1992, then served as general counsel for the South Bronx Overall Economic Development Corp. in 1992. Torres served as a law clerk for the Justice Elliott Wilk of the Supreme Court of the State of New York from 1992 to 1999. She was a commissioner with the New York City Planning Commission from 1993 to 1995. She served as a judge in New York City courts from 2000 to 2004 and a justice of the Supreme Court of the State of New York, Criminal Term, from 2004 to 2013. President Barack Obama nominated and the Senate confirmed her for the position of judge on the U.S. District Court for the Southern District of New York in 2013.

Ernest C. Torres (1941–)

Born in 1941 in New Bedford, Massachusetts, Ernest Torres graduated from Dartmouth College in 1963 and received his law degree from Duke University School of Law in 1968. He was in private practice from 1968 to 1974. In 1975, Torres was elected to the Rhode Island House of Representatives, where he served until 1980. He served as an associate justice of the Rhode Island Superior Court from 1980 to

1985. Torres was appointed by President Ronald Reagan in 1988 to the U.S. District Court for the District of Rhode Island. He served as chief judge from 1999 to 2006, becoming a senior judge on December 1, 2006. He retired on June 1, 2011.

Juan Torruella (1933–2020)

Born on June 7, 1933, in San Juan, Puerto Rico, Juan Torruella received his B.A. degree from the University of Pennsylvania in 1954 and his LL.B. degree from Boston University in 1957. He received a master of public administration from the University of Puerto Rico School of Public Administration in 1984 and subsequently a master of studies from Oxford University. He was in private practice of law in San Juan from 1959 until 1974, when President Gerald Ford appointed him to the U.S. District Court for the District of Puerto Rico. He served as the judge of that court from 1982 until 1984, when President Ronald Reagan appointed Torruella to the U.S. Court of Appeals for the First Circuit. He served as chief judge from 1994 to 2001. Torruella died on October 26, 2020.

John Michael Vázquez (1970–)

Born on May 11, 1970, in Honolulu, Hawaii, John Michael Vázquez graduated from Rutgers University with a B.A. in 1992 and Seton Hall University School of Law with a J.D. in 1996. He was in private practice in West Orange, New Jersey, from 1997 to 2001 and again in Roseland, New Jersey, from 2008 to 2016. He served as an assistant U.S. attorney for the District of New Jersey from 2001 to 2006 and served in the Office of the Attorney General, Department of Law and Public Safety, State of New Jersey, from 2006 to 2008. He was special assistant to the attorney general from 2006 to 2007 and then first assistant attorney general from 2007 to 2008. President Barack Obama nominated and the Senate confirmed him to the position of judge on the U.S. District Court for the District of New Jersey in 2016.

Martha A. Vázquez (1953–)

Born in 1953 in Santa Barbara, California, Martha Vázquez received both her B.A. (1975) and her law degree (1978) from the University of Notre Dame. She began her career as a public defender for the State of New Mexico and then went into private practice, becoming a partner in her Sante Fe firm in 1984. President Bill Clinton appointed Vázquez to the U.S. District Court for the District of New Mexico in 1993. She served as chief judge of the court from 2003 to 2010. She became a senior judge on December 21, 2021.

Filemón B. Vela (1935–2004)

Born on May 1, 1935, in Harlingen, Texas, Filemón Vela served as a private in the U.S. Army from 1957 to 1959. He graduated from the University of Texas and received a J.D. degree from St. Mary's University in 1962. He was in private practice from 1962 to 1975 and also served as an attorney for the Mexican American Legal Defense and Educational Fund (MALDEF) from 1962 to 1975. He was a Texas district court judge from 1975 to 1980. He was a city commissioner in Brownsville from 1971 to 1973. He was a judge of the 107th Judicial District in the Texas counties of Cameron and Willacy from 1975 to 1980. President Jimmy Carter appointed Vela to the U.S. District Court for the Southern District of Texas in 1980. He died on April 13, 2004.

Frank R. Zapata (1944–)

Born on July 1, 1944, in Safford, Arizona, Frank Zapata graduated from Eastern Arizona College with an A.A. degree in 1964, the University of Arizona with a B.A. in 1966, and the University of Arizona College of Law with a J.D. in 1973. He worked as a staff attorney for the Pima County Legal Aid Society from 1973 to 1974 and as an assistant federal public defender for the District of Arizona from 1974 to 1994; he was chief assistant federal public defender from 1984 to 1994. He served as a U.S. magistrate judge for the U.S. District Court for the District of Arizona from 1994 to 1996. President Bill Clinton nominated and the Senate confirmed him for the position of judge on the U.S. District Court for the District of Arizona in 1996. He became a senior judge in 2010.

LATINOS IN THE PUBLIC INTEREST

A great number of Latino attorneys have chosen a career in the public interest. Many serve at government posts or with nonprofit legal organizations established to aid underprivileged and disenfranchised clients. Many attorneys who enter service in the public interest do so because they have a desire to aid other Latinos with legal, social, and cultural problems.

In public interest service, Latino attorneys have the opportunity to make gains for not only themselves and their community but also all Americans. They take pride in the victories made in the struggle for equal rights at a time when the tide is running against civil rights efforts of minorities. Public interest firms often act as watchdogs that monitor government action to see that public resources are effectively channeled into the Latino community. By monitoring these agencies, they can ensure that programs they devise realistically account for the needs of Latinos. However, public interest firms and organizations are plagued by insufficient funding and staff. Despite these limitations, those people who join the public interest have achieved a great deal in this country.

Issues often monitored by public interest groups include immigration, employment, education, housing, voter registration and elections, public funding, discrimination, and civil rights. In the past fifty years, there has been dramatic growth in the number of public interest organizations specifically created to assist Latinos with legal problems and to advocate political involvement. Some of the most well known and effective national public interest groups in the United States include local offices funded by the Legal Services Corporation, Migrant Legal Action Program, Mexican-American Legal Defense and Educational Fund, Puerto Rican Legal Defense and Education Fund, UnidosUS, and the National Immigration Law Center.

Michael J. Aguirre (1940–)

Born in San Diego, California, on September 12, 1949, Michael Aguirre was educated in California and attained a bachelor of science degree at Arizona State University in 1971, a law degree from the University of California, Berkeley, in 1974, and a master of public administration degree from Harvard University in 1989. He worked as deputy legislative counsel for the California legislature from 1974 to 1975; as assistant U.S. attorney from 1975 to 1976; assistant counsel for the U.S. Senate Subcommittee on Investigations from 1976 to 1977; and as special reports legal counsel for the CBS network in 1977. Since that time he has worked in private practice. Since 1980, he has been the president of his own law firm, Aguirre & Meyer, A.P.C., which specializes in civil litigation. He has also been an adjunct law professor and lecturer at the University of California, San Diego, and at the University of Southern California. Aguirre is active in the community and has also been the author of various laws passed by the California legislature. His awards include the Willie Velásquez Community Service Award, given by the Chicano Federation in San Diego in 1989. In 1987, he was voted the most distinguished name in the San Diego legal community by the readership of the *San Diego Daily Transcript*.

Joaquín Avila (1948–2018)

Born in Los Angeles, California, on June 23, 1948, Joaquín Avila graduated with a B.A. in political science from Yale University in 1970 and received his law degree from Harvard University Law School in 1973. He had served as an editor of the *Harvard Civil Rights–Civil Liberties Law Review*. Avila devoted his career to combating voting rights discrimination against Latinos and other minorities, including a successful effort to ensure greater political representation through census counts. Avila served as president and general counsel for the Mexican American Legal Defense and Educational Fund (MALDEF) from 1982 to 1985, and after leaving MALDEF he continued to work to secure voting rights for minorities. Avila is credited with helping increase the number of Spanish-speaking social workers in Los Angeles; Latino firefighters in Salinas, California; and Latina women working as electrician apprentices and border guards. Under his leadership MALDEF was instrumental in the 1982 Supreme Court case *Phyler v. Doe*, which struck down a Texas law that allowed the state's school districts to ban undocumented immigrants from public school or to charge them tuition; the decision guaranteed those children a constitutional right to a free public education. Avila was involved in more than seventy voting rights cases. In 1980, he succeeded in having the U.S. Census Bureau include a box to indicate Latino heritage.

Wilfredo Caraballo (1947–)

Wilfredo Caraballo was born in Yabucoa, Puerto Rico, in 1947 and grew up in a tough neighborhood of New York City. Caraballo attended St. Joseph's University and went on to New York University Law School and received his law degree in 1974. He then worked the streets of New York City as a community activist and a legal aid lawyer. Caraballo was also active in the Puerto Rican Legal Defense and Education Fund. In 1975, he joined Seton Hall Law School in Newark, New Jersey, as a clinical professor. During his fifteen years at Seton Hall, Caraballo specialized in teaching contract, commercial, and bankruptcy law. He was a visiting professor at New York University, the City University of New York, and Pace College law schools. In 1982 he was named associate dean of Seton Hall Law School. Caraballo took a leave of absence in 1990, when New Jersey governor James Florio appointed Caraballo the state's public advocate and public defender, a cabinet post. Caraballo stated that one of the reasons he was so enthusiastic about becoming New Jersey's fourth public advocate is that the post gave him an opportunity to deal with the same kinds of public interest problems he faced firsthand as a young man growing up on the streets of Brooklyn and the South Bronx. Caraballo served as public advocate until 1992. Caraballo became politically active and ran for office; he served in the New Jersey General Assembly from 1996 to 2008, after which he returned to teach law at Seton Hall.

Linda Corchado

Linda Corchado was born in El Paso, Texas, to immigrant parents who were fieldworkers in California before moving to El Paso and opening Freddy's Café. She attended Burges High School, where she was a statewide award-winning editor of her newspaper. She went on to major in political science and minor in Latin American studies at Swarthmore College,

graduating in 2008. She received her J.D. from the Benjamin N. Cardozo School of Law in New York City in 2012 and returned to El Paso, where she obtained a master's in business administration from the University of Texas at El Paso in 2015. She has been practicing immigration law with a particular focus on asylum and the detention of asylum seekers since 2014. That year, she became a managing attorney for Las Americas Immigrant Advocacy Center (Las Américas). In 2019, she became the legal director at Las Américas, engaging in direct representation of noncitizen clients and supervising attorneys and other staff who represent individuals detained during immigration proceedings. Her responsibilities include overseeing the involvement of Las Americas in the El Paso Immigration Collaborative, which provides legal support to detained individuals seeking release from detention centers in the El Paso region.

Miguel Domínguez (?–)

Born in the South Bronx, New York, Miguel Dominguez graduated from the University at Buffalo with a B.A. in psychology and became a social worker at an Atlanta nonprofit organization, providing case management services for homeless and mentally ill clients. Dominguez furthered his education and obtained his law degree from the Thomas M. Cooley Law School in 2008. He then served as a judicial law assistant at the Georgia Court of Appeals, as an assistant district attorney in Rockdale and Clayton counties, and as an assistant to the DeKalb County solicitor-general before entering private practice. Later, he became a criminal defense attorney before leaving his practice to become a state prosecutor. He was the first Latino prosecutor in the history of several metro Atlanta judicial circuits. Domínguez is cochairman of Atlanta's Criminal Justice Reform Commission. He provides pro bono legal services to victims of domestic violence as well as to youthful offenders, using his experience as a prosecutor to provide them a second chance at becoming productive members of society by way of having their criminal records expunged. Domínguez has been recognized as one of *Georgia Trend* magazine's 40 under 40 Best and Brightest, Super Lawyers' Rising Stars, and the National Bar Association's 40 under 40 Nation's Best Advocates.

Daniel García (1947–)

Born in Los Angeles in 1947, Daniel García was educated in Los Angeles and attended Loyola University, where he received a degree in business in 1970. He went on to the University of Southern California and earned his M.B.A. in 1971. García then attended UCLA School of Law and was awarded a law degree in 1974. García joined the prestigious firm of Munger, Tolles & Olson in Los Angeles, where he is now a partner. He served as a member of the board of the Mexican-American Legal Defense and Education Fund and was active in Los Angeles politics. García was a member of the Los Angeles Planning Commission from 1976 to 1988 and was its president from 1978 to 1988. Of Latino participation in the legal profession, García believes that in recent years Latino attorneys have done much better in breaking barriers to join the nation's largest firms. García himself is among that group. Currently García is senior vice president and chief compliance and privacy officer for Kaiser Foundation Hospitals and Kaiser Foundation Health Plan, Inc. He is responsible for ensuring that Kaiser Permanente meets or exceeds compliance, ethics, and integrity standards with respect to all applicable laws, regulations, and accreditation requirements.

Gustavo García (1915–1964)

Born on July 27, 1915, in Laredo, Texas, Gustavo Garcia was raised and schooled in San Antonio. He graduated with a B.A. from the University of Texas in 1936 and received his law degree from the same institution in 1938. Before being drafted into the Army in 1941, he worked in the district attorney's office and with the city attorney. After the war, García contributed to the founding of the United Nations in San Francisco. After he returned to San Antonio, he and other lawyers filed and won suits against school districts in 1947 and 1948 to desegregate schools for Mexican Americans and during the following years pressured the Texas State Board of Education to enforce desegregation. In 1952 and 1953 he worked with the American G.I. Forum, a civil rights organization founded by Mexican American war veterans, and helped pass an antidiscrimination bill in Texas. Most important and influential of all his civil rights work was the case he and two other Mexican American lawyers brought before the U.S. Supreme Court, *Hernandez v. Texas* (1954), in which they prevailed to have juries in the State of Texas desegregated. They were the first Mexican American attorneys to argue a case before the U.S. Supreme Court, and the decision became a precedent for many other cases, including *Brown v. Board of Education* (1954), which desegregated public education throughout the United States. After the landmark case, García's life unfortunately went into a tailspin involving alcoholism and ultimate disbarment. He died on June 3, 1964. The League of United Latin American Citizens created the Gus C. Garcia Memorial Fund in 1964, and a middle school in San Antonio was named in his honor in 1983.

Ricardo García (?–)

Born in Los Angeles to immigrant parents from Mexico, Ricardo García received his bachelor of arts degree in politics in 1991 from the University of California, Santa Cruz and his juris doctorate in 1995 from the University of California, Berkeley, Boalt Hall School of Law. García started his legal career in 1995 with the San Diego Public Defender's Office. In 1998, he was recruited to the Alternate Public Defender's Office as the youngest attorney in that office. In 2004, García was named director of criminal justice for the American Civil Liberties Union of Southern California. There, he worked on public policy issues in conjunction with city, county, and state agencies. From 2007 to 2009, García supervised the South Bay Branch of the Alternate Public Defender's Office. In 2008, he was awarded the Dale Melvin Ray Memorial Award for excellence in the representation of the indigent. In February 2009, García accepted a position with the Multiple Conflicts Office–Major Cases, a unit of highly regarded attorneys. García was awarded Trial Lawyer of the Year by the Criminal Defense Association of San Diego. In 2018, García became the first Latino public defender for Los Angeles County. García has significant expertise and experience with criminal street gang cases throughout San Diego County, and he lectures regularly on the subject. He is a guest lecturer and adjunct professor at California Western School of Law in its Criminal Justice LLM and ACCESO programs, work that takes him to Mexico,

Chile, and Peru to educate and train judges, prosecutors, and defense attorneys.

Raed González (1963–)

Born on September 27, 1963, in Puerto Rico, Raed González earned his B.A. *cum laude* in 1992 and his J.D. *cum laude* in 1996 from the Inter American University of Puerto Rico in San Juan, and he began practicing law in 1997. He then received his L.L.M. in health law from the University of Houston Law Center in 1998. González is the founder and chief executive officer of González Olivieri, LLC, a highly regarded immigration law firm. He leads a large team of attorneys and staff devoted to providing legal services to Houston's large, diverse immigrant community. His record includes four victories before the U.S. Supreme Court and numerous other published circuit court precedential decisions. González was selected to Super Lawyers for 2013–2020. González and his staff frequently volunteer their time to assist with planning and hosting community citizenship drives, DACA forums, and law enforcement public forums.

José Angel Gutiérrez (1944–)

Born on October 25, 1944, in Crystal City, Texas, the son of a medical doctor, José Angel Gutiérrez grew up witnessing the discrimination and exploitation of farm workers in South Texas. He received a B.A. from Texas A&M University in Kingsville in 1966, an M.A. in political science from St. Mary's University in San Antonio in 1969, a Ph.D. from the University of Texas at Austin in 1976, and a law degree from the University of Houston Law Center in 1988. While at St. Mary's, he met other incipient civil rights activists, who together founded Mexican American Youth Organization (MAYO), a university-based activist organization that spread to campuses throughout the Southwest among the first large generation of Mexican Americans to attend college. After receiving his M.A. degree in political science in 1969, he returned to and supported students in a protest walkout that he helped promote to the larger community of Mexican Americans. In April 1970 the movement was successful in electing Mexican Americans to local city councils and school boards, and they formed a political party called La Raza Unida (The

United People). From this humble beginning, La Raza Unida opened chapters in seventeen states and the District of Columbia. In 1972, Gutiérrez was elected national party chairman, and under his leadership the party went on to challenge the Democratic and Republican parties, which had continued to ignore Mexican American voters and their needs. Under the banner of La Raza Unida, Gutiérrez served as an elected trustee and president of the Crystal City Independent School District (1970–1973), urban renewal commissioner for Crystal City, Texas (1970–1972), and county judge for Zavala County, Texas (1974–1981). After the demise of La Raza Unida Party, Gutiérrez moved to Oregon in 1980 and taught at various colleges until 1985; he also served as the director of Minority Student Services, the director of the Hispanic Services Project for the United Way, and the executive director of the Commission on Economic Development Subcommittee of the National Catholic Conference's Campaign for Human Development. In 1984 he unsuccessfully ran for Oregon state representative. In 1986, he returned to Texas, where he served as an administrative law judge for the City of Dallas and a member of the Dallas Ethics Commission (1999–2000), while teaching at the University of Texas at Arlington, where he founded the Mexican American Studies program and also successfully sued the university for discrimination. From 2000 to 2003 he served as the Texas chair of the National Association of Hispanic and Latino Studies. After retiring form UT-Arlington, he dedicated much of his time to writing; in all he has written thirteen books over the years.

Antonia Hernández (1948–)

Born on May 30, 1948, in Torreón, Coahuila, Mexico, Antonia Hernández immigrated to the United States in 1956. She earned her B.A. at UCLA, a teaching credential at the university's School of Education, and her law degree at the UCLA School of Law in 1974. Hernández began her legal career as a staff attorney with the Los Angeles Center for Law and Justice that same year. In 1977, she became the directing attorney for the Legal Aid Foundation office in Lincoln Heights. An expert in civil rights and immigration issues, Hernández worked with Senator Edward M. Kennedy and the U.S. Senate Committee on the Judiciary in 1979 and 1980. She was also the Southwest regional political coordinator of the Kennedy for President campaign in 1980. Hernández was the president and general counsel of MALDEF from 1985 to 2004, served as its vice president from 1984 to 1985, as employment program director from 1983 to 1984, and as an associate counsel from 1981 to 1983. As president of MALDEF, she directed all litigation and advocacy programs, managed a $4.5 million budget and a 65-person staff, and was responsible for the organization's long-range plans and goals. Among the notable victories of MALDEF led by Hernández was the case against the State of Texas underfunding schools in minority districts, because Texas public school funding led to economic and racial disparities between school districts. MALDEF's suit was successful when the Texas Supreme Court ruled that the Texas Legislature had to require shared funding between school districts. MALDEF then won a similar case in California, where urban schools were receiving less funding than suburban schools. Hernández also led MALDEF in the establishment of bilingual and multicultural programs for Latino students in Denver, Colorado, led Texas to expand higher education programs for Latinos in South Texas, and advocated for undocumented students in California to pay the same tuition as other in-state students at public universities. In 2004, Hernández became the president of the California Community Foundation. Hernández has led the foundation in fundraising and in expanding its grant program to work in the areas of civic engagement and public policy initiatives, notably creating programs for immigrants. In 2013, the National Committee for Responsive Philanthropy awarded its Impact Award for Grantmaking Public Charity to the foundation, citing Hernández's leadership.

Gerald P. López (1948–)

Born in 1948, Gerald López grew up in Southern California, the son and grandson of immigrants who came to the United States to work in mining. López's father died when the boy was fourteen, so

López had to support the family through a variety of menial labors. He attended the University of Southern California. He received his law degree from Harvard Law School in 1974. López then served as law clerk to U.S. District Court judge Edward Schwartz from 1974 to 1975 in San Diego. López has taught at California Western School of Law, UCLA Law School, and Harvard Law School. He has been a professor at Stanford School of Law since 1985. Among the books he has published are *Rebellious Lawyering: One Chicano's Vision of Progressive Law Practice* (1992) and *The Center for Community Problem Solving Guide to a Fair and Just Workplace* (2006). López is a cofounder of the Rebellious Lawyering Institute, which expounds on and trains lawyers in his legal philosophy on the practice of civil-rights and poverty law. The institute has sponsored a number of law conferences in New Mexico and San Francisco beginning in 2008. López's strategies have been applied to immigration law, racial discrimination, mass incarceration, environmental justice, and education reform.

Vilma S. Martínez (1943–)

Vilma Martínez is a partner in the firm of Munger, Tolles & Olson in Los Angeles. Martínez was born in San Antonio, Texas, in 1943. She attended the University of Texas and went on to the Columbia University Law School, where she received her law degree in 1967. As general counsel of MALDEF from 1973 to 1982, Martínez was an influential advocate during the congressional hearings for the Voting Rights Act of 1975, which opened the door to greater access to political participation by Latinos. Martínez also served as a consultant to the U.S. Commission on Civil Rights from 1969 to 1973. From 2009 to 2013, she served as U.S. ambassador to Argentina, the first woman to hold that post.

Miguel Angel Méndez-Longoria (1942–2017)

Born on December 25, 1942, in Brownsville, Texas, to a Mexican American mother and a Mexican father, Miguel Méndez-Longoria attended Texas Southmost College and received his law degree from George Washington University Law School in 1968. Méndez-

Longoria served as a law clerk for the U.S. Court of Claims in Washington, D.C., from 1968 to 1969. He then was legal assistant to U.S. senator Alan Cranston (D-CA) from 1969 to 1971. Méndez-Longoria was a staff attorney for the Mexican American Legal Defense and Educational Fund (MALDEF) in San Francisco from 1971 to 1972 and was deputy director of California Rural Legal Assistance in San Francisco from 1972 to 1974. Méndez-Longoria served as deputy public defender for Monterey County, California, from 1975 to 1976. Beginning in 1976 Méndez-Longoria taught law at the University of Santa Clara Law School, University of California at Berkeley Law School (Boalt Hall), Vermont Law School, University of San Diego Law School, and Stanford University Law School until his retirement in 2009.

Mario G. Obledo (1932–2010)

Born in San Antonio, Texas, one of twelve children to Mexican immigrant parents, Mario Obledo attended the University of Texas, where he was awarded a degree in pharmacy. After serving in the Korean War, he returned to Texas and received his law degree from St. Mary's University Law School in 1961. Obledo was active in Latino affairs for over thirty years. He cofounded the Hispanic National Bar Association (HNBA) and the Mexican-American Legal Defense and Educational Fund (MALDEF), and in the League of United Latin American Citizens (LULAC), he held local, district, state, and national offices, including the presidency. He was also active in the Southwest Voter Registration Project. Obledo was active in government and was a secretary of the California Health and Welfare Agency, where he was instrumental in bringing thousands of Latinos into state government. He also served as California's secretary of health and welfare from 1975 to 1982. Obledo was also an assistant attorney general for Texas. President Bill Clinton presented Obledo with the Presidential Medal of Freedom in 1998.

Michael A. Olivas (1951–)

Born on February 14, 1951, in Tokyo, Japan, while his father was in the Army, Michael Olivas and his family resettled in New Mexico where generations of Olivases had lived. Olivas attended Pontifical College in Columbus, Ohio, where he was awarded a B.A. in 1972 and an M.A. in 1974. He then went on to Ohio State University and received his Ph.D. in 1977. Olivas received his law degree from Georgetown University Law School in 1981. Olivas served as director of resources for the League of United Latin American Citizens (LULAC) Education Resource Center in Washington, D.C., from 1979 to 1982. In 1982, he was named the William B. Bates Distinguished Chair in Law at the University of Houston Law School, where he founded and directed the Institute for Higher Education Law and Governance until his retirement in 2020. He served as associate dean from 1990 to 1995. Since 2002, he has served as a director on the MALDEF Board. He has a substantial and varied legal consulting practice, including representing faculty, staff, institutional, and state clients, serving as an expert witness in federal and state courts (including the U.S. Supreme Court, Circuit Courts of Appeals, and federal district courts) and joining as a member of litigation teams in educational, finance, and immigration matters. From February 2016 until May 2017, Olivas served as the president of the University of Houston–Downtown on an interim basis. Recognized as a national leader in immigration law, higher education law, and discrimination, Olivas is the author or coauthor of fifteen books, including *The Dilemma of Access* (1979), *Latino College Students* (1986), *Prepaid College Tuition Programs* (1993), *The Law and Higher Education* (4th edition, 2015), *"Colored Men" and "Hombres Aquí"* (2006), *Education Law Stories* (2007), *No Undocumented Child Left Behind* (2013), *In Defense of My People: Alonso S. Perales and the Development of Mexican-American Public Intellectuals* (2013), and *Suing Alma Mater* (2019). In 2011, he served as president of the Association of American Law Schools, and in 2018, AALS gave him its Triennial Award for Lifetime Service to Legal Education and the Law. Olivas retired in 2020.

Alonso S. Perales (1898–1960)

Born on October 17, 1898, in Alice, Texas, Alonso Perales became an orphan when he was six years old, and from then on he mostly had to fend for himself. After graduating from high school in

Alice, Perales attended Draughn's Business College in Corpus Christi, after which he was drafted into the U.S. Army during World War I. After the war, he graduated from the Prepatory School in Washington, D.C., and later received a B.A. in the School of Economics and Government at the National University. In 1926 he received a law degree from National University. Throughout the next decades he served on many U.S. diplomatic missions in such countries as Chile, Cuba, the Dominican Republic, Mexico, and Nicaragua. But his diplomatic ventures were far outshined by his civil rights work; as Michael Olivas has said, Perales was a civil rights activist before the concept even existed. After becoming a lawyer—it would have been more difficult in Texas for a Mexican American to achieve this than in Washington, D.C.—he returned to San Antonio, and he founded or led various civil rights organizations; lobbied at all governmental levels for the improvement of the educational, employment, and living conditions of Mexican Americans; wrote columns and broadcast radio programs defending their civil rights and encouraging their political organizing; and even took on several civil rights court cases himself. He cofounded the League of United Latin American Citizens (LULAC) in 1929 and served as its third president; the organization is still very active today. In the early 1930s, he also was one of the founders of the Independent Voters Association, an organization to empower Mexican American voters. In the 1940s and into the 1950s he lobbied unsuccessfully for the passage of a bill in the Texas legislature to prohibit discrimination based on race. An untiring essayist, columnist, and letter-writer, Perales published three books and had others in manuscript form that were never published. Much of his political and antidiscrimination thought can be found in the two volumes of *En Defensa de Mi Raza* (1936, 1937, In Defense of My People). In another book, he challenged the mistreatment of Latinos during the time when the Franklin Roosevelt administration was promoting U.S. policy in Latin America: *Are We Good Neighbors?* (1948). In 1977 an elementary school in the Edgewood Independent School District, next to San Antonio, was named for Alonso S. Perales.

Anthony D. Romero (1965–)

Born on July 9, 1965, in Bronx, New York to Puerto Rican parents, Anthony Romero was the first in his family to receive a high school education. After high school in New Jersey, Romero went on to graduate with a B.A. degree from Princeton University's Woodrow Wilson School of Public and International Affairs in 1987 and a J.D. from Stanford University Law School in 1990. Romero began his career by working on civil rights issues at the Rockefeller and Ford Foundations. In 1996 he became the director of the Ford Foundation's Civil Rights and Social Justice Program. He later directed the Human Rights and International Cooperation Program, making it the largest in the foundation. In September 2001 he became the executive director of the American Civil Liberties Union (ACLU), the largest and most prominent civil rights organization in the United States; he was the first Latino to lead the organization. Under his leadership the ACLU has experienced the fastest and largest growth in its history, with a generously increased budget that allows it to address issues of racial justice, religious freedom, privacy rights, reproductive freedom, LGBT rights, and governmental policies on immigration, children's detention at the southern border, and refugees.

Gerald Torres (1952–)

Gerald Torres was born in Victorville, California. He attended Stanford University, where he received his B.A. in 1974. He received his J.D. degree from Yale Law School in 1977 and his LL.M. degree from the University of Michigan Law School in 1980. He was admitted to the bar in 1978. Torres was staff attorney for the Children's Defense Fund in Washington, D.C., from 1977 to 1978. He began teaching law in 1980 and has taught at the University of Pittsburgh Law School, the University of Minnesota Law School, Harvard Law School, the University of Texas School of Law, and Yale University, where he was appointed professor of environmental justice in the Yale

School of Forestry & Environmental Studies in November 2019. Torres served as U.S. deputy assistant attorney general for environmental and natural resources and Indian affairs, where he established the Office of Tribal Justice. He served on the board of the Environmental Law Institute and on the Environmental Protection Agency's National Environmental Justice Advisory Council. In addition to publishing numerous law review articles, Torres coauthored *The Miner's Canary: Enlisting Race, Resisting Power, Transforming Democracy* (2002). Torres was honored with the 2004 Legal Service Award from the Mexican American Legal Defense and Educational Fund (MALDEF) for his work to advance the legal rights of Latinos.

Gilbert Paul Carrasco and Nicolás Kanellos

RELIGION

The ancestors of today's Latinos, who were already of mixed Spanish, African, and Indigenous heritages, brought Christianity to Florida and the Southwest more than one hundred years before the Pilgrims landed at Plymouth Rock. The soldiers and colonists who settled in those lands were always accompanied by missionaries and other religious. They named most of the towns and settlements in honor of Catholic saints, such as San Antonio, San Diego, San Francisco, and the Virgin Mary herself—as in La Virgin de los Angeles de Porciúncula (the city of Los Angeles's original name). In the new lands, the missionaries recognized the Indigenous populations as having souls and set about the task of converting them to Christianity, even while appropriating their lands and converting them into workers to produce value for the Spanish Crown. The role of Father Eusebio Kino and Father Junípero Serra in setting up a trail of important missions from Arizona to Northern California was extremely important in laying the basis for the religiosity in the West as well as for establishing towns that have become major cities of the United States. Kino established twenty-nine missions and Serra twenty-one missions. The descendants of the Hispanicized-Christianized Indigenous populations of colonial times also are among the people we consider to be Latinos today. By the early nineteenth century,

the missions were secularized because they had either accomplished their evangelical purpose or the Indigenous had fused with the people in the surrounding towns and ranches.

In the nineteenth century, when the United States expanded westward and to the south through conquest and purchase of lands, the Catholic Church took on the responsibility of integrating Latinos into the mainstream. It thus established national parishes for Latinos, with local churches named for their patron saints or the Virgin Mary and the importation of Spanish-speaking priests from Spain and Spanish America. In 1875, Bishop José Sadoc Alemany established Our Lady of Guadalupe parish as the first national Hispanic parish to tend specifically to the Spanish-speaking residents of San Francisco, California, and to unite that community. When the great migrations took place in the twentieth century, during the Mexican Revolution (1910), the incorporation of Puerto Ricans as U.S. citizens (1917), and the Cuban Revolution (1959), these patterns were still functioning, helping to provide religious services and identities for Latinos in their own language and with their own particular religious customs. The importation of priests from outside the United States was due to the failure of the church to recruit and train U.S. Latinos for the clergy. In 1936,

Our Lady of Guadalupe Church in San Francisco, California, built in 1912, is a San Francisco Designated Landmark.

Mariana S. Garriga was appointed bishop of the diocese of Corpus Christi, Texas, becoming the first U.S. Latino and first Mexican American to be named a Catholic bishop. It was not until 1970 that another U.S.-born Latino priest was ordained as a bishop: Patrick Flores, the son of poor migrant workers from Ganado, Texas. And in 1973, a New Mexico–born Latino, Robert Sánchez, became the first Mexican American archbishop, of Santa Fe. Today, there are twenty-seven active Latino Catholic bishops in the United States. The Protestants, however, were not as quick to elevate Latinos to church leadership; it was not until 1995, for instance, that Reverend Leopoldo Alard was elected a bishop of the Episcopal church, in the Episcopal Diocese of Texas.

The nineteenth century also saw the targeting of Hispanics in Spanish America and the United States for conversion to Protestant religions. As early as 1871, a former Catholic priest, Alejo Hernández, converted to the Methodist faith in Corpus Christi, Texas. Many others followed. As opposed to the national parishes fostered by the Catholics, the Protestants discouraged ethnic churches and, instead, worked for assimilation of the Latinos, often ignoring or not encouraging Latino cultural practices. Becoming Protestant quite often meant "Americanization" of the Latinos. One of the most successful of the mainstream Latino Protestant churches, however, emerged in 1939 as the Rio Grande Conference of Latino Methodists in Texas and New Mexico. Among its leaders was Francisco Ramos, the first Latino to receive a B.D. degree from Southern Methodist University. During the mid- and late twentieth century, furthermore, Southern Baptists and Pentecostals made large inroads into Latino faith communities. Pentecostal popularity—which grew by leaps and bounds, particularly in Puerto Rico—seems to rest among Latinos in the church's small-community atmosphere as well as its respect for Latino identity and cultural practices.

According to a 2007 Pew study of Latino religious tendencies, 68 percent of Latinos are Catholics, 20 percent are Protestants, 3 percent are other types of Christians (Jehovah's Witnesses, Mormons, Orthodox), 1 percent are adherents of other religions, and 8 percent define themselves as secular. Among Latinos nationally, 68 percent of Catholics, 55 percent of evangelicals/Pentecostals, and 35 percent of mainline Protestants were born in Latin America. Overall, the religious affiliations and diverse religious practices of Latinos have been critical to their evolving as ethnic or minority groups in the United States. Part of the Americanization process of Puerto Ricans on the island and on the mainland was their being targeted by Protestant missionaries. An integral part of the practice of Mormonism is the conversion of Latin Americans and Native Americans, thus the need for missionary experience in Latin America for the Church of Jesus Christ of Latter-day Saints. During the Mexican Revolution, the Catholic Church set up its hierarchy in exile, in Texas and Southern California, and this helped to solidify the Catholic identity of Mexicans and Mexican Americans in the United

States. In Mexico, an entire war was fought (and funded in part by religious exiles and immigrant communities in the United States) over the role of religion in Mexican life: the Cristero War, 1926–29. From the 1920s through the 1960s, churches and church societies became the most stable and unifying institutions in the immigrant communities of Cubans, Mexicans, Puerto Ricans, and Spaniards. Quite often, the first institution that immigrants constructed in their new home was that of a church named for their patron saint; affiliated with the churches were the numerous lay organizations they founded. An example of such societies is the Círculo de Obreros Católicos San José in East Chicago, Indiana, in the 1920s and 1930s, which preserved language, faith, and culture by performing plays, sponsoring fundraising dances and bazaars, publishing newspapers, and even organizing civil rights protests.

As much as the historical role of religion in building Latino communities is often unrecognized, even the religious background of civil-rights, land-rights, and workers'-rights movements in the 1960s and 1970s is often ignored or minimized by political scientists and historians. The beginning of the Chicano Movement, with farm-worker strikes and boycotts as well as school walkouts, was largely successful not only because churches and religious personnel, both Catholic and Protestant, offered meeting facilities, guidance, and funding but also because of the spirituality of the leaders and participants themselves, who often openly prayed and invoked religious symbolism to inspire and motivate the participants. Even the most militant struggle to recover ancestral lands in New Mexico was led by a Pentecostal minister, Reies López Tijerina, in the late 1960s. In 1965, furthermore, the Migrant Ministry of the National Council of Churches, a Protestant organization, became the first religious group in the history of labor organizing to support the formation of a labor union, the United Farm Workers Union. And the contem-

Afro-Cuban drummers in Havana perform a toque de santo, a ceremony found in Santería, a Catholic-African religion developed in the Caribbean. The development of salsa music is inconceivable without Santería, which also informs the Nuyorican poetry movement.

porary literary movement, which has helped define Latino identity in the United States, has done so by exploring Hispanic spirituality and religious practices, so clear in such foundational works as Piri Thomas's *Down These Mean Streets* and *Savior, Savior, Hold My Hand*, Tomás Rivera's *… y no se lo tragó la tierra/And the Earth Did Not Devour Him*, Pat Mora's *Chants,* and Rudolfo Anaya's *Bless Me, Ultima.* Numerous other religious beliefs and practices have helped define a Latino identity; for example, the development of salsa music is inconceivable without Santería (a syncretic Catholic-African religion developd in the Caribbean), which also informs the Nuyorican poetry movement, especially as practiced by Sandra María Esteves and Tato Laviera. Similarly, Santería is evident in such Cuban American visual arts as the canvases of Paul Sierra. The devotion to the Virgin of Guadalupe has informed much of Chicano easel and mural art, as practiced among many others by Yolanda López and Judy Valdez, and Chicano theater, especially as pioneered by the movement's founder, Luis Valdez, in such works as *La Carpa de la Familia Rascuache* and *La Pastorela.*

> The sheer number Catholic, Baptist, Presbyterian, and Methodist books and periodicals that have circulated in Latino communities and are still available attests to purposeful and intelligent pursuit of religion and spirituality among Latinos.

During the nineteenth and twentieth centuries, Latinos developed an intellectual basis for their religiosity by establishing and maintaining publishing houses that produced hundreds of books and periodicals, many of them founded during the period of exile of the religious from Mexico during the Revolution, but still functioning today, as is the Centro Bautista de Publicaciones (Baptist Publishing Center) in El Paso. The sheer number of Catholic, Baptist, Presbyterian, and Methodist religious books and periodicals that have circulated in Latino communities and that are still available in Paulist, Baptist, and Pentecostal bookstores attests to purposeful and intelligent pursuit of religion and spirituality among Latinos today. These publications are also an indication of the diversity of Latino religiosity in all the varieties of language, from Spanish to English and even Ladino, the archaic Spanish written by the Sephardic Jews.

LEADING LATINO RELIGIOUS FIGURES

Leopoldo J. Alard (1941–2003)

Born on March 11, 1941, in Havana, Cuba, Leopoldo Alard immigrated to the United States in 1961. He graduated from Stetson University in Deland, Florida, and the Episcopal Theological Seminary of the Caribbean in Puerto Rico in 1967 with a master's in divinity. He was ordained in 1968 and served as vicar of St. Mark's in Chattahoochee, Florida. In 1986, Alard became the executive director of the Center for Hispanic Ministries of the Province of the Southwest (VII) in Texas and the Canon for Hispanic Ministries in the Diocese of Texas. In 1995, he became the canon for multicultural ministry and was elected bishop suffragan. In 1996, he received a doctorate from the Episcopal Theological Seminary of the Southwest in Austin, Texas. He was the first Hispanic to be elected bishop in the Episcopal Church, USA.

Minerva G. Carcaño (1954–)

Born on January 20, 1954, in Edinburg, Texas, Minerva Carcaño graduated from the University of Texas–Pan American in 1975 and received a master of theology degree from Perkins School of Theology of Southern Methodist University in 1979. She was ordained an elder in the United Methodist Church in 1979. She subsequently served as pastor in churches in California and Texas. In 1986, she became the first Hispanic woman to be appointed a United Methodist district superintendent, serving in West Texas, New Mexico, and Oregon. From 2004 to 2012, she served as the bishop of the Phoenix Episcopal Area, becoming the first Hispanic woman to be elected to the episcopacy of the United Methodist Church, the second-largest Protestant denomination in the United States. In 2012 she became the resident bishop of the Los Angeles Episcopal Area, providing oversight to the California-Pacific Annual Conference of the United Methodist Church. In 2016, she served in a similar capacity as the resident bishop of the San Francisco Episcopal Area.

Patrick Flores (1929–2017)

Born in Ganado, Texas, on July 26, 1929, to migrant worker parents, Patrick Flores attended St. Mary's Seminary in La Porte, Texas, and St. Mary's Seminary in Houston. He was ordained a Catholic priest on May 26, 1956, and served in a variety of functions in the Houston-Galveston diocese. In 1970, Pope Paul VI appointed him to serve as the auxiliary bishop of San Antonio, becoming the first Mexican American to be elevated to the hierarchy of the church in the United States since 1936. On May 29, 1978, Flores was installed as the bishop of the diocese of El Paso and on October 13, 1979, as archbishop of the archdiocese of San Antonio, the largest ecclesiastical province in the United States. In 1986, he was awarded the Ellis Island Medal of Freedom in honor of the Statue of Liberty's one hundredth birthday. Flores retired in 2004.

Mariano S. Garriga (1886–1965)

Born on May 30, 1886, in Port Isabel, Texas, Mariano Garriga studied at St. Mary College in Kansas City, Kansas, and at St. Francis Seminary in Milwaukee, Wisconsin. He was ordained to the priesthood on July 2, 1911. He then served as assistant chancellor of the Archdiocese of San Antonio until 1912, when he became a curate in Marfa. After serving as a chaplain to the National Guard during World War I, he served from 1919 to 1936 as pastor of St. Cecilia Church in San Antonio. He also served as president of Incarnate Word College. He became a papal chamberlain in October 1934 and a domestic prelate in September 1935.

On June 20, 1936, Garriga was appointed coadjutor bishop of Corpus Christi by Pope Pius XI. He thus became the first Mexican American bishop and the first Catholic bishop of a Texas diocese to be born in the state. In addition to his episcopal duties, he served as pastor of St. Peter Church in Laredo (1936–1948). On March 15, 1949, Garriga became the bishop of Corpus Christi, Texas.

Justo L. González (1937–)

Born in Havana, Cuba, on August 9, 1937, Justo González attended United Seminary in Cuba and received his master of sacred theology, master of arts, and Ph.D. from Yale University. He was the youngest person to be awarded the historical theology doctorate at Yale. González taught at the Evangelical Seminary of Puerto Rico for eight years, followed by another eight years at Candler School of Theology of Emory University in Georgia. González is a leading voice in the growing field of Hispanic theology, one of the few first-generation Latino theologians to come from a Protestant background. He was the cofounder of the first academic journal related to Latino/a theology, *Apuntes*, published by the Mexican American Program of Perkins School of Theology at Southern Methodist University. He also helped to found the Association for Hispanic Theological Education. González is the author of more than twenty books, including *Santa Biblia: The Bible through Hispanic Eyes* (1996), *The Story Luke Tells: Luke's Unique Witness to the Gospel* (2015), *Three Months with Revelation* (2004), *Tres meses en la escuela de Patmos: Estudios sobre el Apocalipsis* (1997, Three Months in the School of Patmos: Studies), and *Introducción a la historia de la iglesia* (2011, Introduction to the History of the Church). He is the recipient of the Ecumenism Award from Washington Theological Consortium in recognition of his ecumenical work to unify churches with a variety of denominational backgrounds.

Guillermo Maldonado (1965–)

Born on January 10, 1965, in Honduras, Guillermo Maldonado received his master of divinity from Oral Roberts University and his doctorate of divinity from Vision International University. He started a church with twelve members in 1996 and eventually became the pastor of El Rey Jesus, a Christian Apostolic and Prophetic church located in Miami, Florida, with a general attendance between fifteen thousand and twenty thousand individuals per week. According to *Christian News Report*, the church is the largest Hispanic church in the United States. Maldonado has written some fifty books, two of which have won the Spanish Evangelical Press Association award for the best original books in Spanish: *La Gloria de Dios* (2012, The Glory of God) and *Cómo Caminar en el Poder Sobrenatural de Dios* (2014, How to Walk in the Supernatural Power of God). Maldonado's international television program *The Supernatural Now* appears regularly on various religious networks.

Nelson J. Pérez (1961–)

Born in Miami, Florida, on June 16, 1961, Nelson Pérez was raised in West New York, New Jersey. He earned a B.A. in psychology from Montclair State University (1983) and a master of divinity and a master of arts in theology in 1988 and 1989, respectively, from Saint Charles Borromeo Seminary in Philadelphia, where he was ordained a priest in 1989. He subsequently served as a pastor at various churches in the Philadelphia area and in 1998 was named chaplain to Pope John Paul II, with the title of monsignor. In 2009, he was named a prelate of honor by Pope Benedict XVI. In 2012, Pope Benedict XVI appointed Reverend Monsignor Pérez auxiliary bishop of the Diocese of Rockville Centre in New York. In 2017, Pérez was appointed by Pope Francis as the eleventh bishop of the Diocese of Cleveland. As a member of the United States Conference of Catholic Bishops, Pérez serves as chair of the Bishops' Standing Committee on Cultural Diversity. In 2020, Pope Francis appointed him the fourteenth bishop and tenth archbishop of the Archdiocese of Philadelphia.

Samuel Rodríguez (1969–)

Born in Puerto Rico on September 29, 1969, Samuel Rodríguez is an Evangelical Christian pastor, movie producer, author, civil rights activist, and television personality. He is the president of the National Hispanic Christian Leadership Conference. In 1992, he became an ordained minister in the Assemblies of God, a Pentecostal denomination. In 2000, he founded the National Hispanic Christian Leadership Conference, the largest Hispanic Evangelical Christian organization in the world, with more than forty thousand Latino Evangelical churches as members. Rodríguez became a member of the board of the National Association of Evangelicals in 2013. In June 2016, his book *Be Light* reached number one on the *Los Angeles Times* bestseller list. *You Are Next*, released in 2019, was a *Publishers Weekly* bestseller. He has also produced commercial films through Twentieth Century-Fox. Under President Barack Obama, he served in the White House Office of Faith-Based and Neighborhood Partnerships initiative and the President's Advisory Council on Faith-Based and Neighborhood Partnerships. He delivered an invocation at the inauguration of Donald Trump on January 20, 2017. *Forbes* called him America's most prominent Latino Evangelical leader.

Gabriel Salguero (?–)

Born in Puerto Rico, Gabriel Salguero received his B.A. in history from Rutgers University and his M.Div. (magna cum laude) from New Brunswick Theological Seminary, and he did postgraduate work in Christian social ethics at Union Theological Seminary in New York. He is the senior pastor of the multicultural Lamb's Church in New York City. His life's work is bringing an ethical framework to public policy and empowering multicultural leadership. He is the founder of P.O.G. International, a ministry focused on diversity leadership empowerment and training. He is also the president of the National Latino Evangelical Coalition. The *Huffington Post* and other media have recognized him as one of the national Latino faith leaders. Salguero is a board member of the National Association of Evangelicals and previously served as the director of the Institute for Faith and Public Life as well as the Hispanic Leadership Program at Princeton Theological Seminary.

Junípero Serra (1713–1784)

Born on November 24, 1713, in Petra, Mallorca, Spain, Miquel Josep Serra i Ferrer was the Franciscan friar who is credited with founding the large chain of Catholic missions during the settlement of California by subjects of the Spanish crown. On July 16, 1769, he established the first mission of what would become Alta California in San Diego. Traveling more than ten thousand miles, Serra eventually founded ten missions and converted more than sixty-eight hundred Native Americans. Many of the missions he and his Franciscan entourage founded became the hub for today's cities. These included Mission Basilica San Diego de Alcalá, July 16, 1769, present-day San Diego; Mission San Carlos Borromeo de Carmelo, June 3, 1770, today Carmel-by-the-Sea; Mission San Antonio de Padua, July 14, 1771; Mission San Gabriel Arcángel, September 8, 1771, today San Gabriel; Mission San Luis Obispo de Tolosa, September 1, 1772, today the city of San Luis Obispo; Mission San Juan Capistrano, November 1, 1776, today San Juan Capistrano; Mission San Francisco de Asís, June 29, 1776, today San Francisco; Mission Santa Clara de Asís, January 12, 1777, today Santa Clara; Mission San Buenaventura, March 31, 1782, today Ventura; and the founding of the Presidio of Santa Barbara, today Santa Barbara, on April 21, 1782. Serra set up the system that produced Indigenous souls for the Catholic Church and economic value for the California settlements and the Crown by administering the labor, cattle, and crops tended by the converted Amerindians. In particular, the cattle hides and tallow produced by the missions were in high demand even in the new American Republic on the coast of North America. Serra was beatified by Pope John Paul II on September 25, 1988, and Pope Francis canonized him on September 23, 2015.

Félix Varela (1788–1853)

Born on November 20, 1788, in Havana, Cuba, Félix Francisco Varela y Morales was raised in St. Augustine, Florida, when it was a colony of Spain. At age fourteen, he entered the San Carlos Seminary in Havana to train for the priesthood. Upon becoming a priest and earning his baccalaureate in 1811, Varela began

teaching philosophy at San Carlos. He became known as Cuba's foremost philosopher, which also led to his involvement in politics, his subsequent exile to the United States, and leadership of the Cuban independence movement. Varela served as the Catholic vicar of New York City, tending principally to Irish immigrants, and pursued a career as a writer and theologian. In fact, many of his numerous works and his actions within the church hierarchy laid the basis for the Catholic Church in the United States, when Catholics were discriminated against as papists and obscurantists. One of his most famous books is *Cartas a Elpidio* (1835, Letters to Elpidio), which is about piety, fanaticism, and superstition. From 1834 to 1843, Varela coedited the monthly *Expositor Católico y Almacén Literario* (Catholic Expositor and Literary Storehouse) and also edited the *Children's Catholic Magazine* (1838), *Young Catholic's Magazine* (1840), and the *Catholic Expositor and Literary Magazine* (1841). In 1850, Varela retired to the town of his childhood, St. Augustine, where he died on February 18, 1853.

Nicolás Kanellos

THE MILITARY

Latinos have served in the military throughout American history. In fact, the ancestors of today's Latinos served as soldiers in the exploration and settlement of large parts of what became the United States. Mestizo, mulatto, and Spanish naval and foot soldiers even participated in the flotilla of General Bernardo de Gálvez (namesake of Galveston, Texas), attacking and blockading British forces in the Gulf of Mexico to safeguard the supply chains up the Mississippi to George Washington's Continental Army during the American Revolution. Gálvez's taking of Pensacola is commemorated on a U.S. postal stamp issued in 1980. A Spanish citizen by the name of Jorge Farragut also fought in the Continental Army and achieved the rank of major. His son, David Farragut, became the first admiral of the U.S. Navy. And so it has been into the present that Latinos have served with distinction in every military enterprise of the United States, including fighting on both sides during the Civil War, serving overseas in both world wars, and fighting in the wars in Vietnam, Korea, and the Middle East. Proportionately, Latinos have been more decorated than other soldiers, beginning with their heroism during World War II. Mexican American soldiers, in particular, were decorated with more Medals of Honor than those of any other ethnic group.

While Latinos more often served in the lowest of ranks and often in all-Latino battalions, beginning with the Korean War, more of them were promoted to higher rank. And in the mid-1970s the military academies began to graduate Latinos into the officer corps. Today Latinos are represented in all ranks and command diverse groups of men and women. In 1964 Horacio Rivero became the first Latino four-star admiral of modern times, and in 1976 Richard E. Cavazos became the first Latino general in the U.S. Army. In 1979 Edward Hidalgo became the first Latino secretary of the Navy. More recently, General Ricardo Sánchez held the top military position in Iraq, commanding the coalition ground forces in the U.S.-led occupation of the country.

OUTSTANDING LATINOS IN THE MILITARY

Christina Alvarado (?–)

Born in Raleigh, North Carolina, Christina Alvarado is a graduate of the Alexandria Hospital School of Nursing in Alexandria, Virginia, and the Columbia University School of Nursing in New York, and she

Bernardo de Gálvez y Madrid, Spanish viceroy of New Spain, became the namesake of Galveston, Texas.

holds a master of health care administration from the University of North Carolina, School of Public Health. She became a rear admiral and was the first nurse to command Naval Reserve (NR) Expeditionary Medical Facility (EMF) Dallas One, a commissioned unit whose mission is expeditionary medicine. Alvarado began her Navy Reserve career as a direct commissioned officer and attended school at the Naval Air Station in Pensacola, Florida. She was called to active duty from 1990 to 1991 in support of Operations Desert Shield and Desert Storm and served in the Neurosurgical Intensive Care Unit at the National Naval Medical Center in Bethesda, Maryland. In January 2002, she was again called to active duty in support of Operations Noble Eagle and Enduring Freedom. She served as the executive officer of the Operational Health Support Unit in Jacksonville, Florida, from 2008 to 2010 and commanding officer of EMF Dallas One from 2010 to 2012. Her military awards include

the Legion of Merit, Meritorious Service Medal, Navy and Marine Corps Commendation Medal (four awards), Navy and Marine Corps Achievement Medal (two awards), Meritorious Unit Commendation (two awards), the Armed Forces Reserve Medal with "M" device, and the National Defense Medal (two awards).

Richard E. Cavazos
(1929–2017)

Born in Kingsville, Texas, on January 31, 1929, Richard Cavazos received a B.S. in science from Texas Tech University and was commissioned a first lieutenant in 1951. During thirty years of military service, he commanded forces in Vietnam and served in the Pentagon. In 1976 he became commanding general of the 9th Infantry Division and post commander of Fort Lewis, Washington—thus becoming the first Latino general in the U.S. Army. From 1982 to 1984 Cavazos served as commander of the U.S. Armed Forces Command in Fort McPherson, Georgia. He retired in 1984; during his career he received the Distinguished Service Cross with oak leaf cluster, the Silver Star with oak leaf cluster, the Defense Superior Medal, the Legion of Honor, the Purple Heart, and numerous other decorations.

Pedro A. del Valle
(1893–1978)

Born on August 28, 1893, in San Juan, Puerto Rico, Pedro del Valle graduated from the U.S. Naval Academy in 1915 and served on the USS *Texas* during World War I. Del Valle rose up through the ranks and in 1942 he was promoted to brigadier general, becoming the first Latino U.S. Marine general. In World War II he served as commanding officer of the 11th Marines and assisted in the seizure and defense of Guadalcanal, Tulagi, Russell, and Florida Islands. In 1944 he served as the commanding general of the Third Corps Artillery, Third Amphibious Corps. Among his many decorations are the Gold Star and the Distinguished Service Medal. After the war del Valle served as inspector general and later as director of personnel for the Marine Corps.

David G. Farragut (1801–1872)

Born in Campbell's Station, Tennessee, the son of Spanish immigrant Jorge Farragut, who had served in the Continental Army during the American Revolution, at the age of thirteen David Farragut served as a midshipman aboard the USS *Essex* in the war of 1812. In 1854 he established the Mare Island Naval Shipyard near San Francisco. During the Civil War he took New Orleans in 1862 and proceeded up the Mississippi to capture Vicksburg after heavy fighting and break the Confederate supply lines. In 1864 he took Mobile, Alabama. It was at the Mobile battle that he uttered the famous words "Damn the torpedoes! Full speed ahead!" Farragut was commissioned admiral of the Navy on July 26, 1866, and thus became the first Latino to achieve such a high rank. This would not be repeated for almost one hundred years.

Belisario D. J. Flores (1926–2018)

Born in Eagle Pass, Texas, on July 22, 1926, Belisario Flores began his career in the Army Enlisted Reserve Corps in March 1944 and was called to active duty in January 1945. From 1946 to 1948 he attended San Antonio College, and in 1950 he obtained a B.B.A. degree from St. Mary's University, whereupon he was commissioned a second lieutenant of artillery. He joined a reserve unit at Dodd Field and served until he was called to active duty in 1951, serving until 1953 as an artillery officer. Flores remained in the Inactive Reserve program until May 1955, when he was appointed in the Texas Air National Guard as supply officer. By 1964 he was promoted to comptroller. In 1966 he was assigned as commander of the 149th Combat Support Squadron, where he served until his appointment as assistant adjutant general on September 1, 1971. In 1974 he became a brigadier general, the first Latino to be promoted to general in the National Guard of Texas. His decorations include the Bronze Star Medal, the Legion of Merit, the Air Force Commendation Medal, and the Air Force Outstanding Unit Award.

Diego E. Hernández (1934–2017)

Born on March 25, 1934, in San Juan, Puerto Rico, Diego Hernández received a bachelor of science degree from the Illinois Institute of Technology in 1955 and an M.S. in international affairs from George Washington University in 1969. Among his important command posts were commanding officer on the aircraft carrier USS *John F. Kennedy* (1980–81) and chief of staff of the Naval Air Forces Atlantic Fleet (1982). Hernández was promoted to vice admiral in 1985. His last assignment on active duty was as deputy commander in chief of the U.S. Space Command (1986–89), dual hatted as vice commander, North American Aerospace Defense Command. Among his decorations are the Distinguished Service Medal with Gold Star, the Distinguished Flying Cross, the Purple Heart, and numerous others. He also held decorations from abroad, including the Venezuelan Naval Order of Merit and the Peruvian Cross of Naval Merit.

Benjamin F. Montoya (1935–2015)

Born on May 24, 1935, in Indio, California, Benjamin Montoya graduated with a B.S. degree in naval science from the U.S. Naval Academy in 1958; he also received a B.S. degree in engineering from Rensselaer Polytechnic Institute in 1960 and an M.S. degree in environmental engineering from the Georgia Institute of Technology in 1968. He received a law degree from Georgetown University in 1981. Montoya's naval career spanned thirty-two years. Beginning with two tours in Vietnam, he rose through the ranks to become commander of Naval Facilities Engineering Command and chief of civil engineers. He served at the Pentagon as the director of the Environmental Protection and Occupational Safety and Health Division. Montoya served as a rear admiral from 1958 to 1989. Among his decorations are the Defense Distinguished Service Medal, two Legions of Merit, the Bronze Star with combat "V" for service in Vietnam, and a number of other citations. In 1989 he was named Hispanic Engineer of the Year.

Horacio Rivero
(1910–2000)

Born on May 16, 1910, in Ponce, Puerto Rico, Horacio Rivero graduated from the U.S. Naval Academy in 1931 and began serving on a variety of cruisers and battleships. During World War II he saw considerable action in the Pacific, participating in the Iwo Jima and Okinawa campaigns and the first carrier raids on Tokyo. He was awarded the Legion of Merit for saving the USS *Pittsburgh* and preventing loss of life during a fierce typhoon in 1945. In 1955 he was promoted to rear admiral; in 1962 he was promoted to vice admiral. In 1964 he was promoted to admiral and became vice chief of naval operations. In 1968 he commanded NATO forces as commander in chief of Allied Forces, Southern Europe. He retired in 1971 and was later named ambassador to Spain.

David M. Rodríguez
(1954–)

Born on May 23, 1954, in Overbrook, Pennsylvania, David Rodríguez graduated from the U.S. Military Academy at West Point, New York, in 1976, and was commissioned an officer. He also received a master of arts in national security and strategic studies from the U.S. Naval War College and a master of military art and science from the U.S. Army Command and General Staff College. Rodríguez accrued extensive combat experience in Operation Just Cause (1989–90); in Desert Shield/Desert Storm (1990–91); and in Afghanistan, where he served as deputy commander and commander of the International Security Assistance Force Joint Command. Rodríguez commanded at every level across the U.S. Army. His assignments included the commanding general of the U.S. Army Forces Command and the International Security Assistance Force–Joint Command. He achieved the rank of four-star general in 2011. His decorations include Defense Distinguished Service Medal with two bronze oak leaf clusters, the Army Distinguished Service Medal, the Defense Superior Service Medal, and the Legion of Merit.

Richard A. Rodríguez (?–)

Born in Pacifica, California, to poor Mexican parents, Richard Rodríguez graduated from the U.S. Naval Academy (USNA) in Annapolis, Maryland, with a B.S. in political science and from Xavier University in Cincinnati, Ohio, with an M.B.A. Rodríguez received his naval commission in 1988 and completed basic underwater demolition/SEAL training in 1989. He served overseas in Operations Desert Shield, Desert Storm, Iraqi Freedom, and Enduring Freedom. Command tours included Navy Reserve (NR) Special Boat Team Twenty, NR Naval Special Warfare Unit 10, and NR Naval Special Warfare Group Three. He also served as commanding officer in the Office of Military Representative to the North Atlantic Treaty Organization Military Committee. In 2017 he was promoted to rear admiral of the U.S. Navy. After retiring from the Navy, Rodríguez has served as a senior executive with several home building and real estate development companies in the United States and abroad.

Angela Salinas
(1953–)

Born on December 6, 1953, in Alice, Texas, Angela Salinas enlisted in the U.S. Marine Corps in May 1974, whereupon she was assigned as a legal services clerk at Camp Pendleton. In 1977 she graduated from Dominican College of San Rafael with a B.A. in history and was commissioned as a second lieutenant. She subsequently worked her way up the ranks, serving in a variety of positions, and in 1993, Salinas became a deputy, a special assistant for general/flag officer matters in the Office of the Director, Joint Staff at the Pentagon. In 1996, she assumed command of the 4th Recruit Training Battalion at Parris Island. In 2006, Salinas was promoted to the rank of brigadier general, becoming the first Latino to hold that rank in the Marines and assuming command of the Marine Corps Recruit Depot San Diego. In 2012 she was promoted to major general. In 2013 she retired as the highest ranking female in the Marines. Her decorations include the Legion of Merit, Navy and Marine Corps

Achievement Medal, and the Global War on Terrorism Service Medal.

Henry Gabriel Sánchez (1907–1978)

Born on December 29, 1907, in New York City, Henry Gabriel Sánchez graduated from the U.S. Naval Academy in 1926 and became a naval aviator. He achieved the rank of commander in 1947 and later advanced to rear admiral upon retirement in 1959. During World War II he commanded the Fighting Squadron Seventy-Two, for which he received the Air Medal, a Gold Star, and the Distinguished Flying Cross. From 1946 to 1949 he served as chief of the Aviation Ships Section in the Office of the Chief of Naval Operations, Navy Department, Washington, D.C. He then served on the staff of the commander in chief, U.S. Naval Forces, Eastern Atlantic Mediterranean. Sánchez also received the Presidential Unit Citation with three stars and the China Service Medal, among others.

Ricardo Sánchez (1953–)

Born on September 9, 1953, in Rio Grande City, Texas, Ricardo Sánchez graduated from Texas A&M University–Kingsville in 1973 majoring in mathematics and history, joined the U.S. Army, and worked his way up the ranks. In 1991 as a lieutenant colonel, Sánchez served as a battalion commander during Operation Desert Storm. In 2001, he was promoted to general and became commander of the 1st Armored Division V Corps; in 2003 he became commander of Combined Joint Task Force 7, the coalition ground forces in the U.S.-led occupation of Iraq. Sánchez held the top military position in Iraq during the most critical period of the war—after the fall of the Hussein regime and when the insurgency began its counterattack. Among his decorations are the Defense Distinguished Medal, Army Distinguished Service Medal with one oak leaf cluster, the Legion of Merit, and the Global War on Terrorism Service Medal.

Alfred A. Valenzuela (1948–)

Alfred Valenzuela was born in Refugio, Texas, in 1948, into a family of modest means that worked as migrant agricultural laborers. He graduated from St. Mary's University in 1970 and was commissioned as a field artillery officer, first stationed in Fort Hood, Texas, but his career took him to Peru, Colombia, Grenada, El Salvador, Korea, Somalia, Kuwait, and other countries. When promoted to major general in 1998, he became the highest ranking Latino in the U.S. military at that time—only one of three Latino generals active. He served during the Cold War, Gulf War, and the Iraq and Afghanistan wars. He served in three combat corps and six infantry divisions. Upon his retirement in 2004 he received the highest peacetime awards: the Defense and Army Distinguished Service Medals. Valenzuela is the author of *No Greater Love: The Lives and Times of Hispanic Soldiers* (2008). President Barack Obama named Valenzuela to be a part of the ten-member World War I Centennial Commission to commemorate and spread awareness of the Great War.

Dennis Vélez (?–)

A native of Adjuntas, Puerto Rico, Dennis Vélez graduated from the U.S. Naval Academy in 1992 with a B.S. in aerospace engineering. He earned a master's degree in information technology management from Touro College in 2006. He held a number of positions at sea, including operations officer and air defense officer aboard the USS *Gettysburg*, assistant to the deputy commander with the Second Fleet/Striking Fleet Atlantic, and commanding officer aboard the USS *Fitzgerald*, and he was forward deployed to Yokosuka, Japan. He also commanded the USS *San Jacinto* and was air defense commander for the Eisenhower Strike Group. He has operational experience in the Pacific, Atlantic, Middle East, Mediterranean, Caribbean, and Southwest Asia theaters. He was an assistant director for political-military affairs, Asia.

More recently, Velez served as senior military assistant to the secretary of the Navy. Now a rear admiral, Vélez assumed the duties of commander, Navy recruiting command in April 2020. He is the recipient of the Navy League of the United States 2016 John Paul Jones Award for Inspirational Leadership. His personal military decorations include the Defense Superior Service, Legion of Merit, Meritorious Service, the Navy Commendation, and the Navy Achievement Medals.

Carmelita Vigil-Schimmenti (1936–)

Born on December 16, 1936, in Albuquerque, New Mexico, Carmelita Vigil-Schimmenti received a degree in nursing from the Regina School of Nursing in Albuquerque (1957) and joined the U.S. Air Force Nursing Corps in 1958. She later received a B.S. in nursing from the University of Pittsburgh (1966). In July 1966, she was assigned to the USAF School of Health Care Sciences, Sheppard Air Force Base, Texas, as an instructor in the Medical Service Specialist Course. In 1974 she earned a master of public health degree from the University of North Carolina. Vigil-Schimmenti served in various positions until March 1983, when she was selected as command nurse, Headquarters Strategic Air Command, Offutt Air Force Base in Nebraska. In October 1985, Vigil-Schimmenti became the first Hispanic female to attain the rank of brigadier general. She became chief of the U.S. Air Force Nurse Corps, Office of the Surgeon General, Headquarters U.S. Air Force, Washington, D.C. Her decorations include the Air Force Distinguished Service Medal, the Legion of Merit, and the Meritorious Service Medal with oak leaf cluster.

Nicolás Kanellos

SCIENCE, TECHNOLOGY, AND MEDICINE

From scientific experiment and medical practice in medieval Spain, often in the hands of the Arabs inhabiting the Iberian peninsula; on through the colonization of the Americas where European science was enriched with the Indigenous knowledge of agronomy, astronomy, and mathematics; and into current times, when Latinos have won Nobel prizes, Latinos have distinguished themselves in the natural sciences, technology, and medicine. It should be remembered that the first universities in the Western Hemisphere—in Santo Domingo, Mexico, and Peru—were founded by the Spanish and have furthered experimentation and knowledge to this day. And such technologies as the printing press, the plow, and mining tools and techniques also facilitated the development of new knowledge systems and their dissemination throughout the hemisphere.

In Spain the Arabic cities of Córdoba, Sevilla, and Toledo became centers of learning in the Early Middle Ages, with universities that drew students from the rest of Europe. Arabs were the inventors of algebra and were able to apply the principles of mathematics to everything they did, including architecture, design, and landscaping. Originating in arid climates, they became superb horticulturalists and agronomists and developed systems of water management and irrigation that survive today in many parts of the Americas, including the United States. Their advances in medical science extended, for example, to mastering delicate corneal operations.

The native peoples of the Americas had also advanced scientific knowledge and technology before the arrival of the Europeans by joining their knowledge with what they had assimilated from Arabic culture and classical knowledge. Native Americans were outstanding horticulturalists and agronomists who developed a type of grass into the corn that became a staple in the diet of millions of people around the world, a product whose oils and sugar content is to be found in myriad foods and technological products. The Indigenous people also contributed the potato, which has become a universal dietary staple. Add beans, tomatoes, and squash to the list of the foodstuffs that the Indigenous peoples developed from wild plants over thousands of years. The Native Americans, in addition, were ecologists and land and game managers who respected the wildlife and all of the natural world in everything they did—an attitude we strive to emulate today to save the planet. In their observations of the natural world, Native Americans were advanced astronomers, whose precise mathematical calculations were achieved without the use of to-

In Spain the Arabic cities of Toledo (pictured), Córdoba, and Sevilla became centers of learning, with universities that drew students from the rest of Europe.

day's sophisticated instrumentation. And the Mayans, who constructed modern-looking observatories, invented the concept of zero, unknown to Europeans at the time of the conquest and colonization.

Much of the exploration and colonization of the New World can be seen as a scientific adventure. The Spaniards, including the Hispanicized Indians, Africans, and their mixed progeny who explored and settled in the Americas, were superb cartographers and geographers, not only describing the physical landscape but also the fauna and flora in the Americas. They discovered and charted the Gulf Stream. They may be considered the first ethnographers and anthropologists in the Americas, studying the Indigenous peoples and their languages and their cultures. Much agricultural technology was introduced to North America by the Spaniards and their mixed descendants, including the breeding and raising of the basic livestock, such as cattle, sheep, horses, hogs, and goats, on which the economy of the southwestern United

States was almost entirely based. They introduced the plow, systems of irrigation, and farmland distribution, often in arid environments where they applied the learning of the Arabs. Mining technology that had been developed in Central Mexico was introduced into what became the U.S. Southwest and West as early as the seventeenth century and helped the region to attract settlers and flourish; it was the same knowledge that helped drive Anglo-American settlers westward during the gold rush in the nineteenth century.

During the nineteenth century, waves of immigrants from throughout the Hispanic world began settling in all parts of the United States, bringing their knowledge and technologies with them, often acquired from universities south and far south of the U.S. border or from overseas. In 1885 Rafael Guastavino (1842–1908) obtained the first of his twenty-five patents, this one for mortars he developed for tiled floor and ceiling vaults. He went on to develop fireproofing innovations and perfected the type of cohesive masonry commonly used throughout the Hispanic world; he built the vaults for New York's Grand Central Station, the Metropolitan Museum of Art, Carnegie Hall, the old Penn Station, and many other historically important edifices. So sturdy and resilient were Guastavino's vaults, domes, and tiled surfaces that they have survived into the present at state capitals, universities, museums, and railway stations.

Today numerous scientists, medical doctors, and technologists from the Hispanic world either immigrate to the United States or are trained at U.S. universities and decide to stay and pursue their careers there. They join homegrown U.S. Latino scientists and technologists, experimenting in U.S. laboratories, teaching at U.S. universities, operating in U.S. surgical theaters, building U.S. bridges, and engineering U.S. spacecraft.

The iconic tiled vaults of the Grand Central Oyster Bar at New York City's Grand Central Terminal are representative of Rafael Guasavino's work, wherein arches are created with interlocking terra-cotta tiles and layers of mortar.

PROMINENT LATINOS IN SCIENCE, TECHNOLOGY, AND MEDICINE

Daniel Acosta Jr. (1945–)

Medicine

Born on March 25, 1945, in El Paso, Texas, Daniel Acosta received his B.A. from the University of Texas in 1968 and his Ph.D. in pharmacology from the University of Kansas in 1974. His research and teaching career started at the University of Kansas, and at the University of Texas he became the Johnson & Johnson Professor of Pharmacology and Toxicology. He later served as the dean of pharmacology at the University of Cincinnati from 1996 to 2012 and was the chair of pharmacy until 2014. He also served as the chair of the Science Advisory Board to the National Center for Toxicological Research (NCTR) for the Food and Drug Administration (FDA). Acosta's research is in cell toxicology, particularly studying the effects of drugs and toxicants at the cellular and subcellular levels; he is especially interested in heart cells and injury to them.

José Ramón Alcalá (1940–)

Anatomy, Biochemistry

Born in Ponce, Puerto Rico, on May 1, 1940, José Ramón Alcalá received B.A. and M.A. degrees in zoology from the University of Missouri in 1964 and 1966, respectively. He received his Ph.D. degree in anatomy from the University of Illinois Medical Center in 1972 and went on to a research and teaching career at Wayne State University, where he became a full professor in 1987. He served as the director of the gross anatomy program in its School of Medicine, where he specialized in the anatomy of the eye, studying the biochemistry and immunochemistry of lens plasma membranes. His research has had great impact in the field of lens research and on the formation of cataracts. In 1992 Alcalá began serving as the chair of the anatomy department at the Ponce School of Medicine in Puerto Rico.

Kenneth B. Alonso (1942–)

Pathology, Nuclear Medicine

Born in Tampa, Florida, on November 26, 1942, Kenneth Alonso received his A.B. degree from Princeton University in 1964 and his M.D. degree from the University of Florida in 1968. In 1976 he became the director of laboratory procedures for Upjohn South Company in Georgia, and from 1978 to 1984 he served as chief of staff and director of pathology for two hospitals; in 1984 he became the director of Lab Atlanta in Riverside, Georgia. Alonso is a physician who has made significant contributions to the understanding and treatment of cancer and of AIDS. Most recently he served as the director of the Community Clinical Oncology Program at the Morehouse School of Medicine in Atlanta, where he was a clinical professor and was a director of the Clinical Trials Program of the Drew-Meharry-Morehouse Cancer Consortium funded by the National Cancer Institute.

Luis Walter Alvarez (1911–1988)

Experimental Physics

Born in San Francisco, California, on June 13, 1911, Luis Alvarez became one of the country's most distinguished and respected physicists. In addition to a B.S. (1932) and a Ph.D. (1936), both from the University of Chicago, Alvarez received a number of honorary degrees from various universities. He produced most of his research work at the University of California, Berkeley, beginning in 1936. From 1954 to 1959 and from 1976 to 1978, he served as associate director of the prestigious Lawrence Berkeley Lab. In 1968 he was awarded the Nobel Prize in Physics; he also received the Collier Trophy (1946), the Scott Medal (1953), the Einstein Medal (1961), the National Medal of Science (1964), and many other awards. Alvarez was a pioneer in particle physics, astrophysics, and air navigation.

Angeles Alvariño de Leira (1916–2005)

Marine Biology

Born on October 3, 1961, in El Ferrol, Spain, Angeles Alvariño received her master's degree (1941) and her doctorates in chemistry (1951) and sciences (1967) from the University of Madrid. She worked as a biological oceanographer at various institutes in Spain until 1957, when she moved to Scripps Institute of Oceanography of the University of California, La Jolla. She became a U.S. citizen in 1966. In 1970 she joined the National Marine Fisheries Service and held positions in England, Mexico, and Venezuela. Alvariño discovered twenty-two new species of ocean animals and made great contributions to the scientific understanding of small marine life forms. She published more than one hundred scientific books, chapters, and articles. She continued conducting research even after retiring in 1987. In 1993 she received the Great Silver Medal of Galicia from King Carlos I and Queen Sophia of Spain in recognition of her scientific contributions. She died in 2005.

Albert Vinicio Báez (1912–2007)

Physics

Born on November 15, 1912, in Puebla, Mexico, Albert Báez received his B.S. degree from Drew University in 1933, his M.A. from Syracuse University in 1935, and his Ph.D. from Stanford University in 1950. Over his long career he taught at various universities, from Cornell to Stanford to MIT, among others, and between 1961 and 1974 he worked for UNESCO in New York and Paris in science education. Throughout his career Báez made important contributions to the early development of X-ray microscopes and later X-ray telescopes, at least one of which was deployed on a U.S. space station. In 1960, working with the Smithsonian Astrophysical Observatory in Cambridge, he developed optics for an X-ray telescope. As a physics educator, he made nearly a hundred films on physics from 1967 to 1974 for the Encyclopedia Britannica Educational Corp. Baez chaired the Commission on Education and Communication of the International Union for Conservation of Nature and Natural Resources from 1979 to 1983. In 1991, the International

Society for Optical Engineering awarded him and Paul Kirkpatrick the Dennis Gabor Award for pioneering contributions to the development of X-ray imaging microscopes and X-ray imaging telescopes.

Mónica Ramírez Basco (1950–)

Psychology, Psychiatry

Mónica Ramírez Basco received her B.S., M.S., and Ph.D. in clinical psychology from the University of Southern California in 1977, 1984, and 1987, respectively. She became a professor, renowned author, and national leader in the sciences, serving as assistant director of President Barack Obama's White House Office of Science and Technology Policy (2011–2017). Before serving in the White House, she was a clinical associate professor of psychiatry at the University of Texas Southwestern Medical Center (2002–2011). She then served as associate director for science policy at the National Institutes of Health until 2017. After that she returned to the University of Texas Southwestern Medical Center as associate professor of psychiatry. Her research deals with studying how the brain works, looking for answers to Alzheimer's and Parkinson's diseases, depression, traumatic brain injury, and more. She has written nine books, including *The Bipolar Workbook: Tools for Controlling Your Mood Swings*, *Learning Cognitive-Behavior Therapy: An Illustrated Guide*, and *Cognitive-Behavioral Therapy for Bipolar Disorder*.

Teresa Bernárdez (1931–2010)

Medicine, Psychiatry

Born on June 11, 1931, in Buenos Aires, Argentina, Teresa Bernárdez earned her M.D. at the University of Buenos Aires Medical School (1956), interned at the Hôpital Vaugirard in Paris, and did her residency and served on the faculty at the Menninger Clinic in Topeka, Kansas (1965–71). She served as a full professor at Michigan State University (1971–89) and was a member of the Michigan Psychoanalytic Council. Bernárdez was an organizer of a mental health panel at the 2nd World Conference on Women in Copenhagen in 1980. She worked extensively with patients facing multiple challenges, women and anger,

group psychotherapy, and feminism. As chair of the American Psychiatric Association's Committee on Women, Bernárdez led a rebellion on the revision in 1985 of the *Diagnostic and Statistical Manual of Mental Disorders*, attempting to remove from that manual three so-called mental disorders: premenstrual dysphoric disorder, paraphiliac rapism disorder, and masochistic personality disorder. She was the author of numerous works and articles in her field and ran many workshops throughout her career. Her awards include the Leadership Workshop Award from the American Medical Women's Association (1977) and the Peace Award from the Pawlowski Foundation (1974).

Caridad Borrás (1942–)

Born on February 18, 1942, in Spain and raised in Barcelona, Caridad Borrás received her M.S. and Ph.D. degrees from the University of Barcelona in 1964 and 1974, respectively. After working in Barcelona hospitals, she moved to the United States, where she worked as an assistant physicist at Thomas Jefferson University in Philadelphia, then at the West Coast Cancer Foundation and at the University of California. From 2000 to 2002, she served as coordinator of essential drugs and technology at the Pan American Health Organization in Washington, D.C. Borrás has studied the radioembryopathological effects of high LET nuclides, as well as the physics of diagnostic radiology and radiation therapy. At the International Organization for Medical Physics, she chaired the Science Committee for nine years, and at the International Union for Physical and Engineering Sciences in Medicine, she cochaired and chaired the Health Technology Task Group. Borrás has written over one hundred publications on radiology services and radiation safety and edited two books.

Rebecca Calisi Rodríguez (1979–)

Born in Dallas, Texas, on September 13, 1979, Rebecca Calisi Rodríguez got her B.A. in art and theater from Skidmore College in 2001, and later while working at a zoo turned to biology and obtained her master's degree in biology from the University of Texas at Arlington in 2006 and her Ph.D. from the University of California, Berkeley in 2010. After doing postdoctoral work, she became an assistant professor of biology at

Barnard College at Columbia University. In 2015 she went to the University of California, Davis, where she became an associate professor in the Department of Neurobiology, Physiology, and Behavior in the College of Biological Sciences. She leads a research team that studies how the brain controls sexual behavior, reproduction, and parental care and how this changes under stress. As the director for science communications at UC Davis, she also studies science communication and is a well-known advocate for inclusivity, equity, and diversity in STEM. Among her awards are the National Geographic Research and Exploration Award (2018) and the Early Career Impact Award–Federation of Associations in Behavioral and Brain Sciences (2019) in recognition of major research contributions to the sciences of mind, brain, and behavior.

Oscar A. Candia (1935–2018)

Biophysics

Born on April 30, 1935, in Buenos Aires, Argentina, Oscar Candia received his M.D. degree from the University of Buenos Aires in 1959. After working as a researcher there, he relocated to the University of Louisville in Kentucky in 1964 as a research associate and moved up the ranks to full professor. From 1918, Candia went on to spend fifty years of his career at Mount Sinai School of Medicine in the Departments of Ophthalmology and Physiology, ultimately serving as director and vice chairman for research in the Department of Ophthalmology. Candia's extensive academic career was intimately associated with the progress and growth of the eye research community. His work furthered the understanding of the physiological and biophysical features of the cornea, lens, and ciliary body; he wrote more than 140 peer-reviewed publications. He was also a key figure in the earliest formal meetings of the Association for Research in Vision and Ophthalmology and served as a member, chairman, and trustee of its Physiology and Pharmacology section.

Fernando Caracena (1936–)

Physics

Born on March 13, 1936, in El Paso, Texas, Fernando Caracena received his B.S. degree from the University of Texas at El Paso in 1958 and his M.S. and Ph.D. from Case Western Reserve in 1966 and 1968, respectively. From 1958 to 1961, he worked as an atmospheric physicist for the Department of Defense at White Sands Missile Range, New Mexico. From 1969 to 1976 he worked his way up from assistant professor to full professor and chair of the Physics Department at Metropolitan State University in Denver. From 1976 to 2005 he worked as a research scientist at the National Oceanic and Atmospheric Administration in the Atmospheric Physics and Chemistry Laboratory. Since 2010 he has served as the principal physicist at Ghyzmo, his own blog on physics. Caracena's research is in air safety, especially clear air turbulence, low altitude wind shear, and the meteorology of wind-shear-related aircraft accidents.

Yarimar Carrasquillo (1979–)

Cell Biology

Yarimar Carrasquillo received her B.S. in biology from the University of Puerto Rico (2000) and her Ph.D. in neuroscience from Baylor College of Medicine (2005), after which she spent nine years in postdoctoral research in the Nerbonne Lab and as a staff scientist at the Washington University School of Medicine. She joined the National Institutes of Health (NIH) in 2014, where she leads the Behavioral Neurocircuitry and Cellular Plasticity Section. The main goal of her lab is to identify anatomical, molecular, and cellular mechanisms that underlie pathological pain states. In her lab, Carrasquillo directs a multifaceted, multidisciplinary research program focused on delineating the anatomical, molecular, and cellular mechanisms that underlie pain perception and modulation.

George Castro (1939–)

Physical Chemistry

Born on February 23, 1939, in Los Angeles, California, Castro received his B.S. in chemistry from the University of California, Los Angeles, in 1960 and his

Ph.D. in physical chemistry from the University of California, Riverside in 1965. After doing postgraduate work at various institutions, he began as a researcher at IBM in 1968; in 1986 he became the manager of Synchrotron Studies at IBM. In 1978 he received the Outstanding Innovation Award from IBM, and in 1990 he was elected as a fellow of the American Physical Society. Castro is the discoverer of the mechanisms of intrinsic charge carriers of organic photoconductors, which eventually found application in photocopying machines and high-speed printers. In 1975 Castro assumed the leadership of the IBM San Jose Research Lab, which is world famous for scientific discoveries, including superconducting polymer, novel organic metals and superconductors, high-resolution laser techniques, and new methods of investigating magnetic materials.

Grace E. Colón (1976–)

Born on February 12, 1976, in Hato Rey, Puerto Rico, Grace Colón received her B.S. in in chemical engineering from the University of Pennsylvania (1988) and her Ph.D. in chemical engineering from the Massachusetts Institute of Technology (1995). Beginning in 2013, she has served as president, chief executive officer, and director of InCarda Therapeutics, Inc., a clinical-stage company developing therapeutics for cardiovascular conditions. In addition to her role at InCarda, since 2016 Colón has also been the executive chair (formerly chief executive officer) of ProterixBio, Inc., and she serves on the board of Cocoon Biotech, Inc. Colón was a cofounder of Pyranose Biotherapeutics, a biologics discovery platform company. She was also the founding president of the Industrial Products Division at Intrexon Corporation. InCarda Therapeutics is a clinical stage drug delivery company pioneering a novel approach of treating acute cardiovascular diseases and conditions by the inhalation route.

Adán Colón-Carmona (1966–)

Biology

Born on March 8, 1966, in Zacatecas, Mexico, at age six Adán Colón-Carmona moved to Southern California with his working-class parents. He grew up in the Los Angeles area, primarily in the communities of Sepulveda and Norwalk. Colón-Carmona completed his undergraduate degree in biology at the University of California, Santa Cruz in 1989 and then earned his Ph.D. at the University of California, Irvine in 1999 in plant cell and developmental biology. He conducted postgraduate work at the Salk Institute from 1995 to 1999. Throughout his career he has focused on projects involving the regulation of the cytoskeleton, plant-microbe interactions, and science education and mentoring. He did his postdoctoral training at the Salk Institute for Biological Studies and UC Davis. Since 2006 he has been the principal investigator for the UMass Boston–Dana-Farber/Harvard Cancer Center Partnership. Also in 2006 he became an associate professor of the Department in Biology at the University of Massachusetts–Boston, and is focusing on providing high quality research in the areas of plant biology, educating the next generation of scientists, and promoting social justice via efforts in education access and equity.

Daniel Alfonso Colón-Ramos (1976?–)

Cell Biology

Born in Hato, Rey, Puerto Rico, Daniel Colón-Ramos obtained his A.B. from Harvard University in 1998 and his Ph.D. from Duke University Medical Center in 2003. He was a postdoctoral fellow at Stanford University in 2008, after which he became an assistant professor at the Yale University School of Medicine. In 2019 he achieved full professor status and is currently the Dorys McConnell Duberg Professor of Neuroscience and Cell Biology at Yale University. Colón-Ramos operates his own lab at the Yale University School of Medicine, which explores how synapses are precisely assembled to build the neuronal architecture that underlies behavior. To address this, his team developed tools in the thermotaxis circuit of *C. elegans*. Their system enables unbiased genetic screens to identify novel pathways that instruct synaptogenesis *in vivo* and single-cell manipulation of these pathways to understand how they influence behavior. In 2012 he received the American Association for the Advancemnet of Science (AAAS) Early Career Award for Public Engagement with Science. He was elected to the National Academy of Medicine in 2020.

France Anne-Dominic Córdova (1947–)

Astronomy, Astrophysics

Born on August 5, 1947, in Paris, France, to an Irish American mother and a Mexican American father, France Córdova graduated from high school in California and received her B.A. degree in English from Stanford. She went on to receive a Ph.D. in physics from the California Institute of Technology in 1979. She worked at the Space Astronomy and Astrophysics Group at the Los Alamos National Laboratory from 1979 to 1989. She was the chair of the Department of Astronomy and Astrophysics at Pennsylvania State University from 1989 until 1993, when she became a NASA chief scientist. Córdova has published more than 150 scientific papers, especially on observational and experimental astrophysics, multispectral research on X-ray and gamma ray sources, and space-borne instrumentation. She went onto a career in academic administration, serving as vice chancellor and chancellor of University of California campuses and in 2007 became the president of Purdue University. Córdova served as the fourteenth director of the National Science Foundation from 2014 to 2020. In May 2021 she was named president of the Science Philanthropy Alliance.

Francisco Dallmeier (1953–)

Wildlife Biology

Born on February 15, 1953, in Caracas, Venezuela, Francisco Dallmeier received his undergraduate degree in biology from the Central University of Venezuela in 1979 and his M.S. and Ph.D. in wildlife biology from the University of Colorado in 1984 and 1986, respectively. From 1973 to 1977 he was the director of the La Salle Museum of Natural History. Since 1986

he has worked at the Smithsonian Institute in Washington, D.C.; from 2005 to 2014 he was the director of the Man and the Biosphere Diversity Program. Currently he is the director of the Center for Conservation Education and Sustainability of the Smithsonian Conservation Biology Institute; he is also an adjunct professor of conservation studies at George Mason University. Dallmeier has a wide range of global experience in conservation, planning for biodiversity-friendly working landscapes, sustainable infrastructure priority setting, and natural resources and protected area management.

Enrique M. De La Cruz (1969–)

Molecular Biology

Born on September 15, 1969, in Newark, New Jersey, the son of Cuban immigrants, Enrique De La Cruz received a B.S. in biology from Rutgers University-Newark. De la Cruz received his Ph.D. in molecular biology from the Johns Hopkins University School of Medicine in 1997. After conducting postdoctorate research at the University of Pennsylvania for four years, he became a professor at Yale and rose up through the ranks to serve since 2020 as the chair of the Molecular Biophysics and Biochemistry Department and since 2017 as the head of Branford College at Yale University. His research involves integrating comprehensive kinetic and thermodynamic analyses of catalytic reaction pathways with computational and mathematical modeling to develop and test predictive models of work output by molecular motor proteins, enzyme function and adaptation, and biopolymer fragmentation. In 2017 he received the Emily Gray Award in Education from the Biophysical Society, and in 2020 he was named to Cell Press's "100 inspiring Hispanic/Latinx scientists in America" list.

Henry Frank Díaz (1948–)

Meteorology

Born on July 15, 1948, in Santiago, Cuba, Henry Díaz moved to the United States in 1961 after the Cuban Revolution triumphed. He received a B.S. from Florida State University in 1971 and an M.S. in atmospheric science from the University of Miami in 1974, after which he began work at the Environmental

Data Center of the National Oceanic and Atmospheric Administration (NOAA). In 1980 he transferred to the Climate Research Program of NOAA in Boulder, Colorado. In 1985 he obtained his Ph.D. in geography and climatology from the University of Colorado. He continued with NOAA until 2007. He was a senior research associate at the Cooperative Institute for Research in Environmental Science (CIRES) at the University of Colorado–Boulder until his retirement in 2016. He has affiliate faculty positions at the University of Hawaii–Manoa and the University of Arizona–Tucson. Díaz has published more than fifty research papers and seven books.

Orlando Figueroa (1955–)
Mechanical Engineering

Born on September 9, 1955, in San Juan, Puerto Rico, Orlando Figueroa received a B.S. in mechanical engineering from the University of Puerto Rico–Mayagüez in 1978 and immediately began his career at NASA, where he was worked to the present, serving in such capacities as manager of the Superfluid Helium On-Orbit Transfer (SHOOT) Shuttle Experiment, manager for the Explorer Program, and director of the Systems, Technology, and Advanced Concepts Directorate. In 2001 he was appointed director of NASA's Mars Exploration Program, at the time the largest program at NASA, which was responsible for all of the space probes of Mars. In 2005 Figueroa was appointed to the position of director for system safety and mission assurance at the Goddard Space Flight Center. In 1993 Figueroa won NASA's Outstanding Leadership Medal. He retired from NASA in 2010 to start Orlando Leadership Enterprise, LLC, an aerospace consulting company.

Marcelo H. García (1959–)
Hydraulic Engineering

Born on April 22, 1959, in Córdoba, Argentina, Marcelo García received his diploma in water resources from Universidad Nacional del Litoral, Argentina, in 1982, and his M.SC. and his Ph.D. in civil engineering from the University of Minnesota in 1985 and 1989, respectively. He has spent most of his career at the University of Illinois in the Department of Civil and Environmental Engineering but has frequently taken visiting positions at universities in Latin America and Europe. At Illinois, he rose to his current position of M.T. Geoffrey Yeh Endowed Chair in Civil Engineering. He served as the editor-in-chief of *ASCE Manual of Practice 110—Sedimentation Engineering* from 1999 to 2008, the editor-in-chief of the *Journal of Hydraulic Research* from 2001 to 2006, and the associate editor of the *International Journal of Infrastructure and Natural Disasters* from 2000 to 2010. Acknowledged internationally as "the river man," García has consulted nationally and internationally in Argentina, Bolivia, Brazil, Canada, Chile, China, Colombia, Costa Rica, Ecuador, Ghana, Hong Kong, Indonesia, and Mexico.

Mónica Guzmán (?–)
Pharmacology

Mónica Guzmán received her B.S. from the University of Guanajuato in 1997 and her Ph.D. from the University of Kentucky in 2002. She started as an assistant professor at Cornell Weill Medical College in New York City in 2009 and has served as an associate professor there since 2016. Her research involves work with cancer stem cells, specifically demonstrating that acute myelogenous leukemia (AML) stem cells exist in a molecular state that is unique from their normal hematopoietic counterparts. She has successfully employed both molecular genetic and small molecule strategies that exploit these differences to selectively ablate AML at the bulk, stem, and progenitor levels.

Juan Martín Maldacena (1968–)
Theoretical Physics

Born on September 10, 1968, in Buenos Aires, Argentina, Juan Martín Maldacena obtained his licenciate in 1991 from the Instituto Balseiro, Bariloche, Argentina, and his Ph.D. in physics at Princeton University after completing a doctoral dissertation titled "Black Holes in String Theory" in 1996. He conducted postdoctoral work at Rutgers University, and in 1997 he joined Harvard University as associate professor, being quickly promoted to full professor of physics in 1999. Since 2001 he has been a professor at the Institute for Advanced Study in Princeton, New Jersey, and in 2016 he became the first Carl P. Feinberg Professor of Theoretical Physics in the Institute's School of Natural Sciences. He has made significant contributions to the foundations of string theory and quantum gravity. Maldacena has won numerous awards, including the Lorentz Medal (2018), the Albert Einstein Medal (2018), the St. Albert Award (2018), and the Galileo Galilei Medal (2019).

Luz Martínez-Miranda (1960s–)

Material Science, Physics

Born in the early 1960s in Bethesda, Maryland, Luz Martínez-Miranda moved with her family back to Puerto Rico when she was five years old. She obtained her education on the island, earning a B.S. and an M.S. in physics from the University of Puerto Rico. She received her Ph.D. in physics from the Massachusetts Institute of Technology in 1985. She is a researcher and teacher in the Department of Materials Science and Engineering at the University of Maryland. Martínez-Miranda began her study in physics in the area of lenses but has since moved to exploring ferroelectric liquid crystals, amorphous carbon films, and nanocrystalline materials. She also has researched the effect of order of the transfer of changes within the liquid crystals in photovoltaics. In addition, Martínez-Miranda has studied X-ray scattering techniques of liquid crystals. She served as the president of the National Society of Hispanic Physicists from 2010 to 2016.

Mario Molina (1943–2020)

Chemistry, Environmental Sciences

Born in Mexico City on March 9, 1943, Mario José Molina-Pasquel Henríquez earned a B.S. degree in chemical engineering from the National Autonomous University of Mexico in 1965 and his Ph.D. in physical chemistry from the University of California, Berkeley in 1972. He taught and conducted research at various universities. In 1992 he became the Lee and Geraldine Martin Professor of Environmental Sciences at the Massachusetts Institute of Technology, where he was teaching when he received the 1995 Nobel Prize in Chemistry for work that led to the international ban on chemicals believed to deplete the ozone protective layer of the Earth; he was one of the first scientists to call attention to the growing hole in the ozone layer over Antarctica. Molina became the first Latino scientist to receiv NASA's Medal for Exceptional Scientific Achievement. Molina won numerous prestigious awards and was named by President Barack Obama to the U.S. President's Council of Advisors on Science and Technology. In 2013 President Obama presented the Presidential Medal of Freedom to Molina. At the time of his death in 2020, Molina was a professor at the University of California, San Diego, and director of the Mario Molina Center for Energy and Environment in Mexico City.

Ellen Ochoa (1958)

Electrical Engineering, Astronautics

Born on May 10, 1958, in Los Angeles, California, Ellen Ochoa received a B.S. in physics from San Diego State University in 1980 and her M.S. and Ph.D. degrees in electrical engineering from Stanford University in 1981 and 1985, respectively. Ochoa began her career as a research engineer at Sandia National Laboratories and NASA Ames Research Center, where she rose to be chief of the information sciences division. After that, she became an astronaut, the first Latina to become one. As an astronaut, she served as a crew member on four space shuttle missions in a variety of roles, including leading onboard scientific activities, operating the robotic arm, and serving as flight engineer during the launch, rendezvous, and entry phases of the mission. After retiring from her astronautic experiences in 2007, Ochoa remained at NASA Johnson Space Center and served as deputy center director for five years; she previously led the Flight Crew Operations Directorate, managing the astronaut office and the aircraft operations divisions. Ochoa became director of the space center in 2013 and served until her retirement. She has three patents in the area of optical information processing and numerous publications in technical journals. She is a fellow of the American Institute of Aeronautics and Astronautics (AIAA), the American Association for the Advancement of Science (AAAS), and the National Academy of Inventors (NAI). She was vice chair of the National Science Board from 2018 to 2020. In 1995 Ochoa won the Albert V. Baez Award for Outstanding Technical Achievement in Service to Humanity.

Christine Ortiz
(1971?–)

Material Science, Engineering

Christine Ortiz received her B.S. from Rensselaer Polytechnic Institute in 1992 and her Ph.D. from Cornell University in 1997, after which she joined the faculty of the Massachusetts Institute of Technology (MIT). Since 1993, she has been the Morris Cohen Professor of Materials Science and Engineering at MIT, and she served as dean of Graduate Education from 2010 to 2016. Ortiz is a distinguished scientist and engineer with over 180 scholarly publications and has received thirty national and international honors, including the Presidential Early Career Award in Science and Engineering, which was awarded to her at the White House by President George W. Bush. Ortiz currently serves on the National Advisory Board of the National Science Foundation Inclusive Graduate Education Network, the Board of Directors of the National GEM Consortium (National Consortium for Graduate Degrees for Minorities in Science and Engineering), and the Scientific Advisory Board of the Max Planck Institute of Colloids and Interfaces (Potsdam, Germany), among many others.

Alfredo Quiñones-Hinojosa (1968–)
Neurology

Born in Baja California, Mexico, on January 2, 1968, Alfredo Quiñones-Hinojosa came to the United States at age nineteen as a farm worker. He was able to leave the fields and receive a degree from the University of California, Berkeley in 1994 and M.D. from Harvard University in 1999. He subsequently worked as a neurosurgeon at Johns Hopkins Medical Center and an assistant professor of neurosurgery and oncology, climbing the ranks from 2005 until 2016, when he became a full professor in the Johns Hopkins Medical School. From 2016 to the present he has been the William J. and Charles H. Mayo Professor and Chair of Neurologic Surgery at Mayo Clinic Florida in Jacksonville. Quiñones-Hinojosa has published more than fifty chapters in science books and his autobiography, and he coauthored *Controversies in Neuro-Oncology: Best Evidence Medicine for Brain Tumor Surgery* with Dr. Shaan Raza. The British Medical Association awarded *Controversies in Neuro-Oncology* first prize in oncology in its medical book awards in 2014.

Alejandro Sánchez Alvarado (1964–)
Molecular Biology

Born in Caracas, Venezuela, on February 24, 1964, Alejandro Sánchez Alvarado received a BS in molecular biology and chemistry from Vanderbilt University in 1986 and received his Ph.D. in pharmacology and cell biophysics from the University of Cincinnati College of Medicine in 1992. He carried out postdoctoral studies from 1994 to 1995 in Baltimore, Maryland, at the Carnegie Institution of Washington, Department of Embryology and was then appointed staff associate at the Department of Embryology to run his own independent research group. Today he is an investigator of the Howard Hughes Medical Institute and the executive director and chief scientific officer of the Stowers Institute for Medical Research. The Sánchez Alvarado Laboratory focuses on understanding the regenerative capabilities of the planarian flatworm *Schmidtea mediterranea*. In 2015 Sánchez Alvarado was elected a fellow of the American Academy of Arts and Sciences, and in 2018 he was elected to the National Academy of Sciences.

Luis Fernando Santana (1968)

Physiology and Membrane Biology

Born in 1968 in Caguas, Puerto Rico, Luis Fernando Santana received his early education in Cayey. He received his B.S. from the University of Puerto Rico–Humacao and his M.S. in marine biology and zoology from the University of Hawaii in 1992 and his Ph.D. in physiology from the University of Maryland School of Medicine in 1996. After conducting postdoctoral work at the University of Vermont, he became an assistant professor in the Institute of Neurobiology at the University of Puerto Rico in 1999. After that he taught at the University of Washington until 2015, when he became professor and chair of the Department of Physiology and Membrane Biology at the University of California–Davis Medical School. His research work centers on the mechanisms underlying calcium signaling and excitation-transcription coupling in cardiac and arterial smooth muscle during health and disease.

C. Francisco Valenzuela (1963?–)

Neuroscience

Born in Bogotá, Colombia, C. Francisco Valenzuela received his M.D. from the Colombian School of Medicine (Universidad El Bosque) in Bogota in 1987 and his Ph.D. from the University of California, Riverside in 1993. He became an instructor at the University of New Mexico School of Medicine in 1996 and since 2013 has been the Regents' Professor in the Department of Neurosciences at the University of New Mexico Health Sciences Center. Research in his laboratory focuses on modulation of developing and mature neuronal circuits by alcohol (ethanol), with the long-term goal of contributing to a better understanding of the neurobiology of alcoholism and fetal alcohol spectrum disorders (FASDs).

Lydia Villa-Komaroff (1947–)

Cellular Biology

Born on August 7, 1947, and raised in Santa Fe, New Mexico, Lydia Villa-Komaroff earned a Ph.D. in cell biology at the Massachusetts Institute of Technology (MIT) in 1975. While doing postdoctoral work at Harvard University, she was the first author of the landmark report showing that bacteria could be induced to make proinsulin—the first time a mammalian hormone was synthesized by bacteria. The research was a milestone in the birth of the biotechnology industry. In 1977 she joined the faculty of the University of Massachusetts Medical School (UMMS), and in 1983 she became a professor at the Harvard Medical School. In a 1995 television documentary, *DNA Detective*, she was featured for her work on insulin-related growth factors. In 1996 Villa-Komaroff became the vice president of research at Northwestern University. In 2003 she became the vice president for research and chief operating officer of the Whitehead Institute in Cambridge, Massachusetts, an affiliated research institute of MIT. Among Villa-Komaroff's awards are the Leadership Award from Women Entrepreneurs in Science & Technology (2011), the Woman of Distinction from the American Association of University Women (2013), the Distinguished Women Scientist from the White House Office of Science and Technology Policy (2015), and the Morison Prize from the MIT Program in Science, Technology & Society (2016).

Nicolás Kanellos

MEDIA

The treatment of one ethnic group by another is quite often influenced by economic or political factors in their nation, state, or region. This is certainly true regarding the relations between Anglos and Latinos. The conflict and cooperation between these groups has been shaped by the political and economic relations between the United States and other Spanish American countries.

The general market mass media, including newspapers, magazines, television, and radio—which so often reflect the prevalent perspectives of the dominant groups in society—have historically replicated those views in their treatment of Latinos. Therefore, an avenue for partially understanding contemporary Latino life is the assessment of messages that the media disseminate about them. First, at all levels of society, general mass market media are the most pervasive sources of news and information. For many people they are also the most relied-upon source for entertainment. Second, the messages presented by the media may have significant effects on the audience, especially regarding events, topics, and issues about which the audience has no direct knowledge or experience. Thus, for millions of people, a significant part of the information they receive and the notions they develop about Latinos may often be products of mass media messages.

TREATMENT OF LATINOS IN GENERAL MARKET MEDIA

Two qualifications are critical to a discussion of the general market media's treatment of Latinos. One of those conditions occurs when viewers do not have other sources of information or experiences that provide a standard against which to assess the media messages. To the extent that non-Latinos live segregated lives with limited opportunities to interact effectively with a variety of Latinos in constructive or productive ways, the media images of Latinos will be among the only sources for non-Latinos to learn and interpret who Latinos are and how they think. Another factor that increases media's influence occurs when the values or views presented by them are recurrent. To date, the values and views presented about Latinos are predominantly negative and recurrent across media and time.

Furthermore, the treatment of Latinos in general market media has its impact on Latinos, who suffer the consequences of the recurring negative imagery. For example, they face the psychological pain that emerges from the negative portrayals and lack of recognition of their own people and values. They also have to endure the social scorn that emerges when the treatment they receive from other people, and sometimes from those of their own ethnic background, is consciously or unconsciously based on stereotyped notions disseminated by the media.

GENERAL MARKET NEWSPAPERS

General market newspapers were probably the first major means of mass communication through which fragmented and distorted news, information, and images of Latinos were created and promoted. While much has changed from the early depictions, the treatment and employment of Latinos in newspapers are still far from adequate in this media institution.

Portrayals

The Anglo image of the Mexican as a bandit is largely an outgrowth of the Manifest Destiny policy of the 1800s. English-language American newspapers in California and Texas reveal how circumstantial events related to economic and political relations between the people who inhabited the expansive Mexican territories of the Southwest and the Anglo-European settlers and gold prospectors led the latter group to create stereotypes of the former to justify the conquest of that region. The political, religious, and economic beliefs of Anglo-European superiority were constantly betrayed as they depicted the Native American and Mexican inhabitants as people destined to be conquered and unworthy of keeping their lands and resources.

After the conquests of the southwestern territories, the general market press of the early twentieth century continued a pattern of false depictions of Latino people, or simply ignored their experiences.

By the end of the nineteenth century, these negative images were also used to portray Latinos from the Caribbean and elsewhere, especially during the dawn of U.S. occupation and colonization of Cuba, Puerto Rico, and Panama.

Changing journalistic standards over the years increased professionalism, balance, and objectivity, which diminished such blatant anti-Latino racism. Yet negative, limited, or inadequate portrayals of Latinos in newspapers of the latter half of the twentieth century have been systematically documented. One of the first studies in this area was a 1969 analysis of Puerto Ricans in the *New York Times* and the *New York Post* compared with coverage in the Spanish-language dailies *El Diario* and *El Tiempo*. The English-language dailies showed little interest in Puerto Ricans, who were referred to with negative attributes and covered primarily in terms of their community needs or problems (for which solutions were infrequently offered). The same was not true in the Spanish dailies, which featured more positive and solution-oriented stories.

Negative and biased coverage of Mexican Americans was also evident in research regarding pretrial criminal news reporting and general reporting, and comparing immigration and deportation news in the *Los Angeles Times* and the Spanish-language daily *La Opinión* during the 1930s, 1950s, and 1970s, which found that the plight of Mexicans was covered much more sympathetically and humanistically in the latter paper.

> Negative, limited, or inadequate portrayals of Latinos in newspapers of the latter half of the twentieth century have been systematically documented.

Yet some improvements have been made, at least according to two recent studies of the general market press. In a 1983 study of the coverage of Latino Americans in the English-language dailies of Santa Fe, Tucson, Salinas, San Bernardino, Stockton, and Visalia, researchers concluded that sports news and photo coverage got high marks for their inclusion of local Latinos and that local news coverage exclusive of sports got a passing grade—good, not excellent, but better than it had received credit for. However, editorial coverage and bulletin listings of Latino people and activities were below average and in need of considerable attention.

A *Washington Post* study of major newspapers in 2019 found that 53 percent of the articles on Latinos or Hispanics contained words related to the negative themes of criminality (37 percent), economic threat (21 percent), and illegal immigration (12 percent). The *Post* also found that the average negative article mentioning Latino crime was *highly* negative.

In spite of this, the prognosis of Latino treatment in general market newspapers has consistently remained culturally insensitive and nonsupportive. From his observations and personal experiences, Charles A. Erickson, founder and editor of *Hispanic Link, Inc.*, in 1981 summarized that "the relationship between 20 million Americans crowded under the umbrella Hispanic and the nation's establishment print media sprawls across the spectrum from nonexistent

to quaint, to precarious, to outright antagonistic." Erickson identified six dimensions of general market press irresponsibility: the press will not allow Latinos to be authorities on general issues; the press will not even allow Latinos to be authorities on issues where Latinos have the obvious expertise; the press still views the Latino community in stereotype; the press fails to provide Latinos with information of critical interest and importance to their welfare and progress; the press does not hire enough Latinos or other reporters and editors with Latino cultural awareness and expertise; and the press tends to smother those Latinos they do hire.

Regarding the press's viewing the Latino community in stereotype, Erickson states, "Traditionally, non-Hispanic reporters have attached negative adjec-

The lack of Latinos in newsrooms and in news management could be a major factor leading to the continued fragmentation and distortion of news about Latinos and other minorities. Pictured here is the Chicago Tribune *newsroom, November 8, 2012.*

tives to the word 'barrio.' For example, Houston's barrios were described in a series one of its papers ran some months ago as places where shoppers haggle and Latin rhythms blare. A Chicago reporter described New York's Spanish Harlem as 'grim, rat-infested.' A *Christian Science Monitor* writer chose the words 'the often-steamy barriors [sic] of East Los Angeles.'"

A decade following Erickson's critique of the general market press, David Shaw's 1990 nine-article series in the *Los Angeles Times* assessing the status of reporting about and hiring minorities found many of the same situations and problems discussed by Erickson. The headline of the first story summarized the issue: "Negative News and Little Else." The story went on to say that "by focusing on crime, poverty and aberrant behavior newspapers fail to give a complete portrait of ethnic minorities." An example of continued stereotyping presented by Shaw is the use of the word "aliens" (which can make Latinos seem "inhuman—strange outcasts from another world") instead of "illegal immigrants" or "undocumented workers."

◆••••
"By focusing on crime, poverty and aberrant behavior newspapers fail to give a complete portrait of ethnic minorities."

A scholarly article by Professor Emily M. Farris published in 2018 demonstrated how the press criminalizes immigrants and concluded, "Our analysis demonstrates a general tendency to frame immigrants in a negative light, consistent with a 'threat' narrative but inconsistent with actual immigrant demographics. Our findings are particularly important in light of research establishing that such portrayals contribute to more hostile attitudes about immigration in the U.S. as well as greater support for punitive immigration policy among Whites." Other research has shown that press coverage between 2000 and 2010 criminalized Latino male migrants and prepared the ground for presidential candidate Donald Trump's racialized and gendered characterization of Latino immigrant men as "bad hombres," one in a continued barrage of attacks that have been repeated in social media and the conservative press that, in turn, have been shown to significantly elevate hate crimes committed against Latinos.

In trying to understand some of the reasons that lead to the continued fragmentation and distortion of news about Latinos and other minorities, those who have written on this subject would probably agree that the lack of Latinos in the newsrooms and in their management is one of the major factors to be considered.

Employment

When the first counts of minority participants in the general market press were conducted in the early 1970s, these groups constituted less than 2 percent of the total. About a decade later, in 1984, the total had only made it to 5.8 percent among the approximately 1,750 daily newspapers in the nation. As low as these figures were, one must realize that they were for all minorities, which means that the situation for Latinos was more dismal. This is a problem that continues even today, according to the most recent surveys of the National Association of Hispanic Journalists (NAHJ) and the American Society of News Editors (ASNE).

According to the Pew Research Center, more than three-quarters (77 percent) of newsroom employees—reporters, editors, photographers, and videographers in the newspaper, broadcasting, and internet publishing industries—were non-Hispanic Whites from 2012 to 2016, and this figure is higher than the 65 percent of workers in all industries in the United States. According to Statista.com, totals were worse for television newsrooms; in 2018, only 11.6 percent of employees in TV newsrooms were Latinos. Newsroom employees are also more likely than workers overall to be male. The numbers were dismal for women in a survey conducted in 2016: according to the ASNE, Hispanic, Black, and Asian women made up less than 5 percent of newsroom personnel at traditional print and online news publications.

Even in cities where the population or market is significantly Latino, such as in Los Angeles, where Latinos make up more than 50 percent of the population, only 15 percent of the *Los Angeles Times* employees identify as Latino. Only 9 percent of *Chicago Tribune* employees are Latinos, whereas the population is 29 percent. The *New York Times*'s Latino employees number 8 percent while the community is 18 percent Latino. Some 7 percent of *USA Today*'s employees are Latino, and of course Latinos make up 18 percent of the national population (a conservative figure).

In addition to the problem of low employment, Latinos who have succeeded in gaining employment in journalism encounter various burdens often related to their ethnicity. Latino reporters face unwarranted challenges of their latitude and credibility as professional journalists. While too often Latinos are considered to lack the intellect to write about issues other than ethnic problems or strife, they are also perceived as too partial for "objective" in-depth reporting about educational, economic, and other types of policy issues of importance to their community. Moreover, many Latino journalists are burdened with requests to be translators in situations beyond their reporting duties—for example, to assist in answering Spanish-language business calls or correspondence not related to their responsibilities. Yet these bilingual abilities usually are exploited without compensatory pay.

Given these current employment figures and practices, one can understand some of the factors related to the inadequate treatment of Latinos in newspapers. Unfortunately, given the slow progress in newsroom integration and the limited sensitivity of many Anglo reporters and editors, it will be some time before Latinos make sufficient inroads to professional positions, which is necessary to help improve the portrayal of their communities. The 2017 ASNE Newsroom Diversity Survey reported that approximately 25 percent of news organizations reported having at least one minority among their top three editors. But if these supposed newsroom leaders were not connected to their diverse communities, it would be likely to lead to more inclusive and accurate, culturally sensitive reporting on Latinos.

At the same time, however, that many newspapers have been hiring more Latinos and other ethnic minority journalists and improving their working environment, especially with respect to training, promotions, and distribution of assignments, newspapers have been losing their readership, and many have been going into bankruptcy. This, of course, makes the competition for those newsroom jobs even more intense and likely to even more adversely affect the hiring of Latinos.

In 2020, the Black Lives Matter (BLM) movement intensified the evaluation of hiring and representation of minorities in the media, including print journalism. However, despite the broad focus and multicultural approach of BLM, the country and the media remain very much in the Black-White binary, and there has been little improvement for the Latinos and other "Brown" people.

Despite these trends and perennial marginalization, there are concerted efforts to improve the situation by such organizations as the National Association of Hispanic Journalists, the National Hispanic Media Coalition, the Latin Academy of Recording Arts and Sciences, and the National Association of Hispanic Publications. Over the years, they have had some success in the push for positive changes and will undoubtedly contribute to improving both the portrayal and employment of Latinos in the media.

GENERAL MARKET TELEVISION

While newspapers were the first mass medium to widely disseminate images of Latinos, their circulation and influence were limited when compared with films or television. Since the inception of moving pictures, stereotypes of minority and ethnic groups have been a standard feature. For a more extensive survey, see the Film chapter.

Not surprisingly, the treatment of Latinos on general market television has not been sharply different from that in the film industry. Although there have been occasional breaks with stereotypical imagery, in some respects the portrayal has been more critical of Latino culture and life. In addition, the situation is worse in the number of Latinos employed in front of or behind cameras. This conclusion is quite evident from even cursory watching of American television.

Portrayals

The masters of television images have been less than fair in their portrayals of Latinos. The first "prominent" Latino male on television was on the *I Love Lucy* show (CBS 1951–61), where Lucille Ball's husband, Desi Arnaz, played Ricky Ricardo, the good-looking, excitable, short-tempered Cuban band leader who spoke with an accent and occasionally rattled off expletives in Spanish. Interestingly, in *Desi and Lucy: Before the Laughter*, a television biography, he is portrayed as an irresponsible Latin lover.

Other Latino male buffoons include Pancho, the sidekick to the Cisco Kid in the syndicated series *The Cisco Kid* (1951–56); José Jiménez, the Puerto Rican bumbling doorman and elevator operator in *The Danny Thomas Show* (NBC 1953–71); and Sgt. García in the *Zorro* series (ABC, 1957–59). The last of the successful (in terms of ratings and continuity) Latino male buffoons on network television was probably Freddie Prinze, who in *Chico and the Man* (NBC, 1974–78) played Chico, a streetwise kid working in a garage with a bigoted old man.

With such exceptions as *Chico and the Man*, which was cancelled a year and a half after Prinze's suicide, Latinos as major comic characters in successful network programs have been few. CBS came up with an innovative strategy to market its "Latino Odd Couple" sitcom *Trial and Error* (1988). It was simulcast in Spanish on Spanish-language radio stations. The show centered

One of the last of the prominent Latino male buffoons on network television was probably Freddie Prinze, who in Chico and the Man *(NBC, 1974–78) played Chico, a streetwise kid working in a garage with a bigoted old man (played by Jack Albertson).*

on two unlikely roommates: Tony (Paul Rodríguez), a T-shirt salesman on Los Angeles's Olvera Street, and John (Eddie Vélez), a newly graduated Puerto Rican lawyer working in an established law firm. The comedy was strained, and the series never gained acceptance. Much more noteworthy was the short-lived *I Married Dora*, which had a brief run on ABC during the fall 1987 season. An admirable attempt to center a situation comedy around a Salvadoran woman, it reversed cultural fields by making Dora (Elizabeth Peña) smart and self-assured and her uptight, "open-minded" Anglo husband the butt of many jokes because of his stereotypical ideas about Latinos. The series dealt meaningfully with Latino immigration to the United States and the misconceptions the two cultures often have about one another. Sadly, it was canceled before establishing a consistent tone and finding an audience.

However, in the twenty-first century, broadcast television has lost its dominance and been overshadowed by cable and internet networks. The market has become so fragmented that new spaces for Latino participation and representation have opened up, including on the four major broadcast networks, whose audiences often do not have access to cable or internet-delivered providers, such as Netflix, Amazon Prime Video, and Hulu. Even more interesting is the internationalization of these providers and, for the first time in history, the provision of easy access to media products in languages other than English. Where in the past Latinos had recourse only to Spanish-language broadcasts on three networks—Univisión, Telemundo, and Galavisión—today they can enjoy material broadcast from Monterrey, Mexico, or San Juan, Puerto Rico, as well as movies and series filmed or taped in Argentina, Chile, Cuba, Mexico, Spain, and the United States. The added competition for Latino viewers has translated to the employment of more Latino actors, directors, and producers on television series and programs. Of course, much of this improved response is due to the fast and large demographic growth of Latinos in the United States.

Under these new twenty-first century determinants, not only are brown faces and Spanish surnames more evident in television programs, but for the first time since *I Love Lucy* and *Chico and the Man*, Latinos are the actual stars and producers of shows, such as with the eighty-five episodes of the ABC comedy-drama series *Ugly Betty* (2006–10), starring América Ferrera. Developed by Silvio Horta and based on Fernando Gaitán's Colombian telenovela *Yo soy Betty, la fea*, actress and producer Salma Hayek, José Tamez, and Silvio Horta combined with other mainstream producers to create the U.S. adaptation of the series. To show the power of Latino acting and audience attraction, Ferrera won the Best Actress Award at various ceremonies in 2007, including the Golden Globe Awards, the Screen Actors Guild Awards, and the Primetime Emmy Awards—a first for a Latina in the category.

Despite these inroads, the doors to the networks need to be opened wider. In 2018 five mainstream broadcast TV networks—ABC, CBS, NBC, Fox, and CW—produced around eighty pilots for selection of shows to air or not. Some thirty shows were picked for airing, but only three—ABC's *Grand Hotel* and CW's *Roswell, New Mexico* and *Charmed*—had Latinos in starring roles. Seven other shows featured at least one Latino actor as part of the main cast. In some thirty-four pilots that were not picked, almost half featured Latino main characters or storylines. This was despite CW's success with CW's *Jane the Virgin* (2014–19). In the 2019 pilot season, these five networks had chosen only two pilots with Latinos starring: a CW spinoff of *Jane the Virgin* titled *Jane the Novela* and an untitled CBS comedy starring Mexican actor Jaime Camil.

However, the cable and internet networks were more sensitive to Latino programming and representational needs. In 2020 Netflix produced a comedy-drama series on gentrification in the East Los Angeles barrio, *Gentefied*, with América Ferrera as the executive producer. Cable network production of Latino features included FX's short series *The Bridge*, starring Demián Bichir and focusing on El Paso-Juárez, Mexico; *Devious Maids* (2014–2016), starring Ana Ortiz, Dania Ramirez, and Roselyn Sánchez; and FX's *Mayans M.C.* (debuted in 2018 and still running in 2022), starring J. D. Pardo, Clayton Cardenas, Edward James Olmos, and Sarah Bolger. Some of these were subsequently carried on the Hulu streaming network, which itself produced with an almost entire Latino cast *East Los High* (2013–14), Hulu's first and only series with an all-Latino cast and crew, mostly filmed

A Dora the Explorer balloon passes Times Square at the Macy's Thanksgiving Day Parade on November 26, 2009, in Manhattan.

in East Los Angeles. Netflix, not to be outdone, produced a Latino-family sitcom remake of producer Norman Lear's 1970s sitcom *One Day at a Time* (2017–19), starring Justina Machado, Todd Grinnell, Isabella Gomez, and Marcel Ruiz. However, the most successful cable or broadcast production of all has been Nickelodeon's *Dora, the Explorer*, an animated series about an eight-year-old girl who sets off with friends to explore the world, freely interspersing Spanish with English, and featuring the voices of Caitlin Sánchez, Fátima Ptacek, Kathleen Herles, and Harrison Chad. Original episodes aired from 1999 to 2019. A spinoff, *Go, Diego, Go!* ran from 2005 to 2010.

Prevailing Stereotypes

Despite the advances in representation of Latinos on television in some of the programs listed in

the previous section, shows that predominantly link Latinos to drugs and crime continue to light up television screens, even in such series that employ numerous Latino actors, such as *Mayans M.C.* and *The Bridge*. They continue the stereotype of the Latino bandido—bandit, criminal, lawbreaker, and drug smuggler—that has even negatively colored the portrayal of Latino immigrants as criminals on the screen, in popular culture, and in politics. The stereotype, whose origin can be traced to the dime novels written in the nineteenth century as an ideological product of Manifest Destiny, was immediately reproduced in early cinema and subsequently was also adapted promptly and prominently by television. The stock bandido, Latina spitfire (a sexualized hot-tempered peasant girl), or peon were common in innumerable western cowboy films and series. Also, the numerous urban counterparts have been constantly present, starting with *Dragnet* (NBC 1951–59; 1967–70) and *Naked City* (ABC 1958–59; 1960–63), as part of the detective and police dramas. They were continued in the underworld activities (especially regarding drug traffic and dealings) in *Hill Street Blues* (NBC 1981–86) and *Miami Vice* (ABC 1984–89), and to this day are prevalent in *Mayans M.C.* and others, as mentioned above.

General market television has allowed a few law-enforcer or lawmaker Latino stereotypes. *The Cisco Kid, Zorro, CHiPs, Miami Vice,* and *L.A. Law* have included some relatively positive Latino male figures. One notable early example was Walt Disney's *The Nine Lives of Elfego Baca* (1958). Based on the exploits of the legendary Mexican American lawman, the miniseries was an all-too-rare instance of television depicting a Chicano hero. More often, Latinos have been cast in secondary or insignificant roles. For example, on *Hill Street Blues* the Latino lieutenant who was second in command was often given little to do and was generally dull.

Most attempts at centering a law enforcement series around a Latino character have been disappointing. *Juarez* (1988) was conceived as a gritty portrayal of the life of a Mexican American border detective. ABC lost confidence in the project, however, and suspended production shortly after only two episodes were completed. NBC's *Drug Wars: The Camarena Story* (1990) was replete with updated bandido stereotypes and so offensive to Mexicans that Mexico issued formal complaints about the miniseries, which went on to win an Emmy. Paul Rodríguez's private investigator in *Grand Slam* resulted in little more than yet another instance of the comic buffoon. More recently, Demián Bichir in *The Bridge* is a generally positive and attractive lawman, but he is far overshadowed by the numerous bandidos who run the Mexican cartels and commit heinous crimes.

In contrast, Edward James Olmos's Lieutenant Martin Castillo in *Miami Vice* was one of the most positive Latino characters in television history. Olmos was initially reluctant to take the part (he turned down the role several times before finally accepting), and the show's producers ultimately gave him control over the creation and realization of Castillo. He fashioned a dignified, honorable character of quiet strength and considerable power, thereby helping to offset the show's facile stereotyping of villainous Latin American drug smugglers. Another major impact was in the formidable presence of Jimmy Smits playing Victor Sifuentes on *L.A. Law*, who provided the law firm (and the series) with a healthy dose of social consciousness. He reprised this dignity as the head of a law firm in *Bluff City Law* (2019), but he plays a character not identified as Latino.

Other stereotypes of Latinos on television could be examined, as could the occasions when some Latino actors (for example, Ricardo Montalbán) and actresses (for instance, Rita Moreno) have been called upon to play a variety of roles beyond the usual stereotypes. What has been most neglected, however, is regular positive roles for Latinas and, equally important, the Latino family. This is one area in which Latinos on television have been worse off than in film.

During the early 1950s Elena Verdugo starred in the comedy series *Meet Millie*, but not as a Latina woman. Instead, she played an "all-American girl." The image of the Latina woman has been usually relegated to the overweight mamacita, the spitfire or hot-tempered sexy señorita, the suffering mother, or gang member's girlfriend. But today, more than any other character type, Latinas appear as stereotyped maids and have inherited the role of the African American "mammy," accounting for as much as 69 percent of Latina TV roles. Images of strong, self-reliant, attractive, all-knowing Latina females were notable in Linda Cristal's role as Victoria Cannon in *The High Chaparral* (NBC 1967–71) and Verdugo as nurse Consuelo in *Marcus Welby, M.D.* (ABC 1969–76). More recently this shortage of strong Latina characters remains the predominant pattern. Exceptions in the past were Elizabeth Peña's roles on the previously discussed *I Married Dora* (ABC 1987) and *Shannon's Deal* (NBC 1989–90) and the character of Pilar in *Falcon Crest* (CBS 1987–89). The latter managed to be more than a simple one-dimensional love interest and was a forceful businesswoman. And, of course, today, such roles that América Ferrera in *Ugly Betty* and Justina Machado in *One Day at a Time* are current exceptions.

Latina families have also been absent from the center stages of general market network television. In *The High Chaparral*, which ran from 1967 to 1971, a Mexican cattle-ranching family was portrayed along-

Henry Darrow as Manuelito Montoya and Aspa Nakapoulou as Angelina from the television program The High Chaparral.

side the gringo family. After that series, consequential inclusions of Latino families have eluded long runs on the small screen. *Viva Valdez*, a poorly conceived and received situation comedy about a Chicano family living in East Los Angeles, was aired on ABC during the summer of 1976.

It was not until the spring of 1983, when ABC aired *Condo*, that a middle-class urban Latino family was first introduced to TV viewers in the United States. That situation comedy series featured a stereotyped WASP and an upwardly mobile Latino who found themselves as condominium neighbors on opposite sides of almost every question, but who were faced with impending family ties. This modern-day Romeo and Juliet—in the very first episode, the oldest Anglo son and a Latino daughter elope—was also short-lived as its quality declined and ratings faltered against the competition of CBS's *Magnum, P.I.* and NBC's *Fame*. Yet during *Condo*'s twelve episodes, another TV first was set as the featured Mexican American family was shown interacting as equals with an Anglo family that sometimes acceptingly participated with them as Latinos.

In March 1984 ABC tried Norman Lear's *a.k.a. Pablo*, another situation comedy centered on Latino comedian Paul Rodríguez. This show also featured his working-class family. Unfortunately, Pablo's pungent jokes, often about Mexicans and Latinos in general, irked enough Latinos and others that their strong protest to the network contributed to the show's cancellation after only six episodes. As of this writing, the Latino family as subject has reappeared with credible products, as mentioned: *One Day at a Time, Gentefication,* and *Ugly Betty*. All three shows portray diverse Latino families with realism and cultural sensitivity—once again reflecting the changing times of a large Latino viewing audience and generations of Latinos who consume entertainment in English.

Until very recently, the absence of notable Latino female figures and families was also evident in the daytime soap opera genre, which generally neglects Blacks, Latinos, and most other ethnic minorities. *Santa Barbara* was the only ongoing contemporary soap with recurring roles for Latinos. That show made a commitment to have a Latino family to reflect the large numbers of Latinos in Santa Barbara. The twenty-first century, however, has seen the introduction of Latino characters in many of the most popular and longest running American soap operas, although these characters are often the only Latinos featured in those shows. Andrés Zuno was the first to star in an American soap: *The Bold and the Beautiful*. Others to break into the daytime drama market are Vincent Irizarry in *All My Children* and *The Young and the Restless*; Eva LaRue, Eddie Matos, Mark Consuelos, and J. R. Martínez in *All My Children*; Gabriela Rodríguez and Gina Gallego in *The Days of Our Lives*; Camila Banus and David Fumero in *One Life to Live*; Vanessa Marcil and Erik Valdez in *General Hospital*; and Marisa Ramírez in *The Young and the Restless*.

Studies originating from government, academic, and professional circles corroborate the previous findings and reveal additional shortcomings about the treatment of Latinos on general market television. In 1977 and 1979, the U.S. Commission on Civil Rights published two reports on the portrayals and employment of women and minorities in television. While many results were reported with aggregated data on all minorities, specific findings about "people of Spanish origin" [sic] were noted in the 1977 report. For example, from the content analysis of one sample week of programming during the fall of 1973 and 1974, only three Latinos, all males, were found in "major" roles; twelve Latino males and one female were found playing minor roles. The highest-status occupation shown was a lawyer in a minor role. Unfortunately, the U.S. Commission on Civil Rights has not conducted any follow-up studies.

The first academically based systematic analysis of this subject examined sample weeks of commercial fictional programming during three television seasons (1975–78). Among the 3,549 characters with speaking roles observed in the 255 episodes coded, they were able to find only fifty-three different individuals who could reliably be identified as Latinos—slightly less than 1.5 percent of the population of speaking TV characters. Those characters were hard to find; mostly males of dark complexion, with dark hair, most often with heavy accents; women were absent and insignificant; the characters were gregarious and pleasant, with strong family ties—half worked hard, half were lazy, and very few showed much concern for their futures; most had very little education, and their jobs reflected that fact.

General market television's neglect of Latinos was similarly documented in a report commissioned by the League of United Latin American Citizens (LULAC) and prepared by Public Advocates, Inc. In the Public Advocates audit of all sixty-three prime-time shows during the first week of the fall 1983 television season, Latinos played 1/2 of 1 percent (3 characters out of 496) of the significant speaking roles and only 1 percent (10 characters out of 866) of those who spoke one or more lines. With the exception of Geraldo Rivera, there was an absence of positive Latino characters. On ABC, two-thirds of all speaking parts for Latinos were criminals; on CBS, no Latinos were in any significant speaking roles; and on NBC only one of its 189 (1/2 of 1 percent) significant roles included a Latino.

The very low percentage of Latino participation in television was also found in a study analyzing 620 episodes of prime-time series randomly selected from the Library of Congress's holdings from 1955 to 1986. Findings showed that since 1975, nearly one in ten characters have been Black (from a low of under 1 percent in the 1950s), while Latinos have hovered around the 2 percent mark for three decades. Furthermore, in almost every comparison made of the social background (for example, education and employment) and plot functions (starring role, positive/negative portrayal, having committed a crime, and so on) of the White, Black, and Latino characters, the latter group was consistently worst off.

A survey conducted and a thesis written in 2017 for San Jose State University by Gloria Arellano concluded, "Although Latinos comprise 17 percent of the U.S. population, only 7.4 percent of the representations in primetime on ABC and CBS were Latino. This percentage is higher compared to the 0.6 percent to 6.5 percent found by Fullerton and Kendrick in the year 2000. The Latino population is rapidly growing and it has become the largest minority group in the United States. Of the 403 characters analyzed in English-language TV, only 30 were Latinos. Only seven Latino characters had recurring roles in which they appeared in every episode of a show. Latinos have the least representation in primetime television, as compared with all other minority groups in the United States."

Public television has fared just slightly better than the commercial networks. *Sesame Street*, *3–2–1 Contact*, and *The Electric Company*, programs produced by the Children's Television Workshop for PBS, regularly feature Latino role models, adults as well as children. PBS also has featured Latino themes, dramas, and films such as Jesús Salvador Treviño's *Seguín*, Robert M. Young's *Alambrista*, Moctesuma Esparza and Robert M. Young's *The Ballad of Gregorio Cortez*, and Gregory Nava's *El Norte*.

Happily, this trend has continued. Over the years, PBS has broadcast Luis Valdez's *Corridos!* (1987), dramatizations of traditional Mexican narrative ballads; Jesús Salvador Treviño's *Birthright: Growing Up Latino* (1989), interviews with leading Latino writers; Isaac Artenstein's *Break of Dawn* (1990), a docudrama based on the life of singer and Los Angeles radio personality Pedro J. González; and Héctor Galán's hard-hitting documentaries *New Harvest, Old Shame* (1990), *Los Mineros* (1991), and *In Search of Pancho Villa* (1993). However, exemplary series such as *Villa Alegre*, *Carrascolendas*, and *Qué Pasa, U.S.A.* were canceled due to lack of funds or low ratings.

A new vehicle to improve funding and the production of Latino-oriented CPB programs was created in 1998: Latino Public Broadcasting (LPB). Pioneered by Edward James Olmos and Marlene Dermer, who served as its first executive director, LPB functions as a nonprofit corporation that is funded by the CPB and philanthropic organizations to fund the development, production, postproduction, acquisition, and distribution of noncommercial educational and cultural television related to Latino subjects. The LPB dramas, documentaries, comedies, satire, and animated productions are then distributed to Public Broadcasting Services (PBS) stations that request them throughout the United States. As of the year 2020, LPB pro-

> A new vehicle to improve funding and the production of Latino-oriented CPB programs was created in 1998: Latino Public Broadcasting (LPB).

ductions have won some 125 awards, including two George Foster Peabody Awards, Emmys, Imagen Awards, and the Sundance Film Festival Award for Best Documentary Director. Recent program highlights include the PBS *Great Performances/VOCES* special *John Leguizamo's Road to Broadway*; the *American Masters/VOCES* special *Raúl Julia: The World's a Stage*; the *Frontline, Independent Lens* and *VOCES* copresentation *Marcos Doesn't Live Here Anymore*; the POV broadcast documentary *The Silence of Others*; and the Independent Lens broadcast *Harvest Season*. Other highlights include *Farewell, Ferris Wheel* and *Personal Statement*, nominated in 2017 and 2019, respectively, for the Outstanding Business and Economic Documentary Emmy Award; and *Don't Tell Anyone*, winner of the 2015 George Foster Peabody Award, among many others. As of 2020, LPB has awarded $12.6 million in funds, distributed 255 hours of programming, and presented five seasons of VOCES, the acclaimed PBS documentary series that explores the richly complex Latino experience.

News Coverage

The final area of interest regarding the images of Latinos in general market television is news coverage. Ironically, researchers of media news content have themselves shown little concern for this population. Among the scores of articles published about the characteristics and biases of television news, not even one has given systematic attention to the portrayal of Latinos in newscasts. For studies that have focused on the major network news, part of the problem may be the few stories broadcast about Latinos.

One study, "The Latino Media Gap," produced by Frances Negrón-Muntaner et al. for the National Association of Latino Independent Producers and Columbia University's Center for the Study of Ethnicity and Race, concluded that "stories about Latinos constitute less than 1 percent of news media coverage, and the majority of these stories feature Latinos as lawbreakers. Moreover, Latino participation in front of and behind the camera is extraordinarily low: As of 2013, there were no Latino anchors or executive producers in any of the nation's top news programs. According to available data, only 1.8 percent of news producers are Latinos." But none of the twenty-one top news executive producers were Latinos.

Not only are Latinos underrepresented at 1 percent of all news stories—with 66 percent of those related to crime or "illegal" immigration—but Latinos only make up 3 percent of opinion in the form of guests on talk shows. And the trend is to have non-Latinos expressing opinions on Latino people and their issues. This is true on broadcast as well as cable news and opinion shows.

One view is that in essence, it seems that general market television has yet to do much with, or for, the Latino either as a television character or as a viewer. It might be improper to characterize them as invisible, except for criminality.

Behind the cameras and in the offices, the treatment of Latinos is likewise inadequate. From the first reports of the U.S. Commission on Civil Rights (1977, 1979) to more recent configurations of minority employment in the broadcasting industry, Latino participation has been and continues to be extremely small, much below Latino population proportions, and it is inferior to that of Afro-Americans.

Overall, Latinos have been neglected and poorly depicted in a television industry oriented to the dominant society. The future treatment of Latinos in this medium may be contingent on some inroads that individual actors and actresses make. It may also depend on the continued process of organized activities being carried out by advocacy and Latino community groups.

Given the dismal record of authentic representation and of employment of Latinos in television news, Latinos are more and more abandoning TV news shows for news on the internet. According to a 2016 survey conducted by the Pew Research Center, three-quarters of U.S. Latinos get their news from in-

> Given the dismal record of authentic representation and of employment of Latinos in television news, Latinos are more and more abandoning TV news shows for news on the internet.

ternet sources, nearly equal to the share who do so from television. TV has been the most commonly used platform for news among Latinos, but the proportion getting their news from TV has declined, from 92 percent in 2006 to 79 percent in 2016. That same year, 74 percent of Latinos reported that they used the internet—including social media or smartphone apps—as a source of news, up from 37 percent in 2006. (Newspapers as a news source declined from 58 percent in 2006 to 34 percent in 2016.) And the downward trend will intensify with millennials, 91 percent of whom in 2016 already got their news from the internet.

Another alternative, especially where some Spanish is employed in the home, is Spanish-language television. According to the National Association of Broadcasters, in 2016 the Univisión broadcast network was one of the top five networks in the United States, reaching 93 percent of Latino television households and 83 million unduplicated media viewers. Univisión's sister network, UniMás, was also available in 87 percent of Latino television homes, and Telemundo network reached viewers in forty-seven markets, including all of the top ten Hispanic markets. MundoMax reached nineteen television markets across the country, and Estrella TV reached fifteen television markets across the United States. Azteca America was viewed by more than twenty-one million people across the United States. Local Spanish-language stations are also witnessing substantial audience expansion. In December 2015, the finale of *La Banda* on Univisión recorded 5.1 million total viewers nationally and outperformed ABC and CBS stations with viewers aged 18–49 in Los Angeles, New York, Dallas, Miami, and Houston. The Univisión network is number one in the major media markets of Los Angeles, Houston, Miami, and New York, regardless of language.

Advertising

For years Latinos have been practically invisible in general market advertising and by extension in employment in this industry. When Latinos have been included in ways palatable to the Anglo majority society, their images have often been quite offensive to fellow Latinos.

Perhaps the most controversial advertisement with a "Latino character" was the Frito Bandito, the Mexican bandit cartoon figure utilized repeatedly by the Frito-Lay Corporation in its television and print promotions of corn chips. In discussions about advertising racism and mistreatment of Latinos, this example is often cited because of the complaints it generated, especially among Chicano activist and civic groups. Thanks in part to the public protests against Frito-Lay and activists threatening boycotts of television stations airing the commercials, the Frito Bandito figure was discontinued in 1971. The public objections by Latinos during the 1970s led to some positive changes in the media during the 1970s, just at the dawn of the so-called Latino decade. As advertising and marketing companies began to recognize the profitability of this growing sector of society, Latino-oriented strategies began to emerge in these industries.

LATINO-ORIENTED PRINT MEDIA

Unlike other ethnic groups, Latinos have had a broad range of mass media directed at them. Beginning with the border newspapers of the 1800s up to present-day inroads in telecommunications, Latinos have worked hard at establishing and maintaining print and electronic channels through which they can be informed and entertained in ways relevant to their particular populations and cultures. While most of the Latino-oriented media have been in the Spanish language, many have been bilingual and, in more recent times, fully English-language products specifically directed at Latinos. Likewise, Latinos have been owners and producers of a number of mass media institutions oriented to them. However, a significant part of such media have been wholly or partially owned and operated by Anglo individuals or corporations. Whatever the language or ownership, one of the common aspects of all these media is that in their portrayals via images or words, and in their general employment practices, Latinos have been treated much more adequately. In these media, Latino life in the United States has been and continues to be presented and reflected more thoroughly, appropriately, and positively.

The Spanish-language press within the United States had its beginnings in 1808 in New Orleans, Louisiana, with *El Misisipí*, a four-page commercial- and trade-oriented publication. The paper, which was started by the Anglo firm of William H. Johnson & Company, appeared to be a business venture. Its content was heavily influenced by events outside the United States, and it was directed toward Spanish-speaking immigrants—characteristics that were similar to those of other Latino-oriented publications that followed. More importantly, it expressed the political views of the Latino community, in this case against the Napoleonic invasion of Spain and the need for autonomy or independence of Spain's colonies in the Americas.

After the inauguration of *El Misisipí*, hundreds of Spanish-language newspapers and periodicals were founded by Latino natives and immigrants, wherever Latinos lived, from the Southwest to the Northeast, including in the territories belonging to Mexico until the 1850s. Among the first newspapers published in various states and territories were Spanish-language periodicals: *La gaceta de Texas* (Nacogdoches, Texas, 1813), *El Telégrafo* (Fernandina, Florida, 1817), and *El Crepúsculo* (Santa Fe, New Mexico, 1834). It is estimated that more than two thousand Spanish-language newspapers were published before World War II, and the postwar period to the present has seen thousands across the United States. The tradition of printing and publishing in all of the Americas, in fact, was started in Spain's colonies, with the very first printing press in the New World brought to Mexico from Spain in 1535.

Contemporary Newspapers

At present, Spanish-language daily and weekly newspapers are published in cities throughout the United States. One of the oldest running dailies, Los Angeles's *La Opinión*, began publishing on September 16, 1926. It was founded by Ignacio E. Lozano Sr., a Mexican national who wanted to provide news of the native homeland as well as of the new country for the growing Mexican population in Southern California. Lozano went to Los Angeles after working during four years for two Texas newspapers and owning and editing his own paper, San Antonio's *La Prensa*, from 1913 to 1926 (his family continued to own and publish *La Prensa* until its demise in 1963). The move to California was the result of Lozano's view that there were greater Mexican readership needs and opportunities on the West Coast.

From its beginning, *La Opinión* was owned and operated by Lozano and his family, which in 1926 formed Lozano Enterprises, Inc. This company also published *El Eco del Valle*, a weekly tabloid distributed in the San Fernando Valley from 1987 to 1991. On September 28, 1990, 50 percent interest in Lozano Enterprises was purchased by the Times Mirror Company. This major media conglomerate has interests in broadcasting and cable television and in book and magazine publishing; it publishes the *Los Angeles Times*, *Newsday* (New York), and five other newspapers nationwide. With this association, *La Opinión* acquired financial resources to continue improving its product. In spite of this new financial affiliation, the Lozano family maintained a majority on the board of directors and continued its full editorial policy and operational control. In 2004, ImpreMedia, chaired by Mónica Lozano, bought the Tribune Company out and regained full control over *La Opinión*. In November 2007, *La Opinión* ranked number one in net daily paid circulation growth among the two hundred largest newspapers, but by 2008 *La Opinión* and ImpreMedia had downsized, and circulation had suffered, mirroring the fate of most newspapers in the United States. In 2012, a subsidiary of the Argentine newspaper *La Nación* purchased a majority share of ImpreMedia and *La Opinión*. Today, more readers have access to *La Opinión* online: its website, laopinion.com, is the most read newspaper website in the United States, reaching more than six million readers each month. *La Opinión* has more than a half million followers on Facebook.

La Opinión, being the largest Spanish-language daily, is the lead periodical and market of ImpreMedia,

> Today, more readers have access to *La Opinión* online: its website, laopinion.com, is the most read newspaper website in the United States, reaching more than six million readers each month.

which provides content for its newspaper members reaching out to a multigenerational Hispanic audience. Among its members are powerhouses of Latino periodical publishing: *La Opinión* in Los Angeles, *El Diario La Prensa* in New York, *La Raza* in Chicago, *El Mensajero* in San Francisco, *La Prensa* in Orlando, and Rumbo Digital in Houston. ImpreMedia boasts a strong local presence and recently has expanded to include digital-only products, such as *Quiero Más Fútbol* and *Chica Fresh*. It also operates IMPOWER!, a premium content network that increases it broad reach. With more than eight million monthly unique users, IMPOWER! is in Comscore's Hispanic Ad Focus's top ten.

El Diario La Prensa (New York) started in the summer of 1963 from the merger of two newspapers, *La Prensa* and *El Diario de Nueva York*. The former had been operating since 1913 under the ownership of José Campubrí, a Spaniard who kept the paper until 1957, when it was purchased by Fortune Pope. Pope, whose brother was the owner of the *National Enquirer*, was also the owner of the New York Italian paper *Il Progresso* and of WHOM-AM, which later became WJIT-AM, one of the most popular Spanish-language radio stations in New York. In 1963, Pope sold *La Prensa* to O. Roy Chalk, who bought *El Diario de Nueva York* in 1961 from Porfirio Dominici, a Dominican who had started the paper in 1948. With both papers under his control, Chalk, president of Diversified Media, merged *El Diario* and *La Prensa*. In 1981, he sold it to Gannett, which at the time owned a chain of ninety English-language papers. In 1989 El Diario Associates, Inc., was formed by Peter Davidson, a former Morgan Stanley specialist in newspaper industry mergers and acquisitions. This new company then bought *El Diario La Prensa* from Gannett in August 1989 for an estimated twenty million dollars.

Carlos D. Ramírez, a Puerto Rican from New York who had been publisher of this newspaper since 1984, stayed on board to participate as a partner of El Diario Associates. *El Diario* merged with the Los Angeles–based *La Opinión* in 2004 to form ImpreMedia. *El Diario*'s chief competitor in New York was *Hoy*, with 180,000 readers, but in 2007, ImpreMedia purchased *Hoy* from the Tribune Company.

Since their beginnings, *La Prensa* and *El Diario de Nueva York* had been primarily directed at the Puerto Rican, Spanish, and Dominican communities in New York. Presently, *El Diario La Prensa* caters to a more diverse Latino population that, although still principally Puerto Rican, is increasingly more Dominican, Mexican, and Central and South American. It is the largest Spanish-language newspaper in the United States and has 294,769 daily readers and 676,570 unique readers, print and online; its daily circulation is 35,615.

Noticias del Mundo (New York) began publishing on April 22, 1980, under the ownership of Sun Myung Moon's News World Communications, Inc., which also publishes the *Washington Times*, the *New York City Tribune*, and various other publications, including *Últimas Noticias*, a daily newspaper in Uruguay. *Noticias del Mundo*'s circulation hovered around thirty-two thousand in the New York metro area; however, this newspaper ceased publication in the early 1990s.

El Nuevo Herald (Miami) was started on November 21, 1987, as a new and improved version of *El Miami Herald*, which had been continuously published since March 29, 1976, as an insert to the *Miami Herald*. Both the Spanish-language and the English-language newspapers are owned by the Miami Herald Media Company, a subsidiary of the McClatchy Company. In 1987, the Miami Herald Publishing Company (as it was called) recognized the geometric growth of the Latino populations in south Florida and, with the support and approval of the McClatchy Company, began assessing what Latino readers wanted in their Spanish-language daily. The outcome of the study was *El Nuevo Herald*, which moved to a separate building from that of its English-language counterpart to begin publishing from a location closer to the Latino community. Other improvements included a 150 percent increase of the daily news space, better coverage of the Cuban and Latin American events and communities, and the use of color with modern format, graphics, and layout.

As might be expected, given the demographics of Miami and southern Florida, since its beginnings the principal readers of *El Nuevo Herald* have been immigrant Cuban and Latin American populations residing in that area. This broadsheet paper, in contrast to its New York counterparts, reaches the majority of its readers via home delivery. Its daily circulation is approximately 53,924, and its Sunday circulation is

68,781, which is the largest Sunday readership of any Spanish-language newspaper.

Aside from the news gathering by its own staff, *El Nuevo Herald* can benefit from the work of its English-language partner, including the use of translated stories from the international correspondents. For major stories, *El Nuevo Herald* may send its own reporters to Latin America. Thus, the *Miami Herald* may use stories gathered by *El Nuevo Herald*'s foreign or local reporters. *El Nuevo Herald* was deemed Best Hispanic Daily, from 1990 to 1999 and 2004 to 2006, by the National Association of Hispanic Publications.

El Diario de las Américas (Miami) was founded on July 4, 1953, by Horacio Aguirre, a Nicaraguan lawyer who had been an editorial writer for a Panamanian newspaper, *El Panamá-América*, edited by Harmodio Arias, a former president of that country. Part of the financial support needed for starting *El Diario de las Américas* was made possible thanks to a Venezuelan builder-investor and two Pensacola, Florida, road builders who also believed in the founder's mission. The paper was published by the Americas Publishing Company, owned by the Aguirre family until 2012, when the newspaper was acquired by the Mezerhane Group, whose president is the businessman of Venezuelan origin. As online news expanded, *El Diario de las Américas* cut back on print publication and by 2018 became a weekly appearing in print only on Saturdays. In November 2019, Cuban journalist Iliana Lavastida was appointed executive director. *El Diario de las Américas* remains the only Spanish-language daily owned and operated by Latinos without full or partial partnership by Anglo corporations. The Cuban and Latin American interests of their readership are evidently reflected in the strong international—particularly Latin American—news coverage of the paper.

In addition, other daily publications serve Latino communities. The oldest is the Spanish-language page of the *Laredo Morning Times*. This daily news page has been published continuously since 1926. Also produced in the United States is *El Nuevo Heraldo*, the sister publication to the *Brownsville Herald*, serving the Rio Grande Valley region in Texas. *El Nuevo Heraldo* appears to be a continuation of the former *El Heraldo de Brownsville* (Texas), which was published seven days

a week by the *Brownsville Herald*. That paper was inaugurated on November 11, 1934, by Oscar del Castillo, who was the founder and editor from its beginning until his death on January 19, 1991. Marcelino González then edited the paper until 1999.

Other Spanish-language newspapers affiliated with English-language dailies include *La Voz de Houston*, distributed by the *Houston Chronicle*, and *Hoy*, distributed by the *Chicago Tribune*. The daily newspapers *El Fronterizo*, *El Mexicano*, and *El Continental* are distributed respectively in morning, afternoon, and evening editions published by the Compañia Periodística del Sol de Ciudad Juárez. *El Fronterizo*, published since 1943, is the largest of the three, with six daily sections each of approximately eight pages. *El Mexicano*, published since 1950, is more condensed and contains about ten pages; its circulation figures are twenty-nine thousand Monday through Saturdays. *El Continental*, founded in 1933, has only eight pages and a Monday through Saturday circulation of eight thousand. While all three newspapers have as major clients the Mexicans and Latinos in El Paso and surrounding communities, they are published in Ciudad Juárez by the Organización Editorial Mexicana, representing seventy-eight newspapers in that country.

Magazines and Periodicals

Long before the turn of the century, a variety of publications that can be classified as Latino-oriented magazines were produced. The rich history of these publications can be observed in the holdings of major libraries such as the Nettie Lee Benson Latin American Collection at the University of Texas at Austin and the Chicano Studies Collections of the University of California, Berkeley, Los Angeles, and Santa Barbara. While a comprehensive anthology of all such publications is still lacking, even a cursory review of the titles shows that culturally oriented magazines have abounded, as have many with political, social, education, business, and entertainment topics. More than eighty Latino consumer magazines circulate throughout the United States today.

Actually, the publication of general interest and illustrated Latino magazines goes back to the nineteenth century, when there was an emerging leisure and middle class of Latinos, and women in particular found the time to engage in this type of reading. Among the many such periodicals that appeared and had some staying power were New York's *El Ateneo: Repertorio Ilustrado* (1874–77), *La Ilustración Norteamericana* (c. 1890s), and *La Revista Ilustrada de Nueva York* (1882–?); Albuquerque, New Mexico's *La Revista de Albuquerque* (1881–188?); and El Paso, Texas's *Revista Ilustrada* (1917–?). These magazines, which were beautifully illustrated with drawings and photographs, drew on the works of the most famous writers of the Hispanic world.

One of the oldest contemporary Spanish-language magazines was *Temas*, founded in November 1950 and published until 1997. It circulated more than 110,000 copies per month. *Temas* featured articles on culture, current events, beauty, fashion, home decoration, and interviews with personalities of various artistic and academic backgrounds of interest to Latinos. This general-interest, family-oriented magazine was founded by publisher and editor José de la Vega, a Spaniard, who indicated that *Temas* was the only national magazine published in Castilian Spanish without trendy "idioms." Given this editorial style, many of its articles were widely reprinted in high school and university reading packages across the country.

> The publication of general interest and illustrated Latino magazines goes back to the nineteenth century, when there was an emerging leisure and middle class of Latinos.

Another notable magazine, *Réplica*, was founded in 1963 by Alex Lesnik, a Cuban refugee, who once ran a propaganda network that helped Fidel Castro come to power. From its base in Miami, this monthly magazine had a circulation of 111,000 nationwide, of which approximately 96 percent was targeted to reach bilingual, bicultural, affluent opinion makers and other influential Latinos in the United States. It included a variety of articles on topics such as travel, fashion, sports, entertainment, and news events related to Latin America and the Caribbean Basin, and it regularly carried Lesnik's commentary on Cuba and the Revolution. *Réplica*'s offices in Little Havana were bombed eleven times, mostly in the mid-1970s. Lesnik eventually shut down *Réplica* in the early 1980s because of death threats aimed at him, his advertisers, and businesses that carried the magazine.

Latina Style magazine was founded by Anna María Arias in 1994 in Los Angeles; it claims to be "the first national magazine dedicated to the needs and concerns of the contemporary Latina professional working woman and the Latina business owner in the United States." Its current circulation is 150,000 with a readership of nearly 600,000. *Latina Style* is aimed at both the professional Latinas and young Latinas entering the workforce for the first time. It showcases successful Latinas in all areas, including business, science, civic affairs, education, entertainment, sports, and the arts. It also offer technology tips and reviews, entertainment reviews, travel recommendations, investment guidance, beauty tips, food and drink recipes, automotive updates, and career advice. Each year the magazine publishes the *LATINA Style 50 Report* to recognize the top fifty companies for inclusion and best treatment of Latinas in their professional careers; this is the way they recruit, promote, provide benefits, and create programs for the betterment of their employees who are Latina professionals. Beginning in 2014, the magazine has brought together Latina leaders from throughout the nation for a "National LATINA Symposium" to discuss in panels and roundtables the status of the Latina working woman in the United States.

Latina magazine was founded in 1996 by Christy Haubegger under Latina Publications, LLC, but was later purchased by Latina Media Ventures (LMV), which is wholly focused on celebrating the "culture, honoring the past and enriching the future of Latina women in the United States." In 2010, LMV named editorial director Galina Espinoza and publisher Lauren Michaels copresidents of the company. At the time it had a readership of two million people and was the largest magazine edited by and for Latina women. *Latina* was named Best Magazine by *Advertising Age* in 2000. Despite all of its success, its new owner, Solera Capital, announced financial difficulties in 2018, and then *Latina* ceased operations. In 2021, however, LMV announced a relaunch of *Latina* as a digital publication to be led by Camila Legaspi as the chief content officer and Verky Baldonado as editor at large.

Latino Leaders was founded by Raúl and Jorge Ferráez, two Mexican businessmen, in 1999 to publish stories of successful Latinos with a focus on the leadership or high end of the market. The magazine has grown its readers from 17,000 in 2000 to more than 240,000 currently. It claims 778,600 average readers per print and online edition. The market segment it reaches has 45 percent of the total purchasing power of the entire Latino market (estimated at more than a trillion dollars in 2018). *Latino Leaders*, in print and online, aims at connecting leaders and inspiring future leaders. By promoting and publishing stories of Latino success, *Latino Leaders* strives to showcase stories not often seen in the mainstream media. At the same time, it demonstrates the influence Latinos maintain in the United States.

Three English-language magazines of particular note are *Hispanic*, *Hispanic Business*, and *Hispanic Link*, all of which no longer publish. Founded in 1988 and closed down in 2010, *Hispanic*'s major focus was on contemporary Latinos and their achievements and contributions to American society; it targeted upwardly mobile Latinos. The stories covered a broad range of topics, such as entertainment, education, business, sports, the arts, government, politics, literature, and national and international personalities and events that may be of importance and interest to Latinos in the United States. It was a family company of chairman and founder Fred Estrada, a native of Cuba, whose son, Alfredo, was the publisher until 2003, when Sam Verdeja's Hispanic Publishing Group bought the magazine. The original publisher had been Jerry Apodaca, a Mexican American and former governor of New Mexico. Published monthly, *Hispanic* had an ABC-audited circulation of 315,000 at its height.

Hispanic Business was run by editor and publisher Jesús Chavarría, a Mexican American who started the magazine in 1979 as a newsletter. In 1982 it became a monthly publication; with a BPA-audited primary circulation of 265,000 and a total audience of more than one million readers, *Hispanic Business* reached CEOs, business owners, corporate decision makers, and professionals in all sectors, including business, law, accounting, health care, government and engineering. One of its regular departments covered news related to "Media/Marketing." Special monthly topics included, among others, statistics and trends in the Latino media markets (December); the Latino "Business 500"—the annual directories of the leading Latino-owned corporations in the United States (June); and Latinos in the general market television, film, music, and related entertainment businesses (July).

Another English-language Latino-oriented publication was *Hispanic Link*. Although it was a newsletter, it was an influential publication that provided a succinct summary of the major issues and events related to education, immigration, business, legislative, political, policy, and economic concerns of the Latino populations. Weekly summary columns included "Arts and Entertainment" and a "Media Report." *Hispanic Link* was founded by Charles A. Erickson and his wife, Sebastiana Mendoza, in February 1980 as a column service for newspapers. In September 1983 it became a regular newsletter. Although it only claimed approximately twelve hundred subscribers, its circulation and readership were much higher as it reached many libraries, Latino organization leaders, people in corporations with major responsibilities toward Latinos, journalists, Latino advocacy groups, and influential government officials working with or interested in legislation and policy issues related to Latinos. *Hispanic Link* solicited columns from various journalists and experts on subjects concerning Latinos and provided those articles as a syndicated service of three columns per week to more than eighty-five newspapers across the country via the *Los Angeles Times* syndicated news service. However, for some time now, it has only existed online as *Hispanic Link D.C.*

Two notable bilingual magazines in the late twentieth and early twenty-first centuries were *Vista* and *Saludos Hispanos*. *Vista* started in September 1985 as a monthly supplement insert to selected Sunday newspapers in locations with large Latino populations. Although *Vista* was published in English on a weekly basis from late 1989 through June 1991, financial problems resulting from the general national economic situation, particularly insufficient advertising support, made it return to its monthly schedule. Beginning in June 1991, in addition to its English-language articles, it incorporated *Mosaic*, a Spanish-language supplement with three stories. *Vista* was aimed at informing, educating, and entertaining Latino readers with stories that focused on Latino role models, positive portrayals of Latinos, and their cultural identity. By July 1994, *Vista* was inserted in thirty-eight different newspapers in seven states: Arizona, California, Florida, Illinois, New Mexico, New York, and Texas, and its readership exceeded one million. In 1991 the magazine was purchased by Fred Estrada and his Latino Publishing Corporation, where it remained until its demise in 2005.

Saludos Hispanos, "the official publication of the United Council of Spanish Speaking People," was owned by Rosemarie García-Solomon, a Mexican American. A significant part of its approximately three hundred thousand circulation went to about three thousand schools, universities, and various institutions in California, Florida, Illinois, New York, and Texas, which used the magazine for educational purposes. One reason for *Saludos Hispanos*'s educational value was that it published side-by-side Spanish and English versions of most of its stories. Furthermore, it stressed positive role models for and about Latinos. In addition to articles on the feature topic, the regular departments included, among others, role models, music, careers, earth watch, university profile, fashion, law and order, museums, and food. Another educational distinction of this publication company was its *Saludos Hispanos Video Magazín*, a three-part video program that was used by more than four thousand schools and organizations for recruitment and retention of Latino youth in the educational system. The video, available in English and a Spanish-language dubbed version, was designed to motivate Latino youth to stay in school, to improve relationships, and to stress the importance of cultural pride and self-esteem as keys to success. Still publishing today, its mission has changed somewhat to a career recruitment and placement service both in print and online at saludos.com.

> *Siempre Mujer* magazine, since its founding in 2005 by Meredith Corporation, has been published entirely in Spanish for Latinas throughout the United States and Puerto Rico.

Siempre Mujer magazine, since its founding in 2005 by Meredith Corporation, has been published entirely in Spanish for Latinas throughout the United States and Puerto Rico. Its leadership includes publication director Enedina Vega-Amáez, editorial director Alberto Oliva, and editor María Cristina Marrero. Its mission has been to inform and motivate Latinas to maintain their traditions while adapting to the culture of the United States. It offers articles on homemaking, family, and beauty so that Latinas can feel complete while attending to their varied roles as mothers, wives, daughters, and friends. The overall emphasis is on self-improvement.

Dozens of Spanish-language consumer magazines cover specialized topics related to parenthood, fashion, hobbies, and social, cultural, business, and political interests. All are readily available in the United States via subscriptions or magazine racks in Latino communities in major cities. Some of the most popular are *Buenhogar*, *Cosmopolitan*, *Geomundo*, *Hombre*, *Harper's Bazaar en Español*, *Mecánica Popular*, *People en Español*, *Selecciones del Reader's Digest*, *Tu Internacional*, and *Vanidades Continental*. As can be observed by the titles, some are Spanish-language editions of English-language publications. Regardless of whether these are produced in Spain, the United States, or Latin America, they have as primary clients any and all Spanish-speaking populations.

Other specialized magazines in Spanish and/or English are produced with the Latino as the primary client, for example, *Abasto*, *Automundo*, *Buena Salud*, *Career Focus* (also targeted to African Americans), *Embarazo*, *Hispanic Executive*, *Hispanic Outlook in Higher Education*, *Parents Latina Magazine*, *Latino Youth-USA*, *Mi Bebé*, *Ser Padre*, *Teleguía*, *TV y Novelas USA*, *Una Nueva Vida*, the northeastern U.S. edition of *Imagen*, and the Latino youth-oriented automobile publication *Lowrider*.

Furthermore, there are journals with specialized topics related to academia, professions, and organizations. Among the current academic journals are *Aztlán*, *Centro*, the academic journal of the Centro de

Estudios Puertorriqueños-Hunter College, the *Latino Journal of Behavioral Sciences*, *Harvard Journal of Hispanic Policy*, and *Latino Studies*.

Finally, there are state and regional publications aimed at the respective Latino or Spanish-speaking populations. Examples of these are *Adelante* (Washington, D.C.), *Avance Hispano* (San Francisco), *Cambio!* (Phoenix), *La Voz de Houston* (Houston), *La Voz* (Seattle), *Miami Mensual*, and *Bienvenidos a Miami*, *Tele Guía de Chicago* and *Lea* (directed at Colombians residing in the United States). In these cities and dozens of others with large Latino concentrations, one can even find Spanish or Latino yellow pages.

LATINO-ORIENTED ELECTRONIC MEDIA

The number of stations, companies, and organizations related to Spanish-language radio and tel-

evision in this country has grown, as has the content they offer. Radio, for example, not only offers *rancheras* and salsa, but also Top 40, mariachi, *norteña*, Tex-Mex, Mexican hits, adult contemporary, contemporary Latin hits, international hits, Spanish adult contemporary, romantic, ballads, traditional hits and oldies, folkloric, regional, *boleros*, progressive *tejano*, merengue, and even bilingual contemporary hits. Television is no longer song-and-dance shows with some *novelas* and old movies. It also offers drama, talk shows, comedy, news, investigative journalism, sports, contemporary movies, entertainment magazines, dance videos, and many specials from all over the world. All of these options have been brought by the search for new markets by both Latino and Anglo entrepreneurs, and the combined growth of the Latino population and its purchasing power.

In some markets the Latino audience for selected Spanish-language radio and television stations is larger than that of many well-known English-language stations; for example, in Los Angeles, KLVE-

Two films have been made about Spanish-language radio pioneer Pedro J. González (left, with attorney Anna Zacsek in Los Angeles, 1935).

FM and KWKW-AM have more listeners than KNX-AM and KROQ-FM. Radio directed especially to the Latino market has grown from an occasional voice heard on isolated stations in the Southwest and on big city multilingual stations to a multimillion-dollar segment of the broadcast industry.

Radio: The Early Years

Spanish-language radio programs transmitted from within the boundaries of the United States began as early as the mid-1920s, almost immediately after the inauguration of commercial broadcasting in this country. While Latino-oriented radio is now quite diversified and can be found in almost every community with an established Latino population, its development has been difficult. Spanish-language radio started in the mid-1920s when English-language radio stations began selling time slots to Latino brokers. During the early days of radio, the stations that sold these slots and the time frames that were made available to brokers depended on the local market competition among stations and the profitability of the various airtimes. Invariably, space for foreign-language programming was provided primarily during the least profitable time (early mornings or weekends) and by stations seeking alternative avenues for revenue.

One of the most well known pioneers of Spanish-language radio in California was Pedro J. González, about whom two films have been made: the documentary *Ballad of an Unsung Hero* (1984, Paul Espinosa, writer and producer) and the full-length feature *Break of Dawn* (1988, Isaac Artenstein, director). Between 1924 and 1934 González was responsible for shows such as *Los Madrugadores* (The Early Birds). This program was broadcast from 4:00 to 6:00 a.m., primarily on Los Angeles station KMPC, which, thanks to its one-hundred-thousand-watt power, could be heard at that time all over the Southwest—even as far as Texas—thus reaching thousands of Mexican workers as they started their day. The dynamics of González's show and his progressive political stands made him a threat to the establishment, resulting in trumped-up rape charges against him in 1934. He was convicted and condemned to six years in San Quentin prison, released in 1940, and immediately deported

to Mexico. In Tijuana he reestablished and continued his radio career until the 1970s, when he retired to the United States. Many others across the Southwest followed González's footsteps in the new medium.

Even through the early brokerage system, Spanish-language radio thrived. By the late 1930s, numerous stations carried Spanish-language programs either full-time or part-time. In response to the market demands, in 1939 the International Broadcasting Company (IBC) was established in El Paso, Texas, to produce and sell Spanish-language programming to various stations and brokers across the country. As a result of the efforts of services like the IBC and the work by dozens of independent brokers, by 1941 it was estimated that 264 hours of Spanish were being broadcast each week by U.S. broadcasters.

In Texas, Raúl Cortez was one of the earliest Chicano brokers and eventually was successful enough to establish and operate his own full-time Spanish-language station—KCOR-AM, a one-thousand-kilowatt "daytime only" station in San Antonio—which went on the air in 1946. Nine years later, Cortez ventured into the Spanish-language television industry. After World War II, Anglo station owners and Latino brokers saw increasing opportunities in the Latino market via Spanish-language radio. This allowed some brokers to follow Cortez's lead and become owners of full-time stations. Most, however, were made employees of the stations they had been buying time from.

From the 1950s to the 1970s, Spanish-language radio was in transition. During those decades, this radio format continued to grow but began moving away from the brokerage system in favor of the more independent, full-time stations in AM and subsequently in FM—many transmitting up to twenty-four hours per day. In terms of the content, the early "broker" years were characterized by poetry, live drama, news, and live music programming. Most of the live music was "Mexican" and the majority of the news was from foreign countries, predominantly Mexico. As musical recordings became more common, this less expensive form of programming replaced the live music, allowing brokers and the stations to keep more of their profits for themselves. During the transition years, "personality radio" was at its best; brokers and announcers who had control over their programs and commercials became popular themselves. By the late 1960s, the format became more tightly packaged and was less in the hands of individual radio stars. Music was selected by the station management to give a consistent sound throughout the programs. These broadcasts had less talk than before and were very much like other music-oriented English-language programs. In the 1970s, the stations' growth also brought increased attention to format programming on the air and to sophisticated marketing techniques on the business side.

Today, the station formats are more varied: 44.16 percent have a programming of religious content; 26.43 percent a regional Mexican format; 18.25 percent a popular/contemporary format; 2.72 percent a programming centered on sports; 2.72 percent tropical rhythms; 2.72 percent includes some variety within their daily spaces; 1.09 percent is dedicated to information; 1.09 percent based their programming on oldies; and 0.82 percent issued in *Tejano* format.

Contemporary Spanish Radio

In the 2020s, the number of Spanish-language radio stations in the United States exceeds fifteen hundred and increases almost monthly. In addition to these, there are a number of bilingual broadcasters. They are broadcasting in at least forty-one of the fifty states, and California, Florida, Illinois, New York, and Texas have scores of the stations in the major cities. In fact, for Latinos, radio is the hottest medium, accompanying workers on the job through the workday, bringing soccer and baseball games into homes and job sites, and promoting radio talk show moderators and disc jockeys as members of the family and neighborhood. Studies by Nielsen of Latino listenership show that Latinos tune into radio more than television, smartphones, or tablets. Spanish-language radio is a powerful and growing medium in the United States. According to the Nielsen service, there were 40.4 million Latino radio listeners in 2015. According to another Nielsen study in 2018, 98 percent of Latinos age twelve or older tuned in each week. That compared to 93 percent of Americans overall. The average weekly listening time was twelve hours and thirty-five minutes; 69 percent of Latinos who tuned in to their favorite station during the day did it away from home. Spanish-dominant listeners spent thirteen hours and twelve minutes each week with radio, compared with eleven hours and forty-eight minutes for English-dominant Latinos.

While these numbers attest to a remarkable growth of the Latino-oriented radio industry, Latino ownership of these radio stations has not followed similar patterns. In 1980 of the sixty-four primary Spanish-language radio stations identified in their study, only 25 percent were owned by Latinos. In the top ten markets (for example, New York, Los Angeles, Chicago, Miami, and San Antonio), Latinos owned only about 10 percent of these types of stations. Primary Spanish-language radio (PSLR) stations are those that transmit in Spanish 50 percent or more of their broadcast day. Latino radio is closely aligned with Hispanic television. All of the top five Hispanic radio station groups are affiliated with a Spanish-language broadcast or cable property, with the exception of iHeartMedia. Many Spanish-language radio stations are affiliates of ABC, CBS, CW, ESPN, Fox, ION, NBC, and NPR. But within the Latino media market there are specific groups with the largest market sectors: Univisión, Entravisión, Estrella Media, iHeart Media, and Spanish Broadcasting System (SBS). SBS, which was started in 1983 by Raúl Alarcón Jr., is the only radio group company whose proprietors are Latinos.

Univisión is the largest Latino-oriented media group in the United States; with approximately ten million weekly listeners, Univisión Radio owns and operates sixty-eight radio stations in seventeen of the top twenty-five U.S. Latino markets and four radio stations in Puerto Rico. Three of the top radio stations broadcast to Los Angeles, and Univisión owns two of them. The Latino radio markets are very diverse ethnically and geographically. New York's Spanish-language radio stations serve a community of 57 percent foreign-born Latinos. In Los Angeles, half are U.S.-born. Mexican Americans along the Rio Grande Valley overwhelmingly claim Mexican American heritage. Over half of Orlando's Latinos are Puerto Ricans. And Miami stations serve a Latino community that is 75 percent foreign born.

Entravision has fifty-eight television channels and more than fifty radio stations with a digital presence. Estrella Media, formerly known as Liberman

The Univisión float at the Dominican Day Parade in New York City, August 9, 2009. Univisión is the largest Latino-oriented media group in the United States.

Broadcasting Inc., founded by José Liberman, is located in California and is considered the largest privately owned minority company in the United States. iHeartMedia, formerly Clear Channel, is the largest media company in the country and has some thirty Spanish-language stations. SBS is the largest public-owned Latino company in the United States and has some twenty stations.

Such concentration of media under very few owners or corporations has become an important issue, working against diversity and local Latino cultures. In fact, in 2003 two of the giants in radio, Univisión and Hispanic Broadcasting Corporation (HBC), merged, concentrating the market as never before. HBC was previously the oldest and largest, operating as Tichenor Media System, Inc., a family-owned private company

headquartered in Dallas, Texas. Started in 1940 by McHenry Tichenor, a successful Anglo newspaperman, in 1941 he bought his second radio station in South Texas, an English-Spanish bilingual station. This was the family's first venture into the Latino market. The expansion into the Spanish radio field began in 1984 with the formation of Tichenor Spanish Radio. At that time, the non-Spanish-language broadcast properties, including television, were divested to allow for the new ventures into the Latino market. In 1990, Spanish Radio Network was formed in partnership with SRN Texas, Inc. (a wholly owned subsidiary of Tichenor Media System) and Radio WADO, Inc., in order to purchase the Miami and the New York stations. In 2004, shortly after the merger with Univisión, McHenry (Mac) Tichenor Jr. resigned his position as president of Univisión Radio.

Lotus Communications Corporation owns seventeen stations, mostly in California and Arizona. The flagship operation is KWKW-AM, a station that has been serving the Latino community in Los Angeles and vicinities since 1942. It was purchased by Lotus in 1962 for approximately one million dollars. The price was a reflection of the large audience it attracts, especially among the Mexican and Mexican American populations of that region. In addition, under Lotus Latino Reps, the company is sales representative to approximately one hundred Spanish-language radio stations in the United States. The president of Lotus Communications is Jim Kalmenson, who was named the 2018 Broadcaster of the Year by the Hispanic Radio Conference. While Kalmenson and the other owners are Anglos, the executive vice president is Joe Cabrera, a Latino, as are the respective station managers.

A fourth Spanish-language radio group is Radio América, founded in 1986 when brothers Daniel and James Villanueva, of Mexican heritage, bought KBRG-FM in the San Francisco Bay area. In 1988, they acquired KLOK-AM in the San Jose/San Francisco area. And under a separate company called Orange County Broadcasting, the Villanuevas purchased KPLS-AM in Los Angeles. A distinctive characteristic of this station, with 20 percent ownership by Fernando Niebla, also of Mexican descent, is that it is the first "all talk" Spanish-language station in the Los Angeles and Southern California area (there are four "talk" stations in the Miami market). Daniel Villanueva also has minority (20 percent) interests in Washington, D.C.'s Los Cerezos Broadcasting Company, which owns WMDO-AM.

Yet another Spanish-language radio group is the Viva América company, which was started in 1989 with 49 percent owned by Heftel Broadcasting and 51 percent owned by Mambisa Broadcasting Corporation. Heftel owned stations in Los Angeles (KLVE-FM and KTNQ-AM). Mambisa was divided among Amancio V. Suárez, his son Amancio J. Suárez, and cousin Charles Fernández, all of whom were of Cuban descent. In Miami, the Viva America Media Group owned two stations (WAQI-AM and WXDJ-FM). In addition, under the corporate heading of the Southern Media Holding Group, presided over by Amancio V. Suárez, it was linked to *Mi Casa*, a monthly Spanish-language newspaper. Viva América earned $10.1 million in billings in 1991, almost doubling the figure of the previous year; the two Heftel stations were the top in the Spanish-language radio market, totaling $16.3 million for the same year. Eventually Heftel merged with Clear Channel and Tichener to accelerate the pace of media concentration.

A final group of stations that are especially distinct from the aforementioned ones are administered by the nonprofit Radio Bilingüe (Bilingual Radio) network in California. Efforts to establish this network date to 1976, when Hugo Morales, a Harvard Law School graduate of Mexican Mixtec Indian heritage, and Lupe Ortiz and Roberto Páramo, in collaboration with a group of Mexican peasants, artists, and activists, sought to use radio to improve life and sustain the cultural identity of farm workers of the San Joaquin Valley. Radio Bilingüe grew out of a single nonprofit station founded in California's San Joaquin Valley as La Voz que Rompió el Silencio—The Voice That Broke the Silence. With the significant backing of a grant from a Catholic charity, KSJV-FM was launched as "Radio Bilingüe" in Fresno, California, on July 4, 1980. It transmits a variety of music programs, plus a diversity of information related to health, education, immigration, civic action, and the arts. Supported primarily by donations from community members, businesses, and some foundations, Radio Bilingüe owns and operates thirteen of its own full-power FM noncommercial stations in California and the Southwest and produces the first—and only—daily national Spanish-language news and public affairs programs in public broadcasting. Scores of affiliate stations throughout the nation carry the award-winning journalism of Radio Bilingüe's Noticiero Latino news show and Línea Abierta call-in talk show—unmatched in public or commercial broadcasting. It also offers Edición Semanaria, the only national Spanish-language weekly news magazine. Radio Bilingüe broadcasts its twenty-four-hour service via national satellite; all of its programming is also streamed live at radiobilingue.org. In Southern California, some of the network's programs are also aired by affiliate KUBO-FM, which started in El Centro in April 1989, producing some of its own independent programming. Radio Bilingüe also sponsors the "Viva El Mariachi" (Long Live the Mariachi), a music festival that serves as an important fundraiser for the network. One of the distinctive features of this network is the operational and programming support it receives from innumerable volunteers who produce diverse music and public service programs in English, Spanish, and bilingual format.

Due to increased pressures in the commercial and public radio markets, two organizations serving the interests of this sector were established. In 1991, the first was the American Latino-Owned Radio Association (AHORA), which started with sixty Latino station owners concerned with competition for the Latino market and with the rapid pace at which Spanish-language radio stations are being bought by non-Latinos. AHORA, under the direction of Mary Helen Barro (majority owner of KAFY-AM in Bakersfield, California), sought to increase the number of business opportunities for Latino broadcasters and to attract more Latino talent to broadcasting; its agenda also included encouraging the government to include Spanish-language radio stations in government media buys. AHORA has testified before congressional committees and the FCC to protect the interests of Latino radio broadcasters and against further consolidation of the industry.

In August of 2007 the Latino Public Radio Consortium (LPRC) was founded by Latino leaders and their allies from public radio who gathered in Boulder, Colorado, at the National Federation of Community Broadcasters (NFCB) to develop strategies that would significantly increase Latino participation in public broadcasting. The meeting was funded by the Corporation for Public Broadcasting (CPB). The founders of the LPRC served as the initial board of directors: Silvia Rivera, Raúl Ramírez, Hugo Morales, Victor Montilla, Florence Hernández-Ramos, and Ginny Berson. In 2008 the group drafted a "brown paper" outlining how the public media system could better serve Latinos. The document was then distributed throughout the public broadcasting system. These are the bullet points in the document, which may serve as a manifesto for all radio wishing to reach Latinos:

- In designing services for Latino audiences, recognize that their interests in news and cultural information vary widely depending on their primary language, country of birth, edu-

cation level, and household income. The paper cites the youth-training programs of Radio Arte and Puerto Rican Public Radio, as well as Radio Bilingüe's national news service, as blueprints for a culturally diverse service.

- Offer diverse programming in both Spanish and English. No single format or single-language service will universally address Latinos, and public media in either language must directly address their needs and interests.

- Support distribution of multiple program streams. Both Radio Bilingüe and Native Voice One are distributed free over the public-radio interconnection system, and the paper calls for "additional alternatives for production and sustainability" if public radio is to address the many different needs and tastes of Latino audiences.

- Assist existing Latino-controlled stations, which need resources to build their capacity, and help them develop new financial models. These stations primarily serve low-income communities and cannot sustain themselves with listener-based revenues.

- Engage Latinos as participants and contributors, not just as listeners. The paper asks public radio to assess how stations identify and respond to issues relevant to Latinos.

With CPB's assistance, in May 2008 the LPRC hired Florence Hernández-Ramos as project director and began developing a strategic plan. Since that time, the LPRC has developed numerous projects that have resulted in more Latino radio programming on the CPB and public stations around the United States.

Radio News and Other Program Providers

Although some stations produce everything they broadcast, including news and commercials, many stations depend on various companies dedicated to packaging programs for the Spanish-language radio market. Although radio has become less important than internet-based distribution in the twenty-first century, two types of providers nonetheless merit special attention: those that provide news services and the ones that provide "full service."

The news service provider Spanish Information Systems (SIS) was inaugurated in 1976. From its headquarters in Dallas, Texas, it distributed Spanish-language news programs via satellite. They also transmitted *SIS al Día* (SIS to Date), a fifteen-minute radio magazine that included segments on current affairs, cooking, health, and sports. SIS became a division of Command Communications, Inc., an Anglo-controlled company that also owned Texas State Network, a subsidiary of iHeart that served as a nationwide English-language information service and sports news network.

Another radio news provider was Radio Noticias (News Radio), which began in 1983 as a division in Spanish of United Press International (UPI), once one of the major wire services in the world. From its base in Washington, D.C., Radio Noticias distributed its news program on an hourly basis.

A third news provider is Noticiero Latino, the first—and only—national Spanish news program in public broadcasting. Produced by Radio Bilingüe in Fresno, California, since 1985, each weekday Noticiero Latino broadcasts a five-minute newscast of reports by Latino producers and reporters based around the nation. It is unique in that it is the only Spanish news service produced by a nonprofit network in the United States whose proprietaries and coordinators are Latino residents of this country. It is also unique because it is exclusively dedicated to informing and helping to interpret events in the United States, Latin America, and the Caribbean that are related to Latinos—for example, immigration, civil rights, health, education, culture, and successes of Latinos. Using information gathered by its local reporters and network of correspondents in the United States, Mexico, and Puerto Rico, Noticiero Latino offers a daily news program. It is carried by seventy-five stations in the United States and ten in Mexico.

Among the "full service" providers of Spanish-language programming, the oldest and one of the largest was Cadena Radio Centro (CRC), a network founded in 1985 in Dallas, Texas. CRC was a subsidiary of Organización Radio Centro, a Mexican company founded and controlled by the Aguirre family since 1946. The network owned forty-five stations in Mexico and the United States. In 1994, it bought and promptly divested part ownership in Univisión Radio in the United States. In 2012 it acquired 25 percent of KXOS-FM in Los Angeles and in 2016 took control of four Univisión Radio stations in El Paso, Texas. This U.S. radio network offered its news services to affiliated Spanish-language stations linked via satellite. After years of financial difficulties and overburdening debt, the company, which was once listed on the New York Stock Exchange, in 2020 planned to shut down or sell at least twenty stations, including those in the United States.

Another major provider of Spanish-language radio programs was CBS Hispanic Radio Network (CBSHRN), which focused on sports and entertainment special events. CBS Hispanic Radio Network started its Spanish-language programming in Latin America in the mid-1970s with baseball specials. When it began in the United States, it was affiliated with Caballero Latino media representatives to provide such programs to the stations represented by Caballero, but in 1990 it established its own syndication network. By 2014, faced with increased competition, CBS Latino merged its stations with Univisión radio, with some thirteen stations now branded as Univisión radio.

LATINO-ORIENTED TELEVISION

As was the case for radio, Spanish-language television transmissions started almost as soon as English-language ones did. Since the 1940s, entrepreneurs have found a significant market and profits transmitting to the Latino populations in the United States. Spanish-language television has grown enormously from the early days of a few brokered hours on some English-language stations in San Antonio and New York. In 2018, over $9.4 billion in advertising was spent in national network, local, and digital Spanish-language television.

The Early Years

The first Spanish-language television station in the United States was San Antonio's KCOR-TV Channel 41, which began some evening programs in 1955. But a few years before KCOR and similar stations started, several Spanish-language radio entrepreneurs recognized the potential of the Spanish-speaking television audiences and pioneered the way by producing special TV programs. Following the pattern used in the early stages of Spanish-language radio, time was brokered for these programs in the nascent English-language stations in selected cities.

During the 1960s, part-time Spanish-language programs on English-language stations emerged in various cities with large concentrations of Latinos, such as Los Angeles, Houston, Miami, Phoenix, Tucson, and Chicago. Most often such programs—sponsored primarily by a local company—would be the outcome of personal efforts of Latino entrepreneurs, many of whom had experience with radio. Some stations provided time for these in order to seek alternative sources of profits or to comply with Federal Communications Commission (FCC) requirements of public service programs.

From Spanish International Network to Univisión

The experiences of Latino entrepreneurs and their part-time Spanish-language television programs eventually led the way to establishing separate stations especially directed at Latino viewers. The pioneer behind the KCOR-TV effort was Raúl Cortez, also the owner of KCOR-AM, which was itself the first Latino owned and operated Spanish-language radio station in the United States. KCOR-TV began in 1955, broadcasting from 5:00 p.m. to midnight. The late Emilio Nicolás, one of the first general managers of the station, recalled that approximately half of the programs were live variety and entertainment shows that featured a host of the best available talent from Mexico. Many of these shows took place in the studios of Cortez's radio station, which aired these programs simultaneously. Movies and other prerecorded programs imported primarily from Mexico accounted for the rest of the early offerings of Channel 41.

Although the station was very popular among the Mexican and other Spanish-speaking residents of San Antonio and vicinities, Nicolás recalled that advertisers did not acknowledge this market and failed to use it extensively for commercial promotions. During those early years of the medium, Latino viewers were not accounted for in the standard ratings services. One reason for this, according to Nicolás, was that in the 1940s and 1950s Mexicans were hesitant to acknowledge their heritage or exposure to Spanish-language media for fear of blatant discriminatory practices. Thus, Cortez, after spending heavily on the live talent imported from Mexico and receiving limited financial support from the advertising agencies, was forced to sell the television station to an Anglo. He kept the KCOR call letters for his radio station, but KCOR-TV changed to KUAL. The station continued some Spanish-language programs, and in 1961 these call letters changed again to KWEX when Channel 41 was sold to Don Emilio Azcárraga Vidaurreta and his financial partners, who then went on to establish the first Spanish-language television network.

Until his death in 1972, Azcárraga Vidaurreta was the most prominent media magnate in Mexico. With his family, he owned and operated a significant part of the country's commercial radio system and the emerging Telesistema Mexicano S.A. (Sociedad Anónima) broadcasting empire. In the United States, Don Emilio, his son Emilio Azcárraga Milmo, and Reynold (René) Anselmo became central figures in not only the purchase of San Antonio's Channel 41 but also in the establishment of the largest and most influential businesses related to Spanish-language television broadcasting.

The most significant development of Spanish-language television in the United States began when Spanish International Communications Corporation (SICC) was initiated and organized by René Anselmo and bankrolled by Emilio Azcárraga Vidaurreta, along with minority investors having U.S. citizenship. Since SICC (which at one point was called Spanish International Broadcasting Corporation [SIBC]) was to hold the licenses of the stations, the corporation was structured so that Azcárraga Vidaurreta, a Mexican citizen, would own only 20 percent of the company. Most of the other partners were U.S. citizens so as to conform with Federal Communications Act Section 310, which "prohibits the issuing of broadcast licenses to aliens, to the representatives of aliens, or to corporations in which aliens control more than one-fifth of the stock."

Although there is a limitation in the amount of stock a foreign national can hold in a broadcast license, there apparently is no such restriction on U.S. television networks. Thus, in 1961 Don Emilio and Anselmo established the sister company Spanish International Network (SIN) to purchase and provide programming, virtually all of which originated from Azcárraga Vidaurreta's production studios at Telesistema (later known as Televisa) in Mexico. The other function of SIN was to provide advertising sales for the SICC stations.

Over the next ten years the licensee corporation went through a series of expansions, mergers, and reorganizations as it added three other stations: WXTV Channel 41 in New York (1968); WLTV Channel 23 in Miami (1971); and KFTV Channel 21 in Fresno/Hanford (1972). The network was also extended with stations owned by some principals of SICC/SIN: under the Bahía de San Francisco company, it was KDTV Channel 14, San Francisco (1974), and under Legend of Cibola (later known as Seven Hills Corporation), it was KTVW Channel 33, Phoenix (1976). In addition, SIN had the affiliation of five stations owned and operated by corporations not related to SIN/SICC; these were located in Albuquerque, Chicago, Corpus Christi, Houston, and Sacramento. Furthermore, SIN had four stations owned and operated by this company's parent corporation, Televisa, S.A. From their locations on the Mexican border at Juárez, Mexicali, Nuevo Laredo, and Tijuana, these stations served the U.S. cities of, respectively, El Paso, El Centro, Laredo, and San Diego.

Until the mid-1970s, most of these stations shared the programming, which primarily came from Mexico's Productora de Teleprogramas (ProTele, S.A.), a company created and controlled by Televisa as its export subsidiary. SIN imported and licensed taped shows, movies, and other programs that were transported to the Los Angeles station, sent to San Antonio, and then passed along in a "bicycle type network" to the other owned and affiliated stations. In September 1976, SIN became the first major broadcasting company, preceding CBS, ABC, and NBC, to distribute programming directly to its affiliates via domestic satellite.

In 1979, as cable connections became more readily available, another precedent was established as SIN began paying cable franchise operators to carry its satellite signals. Then in early 1980, SIN's outlets expanded further as the network was granted permission to establish low-power television (LPTV) stations (those whose signals only reach a radius of approximately twelve to fifteen miles). Altogether, by 1983 the Spanish-language television stations represented by SIN/SICC were reaching over 3.3 million Latino households across the United States. Advertising for the stations was sold in the United States, Mexico, and other Latin American countries.

Most of the programming broadcast by Univisión has been provided by Mexico's Televisa, with additional programs imported from Venezuela, Spain, Argentina, Brazil, and, occasionally, Puerto Rico and other countries. Telenovelas continue to be very popular with the Latino audiences in the United States and elsewhere. However, game and variety shows, music festivals, comedies, and sports are also big attractions in this network. Since 1970, Univisión has had exclusive rights to broadcast the World Cup soccer championship in the U.S. Spanish-language market.

From the 1960s to the 1970s, Latino programs made within the United States usually consisted of public affairs programming and local newscasts, some of which were acclaimed for their excellent coverage of issues of concern to the local Latino communities.

A notable accomplishment of SIN (and Univisión) news has been its coverage of U.S. and Latin American political developments. The first U.S. national election night coverage in Spanish was in 1968; similar reports followed in subsequent years. Starting with the 1981 elections in Miami, in which two Latino candidates were finalists for mayor of that city, "Noticias 23" (News 23) and "Noticiero SIN" at the national level began giving ample time to present and

> A notable accomplishment of SIN and Univisión news has been their coverage of U.S. and Latin American political developments.

analyze in Spanish the campaigns, issues, and personalities of the time. Pre- and post-exit polls were conducted by the stations and the network to share their projections and predictions of the electoral outcomes, especially among the Latino populations. At each station and at the network level, there was also a very strong campaign for voter registration.

In 1984, SIN launched "Destino '84" (Destiny '84), which further promoted voter registration and, through a series of special programs and reports, gave ample coverage to the presidential elections in the United States. Since then, Univisión has produced "Destino" programs for every presidential and congressional election year. Reporters follow up the trends in Latino voting at the national level. Similar coverage is given to elections in Latin America, including polling activities beginning with the 1984 congressional and presidential elections in El Salvador, where their surveys were quite accurate in predicting the voting results. In subsequent years ample coverage was given to and more exit polls were conducted of elections in Guatemala, Peru, Honduras, Colombia, Costa Rica, and many other locations.

Most of the SICC stations did not operate in the black until a decade or more after they began operations. Nevertheless, the Azcárraga Vidaurretas and their fellow investors recognized the growth potential of the Spanish-speaking television audience and market in the United States and were willing to subsidize the station group. When SICC did eventually generate profits, many of them found their way back to Mexico through the SIN pipeline. A falling out between Frank Fouce, one of SICC's principal investors, and René Anselmo, one of the creators and president of both SICC and SIN, led to a long, bitter stockholder derivative lawsuit that took more than ten years to settle. A second legal action against SICC was initiated at the FCC in 1980 when a group of radio broadcasters (the now-defunct Spanish Radio Broadcasters Association) charged that the company was under illegal foreign control. In January 1986, a judge appointed by the FCC ruled not to renew the licenses of the thirteen SICC stations and ordered their transfer to U.S.-based entities. This decision was followed by numerous legal appeals and challenges.

An intense and controversial bidding war in the same court that had heard the stockholder suit culminated in July 1986. Hallmark Cards, Inc., and its 25 percent partner, First Capital Corporation of Chicago, won with a $301.5 million bid for the SICC licenses and properties. The losing bidder was TVL Corporation, directed by a group of Latino investors who submitted a higher bid ($320 million) but whose financing was less secure. Legal challenges of the sale process brought by losing bidders were not resolved until April 1991.

As various appeals were being deliberated in federal court and at the FCC, SIN and SICC were renamed Univisión on January 1, 1987. In February, the cable service Galavisión, which was not included in the deal, split from Univisión and remained under the control of Televisa and Univisa. Univisa was Emilio Azcárraga Vidaurreta's new enterprise established to house Galavisión and his remaining U.S. companies. In July of that year, Hallmark and First Capital paid $286 million for the five original SICC stations and in August obtained actual control of the channels. Later, San Francisco station KDTV was purchased for an additional $274.5 million. With the transition, both the station group and the network continued operations under the name Univisión Holdings, Inc., of which Hallmark became sole owner February 15, 1988.

In spite of its expansions and changes, by late 1991 Hallmark Cards Corporation was dissatisfied with its returns on its investments. Thus, in the spring of 1992 it sold the network to a group comprised of A. Jerrold Perenchio (a previous owner of the Spanish-language station WNJU in New Jersey and an unsuccessful bidder for Univisión when Hallmark purchased it in 1986) and three of the richest and most influential media magnates in Latin America, Emilio Azcárraga Milmo (the controlling owner of the Mexican media conglomerate Televisa) and Gustavo and Ricardo Cisneros (of the powerful Venezuelan broadcast coporation Venevisión). The arrangement was announced in April 1992 and approved by the FCC in September 1992. Perenchio had 76 percent ownership of the television station group and 50 percent ownership of the network, with Azcárraga Milmo and the Cisneroses each holding 12 percent of the station group (to conform with U.S. foreign ownership laws) and 25 percent of the network.

This ownership change caused protest within and outside the industry and led to numerous changes among the top executives of Univisión. For example, network president Joaquín Blaya had not been forewarned of the sale and within two months left his post to become president of Telemundo.

In 2002, Univisión acquired Dallas, Texas–based Hispanic Broadcasting Corp., which owned Spanish-language radio stations in the major markets of New York City, Los Angeles, San Antonio, Dallas, and elsewhere for $3.5 billion in stock. Univisión then renamed the group Univisión Radio.

In 2007 the FCC approved Univisión Communications' sale to Broadcasting Media Partners Inc.—a consortium made up of Saban Capital Group, TPG Capital, L.P., Providence Equity Partners, Madison Dearborn Partners, and Thomas H. Lee Partners—for $13.7 billion, plus taking on $1.4 billion in debt. Heavy with debt, in 2008 Univisión sold the Univisión Music Group to Universal Music Group, which was rebranded as Universal Music Latin Entertainment.

Currently, Univisión is by far the largest Spanish-language media company in the United States. Its flagship is the Univisión Network, which is the most watched Spanish-language broadcast television network in the United States, reaching 98 percent of Latino households. Its other properties are UniMás, a general interest Spanish-language broadcast television network it launched as TeleFutura Network in 2002 that reaches 86 percent of U.S. Hispanic households; Galavisión, the largest Spanish-language cable network; Univisión Television Group, which owns and operates sixty-two television stations in major U.S. Hispanic markets and Puerto Rico; the Univisión Radio network studied above; and Univisión Online, the most accessed Spanish-language internet site. Univisión also has a nonvoting 14.9 percent interest in Entravision Communications Corporation. In 2002 revenues exceeded one billion dollars for the first time. Today, Univisión news programs reach far more viewers than its Spanish-language competitors, and its early-evening edition of *Noticiero Univisión* outranks

its English-language rivals, such as *NBC Nightly News, ABC World News Tonight,* and the *CBS Evening News,* in the 18–49 demographic. In major media markets, such as New York, Los Angeles, and Houston, Univisión stations have a larger viewership than any of the big four English-language networks. As of 2018 the Univisión network reached 58.35 percent of all households in the United States (or 182,330,440 Americans with at least one television set), making Univisión the largest U.S. broadcast television network.

Telemundo

While SIN and SICC were developing their powerful and far-reaching dominion, the growth and market potential of the Latino audience was being recognized by other interested parties, such as Saul Steinberg, chairman of the board and chief executive officer (CEO) of Reliance Capital Group, L.P., and Henry Silverman, the eventual president, CEO, and director of Telemundo. Together with their investment partners, they founded the Telemundo Group, Inc., which is currently the second-largest Spanish-language television network in the United States.

> Univisión Network is the most-watched Spanish-language broadcast television network in the United States, reaching 98 percent of Latino households.

The organization of the Telemundo Group began in May 1986, when Reliance Capital Group acquired John Blair & Company, a diversified communications business. Blair had fallen prey to corporate raiders after an attempt at expansion left it overburdened with debt. Telemundo, as the successor to Blair, thus obtained stations WSCV Channel 51 in Miami and WKAQ Channel 2 in San Juan, Puerto Rico, which had been purchased by Blair in 1985 and 1983, respectively. Prior to its acquisition by Blair, WSCV was an English-language subscription television station. The station in Puerto Rico had been a major component of the Fundación Angel Ramos media enterprises and had its own island-wide retransmitter and affiliation network under the name adopted for the U.S. group—Cadena Telemundo. The change of name to Telemundo Group, Inc., was officially established on April 10, 1987. The company went public

The organization of the Telemundo Group, the second-largest Spanish-language television network in the United States, began in May 1986.

Spanish. The remaining hours were sold to other programmers. In 1980 KBSC offered a pay-television service (ON-TV) in English at night and switched to full-time Spanish-language programs during the day. Much of that station's Spanish-language programming was supplied by government station Channel 13, of Mexico. When KBSC was put on the market in 1985, Reliance Capital, a large shareholder of Estrella Communications, purchased a greater proportion of the stock for $38 million and began operating the station with the new call letters KVEA. By December 1986, Reliance had spent $13.5 million to buy out the remaining minority holders of Estrella Communications, including some shares held by Hallmark Cards.

The third major component of the Telemundo Group was WNJU Channel 47, licensed in Linden, New Jersey, and serving the metropolitan New York area. It was because of the strength of its Spanish-language programs and Latino audience that WNJU was bought for approximately $75 million in December 1986 by Steinberg and his Reliance Capital Group.

The growth of Steinberg's television network continued in August 1987, when Telemundo bought out (for $15.5 million) National Group Television, Inc., the license holder of station KSTS Channel 48, serving the San Jose and San Francisco area. For the Houston/Galveston market, Telemundo invested $6.428 million to obtain the outstanding stock of Bluebonnet, which operated KTMD Channel 48 in that area in 1988. Another significant Latino market penetration came that year when Telemundo won over the affiliation of Chicago's WSNS Channel 44, which had been associated with Univisión. Until then, Telemundo's link to Chicago had been WCIU Channel 26. A year later, entry was made into San Antonio with the affiliation of KVDA Channel 60. In August 1990, Telemundo paid $2.975 million to purchase 85 percent of the stock of Nueva Vista, which operated KVDA. With these stations, its affiliations, and cable linkages, the Telemundo network was firmly established and available to more than 80 percent of Latino households.

with offerings of common stock and bonds during the summers of 1987 and 1988.

Prior to forming the Telemundo Group, Reliance had entered the Latino media market in April 1985 with its ownership interests in Estrella Communications, Inc., which had been formed in January of that year for the purpose of buying Channel 52 in Los Angeles. Under the call letters KBSC and the corporate name SFN Communications, Inc., this station was owned by Columbia Pictures and A. Jerrold Perenchio, who had launched it in the late 1970s to compete with KMEX for Los Angeles's Latino audience. At the time, KBSC split its broadcast schedule, offering approximately ninety-five hours a week in

In 1998, Sony Pictures and Liberty Media formed Telemundo as a 50/50 joint venture now named Telemundo Communications Group. Peter Tortorici became president and CEO and Nely Galán president of entertainment. Under this new leadership, Telemundo explored expanding into the bilingual market under a campaign slogan of "Lo Mejor de los Dos Mundos" (The Best of Two Worlds). Telemundo began targeting the more "assimilated" bilingual Latinos and revamped its production and scheduling. It removed telenovelas from prime time and included several new sitcoms, traditional scripted dramas, and game shows with higher production values. They also included remakes of English-language shows, such as *Charlie's Angels*, *Who's the Boss?*, and *One Day at a Time* and developed versions of *The Dating Game*, *The Newlywed Game* and *Candid Camera*. It also added movies to prime time, many of them dubbed versions of recent Hollywood productions from the Sony movie library. Despite all of these upgrades, ratings plummeted, and by 1999, Tortorici resigned as president. Under new president Jim McNamara, the network reverted to more traditional fare, acquiring telenovelas from TV Azteca for up to three hours in prime time. In 2001, NBC purchased Telemundo Communications Group from Sony and Liberty Media.

Today, Telemundo is owned by NBCUniversal Television and Streaming, a division of NBCUniversal, which in turn is owned by Comcast (as of 2022). While Univisión reaches more households than Telemundo, Telemundo provides more Spanish-language content nationally, and its programming is syndicated worldwide. Telemundo's NBC Universo is its channel directed toward young Hispanic audiences, and Telemundo Digital Media distributes original programming content on the internet. During the second decade of the twenty-first century, Telemundo produced new, hit telenovelas, recruited popular on-air personalities from Univisión, and increased its ratings and narrowed the gap somewhat between its and Univisión's audiences. In an effort to expand its reach, Telemundo provides English subtitles via closed captioning during its prime-time programming. Today, Telemundo owns and operates twenty-eight stations; it has some sixty-six affiliate stations in forty-nine states, the District of Columbia, and the U.S. possession of Puerto Rico. In 2018, the network had an estimated national reach of 57.23 percent of all households in the United States.

Galavisión

A third major player in Spanish-language television in the United States is Galavisión. This television company was launched in 1979 under parent company Univisa, Inc., a subsidiary of Mexico's Televisa. At that time, Galavisión was a premium cable service, offering recently produced Spanish-language movies along with coverage of select sporting events and special entertainment shows. In early 1988, it had only 160,000 subscribers. But in September of that year, after the entry of the Telemundo network and the consolidation of Hallmark's Univisión network, Univisa started to convert Galavisión's cable operations to an advertising-based basic cable service. This change expanded Galavisión's audience substantially as potentially two million cable subscribers were able to receive Galavisión's programs.

The new format offered continuous programming via a network feed provided by the Galaxy I and Spacenet 2 satellites. Galavisión expanded to over-the-air offerings when it affiliated stations KWHY Channel 22 in Los Angeles, KTFH Channel 49 in Houston, KSTV Channel 57 in Santa Barbara, and low-power retransmitters in seven other cities. KWHY and KTFH were converted from English-language stations; KSTV was licensed for the first time for Galavisión.

Galavisión, operating under the separate entity of SIN, Inc., was not included in the sales of SICC and SIN to Hallmark. Shortly after Televisa regained control of Univisión, Galavisión was placed under the management of Univisión. To avoid competition with its new sister network, contracts were terminated with the few stations that carried Galavisión over the air (except the Houston broadcast affiliate); it thus became an almost exclusively cable delivery service. In May 1993 Galavisión announced its move to the Galaxy 1–R satellite as well as the addition of four new Spanish-language cable-exclusive netowrks: Telehit, a pop music video network; Telenovelas, a continuous soap opera channel; ECO, a twenty-four-hour news channel; and Ritmosón, a video channel featuring nonstop Latin dance hits.

As of this writing, Galavisión broadcasts continuously, reaching approximately 28 percent of Latino households (1.5 million) via three hundred cable affiliates and its broadcast affiliate, KTFH Channel 49 in Houston. Executives include J. Manuel Calvo, vice president and general manager, and María Elena Diéguez, director of programming.

Other Latino-Oriented Television Companies and Program Ventures

It could be expected that the aforementioned networks would capture the majority of the Latino audience in terms of general programming. However, several companies sought their own niche in this market. One of them was International TeleMúsica, Inc., which produced a show featuring international music videos, entertainment news, promotions, and lifestyle segments. The programs, hosted by Alex Sellar, a Spaniard, and Pilar Isla, a native of Mexico, were produced in Hollywood using various California landscapes for settings. The target audience was Latino and Latin American youth. In 1990, Jesús Garza Rapport, executive vice president of Telemusica, started the company with full financial backing from Radio Programas de México (RPM). A Mexican company, RPM owned thirty and operated fifty radio stations in that country in the 1990s, and it owned one television station in Guadalajara, Mexico.

Home Box Office's Selecciones en Español (Selections in Spanish) was another significant venture to capture a niche in the U.S.-Latino television audience. In January 1989, this service was inaugurated to provide to HBO and Cinemax cable subscribers the option of Spanish-language audio for the telecast motion pictures and even some sporting events, such as boxing matches. This service was the brainchild of Lara Concepción, a native of Mexico, who after eight years of trying was able to persuade HBO's executives that there was a viable Latino market for such a service. The turning point for Concepción came shortly after the box office success of the Latino-themed movie *La Bamba*. Following a market study that further convinced HBO that it could expand its business with the Spanish-speaking audience, HBO scheduled about ten Spanish-dubbed movies per month in 1989. At first, Selecciones en Español was provided to twenty HBO and Cinemax cable op-

erators in five cities: El Paso, Miami, New York, San Antonio, and San Diego. Shortly thereafter, the service was requested by an additional thirty-five cable firms and later by another fifteen. By the end of 1989, HBO expanded its dubbed activities and was offering an average of twenty movies per month in Spanish. In 1991, Selecciones en Español was carried by 182 cable systems within the United States. HBO and Cinemax cable operators had three methods for delivering this service: a channel dedicated to Selecciones, a Second Audio Program (SAP) channel available for stereo television sets or videocassette recorders with multiple channel television sound (MTS), and an FM tuner in which the affiliates can transmit the second audio feed via an FM modulator (that is, cable subscribers listen to the Spanish soundtrack on their FM radio).

Following up on its formidable success with the U.S. Spanish-speaking audience, HBO in October 1991 launched HBO-Olé pay-cable service in Latin America and the Caribbean Basin. This allowed cable subscribers in more than twenty Latin American countries prompt access in Spanish to HBO's movies and other shows, which are supplied by Warner Brothers, Twentieth Century-Fox, and Columbia TriStar International Television, which provides feature films from Columbia Pictures and TriStar Pictures.

In 2000 Selecciones en Español became a set HBO channel: HBO Latino, which includes HBO original productions, Spanish and Portuguese series sourced from HBO Latin America, dubbed versions of American theatrical releases, and domestic and imported Spanish-language films. HBO Latino largely acts as a de facto Spanish-language simulcast of the primary HBO channel. (All other HBO multiplex channels provide alternate Spanish audio tracks of most of their programming via second audio program feeds.)

Long before HBO started applying the Spanish-language audio and related technologies to establish its particular niches in the Latino market, other Anglo television businesses had successfully used SAP to provide selected programs to their audiences. In Los Angeles, one of the most successful ventures with SAP was CW affiliate KTLA Channel 5. This station, now owned by the Nexstar Media

Group, was the pioneer in taking advantage of the Federal Communication Commission's 1984 rule authorizing broadcasters and cable providers to split up the single soundtrack into four audio channels. Henceforth, the first track was for the English audio, the second for stereo, the third for any alternate language, and the fourth for data transmission. In October 1984 KTLA broadcast the movie *2001: A Space Odyssey* and began offering the *The Love Boat, McMillan & Wife, Columbo,* and *McCloud* in Spanish via the third audio channel. Dubbed editions of these programs were readily available because some Hollywood producers had a long-standing policy of dubbing many of their programs for their Latin American markets. Then, in February 1985, KTLA hired Analía Sarno-Riggle to be the Spanish interpreter of *News at Ten,* airing Monday through Friday from 10:00 to 11:00 p.m. While in 1984 the pilot program with three other interpreters had not succeeded, the public response to Sarno-Riggle was formidable, as she developed an accurate technique to provide the Spanish-speaking viewers an adequate representation of what they were getting on the screen. She also strived to establish her own "audio personality," not just mimic the people she was interpreting.

Given her success, especially as evidenced by ratings among Latino viewers, by July 1985, KTLA had made Sarno-Riggle a regular staff employee and committed to continue the service. She stayed in that role until December 2006. Sarno-Riggle, a native of Argentina and now an interpreter for the U.S. government, considered her own simulcast interpretations an alternative to Univisión's and Telemundo's news. She believes it offered access to a larger and more diverse amount of local news, which may be preferred by some assimilated Latinos or by those who simply wish to be informed on the same issues their neighbors are tuned into. In addition to her news role, KTLA assigned her to the Hollywood Christmas parade and various other specials. The station also expanded its offerings of Spanish-language audio for more of its prime-time programs, such as *Airwolf, Magnum P.I.,* and *Knight Rider.* These programs were also among those dubbed for foreign distribution by their producers. Currently, KTLA schedules approximately twenty hours per week of Spanish-language audio.

The Latino audience ratings of KTLA did not go unnoticed by other stations and networks in Los Angeles and elsewhere. SAP was adopted by various other Anglo broadcasters in large Latino markets, including the Tribune Broadcasting Company's Chicago and New York stations WGN Channel 9 and WPIX Channel 11. Even some nonprofit stations began this language option. For example, KCET Channel 28 hired Sarno-Riggle for ten months to do the Spanish-language audio for *By the Year 2000,* a weekly half-hour public affairs program for Southern California. Also under Sarno-Riggle's guidance, on January 14, 1991, New York station WNET Channel 13 began the second audio for *The MacNeil/Lehrer NewsHour* (later renamed *PBS NewsHour*). Bolivian native Oscar Ordenes became the Spanish-language voice for this show, which in the United States was carried by thirty-three Public Broadcasting System stations either via SAP or as a separate show repeated later in the evening. In addition, thirty-two cities in twenty-six Latin American countries received videos of this version of *The MacNeil/Lehrer NewsHour* by way of the United States Information Agency's Worldnet information program.

Finally, English-language musical programs specifically oriented toward Latinos made their debut. In June 1991, MTV launched *Second Generation,* a half-hour mix of videos, comedy, and entertainment news aimed primarily at second-generation Latinos in the United States. Hosted by New York Puerto Rican Andy "Panda" Tripoli and Colombian Tony Moran, this program was broadcast by thirty-one primarily English-language stations from the East to the West Coast. In 1998, MTV launched a twenty-four-hour digital cable channel, MTV S (the "S" standing for "Spanish"). In 2001, the channel was relaunched as MTV Español, focusing on music videos by Latin rock and pop artists. In 2005, Viacom acquired Más-Música TV and ten of the network's affiliated stations, and then in 2006 launched MTV Tres (also styled as MTV Tr3s), which merged MTV Español with Más-Música TV. In 2010, MTV Tres dropped the MTV name from its logo and name and rebranded as Tres.

Federico A. Subervi-Vález
and Nicolás Kanellos

SELECTED LATINOS IN MEDIA

Desi Arnaz (1917–1986)

Television Producer, Actor, Singer

Desiderio Alberto Arnaz was born on March 2, 1917, in Santiago, Cuba, and went on to make television history as the producer-writer and performer of the longest-running sitcom of its time, *I Love Lucy*, which starred his wife, Lucille Ball. Arnaz immigrated to the United States with his family as political exiles during the Fulgencio Batista regime. After finishing high school near Tampa, Arnaz formed an Afro-Cuban music band, whereupon he was discovered by the famed orchestra leader Xavier Cugat, who recruited Arnaz to play the conga. Arnaz went on to start his own Desi Arnaz Orchestra and rose to fame in New York's nightclub scene. There he performed in a Rodgers and Hart musical that eventually became a Hollywood film, *Too Many Girls*. Arnaz's motion picture career was launched, and he met Ball. He served in the Army during World War II, where he also entertained, and after the war his orchestra was featured on comedian Bob Hope's radio program *The Pepsodent Show* (1946–47). In 1951 he had his own show on CBS radio, *Your Tropical Trip*, which ended when *I Love Lucy* premiered that year. For *I Love Lucy* Arnaz played a fictionalized version of himself as a nightclub band leader and conga player. The show was an overwhelming hit with the outstanding comedy antics of Ball. But also, TV audiences were titillated subconsciously at a time when little Black representation was allowed on television; here was a "Latin" of dubious mixed racial heritage playing Afro-Cuban music and married to a very White, red-headed midwesterner—and the series took audiences into the chaste bedroom with twin beds. The show became a model for numerous sitcoms to follow in which an American upper-class Anglo was paired with a non-Anglo love interest, such as *Who's the Boss?* and *The Nanny*. The show also pioneered the use of the multiple-camera setup production style by using adjacent sets in front of a live audience, which soon became the norm for situation comedies. Arnaz and Ball's Desilu Productions, founded in 1950, retained the rights to the films of their show and pioneered the business of reruns and syndication, which brought in much additional revenue for their company. With the resources it accumulated, Desilu was able to produce a number of other popular shows, such as *The Ann Sothern Show*, *Those Whiting Girls*, *The Untouchables*, *The Dick Van Dyke Show*, and *The Andy Griffith Show*. Their greatest hits made television history and have lived on to today in remakes and sequels: *Mission: Impossible* and *Star Trek*. Arnaz has two stars on the Hollywood Walk of Fame and is in the Television Hall of Fame.

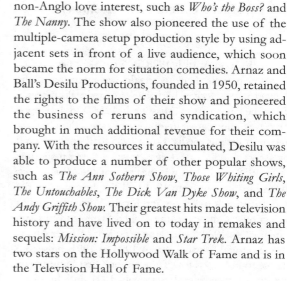

Mary Helen Barro (1938–)

Radio Broadcasting

Born on June 17, 1938, in Culver City, California, Mary Helen Barro was educated in California, received a degree in management systems and procedures from the University of California at Los Angeles in 1967, and began a career in radio broadcasting. After working at various on-air and management positions in radio and television, from 1985 to 1986 she served as the general manager of the King Videocable Corporation. In 1986, she became a founder and partner of McGavren-Barro Broadcasting Corporation, serving as vice president and general manager. She also became vice president/general manager of Station KAFY in 1987. She beame the president of the bilingual media consultant Up Front Productions in Citrus Heights, California, in 1974. She has been an outstanding figure in broadcasting and a pioneer in creating emergency broadcasting procedures for the Spanish-speaking in the Los Angeles area. Her honors include the Mexican American Opportunity Foundation's Woman of the Year Award in 1972 and resolutions honoring her achievements from the city of Los Angeles (1972) and the California state legislature (1976). In 2018, she ran unsuccessfully for Congress.

Harry Caicedo (1928–2004)

Journalism

Born on April 1, 1928, in New York City to Colombian parents, Harry Caicedo was educated in the United States, received his bachelor of journalism degree from the University of Missouri in 1954, and developed an outstanding career in journalism as an editor and director in various media. From 1955 to 1958, he served as associate editor of *Latin American Report* magazine; from 1958 to 1959, he was the chief of the *Miami Herald* news bureau; and from 1961 to 1978, he served in the U.S. Information Agency and for the Voice of America in various positions in the United States and in Latin America. In 1984, he became president of Inter American Editorial Services. From 1984 to 1991, he served as the founding editor of the nation's first Latino mass circulation magazine, *Vista*. From 1991 until his death in 2004, Ciacedo worked as a media consultant.

Lynda Córdova Carter (1951–)

Television, Film

Born on July 24, 1951, in Phoenix, Arizona, Lynda Carter began her show business career as a nightclub singer and dancer after finishing high school; she later attended Arizona State University. In 1970, she was crowned Miss World USA, which led her to Hollywood. She became a successful television actress, her most famous role being Wonder Woman, from 1976 to 1979. She also starred in various made-for-television movies, including *Stillwatch* and *Born to Be Sold* in 1981 and *Rita Hayworth: The Love Goddess* in 1983. During the 1980s, Carter also starred in her own variety shows, which highlighted her singing and dancing: *Lynda Carter Celebration, Lynda Carter: Body and Soul,* and *Lynda Carter: Street Life*. In 1993, she was the founder of Potomac Productions, which launched new television programs. During the 2000s, Carter appeared in live theater, numerous TV programs, and some feature films, and recorded voiceover for a new medium: video games. She also recorded a number of music albums singing many of her own compositions. Today, she continues to tour performing in her own concerts far and wide. Included among her honors were the Golden Eagle Award for Consistent Performance in Television and Film and Mexico's Ariel Award as International Entertainer of the Year. In 2014, she received a Golden Palm Star on the Palm Springs, California, Walk of Stars, and in 2018, she received a star on the Hollywood Walk of Fame.

Ricardo Chavira (1951–)

Journalism

Born to a fourth-generation Mexican family in Los Angeles, Ricardo Chavira obtained a B.A. in journalism and an M.A. in mass communication from California State Long Beach and California State Northridge, respectively. He went on to work for thirty years as a reporter for such publications as the *San Diego Union, Time* magazine, and the *Dallas Morning News*, specialized in international affairs, with an emphasis on Latin America. He also covered the U.S.-Mexico border extensively. He served as a correspondent for the historically important *Nuestro* magazine. As a diplomatic correspondent for *Time* in the mid-1980s and early 1990s, he reported hundreds of stories from more than forty countries. Unlike many of his contemporary journalists, he spoke Spanish and was able to interview the likes of Fidel Castro and venture into the jungles of Central America with revolutionaries and Contras. In 1994 he was part of a *Dallas Morning News* team awarded the 1994 Pulitzer Prize for international reporting, which documented the plight of women around the world who suffered systematic violence. From 2006 to the present, he has taught courses on media writing, international journalism, U.S.-Mexico border perspectives, Mexican politics, and American culture at the University of California, Irvine. In 2021, his memoir *We Were Always Here* was published by Arte Público Press of the University of Houston.

Ingrid Ciprián-Matthews (?–)

TV Journalism

Born in Santo Domingo, the Dominican Republica, Ingrid Ciprián-Matthews immigrated to the

United States as a child and obtained a B.A. from Barnard University (1981) and an M.A. in journalism from New York University (1984). After starting her career as a general assignment reporter for the National Public Radio Spanish-language news program *Enfoque Nacional*, she worked at CNN from 1984 to 1993 as a field producer, assignment manager, assignment editor, and managing editor of CNN's New York bureau. She has spent the rest of her career at CBS News, where she began in 1993 as a senior producer for live segments on *CBS This Morning*. She subsequently ascended to serving as the deputy bureau chief for the CBS News London bureau from 1998 to 2000; senior broadcast producer for the *CBS Evening News* (2004–6); vice president of news (2011–15); senior vice president of news administration (2015–18); and executive vice president of news (2018–19)—the first Latina to achieve such a lofty position in mainstream English-language television journalism. Since 2019, Ciprián-Matthews has worked as executive vice president of strategic professional development and acting Washington bureau chief.

María Antonieta Collins (1952–)

Television Journalism

Born on May 12, 1952, in Coatzacoalcos, Veracruz, Mexico, María Collins began her journalism career in 1974 in Mexico as a reporter for Televisa, which sent her in 1979 to serve as a general assignment journalist in Southern California. In 1986 she began working for the Spanish International Network, which became Univisión, and worked there as a correspondent until 1993, when she became the senior correspondent on Univisión for the *Aquí y Ahora* news magazine. From 2005 to 2008, for Telemundo she hosted the morning show *Cada Día con María Antonieta Collins*. In May 2020 she became one of the hosts of the Univisión morning show *Despierta América*, immediately after working on the network with Jorge Ramos to offer day-to-day coverage of the emerging COVID-19 pandemic. Among the diverse stories she has covered were the September 11, 2001, destruction of the World Trade Center, the Pope's 2012 visit to Mexico, and the 2014 World

Cup in Brazil. In addition to her journalism work, Collins is the author of more than a half dozen self-help and inspirational books.

Nely Galán (1963–)

Producer, Media Entrepreneur

Born in 1963 in Santa Clara, Cuba, Nely Galán (birth name Arnely Alvarez) immigrated with her parents to Teaneck, New Jersey, when she was five years old. The precocious Galán started wrting for *Seventeen* magazine while she was in high school. By age twenty-two she was the youngest TV station manager in history, of WNJU-TV Channel 47 in New York, and that station became the basis for what grew into the Telemundo network. Since then, she has started businesses in media, launching channels, television production, and real estate investment and development. In 2008 she returned to school to eventually earn master's and doctorate degrees in clinical psychology from Pacific Graduate Institute. Galán is an Emmy Award–winning producer of over seven hundred episodes of television in Spanish and English, including the hit Fox reality series *The Swan*. Galán has owned and operated her own media company, Galán Entertainment, since 1994; it helped launch ten television channels in Latin America and also produced hundreds of episodes of programming in various genres, from reality series to sitcoms, telenovelas, and talk shows in both English and in Spanish.

Juan González (1947–)

Journalism

Born on October 15, 1947, in Ponce, Puerto Rico, Juan González grew up in East Harlem and Brooklyn, New York, and attended Columbia University. A student activist, he protested the Vietnam War, was a member of Students for a Democratic Society that took over buildings at Columbia, and served as the education minister for the Young Lords grassroots political-educational organization. In 1978 he began his journalism career as a reporter for the *Philadelphia Daily News*, continued as a reporter for New York's *Village Voice* in 1987, and left that position to become a columnist for the *New York Daily News*. Until recently, González continued with the *Daily News*, notably being the first investigative reporter to report on the adverse health effects from the destruction of the World Trade Center, which he also documented in his book *Fallout: The Environmental Consequences of the World Trade Center Collapse* (2002). He has served for more than twenty years as the cohost with Amy Goodman of the nationally syndicated Pacifica radio network program *Democracy Now!* When he was president of the National Association of Hispanic Journalists, he established the Parity Project to help news organizations recruit and retain Latino reporters and managers. Since 2018, he has held the post of professor of professional practice at Rutgers University–New Brunswick's School of Communication and Information. Among his awards are two George Polk Awards for his reporting and his induction into the New York Journalism Hall of Fame.

María Hinojosa (1961–)

Journalism, Radio

Born on July 2, 1961, in Mexico City, María Hinojosa moved with her parents to Chicago when she was one year old; her father had been recruited as a surgeon for the University of Chicago medical faculty. She graduated with a B.A. in Latin American studies from Barnard College in 1985. Hinojosa's professional career in broadcast journalism started when she worked for CNN's New York City bureau for eight years, reporting on urban issues. In 1992, Hinojosa was one of the founders and the host of *Latino USA*, one of the first nonprofit radio programs covering Latinos to be carried on public stations across the United States. Since 2000 she has also served as the executive producer of the radio magazine. In 2010 she founded Futuro Media Group, which took over production of *Latino USA*. Along the way, Hinojosa had her own interview talk show on PBS, *Maria Hinojosa: One-on-One*, and even had a short run as a host for the WNBC-TV public affairs show *Visiones*. In 2020, she published her autobiography, *Once I Was You: A Memoir of Love and Hate in a Torn America*. As the *New York Times* stated in reviewing her book, "Hinojosa has made it her mission to shed light on the lives and stories that others refuse or aren't equipped to see." Among her many awards are the John Chancellor Award for Excellence in Journalism and the Robert F. Kennedy Journalism Award for Reporting on the Disadvantaged. She has also won four Emmys for reporting on the poor and disadvantaged as well as on terrorism.

John Lantigua (1947–)

Journalism

John Lantigua was born in the Bronx in 1947 to a Puerto Rican mother and a Cuban father. Lantigua got his first job as a reporter at age twenty-one at the *Hartford Courant*. At age twenty-five he moved to Oaxaca, Mexico, and performed a variety of jobs, after which he landed work for United Press International in Honduras in 1982 as the Central American civil wars were heating up. In 1983 he started reporting for the *Washington Post* and other periodicals on the wars. He worked in Florida for the *Miami Herald* from 1993 to 1999, during which time he was awarded the 1999 Pulitzer Prize for investigative reporting on voter fraud. In 2002 he began working freelance and placed some of the most important stories of the day in the *Nation*, the *Washington Post*, *Newsweek*, and other outlets. These included the Elián González controversy and the Bush-Gore election debacle in Florida. While working at the *Palm Beach Post*, he won the Robert F. Kennedy Journalism Award in 2004 and 2006 and the National Hispanic Journalists Award for investigative reporting in 2004 and 2006 for reporting on immigration. In 2017 he published his account of going undercover in the migrant stream from Mexico, based on the reports that won him the John F. Kennedy Award, as *Smuggled across the Mexican-U.S. Border*. From 2017 to the present Lantigua has worked as an investigative reporter for the American Civil Liberties

Union (ACLU) of Florida. Lantigua is also a writer of eight detective novels, each of which deals with a different U.S. Latino ethnic culture and the characters' homelands in the Americas. He has won awards for some of these efforts, including the Edgar Allan Poe Award. His latest novel in the Willie Cuesta detective series is *Remember My Face* (2020).

Eva Longoria
(1975–)
Actor, Producer

Eva Jacqueline Longoria was born on March 15, 1975, on a ranch near Corpus Christi, Texas, to Mexican American parents. Longoria attended Texas A&M University–Kingsville, where she received a bachelor of science degree in kinesiology. She received a master's degree in Chicano studies from California State University, Northridge in 2013. After graduating from college, she moved to Los Angeles, where she was signed by an agent. After landing roles on *The Bold and the Beautiful* and *General Hospital* and costarring on *Beverly Hills 90210,* she auditioned for and won the role of Isabella on the popular series *The Young and the Restless*. But Longoria's national fame was cemented by her role of the spunky, wily Gabrielle Solís in the hit series *Desperate Housewives* (2004–2012), for which she was nominated for the Golden Globe and Screen Actors Guild Award. Her face also became nationally familiar as an advertising model for L'Oreal, which led to her being named one of the most beautiful people. From 2015 to 2016, Longoria starred as Ana Sofia Calderón in the NBC sitcom *Telenovela* while also serving as the executive producer for the hit Lifetime series *Devious Maids*. She has also served as an executive producer of social issue documentaries, including *Food Chains* and *The Harvest*. In 2006 Longoria starred in her first major film role in *The Sentinel*, opposite Michael Douglas. Longoria has acted in more than two dozen films, her latest being *Sylvia's Love* (2020), and numerous episodes of television series. Since 2008 she has had steady work in both each year. She has been an executive producer on some ten shows, the latest being *Grand Hotel* (2019), and directed a dozen episodes of television series. In 2018 her star was added to the Hollywood Walk of Fame.

George López
(1961–)
Television Comedian, Actor

Born on April 23, 1961, in Mission Hills, Los Angeles, California, the son of migrant workers, George López was abandoned by his parents and raised by his grandmother. After performing for a number of years as a stand-up comic, he got his first television opportunity in 2002 to star in and produce his own *George Lopez* show, which aired until 2007 on ABC. From there he went on to appear as a guest and act on various broadcast and cable talk shows and dramatic series. In 2014 he had another opportunity to star in his own *Saint George* show, but due to low ratings it was cancelled in its first season. Since then López has continued to appear in movies and on television. He has acted in more than thirty films, his latest being the crime thriller *The Tax Collector* (2020), and he continues to tour his stand-up comedy routines. In 2007 a documentary was filmed on his life and struggles: *Brown Is The New Green: George Lopez and the American Dream*. In 2004 López was presented the Artist of the Year and Humanitarian Award by the Harvard University Foundation. Also in 2004 he published his autobiography, *Why You Crying?*

Roberto Lovato
(1963–)
Journalism

Born in the Mission District of San Francisco to Salvadoran immigrant parents, Roberto Lovato has been a freelance journalist and columnist published internationally. His articles and columns have appeared in *Guernica Magazine*, the *Boston Globe*, *Columbia Journalism Review*, *Foreign Policy* magazine, the *Guardian*, the *Nation*, the *Los Angeles Times*, *Der Spiegel*, *La Opinión*,

Dignidad Literaria founders Myriam Gurba, David Bowles, and Roberto Lovato meet in New York City, January 2020.

and many other national and international publications. He is a socially and politically committed journalist who has a take on many public issues of concern to Latinos, such as the struggle against Proposition 187 in California, immigration, the border, and the wars in Central America. With cofounders Myriam Gurba and David Bowles he is leading #Dignidad-Literaria, a movement to pressure publishing houses and the whole book industry to publish and distribute the writing of U.S. Latinos. He is also the author of *Unforgetting: A Memoir of Family, Migration, Gangs, and Revolution in the Americas* (2020).

Rubén Martínez (1962–)

Rubén Martínez, a nonfiction writer of Salvadoran and Mexican heritage, was born on July 9, 1962, in the Los Angeles neighborhood of Silver Lake. He has distinguished himself as a journalist as well as an author of feature articles and books. An associate editor of the Pacific News Service and a

Loeb Fellow of Harvard University's Graduate School of Design, Martínez is also a pioneer in what has been called the "non-fiction novel," a narrative that re-creates lives and events based on historical and journalistic research. His most renowned work in this genre is *Crossing Over: A Mexican Family on the Migrant Trail* (2001), which traces the lives of an extended family of migrants during several years and through thousands of miles of their treks. Among Martínez's other works are *The Other Side: Notes from the New L.A., Mexico City, and Beyond* (1992), a collection of poetry and essays, and *Eastside Stories: Gang Life in East Los Angeles* (1998). Martínez's latest full-length book is *Desert America: Boom and Bust in the New Old West* (2012). In 2004, he published four essays on immigrant life in the United States in *The New Americans*, coauthored with Joseph Rodríguez, to accompany a PBS series of the same title. His reportage, opinion pieces, and essays have been published nationwide, from the *New York Times* to the *Los Angeles Times*, as well as in Mexico. Martínez was awarded an

Emmy for hosting the politics and culture series *Life & Times* (1995) on Los Angeles's KCET-TV. He is also the recipient of the Freedom of Information Award from the American Civil Liberties Union (1994), the University of California, Irvine prize in poetry (1990) and the Lannan Literary Fellowship (2002). As a poet, Martínez has delivered many spoken word performances and participated in public schools as an artist-in-residence.

Sonia Nazario (1960–)

Journalism

Born on September 8, 1960, in Madison, Wisconsin, Sonia Nazario was raised in Kansas and in Argentina. She graduated with a B.A. in history from Williams College in 1982 and went on to get a master's degree in Latin American studies from the University of California, Berkeley, in 1988. Completely bilingual, Nazario has written in both English and Spanish and worked for publications in both the United States and abroad. Her reporting career started in Spain at *El País* in 1980, and from 1982 to 1993 she worked at the *Wall Street Journal*, switching offices from New York to Atlanta, Miami, and Los Angeles. From 1993 to 2008 she carried out special projects and reported on urban affairs, social issues, and social justice issues for the *Los Angeles Times* and to the present has worked as a freelancer, writing books and speaking around the country. Since 2014 she has also served as an opinion writer for the *New York Times*. Nazario is one of the most recognized and acclaimed Latino journalists, having won numerous journalism and humanitarian awards, including three Pulitzer Prizes (1994, 1998, and 2003), two George Polk Awards (1994 and 2004), and the Robert F. Kennedy Journalism Award for Outstanding Coverage of the Problems of the Disadvantaged (2002). Her most impactful reportage was her book *Enrique's Journey: The Story of a Boy's Dangerous Odyssey to Reunite with His Mother*, which was a compilation of her *Los Angeles Times* series (2002) that became a national best-selling book in 2006. The story, which also became the basis of a video documentary, charted the struggles of a young boy leaving his home in Honduras to trek and face the dangers of riding "La Bestia" train and confronting the dangers of migrating to the United States alone.

Freddie Prinze (1954–1977)

Comedian, Actor

Born on June 22, 1954, in New York City to a Puerto Rican mother and a German immigrant, Freddie Prinze (born Frederick Karl Pruetzel) studied acting at LaGuardia High School of Performing Arts but dropped out to work as a stand-up comic, specializing in self-deprecating ethnic humor. In 1973 he got two breaks that introduced him to the viewing nation: appearances on *Jack Paar Tonite* and *The Tonight Show Starring Johnny Carson*. From there he repeatedly performed stand-up comedy on a variety of television shows. From 1974 to 1977 he starred in the historically important *Chico and the Man* opposite Jack Albertson; it was the first time after *I Love Lucy* that a Latino starred in a television sitcom. In 1975 he recorded a hit album, *Looking Good,* a catch phrase from his portrayal of Chico. Before he committed suicide on January 29, 1977, Prinze signed a five-year contract with NBC for $6 million, a fortune in those days. Prinze received a star on the Hollywood Walk of Fame on December 14, 2004.

Geraldo Miguel Rivera (1943–)

Television Journalism

Born on July 4, 1943, in New York City, Geraldo Rivera studied at the University of Arizona and Brooklyn Law School and received his law degree from the University of Pennsylvania and a degree in journalism from Columbia University. Rivera went on to become one of the nation's most celebrated and respected investigative television journalists, writing and producing various award-winning documentaries. In 1972, he won a Peabody Award for his report on the abuse of mentally impaired patients at Willowbrook State School in Staten Island and began appearing on national TV programs such as *20/20* and *Nightline*. After beginning his career as a reporter for WABC-TV in New York in 1970, he went on to become a reporter, producer, and host for various television news and entertainment shows. From 1973 to 1977, Rivera hosted *Good Night America*, a newsmagazine that he also executive produced. In 1987, he began hosting and producing his own *Geraldo* talk show, which was nationally syndicated until 1998. In 1991 Rivera published his controversial autobiography, *Exposing Myself*. From 1994 to 2001, Rivera hosted *Rivera Live* on CNBC. From 2001 to 2003, he worked as a war correspondent in Afghanistan. In 2008, Rivera published a book, *HisPanic: Why Americans Fear Hispanics in the U.S.*, a history and opinion about Latinos in the United States. In 2020, Rivera received widespread criticism for defending President Donald Trump and some of his associates during the COVID-19 pandemic. Today, Rivera hosts the newsmagazine program *Geraldo at Large* on the Fox News Channel. He remains one of the most visible and successful Latinos in media and entertainment.

Jorge Ramos (1958–)
Television Journalism

Born on March 16, 1958, in Mexico City, Jorge Gilberto Ramos Avalos received his B.A. in communications from the Unviersidad Iberoamericana and his M.A. in international studies from the University of Miami. In 1982, he worked briefly for Grupo Televisa in Mexico City and then moved to Los Angeles, where he was employed by KMEX-TV, the affiliate of the Spanish International Network that would become Univisión. Soon he was promoted to Univisión's national team. From 1987 to the present, Ramos has served as anchorman for the national broadcast *Noticiero Univisión*, which has made his a household name among most Latino families in the United States. Ramos also hosts *Al Punto*, a weekly public affairs program on Univisión. Ramos is one of the very few Spanish-language newsmen to cross over to English-language television: he hosts *America with Jorge Ramos*, a newsmagazine on Fusion TV. Since his days at Televisa in Mexico, Ramos has never shrunk back from telling the truth to powerful figures: in

2019, he was first detained and then deported by Venezuelan president Nicolás Maduro in Caracas; Ramos was also a thorn in the side of Donald Trump, beginning in 2015, when presidential candidate Trump reacted by banning him from a news conference, and once in the White House Trump continuously attacked him. Ramos in his career has reported on major world events, such as the fall of the Berlin Wall, the wars in Central America and the Middle East, terrorist attacks, and many others. Ramos writes a column in Spanish and English that is syndicated internationally, and he appears as a pundit on major English-language networks, such as CNN. Ramos is the recipient of eight Emmy awards.

Paul Rodríguez (1955–)
Entertainment

Paul Rodríguez is one of the most recognized and popular Latino comedians in the United States. Born on January 19, 1977, in Culiacán, Sinaloa, Mexico, Rodríguez came to the United States as the son of immigrant farm workers. "My family never thought that being a comedian or an actor was an obtainable goal. Being farm workers, all they wanted for their children was a steady job. But I knew I had to give it a chance." In 1977, after a stint in the air force, Rodríguez entered Long Beach City College on the G.I. Bill, where he received an associate arts degree, and then he enrolled in California State University, Long Beach, with the objective of becoming an attorney. During theater classes at the university, Rodríguez's comic talent became obvious to his professor, who led him to become associated with the Comedy Store in Los Angeles, and thus his stand-up comic career was launched. Rodríguez has worked in three television major network sitcom series and various movies. He was the host and star of the immensely popular *El Show de Paul Rodríguez* on the Univisión Spanish-language network from 1980 to 1993. Rodríguez was the head of his own company, Paul Rodríguez Productions, which produced the one-hour special *Paul Rodríguez behind Bars* that aired nationally on the Fox Network in 1991. His earlier special *I Need a Couch* had one of the highest ratings in the history of HBO comedy specials. From 2010 to 2011, Rodriguez hosted two seasons of the MTV Tr3s comedy home video series *Mis Videos Locos*. His largest role was starring in the film *A Million to Juan* (1994), which he also directed. In addition to his film and television work, Rodríguez was a comedy headliner at Las Vegas and Atlantic City, and in 1986 he released his first comedy album, *You're in America Now, Speak Spanish* and in 1997 *Cheese and Macaroni*.

María Elena Salinas (1954–)

Television Journalism

Born in 1964 in Los Angeles to Mexican immigrant parents, in 1981 Salinas started reporting for KMEX-TV, the Univisión affiliate in Los Angeles, and in 1987 became a coanchor for Univisión's *Noticiero Univisión*, eventually serving for three decades. She also was a cohost for Univisión's news magazine *Aquí y Ahora*. She became the most well-known Latina on television, earning numerous awards during her career, including Emmys, Gracie Awards, a Peabody, the Edward R. Murrow Award, and the Walter Cronkite Award for Excellence in Television Political Journalism. In 2012, with her coanchor Jorge Ramos, she received an Emmy Award for Lifetime Achievement from the National Academy of Television Arts and Sciences. She is known to have interviewed all of the U.S. presidents during her tenure at Univisión and was one of the first female journalists in wartime Baghdad; in 2007 she cohosted the first Democratic and Republican presidential candidate forums in Spanish for Univisión. Salinas left the network in 2017, and in 2018 became the host of *The Real Story with Maria Elena Salinas*, a crime series for Investigation Discovery. In 2019 she signed with CBS News to contribute reports and to appear during coverage of the run-up to the 2020 election. In 2006, she published her autobiography, *Yo Soy la Hija de mi Padre* (I Am My Father's Daughter).

Luis Santeiro (1947–)

Television Writer, Playwright

Born on October 9, 1947, in Havana, Cuba, Luis Santeiro immigrated to Miami with his parents in 1960. He received a B.A. degree in sociology from Villanova University in 1969 and an M.A. degree in communications from Syracuse University in 1970. He became a freelance writer and, beginning in 1978, served as a writer for the award-winning Children's Television Workshop and as the producer of *Sesame Street*. Among the many shows he has written for television are thirty episodes of the bilingual comedy *Qué Pasa, USA?* (1977–80) and numerous episodes of the PBS series *3–2–1 Contact!*, *Oye, Willie!*, *Carrascolendas*, and the ABC "After School Specials." *Qué Pasa, USA?* was the first English-Spanish bilingual program broadcast in the United States. Santeiro is among the most recognized Latinos behind the scenes in television; he has won fourteen Emmy Awards for his writing on *Sesame Street*. Santeiro is also a recognized dramatist with plays successfully produced in New York and Miami. In 2017 Santeiro published his memoir, *Dancing with Dictators: A Family's Journey from Pre-Castro Cuba to Exile in the Turbulent Sixties*.

Cristina Saralegui (1948–)

Television, Journalism

Cristina Saralegui was born on January 29, 1948, in Havana, Cuba, into a distinguished family of journalists. Her grandfather, Francisco Saralegui, was known throughout Latin America as the "paper czar"; he initiated his granddaughter into the world of publishing through such popular magazines as *Bohemia*, *Carteles*, and *Vanidades*. In 1960, she immigrated to Miami's Cuban exile community and furthered the family profession by majoring in mass communications and creative writing at the University of Miami. In her last year at the university, she began working for *Vanidades*, the leading ladies' service magazine in Latin America. By 1979, she was named editor-in-chief of the internationally distributed *Cosmopolitan-en-Español*. In 1989, she resigned that position to become the talk show host for *El Show de Cristina* on Univisión, which became the number-one rated daytime show on Spanish-language television in the United States. It lasted twenty years until it was cancelled in 2010. Beginning in 1991, Saralegui was also the host for a daily nationally syndicated radio show, *Cristina Opina* (Cristina's Opinions), and the editor-in-chief of her monthly magazine, *Cristina—La Revista* (Cristina—The Magazine), published by Editorial América in Miami. At her peak, through radio and television, *Cristina* reached 6.5 million Latinos daily throughout the United States and in twelve Latin American countries. After she left Univisión, she worked for a while for Telemundo, and in 2012 Saralegui began Cristina Radio on Sirius XM. Currently, she produces *Amigos Live! On the Internet* for AARP.

Ray Suárez (1957–)
Broadcast Journalism

Born on March 5, 1957, in Brooklyn, New York, to Puerto Rican parents, Rafael Suárez Jr. graduated from high school in Brooklyn and went on to earn a B.A. in African history from New York University and an M.A. in the social sciences from the University of Chicago. From 1993 to 1999 he served as the host of the National Public Radio program *Talk of the Nation*. From 1999 to 2013, Suárez was chief national correspondent and at times served as anchor on the nationally broadcast *PBS NewsHour*. From 2008 to 2011 he hosted *Destination Casa Blanca*, a program that covered Latino politics and other important issues. He was also host for *America Abroad* for Public Radio International. In 2019, Suárez became the interim host for WMHT's statewide public affairs program *New York NOW*. Currently, he is cohost of KQED's *World Affairs* nationally syndicated radio broadcast.

Roberto Suárez (1928–2010)
Journalism

Born in Havana, Cuba, on May 5, 1928, Roberto Suárez received his primary and secondary education there. For political reasons, he went into U.S. exile twice: once under the Fulgencio Batista regime and the second and final time under Fidel Castro. He ob-

tained a bachelor's degree in economics and finance from Villanova University in 1949. After returning to Havana, from 1959 to 1960 he was active in real estate, construction, and finance. In 1962, he went to work for the *Miami Herald* as a part-time mailer. He advanced to controller of the Knight-Ridder subsidiary operations. In 1972, he joined Knight Publishing Company in Charlotte, North Carolina, as controller and was named vice president and general manager in 1978. He was named president in 1986. In 1990, he became president of the *Miami Herald* and publisher of *El Nuevo Herald*, the Spanish-language newspaper published by the *Herald* since 1987. His awards included the 1989 Gold Medal for Excellence as the most distinguished executive of all Knight-Ridder companies, the 1990 Latino Alliance Heritage Award for Media, and the 1991 Leadership Award from ASPIRA. He died in 2010.

Jesús Salvador Treviño (1946–)
Television Director, Producer, Writer

Born on March 26, 1946, in El Paso, Texas, as a child Jésus Treviño moved with his family to East Los Angeles, where he obtained his primary and secondary schooling. He graduated with a B.A. in philosophy from Occidental College in 1968, whereupon he went to work for KCET-TV in Los Angeles producing the nightly Mexican American talk show *Ahora!*. The show did not survive, but he stayed on as a producer at KCET-TV while also writing, producing, and directing three documentaries: *Soledad*, about prisoners at the Soledad jail; *America Tropical*, about artist David Siqueiros; and *Yo Soy Chicano*, a history of the Chicano people. As such, he became the primary videographer for the Chicano Movement. In 1975 he wrote, directed, and produced a fictional film, *Raíces de Sangre*, which in 1991 was named one of the top twenty-five Latin American films of all time at the 36th Annual International Film Festival of Valladolid, Spain. Treviño has worked as a director and producer of many projects over the years, including the television series *Infinity Factory* as executive producer, 1975–76; as a director or producer during the 1970s for Conacine Productions in Mexico City, New Vista Productions, and KLCS-TV; and as a producer, writer, and director in the 1980s for Inter-American Satellite, Inc., and KAET. He is probably most highly regarded for the latter part of his career, during which he was a highly successful director of episodes for major television dramas, such as *Star Trek: Deep Space Nine, NYPD Blue, Chicago Hope, ER, Star Trek: Voyager, The Pretender, Dawson's Creek, Martial Law,* and *Resurrection Blvd.* Among his numerous awards are the Directors Guild of America (DGA) Award for Outstanding Directorial Achievement in Dramatic Shows–Daytime, for *Gangs,* 1988, and the DGA Award for Outstanding Directorial Achievement in Dramatic Shows–Daytime, for *P.O.W.E.R.: The Eddie Matos Story,* 1995. Treviño chronicled his involvement in and coverage of the Chicano Movement in his memoir, *Eyewitness: A Filmmaker's Memoir of the Chicano Movement* (2001), and he has published three volumes of interrelated short stories: *The Skyscraper That Flew and Other Stories* (2005), *The Fabulous Sinkhole and Other Stories* (2011), and *Return to Arroyo Grande* (2015).

ART

What is Latino art? What are its sources? When and where did it begin? What are its characteristics? How has it changed over time? What forces altered or determined its direction? How does it differ from the art of other groups of people? These and related questions are examined here to provide a historical framework for the art of Latinos.

Each region in Spanish America developed its own national culture as a result of local conditions, resources, and people. Mountains, jungles, and other natural barriers isolated settlements and affected communications between them. The cultural differences were also the result of differences in the size of the Indigenous populations and their level of civilization at the time of European contact. Finally, the history of the areas determined how the peoples of Spanish America developed as nations following their independence from Spain in the early nineteenth century. The result is that Latino cultures have been tempered by European, Indigenous, and African peoples, and their art reflects those conditions.

The sources of Latino art in the United States are found primarily in Mexico and the Caribbean basin as well as in the regions where most Latinos reside (Texas, Colorado, New Mexico, Arizona, California, New York, and Florida). The countries or territories to the immediate south of the United States—Mexico, Puerto Rico, and Cuba—have had a greater influence on the art of Latino Americans than others because of their geographical proximity and the result of wars between Spain, Mexico, and the United States in the nineteenth century. There are fewer people from other parts of Latin America, and as a result, their impact on Latino art in the United States has not been as great.

NEW SPANIARDS AND MEXICANS: 1599–1848

Missions

The missions built from Texas to California in the seventeenth and eighteenth centuries were intended to serve as Christianizing outposts as well as economic, social, and political units. The Franciscan friars in charge of the northernmost missions were sometimes the sole Europeans along the frontier. The missions, therefore, had to serve many assigned functions and be relatively independent, self-contained units.

The northern missions are related to the architectural complexes built by the friars in central New Spain in the sixteenth century. These complexes, known as *conventos*, always included a single-nave church and the various units associated with it, such as the sacristy (a small room next to the altar for storage of religious vestments), the friars' quarters, the cloister, the refectory or dining room, the kitchen, and other areas. The friars also included a large open space in front of the church, known as the *atrio* (atrium), with small chapels called *posas* at each of the four corners and a cross in the center. The *posas* were used for religious processions, and the cross was used to teach the Native Americans about the new religion.

The seventeenth- and eighteenth-century missions in the Amerindian pueblos of New Mexico follow the same arrangement used in the *conventos* of central New Spain. Examples are found in New Mexico at the Amerindian pueblos of Laguna (San José, about 1700) and Acoma (San Esteban del Rey, 1629–1641).

By the eighteenth and early nineteenth centuries, the standard arrangements seen in the sixteenth-century *conventos* were no longer strictly followed in the northern territories. They varied from region to region. The church no longer seemed to be the focal point of the complex, since the various units were not clustered around it as in central New Spain, nor did they have the standard east-west orientation of the earlier churches. Most churches had Latin cross plans, which also correspond to examples found in central New Spain. Examples are seen in the churches of Nuestra Señora de la Purísima Concepción (1755) in San Antonio, Texas; San Xavier del Bac (1783–1797), south of Tucson, Arizona; San Juan Capistrano (1796–1806) in California; and San Francisco de Assís (1813–1815) in Ranchos de Taos, New Mexico.

The north corridor of the Mission San Juan Capistrano in Orange County, California, photographed in 2013.

The facades of the mission churches also followed examples seen in the churches of central New Spain. The early *convento* churches have a vertical extension of the facade sometimes used as a belfry (*espadaña*), as in the churches of the Amerindian pueblos of Laguna and Picuris, New Mexico, and in the San Francisco de la Espada church in San Antonio. Another type of belfry is the bell wall (*campanario*), a wall with one or more openings for bells. A *campanario* was added to one of the walls of the nave of the San Juan Capistrano church in San Antonio. Another was built as an independent tower or wall adjacent to the facade but not part of it, as in the churches of the San Diego, San Gabriel, and Santa Inés missions in California.

The bell towers of the later colonial period and a dome over the crossing of the nave and transept are seen in the San José and Concepción churches in San Antonio, and the San Xavier church in Arizona. Bell towers but not the domes are seen in the Acoma and Ranchos de Taos churches in New Mexico, and the Santa Barbara, Carmel, San Buenaventura, and San Luis Rey churches in California.

Although the missions of the Southwest have *espadañas*, *campanarios*, bell towers, and domes, each region or mission field has its own characteristics due to the local conditions and the time the building programs began. The style of the New Mexico missions, built in adobe, remained unchanged over a period of several hundred years. The others differ only slightly, owing to the differences in style (baroque in Texas and Arizona and neoclassical in California) and distance from the central part of New Spain.

The primary function of the mission churches and chapels was to provide an area for religious celebrations carried out on a daily, weekly, and annual basis. The images on the exterior portal facades and the altarpieces placed inside these sacred areas were meant to be viewed and experienced for their religious meaning, with the devout using them for veneration and supplication purposes. Thus, purpose and function were related to the religious content and meaning the images conveyed, rather than their being created for purely artistic or aesthetic reasons.

The best examples of portal facades with figural and architectural sculptures are found in the mission churches of San José y San Miguel de Aguayo (1768–1782) in San Antonio and San Xavier del Bac (1783–1797) near Tucson. Figural sculptures are placed in niches framed by columnar supports, known as estipites, at San Xavier and on pedestals placed within niche-pilasters at San José. The pilaster is so named because it functions as a background for the sculptures.

San José y San Miguel de Aguayo

The architectural frame of the San José church portal has a single bay that spans its two stories. The entablature of the first story establishes its width, and the niche-pilasters provide its outer frame. Inner pilasters extend up to the entablature beyond the jambs of the doorway, which has a mixtilineo arch. The second-story bay, narrower than the first, has an entablature with supporting pilasters and a choir window, which are in line with the inner dimensions of the main doorway. The pedestals with sculptures are in line with the inner pilasters of the first story. Mixtilineo brackets provide the frame for the ensemble and a transition to the cornice topped by a stone cross.

Figural sculptures are on each side of the doorway, and above it under the cornice of the entablature. The same arrangement is seen around the choir window of the second story.

The main doorway is flanked by sculptures of Saint Joachim on the left and Saint Anne on the right. A sculpture of Our Lady of Guadalupe is seen over the doorway. There is a sculpture of Saint Dominic on the left side of the choir window and one of Saint Francis on the right. A sculpture of Saint Joseph holding the Christ Child is seen above the choir window. The arrangement of the sculptures by threes at each level of the portal is in keeping with other similar ones found throughout New Spain. There is no other example like this one in the mission churches of New Mexico, Arizona, or California. The closest to this arrangement is found at San Xavier, where the sculptures are located in niches on each side of the door and choir window. However, there are no sculptures along the central axis.

The portal facade on the mission church of San José y San Miguel de Aguayo (1768–1782) in San Antonio, Texas, features figural and architectural sculptures.

San Xavier del Bac

The estipite columns and the entablatures of the San Xavier portal are arranged in a rectangular grid. This is contrasted by the third story, framed by the curvilinear frame known as a reretted cornice. There is a sculpture of Saint Francis of Assisi in the central part of the cornice, known as a chamfered center. The sculptures on either side of the doorway are Saint Catherine of Siena on the left and Saint Lucy on the right. The sculptures on the second story are Saint Barbara on the left and Saint Cecilia on the right. These are much smaller in relation to their surrounding spaces than those at San José.

Other Mission Church Portals

The few sculptures that may have been placed in the portal niches of the California mission churches have long since disappeared. As an example, the three sculptures on the portal of the Santa Barbara church are modern replacements of those that were destroyed by an earthquake in 1925. The sculptures of the San Luis Rey church have disappeared. Those that were undoubtedly on the portal of the San Juan Capistrano church were destroyed by the earthquake of 1812. And finally, the sculpture in a niche on the portal of the San Gabriel church is a modern addition.

The mission churches of New Mexico did not have figural or architectural sculptures on the facades, owing to the use of adobe, which does not lend itself to this type of decoration. The primary focus in these churches was on the interior walls used for paintings and individual panels hung as pictures. Every church had an altar screen, known as a *reredos* in New Mexico (and *retablo* in Mexico), on the back wall of the sanctuary and numerous freestanding sculptures of holy images, known as *santos* (literally, saints), placed in front of it on altar tables.

Architectural Polychromy

Some of the mission churches also had painted decorations on the exterior surfaces to enhance their appearance, particularly in those cases where it was too expensive to add architectural and figural sculptures on the portals. A good example of this practice is seen on the facade of Nuestra Señora de la Purísima Concepción de Acuña Mission (1755) in San Antonio. All the windows and the portal and tower bases and the belfries were painted to simulate stone masonry frames and belfry arches. Simulated masonry was also painted on each side of the portal to give the illusion of tower bases. Simulated fluted pilasters were painted near the corners of each side of the belfry towers.

Finally, a sun and a moon were painted on the upper part of the portal. Other examples are found at San José mission church, where a quatrefoil pattern was painted over the entire facade along with simulated block frames on the tower base windows and zigzags on the dome. Examples of architectural painting in California are seen in the mission churches of Santa Clara de Assís (1822–23) and Santa Inés.

The use of colors on the facades of the Texas and California churches reflects the interest in creating dramatic effects of light and color seen in the churches of central Mexico (New Spain), where glazed tiles were used on domes and, on occasion, on facades as well. The best example of this practice is seen at the church of San Francisco Acatepec, Puebla.

Altarpieces

Few of the mission churches in Texas and California have sculptures or paintings on canvas that are original or date from the mission period. Those seen in some of the churches may not be from that period but are recent additions. Others that are from the mission period, as in the case of the San Antonio missions, are no longer in their original locations because the altarpieces in which they were placed disappeared in the nineteenth century.

Only the church of San Xavier del Bac in Arizona and others in New Mexico have their original altar screens in place. Those at San Xavier cover the altar area and the transepts (the arms of a Latin cross). The apostles are represented in the nave and chancel (the area in front of the altar at the crossing of the transepts and the nave). The focus is on human salvation (entrance to the chancel), and within the chancel are references to the missionary work of Saint Francis Xavier, the birth of the Virgin Mary, the earthly experience of Adam's offspring, and God the Father giving his benediction.

The altarpieces of the New Mexico mission churches were painted by local artisans in a folk art style. The sculptures made of wood and painted in different colors were also done by local artisans. Some mission altar screens are now found in the Museum of New Mexico (Santa Fe) and Taylor Museum (Colorado Springs, Colorado).

Alteration and Restoration of the Mission Churches

Many of the original churches have been altered over the years as a result of neglect and, in some cases, restorations carried out in the nineteenth and twentieth centuries. In the nineteenth century, some of the New Mexico churches were altered when Victorian-style decorations were added to the adobe structures. Most of these additions were removed in the twentieth century and efforts made to restore the churches to their original configurations. Unfortunately, the need to continually maintain the adobe surfaces because of the fragile nature of the material has led to unintended changes in the details of the structures.

The main altar at Mission San Xavier del Bac near Tucson, Arizona, features intricate carving and sculptures.

More durable materials were used in Texas and Arizona, and to some extent in California. It is on the portal facades of these structures that figural and architectural sculptures are more apt to be found than on the adobe churches of New Mexico. However, these sculptures suffered as a result of abandonment and vandalism in the nineteenth century. This began when the missions were secularized a few years after Mexico gained its independence from Spain in 1821. Political turmoil and war between Texas and Mexico eventually led to the partial destruction of some of the sculptures found on these facades. Some of them were restored in the twentieth century.

New Mexico Santeros

The relatively isolated New Mexicans developed a folk art independent of academic models far to the south during the first half of the nineteenth century. That style, generally dated from 1810 to 1850, is characterized by the work of holy image makers known as *santeros* (literally, makers of saint images—sculptures and paintings). The paintings on panels were called *retablos*; the sculptures were called *bultos*. However, they were not totally isolated. Works by masters from the metropolitan cities were available in such places as the church at Pecos Pueblo and the church of Our Lady of Guadalupe in Santa Fe. In addition, the earlier paintings and sculptures produced in New Mexico during the eighteenth century are derivative of academic styles.

In the twentieth century there was a new emphasis on *santo* making, at times encouraged by a number of American artists who began to arrive in Santa Fe and Taos. The craftsmen were encouraged to continue making furniture and other domestic products as well as sculptures that were similar to the traditional *santos* of the nineteenth century. Unlike the earlier pieces, however, the new *santos* were not painted in different colors, nor were they intended for chapels or churches. They were produced for collectors and tourists who acquired such objects as mementos of a trip through the area. Another change was seen in the production of the *santos*. Entire families were now involved in making *santos*, in contrast to the production of works by single artists in the past.

The revival of *santo* making took place primarily in the small community of Cordoba, New Mexico. However, the impetus for it can be found in Santa Fe, where the needed mechanisms were instituted starting in 1919 with the "revival" of the Santa Fe Fiesta and culminating in 1929 with the incorporation of the Spanish Colonial Arts Society, which had an impact on the making of *santos* in northern New Mexico. An annual fiesta exhibition was adopted in the late 1920s in which the works of Latino craftsmen were included. These exhibitions were variously called Spanish Colonial Handicrafts, Spanish Fair, and Spanish Arts and Crafts Exhibition. In 1929 the Spanish Arts Shop was established by the Spanish Colonial Arts Society in Sena Plaza, Santa Fe. During the time it lasted, through the early 1930s, it served as an impetus to some of the santeros, such as José Dolores López and others, who began to concentrate on the production of objects that were acceptable to Anglo patrons. As patrons, the Anglos determined questions of quality and originality of craftsmanship. *Santos* were no longer produced on the basis of the Latinos' own understanding of their heritage.

The Laguna Santero

The unique style of painting and sculpture in New Mexico began with the work of an anonymous Laguna santero who worked there from 1796 to 1808. The design of his altar screens and paintings indicate that he may have been from the provinces of Mexico. His work is clearly derived from Mexican provincial sources, specifically paintings and engravings, but is simplified to such an extent (all the forms are flattened out) that the figures appear weightless. The facial expressions are neutral in contrast to the more animated baroque examples from central New Spain. The baroque image and its variety of poses and expressions were meant to accentuate the ecstasy or other states of the saintly or holy person portrayed. The expression of religious piety in the works by the Laguna santero are closer to the images of medieval Europe.

A good example of the santero's work is the Laguna altar screen, dated 1800 to 1808. It has three bays on the first story and a single one on the second story. Solomonic columns frame each of the side bays, and solomonic balusters top the two outer columns on the second story. (Other santeros painted altar screens in a similar style; that is, they emphasized the architectural frame for the images as in the examples found in central New Spain.) Altar screens attributed to the Laguna santero are found in Pojoaque (about 1796–1800), Santa Fe (around 1796 and 1798), Zia and Santa Ana (both about 1798), and Acoma (1802). The altar screens have three bays and usually two stories.

The Laguna santero had several followers, among them Molleno, who may have worked in the santero's workshop. Among Molleno's works is the altar screen at the church in Rio Chiquito (1828). Another santero, known as the Quill Pen santero, was a follower of Molleno. These two artists, like the Laguna santero, emphasized the linear treatment of all forms and details.

José Aragón

José Aragón differed from the other santeros because he could read and write, and this ability was reflected in his work. He used engravings as models for his paintings, signed them, and even included lengthy prayers in them. While his work can be considered folk in style, it has a relationship to academic sources. It is sophisticated in its definition of form and the proportions of the human figure.

A good example of Aragón's *reredos* (altar screen) paintings is the one of Our Lady of Guadalupe, now in the Taylor Museum in Colorado Springs. The iconographic program is clearly based on the well-known conventional sources, but Aragón emphasized the formal rather than the narrative qualities of the image. There is a fine linearity that permeates all of the narrative panels and the spaces between them as well as the frame that contains them all. The Virgin is represented in the center, and her appearance to Juan Diego and the events subsequent to it are depicted in the four corners of the painting. Christ is seen in the top center, and the church that the Virgin ordered built in her honor is seen at the bottom center.

The Truchas Master

Another of the anonymous santeros working in the first quarter of the nineteenth century was initially identified as the Dot-Dash Painter, then later as don Antonio Fresques, and more recently as the Truchas Master. Works by this artist are dated between 1790 and 1830.

The reredos painting of Our Lady of Guadalupe, now in the Taylor Museum in Colorado Springs, is a good example of the Truchas Master's work. This painting is unlike most representations of the Virgin, which are based on the original in the basilica of Guadalupe near Mexico City. The artist ignored the standard proportions of the slender figure of the Virgin and did away with all semblance of naturalism in the depection of her downward gaze. The eyes are simple crescent shapes, and each iris is indicated by a black dot. The other features are defined with an equal economy of means.

Nuestra Señora del Carmen (Our Lady of Mount Carmel) by José Aragón, water-based paint on wood, c. 1830.

LATINO ARTISTS IN THE TWENTIETH CENTURY

The art of Mexican American and other Latino artists in the twentieth century reflects the many current styles of art of the period, from figurative to abstract, and from pop, op, and funk to destructive. However, the 1960s was also an important turning point for all Latino arts in the United States. Among the Mexican American artists who matured in the 1960s are Michael Ponce de León of New York; Eugenio Quesada of Phoenix; Peter Rodríguez of San Francisco; Melesio Casas of San Antonio; Manuel Neri of San Francisco; Ernesto Palomino of Fresno, California; and Luis Jiménez of Hondo, New Mexico. Puerto Rican artists who matured during the same period include New York–based artists Olga Albizu, Pedro Villarini, Rafael Montañez-Ortiz (Ralph Ortiz), and Rafael Ferrer. There were many other artists from Latin America working in New York and other U.S. cities at the time, but their work falls outside the confines of this study because their formative years as artists were spent in their countries of origin. Their presence, however, has not gone unnoticed by Latino and other American artists. Some remained in the United States for many years and then returned to their native countries. Others stayed to continue their careers.

Among those who stayed and attained national and international status for their work is the Argentine printmaker Mauricio Lasansky, who immigrated to the United States in 1943 and taught printmaking at Iowa State University until his death in 2012. He influenced generations of American printmakers through his teaching and his work. He was born in Buenos Aires in 1914 and became a U.S. citizen in 1952. Marisol Escobar, born to Venezuelan parents in Paris in 1930, resided in New York City from 1960 until her death in 2016. She became internationally famous in the 1960s with her sculptures of well-known personalities, such as Lyndon B. Johnson and John Wayne. Fernando Botero, known for his paintings of overblown figures used in satirical contexts, arrived in New York City in 1960. He was born in Medellín, Colombia, and now resides in New York City and Paris.

NOTABLE LATINO ARTISTS

José Aceves (1909–1968)

José Aceves painted murals (framed oil paintings) for the post offices in Borger and Mart, Texas (both in 1939). The mural in Borger, titled *Big City News*, deals with the mail service's delivering news to the most remote and isolated regions of the country. The mural in Mart, titled *McLennan Looking for a Home*, focuses on the arrival in 1841 of Neil McLennan and his family in the Bosque River Valley, eight miles east of Waco, Texas. The latter is typical of the idealized portrayals of the pioneers in the Southwest seen in post office murals of that period. Aceves was influenced by the muralist Edward Holslag in the development of the western subject matter in the Mart painting.

ADÁL (1948–2020)

Born in Utuado, Puerto Rico, Adál Alberto Maldonado (known as ADÁL) moved to New York City when he was seventeen; in the 1970s he studied photography and printmaking at the San Francisco Art Institute. Back in New York he became associated with the Nuyorican cultural movement and often worked with such writers as Pedro Pietri. In 1975 he cofounded and codirected Foto Gallery in Soho. In the 1970s and early 1980s, ADÁL experimented with surreal portraiture and out-of-focus photography, often attributed to his bicultural psychology. He frequently created visual puns in his work, comparable to code-switching in Nuyorican language and poetry. ADÁL's exhibitions have been published as books: *The Evidence of Things Not Seen ...* (1975), *Falling Eyelids: A Foto Novela* (1980), *Portraits of the Puerto Rican Experience* (1984), *Mango Mambo Galería Luiggi Marrozzinni* (1987), *Out of Focus Nuyoricans* (2004), and his auto-portraits, *I Love My Selfie* (2017). ADÁL's photos are collected in major museums around the United States and abroad. He had two major retrospectives of his work: in 2004 at the David Rockefeller Center for Latin American Studies,

Harvard University, and in 2017 at the Museo de Arte Contemporáneo in Santurce, Puerto Rico. In 2016 he moved back to Puerto Rico, where he executed his series *Los ahogados/Puerto Ricans Underwater*, distributed only on the internet.

Olga Albizu (1924–2005)

Olga Albizu was born in Ponce, Puerto Rico, in 1924 and graduated from the University of Puerto Rico in 1946. She first arrived in New York City in 1948 with a University of Puerto Rico fellowship for postgraduate study at the Art Students League, where she studied with the well-known abstract expressionist Hans Hoffmann until 1951; that experience is evident in her work. She also studied in Paris and Florence in 1953, when she returned to New York City. Albizu is remembered as an abstract painter who became widely known for her paintings for RCA record covers for the music of Stan Getz in the late 1950s. Albizu had her first solo exhibition in Puerto Rico, where she is canonized as a pioneer in abstract expressionism. She stopped painting in 1984. In 1996 Albizu was given a solo show at the Pan American Union in Washington, D.C. Upon her death in 2005 an exhibition of her works, "El Legado de Olga Albizu," was held at Biaggi & Faure Fine Art in San Juan, Puerto Rico.

Carlos Alfonzo (1950–1991)

Carlos Alfonzo was born in Cuba in 1950. He studied painting, sculpture, and printmaking at the Academia de Bellas Artes San Alejandro in Havana from 1969 to 1973 and art history at the University of Havana from 1974 to 1977. He began a teaching career at the Academia San Alejandro as instructor in art history from 1971 to 1973 and then taught studio courses in art schools of the Ministry of Culture during 1973 and 1980. He immigrated to the United States in 1980 for ideological and professional reasons. Alfonzo, a Miami-based Cuban American artist, drew his images from the Afro-Cuban religious tradition. Among the motifs he used was the knife, which stands for protection against the evil eye. The knife through the tongue is intended to keep evil quiet. He used such motifs for their connotations as well as for formal reasons. His paintings include numerous references

to the human figure presented in simplified configurations that recall the jungle paintings (1943) of Wifredo Lam. They are shown within a flattened-out visual field full of crescent shapes that can be used to define large mouths with toothy grins, tongues, large leaves, and eye masks. Alfonzo's works form part of the permanent collections of the Whitney Museum of American Art, the Museum of Fine Arts in Houston, and the Smithsonian Institution, among many others. He died of AIDS in Miami in 1991. The year before he died, he had solo exhibitions in Miami, Miami Beach, and Washington, D.C.

Carlos Almaraz (1941–1989)

Carlos Almaraz was born in Mexico City in 1941. His family moved to Chicago when he was one year old and to California when he was eight. He attended Loyola University in New Orleans, California State University at Los Angeles, East Los Angeles College, and Los Angeles Community College. He also attended the New School of Social Research and the Art Students League in New York City. Almaraz received his master of fine arts degree from the Otis Art Institute in 1974. He exhibited as a member of Los Four in 1974 at the University of California, Irvine and the Los Angeles County Museum. He was deeply involved with the Chicano movement in the 1970s, doing volunteer work with the United Farm Workers Union from 1972 to 1974 and graphic designs for El Teatro Campesino, which was formed to promote the farm worker cause. He was also a counselor and program director for the All Nations Neighborhood Center, helping "hard core" youth from 1974 to 1976. He painted murals in East Los Angeles during the same period until 1978. Starting in the 1980s he concentrated on painting nonmural works of art that focus on his background as a Chicano. A good example of his nonmural work is the painting *Europe and the Jaguar* (1982), in which the two major strands of Mexican and Mexican American or Chicano culture—the European and the Indigenous—are woven into a complex pictorial statement. A woman and a jaguar walking hand in hand are in front of a backdrop full of isolated motifs—a house, a train, a quarter moon, human heads in profile—painted in an explosive style. A man between them on a lower level stands calmly smoking a cigarette. The backdrop seems to be full of multicolored sparks that give the surface a luminous effect. Almaraz died of AIDS in 1989. Today, his works are part of the permanent holdings of the Smithsonian American Art Museum in Washington, D.C., the Los Angeles County Museum of Art, and the Whitney Museum of American Art in New York, among others.

Celia Álvarez Muñoz (1937–)

Born in El Paso, Texas, in 1937 to a family whose father was deployed repeatedly far from home, Celia Alvarez Muñoz was raised mostly by her mother and grandmother in the U.S.-Mexico border culture. She graduated with a B.A. after taking many courses in art from Texas Western University (now the University of Texas at El Paso) and worked as a teacher and fashion illustrator. She studied at North Texas State University (now the University of Texas of North Texas) and received her M.F.A. in 1977. Álvarez Muñoz is a celebrated conceptual multimedia artist, the creator of photographic work and installations and various other forms of public art. The dominant themes in her work over the years deal with all types of border: physical, linguistic, political, geographic, psychological, and social. She has had a half dozen solo exhibitions from El Paso to Providence, Rhode Island, and been included in numerous group shows nationally and internationally. She has had the distinction of having a book published on her artistic career: Roberto Tejada's *Celia Álvarez Muñoz*. Her awards include two National Endowment for the Arts grants (1988, 1991) and the Honors Award for Outstanding Achievement in the Visual Arts from the Women's Caucus for Art (1995).

José Rafael Aragón (1796–1862)

José Rafael Aragón was born in 1796 or 1797 and died in 1862. His earliest dated altar screen (1825) is found in the pueblo church of San Lorenzo de Picuris. Other works are in Chimayo, Taos, Talpa, and the Cordoba/Santa Cruz area.

Aragón was the major artist from around 1820 to 1860, and his *reredos* panel paintings, altar screens, and sculptures are the finest examples of the local folk art style.

Aragón took all the abstracting tendencies of his predecessors and created even finer examples of this type of art. His work is known for his bold use of line and pure color, and although he used late baroque models, his work was not dependent on them. Typical of his mature work is the altar screen originally in the chapel of Our Lady of Talpa (near Taos) and now in the Taylor Museum. It was completed in 1838. The style is softer than his earlier works. The faces tend to be round instead of elongated ovals, and the figures are relatively static in presentation.

A fine example of Aragón's sculpture is a *bulto* (religious sculpture) from the Talpa chapel, now in the Taylor Museum collection of Our Lady of Talpa. She is crowned and holds the Christ Child in her left arm. As in the *retablo* and altar screen paintings, the artist created a fine balance between the decorative and figural elements in the sculpture.

Luis Cruz Azaceta (1942–)

Born on April 5, 1942, in Havana, Cuba, Luis Cruz Azaceta arrived in the United States in 1960 and settled in Hoboken, New Jersey. He began to take life-drawing lessons at an adult center in Queens in the mid-1960s. While working nights as a clerk in the library of New York University, he enrolled in the School of Visual Arts in 1966 and received the equivalent of a bachelor of arts degree in 1969. He had his first solo show at the Allan Frumkin Gallery in Manhattan. In 1992 he relocated to New Orleans, and he incorporated a new materiality in his works: twisted metal studs, nails, wood, board, plastic barricade fencing, and weathered sheet metal. He taught at the University of California, Davis in 1980; Louisiana State University, Baton Rouge in 1982; the University of California, Berkeley in 1983; and Cooper Union, New York in 1984. He lives in Queens. Azaceta, like other Latino artists, was first concerned with portraying the brutalizing effects of violence in his work, in which cartoonlike characters were often presented as victims. According to Azaceta, "My art takes the form of violence, destruction, cruelty, injustice, humor, absurdity and obscenity, as a revolt against our condition and man's evil instincts. I want my paintings and drawings to be an outcry, to awaken man's deepest feelings. Feelings of love, nobility and brotherhood." A dominant theme across his many styles, materials, and experiments has been exile, and he has adjusted with the evolution of culture and current events to deal with the AIDS epidemic, Hurricane Katrina, the mass shooting at Sandy Hook Elementary School, and the Boston Marathon bombing. His 2011–2012 series *Shifting States* was dedicated to various recent shocks experienced in the world, such as the Great Recession, revolutions, wars, social injustice, and climate change, among others. Azaceta's work has been presented in more than one hundred solo exhibitions in the United States, Europe, and Latin America, and his works are part of the permanent collections of numerous museums.

Judy Baca (1946–)

Judith F. Baca was born in Los Angeles on September 20, 1946, to working-class parents and was raised in an all-female household; she is a leading feminist among Chicana artists. Baca attended California State University, Northridge, where she received her bachelor of arts degree in 1969. She also did work toward a master of art education degree and completed an intensive mural techniques course in Cuernavaca, Mexico. Baca is one of the pioneers of the mural movement in Los Angeles. She founded the first City of Los Angeles mural program in 1974, and in 1976 she cofounded the Social and Public Art Resource Center (SPARC) in Venice, California, where she still serves as its artistic director. Her best-known work is *The Great Wall of Los Angeles*. Painted over five summers, the half-mile-long mural employed forty ethnic scholars, 450 multicultural neighborhood youth, forty assisting artists, and more than one hundred support staff. In 1987 Baca started painting *The World Wall: A Vision of the Future without Fear*, a painting depicting the world with no violence; it includes issues of war, peace, cooperation, interdependence, and spiritual growth, and it consists of seven portable panels that measure ten feet by thirty feet each. The idea behind the project was for the mural to travel inter-

nationally, and each host country would add a panel to the mural. In 1996 Baca created *La Memoria de Nuestra Tierra* ("Our Land Has Memory") for the Denver International Airport, an indoor mural that has the pride of place and is visited by thousands daily. Baca is a pioneer in creating portable murals, with techniques borrowed from billboard printing; part of SPARC's services is to photograph and print portable murals. Baca and SPARC also have been able to professionalize the licensing of mural art, maintaining large databanks of mural photos and issuing contracts for printed, film, and internet reproductions of the art, and thus providing the creators with compensation. Baca is a distinguished professor emeritus of the Chicana/o Studies Program of the University of California, Los Angeles, and continues to teach at the University of California, Irvine and California State University, Monterey Bay. In 2010 Baca was conferred with the National Award in Public Art by Americans for the Arts; in 2011 a Los Angeles school was named in her honor, the Judith F. Baca Arts Academy; and in 2016 she received a prestigious United States Artist Fellowship.

Patrociño Barela (1908–1964)

The work of Patrociño Barela, a Taos wood carver, was supported by the Federal Art Project (FAP), part of the Works Progress Administration, from 1936 to 1943. He began to carve *santos* in 1931, and his work was later exhibited nationally under the auspices of the FAP. His benefactors had a great impact on his work. Barela broke away from the *santero* tradition and began to carve figurative works that have an overall organic quality usually suggested by the grain of the woods he used for his works. A good example of Barela's work is *Saint George*, in the National Museum of American Art (Washington, D.C.). It was carved from a single piece of cedar. The helmet-like nose and brow of the saint form one continuous shape that is echoed by the figure's crown, just as the V-neck of the tunic mirrors the shape created by the position of the figure's legs. The saint's expression is characterized by a stern projecting chin and the gentle slit of the mouth, set off to one side. Through a dynamic series of directions and counter directions—created by the play between positive and

Woodcarver Patrociño Barela in Taos County, New Mexico.

negative form and space—Barela adroitly depicts the slaying of the dragon.

Santa Barraza (1951–)

Born on April 7, 1951, in Kingsville, Texas, to working-class Mexican American parents, Santa Barraza enrolled at Texas A&I University (now Texas A&M Kingsville) and became involved in the Chicano movement, principally as a member of the Mexican American Youth Organization (MAYO). Barraza later transferred to the University of Texas, Austin and earned a B.F.A. in 1975, after which she became affiliated with Chicana feminist arts groups, especially Mujeres Artistas del Suroeste, which survived into the 1980s. In 1982 she received her M.F.A. from the University of Texas. Barraza accepted her first teaching positon at La Roche College in Pittsburgh, the first of

a number of such jobs she would have, eventually making her way back to Kingsville to teach for many years at Texas A&M, where she has served as the chair of the art department since 1998. Barraza is a mixed-media artist who blends traditional Mexican and Indigenous styles and iconography with social and political visual commentary. Her work incorporates Mayan, Aztec, and folk art motifs along with Catholic religious symbolism and ritual, as in her depictions of the Virgin of Guadalupe. Barraza works in easel art and constructions as well as large-scale murals, such as her commission for the Biosciences rotunda at the University of Texas at San Antonio in 1996. Her awards include the Lifetime Achievement Award in the Visual Arts from the Mexic-Arte Museum in 2014 and the Heroes for Children Award from the State of Texas Board of Education in 2008. Her work has been exhibited internationally; noteworthy was her solo exhibition at the Casa de América in Madrid, Spain, in 2014. In 2020 Barraza opened her own gallery, Barraza Fine Arts, in Kingsville's historic district; the first exhibition was of twenty-five artists who represent the spiritual creativity of the borderlands.

Jean-Michel Basquiat (1960–1988)

Born on December 22, 1960, in New York to a Haitian father and a Puerto Rican mother, Jean-Michel Basquiat ran away from home when he was fifteen and in the 1980s became a celebrated mixed-media artist, working often on graffiti murals, among the intelligentsia of Manhattan, and even in collaboration with Andy Warhol. Basquiat had his first solo show at a gallery in Modena, Italy, in 1981. That same year, when Baquiat was twenty-one, he became the youngest artist ever to take part in the famed *Documenta* exhibition in Kassel, Germany, and then at twenty-two, he was the youngest artist to be included in the Whitney Museum of American Art's Biennial. He had his first American one-man show in 1982. On February 10, 1985, he was featured on the cover of the *New York Times Magazine* and profiled in the article "New Art, New Money: The Marketing of an American Artist." Throughout the following years until his death, Basquiat exhibited internationally, including in Europe, Africa, and the South Pacific. He died of a heroin overdose on August 12, 1988. In 1992 the Whitney gave him a posthumous retrospective. Basquiat's works were a mélange of drawing, painting, poetry, historical information, and political commentary often from the vantage point of society's have-nots. His messages dealt with race and social class, even while he was celebrated by the White elite of society. Basquiat produced at a feverish pace during his ten years as an artist: creating some fifteen hundred drawings, six hundred paintings, and numerous sculptures and mixed-media works. His works continue to appreciate in value; they are among the highest priced of contemporary artworks.

Barbara Carrasco (1955–)

Barbara Carrasco was born in El Paso, Texas, in 1955 to Mexican American parents and was raised in the community of Mar Vista Gardens, near Culver City, California. She received her B.F.A. from the University of California, Los Angeles in 1978, and her M.F.A. from the California Institute of the Arts in 1991. She was the first woman editor of the UCLA newspaper *La Gente*. At age nineteen Carrasco became associated with César Chávez and the United Farm Workers of America (UFW), for which she designed and created flyers and banners. In 1981 Carrasco was commissioned by the Community Redevelopment Agency to create a sixteen-by-eighty-foot portable mural titled *The History of Los Angeles: A Mexican Perspective*. The mural resulted in a backlash because of its images of Japanese and Japanese Americans interned by the United States during World War II, as well as of the Zoot Suit Riots and other political issues. The mural, which depicted fifty-one events, was displayed only once, at Union Station in downtown Los Angeles. Carrasco is a mixed-media artist and created an animation titled *Pesticides!* (1989) for the Spectacolor light board in Times Square, New York. This computer artwork depicted farm workers being exposed to toxic pesticides, which led to the display being censored and two scenes being replaced. In 1999 she created one of her most iconic prints, *Dolores*, depicting, in a pop art aesthetic, the UFW activist Dolores Huerta. Carrasco has stated that because her art is so political, it has not been taken seriously. Carrasco's original mural sketches and drawings have been archived in the Permanent Collection of Works on Paper at the Library of Congress in Washington, D.C.

Melesio Casas (1929–2014)

Melesio Casas was born in El Paso, Texas, in 1929. He received his primary and secondary education in the city and later served in the Korean War from 1950 to 1953, where he was injured. Upon his return, Casas went to college on the G.I. Bill. He received a B.A. in art in 1956 from Texas Western University and an M.A. from the University of the Americas in Mexico City in 1958. He taught art for twenty-nine years at San Antonio College until his retirement; he died in

2014. Casas had a strong impact on the training and education of many Chicano artists in the Southwest. Casas was among the pioneers of the Chicano art movement, being a leading member as well of the highly influential art collective Con Safos. Although he began to include references to the United Farm Workers' eagle logo and pre-Columbian motifs in his work as early as 1970, the way in which these were used reflects the pop art style of the early 1960s. Typical of these works is the 1970 painting *Brownies of the Southwest*. However, he is best known for his series of 153 large-scale paintings called *Humanscapes* that were painted between 1965 and 1989. The series, organized like glimpses at a drive-in movie while driving by, deals with Chicano politics and identity, among other topics, and uses satire, pop culture, and folk art.

Edward Chávez (1917–1995)

Edward Chávez was born into a sheep-raising family near Wagonmound, New Mexico. Although he studied at the Colorado Springs Fine Arts Center, he considers himself to be largely self-taught as an artist. He taught at the Art Students League, New York City, in 1954 and from 1955 to 1958; Colorado College, Colorado Springs, in 1959; Syracuse University in New York from 1960 to 1961; and Dutchess Community College, Poughkeepsie, New York, in 1963. He was appointed artist in residence at the Huntington Fine Arts Gallery in West Virginia in 1967. Chávez painted murals for post offices and other government buildings from 1939 to 1943 in Denver, Colorado; Geneva, Nebraska; Center, Texas; and Fort Warren, Wyoming. His murals deal with a direct portrayal of life and industry in each of the areas where he received commissions for his work. He turned to abstraction in the 1950s and 1960s. For the Denver Center High School panels, titled *The Pioneers* (1939), Chávez focused on the daily chores of tending the oxen on the wagon trail and chopping down trees. He chose the actual building of a sod house as the subject for his Geneva, Nebraska, mural, *Building a Sod House* (1941). He portrayed the early method of hauling logs in the lumber industry around Center, Texas, for that city's post office mural, *Logging Scene* (1941). He focused on the American Indians and the first White men in Wyoming for the mural in Fort Warren, *Indians of the Plains* (1943). All his works were painted with oil on canvas except for the one in Wyoming, which was painted with egg tempera on plywood. The mural has numerous scenes in which hunting and other everyday activities of the Amerindians are depicted in two horizontal registers to the left and right of the large Indian.

Rafael Colón-Morales (1941–)

Rafael Colón-Morales, born in 1941 in Trujillo Alto, Puerto Rico, obtained his B.A. from the Universidad de Puerto Rico (1964). He pursued graduate study at the American University in Washington, D.C. (1965–66) and at Academia de Bellas Artes de San Fernando in Madrid, Spain (1966–67). He has taught art at the Universidad de Puerto Rico, Brooklyn Community College, and the Art School from El Museo del Barrio in New York. He has lived in New York since 1970. Colón-Morales was a member of Borinquen 12, an artists' group formed in New York to find venues for their work. The artists did not have a unifying goal in their work other than a practical aim to have their art exhibited, and the group no longer exists. Colón-Morales's early work was primarily geometric abstraction. His later works bear a resemblance to that of the Cuban surrealist painter Wifredo Lam, with crescent shapes and spiked projections within a dense thicket of forms. An example is *Apestosito* (Little Stinker, 1969). In his early career he became known by experimenting in mediums and techniques in his paintings, especially through the application of layers of acrylic polymers that he then removed to create textures and chromatic transparencies in his work. In fact, throughout his career he has explored new techniques. His 2004 series *Visitando a los Maestros* is a contemporary gloss on the grand masters by applying new techniques in the re-creation of their works, especially those of Caravaggio. From 1995 to 1996 he served as the curator of Pre-Columbian art at the Museo de Arte Puertorriqueño; from 1984 to 1989 he worked as an administrator at the Museo del Barrio.

Frank Espada (1930–2014)

Francisco Luis Espada Roig was born in Utuado, Puerto Rico, on December 21, 1930. His family moved to New York City in 1939. After high school he attended City College of New York but soon left without finishing his studies, instead joining the U.S. Air Force during the Korean War. After the war, he attended the New York Institute of Photography. In the 1960s and 1970s he was a civil rights activist. In 1979 Espada was awarded a grant from the National Endowment for the Humanities, which allowed him to focus on documenting the struggle of Puerto Rican communities in the United States; more than any other photographer, he produced indelible and iconic photos of Puerto Rican life and culture on the continent. His published collection *The Puerto Rican Diaspora: Themes in the Survival of a People* (2006) presents his documentary photography from the early 1960s to the mid-1980s. Later in his career, Espada became known for documenting the devastating effects of the AIDS plague on minority populations. Espada taught photography at the University of California, Berkeley, the Academy of Art University, and the San Francisco Art Institute. Espada was the father of the renowned poet Martín Espada.

Rafael Ferrer (1933–)

Rafael Ferrer was born in Santurce, Puerto Rico, in 1933. He studied at the Shunton Military Academy, Virginia, from 1948 to 1951 and at Syracuse University, New York, from 1951 to 1953. He abandoned his studies at Syracuse to study art in Puerto Rico, where he was introduced to the work of the surrealists by the Spanish painter E. F. Granell. From then on he spent part of the year in Puerto Rico and part in the United States until 1966. In the 1960s Ferrer was at the forefront of the movement in New York City that dealt with temporary installations and other ephemeral works and deemphasized "the object" as a work of art. He experimented with a variety of media and methods, from assemblages, constructions, and freestanding sculpture to lengths of chain-link fence, blocks of ice, bales of hay, and masses of dry leaves used to create environments for indoor and outdoor exhibitions. These temporary installations were related to the non-object events of conceptual art of the early 1970s and took place in such venues as the Museum of Modern Art in New York, the Whitney Museum of American Art in New York, the Corcoran Gallery in Washington,

D.C., the Stedelijk Museum in Amsterdam, and the Museums of Contemporary Art in both Philadelphia and Chicago. In the early 1970s Ferrer began to focus on imaginary voyages and the apparatus used to carry them out—maps, kayaks, tents, and boats—in works assembled or constructed of steel, wood, and other materials. In the 1980s he began producing expressionistic paintings of his native Caribbean, focusing on the beauty of the tropics and breaking tourists' stereotypes. He also produced sculptures for important commissions, such as *Puerto Rican Sun* erected in the South Bronx in 1979 and *El Museo Rodante* (The Rolling Museum) of five bronze sculptures in La Parguera, Puerto Rico—reinstalled in San Juan in 2005. Ferrer had major solo exhibitions at El Museo del Barrio in 2010, titled *Retro/Active*, and a *Survey of Works on Paper* at the Lancaster Museum of Art in 2012.

Antonio García (1901–1997)

Antonio García, born in Monterrey, Mexico, on December 27, 1901, used the Spanish conquest of Mexico as a theme in a work titled *Aztec Advance* (1929), and he portrayed a Mexican national and religious icon in a mural titled *Our Lady of Guadalupe* (1946–47). Beginning in 1914 he resided in San Diego, Texas, as a refugee from the Mexican Revolution, and he graduated from high school there. García studied at the Chicago Art Institute from 1927 to 1930 and taught art at Del Mar College in Corpus Christi, Texas, from 1950 to 1970. He painted murals in Texas beginning in the 1920s, including five frescoes at Sacred Heart Catholic Church in Corpus Christi and *March on Washington*, which he painted for the Dallas Museum through the Public Works Administration in 1933. At the end of his career in the 1990s, he was legally blind and had to give up painting. García died in 1997 in Florida.

Rupert García (1941–)

Rupert García was born in French Camp, California, in 1941. He attended Stockton College and San Francisco State University, where he received his bachelor of arts degree in painting in 1968 and a master of arts degree in printmaking (silk-screen) in 1970. He pursued his doctoral studies in art education at the University of California, Berkeley, from 1973 to 1975, and received another master of arts degree in the history of modern art in 1981. He taught at San Francisco State University from 1969 to 1981; the San Francisco Art Institute from 1973 to 1980; the University of California, Berkeley beginning in 1979; Mills College in 1981; Washington State University in 1984; the Mexican Museum, San Francisco, in 1986, and San Jose State University from 1988 to 2010, when he retired and was named professor emeritus of art. The precisely defined flat areas that are characteristic of the silkscreen process make the work of Rupert García immediately recognizable. The unvarying fields of color, which are also part of this process, carry over into some of his painting. This aspect of his work is so strong that a design he provided for a mural in Chicano Park, San Diego, retained the look of a silk-screen print. The pylon mural, actually painted by Víctor Ochoa and the Barrio Renovation Team, focuses on Los Tres Grandes (Diego Rivera, José Clemente Orozco, and David Alfaro Siqueiros) and Frida Kahlo (1978). García's silk screens have been included in most exhibitions of Chicano art, most recently in 2013 with *Empujando Tinta: Ten Years of Collaborative Activism* celebrating the tenth anniversary of Taller Tupac Amaru, a collective art studio founded in Oakland in 2003 (*taller* means "workshop" in Spanish). His most recent one-man show was *Rupert García: Rolling Thunder* at the Rena Bransten Gallery in San Francisco in 2018.

Scherezade García (1966–)

Born Scherezade García Vázquez in Santo Domingo, Dominican Republic, García graduated with an A.A.S. from the Altos de Chavón School of Design, a Parsons School of Design affiliate in the Dominican Republic in 1986, and won a scholarship to Parsons in New York City. After receiving her B.F.A. from Parsons in 1988, she earned an M.F.A. in sculpture at City College of New York in 2011. She has taught at Parsons since 2010. García's interdisciplinary art explores the culture of colonialism, immigration, and politics as well as the Afro-European culture of Dominicans and other Latinos, including allusions to syncretic religious practices. She has stated, "Almost everything that I'm interested in has to do with diversity and freedom and what is new. What does that have to do with Dominicans? I will tell you. In this country we love to talk about diversity and freedom, freedom of speech, freedom of thought. We have to have tokens of diversity all over, which is almost fake, in that we have to work on it." García has had more than twenty-five solo exhibitions, mostly in New York and Santo Domingo, and has been included in even more group shows internationally.

Carmen Lomas Garza (1948–)

Garza was born in Kingsville, Texas, in 1948. She attended Texas A&I University in Kingsville (now Texas A&M University–Kingsville), where she received her bachelor's degree in education in 1972 and subsequently became a certified teacher. She attended Antioch Graduate School of Education, Juarez Lincoln Extension (Austin), where she received her master of arts degree in 1973. She received another master of arts degree from San Francisco State University in 1980. She currently resides in San Francisco. A painter and printmaker, Garza uses her Chicano background as the primary focus of her work. Her images, based on recollections of her childhood in South Texas, are used to heal the wounds she suffered as a result of racism and discrimination. One of Garza's most widely known series is the one based on the game *Lotería* (The Lottery). In the work, titled *Lotería-Tabla Llena*, she consciously uses an exaggerated perspective, reminiscent of the works of native artists, because it allows her to present all the thematic elements (motifs) in the work in as clear a fashion as possible. The large table is presented as if seen from above, and everything else—the figures, the animals, furniture, plants, and trees—is represented as if seen head-on. The only exception is the walkway at the bottom of the print, also shown as if seen from above. Garza's work has been published extensively and included in numerous exhibitions, including in the Smithsonian American Art Museum's "Our America:

The Latino Presence in American Art" in 2013. The San Jose Museum of Art organized "Carmen Lomas Garza: A Retrospective" in 2001. She has also written children's books illustrated with her art; her *Family Pictures/Cuadro de Familia* was chosen by the Library of Congress as one of the best books of 1990. Two other books won Bura Pelpré Prize honors: *In My Family/En Mi Familia* (1998) and *Magic Windows* (2000).

José González (1933–)

José González, born in Iturbide, Nuevo León, Mexico, in 1933, and raised in East Chicago, Indiana, has lived most of his life in the United States. He studied and received a diploma from the Chicago Academy of Fine Arts in the mid-1950s and continued his studies at several institutions in the 1960s: the Instituto Allende in San Miguel Allende, Mexico; the University of Chicago; the School of the Art Institute of Chicago, where he received his bachelor of fine arts degree in 1970; and the University of Notre Dame, where he received his master of fine arts degree in 1971. He devoted all his energies to the Chicano movement throughout the 1970s and 1980s as a muralist, organizer of exhibitions, and founder of organizations, such as Movimiento Artístico Chicano (MArCh) and others. González is a multitalented painter, photographer, and arts administrator who has been at the forefront of the muralist movement in that city since the early 1970s. He was the art director for the quarterly magazine *Revista Chicano Riqueña* (later the *Americas Review*), published first in Gary, Indiana, and later in Houston by Arte Público Press. Among the designs by González for the *Americas Review* is one titled "Barrio Murals" (1976). The cover design is a photo collage composed of the many murals painted in Chicago in the early 1970s. González painted various murals in East Chicago, Indiana, that are in large disrepair today. González is known for a series of charcoal drawings and portraits inspired by the techniques of the Mexican masters. However, his artistic productivity was limited due to his untiring efforts to promote Latino art and artists, organizing exhibitions, fighting the powers that be for Latino arts representation, and nurturing young artists. In 2010 he published his autobiography, *Bringing Aztlán to Mexican Chicago*.

Xavier González (1898–1993)

Xavier González was born in Almería Spain, in 1898, and received his art training at the Chicago Art Institute from 1921 to 1923. He taught art in San Antonio, Texas, in the early 1920s and at Newcomb College, Tulane University, from 1929 to 1943. In 1930 González won third prize in a national competition for murals on the subject "The Dynamic of Man's Creative Power." The winning entries were installed in the Los Angeles Museum. He painted murals for the post offices in Hammond and Covington, Louisiana (1936 and 1939); the federal courtroom in Huntsville, Alabama (1937); and the post offices in Kilgore and Mission, Texas (1941 and 1942). He later became the director of the art school at Sul Ross State Teachers College in Alpine, Texas. His works have been included in exhibitions at the Corcoran Gallery of Art, the Whitney Museum of American Art, and the Metropolitan Museum of Art.

Ester Hernández (1944–)

Ester Hernández was born in Dinuba, California, in 1944 to farm-worker parents of Mexican and Yaqui heritage. She moved to the San Francisco Bay area in 1971 to continue her studies and became active in the Chicano movement. She received her B.A. from the University of California, Berkeley in 1976 and began teaching art at schools in the area while furthering her art; by 1977 she had completed eleven murals there. In the Bay Area, she met and worked with other Chicano artists, among them Malaquías Montoya, and became involved with Mujeres Muralistas (Women Muralists). Hernández has used her painting and graphic work to make statements about Chicano culture and the economic forces that have had a negative impact on one segment of it: the farm-working communities in California. One of the most controversial works by Hernández is a print that was published on the cover of *En frecuencia*, a guide for public radio in Santa Rosa, California. The primary focus of the image was on Our Lady of Guadalupe, but instead of using the traditional image of the Virgin she used a woman in a karate stance to make a statement about the liberation of Chicanas. Artist Amalia Mesa-Bains has said of Hernández, "She subverts, re-contextualizes, and transforms culturally traditional images into a series of feminist icons." Hernández's works have been exhibited nationally and internationally, and they have been included in the permanent collections of the National Museum of American Art, the Smithsonian Institution, the Library of Congress, the Museum of Modern Art and the Mexican Museum in San Francisco, the Mexican Fine Arts Center Museum in Chicago, and the Frida Kahlo Studio Museum in Mexico City. In 2009 she won the Lifetime Achievement Award presented by the Women's Caucus for Art, New York City. In 2016 she was presented with the Sor Juana Award by the National Museum of Mexican Art in Chicago.

Carmen Herrera (1915–2022)

Born on May 31, 1915, in Havana, Cuba, the daughter of a newspaper editor, Carmen Herrera studied at the University of Havana but married an American teacher and moved to New York in the 1930s. She studied at the Art Students League of New York in 1943 and later moved to Paris to pursue her art, unsuccessfully, from 1948 to 1953. Back in New York, she continued to receive rejection from the critics; it was only late in life, beginning in the 2000s, that she was favorably discovered by the critics and included in many shows, especially of structuralists and minimalists. Thus, her career as a Cuban American artist spanned nine decades, during which time she worked on expanding the boundaries of geometric abstraction. In 2016, fifty of Herrera's works were gathered in "Carmen Herrera: Lines of Sight" at the Whitney Museum of American Art, her first museum exhibition in almost two decades. In October 2020 she received a major retrospective at the Museum of Fine Arts, Houston: "Carmen Herrera: Structuring Surfaces"; she had turned 105 years old in May of that year. "Structuring Surfaces" revealed Herrera's elaborate artistic process, by which she structured the surfaces of her supports to produce dynamic spatial tension. The exhibition showcased more than thirty works from the 1960s onward, including paintings, drawings, prints, wall structures, and objects. Influenced by her early architectural training, Herrera began to conceptualize her early two-dimensional paintings as objects through a series of drawings produced in 1966. Five years later, she transformed these drawings into wall reliefs that she called *Estructuras* (Structures). Hovering between painting and sculpture, these works directly influenced other areas of Herrera's artistic production, as she consistently structured her compositions to physically manifest the hard edges and lines of her works. "Structuring Surfaces" investigated the various formats these constructions assumed as Herrera seamlessly moved between media to generate tension between planarity and three-dimensionality, line and form, and positive and negative space. Herrera died in New York City on February 12, 2022.

Miguel Herrera (1835–1905)

Miguel Herrera, a resident of Arroyo Hondo in Taos County, was among the several santeros serving the needs of the Penitentes and others in the area. He worked in the 1870s, 1880s, and possibly later as a *bulto* maker. (No *retablos* are known to have been produced by him, but this is not surprising, since religious prints were readily available.) The tall figures with attention paid only to the head and hands were meant to be dressed in fabric clothing. His *santos* are noted for small seashell ears set too low on the head. Much of his work was done for the *moradas* of the Penitentes. A fine example of his work is the *Christ in the Holy Sepulchre*, in the Taylor Museum collection. It is life-size, and its knees, shoulders, neck, and jaw are articulated.

Luis Jiménez (1940–2006)

Luis Jiménez was born in El Paso in 1940. He attended the University of Texas, Austin, where he received his bachelor of fine arts degree in 1964. After finishing fellowship study at the National University of Mexico, in 1966 he moved to New York, where he worked and exhibited in several galleries. He made his permanent residence in Hondo, New Mexico, while teaching one semester each year as an endowed professor of art at the University of Houston. While influenced by the great Mexican muralists, Jiménez is generally considered within the genre of pop art, largely because of the materials and techniques he used. Jiménez is primarily known for his sculptures made of resin epoxy coated with fiberglass. Jiménez paraphrased Mexican art and American western art and used pre-Columbian concepts in his works of the late 1960s and early 1970s. After that, he concentrated on the Southwest for a series of sculptures and colored-pencil drawings. Among the early works are *Man on Fire* (1969–70), *The End of the Trail* (1971), *The American Dream* (1967–69), and *Indians to Rockets* (1972). Jiménez initially selected the many post office murals found all over the country as a source for the imagery in the *Indians to Rockets* project. The murals in the Southwest invariably deal with the history of the region or its industries. What struck the artist most was the emphasis in all of these murals on the notion of progress, exemplified by the machine. Starting in the early 1970s, he did studies on the history of the Southwest that were eventually used for a series of sculptures on that subject, titled *Progress I*, *Progress II*, and so on. His *Vaquero* (1990), a cowboy on a bucking horse, stood for many years outside the front door of the National Museum of American Art in Washington, D.C. His last sculpture was of a thirty-two-foot horse, *Mustang*, rearing on its hind legs. Ironically, it is his most viewed, given that it stands at the entrance to the Denver International Airport. Toward the end of the 1970s, Jiménez began to concentrate more specifically on regional subjects in which the Chicano, the Anglo, and others were represented in their natural surroundings. A good example of these works is the drawing of a man and woman dancing while an onlooker watches, titled *Honky Tonk* (1981–86). In 1993 Jiménez received the New Mexico Governor's Award for Excellence in the Arts and in 1998 the Distinguished Alumni award from the University of Texas. In 2006 Jiménez died in his studio when a piece of *Mustang* fell on him, crushing him to death. The statue was completed by his staff, family, and volunteers, and installed in 2008.

Alma López (1966–)

Alma López was born in Los Mochis, Sinaloa, Mexico, in 1966 and immigrated to Los Angeles with her parents when she was a child. She received a B.A. from the University of California (UC), Santa Barbara; an

M.F.A. from UC Irvine in 1978; and a photography certificate from UCLA Extension. López teaches art at UCLA and in 2018 received a faculty research grant from the institution. López, in her experiments with Chicano/Latino icons from a feminist/lesbian perspective, has often used Our Lady of Guadalupe in various series of works that emphasize Chicano culture and identity. She substituted human figures and an Aztec deity for Our Lady of Guadalupe in several works, including her grandmother, Tonantzin (*Our Mother*), a small sculpture of Coatlicue (*Serpents Her Skirt*), an Amerindian woman nursing her child, and the artist herself. Her self-portraits include a performance piece and a painting. In the former, the artist was photographed moving toward the viewer armed with paint brushes and wearing blue shorts, a sleeveless undershirt with stars painted on it, and sneakers. In the latter, the artist is shown appropriating the attributes of Our Lady of Guadalupe and her pre-Columbian counterpart. She runs toward the observer with an expression of triumph while holding a serpent in one hand and a mantle with a star-studded blue field in the other. Among her awards are the 2013 Richard T. Castro Distinguished Visiting Professorship, Metropolitan State University, Denver, Colorado; the 2005 Outstanding Community Activist, Los Angeles LGBT Center; and the 1999 Premio Pollock-Siqueiros Binacional.

Carlos López (1908–1953)

Carlos López was born in Havana, Cuba, in 1908, spent his early years in Spain, and lived in South America before immigrating to the United States when he was eleven years old. He studied at the Art Institute of Chicago and the Detroit Art Academy. López's first exhibition took place in Detroit in January 1932, and he became the director of the Detroit Art Academy from 1933 to 1937. He taught at the Meinzinger School of Art in Detroit from 1937 to 1942. In 1945 López became a professor of art at the University of Michigan, where he served until his death in 1953. López painted murals under the Works Progress Art Project (WPAP) from 1937 to 1942. His first mural was painted in Dwight, Illinois (1937), followed by three others in the Michigan cities of Plymouth (1938), Paw Paw (1940), and Birmingham (1942). Throughout the 1940s, López received numerous commissions from several federal agencies and from private companies to portray various aspects of American life: American industries at war for the War Department, a pictorial record of the war for *Life* magazine, the amphibious training activities for the U.S. Navy, and the project "Michigan on Canvas" for the J. L. Hudson Company. After World War II, López's work turned toward fantasy and symbol, conveyed by figures that always appear to stand alone, lonely and sad.

Félix A. López (1942–) and Luis Tapia (1950–)

Typical of the new style of *santos* are the sculptures of Saint Michael by Félix A. López and Luis Tapia. López's *San Miguel* (1984), in a private collection, shows the saint with his sword in one hand and the scales in the other. This is the traditional image of the saint. The other way in which Saint Michael was portrayed is seen in the elaborate image of St. Michael and Tapia's *Dragón* in the collection of the Museum of International Folk Art. These and other pieces by these santeros are generally larger than the unpainted *santos* made in Cordova and are meant to be taken more seriously as images related to the Latino tradition in New Mexico. Tapia was innovative in using acrylic paints on his *santos* and also broke with tradition on making them relevant to social and political issues. Critic Lucy Lippard stated, "Tapia is famous for breaking away from stylistic confinement while maintaining cultural continuity. He has disrupted the expectations of his genre while creating an art responsive to its own times, a complex task acknowledging and exploring the contradictions of modern life, or *la vida loca*." López was born in Gilman, Colorado, in 1942. He attended New Mexico Highlands University, where he received his bachelor's degree with a major in Spanish and a minor in German in 1965. He taught high school in Corcoran and Orange, California, in the late 1960s. He continued his studies and received his master's degree in Spanish literature in 1972 from the University of New Mexico, Albuquerque. He began making *santos* in 1977. Today he teaches wood carving at Santa Fe Community College. Tapia was born in the village of Agua Fria, outside of Santa Fe, New Mexico, in 1950. He attended New Mexico State University for a year and began making *santos* around

1970 when he became aware of the Latino issues related to the civil rights movement. Unlike the earlier santeros, he began to use bright colors for the figures; this was shocking to viewers in the early 1970s. He also paints altar screens in the old style. In 1996 Tapia received the New Mexico Governor's Award for Excellence in the Arts.

George López (1900–1993)

The increased markets and competition between artists led to an increase in the number of people making *santos* in the 1930s. The children of José Dolores López began to make *santos* at this time. Among them was George López, who was born on April 23, 1900, in Cordova and began carving objects in 1925 but was not able to devote full time to it until 1952, after years of working jobs related to the railroad. Eventually, his work became more widely known than that of the other Cordova santeros. By the 1960s he was considered the best of the santeros. He preferred the traditional saints for his carvings—St. Francis, St. Joseph, San Ysidro Labrador, St. Michael, the Virgin of Guadalupe, and Santo Niño de Atoche—and was highly influenced by Penitente practices. He was awarded the National Heritage Fellowship by the National Endowment for the Arts in 1982. López was the sixth generation of a santero family, but he did not have children to carry on the tradition.

José Dolores López (1868–1937)

One of the most important of the new santeros was José Dolores López, whose works date from about 1929 to 1937, the year of his death. He was primarily a furniture maker from 1917 to about 1929. He also did carpentry work—window and door frames, roof beams and corbels, crosses for grave markers, coffins, and chests—and made small wooden figures, primarily for relaxation and as gifts for neighbors and relatives. He began to carve birds and animals as well as *santos* after 1929 because he could no longer earn a living from his fields and livestock and his carpentry work. This new endeavor coincided with the emerging interest in Latino culture and handicrafts generated by a few Anglo artists. They were interested in revitalizing Latino "traditional," "colonial," and

"Spanish" crafts. These external factors created new markets for Latino crafts and competition between artists. At the same time, the new patrons taught the Latino artists to be "selective" in their work—that is, to produce objects for the non-Latino market.

López made several changes in his work during the period of transition from an older Latino tradition to the new one created by Anglo patrons. The furniture he produced in painted and unpainted versions was changed exclusively to the latter because the painted pieces were too "gaudy" for Anglo patrons. He then turned to making unpainted *santos* at the prodding of Frank Applegate, who was in charge of arts and crafts for the Spanish Colonial Arts Society. Among the subjects López portrayed in his work are Saint Anthony, Saint Peter, Saint Michael with the dragon, a *nacimiento* (nativity) in which all the appropriate figures are included, a *muerte* (death cart), and Adam and Eve, in which the Garden of Eden and the Tree of Life with the serpent are included. The latter is a formal extension of earlier trees with birds made by the artist. A good example of the Adam and Eve theme is a piece in the Taylor Museum collection titled *Adam and Eve in the Garden of Eden*. López made other elaborate *santos*, such as *The Expulsion from the Garden of Eden*, in the collections of the Museum of International Folk Art (Santa Fe); *Michael the Archangel and the Dragon*, in the Taylor Museum; *The Expulsion from Paradise*, in the collections of the Museum of International Folk Art; and in the same museum, *The Flight into Egypt*.

Gilbert Sánchez Luján (Magú) (1940–2011)

Gilbert Sánchez Luján was born in French Camp (Stockton), California, on October 16, 1940. After serving in the Air Force, in 1962 he returned to California and attended East Los Angeles Junior College and Long Beach State College, where he received his bachelor of arts degree in 1969. He received his master of fine arts degree at the University of California, Irvine in 1973. In 1969, he became the art director for the famous Chicano art and culture magazine, *Con Safos*, and was deeply involved in the Chicano movement. He joined Almaraz and Romero to form the

exhibiting group known as Los Four. Their first show went up at Irvine in 1974. He taught in the La Raza Studies Department at Fresno City College from 1976 to 1981, becoming department chair in 1980. Then he returned to Los Angeles, where he taught at the Municipal Art Center at Barnsdall Park. From 1999 to 2007, Luján operated his art studio at the Pomona Art Colony and in 2005 became a professor at Pomona College. Luján is known for his pastel paintings and painted wood sculptures that deal with barrio life in Southern California. In some of the wood sculptures, he combines brightly colored cactus and palm trees in tableaus that include smartly dressed figures with dog faces. Their activities on the street, at the beach, or elsewhere in the barrio strike a responsive chord in the viewer who reacts to the humor in the scenes. A good example of his work is the sculpture *Hot Dog Meets La Fufu con su Poochie* (1986). The wood cutouts of the two figures, the dog, the plants, and the small fence were painted in different colors and constructed to create a whimsical street scene with two young people in the barrio reacting to each other. Luján died of prostate cancer at age seventy.

César Martínez (1944–)

César Martínez was born in Laredo, Texas, in 1944. He attended Texas A&I University in Kingsville, where he received his bachelor of science degree in 1968. In the late 1970s Martínez dealt with specific Chicano motifs other than the usual Huelga eagle and the Chicano triface. He was fascinated with the *pachuco* (zoot suiter) as an important icon in Chicano culture. As a teenager in the 1950s and 1960s, he saw individuals who adopted the dress of the *pachucos*. He also included other figures in his works that he classified as *batos locos* (*pachucos*) and *rucas* (female *pachucos*). Since he did not have any visual information other than his memory and photographs (snapshots and high school annual pictures), he used them as sources for some of his paintings. He was interested in these types as individuals rather than as a social phenomenon. An example of these works is *La Pareja* (The Couple, 1979). Aside from these Chicano subjects, Martínez also did a painting of Our Lady of Guadalupe under the guise of Leonardo da Vinci's *Mona Lisa*; it was a bizarre juxtaposition of motifs. The work, titled *Mona*

Lupe, demonstrates the power that each of its sources has to evoke emotions and to function within several levels of meaning. First of all, there is the antiart posture first articulated by Marcel Duchamp in his work of 1919 titled *L.H.O.O.Q.* (a reproduction of Leonardo da Vinci's *Mona Lisa* with a mustache and beard added in pencil), and second, there is the entire realm of Chicano identity, exemplified by the religious, national, and political icon of Our Lady of Guadalupe.

Octavio Medellín (1907–1999)

Octavio Medellín dealt with the entire scope of Mexican history, from pre-Columbian times to the revolution to the 1940s with a sculpture titled *History of Mexico* (1949), and he treated the pre-Columbian Maya and Toltec in a series of prints titled *Xtol: Dance of the Ancient Maya People* (1962) based on research he carried out in Yucatán in 1938. Medellín was born

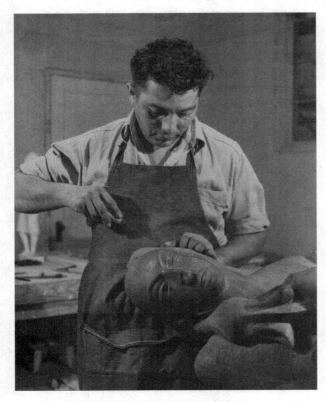

Octavio Medellín in his studio in Grand Prairie, Texas, in 1945, working on one of his art pieces.

the son of an Otomí Indian mine worker in Matehuala, Mexico, in 1907, and moved to San Antonio in 1920, where he studied painting under José Arpa and drawing under Xavier González at the San Antonio School of Art from 1921 to 1928; he studied at the Chicago Art Institute in 1928. He traveled the Gulf Coast of Mexico from 1929 to 1931 and the Yucatán in 1938. He taught at North Texas State College (now the University of North Texas), Denton, from 1938 to 1942, and at Southern Methodist University, Dallas, from 1945 to 1966. In 1966 he opened his own Medellin School of Sculpture in Dallas.

Ana Mendieta (1948–1985)

Born in Havana, Cuba, on November 18, 1948, Ana Mendieta came with her sister to the United States in 1961 through Operation Peter Pan as unaccompanied child refugees from the Cuban Revolution; her parents were not able to leave Cuba until years later—her father was a political prisoner for eighteen years. She was educated in Iowa schools and earned a B.A. in 1972 and an M.A. in painting and an M.F.A. (1972–1977) from the University of Iowa. Inspired by her life story, she continually addressed dislocation from and reconnection to the land in her art. She also focused on blood and violence toward women as well as spiritualism and religious subjects. She often used her own body as subject and material for her works. Her best-known series, *Silueta Series* (1973–1980), depicted her nude body or traced silhouette in natural environments (mud, sand, grass), making body prints and outlines on a wall. She frequently referenced the portrayal of women as ancient goddesses, fertility symbols, and Catholic saints; she also explored the Afro-Cuban syncretic religion of *santería*, as in her pieces *Untitled (Ochún)* (1981) and *Náñigo Burial* (1976). In 1978 Mendieta became a member and administrator of Artists in Residence Inc. (A.I.R. Gallery) in New York, the first gallery for women's art established in the United States. Mendieta's work was exhibited or installed in numerous museums and galleries; her work is collected by major museums domestically and abroad. In 2004 the Hirshhorn Museum and Sculpture Garden in Washington, D.C., organized "Earth Body, Sculpture and Performance," a major retrospective that traveled to important venues around the United

States. She died in New York City on September 8, 1985, either in a fall or thrown out of a thirty-third-story window.

Amalia Mesa-Bains (1943–)

Born on July 10, 1943 in Santa Clara, California, Amalia Mesa-Bains received a B.A. in painting from San Jose State University and later an M.A. in inter-disciplinary education from San Francisco State University and a Ph.D. in clinical psychology from the Wright Institute in Berkeley, California; thereafter she worked for some twenty years as an ESL (English as a second language) teacher and a school psychologist. Mesa-Bains first exhibited an altar in the annual show at the Galería de la Raza in 1976 and later at the San Francisco Museum of Art in 1980. She has since exhibited altars in several national and international exhibitions. Mesa-Bains received her Ph.D. in psychology with an emphasis on culture and identity. Although her altar installations are not directly religious in content, their format has allowed her to attain a spiritual sensibility that is in tune with her personal and cultural life. She has used these altars to pay homage to ancestors and Mexican historical figures in the arts, religion, and the cinema, such as Frida Kahlo, Sor Juana Inés de la Cruz, and Dolores del Río. Mesa-Bains uses Mexican symbols in her altars, such as *calaveras* (skulls), *corazones* (hearts), crosses, and images of the Virgin in her many manifestations. She also cuts her own paper (*papel picado*), makes the altar cloths and paper flowers, and builds the *nichos* and the *retablo* boxes with the help of a carpenter. One of her major works, *Altar for Sor Juana Inés de la Cruz* (1981), a mixed-media construction, was shown in the "Made in Aztlán" exhibition at the Centro Cultural de la Raza in San Diego in 1986. Her works have been included in exhibitions at the Smithsonian American Art Museum; the Whitney Museum of American Art; the San Francisco Museum of Modern Art; Williams College Museum of Art; the Queens Museum in New York; the Contemporary Exhibition Center of Lyon, France; the Kulturhuset in Stockholm, Sweden; the Museum of Modern Art in Dublin, Ireland; and the Culterforgenin in Copenhagen, Denmark. In 1992 Mesa-Bains received a MacArthur Foundation fellowship.

Raphael Montañez-Ortiz (1934–)

Raphael Montañez-Ortiz (known for a time as Ralph Ortiz) was born in New York City in 1934. He studied at the High School of Art and Design, the Brooklyn Museum of Art, and the Pratt Institute, where he received a bachelor of science degree and a master of fine arts degree in 1964. He received his doctorate of fine arts and of fine arts higher education degrees from Columbia University in 1967. He taught at New York University in 1968 and was an adjunct professor at Hostos Community College in the Bronx in 1970. Since 1972 he has been a professor of art at Rutgers University in New Jersey. The work of Montañez-Ortiz was part of the European and American movement known as destructive art. His best-known piece, *Piano Destruction Concert*, was performed on BBC television in 1966 and later presented on national and local television in the United States. The extreme gestures in Monatñez-Ortiz's work have their source in the work of the European Dadaists, who emerged during World War I. In one of their events, they invited viewers to use an ax placed next to a small exhibit to destroy the art. This was only one of many antiart gestures of the Dadaists. Montañez-Ortiz focused on the violence itself in order to emphasize its pervasive presence in our lives. This was unlike the "happenings" of Claes Oldemburg, Allan Kaprow, and others, which were essentially formalist events. Montañez-Ortiz also used pre-Columbian references in a series he called *Archaeological Finds* to focus on his non-European roots and the destruction wrought by the first Europeans who arrived in the Americas. A typical piece in this series is an upholstered chair that was torn apart and destroyed with the title of *Tlazolteotl* (1963), a manifestation of the Aztec earth goddess. In 1988 El Museo del Barrio gave him a retrospective: *Rafael Montañez Ortiz: Years of the Warrior, Years of the Psyche, 1960–1988.*

Delilah Montoya (1955–)

Born on December 10, 1955, in Fort Worth, Texas, and raised in Omaha, Nebraska, Montoya earned her B.A., M.A., and M.F.A. from the University of New Mexico. After teaching at the University of New Mexico and the California State University, she has spent most of her career at the University of Houston, where she is a tenured professor and a noted arts activist in the community. Montoya is a Chicana feminist artist who explores Catholic iconography, Mexican myth, feminine prowess, and ethnic families in her photographic essays. One such series is her *Women Boxers: The New Warriors* (Arte Público Press, 2006), a traveling exhibition and book studying professional women boxers in the ring and in family settings. Other times, her work takes the form of mixed-media installations, as in her *La Guadalupana* (1998), which portrays the Virgen de Guadalupe. Her most recent endeavor was the traveling show, also accompanied by a book, *Contemporary Casta Portraiture: Nuestra Calidad* (Arte Público Press, 2017), in which she updated the Spanish colonial painting depictions of mixed racial categories in the Americas by studying today's families in the Southwest and including the DNA maps of their lineage in the world by percentage. Major museums have collected her works, such as the Smithsonian American Art Museum, the Los Angeles County Museum of Art, the New Mexico Museum of Art, the Mexican Museum, the Bronx Museum of the Arts, and the Museum of Fine Arts, Houston.

Francisco Luis Mora (1874–1940)

Francisco Mora was born in Montevideo, Uruguay, in 1874, and his family immigrated to the United States in 1880. He studied with his father, a sculptor, at the Museum of Fine Arts School in Boston and the Art Students League in New York. He taught painting and drawing for many years at the Chare School and the Art Students League in New York. Mora painted murals for the Orpheum Theatre in Los Angeles; the reading room of the Lynn Public Library in Lynn, Massachusetts; the central building of the Red Cross in Washington, D.C.; and in Clarksville, Tennessee (1938). Among his earliest public works was a large decoration for the Missouri State Building for the Saint Louis Fair of 1904, for which he received a Bronze Medal. He also developed a lucrative career as an illustrator for books and popular magazines. Mora won numerous awards in New York, including the Rothschild Prize, the Carnegie Prize, and the Shaw Purchase Prize at the Salmagundi Club. In 1915 he won a gold medal at the Panama Pacific International Exhibition in San Francisco. Mora's works are in the collections of more than thirty museums, including the Metropolitan Museum of Art in New York (eight works) and the Smithsonian American Art Museum.

Jesús Bautista Moroles (1950–2015)

Born on September 22, 1950, in Corpus Christi, Texas, Jesús Moroles earned an associate's degree from El Centro College in Dallas, Texas, in 1975 and a bachelor of fine arts degree from the University of North Texas in 1978; that same year he worked as an apprentice to sculptor Luis Jiménez. But his work could not be more different from Jiménez's colorful epoxy creations; Moroles was a monumental sculptor exploring geometric creations in granite. Moroles developed a national reputation that resulted in major commissions around the United States, from his *Floating Mesa Fountain* for the Albuquerque Museum to the *Gateway Stele* at Lubben Plaza in Dallas, Texas. In 1987, he created one of his best-known pieces, *Lapstrake*, for CBS Plaza in New York City. His works have been collected at major museums throughout the country, including the Museum of Fine Arts in Houston and the Smithsonian Museum, and they have been included in more than three hundred exhibitions internationally. In 2007 he was awarded the Texas Medal of the Arts, and in 2008 Moroles was awarded the National Medal of Arts. In 2011 he was designated a Texas State Artist by the Texas Commission on the Arts. He died in a tragic car accident on June 15, 2015.

José Moya del Pino (1891–1969)

José Moya del Pino was born in Piegro de Cordova, Spain, in 1891, studied at the Royal Academy of Fine Arts of San Fernando in Madrid, and settled in San Francisco in 1928. Most of his work was done in California. Throughout the 1930s, Moya del Pino painted murals under the auspices of the Works Progress Art Project (WPAP) and for private corporations. In 1933 he painted murals and did the decorations, in Aztec and Mayan motifs, for the rathskeller of the Aztec Brewery in San Diego, California. In the mid-1930s he worked on the WPAP-sponsored murals painted in San Francisco's Coit Tower. He also painted

José Moya del Pino created this study for the mural Flower and Vegetable Farming *for the Works Progress Administration.*

murals in Stockton (1936), Redwood City (1937), and Lancaster, California (1937), and in Alpine, Texas (1940). In 1988 Moya del Pino's murals and decorations at the Aztec Brewery were threatened with destruction when the brewery was targeted for demolition to make way for the construction of a $10 million concrete warehouse. When Salvador Roberto Torres, a leading Chicano activist from the Barrio de la Logan, learned of the demolition, he managed to save the murals; after years of being in storage and having undergone restoration, they are now installed at the Logan Heights Library in San Diego. Moya del Pino died in Ross, California, in 1969.

Manuel Neri (1930–2021)

Manuel Neri was born in Sanger, California, in 1930, and received all his early schooling in Los Angeles. He studied ceramics from 1949 to 1953 at San Francisco City College, the University of California, and the Bray Foundation in Helena, Montana. He also studied at the Oakland School of Art and Crafts from 1955 to 1957 and at the California School of Art, now the San Francisco Art Institute, from 1957 to 1959. Neri taught sculpture and ceramics at the California School of Fine Arts from 1959 to 1965, the University of California, Berkeley from 1963 to 1964, and the University of California, Davis from

1965 to 1999. Neri was at the forefront of the art movements of the 1960s, especially funk art. Neri's early works included paintings and mixed-media sculptures based on abstracted figurative or architectural forms. Overall, his work is based primarily on the human figure defined in plaster and selective polychromy; he at times referred to pre-Columbian architectural forms, such as the pyramid, in other works. His works are collected in major museums throughout the United States. Neri was the recipient of many distinguished awards, including the International Sculpture Center's Lifetime Achievement Award in Contemporary Sculpture in 2006. Neri died in 2021.

Víctor Ochoa (1948–)

Born in South Central Los Angeles on August 2, 1948, Victor Ochoa was deported with his Mexican immigrant family when he was seven years old. Ochoa graduated from high school in San Diego, California, and studied technical illustration at City College. In 1974 he graduated with a B.A. from San Diego State University. Ochoa was one of the pioneers of the Chicano art movement in San Diego, concentrating primarily on mural painting. A good example of his work is the mural *Gerónimo* (1981) on one part of the wall of the Centro Cultural in Balboa Park, for which he was one of the founders, as he was of the Chicano

Park group of murals on the supports for the highway built over the Mexican barrio. A gigantic depiction of the late-nineteenth-century Apache warrior Gerónimo, it is a faithful rendition of a well-known photograph of the Apache leader. Ochoa saw him as a freedom fighter, with whom he identified as a Chicano fighting for his rights in his community. This is in contrast to the Anglo-American view of Gerónimo as a renegade. The other figures on either side are also rendered from photographs. There is a potter on the left and a woman in a skeletal costume on the right. Behind her is a view of Chicano Park with the kiosk where celebrations take place. The Coronado Bridge is seen in the background. Ochoa has taught at Grossmont College for a couple of decades, as well as at the University of California San Diego and San Diego Mesa College.

José Benito Ortega (1858–1941)

José Benito Ortega traveled from town to town, a true itinerant artist, to seek out potential patrons. He was one of several such artists serving the needs of the Hispanos in northern New Mexico. When Ortega received an order, he stayed in the town until he finished the work. He also made death figures for use in the *moradas*. His *santo* figures are very simple and stylized with sharply defined Spanish features and painted in bright colors.

An example of Ortega's work is *San Isidro Labrador* (Saint Isidro the Farmer) in the Denver Art Museum, made of wood and gesso, and painted. The work is modeled on the traditional representations of this saint in the tin paintings of northern Mexico, in which the size of the figures is based on their importance rather than on how they would appear in nature. The saint towers over all the other figures in the group. The winged angel behind the plow is slightly less than half the size of Saint Isidor. The oxen are also less than half the size of the angel, thereby creating a pronounced distortion of scale in the work.

Ernesto Palomino (1933–)

Ernesto Palomino, born in Fresno, California, in 1933, has spent most of his life in that city as an artist and has been a professor at Fresno State University since 1970. He attended the San Francisco Art Institute in 1954, Fresno City College in 1957, and San Francisco State University from 1960 to 1965, earning a B.A. and and M.A. in fine arts. Palomino was an activist artist during the Chicano movement and worked with and nurtured many other artists, especially through the group La Brocha del Valle (the Valley Brush), which he founded. He was among the first of the Chicano muralists to use pre-Columbian and Mexican as well as Chicano motifs in murals, such as the one he painted in Fresno in 1971. In 1973 Palomino led the Inner City Mural Project of Fresno and, with support from the National Endowment for the Humanities, assisted in the creation of the Malaga Community Park mural titled *Humanities Mural*. Palomino considers the culmination of his career the bronze statue of Coatlicue, entitled *Viva la Raza*, installed in front of Arte Américas museum in downtown Fresno's center in 2016; it is eight feet tall, eight feet by six feet thick, and weighs approximately one ton. In 2017 Palomino received an honorary doctorate from California State University in Fresno.

Michael Ponce de León (1922–2006)

Michael Ponce de León was born in Miami, Florida, in 1922 and spent his early years in Mexico City, where he studied at Universidad Nacional Autónoma de México. He joined the U.S. Air Force during World War II. After working as a cartoonist in New York in the 1940s and early 1950s, he turned to printmaking in the late 1950s and later went on to teach printmaking at New York's Pratt Graphic Center, among many other universities. As a printmaker, Ponce de León was in keeping with the new styles of the 1960s. His fame was at its peak when in 1966 he had a solo exhibition at the Corcoran Gallery of Art in Washington, D.C. He used a raised surface (relief) and objects to create works that were expressive of his feelings toward words, places, conditions, and events. His prints and paintings are in the permanent collections of the Art Institute of Chicago, the Museum of Modern Art, the National Gallery of Art, the Smithsonian American Art Museum, and the Walker Art Center, among others.

La Nuestra Señora (Virgin Mary) by José Benito Ortega, c. 1900.

Marcos Raya (1948–)

Marcos Raya was born in Irapuato, Guanajuato, Mexico, and moved to Chicago in 1964. He studied drawing and painting for two years with Alan Thielker. A highly prolific painter of murals and easel pictures, Raya was a full participant in the Chicano mural movement in Chicago and also made altars with secular subjects, such as *Frida and Her Nurse* (1987). Raya's murals deal with political issues in Chicago and abroad, with particular emphasis on Central America. This is seen in his panel for the mural program Stop World War III (1980), in which six other artists participated. The mural project was initiated by the Chicago Mural group under the leadership of John Weber. The block-long mural includes different panels framed in accordance with a series of curvilinear formats. Raya's work is seen on the upper left of the mural. The motifs include the fallen statue of a Central American dictator

and a group of figures above it holding banners and flags with the image of Che Guevara and references to El Salvador and Guatemala. Raya's works have been included in shows at the Museum of Contemporary Art in Chicago, the Museum of Fine Arts in Houston, the Museum of Modern Art in Mexico City, the Smart Museum of the University of Chicago, the Snite Museum of the University of Notre Dame, and the National Museum of Mexican Art in Chicago. He had a major retrospective at Hospicio Cabañas Mural gallery in Guadalajara, Mexico, and a one-man London show in 2013.

Arnaldo Roche Rabell (1955–2018)

Arnaldo Roche Rabell was born in Puerto Rico in 1955. He studied at the Luchetti School of Art in San Juan, Puerto Rico, and studied architecture at the University of Puerto Rico, only to give it up for painting. He obtained a B.A. and an M.F.A. from the Art Institute of Chicago in 1982 and 1984, respectively. He lived much of the year in Chicago and the rest in Puerto Rico. Considered a neo-abstract expressionist, Roche Rabell had a unique style of painting in which the figures and their surroundings are almost overwhelmed by a densely painted surface. An overall fur-like effect is the result of the paint being applied and then scratched with a sharp instrument. Rubbings and projections are the two methods he used in his work. He would lay a piece of canvas or paper over a model or an object that has been smeared with paint. He then rubbed it and elaborated upon the distorted image. His projections of face-only self-portraits are presented in frontal view. His works are part of the permanent collections of the Miami Museum of Art, the Museum of Contemporary Art in San Juan, and the Metropolitan Museum of Art in New York. Roche Rabell's works have been exhibited internationally, from Mexico to Germany; in 2008 Roche Rabell received a solo exhibition at the Museum of Latin American Art in Long Beach, California. In 1998 he received the Grand Prix in Painting at the International Biennial of Art of Cumaná, Museo de Arte Contemporáneo de Cumaná, Venezuela; in 2006 his exhibition received the Best Museum Solo Show Award from the Asociación Internacional de Críticos de Arte, Puerto Rico Chapter, San Juan.

Patricia Rodríguez (1944–)

Patricia Rodríguez was born in Marfa, Texas, in 1944 and was raised by her grandparents. At age eleven she lived with her parents, who worked as migrants throughout the Southwest. At age thirteen, in the 1950s, she attended public schools in California. She later attended junior college and the San Francisco Art Institute on a scholarship. She taught at the University of California from 1975 to 1980, as well as other institutions in the San Francisco Bay area; she was the first to teach Chicano art history at the University of California. From 2001 to 2009, Rodríguez worked as a gallery coordinator at the Mission Cultural Center for Latino Arts in San Francisco. Rodríguez was one of the leading muralists in the San Francisco Bay area in the 1970s. She later went on to teach art for five years at colleges in the Santa

Fe, New Mexico, area. In 1972 she and Graciela Carrillo, Consuelo Méndez, and Irene Pérez organized the group known as Mujeres Muralistas that painted murals from 1972 to 1977. In 1980 she began working on box constructions, inspired by the traditional *nichos* that serve a religious function for the Chicano family. She focused on religious prejudice, cultural identity, and the world around her. The boxes, or *nichos*, made with found and handmade objects, are based on Catholic traditions as well as on the myths, legends, and magic of Mexican culture dating back to the Aztecs and the Mayans.

Peter Rodríguez (1926–2016) and Eugenio Quesada (1927–2011)

Peter Rodríguez of California and Eugenio Quesada of Arizona spent several years in Mexico, and their work reflects that experience. Rodríguez used Mexican place-names in some of his abstract works, such as *Tlalpan*. In addition, he often concentrated on making altars that had a close relationship to his background as a Chicano in Northern California. Quesada's drawings of Mexican American children are similar in form and subject to the paintings and drawings of Mexican artists such as Raúl Anguiano. Rodríguez was born to Mexican immigrant parents in Stockton, California, in 1926 and received all his schooling in that city. As a cofounder of the Mission District's Galería de la Raza and of the Mexican Museum in San Francisco in 1972, he had a great impact on the development of the Chicano art movement in the San Francisco Bay area. Quesada, born in Wickenburg, Arizona, in 1952, studied at Mesa Community College and Arizona State University, where he received a bachelor of arts degree in 1972. He taught at Santa Paula High School, California, in 1954; Glendale Community College, Arizona, in 1972; and Arizona State University from 1972 until his retirement in 1989. During his years in Mexico he painted murals and also began his characteristic charcoal drawings of children. Quesada had numerous one-person shows in Mexico and the U.S. Southwest during the 1970s and 1980s. A major retrospective of his fifty years in art was held in San Diego, California, in 2010. He died the next year in his native Wickenburg.

Alejandro Romero (1948–)

Alejandro Romero was born in Tabasco, Mexico, in 1948, but was raised and educated in Mexico City. Beginning in 1967 Romero studied at Mexico City's famed Academy of San Carlos and came into contact with many of the giants of Mexican art, including Diego Rivera, José Clemente Orozco, and Juan O'Gorman. He studied in the workshop of muralist David Alfaro Siqueiros, from 1969 to 1970, whose style and political commitment highly influenced Romero. He also took courses in Paris and at the Art School of Vincennes, the Artists' Collective in Taos, New Mexico, and the Art Institute of Chicago. Romero moved to Chicago in 1975 and became part of the Latino mural and easel painting movement, where in addition to painting works for sale and creating commissioned murals, he painted more than seventy-five event posters placed all around the city. He has had exhibitions in Mexico, Italy, Canada, and the United States, as well as group shows in Japan, Germany, Yugoslavia, Spain, Portugal, and Puerto Rico. His works are part of the permanent collections of the Museum of Contemporary Art, the Art Institute of Chicago, and the Mexican Fine Arts Center Museum in Chicago; the Museum of Modern Latin American Art in Washington, D.C.; the Museum of the Print in Mexico City; and the Hermitage in Saint Petersburg, Russia. In addition, Romero has designed about a dozen book covers for the leading Latino publisher Arte Público Press.

Frank Romero (1941–)

Frank Romero was born in East Los Angeles in 1941. He attended the Otis Art Institute and California State University, Los Angeles, where he met Carlos Almaraz in the 1960s. He met Gilbert Luján and Beto de la Rocha in 1969 during a sojourn in New York (1968–69) where he stayed with his friend Almaraz. Throughout the early 1970s, he was involved in the Chicano movement. Romero was a member of the pioneering Los Four group of Chicano painters. He often focused on street scenes in his paintings, in which automobiles are prominently displayed. Sometimes he makes a statement about barrio life in Los Angeles. He works in various media other than paint-ing and drawing-photography, graphics, ceramics, and textile design. A good example of his work is the painting *The Closing of Whittier Boulevard* (1984). The night scene includes a bird's-eye view of a street corner in East Los Angeles where the police have set up barricades to stop the flow of traffic. The two streets leading up to the corner are filled with cars with their lights illuminating the police behind the barricades, who are holding billy clubs. The toy-like appearance of the figures and the cars gives the entire scene an eerie effect. Romero's work has been exhibited in many solo and group shows including the national exhibitions "Contemporary Hispanic Art in the U.S." and "Chicano Art: Resistance and Affirmation."

Emilio Sánchez (1921–1999)

Emilio Sánchez was born in Camagüey, Cuba, in 1921 to a wealthy family, and his upbringing was one of privilege. He lived in Cuba, Mexico, and the United States when growing up. He studied at Yale University and, from 1941 to 1943, the University of Virginia. In 1944 Sánchez moved to New York City to attend the Art Students League and subsequently the Columbia University School of the Arts. In 1949 he had his first solo exhibition, to be followed by many others internationally. Among his awards was the first prize at the 1974 Biennial in San Juan, Puerto Rico. Sánchez is an architectural painter whose work predominantly studies the lines, light, and contrast of the geometric shapes in buildings, whether depicting a bodega in New York's El Barrio or modest homes in tropical Cuba. Sánchez was an active painter until he died in Warwick, New York, in 1999. After his death, his works continued to benefit from solo exhibitions around the United States. Sánchez's works are in major museums around the United States and abroad, including the Metropolitan Museum of Art in New York, which has two hundred drawings or prints. In summer 2021, the U.S. Postal Service issued four Forever stamps featuring the paintings of Emilio Sánchez.

Rufino Silva (1919–1993)

The work of Rufino Silva, a Chicago-based artist, belongs to the Chicago school of social realism in a surrealistic vein. Silva was born in Humacao, Puerto

Rico, in 1919. He studied at the Chicago Art Institute from 1938 to 1942 on a fellowship from the Puerto Rican government. He taught at the Layton School of Art, Milwaukee, from 1946 to 1947 and studied abroad for four years, from 1947 to 1951, in Europe and South America on grants from the Art Institute. He returned to Chicago in 1952 and taught at the Art Institute until he retired in 1982. His work at times has been considered realist and other times surrealist. Figurative art in his easel paintings and murals is prominent, often with numerous human bodies intersecting and forming a type of collage of body types and facial features. He died in Sedro Woolley, Washington, in 1993.

Jorge Soto Sánchez (1947–1987)

Jorge Soto Sánchez was born and raised in East Harlem, New York City to Puerto Rican parents. In his childhood, art was Soto Sánchez's refuge from the violence and chaos that surrounded his family's existence in poverty. Largely self-taught, he became one of the most intellectual artists of the Nuyorican school, exploring the physiology of African peoples to graphically represent their Puerto Rican descendants in his elaborate, baroque-style pen-and-ink drawings on rice paper. What he did not get in formal schooling, he assimilated through his long association with other Puerto Rican painters at the Taller Boricua. One of Soto Sánchez's large, highly regarded pieces is *El Velorio* (1974), a redrafting of the classic 1893 piece by the same name by the famous nineteenth-century Afro–Puerto Rican painter Francisco Oller, in which he resituates the poor shack where a child's wake is held to Manhattan and elaborates a magic-realist dreamlike scene. Soto Sánchez only worked in black and white and was able to create great psychological depth in the numerous self-portraits he effected in his favorite medium. Soto Sánchez had solo exhibitions in New York and Puerto Rico; his last major show was at the Museo del Barrio in 1979. Never really accorded the fame or respect he deserved, Soto Sánchez did not outlive the environment in which he lived as a child; he was a drug addict who died an untimely death in White River Junction, Vermont. In 2015, a large collection of his works was exhibited at Hostos Community College's Longwood Art Gallery.

Leo Tanguma (1941–)

Born in 1941 in Beeville, Texas, to farm-worker parents, Leopoldo Tanguma was raised in the small agricultural town in southeast Texas. He quit school in the sixth grade and at age fourteen moved to Pasadena, Texas, where he worked as a custodian. He later served in the Army, where he began experimenting with mural art, and when discharged, he enrolled in Lee College in Pasadena, an industrial suburb of Houston; this led to his involvement in the Chicano movement, which was at its peak in the late 1960s and the 1970s. Tanguma worked at a variety of jobs in the Houston area, when he began his first monumental mural, "The Birth of Our Nationality," a 240-linear-feet mural (18 feet high) that took him a year to finish; he barely had support to buy the paint needed for the work. Emerging from the petals of a central rose is a Chicano couple who represent the birthing of the new nationality. Marching toward them in various stages of the pageant of Mexican and Mexican American history are some seventy fully depicted figures. A book without pages symbolizes the unwritten literature and art of Mexican Americans, whose expression was truncated when the United States took over the northern part of Mexico. Tanguma struggled throughout the 1970s because of lack of support for his art and that of other Latinos in Houston, and in 1983 he abandoned the city in frustration. He relocated to Denver, where to this date his art has been revered, as exemplified by the import mural commissions he has received. Tanguma has painted murals in schools, libraries, and prisons. In 1988, he was commissioned by the Denver Art Museum to paint *The Torch of Quetzalcoatl*. In 1994, he executed two murals at the Denver International Airport: *In Peace and Harmony with Nature* and *Children of the World Dream of Peace*, the latter pleading for the abolition of violence in society. In 2018, finally appreciated by the Houston community, the Houston Arts Alliance provided $105,000 for the restoration of *The Birth of Our Nationality* at the hands of Gonzo247, a graffiti muralist, under the supervision of Tanguma.

Jesse Treviño (1946–)

Jesse Treviño was born in Monterrey, Mexico, in 1946, and four years later his family moved to San photorealism exhibitions in San Antonio and elsewhere. An example of the very matter-of-fact portrayals of the barrio is the painting *La Panadería* (The Bakery). Treviño's best-known mural looms over San Antonio: his nine-story-tall hand-cut tile mural on the side of the Children's Hospital of San Antonio, entitled *The Spirit of Healing*. In 2019, Texas A&M University Press published his biography, *Spirit: The Life and Art of Jesse Treviño.*

Rudy Treviño (1953?–)

Rudy Treviño was born in Eagle Pass, Texas, and moved to San Antonio when he was fourteen. He graduated from Fox Technical High School and then studied with pioneering Chicano painter Mel Casas at San Antonio College, earning an associate of arts degree. Treviño received a B.F.A. from the University of Texas in Austin in 1973 and an M.F.A. from the University of Texas, San Antonio in 1976. He worked as a high school art teacher for twenty-three years. Treviño worked in an abstract style in the 1960s and in a more figurative one in the 1970s and 1980s in which he used pre-Columbian, Mexican, and Chicano subjects. An example of Chicano iconography is his work titled *George Zapata*. The work refers to the Mexican revolutionary hero Emiliano Zapata and to the American revolutionary hero George Washington, both of whom are components of Chicano culture and identity. Since the 1970s Treviño's works have been included in numerous nationally touring exhibitions, especially of Chicano and Latino art. In 2015 Treviño was named executive director of special projects for the Entertainment Legends of San Antonio (E.L.S.A.) Foundation, an organization whose mission includes the preservation fostering and promotion of Tejano/Latino culture through art, music, film, dance, comedy, radio, television, and any future media.

Patssi Valdez (1951–)

Born in 1951 in East Los Angeles, Patssi Valdez received a B.F.A. from Otis Art Institute in 1985. Valdez started working with the Asco art collective when she graduated from high school in 1970, and since then her art has been diverse, not only incorporating

Mosaic in half-relief, depicting the Virgin Mary, at the Guadalupe Cultural Arts Center in San Antonio, Texas, created by Jesse Treviño (2004).

Antonio, Texas. He attended the Art Students League in New York City on an art scholarship and studied portrait painting under William Draper from 1965 to 1966. He attended Our Lady of the Lake University in San Antonio, where he received his bachelor of arts degree in 1974, and the University of Texas, San Antonio where he received his master of fine arts degree in 1979. Treviño served in Vietnam and lost his right hand (his painting hand) in combat but relearned drawing and painting with his left hand. Treviño has been seen as the quintessential San Antonio artist. He has used everyday scenes and places in the barrio for works that have been included in painting, photography, film, and installations, but also street performance; she and the group became a very important and hip part of the Chicano movement of the 1970s and 1980s for their social and political commentary. From the 1990s to the present, Valdez has developed a feminist ethos, commenting visually on violence against women, the nurturing of girls, and other related women's issues in her work that still combines techniques drawn from both painting and photography. Her works have been collected by the Smithsonian American Art Museum, the National Hispanic Cultural Center Collection, the National Museum of American Art, the Tucson Museum of Art, the San Jose Museum of Art, and the El Paso Museum of Art. In 2005 she was named the "Latina of Excellence in the Cultural Arts" by the U.S. Congressional Hispanic Caucus. Her other awards include a Brody Art Fellowship in Visual Arts (1988), an artist-in-residence grant from the National Endowment for the Arts (1994), and a J. Paul Getty fellowship (1998); in 2013 she was named Regent's Lecturer at the University of California, Berkeley.

Camilo José Vergara (1944–)

Born in Santiago, Chile in 1944, Camilo Vergara received a B.A. in sociology from the University of Notre Dame in 1968 and an M.A. in sociology from Columbia University in 1977. He began photographing the streets of New York in the 1970s and eventually developed a methodology of photographing the same buildings and scenes at various times over

Self-portrait of Camilo José Vergara, apparently taken in a Lufthansa bathroom, May 2005.

the years to document the changes in the urban landscape, from flourishing to decay and even ruins, as well as gentrification. Vergara published a book of his photographs with commentary as *The New American Ghetto* in 1995 with Rutgers University Press, for which he received the Robert E. Park Award of the American Sociological Association in 1997. Vergara's work was the subject of a 1999 exhibition at the National Building Museum, "El Nuevo Mundo: The Landscape of Latino Los Angeles." The exhibition was shown later in 1999 at the Cooper-Hewitt, Smithsonian Design Museum. With his second major book, *American Ruins*, Vergara's reputation as a documentary photographer was fully established; he won a MacArthur Foundation Fellowship in 2002. Since 2004, Vergara shows his main work on his website, "Invincible Cities." His recent books are *Harlem: The Unmaking of a Ghetto*, published in 2013 by the University of Chicago Press, and *Detroit Is No Dry Bones*, published by the University of Michigan Press in 2016. In 2010, Vergara was awarded a Berlin Prize fellowship and spent the academic spring semester at the American Academy in Berlin. On July 10, 2013, Vergara received the National Humanities Medal from President Barack Obama in a ceremony at the White House.

Pedro Villarini (1933–2009)

Pedro Villarini was born on May 19, 1933, in Hato Ray, Puerto Rico. A self-taught painter, Villarini lived and worked in East Harlem, New York City, from 1947 until his death in 2009. As a folk painter, his work exhibited nostalgia for the lost homeland, often taking the form of romanticized landscapes, as in his *Villa Playita* (Town Beach). Villarini defined all the motifs in his paintings with great precision. There is a stillness and an air of calm in his painting *La Fortaleza* (1968). The peaceful effect is enhanced by the horizontal directions established by the fortress wall and the buildings in the middle ground and by the clouds in the sky. They are balanced by the turret of the fortress on the left side of the painting. Villarini believed that true Puerto Rican art had to always reference the island and should not accept influences from "American" art.

Jacinto Quirarte and Nicolás Kanellos

LITERATURE

Latino literature of the United States is the literature written by Americans of Latino descent. It includes the Spanish-language literature of what became the U.S. Southwest before that territory was incorporated through war and annexation. It thus incorporates a broad geographic and historical space, and it even includes the writings of early explorers of the North American continent as well as Spanish-speaking immigrants and exiles who made the United States their home. It is a literature that reflects the diverse ethnic and national origins of Latinos, and thus includes writers of South and Central American, Caribbean, and Spanish descent, as well as writers of Afro-Latino and Indo-Latino literatures; it may also include writers of Sephardic origins—exiled Spanish Jews—who identified themselves as Latino, should their works be brought to light in the future. Finally, Latino literature also reflects the linguistic diversity of the people and has been written and published in Spanish, English, and bilingually.

THE COLONIAL PERIOD

The roots of Latino literature were planted north of the Rio Grande quite some time before the landing of the *Mayflower* at Plymouth Rock. The Spanish colonization of Florida in the early sixteenth century and Juan de Oñate's 1598 colonizing expedition up from Zacatecas, Mexico, into what is today New Mexico are doubly important as the beginnings of a written and oral literary tradition in a European language, Spanish. The written tradition is represented by the landmark epic poems *La Florida*, by the Franciscan missionary Alonso Gregorio de Escobedo, and *La conquista de la Nueva México* (The Conquest of the New Mexico), by one of the soldiers on the expedition, Gaspar Pérez de Villagrá. The oral Spanish literary tradition was introduced with the improvised dramas, songs, ballads, and poetic recitations of the soldiers, colonists, and missionaries, some of which have survived in New Mexico and the Southwest to this date.

The Northeast of what is today the United States, on the other hand, can point to its earliest written and oral expression in Spanish with the founding of the colony of Sephardic Jews in New Amsterdam in 1654. The Northeast, the Southwest, and parts of the South can boast an unbroken literary tradition in Spanish that predates the American Revolutionary War. Much of this early literary patrimony from the colonial period has been lost or has not been collected and studied; the same can be said of all periods of the literature except for contemporary Latino literature in the United States. A missionary and colonial literature of historical chronicles, diaries, and letters and an oral literature developed in the Southwest until the Mexican-American War of 1846–48.

The Southwest

Following the Mexican-American War and up to 1910, the foundation was laid for the creation of a true Mexican American literature, a U.S. Latino literature, with the resident population of the Southwest adapting to the new U.S. political and social framework. It was the period when many Spanish-language newspapers began publishing throughout the Southwest and when they and the creative literature they contained became an alternative to Anglo-American information and cultural flow. During this period the important commercial centers of San Francisco and Los Angeles supported numerous newspapers, which, besides fulfilling their commercial and informational functions, also published short stories, poetry, essays, and even serialized novels, such *Las aventuras de Joaquín Murieta* (The Adventures of Joaquín Murieta), a novel of the legendary California social bandit, published in 1881 by the Santa Barbara newspaper *La gaceta*. Among the more important newspapers in California were Los Angeles's *El clamor público* (The Public Clamor) and *La estrella de Los Angeles* (the Los Angeles Star), issued in the 1850s, and *La crónica* (the Chronicle), from the 1870s to the 1890s, and San Francisco's *La voz del Nuevo Mundo* (the Voice of the New World), *La sociedad* (Society), *La cronista* (the Chronicle), and *La República* (the Republic), issued during the last four decades of the century. In New Mexico, *El clarín mexicano* (the Mexican Clarion) and *El fronterizo* (the Frontier), in the 1870s, *El nuevomexicano* (the New Mexican), from the 1850s to the turn of the century, and *El defensor del pueblo* (the People's Defender), in the 1890s, were important. Among Texas's contributions during this period were San Antonio's *El bejareño* (the Bejar County) during the 1850s, El Paso's *Las dos Américas* (the Two Americas) in the 1890s, and *El clarín del norte* (the Northern Clarion) in the 1900s. These were but a few of the literally hundreds of newspapers that provided for the cultural enrichment and entertainment of the Mexican American communities while they provided information, helped to solidify the community, and defended the rights of Mexican Americans in the face of the growing influence of Anglo-American culture.

During the latter part of the nineteenth century various literary authors were published in book form. In Southern California, María Amparo Ruiz de Burton was the first writer to contribute important novels in the English language. Writing under the pseudonym C. Loyal, she published *The Squatter and the Don* in 1881, a novel that effectively exploits the genre of the romance to document the loss of family lands by many Californios to squatters and other interests supported by the railroads, corrupt bankers, and politicians in the newly acquired American territory of California. From a wealthy Californio family herself, she underwrote the cost of publication of *The Squatter*

The long life of Eulalia Pérez (c. 1766–1878; also spelled Ulialia Peres and other variations) is recorded in Una vieja y sus recuerdos *(An Old Woman and Her Memories), transcribed by historian Hubert H. Bancroft in 1877.*

and of her other novel, *Who Would Have Thought It?* (1872), which she published under her own name.

Also in 1881, New Mexican Manuel M. Salazar published a novel of romantic adventure, *La historia de un caminante, o Gervacio y Aurora* (The History of a Traveler on Foot, or Gervacio and Aurora), which creates a colorful picture of the pastoral life in New Mexico at this time. Another New Mexican, Eusebio Chacón (1869–1948), published two short novels in 1892 that are celebrated today: *El hijo de la tempestad* (Child of the Storm) and *Tras la tormenta la calma* (The Calm after the Storm). New Mexican Miguel Antonio Otero (1859–1944) issued a three-volume autobiography, *My Life on the Frontier* (1935), in English, in which he covers his life from age five until just after his term as governor of the New Mexico territory ended in 1906.

During the late 1870s California bookseller and historian Hubert H. Bancroft had numerous autobiographies transcribed from oral dictation in his research for writing the history of California. In the process, some fifteen Latina women of early California were able to dictate their autobiographies, some of which are literary documents that reveal women's perspectives on life, culture, politics, and gender roles. Notable among those autobiographies are those of María Inocenta Avila's *Cosas de California* (California Subjects), Josefa Carrillo de Fitch's *Narración de una californiana* (Narration by a California Woman), Apolinaria Lorenzana's *Memorias de la Beata* (Memories of a Pious Woman), Eulalia Pérez's *Una vieja y sus recuerdos* (An Old Woman and Her Memories), and Felipa Osuna de Marrón's *Recuerdos del pasado* (Memories of the Past).

Apolinaria Lorenzana was a woman who came to Alta California as an orphan, worked as a servant in various homes, and as an adult worked at the San Diego Mission up until the time of the U.S. invasion and occupation of California. At the mission she became a teacher, nurse, and supervisor of the Indian seamstresses and came to own three ranches herself. Similarly, Eulalia Pérez was the housekeeper for the richest mission in California, the San Gabriel Mission, where she was in charge of all of the Indian domestic workers and oversaw the distribution of provisions for the mission. Both of their autobiographies are especially important because of their perspective of self-made and important women who functioned in positions of power in a society dominated by men.

Among the most frequently published poets were the Texan E. Montalván in *El bejareño*, Felipe Maximiliano Chacón and Julio Flores in New Mexico papers, and Dantés in Santa Barbara's *La gaceta* (the Gazette). One of the most interesting poets of the turn of the century was Sara Estela Ramírez, who published her poems and some speeches in Laredo's *La crónica* (the Chronicle) and *El demócrata* (the Democrat) and in her own literary periodicals, *La corregidora* (the Corrector) and *Aurora*, between the years 1904 and 1910. In her life and in her literary works, Ramírez was an activist for the Mexican Liberal Party in its movement to overthrow dictator Porfirio Díaz, and for workers' and women's rights. But much work needs to be done in collecting and analyzing Ramírez's works and the thousands upon thousands of other poems that were published throughout the Southwest during the nineteenth century.

On the other hand, the late nineteenth century is the period when the Mexican *corrido* (a folk ballad related to the *romance* introduced by the Spanish colonists and missionaries) came into maturity and proliferated throughout the Southwest. The corrido increased its popularity in the twentieth century and became a living historical and poetic document that records the history of the great Mexican immigrations and labor struggles between the two world wars.

The Northeast

Miguel Teurbe Tolón.

During the nineteenth century, the New York area sustained various Latino literary activities and cultural institutions. Again the newspapers came to play a key role in providing a forum for literary creation for a community that at that time was made up principally of Spaniards and Cubans. During the late 1820s and 1830s such weekly newspapers as *El menasajero semanal* (the Weekly Messenger) and *El mercurio de Nueva York* (the New York Mercury) published news of the homeland, political commentary and poetry, short stories, essays, and even excerpts of plays. Two other early newspapers were *La crónica* (the Chronicle) and *La voz de América* (the Voice of America), appearing in the 1850s and 1860s, respectively. Among the poets publishing at this time were Miguel Teurbe Tolón (1820–1858), who was born in the United States, educated in Cuba, and became a conspirator for Cuban independence from Spain. One of the few books of poetry in Spanish was published in 1828: *Poesías de un mexicano* (Poems by a Mexican), by Anastacio Ochoa y Acuña.

But it was not until the late nineteenth century that newspaper, magazine, and book publishing really began to expand, because of increased immigration and the political and cultural activity related to the Cuban, Puerto Rican, and Dominican independence movements and the Spanish-American War. In this regard, the most noteworthy institution was the Cuban newspaper *Patria*, in whose pages could be found essays by the leading Cuban and Puerto Rican patriots. Furthermore, numerous essays, letters, diaries, poems, short stories, and literary creations by some of Puerto Rico's most important literary and patriotic figures were written in New York while they worked for the revolution. Included among these were Eugenio María de Hostos, Ramón Emeterio Betances, Lola Rodríguez de Tió, and Sotero Figueroa. Active as well in literature and political organizing were the revolutionary leaders Francisco Gonzálo "Pachín" Marín, a Puerto Rican, and the Cuban José Martí. Marín, a typesetter by trade and an important figure in Puerto Rican poetry for his break with romanticism, left us an important essay, "Nueva York por dentro; una faz de su vida bohemia" (New York on the Inside; One Side of Its Bohemian Life), in which he sketches New York from the perspective of a disillusioned immigrant; this is one of the earliest documents in Spanish that takes this point of view and can be perhaps considered a beginning of Puerto Rican immigrant literature. Martí was an international literary figure in his own right, and his writings are still studied today in Latin American literature classes throughout the world; he has left us a legacy of many essays and other writings that relate directly to his life in New York and elsewhere in the United States.

Also of importance as the most widely circulated weekly was *Las novedades* (the News) (1893–1918), whose theater, music, and literary critic was the famed Dominican writer Pedro Henríquez Ureña. An early Puerto Rican contribution was *La gaceta ilustrada* (the Illustrated Gazette), edited in the 1890s by writer Francisco Amy. Many of the Spanish-language literary books published in New York were also related to the Cuban independence struggle, such as Luis García Pérez's *El grito de Yara* (The Shout at Yara, 1879) and Desiderio Fajardo Ortiz's *La fuga de Evangelina* (The Escape of Evangelina, 1898), the story of Cuban heroine Evangelina Cossío's escape from incarceration by the Spaniards and her trip to freedom and the organizing effort in New York.

THE EARLY TWENTIETH CENTURY

The Southwest

The turn of the century brought record immigration from Mexico to the Southwest and Midwest because of the Mexican Revolution of 1910. During the period from 1910 until World War II, immigrant workers and upper-class and educated professionals from Mexico interacted with the Mexican-origin residents of the Southwest, who had been somewhat cut off from the evolution of Mexican culture inside Mexico. During this period Latino newspaper and book publishing flourished throughout the Southwest. Both San Antonio and Los Angeles supported Spanish-language daily newspapers that served diverse readerships made up of regional groups from the Southwest, immigrant laborers, and political refugees from the revolution. The educated political refugees played a key role in publishing, and in light of their upper social class, they created an ideology of a Mexican community in exile, or *México de afuera* (Mexico on the Outside).

In the offices of San Antonio's *La prensa* (the Press) and Los Angeles's *La opinión* (the Opinion) and *El heraldo de México* (the Mexican Herald), some of the most talented writers from Mexico, Spain, and Latin America earned their living as reporters, columnists, and critics. These included Miguel Arce, Esteban Escalante, Gabriel Navarro, Teodoro Torres, Daniel Venegas, and many others, who wrote hun-

Refugees of the Mexican Revolution in a tent camp, 1913 or 1914.

dreds of books of poetry, essays, and novels. Many of these were published in book form and marketed by the newspapers themselves via mail and in their own bookstores. Besides the publishing houses related to these large dailies, there were many other smaller companies, such as Laredo Publishing Company, Los Angeles's Spanish American Printing, and San Diego's Imprenta Bolaños Cacho Hnos.

Mariano Azuela, author of Los de abajo (The Underdogs).

The largest and most productive publishers resided in San Antonio. Leading the list was the publishing house founded by the owner of *La prensa* and Los Angeles's *La opinión*, Ignacio Lozano. The Casa Editorial Lozano was by far the largest publishing establishment ever owned by a Latino in the United States. Among the San Antonio publishers were the Viola Novelty Company, probably a subsidiary of P. Viola, publisher of the satiric newspapers *El vacilón* (the Joker) and *El fandango* (the Fandango), active from 1916 until at least 1927; the Whitt Company; and the Librería Española, which still existed until 1999 as a bookstore. Many of the novels produced by these houses were part of the genre known as "novels of the Mexican Revolution"; the stories were set within the context of the revolution and often commented on historical events and personalities. In the United States, the refugees who wrote these novels were very conservative and quite often attacked the revolution and Mexican politicians, which they saw as the reason for their exile. Included among these were Miguel Bolaños Cacho's *Sembradores de viento* (Sewers of the Wind, 1928), Brígido Caro's *Plutarco Elías Calles: dictador volchevique de México* (Plutarco Elías Calles: Bolshevik Dictator of Mexico, 1924), and Teodoro Torres's *Como perros y gatos* (Like Cats and Dogs, 1924). The most famous author of this genre has become Mariano Azuela, author of the masterpiece that is one of the foundations of modern Mexican literature, *Los de abajo*

(The Underdogs), which was first published in 1915 in a serialized version in El Paso's newspaper *El paso del norte* (The Northern Pass) and was issued later by the same newspaper in book form.

Although most of the novels published during these years gravitated toward the political and counterrevolutionary, there were others of a more sentimental nature and even some titles that can be considered forerunners of the Chicano novel of the 1960s in their identification with the working-class Mexicans of the Southwest, their use of popular dialects, and their political stance in regard to U.S. government and society. The prime example of this new sensibility is newspaperman Daniel Venegas's *Las aventuras de Don Chipote, o Cuando los pericos mamen* (The Adventures of Don Chipote, or When Parakeets May Suckle Their Young, 1928), a humorous account of a Mexican immigrant, Don Chipote, who travels through the Southwest working here and there at menial tasks and running into one misadventure after the other, suffering at the hands of rogues, the authorities, and his bosses while in search of the mythic streets of gold that the United States is supposed to offer immigrants. Don Chipote is a novel of immigration, a picaresque novel, and a novel of protest all wrapped into one, and furthermore, it is the one clear forerunner of today's Chicano literature.

> Jorge Ulica satirized women who threw American-style surprise parties and celebrated Thanksgiving, and he criticized their taking advantage of greater independence and power at the expense of men's machismo.

One of the most important literary genres that developed in the newspapers at this time was *la crónica* (chronicle). It was a short satirical column that was full of local color, current topics, and observation of social habits. In the Southwest it came to function and serve purposes never before thought of in Mexico or Spain. From Los Angeles to San Antonio, Mexican moralists satirized the customs and behavior of the colony, whose very existence was seen as threatened by the dominant Anglo-Saxon culture. It was the *cronista*'s (chronicler's) job to enforce the ideology of *México de afuera* and battle the influence of Anglo-American culture and the erosion of the Spanish language caused by the influence of speaking English. The *cronistas*, using such pseudonyms as El Malcriado (the Spoiled Brat—Daniel Venegas), Kaskabel (Rattler—Benjamín Padilla), Az.T.K. (Aztec), and Chicote (the Whip), were literally whipping and stinging the community into conformity, commenting on or simply poking fun at the common folks' mixing of Spanish and English and Mexican women adapting American dress and more liberalized customs, such as cutting their hair short, raising hemlines, and smoking.

First and foremost behind the ideology of the *crónica* writers and the owners of the newspapers was the goal of returning to the homeland; as soon as the hostilities of the revolution ended, the immigrants were supposed to return to Mexico with their culture intact. Quite often the targets of their humorous attacks were stereotyped country bumpkins, like Don Chipote, who were having a hard time getting around in the modern American city. They also poked fun at the Mexican immigrants to the United States who became impressed with the wealth, modern technology, efficiency, and informality of American culture, to the extent that they considered everything American superior and everything Mexican inferior. In some of his chronicles, the pseudonymous Jorge Ulica satirized women who made much to-do about throwing American-style surprise parties and celebrating Thanksgiving, and criticized their taking advantage of greater independence and power at the expense of men's machismo. The *cronistas* quite often drew from popular jokes, anecdotes, and oral tradition to create these tales. Two of the most popular *cronistas*, who saw their columns syndicated throughout the Southwest, were the aforementioned Benjamín Padilla, an expatriate newspaperman from Guadalajara, and Julio Arce, who was also a political refugee from Guadalajara and used the pseudonym Jorge Ulica for his *Crónicas Diabólicas* (Diabolical Chronicles). So popular was this type of satire that entire weekly newspapers, usually of no more than eight pages in length, were dedicated to it. Daniel Venegas's weekly *El Malcriado* (the Brat) and P. Viola's *El vacilón* (the Joker) are prime examples of these.

Clustered around the publication of newspapers in the Southwest were communities of women intellectuals who not only aimed their journalism at the service of the Mexican Revolution and women's empowerment but also penned and published some of the most eloquent editorials, speeches, and poems in support of their liberal causes. Most noteworthy were Sara Estela Ramírez's newspapers and magazines, mentioned above; Teresa Villarreal's *El obereo* (the Worker), founded in San Antonio in 1910; Isidra T. de Cárdenas's *La voz de la mujer* (the Woman's Voice), founded in El Paso in 1907; and *Pluma Roja* (Red Pen), edited and directed by Blanca de Moncaleano from 1913 to 1915 in Los Angeles. In the anarchist *Pluma Roja* there was a consistent editorial articulation of reconfiguring the role of women in society as central to the struggle for social, political, and economic freedom; it was presented as an integral part of the ideal of anarchism. Moncaleano addressed both men and women, urging them to free women of their enslavement and to encourage their education and politicization. In a February 1, 1914, editorial entitled "Hombre, educad a la mujer" (Man, Educate Women), she pleads for men to allow women to obtain an education. Her speech "Manifiesto a la Mujer" (Manifesto for Women, 1915), published in the Boston anarchist periodical *Fraternidades*, exhorts women to rebel against the patriarchy and take the leadership of social revolution, violently if need be.

One of these women activists, Leonor Villegas de Magnón (1876–1955), was born and raised in Mexico but immigrated to Laredo, Texas. She provided one of the very few autobiographies of the Mexican Revolution to be written by a woman: *The Rebel*, which was finally published posthumously in 1994 after the author was unsuccessful in having it published in Spanish or English versions during her lifetime. Villegas de Magnón was associated with the ideological precursors of the Revolution, the Flores Magón Brothers, and in fact spent her inherited fortune in support of the Revolution. Villegas de Magnón was the founder of a women's nursing corps, made up mostly of women from the Texas side of the border, which tended to the wounded in Venustiano Carranza's army. As such, she worked side-by-side with the future victor

> Leonor Villegas de Magnón (1876–1955) provided one of the very few autobiographies of the Mexican Revolution to be written by a woman: *The Rebel*.

of the Revolution and president of the republic. Upon seeing how fast official sources had ignored the women's contribution, she specifically created her two autobiographies to document the role of women in Mexico's cataclysmic insurgency. Villegas de Magnón was both a heroic figure and a dramatic writer, one who wrote with documentary care but with literary style and flair.

Much of this literary activity in the Mexican American Southwest came to an abrupt halt with the Great Depression and the repatriation, forced or voluntary, of a large segment of that society back to Mexico. Some writers during the Depression, such as Américo Paredes, began to write in both Spanish and English and to express a very pronounced and politicized Mexican American sensibility. His English-language novel *George Washington Gómez* was written from 1936 to 1940 (but not published until 1990), and during the 1930s and 1940s he was a frequent contributor of poetry in Spanish, English, and bilingual format to newspapers in Texas, including *La prensa*. In 1937, at the age of twenty-two, he published a collection of poems, *Cantos de adolescencia* (Songs of Adolescence), but it was not until 1991 that his collected poems were issued under the title *Between Two Worlds*, which contained works selected from his writings from the late 1930s to the 1950s.

Another very important literary figure who emerged during the Depression and began to publish poetry and tales based on New Mexican folklore was Fray Angélico Chávez. A Franciscan monk, Chávez's poetry books are principally made up of poems to Christ and the Virgin Mary: *Clothed with the Sun* (1939), *New Mexico Triptych* (1940), *Eleven Lady Lyrics and Other Poems* (1945), *The Single Rose* (1948), and *Selected Poems with an Apologia* (1969). From the 1930s to the 1950s there appeared a number of short story writers who succeeded in publishing their works in general market English-language magazines. Most of these, such as Texas's Josefina Escajeda and Jovita González, based their works on folktales, oral tradition, and the picturesque customs of Mexicans in the Southwest. Robert

Herman Torres, who published some of his stories in *Esquire* magazine, focused his works on the cruelty and senselessness of the revolution in Mexico. Despite the significance of Chávez, Paredes, and others, it was not until the 1960s that there was a significant resurgence of Mexican American literary activity, except that by the end of that decade it was called Chicano literature.

Josephina Niggli was successful in having a number of her works published by general market presses in the United States. While writing as an adult, Niggli was able to vividly re-create the small town settings of her rural upbringing in Mexico. Although born in 1910, she was somewhat of a nineteen-century regionalist in her descriptions and evocations. Her *Mexican Village* (1945), for example, portrays the power of land and locale over individuals and community, in this case a fictional town on the northern border of Mexico. Like many of the New Mexico writers, Niggli was also concerned with tradition and the passage of customs and worldview from one generation to the other.

Adelina "Nina" Otero-Warren, homesteader, suffragist, and writer.

Emerging in the English-language literary world at the same time as Angélico Chávez was a group of New Mexican women writers who sought to examine the colonial and territorial past and preserve the folkways and customs that were fast passing away. Their contributions ranged from fiction and literary folklore to personal narrative and social history. Included among their works are Adelina "Nina" Otero-Warren's *Old Spain in Our Southwest* (1936); Cleofas Jaramillo's *The Genuine New Mexico Tasty Recipes: Old and Quaint Formulas for the Preparation of Seventy-five Delicious Spanish Dishes* (1939), a kind of culinary autobiography; Aurora Lucero-White Lea's *Literary Folklore of the Hispanic Southwest* (1953); and Fabiola Cabeza de Baca's *The Good Life: New Mexico Traditions and Food* (1949) and *We Fed Them Cactus* (1954). Many of the personal reminiscences in these books are framed within the traditional practices of telling stories within the family, of passing recipes down from mother to daughter and relating them to life experiences and family history, and of preserving the songs and other oral lore of the family and the region. In these women, we find a somewhat nostalgic re-creation of the past that is an embryonic resistance to the Anglo-American ways that were eroding traditional New Mexican culture.

An English-language short fiction writer, María Cristina Mena (1893–1965), was also born and raised in Mexico and moved to the United States at age fourteen. In New York from 1913 to 1916, Mena published a series of short stories in *The Century Illustrated Monthly Magazine*. In 1927, many of these stories, along with new ones, were published in a collection under her husband's name, Henry K. Chambers, a dramatist and journalist. In the 1940s she developed into a prolific novelist: *The Water Carrier's Secret* (1942), *The Two Eagles* (1943), *The Bullfighter's Son* (1944), *The Three Kings* (1946), and *Boy Heroes of Chapultepec: A Story of the Mexican War* (1953). Behind all of her writings was the desire to inform the public in the United States of the history and culture of Mexico, proposing to correct the negative image that Mexico has held in the popular media.

The Northeast

In New York, the period from the turn of the century up into the Great Depression was also one of increased immigration and interaction of various Latino groups. It was a period of increased Puerto Rican migration, facilitated by the Jones Act of 1917, which declared Puerto Ricans to be citizens of the United States, and later of immigration of Spanish workers and refugees from the Spanish Civil War. Artistic and literary creation in the Latino community quite often supported the Puerto Rican nationalist movement and the movement to reestablish the Spanish republic. At the turn of the century, Cuban and Spanish writers and newspapers still dominated the scene. The first decade of the century witnessed the founding of *La prensa* (the Press), whose heritage continues today in *El Diario La prensa* (the Daily the Press), born of its 1963 merger with *El Diario de Nueva York*. Also publishing during the decade were *Sangre latina* (Latin Blood) out of Columbia University, *Revista Pan-Americana* (Pan American Review), and *La paz y el trabajo*

(Peace and Work), a monthly review of commerce, literature, science, and the arts. Even places as far away as Buffalo began to support their own publications, such as *La hacienda* (the State), founded in 1906.

Spanish-language literary publishing did not begin to expand until the late 1910s and early 1920s. By far the most interesting volume that has come down to us from the 1910s is an early example of the immigrant novel. Somewhat similar in theme to *Don Chipote*, Venezuelan author Alirio Díaz Guerra's *Lucas Guevara* (1914) is the story of a young man who comes to the city seeking his fortune but is ultimately disillusioned. While *Lucas Guevara* was probably self-published at the New York Printing Company, there were Spanish-language publishing houses functioning during the 1910s in New York. One of the most important and long-lived houses, Spanish American Publishing Company, began issuing titles at this time and continued well into the 1950s. It too was an early publisher of books on the theme of Latinos in New York, such as Puerto Rican playwright Javier Lara's *En la metrópoli del dólar* (In the Metropolis of the Dollar), circa 1919. *Las novedades* newspaper also published books, including Pedro Henríquez Ureña's *El nacimiento de Dionisos* (The Birth of Dionysus, 1916).

Although during the 1920s the Spanish American Publishing Company, Carlos López Press, the Phos Press, and others were issuing occasional literary titles, it was not until the late 1920s and early 1930s that there was an intensification of activity. To begin with, various specialized newspapers began to appear. Probably as an outgrowth of the very active theatrical movement that was taking place in Manhattan and Brooklyn, *Gráfico* (Graphic) began publishing in 1927 as a theater and entertainment weekly newspaper under the editorship of the prolific writer Alberto O'Farrill, who was also a playwright and a leading comic actor in Cuban blackface farces (*teatro bufo cubano*). As was also the custom in the Southwest, *Gráfico* and the other newspapers and magazines published numerous poems, short stories, literary essays, and *crónicas* by the leading New York Latino writers. Among the most notable *cronistas* were those unknown writers using the pseudonyms *Maquiavelo* (Machiavelli) and *Samurai*; O'Farrill himself was an important contributor to the tradition, signing his columns "Ofa." One stood out

among the *cronistas* of both sexes for her daring stances on gender roles, her opposition to war, and her superior command of a broad range of subjects: the Puerto Rican Clotilde Betances Jaeger, who wrote hundreds of columns in various newspapers and magazines from the 1930s through the 1950s. As in the Southwest, these *cronistas* labored in their writings to solidify the Latino community, which in New York was even more diverse than in the Southwest, drawing from many ethnic and national backgrounds. They too were protecting the purity of Latino culture against the dangers of assimilation, as they voiced the political and social concerns of the community and corrected and satirized current habits. While in the Southwest the *cronistas* promoted a *México de afuera*, in New York they often attempted to create a *Trópico en Manhattan* (Tropical [or Caribbean] Culture in Manhattan).

Unlike in the Southwest, there were no massive repatriations and deportations disrupting the cultural life in the Latino community during the Great Depression. In fact, New York continued to receive large waves of Latinos during the Depression and World War II: refugees from the Spanish Civil War, workers for the service and manufacturing industries flown in from Puerto Rico during World War II in the largest airborne migration in history, and Latinos from the Southwest. Newspapers were founded that reflected this renewed interest in Spanish, Puerto Rican, and working-class culture: *Cultura Obrera* (Worker Culture, 1911–27), *Alma boricua* (Puerto Rican Soul, 1934–35), *España libre* (Free Spain, 1839–1977), and *Cultura proletaria* (Proletariat Culture, 1927–53). The pages of these newspapers are valuable sources of an important body of testimonial literature that reflected the life of the immigrant. They frequently took the form of autobiographical sketches, anecdotes, and stories, quite often in a homey, straightforward language that was also replete with pathos and artistic sensibility. Despite the many sources available in print, a large part of Puerto Rican, Cuban, Dominican, and Spanish literature in New York is an oral literature—a folk expression completely consistent with and emerging from the working-class nature of the immigrants.

As the Puerto Rican community grew in the late 1920s and into World War II, Puerto Rican literature began to gain a larger profile in New York, but within a decidedly political context. It also seems that the literature with the most impact for the Puerto Rican community was the dramatic literature, if published books are a measure. Poet Gonzalo O'Neill (1867–1942) was a businessman who during the 1920s and 1930s was at the hub of Puerto Rican and Latino cultural life, not only as a writer but as a cultural entrepreneur, investing his money in the theater and protecting and offering support to other writers. O'Neill began his literary training and career in Puerto Rico as a teenager in association with a magazine, *El palenque de la juventud* (the Young People's Arena), which featured the works of some of the most important writers in Puerto Rico, such as Luis Muñoz Rivera, Lola Rodríguez de Tió, Vicente Palés, and many other notables. O'Neill's first published book was a dramatic dialogue in verse, more appropriate for reading aloud than staging: *La indiana borinqueña* (The Puerto Rican Indians, 1922). Here O'Neill revealed himself to be intensely patriotic and interested in Puerto Rican independence from the United States. His second published book was the three-act play *Moncho Reyes*, named after the central character, issued by Spanish American Publishing in 1923. In 1924, O'Neill published a book of nationalistic poetry, *Sonoras bagatelas o sicilianas* (Sonorous Bagatelles or Sicilian Verses), for which Manuel Quevedo Baez stated in the prologue that "Gonzalo is a spontaneous and ingenuous poet…. He is a poet of creole stock, passionate, tender, and as melancholic as Gautier Benítez" (Gautier Benítez was at the time considered Puerto Rico's greatest poet). Although all of his plays, even *La indiana borinqueña*, enjoyed stage productions, it was his third play, *Bajo una sola bandera* (Under Only One Flag, 1928), that went on to critical acclaim and various productions on stages in New York as well as in Puerto Rico. *Bajo una sola bandera* examines the political options facing Puerto Rico, as personified by down-to-earth flesh-and-blood characters. (A more extensive study of O'Neill's plays is in the Theater chapter.) A glowing review in San Juan's *La democracia* (Democracy) on April 16, 1929, marveled at O'Neill's

> Despite the many sources available in print, a large part of Puerto Rican, Cuban, Dominican, and Spanish literature in New York is an oral literature—a folk expression completely consistent with and emerging from the working-class nature of the immigrants.

conserving perfect Spanish and his Puerto Rican identity, despite having lived in the United States for forty years. O'Neill certainly continued to write, although the remainder of his work is unknown or has been lost. Newspapers report that another play of his, *Amoríos borincanos* (Puerto Rican Loves), was produced for the stage in 1938.

Following the example of Gonzalo O'Neill, there were many other Puerto Ricans who wrote for the stage and even published some of their works from the late 1920s to the 1940s, such as Alberto M. González, Juan Nadal de Santa Coloma, José Enamorado Cuesta, Frank Martínez, and Erasmo Vando. But one poet-playwright stands out among the rest as a politically committed woman, although the major portion of her work has been lost: Franca de Armiño. Armiño (probably a pseudonym) wrote three works that have been lost and are inaccessible today: *Luz de tienieblas* (Light of Darkness), a book of poems on various themes; *Aspectos de la vida* (Aspects of Life), philosophical essays; and *Tragedia puertorriqueña* (Puerto Rican Tragedy), a comedy of social criticism. Her one published and available play, *Los hipócritas: comedia dramática social* (The Hypocrits: A Social Drama), self-published in 1937 at the Modernistic Editorial Company, is a major work that demands critical attention. Dedicated to "the oppressed and all those who work for ideas of social renovation," the work is set in Spain during the time of the republic and is openly anti-Fascist and revolutionary, calling for a rebellion of workers. *Los hipócritas*, which begins with the 1929 stock market crash, deals with a daughter's refusal to marry her father's choice, the son of a duke. Rather, she is romantically involved with a son of the working class, Gerónimo, whom her father calls a Communist and who has led her into atheism. The plot is complicated, with Gerónimo organizing workers for a strike, a Fascist dictatorship developing in Spain, and a corrupt priest trying to arrange for Gloria to become a nun so that the church will receive her dowry. The play ends with Gloria and Gerónimo together, the traitors unmasked, and the workers' strike prevailing over police, who attack them brutally. While full of propaganda and stereotyped characters, *Los hipócritas* is a gripping and entertaining play that reflects the tenor of the times, as far as the Great Depression, labor organizing, and the Spanish Civil War are concerned.

A cigar roller who settled in New York in 1916, Bernardo Vega reconstructed life in the Puerto Rican community during the period between the two great wars. Written in 1940, his *Memorias de Bernardo Vega* was published in 1977, and its translation was published in English as *The Memoirs of Bernardo Vega* in 1984. Valuable as both a literary and a historical document, Vega's memoirs make mention of numerous literary figures, such as poet Alfonso Dieppa, whose works were either not published or are lost to us. Vega is an important forerunner of the Nuyorican writers of the 1960s because he wrote about New York as a person who was there to stay, with no intention to return to live in Puerto Rico.

A figure similar to the women activists of the Latino Southwest was anarchist Luisa Capetillo, who came to New York from Puerto Rico in 1912 and wrote for various labor publications. In *Cultura Obrera* (Worker Culture), she consistently built a case for women's emancipation. She reemerged in the cigar factories of Tampa and Ybor City and continued her intellectual as well as her activist life. In Tampa she published the second edition of her book *Mi opinion sobre las libertades, derechos y deberes de la mujer* (My Opinion on the Rights and Responsibilities of Women, 1913) and published a new book of essays, *Influencia de las ideas modernas* (The Influence of Modern Ideas, 1916).

Newspaper columnist and Communist supporter Jesús Colón.

The literature of this period is also represented by a newspaper columnist who wrote in English and was very active in the Communist party: Jesús Colón, author of columns for the *Daily Worker*. Colón's was a heroic intellectual battle against the oppression of workers and racial discrimination; he nevertheless wrote about and supported Puerto Rican culture

and literature, even to the extent of founding a small publishing company that has the distinction of issuing some of the first works of the great Puerto Rican novelist and short story writer José Luis González. In 1961, Colón selected some of the autobiographical sketches that had appeared in newspapers and published them in book form in *A Puerto Rican in New York*, which was perhaps the one literary and historical document that was accessible to young Nuyorican writers and helped to form their literary and social awareness, as well as stimulate their production of literature. Colón, a Black Puerto Rican, had created a document that, tempered with his political ideology, presented insight into Puerto Rican minority status in the United States, rather than just immigrant or ethnic status. In this it was quite different from all that had preceded it.

WORLD WAR II TO THE PRESENT

Chicano Literature

Scholars consider the year 1943 as the beginning of a new period in Mexican American history and culture. This is the year when the so-called Zoot Suit Riots occurred in June in the Los Angeles area, when U.S. servicemen and other White Americans attacked Latinos and other young people wearing zoot suits, considering the clothing unpatriotic. This marked a stage in the cultural development of the Mexican American in which there was a consciousness of not belonging to either Mexico or the United States, and there was an attempt to assert a separate independent identity, just as the zoot suiters in their own subculture were doing by creating their own style of dress, speech, and music. Then, too, Mexican American veterans serving in and returning from World War II, where they disproportionately suffered more casualties and won more medals for valor than any other group in U.S. society, now felt that they had earned their rights as citizens of the United States; they were prepared to assert that citizenship and to reform the political and economic system in order to participate equitably. Thus, the quest for identity in modern American society was initiated, and by the 1960s, a younger gener-

Men wearing zoot suits line up outside a Los Angeles jail on the way to court after attacks by sailors that became known as the Zoot Suit Riots, June 9, 1943.

ation made up of the children of the veterans not only took up this pursuit of democracy and equity in the civil rights movements but also explored the question of identity in all of the arts.

Because of the interruption caused by the Depression, repatriation, and World War II, and the decreased production of literature that ensued during the 1940s and 1950s, the renewed literary and artistic productivity that occurred during the 1960s has often been considered a Chicano renaissance. In reality it was an awakening that accompanied the younger generation's greater access to college and its participation in the civil rights movements, the farm worker labor struggle, and the protest movement against the Vietnam War. For Chicano literature the decade of the 1960s was characterized by a questioning of all the commonly accepted truths in the society, fore-

most of which was the question of equality. The first writers of Chicano literature in the 1960s committed their literary voices to the political, economic, and educational struggles. Their works were frequently used to inspire social and political action, quite often with poets reading their verses at organizing meetings, at boycotts, and before and after protest marches. Of necessity many of the first writers to gain prominence in the movement were the poets who could tap into an oral tradition of recitation and declamation, such as Abelardo Delgado, Ricardo Sánchez, and Alurista (Alberto Urista), and create works to be performed orally before groups of students and workers, to inspire them and raise their level of consciousness.

The most important literary work in this period that was used at the grass roots level as well as by uni-

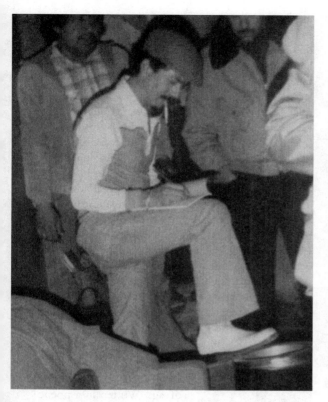

Chicano poet Alurista signs books after a reading at Colegio César Chávez in Mount Angel, Oregon, c. 1982.

to give his blessings in the form of readings at all cultural and Chicano movement events.

The 1960s was an era of intense grassroots organizing and cultural fermentation and along with this occurred a renewed interest in publishing small community and workers' newspapers and magazines, such as the California farm workers' *El Malcriado* (the Brat) and Houston's *Papel Chicano* (Chicano Newspaper), which were now quite often published bilingually. During the late 1960s and early 1970s, literary magazines proliferated, from the academic, such as Berkeley's *El grito: A Journal of Contemporary Mexican-American Thought* (The Shout [for independence]), to the grassroots type printed on newsprint and available for twenty-five cents, such as San Antonio's *Caracol* (Shell), to the artsy, streetwise, avant-garde, and irreverent, such as Los Angeles's *Con Safos* (Safety Zone).

In 1967 appeared the most influential Chicano literary magazine, *El grito*, which initiated the careers of some of the most prominent names in Chicano literature. Along with the publishing house Editorial Quinto Sol, which it established in 1968, *El grito* began to delineate the canon that is the official identity of Chicano literature by publishing those works that best exemplified Chicano culture, language, themes, and styles. The very name of the publishing house emphasized its Mexican/Aztec identity, as well as the Spanish language; the term *quinto sol* (fifth sun) referred to Aztec belief in a period of cultural flowering that would take place some time in the future, in a fifth age that conveniently coincided with the rise of Chicano culture. Included in its 1968 anthology, *El espejo/The Mirror*, edited by the owners of Quinto Sol, Octavio Romano and Herminio Ríos, were such writers as Alurista, Tomás Rivera, and Miguel Méndez, who are still models of Chicano literature. *El espejo* recognized the linguistic diversity and the erosion of Spanish literacy among the young by accompanying works originally written in Spanish with an English translation; it even included Miguel Méndez's original Yaqui-language version of his short story "Tata Casehue." In *El espejo* and in later books that Quinto Sol published, there was a definite insistence on working-class and rural culture and language, as exemplified in the works of Tomás Rivera, Rolando Hinojosa, and most of the other authors published in book

versity students to provide a sense of history, mission, and Chicano identity was an epic poem written by an ex-boxer in Denver, Colorado: Rodolfo "Corky" González's *I Am Joaquín/Yo Soy Joaquín* (1967). The short, bilingual pamphlet edition of the poem was literally passed from hand to hand in the communities; it was read from at rallies, dramatized by street theaters, and even produced as a slide show on film with a dramatic reading by Luis Valdez, the leading Chicano director and playwright. The influence and social impact of *I Am Joaquín* and poems such as "Stupid America" by Abelardo Delgado, which was published and reprinted in community and movement newspapers throughout the Southwest, then cut out of those papers and passed hand to hand, is inestimable. "Stupid America" was included as well in Abelardo's landmark collection, *Chicano: 25 Pieces of a Chicano Mind* (1969). This period was one of euphoria, power, and influence for the Chicano poet, who was sought after, almost as a priest, form. Also, there was not only a tolerance but a promotion of works written bilingually and in caló, the linguistic code of street culture, switching between both English and Spanish and various social dialects of each one in the same literary piece, as in the poems of Alurista and the plays of Carlos Morton.

In 1970, Quinto Sol reinforced its leadership in creating the concept of Chicano literature by instituting the national award for Chicano literature, Premio Quinto Sol (Fifth Sun Award), which carried with it a one-thousand-dollar prize and publication of the winning manuscript. The first three years of prizes went to books that today are still seen as exemplary Chicano novels and, in fact, are still among the best-selling Chicano literary texts: Tomás Rivera's ... *y no se lo tragó la tierra* (... And the Earth Did Not Part, 1971), Rudolfo Anaya's *Bless Me, Ultima* (1972), and Rolando Hinojosa's *Estampas del valle y otras obras/Sketches of the Valley and Other Works*. Rivera's outwardly simple but inwardly complex novel is much in the line of experimental Latin American fiction, demanding that the reader take part in unraveling the story and in coming to his own conclusions about the identity and relationships of the characters, as well as the meaning. Drawing upon his own life as a migrant worker from Texas, Rivera constructed a novel in the straightforward but poetic language of migrant workers in which a nameless central character attempts to find himself by reconstructing the overheard conversations and stories as well as events that took place during a metaphorical year, which really represents his whole life. It is the story of a sensitive boy who is trying to understand the hardship that surrounds his family and community of migrant workers; his path is first one of rejection of them only to embrace them and their culture dearly as his own at the end of the book. In many ways, ... *y no se lo tragó la tierra* came to be the most influential book in the Chicano search for identity.

Rivera, who became a very successful university professor and administrator—he rose to the position of chancellor of the University of California, Riverside, before his death in 1984—wrote and published other stories, essays, and poems. Through his essays, such as "Chicano Literature: Fiesta of the Living" (1979) and "Into the Labyrinth: The Chicano in Literature" (1971), and his personal and scholarly activities, he was one of the prime movers in the promotion of Chicano authors, in the creation of the concept of Chicano literature, and in the creation of Chicano literature and culture as legitimate academic areas in the college curriculum. In 1989, his stories were collected and published under the title *The Harvest*, which was also the title of one of his stories, and in 1990 his poems were collected and published under the title *The Searchers*, both by Arte Público Press, which has kept his first novel in print and also published *Tomás Rivera: The Complete Works* (1990). In 1987, ... *y no se lo tragó la tierra* was given a liberal translation into Texan dialect under the title *This Migrant Earth* (1987) by Rolando Hinojosa; the translation that accompanies the Arte Público bilingual edition was done by poet Evangelina Vigil-Piñón. By any accounts, Tomás Rivera remains the most outstanding and influential figure in the literature of Mexican peoples in the United States, and he also deserves a place in the canon of Spanish-language literature in the world.

Rudolfo Anaya.

Rudolfo Anaya's *Bless Me, Ultima* is a straightforward novel about a boy's coming of age. Written in a poetic and clear English, it has reached more readers, especially non-Chicano readers, than most other Chicano literary works, possibly only eclipsed by Sandra Cisneros's *The House on Mango Street* and Victor Villaseñor's *Rain of Gold*. In *Bless Me, Ultima*, again we have the search for identity, but this time the central character, Antonio, must decide between the more Spanish heritage of the plainsman-rancher or the more Indian heritage of the farmer; he is guided and inspired in his attempts to understand good and evil and his role in life by a larger-than-life folk healer, Ultima, who passes on many of her secrets and insights about life to Antonio. Anaya puts to good use his knowledge of the countryside of New Mexico, its romance and picturesque qualities, in fashioning this novel full of mystery and references to the symbols and folk knowledge of American Indian, Asian, and Spanish cultures. Anaya went on to become celebrated in his home state and to head the creative writing program at the University of New Mexico. His subsequent novels, all dealing with Chicano/Indian culture in New Mexico, were not as well received by the critics: *Heart of Aztlán* (1976), *Tortuga* (Tortoise) (1979), *The Silence of the Llano* (1982), *Lord of the Dawn: The Legend of Quetzalcoatl* (1987), *Alburquerque* (1992), *Jalamanta: A Message from the Desert* (1996), *Serafina's Stories* (2004), *The Man Who Could Fly and Other Stories* (2006), *Randy Lopez Goes Home: A Novel* (2011), *The Old Man's Love Story* (2013), and *The Sorrows of Young Alfonso* (2016). He also published four novels in the Sonny Baca detective series, ten children's books, and a few plays, as well as some nonfiction works and anthologies.

As can be seen from these titles, Anaya was a promoter of the concept of Aztlán, the mythical place of origin of the Aztecs, supposedly located in what has become the five states of the Southwest. He and numerous other Chicano writers have derived both poetic inspiration and a sense of mission in reviving the cultural glories of Mexico's Indigenous past. For Anaya and especially for poets and playwrights such as Alurista and Luis Valdez, the Aztec and Mayan past has been a source of imagery, symbols, and myths that have enriched their works.

Rolando Hinojosa.

Rolando Hinojosa is the most prolific and probably the most bilingually talented of the novelists, with original creations in both English and Spanish published in the United States and abroad. His Quinto Sol Award–winning *Estampas del valle y otras obras/Sketches of the Valley and Other Works* is a mosaic of the picturesque character types, folk customs, and speech of the bilingual community in the small towns along Texas's Rio Grande Valley. His sketches and insights at times reminiscent of the local color of the *crónicas* of the 1920s, Hinojosa's art is one of the most sophisticated contributions to Chicano literature.

Estampas was just the beginning phase of a continuing novel that has become a broad epic of the history and culture of the Mexican Americans and Anglos of the valley, centered in the fictitious Belken County and around two fictitious characters and a narrator—Rafa Buenrostro, Jehú Malacara, and P. Galindo—all of whom may be partial alter egos of Hinojosa himself. What is especially intriguing about Hinojosa's continuing novel, which he calls the Klail City Death Trip Series, is his experimentation with various forms of narration—derived from Spanish, Mexican, English, and American literary history—in the respective installments of the novel. *Klail City y sus alrededores* (Klail City and Surroundings, 1976) owes much to the picaresque novel; *Korean Love Songs* (1980) is narrative poetry; *Mi querido Rafa* (Dear Rafe, 1981) is part epistolary novel and part reportage; *Rites and Witnesses* (1982) is mainly a novel in dialogue; *Partners in Crime* (1985) and *Ask a Policeman* (1998) are detective novels; *Claros varones de Belken* (Fair Gentlemen of Belken, 1986) is a composite; *Becky and Her Friends* (1990) continues the novel in the style of reportage but with a new unnamed narrator, P. Galindo having died; *The Useless Servants* (1993) is a war novel; and *We Happy Few* (2006) is a satire of academia.

While there have been translations by others of his works, Hinojosa has penned and published recreations in English and Spanish of almost all of these books, except for the English titles *Korean Love Songs, Rites and Witnesses, Partners in Crime, Ask a Policeman,* and *We Happy Few. Mi querido Rafa* is especially important because it represents the first novel to experiment with bilingual narration and demands of the reader a good knowledge of both English and Spanish and their South Texas dialects.

Because of his many awards—including, in 1976, the international award for Latin American fiction given in Cuba: the Premio Casa de las Americas award—his academic background and doctorate in Spanish, and the positive response to his sophisticated art from critics and university professors, in particular, Hinojosa was one of the first Latino writers in the country to teach in creative writing programs at a high level. In holding the distinguished title Ellen Clayton Garwood Professor of English and Creative Writing at the University of Texas before his retirement in 2018, Hinojosa is the most recognized and highest-ranking Chicano/Latino author in academia.

In 2013 he became the first and to date only Latino to win the Ivan Sandrof Lifetime Achievement Award of the National Book Critics Circle.

It was not until 1975 that the Quinto Sol Award was given to a woman, Estela Portillo Trambley, for her short story collection *Rain of Scorpions*, and it marked the ascendancy of women's voices in Chicano literature, which had been too dominated by males. Portillo Trambley's strong feminist and irreverent stories did much both to sensitize the publishing powers in Chicano literature and to encourage a new generation of women writers to persevere in getting their works published; their works were soon to change the character of Chicano literature in the 1980s.

In nine finely crafted stories and a novella, *Rain of Scorpions* presents a series of female characters who draw from an inner strength and impose their personalities on the world around them. In the novella that gives title to the collection, an overweight and unattractive central character overcomes her own dreams of beauty and the set roles that society has for her to prevail as a woman who from behind the scenes controls and determines the action around her. She has chosen her life and how to live it; it will not be imposed upon her by others. In the most feminist of the short stories, "If It Weren't for the Honeysuckle," the eldest of three women being oppressed and enslaved by a drunk and irrational male succeeds in poisoning him and freeing the women. In this as in the other stories, as well as in her books to follow— *The Day of the Swallows* (1971), the collection of plays *Sor Juana* (Sister Juana, 1983), and the novel *Trini* (1986)—Portillo Trambley created strong women who prevail in a male-dominated world. *Trini* is the story of a Tarahumara woman who leaves her Indian life behind and, after numerous tragedies and betrayals, crosses the border to give birth to her child in the United States, where she is able to control her life for herself and even become a landowner. In all of her work, Portillo Trambley demonstrated an uncompromising pursuit for equality and liberation for women.

By the end of the 1970s most of the literary magazines and Chicano literary presses had disappeared, including Editorial Quinto Sol and *El grito*. Fortunately, since 1973 a new Latino magazine, *Revista Chicano-Riqueña* (Chicano-Rican Review), edited by Nicolás Kanellos and Luis Dávila in Gary, Indiana, had been operating and making greater incursions into academia than any other Latino literary publication. In 1979, Kanellos founded Arte Público Press as an outgrowth of the magazine and relocated both to Houston, Texas, just in time to carry on where Quinto Sol had left off and to assume the leadership in publishing the works of a blossoming Latino women's literary movement. During the 1980s, Arte Público published books of poetry by San Antonio poets Evangelina Vigil and Angela de Hoyos, Chicago poets and prose writers Ana Castillo and Sandra Cisneros, San Francisco Bay area novelist and poet Lucha Corpi, Los Angeles short story writer and former editor of the magazine *ChismeArte* Helena María Viramontes, and New Mexico novelist and playwright Denise Chávez, who were to produce some of the best-selling and most highly reviewed Chicano books of the decade. It was this generation of women who were to cross over to mainstream commercial publishing in the United States.

At the University of Houston, Arte Público was able to launch prose fiction and memoir books that made the transition into mainstream commercial publishing for such authors as Ana Castillo, Sandra Cisneros, Judith Ortiz Cofer, Gary Soto, and Helena María Viramontes, among many others. But it was not until 1991, with Victor Villaseñor's *Rain of Gold*, that Arte Público registered its first best seller. The book was successfully auctioned off for paperback rights to the largest U.S. publisher at that time, Bantam Doubleday Dell. Since those heady days, Arte Público Press has diversified, going into nonfiction, reference, and children's publishing, to name a few of its lines. In the early twenty-first century, Arte Público also launched an extensive series of books on the history of Latino civil rights struggles since the nineteenth century. Included among the titles are biographies of such leaders as Héctor P. García, César Chávez, Antonia Pantoja, Alonso S. Perales, Reies López Tijerina, and Willie Velásquez. The series also documents and studies important court cases, such as *Hernández v. Texas*, as well as such perennial issues as farm labor abuses and the history of such organizations as the American G.I. Forum.

As part of the ongoing efforts to bring Hispanic literature to schools at every level of the curriulum and to mainstream audiences, Arte Público Press launched the Recovering the U.S. Hispanic Literary Heritage Project in 1992. Now arriving at its third decade, the Recovery project is the largest ongoing program to recover, index, and publish lost Latino writings that date from the American colonial period through 1980.

The notion of an imprint dedicated to the publication of literature for children and young adults was Arte Público's response to an urgent public demand for books that accurately portray U.S. Hispanic culture. In 1994, a grant from the Mellon Foundation allowed Arte Público Press to transform the dream into a reality. With its bilingual books for children and its entertaining novels for young adults, Piñata Books has made giant strides toward filling the void in the literary market created by an increased awareness of diverse cultures, with award-winning books by such authors as Jorge Argueta, Diane Gonzales Bertrand, Pat Mora, Victor Villaseñor, and many more.

Along with Arte Público and *Revista Chicano-Riqueña*, which in 1987 became *The Americas Review* and was edited by Julián Olivares and Evangelina Vigil, another magazine/book publisher was founded in Indiana in 1980 and relocated to the University of California, Berkeley, in 1985: *Third Woman*, directed by Norma Alarcón. Around the same time, another Latino book publisher with an academic base, Bilingual Review Press, also relocated, from Binghamton, New York, to the Southwest, to Arizona State University in Tempe. Supported by these three establishments and various other presses that were occasionally issuing women's titles, this first full-blown generation of Chicana writers flourished, finding a welcome space for their books in the academic curriculum, not only in Chicano literature courses but also in women's studies programs and American literature courses. The majority of the women were more educated than the 1960s and 1970s writers; most of them were college graduates. Two of its representatives, Denise Chavez and Sandra Cisneros, had even obtained master's degrees in creative writing. Most of the women wrote in English, thus the Spanish language was no barrier to their works' entering literature courses and becom-

ing accessible to broader circles of the reading public. As a whole, they were thoroughly versed in the general feminist movement while preserving their own Chicana identities and culture and developing their literature from it.

Pat Mora.

At the close of the decade, general market textbook publishers were finally responding to the reform movements occurring in academia and to the new demographic statistics relating to the public school markets in the most populous states, which convincingly showed overwhelming Latino enrollments then and into the twenty-first century. As a result, most of the textbook publishers have begun to desperately search out and include Latino writers for inclusion, if not major promotion. In 1990, the nation's largest textbook publisher at that time, Harcourt Brace Jovanovich, even went so far as to issue a high school English anthology titled *Mexican American Literature*, which included selections of works from the colonial period to the present in its more than seven hundred pages. Some of the most successful writers chosen for the general American literature textbooks and for such canonizing texts as *The Norton Anthology of American Literature* now included Pat Mora and Denise Chávez. Mora at the time was the author of three books of poetry, her first two winning the Southwest Book Award: *Chants* (1984), *Borders* (1986), and *Communion* (1991). Drawing upon the desert landscape and a Mexican Indian sensibility, *Chants* is a richly textured exploration, in beautiful whispered tones, of the desert as a woman and of women as holders of the strength and endurance of the desert. In *Borders*, Mora, an El Paso native, continued in the same vein, drawing upon folk customs and the insight of healers as she explored all types of borders: the political and cultural ones between the United States and Mexico, the borders between the sexes, and so forth. *Communion* was about communion with other women and other peoples of the earth as Mora expanded her vision to Asia and Africa. Mora went on to be the most prolific Latino writer of children's books, as well as to publish various other books of poetry and essays. In 1997 she also founded the American Library Association's Día de los niños/El Día de los Libros, a celebration and promotion of literacy and reading for all children.

Denise Chávez is a talented actress and a prolific playwright, but it is as a novelist that she has gained a deserved place in Chicano and American literature as a whole. For Chávez, as for Rolando Hinojosa, literature is very much the art of writing about lives, about individuals, and about the stories they have to tell. Her novels *The Last of the Menu Girls* (1986) and *Face of an Angel* (1993) present series of lives and characters talking for themselves within a loose biographic structure. In the case of her first novel, the unifying structure is the life of Rocío Esquivel, who, through a series of interconnected stories, gains maturity by rebelling against the social roles created for her. *Face of an Angel*, on the other hand, centers on the life of a waitress and the unfortunate and tragicomic amorous relationships that she has with men; in the midst of the narration are brought in various types of unlikely elements, such as a manual on how to become a good waitress that the protagonist is writing. Chávez produced two more novels in her career—*Loving Pedro Infante* (2001) and *The King and Queen of Comezón* (2014)—as well as about a dozen plays.

Both Mora and Chávez have won attention from the world that was previously off-limits to Chicano writers: the pages of the *New York Times Book Review* and the Norton anthologies, important fellowships, and awards.

While women were ascending in the world of Chicano literature, so was a younger generation of male writers who were the products of creative writing programs at universities, through which they gained access to opportunities for study, travel, and publishing never before had by Chicanos (nor Chicanas). To date, theirs is the only Chicano poetry that has begun to become part of the American literary establishment. Of this new cadre of American poets who no longer speak or write in Spanish and no longer derive sustenance from the oral tradition, recitation, and political action, the most famous and prolific is Gary Soto, who was once a tenured associate professor in creative writing and

ethnic studies at the University of California, Berkeley, but was successful in sustaining his life as a professional writer—something very few Latino writers can do even today. He is the winner of numerous prestigious awards, including the Academy of American Poets Prize (1975), the Discovery-Nation Award (1975), a Guggenheim Fellowship (1979), an American Book Award, and many other prizes. His poetry is finely crafted, down-to-earth, and rigorous, mostly inspired by the life of the common working man in the fields and factories.

Gary Soto.

Quite often, as in his book *The Elements of San Joaquin*—published, as are most of his other poetry books, as part of the prestigious University of Pittsburgh Press's Pitt Poetry Series—his work is a recollection of growing up in Fresno. While dealing with very real and concrete pictures of life in a particular time and setting, such as his youth in the agricultural San Joaquin Valley, Soto frequently approaches his subject from a classical frame of reference. For instance, in the second section of the book, the Valley is envisioned according to the four universal elements of the Greek philosophers: earth, air, water, and fire. He takes these elements and transforms them into the particular sights, smells, and labors of the Valley. Among Soto's other books of poetry are *The Tale of Sunlight* (1978), *Where Sparrows Work Hard* (1981), *Black Hair* (1985), *Who Will Know?* (1990), *Home Course in Religion* (1991), *Neighborhood Odes* (1992), *Canto Familiar/Familiar Song* (1994), *New and Selected Poems* (1995), *Junior College* (1997), *A Natural Man* (1999), *One Kind of Faith* (2003), *A Simple Plan* (2007), *Partly Cloudy: Poems of Love and Longing* (2009), and *Sudden Loss of Dignity* (2013).

In 1985, Soto also began publishing autobiographical prose essays, which have met with a great deal of success, his first three books winning an American Book Award: *Living Up the Street* (1985), *Small Faces* (1986), and *Lesser Evils: Ten Quartets* (1988). These led Soto to explore the children's and young adult fiction; he has since become the most prolific Latino writer of young adult fiction, producing titles including the following: *Baseball in April* (1990), *A Fire in My Hands* (1991), *Taking Sides* (1991), *Pacific Crossing* (1992), *Too Many Tamales* (1992), *The Skirt* (1992), *The Pool Party* (1993), *Local News* (1993), *Jesse* (1994), *7th Grade* (1995), *Crazy Weekend* (1994), *Boys at Work* (1995), *Summer on Wheels* (1995), *Canto Familiar* (1995), *Buried Onions* (1997), *The Cat's Meow* (1997), *Jessie De La Cruz: A Profile of a United Farm Worker* (2000), *Fearless Fernie* (2002), *If the Shoe Fits* (2002), *Marisol* (2005), and *When Dad Came Back* (2011).

Among other writers who have made it into university creative writing programs as professors are Arizonan Alberto Ríos and Californians Ernesto Trejo and Lorna Dee Cervantes. Cervantes did not follow the usual trek through master of fine arts programs in creative writing for entrance into her career. She was very much a product of the 1970s and the Chicano literary movement of those days, in which she began reading her poetry in public at a theater festival in 1974, published her first works in *Revista Chicano-Riqueña* in 1975, and shortly thereafter founded and edited a literary magazine, *Mango*, which was free-form and experimental and not limited to publishing Chicanos. By 1981, her first book of poems, *Emplumada* (Plumed), was published by the University of Pittsburgh Press. Despite many publications in magazines and success as a performer of poetry, it was not until 1986 that she finished her B.A. degree. In 1990, she earned a Ph.D. in the history of consciousness at the University of California, Santa Cruz. She went on to teach creative writing at the University of Colorado and various other institutions.

Perhaps better than anyone else, Lorna Dee Cervantes has described the pain of separation from the tongue and culture of family in such poems as "Refugee Ship" and "Oaxaca, 1974." Her work also deals with the dehumanizing landscape and the dehumanization that is caused by racism and sexism. Today she is still very much a hard-driving poet who takes risks and is not afraid to deal with taboo topics and violence, whether it be racist, sexist, or psychological, as can be seen in her book *From the Cables of Genocide* (1991). Her other books include *DRIVE: The First Quartet* (2006), *Ciento: 100 100-Word Love Poems* (2011), and *Sueño: New Poems* (2013).

In the 1980s there emerged among Chicana feminist writers, subsequently spreading throughout all of Latino literature, a very strong LGBTQ+ movement that persists to this day. While gay and gender diverse writers have always existed among Latinos, going back into the nineteenth century, it was in the 1980s that their identity and aesthetic first became articulated in such groundbreaking books as *This Bridge Called My Back: Writings by Radical Women of Color* (1981), edited by eminent essayists Cherríe Moraga and Gloria E. Anzaldúa, both of whom through literary genres were able to forefront the intersectional identity determinants of Latinas while celebrating their own lesbian identities. While Moraga's first book, *Loving in the War Years: Lo que nunca pasó por sus labios* (1983), wove English and Spanish through her essays and mixed-genre work, her signal contribution over the years has been through drama, while poet Anzaldúa developed more than two decades of essays and books that traced her evolution from a lesbian consciousness to exploring all of the facets of border culture—physical, geographic, ethnic, gender, and psychological—through such books as *Borderlands/La Frontera: The New Mestiza* (1987), *Making Face, Making Soul/Haciendo Caras: Creative and Critical Perspectives by Feminists of Color* (1990), and *Light in the Dark/Luz en lo Oscuro: Rewriting Identity, Spirituality, Reality* (2015). In 1987, Juanita Ramos's *Compañeras: Latina Lesbians* broadened the movement to connect to other Latinas and Latin American women. Third Woman Press and its magazine were central to movement among Latinas, publishing such works as *Chicana Lesbians: The Girls Our Mothers Warned Us About*, edited by Carla Trujillo (1991), and *The Sexuality of Latinas*—first appearing as volume 4 of *Third Woman* magazine and as a free-standing book in 1992—edited by Norma Alarcón, Ana Castillo, and Cherríe Moraga. Most recently, Lourdes Torres and Inmaculada Pertusa's *Tortilleras: Hispanic and U.S. Latina Lesbian Expression* (2003) and *Jota* (2020), edited by T. Jackie Cuevas, Anel Flores, Candace López, and Rita E. Urquijo-Ruiz, are anthologies that proudly assert queer Latina identities in prose, poetry, and art.

While the Chicana lesbian writers have cultivated many important books of essays and memoirs, they have also broken ground with their novels. Considered the first Chicana lesbian novel, Sheila Ortiz Taylor's *Faultline* (1982) deals with the subject of a lesbian mother's custody hearing. In 1990 Taylor published its sequel, *Southbound*, and went on to publish a steady stream of works throughout the 1980s and 1990s. One of the most distinguished and hailed novels, postulating a lesbian tradition across the ages, is Alicia Gaspar de Alba's *Sor Juana's Second Dream* (1999), which constructs the famous poet-nun of colonial times as a lesbian. Gaspar de Alba's *Desert Blood: The Juarez Murders* (2005) is a detective mystery set among the misogynistic femicides on the El Paso–Juarez border; it was the recipient of the 2005 Lambda Literary Award for Best Lesbian Mystery. Scholar-essayist Emma Pérez's three novels are considered today as landmarks of lesbian narrative: *Gulf Dreams* (Third Woman Press, 1996), an autobiographical coming-of-age story; *Forgetting the Alamo, or Blood Memory* (2009), a historical western featuring a cross-dressing female hero; and *Electra's Complex* (2015), an erotic murder mystery. *Forgetting the Alamo* won the Christopher Isherwood grant in 2009 and was a finalist for the Lambda Literary Awards in 2010.

Chicano gay writers have been publishing since John Rechy's classic novel *City of Night* (1963), but his writing and identity were not embraced or seen as part of Chicano literature until the 1980s, when it became more acceptable or perhaps safer to identify oneself as queer in Chicano and Latino communities. Rechy has stated to the *New York Times*, "For years, people didn't consider me a Mexican-American. A couple of Chicano writers got annoyed and angry for me claiming to be Mexican-American. It's been more difficult for me to come out as a Mexican-American than come out as gay." And in fact, there has been a paucity noted of openly gay Chicano works, when compared to the proliferation of works by Chicana lesbians. It was, as noted above, the women who broke ground in coming out through Chicano literature. Nevertheless, from the 1980s to the present there has been a steady stream of important literary works published by gay Chicanos and featuring gay themes and characters. Poets Francisco X. Alarcón, Juan Pablo Gutiérrez, and Rodrigo Reyes founded Las Cuarto Espinas (The Four Thorns), the first gay Chicano poets collective, in 1985, and their aesthetic and worldview were articulated through their anthology of poetry titled *Ya Vas Carnal* that same year. Alarcón, the group's leader, published numerous books of poetry and chapbooks in original Spanish and bilingual editions, including *Tattoos* (1985), *Body in Flames/Cuerpo*

en llamas (1990), *De amor oscuro/Of Dark Love* (1991), *Poemas zurdos* (1992), *Snake Poems: An Aztec Invocation* (1992), *Sonnets to Madness and Other Misfortunes / Sonetos a la locura y otras penas* (2001), *From the Other Side of Night/Del otro lado de la noche: New and Selected Poems* (2002), and *Ce Uno One: Poems for the New Sun/Poemas para el Nuevo Sol* (2010). Among the first, most prominent works were Arturo Islas's highly autobiographical novels *The Rain God* (1984) and its sequel, *Migrant Souls* (1991), which explored the patriarchal suppression of the male protagonist's sexuality. Following on Islas's breakthrough, various gay novelists have been published to rising acclaim. Foremost among them is an ex-priest, Benjamin Alire Saenz, who writes novels, poetry, and children's books that have won national awards, including the Americas Book Award, the Paterson Book Prize, the J. Hunt Award, and the PEN Faulkner Award. Likewise, poet and memoirist Rigoberto González has developed a distinguished career, recognized by both the Chicano and mainstream literary communities. His memoir, *What Drowns the Flowers in Your Mouth: A Memoir of Brotherhood*, was a finalist for the National Book Critics Circle Award; he also won the 2015 Bill Whitehead Award for Lifetime Achievement from the Publishing Triangle and the 2020 PEN/Voelcker Award for Poetry.

Today, as greater opportunities in academia have opened up for both Latino students and writers, the larger commercial world of publishing is beginning to open its doors to a few more Chicano writers. Under the leadership of writer-scholars, such as Tomás Rivera and Rolando Hinojosa, and publishers like Arte Público Press and Bilingual Review Press, Chicano literature has created a firm and lasting base for itself in academia. The larger society of readers and commercial publishing represent the new frontier for the twenty-first century. A strong beginning is represented by the publication in 1991 of Victor Villaseñor's generational family saga, "the Chicano Roots," entitled *Rain of Gold*, which was the first-ever best seller published by a Latino small press, Arte Público Press. Under development as a five-part television miniseries for years, Arte Público Press auctioned off the paperback rights to Bantam Doubleday Dell. Subsequently, Villaseñor published other books in his family autobiography series in large commercial houses: *Wild Steps of Heaven* (1997), *Thirteen Senses: A*

Memoir (2001), *Burro Genius* (2006), and *Crazy Loco Love* (2008). In 1975, Villaseñor's novel *Macho* was published but barely promoted by Bantam Books; in 1991, it was reprinted by Arte Público Press and made into a feature film for commercial release. In 1990, the commercial publisher Chronicle Books issued two books of poetry by Chicanos, Gary Soto and Francisco Alarcón, and Random House in 1991 issued two books by Sandra Cisneros. Finally, in 1991 the long-awaited filming of *Bless Me, Ultima* began, with Luis Valdez as director.

Since then a younger generation of Chicano writers has come on the scene, with a new aesthetic that, while still committed to exploring themes, issues, and characters that emerge from Mexican American communities, takes the form of more commercially viable narratives. Nevertheless, there is no Chicano author as yet in the twenty-first century who is more than a mid-list author. The commercial publishing industry, still overwhelmingly White and Eurocentric, has not invested in top-of-the-list promotion of the Chicano works it does publish. Notable among the writers to emerge in the last twenty years are Daniel Chacón, Diana Noble, Daniel Peña, Sergio Troncoso, and Gwendolyn Zepeda, most of whom are graduates of university creative writing programs.

Nuyorican Literature

In 1898, Puerto Rico became a colony of the United States; since 1917, Puerto Ricans have been citizens of the United States. Since that latter date, Puerto Ricans have never really been immigrants to the United States but rather migrants. Puerto Ricans on the island and those on the continent, despite geographic separation, hold in common their ethnicity, their history, and their religious and cultural traits and practices. They also both deal with the confrontation of two languages and cultures. Thus, whether they reside in the continental United States or on the island of Puerto Rico, Puerto Ricans are one people. That is true whether they prefer the Spanish language or English, whether they were born on the island or not. The island experience and the experience on the continent are two sides of the same coin. Thus, most attempted divisions of the people are for vested interests, whether political or prejudicial.

Puerto Rican culture today is the product of the powerful political, economic, and social forces that descend on small native populations and attempt to evangelize, assimilate, decimate, or otherwise transform them. In the case of Puerto Rico, in 1493 Christopher Columbus initiated the process that forever would make the island's people a blend of the cultures and races of Europe, Africa, and the Americas. It was this act of "discovery" that also resulted in Puerto Rico's becoming a colony in the Spanish Empire until 1898, when it passed into the possession of the next empire to dominate the hemisphere: the United States. It is therefore a land that has been and still is subject to overseas rule—politically, economically, and artistically.

Despite being an island geographically cut off from the rest of Latin America and despite being ruled as a colony and not enjoying complete self-determination, Puerto Rican literature has been rich, for it has developed out of the many cultures and experiences that make up its peoples. From the middle of the nineteenth century, it first assumed a creole, Latino-American identity, emphasizing the new speech and customs and history of people in this hemisphere as opposed to the Spanish in Europe—Puerto Rico and Cuba were among the very last remnants of Spain's colonial empire, the rest of Spanish America having gained its independence at the beginning of the century. After 1898, Puerto Rico emphasized its Latin American, Spanish-speaking identity as separate from the Anglo-American United States. While the reaction of Puerto Rican artists to the Spanish identity and tastes was to create a nationalism or an ethnic identity based on *mestizaje*, a blending of the cultures and the values of the New World, the reaction to the powerful presence of the United States has come as an insistence on the use of the Spanish language itself and on the relationship to Latin America and its cultures and arts.

At the turn of the century, the island's literature was developing along the lines of Latin American modernism, which was heavily influenced by French, peninsular Spanish, and Latin American models. As was the case in Mexico, Peru, Argentina, and Cuba, the artists and writers of Puerto Rico turned to the Indigenous people of the island, their folklore, and national models in an effort to discover the true identity of the national culture. The mestizo highlander, or *jíbaro*, and the Black and mulatto became cultural types that related Puerto Rico to the other island cultures of the Caribbean and thus created a space that was identifiable as home, while it challenged the imposition of the English language—which was done officially under U.S. military rule of the island—and the purported benefits of Yankee customs and economic power.

Although he was one of Puerto Rico's master poets, Luis Lloréns Torres (1876–1944) was a Euro-

Luis Palés Matos, commemorated with this bust in Guayama, Puerto Rico, developed a poetic style inspired by the rhythms and languages of Africa and the Black Caribbean.

pean-educated intellectual who adapted the verse forms of the plaintive mountain songs (*décimas*) and folk speech of the *jíbaros* in poems that took pride in rural life and its values rather than in the sophistication and modern advances of the city. His *jíbaros* were always skeptical and unmoved by the bragging and showing off of Americanized Puerto Ricans who believed in Yankee ingenuity and progress. Puerto Rico's greatest and most universally studied poet, Luis Palés Matos (1898–1959), was the first Puerto Rican literary figure to achieve a lasting impact on the evolution of Latin American literature, principally through the development of a poetic style that was inspired by the rhythms and languages of Africa and the Black Caribbean. His landmark book, *Tun tun de pasa y grifería* (1937), whose onomatopoetic title has no translation, openly claimed a Black African heritage and presence for the cultural makeup of Puerto Rico. But the primitivism, vigor, and freedom of his Black verses was only a point of departure for his critical stance toward Europe and the United States. In Palés Matos's master poem, "La plena de menéalo" ("The Dance of Shake It"), Puerto Rico is personified by a seductive *mulata* who sweats rum as she erotically dances close to, but just out of reach of, a drooling Uncle Sam.

Two figures are essential in recognition of the transition of Puerto Rican literature from the island to the continent: Julia de Burgos (1914–1953) and René Marqués (1919–1979). De Burgos cultivated beautiful, sensuous verses—odes to her beloved countryside—only to die tragically on the streets of New York. Her lyricism served the parallel desires for personal and national liberation. Marqués, the most widely known Puerto Rican playwright, spent time in New York as well and was able to capture the true meaning of the dislocation of the native populations from Puerto Rico and their relocation to foreign lands and values. Even more moving than John Steinbeck's *Grapes of Wrath* is the plight of the family of displaced mountain folk in Marqués's *La carreta* (The Oxcart), which was first produced on stage in New York in 1953 and then published in Spanish in 1961 and in English in 1969. *La carreta*, which dramatizes the tragic life of this family as they are forced to move from their farm to a San Juan slum and then to New York, ends with an appeal to Puerto Ricans not to leave their homeland and to return to the island and the values of the countryside.

To a great extent, today's major Puerto Rican writers on the island still draw upon Marqués's spirit, style, and message in their attempt to preserve the integrity of the Puerto Rican culture and in their call for the political independence of the island. Prose writers like José Luis González, Pedro Juan Soto, Luis Rafael Sánchez, and Jaime Carrero satirize the complacency of the Americanized middle class, which would like Puerto Rico to become a U.S. state. They also develop the themes of Puerto Rico's past as Edenic and the *jíbaro* as a child of nature, with his intense code of honor and decency. Most of today's island novelists, while romanticizing the island's past, have,

however, also created a one-dimensional image of Puerto Ricans in New York, only focusing on the tragedy of the rootlessness, poverty, and oppression of the second-class citizens who seem to be lost in the labyrinth of the monster city.

Puerto Rican writing in New York dates back to the end of the nineteenth century, and writing in English begins about the time that Jesús Colón was writing his columns for the *Daily Worker*. This seems to be a rather appropriate beginning, given that most of the Puerto Rican writers in English that followed identify with the working class. Unlike the writers of the island, who largely are members of an elite, educated class and many of whom are employed as university professors, the New York writers, who came to be known as

The Nuyorican Poets Café, a New York City home for poetry, music, theater, and visual arts, was founded in 1973 in an East Village apartment and moved to its present location on East Third Street in 1981.

Nuyoricans, are products of parents transplanted to the metropolis to work in the service and manufacturing industries. These writers are predominantly bilingual in their poetry and English-dominant in their prose; they hail from a folk and popular tradition heavily influenced by roving bards, reciters, storytellers, salsa music composers, and the popular culture and commercial environment of New York City.

Thus Nuyoricans are typically the children of working-class Puerto Rican migrants to the city; they are generally bilingual and bicultural, and so is their literature. During the search for ethnic roots and the civil rights movements of the 1960s, young Puerto Rican writers and intellectuals began using the term "Nuyorican" as a point of departure in affirming their own cultural existence and history as divergent from that of the island of Puerto Rico and that of mainstream America, much as the Chicanos were doing. A literary and artistic flowering in the New York Puerto Rican community ensued in the late 1960s and early 1970s as a result of greater access to education for Puerto Ricans raised in the United States and as a result of the ethnic consciousness movement. Although the term "Nuyorican" was first applied to literature by playwright-novelist Jaime Carrero in his poem "Neo-Rican Jetliner/Jet neorriqueño" in the late 1960s when he resided in New York, and the term finds some stylistic and thematic development in his plays *Noo Jall* (a blending of the Spanish pronunciation of "New York" and the word "jail") and *Pipo Subway no sabe reír* ("Pipo Subway Doesn't Know How to Laugh"), it was a group of poet-playwrights associated with the Nuyorican Poets Café in the Lower East Side of New York who later really defined and exemplified Nuyorican literature in their works. Included in the group were Miguel Algarín, Lucky Cienfuegos, Sandra María Esteves, Tato Laviera, and Miguel Piñero. Two members of the group, Cienfuegos and Piñero, were ex-convicts who had begun their writing careers while incarcerated and associating with Afro-American convict-writers; they chose to concentrate on prison life, street life, and the culture of poverty and to protest

the oppression of their peoples through their poetry and dramas. Algarín, a university professor and owner and operator of the Nuyorican Poets Café, contributed more of a spirit of the avant-garde for the collective and managed to draw into the circle such well-known poets as Allen Ginsberg. Laviera, a virtuoso bilingual poet and performer of poetry (*declamador*), contributed a lyricism and a folk and popular culture tradition that derived from the island experience and the Afro-Caribbean culture but was cultivated specifically in and for New York City.

It was Miguel Piñero's work (and life), however, that became most celebrated, his prison drama *Short Eyes* having won an Obie and the New York Drama Critics Award for Best American Play in the 1973–74 season. His success, coupled with that of the autobiography of fellow Nuyorican writer and ex-convict Piri Thomas and that of poet Pedro Pietri, who developed the image of a street urchin always high on marijuana, resulted in Nuyorican literature and theater's often being associated with crime, drugs, abnormal sexuality, and generally negative behavior. Thus, many writers who in fact were affirming Puerto Rican working-class culture did not want to become identified with the movement. Still others wanted to hold onto their ties with the island and saw no reason to emphasize differences but, rather, wanted to stress similarities. What exacerbated the situation was that the commercial publishing establishment in the early 1970s was quick to take advantage of the literary fervor in the Puerto Rican community by issuing a series of ethnic autobiographies that insisted on the criminality, abnormality, and drug culture of New York Puerto Ricans. Included in this array of mostly paperbacks was, of course, Thomas's *Down These Mean Streets* (1967, issued in paperback in 1974), Thomas's *Seven Long Times* (1974), Thomas's *Stories from El Barrio* (1978, issued in paperback in 1980), Lefty Barreto's *Nobody's Hero* (1976), and a religious variation on the theme: Nicky Cruz's *Run Baby Run* (1968).

This very seamy underside of Puerto Rican barrio life and the pursuit of identity in Nuyorican and

> Puerto Rican barrio life and the pursuit of identity in Nuyorican autobiographies were satirized in Ed Vega's *The Comeback* (1985), the story of a confused college professor who creates the identity of a Puerto Rican–Eskimo ice hockey player.

other ethnic autobiographies were satirized in Ed Vega's *The Comeback* (1985), the story of a confused college professor who creates for himself the identity of a Puerto Rican–Eskimo ice hockey player; he suffers a nervous breakdown and is treated for the classical symptoms of an identity crisis. Throughout the novel are satirized all types of characters that populate the barrio as well as popular culture, such as Puerto Rican revolutionaries, psychiatrists, and a Howard Cosell–type sportscaster. In his interrelated collection of stories told by fictitious narrator Ernesto Mendoza, *Mendoza's Dreams* (1987), Vega surveys the human comedy of everyday barrio life and relates tales of success in small ways in reaching for the American Dream. In his collection *Casualty Report* (1991), he shows us the inverse: the physical, psychological, and moral death of many who live within the poverty and deprivation of the Puerto Rican barrio, as well as in the larger ghetto of a racist society.

More than anything else, the first generation of Nuyorican writers was one that was dominated by poets, many of whom had come out of an oral tradition and had honed their art through public readings; thus the creation of the Nuyorican Poets Café was a natural outcome of the need to create a specific space for the performance of poetry. Among the consummate performers of Nuyorican poetry were Victor Hernández Cruz, Tato Laviera, Sandra María Esteves, Pedro Pietri, Miguel Piñero, and Miguel Algarín. Like his fellow poets, Cruz's initiation into poetry was through popular music and street culture; his first poems have been often considered to be jazz poetry in a bilingual mode, except that English dominated in the bilingualism and thus opened the way for his first book to be published by a general market publishing house: *Snaps: Poems* (Random House, 1969). It was quite a feat for a twenty-year-old from an impoverished background. Already announced in *Snaps* were the themes and styles that would dominate and flourish in his subsequent books. In all of Hernández Cruz's poetry of sound, music and performance are central. He experiments with bilingualism as oral poetry (and written symbols of oral speech), and he searches for identity through these sounds and symbols. Thus, his next two books are odysseys that take the reader back to Puerto Rico and primordial Indian and African music and poetry (*Mainland*, 1973) and across the

United States and back to New York, where the poet finds the city transformed by its Caribbean peoples into their very own cultural home (*Tropicalization*, 1976). *By Lingual Wholes* (1982) is a consuming and total exploration of the various linguistic possibilities in the repertoire of a bilingual poet, and *Rhythm, Content and Flavor* (1989) is a summary of his entire career.

Tato Laviera has said in a 1980 interview with the author of this chapter, "I am the grandson of slaves transplanted from Africa to the Caribbean, a man of the New World come to dominate and revitalize two old world languages." And, indeed, Laviera's bilingualism and linguistic inventiveness have risen to the level of virtuosity. Laviera is the inheritor of the Spanish oral tradition, with all of its classical formulas, and the African oral tradition, with its wedding to music and spirituality; in his works he brings both the Spanish and English languages together as well as the islands of Puerto Rico and Manhattan—a constant duality that is always just in the background. His first book, *La Carreta Made a U-Turn* (1979), was published by Arte Público Press, which is the leading publisher of Nuyorican literature, despite its location in Houston. *La Carreta Made a U-Turn* uses René Marqués's *Oxcart* as a point of departure and redirects it back to the heart of New York, instead of back to the island, as Marqués had desired; Laviera is stating that Puerto Rico can be found here too. His second book, *Enclave* (1981), is a celebration of diverse heroic personalities, both real and imagined: Luis Palés Matos and salsa composers, the neighborhood gossip and John Lennon, and Miriam Makeba and Tito Madera Smith—the latter being a fictional, hip offspring of a *jíbara* and a southern American Black. *AmeRícan* (1986) and *Mainstream Ethics* (1988) are surveys of the lives of the poor and marginalized in the United States and a challenge for the country to live up to its promises of equality and democracy. *Mixturao and Other Poems* (2008) is a celebration of *mestizaje*, of neither being one nor the other race or ethnicity, of being an immigrant that belongs not here nor there, of affirming the advantages of bilingualism and biculturalism.

One of the few women's voices to be heard in this generation is a very strong and well-defined one, that of Sandra María Esteves, who from her teen years has been very active in the women's struggle, Afro-American liberation, the Puerto Rican independence movement, and, foremost, the performance of poetry. In 1973, she joined El Grupo, a New York–based touring collective of musicians, performing artists, and poets and the cultural wing of the Puerto Rican Socialist Party. By 1980, she had published her first collection of poetry, *Yerba Buena*, which is a search for identity of a colonized Latino woman of color in the United States, the daughter of immigrants from the Caribbean. All three of her books, *Yerba Buena, Tropical Rains: A Bilingual Downpour* (1984), and *Bluestown Mockingbird Mambo* (1990), affirm that womanhood is what gives unity to all of the diverse characterizations of her life. Beginning in the 1990s, Esteves took publication and distribution of her work into her own hands and self-published a series of chapbooks; she also found a way to preserve and distribute her spoken-word poetry by issuing two CDs: *Wildflowers* (2009) and *DivaNations* (2010).

> Sandra María Esteves, from her teen years, has been very active in the women's struggle, Afro-American liberation, the Puerto Rican independence movement, and, foremost, the performance of poetry.

The most productive and recognized Nuyorican novelist is Nicholasa Mohr. Her works *Nilda* (1973), *El Bronx Remembered* (1975), *In Nueva York* (1977), *Felita* (1979), and *Going Home* (1986) were all published in hardback and paperback by major commercial publishing houses and are all still in print, three of them having been reissued by Arte Público Press. Her books have entered the general market, as have a few other books by Latino authors of the United States. They have won such awards as the *New York Times* Outstanding Book of the Year, the *School Library Journal* Best Children's Book, and many others, including a decree honoring her by the state legislature of New York. Her best-loved novel, *Nilda*, traces the coming of age of a young Puerto Rican girl in the Bronx during World War II. Unlike many other such novels of development, *Nilda* gains awareness of the plight of her people and her own individual problems by examining the racial and economic oppression that surrounds her and her family, in a manner that can be compared to Tomás Rivera's central character in ... *y no se lo tragó la tierra*.

In two of her other books, *In Nueva York* and *El Bronx Remembered*, Mohr examines through a series of stories and novellas various Puerto Rican neighborhoods and draws sustenance from the common folks' power to survive and still produce art, folklore, and strong families in the face of oppression and marginalization. *Rituals of Survival: A Woman's Portfolio* (1985), in five stories and a novella, portrays six strong women who take control of their lives, most of them by liberating themselves from husbands, fathers, or families who attempt to keep them confined in narrowly defined female roles. *Rituals* is the book that the general market houses would not publish, wanting to keep Mohr confined to what they saw as immigrant literature and children's literature, as in her *Felita* and *Going Home*.

While not banding together with groups and collectives, Mohr has been one of the most influential of the Nuyorican writers out of sheer productivity and accomplishment. She has also led the way to greater acceptance of Nuyorican and Latino writers in creative writing workshops, such as the Millay Colony; in PEN International; and on the funding panels of the National Endowment for the Arts and the New York State Council on the Arts.

Another Nuyorican writer who neither participated nor benefited from collective work is Judith Ortiz Cofer, who grew up in Paterson, New Jersey, and lived much of her adult life in Georgia and Florida. Cofer was one of the few Nuyorican products of the creative writing programs, and much of her early poetry was disseminated through establishment small presses in the South that may have been intrigued by the exoticism of her Puerto Rican subjects, packaged in finely crafted verses, with a magic and mystery that is similar to that of Pat Mora's poetry.

Her first book of poems, *Reaching for the Mainland* (1987), was a chronicle of the displaced person's struggle to find a goal, a home, a language, and a history. In *Terms of Survival* (1987), she explored the psychology and social attitudes of the Puerto Rican dialect and how it controls male and female roles; in particular she carried on a dialogue with her father throughout the poems of the book. In 1989, Cofer published a highly reviewed novel of immigration, *Line of the Sun*, through the University of Georgia Press and in 1990 an even more highly reviewed book, made up of a collection of autobiographical essays in the style of Virginia Woolf, *Silent Dancing: A Remembrance of Growing Up Puerto Rican*, through Arte Público Press. It was the recipient of the PEN–Martha Albrand Special Citation in Nonfiction and of the 1990 Pushcart Prize; in 1991 the titular chapter, "Silent Dancing," was selected for *The Best American Essays 1991*. In the last decade of her life—she died in 2014—Cofer wrote children's and young adult books, including the YA titles *The Meaning of Consuelo* (2003), *Call Me Maria* (2004), and *If I Could Fly* (2011); and the children's books *A Bailar!/Let's Dance* (2011), *The Poet Upstairs* (2012), and *Animal Jamboree: Latino Folk Tales/La Fiesta De Los Animales: Leyendas* (2012).

In 1988, Cofer and five other writers discussed earlier—Nicholasa Mohr, Tato Laviera, Rolando Hinojosa, Alberto Ríos, and Lorna Dee Cervantes—were featured reading and performing their works in a historic documentary, *Growing Up Latino*, directed by Jesús Treviño, presented on national television by the Corporation for Public Broadcasting. At that point, the future of Latino literature in the United States promised to be very fruitful, with more and more segments of the population getting the message; however, in the twenty-first century, Latino literature is unfortunately still a phenomenon of small presses, with the large commercial industry neglecting to adequately publish the works of Latino authors.

Cuban American, Dominican American, and Central-American American Literature

Cuban American Literature

As mentioned previously, Cuban culture and literature in the United States date back to the nineteenth century when writer-philosopher José Martí and other patriots plotted from the U.S. mainland for Cuban independence from Spain. During the first half of the twentieth century, Cubans and Spaniards dominated Latino arts and media in New York. While Cuban culture was on the ascendancy in New York,

its island literature had already joined that of Mexico and Argentina in the leadership of Spanish American letters since the nineteenth century, with such internationally acknowledged masters as Martí, Gertrudis Gómez de Avellaneda, José Echeverría, and Julián del Casal, and in the twentieth century with such leaders as patriarch Nicolás Guillén, who took Spanish American poetry from a markedly Afro-Caribbean to a Pan Latino vision in support of universal socialist revolution. Cuban writers who have contributed to the Latin American literary boom include Alejo Carpentier, José Lezama Lima, and Gabriel Cabrera Infante.

It is no wonder then that the inheritors of such a rich and dynamic tradition would contribute so greatly to Latino culture in the United States, especially given the fact that their mass immigration took place so recently, beginning in 1959 as refugees from the Cuban Revolution. In contrast, whereas Puerto Rican mass migration really had begun during World War II, when the American economy drew heavily on its island territory for workers, the Cubans came as political refugees from a land that had never been a colony of the United States, although it had been a protectorate and an economic dependent since the Spanish-American War. Most of the Puerto Ricans had come as workers and generally had neither the level of education nor the financial resources and relocation services that the Cubans did. This first mass of Cubans came with an outstanding written tradition well intact. And the Cuban literary aesthetic, unlike the Puerto Rican one, had never been so obsessed with protecting the Spanish language and Latino culture while defending itself against Anglo-American culture and language. Numerous writers and intellectuals immigrated to the United States as refugees; many of them were able to adapt to and become part of Latino and general U.S. cultural institutions.

Today, after six decades of new Cuban culture in New York, New Jersey, Miami, and dispersed throughout the United States—in contrast to the older Cuban communities in New York City and Tampa—a Cuban American literary and artistic presence has developed. Younger writers are no longer preoccupied with exile, with eyes cast only on the island past; instead, they are looking forward to participating in general English-language society or serving the intellectual and cultural needs of the U.S. Cuban and Latino communities. Thus there has developed a definite separation of purpose and aesthetics between the younger immigrants or children of the exiles—Roberto Fernández, Iván Acosta, Virgil Suárez, and Oscar Hijuelos, for instance—and the older writers of exile—Lydia Cabrera, Matías Montes Huidobro, José Sánchez-Boudy, and so on. Also, there continues to be an influx of exiled writers, disaffected with Cuban communism, such as Heberto Padilla, who must be viewed differently from the earlier generation of exiles who already created for themselves a solid niche within Latino and general market institutions such as publishing houses and universities.

Immediately after the Cuban Revolution of 1959 arose a literature that almost exclusively attacked the revolution, Fidel Castro, and Marxism. The novel of exile became another weapon in the counterrevolutionary struggle. Following the first antirevolutionary novel, *Enterrado vivo* (Buried Alive), published in Mexico in 1960 by Andrés Rivero Collado, were a host of others published in the United States and abroad by minor writers, such as Emilio Fernández Camus, Orlando Núñez, Manuel Cobo Souza, Raúl A. Fowler, Luis Ricardo Alonso, and many others. When they were not openly propagandistic and rhetorical, they were nostalgic for the homeland to the point of idealization. Poetry and drama followed the same course, for the most part. Later, political verse would come to form a special genre of its own, what has been called by critic Hortensia Ruiz del Viso "poesía del presidio político" (political prisoner poetry), as in the works of Angel Cuadra, Heberto Padilla, and Armando Valladares, the latter who resided in Spain but was quite active in the United States.

A key figure in providing a new direction for Cuban literature in the United States has been Celedonio González, who, beginning with *Los primos* (The Cousins, 1971), changed his focus to concentrate on Cuban life and culture in the United States. Later, in

Los cuatro embajadores (The Four Ambassadors, 1973) and *El espesor del pellejo de un gato ya cadáver* (The Thickness of the Skin on a Cat Already a Corpse, 1978), he not only examined culture shock and conflict between Cubans and Americans, but he also covered a very taboo topic: criticism of the economic system of the United States, especially in its exploitation of Cuban workers. González presented us with Cubans who did not yet see themselves as Americans but who were also conscious that Cuba was no longer theirs.

Ironically, one of the most important writers in forging a Cuban American literature and in breaking new ground in his use of the English language is a professor of Spanish, Roberto G. Fernández. Through his novels, Fernández not only touches upon all the taboo subjects in the Cuban community of Miami—the counterrevolutionary movement in the United States, racism, acculturation, and assimilation—but also helps the community to take them in a less serious vein and to laugh at itself. In his two open-form mosaic-like novels, *La vida es un special* (Life Is on Special, 1982) and *La montaña rusa* (The Roller Coaster, 1985), Fernández presents a biting but loving satire of a community transformed by the materialism and popular culture of the United States, but somewhat paralyzed by the nostalgia and political obsession with a Communist Cuba. In 1988, Fernández continued the community saga in English, with the publication of *Raining Backwards* and followed it up in 1997 with *Holy Radishes*, which have become his most known and highly regarded novels. In them as in his other works, the hilarious parade of characters, language styles—with quite a bit of bilingual humor—and diverse social events are aimed at encouraging the community to take stock of its present circumstances and reckon with a future here in the United States. In his latest writing, Fernández has made an unforeseen return to writing in Spanish, this time with his historical novel *El príncipe y la bella cuana: Los amores de don Alfonso de Borbón y Battenberg y Doña Ana Edelmira Sapmedro y Robato*, an extended look at a trans-Atlantic, Spain–Cuba–New York love affair of a Spanish royal with a Cuban woman.

> ◆ ••••
> **Immediately after the Cuban Revolution of 1959 arose a literature that almost exclusively attacked the revolution, Fidel Castro, and Marxism. The novel of exile became another weapon in the counterrevolutionary struggle.**

One of the most influential magazines of Cuban literature in the United States has been *Linden Lane*, which has been published in Spanish since 1982. Founded by writer Heberto Padilla and edited by poet Belkis Cuza Malé, back when she was a professor at Princeton University, the magazine has created a forum for the whole Cuban writing community, both the generation of exiles and the Cuban American generation. In 1990, the magazine formally announced the advent of a Cuban American literature with its publication of an anthology containing works in both English and Spanish and entitled *Los atrevidos: Cuban American Literature*, edited by Miami poet Carolina Hospital, also an editor at *Linden Lane*. In 1991, Arte Público Press published an anthology that also proclaimed a Cuban American identity, *Cuban American Theater*, edited by critic Rodolfo Cortina. Both collections draw upon writers dispersed throughout the United States, not just from the Miami and New York communities.

Among the new generation of Cuban American writers growing up in the United States, there are a few who have gone through creative writing programs at universities and who thus have had access to general market publishing opportunities. A graduate of the important writing program at Louisiana State University, Virgil Suárez has had two novels published in major commercial houses, *Latin Jazz* (1989) by Morrow and *The Cutter* (1991) by Ballantine Books, as well as novels, poetry, essays and anthologies published by small presses, such as Arte Público Press. His third book, a very fine collection of short stories, *Welcome to the Oasis*, was not accepted by commercial publishers who prefer novels; it was published in 1991 by Arte Público Press. *Latin Jazz* is a somewhat different type of ethnic biographical novel, portraying a whole Cuban family, instead of just one individual; in alternate chapters devoted to each of the family members, Suárez provides their respective histories, hopes, and desires as they wait for a missing family member to arrive in Miami with the Mariel boatlift. In 1996 he published *Going Under*, what perhaps would have been anathema to the previous generation: the desperate protagonist gives up on life in Miami, Florida, and plunges into the Atlantic to swim back to Cuba.

Oscar Hijuelos.

Probably the most important of the Cuban American writers to come out of the creative writing schools was Oscar Hijuelos, who was not the son of refugees from the Cuban Revolution but rather of earlier immigrants to New York. Nevertheless, Hijuelos's first offering, *Our House in the Last World* (1983), is a typical ethnic autobiography and may be seen as a symbol of Cuban assimilation; it is one of the few novels that negatively portrays the island culture, as personified by an alcoholic, macho father, while it develops the tried-and-true theme of the American dream in the United States. His novel *The Mambo Kings Play Songs of Love* (1990) made history; it is the first novel by a Latino writer of the United States to win the Pulitzer Prize. It was also the first time that a major publishing house, Simon and Schuster, ever invested heavily in a novel by a Latino writer, bringing it out at the top of its list and promoting the book very heavily. *The Mambo Kings* is the story of two musician brothers during the heyday of the mambo and during the time when at least one Cuban had captured the attention of the United States: Desi Arnaz on the *I Love Lucy* show. The novel thus has a historical background that lends it a very rich texture; it allows us to see a portion of American popular culture history through the eyes of two performers very wrapped up in the euphoria of the times and then the waning of interest in things Latin in the United States. The story of the tragic ending of the duo is very touching, but it offers hope for the potential of Latino culture to influence the general society. In fact, Hijuelos's book and the recognition that it has won offered hope of opening the door to mainstream publishing for other Latino writers, but of course that has not really happened to an appreciable degree. Before his premature death in 2013, Hijuelos went on to publish a stream of novels in mainstream presses, not all of which had Latino themes: *The Fourteen Sisters of Emilio Montez O'Brien* (1993), *Mr. Ives' Christmas* (1995), *Empress of the Splendid Season* (1999), *A Simple Habana Melody (from When the World Was Good)* (2002), *Dark Dude* (2008), *Beautiful Maria of My Soul*

(2010), and the posthumous *Twain & Stanley Enter Paradise* (2015).

Among the new generations of Cuban American writers who have been successful in mainstream commercial publishing houses are Cristina García, Ruth Behar, Achy Obejas, and Carolina García Aguilera, a cadre of women who explore ethnic autobiography as well as genre literature. Cristina García, who has had a successful career as a journalist, has cultivated ethnic autobiography, dealing with the development of her female characters in Cuba and the United States. Her *Dreaming in Cuban* was a finalist for the 1992 National Book Award. Her most recent of seven novels, *Here in Berlin*, was chosen as one of the ten Best Books of 2017 by the BBC and as a *New York Times Book Review* Editor's Choice. Ruth Behar, as well, has been hailed by the *New York Times*. Her literary books—she also writes anthropological studies—are ethnic autobiographies in the form of novels and memoirs exploring her Cuban Jewish upbringing: *An Island Called Home* (2007), *Traveling Heavy* (2013), *Lucky Broken Girl* (2017), and *Letters from Cuba* (2020). Achy Obejas is a fiction writer, poet, journalist, and essayist who explores her Cuban upbringing as well as immigration, accommodation, and the stresses of lesbian sexuality. Her three novels are *Memory Mambo* (1996), *Days of Awe* (2001), and *Ruins* (2009); in 1994 she published a very popular collection of short stories, *We Came All the Way from Cuba So You Could Dress Like This?* Carolina García Aguilera is one of the very few Latina writers to have a successful detective series; her protagonist, Lupe Solano, is a "Cuban American princess" from a well-to-do Miami family and is indomitable in her "feminine wiles" approach to solving mysteries as a private investigator. García Aguilera's "Lupe Solano" series includes *Bloody Waters* (1996), *Bloody Shame* (1997), *Bloody Secrets* (1998), *A Miracle in Paradise* (1999), *Havana Heat* (2000), *Bitter Sugar* (2001), and *Bloody Twist* (2010).

Dominican American Literature

The Dominican-origin population had grown significantly by the end of the twentieth century, and a generation of writers born or raised in the United States, particularly on the East Coast and close to the publishing center of the United States, has achieved access to major publishing opportunities. One beneficiary of elite creative writing programs (an MFA from Cornell University) and professional mentoring is Junot Díaz, whose first slim book of short stories, *Drown* (1995), was celebrated throughout the publishing industry and led the way to the major publishing and promotional effort that took his first novel, *The Brief Wondrous Life of Oscar Wao,* to the 2008 Pulitzer Prize and a MacArthur Fellowship in 2012. Another creative writing program graduate and member of the first generation of Latinas to cross over to mainstream publishing is Julia Alvarez, whose books have not only been celebrated nationally but have also had Hollywood film versions. Her novels include *How the García Girls Lost Their Accents* (1991), *In the Time of the Butterflies* (1994), and *Yo!* (1997). Whereas Alvarez hailed from a comparably privileged background—her father was an exiled physician associated at one point with the Rafael Trujillo regime—among the working-class originated Dominican American writers, Angie Cruz has become a distinguished voice, with various books in major presses, including *Soledad* (2001), *Let It Rain Coffee* (2005), and *Dominicana* (2019). The youngest of the group, Elizabeth Acevedo, born in 1988, grew up in working-class Morningside Heights, New York City, and has become a best-selling author of adult and young adult fiction. Her *The Poet X* was a *New York Times* best seller, won the 2018 *Boston Globe–Horn Book* Award, the Walter Dean Myers Award for Outstanding Children's Literature, and the 2018 National Book Award for Young People's Literature.

Central-American American Literature

Much of the Central-American American literature produced by authors born or raised in the United States is still very close to the traditions of exile and immigration. Guatemalan Arturo Arias is an elder statesman and transitional author from Central America who immigrated as an adult to the United States. Many of his novels and nonfiction works deal with political upheaval, especially as it has affected the Indigenous peoples in the country of his birth, including *Después de las bombas* (1979; *After the Bombs*, 1990), *Itzam Na* (1981, winner of Cuba's Casa de las Américas Award for best novel), and *Jaguar en llamas* (1989). The civil wars in Central America, however, have been so defining that they have become the fiction and nonfiction themes of even the next generation, represented on the one hand by the son of a Guatemalan immigrant and a Jewish American father, Francisco Goldman, in *The Long Night of White Chickens* (1992) and *The Art of Political Murder: Who Killed the Bishop?* (2014), and on the other hand by the son of Guatemalan immigrants, Los Angeles native Héctor Tobar, who set his novel *The Tattooed Soldier* (1998) in the impoverished immigrant barrios of Los Angeles and explores the Central American diaspora. An American-born poet with Guatemalan roots and a product of university creative writing courses is Maya Chinchilla, a founder of EpiCentroAmerica, a place for Central American youths to develop their cultural identity, and the author of *The Cha Cha Files: A Chapina Poética*, which explores the Central American diaspora.

Salvadoran immigrant Mario Bencastro made the transition from his early exilic literature condemning government tyranny, as in *El árbol de la vida* (1983, *Tree of Life*, 1997) and *Disparo en la cathedral* (1997, *Shot in the Cathedral*, 2011), to giving a voice to Salvadoran immigrants in U.S. cities, as in his *Odisea al norte* (2011, *Odyssey to the North*, 2011) and *Viaje a la Tierra del Abuelo* (2003, *A Promise to Keep*, 2015). Salvadoran poet Jorge Tetl Argueta writes about his exile as a youth and odyssey through the United States in *En carne propia: Memoria poética/Flesh Wounds: A Poetic Memoir* (2017) and writes children's books from the vantage point of his Nahua culture. The U.S.-raised Salvadoran poet Leticia Hernández-Linares is the author of *Mucha Muchacha, Too Much Girl* (2015) and is coeditor of *The Wandering Song: Central American Writing in the United States* (2017). Another Salvadoran poet raised in the United States who was trained in a university creative writing program and writes in English is William Archila, author of *The Art of Exile* (2009) and *The Gravedigger's Archaeology: Poems* (2015). One of the few Honduran writers publishing in the United States is Roberto P. Quezada, author of novels that satirize immigration and the American Dream concept that dominates so much U.S. ethnic literature. Among his half dozen novels, *The Big Banana* (1999) takes on the theme of immigration from the vantage point of a picaresque wannabe artist from Tegucigalpa, and his *Nunca entres por Miami* (2002, *Never through Miami* 2002)

is a raucous romp through the Customs and Border Control system at U.S. airports.

OUTSTANDING LATINO LITERARY FIGURES

Marjorie Agosín (1955–)

Jewish-Latina poet Marjorie Agosín was born in Bethesda, Maryland, on June 15, 1955, to Moses and Frida Agosín. Shortly after her birth, her parents moved to Santiago, Chile, where she was partly raised, until 1996, when her parents moved back to the United States. Agosín has plumbed her diverse background to fill her poems with a humanitarian tenor that revisits the Holocaust and Latino and women's struggles in the United States and Latin America. She graduated with a major in philosophy from the University of Georgia (1976) and a Ph.D. in Spanish from Indiana University (1982). From then on, Agosín proceeded to become one of the most prolific producers of Latino poetry in the United States, publishing more than twenty books. The majority of her poetry is originally written in Spanish in order for Agosín to preserve her Spanish American identity; this identity has also been kept refreshed by her frequent travels to South America and her teaching Spanish American literature at Wellesley College since 1982. Her preoccupation with the poor and oppressed is continued in many of her essays and short stories. These have appeared in numerous books that she has published, including *Mujeres melodiosas* (1997, *Melodious Women*), *Always from Somewhere Else: A Memoir of My Chilean Jewish Father* (1998), *Uncertain Travelers: Conversations with Jewish Women Immigrants to America* (1999), *The Alphabet in My Hands: A Writing Life* (2000), *Secrets in the Sand: The Young Women of Juárez* (2006), *The Light of Desire / La Luz del Deseo* (2010), and *I Lived on Butterfly Hill* (2014).

Francisco X. Alarcón (1954–2016)

Francisco Alarcón was born in Wilmington, California, on February 21, 1954. As a child he lived with his family just outside Los Angeles, as well as with his Tarrascan-Indian grandfather in Michoacán and other relatives in Guadalajara, Mexico. Later on his family moved back to California, where he lived since he was eighteen years old. Alarcón graduated with a B.A. in Spanish and history from California State University, Long Beach (1977) and later obtained a Ph.D. in Spanish from Stanford University (1980). He was a poet, an educator, and an author of multiple volumes of poetry, including *Loma Prieta* (1990, Dark Hill), *Snake Poems: An Aztec Invocation* (1992), *Poemas Zurdos* (1992, Left-Handed Poems), *No Golden Gate for Us* (1993), *Sonnets to Madness and Other Misfortunes* (2001), *Iguanas in the Snow and Other Winter Poems* (2001), *From the Other Side of Night* (2002), and *Ce Uno One: Poems for the New Sun / Poemas para el Nuevo Sol* (2010). An early recognition of his work was the winning of the Rubén Darío Latin American Poetry Prize from the Casa Nicaragua in San Francisco. He was also the winner of the Josephine Miles Literary Award of PEN Oakland, the Pura Belpré Honor Award, and the American Book Award of the Before Columbus Foundation. Alarcón was a founder of Las Cuarto Espinas (The Four Thorns), the first gay Chicano poetry group, in 1985, which published an anthology titled *Ya Vas Carnal* (You're Leaving, Brother).

Miguel Algarín (1941–2020)

Born in Santurce, Puerto Rico, on September 11, 1941, Miguel Algarín grew up in a hardworking family whose parents loved music and the arts and gave to their children an early appreciation of opera and classical music; Miguel's father taught him to play the violin. The Algaríns moved to New York City in the early 1950s and settled in Spanish Harlem for a while, and then moved to Queens. Miguel Alagarín began his higher education at City College and finished his B.A. degree at the University of Wisconsin in 1963; in 1965, he graduated with a master's degree in English from Pennsylvania State University. After teaching English literature at Brooklyn College and New York University for a time, Algarín went on to teach at Rutgers, where he was an associate professor in the English department for many years before he retired. In 1973 Miguel Algarín cofounded and became proprietor of the Nuyorican Poets Café, which is dedicated to the support of writers performing their art orally. It was especially important as a gathering place

Miguel Algarín sits in front of Nuyorican Poets Café in Manhattan in August 2007.

of young writers during the early 1970s when Nuyorican literature was being defined. Algarín played an important leadership role in that definition by also compiling, with Miguel Piñero, an important anthology, *Nuyorican Poetry: An Anthology of Puerto Rican Words and Feelings* (1975). He also founded a short-lived publishing house, the Nuyorican Press, which only issued one book, his own *Mongo Affair* (1978). One year later, he took part in the launching of Arte Público Press, which became the leading publisher of Nuyorican literature. Algarín wrote plays, screenplays, and short stories, but was principally known as a poet. In addition to *Mongo Affair*, his books included *On Call* (1980), *Body Bee Calling from the 21st Century* (1982), *Time's Now / Ya es tiempo* (1985), *Love Is Hard: Memorias de Loisaida / Poems* (1997), and *Survival / Supervivencia*

(2009). Algarín's poetry runs the gamut from jazz-salsa poetry to the mystical and avant-garde. He was one of the foremost experimenters with English-Spanish bilingualism and even penned trilingual works that incorporated the French language.

Isabel Allende (1942–)

Born on August 2, 1941, in Lima to Chilean parents, Isabel Allende was raised from the age of three by her divorced mother in Santiago, Chile. In Santiago, Allende became a journalist and editor of the magazine *Paula* and also worked in television. Her family's work in politics and diplomacy resulted in her exile after her father's cousin, Chilean president Salvador Allende, was assassinated in 1972. Her significant literary career was launched while she resided in exile in Venezuela; it was there that she published her most successful novel, *La casa de los espíritus* (1980, The House of the Spirits), which made her an international literary superstar. Other novels followed—*De amor y sombra* (1984, Of Love and Shadow), *Eva Luna* (1988)—in which her credentials as a feminist were underscored. In 1988, she made a transition to living in the United States. In the San Francisco Bay area, she has continued her productivity, also making a transition to becoming an immigrant both as an individual and as a writer. Some of her novels relate to California in one way or another: *El plan infinito* (1991, The Infinite Plan), *Hija de la fortuna* (2003, The Daughter of Fortune), *Retrato en sepia* (2000, Portrait in Sepia), and *Zorro* (2005). Others relate to immigration to the United States in the past, as in *Island Beneath the Sea/La isla bajo el mar* (2010), or the present, as in *In the Midst of Winter/Más allá del invierno* (2017). Many deal with political upheaval and exile, such as *The Japanese Lover/El amante japonés* (2015) and *A Long Petal of the Sea/Largo pétalo de mar* (2019). Allende is one of the few Spanish American writers to have all of her works translated to English and published in the United States. Allende has published two types of memoirs: a memoir through interviews with her friend Celia Correas de Zapata, *Isabel Allende:*

Life and Spirits (2002), and *My Invented Country* (2003), in which she explores the role of politics, myth, and magic in shaping her life. Allende explores the historical past in many of her works, including her novel based on the life of Doña Inés Suárez (1507–1580), a poor Spanish girl who eventually married the founder of colonial Chile and hoped to create an egalitarian society: *Inés del alma mía: Una novela/Ines of My Soul: A Novel* (2010). Allende has won numerous prestigious awards around the world, including the Book of the Year (Germany, 1984), the *Grand Prix d'Evasion* (France, 1984), *Library Journal*'s Best Book (United States, 1988), the U.S. Hispanic Heritage Award in Literature (1996), Chile's National Prize for Literature (2010), the U.S. Presidential Medal of Freedom (2014), and the U.S. National Book Foundation Medal for Distinguished Contribution to American Letters (2018).

Alurista (1947–)

Alurista (Alberto Baltazar Urista Heredia) is considered one of the pioneers of Chicano literature. He was one of the first poets to support the Chicano movement through his poetry, a writer and signer of important manifestoes of the movement, a founder of the Movimiento Estudiantil de Aztlán (MECHA, Chicano Student Movement of Aztlán) in 1967, and one of the first to establish the concept of Aztlán in literature, which forecasts a return to the glories of Aztec civilization by the Chicanos in the mythic homeland of the Aztecs, what is today roughly the five states of the Southwest. Born in Mexico City on August 8, 1947, Alberto Baltazar Urista Heredia spent his early years in the states of Morelos and Guerrero. At age thirteen he immigrated to the United States with his family, which settled in San Diego, California. He graduated from San Diego State University in 1970 with a B.A. degree in psychology and later obtained an M.A. degree from that institution and a Ph.D. degree in literature from the University of California, San Diego, in 1983. Around 1966, he began writing poetry seriously for publication and assumed the pen name Alurista, which is virtually the only name he uses now. Alurista was the founder and co-editor, with his wife, Xelina, of the literary magazine *Maize* and the publishing house associated with it;

both ceased to exist after he became a professor at various universities. Alurista's bilingualism opened new frontiers in poetry, with his free experimentation in combining the sounds, meanings, and graphic representations of Spanish and English in the same poem, quite often achieving surprising and beautiful effects. Alurista has published ten books of poetry, including *Floricanto en Aztlán* (1971), *Nationchild Plumaroja, 1967–1972* (1972), *Timespace Huracán: Poems, 1972–1975* (1976), *A'nque* (1979), *Spik in Glyph?* (1981), *Return: Poems Collected and New* (1982), *Z Eros* (1995), *Et Tu … Raza* (1996), *As our barrio turns: who the yoke b on?* (2000), and *Tuna Luna* (2010).

Julia Alvarez (1950–)

Novelist and poet Julia Alvarez was born on March 27, 1950, in New York City; however, her parents returned to their native Dominican Republic when she was just three months old. Alvarez's parents were politically connected to the Rafael Leonidas Trujillo dictatorial regime, but when her father fell out of favor, he took the family into exile in New York City, when she was ten years old. Alvarez graduated with a B.A. in English from Middlebury College in 1971, and in 1975 she earned a master's degree in creative writing from Syracuse University. She went on to develop a career as a poet and fiction writer and became a tenured professor at Middlebury College. Alvarez's narratives are loosely based on growing up between the two cultures of the United States and the Dominican Republic, although her perspective has always been one of growing up in privilege as the daughter of a successful doctor and politically connected exile. After publishing poems and stories in literary magazines, she published a book of verse, *Homecoming* (1984), and her first novel, *How the García Girls Lost Their Accents* (1991); in so doing, she joined a wave of Hispanic writers breaking into mainstream presses with their tales of immigration and growing up within the United States. In 1994, she published the novel *In the Time of Butterflies*, which was later made into a feature film, and, in 1995, another collection of poems, *The Other Side/El Otro Lado*. In 1995, Alvarez published a collection of autobiographical essays, *Something to Declare: Essays*. Among Alvarez's other novels are *In the Name of Salomé* (2001), *Before We Were Free* (2002), and *Saving the World* (2006). In the latter, Alvarez compares and intertwines the lives of two Dominican women separated by a century: one is a nineteenth-century missionary and the other a Dominican female writer in Vermont chronicling the struggle of the former in battling smallpox in the Dominican Republic. Alvarez has also been a productive poet. Among her poetry books are *Homecoming: New and Collected Poems* (1996) and *The Woman I Kept to Myself* (2004), a collection of seventy-five autobiographical poems that chronicle such major events in her life as love, marriage, divorce, and religion. Alvarez's most recent fiction volumes include *In the Name of Salomé* (2000), *Saving the World: A Novel* (2006), and *Afterlife: A Novel* (2020). Alvarez's awards include the Benjamin T. Marshall Prize in Poetry (1968 and 1969), the American Academy of Poetry Prize, 1974), the National Book Critics' Award, the Fitzgerald Award for Achievement in American Literature (2009), and various others.

Gloria Anzaldúa (1942–2004)

Born on September 26, 1942, on the Jesús María ranch settlement near Edinburg in South Texas, Gloria Evangelina Anzaldúa became a leading figure in Latina feminist and lesbian literature. A member of the seventh generation of her family in Texas, Anzaldúa grew up doing agricultural field work on large farms and ranches. Despite her family's discouragement, Anzaldúa developed a love of reading and learning. She nevertheless continued supporting herself as a farm worker until she graduated from Pan American University with a B.A. in English in 1969. In 1972, she received an M.A. in English and education from the University of Texas at Austin, after which she worked as a teacher, often for migrant children. During the late 1970s and early 1980s, Anzaldúa began teaching at colleges in Texas and California and studying for awhile in the Ph.D. programs at the University of Texas and the University of California at Santa Cruz, where she concentrated on feminist theory and cultural studies; she was never able to complete these doctoral programs. She nevertheless made her way as a poet, essayist, and intellectual, and taught courses at the University of California, Santa Cruz from 1982 to 1986. Many other university positions were in her future, subsequent to her pioneering publications and public presentations. In 1981, Anzaldúa teamed up with Cherríe Moraga in compiling the highly influential anthology *This Bridge Called My Back*, which is a landmark in announcing a multicultural feminism and aesthetic. Anzaldúa's own first and highly influential book, *Borderlands/La Frontera: The New Mestiza* (1987), blends literary genres and the English and Spanish languages as well as memoir and feminist analysis. One of the most salient achievements of the book was using the border as a metaphor for gay and lesbian sexuality as well as for Chicano and other Latino culture in the United States. Anzaldúa also published *Making Face, Making Soul/Haciendo Caras: Creative and Critical Perpsectives by Feminists of Color* (1990), which won the Lambda Literary Best Small Press Award; it is a compilation of essays engaging diverse topics from sexisim and racism to spirituality. In 2000, Anzaldúa compiled a memoir-like collection of interviews, *Interviews/Entrevistas*, and, in 2002, collaborated with AnaLouise Keating in compiling the anthology *This Bridge We Call Home: Radical Visions of Transformation*, a collection of essays, poetry, and artwork directed at promoting societal acceptance of marginalized populations. Anzaldúa was the recipient of the 1991 Lesbian Rights Award, the 1992 Sappho Award of Distinction, and the American Studies Lifetime Achievement Award.

Reinaldo Arenas (1943–1990)

Cuban novelist, poet, and memoirist Reinaldo Arenas is most known as a severely persecuted writer under the Fidel Castro regime, who became an exile in the United States. He was diagnosed with AIDS in 1987 and died of suicide three years later. Born in rural Oriente Province, Arenas was raised in poverty by his mother and a succession of other women; he nevertheless became a poet in childhood and, at age nineteen, won a scholarship to the University of Havana. While there, he published his first novel, *Celestino antes del alba* (1967, *Singing from the Well*, 1987). When his award-winning biography of Friar Servando Teresa de Mier was refused publication by government authorities, Arenas began sending his works

abroad to avoid state-sponsored censorship. After the publication of two books in Mexico, his international reputation began to increase, and in 1969, critics in France named him the best foreign novelist. Arenas was continuously persecuted by Cuban authorities for his homosexuality and his literary work. In 1970, Arenas was sent to a sugar plantation for forced labor; while there he wrote a poem about the sugar mill, and the poem was smuggled out of the country to be published in Spain. His next novel, *Otra vez el mar* (Again the Sea), went through two editions (1969, 1971) in Cuba, which were taken out of circulation by authorities. It was eventually republished in 1982 and translated to English as *Farewell to the Sea* in 1986. From 1974 to 1976, Arenas was imprisoned on moral charges; he was not allowed to leave prison until confessing to having conducted counterrevolutionary activities and swearing to write only "optimistic" novels. In 1980, Arenas went into exile in the United States, eventually ending up in New York, where he was able to publish his work freely. Arenas's writing was supported in 1982 with a Guggenheim Fellowship and in 1987 with a Woodrow Wilson Fellowship. In 1993, Arenas published *Asalto* (*Assault*), a passionate attack on Fidel Castro and postrevolutionary Cuba. Arenas's best-known work, probably because it was made into an award-winning movie in 2000, was his posthumously published autobiography, *Antes que anochezca* (1993, *Before Night Falls*, 1994), which documented his trials in Cuba and his continued unhappiness in United States exile. The book also announced his imminent suicide. Another posthumously published book, *Hallucinations: or, The Ill-Fated Peregrinations of Fray Servando* (2001), published first in Mexico as *El mundo halucinante*, features an unforgettable literary creation in Fray Servando, a priest, blasphemer, dueler of monsters, lover, and prophet whose adventures take place in eighteenth-century Europe and the Americas. An activist leader in Cuban exile literary circles, Arenas was a member of the editorial board of *Linden Lane* literary magazine and founded, in 1983, the magazine *Mariel*.

Jorge Argueta (1960–)

Jorge Argueta is a poet in exile from El Salvador, award-winning children's author, and advocate of Latino literacy and reading. He was born in El Salvador on November 26, 1960. In 1980, after Argueta became somewhat involved in the Salvadoran resistance movement and went into exile, he eventually settled in San Francisco, California, where he soon met and associated with Latino writers. There, he began reading his poetry at workshops, cafés, and public events, and his poems began appearing in local newspapers and magazines. After publishing some chapbooks, including *Del Ocaso a la alborada/From Sundown to Dawn* and *La puerta del diablo/The Devil's Gate* and his first complete collection of poems, *Corazón del barrio* (1994, Heart of the Barrio), he became a member of writers-in-the-schools programs and began writing children's stories, some based on the immigrant experience and others on the lore and culture passed on to him as a child by his Nahua grandmother. The Indigenous way of life has since become a major theme in his children's writing. Argueta published his first bilingual children's book, *Una película en mi almohada/A Movie in My Pillow*, in 2001; this first experiment won the America's Book Award for Latin American Literature, the IPPY Award for Multicultural Fiction–Juvenile/Young Adults, and the Skipping Stones Honor Award for Multicultural and International Books. This recognition encouraged him to hone his writing for children and dedicate himself wholeheartedly to the genre. In 2003, Argueta published three more titles: *Los árboles están colgando del cielo/Trees Are Hanging from the Sky*, *El Zipitio/Zipitio*, and *Xochitl la niña de las flores/Xochitl and the Flowers*. Argueta's *Xochitl and the Flowers/Xochitl, la niña de las flores* was an Américas Award Commended Title and a 2004 Independent Publishers Award Finalist. In 2005, the book inspired by his daughter Luna, *Looney Luna/Luna, Lunita Lunera*, was awarded the Nappa Gold Award. Argueta's other books include *La fiesta de las tortillas/The Fiesta of the Tortillas* (2005), *La Gallinita en la Ciudad/The Little Hen in the City* (2006), *Talking with Mother Earth/Hablando con Madre Tierra: Poems/Poemas* (2006) and *Alfredito regresa volando a su casa* (2007, *Alfredito Flies Home*). In 2017, he embarked on a major, Nahua-based cycle of children's books based on water, fire, earth, and air. The first in the series, *Agua Agüita/Water Little Water*, won the children's poetry award from the North American Academy of the Spanish Language. That was followed with *Fuego Fueguito/Fire Little Fire* in 2019, and so on. In 2017

Argueta published his autobiography in poetry, *En carne propia: Memoria Poética/Flesh Wounds: A Poetic Memoir.*

Rudolfo Anaya (1937–2020)

Rudolfo A. Anaya was born on October 30, 1937, in the village of Pastura, New Mexico, in surroundings similar to those celebrated in his famous novel about growing up in the rural culture of New Mexico: *Bless Me, Ultima*. He attended public schools in Santa Rosa and Albuquerque and earned both his B.A. (1963) and his M.A. (1968) degrees in English from the University of New Mexico. In 1972, he also earned an M.A. degree in guidance and counseling from the same university. From 1963 to 1970, he taught in the public schools, but in 1974 he became a member of the English department of the University of New Mexico. With the success of his writing career, Anaya rose to become the head of the creative writing program at the University of New Mexico. Included among his many awards are an honorary doctorate from the University of Albuquerque, the New Mexico Governor's Award for Excellence, the President's National Salute to American Poets and Writers in 1980, and the Premio Quinto Sol in 1972 for his novel *Bless Me, Ultima*. Anaya was also a fellow of the National Endowment for the Arts and the Kellogg Foundation, through whose auspices he was able to travel to China and other countries for study. Anaya was very much a believer and promoter of a return to pre-Columbian literature and thought through the reflowering of Aztec civilization in Aztlán, the mythic homeland of the Aztecs, which corresponds to the five states of today's Southwest. He saw his role in literature as that of the shaman; his task as a storyteller was to heal and reestablish balance and harmony. These ideas are present throughout his works but are most successfully represented in his prize-winning novel *Bless Me, Ultima*, in which the folk healer Ultima works to reestablish harmony and social order in the life of the Mares family and to bring psychological well-being to Antonio, the protagonist, who is struggling to understand the roles of good and evil in life. Anaya's other books include *Heart of Aztlán* (1976), *Tortuga* (1979), *The Silence of the Llano* (1982), *The Legend of La Llorona* (1984), *The Adventures of Juan Chicaspatas* (1985), *A*

Chicano in China (1986), *Lord of the Dawn: The Legend of Quetzalcoatl* (1987), *Alburquerque* (1992), *Jalamanta: A Message from the Desert* (1996), *Serafina's Stories* (2004), *The Man Who Could Fly and Other Stories* (2006), *Randy Lopez Goes Home: A Novel* (2011), *The Old Man's Love Story* (2013), and *The Sorrows of Young Alfonso* (2016). In addition to this prolific output, Anaya authored the Sonny Baca detective series: *Zia Summer* (1995), *Rio Grande Fall* (1996), *Shaman Winter* (1999), and *Jemez Spring* (2005).

Arturo Arias (1950–)

Born in Guatemala City in 1950, Arturo Arias is director of Latin American Studies at the University of Redlands. Cowriter for the screenplay for *El Norte* (1984), he is the author of six novels in Spanish—*Después de las bombas* (1979; *After the Bombs*, 1990), *Itzam Na* (1981), *Jaguar en Llamas* (1989, Jaguar on Fire), *Los caminos de Paxil* (1991, The Roads of Paxil), *Cascabel* (1998, *Rattlesnake*, 2003) and *Sopa de caracol* (2002, Snail Soup)—and winner of the Casa de las Americas Prize twice and the Anna Seghers Prize. *Itzam Na*, named after a Mayan deity and the winner of the Américas Award, deals with a group of young rebels in Guatemala who struggle to launch an effective movement against the bourgeoisie and their nation's conservative and corrupt government. In such works as *After the Bombs*, Arias explores revolutionary history and culture in Central America, in this case through the tale of an ex-revolutionary who invites friends to a dinner where, through the technique of magic realism, he will be the main course. In *Rattlesnake*, Arias changed direction and explored a more popular genre, the thriller; here he spins the tale of a CIA intrigue in Guatemala, kidnappings by guerrillas, and romance. Working in another medium, Arias coscripted the film *El Norte* (1986, The North), which was nominated for an Academy Award. In 2008, Arias was awarded Guatemala's most prestigious prize, the Miguel Angel Asturias National Award for Lifetime Achievement in Literature.

Ron Arias (1941–)

Born on November 30, 1941, in Los Angeles, California, Ron Arias was raised principally by his maternal grandmother because his parents were constantly on the move due to his father's military career. After becoming interested in journalism in high school, Arias furthered his study of that field at universities in the United States, Argentina, and Spain. He earned his B.A. in journalism from the University of California, Berkeley in 1967, and in 1968, he earned his master's degree in journalism from the University of California, Los Angeles. Sent to Argentina with an Inter-American Press Association scholarship, Arias began publishing important series of articles in the *Buenos Aires Herald* and the *Caracas Daily Journal*. After a stint in Peru with the Peace Corps, in 1967 Arias returned to California to continue his education and write for several newspapers. Throughout the 1970s, Arias published short stories in magazines throughout the United States and emerged as an important Chicano author. In 1975, he published his magic realist novel *The Road to Tamazunchale*, which was nominated for a National Book Award. During the 1980s and 1990s, Arias concentrated on his journalism, serving as senior editor of *People* magazine, and on nonfiction writing; in 1989, he authored a nonfiction documentary, *Five against the Sea*, about a group of castaways. In 2002, he published *Moving Target*, an autobiography that begins with a detailed history of his parents and follows his development as a writer. In 2016 a collection of his previously published and new short stories, *The Wetback and Other Stories*, was published and was accorded the Peace Corps Award.

Jimmy Santiago Baca (1952–)

Jimmy Santiago Baca is one of the most successful Chicano poets to come out of the oral tradition, tempered by prison experiences and the Chicano Movement; in this and other aspects, his background is similar to that of Ricardo Sánchez. Baca was born in Santa Fe, New Mexico, on January 5, 1952, to Mexican and Apache-Yaqui parents who abandoned him to be raised by his Indian grandparents; he was later raised in an orphanage. In 1973, Baca was sentenced to five years in prison for narcotics possession. In a maximum security prison in Arizona,

Baca taught himself to read and write, and he passed his G.E.D. exam. In prison, Baca discovered poetry and began penning his first compositions. While he was still serving time, his book *Immigrants in Our Own Land* was accepted for publication by the prestigious Louisiana State University Press, which issued the book in 1979, the same year Baca was released from prison. Baca's poems were highly polished but naturalistic, and met with immediate critical approval; the accolades from mainstream critics expanded with his next books: *Swords of Darkness* (1981), *What's Happening* (1982), *Poems Taken from My Yard* (1986), *Martin and Meditations on the South Valley* (1987), and *Black Mesa Poems* (1989). During this publishing flurry, Baca was able to earn a B.A. in English from the University of New Mexico. In 1992, Baca also published a book of autobiographical essays, *Working in the Dark: Reflections of a Poet in the Barrio,* and in 1993 wrote a screenplay for a film, *Blood In Blood Out,* which was released by Disney's Hollywood Pictures. In his award-winning memoir, *A Place to Stand: The Making of a Poet* (2001), Baca traces his life from rural upbringing to incarceration for dealing drugs and his learning to read and write in prison, which led to his transformation and salvation through pursuing the written word. Baca continued to produce volumes of well-received poetry, including *Healing Earthquakes: A Love Story in Poems* (2001) and *Winter Poems along the Rio Grande* (2004). Baca began publishing short stories in the new millennium; his efforts include *C-Train and Thirteen Mexicans: Dream Boy's Story* (2002), gritty, realist tales of a brutal world of addiction, crime, and injustice, and *The Importance of a Piece of Paper* (2004), which populates the southwestern landscape with drug dealers, convicts, and other unsavory characters while also offering the hope of redemption. Both books illustrate how far the American Dream is from the Mexican American underclass. His most recent book, *American Orphan* (2020), is a highly autobiographical novel that passionately indicts the prison and child welfare system that he knew firsthand. For *Black Mesa Poems,* Baca became the first Latino poet to win the important Wallace Stevens Poetry Award. He is also the winner of the Pushcart Prize, the Before Columbus American Book Award, a National Endowment for the Arts Fellowship, the Southwest Book Award, the Vogelstein Foundation Award, and other honors.

Josefina Báez (1960–)

Josefina Báez is a leading poet, playwright, and prose writer who was born in La Romana, Dominican Republic, and immigrated with her family to New York in 1972. In New York Báez attended the Latino Playwright Lab at the Public Theater in New York City, where she developed various minor dramatic works, including *It's a New York Thang; You Will Understand,* for a staged reading. She went on to write and see a number of plays produced, including her best-known, *Lo mío es mío* (What's Mine Is Mine 1994), a story about Dominican migration to the United States. In 1986, Báez founded and directed the AY Ombe Theater in New York City. Báez has found an audience for her poetry, as well, which has been published in *Forward Motion* (1996), *Brújula/Compass* (1998), *Caribbean Connections: Moving North* (1998), and *Caribbean Connections: The Dominican Republic* (2005), among other venues. In 2000, she published *Dominicanish,* a poetry collection that can also be performed orally and dramatically; it brings together her admiration for African American literature and her wide and diverse travels, including to India. Other books of poetry for performance by Báez include *Comrade, Bliss Ain't Playing* (2013) and *Ay Ombe Dramaturgia* (2014). In 2015, her works were collected in *As Is É: Textos reunidos de Josefina Báez.*

Ruth Behar (1956–)

Born in Havana to a Polish Jewish mother and a Sephardic father from Turkey, Jewish Cuban American anthropologist and writer Ruth Behar moved to New York with her family in 1962. Her higher education consisted of a B.A. in letters from Wesleyan University (1977) and an M.A. and a Ph.D. in cultural anthropology form Princeton (1980 and 1983, respectively). Behar went from publishing anthropological studies, such as her *The Presence of the Past in a Spanish Village: Santa María del Monte* (1986) and *Translated Woman: Crossing the Border with Esperanza's Story* (1993), to publishing literary works, such as her bilingual collections of poetry, *Poemas que vuelven a Cuba/Poems Returned to Cuba* (1995)

and *Everything I Kept/Todo lo que guardé* (2001)—works that reveal a sense of loss and the longing for her place of birth. While much of her anthropological work develops autobiographical themes and concerns, her more literary memoir, conversely, delves into memoir, as in *Bridges to Cuba/Puentes a Cuba*, which combines personal essays, poetry, short fiction and painting, interviews, performance pieces, and images to nationalism, transnationalism, and homeland. *An Island Called Home: Returning to Jewish Cuba* (2007) narrates her journey back to Cuba in search of the new Jewish community that has developed since Castro's takeover. Her most recent, *Letters from Cuba* (2020), narrates her family's history as refugees from Poland to Cuba and eventually to the United States. Behar is the recipient of the following fellowships: MacArthur (1988), John Simon Guggenheim (1995), and a Fulbright (2007).

Mario Bencastro (1949–)

Born in Ahuacapán, El Salvador, Bencastro has become the leading novelist of Salvadoran immigration to the United States. Initially trained as a painter, Bencastro gave up his brushes and canvas when they were incapable of recording and expressing the tragedy of civil wars in his country. He began writing stories about the wars and immigrated to the United States in 1978, the same year he experienced the highest success of a painter in El Salvador: the National Exposition Hall presented twenty-five of his paintings. From 1979 on, Bencastro has concentrated on writing to reflect the social and political life of his communities, both in El Salvador and in the United States. In 1989, his first novel, *Disparo en la catedral* (Shot in the Cathedral), was a finalist in the Novedades-Diana International Literary Prize and was published in the original Spanish in Mexico. His short fiction collection, *Arbol de la vida: historias de la guerra civil* (Tree of Life: Stories from the Civil War), was published in Spanish in El Salvador in 1993, followed by some of the stories being transformed into plays and staged and others being chosen for various anthologies. Both books were translated to English and published in the United States, in 1996 and 1997, respectively. His best-known novel, *Odisea del Norte* (Odyssey to the North, 2000), published in 1999 and in English in the following year, is a classical novel of immigration, following economic

and political refugees from their homes in Central America and Mexico into poorly paying and hazardous jobs in the Washington, D.C., area. In 2005, Bencastro developed a young adult book based on his engaging Salvadoran youngsters in high schools in Los Angeles and Houston. In their name he produced *Viaje a la tierra del abuelo* (2004, *A Promise to Keep*, 2005), a novel that focuses on the challenges faced by Salvadoran youths in high school and the relationship they have with their parents' country. Recently, in the face of the tragedies attending to child migration from Central America, Bencastro has turned to children's literature and published *Un tren llamado Esperanza/A Train Called Hope* (2021).

Antonio Benítez-Rojo (1931–2005)

Born in Havana on March 14, 1931, novelist, essayist, and literary critic Antonio Benítez-Rojo received most of his schooling in Havana, with a stint at the American University in Washington, D.C., to study labor economics, and, after the Cuban Revolution, ascended to important administrative positions in the cultural bureaucracy of Cuba. In 1967, he was awarded the Casa de las Américas international prize for his short story collection *Tute de reyes* (1967, All Kings [from a card game]). His second collection followed soon thereafter, *El escudo de hojas secas* (1969, The Shield of Dried Leaves), and his literary career was on a solid path. After his wife left Cuba to obtain medical care for their daughter, and since Benítez-Rojo was not an openly declared supporter of Fidel Castro, he was denied publication after *El escudo* for some seven years. Apparently coming back in to the good graces of the Castro administration, he was able to resume publishing after ten years: the short story collection *Heroica* (1976, Heroic), the short novel *Los inquilinos* (1976, The Tenants), the story collection *Fruta verde* (1978, Green Fruit), the historical novel *El mar de las lentejas* (1979, Sea of Lentils), and the adventure novel *El enigma de los Esterlines* (1980, The Engima of the Sterlings). Of these, *Sea of Lentils* is his most famous, including four separate plots encompassing Spain, the Canary Islands, Florida, and Hispaniola. In 1980, he was successful in leaving Cuba via the Mariel boatlift and since then has worked as a professor in various universities, eventually achieving an endowed chair at Amherst College in Massachusetts. Among his books of creative literature are *Tierra y cielo* (1978, Land and Sky), *Estatuas sepultadas y otros relatos* (1984, Buried Statues and Other Stories), *Piratas y galeones* (1985, Pirates and Galleons), *Antología personal Antonio Benítez Rojo* (1997, Personal Anthology), *El paso de los vientos* (1999, The Passing of the Winds), and *Mujer en traje de batalla* (2005, Woman in Battle Uniform). Benítez-Rojo is also the editor of the widely hailed *The Repeating Island: The Caribbean and the Postmodern Perspective* (1989), a collection of essays that bring new understanding to the writers and culture of the Caribbean islands.

Diane Gonzales Bertrand (1956–)

Diane Gonzales Bertrand is one of the most prolific authors of Hispanic children's and young adult literature, producing books for three age groups: children learning to read, middle readers, and young adults. Born on March 12, 1956, in San Antonio, Texas, Bertrand began writing at an early age as a means of establishing her identity. Bertrand earned a bachelor's degree in English from the University of Texas at San Antonio (1978) and her master's in English in 1992. During graduate school, Diane wrote and published three novels with Avalon Books. The main characters were Mexican Americans, something new in popular romantic fiction. Her novels include *Sweet Fifteen* (1995), *Alicia's Treasures* (1996), *Lessons of the Game* (1998), *Trino's Choice* (1999), *Trino's Time* (2001), *Close to the Heart* (2002), and *There's a Name for This Feeling/Hay un nombre para lo que siento* (2013). Her children's picture books include *Sip Slurp Soup Soup* (1997), *Family, Familia* (1999), *The Last Doll* (2000), *Uncle Chente's Picnic/El Picnic de Tío Chente* (2001), *The Empanadas That Abuela Baked* (2003; winner of the 2004 Latino Literary Award), *My Pal, Victor/Mi Amigo, Victor* (2004; winner of the Schneider Family Picture Book Award), *We Are Cousins/Somos Primos* (2007), *Sofia and the Purple Dress/Sofía y el vestido morado* (2012), and *Cecilia and Miguel Are Bestfriends/Cecilia y Miguel son mejores amigos* (2015). Gonzales Bertrand has also produced books for middle readers, including *Alicia's Treasures* (1996), *Upside Down and Backwards/De cabeza y al revés* (2004, which received Special Mention of the Patterson Prize for Young People), *The Ruiz Street Kids/Los Muchachos de la Calle Ruiz* (2006), and *The Taco Magician and Other Poems for Kids/El mago de los tacos y otros poemas para niños* (2019). Bertrand creates characters and plots grounded in Latino barrio life and culture, presented in a positive light that empowers readers to believe in their ability to control life forces and achieve their goals in a multicultural society.

Lydia Cabrera (1899–1991)

Short story writer and folklorist Lydia Cabrera was born on May 20, 1899, in Havana, Cuba. Cabrera was home-schooled because of illness, eventually earned a college degree, and became one of Cuba's preeminent scholars of Afro-Cuban folklore and religion. She immigrated to the United States in 1960 after the Cuban Revolution triumphed. Throughout her career both in Cuba and in Miami, where she resided since 1960, Cabrera collected, studied, and published Afro-Cuban legends and tales. She also studied and documented Náñigo secret societies and other manifestations of African religious and Catholic syncretism. Most of Cabrera's fiction is also based on the Afro-Cuban folklore that surrounded her when she was growing up. In addition, her narrative style is direct and owes much to the modes of oral performance and delivery of Afro-Cuban folklore. In both Cuba and the United States, Cabrera's work has had an enriching impact on literature by introducing the themes and culture of a previously ignored and misunderstood base of Cuban and Caribbean literature and culture. Her first, most groundbreaking collection, *Cuentos negros de Cuba* (Black Tales from Cuba), was published in Havana in 1940, although it was written and already circulating as early as 1936. Among her most important fiction works are the following: *Ayapá: Cuentos de Jicotea* (Ayapá: Turtle Stories) in 1971, *Francisco y Francisca: Chascarrillos de negros viejos* (Francisco y Francisca: The Spicy Anecdotes of Old Black Folk) in 1976, *Cuentos para adultos, niños y retrasados mentales* (Stories for Grown-Ups, Children and the Mentally Retarded) in 1983, and *Cuentos negros de Cuba* in 1993.

Rafael Campo (1964–)

Born in Dover, New Jersey, to an Italian American mother and a Cuban father, Rafael Campo attained a prestigious and privileged education, not only earning the degree of medical doctor from Harvard Medical School (1992) but also serving as a Rhodes Scholar at Oxford University (1986). His career as a poet began as an undergraduate at Amherst College, where he created a collection of poems as a creative writing honors thesis while also majoring in neuroscience. From then on his career has been replete with writing awards, including a George Starbuck Writing Fellowship to Boston University (1990), the Agni Poetry Prize (1991), and the *Kenyon Review* Writer of the Year award (1992). Campo has published his poems and belles lettres in numerous magazines, including the *Paris Review*, the *Partisan Review*, and *Prairie Schooner*. His first collection of poems, *The Other Man Was Me: A Voyage to the New World* (1990), explored Latino ethnicity, gay identity, the responsibility of doctors in the age of AIDS, and the meaning of family. It won the National Poetry Series 1994 Open Competition. Campo's other poetry collections include *What the Body Told* (1996), a Lambda Literary Award winner; *Diva* (1999), which was a finalist for the National Book Critics Circle Award and the Paterson Poetry Prize; *Landscape with Human Figure* (2002), which won the Gold Medal from *ForeWord*; *The Healing Art: A Doctor's Black Bag of Poetry* (2003); and his latest work, *The Enemy* (2007). *The Enemy*, conceived in the aftermath of 9/11, takes on some of the most tendentious issues in American cultural life, including the "War on Terrorism," AIDS, feminism, gay marriage, and immigration. *The Poetry of Healing: A Doctor's Education in Empathy, Identity, and Desire* (1997) was also a Lamba Award winner. Among his nonfiction works is *The Healing Art: A Doctor's Black Bag of Poetry* (2003).

Viola Canales (1957–)

After starting school in McAllen, Texas, where she was born, Viola Canales learned English and became a model student, so much so that she went on to college at Harvard University, graduating in 1986, and the Harvard Law School, receiving her J.D. in 1989. Despite her successful career as a lawyer, practicing in a Los Angeles firm and serving in the Small Business Administration under President Bill Clinton, Canales decided to return to her early love of writing, which she had cultivated as a means of remembering

and retaining her life on the border when she was a scholarship student in an Episcopal boarding school in Austin, Texas. In 2001, she published her first collection of stories dealing with border lore and culture, *Orange Candy Slices and Other Secret Tales*. This was followed by her novel *The Tequila Worm* (2005), a highly autobiographic young adult narrative with a fictional protagonist who, like Canales, while away at a boarding school writes narratives about the folk culture, rituals, and traditions of her home town. The coming-of-age tale features a traditional storyteller, *curanderas* (healers), and other picturesque characters and practices of the informal and underground culture of poor people on the border. *The Tequila Worm* received the 2006 PEN "Best in the West" and the Pura Belpré awards. It was also an honorable mention for the Americas Award. In 2014 she published a collection of poems in English and Spanish inspired by the Mexican bingo game, *The Little Devil and the Rose: Lotería Poems/El diablito y la rosa: Poemas de la lotería*, and in 2021 an ingenious young adult novel exploring folk traditions, spiritualism, and the Day of the Dead, *Cecilia's Magical Mission*.

Norma Elia Cantú (1947–)

Born in Nuevo Laredo, Mexico, on January 3, 1947, Norma Cantú was raised in Laredo, Texas, where she was able to mediate the conflicts and synergies of life on both sides of the border. An early love of writing poetry in elementary school inspired Cantú to pursue a career in education as a teacher of literature; in 1973 she earned a B.S. in English and education, and in 1976 a master's degree in English from Texas A&M University–Kingsville. In 1980, she began teaching at Texas A&M International University in Laredo, and she earned a Ph.D. from the University of Nebraska in 1982. Cantú is known for writing personal essays, memoir, and poetry. By far, her most widely known and respected work is her memoir, *Canícula: Snapshots of a Childhood en la Frontera* (1995), where she elaborates on her personal experience from the 1940s to the 1960s of the environment, culture, and especially women's perspectives on life between two societies, countries, and cultures that the border represents. *Canícula* won the Premio Aztlán Literary Prize in 1996. In 2019 Cantú published her first collection of autobiographical poetry: *Meditación Fronteriza: Poems of Love, Life, and Labor.* That same year she published her latest novel *Cabañuelas: A Novel,* in which a young woman from Laredo goes to Spain to search for her roots. Cantú is a professor at San Antonio's Trinity College.

Ana Castillo (1953–)

Born in Chicago to working-class Mexican American parents, Ana Castillo made her way into print during the 1970s as a Chicana feminist poet, first in such magazines as *Revista Chicano-Riqueña* (Chicano-Puerto Rican Review) and later by self-publishing her own chapbooks, *Otro Canto* (1977, Another Song) and *The Invitation* (1979). In 1984, Castillo published her first full-length collection of poems, *Women Are Not Roses,* with Arte Público Press, which launched her soon-to-be extensive touring career. During the late 1980s and to the present, Castillo has developed into a respected fiction writer, publishing novels with the independent small press Bilingual Review Press, and later with W. W. Norton: *The Mixquihuala Letters* (1986), *So Far from God* (1993), *Sapogonia: An Anti-romance in 3/8 Meter* (1994), and *Peel My Love Like an Onion* (2000). In 1991 and 1995, respectively, Castillo published two feminist tracts, *Massacre of the Dreamers: Essays on Xicanisma* and *The Sexuality of Latinas* (with Cherríe Moraga and Norma Alarcón), which are often cited, along with her work on the Spanish version of *This Bridge Called My Back,* as standard texts on Chicana literary theory. Other works in various genres include *My Father Was a Toltec and Selected Poems* (poetry, 1995), *Ask the Impossible* (poetry, 2001), *Goddess of the Americas/La Diosa de las Américas* (essays, 1996), *Loverboys* (short stories, 1996), *My Daughter, My Son, the Eagle the Dove: An Aztec Chant* (2000), *Watercolor Women, Opaque Men: A Novel in Verse* (2005), *The Guardians* (2007), *Give It to Me* (2014), and *Black Dove, Mamé, M'hijo and Me* (2016).

Lorna Dee Cervantes (1954–)

Of Mexican and Amerindian ancestry, Lorna Dee Cervantes was born into a very economically deprived family, but she discovered the world of books at a very early age. Born on August 6, 1954, in the Mission District of San Francisco, at age five she moved with her mother and brother to San Jose to live with her grandmother when her parents separated. Cervantes began writing poetry when she was six years old; poems written when she was fourteen were eventually published in a magazine after Cervantes had established her career as a writer. Cervantes was very much involved in the Chicano literary movement of the 1970s, founded the *Mango* literary magazine to promote poets, and issued chapbooks under the same imprint. Cervantes later attended college but did not finish her B.A. degree from California State University until after she had initiated her writing career; in 1990 she obtained a Ph.D. degree from the University of California, Santa Cruz, where she studied philosophy and aesthetics. She then went on to teach creative writing at the University of Colorado in Denver. *Emplumada* (Plumed, 1981), Cervantes's first collection of poems, is made up of works published in literary magazines throughout the Southwest. The book's popularity has made it the best-selling title in the University of Pittsburgh's prestigious poetry series. *Emplumada* presents a young woman coming of age, discovering the gap that exists in life between one's hopes and desires and what life eventually offers in reality. The predominant themes include culture conflict, oppression of women and minorities, and alienation from one's roots. Cervantes's poetry is very well crafted and has the distinction of using highly lyrical language and being direct and powerful. The same can be said of her second book, *From the Cables of Genocide* (1991), which is very much the work of a mature poet dealing with the great themes of life, death, social conflict, and poverty. Her other books include the voluminous collection *DRIVE: The First Quartet* (2006), *Ciento: 100 100-Word Love Poems* (2011), and *Sueño: New Poems* (2013). Considered one of the greatest Chicano poets, Cervantes has won numerous awards, including the Patterson Prize for Poetry, the Battrick Award for Poetry, and the Pushcart Prize (twice).

Fray Angélico Chávez (1910–1996)

Fray Angélico Chávez was one of the most renowned religious poets in the United States. The author of some nineteen books, Chávez was also a historian of his order, the Franciscan brothers, and of the Catholic church in New Mexico. Born on April 10, 1910, in Wagon Mound, New Mexico, he was named Manuel Chávez by his parents. Chávez attended St. Francis Seminary in Cincinnati, Ohio, and colleges in the Midwest. In 1937, he became the first New Mexican to become a Franciscan friar. From the time of his ordination at age twenty-seven until age sixty-two, he served as a pastor in several towns and Indian pueblos of New Mexico. What unifies Chávez's large output as a poet and historian is his interest in New Mexico's past, the work of his order in New Mexico, and his own Catholicism. Beginning as essentially a religious poet, he later took an interest in historical fiction and, finally, in the history of the region itself, as in his most famous historical essay, *My Penitente Land: Reflections on Spanish New Mexico* (1974). His works of historical fiction include *New Mexico Triptych: Being Three Panels and Three Accounts: 1. The Angel's New Wing, 2. The Penitente Thief, 3. Hunchback Madonna* (1940), *La Conquistadora: The Autobiography of an Ancient Statue* (1954), *From an Altar Screen / El retablo: Tales from New Mexico* (1957), and *The Lady from Toledo* (1960). Chávez's reputation as a creative writer rests upon an important body of poetic works that include *Clothed with the Sun* (1939), *Eleven Lady Lyrics, and Other Poems* (1945), *The Single Rose; the Rose Unica and Commentary of Fray Manuel de Santa Clara* (1948), and *The Virgin of Port Lligat* (1959). Although Chávez's poetry and all of his works are grounded in New Mexico Catholicism, his poems are not local-color pieces celebrating New Mexico's picturesque landscape; instead, they depict Chávez's inner life. In *The Single Rose*, Chávez was so intent on communicating the poems' inner religious meaning that he included commentary in the book, which studies the rose as an allegorical figure for human and divine love. The last poetry collection

Chávez published while alive was *Selected Poems, with an Apologia* (1969), which brought together some of his most successful poems along with an apologia that announced that he would no longer publish poetry, due to changing fashions in poetry and his loss of excitement in writing verse. Other previously uncollected works were published in 2000: *Cantares: Canticles and Poems of Youth, 1925–1932*.

Denise Chávez (1948–)

Denise Chávez is a novelist, playwright, and poet who, through her writings, has brought to life entire populations of memorable characters of the Southwest, both Mexican American and Anglo-American. Born on August 15, 1948, in Las Cruces, New Mexico, Chávez was raised principally by her mother, Delfina, a teacher, because her father had abandoned the family while she was still young. After attending schools and colleges in Las Cruces, Chávez obtained a master's degree in theater arts from Trinity University in San Antonio, Texas, in 1974, and a master's degree in creative writing from the University of New Mexico in Albuquerque in 1984. As a playwright, Chávez has written and seen produced numerous unpublished plays, including *Plaza* (1984), *Novena Narrativa* (A Narrative Novena, 1986), *The Step* (1987), *Language of Vision* (1987), and *The Last of the Menu Girls* (1990). Despite Chávez's high productivity as a playwright, it is her published works of fiction that have contributed most to her national reputation, including *The Last of the Menu Girls* (1986), *Face of an Angel* (1993), *Loving Pedro Infante* (2002), and *The King and Queen of Comezón* (2014). Where all of these are straightforward narratives of the lives of humble female protagonists, her novel *Face of an Angel* is unrestrained, bawdy, irreverent, and hilariously funny as it explores some of the major themes of the women's liberation movement as represented in the life of a waitress, who is an author of a manual on waitressing. Soveida Dosamantes, it seems, is one of those people who are destined to repeat over and over the same mistakes in their choice of a male partner. The novel thus consists of her experiences with a number of lazy, good-for-nothing men who are irresistible to her. But *Face of an Angel* is also populated with a host of other humorous and tragic figures who represent a cross section of life in the Southwest.

Sandra Cisneros (1954–)

Mexican American poet Sandra Cisneros became the first Hispanic writer to win the prestigious MacArthur Award (1995). Cisneros is a short story writer, essayist, and poet who has brought Chicana writing into the mainstream of literary feminism. She is also the first Chicana writer to be published and promoted by mainstream commercial publishing houses. Born on December 20, 1954, in Chicago into a Mexican American working-class family, Cisneros nevertheless benefited from a private education, graduating with a B.A. in English from Loyola University (1976) and later with an M.F.A. in creative writing from the prestigious Iowa Workshop (1978). Cisneros's first novel, *The House on Mango Street* (1983), remains her most important contribution in that it captures the hopes, desires, and disillusionment of a young female writer growing up in the city. In *Mango Street*, Esperanza Cordero functions in a similar manner to the unidentified narrator in Tomás Rivera's classic … *y no se lo tragó la tierra*, observing the behavior and attitudes of the people who populate their environments. In Esperanza's urban Chicago world, children naively internalize the attitudes about gender and class of their adult Latino models; however, somehow the spirit of independence and creativity grows in Esperanza and leads her to escape the barrio in search of a house of her own—her own personality and identity, presumably through literature. Cisneros published her first full-length collection of poems, *My Wicked Wicked Ways*, in 1987 with Third Woman Press and followed it up with *Loose Woman: Poems*. In 1991, Random House issued Cisneros's collection of essays and short stories, *Woman Hollering Creek and Other Stories*, which did not surpass the critical acclaim of *Mango Street*, which had assumed a secure place in college and high school curricula. In 2002, Cisneros published her long-awaited generational novel of Mexican immigration and accommodation in the United States: *Caramelo*. Using a woven Mexican shawl as a trope, Cisneros weaves the intricate tale of the various members of the Reyes family and their generational journey from Mexico City to the United States. Among her other published books are *Vintage Cisneros* (2004), *Have You Seen Marie?* (2012), *A House of My Own* (2015), *Puro Amor* (2018), and *Martita, I Remember You/Martita, te recuerdo* (2021). Cisneros's works are among the most anthologized of any Latino writer. In 2015 she was awarded the National Medal of Arts and in 2019 the PEN/Nabokov Award for Achievement in International Literature.

Uva Clavijo (1944–)

Uva A. Clavijo (also known as Uva de Aragón) was born in Havana, Cuba, in 1944. Having left Cuba with her refugee parents, she resided in Washington, D.C., from 1959 to 1978. Clavijo received a Ph.D. in Spanish from the University of Miami. She published her first article in the *Diario de las Américas* (the Americas Daily) at the age of seventeen and continued to work as a journalist for exile newspapers. She also published poetry and essays widely in the Cuban exile press and books in Spanish in the United States and abroad, including *Eternidad* (1972, Eternity), *Ni verdad ni mentira y otros cuentos* (1976, Not Truth nor Fiction and Other Stories), *No puedo más y otros cuentos* (1989, I Can't Anymore and Other Stories), and *Memoria del silencio* (2002, Memory of Silence). Her poetry books include *Entresemáforos* (1980, Between Stoplights) and *Los nombres del amor* (1996, The Names of Love), among others. Her books of essays include *El caimán ante el espejo: Un ensayo de interpretación de lo cubano* (1993, The Gator in the Mirror: An Essay Interpreting Cubanness) and *Alfonso Hernández Catá: Un escritor cubano, salmantino y universal* (1996, Alfonso Hernández Catá: A Cuban, Salamancan and Universal Writer). Clavijo also teaches and is the adjunct director of the Cuban Research Institute at Florida International University. Among the many awards Clavijo has won are the Premio de Poesía de Federico García Lorca, the Premio Simón Bolívar essay prize, the Alfonso Hernández-Catá short story prize, and the Sergio Carbó journalism award. Recently, Clavijo has been writing mystery and detective novels, including *The Miracle of Saint Lazarus: A Mystery Twenty Years in the Making* (2019) and *El crimen de Biltmore Way: Un caso de la detective María Duquesne* (2020, The Crime of Biltmore Way: A María Duquesne Case).

Judith Ortiz Cofer (1952–2016)

Judith Ortiz Cofer was born in Puerto Rico in 1952 into a family that was destined to move back and forth between Puerto Rico and Paterson, New Jersey, because her father was a Navy man. In 1968, after her father had retired from the Navy with a nervous breakdown, the family moved to Augusta, Georgia, where she attended high school and Augusta College. She met John Cofer at the college, and they were married. After graduation and the birth of her daughter, they moved to West Palm Beach, Florida, and she earned an M.A. degree at Florida Atlantic University. Her collections of poetry include four chapbooks—*Latin Women Pray* (1980), *Among the Ancestors* (1981), *The Native Dancer* (1981), and *Peregrina* (1986)—and three full-length books—*Reaching for the Mainland* (1987), *Terms of Survival* (1987), and *A Love Story Beginning in Spanish* (2005). Her well-crafted poetry reflects her struggle as a writer to create a history for herself out of the cultural ambiguity of a childhood spent traveling back and forth between the United States and Puerto Rico. Through her poetry she also explores from a feminist perspective her relationship with her father, mother, and grandmother, while also considering the different expectations for the males and females in Anglo-American and Latino cultures. In particular, her book of autobiographical essays, *Silent Dancing: A Remembrance of a Puerto Rican Childhood* (1990), pursues this question. Her novel *The Line of the Sun* (1989) is based on her family's gradual immigration to the United States and chronicles the years from the Great Depression to the 1960s. *The Latin Deli* (1993) is a collection of poetry, personal essays, and short fiction. *The Year of Our Revolution: New and Selected Stories and Poems* (1998) is a sequel to *Silent Partners*. In addition, like so many other writers in her cohort when they they began having children or grandchildren, Cofer wrote a number of young adult and children's books. Her young adult titles include and *An Island Like You: Stories of the Barrio* (1995), *The Meaning of Consuelo* (2003), *Call Me María* (2004), and *If I Could Fly* (2011). Her children's books are *A Bailar!/Let's Dance* (2011), *The Poet Upstairs* (2012), and *Animal Jamboree: Latino Folk Tales/La fiesta de los animales: leyendas* (2012). She won the 1990 PEN/Martha Albrand Special Citation in Nonfiction for *Silent Dancing: A Partial Remembrance of a Puerto Rican Childhood;* her essay "More Room" was awarded the Pushcart Prize (1990); her essay "Silent Dancing" was selected for *The Best American Essays 1991*; she was the first Latino to win the O. Henry Prize for the story "The Latin Deli" (1994); *An Island Like You: Stories of the Barrio* was named one of the best books of the year for young adults by the American Library Association (1995); and she was inducted into the Georgia Writers Hall of Fame (2010).

Jesús Colón (1901–1974)

Jesús Colón's writings are considered to be landmarks in the development of Puerto Rican literature in the continental United States because he is one of the first writers to become well known through his use of English, because of his identification with the working class, and because of his ideas on race. These three factors in the essays that he was already writing in the 1940s and 1950s make him a clear forerunner of the Nuyorican writers who began to appear two decades later. Colón was born into a working-class family in Cayey, Puerto Rico, in 1901. At age sixteen, he stowed away on a ship that landed in Brooklyn. In New York, he worked in a series of jobs that exposed him to the exploitation and abuse of lower-class and unskilled workers. Colón became involved in literary and journalistic endeavors while working as a laborer, trying to establish a newspaper and writing translations of English-language poetry. As he strived to develop his literary and journalistic career, he encountered racial prejudice, mainly because of his skin color, for Colón was of Afro–Puerto Rican heritage. Despite discrimination, Colón became active in community and political activities. He became a columnist for the *Daily Worker*, the publication of the national office of the Communist Party, as an outgrowth of these activities and his literary interests. Colón also founded and operated a publishing house, Latino Publishers (Editorial Hispánica), which published history and literary books, as well as political information in Spanish. In 1952 and 1969, he ran for public office on the Communist Party ticket but was unsuccessful. A selection of Colón's newspaper columns and essays was collected and published in 1961 in book form under the title *A Puerto Rican in New York and Other Sketches.*

In this work, Colón's major themes are (1) the creation and development of a political consciousness, (2) his own literary development and worth, (3) advocacy for the working-class poor, and (4) the injustices of capitalist society in which racial and class discrimination is all too frequent and individual worth does not seem to exist. The collection as a whole is richly expressive of a socially conscious and humanistic point of view. His many newspaper columns and essays were compiled and published by Arte Público Press's Recovering the U.S. Hispanic Literary Heritage program in two volumes: *Lo que el pueblo me dice: Crónicas de la colonia puertorriqueña en Nueva York*, edited and with an introduction by Edwin Karli Padilla Aponte (2001) and *The Way It Was, and Other Writings: Historical Vignettes about the New York Puerto Rican Community*, edited with an introductory essay by Edna Acosta-Belén and Virginia Sánchez Korrol (1993).

Lucha Corpi (1945–)

Born in the small tropical village of Jáltipan, Veracruz, Mexico, in 1945, Lucha Corpi married young and moved with her husband to Berkeley, California, when he began his studies at the University of California. At the time of their emotional divorce in 1970, Corpi too was a student at the university and was heavily involved in the Free Speech Movement and the Chicano Civil Rights Movement. She eventually earned both a B.A. and an M.A. in comparative literature and in 1977 became a tenured teacher in the Oakland Public Schools Neighborhood Centers Programs, where she specialized in adult education. She is also a founding member of the cultural center, Aztlan Cultural, which later merged with a center for writers, Centro Chicano de Escritores.

During the 1970s, Corpi began publishing Spanish poetry in small magazines; it is a poetry that is luxuriant, sensual, and reminiscent of her tropical upbringing. In 1976, a group of her poems, along with those of two other poets, was issued in book form in *Fireflight: Three Latin American Poets*. By 1980 Corpi's collected poems were published in her first book, *Palabras de mediodía/Noon Words*, along with their translations by Catherine Rodríguez-Nieto. In 1990, Corpi published a third collection, *Variaciones sobre una tem-*pestad/*Variations on a Storm*, again with translations of her poems by Rodríguez-Nieto.

In the early 1980s, Corpi made the transition to prose and to writing in English with the publication of various short stories in magazines. In 1984, she published her first novel, *Delia's Song*, based on her involvement in the Chicano Movement and campus politics at the University of California. *Delia's Song* is one of the very few novels that deal with that historical period, which is so important in the making of the modern Chicano.

It was not until 1992 that Corpi's writing career took another turn with her creation of an ongoing series of detective novels. In *Eulogy for a Brown Angel*, Corpi introduced the astute Chicana detective Gloria Damasco, who unravels the mysterious assassination of a young boy during the 1970 Chicano Moratorium against the Vietnam War. Described as a feminist detective novel, *Eulogy* is fast-paced, suspenseful, and packed with an assortment of interesting characters. The feminist protagonist Damasco is somewhat of a clairvoyant who is able to use more than reason and logic in solving a puzzling crime. *Eulogy* was awarded the PEN Oakland Josephine Miles award and the Multicultural Publishers Exchange Best Book of Fiction award. In 1995, the Damasco character returned in *Cactus Blood*, a mystery set against the background of the United Farm Workers Movement in California. Historic settings, California panoramas, and Hispanic culture give texture to this suspenseful search for a ritualistic assassin. In 1999, Corpi continued with the series in *Black Widow's Wardrobe*, a mystery inspired in the Mexican rituals of the Day of the Dead, which leads Gloria Damasco once again into the historical past and on a trip to Cuernavaca, Mexico, and Indigenous culture.

In *Crimson Moon* (2004) Corpi expanded her focus to include two detective associates of Damasco on the hunt for an FBI infiltrator of the Chicano Movement who may have committed a rape. Lucha Corpi's bilingual artistry has manifested itself differently from other writers who either use Spanish-English code switching or create two separate versions of their works (one in Spanish, the other in English). Throughout the body of her highly symbolic, intimate poetry and in her short fiction for children, Corpi uses the language of her early upbringing and education in Mexico: Spanish. Her prose fiction, on the other hand, is written in the language of her professional life and education in California: English. In 2014 Corpi published a memoir in the form of essays, *Confessions of a Book Burner: Personal Essays and Stories*.

Victor Hernández Cruz (1949–)

Victor Hernández Cruz is one of the Nuyorican poets most recognized and acclaimed by the mainstream. Born on February 6, 1949, in Aguas Buenas, Puerto Rico, he moved with his family to New York's Spanish Harlem at age five. Cruz attended Benjamin Franklin High School, where he began writing poetry. In the years following graduation, his poetry began to appear in *Evergreen Review*, *New York Review of Books*, *Ramparts*, *Down Here*, and small magazines. In 1973, Cruz left New York and took up residence in San Francisco, where he worked for the U.S. Postal Service. In 1989, he moved back to Puerto Rico, where he currently resides. Cruz's poetry books include *Papo Got His Gun* (1966), *Snaps* (1969), *Mainland* (1973), *Tropicalization* (1976), *By Lingual Wholes* (1982), *Rhythm, Content and Flavor* (1989), *Red Beans* (1991), *Panoramas* (2001), *Maraca: New and Selected Poems, 1966–2000* (2001), *The Mountain in the Sea: Poems* (2006), *In the Shadow of Al-Andalus* (2011), and *Beneath the Spanish* (2017). Classifying his poetry as Afro-Latin, Cruz has developed as a consummate bilingual poet and experimenter who consistently explores the relationship of music to poetry in a multiracial, multicultural context. Cruz has often been considered a jazz poet or an Afro-American poet. The April 1981 issue of *Life* magazine included Cruz among a handful of outstanding American poets.

Abelardo Delgado (1931–2004)

Abelardo "Lalo" Delgado was one of the most renowned and prolific Chicano poets, a pioneer of bilingualism in Latino poetry and a consummate oral performer of his works. Delgado was born in the small town of La Boquilla de Conchos in northern Mexico on November 27, 1931. At age twelve he and his mother immigrated to El Paso, Texas, where he lived in a poor Mexican barrio until 1969. He graduated from the University of Texas, El Paso, in 1962 and then began earning his living as a counselor for migrant workers and as a teacher in Texas and later in Colorado. During the late 1960s and throughout most of the 1970s, Delgado was also one of the most popular speakers and poetry readers in the Southwest, which translated into a life of frequent tours and engagements. This was the height of the Chicano movement, and Delgado was one of its most celebrated animators and poet laureates. Besides writing numerous poems, essays, and stories that were published in literary magazines and anthologies nationwide, Delgado was the author of some fourteen books and chapbooks; many of these were published through his own small printing operation known as Barrio Press. Delgado's first book, *Chicano: 25 Pieces of a Chicano Mind* (1969), is his best known, containing many of the poems that were performed personally in the heat of the protest movement and that subsequently received widespread distribution through small community newspapers and hand-to-hand circulation throughout the Southwest. Poems such as his "Stupid America" not only embodied the values of life in the barrio but also called for the types of social reform that became anthems for the Chicano movement. Other noteworthy titles include *It's Cold: 52 Cold-Thought Poems of Abelardo* (1974), *Here Lies Lalo: 25 Deaths of Abelardo* (1979), and his book of essays, *Letters to Louise* (1982), which ponder the feminist movement and gender roles and was awarded the Premio Quinto Sol, the national award for Chicano literature. In 2011, Arte Público Press published a posthumous volume, *Here Lies Lalo: The Collected Poems of Abelardo Delgado*. In all, Delgado was a remarkably agile bilingual poet, an outstanding satirist and humorist, an undaunted and militant protester and pacifist, and a warmhearted and loving narrator and chronicler of the life and tradition of his people.

Juan Delgado (1960–)

Born on February 28, 1960, in Guadalajara, Mexico, and raised in Colton, California, Juan Delgado did not become a naturalized citizen until 1989. He earned a B.A. in English from California State University in 1983 and an M.F.A. in creative writing from the University of California, Irvine in 1985. Delgado went on to make a life for himself as a professor and academic administrator, but his first love was poetry. He has distinguished himself by publishing his poems in magazines throughout the United States and authoring four important collections of poems: *Green Web* (1994), *El Campo* (1998, The Country), *All Too Familiar* (2002), and *Rush of Hands (Camino del Sol)* (2003). In addition to various fellowships and distinctions, Delgado was the first Chicano to have a manuscript win the Contemporary Poetry Series contest, resulting in *Green Web* being published by the University of Georgia Press. He was also awarded the Whittenberger Fellowship in 2000. Delgado is a poet of both the urban and the rural scene. His *El Campo* explores the lives of Mexican farm workers, their joys and sorrows, while *Rush of Hands* confronts such urban realities as gang violence, labor organizing, and illegal immigration. In 2013 he published *Vital Signs*, a book about his hometown of San Bernardino; it won the American Book Award, given by the Before Columbus Foundation.

and an American Library Association Notable Book. After dealing with fame and many false starts on two novels, in 2007 Díaz published his long-awaited novel, *The Brief Wondrous Life of Oscar Wao*, about a Dominican nerd growing up in a New Jersey barrio who wants to become a writer and win the love of a sweetheart but must overcome his family's curse. More than just the protagonist Oscar's story, the novel also narrates the lives of the members of his immediate family. *The Brief Wondrous Life of Oscar Wao* made the *New York Times* best seller list in September, was chosen one of the Best Books by *Publishers Weekly,* and won the Pulitzer Prize—these were just three distinctions out of many—thus fulfilling all of the high expectations of his early critics. A poll of literary critics in the United States named Díaz's *The Brief Wondrous Life of Oscar Wao* as "the best novel of the 21st century to date." In 2012 he published a sequel to this winning novel, *This Is How You Lose Her.* Currently, Díaz teaches creative writing at the Massachusetts Institute of Technology in Boston.

Junot Díaz (1968–)

Born on December 31, 1968, in the Dominican Republic, fiction writer Junot Díaz came to the United States with his parents when he was six. Raised in a low-income neighborhood in Parlin, New Jersey, by his house-cleaner mother and forklift driving father, Díaz himself became a mill worker after high school but soon decided to go on for a college education. He received a B.A. in English from Rutgers University and an M.F.A. in creative writing from Cornell University in 1995. At Cornell he began writing his breakthrough collection of stories, *Drown* (1996), which received wide national acclaim for its depiction of the grit and dreariness of urban life, very much experienced by him as a laborer before attending college; despite the presence of gang bangers, drug dealers, and immigrants, Díaz is able to convey a sense of piety and pride in survival. *Drown* was selected as a Barnes and Noble Discover Great New Writers Award

Roberto G. Fernández (1951–)

Born in Sagua la Grande, Cuba, on September 24, 1951, just eight years before the Cuban Revolution, Roberto Fernández went into exile with his family at age eleven. His family settled in southern Florida, not in the Cuban community of Miami but in areas where Anglo-American culture was dominant. This led to periods of adjustment to what seemed like a hostile environment to the young boy, an impression that accounts for some of the culture conflict that is narrated in his writings. The Fernández family nevertheless maintained close ties with the Miami community, and this too became subject matter for the writer. Fernández became interested in writing as an adolescent, and this interest led him to college and graduate school. In 1978, he completed a Ph.D. degree in linguistics at Florida State University; by that time he had already published two collections of stories, *Cuentos sin rumbo* (Directionless Tales, 1975) and *El jardín de la luna* (The Garden of the Moon, 1976). At this point he also began his career as an academic, teaching linguistics and Latino literature at Florida State University in Tallahassee. Roberto Fernández is the author of four open-formed novels that have created for him the reputation of being a satirist and humorist of the Miami Cuban community. In all four, he is also a master at capturing the nuances of Cuban dialect in Spanish and English: *La vida es un special* (Life Is on Special, 1982), *La montaña rusa* (The Roller Coaster, 1985), *Raining Backwards* (1988), and *Holy Radishes* (2001). All four are mosaics made up of monologues, dialogues, letters, phone conversations, speeches, and other types of oral performance that, in the composite, make up a continuing tale of the development of the exile community and its younger generations of increasingly acculturated Cuban Americans. Through the pages of these books, the author charts the goings-on at social clubs and coming-out parties, follows counterrevolutionary guerrilla movements in the Florida swamps and the emergence of a Cuban pope, plots a mystery novel, discusses a poetry and art contest, and gives many other episodic bits and pieces that create a broad and epic spectrum of a dynamic community caught between two cultures, two sets of values, two languages, and two political systems. After a long hiatus from writing novels, Fernández came back on the scene with novelistic writing in a completely different direction: *El Príncipe y la bella cubana: Los amores de don Alfonso de Borbón y Battenberg y doña Edelmira Sampedro y Robato* (The Prince and the Cuban Beauty: The Loves of Lord Alfonso de Borbón y Battenberg and Lady Edelmira Sampedro y Robato, 2014), an historical novel about the romantic relationship of a member of Spanish royalty with a Cuban aristocratic woman.

Rosario Ferré (1938–2016)

Born on September 28, 1938, in Ponce, Puerto Rico, into one of the leading families (her father was governor for four years), Rosario Ferré was one of the island's most successful novelists, one of the very few who was able to enjoy success through translations to English in major New York publishing houses. After graduating from Manhattanville College in New York with a major in English, she received a master's degree in Spanish and Latin American literature from the University of Puerto Rico in 1985 and a Ph.D. from the University of Maryland in 1987. Ferré began writing in 1970, when she edited the magazine *Zona de carga y descarga* (Loading and Unloading Zone), which

was instrumental in launching the careers of various young Puerto Rican writers. Ferré explored poetry, children's literature, and adult fiction, but it was as a novelist with a critical eye to the governance of Puerto Rico by an elite class that furthers its colonial status that she made her mark. Ferré was also considered one of the leaders of Puerto Rico's literary feminism, starting with the publication of her first book, *Papeles de Pandora* (1976, *The Youngest Doll*, 1991). In 1976 she received the Ateneo Puertorriqueño (Puerto Rican Atheneum) and the Casa de las Américas (House of the Americas) awards for her short stories. In 1982 she published a book of feminist essays, *Sitio a Eros* (A Siege in Eros), and in 1984 she published her first book of poems, *Fábulas de la garza desangrada* (Fables of a Bled Heron). In 1994, both *La batalla de las vírgenes* (The Battle of the Virgins), a novella, and a selected collection of her poems, *Antología Personal* (Personal Anthology), were published. In 1997, her story collection *Maldito amor* (1998, published in English as *Sweet Diamond Dust and Other Stories* in 1996), in which she indicts the United States for the island's colonial condition, employs a feminist analysis. In 1998, her novel *Eccentric Neighborhoods*, which takes the form of a fictitious memoir of a young woman trying to come to terms with the death of her mother, was published and translated to a half dozen foreign languages. Most of Ferré's books have been published in English, in some cases before their Spanish originals are available. Her most highly acclaimed novel, *A House on the Lagoon* (1996), was a National Book Award Finalist; it narrates the history of a family full of secrets, conflicts, and mysteries that relate to the history of Puerto Rico itself. In 1992, Ferré received the Liberatur Prix in Frankfurt, Germany, for her novel *Kristalzucker*, a translation of *Sweet Diamond Dust* into German, published in Switzerland. Her final novel is *Flight of the Swan*, the story of a world-famous Russian prima ballerina who finds herself stranded on a Caribbean island in 1917 due to political upheavals in her own country.

Víctor Fernández Fragoso (1944–1982)

Born and raised in San Juan, Puerto Rico, Víctor Fernández Fragoso came to the United States in 1965 as a student. He received a Ph.D. from the University of Connecticut and became a staff member of the

Puerto Rican Traveling Theater in New York City. During his life in Connecticut, New York, and New Jersey (where he worked as an associate professor in the Spanish Department at Rutgers University), he wrote plays based on the works of Puerto Rican Julia de Burgos, Dominican Pedro Mir, and Chilean Pablo Neruda. He published poetry in a number of magazines both in the States and on the Island, most notably in *Zona de carga y descaraga* (Loading and Unloading Zone) and in *Claridad* (Clarity), the Communist newspaper. He founded a literary group in New York, La Nueva Sangre (the New Blood), that not only held readings but also published a magazine intermittently as well as chapbooks. Among the members were Dolores Prida and Roger Cabán. Of the numerous poems he wrote and half dozen manuscripts he completed, Fragoso only published two books: *El reino de la espiga: Canto al coraje de Walt y Federico* (1973, The Kingdom of the Wheat Stalk: A Song to the Ire of Walt and Federico) and *Ser islas/Being Islands* (1976). The invocation of Walt Whitman and Federico García Lorca in his first volume is a homage not only to their poetic art but also to their homosexuality. The poet was completely bilingual, and this second volume reflected that. In both books, Fragoso deals openly with his homosexuality and takes both cultural and political stands on the issue. In the latter of the two books, he compares the lack of freedom of Puerto Rico to the oppression of gays and lesbians. All of his work, however, is grounded in the personal and avoids the merely rhetorical. Fragoso died of AIDS in 1982, and Rutgers University named a scholarship in his honor. Fragoso left a number of complete manuscripts unpublished at his death.

Cristina García (1958–)

Cristina García is the first Cuban American woman to experience mainstream success as a novelist in the United States, through the publication of her first novel, *Dreaming in Cuban*. Her journalistic background and her interest in politics led her into the world of writing and the examination of her Cuban American circumstances, which have been shaped by the political history of the United States and Cuba. García was born in Havana, Cuba, on July 4, 1958, and was brought to the United States when her parents went into exile after the triumph of the Cuban Revolution. García graduated from Barnard College with a degree in political science in 1979 and from the Johns Hopkins University with a master's degree in Latin American Studies in 1981. She landed a coveted job as a reporter and researcher with *Time Magazine*, where she was able to hone her writing skills. She quickly ascended to bureau chief and correspondent at *Time* but left the magazine in 1990 to pursue her career as a creative writer. Her highly acclaimed *Dreaming in Cuban* was the first novel by a woman to give insight into the psychology of the generation of Cubans born or raised in the United States and living between two cultures. *Dreaming in Cuban* chronicles three generations of women in the Pino family, and in so doing compares the lives of those who live in Cuba with those living in the United States. *Dreaming in Cuban* was awarded the National Book Award in 1992. García's second novel, *The Agüero Sisters* (1997), is a novel of family history and myth, which contrasts the lives of two sisters, one in Cuba and the other in the United States. In García's following novel, *Monkey Hunting* (2003), she once again explores the search for identity, this time centering on a Chinese-Cuban family. In her novel *A Handbook to Luck* (2007), García explores alienation among three young immigrants from diverse backgrounds—Cuban, Salvadoran, and Iranian—who struggle with alienation and a sense of homelessness. Her other novels include *The Lady Matador's Hotel: A Novel* (2010), *King of Cuba: A Novel* (2013), and *Here in Berlin* (2017). García served as chair of creative writing at Texas State University in San Marcos in 2012–14.

Lionel G. García (1935–)

Lionel G. García is a novelist who has created some of the most memorable characters in Chicano literature in a style that is well steeped in the traditions of Texas tall tale and Mexican American folk narrative. Born on August 20, 1935, in San Diego, Texas, García grew up in an environment in which Mexican Americans were the majority population in his small town and on the ranches where he worked and played. After graduating with a degree in biology from Texas A&M University in 1935, he attempted to become a full-time writer but was unsuccessful in getting his works published. He served in the Army, and after being discharged honorably, he returned to Texas A&M and graduated from that institution in 1969 as a doctor of veterinary science. He subsequently developed a successful career as a veterinarian but continued to write. In the early 1980s, he once again attempted to publish, and he found that there were many more opportunities at hand. In 1983, he won the PEN Southwest Discovery Award for his novel in progress, *Leaving Home*, which was published in 1985. This and his second novel, *A Shroud in the Family* (1987), drew heavily on his family experiences and small-town background. In part, *A Shroud in the Family* also demythologized the "great" Texas heroes, such as Sam Houston and Jim Bowie, who are symbols of Anglo-Texans' defeat of and superiority over Mexicans; this was García's contribution to the Texas sesquicentennial celebrations. His novel *Hardscrub* (1989) is a departure from his former works; it is a realistically drawn chronicle of the life of an Anglo child in an abusive family relationship. García has also published short stories in magazines, newspapers, and anthologies. Among his other works are the novel *To a Widow with Children* (1994), the story collection *I Can Hear the Cowbells Ring* (1994), *The Day They Took My Uncle, and Other Stories* (2001), and his collection of poetry, *Brush Country* (2004).

Carolina García-Aguilera (1949–)

Mystery novelist Carolina García-Aguilera was born in Cuba on July 13, 1949, and immigrated to the United States with her refugee parents in 1960. She received a B.A. in history from Rollins College in 1971 and an M.B.A. in finance from the University of South Florida in 1983. After graduating, she took a radical departure and became a private investigator in Miami. After operating her own agency for ten years, she quit to dedicate herself to writing mystery novels. In addition to using her detective know-how, García-Aguilera draws heavily from her family's experiences as political refugees. Not really a "gumshoe" (for she only wears designer shoes), her protagonist, Cuban American detective Lupe Solano, is at once a Cuban American Princess, known to Miami culture as a "CAP," and intensely feminist, sexually liberated, obsessively independent, and dressed to the nines. She strives for these values even while trying to be a good Catholic and loyal to her family. In the first of the Lupe Solano series, *Bloody Waters* (1996), a Cuban couple employs Solano to find a bone marrow match for their dying daughter. The next installments include *Bloody Shame* (1997), an intimate tale involving the death of Lupe's best friend and a love triangle; *Bloody Secrets* (1998), which deals with political intrigue and a rereading of Cuban history; *A Miracle in Paradise* (1999), a mystery surrounding a weeping statue of the Virgin of Charity, Cuba's patron saint; *Havana Heat* (2000), in which Solana is on the trail of a valuable, historic tapestry believed to have been given to Queen Isabella La Católica; and *Bitter Sugar* (2001), which reveals the world of Cuban sugar culture and its intersection with the Communist regime in Cuba and expatriates in Miami. *One Hot Summer* (2002) is a departure from the mystery series in that it explores a conundrum of mothers who have to decide on whether to return to work or stay at home after having a child. *Luck of the Draw* (2004) is also a departure from the series and features a Cuban American woman, Esmeralda Navarro, in search of her missing sister in Las Vegas; the plot is tied to her family's past ownership of a casino in Havana and their attempts to somehow recover it.

Alicia Gaspar de Alba (1958–)

Born on July 29, 1958, and raised in El Paso, Texas, Alicia Gaspar de Alba is the quintessential bilingual/bicultural writer, penning poetry, essays, and narrative with equal facility in English and Spanish. Gaspar de Alba earned bachelor's (1980) and master's degrees (1983) in English from the University of Texas at El Paso and a Ph.D. in American studies from the University of New Mexico (1994). Gaspar de Alba is the author of a short story collection, *The Mystery of Survival* (1993), which won the Premio Aztlán, and the highly acclaimed historical novel *Sor Juana's Second Dream* (1999), which has been translated to Spanish and to German. Gaspar de Alba's major fiction project bore fruition in 2006: *Desert Blood: The Juárez Murders*. After years working with activist groups protesting the assassination and disfigurement of working women in Juárez, Mexico, Gaspar de Alba set about researching the causes of the more than four hundred mysterious murders and border authorities' reactions to them, including corrupt investigations and indifference. Her meticulous details of the atrocities form the background for a gripping mystery novel in which the protagonist, a lesbian graduate student, desperately follows the trail of the abductions and murders in an attempt to save her suddenly missing little sister from a similar end. *Desert Blood* was awarded the Lamba Literary Award and chosen for the Latino Literary Hall of Fame. Her other fiction narratives include *Calligraphy of the Witch* (2007), which extends her Southwest vision into Salem, Massachusetts, and *The Curse of the Gypsy: Ten Stories and a Novella* (2018), which is a collection of interrelated stories of generations of a family that extends from Spain to Mexico to Los Angeles and a novella set in Medieval Spain that deals with a bearded saint and her eight twins. Gaspar de Alba is also a renowned poet and essayist whose works have been published widely in magazines and anthologies. In 1989, her poetry was featured in an anthology of the works of three poets, *Three Times a Woman: Chicana Poetry,* and in 2003, she published her selected poems and essays in *La Llorona on the Longfellow Bridge: Poetry y Otras Movidas, 1985–2001.* Her incisive and controversial book-length essay, *Chicano Art Inside/Outside the Master's House: Cultural Politics and the CARA Exhibition,* was published in 1998. In all of her work, Gaspar de Alba is one of the most eloquent exponents of a lesbian aesthetic and a promoter of the empowerment of women.

Dagoberto Gilb (1950–)

Born in Los Angeles to a Mexican mother and an Irish American father, Dagoberto Gilb earned a B.A. (1973) and an M.A. (1976) from the University of California, Santa Barbara. Until becoming an established writer, Gilb worked as a carpenter, which has lent his fiction writing a common-man perspective. It was not until the mid-1980s that Gilb's stories began to garner the attention of critics and academics for their fine craft and down-to-earth attitude. After publishing noteworthy short story collections in the 1990s, Gilb began taking visiting professorships in creative writing departments at universities and in 1997 became a tenured associate professor

at Southwest Texas State University in San Marcos, Texas; today he has a similar position at the University of Houston, Victoria, Texas. Gilb's short story collections include *Winners on the Pass Line* (1985), *The Magic of Blood* (1993), and *Woodcuts of Women* (2001). In 2004, he published a volume of essays, *Gritos* (Shouts), which often explore what it was like growing up as a mixed-race child in Los Angeles, as well as other themes of Mexican American life. In 1994, Gilb published his first novel, *The Last Known Residence of Mickey Acuña.* In 2007, he departed somewhat from the previous completely serious tone of his stories and novel to publish *The Flowers* (2008), a novel focusing on a wide variety of characters living in and around the Flores Apartment and satirizing and poking fun at an array of racial prejudices held by them. In 2011 he published *Before the End, After the Beginning.* Some of these books have been translated to French, German, Italian, and Japanese, as well as reprinted in the United Kingdom and Australia. Since 2011, Gilb has concentrated on publishing stories and essays in mainstream magazines, such as *Harper's.* Gilb's awards include the Ernest Hemingway Foundation/PEN Award (1994), a Guggenheim Fellowship (1995), a National Endowment for the Arts Fellowship (1992), and a PEN Southwest Award (2008).

Isaac Goldemberg (1945–)

Born on November 15, 1945, in Chepén, Peru, to a Russian Jewish father and a Peruvian mother, Isaac Goldemberg was until the age of eight raised by his Catholic mother. However, in 1953 he went to live with his father, attended a Jewish school, and became immersed in the Jewish metropolitan culture of Lima. At age seventeen, he went to Israel and lived in a kibbutz for almost two years. After marrying an American citizen and having a child, Goldemberg immigrated to the United States in 1964 and developed into a leading voice of Hispanic immigrant writers as well as Hispanic Jewish literature. He has been able to develop his literary career while earning a living as a Distinguished Professor of Humanities at Hostos Community College of the City University of New York. He has also served as director of the Latin American Writers Institute and editor of the *Hostos Review,* an international journal of culture. Faced with the challenges of multiple identities, Goldemberg's characters search for an ever-elusive spiritual, if not physical home, in such novels as *The Fragmented Life of Don Jacobo Lerner* (1976, translated by Robert S. Picciotto in 1999), *Tiempo al tiempo; o, La conversión* (1983, Time for Time, or The Conversion), and *En el nombre del padre/The Name of the Father* (2002), as well as in his poetry collections: *Tiempo de silencio* (1970, Time of Silence), *De Chepén a La Habana* (1973, From Chepén to Havana), *Hombre de paso/Just Passing Through* (1981, translated by David Unger), *La vida al contado* (1991, Life Paid in Full), *Cuerpo del amor* (2000, Body of Love), *Las cuentas y los inventarios* (2000, The Accounts and the Inventory), *Peruvian Blues* (2001), *Los autorretratos y las máscaras* (2002, Self-Portraits and Masks), *El amor y los sueños* (2003, Love and Dreams), *Crónicas del exilio* (2003, Chronicles of Exile), and *Los Cementerios Reales* (2004, The Royal Cemeteries). Books of various genres include *Diálogos conmigo y mis otros* (2013, Dialogs with Myself and Others), *Acuérdate del escorpión* (2016, Remember the Scorpion, 2015), and *Libro de reclamaciones* (2018, Book of Complaints). He has also published two plays: *Hotel AmeriKaKa* (2000, AmeriCaCa Hotel) and *Golpe de gracia: farsa en un acto* (2003, Coup de Gras: A Farce in One Act). *The Fragmented Life of Don Jacobo Lerner* was chosen by the National Yiddish Book Center of the United States as one of the best 100 Jewish works of the last 150 years.

Francisco Goldman (1954–)

Son of a Guatemalan mother and an American Jewish father, Francisco Goldman was born in Boston in 1954. He grew up in Needham, Massachusetts, and Guatemala City, but English is clearly his first and preferred language. Goldman has been able to enter elite establishment worlds where few Latinos have been accepted, such as the pages of the *New York Review of Books*, *Harper's*, and the *Sunday New York Times Magazine*, with his elegant prose style and knowledge of Latin America. A 1997 graduate of the University of Michigan, Goldman has made a living by writing award-winning novels, placing essays and journalistic pieces in magazines, and teaching creative writing at Trinity College in Hartford, Connecticut. His first novel, *The Long Night of White Chickens* (1992), won the American Academy of Arts and Letters' Sue Kaufman Prize for First Fiction and was a finalist for the PEN/Faulkner Award. As a detective novel, it follows American Roger Graetz to Guatemala City in his effort to solve the mystery of the murder of his former housekeeper; on another level, the novel is a love story and a tale about a boy growing up in two cultures. His second, *The Ordinary Seaman* (1997), was a finalist for the PEN/Faulkner Award and the *Los Angeles Times* Book Prize; based on a true story, it is the tale of fifteen Central American men who make their way to New York to work on a rusting old ship in dry dock. His third, *The Divine Husband* (2004), is a historical novel that follows José Martí from New York to Central America and explores his romantic relationship with a nun amidst political intrigue and turbulence. Goldman's first nonfiction work is *The Art of Political Murder: Who Killed the Bishop?* (2007), based on the assassination of human rights leader Bishop Juan Gerardi in Guatemala. The extensively researched book reveals the U.S. role in the Central American civil wars and the legacy of violence and corruption. His other books include *Say Her Name* (2011), *The Interior Circuit: A Mexico City Chronicle* (2014), and *Monkey Boy* (2021). His novels have been published in ten languages.

Celedonio González (1923–2006)

Celedonio González has been known as *el cronista de la diáspora* (the chronicler of the Cuban diaspora or flight from Cuba). Of all of the Cuban exile novelists, he is the one who turned his attention most to the trials, tribulations, and successes of the Cuban refugees and their children in the United States. Born on September 9, 1923, in La Esperanza, Cuba, González worked in his family's farming enterprises, which he eventually came to manage. He was a supporter of progressive causes and of Castro's revolution, but by 1960 he had become disillusioned with the revolution and was imprisoned for two months as a counterrevolutionary. Upon release, he immigrated to the United States with his wife and children. In Miami he eked out a living at a number of odd jobs. In 1965, he and his family resettled in Chicago in search of a better living. It was there that he began writing, but it was not until his return to Miami at age forty-one that he wrote his first successful novel, *Los primos* (The Cousins, 1971), a mirror of Cuban life in Miami during the 1960s. That same year, his short stories depicting the loneliness of Cuban exile life in the United States, *La soledad es una amiga que vendrá* (Solitude Is a Friend Who Will Come), were published in book form. His novel *Los cuatro embajadores* (The Four Ambassadors, 1973) criticizes American capitalism and the dehumanization in American life. His greatest work was *El espesor del pellejo de un gato ya cadáver* (The Thickness of Skin of a Dead Cat, 1978), a call for Cubans to give up their dreams of returning to the island of their birth and to make the best of life in the United States. González's short stories also deal with life in the United States from the vantage point, quite often, of the Cuban laboring classes and small-scale shopkeepers.

José Luis González (1926–1996)

Puerto Rico's greatest fiction writer, José Luis González was born in Santo Domingo, the Dominican Republic, to a Puerto Rican father and a Dominican mother. The family migrated to Puerto Rico when González was four; he was raised and educated on the island. Before graduating from the University of Puerto Rico in 1946, he had already published two collections of stories, the second of which, *Cinco cuentos de sangre* (1945, Five Bloody Tales), won the Instituto de Literatura Puertorriqueña Prize. After graduating, González moved to New York City and attended the graduate New School for Social Research; during this time he became involved in the Puerto Rican community and with writer Jesús Colón, who published one of González's books in his small press. In 1948, González returned to Puerto Rico and became politically active in the socialist and independence movements and published *El hombre en la calle* (The Man on the Street), which protested the oppression of the urban poor in Puerto Rico. In 1950, González published his famous novel *Paisa*, which was a poetic but realistic portrayal of Puerto Rican life in New York City. In 1953, González renounced his American cit-

izenship in protest of American colonialism and moved to Mexico, where he spent the rest of his life, writing and working with some of the leading figures in Latin American fiction. In 1972, González published his short novel *Mambrú se fue a la Guerra* (Mambrú Went to War), a remarkable piece of antiwar fiction. In 1978, he became the first Puerto Rican novelist and short story writer to win Mexico's most prestigious literary award, the Xavier Villaurrutia Prize for Fiction, for his novel *Balada de otro tiempo* (1978, Ballad of Another Time), which is set to the background of the U.S. invasion of Puerto Rico during the U.S. war with Spain. However, *Paisa* and the short story collection *En Nueva York y otras desgracias* (1973, In New York and Other Disgraces) remain his most famous works from the perspective of Hispanic immigration to the United States.

Rigoberto González (1970–)

Born on July 18, 1970, in Bakersfield, California, and raised in Michoacán, Mexico, Rigoberto González is a poet, novelist, and book critic. Raised to be a farm worker, he nevertheless obtained an education, earning a B.A. from the University of California at Riverside (1992), a master's from the University of California at Davis, and a master of fine arts from Arizona State University (1997). He is the author of three books of poetry, *So Often the Pitcher Goes to Water until It Breaks* (1999), a selection of the National Poetry Series, and two collections of stories: *Other Fugitives and Other Strangers* (2006) and *Men without Bliss: Stories* (2008). The recipient of a Guggenheim Memorial Foundation Fellowship and writing residencies to Spain and Brazil, he has also written two bilingual children's books: *Soledad Sigh-Sighs* (2003) and *Antonio's Card/La tarjeta de Antonio* (2005), which was a finalist for the Lambda Literary Award. His novel *Crossing Vines* (2003), which deals with farm worker life and the struggle to unionize, was winner of *Fore-Word Magazine*'s Fiction Book of the Year. In 2006, he published a memoir of growing up gay in a family of farm workers, *Butterfly Boy: Memories of a Chicano Mari-*

posa. His other memoirs and nonfiction books include *Red-Inked Retablos: Essays* (2013), *Autobiography of My Hungers* (2013), *Pivotal Voices, Era of Transition: Toward a 21st Century Poetics* (2017), and *What Drowns the Flowers in Your Mouth: A Memoir of Brotherhood* (2018). His collections of poetry include *Black Blossoms* (2011), *Unpeopled Eden* (2013), and *The Book of Ruin*. In 2008 he published his second collection of short stories, *Men without Bliss*. González is on the board of directors of *Poets & Writers Magazine* and the National Book Critics Circle Award. He has taught at Queens College of the City University of New York, the University of Illinois, and Rutgers University.

Rodolfo "Corky" Gonzales (1928–2005)

Rodolfo "Corky" Gonzales was born on June 18, 1928, in Denver, Colorado, to parents who were seasonal farm workers. Because of the instability of migrant work, Gonzales received both formal and informal education. Gonzales used boxing to get out of the barrio, becoming the third-ranked featherweight in the world. Eventually, he quit boxing and became a successful businessman, political leader, and director of poverty programs. In 1967 Gonzales authored the famous and influential epic poem "I Am Joaquín/Yo Soy Joaquín," which weaves myth, memory, and hope as a basis for a Chicano national identity. The poem was reprinted in Mexican American neighborhood newspapers across the Southwest, recited repeatedly at activist meetings, and made into a film produced by El Teatro Campesino and recited by Luis Valdez, which made it one of the most well-known pieces of Chicano literature during and after the Chicano Movement. It thus helped to reinforce the terms of Chicano nationalism in the Southwest. Gonzales has stated, "Nationalism exists … but until now, it hasn't been formed into an image people can see. Until now it has been a dream.… Nationalism is the key to our people liberating themselves. I am a revolutionary … because erecting life amid death is a revolutionary act.… We are an awakening people, an emerging nation, a new breed." During the Chicano Movement, Gonzales was a prolific poet as well as a playwright whose plays were produced at the Crusade for Justice and elsewhere. Such plays as *The Revolutionist* and *A Cross for Maclovio* (1966–67) were an early call to mili-

tancy and nationalism for Chicanos. Gonzales's political and inspirational speeches can also be considered in the body of Chicano literature. Many of his poems, speeches, and plays were collected and published in *Message to Aztlan: Selected Writings of Rodolfo "Corky" Gonzales* (2001).

Reyna Grande (1975–)

Born on September 7, 1975, in Iguala, Guerrero, Mexico, Reyna Grande came to the United States at age ten undocumented; she and her siblings waited eight years to be reunited with their parents, who were working in the country without papers. She learned English well enough to eventually earn a degree in creative writing from the University of California, Santa Cruz; she later obtained an M.F.A. in writing from Antioch College. Most of her fiction and nonfiction writing is based on her and her family's experiences immigrating to the United States. Her works include her first novel, *Across a Hundred Mountains* (2006), the novel *Dancing with Butterflies* (2009), and her memoir *The Distance between Us* (2012). In 2018 she published her memoir's sequel, *A Dream Called Home*. In 2016, *The Distance between Us* was adapted for a young adult audience, and along with her other books, it has been used in community, city, and school reading programs. Reyna Grande maintains a busy speaking and reading schedule, almost constantly on tour throughout the United States.

Juan Felipe Herrera (1948–)

Born on December 27, 1948, in Fowler, California, and despite the interruptions in his education that resulted from his parents' migrant work, Juan Felipe Herrera was able to graduate from high school in San Diego (1967) and later receive a B.A. in anthropology from the University of California at Los Angeles (1972). In 1990 he received his M.F.A. in creative writing from the University of Iowa and soon began a career as a professor of Chicano and Latin American studies at Fresno State University. Beginning in the late 1960s, Herrera wrote poetry and became one of the most experimental poets during the Chicano Movement, taking inspiration for his work from the pre-Columbian past and from other media, such as weaving tapestry, as in his first book *Rebozos of Love/We Have Woven/Sudor de Pueblos/On Our Back* (1974), and in photography, as in his poetry book *Exiles of Desire* (1983). Included among Herrera's other books are *Facegames* (1987), *Zenjosé: Scenarios* (1988), *Akrílica* (1989), *Night Train to Tuxla* (1994), *Border-Crosser with a Lamborghini Dream (Camino del Sol)* (1999), *Thunderweavers/Tejedoras de Rayos* (1999), *Giraffe on Fire* (1991), and *Notes of a Bilingual Chile Verde Smuggler* (2005). In 1997, Herrera crossed the boundaries of genres (poetry, narrative, drama), geography, chronology, and political borders to confront the situation of Mayas in history and the present as part of his own discovery of self in *Mayan Drifter: Chicano Poet in the Lowlands of America.*

Herrera has also produced a number of young adult fiction and poetry works, including *Coralito's Bay* (2004), *Featherless/Desplumado* (2004), and *Cinnamon Girl: Letters Found inside a Cereal Box* (2005), a pastiche of poetry and letters; and two novels in verse: *Crashboomlove* (2001) and *Downtown Boy* (2005). Recent books include *187 Reasons Mexicanos Can't Cross The Border: Undocuments 1971–2007* (2007), *Half the World in Light* (2008), *Notes on the Assemblage* (2015), and *Every Day We Get More Illegal* (2020). In this voluminous body of work, Herrera has moved from recovering and reinvigorating the pre-Columbian native past and political protest to an exploration of the urban life of Latinos to crossing borders of all kinds, from the linguistic and cultural to the geographic and psychological. Herrera was chosen as the poet laureate of the United States by President Barack Obama in 2015. Among Herrera's awards are two University of California–Irvine Chicano Literary Prizes (1979, 1985), an American Book Award (1987), the Tomás Rivera Mexican American Children's Book Award (2007), and the National Book Critics Circle Award in Poetry for *Half the World in Light* (2008). In 2011, Herrera was elected a chancellor of the Academy of American Poets.

Oscar Hijuelos (1951–2013)

Oscar Hijuelos was the first Latino writer to win the Pulitzer Prize for Fiction (1990). Born on August 24, 1951, to Cuban-American working-class parents in New York City, Hijuelos was educated in public schools and obtained a B.A. degree in 1975 and an M.A. degree in 1976, both in English, from City College of the City University of New York. When Hijuelos started publishing, he was one of the few Latino writers to have formally studied creative writing and to have broken into the Anglo-dominated creative writing circles, participating in prestigious workshops such as the Breadloaf Writers Conference and benefiting from highly competitive fellowships, such as the American Academy in Rome Fellowship (1985), the National Endowment for the Arts Fellowship (1985), and the Guggenheim Fellowship (1990). Hijuelos was the author of various short stories and novels: *Our House in the Last World* (1983); *The Mambo Kings Play Songs of Love* (1989), which won the Pulitzer Prize; *The Fourteen Sisters of Emilio Montez O'Brien* (1993); *Mr. Ives' Christmas* (1995); *Empress of the Splendid Season* (1999); *A Simple Habana Melody (from When the World Was Good)* (2002); *Dark Dude* (2008); and *Beautiful Maria of My Soul* (2010). He also published *Thoughts without Cigarettes: A Memoir* (2011). His first novel follows in the tradition of ethnic autobiography and the novel of immigration, as it chronicles the life and maladjustment of a Cuban immigrant family in the United States during the 1940s. *The Mambo Kings Play Songs of Love*, more than just a story of immigration, examines a period in time when Latino culture was highly visible in the United States and was able to influence American popular culture: the 1950s during the height of the mambo craze and the overwhelming success of Desi Arnaz's television show, *I Love Lucy*. Written in a poetic but almost documentary style, the novel follows two brothers who are musicians trying to ride the crest of the Latin music wave. While providing a picture of one segment of American life never seen before in English-language fiction, the novel also indicts, as does *Our House in the Last World*, womanizing and alcoholism as particularly Cuban flaws.

Rolando Hinojosa-Smith (1929–)

Rolando Hinojosa-Smith is the most prolific and bilingual of the Latino novelists of the United States.

Not only has he created memorable Mexican American and Anglo characters, but he has completely populated a fictional county in the lower Rio Grande Valley of Texas through his continuing generational narrative that he calls the Klail City Death Trip Series. Hinojosa was born in Mercedes, Texas, on January 21, 1929, to a Mexican American father and a bilingual Anglo mother; his paternal ancestors arrived in the lower Rio Grande Valley in 1749 as part of the José de Escandón expedition. Hinojosa was educated at first in Mexican schools in Mercedes and later in the segregated public schools of the area, where all his classmates were Mexican Americans. He only began integrated classes in junior high. It was in high school that Hinojosa began to write, with his first pieces in English published in an annual literary magazine, *Creative Bits*. Hinojosa left the valley in 1946 when he graduated from college, but the language, culture, and history of the area form the substance of all his novels. The ensuing years saw a stretch in the Army, studies at the University of Texas, reactivation into the Army to fight in the Korean War (an experience that informs his poetic narrative *Korean Love Songs*), graduation from the University of Texas in 1954 with a degree in Spanish, back to Brownsville as a teacher, a variety of other jobs, and finally on to graduate school. In 1969 he obtained his Ph.D. degree in Spanish from the University of Illinois and returned to teach at Texas colleges.

Although he wrote throughout his life, Hinojosa did not publish a book until his *Estampas del Valle y otras obras* (which he re-created in English and published as *The Valley* in 1983) was published in 1973. The book won the national award for Chicano literature, Premio Quinto Sol. From that time on he has become the most prolific Chicano novelist, publishing one novel after another in his generational narrative that centers around the lives of two of his alter egos, Rafe Buenrostro and Jehú Malacara, in individual installments that vary in form from poetry and dialogue to the picaresque novel and the detective novel. His titles in English alone include *Korean Love Songs* (1980), *Rites and Witnesses* (1982), *Dear Rafe* (1985), *Partners in Crime: A Rafe Buenrostro Mystery* (1985), *Claros varones de Belken/Fair Gentlemen of Belken County* (1986, bilingual edition), *Klail City* (1987), *Becky and Her Friends* (1989), *Ask a Policeman* (1998), *We Happy Few* (2006), and *A Voice of My Own: Essays and Stories* (2011). His original Spanish version

of *Klail City*, entitled *Klail City y sus alrededores* (1976), won an international award for fiction, Premio Casa de las Américas, from Cuba in 1976; it was issued there under this title, and a year later a version was published in the United States under the title *Generaciones y semblanzas*. The book was also published in German two years later. Hinojosa has also published short stories and essays widely, as well as installments of a satirical running commentary on life and current events in the United States, known as "The Mexican American Devil's Dictionary," supposedly created by another of his alter egos who is also one of the narrators of the Klail City Death Trip Series: P. Galindo (meaning "right on target" in Spanish). Hinojosa has been hailed as a master satirist, an acute observer of the human comedy, a Chicano William Faulkner for his creation of the history and people of Belken County, and a faithful recorder of the customs and dialects in Spanish and English of both Anglos and Mexicans in the lower Rio Grande Valley.

Angela de Hoyos (1940–2009)

Angela de Hoyos was born on January 23, 1945, into a middle-class family in Coahuila, Mexico. Her childhood education was informal. In the late 1960s, de Hoyos began publishing poetry and entering her work in international competitions, for which she won such awards as the Bronze Medal of Honor of the Centro Studi a Scambi Internazionale (CSSI), Rome, Italy, 1966; the Silver Medal of Honor (literature), CSSI, 1967; the Diploma di Benemerenza (literature), CSSI, 1968; and the Diploma di Benemerenza, CSSI, 1969 and 1970. During the 1970s, her interest in literature and her awareness of the lack of opportunity for Chicano writers led her to establish a small press, M&A Editions, in San Antonio, through which she issued not only her own work but also that of such writers as Evangelina Vigil-Piñón. During the 1980s, de Hoyos also founded a cultural periodical, *Huehuetitlan*. In addition to this intense literary life, de Hoyos developed a successful career as a painter. Her works, also inspired by Mexican American culture, are widely exhibited and collected in Texas. De Hoyos cultivated free-verse, terse, conversational poetry—which at times takes dialog form—that provides a context for cultural and feminist issues within a larger philosophical and literary framework. De Hoyos's poetry is socially engaged while at the same time humanistic in the best sense of the word. Her particular concerns were poverty, racism, and disenfranchisement, whether of her people, of children, or of women. Her particular mission was to give voice to those who cannot express themselves. De Hoyos was also a poet of humor and wit, creating piquant exchanges in verse between lovers and enemies, as is exemplified in her dialogues between Hernán Cortes and La Malinche. Her most important book, *Woman, Woman*, deals with the roles that society has dictated for women and their struggle to overcome the limits of those roles. De Hoyos surveyed history, from Aztec days to the present, and even cast an eye on the image of women in fairy tales, as in her poem "Fairy-Tale: Cuento de Hadas." Throughout *Woman, Woman*, de Hoyos sustains the dynamic tension that both unites and separates male and female. In her poetry, that tension is always erotically charged, always threatening to one or the other, always reverberating in the political. In *Woman, Woman*, de Hoyos also perfected her bilingual style, innovatively mixing the linguistic codes of English and Spanish to reach beyond the merely conversational to the more philosophical—the choice of language and lexicon is not just a sociolinguistic one, it is also a deeply cultural one. Angela de Hoyos's other books and chapbooks include *Selecciones* (1976, Selections), *Poems/Poemas* (1975), *Chicano Poems from the Barrio* (1975), *Arise Chicano: And Other Poems* (1975), and *Linking Roots* (1993). In 2015 *Selected Poems of Angela de Hoyos* was published posthumously from her archive at Arte Público Press/University of Houston.

Arturo Islas (1938–1991)

Born on May 24, 1938, in El Paso, Texas, novelist, poet, and essayist Arturo Islas grew up dealing with the conflict between his homosexuality and the familial and social environment. Early on he developed the discipline to survive and to become an outstanding student, which resulted in his attending Stanford University on a scholarship. In 1960, Islas graduated from Stanford as a Phi Beta Kappan and went on to earn a Ph.D. at Stanford in 1971 and become a member of the faculty. He was a pioneer in teaching Chicano literature and Chicano creative writing courses at that institution. Islas began writing in elementary school and by the time he reached college was already penning excellent stories and essays. Despite his excellent prose and academic credentials, Islas had difficulty placing his works with the New York commercial presses; thus his first book, *The Rain God: A Desert Tale* (1984), was issued by a small press in California. Nevertheless, *The Rain God* achieved outstanding reviews and went through twelve printings by the time his next novel, *Migrant Souls*, was ready; it was finally accepted and issued by a mainstream publisher in 1990, a year before his untimely death due to AIDS. In both his novels, Islas examines family relationships, border culture, and the omnipresence of death—Islas had faced death battling intestinal cancer for a number of years. Also embedded in these novels is a critique of patriarchy and traditional views of gender and homosexuality. The larger part of Islas's writings, including a large body of poems and stories, an unfinished novel, and essays, were left unpublished at his death but were published posthumously; the novel was issued under the title of *La Mollie and the King of Tears: A Novel* (1996) and the remaining works as *Arturo Islas: The Uncollected Works* (2002).

Maya Islas (1947–)

A poet of symbolism and metaphysics, Maya Islas was born on April 12, 1947, in Cabaiguán, Las Villas, Cuba, and came to the United States in 1965. She earned bachelor's and master's degrees in psychology from Fairleigh Dickinson University and Montclair State University in 1972 and 1978, respectively, and had a career as a counselor in institutions of higher education. She served as the coordinator of supportive services for the New School University in New York City. Her books of poetry include *Sola, Desnuda ... sin Nombre* (1974, Alone, Naked ... without a Name), *Sombras-Papel* (1978, Shadow-Paper), *Altazora acompañando a Vicente* (1989, Altazora Accompanying Vicente), *Merla* (1991), *Lifting the Tempest at Breakfast* (digital, 2001), *Altazora dos* (2013, Altazora Two), and *La divinidad que devora* (2016, Divinity that Devours). Her poetry has appeared in numerous anthologies and magazines. Her books have been finalists in the Premio Letras de Oro (1986–87, 1990, 1991) and awarded the Latino Literature Prize 1993. In 1978,

Islas won the Silver Carabel Poetry Award in Barcelona, Spain, where she has published three of her poetry books. Islas was awarded a Cintas Fellowship in 1991 to continue her writing. She has also served as the editor of the literary magazine *Palabra y Papel* (Word and Paper) during the 1980s. Islas's major themes deal with women archetypes, mythology, and the exploration of symbols; she poses existential questions and answers them metaphysically. She is also a talented graphic artist, who quite often juxtaposes plastic works with poetry or uses one form to inspire or comment on the other. Such is the case in her online book *Lifting the Tempest at Breakfast*, which is made up of thirty-five stream-of-consciousness poems and thirty-five collages.

Nicolás Kanellos (1945–)

Born on January 31, 1945, in New York City to working-class Puerto Rican and Greek parents, Nicolás Kanellos spent long spells in Puerto Rico as a child—so much that he forgot how to speak English twice and had to relearn it. While living in the industrial area of Jersey City as a child, he discovered discarded signatures (large uncut and unfolded printed sheets that are bound into books) in the trash of a local bindary and began to make his own books with them; little did he know that he would become a publisher as an adult and the most senior editor of Latino literature. Kanellos studied in the United States, Mexico, and Portugal; he received a B.A. in Spanish from Fairleigh Dickinson University (1966) and an M.A. (1968) and a Ph.D. (1974) from the University of Texas. In 1973, he founded *Revista Chicano-Riqueña* (Chicano Puerto Rican Review) with coeditor Luis Dávila. In 1979 Kanellos founded Arte Público Press (APP), which has become the nation's oldest and largest publisher of Latino literature. Over the years, APP has published the works of most of the leading Latino authors, from Alurista and Sandra Cisneros to Helena María Viramontes and Victor Villaseñor. In 1992 APP initiated its Recovering the U.S. Hispanic Literary Heritage program, which is a large, archival print and electronic publishing program of the hundreds of thousands of texts created by Latinos from the colonial period to the present. In 2019 APP was only the fourth press in history to receive the Ivan Sandroff

Lifetime Achievement Award of the National Book Critics' Circle. Kanellos is the Brown Foundation Professor of Hispanic Studies at the University of Houston. His awards include the PEN Southwest Book Award for *Hispanic Immigrant Literature: El Sueño del Retorno* (2011), the Enrique Anderson Imbert Prize of the North American Academy of the Spanish Language for Lifetime Achievement for contributing to the knowledge and dissemination of the Spanish language and Hispanic culture in the United States (2014), the Cross of the Order of Isabella the Catholic Queen presented by the king of Spain (2016).

José Kozer (1940–)

José Kozer was born in Havana, Cuba, to Jewish immigrant parents from Poland and Czechoslovakia. Kozer became a refugee of the Cuban Revolution in 1960 and settled in New York, where he received a B.A. from New York University in 1965. He is one of the most prolific Latino poets writing and publishing in Spanish. His work is very experimental, considered by critics to be "neo-baroque." Kozer claims to have written some six thousand poems; he has won many awards, and his work has been translated into various languages. Among his numerous books are *Padres y otras profesiones* (1972, Fathers and Other Professions), *Este judío de números y letras* (1975, This Jew of Numbers and Letters), *Y así tomaron posesión en las ciudades* (1978, And That's How They Took Possession in the Cities), *Jarrón de abreviaturas* (1980, A Pitcher of Abbreviations), *La rueca de los semblantes* (1980, The Loom of Appearances), *The Ark upon the Number* (1982), *Bajo este cien* (1983, Under These Hundred), *Nuevas láminas* (1984, New Laminations), *El carillón de los muertos* (1987, Carillon of Dead People), *Carece de causa* (1988, Missing a Cause), *Prójimos / Intimates* (1990), *De donde oscilan los seres en sus proporciones* (1990, Where Beings Oscillate in Their Proportions), *Trazas del lirondo* (1993, Clean Traces), *La maquinaria ilimitada* 1998, Unlimited Mechanisms), *Dípticos* (1998, Diptyches), *Farándula* (1999, Theater World), *Mezcla para dos tiempos* (1999, A Mix for Two Time Periods), *Anima* (2002,

Spirit), *No buscan reflejarse* (2002, They Do Not Look to Reflect Themselves), *Una huella destartalada* (2003, A Messy Footprint), *Y del esparto la invariabilidad: Antología, 1983–2004* (2005, And from Fiber a Lack of Variety: Anthology)*, Stet* (2006), *La garza sin sombras* (2006, The Heron without Shade), *De dónde son los poemas* (2007, From Whence Come the Poems), *Tokonoma* (2011), *Of Such Nature/Indole* (2018), and *Carece de Causa/No Known Cause* (2020). In 2013, Kozer won the most prestigious prize in poetry of the Hispanic world, the Pablo Neruda Prize.

John Lantigua (1947–)

Born in the Bronx, New York, to a Puerto Rican mother and a Cuban father, John Lantigua was rasied in Ridgewood, New Jersey. His career in journalism, which would eventually lead to a Pulitzer Prize, began in his early twenties at the *Hartford Courant* in Connecticut, but he left the United States shortly thereafter to travel in Mexico and ultimately stayed for five years. He returned to the United States to work in a series of low-level jobs, and then he returned to Latin America to resume work as a journalist; he covered the Contra War for United Press International and later for the *Washington Post*, while living in Honduras and Nicaragua. Lantigua began producing detective novels in 1990 and has continued with his main character, the Miami ex-cop and now P.I. Willie Cuesta in *Twister* (1992), *Player's Vendetta: A Little Havana Mystery* (1999), *The Lady from Buenos Aires* (2007), *On Hallowed Ground* (2011), and *Remember My Face* (2020). The modus behind the Willie Cuesta series is Lantigua basing the novels on the culture of the diverse Latin Americans making Miami their home and tracing the crimes and mysteries back to each homeland, such as refugees from the Cuban revolution, the "dirty war" in Argentina, the narcotics trade in Colombia, and migrant workers coming up from Mexico. *Heat Lightning* (1987), about the Salvadoran civil war, was nominated for the Edgar Prize by the Mystery Writers Association of America. It is not a part of the Willie Cuesta series. While writing these novels, Lantigua was employed by major newspapers. In addition to the Pulitzer, he is the recipient of the Robert F. Kennedy Journalism Award in 2004 and 2006, as well as the World Hunger Year Award in 2004.

Jesús Abraham "Tato" Laviera (1950–2013)

Born in Santurce, Puerto Rico, on September 5, 1950, Jesús Abraham "Tato" Laviera migrated to New York at age ten with his family, which settled in a poor area of the Lower East Side. After finding himself in an alien society and with practically no English, Laviera was able to adjust and eventually graduate from high school as an honor student. Despite having no other degrees, his intelligence, aggressiveness, and thorough knowledge of his community led to his developing a career in the administration of social service agencies. After the publication of his first book, *La Carreta Made a U-Turn* (1979), Laviera gave up administrative work to dedicate his time to writing. Beginning in 1980, his career included not only writing but touring nationally as a performer of his poetry, directing plays, and producing cultural events. In 1980, he was received by President Jimmy Carter at the White House gathering of American poets. In 1981, his second book, *Enclave*, was the recipient of the American Book Award of the Before Columbus Foundation. All of Laviera's books have been well received by critics, most of whom place him within the context of Afro-Caribbean poetry and U.S. Latino bilingualism. *La Carreta Made a U-Turn* is bilingual jazz or salsa poetry that presents the reader with a slice of life drawn from the Puerto Rican community of the Lower East Side. In *Enclave*, Laviera celebrates such cultural heroes, both real and imagined, as Alicia Alonso, Suni Paz, John Lennon, Miriam Makeba, the fictitious half–southern Black, half–Puerto Rican Tito Madera Smith, the barrio gossip Juana Bochisme, and the neighborhood tough Esquina Dude. *AmeRícan* (1986), published on the occasion of the centennial celebration of the Statue of Liberty, is a poetic reconsideration of immigrant life in New York City and the United States. *Mainstream Ethics* (1988) proposes transforming the United States from a Eurocentric culture to one that is ethnically and racially pluralistic in its official identity. *Mixturao and Other Poems* (2008) celebrates bilingualism-biculturalism as defining Latino identity while at times lamenting alienation from both Latin American countries and mainstream U.S. society. In 2014, Arte Público Press published his collected works posthumously: *Bendición: The Complete Poetry of Tato Laviera*. For Laviera, included in the oral tradition of his performances were the structures, spirit, and rhythms of popular and folk music, especially those drawn from Afro–Puerto Rican music. In 2018 a new theater in East Harlem was named in his honor.

Aurora Levins Morales (1954–)

Born in Maricao, Puerto Rico, on February 24, 1964, to a Puerto Rican mother and a Jewish American father, Aurora Levins Morales is an award-winning writer, essayist, and historian who writes and speaks about multicultural histories of resistance, feminism, uses of history, cultural activism, and the ways that racism, anti-Semitism, sexism, class, and other systems of oppression interlock. She was one of the writers included by Cherríe Moraga and Gloria E. Anzaldúa in the groundbreaking anthology *This Bridge Called My Back* (1981). Her diary-like *Getting Home Alive* (1986), alternating her own voice with that of her mother, is a collection of sketches, short stories, and poems that celebrate the lives of mothers, daughters, grandmothers, sisters, and other female relatives across continents and back through history. As a passionate, poetic evocation of a feminist world view, *Getting Home Alive* is her most famous work. Levins Morales's most recent works are *Medicine Stories: Writings on Cultural Activism* (1998) and *Remedios: Stories of Earth and Iron from the History of Puertorriqueñas* (1998). The first is a collection of essays on culture and politics; the latter, coauthored with her mother, is, like her first mother-daughter collaboration in *Getting Home Alive*, a dialogue in prose and poetry about identity, family, and the immigrant experience. A major theme in Levins Morales's work is her identity as a lesbian of biracial, bicultural, and bireligious heritage. In all of her works, language and reading are the keys to remembering and memory in order to integrate one's history and sense of identity and place in the world. Her other books include *Remedios: Stories of Earth and Iron from the History of Puertorriqueñas* (1998), *Kindling: Writings on the Body* (2013), *Cosecha and Other Stories* (with Rosario Morales; 2014), *Medicine Stories: Essays for Radicals* (2019), and *Silt: Prose Poems* (2019).

Graciela Limón (1938–)

Born on August 2, 1938, in Los Angeles to Mexican immigrant parents, Graciela Limón began writing prose fiction only after having achieved success in her career as a professor of Latin American history and culture. With an M.A. from the Universidad de las Américas in Mexico City (1969) and a Ph.D. from the University of California at Los Angeles (1975), Limón developed a long career at Los Angeles's Loyola Marymount University. Only in her forties did she begin to sketch out novels based on Mexico's pre-Columbian history. "I saw what the years had given me in experience and emotions, in the many people and places that had crossed my life. I realized that I had the material I needed to become what I had always wanted to be. A novelist." Her first critical acclaim was achieved with *In Search of Bernabé*, named a *New York Times* Notable Book for 1993 and a finalist for the *Los Angeles Times* Book Award. Inspired in her official visits to El Salvador during its civil war, *In Search* chronicles a desperate mother's search for her son after after being separated from him during the war; both eventually end up in Los Angeles. Her second novel, *The Memories of Ana Calderón* (1994), is a novel of immigration that follows the trials and tribulations of a young woman who rises from the working classes to business success but ultimately experiences disillusionment after battling the forces of family, church, and the justice system in the United States. One of her most popular novels, *The Song of the Hummingbird* (1996), deals with the pre-Columbian world at the time of the Spanish conquest; Limón successfully portrays this time of conflict and synthesis of cultures through the eyes of an Aztec woman who was captured and forced to deal with Christianity. Limón updated her chronicling of the conflict between Spanish and Indian cultures, as well as the evolution of racism, in her *The Day of the Moon*, which sets the conflict within a tale of forbidden love. After visiting Chiapas, Mexico, and researching the history of the Mayan conflict that erupted into the 1994 revolt of the Zapatistas, Limón again took on the conflict of Indigenous peoples with authorities in her *Erased Faces* (2001), which explores this conflict from the perspective of women and amorous relationships in conflict with ancestral patriarchal traditions. *Erased Faces* was named the 2002 winner of the Gustavus Myers Outstanding Book Award in recognition of the novel's success in extending our understanding of the root causes of bigotry and the range of options we as humans have in constructing alternative ways to share power. In *Left Alive* (2005), Limón takes on the difficult task of writing from within the mind of a mentally ill narrator and pondering the motives for why certain women become family annihilators. Limón continues to publish novels, including *The River Flows North* (2009), the historical novel *The Madness of Mamá Carlota* (2012), and *The Intriguing Life of Ximena Godoy* (2015).

Jaime Manrique (1949–)

Born in Colombia on June 16, 1949, Jaime Manrique moved to the United States as a teenager and has made a significant contribution to gay and lesbian Latino/a literature with his novels, criticism, and memoirs. His autobiographical novel *Latin Moon in Manhattan* (1992) depicts the life of a young Colombian boy, Santiago Martínez (a.k.a. Sammy), who comes to New York City with his mother. The novel discusses the problems Sammy faces after being transported from Bogotá to Times Square. These problems include drugs, violence, his adaptation to a new culture, his relationship with his family, and his sexuality. For Sammy there is a conflict between being gay and being Colombian. Manrique's second novel published in English in the United States, *Twilight at the Equator* (1997), is a transnational novel that takes places in Colombia, the United States, and Spain. The protagonist is Santiago Martínez, who deals with homophobia and fights against it. In *Eminent Maricones* (1999), Manrique takes on an extremely important project, tracing what could be called a genealogy of literary *maricones* (gays) in the United States—a historical tract that explores expressions of queer male sexuality in several Latin American or Spanish authors. Manrique recounts his own interactions with Cuban author Reinaldo Arenas and Argentinian author Manuel Puig, both of whom he met while they were living in New York. He also examines what he sees as the internalized homophobia and repressed yearnings of Federico García Lorca. His recent works include *El libro de los muertos, poemas selectos 1973–2015* (2016, The Book of the Dead, Select Poetry 1973–2015) and *Como esta tarde para siempre* (2018; *Like This Afternoon Forever,* 2019).

Patricia Preciado Martin (1939–)

Patricia Preciado Martin was born in the small mining town of Humboldt, Arizona, on July 6, 1939; she received her early education in Tucson, where because of her love of reading, she excelled as a student. Martin's early enjoyment of folklore and fairy tales, often narrated by her mother, led her to writing and to study literature at the University of Arizona. She began her own writing in the late 1970s and early 1980s. From then on she authored numerous stories for children and young adults, many of them based on the folklore she studied. Her first book, *The Legend of the Bellringer of San Agustín* (1980), came out of this effort; it recalls a quaint and somewhat idealized past in Mexican history and culture. In 1988, Martin published a well-received book of short stories, *Days of Plenty, Days of Want*, whose eight stories capture the flavor and deep culture of a Mexican barrio in Arizona. Two of Preciado's books are collections of oral interviews that she conducted in the Tucson barrio: *Images and Conversations: Mexican Americans Recall a Southwestern Past* (1983) and *Songs My Mother Sang to Me: An Oral History of Mexican American Women* (1992). The former is accompanied by artistic photographs of the interlocutors taken by Louis Carlos Bernal. Martin published two additional story collections, *El Milagro and Other Stories* (1996) and *Amor Eterno: Eleven Lessons in Love* (Eternal Love), which once again utilize personal experience narratives from the elderly as an inspiration for creative fiction. However, *Amor Eterno* is the most lyrical and intimate of Martin's books. In 1997, Martin was named Arizona Author of the Year. She was also the winner of the University of California–Irvine Award for Chicano/Latino Literature in 1989 for her short story "María de las Trenzas" (María of the Braids).

Demetria Martínez (1960–)

Activist, journalist, and creative writer Demetria Martínez was born on July 10, 1960, in Albuquerque,

New Mexico. She received a bachelor's degree in public policy from Princeton University in 1982 and began publishing her poems in 1987. The very next year, she was indicted for smuggling refugee women into the United States, and the government attempted to use one of her poems against her as evidence: "Nativity for Two Salvadoran Women." Martínez was acquitted, based on first amendment rights. In 1990, she became a columnist for the *National Catholic Reporter* in Kansas City but soon lost interest and returned to poetry and creative writing. Her plan soon came to fruition as her first novel, *Mother Tongue*, won the Western States Fiction Award; it is the tale of a young woman who comes to know herself through her love of a Salvadoran refugee smuggled into the United States during the Sanctuary Movement. Her two books of poetry, *Breathing between the Lines* (1997) and *The Devil's Workshop* (2002), address good and evil in the human condition. Her *Confessions of a Berlitz-Tape Chicana* (2005) is a collection of passionate essays, newspaper columns, speeches, and poems that reveal Martínez's ethos for activism, from prayer to social and political intervention.

Michele Martínez (1962–)

Crime/legal thriller author Michele Martínez is the daughter of a Puerto Rican father and a Jewish Russian mother. Born and raised in New York, she graduated from Stanford University with honors and went on to earn a law degree from Harvard University. Subsequently she worked for a top law firm in New York City but decided to render public service by becoming an assistant U.S. attorney in the Eastern District of New York, a district of rampant gang and illegal drug activity. During the next eight years, Martínez prosecuted criminals, became a mother of two children, and sought a change of career, dedicating herself to writing about the subject that had recently dominated her professional life: crime. Martínez thus invented her literary surrogate, Melanie Vargas, a prosecutor who not only takes on criminals in court but also becomes involved in solving murder mysteries and puts her own life at risk. Vargas has become the protagonist so far in a series of four novels: *Most Wanted* (2005), which deals with murder and arson; *The Finishing School* (2006), named Best Mystery &

Suspense Novel by *Romantic Times Magazine*, which deals with two teen murders in an elite private school; *Cover-Up* (2007), which investigates the murder in Central Park of a ruthless society reporter; and *Notorious* (2008), in which Vargas brings a rap star to justice and witnesses a car bombing. Martínez's books have ascended the best-seller charts and been translated to other languages.

Julio Marzán (1946–)

Puerto Rican poet, translator, and academic Julio Marzán was born on February 2, 1946, and came to New York when he was four months old. Despite receiving his education in English-dominant schools, Marzán maintained his Spanish and today is completely bilingual in his poetry and one of the few translators who can translate equally well from either language to the other. Marzán received a B.A. from Fordham University (1967), an M.F.A. in creative writing from Columbia University (1971), and a Ph.D. from New York University (1986). He has taught English at Nassau Community College for many years, except for the 2006 school year, when he was a visiting professor at Harvard University. While Marzán has published poems and translations in magazines and anthologies far and wide, he has also published two books of poems, *Translations without Originals* (1986) and *Puerta de tierra* (1998, Gateway), which may not fit the mold of Nuyorican writing in its classical/canonical referents and command of craft as perfected in the academy. In 2005, Marzán published his first novel, *The Bonjour Gene*, dealing with a generational curse of womanizing among the members of the Bonjour family in both Puerto Rico and New York. Marzán's first major translation project was *Inventing a Word: An Anthology of Twentieth-Century Puerto Rican Poetry* (1980). Perhaps his greatest translation feat was that of taking the onomatopoetic works of poet Luis Palés Matos and rendering them in a sonorous English rendition in *Selected Poems/Poesía Selecta: The Poetry of Luis Palés Matos* (2001). This effort was eclipsed, however, by his feat in 2011 of translating William Carlos Williams's Spanish-language poems in *By Word of Mouth: Poems from the Spanish, 1916–1959*. Marzán, a lifelong resident of Queens, New York City, served as poet laureate of Queens County from 2007 to 2010.

Pablo Medina (1948–)

Pable Medina was born in Havana on August 9, 1948, into a middle-class family of Spanish descent. As he grew up in Havana during the 1950s, events of the Cuban Revolution unfolded before him: sabotages, dictator Fulgencio Batista's henchmen rounding up suspects, and dead bodies at a park. All of these images he depicts in his *Exiled Memories: A Cuban Childhood* (1990). After Fidel Castro's triumph in 1959, Medina and his parents went into exile, settling in New York City in 1961. Medina earned a B.A. in Spanish (1970) and an M.A. in English (1972) from Georgetwon University. In 1975, he produced the first collection of poems written directly into English by a Cuban-born writer: *Pork Rind and Cuban Songs*. This was followed by two poetry collections, *Arching into the Afterlife* (1991) and *Floating Island* (1999). In 1994, he published his first novel, *The Marks of Birth*, about the revolution and Castro's dictatorship. In 2000, he published his second novel, *The Return of Felix Nogara*. Other titles include *Todos me van a tener que oír/Everyone Will Have to Listen* (1990), translations, with poet Carolina Hospital, from the Spanish of Cuban dissident Tania Díaz Castro; *Puntos de Apoyos* (2002, Supporting Points), poems written in Spanish; a new and updated edition of *Exiled Memories* (2002); *The Cigar Roller: A Novel* (2005); and *Points of Balance*, a bilingual poetry collection (2005). Medina's recent books are *The Man Who Wrote on Water* (2011, poems), *Cubop City Blues* (2012, novel), *Calle Habana* (2013, poems), *The Weight of the Island* (2015, poems in translation), *Island History: Poems* (2015), and *The Cuban Comedy* (2019, novel).

Miguel Méndez (1930–2013)

Born on June 15, 1930, in Bisbee, Arizona, into a working-class family during the Depression, Miguel Méndez moved with his family back and forth across the border as they searched for employment. Méndez received six years of grammar schooling in Sonora, Mexico, the only formal education he received in his entire life. Nevertheless, Méndez became an omnivorous reader and a self-taught writer, all the while working as a laborer, farm worker, and brick layer. By the age of eighteen, he was outlining novels and trying his hand at writing stories, but his career as a writer did not take off until the Chicano Movement of the late 1960s. After the publication of his stories in periodicals and anthologies, notably those issued by Editorial Quinto Sol, Méndez was hired as a teacher of writing at Pima Valley College in 1970. He later became a distinguished professor at the University of Arizona, and in 1984 he received an honorary doctorate from that university. Méndez's greatest work is *Peregrinos de Aztlán* (1974, *Pilgrims in Aztlán*, 1993), in which he faithfully depicts border culture and class strife in a baroque Spanish style full of neologisms and regional dialects, as well as elevated diction. His most famous story, "Tata Casehua," was written by him in Yaqui as well as Spanish. Among his many other publications are *Los criaderos humanos (épica de los desamparados) y Sahuaros* (1975, Human Flesh Pots [An Epic of the Wretched] and Sahuaro Cacti), *Tata Casehua y otros cuentos* (1980, Tata Casehua and Other Stories), *Que no mueran los sueños* (1991, Don't Let the Dreams Die), *El sueño de Santa María de las Piedras* (1993, The Dream of Saint Mary of the Stones), *Los muertos también cuentan* (1995, The Dead Also Matter) and *Río Santacruz* (1997, Santa Cruz River). Méndez had three of his books translated to English and a pair of them published in Mexico. He also produced stories for children, such as those included in his *Cuentos para niños traviesos: Stories for Mischievous Children* (1979). Included among his awards is the José Fuentes Mares National Award for Mexican Literature.

Nicholasa Mohr (1935–)

Nicholasa Mohr was one of the first Latina women to develop a long career as a creative writer for major publishing houses. Since 1973, her books for such publishers as Dell/Dial, Harper & Row, and Bantam Books, in both the adult and children's literature categories, have won numerous awards and outstanding reviews. Part and parcel of her work is the experience of growing up a female, a Latina, and a minority in New York City. Born on November 1, 1935, in New York City, Mohr was raised in Spanish Harlem. Educated in New York City schools, she finally escaped poverty after graduating from the Pratt Center for Contemporary

Printmaking in 1969. From that date until the publication of her first book, *Nilda* (1973), which has gone through multiple editions, Mohr developed a successful career as a graphic artist. *Nilda* is still her best-known work. A novel that traces the life of a young Puerto Rican girl confronting prejudice and coming of age during World War II, it won the Jane Addams Children's Book Award and was selected by *School Library Journal* as a Best Book of the Year. After *Nilda*'s success, Mohr was able to produce numerous stories, scripts, and the following titles: the *New York Times* Outstanding Book awardee *El Bronx Remembered* (1975), *In Nueva York* (1977), *Felita* (1979), *Rituals of Survival: A Woman's Portfolio* (1985), *Going Home* (1986), and *A Matter of Pride and Other Stories* (1997). Selections from all these story collections have been reprinted widely in a variety of anthologies and textbooks. Her other children's books are *The Song of el Coquí and Other Tales of Puerto Rico/La canción del coquí y otros cuentos de Puerto Rico* (1995), *The Magic Shell* (1995), *El regalo mágico* (1996), and *Old Letivia and the Mountain of Sorrows/La vieja Letivia y el Monte de los Pesares* (1996).

Mohr's works have been praised for depicting the life of Puerto Ricans in New York with empathy, realism, and humor. In her stories for children, Mohr has been able to deal with the most serious and tragic of subjects, from the death of a loved one to incest, in a sensitive and humane way. Mohr has been able to contribute to the world of commercial publishing—where stereotypes have reigned supreme—some of the most honest and memorable depictions of Puerto Ricans in the United States. In this and in her crusade to open the doors of publishing and the literary world to Latinos, Nicholasa Mohr is a true pioneer. In 1996 she received the Lifetime Achievement Award from the National Congress of Puerto Rican Women and in 2005 the New York State Hispanic Heritage Month Award.

Pat Mora (1942–)

Pat Mora has developed the broadest audiences for her poetry of all of the Latino poets in the United States. Her clean, crisp narrative style and the healing messages in her verse have allowed her poetry to reach out to both adults and young people. Mora's poems have been reprinted in more elementary, middle school, and high school textbooks than any other Latino poet's. Mora was born on January 19, 1942, in El Paso, Texas. She received all of her higher education, including college, in this border city. After graduating from the University of Texas at El Paso in 1963, she worked as an English teacher in public schools and college. A writer since childhood, Mora published her first, award-winning book of poems, *Chants*, in 1984. It was followed by other poetry collections: *Borders* (1986), *Communion* (1991), *Agua Santa/Holy Water* (1995), *Carmen's Book of Practical Saints* (1997), *My Own True Name* (2000), *Adobe Odes* (2006), and *Encantado: Desert Monologues* (2018). Mora is also well known for her children's picture books, including *A Birthday Basket for Tía* (1992), *Listen to the Desert* (1993), *Pablo's Tree* (1994), *The Gift of the Poinsettia* (1995), *The Big Sky* (1998), *The Rainbow Tulip* (1999), *The Night of the Full Moon* (2000), *The Bakery Lady* (2001), *A Library for Juana: The World of Sor Juana Inés* (2002), *Doña Flor: A Tall Tale about a Giant Woman with a Great Big Heart* (2005), *The Song of Francis and the Animals* (2005), *The Remembering Day/El día de los muertos* (2015), *Water Rolls, Water Rises/El agua rueda, el agua sube* (2014), and *Bookjoy, Wordjoy* (2018). A number of her children's works, such as *The Desert Is My Mother* (1994), *Delicious Hullabaloo* (1999), *The Big Sky* (2002), and *Adobe Odes* (2004), are made up of poems as opposed to the narrative technique used in most of her other children's books. In 1993, she published autobiographical essays in *Nepantla: Essays from the Land in the Middle* and, in 1997, issued an unconventional memoir of her family, *House of Houses*, in which she uses the voices of her ancestors and family members to tell their own stories. Mora's awards include fellowships from the Kellogg Foundation (1986) and the National Endowment for the Arts (1994), Southwest Book Awards (1985 and 1987), the Skipping Stones Award (1995), and the Pura Belpré Honor Award (2006). In 2002, *A Library for Juana* was a "Commended" title of the Americas Award for Children and Young Adult Literature. Also in 2002, she received the Civitella Ranieri Fellowship from Umbria, Italy.

Cherríe Moraga
(1952–)

The works of Cherríe Moraga have opened up the world of Chicano literature to the life and aesthetics of feminism and lesbians. Moraga's works are well known in both feminist and Latino circles for their battles against sexism, classism, and racism. Born in Whittier, California, on September 25, 1952, to a Mexican American mother and an Anglo father, Moraga was educated in public schools in the Los Angeles area, after which she graduated from Immaculate Heart College with a B.A. degree in English in 1974. While working as a teacher she discovered her interest in writing, and in 1977 she moved to the San Francisco Bay area, where she became acquainted with the Anglo lesbian literary movement. In part to fulfill the requirements for a master's degree at San Francisco State University, Moraga collaborated with Gloria Anzaldúa in compiling the first anthology of writings by women of color, *This Bridge Called My Back: Writings by Radical Women of Color* (1981), which has become the most famous and best-selling anthology of its kind and has inspired a movement of Latina feminist and lesbian writers. In her writings here and in other books, Moraga explains that her understanding of racial and class oppression suffered by Chicanas only came as she experienced the prejudice against lesbians. In 1983, Moraga edited another groundbreaking anthology with Alma Gómez and Mariana Romo-Carmona, *Cuentos: Stories by Latinas. Cuentos* attempts to establish a poetics or a canon of Latino feminist creativity, a canon where there is room for and, indeed, respect for the insights of lesbianism. In 1983, Moraga published a collection of her own essays and poems dating back to 1976, *Loving in the War Years: Lo que nunca pasó por sus labios* (What Never Passed through Her Lips), in which she explores the dialectical relationship between sexuality and cultural identity. Her conclusion here, as elsewhere, is that women must be put first. Moraga is also a playwright whose works have been produced around the country and widely anthologized. One of her most famous plays, *Giving Up the Ghost*, was produced in 1984 and published in 1986. *The Shadow of a Man* was published in 1991. In 1996 her play *Watsonville: Some Place Not Here* won the Fund for New American Plays Award from the Kennedy Center for the Performing Arts in Washington, D.C. Her books include *The Last Generation: Prose and Poetry* (1993), *Heroes and Saints and Other Plays* (1994), *Waiting in the Wings: Portrait of a Queer Motherhood* (1997), *A Xicana Codex of Changing Consciousness: Writings, 2000–2010* (2011), and *Native Country of the Heart: A Memoir* (2019).

Alejandro Morales (1944–)

Born in Montebello, California, on October 14, 1944, Alejandro Morales grew up in East Los Angeles and received his B.A. degree from California State University, Los Angeles. He went on to complete an M.A. degree (1973) and a Ph.D. degree (1975) in Spanish at Rutgers University in New Jersey. In his novels Morales is at once a recorder of the Chicano experience, basing many of his narratives on historical research, and an imaginative interpreter of that experience by creating memorable and dynamic characters and language. His first books were written in Spanish and published in Mexico due to the lack of opportunity in the United States. *Caras viejas y vino nuevo* (1975, translated as *Old Faces and New Wine*, 1981) examines the conflict of generations in a barrio family. *La verdad sin voz* (1979, translated as *Death of an Anglo*, 1988) is a continuation of the earlier novel but is created against the backdrop of actual occurrences of Chicano-Anglo conflict in the town of Mathis, Texas. The novel also includes autobiographical elements in the form of a section that deals with racism in academia, which comes to a head when a Chicano professor goes up for tenure. *Reto en el paraíso* (*Challenge in Paradise*, 1983) is based on more than a hundred years of Mexican American history and myth, as it centers on a basic comparison of the decline of the famed Coronel family of Californios and the rise of the Irish immigrant Lifford family. The novel charts the transfer of power and wealth from the native inhabitants of California to the gold- and land-hungry immigrants empowered by Manifest Destiny. *The Brick People* (1988) traces the development of two families connected with the Simons Brick Factory, one of the largest enterprises of its type in the country. Again, Morales uses the technique of comparing Anglo and Mexican families, that of the owners of the factory and that of an immigrant laborer. Morales's novel *The Rag Doll Plagues* (1991), while still incorporating a historical structure, follows the development of a plague and a Spanish-Mexican doctor who is forever caught in mortal battle with this plague in three time periods and locations: colonial Mexico, contemporary Southern California, and the future in a country made up of Mexico and California united together. Morales has continued crafting novels and short stories to the present, including *The Captain of All These Men of Death* (2008), *Little Nation and Other Stories* (2014), and *River of Angels* (2014). The latter is a generational saga that traces the development of Los Angeles from Indigenous and colonial times to the present by following the fortunes of a mestizo Mexican family and an Anglo family in the area and how their lives intersect. In all, Morales is a meticulous researcher and a creator of novelistic circumstances that are symbolic of Mexican American history and cultural development. His novels have an epic sweep that is cinematic and highly literary. In 2007 Morales won the Luis Leal Award for Distinction in Chicano/Latino Literature.

Elías Miguel Muñoz (1954–)

Born on September 19, 1954, in Cuba and raised in the United States, where he earned a Ph.D. in Spanish from the University of California, Irvine (1984), Elias Miguel Muñoz is one of the most accomplished bilingual novelists, penning original works in either English or Spanish, based on accommodation of Cuban immigrants to life in the United States. Within that overarching theme of culture conflict and synthesis is the conflict of homosexual identity with societal norms in Hispanic and Anglo-American cultures. After receiving his Ph.D. and becoming a professor of Spanish at Wichita State University, Muñoz gave up on the restricted world of university teaching in 1988 to become a full-time writer. He has been a prolific writer of poetry, stories, and novels. His books include *Los viajes de Orlando Cachumbambé* (1984, The Voyages of Orlando Cachumbambé), *Crazy Love* (1988), *En estas tierras/In This Land* (1989), *The Greatest Performance* (1991), and *Brand*

New Memory (1998). In all, the joys and fears of sexual awakening are set to the backdrop of popular music and film during the time period evoked. In the 1990s, he began publishing textbook readers in various editions for learners of Spanish, such as *Viajes fantásticos* (1994), *Ladrón de la mente* (1995), and *Taína, isla de luz* (2016). In the twenty-first century, Múñoz has returned to writing fiction in Spanish; *Vida Mía* (2006, Life of Mine) is a highly autobiographical novel of first love and a chronicle of life in Cuba during the 1960s, evoking the music and popular culture of the times.

Alejandro Murguía (1949–)

Prose fiction writer, poet, and editor Alejandro Murguía was born in California on August 15, 1949, but was raised in Mexico City. He returned to the United States and, after two decades of being a literary and social activist, obtained a B.A. in English and an M.F.A. in creative writing from San Francisco State University in 1990 and 1992, respectively. One of the prime movers of the Latino cultural movement in the San Francisco Bay area during the early 1970s, Murguía was one of the founding editors of the iconic literary and arts magazine *Tin-Tan: Revista Cósmica* (1975–1979, Cosmic Review), in which various pioneers of Latino poetry, such as Victor Hernández Cruz, Rafael Jesús González, and Roberto Vargas, published their works. He also participated in the Editorial Pocho Che publishing group, along with Cruz, José Montoya, and Raúl Salinas. Murguía and Nicaraguan Vargas became involved in the Nicaraguan liberation movement and became soldiers in that civil war. This experience was reflected in his collection of short stories, *Southern Front* (1979), winner of the Before Columbus American Book Award. But Murguía's first book was a collection of poems, *Oración a la Mano Poderosa* (1972, Prayer to the Powerful Hand). In 1980, he published another collection of short stories, *Farewell to the Coast,* and, in 2002, *This War Called Love: Nine Stories*. In 2002 Moruguía published *The Medicine of Memory: A Mexica Clan in California*, a book of creative nonfiction in which Murguía traces his family history back to the eighteenth century in an attempt to reconstruct the Chicano-Indigenous history of California. Among his honors is winning first prize in the *San Francisco Guardian* Short Story Competition (1995) and an Editor's Fellowship from the Coordinating Council of Literary Magazines (1980). In 2012, Murguía was named poet laureate of San Francisco.

Michael Nava (1954–)

Mystery writer Michael Nava was born on September 16, 1954, in Stockton, California. He is a Stanford University–trained attorney who has worked as a prosecutor and a defense lawyer, and is thus very familiar with the world of crime and detective work. Beginning with his first mystery novel, *The Little Death* (1986), he has created a popular series starring homosexual detective Henry Rios, an emotionally and psychologically conflicted protagonist who becomes involved in solving complex cases related to controversial issues, such as ethnicity, sexuality, domestic abuse, and AIDS. The series includes *Golden Boy* (1988), *How Town* (1990), *The Hidden Law* (1992), *The Death of Friends* (1996), *The Burning Plain* (1997), *Rag and Bone* (2001), *Lay Your Sleeping Head* (2016), and *Carved in Bone* (2019). What distinguishes Nava's detective from other protagonists of the hard-boiled genre is that he becomes emotionally involved in each case, taking it personally. For his innovative writing and defense of gay life in his novels, Nava has received five Lambda Literary Awards.

Achy Obejas (1956–)

Born on June 28, 1956, in Havana, Cuba, Achy Obejas and her family left Cuba clandestinely on a boat when she was only six years old. After spending a brief time in Miami, she and her family relocated to Michigan City, Indiana, where Obejas was raised. In 1979, she moved to Chicago, where she became a journalist for the *Chicago Sun-Times*. Before publishing her novels, Obejas published her poetry and short stories widely in small magazines and in anthologies. For more than a decade, Obejas was the author of a weekly column, "After Hours," for the *Chicago Tribune* and contributed regularly to other Chicago periodicals, as well as such national, mainstream ones as *Vogue* and *The Voice*. In 1993, Obejas obtained a master of fine arts degree from Warren Wilson College with a collection of short stories for her master's thesis. In 1994, Obejas published her first book, *We Came All the Way from Cuba So You Could Dress Like This: Stories*, which is made up of personal memoirs, essays, and fiction; the book is held together by the constant perspective of the outsider, political exile, or economic refugee. In her novels *Memory Mambo* (1996) and *Days of Awe* (2001), Obejas explores the themes of identity conflict from ethnic, religious, and sexual perspectives—Obejas is not only a gay Latina but also a member of the Jewish minority within Latino culture. Among her most recent, diverse writings is a novel, *Ruins* (2009); a collection of poems, *This Is What Happened in Our Life* (2007); and a short story collection, *The Tower of the Antilles* (2017). Obejas also edited a collection of noir detective/mystery stories, entitled *Havana Noir*, in 2007. Both *Memory Mambo* and *Days of Awe* were honored with Lambda Awards for Best Lesbian Fiction. In addition to her awards for fiction, Obejas has received a Pulitzer Prize for team investigation for the *Tribune*, the Studs Terkel Journalism Prize, and the Peter Lisagor Award for political reporting from Sigma Delta Chi/Society for Professional Journalists.

Daniel Olivas (1959–)

Daniel Olivas was born on April 8, 1959, in Los Angeles, the grandson of Mexican immigrants. He graduated with a B.A. in English from Stanford University in 1981 and from the UCLA School of Law in 1984. After spending a decade writing legal articles and pursuing his career in law—becoming a senior assistant attorney general for the State of California—in the new century Olivas began writing fiction. In 2000, he published his first work of fiction, *The Courtship of María Rivera Peña: A Novella*, which was followed by *Assumption and Other Stories* (2003), *Devil Talk: Stories* (2004), *Anywhere but L.A.: Stories* (2009), and *The King of Lighting Fixtures* (2017). In 2011 he published his first novel, *The Book of Want*, which like many of his stories is in the tradition of magical realism. Olivas also took on children's literature, writing freelance for the *Los Angeles Times*'s Kids' Reading Room section and publishing a children's picture book on the similar experiences of Jewish and Latino immigrants, *Benjamin and the Word* (2005). In 2017 Olivas crossed over into poetry with his book *Crossing the Border: Collected Poems* and, in 2018, play writing with his Samuel Beckett–inspired *Waiting for Godínez*. Olivas is a prolific writer of fiction, poetry, essays, and book reviews, many of which have appeared in the *New York Times*, the *Los Angeles Times*, the *El Paso Times*, the *MacGuffin*, *Exquisite Corpse*, *Jewish Journal*, *THEMA*, and the *Pacific Review*, among others.

Sheila Ortiz-Taylor (1939–)

Born on September 25, 1939, in Los Angeles into a Mexican American family, Sheila Ortiz-Taylor began writing poetry and plays in junior high school. One year after starting high school, she dropped out to get married and moved to Iowa, where she had two children. She later returned to Los Angeles and was able to major in English and graduate from California State University, Northridge (1963). She went on to obtain her M.A. and Ph.D. in English from the University of California, Los Angeles in 1964 and 1972, respectively. Ortiz-Taylor spent her complete career as a professor at Florida State University, where she became an endowed professor; currently she is a professor emeritus. Ortiz-Taylor is the author of what is believed to have been the first novel to feature an outed Chicana lesbian as the protagonist: *Faultline* (1982). This was the first of six novels, followed by *Spring Forward/Fall Back* (1985), *Southbound: The Sequel to Faultline* (1990), *Coachella* (1998), *Outrageous* (2006), and *Assisted Living* (2007). In 1996, Ortiz-Taylor published *Imaginary Parents,* a literary and artistic collage executed with her sister Sandra. It is a mystery novel set in the California desert and populated by a host of unlikely idiosyncratic characters. *Slow Dancing at Miss Polly's* (1998) is Ortiz-Taylor's only book of poetry. Ortiz-Taylor has won numerous awards, including the Martin Luther King Jr. Distinguished Service Award (1997) and the Alice B. Award for writers of outstanding lesbian portrayals in literature (2007).

Heberto Padilla (1932–2000)

Poet and journalist Heberto Padilla was born in Puerta de Golpe, Pinar del Río, Cuba, on January 20, 1932, the son of a lawyer and a homemaker. After college, Padilla sought to participate in the construction of a new Cuba with the triumph of the Castro Revolution. From 1959 to 1968, he worked for the state-sponsored newspaper, *Revolución* (Revolution), and then for the government newspaper, *Granma*. As the Castro government progressively restricted and controlled artists, especially writers, Padilla became more and more disillusioned with that government. As Padilla was singled out for his resistance to the government aesthetic and ideological dictums, Padilla lost his job with *Granma* in 1969, and his poetry fell into relative obscurity without outlets for publication. In 1971 Padilla was imprisoned for one month after reading some of his works in public, which led to hundreds of protests internationally and his example enshrined as the "Padilla Case." In 1980 with the assistance of U.S. author Bernard Malamud and Senator Edward Kennedy, Padilla was exiled to the United States, where he continued to write poetry and founded a literary magazine, *Linden Lane Magazine*. Among his most successful works published in the United States are *Legacies: Selected Poems* (1982), *Heroes Are Grazing in My Garden* (1984), *Self-Portrait of the Other* (1990), and *A Fountain, a House of Stone: Poems* (1991). *Self-Portrait* is a memoir of his life from 1959 to 1981, charting his estrangement from Communism in Cuba, his persecution under that regime, and his exile. His works have had original Spanish-language editions published in Spain.

Ricardo Pau-Llosa (1954–)

Poet and painter Ricardo Pau-Llosa was born on May 17, 1954, in Havana, Cuba, into a middle-class family that had struggled to emerge from poverty in Cuba. After the Cuban Revolution, the family went into exile in 1960, when Pau-Llosa was just six years old, first to Chicago and later to Tampa. Although he was educated in American schools, Pau-Llosa continues to cultivate the theme of exile in his poetry and art and to balance nostalgia for the homeland he barely new with the overwhelming reality of a U.S. culture that has made him feel foreign since his childhood. His poetry collections include *Sorting Metaphors*, which won the Anhinga Poetry Prize (1983); *Bread of the Imagined* (1992); *Cuba* (1993); *Vereda Tropical* (1999, Tropical Path); *The Mastery Impulse* (2003); and *Parable Hunter* (2008). He has also published individual poems in numerous magazines throughout the United States. In addition, Pau-Llosa has published essays and short stories in magazines and anthologies and is a renowned critic of the visual arts, particularly twentieth-century Latin American painting and sculpture. In 1984, Pau-Llosa was awarded the Cintas Fellowship for Literature, and in 1998, *Miami News Times* named him "the best local poet." He also won the *Linden Lane Magazine* English-Language Poetry Prize (1987).

Terri de la Peña (1947–)

Born on February 20, 1947, in Santa Monica, California, Terri de la Peña is a novelist and prolific short story writer who explores the Chicana and Lesbian identity through her works. A graduate of Santa Monica Community Collage, Peña is a self-taught writer who, although she began writing during her teens, did not publish her first work until after her fortieth birthday. Her first novel, *Margins: A Novel* (1992), narrates the gradual self-awareness of Verónica, a graduate student who begins to deal with her lesbian and Chicana identities. In *Latin Satins* (1994), Peña deals with the world of four Chicana singers who make a living satirizing "golden oldies"; enriched by lyrics in Spanish and English, the novel deals with racial discrimination, the mass media, and the Chicano and lesbian communities. *Faults: A Novel* (1999) charts the troubled waters of five Chicanas united by blood or love trying to make their way through various types of social and psychological problems, inluding spousal abuse, alcoholism, and poverty. Peña's short stories have been published widely in magazines and such anthologies as *Lesbian Bedtime Stories* (1989 and 1990), *Chicana Lesbians: The Girls Our Mothers Warned Us About* (1991), *Lesbian Love Stories* (1991), *Childless by Choice: A Feminist Anthology* (1992), *Out of the Closet* (1994), and *Dyke Life* (1995). In 1986, Peña won the University of California–Irvine Chicano/Latino Prize for her short story "A Saturday in August." In 1990 she won an Artistic Excellence in Writing Award from VIVA: Lesbian and Gay Latinos in the Arts, and in 1993, the Distinguished Recognition for Outstanding Contributions to the Arts, Academia, and the Community from the National Association of Chicana and Chicano Studies.

Prudencio de Pereda (1912–1973)

Novelist and short story writer Prudencio de Pereda was born to Spanish cigar workers in Brooklyn, New York, on February 18, 1912. He graduated from the City College of New York with a Spanish major in 1933 and published his first story in 1936, when he was engrossed in the Republican cause of the Spanish Civil War. During this time, he met Ernest Hemingway and collaborated on two films with him: *Spain in Flames* and *The Spanish Earth*. Involved with many activists in the United States for the Republican cause, Pereda published numerous stories of a leftist inclination for such magazines as *Commentary*, *The New Republic*, and *Nation*. His stories were selected for the *O. Henry Memorial Prize Volume* (1937) and *O'Brien's Best Short Stories* (1938, 1940). Pereda served in the U.S. Army during World War II as a language censor of letters and after the war began producing novels and stories: *All the Girls We Loved* (1948); *Fiesta, a Novel of Modern Spain* (1953), which deals with a failing marriage during the Spanish Civil War; and *Windmills in Brooklyn* (1960). *Fiesta* was so successful that it was adapted as an opera and a radio play. *All the Girls We Loved* is an interconnected group of short stories that follows soldier Al Figueira and his comrades in training for World War II and the girls they thought they loved. The highly autobiographical *Windmills of the Mind* is a comic novel that reminisces about the Spanish colony in Brooklyn just before World War I and features a wise old grandfather, Agapito, who tells his grandson, the narrator, about the adventures and misadventures of selling cigars door to door. De Pereda retired to Sunbury, Pennsylvania, and died in 1973.

Victor Perera (1934–2003)

Guatemalan-born novelist and journalist Victor Perera was the son of Sephardic parents who had moved from Jerusalem to Guatemala City in the 1920s.

The family moved to New York City when Perera was twelve years old, but his early nurturing and his Guatemalan youth stayed with him through his reporting, creative writing, and memoir, *The Cross and the Pear Tree: A Sephardic Journey* (1995). His novels and stories have been filled with the world of ancient Central American tribes and rain forests and an apocalyptic vision for modern civilization. Perera authored what is considered the definitive book about the Native Americans of southern Mexico, *The Last Lords of Palenque: The Lacandon Mayas of the Mexican Rain Forest* (1995). Perera graduated from Brooklyn College and later received a master's degree in English from the University of Michigan. After returning to New York City, Perera began a long relationship with some of the most renowned forums for creative and intellectual writing in the United States: the *New Yorker*, the *New Republic*, and the *New York Times Magazine*. From 1972 to 1979 he taught journalism and creative writing at the University of California, Santa Cruz, and at the Graduate School of Journalism at the University of California, Berkeley from 1993 to 1998. Although Perera was somewhat ambiguous about his Jewish heritage, three of his books were an attempt to explain to himself why his family had ended up in Guatemala. The first, *The Conversion* (1970), was a historical novel. The second, *Rites: A Guatemalan Boyhood* (1986), was an early memoir, and *The Cross and the Pear Tree* was his final inquiry into that question. *The Cross and the Pear Tree* is not just a family autobiography but rather an entire history of the Sephardim. Through this and other writing, Perera is considered to have had an immense impact on Sephardic culture in the United States. He was the cofounder of Ivri-NASAWI, a national Sephardic cultural organization, and served as a volunteer advisor to the University of California, Santa Cruz quarterly magazine *Leviathan*.

Emma Pérez (1954–)

Emma Pérez is a highly respected historian and theorist of gender as well as a novelist; in both roles she has revolutionized Chicano/a and Third-World literary and historical discourse. Born on October 25, 1954, in the small, rural, and Anglo-dominated town of El Campo, Texas, where she received most of her primary and secondary education, Pérez escaped the provincialism of her intellectual environment by relocating to Los Angeles. She was not only liberated to live her life as a lesbian but also to pursue academic study at the highest level: at the University of California, Los Angeles, Pérez received her B.A. in political science and women's studies (1979) and her M.A. (1982) and Ph.D. (1988) in history. As a historian, Pérez has written one of the fundamental texts of Third-World feminism in the United States, *The Decolonial Imaginary: Writing Chicanas into History* (1999), in which she argues that the writing of Chicano history, like that of most other narratives of people emerging from colonialism, adopts the theoretical tools and perspectives formerly used by the colonial masters, and eliminates gender considerations from the historiography. Although Pérez had been interested in literature since her childhood and had, in fact, written creatively on and off during those years, it was precisely the failure of history to record women's voices that drove her to begin writing novels. She has stated, "I write fiction not only because I have a passion for literature, but also because I am frustrated with history's texts and archives. I've always wanted to find in the archives a queer *vaquero* (cowgirl) from the mid-nineteenth century whose adventures include fighting Anglo squatters and seducing willing señoritas." In addressing the motives for writing her historical novel *Forgetting the Alamo, or Blood Memory* (2009), she states, "Impatience led me to create a Tejana baby butch, named Micaela Campos, who must avenge her father's death at the battle of San Jacinto, just a month after the fall of the Alamo." Nevertheless, Pérez's first novel, *Gulf Dreams*, issued by the feminist Third Woman Press in 1996, is highly autobiographical in lyrically re-creating the struggles of a young woman growing up in South Texas while trying to find her own identity amid the constraining gender roles foisted upon her by her family and society. Pérez's 2015 novel, *Electra's Complex,* is a murder mystery involving a professor whose academic and lesbian lives intertwine and conflict. In addition to her books, Pérez has produced a solid body of essays on Chicana and lesbian culture that have highly influenced academics as well as creative writers across ethnicities in the United States.

Loida Maritza Pérez (1963–)

Born in the Dominican Republic, Loida Maritza Pérez writes about what she knows: a poor Dominican family migrating to the United States and attempting to adjust to the new culture in the big city, in this case Brooklyn. Her highly autobiographical novel *Geographies of Home* (1999) deals with the stress the recently arrived family feels and the strains upon relationships that ultimately become abuse: mental, physical, and sexual. The rape, mental illness, and family disintegration are shown not only to be parts of life in the big city but are also traced back to the abuse that existed in the Dominican Republic under dictator Rafael Leónidas Trujillo. Another theme in the novel is one that Pérez has struggled with herself: being Afro-Dominican, she has had to struggle to identify herself within the United States as either Afro-American or Latina. Pérez discovered literature in high school and went on to get a degree in English from Cornell University (1987). Included among her awards are a New York Foundation for the Arts grant (1991), a Ragdale Foundation grant (1994), and a Pauline and Henry Gates fellowship (1996). Pérez has published a number of short stories in such magazines as *Bomb*, *Latina*, and *Callaloo*.

Raymundo "Tigre" Pérez (1946–1995)

One of the prime movers of the Chicano poetry movement in South Texas, Raymundo "Tigre" Pérez was an angry, militant activist whose personal experience of racial and judicial oppression dominated his poetry. Born in utter poverty on March 15, 1946, in a garage in Laredo, Texas, to a Mexican American boxer and stevedore and a Tarascan Indian mother from Michoacán, Mexico, Pérez was a street urchin who, out of force of will and interest in poetry from his junior high school days, managed after various false starts to earn a bachelor's degree in political science from Oberlin College in Ohio. Pérez used his poetry as a rallying cry for the Chicano Movement and became a roving troubador who lent his poetic voice to demonstrations and boycotts throughout the Southwest during the early 1970s. He also published his poems in many ephemeral magazines and community newspapers as well as in such venues as *Revista*

Chicano-Riqueña, *Caracol*, and other Chicano journals. Pérez himself founded and edited a number of underground newspapers, including *Los Muertos Hablan* (the Dead Speak), *Valley of the Damned*, and *Tierra Caliente* (Hot Earth). Often associated with other such movement poets as Abelardo Delgado, Nephtalí De León, and Ricardo Sánchez, who at times assumed similarly militant stances, Pérez saw some of his books published through the assistance of these writers. His books include *Free, Free at Last* (1970), *Los Cuatro* (1970), *Phases* (1971), and *The Secret Meaning of Death* (1972). *Free, Free at Last*, written after his tour of duty in Vietnam, was dominated by his protest against the war and the military. The other collections monitor and respond to the progress of the Chicano Movement, including the farm worker struggle, with the last installment becoming more intimate and personal as to his motivation, hopes, and foreseeing his death. Pérez disappeared for awhile from the annals of Chicano literature and resurfaced in the 1980s as part of a Native American movement, now with the new title of *Chief* Raymundo "Tigre" Pérez, the medicine man; he is credited with founding a yearly festival "Kanto de la Tierra" (Song to the Earth), now known as "Roots of the Earth."

Gustavo Pérez Firmat (1949–)

Gustavo Pérez Firmat was born in Havana, Cuba, on March 7, 1949, and relocated with his family to Miami after Castro came to power in Cuba. Pérez Firmat received most of his formal education in Miami, obtaining a B.A. and an M.A. in Spanish from the University of Miami in 1972 and 1973, respectively, and a Ph.D. in comparative literature from the University of Michigan in 1979. A poet, fiction writer, and scholar, Pérez Firmat is the author of ten books and over seventy essays and reviews. Pérez Firmat's basic condition—born in Cuba and transplanted to American soil in his youth—made him a member of the new "Cuban American" generation and led to his theories about the dual perspective held by what he terms a "transitional" generation. For this poet/theorist, Cuban Americans of his generation can be equally at home or equally uncomfortable in both Cuba and the United States. They are cultural mediators, who are constantly translating not only language but also the differences between the Anglo-American and Cuban/Cuban American worldviews. In his groundbreaking book-length essay *Life on The Hyphen: the Cuban American Way* (1993), Pérez Firmat maintains, however, that this is only a transitional stage and that the next generation will follow a path similar to that of the children of European immigrants, who are simply considered ethnic Americans. Themes of biculturalism are ever present in Perez Firmat's three collections of poetry—*Carolina Cuban* (1987), *Equivocaciones* (1989), and *Bilingual Blues* (1995)—which are full of code switching and bilingual-bicultural double entendres and playfulness. His tour-de-force exploration of bilingualism and biculturalism as a critic and writer, *Tongue Ties: Logo-Eroticism in Anglo-Hispanic Literature*, was published in 2003. In his book-length memoir, *Next Year in Cuba* (1995), which was nominated for a Pulitzer Prize, Pérez Firmat documents the tension his generation feels between identifying with other Americans their age and identifying with their parents, who always looked forward to returning to Cuba. True to form, Pérez Firmat re-created the memoir in Spanish in 1997 as *El año que viene estamos en Cuba*. His novel *Anything but Love* (2000) is Pérez Firmat's tour de force of culture conflict revolving around love, marriage, and sex roles, all articulated with that inimitable rhapsodic excess that is the author's trademark. In 2005, Pérez Firmat published a memoir, *Scar Tissue*, in prose and verse in which he chronicles his dealing with the death of his father and with his own prostate cancer. In retirement Pérez Firmat has continued to write prolifically. Among his newer works is a bilingual book of poems, *Sin lengua, deslenguado* (2017, Without a Tongue, Detongued), with his typical linguistic play.

Pedro Pietri (1944–2004)

Pedro Pietri was born in Ponce, Puerto Rico, on March 21, 1944, and was just two years old when his family migrated to New York. He was orphaned while still a child and raised by his grandmother. Pietri attended public schools in New York City and served in the Army from 1966 to 1968. Other than his having taught writing occasionally and participated in workshops, very little else is known about this intentionally mysterious and unconventional figure. Pietri is famous for the literary persona of street urchin or skid-row bum that he created for himself. His works are characterized by the consistent perspective of the underclass in language, philosophy, and creative and psychological freedom. Pietri published collections of poems and poetry chapbooks: *The Blue and the Gray* (1975), *Invisible Poetry* (1979), *Out of Order* (1980), *Uptown Train* (1980), *An Alternate* (1980), and *Traffic Violations* (1983). It was his first book of poetry, *Puerto Rican Obituary* (1971), that brought him his greatest fame and a host of imitators. In 1973, a live performance by him of poems from this book was recorded and distributed by Folkways Records. In 1980, Pietri's short story *Lost in the Museum of Natural History* was published in bilingual format by the University of Puerto Rico. Pietri also had numerous unpublished, but produced, plays and one published collection, *The Masses Are Asses* (1984). Always a master of the incongruous and surprising, Pietri created unlikely but humorous narrative situations in both his poetry and plays, such as that in his poem "Suicide Note from a Cockroach in a Low Income Housing Project" and in a dialogue between a character and her own feces in his play *Appearing in Person Tonight—Your Mother*. Pietri's work is one of a total break with conventions, both literary and social, and it is subversive in its open rejection of established society and society's hypocrisies. His poems were collected and published posthumously in *Pedro Pietri: Selected Poems*, edited by Juan Flores and Pedro López Adorno in 2015.

Mary Helen Ponce (1938–)

Born on Janurary 24, 1938, in Pacoima in the San Fernando Valley of California, Mary Helen Ponce first began writing in grammar school and in the eighth grade wrote a play that was produced. Continuing to envision herself as a writer throughout her education, Ponce received a B.A. and an M.A. in Mexican American studies from California State University in 1978 and 1980, respectively. She earned a second M.A. in history in 1984 from the University of California, Los Angeles and eventually a Ph.D. at the University of New Mexico in 1988. Throughout these years she developed her literary career and taught at colleges in the Los Angeles area. From her very first self-published collection of stories, *Recuerdo: Short Stories of the Barrio*

(1983) to her later books published by university-based presses, Ponce has been faithful to the people she grew up with, especially the women, in recording and immortalizing their lives in fine stories and novels. *Taking Control* (1987) followed in the same vein, while *The Wedding* (1989) studied in depth with humor and empathy the community folklore, rituals, and expectations involved in a Pachuco wedding. Ponce penned her autobiography, *Hoyt Street: Memories of a Chicana Childhood*, in 1993; beyond recounting the details of her own upbringing, Ponce's memoir is particularly acute in portraying the racial tensions that dominated her community of Pacoima during the 1940s. In 2001, Mary Helen Ponce received the Lifetime Commitment to Literacy Award from the Friends of the San Fernando Library and, in 2002, the Latino Spirit Award from Governor Gray Davis of California.

Roberto Quesada (1962–)

Born on April 17, 1962, in Olanchito, Honduras, and immigrated to the United States in the early 1980s, Roberto Quesada has become the humorist of immigrant literature, satirizing both the reasons for Latin Americans to leave their home countries and the reception they receive in their new home. After relocating to the United States in 1989, Quesada was one of the fortunate few immigrant writers to have access to English-language publishers in the United States, who translated his novels to English, including *The Ships: A Novel* (1992), *The Big Banana* (1999), and *Never through Miami* (2002). Quesada has also published works abroad, such as *El desertor* (1985, The Deserter) published in Honduras; *El humano y la diosa* (1996, The Human Being and the Goddess), which received the Latin American Writers Institute of the United States Award and was published in the Dominican Republic; *Nunca entres por Miami* (2001), which was published in Spain; and *La novela del milenio pasado* (2004, The Novel of the Past Millenium), which appeared in Lima, Peru. Quesada has also been the editor of the magazine *Nosotros los latinos,* and in 1986 he founded the literary review *Sobre Vuelo* (Over Flight), both in New York. To date, his most accomplished work has been *The Big Banana*, a humorous picaresque novel in the tradition of immigrant literature, which focuses on the life of an aspiring actor who leaves his native Honduras to make it on the stages of New York City. Quesada is particularly deft at creating idiosyncratic characters obsessed with achieving their dreams. *Never through Miami* continues in the same vein of coming to the United States to achieve one's dreams and confronting numerous barriers. *The Ships* is a love story set to the background of the Nicaraguan revolution.

Ernesto Quiñónez (1969–)

Raised in New York City by an Ecuadorian father and a Puerto Rican mother, Ernesto Quiñónez has based his writing on life in Spanish Harlem. Racial and class conflict in the barrio are themes elaborated in his first novel, *Bodega Dreams* (2000). Educated in the New York public schools, Quiñónez attended City College of New York, where he decided on a career in writing. *Bodega Dreams* was a resounding success, with the *New York Times* pronouncing it "a new immigrant classic"—of course, Quiñónez is hardly an immigrant. Quiñónez's second novel, *Changó's Fire* (2004), followed in the same vein but did not accrue the critical acclaim of *Bodega Dreams*. *Taína* (2019), which could be considered a young adult novel, includes sexually explicit episodes and language in its profile of a young unwed mother. Quiñónez is a prolific writer for magazines, including the *New York Times Magazine* and *Esquire*. He has won residencies at Wesleyan Writers Conference (2001) and Bread Loaf Writers' Conference (2002), and he was a visiting screenwriter at the Sundance Screenwriters Lab. He currently teaches creative writing at Cornell University.

Leroy V. Quintana (1944–)

Leroy V. Quintana is one of the most renowned poets to memorialize Hispanic participation in the Vietnam War. Born on June 10, 1944, in Albuquerque, New Mexico, Quintana obtained a B.A. in English in 1969 from the University of New Mexico after serving for two years in the war. In 1974, he obtained a master's degree in English from New Mexico State University and began publishing poems in literary magazines. By 1976, he published his first book, *Hijo del Pueblo: New Mexico Poems* (Son of the People), a highly autobiographical collection of verse. While working as an English instructor in area colleges and universities, Quintana published his next book, *Sangre* (1981, Blood), which won the Before Columbus American Book Award. Quintana experienced a career change, and after obtaining a master's in counseling from Western New Mexico University, he became a psychological counselor in San Diego, California. He continued writing and in 1990 published *Interrogations*, a collection of poems about the Vietnam War, and in 1993 published *The History of Home*, which again memorializes growing up in poverty in New Mexico by casting each poem in the voice of a hometown personality. *The History of Home* was Quintana's second American Book Award winner. His *My Hair Turning Gray among Strangers* (1996) explores emotional and spiritual exile and the need to return home to New Mexico. His *Great Whirl of Exile* (1999) again explores New Mexico life and war experiences. His collection of short stories, *La Promesa and Other Stories* (2002), follows protagonists Mosco Zamora and Johnny Barros through a series of interrelated tales set in the fictional New Mexico town of San Miguel and in Vietnam. Quintana teaches at San Diego Mesa College.

Manuel Ramos (1948–)

Born in Florence, Colorado, on March 6, 1948, Manuel Ramos earned a bachelor's degree in political science from Colorado State University (1970) and a law degree from the University of Colorado (1973). Ramos has practiced law since then. In the late 1980s, he started writing; it was a natural for him to make the transition from his interest in the law to writing detective fiction. In 1993, Ramos published his first book in the Luis Montez series, *The Ballad of Rocky Ruiz*, in which the burned-out lawyer and middle-aged ex-Chicano Movement activist Montez narrates his involvement in unraveling the mystery surrounding the murder of activist Rocky Ruiz some twenty years earlier. In the next installment, *The Ballad of Gato Guerrero*, Montez is called upon to protect a deceased friend's family from a criminal gang. As in *Rocky Ruiz*, the setting is Denver and its Latino barrios, but here instead of the Chicano Movement, the plot harkens back to the Vietnam War. In *The Last Client of Luis Montez* (1996), Montez has to solve the murder of a legal client, which gives Ramos the excuse of reviewing and critiquing American life

and culture in the 1990s. Despite the title of the former installment, Luis Montez lives on to continue detective work in *Blues for the Buffalo* (1997) as he searches for a Chicana writer, Rachel Espinoza, who has disappeared in Mexico; the plot takes a surprise turn for literary enthusiasts when her disappearance becomes linked to the real-life disappearance of Chicano writer Oscar Zeta Acosta in 1974. In *Brown-on-Brown* (2006), Montez gets involved in the Anglo-Hispanic conflict over water rights in the Colorado sand-dune country. Ramos departed from the Montez mysteries in his *Mooney's Road to Hell* (2002), which now features private eye Danny Mora (Mooney) investigating the murder of an illegal immigrant in Denver; this allows Ramos to explore the whole underworld of labor smuggling, as well as revisit themes from the Chicano Movement. In 2013, Ramos returned to his Denver noir writing with Gus Corral, an ex-con protégé of Ramos's first detective/lawyer Luis Montez in *Desperado: A Mile High Noir*; this time, however, Corral is an antihero who always finds his way into trouble of one sort or another and quite often has to be rescued by his pragmatic motherly sister. The series continues with *My Bad: A Mile High Noir* (2016), *The Golden Havana Night: A Sherlock Homie Mystery Havana* (2018), and *Angels in the Wind* (2021). The *Denver Post* wrote of the second installment: "*My Bad* is arguably Ramos' finest novel.... Ramos brings to life the old Northside, its culture, its people, its music and color. This is all authentic stuff. Ramos writes about North Denver better than anybody. *My Bad* is a fine mystery with an unexpected ending, but it is also a view by an insider into the life of one of Denver's unique neighborhoods that may one day disappear." In 2015, Ramos published a collection of short stories from various years in his career, *The Skull of Pancho Villa and Other Stores*, a couple of them eventually found themselves recast into his complete novels. Among the awards garnered by Ramos are the University of California Irvine Chicano/Latino Prize (1991), a nomination for the Edgar Allan Poe Award given by the Mystery Writers of America (1993), and a Colorado Book Award (1994).

Manuel Ramos Otero (1948–1990)

Novelist, short story writer, and poet Manuel Ramos Otero was born on July 20, 1948, in Manatí,

Puerto Rico. After graduating with a degree in social sciences from the University of Puerto Rico (1968), he moved to the United States to pursue his literary and theatrical career as well as to experience the greater freedom for gays on the continent. After studying with Lee Strasberg in 1970, Ramos Otero went on to establish his own theater workshop, Aspaguanza, where he worked with experimental Puerto Rican drama. In 1969, he earned an M.A. in Spanish and Latin American literature from New York University and began teaching in New York–area colleges and universities. From 1973 to 1975, Ramos Otero served as the editor of the literary magazine *Zona de carga y descarga* (Loading and Unloading Zone). In 1976, he founded a small literary press, El Libro Viaje (the Book Trip), which published several books of poetry and Ramos Otero's own experimental novel *La novelabingo* (1976, The Bingo Novel). His other books include *El cuento de la mujer y el mar* (1979, The Story of the Woman and the Sea) and *El libro de la muerte* (1985, The Book of Death). In 1990, he resettled in Puerto Rico and shortly thereafter died of AIDS on October 7, 1990. In the last months before his death, he wrote a memoir of his life with AIDs and coming death; it was published as *Inviatación al polvo* (Invitation to Dust) in 1991. His last collection of stories and poems, *Página en blanco y staccato* (2000, Blank Page in Staccato), was published posthumously and given a special award by the PEN Club of Puerto Rico. Ramos Otero's work was always very experimental and challenging to readers, often mixing literary genres in the same piece. Throughout his work, he addressed numerous themes of modernity: modern technology, ethnic consciousness and identity, and the rationality of the world are but a few of the topics elaborated in his diverse universe.

John Rechy (1931–)

One of the earliest of the contemporary Chicano novelists to gain a national following, and the first to base his narratives on gay life and culture, John Rechy was not at first recognized as a Chicano, in part, apparently, because of his un-Spanish-sounding surname and because his ethnicity was not evident in his themes and gay approach to writing. Born on March 10, 1931, to a Mexican mother who did not speak English and a Scottish father who was a musician, Rechy was raised in poverty in El Paso, Texas. Rechy himself is believed to have become a male hustler, and his first novel, *City of the Night* (1963), is believed to be highly autobiographical. Today it is considered a classic among gay literature and has been named as one of the twenty-five all-time-best gay novels. His rhapsodic style and his protagonist's outlandish sexual adventures were very much ahead of their time in this graphic account of the underworld of gay prostitution; his "youngman" character seeks to find himself on the move from El Paso to New York and France. Among his many other works are *Numbers* (1967), *The Day's Death* (1969), *The Vampire* (1971), *The Fourth Angel* (1972), *Rushes* (1979), *Bodies and Souls* (1983), *Marilyn's Daughter* (1988), *The Miraculous Day of Amalia Gomez* (1991), *Our Lady of Babylon* (1996), *The Coming of the Night* (1999), and *The Life and Adventures of Lyle Clemens* (2003). In 1977, Rechy published *The Sexual Outlaw: A Documentary*, a nonfiction book that alternates chapters of the author's sexual experiences with analysis of homophobic laws, practices, and prejudices. The book was named by the *San Francisco Chronicle* as one of the best one hundred nonfiction works of the century. Rechy's essays have been anthologized in *Beneath the Skin* (2004). Rechy's most recent books are *After the Blue Hour* (2017) and *Pablo!* (2018), the latter actually his very first novel that was rejected for publication at the beginning of his career. Rechy has also published plays and short stories and has been recognized with a number of awards. He received the PEN-USA West's Lifetime Achievement Award (he was the first novelist to be awarded the prize) and the Publishing Triangle's William Whitehead Lifetime Achievement Award. In 2006, he was awarded the One Culture Hero Award in Los Angeles in recognition of writing, teaching, and activism in the gay, lesbian, bisexual, and transgender community. In 2000, a CD biography of his life, *Memories and Desires: The Worlds of John Rechy*, was produced and shown at the Museum of Modern Art in Los Angeles. In 2007, Rechy published his own memoir of growing up biracial and gay on the El Paso border, *About My Life and the Kept Woman*. He currently teaches at the University of Southern California.

Alberto Álvaro Ríos (1952–)

Born in Nogales, Arizona, on September 18, 1952, to a Mexican father and an English mother, Alberto Álvaro Ríos was one the first Latino writers to forge a respected career for himself in the academic creative writing establishment. He not only won prestigious awards for his poetry, but he also became a tenured professor at the University of Arizona. Ríos graduated from the University of Arizona with a B.A. in English and creative writing (1974) and an M.F.A. in creative writing (1979). In 1975, he earned another B.A. in psychology. After achieving national success, Ríos earned tenure at Arizona State University in Tempe (1985) and, in 1994, was appointed a Regent's Professor there. During his career, he has been a writer in residence at various colleges, including Vassar (1992). Ríos's first poetry chapbook, *Elk Heads on the Wall*, was issued in 1979; his first full-length poetry book was *Sleeping on Fists*, published in 1981. Ríos is the author of more than a dozen books of poetry and short stories, including the following: *Whispering to Fool the Wind* (1982), winner of the Academy of American Poets Walt Whitman Award; *The Iguana Killer: Twelve Stories of the Heart* (1984), winner of the Western States Foundation Award for Fiction; *Five Indiscretions* (1985); *The Warrington Poems* (1989); *Teodoro Luna's Two Kisses* (1990), which was nominated for the Pulitzer Prize in poetry; *Pig Cookies and Other Stories* (1995); *The Curtain of Trees: Stories* (1999); *The Smallest Muscle in the Body* (2002); *Theater of the Night* (2006); *The Dangerous Shirt* (2009); and *A Small Story about the Sky* (2015). In 1999, Ríos revisited his childhood in *Capirotada: A Nogales Memoir*, and in 2020 he published the well-received *A Good Map of All Things: A Picaresque Novel*. Ríos's works have been selected for the Best American Poetry, 1996 and 1999, as well as the Best American Essays, 1999. He also bears the distinction of having won Pushcart Prizes in both poetry (1988, 1989, 1995) and fiction (1986, 1993, 2001). In 2007, Ríos was presented with the PEN Beyond Margins Award and the Arizona Literary Treasure Award. In 2013, Ríos served as Arizona's first poet laureate, and in 2014 he was elected a chancellor of the Academy of American Poets.

Beatriz Rivera (1957–)

Beatriz Rivera was born on September 17, 1957, in Havana, Cuba, and accompanied her parents into exile while she was a child. Educated in public schools in Miami, she went on to the equivalent degrees of bachelor's and master's in philosophy from Paris IV Sorbonne in 1977 and 1979, respectively. She later obtained a Ph.D. in comparative literature from the CUNY Graduate Center in New York City in 2000. Rivera is a novelist who satirizes the foibles and conflict within the Cuban communities in the United States. She writes from and about her location in New York and New Jersey, often centering her stories and novels on the Cuban community in Union City, New Jersey. As such, she charts the contradictions of biculturalism and the need to "make it" in the United States, even to the extent of graft and criminality, as in her novel *When a Tree Falls* (2010). Rivera's first book was a collection of short stories, *African Passions and Other Stories* (1995). Her next three books were novels: *Midnight Sandwiches at the Mariposa Express* (1997), *Playing with Light* (2000), and *Do Not Pass Go* (2006), the latter winning the Paterson Prize. In each of these novels, Rivera creates a funny yet realistic portrait of Cuban Americans struggling to find their place in the American Dream.

Louis Reyes Rivera (1945–2012)

Nuyorican poet Louis Reyes Rivera was known for the dramatic recitations of his narrative poetry, including his ability to recite from memory thousands of lines of his often epic-like compositions. The author of various poetry collections that captured the nuance and immediacy of his spoken verse, Rivera was born on May 19, 1945, in Brooklyn and raised in the African American community of Bedford-Stuyvesant; he thus related to both the Puerto Rican and Afro-American communities, both of whose cultures are reflected in the English-language diction and spirit of his poems. The outlets for his verse also reflected this duality, with his work appearing in such magazines as *Areito* (Arawak Dance-Drama-Poetry) and *Black Nation*. Rivera founded and edited his own press, Shamal Books, which also published poets from both communities, in addition to some of his own books. The graduate of the City

University of New York (1974) was also a founder of the Black Writers Union. In his poetry, however, Rivera was the poet of not just Nuyoricans and Afro-Americans but also of Third World peoples everywhere. His outrage at oppression of the poor, racism, colonialism, and disenfranchisement was declaimed passionately in most of his work. In an interview for *Chicken Bones*, he stated, "There's no corner of this hemisphere that was not invaded, conquered, enslaved. There is equally no corner of this hemisphere, from the borders of Canada to the tip of Chile, where Africans were not kidnapped to, for purposes of supplementing and/or complementing slave labor forces." Rivera was the author of three collections of poetry: *Who Pays the Cost* (1977), *This One for You* (1983), and *Scattered Scripture* (1996). *Scattered Scripture*, in which he translated history into poetry and included thirty pages of notes to the poems, was the winner of the 1997 Poetry Award from the Latin American Writers' Institute. Rivera won some twenty other awards, including the CCNY 125th Anniversary Medal (1973), a Special Congressional Recognition Award (1988), and a Lifetime Achievement Award (1995).

Tomás Rivera (1935–1984)

Mexican American novelist Tomás Rivera was one of the principal founders of the Chicano literary movement and was the author of one of the foundational works of that movement, … *y no se lo tragó la tierra/And the Earth Did Not Devour Him* (1971). Born into a family of migrant workers in Crystal City, Texas, on December 22, 1935, Rivera had to fit his early schooling as well as his college education in between the seasons of work in the fields. He nevertheless achieved an outstanding education and became a college professor and administrator. He became chancellor of the University of California–Riverside in 1978, the position he held when he died of a heart attack on May 16, 1984. Rivera's outwardly simple but inwardly complex novel, … *y no se lo tragó la tierra*, is much in the line of experimental Latin American fiction, demanding that the reader take part in unraveling the story and in coming to his own conclusions about the identity and relationships of the characters, as well as the meaning. Drawing upon his own life as a migrant worker from Texas, Rivera constructed a novel in the straightforward but poetic language of migrant workers in which a nameless central character attempts to find himself by reconstructing the overheard conversations and stories and the events that took place during a metaphorical year, which really represents the protagonist's entire lifetime. It is the story of a sensitive boy who is trying to understand the hardship that surrounds his family and community of migrant workers; his path is first one of rejection of them only to embrace them and their culture dearly as his own at the end of the book. In many ways, … *y no se lo tragó la tierra* came to be the most influential book in the Chicano's search for identity. Before his death, Rivera wrote and published other stories, essays, and poems. Through his essays, such as "Chicano Literature: Fiesta of the Living" (1979) and "Into the Labyrinth: The Chicano in Literature" (1971), and his personal and scholarly activities, he was one of the prime movers in the promotion of Chicano authors, in the creation of the concept of Chicano literature, and in the creation of Chicano literature and culture as legitimate academic areas in the college curriculum. In 1989 his stories were collected and published under the title of *The Harvest*, which was also the title of one of his stories, and in 1990 his poems were collected and published under the title of *The Searchers*. In 1990, all of his works were collected and published in *Tomás Rivera: The Complete Works*, the only volume of a Chicano author's complete works published to date. By all accounts, Tomás Rivera remains the most outstanding and influential figure in the literature of Mexican peoples in the United States, and he deserves a place in the canon of Spanish-language literature in the world.

Abraham Rodríguez Jr. (1961–)

Born to Puerto Rican parents in the South Bronx and raised there and in Spanish Harlem, Abraham Rodríguez Jr. experienced success at a young age in writing fiction based on the seedier side of poverty in the South Bronx. With a finely tuned ear for dialect, Rodríguez creates believable characters who fight to survive the mean streets' squalor, drugs, and poverty; it is precisely that naturalistic slice of life that brought Rodríguez to the attention of mainstream publishers and even led to Hollywood film options on his books. An outspoken critic of other Puerto Rican and Nuyorican writers, Rodríguez actually benefited from an excellent education at the City College of New York—despite his having been a high school dropout who earned a high-school equivalency diploma. In 1993 Rodríguez published his first collection of stories: *Boy without a Flag: Tales of the South Bronx*. The book was designated a *New York Times* Notable Book of the Year. His novel *Spidertown*, published in 1995, won an American Book Award from the Before Columbus Foundation and was optioned by Columbia Pictures. In 2001, Rodríguez issued *The Buddha Book: A Novel*, which continued his favorite theme of Puerto Rican teenagers searching for identity in the South Bronx. In 2008 he published *South by South Bronx*, a gritty profile of the Bronx itself and its urban dwellers. In the characters Rodríguez creates, along with their desperation and oftentimes sordid pursuits and environment, he offers very little that cannot be found in television crime drama that focuses on the culture of poverty of Latinos; they are the same cultural depictions that became commonplace after anthropologist Oscar Lewis documented them in *La Vida* and were repeated in books during the 1960s and 1970s.

Luis J. Rodríguez (1954–)

Luis J. Rodríguez was born on July 9, 1954, in El Paso as the son of Mexican immigrants and raised in Los Angeles, where he became a gang member, petty thief, and drug addict and was sentenced to a six-year prison term. He escaped the life on the streets out of the force of will and began working in heavy industry as well as keeping journals and writing. By the 1980s, he became active in Latino arts and cultural circles and served as director of Los Angeles's Latino Writers Association. In 1985, he moved to Chicago and became the editor of the *People's Tribune*, a weekly progressive newspaper. When he perceived the lack of access to publication for Latino and minority writers, Rodríguez in 1989 founded Tía Chucha Press, at first a publisher of

chapbooks. He published his own *Poems across the Pavement* with Tía Chucha that same year. His second book of poetry, *The Concrete River*, won the PEN Oakland/Josephine Miles Award in 1991. These were followed by *Trochemoche* (1989, Helter Skelter), a mélange of various style of urban spoken word and more intimate and affecting verse, and *My Nature Is Hunger: New and Selected Poems* (2005), the latter being a compilation of some of his earlier poems along with twelve new ones. When Rodríguez noted that his son was being drawn into street gang life and culture in Chicago, he wrote *Always Running: La Vida Loca, Gang Days in L.A.* to document the wasted life and dead-end machismo that awaited his son if he continued on the streets. His *The Republic of East LA* (2003) assembles twelve stories of diverse characters who struggle to survive crime, poverty, and deprivation in East Los Angeles barrio. In the 1990s, Rodríguez turned to producing children's and young adult literature, including *America Is Her Name (La llaman América)* in 1998, which won the Paterson Books for Young People Award as well as others, and *It Doesn't Have to Be This Way: A Barrio Story (No tiene que ser así: Una historia el barrio)* (2004), which was a Parents' Choice Approved Winner for Children's Books and an Américas Award Commended Title. Both books deal with the evils and dangers of inner-city life.

After returning to Los Angeles, in 2001 Rodríguez, his wife, Trini, and his friend Enrique Sánchez opened Tía Chucha Café Cultural, a cultural arts center and book store. That same year, he published *Hearts and Hands: Creating Community in Violent Times*, and in 2002 he founded Dos Manos Records to produce music and poetry CDs. His next book, *The Republic of East L.A.: Stories*, won the PEN Oakland Josephine Miles Book Award. In 2005, *Music of the Mill: A Novel*, his first historical novel, received the Latino Book Award for fiction. That same year, he published *My Nature Is Hunger: New & Selected Poems, 1989–2004*. In 2016 he published the collection *Borrowed Bones: New Poems from the Poet Laureate of Los Angeles*. In 2020 he collected his diverse genres in *From Our Land to Our Land: Essays, Journeys, and Imaginings from a Native Xicanx Writer*. In 2001 the Dalai Lama named Rodríguez as one of fifty Unsung Heroes of Compassion. In 2014 Rodríguez was named poet laureate of Los Angeles.

Richard Rodriguez (1944–)

Essayist Richard Rodriguez was born on July 31, 1944, in San Francisco, the son of Mexican immigrants. Having begun school as a Spanish speaker, he had to make the difficult transition to English to progress in school. As he recalled in his autobiographical essay *Hunger of Memory: The Education of Richard Rodriguez,* Rodríguez came to believe that English was the language of U.S. education and society and that the Spanish language and Latino culture were private matters, for the home. Rodriguez received a B.A. in English from Stanford University in 1967 and an M.A. from Columbia University in 1969; he began doctoral work at the University of California but never completed it, focusing instead on his writing career. In 1981, Rodriguez published *Hunger of Memory,* which received praise from mainstream critics across the nation for its elegant and passionate prose and for its rejection of bilingual education and affirmative action programs. Rodriguez immediately was seen by Latinos as an Uncle Tom or Tío Taco for having bought success at the price of attacking Hispanic language, culture, and bilingual programs aimed to assist Hispanics in education and employment. To this date, despite a successful career as an essayist, television commentator, and opinion writer for newspapers, Rodriguez is not embraced by Latino critics as an authentic or valuable voice.

His second book, *Days of Obligation: An Argument with My Mexican Father* (1992), which does not have the political content of *Hunger of Memory,* received fewer, but generally good reviews and garnered very little criticism from Latino quarters. In 2003, he published *Brown: The Last Discovery of America,* a meditation on race and ethnicity as well as gender identity in the United States; in addition to the usual tough subjects treated by Rodriguez, his gay identity is also pondered. Rodriguez's most recent book, *Darling: A Spiritual Autobiography* (2013), continues in the vein of his self-reflection.

Benjamin Alire Sáenz (1954–)

Born in the farm town of Old Picacho, New Mexico, on August 16, 1954, Benjamin Alire Sáenz is one of the few Mexican American novelists to see many of his works published by major, commercial presses in the United States. Raised by devout working-class parents near Mesilla, New Mexico, Sáenz studied for the Catholic priesthood, earning a master's degree in theology in 1980 from the University of Louvain in Belgium and becoming ordained in 1981. Despite his lifelong religiosity, Sáenz left the priesthood and decided to pursue a career in writing; he received a master's degree in creative writing from the University of Texas at El Paso in 1988. He later attempted a Ph.D. degree in English at Stanford University with a Stegner Fellowship but never finished. Sáenz published his first book, *Calendar of Dust* (1991), a poetry collection commemorating the diverse peoples and their migrations in the borderlands, with a small press, Broken Moon, located in Seattle. It immediately won the Before Columbus American Book Award. Based on this initial work, he was awarded a Lannan Poetry Fellowship in 1992. That same year, Sáenz published a collection of short stories, *Flowers for the Broken,* again exploring the peoples and culture of the U.S.-Mexico border. His short-story collection *Everything Begins and Ends at the Kentucky Club* won the PEN/Fualkner Award for Fiction in 2013. The prolific Sáenz went on to publish another poetry collection, *Dark and Perfect Angels,* in 1995; the poems contained in this deeply spiritual and personal anthology eulogize deceased friends and relatives as well as fictionalized strangers. That same year, Sáenz broke into publishing with a commercial house, Hyperion, for his novel *Carry Me Like Water,* which follows twelve disciple-like characters who in the margins of urban life in El Paso and San Francisco learn of human trials and tribulations—such as the spread of AIDS, sexual abuse, homophobia, racism, and poverty—and learn how to teach, heal, and deal with these ills. As usual, the narrative and its symbols have direct references to the Old and New Testaments. In *The House of Forgetting* (1997)—this and his subsequent novels were all published by Harper-Collins—Sáenz produced an even more commercially viable novel, this one exploring the psychological thriller genre. In *The House of Forgetting*, the rearing of a kidnapped Chicana from the border leads to a police procedural drama as well as a consideration of the love-hate relationship the girl develops with the kidnapper, a professor who has held her captive in Chicago. Again, Catholic symbols and ritual enrich the narrative, which also positively identifies spirituality with Mexican culture. Sáenz's latest novel, *In Perfect Light* (2005), the first also to be issued simultaneously in Spanish translation, enters the world of child molestation, the Juárez underworld, and the breaking apart of an El Paso Chicano family. His novel *Names in a Map* (2008) explores how an El Paso family is divided by their reaction to the Vietnam War. In 2002 and 2006, respectively, Sáenz returned to small presses to issue his third and fourth books of poems, *Elegies in Blue* and *Dreaming the End of War*. The first of these is a series of twelve prose poems in elegiac tone dealing with issues of family, childhood, life, and death; the latter is a poetic examination of male identity, especially as related to violence and war. His most recent book of poems is *The Book of What Remains* (2010).

Floyd Salas (1931–2021)

Floyd Salas was born on January 24, 1931, in Walsenburg, Colorado, into a family that traces both its maternal and paternal lines back to the original Spanish settlers of Florida and New Mexico. When he was still very young, the family relocated to California in pursuit of work opportunities. Following the death of his mother when he was a teenager, Salas became a juvenile delinquent and wound up spending 120 days on the Santa Rita Prison Farm; it was a grueling experience that led him to foreswear his delinquent ways to avoid problems with the law. The experience also served as material for his first novel, which graphically depicts prison life. In 1956, Salas won the first boxing scholarship ever given to the University of California, Berkeley, where he discovered literature. A number of writing scholarships and fellowships followed, including a Rockefeller grant to study at the Centro Mexicano de Escritores in Mexico City in 1958. Upon returning to California from Mexico, Salas worked on Bay Area campuses as a creative writing instructor, became active in the campus protest movement, and immersed himself in the drug and hippie subcultures. These experiences later became grist for his novels *What Now My Love* (1970) and *State of Emergency* (1996). His first published book, *Tattoo the Wicked Cross* (1967), however, was made possible by his winning the prestigious Joseph Henry Jackson Award and a Eugene F. Saxton Fellowship, which were awarded to him based on his early drafts of that novel. *Tattoo the Wicked Cross* is an exposé of the brutality of juvenile jail, as seen by a street youth (*pachuco*) who is raped and abused; the brutalized protagonist ends up committing murder. Salas's next novel was of modest proportions, *What Now My Love?* (1970); it told the story of the escape of three hippies involved in a drug bust where policemen were shot. His next novel followed the hippie trail from San Francisco to Marrakesh in *Lay My Body on the Line* (1978). In the early 1990s, through writing his memoir *Buffalo Nickel*, Salas came to terms with his family's dramatic history of widespread drug addiction and suicides (a total of six). The work depicts his own agonizing love-hate relationship with his older brother, a small-time prizefighter, drug addict, and petty criminal. In 2006 he published *Love Bites: Poetry in Celebration of Dogs and Cats* (2006), a celebration of many types of love. In 2012 Salas was recognized with an American Book Award for Lifetime Achievement from the Before Columbus Foundation.

Luis Omar Salinas (1937–2008)

Born in Robstown, Texas, on June 27, 1937, Luis Omar Salinas spent some of his early years in Mexico and by age nine had moved to live with an aunt and uncle in California. He began college at Fresno State University, but he never received his diploma. During the 1960s, Salinas was hospitalized on various occasions for nervous breakdowns, and these breakdowns continued throughout hs life. In 1970 he published his first book of poetry, *Crazy Gypsy*, a highly artistic work that became an anthem for Chicano activists. Many of the poems were included in the first anthologies of Chicano literature and have become canonized in U.S. Latino literature, including "Crazy Gypsy," "Aztec Angel," "Nights and Days," "Mexico, Age Four," and others. In *Crazy Gypsy* Salinas introduces themes that are evident in all of his works:

alienation and loneliness, death, and the defamiliar-ization of the world around us. In *Darkness under the Trees: Walking behind the Spanish* (1982), and in the works that follow, Salinas heightened the note of sorrow and melancholy as he attempted to rationalize his unjust fate. The themes of love, death, and madness dominated. The second part of the book pays homage to the Spanish Civil War poets who have served as his models, including Federico García Lorca. Salinas is the most lyric, most imaginative, deepest, and most humane Chicano/Latino poet. He is nevertheless generally overlooked by the academy, often passed over not only by readers but by other Latino writers, perhaps because his illnesses did not permit him to tour and engage in exchanges with editors and other writers, or perhaps because he was shy and had not done anything to promote himself. Salinas, who supported himself with a variety of blue-color jobs, won some of the most prestigious awards for writing, including the California English Teachers citation, 1973; Stanley Kunitz Poetry Prize (for *Afternoon of the Unreal*), 1980; Earl Lyon Award, 1980; and General Electric Foundation Award, 1983. In 1986, Salinas's best poems were collected in a hefty volume entitled *The Sadness of Days: New and Selected Poems*. This volume was followed by *Sometimes Mysteriously* (1997); *Elegy for Desire* (1997), a collection of odes, elegies, and cantos; and another compilation, *Greatest Hits, 1969–1996* (2002). His last book of poems, *Elegy for Desire*, was published in 2005.

Raúl Salinas (1934–2008)

Born on March 17, 1934, in San Antonio and later a resident of Los Angeles, Raúl Salinas spent eleven years imprisoned in Soledad State Prison, during which time he raised his political and social consciousness and discovered poetry as an outlet for his frustrations, the agony of memory, and his political commitment. After being transferred to Leavenworth penitentiary, Salinas founded and edited two journals: *Aztlán de Leavenworth* and *New Era Prison Magazine*. After his release, he became one of the most noteworthy ex-convict poets, even elevating prison to a metaphor in his poetry; appropriately one of his most famous poems (originally published in *Aztlán de Leavenworth* in 1970) and the title of his first book reveal

this aesthetic: *Un Trip through the Mind Jail y Otras Excursions* (1980). Through assistance from students and professors at the University of Washington, Salinas was released early and in 1972 took courses at the university and became involved in the Chicano and Native American movements. In addition to publishing his work widely in magazines, Salinas was the author of a second book of poems, *East of the Freeway: Reflections de Mi Pueblo* (1995). In 1999, Arte Público Press reissued *Un Trip* and hailed Salinas as a pioneer of Latino literature in the United States. While residing back in Austin, Texas, Salinas was the owner and operator of Resistencia Bookstore and the publisher of Red Salmon Press, which he founded in 1983. In 2006, with the assistance of editor Louis G. Mendoza, Salinas published *raúlrsalinas and the Jail Machine: My Weapon Is My Pen*, his collection of journalism and personal correspondence, especially focusing on the years of his incarceration. That same year, he published *Indio Trails: A Xicano Odyssey through Indian Country*.

Ricardo Sánchez (1941–1995)

Born the youngest of thirteen children on March 21, 1941, in the notorious Barrio del Diablo (Devil's Neighborhood) in El Paso, Texas, Ricardo Sánchez became a high school dropout, an army enlistee, and later a repeat offender sentenced to prison terms in Soledad Prison in California and Ramsey Prison Farm Number One in Texas. At these prisons he began his literary career before his last parole in 1969. Much of his early life experience of oppressive poverty and overwhelming racism, as well as his suffering in prisons and his self-education and rise to a level of political and social consciousness, is chronicled in his poetry, which, although very lyrical, is the most autobiographical of all the Latino poets. Sánchez was a founder of the short-lived Mictla Publications in El Paso, editor of various special issues of literary magazines, such as *De Colores* and *Wood/Ibis*, a columnist for the *San Antonio Express*, a bookseller, and a migrant worker counselor. Throughout his life, he was an active performer of his poetry on tours in the United States and abroad. Sánchez's poetry is characterized by an unbridled linguistic inventiveness that not only calls upon both English and Spanish lexicon but also is a source of neologisms and surprising combinations of the sounds and symbols of both languages in single works. Sanchez was the autobiographical poet who cast himself as a Chicano Everyman participating in the epic history of his people. Sánchez was the author of the following collections: *Canto y grito mi liberación (y lloro mis desmadrazgos)* (I Sing and Shout for My Liberation [and Cry for My Insults], 1971), *Hechizospells: Poetry/Stories/Vignettes/Articles/Notes on the Human Condition of Chicanos & Pícaros, Words & Hopes within Soulmind* (1976), *Milhuas Blues and Gritos Norteños* (1980), *Amsterdam cantos y poemas pistos* (1983), *Brown Bear Honey Madness* (1981), *Selected Poems* (1985), *Bertrand and the Mehkqoverse* (1989), *Eagle-Visioned/Feathered Adobe* (1990), and *Amerikan Journeys: Jornadas Americanas* (1994). In 2016 Arnoldo Vento collected his works and published *The Posthumous Poetry of Ricardo Sanchez: Journeys through the Pass: Bloodied Tracks and Desertland Poems*.

José Sánchez-Boudy (1928–2016)

Born on October 17, 1928, in Havana, Cuba, José Sánchez-Boudy was the son of a wealthy Spanish immigrant and a French Cuban mother. Sánchez-Boudy studied for two years in New Hampshire and the University of Detroit but returned to Cuba for a law degree, which he obtained from the University of Havana in 1953. Sánchez-Boudy became a noted criminal attorney, but in 1961 he abandoned Cuba for Miami and then Puerto Rico after the Castro takeover. In 1965, he took his wife and children to Greensboro, North Carolina, where he spent the rest of his career as a professor at the University of North Carolina, Greensboro. Sánchez-Boudy became one of the most distinguished authors and critics of Cuban exile literature, devoting almost all of his creative work to reliving the Cuban past and the effects of the Cuban Revolution. His poetry, in particular, is nostalgic for the sights and sounds of Havana street culture and, in particular, Afro-Cuban dialect and customs. His collections of poems are heavily inspired in Afro-Cuban poetry: *Aché, Babalú, Ayé* (1975), *Ejué, Abankué Ehué* (1977), and *Ritos Náñigos* (1977, Afro-Cuban Rites). Included among his most famous works are *Cuentos grises* (1966, Grey Stories), *Cuentos del hombre* (1969, Stories about Man), *Tiempo congelado (Poemario de una isla ausente)* (1979, Frozen Weather [Poetry about an Absent Island]), *Cuentos de la niñez* (1983, Stories

from Childhood), and *La patria no ha muerto, no, está en el viento* (1986, The Fatherland Has Not Died, No, It's in the Wind). His novels *Liliyando* (1971) and *Liliyando pal tu* (1978), titles in Sánchez-Boudy's invented language, principally have language as their protagonist, as they are made up of conversations among nameless characters before the outbreak of the Cuban Revolution. His novels *La soledad de la Playa Larga* (1971, The Loneliness of Long Beach) and *Los cruzados de la aurora* (1973, Those Who Crossed at Daybreak) are anti-Castro narratives, the former dealing with the failed Bay of Pigs Invasion of 1961.

Esmeralda Santiago (1948–)

Born on May 17, 1948, in Puerto Rico, Esmeralda Santiago moved with her family to Brooklyn, New York, when she was thirteen. Despite the poverty of her background, Santiago was able to receive a bachelor's degree from Harvard University and an M.A. from Sarah Lawrence College. First dedicated to documentary filmmaking, Santiago shifted her artistic career to writing, when in 1993 she published her acclaimed memoir of growing up in Puerto Rico and moving to New York: *When I Was Puerto Rican*. In 1998, she published *Almost a Woman*, the sequel that covers her maturing in the big city, exploring the immigrant's typical struggle to adapt and establish an identity, as well as the adolescent's fight for independence from a strong-willed mother who retains the old customs. In these and her novel of immigration, *America's Dream* (1997), Santiago revived the 1960s and 1970s themes of culture clash, racial identity, and the culture of poverty, although from a feminist perspective. In addition to these themes, Santiago explores the relationship between mothers and daughters and the cycles of womanhood. In *Almost a Woman*, Santiago charts her adaptation to American society. The book was such a success that it was adapted into a screenplay for the Public Broadcasting System and aired on Masterpiece Theater in 2001; the drama was awarded a George Foster Peabody Award for excellence in broadcasting. Her most recent novel is *My Turkish Lover* (2004), a memoir of an abusive relationship with a film maker. In 2005 after recovering from a stroke, Santiago was able to publish her epic, historical novel, *Conquistadora*, which follows the life of Ana, a fictional Spaniard who moves to Puerto Rico and ascends in the sugar industry.

John Phillip Santos
(1957–)

Born and raised in San Antonio, Texas, in 1957, John Phillip Santos was a Rhodes Scholar and earned degrees in English literature and language from Oxford University and philosophy and literature from the University of Notre Dame (1979). He served as an appointed member of the Presidential Advisory Commission on Excellence in Education for Hispanic Americans and worked as a program officer at the Ford Foundation in the Media, Arts and Culture Program. Santos's reputation as writer depends largely on his family memoir, *Places Left Unfinished at the Time of Creation*, which was a finalist for the 1999 National Book Award. *Places* projects the story of Santos's family onto the epic of the Mexican people and their immigration to the United States. The family saga is rich in adventure and tragedy, dealing with Indian kidnappings, a family member who suffers from epilepsy, and a grandfather's suicide in San Antonio. Santos wrote a sequel to this memoir, *The Farthest Home Is in an Empire of Fire: A Tejano Elegy*, in 2010. In 2007, he published a collection of poems, *Songs Older Than Any Known Singer*, that combine memoir, pre-Columbian myth, and even political commentary. Santos was a recipient of the Academy of American Poets' Prize at Notre Dame and the Oxford Prize for fiction.

Gary Soto (1952–)

Born to Mexican American parents in Fresno, California, on April 12, 1952, Gary Soto attended Fresno City College and California State University in Fresno. He graduated from California State University in 1975, and in 1976 he earned an M.F.A. degree in creative writing from the University of Cali-

fornia, Irvine. Soto has more prestigious awards than any other Latino poet in the United States; these include the Academy of American Poets Prize (1975), the Discovery-Nation Award (1975), the United States Award of the International Poetry Forum (1976), the Bess Hopkins Prize from *Poetry* magazine (1977), the Guggenheim Fellowship (1979), and the Levinson Award from *Poetry* magazine (1984). Soto's books of poetry include the following: *The Elements of San Joaquin* (1977), *Father Is a Pillow Tied to a Broom* (1980), *Where Sparrows Work Hard* (1981), *Black Hair* (1985), *Who Will Know Us?* (1990), *One Kind of Faith* (2003), *A Simple Plan* (2007), *Partly Cloudy: Poems of Love and Longing* (2009), and *Sudden Loss of Dignity* (2013). Soto has also published three collections of autobiographical essays and stories: *Living Up the Street: Narrative Recollections* (1985), *Small Faces* (1986), and *Lesser Evils: Ten Quartets* (1988). He has written too many young adult novels to include here, but among them are *Baseball in April* (1990), *Jesse* (1994), *Fearless Fernie* (2002), *If the Shoe Fits* (2002), *Marisol* (2005), and *When Dad Came Back* (2011). All of Soto's works are highly autobiographical and characterized by a highly polished craft. In his poetry and prose, great attention is paid to narration and characterization; whether he is writing a poem or an essay, Soto is always cognizant of telling a story. Critics have always stated that Soto has something important and human to say, and it is poignantly said in well-crafted writing.

Pedro Juan Soto
(1928–2002)

Born on July 11, 1928, in Cataño, Puerto Rico, to a barber father and a spiritualist mother who ran séances at home, Pedro Juan Soto became a distinguished Puerto Rican short-story writer, novelist, and dramatist. He moved to New York to study premedicine at Long Island University but eventually graduated as an English major. He earned his bachelor's degree in English in 1950 and was drafted and sent to fight in Korea. After returning to the United States, Soto earned a master's degree at Columbia University in 1953. In 1976, Soto earned a Ph.D. in literature from the University of Toulouse in France. All along he had been writing short stories, many of them based on the discrimination against Puerto Ricans he witnessed in New York and in the Army. Finally, after completing his master's degree, he began writing as a professional for *Visión* (Vision) magazine, *Temas* (Themes), and *Ecos de Nueva York* (New York Echoes) in New York. In 1954 he received the first prize for a short story from the Ateneo Puertorriqueño. In 1954 or 1955, Soto returned to Puerto Rico to work in the Division of Publications of the Puerto Rican Department of Education. From then on, he wrote and published a steady stream of short stories and novels, which made him one of the most famous and respected Puerto Rican literary figures. In 1956, Soto published his definitive collection of stories centering on Puerto Rican life in New York: *Spiks*. Ever attracted by marginality, his first published novel, *Usmail* (1958), portrayed a Puerto Rican mulatto living on the island of Vieques. Two other novels reflect his feelings of marginality, probably ingrained since his experience in New York: *Ardiente suelo, fría estación* (1961, Burning Soil, Cold Season), narrating the culture conflict a Puerto Rican faces when he returns to the Island after being gone a long time; and *El francotirador* (1969, The Sniper), dealing this time with a Cuban exile living in Puerto Rico. Other novels include *Temporada de duendes* (1970, Ghost Season), *Un oscuro pueblo sonriente* (1982, A Dark Smiling People), and *Memoria de mi amnesia* (1991, Memory of My Amnesia). For *Un oscuro pueblo sonriente*, Soto received Cuba's international award, Premio Casa Las Américas (America's House Prize).

Clemente Soto Vélez
(1905–1993)

Born in Lares, Puerto Rico, in 1905, Clemente Soto Vélez dedicated himself and his poetry to freeing Puerto Rico from U.S. colonial rule. He studied business and engineering at the Ramírez Commercial School in San Juan but nevertheless became involved in writers' groups and participated in events at the Ateneo Puertorriqueño (Puerto Rican Atheneum). In 1928, he began working as a journalist and editor at *El Tiempo* (Time) newspaper and began publishing poetry. In 1929 he was a leader of the iconoclastic *Atalaya de los Dioses* (Watchtower of the Gods), a poetry movement that, while mainly aesthetic in its innovation and desire to break with all literary tra-

dition, led to political activism. Many of the *atalayistas*, including Soto Vélez, became radicalized and joined the Puerto Rican nationalist movement. In 1936, Soto Vélez was indicted with other nationalist leaders for inciting the overthrow of the U.S. government; he was found guilty and served seven years in prison. Upon release in 1942, he moved to New York, as his return to Puerto Rico had been prohibited in his parole. He spent the rest of his life in New York, where he continued his writing and his political activism. He organized Hispanic merchants into a society and also was the founder of Club Cultural del Bronx (Bronx Cultural Club) and Casa Borinquen (Puerto Rico House); he also served as president of Círculo de Escritores y Poetas Iberomericanos (Ibero-American Writers and Poets Circle) and was a member of various other cultural associations, for which he organized literary events. During the 1940s, he also served as an editor for his fellow Communist Juan Antonio Corretjer's newspaper, *Pueblos Hispanos* (Hispanic Peoples). After years of publishing his poetry in periodicals on the island and in New York, in 1954 Soto Vélez published his first book of poetry, *Abrazo interno* (Internal Embrace). Other books followed, including *Árboles* (Trees, 1955), *Caballo de palo* (Wooden Horse, 1959), and *La tierra prometida* (The Promised Land, 1979), which are book-length narrative poems that continue his experiments with aesthetics and language. In 1976, his importance as a national writer was recognized by the Institute of Puerto Rican Culture with its reprint of *Caballo de palo*.

Carmen Tafolla
(1951–)

Born on July 29, 1951, in San Antonio, Tafolla came to prominence in the late Chicano Movement of the mid-1970s. She is the holder of a B.A. in Spanish and French (1972) and an M.A. in education (1973) from Austin College and a Ph.D. in bilingual education from the University of Texas (1982). Despite her educational accomplishments, Tafolla is an oral poet and performer who bases her work on the bilingualism and bicul-turalism of working-class Mexican American neigh-borhoods. A folklorist at heart, she has preserved many of the folkways and much of the worldview of common folk in her verse. Among her poetry collections are *Curandera* (1983, Faith Healer), *To Split a Human: Mitos, Machos y La Mujer Chicana* (1985), *Patchwork Colcha: Poems, Stories and Songs in English and Spanish* (1987), *Sonnets and Salsa* (2001), *This River Here: Poems of San Antonio* (2014), and *Carmen Tafolla: New and Selected Poems* (2015). What comes to the fore in *Curandera* is a constant in Tafolla's aesthetic, which derives directly from oral lore and wisdom passed on by women. In 1989, her *Sonnet to Human Beings* won the University of California–Irvine award for Chicano literature, and in 2001 she published a well reviewed collection, *Sonnets and Salsa*. Tafolla has also written works for children, including *My House Is Your House: Mi casa es su casa* (2000), *That's Not Fair: Emma Tenayuca's Struggle for Justice* (2008), *The Amazing Water Color Fish* (2018), and *Fiesta Babies* (2020). Tafolla has won the Tomás Rivera Mexican-American Award for Children's Books (2009 and 2010), the Américas Award for Children's and Young Adult Literature (2010), and the Charlotte Zolotow Award for Best Children's Picture Book (2010). She served as San Antonio's first poet laureate from 2012 to 2014.

Piri Thomas
(1928–2011)

Born on September 30, 1928, in New York City to a Puerto Rican mother and a Cuban father, Piri Thomas grew up during the Great Depression, facing both poverty and racism in New York's East Harlem. Thomas entered a life of theft, gang vio-lence, and criminality in adolescence, and he met his inevitable fate of imprisonment. After serving seven years of a fifteen-year term, he was paroled at age twenty-eight. While in prison he had obtained his high school equivalency diploma and also had begun to learn to express himself in writing; he also devel-oped a sense of dignity and self-respect. All of Thomas's literary works are highly autobiographical, dealing mostly with his upbringing in the poverty, racism, and culture conflict of the barrio. In addition

to his well-known *Down These Mean Streets* (1967), Thomas also wrote a sequel, *Savior, Savior Hold My Hand* (1972), and a book on his seven-year impris-onment from 1950 to 1956, *Seven Long Times* (1974). He also published *Stories from el Barrio* (1978). In ad-dition, Thomas published numerous articles and es-says and wrote plays that were produced on stage. Thomas's work is important for having been among the first to break through to the mainstream, with all of his books having been issued by major pub-lishers and *Down These Mean Streets* so highly reviewed that it projected Thomas into the television talk-show circuit and instant celebrity. A powerful and charming speaker, Thomas became an important spokesperson for the Puerto Rican community.

Edwin Torres (1931–)

Born in 1931 in New York City's Spanish Harlem to poverty-stricken Puerto Rican parents, Edwin Torres is one of the most prolific and commercially successful Latino writers. After graduating from Stuyvesant High School and City College, Torres obtained his law degree from the Brooklyn Law School in 1958. In 1959, he worked in the city attorney's office, where he partici-pated in the prosecution of Mafia figures. Shortly there-after, he became a criminal defense attorney, an experi-ence that would serve him well in portraying the criminal mind in his works of fiction. In 1977, the same year as the publication of his second crime novel, Torres was appointed to the New York State Criminal Court, and in 1980, he was elected to the New York State Supreme Court in the Twelfth Judicial District. A master of crime fiction, Torres has seen his works transformed into acclaimed Hollywood productions starring some of the greatest film actors of the twen-tieth century. A judge in the New York City courts by day, Torres has produced an unending stream of stories for such magazines as *Alfred Hitchcock's Mystery Magazine*, *Crimespree*, *Demolition*, *Shred of Evidence*, and *SHOTS*. His novels include *Carlito's Way* (1975), *Q & A* (1977), and *After Hours* (1979), the latter a sequel to *Carlito's Way*. Torres's most acclaimed and renowned work is *Carlito's Way*, a gritty and dark tale of a street criminal, drug dealer, and murderer who rises to power and in his aging sees a new breed of thugs taking over and bringing about his own decline.

Edwin Torres (1958–)

The child of Puerto Rican parents who settled in Bronx, New York, poet Edwin Torres is a spoken-word artist. His books include *SandHommeNomadNo* (1997, a self-published chapbook), *Fractured Humorous* (1999), *The All-Union Day of the Shock Worker* (2001), and *Lung Poetry* (2002), which are highly experimental in their use of graphic and sound juxtapositions in their attempt to represent Torres's oral/aural performances in writing. His poetry is irreverent and humorous in its frequent use of bilingual puns and surprising in its fluid incorporation of so many disparate references, sounds, and concepts. His poetic style, paradoxically, was called "frenetic" as well as "elegant" in a 1999 *Publishers Weekly* article. His other books include *Yes Thing No Thing* (2011), *One Night: Poems for the Sleepy* (2012), and *Ameriscopia* (2014). Torres also produced a CD, *Holy Kid* (1998), featuring his oral performances. From 1993 to 1999, Torres toured nationally and internationally performing and offering workshops as a member of Real Live Poetry (formerly Nuyorican Poets Café Live), a collective of spoken-word artists. In 2003, he coedited a special issue of *Rattapallax Magazine*, featuring spoken-word artists, singers, and composers, with an accompanying CD: *Rattapallax 9*. Based on the success of this experiment, three more issues of the magazine/CD followed, featuring Torres and some of the same Nuyorican and Brazilian poets and performers.

Steven Torres (1969–)

The Bronx, New York–born Steven Torres graduated from Stuyvesant High School in New York and received a B.A. in English from Hunter College in 1994. In 2002, he received his Ph.D. in English from CUNY Graduate Center. Torres is the author of a successful series of detective novels featuring his small-town sheriff Luis Gonzalo, whose beat is Angustias, a fictional mountain village similar to Moca, Puerto Rico, where Torres lived for a while. The series includes the following titles: *Precinct Puerto Rico: Book One* (2002), *Death in Precinct Puerto Rico: Book Two* (2003), *Burning Precinct Puerto Rico: Book Three* (2004), *Missing in Precinct Puerto Rico: Book Four* (2006), and *Blackout in Precinct Puerto Rico* (2010). In 2011, he issued two collections of short stories: *Killing Ways: Stories* and *Killing Ways 2: Urban Stories*. Throughout this police procedural series, the initial mysteries—set in the local color of rural Puerto Rico with idiosyncratic and folksy character types—to be unraveled by Gonzalo led to larger, more international criminal activities and conspiracies. In 2007, Torres departed from the series to turn his attention to New York City as the site of his fiction in *The Concrete Maze*. Torres's short fiction has appeared in *Alfred Hitchcock's Mystery Magazine, Crimespree, Demolition, Shred of Evidence,* and *SHOTS,* among other periodicals.

Estela Portillo Trambley (1926–1998)

Born in El Paso, Texas, on January 16, 1926, Estela Portillo Trambley was raised and educated in El Paso. She received a B.A. degree (1957) and her M.A. degree (1977) from the University of Texas at El Paso and became a high school English teacher. Trambley was the first woman to win the national award for Chicano literature, Premio Quinto Sol, in 1973, for her collection of short stories and novela, *Rain of Scorpions and Other Writings*. Besides stories and plays published in magazines and anthologies, Trambley wrote a collection of plays, *Sor Juana and Other Plays* (1981), and a novel, *Trini* (1983). In both her prose and drama, Trambley developed strong women who resist the social roles that have been predetermined for them because of their sex. In her fiction, women command center stage and achieve a level of self-determination and control over social and cultural circumstances. The culmination of her pursuit of strong women is represented in her exploration of the life of the eighteenth-century poet and essayist Sor Juan Inés de la Cruz in her play *Sor Juana*. The protagonist of her novel, *Trini*, is a fictional character who struggles against poverty and adversity to make her way in life; she eventually leaves Mexico and crosses the border illegally to find the power over her own life for which she has been searching. Among her many plays, the following were produced on stage: *Morality Play* (1974), *Black Light* (1975), *El Hombre Cósmico* (1975, The Cosmic Man), *Sun Images* (1976), and *Isabel and the Dancing Bear* (1977).

Sergio Troncoso
(1961–)

Born on January 1, 1961, in El Paso to Mexican immigrant parents, Sergio Troncoso received his B.A. from Harvard University and his M.A. in international relations and philosophy from Yale University. With such a background, rich in academic exploration, it is no wonder that Troncoso is one of the most intellectual of the Mexican American writers. His first book, *The Last Tortilla and Other Stories* (1999), immediately garnered him attention and won the Premio Aztlán and the Southwest Book Award. The stories in *The Last Tortilla* examine Mexican identity and masculinity on the border as well as more intimate themes, such as psychological conflict, morality, and love. His novel *The Nature of Truth* (2003) is a philosophical thriller that examines evil and the implications of the Holocaust. In 2011 he published a highly autobiographical collection of essays, *Crossing Borders: Personal Essays*, some of which deal with crossing not only the U.S.-Mexico border and biculturalism but also Mexican-Jewish ethnic borders. That same year he published the novel *From This Wicked Patch of Dust*, which traces four generations of a family struggling to become American on the border. In 2019 he issued *A Peculiar Kind of Immigrant's Son*, a highly autobiographical collection of stories dealing with cultural conflict and the accommodation of characters from the margin struggling in the heart of America. Troncoso's latest book, *Nobody's Pilgrims* (2021), features runaway teens from the border. In addition to his books, Troncoso's stories have appeared in numerous magazines, anthologies, and such newspapers as *Newsday* and the *El Paso Times*. In 2014, the El Paso City Council voted to name the Ysleta public library branch in honor of Troncoso. In 2020 Troncoso was elected president of the Texas Institute of Letters.

Sabine Ulibarrí
(1919–2003)

Born on September 21, 1919, in the small village of Tierra Amarilla, New Mexico, Sabine Ulibarrí was raised on a ranch by his parents, both of whom were college graduates. His early love for the Spanish language and Latino literature took Ulibarrí to college and eventually to a Ph.D. degree in Spanish. Over the years he taught at every level, from elementary school to graduate school. He had a long and fruitful career as a professor of Spanish at the University of New Mexico, his alma mater. Ulibarrí published two books of poems, *Al cielo se sube a pie* (1966, You Reach Heaven on Foot) and *Amor y Ecuador* (1966, Love and Ecuador), and the following collections of short stories and a memoir in bilingual format: *Tierra Amarilla: Stories of New Mexico/Tierra Amarilla: Cuentos de Nuevo México* (1971), *Mi abuela fumaba puros y otros cuentos de Tierra Amarilla/My Grandma Smoked Cigars and Other Stories of Tierra Amarilla* (1977), *Primeros encuentros/First Encounters* (1982), *El gobernador Glu Glu* (1988, Governor Glu Glu), *Mayhem Was Our Business: Memorias de un Veterano* (1997, a memoir of World War II), *El Cóndor and Other Stories* (1989), *The Best of Sabine R. Ulibarri: Selected Stories* (1993), and *Sueños/Dreams* (1994). In all of his work, Ulibarrí preserved a style, narrative technique, and language that owed much to the oral folk tradition. Through his works he was able to capture the ethos and the spirit of rural New Mexico before the coming of the Anglo.

Luz María Umpierre-Herrera
(1947–)

Born in Santurce, Puerto Rico, on October 15, 1947, Luz María Umpierre-Herrera attended private schools and graduated from the Universidad del Sagrado Corazón with a B.A. in Spanish. She began law school in Puerto Rico but soon gave that up for graduate work in Spanish at Bryn Mawr College. After receiving her Ph.D. from that institution in 1978, Umpierre-Herrera taught Hispanic literature at the University of Kansas, Rutgers University, and various other universities. Umpierre-Herrera published her first book of poems, *Una puertorriqueña en Penna* (1979, A Puerto Rican Woman in Pain/Pennsylvania), protesting her marginalization while at Bryn Mawr and experimenting with the code-switching between Spanish and English that she copied from the Nuyorican writers. Her later books of poems all criticize U.S. society as an outsider and lesbian while also revealing a desire for acceptance as a Latina. These books include *En el país de las maravillas* (1982, In the Land of Marvels), *Y otras desgracias and Other Misfortunes* (1985), *The Margarita Poems* (1987), *For Christine: Poems and One Letter* (1995), *Pour toi/For Moira* (2005), and *Our Only Island—for Nemir* (2009). Umpierre-Herrera has also published her poetry widely in magazines and anthologies. In 1990, she received the Lifetime Achievement Award from the Coalition of Lesbians and Gays of New Jersey.

Luis Alberto Urrea (1955–)

Born on August 20, 1955, in Tijuana, Baja California, Mexico, to an American mother and a Mexican father who moved with him to San Diego in 1958, Luis Alberto Urrea grew up experiencing conflicts within his bicultural family and psyche, many of which he related in his memoir, *Nobody's Son: Notes from an American Life* (1977). Urrea graduated from the University of California at San Diego in 1977 and until 1982 worked with an American missionary group among poor people at the Tijuana dumps, an experience described in *Across the Wire: Life and Hard Times on the Mexican Border* (1992) and *By the Lake of the Sleeping Children* (1996). He earned a master of arts degree in creative writing at the University of Colorado-Boulder in 1997. His big debut in publishing came in 2005 with *The Devil's Highway: A True Story*, for which he was a Pulitzer Prize finalist. This was followed by *The Hummingbird's Daughter: A Novel*, inspired by the life of his great aunt, Teresa Urrea, a famed folk healer known as the Saint of Cabora all along the border. Urrea's books include various genres, from poetry to fiction to nonfiction to memoirs: *Frozen Moments* (1977), *Across the Wire: Life and Hard Times on the Mexican Border* (1992), *In Search of Snow* (1994), *The Fever of Being* (1994), *By the Lake of the Sleeping Children* (1996), *Ghost Sickness* (1997), *Nobody's Son: Notes from an American Life* (1998), *Wandering Time: Western Notebooks* (1999), *Vatos* (with photographer José Galvez, 2000), *Six Kinds of Sky: A Collection of Short Fiction* (2002), *The Devil's Highway: A True Story* (2004), *The*

Hummingbird's Daughter (2005), *The Water Museum* (2015), and *The House of Broken Angels* (2018).

Alisa Valdés-Rodríguez (1969–)

Born on February 28, 1969, in Albuquerque, New Mexico, to a Cuban American father and an Anglo-American mother descended from the founding fathers, Alisa Valdés-Rodríguez is one of a handful of Latinas popularizing a light, lifestyle literature created to appeal to Latina yuppies or aspirants thereof: Latina "chic lit." Valdés-Rodríguez developed a love of writing and earned a master's degree from the Columbia School of Journalism in 1994. After her first job at the *Boston Globe*, Valdés-Rodríguez moved to the *Los Angeles Times* in 1998 and then to the *Albuquerque Journal*. Her first book, *The Dirty Girls Social Club* (2003), is an irreverent and humorous look at the adventures and misadventures of six fictional women friends who gather six years after their graduation from college and decide to celebrate life and freedom. The book became a national best seller and projected Valdés-Rodríguez onto the pages of popular magazines. She was named one of the top eleven women of the year by *Latina* magazine. With her newfound financial success and fame, Valdés-Rodríguez had the courage to establish the Dirty Girls Production film company to make an independent film of her book. She has published some eleven other "chica lit" novels, including *Playing with Boys* in 2004; *Make Him Look Good* in 2006; *Dirty Girls on Top*, a sequel to *The Dirty Girls Social Club*, in 2008; *The Husband Habit* in 2009; *All That Glitters* in 2011; *The Temptation* in 2012; and *Puta* in 2013. In 2013 she published a memoir, *The Feminist and the Cowboy: An Unlikely Love Story*.

Gloria Vando (1936–)

Gloria Vando is the daughter of two Puerto Rican writers, Anita Vélez-Mitchell and Erasmo Vando. Born and raised in New York and educated in the United States (at New York University) and Europe (Amsterdam and Paris), she ultimately received her B.A. from Texas A&I University in 1975. Vando became a respected poet of the English language who for many years dedicated herself to service of the literary field and women's culture, while only occasionally publishing her poems in magazines. Vando was a contributing editor of the *North American Review* and the coeditor of *Spud Songs: An Anthology of Potato Poems*, benefiting Hunger Relief. In 1977, Vando founded a literary magazine and press, Helicon Nine, which published outstanding literary and artistic works by women until 1992. That year, she and her husband, William Hickok, cofounded the Writers Place in Kansas City, Kansas, a venue for writers to come together and discuss their works. While more than fifty anthologies contain her poems, it was not until 1993 that Vando published her first collection of poems, *Promesas: Geography of the Impossible*, which became the first Hispanic book to win the Thorpe Menn Award for literary achievement. In 2002, Vando published her second collection, *Shadows and Supposes*, winner of the 1998 Alice Fay Di Castagnola Award from the Poetry Society of America; the book was also a finalist for the Walt Whitman Poetry Contest. In 2013, Vando published the anthology *Woven Voices: Three Generations of Puertorriqueñas Look at Their American Lives*. Other awards for her work over the years include the Stanley Hanks Memorial Award (1986), the Billee Murray Poetry Prize (1991), and various fellowships and grants from the Kansas Arts Commission. Three of her poems were adapted for the stage under the title *Moving Targets: Three Interpretations of Murder* and were showcased at the Women's Work Festival in New York City in 1999.

Alfredo Véa Jr. (1950–)

Born in the Arizona desert near Phoenix, on June 28, 1950, Alfredo Véa Jr. was raised by his maternal Yaqui-Spanish grandparents while his mother spent most of her time on the road as a migrant farm laborer. He joined his mother in seasonal farm work at the age of ten, which resulted in interrupted and erratic higher education. He was drafted and served in Vietnam during the war; after returning, he took a series of blue-collar and labor jobs while getting his undergraduate and law degrees. In 1978 he obtained

his J.D. from the University of California–Berkeley. After originally beginning as a public defender, Véa established his own practice in 1986 and has continued to support himself in this manner while writing novels. His first novel, *La Maravilla* (1993, The Miracle), is an experimental novel in style and language that follows the development of a young Mexican American protagonist. Highly autobiographical, the novel centers on Beto, the protagonist, and his mystical and real-life education as a Yaqui descendant in a small town in the Arizona desert. Véa's second novel, *The Silver Cloud Café* (1996), is an intricate interweaving of the lives of farm workers of varying ethnicity whose drama results historically from the legacy of both Spanish and American imperialism; along with their struggles, Véa also delves into various types of love relationships, and throughout, a real plot runs parallel to a metaphysical one. In *Gods Go Begging* (1999), Véa recalls his service in Vietnam in a nonlinear exploration of death and violence. His latest novel is *The Mexican Flyboy* (2016), a Chicano version of time travel.

Ed Vega (1936–2008)

Born in Ponce, Puerto Rico, on May 20, 1936, where he lived with his family until they moved to the Bronx, New York, in 1949, Edgardo Vega Yunqué (whose pen name was Ed Vega) was raised in a devout Baptist home, his father having been a minister of that faith. In later life, Vega adopted the Buddhist faith. After moving to New York and going through the public education system, he served in the U.S. Air Force and studied at Santa Monica College in California under the G.I. Bill. In 1963, Vega almost graduated from New York University with a major in political science but was short three hours of credit and did not actually graduate until 1969. Beginning in 1982 Vega devoted himself full-time to writing and became one of the most prolific Latino prose writers—although much of his work remained unpublished. In 1977, his short stories began to be published by Latino magazines, such as *Nuestro*, *Maize*, and *Revista Chicano-Riqueña*. His novel *The Comeback*, a rollicking satire of ethnic autobiography and the identity crisis, as personified by a half-Puerto Rican, half-Eskimo ice hockey player who becomes involved in an underground revolutionary movement for Puerto Rican independence, was published in 1985. A collection of interconnected short stories, *Mendoza's Dreams*, narrated by a warmhearted observer of the human comedy, Alberto Mendoza, was published in 1987. An additional common thread holding these barrio stories together was their charting of various Puerto Ricans on the road to success in the United States; thus, once again we had a Puerto Rican interpretation of the American Dream. Vega's third book, *Casualty Report* (1991), was just the opposite; for the most part the collection of stories included here chronicle the death of dreams, as characters faced with racism, poverty, and crime succomb to despair in many forms: violence, alcohol and drug abuse, withdrawal, and resignation. Vega's novel *No Matter How Much You Promise to Cook or Pay the Rent You Blew It Cauze Bill Bailey Ain't Never Coming Home Again* (2003) was a crossover to mainstream publishing; it won the PEN Oakland/Josephine Miles Literary Award (2004) and the *Washington Post* Book of the Year Award (2004). The novel opened the way for his subsequent works to be issued by major presses: *The Lamentable Journey of Omaha Bigelow into the Impenetrable Loisaida Jungle* (2004) and *Blood Fugues* (2005). They mark a departure, as well, in exploring themes beyond the barrio.

Gloria Velásquez (1949–)

Born on December 21, 1949, in Loveland, Colorado, to migrant worker parents, Gloria Velásquez grew up with her studies interrupted at times due to the exigencies of the migrant stream. She graduated from the University of Northern Colorado (1978) and earned a Ph.D. in Spanish at Stanford University (1985) on the way to becoming a professor of Spanish at California Polytechnic State University in San Luis Obispo. As a poet, Velásquez published her poems of social and political commitment to women and minorities in numerous literary magazines and anthologies. Her two books of poems are *I Used to Be Superwoman* (1997) and *Xicana on the Run* (2005). But Velásquez's acclaim is principally due to her prose fiction works. In 1994, Velásquez began the Roosevelt High School Series of young adult novels set among a multiracial group of teenagers at Roosevelt High, who must face such social and cultural issues as child and spousal abuse, racial prejudice, homosexuality, teen pregnancy, and others. To date, she has produced eight highly acclaimed books in the series: *Juanita Fights the School Board* (1994), *Maya's Divided World* (1995), *Tommy Stands Alone* (1995), *Rina's Family Secret* (1998), *Ankiza's Rainbow* (2000), *Teen Angel* (2003), *Tyrone's Betrayal* (2006), and *Zakiya* (2022). Each one of the installments deals with a separate and distinct teen problem. Her outstanding sensitivity in interpreting teenage angst and social conditions in the series have made Velásquez a popular speaker at high schools throughout the nation and have led some to call her the "Chicana Judy Blume." In 2004, Velásquez was featured in *100 History Making Ethnic Women*, by Sherry York.

Alma Luz Villanueva (1944–)

Born on October 4, 1944, in Lompoc, California, Alma Luz Villanueva was left by her Mexican mother and her German father in the San Francisco Mission district to be raised by her Yaqui Indian grandmother. After her grandmother died when Villanueva was eleven, her mother took up the responsibility of continuing to raise her. Villanueva dropped out of high school and gave birth to a baby boy when she was just fifteen. Before she knew it, she was in a bad marriage to a Marine and raising three children of her own. She divorced and moved with her children to the California mountains and later married Chicano artist Wilfredo Castaño. Villanueva discovered the writing of poetry as a means of knowing herself and achieving peace with her life. Her first collection of poems, *Bloodroot* (1977), relies on women's insight to explore diverse themes. In 1978, Villanueva published *Mother, May I*, a long autobiographical poem charting her trials and tribulations in a patriarchal society as well as her triumphs. In *La Chingada* (1985, The Fucked), Villanueva departed from the personal to explore feminine archetypes through history. In *Lifespan* (1985), she takes a completely celebratory tack on life and love and her destiny. Villanueva began publishing novels with *Ultraviolet Sky* (1988), whose protagonist struggles against odds to create a life of her own; it was awarded the American Book Award of the Before Columbus Foundation. In *Naked*

Ladies (1994), Villanueva explores the myriad ills afflicting women's lives, including sexual violence, oppression, alcoholism, illness, and infidelity. In *Weeping Woman: La Llorona and Other Stories* (1994), she has created a series of stories once again exploring the darkest corners of women's sexuality: rape, prostitution, and incest. In 1998, Villanueva returned to poetry with *Desire* (1998), an exploration of passionate love; however, in her 2002 poetry collection, *Vida*, she paid homage to her Yaqui heritage. Her most recent books are *Soft Chaos* (2009) and *Song of the Golden Scorpion* (2013).

Tino Villanueva (1941–)

Born on December 11, 1941, in San Marcos, Texas, to migrant farm workers, Tino Villanueva grew up in poverty and discrimination. After serving in the Army, Villanueva studied at Southwest Texas State University, where he began to write poetry, graduated in 1968, and went on to graduate school at the State University of New York at Buffalo and Boston University. While studying for his Ph.D. at BU, he published his first book, *Hay Otra Voz: Poems,* in 1972, in which he experimented with bilingual writing and recalled the migrant farm worker and *pachuco* culture. The book led to his widespread acceptance as a leading Chicano poet, and in this leadership role he was able to compile one of the earliest anthologies of Chicano literature and the first to be published in Mexico: *Chicanos, antología histórica y literaria* (1980). In 1981, Villanueva obtained his Ph.D. and began teaching at Wellesley College but was never able to win tenure at that institution. In 1984, Villanueva founded *Imagine: International Chicano Poetry Journal*, which published authors from widespread cultures in various languages. Also in 1984, Villanueva published his second widely acclaimed book of poetry, *Shaking Off the Dark*. Villanueva's other books include *Scene from the Movie GIANT* (1993) and *Chronicle of My Worst Years* (1994), neither of which has had the impact of his earlier works. Villanueva's latest published book of poems is *So Spoke Penelope* (2013). In 2016 his poems were selected and translated to Spanish for a volume entitled *Antología Poética de Tino Villanueva.*

José Antonio Villarreal (1924–2010)

Born on July 20, 1924, in Los Angeles to Mexican immigrant parents who were migrant farm workers,

José Antonio Villarreal served three years in the Navy during World War II and returned to California to earn a B.A. in English from the University of California at Berkeley (1950). Villarreal took various and sundry jobs to support his wife and children and his writing. He finished his first novel, *Pocho*, in 1956 but was not able to find a publisher until 1959. The novel is considered to be the first Chicano novel in contemporary times. *Pocho* is a developmental novel in which the protagonist has a classic identity crisis. It was also the first Chicano novel to be published by a major commercial house: Doubleday. It was reissued by Anchor Books in 1970. Since then, it has become required reading in Chicano and Latino literature classes at universities. Due to rising demand, Villarreal published his second novel, a tale of the Mexican Revolution, *The Fifth Horseman*, with Doubleday in 1974, but it never achieved the status of *Pocho*. Villarreal became an outspoken critic of the Chicano Movement and its writers, attacking the very base that had made his first work so popular. Villarreal's third novel, *Clemente Chacón* (1984), was an American Dream tale of a poor Mexican who crosses the border to rise in riches and social success. This latest Villarreal offering was published not by a mainstream house but by Bilingual Press, a small university-based publisher, and was indicative of Villarreal's struggle to please both mainstream publishers and students of Chicano literature.

Victor Villaseñor (1940–)

Born on May 11, 1940, in Carlsbad, California, the son of Mexican immigrants, Victor Villaseñor was raised on a ranch in Oceanside and experienced great difficulty with the educational system, having started school as a Spanish-speaker and dyslexic. He dropped out of high school and worked on a ranch, in the fields, and as a construction worker. During years of work in California as a construction worker, Villaseñor taught himself to write literary prose and completed nine novels and sixty-five short stories, all of which were rejected for publication except for *Macho!*, which in 1973 launched his professional writing career. His second publishing venture was the nonfiction narrative of the life and trial of a serial killer, *Jury: The People versus Juan Corona* (1977). Negative experiences with stereotyping and discrimination of Latinos in the commercial publishing world led Villaseñor to publish his most important literary effort, *Rain of Gold* (1991), with a university-based, not-for-profit Latino press, Arte Público Press of Houston. *Macho!* tells the tale of a young Mexican Indian's illegal entry into the United States to find work, along the classic lines of the novel of immigration; however, it departs from the model in that, upon return to his hometown in central Mexico, the protagonist has been forever changed, unable to accept the traditional social code, especially as it concerns machismo. *Rain of Gold*, on the other hand, is the nonfiction saga of various generations of Villaseñor's own family, whose members experienced the Mexican Revolution and eventually immigrated to establish themselves in California. The saga is narrated in a style full of spiritualism and respect for myths and oral tradition, derived not only from Villaseñor's growing up in the bosom of his extended working-class family but also from the years of interviews and research that he did in preparing the book. The popularity of *Rain of Gold* has brought to millions of Americans the family stories of the social, economic, and political struggles that have resulted in Mexican immigration to the United States, where new stories of racism, discrimination, and the triumph over some of these barriers continue to develop in the epic of Mexican American life. *Rain of Gold* became a best seller and was auctioned to a major publisher; it continues to be reissued in various editions and translations. Villaseñor kept extending the family autobiography, converting his own life into a continuing autobiography in prequels and sequels issued by mainstream publishers: *Wild Steps of Heaven* (1996), *Thirteen Senses: A Memoir* (2001), *Burro Genius: A Memoir* (2006), and *Crazy Loco Love* (2008).

Marcos McPeek Villatoro (1962–)

Born on February 20, 1962, in the Appalachian Mountains of Tennessee to an Anglo father and a Salvadoran mother, Marcos McPeek Villatoro has comically elaborated his unusual biography in stand-up comedy routines and in his autobiographical novel, *The Holy Spirit of My Uncle's Cojones* (1999). After studying for the priesthood for a while, Villatoro married and worked in various relief organizations in El Salvador, Guatemala, and Nicaragua, at times during the heat of civil war conflicts. After returning to the United States and working with Latino immigrant communities in the South, he earned an M.F.A. degree in creative writing from the University of Iowa (1998). He then moved his wife and four children to Los Angeles and became the Fletcher Jones Endowed Chair in Creative Writing at Mount St. Mary's College. Even before attending the Iowa Workshop, Villatoro was an accomplished writer, publishing his monumental epic of Salvadoran history, *A Fire in the Earth*, in 1996. His reportage of living and working in Central America, *Walking toward La Milpa: Living in Guatemala with Armies, Demons, Abrazos and Death*, followed in 1996. A diverse writer, he has published two bilingual collections of poems on the themes of identity, Salvadoran culture and politics, and the immigrant worldview in *They Say That I Am Two* (1997) and *On Tuesday, When the Homeless Disappeared* (2004). In 2001, Villatoro created his Salvadoran American female detective, Romilia Chacón, in the first installment of a series, *Home Killings*, which was named one of the best books of the year by the *Los Angeles Times*. The intelligent and intrepid Chacón has now solved mysteries in three sequels, *Minos: A Romilia Chacón Mystery* (2005), *A Venom Beneath the Skin* (2006), and *Blood Daughters: A Romilia Chacón Novel* (2011). Shortly after moving to Los Angeles, Villatoro founded and served as host for a literary talk show on Pacifica Radio called *Shelf Life*.

Helena María Viramontes (1954–)

Born on February 26, 1954, in East Los Angeles, one of eight siblings in a working-class family, Helena María Viramontes graduated from Immaculate Heart College with a B.A. in English (1975). Her love of literature led her to study English and creative writing over the next two decades, and she published her first collection of stories, *The Moths and Other Stories*, in 1985. Her work as a writer was put on hiatus when she married and became the mother of two children, to whom she devoted most of her time. In 1994, almost a decade after publication of *The Moths*, she finished her M.F.A. in creative writing at the University of California–Irvine. By the time she had her degree in hand, Viramontes was already a force on the Hispanic literary scene, and her works had been canonized in some of the most important textbooks and anthologies, based on *The Moths and Other Stories* (1985). Viramontes's powerful writing is based on politics and grounded in the sociological reality of workingclass Latinas. In her conscious effort to give voice to women through her stories, she is personally battling and subverting patriarchal practices. Viramontes's stories graphically depict the repression of women and the price they pay in challenging a misogynist society. *Under the Feet of Jesus* (1996), Viramontes's first novel, is an apparently simple and direct narrative that follows the life of a thirteen-year-old migrant worker girl but soon becomes an indictment of corporate agriculture in California and its practices of child labor and pesticide poisoning. The book is narrated from the point of view of the young girl, Estrella, who also questions the limitations placed on her as a female. Viramontes's next novel was published about ten years later, in 2007: *Their Dogs Came with Them: A Novel* follows a group of young women struggling to survive in the gritty barrio of East Los Angeles during the 1960s. Viramontes's awards include the first prize for fiction from *Statement Magazine*, California State University, Los Angeles, 1977; first prize for fiction from the University of California, Irvine Chicano Literary Contest, 1979; Sundance Institute Storytelling Award, 1989; Robert McKee Story Structure Award from the National Latino Communications Center, 1991; National Association of Chicana/o Studies Certificate of Distinguished Recognition, 1993; a John Dos Passos Award for Literature, 1996; and the USA Artists Fellowship, 2007. Viramontes works as a professor of creative writing at Cornell University.

Jose Yglesias (1919–1995)

Born on November 29, 1919, in the Ybor City section of Tampa, Florida, Jose Yglesias was the first writer to express a Cuban American consciousness. He grew up within the tradition of Cuban cigar rollers, but upon graduation from high school, he moved to Greenwich Village in New York City to become a writer. From his early twenties on, he was politically engaged; his politics would initiate him in the groups of writers and artists who militated against fascism in Spain under dictator Francisco Franco, who promoted socialism in the United States, and who were the first supporters of Fidel Castro in Cuba. His early journalistic writing, in the *Daily Worker* and elsewhere, during the late 1940s and early 1950s, eventually led to his writing several journalistic books on Spain and Cuba, such as *The Goodbye Land* in 1967, *In the Fist of the Revolution: Life in a Cuban Country Town* in 1968, *Down There* in 1970, and *The Franco Years* in 1977. But it is Yglesias's work as a novelist that is most enduring, with his very humane narrators, eloquent prose, and sly humor as noteworthy. For more than thirty years, he wrote novels and stories based on Latino life in the United States, and he saw them published by some of the largest and most respected publishing houses in the country. His first novel, *A Wake in Ybor City* (1963), based on the Cuban Spanish community in Tampa, is considered to be a classic of U.S. Latino literature. His other novels include *The Kill Price* (1976) and *Tristan and the Hispanics* (1989). Yglesias was a working writer until his death from cancer in 1995. Two important new and highly received novels were published posthumously: *Breakin* (1996), set in Tampa and exploring the theme of race relations, and *The Old Gent* (1996), set in New York and dealing with the final days of an aging novelist. Two of his stories were included in *Best American Stories* and form a part of his posthumous collection, *The Guns in the Closet* (1996). In all, he wrote ten books of fiction, three of which were published posthumously.

Rafael Yglesias (1954–)

Rafael Yglesias was born on November 30, 1953, and raised in New York City's Washington Heights, the son of Cuban American novelist Jose Yglesias and Jewish American novelist Helen Yglesias. Immersed in the literary environment of his father and his circle, Yglesias published his first novel, *Hide Fox, and After All* (1972), while still in high school, whereupon he dropped out. He continued writing novels and later became a writer of screenplays in Hollywood. His novel *Fearless* (1993) was his first to become a hit film, by the same title. His credits as a screenwriter include landmark films, such as *Death and the Maiden* (1992),

Les Miserables (1996), *Batman Begins* (2005), and *Dark Water* (2005). His other novels are *How She Died* (1973), *The Work Is Innocent* (1976), *The Game Player* (1978), *Hot Properties* (1987), *Only Children* (1988), *The Murderer Next Door* (1992), *Fearless* (1993), and *Dr. Neruda's Cure for Evil* (1998). One of his most well-known works, *Fearless*, follows the lives of two characters, Max and Carla, after they survive a plane crash and come to a new understanding of their lives. *The Murderer Next Door* is a psychologial thriller about a transvestite who kills his wife and retains custody of their child. Yglesias's magnum opus is the 704-page, highly autobiographical novel *Dr. Neruda's Cure for Evil*, a *bildungroman* that charts the psychological development of a child torn between his father's Cuban Spanish literary, highly bohemian but unstable influence and his mother's wealthy Jewish influence, nevertheless tainted by her sexual abuse of her own son; the clash of cultures and personalities makes for confusing identity formation and spawns a psychiatrist in the making who in later life must attend to the mentally challenged while still undergoing his own therapy.

Gwendolyn Zepeda (1971–)

Born on December 27, 1971, in Houston, Texas, to a Chicano father and German/Welsh/Scottish mother, Gwendolyn Zepeda was four when her mother was diagnosed with schizophrenia and institutionalized, leaving Zepeda to grow up with her father's extended family. She received a scholarship to attend the University of Texas at Austin but dropped out in 1993 to begin raising an impromptu family. Suddenly finding herself a housewife in an isolated corner of the Texas Hill Country, Zepeda desperately reached out to others through the internet. She taught herself HTML and created her own web site, www.gwenworld.com, which won her recognition and freelance writing jobs for other sites. This led her to believe that she could succeed as a "real" writer. Now the mother of three children, Zepeda started writing late at night and in temp-agency waiting rooms, compiling the short-story collection that was published as *To the Last Man I Slept with and All the Other Jerks Just like Him* (2004). The collection contains bawdy, irreverent voices of women strong enough to leave behind their tribulations and mistreatment at the hands of men and create their own identities; the volume also contains a mock bodice buster, which is so formulaic that many of the pages are partially blank because the reader knows what happens in the plot. Zepeda's interest in women's voices has led her to experiment with "chica lit" in her latest novels, set among the salsa-dancing singles in Houston: *Houston, We Have a Problema* (2008) and *Better with You Here* (2012). In 2019, she published *Houston Noir*. Zepeda is the author of two books of poetry: *Falling in Love with Fellow Prisoners: Poems* (2013) and *Monsters, Zombies and Addicts: Poems* (2015). She has also produced children's literature in the form of bilingual picture books: *Growing Up with Tamales/Creciendo con tamales* (2008), *Level Up/Cambio de Nivel* (2012), and *Maya and Annie on Saturdays and Sundays* (2019). Zepeda won the Diarist.net Legacy Award for her online journal/blog in 2003. She served as Houston poet laureate from 2012 to 2015.

Nicolás Kanellos

THEATER

ORIGINS TO 1940

The Southwest

The roots of Latino theater in the United States reach back to the dance-drama of the American Indians and to the religious theater and pageants of medieval and Renaissance Spain. During the Spanish colonization of Mexico, theater was placed at the service of the Catholic missionaries, who employed it in evangelizing the Indians and in instructing them and their mestizo descendants in the mysteries and dogma of the church. But the story of Latino theater in the United States is not just one of a folk theater but also of the development and flourishing of professional theater in the areas most populated by Latinos: throughout the Southwest, New York, Florida, and even the Midwest.

Throughout the seventeenth and eighteenth centuries a hybrid religious theater developed in Mexico. It often employed the music, colors, flowers, masks, even the languages of the Indigenous Mexicans while dramatizing the stories from the Old and New Testaments. In Mexico and what eventually became the Southwest, there developed a cycle of religious plays that, while dramatizing the stories from the Bible, nevertheless became so secular and entertaining in their performances that church authorities finally banned them from church grounds and from inclusion in the official festivities during feast days. They thus became folk plays, enacted by the faithful on their own and without official sanction or sponsorship by the church.

At the center of this cycle of folk plays that dealt with Adam and Eve, Jesus's temptation in the desert, and other favorite passages of the Holy Scriptures was the story of the Star of Bethlehem announcing the birth of Jesus Christ to humble shepherds, who then commence a pilgrimage in search of the newborn Christ Child. On the way to Bethlehem, Satan and the legions of hell attempt to waylay and distract the shepherds, and a battle between good, represented by the Archangel Michael, and evil takes place. Among the other various dramatic elements in this shepherd's play, or *pastorela* as it is called in Spanish, are the appearance of a virginal shepherdess, a lecherous hermit, and a comic bumbling shepherd named Bato. *Pastorelas*, presented by the common folk from central Mexico to Northern California, are still performed today, especially in rural areas during the Christmas season. Originally the whole cycle of mystery plays was performed from December 12, when the play that dramatized *Las Cuatro Apariciones de Nuestra Señora de Guadalupe* (the four appearances of Our Lady of Guadalupe) was presented, through the Easter season and its pageants. The famed *Las posadas* is a Christmas pageant dealing with Mary and Joseph looking for shelter and originally belongs to this cycle as well.

In one form or another, these folk plays are still with us today and have especially influenced the development of Mexican American theater in the United States. The most noteworthy parts of the legacy of the *pastorelas* and other religious drama have been their missionary zeal, their involvement of the community of grass roots people, their use of allegory and masks, their totally mestizo nature, and their sense of comicality and slapstick.

The origins of the Spanish-language professional theater in the United States are to be found in mid-nineteenth-century California, where troupes of itinerant players began touring from Mexico to perform melodramas accompanied by other musical and dramatic entertainments for the residents of the coastal cities that had developed from earlier Franciscan missions—San Francisco, Los Angeles, and San Diego. These three cities were more accessible from Mexico than San Antonio, Texas, for instance, because of the regularity of steamship travel up and down the Pacific coast.

Evidence suggests that plays were being performed as early as 1789; however, it was in the 1840s that various troupes of itinerant players visited the ranches and inns around the San Francisco and Monterey areas of Northern California, performing in Spanish for both Spanish- and English-language audiences. During this time at least one semiprofessional theater house existed in Los Angeles. In the following decades various other theaters opened to accommodate both Spanish- and English-language productions: Don Vicente Guerrero's Union Theater existed from 1852 to 1854, don Abel Stearns's Hall from 1859 to 1875, and don Juan Temple's Theater from 1859 to 1892. In the 1860s and 1870s, the Latino community also frequented the Teatro de la Merced, Teatro Alarcón, and Turn Verein Hall. In the 1880s, Spanish-language productions were even held in the Grand Opera House in Los Angeles.

By the 1860s, the professional stage had become so established and important to the Spanish-speaking community that companies that once toured the Mexican republic and abroad began to settle down as resident companies in California. Among the twelve or fourteen companies that were resident or actively touring California during the 1870s and 1880s, the Compañía Dramática Española, directed by Pedro C. de Pellón, and the Compañía Española de Angel Mollá were two resident companies in Los Angeles that extended their tours to Baja California and up to Tucson, Arizona; from there they would return to Los Angeles via stagecoach. During this time Tucson boasted two Spanish-language theater houses: Teatro Cervantes and Teatro Americano. In 1878 Pellón established himself permanently in Tucson, where he organized the town's first group of amateur actors, Teatro Recreo. Thus, the 1870s mark Arizona's participation in Latino professional theater. It is in this decade as well that troupes began to tour the Laredo and San Antonio axis of Texas, first performing in Laredo and then San Antonio in open-air markets, taverns, and later in such German American settings as Muench Hall, Krish Hall, and Wolfram's Garden in San Antonio; but it is only at the turn of the century and afterward that companies touring from Mexico began making San Antonio and Laredo their home bases.

Between 1900 and 1930, numerous Mexican theater houses and halls were established to house Spanish-language performances throughout the Southwest. By 1910, some smaller cities even had their own Mexican theaters with resident stock companies. The more mobile tent theaters, circus theaters, and smaller makeshift companies performed in rural areas and throughout the small towns on both sides of the Rio Grande valley.

> The origins of the Spanish-language professional theater in the United States lie in mid-nineteenth-century California, where troupes of itinerant players performed melodramas accompanied by other musical and dramatic entertainments in San Francisco, Los Angeles, and San Diego.

Theatrical activities expanded rapidly when thousands of refugees took flight from the Mexican Revolution and settled in the United States from the border all the way up to the Midwest. During the decades of revolution, many of Mexico's greatest artists and their theatrical companies came to tour or take up temporary residence; however, some would never return to the homeland. Mexican and Spanish companies and occasional Cuban, Argentine, or other Latino troupes found their most lucrative engagements in Los Angeles and San Antonio. They at times even crisscrossed the nation, venturing to perform for the Latino communities in New York, Tampa, and the Midwest. By the 1920s, Latino theater was becoming big business, and such important companies as Spain's Compañía María Guerrero y Fernando Díaz de Mendoza had its coast-to-coast tours into major Anglo-American theater houses booked by New York agents. The company of the famed Mexican leading lady Virginia Fábregas was of particular importance in its frequent tours because it not only performed the latest serious works from Mexico City and Europe but also because some of the troupe members occasionally defected to form their own resident and touring companies in the Southwest. Fábregas was also important in encouraging the development of local playwrights in Los Angeles by buying the rights to their works and integrating the plays into her repertoire.

> Numerous Mexican theater houses and halls were established to house Spanish-language performances throughout the Southwest. By 1910, some smaller cities even had their own Mexican theaters with resident stock companies.

The two cities with the largest Mexican populations, Los Angeles and San Antonio, became theatrical centers, the former also feeding off the important film industry in Hollywood. In fact, Los Angeles became a talent pool for Latino theater. Actors, directors, technicians, and musicians from

The Teatro Nacional in San Antonio, Texas, built in 1917, hosted live productions through the Great Depression.

throughout the Southwest, New York, and the whole Latino world were drawn there looking for employment. Both Los Angeles and San Antonio went through a period of intense expansion and building of new theatrical facilities in the late teens and early 1920s. Los Angeles was able to support five major Latino theater houses with programs that changed daily. The theaters and their peak years were Teatro Hidalgo (1911–34), Teatro México (1927–33), Teatro Capitol (1924–26), Teatro Zendejas (later Novel; 1919–24), and Teatro Principal (1921–29). As many as twenty other theaters were operating at one time or another during the same time period.

San Antonio's most important house was the Teatro Nacional, built in 1917 and housing live productions up through the Great Depression. Its splendor and elite status were not shared by any of the other fifteen or so theaters that housed Spanish-language productions in San Antonio during this period. While it is true that in the Southwest, as in Mexico, Spanish drama and zarzuela, the Spanish national version of operetta, dominated the stage up until the early 1920s, the clamor for plays written by Mexican playwrights had increased to such an extent that by 1923 Los Angeles had developed into a center for Mexican playwriting unparalleled in the history of Latino communities in the United States. While continuing to consume plays by Spanish peninsular authors, such as Jacinto Benavente, José Echegaray, Gregorio Martínez Sierra, Manuel Linares Rivas, and the Álvarez Quintero brothers, the Los Angeles Mexican community and its theaters encouraged local writing by offering cash prizes in contests, lucrative contracts, and lavish productions. Various impresarios of the Spanish-language theaters maintained this tradition throughout the 1920s, offering at times as much as two hundred dollars in prize money to the winners of the playwriting contests. It was often reported in the newspapers of the time that the Latino theaters drew their largest crowds every time they featured plays by local writers.

The period from 1922 to 1933 saw the emergence and box office success of a cadre of playwrights in Los Angeles composed mainly of Mexican theatrical expatriates and newspapermen. At the center of the group were four playwrights whose works not only filled the theaters on Los Angeles's Main Street but were also contracted throughout the Southwest and in Mexico: Eduardo Carrillo, an actor; Adalberto Elías González, a novelist; Esteban V. Escalante, a newspaperman and theatrical director; and Gabriel Navarro, a poet, novelist, composer, orchestra director, columnist for La Opinión newspaper, and editor of the magazine La Revista de Los Angeles. At least twenty other locally residing writers saw their works produced on the professional stage, not to mention the scores of authors of vaudeville revues and lighter pieces.

The serious full-length plays created by these authors addressed the situation of Mexicans in California on a broad, epic scale, often in plays based on the history of the Mexican-Anglo struggle in California. Eduardo Carrillo's El proceso de Aurelio Pompa (The Trial of Aurelio Pompa) dealt with the unjust trial and sentencing of a Mexican immigrant; it was performed repeatedly on the commercial stage and in community-based fundraising events. Gabriel Navarro's Los emigrados (The Emigrées) and El sacrificio (The Sacrifice) dealt, respectively, with Mexican expatriate life in Los Angeles during the revolution and with the history of California around 1846, the date of the outbreak of the Mexican-American War.

By far the most prolific and respected of the Los Angeles playwrights was Adalberto Elías González, some of whose works were not only performed locally but also throughout the Southwest and Mexico and made into movies and translated into English. His works that saw the light on the stages of Los Angeles ran the gamut from historical drama to dime-novel sensationalism. Two of González's plays dealt with the life and culture of Mexicans in California: Los misioneros (The Missionaries) and Los expatriados (The Expatriates). The sensationalist La asesino del martillo; o, La mujer tigresa (The Assassin with the Hammer; or, Tiger Woman) was based on a real-life crime story reported in the newspapers in 1922 and 1923. A dozen other plays dealt with love triangles and themes from the Mexican Revolution, including La muerte de Francisco Villa (The Death of Francisco Villa) and El fantasma de la revolución (The Ghost of the Revolution).

Adalberto Elías González and these other authors addressed the needs of their audiences for reliving their history on both sides of the border and for reviving the glories of their own language and cultural tradition with the decorum and professionalism befitting the type of family entertainment that the community leaders believed served the purposes of reinforcing Latino culture and morality while resisting assimilation to Anglo-American culture. But with the rise of vaudeville and the greater access of working-class people to theatrical entertainment, vaudeville-type revues and variety shows became more and more popular and gradually displaced more serious theater. But Mexican vaudeville and musical comedy did not avoid the themes that were so solemnly treated in three-act dramas. Rather, the Mexican stage had developed its own type of revue: the *revista*. *Revistas* were musical revues that had developed in Mexico under the influence of the Spanish *zarzuela* and the French revue and vaudeville but had taken on their own character in Mexico as a format for piquant political commentary and social satire. Also, like the *zarzuela*, which celebrated Spanish regional customs, music, and folklore, the Mexican *revista* also created and highlighted the character, music, dialects, and folklore of the various Mexican regions. Under the democratizing influence of the Mexican Revolution, the *revista* highlighted the life and culture of the working classes. During the revolution, the *revista política* in particular rose to prominence on Mexico City stages, but later all *revista* forms degenerated into a loose vehicle for musical and comedic performance in which typical regional and underdog characters, such as the *pelado* (literally, skinned or penniless), often improvised a substantial part of the action.

The Los Angeles stages hosted many of the writers and stars of *revistas* that had been active during the time of formation of the genre in Mexico, including Leopoldo Beristáin and Guz Águila. In the theaters of Los Angeles and the Southwest were staged most of the *revistas* that were popular in Mexico and that were of historical importance for the development of the genre. Such works as *El tenorio maderista* (The Maderist Tenorio), *El país de los cartones* (The Country Made of Boxes), and *La ciudad de los volcanes* (The City of Volcanoes) were continuously repeated from Los Angeles to Laredo. Such innovators of the genre as Beristáin and Águila were for a time a perennial attraction at the Los Angeles theaters.

It is in the *revista* that we find a great deal of humor based on the culture shock typically derived from following the misadventures of naive, recent immigrants from Mexico who have difficulty in getting accustomed to life in the big Anglo-American metropolis. Later on in the 1920s and when the Depression and repatriation took hold, the theme of culture shock was converted to one of outright cultural conflict. At that point Mexican nationalism became more intensified as anti-Mexican sentiments become more openly expressed in the Anglo-American press as a basis for taking Mexicans off the welfare rolls and deporting them. In the *revista*, the Americanized, or *agringado* and *renegado*, became even more satirized, and the barbs aimed at American culture became even sharper. It was also in the *revista* that the raggedly dressed underdog, the *pelado*, came to the fore with his low-class dialect and acerbic satire. A forerunner of characters like Cantinflas, the *pelado* really originated in the humble tent theaters that evolved in Mexico and existed in the Southwest of the United States until the 1950s. With roots in the circus clown tradition and a costume and dialect that embodied poverty and marginality, the *pelado* was free to improvise and exchange witticism with his audiences that often represented working-class distrust of societal institutions and the upper classes. Although the *pelado*, or *peladito* as he was affectionately called, was often criticized for his low humor and scandalous language, theater critics today consider the character to be a genuine and original Mexican contribution to the history of theater.

Unlike Los Angeles, the stages of San Antonio did not attract or support the development of local playwrights, and while they hosted many of the same theatrical companies and performers as did the California stages, theater in the Alamo City did not support as many resident companies. While the story of Los Angeles's Latino theater is one of proliferation of Spanish-language houses, companies, and playwrights, the story of San Antonio is one that illustrates the persistence of resident companies, actors, and directors in keeping Latino drama alive in community and church halls after being dislodged by vaudeville and the movies from the professional theater houses during the Depression. San Antonio's is also the story of the rise of a number of vaudevillians

From the culture conflicts depicted in the carpas, *or tent theaters, of the Southwest arose the stereotype of the* pachuco, *a typically Mexican American figure associated with flashy clothes and jazz music.*

to national and international prominence. Finally, San Antonio also became a center for another type of theater, one that served an exclusively working-class audience: the *carpa*, or tent theater.

Probably because of their small size, bare-bones style, and organization around a family unit, the *carpas* could manage themselves better than large circuses or theatrical companies. They were able to cultivate smaller audiences in the most remote areas. The *carpas* became in the Southwest an important Mexican American popular culture institution. Their comic routines became a sounding board for the culture conflict that Mexican Americans felt in language usage, assimilation to American tastes and lifestyles, discrimination in the United States, and *pocho*, or Americanized status, in

Mexico. Out of these types of conflicts in popular entertainment arose the stereotype of the *pachuco*, a typically Mexican American figure. Finally, the *carpas* were a refuge for theatrical and circus people of all types during the Great Depression, repatriation, and World War II. More important, their cultural arts were preserved by the *carpas* for the postwar generation that was to forge a new relationship with the larger American culture.

From the turn of the century through World War II, San Antonio was home to many *carpas*. Two of the most well-known resident tent shows of San Antonio were the Carpa García and the Carpa Cubana, whose descendants still reside in the Alamo City. The Carpa García was founded by Manuel V.

García, a native of Saltillo, Mexico. He relocated his family to San Antonio in 1914 after having performed with the Carpa Progresista in Mexico. Featured in his Carpa García was the famed *charro* (Mexican-style cowboy) on the tightrope act. In Latin American and U.S. circus history, the Abreu name appears frequently at the end of the nineteenth century and beginning of the twentieth. The Abreu company, directed by Virgilio Abreu, owned and operated the Carpa Cubana—also known as the Cuban Show and the Circo Cubano—that made San Antonio its home base in the 1920s and 1930s. But before that, various members of the family had appeared as acrobats, tumblers, and wire walkers with such famous shows as Orrin, Barnum and Bailey, Ringling Brothers, John Robinson, and Sells Floto. In San Antonio the Cuban circus included trapeze artists, rope walkers, jugglers, clowns, dancers, and its own ten-piece band. Although based in San Antonio, the company toured as far as California and central Mexico by truck and train, but mostly limited its tours to the Rio Grande Valley in the south and Austin to the north during the 1930s.

New York City

Although there is evidence that there were Latino theatrical performances earlier in the nineteenth century, it was during the 1890s in New York that regular amateur and semiprofessional shows began, as the Latino community, made up mostly of Spaniards and Cubans, was growing in size, reflecting once again the patterns of internal conflict in the homeland and immigration to the United States that would be repeated time and again during the development of Latino communities and culture in the United States. Of course, the diaspora brought on by the Mexican Revolution more than any other factor characterized the theater in the Southwest during the first half of the twentieth century. In the 1890s New York became an organizing and staging center for Cuban and Puerto Rican expatriates seeking the independence of their homeland from Spain. Later in the century, heavy migration of Puerto Ricans, now U.S. citizens, and the Puerto Rican nationalist movement in pursuit of independence from the United States also manifested on the city's Latino stages, as did the efforts by exiled Spanish Republicans fighting fascism during the Spanish Civil War in the mid-1930s.

Documentary evidence of the Latino stage in New York begins in 1892 with the *Patria* (Homeland) newspaper reporting on the dramatic activities of actor Luis Baralt and his company. Until 1898, the year of the Spanish-American War, this newspaper, which supported the Cuban revolutionary movement, occasionally covered performances by Baralt and his troupe, which included both amateurs and actors with professional experience. The company had an irregular performance schedule in such auditoriums and halls as the Berkeley Lyceum and the Carnegie Lyceum, where it presented standard Spanish melodramas as well as Cuban plays, such as *De lo vivo a lo pintado* (From Life to the Painted Version) by Tomás Mendoza, a deceased hero of the revolutionary war, and *La fuga de Evangelina* (The Escape of Evangelina) by

Singer and actress María Conesa, portrayed in the Spanish-language magazine Cine-Mundial, in July 1916.

an unknown author, the dramatization of the escape from prison by a heroine of the independence movement. The last performance reported took place at the Central Opera House on January 16, 1899; funds were raised for the sepulcher of the great Cuban philosopher-poet and revolutionary José Martí. After this last performance, there were very few mentions made in surviving newspapers of theatrical performances in Spanish until the advent of a truly professional stage some seventeen years later in 1916.

Unlike the theatrical experience of Los Angeles, San Antonio, and Tampa, in the mid-teens of the new century the New York Latino community could not claim any theaters of its own. Rather, a number of impresarios rented available theaters around town, but mainly those located in the Broadway area, from midtown Manhattan up to the eighties: Bryant Hall, Park Theater, Amsterdam Opera House, Leslie Theater, Carnegie Hall, and so forth. The first impresario to lead companies on this odyssey through New York theater houses was a Spanish actor-singer of *zarzuelas* who had made his debut in Mexico City in 1904: Manuel Noriega. Noriega became a figure in New York who, in many ways, was comparable to Romualdo Tirado in Los Angeles. Like Tirado, he was a tireless and enthusiastic motivator of Latino theater, and for a number of years he had practically the sole responsibility for maintaining Spanish-language theatrical seasons. Noriega found his way to New York in 1916 from the Havana stage to perform with another singer, the famous and charming María Conesa, at the Amsterdam Theater. That very same year he founded the first of his many theatrical companies, Compañía Dramática Española, which performed at the Leslie Theater from June to September and then went on to other theaters in the city. In Noriega's repertoire was the typical fare of Spanish comedies, *zarzuelas*, and comic afterpieces. During the first two years, Noriega had difficulty in getting the Latino community out to the theater, so much so that a community organization, the Unión Benéfica Española, had to have a fundraiser for his poverty-stricken actors. It was in 1918 at the Amsterdam Opera House that Noriega's company began finding some stability, performing each Sunday, with an occasional special performance on Thursdays. By November of that year the company

was so successful that it added matinee showings on Sundays, and by December it began advertising in the newspaper for theatrical artists. As Noriega hired on more actors, mostly Cuban, Spanish, and Mexican, the nature of the company began to change, at times highlighting Galician or Catalonian works, at others Cuban blackface comedy. In 1919 Noriega formed a partnership with Latino, Greek, and Anglo-American businessmen to lease the Park Theater and make it the premier Latino house, rebaptizing it El Teatro Español. After a short performance run, all the parties concerned bailed out of the bad business deal; the Noriega company went on to other theaters to perform in its usual manner until 1921, when Noriega slipped from sight.

The 1920s saw a rapid expansion of the Latino stage in New York, which was now regularly drawing touring companies from Cuba, Spain, Mexico, and the Southwest and which had also developed many of its own resident companies. Most of the companies followed the pattern of renting theaters for their runs and relocating afterward to different neighborhoods or to Brooklyn, New York, Bayonne, or Jersey City, New Jersey, or even Philadelphia. Beginning in 1922 the Latino community was able to lay claim to several houses on a long-term basis, at times even renaming the theaters in honor of the Latino community. The first two theaters that began to stabilize Latino theatrical culture in New York were the Daly's and the Apollo. After 1930, the Apollo no longer offered Latino fare; the leadership then passed in 1931 to the San José/Variedades, in 1934 to the Campoamor, and finally in 1937 to the most important and longest-lived house in the history of Latino theater in New York: El Teatro Hispano.

As in the Southwest, these houses also experienced the same evolution of Latino theater in which melodrama and *zarzuela* reigned at the beginning of the 1920s to be gradually displaced by musical revues and vaudeville, while in the 1930s artists of serious drama took refuge in clubs and mutualist societies— rarely in church auditoriums as in the Southwest. However, the kind of musical revue that was to reign supreme in New York was not the Mexican revista but the *obra bufa cubana*, or Cuban blackface farce, which featured the stock character types of the *negrito* (blackface), *mulata*, and *gallego* (Galician) and relied heavily on Afro-Cuban song and dance and improvised slapstick comedy. Like the *revistas*, the *obras bufas cubanas* often found inspiration in current events, neighborhood gossip, and even politics.

The *bufo* genre itself had been influenced in its development during the second half of the nineteenth century by the *buffes parisiennes* and the Cuban circus. Under the Spanish in Cuba the *bufos* were particularly repressed for being native Cuban, causing many of them to go into exile in Puerto Rico, Santo Domingo, or Mexico.

Beginning in 1932 the Mt. Morris Theater (inaugurated in 1913) began serving the Latino community under a series of various impresarios and names, first as the Teatro Campoamor, then the Teatro Cervantes, and on August 19, 1937, finally metamorphosing into El Teatro Hispano, which lived on into the 1950s. A somewhat mysterious Mexican impresario who never used his given names, Señor Del Pozo, surfaced at the head of a group of backers made up of Latino and Jewish businessmen. Del Pozo administered the theater and directed the house orchestra. Under Del Pozo, besides movies, the Teatro Hispano offered three daily shows at 2:00, 5:30, and 9:00, except Sundays, which featured four shows. To maintain the interest of his working-class audiences, Del Pozo instituted a weekly schedule that included bonuses and surprises: Tuesdays and Fridays, banco was played at the theater and prizes were awarded; Wednesdays, audiences participated in talent shows broadcast over radio station WHOM; Thursdays, gifts and favors were distributed to audiences; and Saturday mornings featured a special children's show. Occasionally, beauty contests, turkey raffles, and such were held. Weekly programs changed on Friday evenings and were billed as debuts. Del Pozo used the radio, his weekly playbills, and personal appearances to promote the theater as a family institution and himself as a great paternal and kindly protector of the community.

Upon opening in August 1937, Del Pozo immediately began to elaborate the formula of alternating shows relating to the diverse Latino nationalities represented in the community. For one week he played to the Puerto Ricans with the revue *En las playas de Borinquen* (On the Shores of Puerto Rico); then he followed in September with an Afro-Caribbean revue, *Fantasía en blanco y negro* (Fantasy in Black and White) and then *De México vengo* (I Come from Mexico); this was followed by the Compañía de Comedias Argentinas, then a week celebrating Puerto Rico's historic proclamation of independence, El Grito de Lares; by the end of September Del Pozo was again announcing Cuban week, featuring a *Cuba Bella* (Beautiful Cuba) revue. Each week a movie was shown to coincide with the country featured in the revue or plays.

In the months and years that ensued, numerous revues and an occasional *zarzuela* were staged, always balancing out the ethnic nationality represented. The Puerto Rican *negrito* Antonio Rodríguez and the Cuban *negrito* Edelmiro Borras became very popular and were

Spanish actress, singer, and songwriter Rosita Rodrigo, portrayed in El Gráfico, *February 14, 1920.*

ever present. The cast at the Teatro Hispano was constantly being reinforced by refugees from the Spanish Civil War, such as Rosita Rodrigo of the Teatro Cómico de Barcelona, and artists from the failing stages of the Southwest, like La Chata Noloesca and even Romualdo Tirado. By 1940 the Teatro Hispano had fixed its relationship to the predominantly working-class community, which by now was becoming Puerto Rican in majority.

By far the most productive playwrights and librettists in New York were the Cubans, especially those riding the crest of popularity of the irreverent, bawdy, satirical *obras bufas cubanas*. Of these, the most prolific and popular were Alberto O'Farrill and Juan C. Rivera. O'Farrill was a successful blackface comic and literary personality who edited the weekly *Gráfico* newspaper and produced *zarzuelas* and *obras bufas cubanas* based on Afro-Cuban themes. All of them debuted at the Apollo Theater. Rivera was a comic actor who often played the role of the *gallego* and is known to have written both melodramas and *revistas*. Only a few of the works by these authors are known by name; it is assumed that they produced a considerable body of works to be staged by the companies in which they acted.

While it is true that Cubans and Spaniards made up the majority of theater artists in New York City and that their works dominated the stage in the 1920s and 1930s, it is also true that Puerto Rican drama emerged at this time and, it seems, accounts for a more serious and substantial body of literature. Two of the first Puerto Rican playwrights to appear were political writers whose dramas supported the Spanish republican cause and working-class movements: José Enamorado Cuesta (1892–1976) and Franca de Armiño (a pseudonym). *La prensa* on May 22, 1937, called Cuesta a revolutionary writer when it covered his play *El pueblo en marcha* (The People on the March); while Armiño was demonstrably an anarchist in her drama *Los hipócritas* (The Hypocrits), staged in 1933 at the Park Palace Theater.

While Franca de Armiño and José Enamorado Cuesta were calling for a workers' revolution, Gonzalo O'Neill was championing Puerto Rican nationalism and independence from the United States. O'Neill was a very successful businessman and somewhat of a protector and godfather to newly arrived Puerto Rican

immigrants. A published poet and literary group organizer, he wrote poetry and plays, some of which he published. From his very first published dramatic work, *La indiana borinqueña* (1922, The Indians of Puerto Rico), O'Neill revealed himself to be intensely patriotic and interested in Puerto Rican independence. His second published play, *Moncho Reyes* (1923), was a three-act biting satire of the current colonial government in Puerto Rico. Although both of these works enjoyed stage productions, it was his third play, *Bajo una sola bandera* (1928, Under Just One Flag), which debuted at the Park Palace Theater in New York in 1928 and at the Teatro Municipal in San Juan in 1929, that deserves the greatest attention for its artistry and thought, which also made it a popular vehicle for the Puerto Rican nationalist cause. Although O'Neill almost certainly wrote other plays, the only other title that is known, *Amoríos borincanos* (Puerto Rican Episodes of Love), appeared at the Teatro Hispano in 1938; O'Neill was one of the investors in that theater house.

Tampa

In the late nineteenth century, the Tampa area witnessed the transplant of an entire industry from abroad and the development of a Latino enclave that chose the theater as its favorite form of art and culture. To remove themselves from the hostilities attendant on the Cuban war for independence from Spain, to come closer to their primary markets and avoid import duties, and to try to escape the labor unrest that was endemic to this particular industry, various cigar manufacturers from Cuba began relocating to Tampa. In the swampy, mosquito-infested lands just east of Tampa, Ybor City was founded in 1886. By the 1890s, the Spanish and Cuban tobacco workers had begun establishing mutual aid societies and including theaters as centerpieces for the buildings they constructed to house these societies. Many of these theaters eventually hosted professional companies on tour from Cuba and Spain, but, more important, they became the forums where both amateurs and resident professionals entertained the Latino community for more than forty years without interruption. These theaters were also the training grounds where numerous tobacco workers and other community people developed into professional and semiprofessional artists, some of whom were able to make their way to the Latino stages of New York, Havana, and Madrid. Also, Tampa played a key role in one of the most exciting chapters of American theater history: it was the site of the Federal Theater Project's only Latino company under the Works Progress Administration.

Unlike Los Angeles, San Antonio, and New York, very little truly commercial theater was active in the Tampa–Ybor City communities. The six most important mutual aid societies—Centro Español, Centro Español de West Tampa, Centro Asturiano, Círculo Cubano, Centro Obrero, and Unión Martí-Maceo— each maintained a *comisión de espectáculos* (show committee) to govern the use of their theaters, a task that included renting the theater to touring companies and others, scheduling events, hiring professional directors, scenographers and technicians, and even purchasing

The Centro Asturiano in Tampa, Florida, was founded in 1902 as a social club for immigrants and continues to function as an auditorium, hosting theater and opera productions.

performance rights to theatrical works. Along with this comisión, which obviously took on the theater management role, most of the societies also supported a *sección de declamación*, or amateur theatrical company, made up mostly of the society's members. For a good part of each year, the company rehearsed on weeknights and performed on Sundays. For the most part, the audiences were made up of tobacco workers and their families.

Of the six societies, the Centro Asturiano was the most important and the longest-lived; in fact, it is still functioning today as an auditorium, hosting theater and even opera companies. While the Centro Español of Ybor City was the oldest society, founded in 1891 and for a time the most prestigious, the Asturiano (the Asturian) founded in 1902 held the distinction of hosting in its twelve-hundred-seat, first-class theater some of the greatest names in Latino theater in the world and even opera companies from New York and Italy during the period before World War II. It was to the Centro Asturiano that Spain's first lady of the stage, María Guerrero, took her company in 1926. That was a stellar year in which, besides producing the works of its own stock company directed by Manuel Aparicio, the Asturiano also hosted the Manhattan Grand Opera Association. But the socially progressive, even liberal, Centro Asturiano—it extended its membership to all Latinos, even Cubans and Italians—held the further distinction of housing the only Spanish-language Federal Theater Project (FTP).

It was during the tenure of the FTP, for eighteen months in 1936 and 1937, that the Centro Asturiano made American theater history by housing the only Latino unit of the Works Progress Administration's (WPA's) national project. It is a chapter in which the two theatrical traditions, the Latino and the Anglo-American, which had existed side by side for so long, finally intersected to produce at times exciting theater but also examples of cultural misunderstanding. From the start, the FTP administration's attitude seems to have been a model of condescension, and ultimately, the Latino unit had to disband because of congressional xenophobia.

The activities sponsored under the FTP were not much different from what was already ongoing in Tampa's Latino theater. The project hired Manuel

Aparicio to direct the Latino unit in the production of what was for the most part a repertoire of well-worn *zarzuelas* and *revistas*. The greatest difference was brought about, however, by the infusion of capital for scenery, properties, and costumes, which were all new and first-rate. And, even more significant, the Latino actors became integrated for the first time into the shows of the Tampa FTP vaudeville unit and, in general, began to associate more and more with non-Latino artists and personnel. It must be stated, however, that when it came time for that integrated vaudeville unit to perform at the Centro Asturiano, the FTP was not able to get Anglos to cross the tracks to see the show. In all, the Latino unit of the FTP produced fourteen shows in Spanish in forty-two performances for more than twenty-three thousand spectators. The unit achieved its greatest success with *El mundo en la mano* (The World in His Hand), a *revista* written by Aparicio and the entire company, which was a musical tour through Spain, Cuba, Italy, Mexico, and China.

Ultimately, because of language differences and misunderstandings about citizenship, the Latino unit lost twenty-five of its members in 1937 when Congress passed the Emergency Relief Administration (ERA) Act, which effectively removed "foreigners" from the WPA. Included among these was Aparicio. Other members, such as Chela Martínez, were lost when they were decertified because their family income was too high. The remaining citizens were integrated into the "American" vaudeville company of the federal project. The Latino unit had met its end.

Another society that offered a unique theatrical experience was the Centro Obrero, the headquarters for the Union of Tampa Cigarmakers, which served as a gathering place for workers and as a vehicle to promote their culture. Through its various classes, workshops, publications, and other activities, the Centro Obrero promoted unionism and, quite often, socialism. While the Centro Obrero also hosted touring and local companies and even frivolous shows of *obras bufas cubanas*, it was within its halls and auspices that plays were developed and shown that promoted workers' interests, using their dialect and ideology. In the Centro's weekly newspapers, *El Internacional* and *La Federación*, many plays were published, including *Julia y Carlota* (Julia and Carlota), in which Julia exhorts

Carlota to break the bonds of family and religion that are meant to keep women in their place, oppressed, and divorced from politics so that they do not help to reform evil laws. Other works were clearly agitational and propagandistic, attempting to inspire workers to action. Finally, the Centro Obrero went all out to support the republican cause in the Spanish Civil War. It sponsored numerous fundraising performances of such plays as *Milicianos al frente* (Militia to the Front), *Abajo Franco* (Down with Franco), and *Las luchas de hoy* (The Struggles of Today), all of unknown authorship.

Tampa's Latino theatrical experience was unique in that it provided a successful example of deep and lasting community support for theater arts, so deep and so strong that private enterprise could not compete with the efforts of the mutual aid societies. And because the Latino stage had become such a symbol of achievement, that legacy lives on today in the memory of the Tampeños, in the Latino theatrical groups that still exist there, and in such actresses as Velia Martínez who still are enjoying careers on the stage and in film.

POST–WORLD WAR II TO THE PRESENT

The Southwest

The post–World War II period has seen the gradual restoration of the amateur, semiprofessional, and professional stages in the Latino communities of the Southwest. From the 1950s on, repertory theaters have appeared throughout the Southwest to produce Latin American, Spanish, and American plays in Spanish translations. In San Antonio, the extraordinary efforts of such actors as Lalo Astol, La Chata Noloesca, and her daughter Velia Camargo were responsible for keeping plays and vaudeville routines alive in the communities, even if they had to be presented for free or at fundraisers. Actors like Astol made the transition to radio and television, usually as announcers, at times as writers and producers. Astol even wrote, directed, and acted in locally produced television drama during the 1950s and 1960s. In Los Angeles veteran actor-director Rafael Trujillo-Herrera maintained a theater group, almost continuously during the war and through the 1960s, made up of his drama students and professionals, who quite often performed at a small theater house that he bought, El Teatro Intimo.

While a few stories remain of valiant theater artists managing to keep Latino theater alive during the war and postwar years, in most cases the tale is of theater houses that once housed live performances becoming cinemas forever, or at least phasing out live performances during the war and through the 1950s by occasionally hosting small troupes of vaudevillians or subscribing to the extravagant *caravanas de estrellas*, or parades of recording stars, that were syndicated and promoted by the recording companies. Through these shows promenaded singers and matinee idols, with former *peladitos* and other vaudevillians serving as masters of ceremonies and comic relief.

The most remarkable story of the stage in the Southwest is the spontaneous appearance in 1965 of a labor theater in the agricultural fields, under the directorship of Luis Valdez, and its creation of a full-blown theatrical movement that conquered the hearts and minds of artists and activists throughout the country. Under the leadership of Luis Valdez's El Teatro Campesino, for almost two decades Chicano theaters dramatized the political and cultural concerns of their communities while crisscrossing the states on tour. The movement, largely student- and worker-based, eventually led to professionalization, Hollywood and Broadway productions, and the creation of the discipline of Chicano theater at universities.

In 1965 the modern Chicano theater movement was born when aspiring playwright Luis Valdez left the San Francsico Mime Troupe to join César Chávez in organizing farm workers in Delano, California. Valdez organized the workers into El Teatro Campesino in an effort to popularize and raise funds for the grape boycott and farm-worker strike. From the humble beginning of dramatizing the plight of farm workers, the movement grew to include small, agitation-and-propaganda (agitprop) theater groups in communities and on campuses around the country and eventually developed into a total theatrical expression that would find resonance on the commercial stage and screen.

By 1968 Valdez and El Teatro Campesino left the vineyards and lettuce fields in a conscious effort to create a theater for the Chicano nation, a people that Valdez and other Chicano organizers of the 1960s envisioned as working-class, Spanish-speaking or bilingual, rurally oriented, and with a very strong heritage of pre-Columbian culture. By 1970 El Teatro Campesino had pioneered and developed what would come to be known as *teatro chicano*, a style of agitprop theater that incorporated the spiritual and presentational style of the Italian Renaissance commedia dell'arte with the humor, character types, folklore, and popular culture of the Mexican theater, especially as articulated earlier in the century by the vaudeville companies and tent theaters that had toured the Southwest.

El Teatro Campesino's *Los vendidos* (The Sell-Outs), a farcical attack on political manipulation of Chicano stereotypes, became the most popular and imitated of the *actos;* it could be seen performed by

This mosaic tribute to Luis Valdez, founder of the modern Chicano theater movement, is found at Mexican Heritage Plaza, San Jose, California.

diverse groups from Seattle to Austin. The publication of *Actos by Luis Valdez y El Teatro Campesino* in 1971, which included *Los vendidos*, placed a ready-made repertoire in the hands of community and student groups and also supplied them with several theatrical and political canons: (1) Chicanos must be seen as a nation with geographic, religious, cultural, and racial roots in Aztlán. Teatros must further the idea of nationalism and create a national theater based on identification with the Amerindian past. (2) The organizational support of the national theater must be from within, for "the corazón de la Raza (the heart of our people) cannot be revolutionized on a grant from Uncle Sam." (3) Most important and valuable of all was the principle that "the teatros must never get away from La Raza.... If the Raza will not come to the theater, then the theater must go to the Raza. This, in the long run, will determine the shape, style, content, spirit, and form of el teatro Chicano."

El Teatro Campesino's extensive touring, the publicity it gained from the farm-worker struggle, and the publication of *Actos* all effectively contributed to the launching of a national teatro movement. It reached its peak in the summer of 1976 when five teatro festivals were held to commemorate the Anglo bicentennial celebration. The summer's festivals also culminated a period of growth that saw some of Campesino's followers reach sufficient aesthetic and political maturity to break away from Valdez. Los Angeles's Teatro Urbano, in its mordant satire of American heroes, insisted on intensifying the teatro movement's radicalism in the face of the Campesino's increasing religious mysticism. Santa Barbara's El Teatro de la Esperanza was achieving perfection, as no other Chicano theater had, in working as a collective and in assimilating the teachings of Bertolt Brecht in their plays *Guadalupe* and *La víctima* (The Victim). San Jose's El Teatro de la Gente had taken the *corrido*-type acto, a structure that sets a mimic ballet to traditional Mexican ballads sung by a singer-narrator, and perfected it as its innovator, El Teatro Campesino, had never done. El Teatro Desengaño del Pueblo from Gary, Indiana, had succeeded in reviving the techniques of the radical theaters of the 1930s in its *Silent Partners*, an expose of corruption in a local city's construction projects.

The greatest contribution of Luis Valdez and El Teatro Campesino was their inauguration of a true grassroots theater movement. Following Valdez's direction, the university students and community people creating *teatro* held fast to the doctrine of never getting away from the *raza*, the grassroots Mexican. In so doing they created the perfect vehicle for communing artistically within their culture and environment. At times they idealized and romanticized the language and the culture of the *mexicano* in the United States. But they had discovered a way to mine history, folklore, and religion for those elements that could best solidify the heterogeneous community and sensitize it to class, cultural identity, and politics. This indeed was revolutionary. The creation of art from the folk materials of a people, their music, humor, social configurations, and environment represented the fulfillment of Luis Valdez's vision of a Chicano national theater.

While Campesino, after leaving the farm worker struggle, was able to experiment and rediscover the old cultural forms—the *carpas*, the *corridos*, the Virgin of Guadalupe plays, the *peladito*—it never fully succeeded in combining all the elements it recovered or invented into a completely refined piece of revolutionary art. *La gran carpa de la familia Rascuachi* (The Tent of the Underdogs) was a beautiful creation, incorporating the spirit, history, folklore, economy, and music of *la raza*. However, its proposal for the resolution of material problems through spiritual means (a superimposed construct of Aztec mythology and Catholicism) was too close to the religious beliefs and superstitions that hampered *la raza*'s progress, according to many of the more radical artists and theorists of people's theater.

The reaction of critics and many Chicano theaters playing at the fifth Chicano theater festival, held in Mexico, was so politically and emotionally charged that a rift developed between them and El Teatro Campesino that never healed. El Teatro Campesino virtually withdrew from the theater movement, and from that point on the Chicano theaters developed on their own, managing to exist as agitprop groups and raggle-taggle troupes until the end of the decade. The more successful theaters, such as El Teatro de la Esperanza, administered their own theater house, created playwriting workshops, and took up leadership of TENAZ, the Chicano theater organization, while taking over El Teatro Campesino's former role as a national touring company. Other groups, such as Albuquerque's La Compañía, set down roots and became more of a repertory company.

The decade of the 1980s saw many Chicano theater groups disbanding, as some of their members became involved in local community theaters, with their own performance spaces and budgets supplied by state and local arts agencies. Although the grass roots, guerrilla, and street theater movement among Chicanos disappeared, these were the years when greater professionalization took place and greater opportunity appeared for Chicano theater people to make a living from their art in community theaters, at universities, and even in the commercial media—the latter facilitated, of course, by the great rise of the Latino population and its spending power.

From the 1980s to the present, professional Latino community theaters have been created throughout the Southwest and Midwest, where once the model thrived, and a diverse corps of Chicano and Latino playwrights has emerged from coast to coast. Numerous playwriting laboratories, workshops, and contests have sprung up, and a major funding organization underwrites many of these efforts. Now, many mainstream companies and theaters, such as the South Coast Repertory Theater and the San Diego Repertory Theater, produce Latino material and employ Latino actors.

New York

During the war years and following, serious theater in the Latino community waned. First vaudeville drove it from the commercial stage, as it did at the Teatro Hispano, and then, as in the Southwest, the movies and the caravans of musical recording stars began to drive even vaudeville from the stage. Under the leadership of such directors as Marita Reid, Luis Mandret, and Alejandro Elliot, full-length melodramas and realistic plays were able to survive in mutual aid societies, church halls, and lodges during the 1940s and 1950s, but only for smaller audiences and for weekend performances. With such attractions as La Chata Noloesca's Mexican Company and Puerto

Rican vaudevillians, including famed recording star Bobby Capó, vaudeville survived into the early 1960s, playing to the burgeoning working-class audiences of Puerto Ricans. One notable and valiant effort was that of Dominican actor-director Rolando Barrera's group Futurismo, which for a while during the 1940s was able to stage four productions a year of European works in Spanish translation at the Master's Auditorium. Beginning in 1950, Edwin Janer's La Farándula Panamericana staged three or four productions a year of classical works, as well as contemporary Spanish, Puerto Rican, and European works at the Master's Auditorium and the Belmont Theater.

In 1953 a play was staged that would have the most direct and lasting impact ever of any theatrical production in New York's Latino community. A young director, Roberto Rodríguez, introduced to a working-class audience at the Church of San Sebastian *La*

Actress Miriam Colón (pictured) and director Roberto Rodríguez joined forces to form the influential New York theater company El Nuevo Círculo Dramático.

carreta (The Oxcart), by an as-yet-unknown Puerto Rican writer, René Marqués, after its first production in Puerto Rico. The play effectively dramatized the epic of Puerto Rican migration to the United States in working-class and mountain dialect.

Roberto Rodríguez joined forces with stage and screen actress Miriam Colón to form El Nuevo Círculo Dramático, which was able to administer a theater space in a loft, Teatro Arena, in Midtown Manhattan. Although other minor and short-lived companies existed, it was El Nuevo Círculo Dramático, along with La Farándula Panamericana, that dominated the New York Latino stage into the early 1960s, when two incursions were made into the mainstream: in 1964 Joseph Papp's New York Shakespeare Festival began producing Shakespearean works in Spanish, and in 1965 an off-Broadway production of *La carreta* was mounted, starring Miriam Colón and Raúl Juliá.

The late 1960s and early 1970s saw the introduction of improvisational street theater similar to Latin American people's theater and Chicano theater, which attempted to raise the level of political consciousness of working-class Latinos. Among the most well-known, although short-lived, groups were the following ensembles, which usually developed their material as a collective: El Nuevo Teatro Pobre de las Américas (The New Poor People's Theater of the Americas), Teatro Orilla (Marginal Theater), Teatro Guazabara (Whatsamara Theater), and Teatro Jurutungo. But the most interesting of the improvisational troupes, and the only one to survive for years, has been the Teatro Cuatro, named so for its first location on Fourth Avenue on the Lower East Side and made up at first of a diverse group of Puerto Ricans, Dominicans, and other Latin Americans. Under the directorship of an Argentine immigrant, Oscar Ciccone, and his Salvadoran wife, Cecilia Vega, the Teatro Cuatro was one of the most serious troupes, committed to developing a true radical art and to bringing together the popular theater movement of Latin America with that of Latinos in the United States. As such Teatro Cuatro became involved with TENAZ, the Chicano theater movement, and teatro popular in Latin America and sponsored festivals and workshops in New York with some of the leading guerrilla and politically active theatrical directors and companies in

the hemisphere. During the late 1970s Teatro Cuatro became officially associated with Joseph Papp's New York Shakespeare Festival and began to organize the biennial Festival Latino, a festival of Latino/Latin American theater. Into the 1980s, Ciccone and Vega managed the Papp organization's Latino productions, including the festival and a playwriting contest, and Teatro Cuatro had gone its own way, functioning as a repertory company in its own remodeled firehouse theater in East Harlem.

The type of theater that has predominated in New York's cosmopolitan Latino culture since the 1960s is that which more or less follows the patterns established by the Nuevo Círculo Dramático and the Farándula Panamericana mentioned previously, in which a corps of actors and a director of like mind work as a repertory group in producing works of their choosing in their own style. Styles and groups have proliferated, so that at any one time since the 1970s to the present various groups have existed with different aesthetics and audiences. Among these theaters, many of which have, or have had, their own houses, are International Arts Relations (INTAR), Miriam Colón's Puerto Rican Traveling Theater, Teatro Repertorio Español, Nuestro Teatro, Duo, Instituto Arte Teatral (IATE), Latin American Theater Ensemble (LATE), Thalia, Tremont Arte Group, and Pregones. New York has over a million Latino inhabitants, and therefore many organizations are able to survive—although many of them do not flourish and some have disappeared. Also, there are state, local, and private institutions that provide financial support for the arts that at times have been generous to these theaters. Compared with other cities and states, the financial support for the arts, and theater in particular, in the capital of the U.S. theater world has been excellent.

The three most important theater companies have been the Puerto Rican Traveling Theater (PRTT), Teatro Repertorio Español, and INTAR. The PRTT, founded in 1967 by Miriam Colón, takes its name from its original identity as a mobile theater that performed in the streets of Puerto Rican neighborhoods. At first it performed works by some of the leading Puerto Rican writers, such as René Marqués, José Luis González, and Pedro Juan Soto, alternating Spanish-language performances with English-language ones.

The company also produced Latin American and Spanish works and in the early 1970s pioneered productions of works by Nuyorican and other U.S. Latino authors, such as those of Jesús Colón and Piri Thomas. In addition to its mobile unit, the theater maintained a laboratory theater and children's theater classes. Its most important development came in 1974 when it took over and remodeled an old firehouse in the Broadway area, on Forty-seventh Street, and opened its permanent theater house. To this day, the PRTT provides the stage, audience, and developmental work for New York Latino playwrights.

Founded in 1969 as an offshoot of Las Artes by exiled members of Cuba's Sociedad Pro Arte, the Teatro Repertorio Español has grown into the only Latino theater in the nation specializing in the production of both classical Spanish works, such as Calderon's *La vida es sueño* and Zorrilla's *Don Juan Tenorio*, and works by contemporary authors from Latin America. It is also one of the few companies in the nation to also stage nineteenth-century *zarzuelas*. Mixed in with the classical fare are works by Latino playrights of New York and the United States; in fact, one of the most popular plays in its repertoire has been Dolores Prida's *Botánica*. Operating today out of the Gramercy Arts Theater, which has a tradition of Spanish-language performances that goes back to the 1920s, the Teatro Repertorio Español caters to both educational and community-based audiences, with productions in both Spanish and English. It is the only New York Latino theater to tour around the country.

INTAR was founded in 1967 as ADAL (Latin American Art Group), dedicated to producing works by Latin American authors. By 1977, under the name INTAR, the company had achieved equity status as a professional theater. After converting a variety of structures into theater spaces, the company currently occupies a theater on West Forty-second Street near the Broadway theater district. Under the direction of founder Max Ferra, the company offered workshops for actors and directors and staged readings for playwrights and a children's theater. Today INTAR is known for its production of classical works in new settings and innovative directing, such as María Irene Fornés's *La vida es sueño* (Life Is a Dream) and Dolores Prida's *Crisp*, based on Jacinto Benavente's *Los intereses creados* (Vested Interests). INTAR also presents works in English, including some standard non-Latino fare. INTAR has been particularly instrumental in developing Latino playwriting through its playwright's laboratory and readings, quite often following up with full productions of plays by local writers.

While the Latino theatrical environment in New York has been of necessity cosmopolitan and has lent itself to the creation of companies with personnel from all of the Spanish-speaking countries, there have been groups that have set out to promote the work and culture of specific nationalities, such as the Puerto Ricans, Cubans, Dominicans, and Spaniards. Most notable, of course, has been the Puerto Rican Traveling Theater but also the Centro Cultural Cubano, which was instrumental in the 1970s in developing Cuban theatrical expression, most significantly in producing the work of Omar Torres and Iván Acosta. Acosta's play *El super* (The Super) was one of the biggest hits to ever come out of a Latino company and even led

A freestyle battle at the Nuyorican Poets Café in Manhattan, April 1998.

to a prize-winning film adaptation. And, in general, Cuban American theater is well represented in almost all the Latino companies of New York, with Dolores Prida, Iván Acosta, Manuel Martín, and Omar Torres included among the most successful playwrights.

Puerto Rican playwriting is also well represented at most of the Latino companies, but during the 1970s an important new focus developed among New York Puerto Ricans that had long-lasting implications for the creation of theater and art in Latino working-class communities; it was called Nuyorican (New York Rican), meaning that it emerged from the artists born or raised among New York's Puerto Rican working classes.

Included in the first group of Nuyorican playwrights were Miguel Algarín, Lucky Cienfuegos, Tato Laviera, and Miguel Piñero, all of whom focused their bilingual works on the life and culture of working-class Puerto Ricans in New York. Two members of the group, Cienfuegos and Piñero, were ex-convicts who had begun their writing careers while incarcerated, and they chose to develop their dramatic material from prison, the street, and underclass culture. Algarín, a university professor and founder of the Nuyorican Poets Café, created a more avant-garde aura for the collective, while the virtuoso bilingual poet Laviera contributed lyricism and a folk and popular culture base. It was Piñero's work (and life), however, that became most celebrated; his prison drama *Short Eyes* won an Obie and the New York Drama Critics Best American Play Award for the 1973–74 season. His success, coupled with that of fellow Nuyorican writers ex-convict Piri Thomas and street urchin Pedro Pietri, often resulted in Nuyorican literature and theater's being associated with a stark naturalism and the themes of crime, drugs, abnormal sexuality, and generally aberrant behavior. This led to a reaction against the term by many writers and theater companies that were in fact also emphasizing Puerto Rican working-class culture in New York.

Today a new generation of New York Puerto Rican playwrights is at work who were nurtured on the theater of Piñero and the Nuyoricans and who have also experienced greater support and opportunities. They quite often repeat and reevaluate many of the concerns and the style and language of the earlier group but with a sophistication and polish that have come from drama workshops, playwright residencies, and university education. Among these are Juan Shamsul Alam, Edward Gallardo, Federico Fraguada, Richard Irizarry, Yvette Ramírez, and Cándido Tirado.

Florida

Today Latino theater still finds one of its centers in Florida. However, most of the theatrical activity in Tampa has disappeared, with only the Spanish Repertory Theater continuing to perform in the old playhouses (Centro Asturiano) with a fare that varies from the standard *zarzuelas* to Broadway musicals in Spanish. With the exodus of refugees from the Cuban Revolution of 1959, Latino theater in Florida found a new center in Miami, where the Cuban expatriates—many from middle-class or upper-class backgrounds and used to supporting live theater in Cuba—founded and supported theater companies and laid fertile ground for the support of playwrights. The Cuban theater of Miami has produced standard works from throughout the Spanish-speaking world and from the theater of exile, which is burdened with attacking communism in Cuba and promoting a nostalgia for the pre-Castro past. While the Cuban playwrights of New York, many of whom were raised and educated in the United States, have forged an avant-garde and openly Cuban American theater, the Miami playwrights have been more traditional in form and content and, of course, more politically conservative. The exile playwrights whose works were most produced from the 1970s through the 1990s in Miami were Julio Matas, José Cid Pérez, Leopoldo Hernández, José Sánchez-Boudy, Celedonio González, Raúl de Cárdenas, and Matías Montes Huidobro. Overall, today the theatrical fare in Miami is eclectic, with audiences able to choose from a variety of styles and genres, from vaudeville to French-style bedroom farce, serious drama, Broadway musicals in Spanish, and Spanish versions of classics, such as Shakespeare's *Taming of the Shrew* and *Othello*.

The twenty-first century has seen the very long tradition of Latino theater bear fruit in mainstream drama, with three Latino plays being chosen for the Pulitzer Prize, the highest award in theater: Nilo Cruz's *Anna in the Tropics* (2003), Quiara Alegría Hudes's

Water by the Spoonful (2012), and Lin-Manuel Miranda's *Hamilton* (2016). The latter play broke box-office records and revolutionized mainstream and Broadway theater culture in multiple ways: by presenting a truly diverse, multicultural cast; by relying on hip-hop and rap for an openly anachronistic approach to historical subject matter; and by presenting a thoroughly minority perspective on hallowed characters of American history, in this case the portrait of the founding fathers. These breakthroughs led to greater integration of Latino dramas, scripts, actors, directors, and other personnel in theater, film, and television.

OUTSTANDING LATINO FIGURES IN THE THEATER

Iván Acosta (1943–)

Iván Mariano Acosta is an outstanding playwright and filmmaker. Born in Santiago de Cuba on November 17, 1943, he immigrated to the United States with his parents as a result of the Cuban Revolution. He is a graduate in film direction and production of New York University (1969), and he also studied theater with Alejandro Jodorowsky of the Living Theater and New York Theater of the Americas. Acosta worked as a playwright and director at the Centro Cultural Cubano and the Henry Street Settlement Playhouse. His play *El super* (The Super), produced at the Centro Cultural Cubano, is probably the most successful Latino play to come out of an ethnic theater house; it not only was highly reviewed and won awards but also was adapted to the screen by Acosta in a feature film that has won twelve awards for best script and best director. *El super* was published in book form in 1982, and four other plays were published in his anthology *Un cubiche en la luna y otras obras* in 1989. After a long hiatus, during which he developed his work as a filmmaker, Acosta returned to writing plays. His play *Cuba, Punto X* (2012) won several Ace Latin Awards, including the Hola Award for Excellence in Theater for best director in 2013. In all, Acosta has written fifteen plays for the theater. His filmography as a director/screenwriter is extensive and includes *El Súper*

(1979), *Amigos* (1986), *How to Create a Rumba* (1999), and *Cándido: Hands of Fire* (2005).

Luis Alfaro (1963–)

Born in Los Angeles on October 9, 1963, Luis Alfaro was the first Latino playwright to receive a MacArthur Fellowship (1999). Alfaro was a resident artist at Los Angeles's Mark Taper Forum, where he codirected the Latino Theater Initiative during the 1990s and was a visiting artist at such venues as the Kennedy Center in Washington, D.C. His plays have been published in numerous anthologies and staged around the country and abroad. In 2002 he was awarded the Kennedy Center Fund for New American Plays twice, for his plays *Electricidad* (Electricity) and *Breakfast, Lunch and Dinner*. *Electricidad* received its world premiere at the Borderlands Theatre in Tucson and was subsequently produced at the Goodman Theatre in Chicago. He was the winner of the 1998 National Hispanic Playwriting Competition and the 1997 Midwest Play Labs for his play *Straight as a Line*. Included among his plays are a Chicano version of Sophocles's *Electra*: *Electricidad*; *Downtown*, which has been produced as far away as London and Mexico City; *No Holds Barrio*; *Body of Faith*; *Straight as an Arrow*, which premiered at the Edinburgh Festival in Scotland and was named by the *Los Angeles Times* as one of the top ten productions of the year; *Oedipus el Rey* (2010); *Alleluia, The Road* (2013); *This Golden State Part One: Delano* (2015); and *Mojada: A Medea in Los Angeles* (2015). In 2000, Alfaro edited *Plays from South Coast Repertory: Hispanic Playwrights Project Anthology*.

Manuel Aparicio (?–?)

Manuel Aparicio was a Tampa cigar roller who, in the 1920s and 1930s, rose to become an outstanding actor and director in Latino theater in Tampa and New York. From the humble beginnings of acting in amateur performances at the mutualist societies in Tampa, Aparicio went on to head up his own theatrical companies and take them on tour to Havana and New

York. Tampa remained his home base even during the Great Depression, which was the economic cataclysm that eventually resulted in his name going down in Latino theater history, for he became the only director of a Latino company under the U.S. Government Works Progress Administration's (WPA's) Federal Theater Project (FTP). In this role he led one of the FTP's most successful theater companies and was even selected for the FTP's conference of directors in Poughkeepsie, New York, in 1937. The Latino troupe of the FTP produced some of its own collectively created material, such as the revue *El Mundo en la Mano*, under his directorship and including his acting and singing talents. Like some twenty-five other actors, Aparicio lost his job when Congress passed the ERA Act of 1937, which prohibited the employment of aliens under the WPA.

Josefina Báez (1960–)

Born in 1960 in La Romana, Dominican Republic, Josefina Báez immgrated with her family to New York in 1972. At first a student of dance at the American Dance School for eight years, she began working in theater with the Buendía Theater in Cuba. She later took workshops at the Latino Playwright Lab of the Public Theater in New York City, where she began writing dramatic pieces. Workshops in writing for the stage led to several dramatic pieces. In 1994, she had her first staged reading there of *It's a New York Thang; You Will Understand*. Among her produced plays are *Lo mío es mío* (1994, What's Mine Is Mine), which narrates the history of the Dominican people and its twentieth-century diaspora. Báez is also a published poet, with numerous poems in magazines and anthologies. In 2000, she published *Dominicanish*, a collection of poems and "performance texts." In 2013, she produced a series of Spanish and English books of performance poetry beginning with *Comrade, Bliss Ain't Playing* and continuing through *Dramaturgia I & II, Como la Una/Como Uma, Levente no, Yolayorkdominicanyork*, and *De Levente* (four texts for theatrical performance).

Miriam Colón (1936–2017)

Miriam Colón was the first lady of Latino theater in New York. She was the founder and artistic director of the Puerto Rican Traveling Theater and a genuine pioneer in bringing Latino theater to broad audiences. Born on August 20, 1936, in Ponce, Puerto Rico, and raised in Ponce and in New York, Colón attended the University of Puerto Rico and the Erwin Piscator Dramatic Workshop and Technical Institute, as well as the famed Actors Studio, both in New York. Colón developed a long and distinguished career on New York stages and in Hollywood films and television series. Included among her stage credits are *The Oxcart* (1953), *The Innkeepers* (1956), *Me, Cándido!* (1965), *Winterset* (1968), *The Passion of Antígona Pérez* (1972), *Julius Caesar* (1979), *Orinoco* (1985), and *Simpson Street* (1985). In 1989 she was made an honorary doctor of letters by Montclair State College in New Jersey; she also received the White House Latino Heritage Award in 1990. In 1993 Colón received an Obie Award for Lifetime Achievement in the Theater. Colón received the National Medal of Arts from President Barack Obama in 2014.

José Corrales (1937–2002)

Exiled poet and playwright José Corrales was born in Guanabacoa, Cuba, on October 20, 1937. He was not able to finish his university studies in Cuba because the University of Havana was shut down by dictator Fulgencio Batista. After the success of the Cuban Revolution, Corrales worked as an editor of children's theater books and penned articles for the weekly *Bohemia* magazine from 1963 to 1964. He subsequently went into exile in Mexico in 1964 and settled in New York City in 1965, where he became associated with the Dumé Spanish Theater and completed his university education at Mercy College (1975). After that, he became associated with the Centro Cultural Cubano in New York. During the 1970s, many of his plays were staged in the Spanish-language theater houses of New York; among them were: *Farramalla* (1971), *El Espíritu de Navidad* (1974, The Christmas Spirit), *Spics, Spices, Gringos y Gracejo* (1976, Spiks, Spices, Gringos and Ungraciousness), *Juana Machete, la muerte en bicicleta* (1978, Juana Machete and Death on a Bicycle) and *The Butterfly Cazador* (1978, The Butterfly Hunter). Corrales's drama, often expressed bilingually, deals in philosophical and abstract terms with the concept of time but more concretely with the lost homeland and the condition of exile. Especially in *Razones y amarguras* his condition of displacement from Cuba and his alienation in the United States comes to bear. Corrales was the author of some twenty works for the stage, many of which were never performed or published due to the limited resources and facilities available to him in exile. In 2001, Corrales was awarded the Palma Espinada Award by the Cuban American Cultural Institute in California, thus becoming recognized as one of the most distinguished writers of the Cuban expatriate community.

Migdalia Cruz (1958–)

Born on November 6, 1958, and raised in the Bronx, New York, of Puerto Rican heritage, Migdalia Cruz's first theater enchantment was the puppet theater her father built for her to house the fanciful plays she created for her relatives and friends. She received her B.A. in fine arts from Lake Erie College in 1980 and her M.F.A. in playwriting from Columbia University in 1984. She also studied at María Irene Fornés's Playwrights' Laboratory. From 1985 to 1988, she served as playwright in residence at Latino Chicago Theater Company. Her plays have been performed from Los Angeles to New York and in Mexico and England. Her awards include two fellowships from the National Endowment for the Arts and a 1996 Kennedy Center Fund for New American Plays Award. Of the more than fifty plays she has written, Cruz has had more than three dozen produced, including *Miriam's Flowers*, which was produced at the Old Red Lion Theatre in London (1991); *Another Part of the House*, a reworking of Federico García Lorca's *The House of Bernarda Alba*; *The Have-Little*, which was runner-up for the Prize for Plays by Women in 2007; *Telling Tales*, which is actually a group of eleven monologues; and *The Story of Frida Kahlo*. Cruz's plays have been translated into Spanish, French, Arabic, Greek, and Turkish. In 2013, Cruz was awarded the New York Community Trust/Helen Merrill Distinguished Playwright's Award.

Nilo Cruz (1960–)

Nilo Cruz is the first Latino to win a Pulitzer Prize for Drama. Born in Matanzas, Cuba, in 1960, he fled with his family into exile in Miami in 1970. He moved to New York City in 1990 to study with Maria Irene Fornés, then to Brown University to work with Paula Vogel. Although Cruz does not think of himself as a political writer, the themes of exile and alienation recur in many of his plays. Before receiving the Pulitzer, Cruz became a seasoned playwright in regional theater, working with such organizations as the New Theater in Coral Gables, Florida, and the Southcoast Repertory Theater in Orange County, California. Cruz is the author of more than ten produced plays. His *Night Train to Bolina* (1994) follows two children caught up in a civil war in a Latin American country, skirting a line between fantasy and reality. In *Dancing on Her Knees* (1996), Cruz deals with transvestism and AIDS. *Two Sisters and a Piano* (1998) is set in the 1999 Pan American Games in Havana as the Russians are abandoning Cuba. In *A Bicycle Country* (1999), three Cuban exiles brave a perilous open journey in their escape toward freedom. *Hortensia and the Museum of Dreams* (world premiere at New Theatre in 2001) explores the theme of the Peter Pan generation: a brother and a sister return to Havana in search of recuperating part of their past. *Beauty of the Father* (2004) deals with a triangle involving a bisexual father, his daughter, and the father's ex-lover. Cruz's recent works include *The Color of Desire* (2010), *Hurricane* (2010), *Sotto Voce* (2014), *Bathing in Moonlight* (2016), and *Exquisita Agonía (Exquisite Agony)* (2018). Cruz's 2003 Pulitzer Prize–winning play, *Anna in the Tropics*, is set in 1929, as Cruz has explained that he wanted audiences to appreciate that Cuban culture in the United States is not new and only related to exiles of the Revoultion. Based on the historical community of Cuban cigar rollers in Tampa, the play is highly literary, exploring numerous background texts and their ability to influence the real life of the plot. *Anna in the Tropics* tells the story of a family of cigar workers whose lives are irrevocably changed by the arrival of a new lector, Juan Julian, who reads *Anna Karenina* to the workers.

Ariel Dorfman (1942–)

Born on May 6, 1942, in Buenos Aires, Argentina, and raised in Chile and the United States (Queens, New York), novelist, poet, playwright, and essayist Ariel Dorfman became a Chilean exile in 1973 when Salvador Allende's democratic government was overthrown by a coup d'état led by General Augusto Pinochet and supported by the CIA. Dorfman's most known and acclaimed literary work in the United States is his play *Death and the Maiden/La muerte y la doncella* (1992), which was a successful Broadway play and well-respected Roman Polanski film. Here as in various other books, Dorfman deals with the human rights violations of the Pinochet dictatorship. In the highly dramatic and stark *Death and the Maiden*, his main character confronts her former torturer. Other politically engaged works by Dorfman include his *Desaparecer/Missing*, published by Amnesty International in 1981; *Máscaras* (1988, Masks); *Los sueños nucleares de Reagan* (1986, The Nuclear Dreams of Reagan); *Más allá del miedo: El largo adios a Pinochet/Exorcising Terror: The Incredible Unending Trial of Augusto Pinochet* (2002); and *Other Septembers, Many Americas: Selected Provocations, 1980–2004*. Completely bilingual and prolific, Dorfman often writes both Spanish and English versions of his books. In 1998, Dorfman published a memoir of his bilingual, bicultural career: *Heading South, Looking North: A Bilingual Journey*. Today, Dorfman is the Walter Hines Page Research Professor of Literature and Professor of Latin American Studies at Duke University in Durham, North Carolina.

José Ferrer (1912–1992)

José Ferrer was one of the most distinguished actors of Latino background to have made a career in mainstream films and on stage in the United States. The star of numerous Hollywood films and many stage productions, he was born in Santurce, Puerto Rico, on January 8, 1912. Raised and educated in Puerto Rico, he graduated from Princeton University in 1933. His stage credits as an actor or director include *Let's Face It* (1942), *Strange Fruit* (1945), *Design for Living* (1947), *Twentieth Century* (1950), *Stalag 17* (1951), *Man of La Mancha* (1966), and *Cyrano de Bergerac* (1975). As an actor, director, or producer, he was associated with some of the most famous Hollywood films, including *Joan of Arc* (1947), *Moulin Rouge* (1952), *The Caine Mutiny* (1954), *Return to Peyton Place* (1962), *Lawrence of Arabia* (1962), and *Ship of Fools* (1966). His awards include the Gold Medal from the American Academy of Arts and Sciences (1949), the Academy Award for Best Actor in *Cyrano de Bergerac* (1950), and induction into the Theater Hall of Fame (1981). In 2012 the U.S. Postal Service issued a stamp in Ferrer's honor.

María Irene Fornés (1930–2018)

María Irene Fornés was the dean of Latino playwrights in New York, having enjoyed more productions of her works and more recognition, in the form of six personal Obie awards, than any other Latino. Born on May 14, 1930, in Havana, Cuba, she immigrated to the United States in 1945 and became a naturalized citizen in 1951. This sets her off considerably from most of the other Cuban playwrights, who immigrated to the United States as refugees from the Cuban Revolution of the 1960s. Since 1960 she worked as a playwright, director, and teacher of theater at a variety of workshops, universities, and schools, including Theater for New York City (1973–78). Fornés had more than thirty plays produced, including adaptations of plays by Federico García Lorca, Pedro Calderón de la Barca, and Anton Chekhov. Her plays were produced on Latino stages, on mainstream off-off-Broadway, off-Broadway, and Broadway, and in Claremont, California, Milwaukee, Minneapolis, London, and Zurich. Fornés's works, although at times touching upon political and ethnic themes, generally dealt with human relations and the emotional lives of her characters. Many of her plays have been published in collections of her work: *Promenade and Other Plays* (1971), *María Irene Fornés: Plays* (1986), and *Lovers and Keepers* (1986). Fornés's plays won nine Obies, and she was awarded the PEN/Laura Pels International Foundation for Theater Award for a Master American Dramatist in 2002.

Anthony J. García (1953–)

Anthony J. García is a well-known leader in the Chicano theater movement, in which he became involved during the early 1970s. Born and raised in Denver, Colorado, and a graduate of the University of Colorado–Denver with a degree in theater, García began performing with Su Teatro (Your Theater) soon after its founding in 1971. He became the theater's director in 1974. To date, he has written more than twenty plays, most of which have not been published. Su Teatro has developed into a cultural arts center, for which he has served as the executive director since 1989. García's play *Introduction to Chicano History 101* was taken to Joseph Papp's New York Latino Theatre Festival and then toured the U.S. Southwest and Mexico. *I Don't Speak English Only!* (1993) by García and José Guadalupe Saucedo also toured throughout the United States. His *Ludlow, Grito de las Minas* is a play that documents the killing of workers, women, and children during the Ludlow, Colorado, labor strike of 1914. His most recently produced plays are *El Río: Las Lagrimas de la Llorona* (2013, The River: Tears of the Crying Woman), *Cuarenta y Ocho* (2014, Forty-Eight), and *La Tierra: El Corazón de Mi Madre* (2015, Land: My Mother's Heart). García's *Serafín: Cantos y Lágrimas* (Serafín, Songs and Tears) was awarded a Rocky Mountain Drama Critics Award. During his executive directorship, Centro Su Teatro was awarded the 1997 Governors Award for Excellence in the Arts.

Quiara Alegría Hudes (1977–)

Born in Philadelphia, the daughter of a Jewish father and Puerto Rican mother, Quiara Alegría Hudes earned a B.A. from Yale University and an M.F.A. from Brown University. Her career as a composer and playwright for the stage has been spectacular. Her first award was for writing the book for Lin-Manuel Miranda's *In the Heights*; it won the won the 2008 Tony Award for Best Musical, among other recognitions. Her play *Yemaya's Belly* won the 2003 Clauder Competition for New England Playwriting and the Paula Vogel Award in Playwriting. *Elliot, a Soldier's Fugue* was a finalist for the Pulitzer Prize in 2007, and *Water by the Spoonful* won the Pulitzer Prize in 2012. The latter was followed by five new plays produced across the country, from California to Illinois to New York: *The Happiest Songs Playlist* (2014), *Lulu's Golden Shoes* (2015), *The Good Peaches* (2016), *Daphne's Dive* (2016), and *Miss You Like Hell* (2016). Four of her plays have been published as books.

Josefina López (1969–)

Born on March 19, 1969, in San Luis Potosí, Mexico, Josefina López immigrated to East Los Angeles with her parents in 1975. She graduated from the Los Angeles County High School for the Arts and from 1985 to 1988 was a member of the Los Angeles Theater Centre's Young Playwrights Lab. Her play *Simply María, or The American Dream* was produced by the California Young Playwrights' Contest in 1988. Later in 1998 she studied in María Irene Fornés's Hispanic Playwrights-in-Residence Laboratory in New York City. Out of her work at the lab came her renowned *Real Women Have Curves*, which went on to be produced in Latino community theaters and on professional stages, eventually becoming a Hollywood film. López eventually obtained an M.F.A. in playwriting from the University of California, Los Angeles. López continues to be a prolific playwright, penning and producing such plays as *Unconquered Spirits*, *Confessions of Women from East L.A.*, *Boyle Heights* (2004), *Hungry Woman in Paris* (2009), *Detained in the Desert* (2012), *A Cat Named Mercy* (2014), and *Piñata Dreams* (2014). In 2000 López founded the CASA 0101 Theater in Boyle Heights, Los Angeles, for which she serves as the artistic director. She founded and administers the theater as a way to extend the arts to the community, teach playwriting, and protest gentrification of the neighborhood.

Matthew López
(1977–)

Born in Panama City to public school teacher parents, Matthew López graduated with a B.A. in theater from the University of South Florida in Tampa. López's first produced play, which debuted in 2006, *The Whipping Man*, moved to off-Broadway in 2011, where it won an Obie, and López himself won the John Gassner New Play Award. The play, which deals with addiction and slavery, had numerous productions throughout the United States between 2012 and 2016. López, who is of Puerto Rican heritage, wrote his next play, *Somewhere* (2011), in somewhat of a dialog with the famed *West Side Story*, featuring a mostly Latino cast. López's off-Broadway *The Legend of Georgia McBride* (2014) is a comedic rendering about a drag queen Elvis impersonator. His *Reverberation* (2015) examines violence against women and the LGBTQ community; it is set in Astoria, New York City. By far, López's greatest hit, one that has established him as a major figure in American drama, is *The Inheritance*, a two-part, seven-hour epic that premiered to rave reviews in London in 2018 and moved to Broadway in 2019. López won the Evening Standard Award and the Critics Circle Theatre Award for Best New Play in 2020, along with numerous other awards and nominations. The play deals sensitively with the topic of being a gay man across ages, generations, and social classes.

Eduardo Machado (1953–)

Born on July 11, 1953, in Havana, Cuba, Eduardo Machado came to the United States when he was eight years old as a member of Operation Peter Pan. His formal training as a playwright was under the tutelage of María Irene Fornés at INTAR and having three plays workshopped at the Ensemble Studio Theater in New York City after he moved there in 1981. Machado has had more different plays produced over a twenty-year period than any other Latino playwright. Among his plays are *Rosario and the Gypsies* (1982); *Broken Eggs* (1984); *Fabiola* (1985); *When*

It's Over (1986); *Stevie Wants to Play the Blues* (1990); *Perricones* (1990); *They Still Mambo in Havana* (1998); *Crocodile Eyes* (1999); *Havana Is Waiting* (2001); *When the Sea Drowns in Sand* (2001); *The Cook* (2003); and *Kissing Fidel* (2005). His latest play, *Celia and Fidel*, was produced at the Arena Stage Theater in Washington, D.C., in 2020. Machado has published two collections of his works in *Once Removed* (1988) and *The Floating Island Plays* (1991).

René Marqués (1919–1979)

Considered Puerto Rico's foremost playwright and writer of short fiction, René Marqués was born on October 4, 1919, in Arecibo into a farming family. In 1948, Marqués received a Rockefeller Fellowship to study playwriting in the United States, which allowed him to study at Columbia University and the Piscator Dramatic Workshop in New York City. After his return to San Juan, he established the Teatro Experimental del Ateneo (the Atheneum Society Experimental Theater). From that time on, Marqués maintained a heavy involvement not only in playwriting but also in the development of Puerto Rican theater. Marqués's best-known work is still the all-important play *La Carreta* (debuted in 1953, published in 1961), which centers on the epic of Puerto Rican immigration to New York. His other published plays include *El hombre y sus sueños* (1948, Man and His Dreams), *Palm Sunday* (1949), *Otro día nuestro* (1955, Another of Our Days), *Juan Bobo y la Dama de Occidente* (1956, Juan Bobo and the Western Lady), *El sol y los MacDonald* (1957, The Sun and the MacDonalds), and the collection *Teatro* (1959), which includes three of his most important plays: *Los soles truncos* (The Fan Lights), *Un niño azul para esa sombra* (A Blue Child for That Shadow), and *La muerte no entrará en palacio* (Death Will Not Enter the Palace).

Julio Matas (1931–2016)

Born in Havana, Cuba, on May 12, 1931, Julio Matas was encouraged to follow in the steps of his father, a judge, and he thus obtained his law degree from the University of Havana in 1955. But he never practiced as an attorney. He had enrolled in the University School for Dramatic Arts, and by the time of his graduation in 1952, he had already organized a drama group called Arena. In his youth he worked on literary magazines and film projects with some of the figures who would become outstanding in these fields, such as Roberto Fernández Retamar, Néstor Almendros, and Tomás Gutiérrez Alea. In 1957 Matas enrolled at Harvard University to pursue a Ph.D. in Spanish literature; however, he remained active as a director, returning to Cuba to work on stage productions. It was during the cultural ferment that accompanied the first years of the Communist regime in Cuba that Matas saw two of his first books published there: the collection of short stories *Catálogo de imprevistos* (1963, Catalog of the Unforeseen) and the three-act play *La crónica y el suceso* (1964, The Chronicle and the Event). In 1965 Matas returned to the United States to assume a position in the Department of Hispanic Languages and Literatures at the University of Pittsburgh, a position that he held until his retirement in 1989.

Oliver Mayer (1965–)

Oliver Mayer is a Los Angeles playwright, born on April 25, 1961, the son of a Mexican American mother, Gloria, an actress who gave up the theater for marriage, and his late father, Alexander, who was a film and television art director. Mayer's education includes studies at Cornell, a B.A. from Oxford, and an M.F.A. in theater from Columbia University. His inspiration for theater was seeing the works of Luis Valdez and El Teatro Campesino; he was especially taken by the Los Angeles production of *Zoot Suit*. Rather than thinking of himself as a Chicano dramatist, he identifies more generally as a Latino playwright. Among his produced plays are *José Louis Blues* (1992), *Conjunto* (1999, Band), *The Road to Los Angeles* (2000), *Joy of the Desolate* (2000), *Ragged Time* (2002), *Young Valiant* (2004), *A Pesar de Todo* (2006, In Spite of Everything), and *Yerma in the Desert* (2017). They have enjoyed productions on both coasts, from the Mark Taper Forum to Joseph Papp's New York Shakespeare Festival. A play that takes Mayer back to the days of incipient Chicano theater, however, is *Conjunto*, his study of Mexican, Japanese, and Filipino farm workers in the post–World War II period. He is the recipient of an Obie award and two Drama Critics' Circle awards, among many others.

Lin-Manuel Miranda (1980–)

The greatest Latino Broadway star ever, Nuyorican playwright, composer, actor, singer, and dancer Lin-Manuel Miranda was born on January 16, 1980, in New York City. His mother was a clinical psychologist and his father was a political consultant. While studying at Wesleyan University in Ohio in 1999, Miranda wrote the first draft of what would become a Broadway hit: *In the Heights*. After graduating in 2000, he reworked the musical with Quiara Alegría Hudes in 2004, and it was produced off-Broadway and then opened on Broadway in 2008, winning four Tonys, including Best Musical and Best Original Score. After leaving the cast, Miranda worked in a variety of acting roles for television, started a hip-hop performance group, wrote a newspaper column, taught high school, and continued to write plays, some of which were produced and toured, such as *Bring It On* (2011). In 2008 Miranda began to improvise rap poetry and music based on the historical figure of Alexander Hamilton and even performed a version at the White House Evening of Poetry, Music, and the Spoken Word on May 12, 2009. The work slowly took shape as a musical drama, and in 2015 *Hamilton: An American Musical* premiered off-Broadway at the Public Theater. It officially opened on Broadway on August 6, 2015, receiving rave reviews and on track to becoming the highest-grossing musical ever. In 2020 the Disney Channel aired the video production of *Hamilton* nationally, which made it accessible to the millions of people who could not afford Broadway's most expensive ticket. *Hamilton* won the Tony Award for Best Musical; Miranda won Tony Awards for Best Original Score and Best Book of a Musical; and the *Hamilton* cast album won the Grammy Award for Best Musical Theater Album. *Hamilton* is a truly revolutionary work of art for the stage in many regards. First, its cast of actors playing the founding fathers was predominantly made up of people of color; second, the entire play is sung and spoken in rap; and third, it presents a subtle message about immigration—Hamilton was an immigrant—to a Broadway audience that is traditionally averse to political messages. After leaving the stage production of *Hamilton*, Miranda worked on various television and film productions, including costarring in 2019 in *Mary Poppins Returns*, writing eight songs for Disney's 2021 animated film *Encanto*, and directing the 2021 Netflix film *Tick, Tick … Boom!* A Hollywood production of *In the Heights* hit movie theaters and HBO in 2021. In 2019 the Smithsonian National Portrait Gallery awarded Miranda the Portrait of a Nation Prize.

Pedro Monge Rafuls (1943–)

Pedro Monge Rafuls was born in Central Zaza, Cuba. In 1961, he went into exile, escaping from Cuba by boat. He moved to the United States and in Chicago cofounded the Círculo Teatral de Chicago (Chicago Theatrical Circle), one of the first Latino, Spanish-language theater groups in the Midwest. In 1977, he founded the journal *Ollantay* and the Ollantay Center in Queens, where he often offers theater seminars, conferences, exhibits, and recitals. His play *Nadie se va del todo* (1991, No One Is Completely Gone) has become a classic on the subject of the Cuban *re-encuentro* (rapprochement) and has been translated and published in German. Among his other published and staged plays are *Cristóbal Colón y otros locos* (1986, Christopher Columbus and Other Crazy Men), *Easy Money* (1989), *Solidarios* (1989, In Solidarity), *Limonada para el Virrey* (1989, Lemonade for the Viceroy), *El instante fugitivo* (1989, The Fugitive Instant), *Trash* (1989), *Recordando a mamá* (1990, Remembering Mother), *La oreja militar* (1993, The Military Ear), *Las lágrimas del alma* (1994, Tears from the Soul), *Soldados somos y a la guerra vamos* (1995, We're Soldiers and We're Marching Off to War), *Simplemente Camila* (1999, Simply Camila), and *Pase adelante si quiere* (1999, Come On In, If You Wish). His plays have been performed in New York, Los Angeles, Lima, Buenos Aires, Bogotá, Rome, Cambridge, and London.

Matías Montes Huidobro (1931–)

Matías Montes Huidobro is a prolific writer of plays, fiction, and poetry, and he has been a theatrical producer and scriptwriter for television and radio. Born in Sagua la Grande, Cuba, Montes Huidobro was educated there and in Havana. In 1952 he obtained a Ph.D. degree in pedagogy from the University of Havana, but from 1949 on he had already begun publishing creative literature and literary criticism. He served as a professor of Spanish literature at the National School of Journalism in Havana, at which point he had a falling out with the political powers and immigrated to the United States. In 1963 he became a professor of Spanish at the University of Hawaii. The dramas of Matías Montes Huidobro vary in style, theme, and format, ranging from expressionism to surrealism, from the absurd to the allegorical and political. His published plays include *Los acosados* (The Accosted) (1959), *La botija* (The Jug) (1959), *Gas en los poros* (1961, Gas in His Pores), *El tiro por la culata* (1961, Ass-Backwards), *La vaca de los ojos largos* (1967, The Long-Eyed Cow), *Funeral en Teruel* (1982, Funeral in Teruel), and *La navaja de Olofé* (1982, Olofé's Blade). Montes Huidobro has also published important novels, including *Desterrados al fuego* (1975, Exiled into the Fire) and *Segar a los muertos* (1980, To Mow the Dead).

Carlos Morton (1947–)

Carlos Morton is one of the most published Latino playwrights in the United States. Born on October 15, 1947, in Chicago, to Mexican American parents, Morton received his education in various states, as his father's assignments in the Army as a noncommissioned officer changed. Morton obtained a bachelor's degree from the University of Texas, El Paso (1975), an M.F.A. degree in theater from the University of California, San Diego (1979), and a Ph.D. degree in drama from the University of Texas, Austin (1987), after which he embarked on a career as a professor of drama. His writing career began much earlier, with the publication of his first chapbook of poems, *White Heroin Winter*, in 1971, followed by the publication of his most famous play, *El Jardín* (The Garden) in an anthology in 1974. The majority of his plays have been produced on stages at universities and Latino community arts centers, with *Pancho Diablo* being produced by the New York Shakespeare Festival and *The Many Deaths of Danny Rosales* by Los Angeles's Bilingual Foundation for the Arts. Most of his plays are contained in three published collections, *The Many Deaths of Danny Rosales and Other Plays* (1983), *Johnny Tenorio and Other Plays* (1991), and *Dreaming on Sunday in the*

Alameda (2004). A collection of his plays was translated to Spanish and published in Mexico and the United States: *Rancho Hollywood y otras obras del teatro chicano* (2017). Morton has had two volumes of his plays translated to Italian and published in Italy.

Mónica A. Palacios (1959–)

Los Angeles playwright and lesbian activist Mónica A. Palacios has performed her one-woman shows and produced her plays in theaters and a wide array of performance spaces. Palacios was a founding member of the highly regarded comedy troupe Culture Clash (1984–85). A Mexican American born on June 14, 1959, in Santa Cruz, California, Palacios earned a B.A. in film, with a concentration in screenwriting. Recognized for her writing and performing against homophobia, in 2002 she was named to *OUT* magazine's "OUT 100" lesbian-bisexual-transgender success stories. That same year, she performed *Queer Soul*, a twenty-year retrospective of her work, in various venues. The Latin Pride Foundation, among other institutions, has honored Palacios. Her plays and productions include *Latin Lezbo Comic* (1991), *Confession … A Sexplosion of Tantalizing Tales* (1994), *La Llorona* (1994, The Crying Woman), *Clock* (1996), *My Body and Other Parts* (1998), *Greetings from a Queer Señorita* (1999), *Bésame Mucho* (2000, Kiss Me Much), *Miércoles Loves Luna* (2013), *Clock* (2014), *I Kissed Chavela Vargas* (2016), and *Say Their Names* (2017).

Miguel Piñero (1946–1988)

Miguel Piñero is the most famous dramatist to come out of the Nuyorican school. Born in Gurabo, Puerto Rico, on December 19, 1946, he was raised on the Lower East Side of New York, the site of many of his plays and poems. Shortly after moving to New York, his father abandoned the family, which forced them to live on the streets until his mother could find a source of income. Piñero was a gang leader and involved in petty crime and drugs while an adolescent; he was a junior high school dropout, and by the time he was twenty-four he had been sent to Sing Sing Prison for armed robbery. While at Sing Sing, he began writing and acting in a theater workshop there. By the time of his release, his most famous play, *Short Eyes* (published in 1975), had already been prepared in draft form. The play was produced and soon moved to Broadway after getting favorable reviews. In 1974, it won an Obie, a Drama Desk Award, and the New York Drama Critics' Award for Best American Play. During the successful run of his play and afterward, Piñero became involved with a group of Nuyorican writers in the Lower East Side and became one of the principal spokespersons and models for the new school of Nuyorican literature, which was furthered by the publication of *Nuyorican Poets: An Anthology of Puerto Rican Words and Feelings*, compiled and edited by him and Miguel Algarín in 1975. During this time, as well, Piñero began his career as a scriptwriter for such television dramatic series as *Baretta*, *Kojak*, and *Miami Vice*. In all, Piñero wrote some eleven plays that were produced, most of which are included in his two collections, *The Sun Always Shines for the Cool; A Midnight Moon at the Greasy Spoon; Eulogy for a Small-Time Thief* (1983) and *Outrageous One-Act Plays* (1986). Piñero is also author of a book of poems, *La Bodega Sold Dreams* (1986). In 2010, Piñero's complete works were gathered and published as *Outlaw: The Collected Works of Miguel Piñero*. In 2001, he was the subject of a Hollywood film depicting his life, *Piñero*.

Dolores Prida (1943–2013)

Dolores Prida was a playwright and screenwriter whose works were produced in various states and in Puerto Rico, Venezuela, and the Dominican Republic. Born on September 5, 1943, in Caibairén, Cuba, Prida emigrated with her family to New York in 1963. She graduated from Hunter College in 1969 with a major in Spanish American literature. Upon graduation she began a career as a journalist and editor, first for Collier-Macmillan and then for other publishers, quite often using her bilingual skills. In the 1970s and 1980s she served as the senior editor of *Nuestro* magazine. In 1977 her first play, *Beautiful Señoritas*, was produced at the Duo Theater. Since then approximately ten of her plays have been produced. Prida's plays vary in style and format and include adaptations of international classics, such as *The Three Penny Opera*; experiments with the Broadway musical formula, as in her *Savings* (1985); and her bilingual play, *Coser y cantar* (To Sew and to Sing, 1981). Her themes involve an examination of the phenomenon of urban gentrification, as in *Savings*; and the generation gap and conflict of culture, as in *Botánica* (1990). Prida's plays, which are written in Spanish or English or bilingually, have been collected in *Beautiful Señoritas and Other Plays* (1991). Prida was also a talented poet who was a leader in the 1960s of New York's Nueva Sangre (New Blood) movement of young poets. Her books of poems include *Treinta y un poemas* (Thirty-One Poems, 1967), *Women of the Hour* (1971), and, with photographer Roger Cabán, *The IRT Prayer Book*.

Guillermo A. Reyes (1962–)

Prolific playwright Guillermo A. Reyes was born in Mulchen, Chile, in 1962 and immigrated with his mother to the Washington, D.C., area in 1971. The pair moved to Los Angeles in 1977, where Reyes attended high school. Reyes went on to study drama at the University of California, Los Angeles and later earned an M.F.A. in playwriting from the University of California, San Diego (1990). In 1988, he served as a dramaturge for the San Diego Repertory Theater. Included among his produced plays are *The Seductions of Johnny Diego* (1990), *Men on the Verge of a His-panic Breakdown* (1994), *The West Hollywood Affair* (1994), *Miss Consuelo* (1997), *We Lost at the Movie* (2005), *Farewell to Hollywood* (2006), *Allende by Pinochet* (2007), and *They Call Me a Hero* (2014). *Men on the Verge* won the Theater L.A. Ovation Award for Best World Premier Play and Best Production 1994. A gay Latino playwright, Reyes has treated the theme of gender identity and its conflicts inside and outside the Latino culture in a number of plays. In 2010, he published a memoir with the University of Wisconsin Press, entitled *Madre and I: A Memoir of Our Immigrant Lives*.

Carmen Rivera (1964–)

Prolific Nuyorican playwright Carmen Rivera was born on October 1, 1964, in the Bronx, New York, and graduated in 1986 from New York University with a double major in economics and Latin American literature. Upon graduation, she became a member of the Puerto Rican Traveling Theater's Professional Playwriting Unit, and in 1990 she began graduate studies in playwriting and theater at the Gallatin School at New York University. She then cofounded the Latino Experimental Fantastic Theatre with director Gloria Zelaya and her husband, playwright/director Cándido Tirado. Soon after receiving her master's degree in 1993, Rivera saw a number of her plays produced. *To Catch the Lightning* (1997), *Julia de Burgos, Child of Water/Julia de Burgos, Criatura del Agua* (1999), *Destiny* (2001), and *La Lupe: My Life, My Destiny* (2002), for which she won an ACE Award, are among the plays that were successfully staged at the Puerto Rican Traveling Theater. Her *The Next Stop/La Próxima Parada* (1997) and *Under the Mango Tree* (2004) were produced at INTAR. For *La Gringa*, produced in 1996 at Teatro Repertorio Español, she received the coveted Obie Award. Among her other produced plays are *La Caída de Rafael Trujillo* (2014, The Downfall of Rafael Trujillo) and *Riding the Bear* (2016). Besides having works produced at theaters around the United States, Rivera has seen her plays performed at festivals in Russia, Chile, Colombia, and Bolivia.

José Rivera (1955–)

José Rivera is one of the most successful Latino playwrights in the United States. A Puerto Rican who writes in English, Rivera was born on March 24, 1955, in Santurce. When he was four, his family moved to a small town in Long Island, New York, where he was raised and educated in the middle-class Anglo-American tradition, receiving very little influence from the Latin American intellectual tradition. However, when he began to discover Latin American literature, it was Gabriel García Márquez's *One Hundred Years of Solitude*

that affected him deeply. Later, he was to study with Márquez at the Sundance Institute. Along the way, Rivera was nurtured by many of the fellowships and workshops that during the 1980s and 1990s were opening up for Latino playwrights, and his plays were workshopped and developed in the South Coast Repertory Theater. He even served as a writer-in-residence at the Royal Court Theatre in London. Rivera's plays have been produced on many of the leading stages in the United States, such as the Mark Taper Forum in Los Angeles, the Goodman Theater in Chicago, and the Public Theater in New York. Among his plays are *The House of Ramón Iglesia* (1983), *The Promise* (1988), *Marisol* (1992), *Cloud Tectonics* (1995), *Each Day Dies with Sleep* (1995), *The Street of the Sun* (1996), *Sueño* (1998), *The Garden of Tears and Kisses* (2014), *Sermon for the Senses* (2014), and *Charlotte* (2014). Two anthologies of his plays have been published: *Marisol and Other Plays* (1997) and *References to Salvador Dali Make Me Hot and Other Plays* (2003). Rivera has also been a successful scriptwriter for the large and small screen. Most notably, he became the first Puerto Rican playwright to be nominated for an Oscar for his *The Motorcycle Diaries* (2004), which was nominated in the category of Best Adapted Screenplay. Included among his awards are Obie awards for *Marisol* and *References to Salvador Dali Make Me Hot* and two Joseph Ketterling Award honorable mentions for *Marisol* and *The Promise*. *The House of Ramón Iglesia* won the FDG/CBS New Play Contest and was produced on the Public Broadcasting System's *American Playhouse*.

Milcha Sánchez-Scott (1953–)

Born in Bali to a Colombian father who was raised in Mexico and a mother of mixed Asian and European ancestry, playwright Milcha Sánchez-Scott was raised in South America and England before her family settled in the San Diego area of Southern California. While studying literature at the University of San Diego, Sánchez-Scott worked at an employment agency for maids; the stories she collected there became part of her first written and produced play, *Latina* (1980), a serious drama with humorous elements and surrealistic episodes that indicts racism among and against Latinos on top of gender discrimination in the employment of maids by rich Anglo-Americans.

After college, Sánchez-Scott honed her playwriting skills through workshops with such pioneers as María Irene Fornés at INTAR (1984–85) and fellowships from the Rockefeller Foundation (1987) and the Mark Taper Forum (1995–96). Her plays were workshopped in various laboratories, such as the South Coast Repertory (1993), and have received such awards as Dramalog Award (1980), the Vesta Award (1983), and Le Compte du Nouy Prize (1985). Her most renowned play is *Roosters* (1987), an energetic and often surrealist drama set on a farm that deals with a father-son confrontation over masculine values. Among her other plays are the one-acts *Dog Lady* (1982) and *The Cuban Swimmer* (1982), which deal with Latino athletes in training; *Evening Star* (1988), a barrio love story; *Stone Wedding* (1989); *El Dorado* (1990); and *The Old Matador* (1993). In 2018 *The Collected Plays of Milcha Sánchez-Scott* was published.

Rubén Sierra (1946–1998)

Born in San Antonio, Texas, on December 6, 1946, into a family whose members had participated in Mexican American traditional theater and had even written plays, Rubén Sierra developed an early interest in the theater. In 1970 Sierra graduated with a bachelor's degree in speech and drama and, shortly thereafter, served in the Army for two years—this later experience informed plays he would write. Sierra received his M.A. in directing from the University of Washington in Seattle in 1974. He taught theater there until 1978, when he founded the Group Theater, which was committed to producing plays representing the various ethnic theater arts in the United States; he also continued to serve as the director of the Ethnic Cultural Center and Theater at the University of Washington. Sierra's first play to be produced was *La Raza Pura, or Racial, Racial*, produced at St. Mary's University in San Antonio in 1968 and later published; it satirized interracial relations and conflict. *The Conquering Father* (1972) was one of his most philosophical: an allegory dealing with the Divinity, death, and organized religion. Sierra's *La Capirotada de los Espejos* (1973, The Potpourri of Mirrors), constructed in Chicano theater style, presented the pageant of Chicano history, beginning with the Aztecs in Aztlán. Sierra's *Manolo* (1975, published in 1979), on the other hand, was a realistic drama drawing on his Army and Vietnam experience; the three-act work deals with the drug addiction of a Vietnam veteran and his responsibility to family and community. *The Millionaire and the Pobrecito* (1979) was Sierra's adaptation of Mark Twain's *Prince and the Pauper* for children's theater. Sierra also adapted Leo Romero's poetry collection, *Celso*, into a one-man play, *I Am Celso* (1985), which saw him tour the country as the actor. *Say Can You See* is Sierra's satirical answer to the American Dream and the melting pot. His final play, *When The Blues Chase Up a Rabbit* (1998), has a young Chicano fighting prejudice in Texas in the 1960s.

Caridad Svich (1963–)

Of a mixed Cuban, Argentine, Spanish, and Croatian ancestry, Latina playwright Caridad Svich was born in Philadelphia, Pennsylvania, on July 30, 1963. Svich received a B.F.A. in theater–performing arts from the University of North Carolina, Charlotte (1985) and then went on for an M.F.A. in theater–playwriting at the University of California, San Diego (1988). Her plays have been produced in commercial and academic venues on both coasts of the United States and as far abroad as Scotland, England, Italy, and Germany. Svich's produced plays include *Gleaning/Rebusca* (1991), *Any Place but Here* (1992, and a revised draft directed by María Irene Fornés in 1995), *Alchemy of Desire/Dead-Man's Blues* (1994), *Fugitive Pieces* (2000), *Iphigenia Crash Land Falls on the Neon Shell That Was Once Her Heart (a rave fable)* (2004), *The Booth Variations* (2004), *Thrush* (2006), *The Tropic of X* (2007), and *The Labyrinth of Desire* (2008). Some fifteen of her plays and translations have been published in anthologies and theater journals. Svich's awards include Cincinnati Playhouse's Rosenthal New Play Prize (1994), an NEA/TCG Playwriting Residency at the Mark Taper Forum for *Prodigal Kiss* (1996–97), a Bunting Fellowship from Harvard University/Radcliffe Institute for Advanced Study (2002–3), a National Latino Playwrights Award (2003), the Whitfield Cook Award for New Writing given by New Dramatists for her as yet unproduced "Lucinda Caval" (2007), and many others. In 2012 Svich received an Obie for Lifetime Achievement. Svich is the founder of NoPassport, the pan-American theater alliance and publishing venture; she is also a contributing editor for *Theatre Forum*.

Cándido Tirado (?–)

The works of Nuyorican playwright Cándido Tirado have been successfully staged in New York since the mid-1980s, many in the leading Latino theaters in New York, including Pergones, the Puerto Rican Traveling Theater, and Teatro Repertorio Español. Tirado's dramas present with gritty realism many of the social and familial problems afflicting poor Puerto Rican families in New York City: incest, prostitution, child abandonment, drugs, gang violence, and more. One play even features a baby refusing to be born into such a horrible and chaotic world. Two exceptions from this dire fare are his musical biography of salsa queen Celia Cruz, *Celia* (2007), coauthored with Carmen Rivera, and his joint interpretation with multiple authors of Calderón de la Barca's classic *La vida es sueño: The Dream Chain* (2007). Tirado's produced plays include *First Class* (1988), *For Love* (1994), *Checking Out/Morir Soñando* (1998), *King without a Castle/Rey sin Castillo* (2000), and *Momma's Boyz* (2006). Tirado has also worked as a successful screenwriter for such television series as *Heroes*, *Lost*, *24*, *Grey's Anatomy*, *House*, *The Simpsons*, *Ugly Betty*, and others.

Omar Torres (1945–)

Omar Torres is an actor, playwright, poet, and novelist. Born and raised in Las Tunas, Cuba, he immigrated to Miami with his family in 1959. Later he attended Queens College in New York and then took acting classes at the New York Theater of the Americas; he graduated from the International Television Arts School. He has had an active career in radio, television, and movies. In 1972 he cofounded, with Iván Acosta, the Centro Cultural Cubano, and in 1974 he founded the literary and arts journal *Cubanacán* (a nonsense word meaning "Cuba"). Torres's produced plays include *Abdala-José Martí* (1972), *Cumbancha cubiche* (Cumbancha Low-Class Cuban; 1976), and *Dreamland Melody* (1982). Torres is the author of three novels— *Apenas un bolero* (Just a Bolero; 1981), *Al partir* (Upon Leaving; 1986), and *Fallen Angels Sing* (1991)—and five books of poetry: *Conversación primera* (First Conversation; 1975), *Ecos de un laberinto* (Echos from a Labyrinth; 1976), *Tiempo robado* (Stolen Time; 1978), *De nunca a siempre* (From Never to Always; 1981), and *Línea en diluvio* (Line in the Deluge; 1981).

Alina Troyano (1957–)

Comedienne, playwright, and widely renowned performance artist Alina Troyano has created and assumed the persona of Carmelita Tropicana, an outlandish, brash, outspoken, and irreverent commentator of the cultural scene as well as satirist of the Latina spitfires, à la Carmen Miranda. Born in Cuba, but from age seven on raised in the United States, Troyano has been a perennial performer on stages and alternative spaces in and around New York City during the 1980s, and by the 1990s she went on to national fame. Her productions include *Carmelita Tropicana: Your Kunst Is Your Waffen (Art Is Your Weapon)* (1994), *Single Wet Female* (2002), *With What Ass Does the Cockroach Sit* (2004), *The Box/Meine Box* (2008), *Post Plastics* (2012), and *Memories of the Revolution: The First Ten Years of the WOW I* (2016). In 1999, Troyano was awarded an Obie for Sustained Excellence in Performance. In 2016 she won a Creative Capital award and in 2021 was named a USA Artists Fellow. In 2000, Troyano published a collection of her one-woman plays, essays, and commentary under the title of *I, Carmelita Tropicana: Performing between Cultures*, in which her bilingual humor, her satire of stereotypes, and her lesbian identity challenge heteronormative culture. In 2003, she was the recipient of the Plumed Warrior writing award from the National Latin Gay Lesbian Bisexual Transgender Organization.

Luis Valdez (1940–)

Luis Valdez is considered the father of Chicano theater. He has distinguished himself as an actor, director, playwright, and filmmaker; however, it was in his role as the founding director of El Teatro Campesino, a theater of farm workers in California, that his efforts inspired young Chicano activists across the country to use theater as a means of organizing students, communities, and labor unions. Valdez was born on June 26, 1940, in Delano, California, into a family of migrant farm workers. He began to work the fields at age six and to follow the crops. Valdez's education

was continuously interrupted; he nevertheless finished high school and went on to San Jose State College, where he majored in English and pursued his interest in theater. While there he won a playwriting contest with his one-act *The Theft* (1961), and in 1963 the drama department produced his play *The Shrunken Head of Pancho Villa*. After graduating from college in 1964, Valdez joined the San Francisco Mime Troupe and learned the techniques of agitprop (agitation and propaganda) theater and Italian commedia dell'arte (comedy of art), both of which influenced Valdez's development of the basic format of Chicano theater: the one-act presentational *acto*.

In 1965 Valdez enlisted in César Chávez's mission to organize farm workers in Delano into a union. It was there that Valdez brought together farm workers and students into El Teatro Campesino to dramatize the plight of the farm workers. The publicity and success gained by the troupe led to the spontaneous appearance of a national Chicano theater movement. In 1967 Valdez and El Teatro Campesino left the unionizing effort to expand their theater beyond agitprop and farm worker concerns. From then on Valdez and the theater have explored most of the theatrical genres that have been important to Mexicans in the United States, including religious pageants, vaudeville with the down-and-out *pelado* (underdog) figure, and dramatized *corridos* (ballads).

During the late 1960s and the 1970s, El Teatro Campesino produced many of Valdez's plays, including *Los vendidos* (1967, The Sell-Outs), *The Shrunken Head of Pancho Villa* (1968), *Bernabé* (1970), *Dark Root of a Scream* (1971), *La carpa de los Rascuachis* (1974), and *El fin del mundo* (1976). In 1978 Valdez broke into mainstream theater in Los Angeles with the Mark Taper Forum's production of his *Zoot Suit*, and a year later a Broadway production of the same play was performed. In 1986 he had a successful run of his play *I Don't Have to Show You No Stinking Badges* at the Los Angeles Theater Center. Valdez's screenwriting career began with early film and television versions of "Corky" González's poem *I Am Joaquín* (1969) and his own *Los vendidos*, and later with a film version of *Zoot Suit* (1982) and such other dramatic works brought to film as *La Pastorela* (1991). His 1987 production for PBS of *Corridos: Tales of Passion and Rev-*

olution won a Peabody Award for excellence in television. But his real incursion into major Hollywood productions and success came with his writing and directing of *La Bamba* (the name of a dance from Veracruz), the screen biography of Chicano rock-and-roll star Ritchie Valens. Valdez's plays, essays, and poems have been widely anthologized. The following are the collections of his plays still in print: *Luis Valdez: Early Works* (1990), which includes the early *actos* that he developed with El Teatro Campesino; his play *Bernabé*; his narrative poem "Pensamiento Serpentino"; *Zoot Suit and Other Plays* (1992); and *Mummified Deer and Other Plays* (2005). In 1994 he was awarded Mexico's highest award for a non-native, the Aguila Azteca (Aztec Eagle), and in 2007 a USA Artists Award. In 2016 he was awarded the National Medal of the Arts by President Barack Obama.

Edit Villareal (1944–)

Born in Brownsville, Texas, on September 7, 1944, and raised in San Antonio and Los Angeles, Edit Villareal received her B.A. in theater from the University of California, Berkeley, in 1967. In 1981, she participated in María Irene Fornés's Hispanic Playwrights Lab in New York City and then went on to obtain her M.F.A. in playwriting from the Yale School of Drama in 1986. Villareal is the author of various plays and screenplays that have been produced. In 1991, her *The Language of Flowers*, an adaptation of Shakespeare's *Romeo and Juliet* set during the Mexican celebration of the Day of the Dead, was produced at California State University, Los Angeles. Probably her best known play is *My Visits with MGM (My Grandmother Marta)*, produced in 1992 at the San Jose Repertory Theater; the play deals with a grandmother returned from death to guide her granddaughter through trials and tribulations. Villareal's other plays include *Crazy from the Heart* (1989), produced by the Yale Repertory Theater; *Marriage Is Forever* (1999); and *Ice* (2001). As a screenwriter, her two produced scripts are *La Carpa* (1993, The Tent, written with Carlos Avila), for PBS's "American Playhouse," and *Broken Sky* (2003), released in theaters. *La Carpa* is particularly interesting because of Villareal's research into the history of Mexican American theater: set in 1938, the play focuses on a tent theater of vaudeville performers, typical of the ones that toured the Southwest during the Depression.

Carmen Zapata (1927–2014)

Carmen Zapata was an actress and producer of Mexican heritage. Born on July 15, 1927, in New York City, she was raised and educated in New York and later attended the University of California, Los Angeles and New York University. Zapata had a very successful career on the stage as a dramatic actress, in Hollywood films, and on television, including children's television. She was most important, however, as the founder and director of the Bilingual Foundation for the Arts in Los Angeles, which is a showcase for Latino playwrights, actors, and directors and has resulted in introducing new talent to the television and movie industries. Included among her awards are the National Council of La Raza Rubén Salazar Award (1983), the Women in Film Humanitarian Award (1983), Latino Women's Council Woman of the Year (1985), Best Actress Dramalogue (1986), and an Emmy (1973).

Nicolás Kanellos

FILM

Depictions of Latinos by the American film industry generally have been less than realistic or sympathetic. A host of early trends and personal contributions combined to create an extraordinarily harsh American style of racial and ethnic characterization, which was reinforced in the 1920s and 1930s with the conglomeration of the American film industry in a fashion that emphasized theatrical distribution, the assembly-line production of many films, the star system, and production formulas that were later turned into a production code.

The early cinematic portrayal of Latinos embodied the prevailing stereotypes of bandidos, buffoons, dark ladies, caballeros, and gangsters. However, the changes in the representation of Latinos and other minority groups brought about by the Great Depression, World War II, and the advent of the "Hollywood social problem film" are quite remarkable. Latino-focused films and Latino actors and filmmakers carved a niche in the industry against the backdrop of important social developments such as the emergence of the civil rights movement and the decline of the production code.

Since the early 1980s, the emergence of Latino film consciousness has broadened, with an emphasis on Chicano productions and films made in Puerto Rico (often with Mexican or Hollywood control) or by Puerto Ricans both on the island and in the continental United States. The filmmaking climate of the twenty-first century indicates that the future of Latino cinema is a bright one, with Latino talent and issues continuing to gain prominence.

DEPICTION OF MINORITY GROUPS IN EARLY AMERICAN FILM

During a period of a few years, primarily between 1903 and 1915, several technological, aesthetic, economic, and cultural developments in the United States came together that were important in determining how American cinema was to depict race and ethnicity for decades to come. An unfortunate filmic style emerged that was much harsher in its depiction of race and ethnicity than the cinema of other nations. American cinema delighted in the depiction of such stereotypes as "chinkers," "Micks," "darkies," "Hebrews," "greasers," "redskins," and "guineas," and actually used these epithets in the titles and publicity or in the films themselves.

Five governing factors converged and interacted with one another around the turn of the century to produce a definable style of racial stereotyping in American cinema: (1) the developing technological sophistication of filmmaking, particularly in projection and editing; (2) the developing philosophy of illusionism that began to gain ascendancy in film aesthetics; (3) the economic necessity in the U.S. film industry to produce westerns and to produce epic, prestige pictures of middle-class appeal; (4) the attitudes toward race and ethnicity that prevailed in society and that governed the popular novel of the period; and (5) the racial attitudes of the most prominent filmmakers of the period, especially D. W. Griffith.

In 1903 Edwin S. Porter produced the landmark film *The Great Train Robbery*. Significantly, the film was a western and reigned for about ten years as the most important American cinematic production, until the emergence of D. W. Griffith's features. *The Great Train Robbery* was of epic proportions for its time, an incredible twelve minutes. By 1915 technological advances and artistic will had stretched the concept of epic to three hours with Griffith's *The Birth of a Nation*. It is in the nature of epics that they deal with race and ethnicity; and it was no coincidence that Griffith's most famous epic was the most ambitious attempt to date, a flawed and racist depiction of ethnic and racial types: tender and sensitive Southern Whites, vain White Northern liberals, vicious or brutal Blacks, merciless Northern soldiers, heroic Ku Klux Klansmen, and evil mulattoes, the result of deplorable mixing of the races. Griffith's films, through their depiction of kidnappings, attempted rapes, destruction of homesteads or Indian villages, and most of all, war, were able to bring forth feelings of outrage, simultaneous horror, and titillating anticipation, pity, and remorse more intensely than other available media—theater, fiction, poetry, or journalism.

The early film directors—Edwin S. Porter, J. Stuart Blackton, Sidney Olcott, and others—quickly discovered that film had a distinct advantage over the stage in presenting melodrama. The devices available

> An unfortunate filmic style emerged in America that was much harsher in its depiction of race and ethnicity than the cinema of other nations.

to create film could generate a reality that was impossible to attain on the stage. Moreover, the early filmmakers—Griffith the leader among them—soon made changes in style based on the aesthetics of illusionism. Film moved from a style based on special optical effects (where the cameraman was supreme) to a photographic record of legitimate theater, to an emotionally heightened superrealism where the auteur/director reigned supreme.

The conscious economic policy of attempting to raise the social respectability of films and consequently attract a middle-class audience also had an important ideological and aesthetic consequence, propelling film toward the classical narrative style of illusionism and, in turn, the depiction of ethnic and racial stereotypes in the distinctive American manner. In 1908 the Motion Picture Patents Company (MPPC) was established with the goals of establishing a controlling monopoly of film distribution and achieving acceptance of the "flickers" by the middle class. To woo the middle class, filmmakers began to produce films with more complicated narrative plots and characterization, films with "educational" or "instructive" values or a "moral lesson," and films with happy endings. These initiatives lent themselves to the creation of racial antagonists (Mexicans, Blacks, American Indians), whose interactions with White males and females, however simplistic and formulistic by contemporary standards, were considerably more complex from a narrative and psychological point of view. Moreover, their defeat could be the basis of a moral lesson for both the character on screen and the audience, and for happy endings evoking the moral and physical superiority of Anglo values over the degenerate or primitive mores of other cultures. The central impetus behind the production of vast numbers of westerns, many using Mexicans or Indians as foils to Anglo heroes and heroines, was a ready international market for such films. The genre became proprietary to the American film industry.

It appears that the filmmakers' racial attitudes that were introduced in westerns were readily passed into American cinema style. These attitudes were embedded in D. W. Griffith's film technique. They were integral to the way he developed many of his plots and the way he developed several of his epic films. American cinema took not only the technical (relatively content-free) contributions from Griffith and other early filmmakers, but also the content-intensive ones. What emerged, partially as a contribution of these racial attitudes and their narrative and thematic elaboration in film, partially from the convergence of technological, aesthetic, economic, and sociocultural factors, was a distinctively American style of racial and ethnic depiction, one that was uniquely derogatory.

THE CONGLOMERATION OF THE FILM INDUSTRY AND THE PRODUCTION CODE

The first wave of ethnic stereotyping that so distinguishes American film from the silver screen of other nations was further reinforced by the development of film as big business. Capital investment in the American film industry became centered not in production but in distribution, particularly in the form of movie theaters. By the early 1930s, power rested with a mere eight major, vertically structured corporations that had consolidated production, distribution, and exhibition in monopolistic fashion: MGM, Warner Brothers, Paramount, Twentieth Century-Fox, Universal, RKO, Columbia, and United Artists. A steady turnover of product was needed to ensure revenue at the box office, which was dependent on regular attendance at many theaters on a continual basis, not on high attendance for any one movie during a single run. From an industry point of view, then, making good pictures was secondary to making a large quantity of pictures.

This assembly-line methodology or homogenization of craft, which governed the "high technology" of the early twentieth century and had a profound influence on the stylistic, thematic, and performance components of U.S. film, is usually known as the Hollywood Formula. With respect to style, film was produced and marketed to the public by genre: western, musical, screwball comedy, horror, gangster, or woman's film. The easily identifiable genres provided variations on familiar movie experiences and made moviegoing a sort of ritual. Repetition of this sort ensured a basically effortless participation by the audience. For example, they absolutely trusted that the hero would prevail and get the girl. It was just a matter of how and when. With respect to performance, typecasting (the human resource analog to the production of standard fenders or automobile bodies) led to the highly salesworthy star system. After several films, the public came to know a star very well, so much so that it became difficult for actors to stray very far beyond their normal range.

Given the circumstances of marketing by the star system, it is small wonder that Latino film actors and actresses had the option of either retaining their Latino identity and being typecast negatively or denying their Latino identity by what the industry euphemistically calls "repositioning" themselves.

> The influence of the Hollywood Formula on the development of movie themes or messages did extreme damage to minority groups, including Latinos.

The influence of the Hollywood Formula on the development of movie themes or messages did extreme damage to minority groups, including Latinos. The two fundamental thematic components of the formula were that the movie should communicate Americanism and that it should provide wish fulfillment. Often films combined both notions—nationalism and hedonism—at the deleterious expense of minorities.

As a result, in American film the ethnic other strictly and almost invariably played the outcast or the evildoer. Film, and for that matter, television in its early period, was an instrument of socialization that took as its guiding premise the assimilation of all racial, ethnic, and religious differences into the harmonizing credo of the American melting pot. No room whatsoever was allowed for divergence from this requirement. Even more painful, those races and ethnicities that could not be readily assimilated because of their difference of color and physiognomy, which would be readily apparent on the black-and-white celluloid—for example, African Americans, Latinos, and Native Americans—were drummed into the fold of evildoers and outcasts, a priori and without recourse. These and other ethnic groups consequently functioned as the slag in the melting-pot alchemy of American film. The usual components of wish fulfillment, such as romance and true love, destroying evil (even as we relish evil actions fiendishly depicted on the screen), rewarding good, happy endings, and so on, ensured that Latino and other minority characters would perform for the assembly line the roles of vamps, seductresses, greasers, gangsters, and the like, ad nauseam.

The formula became Hollywood law in 1934 with the introduction of the production code. The code states in pontifical and hypocritical fashion the moral value system behind the Hollywood Formula, decrying criminal violence and intimate sexuality, upholding the sanctity of marriage and the home and other traditions that had already become heartily compromised in the movies. The code stated that entertainment is "either helpful or harmful to the human race." Because of this, "the motion picture … has special moral obligations" to create only "correct entertainment" that "raises the whole standard of a nation" and "tends to improve the race, or at least to re-create or rebuild human beings exhausted with the realities of life."

In a very broad sense, an ideological vision of the world was acted out in each formula movie. Each individual—of the correct ethnic background, that is—can aspire to success. You are limited only by your own character and energies (if you are of the correct ethnic background, of course). Wealth, status, and power are possible for everyone (Anglo, that is) in America, the land of opportunity where the individual (Anglo) is rewarded for virtue. Such Americana as home, motherhood, community, puritanical love, and the work ethic are all celebrated. All issues are reduced to a good-versus-evil, black-and-white conflict, an us-against-them identification process where good equals the American (Anglo) values and social system ("us"). "Them," the villains, are defined as those who reject and seek to destroy the proper set of American (Anglo) values. Conflict is always resolved through the use of righteous force, with American (Anglo) values winning out.

"Them" not only includes Blacks, Latinos, and Native Americans—that is, those ethnics whose color and racial features overtly identify them as "others"—but usually any ethnic group when it is depicted ethnically.

THE FIRST DECADES: THE BANDIDO, BUFFOON, DARK LADY, CABALLERO, AND GANGSTER

During the first two decades of U.S. filmmaking, the Latino stereotypes were the bandido, the buffoon, and the dark lady. By the 1920s, two additional roles were added to the repertoire: the caballero and the gangster. Typically, in accordance with the traditional role of minorities in American film, the Latino was the one to be killed, mocked, punished, seduced, or redeemed by Anglo protagonists.

The earliest westerns generally followed the conventions of that period's dime novels, with two differences. One is that in some films the greaser was allowed to reform or redeem himself, usually by saving a beautiful Anglo heroine. *The Greaser's Gauntlet* and *Tony, the Greaser* cultivate the theme of Latino redemption through obeisance to the physical and moral splendor of an Anglo-Saxon beauty.

The second way films were different from the dime novels reflected the historical reality of the Mexican Revolution (1910–1920), which the American film industry depicted with the customary quality of cinematic exaggeration, but occasionally showing no Americans at all. These films actually depicted the emergence of revolutionaries from the peon class and treated them as heroes. Thus, in *The Mexican Joan of Arc*, where only Mexican characters are featured, a woman whose husband and son are arrested and murdered by the federales becomes a rebel leader. In a similar film, *The Mexican Revolutionists*, a rebel named Juan is captured but escapes the federales only to help the revolutionaries capture Guadalajara. Films of this type were rare, however. As has been described earlier, American film needed to operate on the basis of stark moral conflicts where whites represented good and nonwhites represented evil. Thus, even the Mexican Revolution provided the backdrop for the famous early actor Tom Mix. In his movies, such as *An Arizona Wooing* and *Along the Border*, the plot features rebels who are really bandidos in masquerade interested in kidnapping a beautiful blonde and providing her with a "fate worse than death." The plot required an Anglo hero to outwit them and give them a suitable punishment.

The Caballero's Way in 1914 marked the first of the Castilian caballero films, promoting personages such as Zorro, Don Arturo Bodega, and later the Cisco Kid. The formula for this cycle of films is very much within the convention of how American film treated ethnicity, since the heroes of these movies, by virtue of their pure Spanish ancestry or Caucasian blood, are able to put down the degraded mestizos who inhabit the Mexican California setting. The caballero cycle owed its inspiration to the North Carolina–born

writer O. Henry (pen name of William Sydney Porter). The Cisco Kid was directly modeled on the writer's story "The Caballero's Way" (1907). O. Henry, whose colorful life included several years in Austin and Houston and a jail sentence for embezzlement from an Austin bank, presented Mexicans in a prejudicial and stereotypical manner. His usual method when writing about the West, aptly reflected in the caballero film cycle, was to spice up his stories with Spanish characters and motifs and to have pure-blooded Castilians thwart the mestizos and Indians. O. Henry's short stories, extremely popular at the time, were ideal for movies.

The "gay caballero" had a few minor variations. The Cisco Kid cycle was the most popular. It began in the silent era with films such as *The Caballero's Way* and *The Border Terror* (1919), and during the sound era large numbers were made. Warner Baxter starred (typically with Hollywood, Anglos first portrayed the role, Latinos only later) in three such films from 1929 to 1939. César Romero did six between 1939 and 1941, Duncan Renaldo did eight between 1945 and 1950, and Gilbert Roland did six between 1946 and 1947. The Cisco character stressed the amorous side of the "gay caballero," a charming brigand who prized a beautiful woman as a gourmet savors a vintage wine (from a contemporary perspective, he was a plain and simple cad). Like his Anglo counterparts of similar western series, his method was to ride in, destroy evil, and ride out, leaving a broken heart or two. If Cisco flirted with Anglo women, his status as a serial hero made marriage inconceivable—it would end the series! The formula worked tremendously on television as well, and this syndicated serial garnered the largest receipts of its time.

Even before the demise of the "gay caballero" series, the popularity of this type of film was outstripped by the appearance of the dark lady films, particularly the Mexican spitfire in the person of Lupe Vélez, who elevated the stereotype from a minor role to star billing. Rita Hayworth also got her start this way. Born Margarita Carmen Cansino of a Spanish-born dancer father and his Ziegfeld Follies partner Volga Haworth, she was discovered at thirteen dancing at Mexican night spots in Tijuana and Agua Caliente. Her early movies, under the name Rita Cansino, included work in the *Three Mesquiteers* series (a takeoff on both *The Three Musketeers* and the mesquite plant),

The popular film and TV character the Cisco Kid was modeled on a character in O. Henry's story "The Caballero's Way."

a seemingly unending cycle of movies featuring trios of cowboys. Everyone did them, including John Wayne, Bob Steele, Tom Tyler, Rufe Davis, Raymond Hatton, Duncan Renaldo, Jimmy Dodd, Ralph Byrd, Bob Livingston, Ray (Crash) Corrigan, and Max Terhune. Rita played, of course, the dark lady, and she was notable in dancing a barroom "La Cucaracha" in *Hit the Saddle* (1937). It was that year that she married the shrewd businessman Edward Judson, who helped her see that being a Latino limited her to work as a cinematic loose woman. Under his guidance she changed her name to Rita Hayworth and was transformed from a raven-haired Latino dark lady into an auburn-haired sophisticate. By the early 1940s she attained Anglo recognition as the hottest of Hollywood's love goddesses. Her picture in *Life* magazine was so much in demand that it was reproduced in the millions and adorned the atomic bomb that was dropped on Bimini. Raquel Welch (formerly Raquel Tejada) had a similar career as a non-Latino and was therefore more acceptable as a love goddess to the mainstream.

Lupe Vélez went the other way and was dead at age thirty-six. Born Maria Guadalupe Vélez de Villalobos in San Luis Potosí, Mexico, in 1910, she was the daughter of an army colonel and an opera singer. Her arrival in Los Angeles was auspicious. She did eight movies in the "Mexican Spitfire" series, had a tempestuous romance with Gary Cooper, married Johnny Weismuller, with whom she had celebrated rows, and committed suicide, reportedly because she could not face the shame of bearing a child out of wedlock to a man she felt bore her no love (actor Harold Ramond). She was five months pregnant. Ironically, her last film was Mexican Spitfire's *Blessed Event* (1943).

In the early 1930s Hollywood began to produce a number of gangster films, and as one might have predicted, there quickly appeared a greaser-gangster subgenre. The greaser gangster differed from the dark heroes of Prohibition and the Great Depression (such as James Cagney, George Raft, and the early Humphrey Bogart) in crucial ways. He was a treacherous coward, oily, ugly, crude, overdressed, unromantic, and with no loyalty even to his criminal peers. Leo Carrillo played the stereotype faithfully as a gambling, murdering, extorting, pimping, often border bandido in some twenty-five or thirty films. In *Girl of the Río*

(1932), he attempted to steal the hand of the glamorous Dolores del Río, a cantina dancer called the Dove. That particular film earned a formal protest on the part of the Mexican government, especially because it portrayed Mexican "justice" as a reflection of who could pay the most for the verdict of their liking.

Ironically, one of the most positive things to happen on behalf of Latinos with respect to animation was the advent of World War II and the need to be sensitive to Latinos during wartime. During World War II, Nelson A. Rockefeller's Office for Coordination of Inter-American Affairs asked Walt Disney to make a goodwill tour of Latin America in support of the Good Neighbor Policy. The result was two films, *Saludos Amigos* (1943), oriented toward Brazil, and *The Three Caballeros* (1945), set in Mexico. The latter film featured Panchito, a sombrero-wearing, pistol-packing rooster.

Lupe Vélez poses in a publicity still for the "Mexican Spitfire" film series.

A bit of the stereotype remained in Panchito, but he was a likable, fun-loving, and highly assertive type who showed *el pato* Pascual (a Latino Donald Duck) and José Carioca (a Brazilian parrot from *Saludos Amigos*) the wonders of Mexico, such as piñata parties, Veracruz *jarochos* (dances), *posadas* (Christmas pageant), and other Mexican folk celebrations. Mexico had never been given such a benign, positive image by Hollywood, wherein in the persons of Donald, José, and Panchito, the United States, Brazil, and Mexico were three pals, none better than the others. Latin American audiences were enchanted by both of these films.

LATINOS IN FILM DURING THE 1930s AND THE ERA OF SOCIAL CONSCIOUSNESS

The Great Depression brought an expansion of the gangster movie genre, which produced a new spate of negative Latino stereotypes. The Depression also brought with it a new genre as well, the "Hollywood social problem film." For the first time, Latinos were portrayed in a somewhat different, and occasionally radically different, light in these Hollywood movies.

The economic breakdown represented by the Depression, the rise of fascism and other totalitarianism movements worldwide, the war against these political forms of oppression, and the idealistic vigor of the post–World War II years (up to the advent of McCarthyism) all fostered concern with social conditions and an impulse toward political change. The theater of Clifford Odets, the novels and screenplays of John Steinbeck, and the songs of Woody Guthrie all found a large public response to their criticism of American society, government, and business during the period.

This era of social consciousness also found reflection in Hollywood social problem films, which usually were produced in accordance with the conventions of the Hollywood Formula. The Hollywood conventions were that America is a series of social institutions that from time to time experience "problems" that, like those of an automobile, need to be tinkered with and corrected. For the most part, the films attacked such problems in order to inspire limited social change or restore the status quo to an "ideal" level of efficiency. While the Hollywood social problem genre places great importance on the surface mechanisms of society, only an indirect or covert treatment is given to the broader social values (those of the family, sexuality, religion, and so on) that function behind and govern the mechanisms.

In depicting Chicanos, Mexicans, and other Latinos, the social problem vehicle produced some noteworthy if flawed films, but a review of the overall film production reveals that the positive depiction of Latinos was still the exception rather than the rule. *Bordertown* (1935, starring Paul Muni in brownface and Bette Davis in her standard performance as a lunatic) is the first Latino social problem film. The central concern is not the oppression of Chicanos but rather who committed a murder. What social comment exists functions as a sedative against militancy by Latinos. The filmic creation of Johnny Ramírez is certainly a more complex one than the standard Hollywood border type. Relative psychological complexity aside, the soothing conventions of the Hollywood Formula determine the finale. The film ends with Ramírez, disillusioned over the corruption and meanness of success, returning to his barrio home. He says his confession to the priest, prays with his mother, and all three walk down the church aisle. The padre asks, "Well, Johnny, what are you going to do now?" and Johnny gives the expected reply, "Come back and live among my own people where I belong." *Bordertown* hypothesizes that for a Chicano, success is fruitless and undesirable, and true virtue lies in accepting life as it is. Ramírez has learned the padre's lesson of patience and no longer holds impractical ambitions. *Bordertown* celebrates stoic acquiescence to the status quo and denigrates the aspiration for social change.

Despite the limitations of the social problem film, it is certainly true that psychologically complex and occasionally resolute and strong characters emerged from this genre. Among them are several Chicano protagonists in *Giant* (1956), including the proud and dedicated nurse María Ramírez, who experiences the racism of Texans; the family of Leo Mimosa, who is buried alive in a New Mexico cave in Billy Wilder's notable *The Big Carnival* (1951), which depicts a tragic act of God turned into a public relations event; and Katy Jurado and Pina Pellicer, the women in *One-Eyed Jacks* (1961, starring Marlon Brando). Occasionally the strong and resolute character is also "evil," as in *Washington Masquerade* (1932), one of the earliest of the "political machine and country crusader" series of films that include *Washington Merry-Go-Round* (1932) and the Frank Capra series: *Mr. Deeds Goes to Town* and *You Can't Take It with You* (1938), *Mr. Smith Goes to Washington* (1939), and *Meet John Doe* (1941). *Washington Masquerade* proclaims that "the running of the U.S. has fallen into bad hands!" and proceeds to identify clearly whose hands they are: Latino ones! Unbelievable as this may be, given the lack of political visibility, much less power, of Latinos in the real world of 1932, the villain is an oily, Latin-like (and hence un-American) lobbyist whose influence extends through all levels of government.

The socially conscious era of the Great Depression and its aftermath brought in a new wave of Anglo Good Samaritans who acted on behalf of innocent and defenseless Mexicans. Some of this character development and plot existed in the silent era as well: *A Mexican's Gratitude* (1909), *Mexicans on the Río Grande* (1914), and *Land Baron of San Tee* (1912). In films such as *Rose of the Rancho* (1936), *Border G-Man* (1938), and *Durango Valley Raiders* (1938), or for that matter in the pertinent films of Hopalong Cassidy, Gene Autry, the Lone Ranger, Roy Rogers, and Tex Ritter—*In Old Mexico*, (1938), *Song of the Gringo* (1936), *South of the Border* (1939), and numerous others—the emphasis changes from the hero as implacable and brutal conqueror of greasers to the hero as implacable and devoted defender of Mexican rights, typically as he tramps tourist-like through the exotic local Latino community, whether it be north or south of the border. Often the Anglo is fighting bad Mexicans on behalf of good, defenseless, passive Mexicans. The acts of these Good Samaritans strongly reinforce the stereotype of Mexicans as people who are unable to help themselves.

The most daring and best realized of the Latino-focused social problem films are *The Lawless* (1950) and *Salt of the Earth* (1954). The former was a low-budget independent released through Paramount, while the latter was made outside the studio system altogether by blacklisted artists, including writer Michael Wilson, producer Paul Jarrico, and director Herbert Biberman.

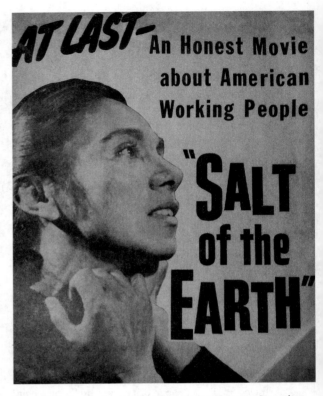

Salt of the Earth, starring Mexican actress Rosaura Revueltas, was a daring and well-realized example of the Latino-focused social problem films of the mid-twentieth century.

It is precisely because neither was made within the confines of the studio that a profounder and more artistically elaborated interpretation of racial oppression is realized. In contrast to the usual treatment, which views racial prejudice against minorities as the product of a White sociopath or other such deranged troublemaker who is then blamed for inciting a mostly ingenuous but somewhat blameless populace, the lynch mob violence in *The Lawless* and the vicious labor strife in *Salt of the Earth* are deemed to be typically middle American. In these films, by stereotyping "spics" as lazy and no-good, people find a scapegoat for their hatreds and a rationale for injustice.

Closely aligned to the social problem films were the historical "message" pictures such as the Warners' Paul Muni biography cycle initiated with *The Life of Emile Zola* (1937), which devoted considerable attention to the Dreyfus affair (but only fleetingly alluded to the anti-Semitic element). Two major films focused on Mexico emerged from this cycle: *Juárez* (1939) and the renowned *Viva Zapata!* (1952). *Juárez* featured Paul Muni in the title role, Bette Davis as Carlotta, and John Garfield as a youthful Porfirio Díaz learning Lincolnesque democracy at the master's feet. This was another film marked by renewed efforts on the eve of the war by Franklin Roosevelt's administration to enhance the Good Neighbor Policy. The passing of the years has not been good to *Juárez*, but despite its faults, which include the cultural chauvinism of an omnipresent Lincoln, the film rises far above the standard degrading stereotypes of Hollywood. *Juárez* reflects relatively accurate documentation of Mexican history and society, and it impressed not only the American audience for whom it was intended but the Mexican public as well.

The clear masterpiece of the "message" biographies, *Viva Zapata!* (screenplay by John Steinbeck, direction by Elia Kazan, and starring Marlon Brando and Anthony Quinn) is also one of the best Hollywood Latino-focused films. The film is not free of problems and stereotypes, many of which relate to turning Zapata into a Hollywood-style "hero" at the expense of historical veracity; nevertheless, it is the most comprehensive and attentive Hollywood film ever produced about the Mexican Revolution—with the possible exception of *Old Gringo* (1989), which is not accurately a "Hollywood" film. One of the reasons for the enduring popularity of the film is precisely the nature and complexity of the message. The film is not only about power and rebellion but also about the ways of corruption and how easy it is for a social movement to be debased. Zapata resists the corruption of his brother, the power-hungry Fernando, who betrays the revolution and goes to the side of Huerta, and he even resists the tendency of the campesinos to look for heroes or leaders to whom they can abdicate their own responsibilities.

In addition to *Viva Zapata!*, John Steinbeck wrote several other treatments of Latino material. His other contributions make for a mixed, but on balance, positive record. In 1941 he wrote the screenplay and collaborated with director/producer Herbert Kline to film *The Forgotten Village*, an artistic semidocumentary about science versus superstition in a small Mexican mountain village. This film, which was done outside the studio system, won numerous prizes as a feature documentary but played only in small independent art theaters because it did not benefit from studio distribution. In 1954 Steinbeck helped write the screenplay for *A Medal for Benny*, adapted from one of his *paisano* (rustic Latino) short stories. Starring Arturo de Córdova and Dorothy Lamour, this comedy treats the hypocrisy of town officials who exploit the posthumous awarding of the Congressional Medal of Honor to a brawling *paisano*. It contains many of the stereotypes of Latinos (drunkenness, immaturity, brawling, but also a chivalric sense of honor) that mark the novel *Tortilla Flat*, which was also adapted into a film in 1942 (starring Spencer Tracy, John Garfield, Hedy Lamarr, Akim Tamiroff, and Academy Award–nominated supporting actor Frank Morgan), but without Steinbeck's participation. *Benny* was a critical and box office success, and Steinbeck and his cowriter received Academy Award nominations. This film, however, is hardly Steinbeck's best effort at depicting Latinos.

The 1948 production *The Pearl* was cowritten by Steinbeck, Emilio "El Indio" Fernández, and Jack Wagner (who also cowrote *Benny*). In addition, Fernández directed it, and it starred Pedro Armendáriz. *The Pearl* was in fact a Mexican movie, the first to be widely distributed (by RKO) in the United States. The film, an adaptation of Steinbeck's novella, is a well-made, sensitive, and genuine treatment of Mexican fishermen, as might be expected of the Mexican director and crew. The plot itself is a parable of a poor Mexican fisherman who learns that wealth brings corruption and death. The critical response and box office receipts for this film were respectable, but it has not endured.

Even as significant Latino films of the social problem and historical message varieties were being produced, in parallel fashion other films of the earlier genres continued unabated. Enormous numbers of westerns were produced in the period between the Great Depression and the civil rights movement. A small fraction of those containing significant Latino elements include the following, in chronological order, concentrating on the more notable westerns: *Billy the Kid* (1930, King Vidor, director), *The Ox-Bow Incident* (1943, William Wellman, director; Anthony Quinn, Henry Fonda), *The Outlaw* (1943, Howard Hughes,

The Pearl, adapted from John Steinbeck's novella, was filmed both in Spanish (as La perla) *and in English by the same cast, for Mexican and U.S. distribution.*

Stanwyck, Gilbert Roland), *Branded* (1951, Alan Ladd), *High Noon* (1952, Gary Cooper, Katy Jurado), *Rancho Notorious* (1952, Fritz Lang, director; Marlene Dietrich), *Ride Vaquero* (1953, Anthony Quinn), *Veracruz* (1954, Robert Aldrich, director; Gary Cooper, Sarita Montiel), *The Burning Hills* (1956, Tab Hunter, Natalie Wood), *The Sheepman* (1958, Glenn Ford), *The Left-Handed Gun* (1958, Arthur Penn, director; Paul Newman), and *Río Bravo* (1959, Howard Hawks, director; John Wayne, Dean Martin, Ricky Nelson).

Billy the Kid, *The Outlaw*, *The Left-Handed Gun*, and much later *Pat Garrett and Billy the Kid* (1973) form part of the cycle on that folk hero; each of these films perpetuates the legend of the Kid as the friend of oppressed Hispanos and the foe of the Anglo cattle barons in New Mexico.

Most of these films perpetuate the three major Latino stereotypes of the western: dark lady, bandido, and buffoon. The more substantial dark lady roles of the westerns of the 1930s through the 1950s have been assigned to mistresses of White gunmen. This is the case in such films as *My Darling Clementine*, *Veracruz*, and, above all, the classic *High Noon*, which is undoubtedly the best of these films.

While some opportunities for Latinos to work in the film industry remained in the western genre between the Great Depression and 1960, notwithstanding the fact that back then many of the parts were played by Anglos, in other genres the Latino presence was, in fact, greatly diminished. Some World War II movies contained a bit part from time to time for a Latino character, presumably to promote patriotism, a sense of unity, and the brotherhood (not yet sisterhood in these self-satisfied times) of races against the fascist menace.

THE DECLINE OF THE PRODUCTION CODE, EMERGENCE OF THE CIVIL RIGHTS MOVEMENT, AND NEW DEVELOPMENTS IN FILM: 1960s AND 1970s

The 1960s witnessed two important social developments that had significant impact on filmmaking:

director; Jane Russell), *My Darling Clementine* (1946, John Ford, director; Linda Darnell, Victor Mature), *Treasure of the Sierra Madre* (1947, John Huston, director; Humphrey Bogart, Alfonso Bedoya), *The Fugitive* (1947, John Ford, director; Henry Fonda, Pedro Armendáriz, Dolores del Río), *The Furies* (1950, Barbara a liberalizing or loosening of social values, often referred to as the sexual revolution, and the emergence of the civil rights movement. The first phenomenon was a factor in the decline of the production code. Beginning in the 1960s, films became much bolder in their depiction of sex, including interracial sex, and violence. However, this was a double-edged sword for Latinos and other minorities because often they were cast in roles where their villainy was far more graphic and horrifying than the snarling but ineffective criminal or would-be rapist of blander times. In this sense, the stereotypes of many Latino characters were actually intensified by the relaxation of Hollywood moral codes.

The 1960s and 1970s were marked by far more diversity in films but also by a group of films that featured even more serious, racially damaging put-downs of Latinos. For example, the bandidos were often engaged in visually explicit and gory violence, and the torrid Latinas were engaged in R-rated loose sex with Anglo heroes or an occasional Black super-stud. The Latino became the toy of Anglo producers, directors, and audiences, all competing in the effort to create for Anglos ever more titillating and vicariously experienced films. As a result, new subgenres of film emerged, such as the fiendish group of plotters (particularly the group western), featuring casual brutality and other actions that Anglos stereotypically and inaccurately identify under the rubric of "macho." The word "macho" entered the Anglo lexicon in a way that is ungrammatical in Spanish as an abstract quality in adjective form ("mucho macho" could be heard from time to time in bars or seen on T-shirts around the nation).

Moreover, by the 1960s there emerged the "good-bad bandidos." An example is Clint Eastwood in *The Good, the Bad, and the Ugly* (1967), where the Anglo hero teams up with the Mexican bandit, Tuco the Terrible (Eli Wallach), to steal gold. In this film, typical of the new, amoral western, both Anglos and Mexicans are equally evil from the moral perspective and good becomes merely identified with technical skills, such as a quick draw or creative thievery.

While in *The Good, the Bad, and the Ugly* the Anglo descends to the level of the stereotypical greaser, the converse is true in the extremely popular group west-ern, *The Magnificent Seven* (1960) (which spawned sequels: *Return of the Seven*, 1966, and *Guns of the Magnificent Seven*, 1969). Unfortunately for Latino actors in this film, which is about the defense of a Mexican village against a Mexican bandit, the stereotypical greaser role is not even played by a Latino but by Eli Wallach, who was to become the new Leo Carrillo, replaying the greaser-style performance in a number of Italian and Spanish "spaghetti" westerns.

This trend toward amorality reached its extremes in the 1960s and 1970s films that revolved around the Mexican Revolution of 1910, taking the image of Latinos and the understanding of those events a giant step backward from the peak that was established by *Viva Zapata!* In the amoral westerns of director Sergio Leone—*A Fistful of Dollars* (1967); its sequel, *For a Few Dollars More* (1967); and *Duck, You Sucker* (1972)—the viewer is given no moral guidelines by which to measure or judge the revolution. Both the *federales* and the rebels are repulsive. If the former are sadistic, pretentious, class-conscious, and stupid, the latter are sadistic, filthy, promiscuous, contemptuous, and stupid.

The cycle of Pancho Villa movies displays the same sort of denigration. The first Villa film of the sound era, *Viva Villa!* (1934), presented the revolutionary hero as a sadistic Robin Hood. Subsequent films, *Villa!* (1958) and *Villa Rides* (1968), stray little from this general depiction. The latest film to depict Villa, *Old Gringo* (1989), based on a novel by Mexican novelist Carlos Fuentes and produced by Jane Fonda with the avowed intention of injecting realism into the relationship between the United States and Mexico, stands in marked positive contrast to the rest of the cycle.

Set against the simplistic, amoral standard of most of the other westerns of these years, the work of Sam Peckinpah—particularly *The Wild Bunch* (1969), *Pat Garrett and Billy the Kid* (1973), and *Bring Me the Head of Alfredo García* (1974)—developed a more sophisticated view of Latinos, particularly in the context of the Mexican Revolution in the case of *The Wild Bunch*. In that film the two Mexicos of the revolution are rendered in the contrast between Angel, the morally pure *villista* who represents Mexican village life, and Mapache, the degenerate revolutionary. In a film that is, ironically, one of the most violent on record, Angel occupies a pivotal role in that by his Christlike

The Ox-Bow Incident, *released in 1943, presents an example of the Latino avenger type.*

example he turns the drifting, amoral Anglo mercenaries to good purpose and sacrifice, thus redeeming them. *The Wild Bunch* is one of the most memorable films of the period, combining outsize violence and explicit sex with a certain sense of high moral purpose and interethnic camaraderie. In its own way, it is a distinctively realized combination of the decline of the moral code and the rise of civil rights.

Sporadic examples of Latino avenger types existed during the silent period, although not usually directed against Anglos but rather against *federales* of the Mexican government. The first major appearance of the type is in the western *The Ox-Bow Incident* (1943). Here Anthony Quinn plays a Mexican who is hanged along with two Anglos for murdering a Nevada cow-

boy. Of the three, he is the only one to die with his dignity and honor intact, subverting the stereotypical role of the cowardly and inept greaser. These pre–civil rights examples, however, have a quite different tone about them, primarily because they were pitched to a non-Latino audience. This is the case, as well, of the films *Death of a Gunfighter* (1969) and *The Outrage* (1964), which also depict assertive Latinos, even though they are not part of the Latino exploitation model. In *Death of a Gunfighter* the aging White marshall (Richard Widmark) has become an embarrassment to a prospering Kansas town that no longer needs him. In the final, shocking scene, the shopkeepers and bankers gun him down, leaving his Chicana mistress without a husband after a last-minute wedding ceremony.

Even with the emergence of the Latino avenger, which somewhat reflected the atmosphere of the civil rights movement, and the emergence of a more sexually titillating dark lady, which primarily reflected the relaxation of the Hollywood production code, the film industry continued to grind out westerns with buffoons and bandidos. *The Sheepman* (1958) provided a comic sidekick to the Anglo played by Glenn Ford, and in *Río Bravo* (1959) we view the antics of Carlos and Consuela, a comedy couple. In *The Train Robbery* (1973), John Wayne's gun quickly turns a Mexican railroad engineer from a "¡No! ¡No!" stance to a "¡Sí! ¡Sí!"

The role of the bandido took on certain variations that reflected Hollywood's exploitation of attitudinal changes. On the one hand, there existed the straight evil bandido, the continuation of the type from the earliest period, except that with the relaxation of the Hollywood morality codes this character suddenly became more "competent." Whereas the earliest version was usually a tame utterer of incomplete curses or hisses who was incapable of really delivering evil, at least on screen—he might tie the girl to the railroad track or inside a house he would set on fire, but the deed was never consummated—the new breed practiced mayhem, sadism, and sex. Anthony Quinn in *Ride Vaquero!* (1953) enjoys killing men and raping women and maims a cattleman for life in a sadistic shooting. The earlier, classic performance of Alfonso Bedoya and his gang, who brawl over their victims' boots in *Treasure of the Sierra Madre* (1947), is another of the same variety. A xenophobic variation on the same theme was John Wayne's (director and star) *The Alamo* (1961). This film, which takes egregious liberties with the facts, not only depicts Mexicans as violent and inept but also was promoted by means of a shamelessly ultrapatriotic advertising campaign. In 1969, Hollywood took another crack at the Alamo with *Viva Max*, starring Peter Ustinov as a bumbling Mexican buffoon who retakes the historic site from the Anglos in contemporary times. This film, without a single Latino in any significant role, was hardly as offensive as the Wayne vehicle, and pitted inept Americans against incompetent Mexicans. In contrast to the patriotic froth associated with *The Alamo*, however,

the latter film inspired minor demonstrations in several cities where it played, a good index of the progress of the civil rights movement over the 1960s.

Beginning in the 1960s and intensifying in the 1970s, changes in American society and consequently American film and television made the roles of dark lady and Latin lover considerably less important. One of these changes related to ethnicity. Particularly in the 1970s, Hollywood and other media centers rediscovered the significance of ethnicity, both from the point of view of plot and of box office. However, the primary ethnicity that was cultivated was the Italian American, and secondarily the Jewish American, Slavic,

George Chakiris (center), a non-Latino, played the Latino leading role in West Side Story *(1961).*

and Afro-American. This period witnessed the rise to stardom of such actors as Robert De Niro, Sylvester Stallone, Al Pacino, Barbra Streisand, and others. However, the cultivation of various U.S. cultures and ethnicities primarily reflected English-speaking groups, not Spanish or other non-English speakers. In the increased attention to multi-ethnicity, the Latino variety played a limited role.

The phenomenon of increased multiculturalism in plots and acting styles combined with yet another factor to the detriment of Latinos in film, namely, the expectation of increased sexuality on the part of actors and actresses, irrespective of their culture. While this expectation produced degrading stereotypes, it also provided considerable work for Latino actors and actresses, who consistently had roles exposing their "hot-blooded" nature. In contrast to the earlier traditions of Anglos and some of the other ethnicities who were expected to be aloof, glacial, and dispassionate, the film expectations of the 1960s to this day cultivate unabashed carnality and hot-bloodedness on the part of all actors and actresses, whatever their national origin.

The civil rights period beginning in the 1960s also marked an important change in hiring patterns in the film industry with respect to directors, camera crew, and other production people. For the first time, an effort was made to bring Latinos into production, and it was this cadre of professionals who were the primary group to go on to make Latino films. However, the introduction of Latino avenger films, group westerns, and other Latino-focused subgenres usually did not carry with it more work for Latino actors. The 1960s and 1970s were not particularly advantageous for Latinos in acting roles, since more often than not, non-Latino actors were awarded the roles of Latino characters. For example, George Chakiris and John Saxon, respectively, got the Latino leading parts in *West Side Story* (1961) and *Death of a Gunfighter*, and Burt Lancaster, Charles Bronson, and Paul Newman were the respective leads in *Valdez Is Coming, Mr. Majestyk,* and *The Outrage. The Young Savages* (1961), starring Burt Lancaster, was about gang war between Italians and Puerto Ricans, the latter played by non-Latino actors. *The Professionals* (1966) featured Claudia Cardinale as María Grant and Jack Palance as Jesús

Raza, who kidnaps her and sweeps her off her feet. *Villa Rides* (1968) featured Yul Brynner as Pancho Villa and Charles Bronson and Herbert Lom in the other significant Latino roles. *Che!* (1969) starred Omar Sharif and Jack Palance in the incongruous roles, respectively, of Che Guevara and Fidel Castro. *Night of the Iguana* (1964), starring Richard Burton, Deborah Kerr, and Ava Gardner all in Anglo roles, exemplified the Hollywood trend of filming on Latin location, but mostly for the purpose of local color, preferring stories reflecting non-Latino characters.

Despite successes in having some stereotypes eliminated, they remained abundant. In addition to the more intensive violence and sadism of Latino characters prevalent in the westerns of the period, gang films also abounded during the 1960s and 1970s. It was probably a factor in a spate of either Latino-focused exploitation, juvenile delinquent or gang films, or films with other premises that brought in Latino gang members for their recognition value, such as *The Pawnbroker* (1965), *Change of Habit* (1969), *Badge 373* (1973), *Assault on Precinct Thirteen* (1976, a multiethnic gang, director, John Carpenter), *Boardwalk* (1979), *Boulevard Nights* (1979, Richard Yñíguez, Danny de la Paz), *Walk Proud* (1979, featuring blue-eyed Robby Benson in contact lenses as a Latino), *The Exterminator* (1980), and many others. With the aid of feverish media attention dedicated to gangs, the cycle has been running strong to the present day.

The urban violence (primarily juvenile gang) film has been exploitative of Anglo willingness to pay for explicit sex and brutality—both premeditated and mindless—and the pleasures of vicariously induced but movie-house-controlled fear of the alien. These films play upon the baser assumptions about Latino youth and mostly do damage to racial relations in our society. To add insult to injury, Latino actors do not even get the top parts in these films. *Boulevard Nights* did, however, rise above the pap. While the film is not without its defects, particularly an inaccurate understanding in some respects of Chicano mores by Japanese American screenwriter Desmond Nakano, it does have an all-Latino cast, reasonably successful use of Chicano and pachuco dialect, and a serious theme and plot development that includes Latino violence against Latinos—an all-too-real phenomenon of gang life. It deserves recognition, within B-movie limitations, as one of the better Hollywood achievements in Chicano-focused film.

In *Badge 373* (1973), a minor follow-up to *The French Connection*, Robert Duvall singlehandedly fights the Mafia as well as Puerto Ricans who are blamed for all sorts of evil and wrongdoing. Whatever might be thought of *Colors* (1988), also starring Duvall, it represents a major advance in the Hollywood understanding of gang psychology. *The Warriors* (1978), although its artistry demands more respect than most of the others, primarily perpetuates the usual stereotypes.

Revolution in Latin America became a common topic of films in the 1970s. Curiously enough, in contrast to the serious and solemn 1980s (*Salvador, Prisoner without a Name, Cell without a Number, Old Gringo, Latino, Missing, Under Fire, Romero*, and so on), many of these films were screwball comedies, a long-standing Hollywood genre now attached to a new environment. In addition to Woody Allen's *Bananas* (1971) was *The In-Laws* (1979), starring Peter Falk. Brothers Luis and Daniel Valdez both had parts in the Richard Pryor comedy *Which Way Is Up?* (1977). In a more common mode, *Viva Max!* appeared in 1969, describing, in opera-buffa style, the Chicano retaking of the Alamo. When Hollywood attempted contemporary Latin American revolutionary topics or other Latin American material in a serious fashion during this period, as in *Che* and *Night of the Iguana*, the results were more uninspired than the comic attempts. *Iguana* was particularly disappointing in its turning of the admittedly minor Mexican characters into mere cutout figures of sexuality.

HOLLYWOOD FILM SINCE 1980

The period from 1980 to the present has been a relatively exhilarating one for Latinos in the film industry, especially over the last few years, primarily because of three sets of closely interrelated events or trends. The first is the increased appreciation of the importance of Latino culture and the Latino population in the United States. It became generally understood that demographics projected that Latinos were to become the largest minority group in the United States sometime early in the twenty-first century. This underlying fact of population power and consequently political, economic, and cultural importance spurred all sorts of film, television, and video initiatives for and by Latinos. It even underlay their national promotion, as exemplified by an extended article in *Time* magazine that featured Edward James Olmos on its cover, the first time in memory that any Latino, much less an actor and filmmaker, had achieved such recognition.

A second factor, somewhat encouraged by the Hollywood appreciation of Latino box office potential, was the emergence of a considerable number of actors and filmmakers who attained star status or national recognition during the contemporary period. These included Olmos, Raúl Juliá, Andy García, and Emilio Estévez. Similarly, film figures who had labored under less recognized conditions in the 1970s also made quantum leaps with respect to their weight in the film industry, including Moctesuma Esparza, Luis Valdez, Ricardo Mestre, and Martin Sheen.

Finally, with more interest in the United States in Latino themes and market penetration and more power and recognition of Latino actors and filmmakers came more control of product within Hollywood. For the first time a Latino, Mestre of Disney, was to run a major studio. Similarly, Esparza established Esparza/Katz Productions, raising tens of millions of dollars for a variety of projects, some but not all Latino-focused. Olmos, García, Joseph P. Vásquez, and comedian Paul Rodríguez all entered the film production business, with considerable diversity in their level of affiliation with or independent from traditional Hollywood sources of backing. Both the number of production outlets and either realized or pending film deals and the number of actors and other filmmakers with national recognition have never been greater, surpassing even a few "silver" years of the silent period when Latin lovers and hot-blooded Latinas were in great demand, albeit with virtually no control over their acting roles. On the other hand, it should be noted that Afro-American filmmakers made even greater strides during the current period, led by Spike Lee, John Singleton, and many others.

The current period also marks the strong emergence of a phenomenon called Latino Hollywood by the mass media. Although Chicano films such as *Zoot Suit* had been released by the mainstream industry before, between the summer of 1987 and spring of 1988 Hollywood released four films that depicted the Chicano experience: *La Bamba* (1987), *Born in East L.A.* (1987), *The Milagro Beanfield War* (1987), and *Stand and Deliver* (1988). The Latino directors, producers, and writers who made these films had typically been in very junior roles in the film and television industry and then began to work as principals in the conceptualization, development, and execution of alternative, independent Latino films, such as *Seguín*, *Alambrista!* (Fence Jumper), and *Once in a Lifetime*. Now they entered the mainstream as well (although not necessarily giving up their commitments to independent, alternative films), bringing Hollywood production values to the creation of strong Latino images that also had (or at least were intended to have) box office appeal and arranging for distribution through mainstream outlets. The cross-pollination and collaboration inherent in the Latino Hollywood phenomenon ran the gamut—from *The Milagro Beanfield War*, where Anglos carried most of the picture (directed by Robert Redford, the script was based on the novel by Anglo connoisseur of New Mexican culture John Nichols) and consequently Latinos had secondary, although highly significant, roles, to *Stand and Deliver*, where essentially the entire film, including scripting, producing, financing, directing, and acting, was conducted by Latinos until the point of distribution, when the appeal of the film earned its release through mainstream industry channels.

Since 1980, several films have focused on Latin America, reflecting the political situation of the region or drug-running or both. These include *Missing* (1982), starring Jack Lemmon and Sissy Spacek, which takes place during the overthrow of Salvador Allende in Chile; *Under Fire* (1983), starring Nick Nolte and Joanna Cassidy as journalists in the midst of the 1979 Sandinista revolution in Nicaragua; *Salvador* (1986), cowritten and directed by Oliver Stone, featuring Jim Belushi; *Latino* (1985), directed by Haskell Wexler, about the anti-Samoza uprising; *Under the Volcano* (1984), featuring Jacqueline Bisset and Albert Finney, an adaptation of Malcolm Lowry's classic novel; and *Havana* (1991), a failed movie starring Robert Redford as a gambler with a heart of gold who becomes embroiled in plots to overthrow dictator Batista in 1959. The poorly done but financially successful *Scarface* (1983), directed by Brian de Palma and starring Al Pacino, more or less feeds at the same trough, although it also focuses on Latino drug runners in the United States.

The 1980s witnessed several films dealing with the *indocumentado* (undocumented worker). Undocumented immigration from Mexico became a movie theme as early as 1932, with *I Cover the Waterfront*, but the undocumented were Chinese being smuggled by sea from Mexico to San Diego. This theme continued into the 1940s; *Hold Back the Dawn* (1941) dramatized the desperate efforts of European refugees living temporarily in Tijuana to enter the United States. Not until the post–World War II era did such films as *Border Incident* (1949), *Borderline* (1950), *The Lawless* (1950), and *Wetbacks* (1956) begin to deal with Mexican immigrants, although the immigrants usually functioned as passive pawns to incite Anglo crime and Anglo crime-fighting. *Border Incident* (1949, directed by Anthony Mann, starring Ricardo Montalbán) is a quite violent, well-made crime story of the social problem era, also rife with the usual stereotypes, as was the original *Borderline* (1950, Fred MacMurray, Claire Trevor), with an unlikely plot featuring law enforcers tracking down dope smugglers on the Mexican border. In the latter part of the twentieth century, as undocumented immigration became a more widely debated public issue, a new wave of films emerged: *Blood Barrier* (1979, Telly Savalas, Danny De La Paz), *Borderline* (1980, Charles Bronson), and *The Border* (1982, Jack Nicholson, Harvey Keitel, Valerie Perrine, Elpidia Carrillo). Nevertheless, the theme of passive Mexican immigrants being saved by noble Anglos has continued to dominate. None of these Hollywood films has ever risen above the mediocre. The films of the 1980s scarcely improved upon the first of the lot in terms of veracity, character development, or aesthetics. Hollywood *indocumentado* pictures have never surpassed the limitations of the social problem genre as originally conceived in the 1930s and 1940s.

In contrast to the stock characterizations of the Hollywood versions, two independently produced Latino works, *Alambrista!* (1979) and *El Norte* (The North,

The comedy duo Richard "Cheech" Marín and Thomas Chong adapted their nightclub act to film in Cheech and Chong's Up in Smoke *(1978) and several sequels.*

1983), shine because of their strong and distinctive plot developments and intriguing characters. Similarly, Cheech Marín's *Born in East L.A.* (1987) shines as a Latino Hollywood exception to the bleakness of the rest, precisely because it combined Latino expertise and sensitivity to Hollywood production values.

In the area of comedy, the late twentieth century was marked by the films of the comic team Richard "Cheech" Marín and Thomas Chong, who began by adapting their nightclub act to film in *Cheech and Chong's Up in Smoke* (1978), featuring stoned hippie routines. The film became the highest-grossing film of the year and spurred a number of 1980s sequels, including *Cheech and Chong's Next Movie* (1980), *Cheech and Chong's Nice Dreams* (1981), *Things Are Tough All Over* (1982), *Yellowbeard* (1983), *Cheech and Chong's The Corsican Brothers* (1984), *Get Out of My Room* (1985), *Cheech & Chong: Roasted* (2008), and *Cheech & Chong's Animated Movie!* (2013).

Despite some innovations that brought Latino actors and filmmakers to the fore, the industry continued, as it has always done, to create more exploitative films. Among these, *Salsa* (1988) was a Latino version of *Dirty Dancing* (1987) that attempted to "out-dirty" it. *The Penitent* (1988, Raúl Juliá, Julie Carmen) was a muddle that featured the eternal triangle set against the local color of New Mexican *penitentes*. *Moon over Parador* (1988, Richard Dreyfuss, Sônia Braga, Raúl Juliá) made liberal use of the usual stereotypes about Latin America and its dictators for uninspired humor. *The Believers* (1987, Martin Sheen, Jimmy Smits) abused Santería in order to make a horror/thriller. *Young Guns* (1988, Emilio Estévez, Lou Diamond Phillips, Charlie Sheen) updated the Billy the Kid cycle, having us believe that the Kid whips up the inherent violence of six young punks, including Latino members. *Bad Boys* (1983, Sean Penn, Esai Morales), in which both Penn and Morales are superb, features a personal vendetta within prison walls. Morales, who has been badly typecast merely as a Latino gang member, got to do his repartee also in *The Principal* (1987), featuring Jim Belushi overpowering the Latino youth warlord, somewhat reminiscent of the way honest Anglo do-gooders used to bring down Latino and other alien power-brokers in the 1940s films. On the other hand, the gang film *Colors* (1988), directed by Dennis Hopper and starring Sean Penn, Robert Duvall, María Conchita Alonso, Rudy Ramos, and Trinidad Silva, is a superior version of the genre, with the notable exception of the misuse of the Alonso romantic subplot. Silva is excellent in this film, as he is in *The Night Before* (1988), an offbeat comedy about a young man at a senior prom who wakes up in an East Los Angeles alley.

THE EMERGENCE OF LATINO FILMS

Chicano Cinema

In a certain sense, the emergence of Chicano cinema has been the result of new, energetic actions on the part of the film industry to increase the participation of Chicanos and other minorities in the craft of filmmaking. In that sense, it was perhaps unexpected—at least by industry executives—and due more to prodding by the courts, by certain sectors of society, such as college students, and above all by the civil rights movement. The film corporations did hire Chicanos, but for general work in the profession and not necessarily for the production of Chicano films.

As Chicano actors, filmmakers, and other professionals began entering the industry and, particularly, receiving their apprenticeships through the production of documentaries on varied subject matter, their sensitivities inevitably turned to the Chicano experience, primarily because the raza story was there, beckoning and untold.

First Films

The Chicanos who entered the studios on the production side were soon producing and directing a series of politically aware documentaries on the Chicano experience. Among the most significant of these are David García's *Requiem-29* (1971), which describes the East Los Angeles riot of 1970 and the circumstances surrounding the suspicious death of Chicano reporter Rubén Salazar. Jesús Treviño's *América Tropical* (1971) is about the whitewashing of a Siquieros mural in Los Angeles. Severo Pérez's *Cristal* (1975) is about Crystal City, "Spinach Capital of the World" and birthplace of the Raza Unida Party. Treviño's *Yo Soy Chicano* (I Am Chicano, 1972) was the first Chicano film to be nationally televised and to deal with the Chicano movement from its roots in pre-Columbian history to the activism of the present. José Luis Ruíz's *Cinco Vidas* (Five Lives, 1972) narrates the lives of five Chicanos and Chicanas of varied backgrounds and experiences. Treviño's *La Raza Unida* (The United People, 1972) covers the 1972 national convention of the Raza Unida Party. Ricardo Soto's *A La Brava* (With Courage, 1973) describes the condition of Chicano convicts at Soledad prison. Rick Tejada-Flores's *Sí Se Puede* (Yes It Can Be Done, 1973) records César Chávez's twenty-four-day fast in Arizona to protest proposed antistrike legislation. Ruíz's *The Unwanted* (1974) depicts the difficulties of the indocumentado population, and Soto's *A Political Renaissance* (1974) examines the contemporary emergence of Chicano political power.

From 1975 to the present, the pace of Chicano documentary cinema has accelerated enormously. Scores of films have been produced. The following are brief notations of some of the most significant documentary productions.

Anthropological and Folkloric Films

Among the most notable documentaries of the anthropological or folkloric type are Esperanza Vázquez and Moctesuma Esparza's *Agueda Martínez* (1977), nominated for an Academy Award in 1978, and Michael Earney's *Luisa Torres* (1981). Both documentaries depict the lifestyles of elderly women in northern New Mexico. Also outstanding are Les Blank's *Chulas fronteras* (Beautiful Border, 1976), and its sequel, *Del mero corazón* (From the Heart, 1979), which beautifully evoke the *norteña* or conjunto music prevalent in the Texas-Mexico border region and throughout the Southwest. Homer A. Villarreal's *Expression: The Miracle of Our Faith* (1978) is about the practices of *curanderismo* (faith healing) in San Antonio and elsewhere in southern Texas. Daniel Salazar's *La tierra* (The Land, screened at the 1981 San Antonio Cine Festival) describes the Chicano lifestyle in Colorado's San Luis Valley. Luis Reyes's *Los Alvarez* (The Alvarez Family, also screened at the 1981 San Antonio Cine Festival) depicts the hopes and dreams of a family living in California's Salinas Valley. Alicia Maldonado and Andrew Valles's *The Ups and Downs of Lowriding* (screened at the 1981 San Antonio Cine Festival) is an investigation of lowriding through the eyes of the cruisers themselves, the general public, and the police department. Ari Luis Palos's *Beyond the Border: más allá de la frontera* (2001) follows a Mexican immigrant crossing the border into the United States.

Ray Téllez's *Voces de yerba buena* (Voices of Mint, screened at the 1981 San Antonio Cine Festival) traces the Latino historical foundations of the San Francisco area and evokes the contemporary Latino influence in the area today. Ken Ausubel's *Los remedios: The Healing Herbs* (screened at the 1983 San Antonio Cine festival) is a review of herbal medicine in the Southwest. Rhonda Vlasak's *Between Green and Dry* (screened at the 1983 San Antonio festival) examines the impact of accelerated economic change in the New Mexican village of Abiquiu. Paul Espinosa's *The Trail North* (1983) follows Dr. Robert Alvarez and his ten-year-old son, Luis, as they re-create the journey their familial ancestors made in immigrating to California from Baja California. Toni Bruni's *Los vaqueros* (The Cowboys, screened at the 1983 San Antonio festival) is about Chicano cowboys, particularly those who participate in the Houston Livestock Show and Rodeo. Rick Tejada-Flores, producer and director of *Low 'N Slow: The Art of Lowriding* (screened at the 1984 San Antonio Cine Festival), both explains the lowriding phenomenon and makes a case for it as an important form of modern industrial folk art. Jack Ballesteros, producer and director of *Mt. Cristo Rey* (screened at the 1984 San Antonio festival), has created a documentary about a priest in a small mining community near El Paso and how he erected a huge sandstone cross and statue of Christ. Toni Bruni's *Long Rider* (1986) is an English-language version of his 1983 *Los vaqueros*. Jesús Treviño and Luis Torres's *Birthwrite: Growing Up Latino* (1989) is a docudrama that recreates the themes of growing up and self-identity in the writing of several Latino writers; and *Del Valle* (From the Valley, 1989), directed by Dale Sonnenberg and Karl Kernberger, evokes traditional and popular Mexican and New Mexican music performed in the central Río Grande Valley of New Mexico. Carlos Sandoval and Peter Miller's *A Class Apart: A Mexican American Civil Rights Story* (2009) narrates the story of the *Hernandez v. Texas* trial at the Supreme Court that resulted in the integration of juries. *Cesar's Last Fast* (2014), directed by Richard Ray Pérez, focuses on the last protest of the farm worker leader, who was failing in health. Peter Bratt's *Dolores* (2017) is the biography of labor leader Dolores Huerta, who cofounded the United Farm Workers.

Films with Political Content

On the matter of politics and the emerging Chicano political movement, several valuable films have been produced. Marsha Goodman's *Not Gone and Not Forgotten* (screened at the 1983 San Antonio festival) depicts how the community of Pico Union in Los Angeles successfully fought the mayor, the city council, and powerful business interests to maintain the integrity of its neighborhood. Richard Trujillo's *Tixerina: Through the Eyes of the Tiger* (1983) is an interview with Reies López Tixerina reviewing the famous courthouse raid of 1967 in Tierra Amarilla and related events. National Education Media's *Decision at Delano* (screened at the 1982 Eastern Michigan University Chicano Film Festival) documents the historic Delano grape workers' strike. Centro Campesino Cultural's *El Teatro Campesino* (screened at the 1982 Eastern Michigan University festival) traces the theater from its beginnings in the fields, boosting the morale of striking farm workers and winning over scabs, to its role as a theater committed to social change. Paul Espinosa and Isaac Artenstein's extraordinary documentary *Ballad of an Unsung Hero* (1984) evokes the political consciousness of an earlier era, depicting the life history of the remarkable Pedro J. González, a pioneering radio and recording star who was jailed on trumped-up charges by the Los Angeles district attorney's office in the midst of the Great Depression.

Coproduced by directors Jesús Treviño and José Luis Ruíz, *Yo soy* (I Am, 1985) reviews the progress that Chicanos made in the 1970s and 1980s in politics, education, labor, and economic development and summarizes the variety of ways that Chicanos are responding to contemporary challenges. *Graffiti* (1986) by Diana Costello, producer, and Matthew Patrick, director, is about a nocturnal wall-sketcher in a militaristic South American country. *Maricela* (1986), by Richard Soto, producer, and Christine Burrill, director, is the story of a thirteen-year-old Salvadoran girl who immigrates to Los Angeles with her mother, seeking to find a new home and a better life. *The Lemon Grove Incident* (1986), by Paul Espinosa, producer, and Frank Christopher, director, is a docudrama that examines the response of the Mexican American community in Lemon Grove, California, to a 1930 school board's attempt to segregate their children in a special school.

Watsonville on Strike (1989), by producer-director Jon Silver, describes an eighteen-month strike by cannery workers that virtually paralyzed a rural California town. Marilyn Mulford and Mario Barrera's *Chicano Park* (1989) is a compelling and moving visual history of the struggle of one community, Barrio Logan, to stake out a place for itself in the metropolis of San Diego. The film shows the process through which

Logan residents begin to effect positive changes in their lives and their community by using the richness of their cultural heritage as the basis around which to educate themselves to gain political power. There have been numerous Chicano documentaries of political and community themes since then; some more recent ones include *Southwest of Salem* (2016), directed by Deborah S. Esquenazi, in which four Chicana lesbians deal with the justice system in San Antonio; and *The Sentence* (2018), in which director Rudy Valdez explores how the justice system failed a Chicano family.

Film Portrayals of Undocumented Workers and Migrant Workers

The plight of *indocumentados* and migrant labor generally has seen extensive filmic treatment, including Ricardo Soto's films *Cosecha* (Harvest, 1976), about migrant labor, *Migra* (1976), on the arrest of *indocumentados*, *Al otro paso* (To Another Pass, 1976), on the economy of the border, and *Borderlands* (1983), which once again explores the complex interrelations of the Mexican-U.S. border. F. X. Camplis's *Los desarraigados* (The Uprooted, 1977) is about the early problems of undocumented workers. Jesús Carbajal and Todd Darling's *Año Nuevo* (New Year, screened at the 1979 San Antonio Cine Festival and 1981 winner of the Eric Sevareid Award for best information program, Academy of Television Arts and Sciences) is about the nearly unprecedented court struggle by twenty-two undocumented workers against their employer, the Año Nuevo Flower Ranch. Jim Crosby's *Frank Ferree: El amigo* (screened at the 1983 San Antonio Cine Festival) depicts a man from Harlingen, Texas, known as the Border Angel, who spent most of his adult life in an untiring effort to aid the poor and dispossessed along the Texas border with Mexico. The Learning Corporation of America's *Angel and Big Jose*, an Academy Award winner for short dramatic film, starring Paul Scorvino, is an outstanding film that depicts the friendship and ultimate parting of a migrant worker youth and a lonely Anglo telephone repairman. The United Farm Workers' *The*

> The plight of *indocumentados* and migrant labor generally has seen extensive filmic treatment.

Wrath of Grapes (1986) is a documentary that depicts the plight of California farm workers exposed to deadly pesticides. Producer-director Susan Ferris has used historical footage, clippings, interviews, and other realia to trace the history of the farm workers' union and to chronicle the experiences of Mexican farm workers in California in *The Golden Cage: A Story of California's Farmworkers* (1989). Paul Espinosa has produced and directed *Vecinos Desconfiados* (Uneasy Neighbors, 1989), evoking the growing tensions between the migrant worker camps and affluent homeowners in the San Diego area. While documentaries on *indocumentados* and farm labor are favorite genres of Chicano film makers, *Enrique's Journey* (2017), based on Sonia Nazario's Pulitzer Prize–winning book documenting in text and photographs the plight of a Honduran boy riding "La Bestia" train to the U.S. border, has had probably more impact than any other such documentary.

Chicano Features

A significant and growing number of Chicano features have been produced since the distribution of what might be considered the first Chicano feature, *Los vendidos* (The Sellouts, 1972), a film adaptation of one of the finest of El Teatro Campesino's *actos*. On the other hand, some of what has been produced, such as the works of Efraín Gutiérrez, have fallen into complete obscurity. If we include some of the dramatic films that were aired on television (*Seguín*) or originally planned for television (*Stand and Deliver*), in addition to the films made for theatrical distribution, the Chicano features include the following, directors noted: *La Vida* (1973, Jeff Penichet), *Please Don't Bury Me Alive! (Por favor ¡No me entierren vivo!*, 1977, Efraín Gutiérrez), *Alambrista!* (1977, Robert M. Young and Moctesuma Esparza), *Amor Chicano es para siempre* (Chicano Love Is Forever, 1978, Efraín Gutiérrez), *Only Once in a Lifetime* (1978, Alejandro Grattan), *Raíces de Sangre* (Roots of Blood, 1978, Jesús Treviño), *Run, Junkie (Tecato, Run,* 1979, Efraín Gutiérrez), *Zoot Suit* (1981, Luis Valdez), *The Ballad of*

Gregorio Cortez (1982, Robert M. Young), *Seguín* (1982, Jesús Treviño), *Heartbreaker* (1983, Frank Zúñiga), *El Norte* (1983, Gregory Nava), *Stand and Deliver* (1988, Ramón Menéndez), *Break of Dawn* (1988, Isaac Artenstein), Puerto Rican filmmaker Joseph B. Vásquez's *Hangin' with the Homeboys* (1991), *Selena* (1997, Gregory Nava), *Tortilla Soup* (2001, María Ripoll), *Spy Kids* and its sequels (2001, 2002, 2003, 2011, Robert Rodríguez), *Real Women Have Curves* (2002, based on Josefina López's play and directed by Patricia Cardoso), *Walkout* (2006, Moctesuma Esparza), *Nothing Like the Holidays* (2008, Alfredo De Villa), *Don't Let Me Down* (2009, Cruz Angeles), *La Mission* (2009, Peter Bratt), *Mosquita y Mari* (2012, Aurora Guerrero), *East Side Sushi* (2014, Anthony Lucero), *Tigers Are Not Afraid* (2017, Issa López), *Coco* (2017, Lee Unkrich and Adrián Molina), *De Lo Mío* (2019, Dominican American Diana Peralta), and various other features as more and more Latinos ascend to directing features. The Latino Hollywood films (combining Latino expertise and often control with Hollywood production values and distribution) usually are more closely affiliated with Chicano independent film than with the average Hollywood production that makes use of Chicano material. This is certainly the case of *La Bamba* (1987) and *Born in East L.A.* (1987).

Chicano feature films have contrasted greatly with contemporary films about Chicanos made by Hollywood directors and producers, even as they have shared some themes, situations, or genres, such as the problems at the U.S.-Mexican border, the western genre, or teenage groups. Some salient characteristics of Chicano film not usually seen in the Hollywood products have been a meticulous attention to the authentic cultural and social conditions of Chicano life, the use of Spanish to produce a bilingual film with considerable switching between languages, the recuperation of Chicano history (in period pieces), close attention to the political dimensions of the topics that are cultivated on screen, commitment to dealing with issues above considerations of box office, and a willingness to employ considerable numbers of Latino actors and Latino production people. Chicano pictures feature plots that may or may not appeal to the mainstream audience but are definitely designed for Chicano filmgoers. They feature Latino actors in genuine situations, usually filmed on location in authentic settings and speaking or singing in a natural, often bilingual environment.

In contrast to the conventional Hollywood pap of the border, Chicano productions such as *Raíces de Sangre* (Roots of Blood), *Alambrista!*, *El Norte*, and *Break of Dawn* (depicting a radio announcer and singer deported to Tijuana) have all evoked the situation at the border with sociological depth and creative distinction. The quality of verisimilitude, heightened by the bilingual (or in the case of *El Norte*, trilingual) script, have caused these movies to stand head and shoulders above their Hollywood contemporaries, such as *Blood Barrier*, *The Border*, and *Borderline*.

> In contrast to the conventional Hollywood pap of the border, Chicano productions have evoked the situation at the border with sociological depth and creative distinction.

Luis Valdez's productions *Zoot Suit* (1981) and *La Bamba* (1987), as well as *Stand and Deliver* (1988, Ramón Menéndez, Tom Musca, and Edward James Olmos) and *Hangin' with the Homeboys* (1991), all deal with various aspects of Chicano or Puerto Rican juvenile and domestic life in the United States. Valdez's works, both of which have an important historical dimension, are fine examples of Chicano filmmaking, with Hollywood support and distribution. The Chicano juvenile films are light-years ahead of Hollywood products such as *Streets of L.A.* (1979), *Walk Proud* (1981), and *Spy Kids* (2001, 2002, 2003, and 2011). The Hollywood films are invariably exploitive in their approach. Whether the Chicanos in these films are a menace to Whites or to themselves, it is strictly the prospect of violence and its description on screen that carries these Hollywood juvenile films. In contrast, *Stand and Deliver* is a stirring story that barely even evokes gang violence. It is primarily about an extraordinary Bolivian mathematics teacher who helps Latino high school students in East Los Angeles learn college-level calculus and get admitted into selective universities. *Hangin' with the Homeboys* (1991), by Puerto Rican director-writer Joseph P. Vásquez, was the cowinner of a screenwriting award at the Sundance Film Festival. *Homeboys* evokes the coming of age of four young male friends, two Puerto Rican, two Afro-American, out on the town during a night in which their futures and relationships with each other are tested.

Puerto Rican Films

Both the film industry in Puerto Rico and Puerto Rican films deserve considerably more attention than they have been given to date. Puerto Rican film dates at least from 1916, with the establishment of the Sociedad Industrial Cine Puerto Rico by Rafael J. Colorado and Antonio Capella. This production company's first work had a *jíbaro* (Puerto Rican rural highlander) focus and was titled *Por la hembra y el gallo* (For Women and Fighting Cocks, 1916), which was followed by *El milagro de la virgen* (The Miracle of the Virgin, 1916) and *Mafia en Puerto Rico* (The Mafia in Puerto Rico, 1916). Because of lack of funds and competition from U.S. film, the Sociedad Industrial was bankrupted, and no prints of its films are known to exist, although still photographs of *Por la hembra y el gallo* remain.

◆····
Puerto Rican film dates at least from 1916, with the establishment of the Sociedad Industrial Cine Puerto Rico by Rafael J. Colorado and Antonio Capella.

In 1917 the Tropical Film Company was organized with the participation of such well-known Puerto Rican literary figures as Luis Lloréns Torres and Nemesio Canales. Although its existence terminated with the entry of the United States into World War I, it did produce *Paloma del monte* (Mountain Dove), directed by Torres. In 1919 the Porto Rico Photoplays company was organized and produced *Amor tropical* (Tropical Love, 1920), with American actors Ruth Clifford and Reginald Denny, a melodrama that was produced for the North American market but failed to penetrate that distribution system, causing the company to go bankrupt.

Juan Emilio Viguié Cajas purchased the equipment of Photoplays and began a long and productive filmmaking career in Puerto Rico, primarily doing newsreels for continental U.S. enterprises, such as Pathé, Fox Movietone, and MGM. Among his works was a film on Charles A. Lindbergh's trip to Puerto Rico in 1927 and another on the San Ciriaco hurricane of 1928. He did many documentaries for private entities and for the government, the first of which was *La colectiva* (The Collective, 1920), about the tobacco industry. His film *Romance tropical* (Tropical Romance, 1934) was the first Puerto Rican feature of the sound period.

For the most part, film languished in Puerto Rico until 1949, when the government established a production facility in Old San Juan. Administered by the División de Educación de la Comunidad (which was part of the Departamento de Instrucción Pública), this unit was able to produce sixty-five shorts and two features by 1975, the year of publication of its last catalog. It counted on the cooperation of many of the best Puerto Rican graphic artists (Homar, Tony Maldonado, Eduardo Vera, Rafael Tufiño, Domingo Casiano, and so on) and writers (René Marqués, Pedro Juan Soto, Emilio Díaz Valcárcel, Vivas Maldonado, for instance). The unit also made considerable use of North American expertise, particularly screenwriter Edwin Rosskam, director Jack Delano, a longtime resident of Puerto Rico, cameraman Benji Doniger, and director Willard Van Dyke. Because these films were produced by a unit of government responsible for education, they generally had a pedagogical or didactic quality. *Los peloteros* (The Ballplayers, 1951) is generally thought to be the best film from this period. Directed by Jack Delano, it is based on a script by Rosskam and features Ramón Ortiz del Rivero (the celebrated comedian Diplo) and Miriam Colón. The premise revolves around a group of children raising money to buy baseball uniforms and equipment.

Viguié Film Productions, founded in 1951 by Juan Emilio Viguié Cajas Jr. and journalist Manuel R. Navas, became the first large Puerto Rican film producer. In 1953 writer Salvador Tió became a partner of the company, which had its own studio and laboratory in Hato Rey. Many filmmakers received their training here or with the División de la Educación de la Comunidad. The company produced both commercials and documentaries for the government and

Juan Emilio Viguié Cajas Jr. (the son of Puerto Rican film pioneer Juan Emilio Viguié Cajas) founded the first large Puerto Rican film producer, Viguié Film Productions, in 1951 with journalist Manuel R. Navas.

tion with Mexican interests began during the 1960s but led to no more than the repetition of old Mexican formula films with Puerto Rican settings. Among the films produced were *Romance en Puerto Rico* (1961), which has the distinction of being the first Puerto Rican color film; *Bello amanecer* (Beautiful Dawn, 1962); *Lamento borincano* (Puerto Rican Lament, 1963); *Mientras Puerto Rico duerme* (While Puerto Rico Sleeps, 1964), which deals with the drug problem; *El jibarito Rafael* (1966), about Rafael Hernández; and *Fray Dollar* (Brother Dollar, 1970). Most of the major actors and directors were not Puerto Rican but rather of Mexican or other Latin American nationalities.

In 1964 Pakira Films was organized, led by television producer Paquito Cordero and with financial backing from Columbia Pictures. It made several films based on the appearances of television comedian Adalberto Rodríguez (Machuchal). These films were financially successful, including *El alcalde de Machuchal* (The Mayor of Machuchal, 1964), *Millionario a-go-go* (Millionaire A-Go-Go, 1965), *El agente de Nueva York* (The New York Agent, 1966), and *El curandero del pueblo* (The Town Healer, 1967). The company also produced its own Mexican formula films, called *churros* by the Mexican industry, such as *En mi viejo San Juan* (In Old San Juan, 1966), *Luna de miel en Puerto Rico* (Honeymoon in Puerto Rico, 1967), and *Una puertorriqueña en Acapulco* (A Puerto Rican Girl in Acapulco, 1968).

Another type of film based on criminals who had captured the popular imagination was produced by Anthony Felton, a Puerto Rican resident of New York. Popular for a while, the public eventually tired of these films with very low budgets, low production values, earthy language, and titillating situations: *Correa Coto, ¡así me llaman!* (Correa Coto, That's What They Call Me!, 1968), *La venganza de Correa Coto* (The Revenge of Correa Coto, 1969), *Arocho y Clemente* (Arocho, 1969), *La palomilla* (The Gang, 1969), and *Luisa* (1970).

In the 1970s the number of Mexican coproductions declined significantly, primarily because of political changes in the film industry. Among the few that were done were *Yo soy el gallo* (I Am the Rooster, 1971), featuring Puerto Rican singer José Miguel Class; *La pandilla en apuros* (The Gang in Trouble, 1977); *¡Qué bravas son las solteras!* (Single Women Are Brave), featuring vedette

private firms. In 1962 the company was associated with the brothers Roberto and Marino Guastella, and what emerged ultimately in 1974 was Guastella Film Producers, currently the largest producer in Puerto Rico. Unfortunately, no film laboratory currently exists in Puerto Rico, so footage is sent to New York.

Beginning in the 1950s, the production of film features accelerated somewhat. A group of investors and actors headed by Víctor Arrillaga and Axel Anderson produced a few films under the Producciones Borinquen. *Maruja* (1959) was the most successful, depicting the love life of a barber's wife and starring Marta Romero and several well-known actors and actresses from Puerto Rican television. A few films were produced in Puerto Rico by North American filmmakers for the continental market. *Machete* (1958) is the best known, primarily for its sexuality. Coproduc-

Iris Chacón; and *Isabel La Negra* (Black Isabel, 1979), by Efraín López Neris, the first superproduction by Puerto Rican standards, featuring José Ferrer, Henry Darrow, Raúl Juliá, and Miriam Colón. This last film is about a notorious madam of a Ponce brothel and is recorded in English. However, the production was both an artistic and financial failure.

While the number of features declined, the number of documentaries increased greatly in the 1970s, spurred in part by the intense political climate of Puerto Rico. A number of *talleres cinematográficos* (movie workshops) were established. Notable among them was Tirabuzón Rojo, which produced *Denuncia de un embeleco* (Charges Filed against a Madman, 1975, Mario Vissepó, director); *Puerto Rico* (1975, Cuban Film Institute and Tirabuzón Rojo), a socioeconomic analysis of present-day Puerto Rico from a nationalist point of view; and *Puerto Rico: Paraíso invadido* (Puerto Rico: Paradise Invaded, 1977, Alfonso Beato, director), an examination of the history and present-day reality of Puerto Rico from a nationalist perspective. Independent filmmakers produced *The Oxcart* (1970, José García Torres, director), a short twenty-minute portrayal of the migration of a Puerto Rican family that is based on the famous play by René Marqués; *Culebra, el comienzo* (Island of Culebra, the Beginning, 1971, Diego de la Texera, director); *La carreta* (1972, José García, Spanish-language version of *The Oxcart*); *Los nacionalistas* (The Nationalists, 1973, José García Torres, director), which surveys the activities of the Puerto Rican Nationalist Party during the 1950s with a special focus on Don Pedro Albizu Campos; *La vida y poesía de Julia de Burgos* (The Life and Poetry of Julia de Burgos, 1974); *Destino manifiesto* (Manifest Destiny, 1977); *A la guerra* (To War, 1979, Thomas Sigel, director), an ode to the Puerto Rican community's war against cultural and racial discrimination in the form of a poem read by its author, Bimbo Rivas; and *The Life and Poetry of Julia de Burgos* (1979, José García Torres, director, Spanish-language version in 1974), a docu-drama on the life and work of the great Puerto Rican poet.

In the 1980s, several features were produced, including *Una aventura llamada Menudo* (An Adventure Called Menudo, 1983, Orestes Trucco, director), featuring the famous young musical group. This film was one of the biggest box office successes in Puerto Rican history; however, its sequel, *Operación Caribe* (Operation Caribbean, 1984), with another very popular juvenile group, Los Chicos, was a financial flop. Also produced, all in 1986, were *Reflejo de un deseo* (Reflection of a Desire, Ivonne María Soto, director), about the director's mother, a poet; *Nicolás y los demás* (Nicolás and the Others, Jacobo Morales, director), a variation on the eternal triangle theme; and *La gran fiesta* (The Great Fiesta, Marcos Zurinaga, director). The first two were low-budget vehicles, done in sixteen millimeters and blown up to thirty-five. They were not financially or artistically successful. On the other hand, *La gran fiesta* was a watershed in Puerto Rican film. Produced with a high budget by local standards (about $1 million) and boasting excellent production values, this period piece with strong political dimensions evokes the handing over of the San Juan Casino to the U.S. military in 1942 amidst considerable turmoil about the possibility of a Nazi invasion, the status of Puerto Rico, and changing attitudes among the upper classes, particularly growers and merchants. This financially successful film was also the first to be produced under the new Ley de Sociedades Especiales (Law of Special Societies, 1985), which was designed to spur filmic production.

In the 1990s, the following were among the features produced: the romantic comedy *Linda Sara* (1994, Jacobo Morales, director); *Angelito Mío* (My Little Angel, 1998, Enrique Pineda Barnet); *Héroes de otra patria* (Heroes of Another Fatherland, 1998, Iván Danile Otiz), about Puerto Rican soldiers in the Vietnam War; and *Pagin Emma*, an English-language thriller set in Puerto Rico (1999, Roberto Busó-García). In the 2000s, the following were among the features: a suspenseful romance *El beso que me diste* (The Kiss You Gave Me, 2000, Sonia Fritz); an English-language romance, *Flight of Fancy* (2000, Noel Quiñones); *12 Horas* (12 Hours, 2001, Raúl Marchand Sánchez), about a night in the life of a taxi driver; *Bala Perdida* (Lost Bullit, 2003, Raúl Marchand Sánchez), a tropical Christmas story; the boxing bio-pic *Bazooka: Las Batallas de Wilfredo Gómez* (Bazooka: Wilfredo Gómez's Battles, 2003, Mario Díaz); the heist flick *El anillo* (The Ring, 2004, Coraly Santaliz); a Vietnam vet cum New York police officer story, *Cayo* (Key Island, 2005, Vicente Juarbe); *Taínos* (2005, Benjamín López), a mystery set among Puerto Rico's archeological ruins; the high school romance *Casi casi*

(Almost, Almost, 2006, Jaime Vallés, Tony Vallés); the circus drama *El clown* (2006, Pedro Adorno and Emilio Rodríguez); the police-legal drama *Ángel* (2007, Jacobo Morales); the family drama *Ladrones & Mentirosos* (Thieves & Liars, 2007, Ricardo Méndez Matta); *Shut Up and Do It!* (2007, Bruno Irizarry), a comedy about the depiction of Latinos in film; the romantic comedy *Mi Verano con Amanda* (My Summer with Amanda, 2008, Benjamin López); and the romantic drama *Christián y Cristal* (2009, Víctor Aldarondo).

Since 2010 there have been a plethora of Puerto Rican features, too numerous to name here. Howver, the following are notable: possibly the first Puerto Rican horror film *Los condenados* (The Condemned, 2012, Roberto Busó-García); the erotic crime thriller *Under My Nails* (2012, Kisha Tikina Burgos), winner of four Latino and Latin American film awards; a romantic comedy with Lin-Manuel Miranda, *200 Cartas* (200 Letters, 2013, Bruno Irizarry); the dramedy *Las vacas con gafas* (The Cows Wearing Glasses, 2014, Alex Santiago Pérez); and the domestic drama *Antes que cante el gallo* (Before the Rooster Crows, 2016, Arí Maniel Cruz).

Among independent filmmakers, primarily with financial support of the Fundación Puertorriqueña de las Humanidades (Puerto Rican Humanities Foundation), the number of documentaries was on the increase in the 1980s. *Retratos* (Portraits, 1980, Stewart Bird, director) chronicles the life stories of four individuals from New York's Puerto Rican community in their attempts to adjust to life in the United States. *Puerto Rico: Our Right to Decide* (1981, Stanley Nelson, director) features interviews with people from various walks of life on Puerto Rico's current problems and aspirations for its political future. *Puerto Rico: A Colony the American Way* (1982, Diego Echeverría, director) examines the island's economic relationship with the United States. *La operación* (The Operation, 1982, Ana María García, director) studies the sterilization of Puerto Rican women. *El arresto* (The Arrest, 1982, Luis Antonio Rosario Quiles, director) dramatizes a major event in the history of the Puerto Rican independence movement. *Ligía Elena* (1983, Francisco López, director) is a color animation that criticizes consumerism, snobbery, and racism, set to a salsa song by Rubén Blades. *Manos a la obra (Let's Get to Work): The Story of Operation Bootsrap* (1983, Pedro Rivera and Susan Zeig, directors) is an examination of the economic development plan Operation Bootstrap, undertaken in the 1950s. *La herencia de un tambor* (The Heritage of a Drum, 1984, Mario Vissepó, director) is about Afro-Caribbean music. *Luchando por la vida* (Fighting for Life, 1984, José Artemio Torres, director) is about Puerto Rican tobacco workers. *Luis Muñoz Marín* (1984, Luis Molina, director) is a biography of the noted governor, and *Corretjer* (1984, Antonio Segarra, director) is a portrait of the noted poet and politician Juan Antonio Corretjer.

La batalla de Vieques (The Battle of Vieques, 1986, Zydnia Nazario, director) examines the U.S. Navy's control and use of the small island of Vieques. *Tufiño* (1986, Ramón Almodóvar, director) evokes the life and work of the eponymous painter. *Raíces eternas* (Eternal Roots, 1986, Noel Quiñones, director) describes the history of Puerto Rico. *Cimarrón* (Cimarron, 1986, Juis Antonio Rosario, director) is a short fiction about an enslaved Black man who escapes his owner's manor and searches for his wife and child in Puerto Rico. *Machito* (1986, Carlos Ortiz, director) is an excellent biographical film that follows salsa musician Machito's career as well as the evolution of Latin jazz from the Cuba of the 1920s to contemporary New York City. *Una historia de los Reyes Magos* (A History of the Three Wise Men, 1988, Producciones Rodadero) is an animation that brings to life a Puerto Rican story inspired by the tradition of the Magi. *Sabios árboles, mágicos árboles* (Wise Trees, Magic Trees, 1988, Puerto Rico Conservation Trust) is an animation that deals with the importance of trees and with man's relationship to nature. *Las plumas del múcaro* (The Feathers of the Múcaro, 1989, Puerto Rico Animation Workshop) is an animated Puerto Rican folktale from the oral tradition. More recently, the following documentaries have been produced: *Aljuriya* (2004, Freddie Marrero Alfonso), awarded Best Docmentary at the San Juna Cinefestival in 2005); *Los 17* (The 17, 2010, Noel Quiñones), about a community uniting to save a rural school; *100,000* (2010, Juan Agustín Márquez), about stray dogs overrunning the island; *Las carpetas* (The Files, 2011, Maite Rivera), an exposé about historical abuses by the authorities; *Aquel rebaño azul* (2012, Guillermo Gómez Álvarez), about police brutality in Puerto Rico; and *The Last Colony* (2015, Juan Agustín Márquez), which examines the colonial relationship of Puerto Rico to the United States.

LATINOS IN FILM: FUTURE DIRECTIONS

The prospects of the independent U.S. Latino film movement are good but are without any perceived fundamental changes in the budgetary and distribution limitations of these films. Independent U.S. Latino filmmakers will enjoy most of the benefits of the trends previously described, including more Latino viewers and more awareness of the importance of U.S. Latino culture; the decline in power and market control of the film studios and more recently of the television networks, as cable and as streaming companies become more popular; more diversity in distribution, particularly through television and streaming; the existence of a small, influential number of benefactors with money or other substantive resources; and perhaps, most of all, the growing number of well-trained and recognized Latino production people and actors and actresses who may not want to make a career out of low-budget productions but are willing to cross over to the independent side periodically.

The outlook is relatively good for U.S. Latino cinema. Both the Latino Hollywood and the independent U.S. Latino film movement will expand, and their productions will tend to be more comparable to each other than to the exploitive films that will also continue to be ground out by the Hollywood film carnival industry. The cadre of Latino talent will continue to expand, fostered by all elements of the film, television, and video industries, even the most crass sectors. However, once these individuals have been initiated into the field and develop their skills, they will be qualified and eager to produce, at least from time to time, a "real" movie about some aspect of U.S. Latino people.

In the twenty-first century, numerous Spanish and Latin American actors and directors have been employed by Hollywood and created outstanding careers. Generally speaking, these professional careers have not been open to U.S. Latinos or to their real stories. As Benjamin Bratt told the *New York Times* in 2020, "The sad reality is that we have been exoticized in American films, purposefully 'othered' as a foreign entity or an encroaching source of menace." Mexican Americans, Puerto Ricans, Cubans, Salvadorans, and other Latin ethnic minorities are still discriminated against, stereotyped or erased by Hollywood. Not a single U.S. Latino director has been afforded the opportunities and access, for instance, of the "Three Amigos," the nickname for the numerous-award-winning Mexican directors Alfonso Cuarón, Alejandro González Iñárritu, and Guillermo del Toro. Often, too, when there are excellent Latino roles and stories, they do not receive the recognition they deserve. As of this writing, no Latino star has been nominated for an Academy Award since Benicio Del Toro for *21 Grams* in 2003. There has never been a U.S. Latino nominated for best director. The curated Blu-ray/DVD archive of acclaimed films, entitled the Criterion Collection, includes only one feature film with a Latino protagonist, *The Ballad of Gregorio Cortez*, and the only Latino director included is Gregory Nava, for his film about Guatemalan migrants, *El Norte*.

OUTSTANDING LATINOS IN THE FILM INDUSTRY

Norma Aleandro (1936–)

An actress, playwright, and director born in Argentina, Norma Aleandro is known best for her performance in the Academy Award–winning *The Official Story* (1985), for which she was named best actress at Cannes. She has also acted in *Gaby—A True Story* (1987), *Cousins* (1989), *Vital Signs* (1990), *Autumn Sun* (1996), *The Lighthouse* (1998), *Son of the Bride* (2001), and *Cama Adentro* (2005). After her last Hollywood English-language film, *The City of Your Final Destination* (2009), she continued acting in Argentine films at least through 2012.

Néstor Almendros (1930–1992)

A photography director born in Barcelona, Spain, who moved to Havana, Cuba, as a teenager,

Néstor Almendros worked as a cameraman or director on several documentaries of the early Castro era, then moved to France, where he worked for television and on film shorts. In the mid-1960s he began collaborating regularly with director Erich Rohmer and later director François Truffaut. He won the Academy Award for cinematography for the 1978 film *Days of Heaven*. He also was nominated for the Academy Award for his work on *Kramer vs. Kramer* (1979), *The Blue Lagoon* (1980), and *Sophie's Choice* (1982). Included among his other films are *The Wild Racers* (1968), *Gun Runner* (1968), *Ma nuit chez Maud* (My Night at Maud's, 1969), *L'enfant sauvage* (The Wild Child, 1970), *Le genou de Claire* (Claire's Knee, 1971), *L'amour l'après-midi* (Chloe in the Afternoon, 1972), and *L'histoire d'Adele* (The Story of Adele H., 1975). In the 1980s Almendros applied his considerable artistic skills in documentaries against Cuban communism and Fidel Castro.

Trini Alvarado (1967–)

Born in New York City on January 10, 1967, Trinidad "Trini" Alvarado debuted in her family's dance troupe at age seven and in pictures at the age of eleven in *Rich Kids* (1979), by Robert Young, and has done considerable work in television and films. Her credits include *Mrs. Soffel* (1984), starring Diane Keaton and Mel Gibson; *Sweet Lorraine* (1987); *Satisfaction* (1988); *Stella* (1990), opposite Bette Midler; *The Babe* (1992); *American Friends* (1991); *Little Women* (1994); *The Perez Family* (1995); *The Good Guy* (2009); and *All Good Things* (2010). In the last two decades she has appeared in numerous episodes of television series.

Pedro Armendáriz (1912–1963)

Born on May 9, 1912, in Mexico City, Pedro Armendáriz was one of Mexico's most successful film stars, appearing in over forty films, many directed by Emilio "El Indio" Fernández. He was internationally recognized for *María Candelaria* (1943) and his work with major directors, including Luis Buñuel and John Ford. His son, Pedro Armendáriz Jr., was also an actor. Included among his films are *María Candelaria* (1943), *La perla* (The Pearl, 1945), *Fort Apache* (1948), *Three Godfathers* (1948), *We Were Strangers* (1949), *Tulsa* (1949), *Border River* (1954), *The Littlest Outlaw* (1955), *The Wonderful Country* (1959), *Francis of Assisi* (1961), and *Captain Sinbad* (1963). His last appearance was in the James Bond film *From Russia with Love* (1963).

Armida (1911–1989)

Born on May 29, 1911, in Sonora, Mexico, Armida Vendrell became a stereotypical Latin lady of Hollywood B pictures of the 1930s and 1940s. Known professionally as Armida, she appeared in the films *Under a Texas Moon* (1913), *Border Romance* (1931), *Border Café* (1940), *Fiesta* (1941), *The Girl from Monterey* (1943), *Machine Gun Mama* (1944), *South of the Rio Grande* (1945), and *Bad Men of the Border* (1946).

Alfonso Bedoya (1904–1957)

Born in Vicam, Mexico, on April 16, 1904, Alfonso Bedoya developed a considerable career as a character actor in Mexican films. He made a notable American film debut in 1948 in John Huston's *The Treasure of the Sierra Madre* as a treacherous, smiling, and mocking stereotypical Mexican bandit. His performance is both recognized and parodied in Luis Valdez's notable play *I Don't Have to Show You No Stinking Badges*. Included among his other films are *La perla* (The Pearl, 1945), *Streets of Laredo* (1949), *Border Incident* (1949), *Man in the Saddle* (1951), *California Conquest* (1952), *Sombrero* (1953), *The Stranger Wore a Gun* (1953), *Border River* (1954), *Ten Wanted Men* (1955), and *The Big Country* (1958).

Rubén Blades (1948–)

Actor, musician, composer, and lawyer Rubén Blades was born in Panama City, July 16, 1948. Known as a leading salsa musician, in 1985 Blades was recognized as cowriter and star of the film *Crossover Dreams* and has gone on to do several film performances, including the role of the sheriff in *The Milagro Beanfield War* (1988). Among his other films are *Critical Condition* (1986), *Fatal Beauty* (1987), *Homeboy* (1988), *Dead Man Out* (1989), *Disorganized Crime* (1989), *The Lemon Sisters* (1989), *The Heart of the Deal* (1990), *Mo' Better Blues* (1990), *One Man's War* (1990), *Predator 2* (1990), *Q & A* (1990), *The Two Jakes* (1990), *Crazy from the Heart* (1991), *The Super* (1991), *Safehouse* (2012), *The Counselor* (2013), and *Hands of Stone* (2016).

Benjamin Bratt (1963–)

Born December 16, 1963, to a Peruvian immigrant mother and an American father, Benjamin Bratt was raised in the Mission District of San Francisco. He received a B.F.A. from the University of California, Santa Barbara in 1986 and began studies toward an M.F.A. but left to star in the television film *Juarez* (1987). Bratt then went on to make a career as a supporting actor in such films as *Bright Angel* (1990), *Demolition Man* (1993), *Clear and Present Danger* (1994), *The River Wild* (1994), *Miss Congeniality* (2000), and *Traffic* (2000). In 2001, Bratt starred in *Piñero*, based on the life of playwright-poet Miguel Piñero. From then on, he was able to secure starring roles in *The Great Raid* (2005), *La Mission* (2009), and *The Lesser Blessed* (2012). His other notable films include *Catwoman* (2004), *The Woodsman* (2004), *Thumbsucker* (2005), *Trucker* (2008), *Snitch* (2013), *The Infiltrator* (2016), and *Ride Along 2* (2016), and he has done voiceover work for such animated films as *Coco* (2007), *Cloudy with a Chance of Meatballs* (2009), and *Despicable Me 2* (2013). Bratt produced the film *Dolores* (2017), which follows the life of civil rights activist Dolores Huerta. Bratt has also had a very active and fruitful career in television dramatic series, including *Law and Order* (1995–1999, 2009), *Homicide: Life on the Street* (1996–1999), and *Private Practice* (2011–2013). Among his awards are a Screen Actors Guild Award (2000) and a Blockbuster Entertainment Award.

Leo Carrillo (1880–1961)

Born on August 6, 1880, in Los Angeles to an old California family, Leopoldo Antonio Carrillo began as a cartoonist before becoming a dialect comedian in vaudeville and later on the stage. Debuting in Hollywood in the late 1920s, he became one of Hollywood's busiest character actors of the 1930s and 1940s, playing the stereotypical Latino buffoon in some features and gangster in others. In the early 1950s, he played Pancho, Duncan Renaldo's sidekick in *The Cisco Kid* TV series. His films include *Mister Antonio* (1929), *Girl of the Rio* (1932), *Viva Villa!* (1934), *Manhattan Melodrama* (1934), *The Gay Bride* (1934), *In Caliente* (1935), *The Gay Desperado* (1936), *Manhattan Merry-Go-Round* (1937), *The Girl of the Golden West* (1939), *Captain Caution* (1940), *Horror Island* (1941), *Sin Town* (1942), *American Empire* (1942), *Gypsy Wildcat* (1944), *Crime Incorporated* (1945), *The Fugitive* (1947), and *The Girl from San Lorenzo* (1950).

Arturo de Córdova (1908–1973)

Born on May 8, 1908, in Merida, Yucatán, Mexico, Arturo de Córdova made his debut in Mexican films in the early 1930s and played Latin lovers in Hollywood during the 1940s, thereafter returning to Spanish-language film. Among his more than fifty films are *Cielito lindo* (1936), *La zandunga* (1937), *For Whom the Bell Tolls* (1943), *Masquerade in Mexico* (1945), *A Medal for Benny* (1945), *New Orleans* (1947), and *Adventures of Casanova* (1948).

Pedro de Córdoba (1881–1950)

Born on September 28, 1881, in New York to Cuban French parents, Pedro de Córdoba began as a stage actor and later played character parts in numerous silent and more than fifty sound films, usually as either a benevolent or malevolent Latin aristocrat. His films include *Carmen* (1915), *Temptation* (1915), *Maria Rosa* (1916), *The New Moon* (1919), *When Knighthood Was in Flower* (1922), *The Bandolero* (1924), *Captain Blood*

(1935), *Rose of the Rancho* (1936), *Anthony Adverse* (1936), *Ramona* (1936), *Juárez* (1939), *The Mark of Zorro* (1940), *Blood and Sand* (1941), *For Whom the Bell Tolls* (1943), *The Keys of the Kingdom* (1945), *Samson and Delilah* (1949), *Comanche Territory* (1950), and *Crisis* (1950).

Linda Cristal (1931–2020)

Born on February 23, 1931, in Buenos Aires and orphaned at thirteen, Linda Cristal played leads in Mexican films from age sixteen and debuted in Hollywood in the mid-1950s in both film and television (*High Chaparral* and episodes of various other series) as a leading lady. Her U.S. films include *Comanche* (1951), *The Perfect Furlough* (1958), *Cry Tough* (1959), *The Alamo* (1960), *Two Rode Together* (1961), *Panic in the City* (1968), *Mr. Majestyk* (1974), and *Love and the Midnight Auto Supply* (1978). She received a Golden Globe Award for her performance in *The Perfect Furlough*.

Rosario Dawson (1979–)

Born on May 9, 1979, in New York City to working-class parents, a Puerto Rican/Cuban mother and an Irish father, Dawson got her start in independent films and videos. In 2002 she made her breakthrough in the 2002 Spike Lee film *25th Hour*. From there she went on to work in numerous films, often opposite the leading men. Among her films are *He Got Game* (1998), *Sidewalks of New York* (2001), *Men in Black II* (2002), *Rent* (2005), *Eagle Eye* (2008), *Unstoppable* (2010), *César Chávez* (2013), *Justice League: Throne of Atlantis* (2015), *Wonder Woman: Bloodlines* (2019), and *Justice League Dark: Apokolips War* (2020). Her awards include an NAACP Image Award (2009), a Women Film Critics Circle Award (2014), and a Behind the Voice Actors Award (2018).

Dolores del Río (1904–1983)

Born on August 3, 1904, in Durango, Mexico, Dolores del Río (Lolita Dolores Martínez Asunsolo López Negrete) was educated in a convent. By age sixteen, she was married to writer Jaime del Río. Director Edwin Carewe was struck by her beauty and invited her to Hollywood, where she appeared in *Joanna* in 1925. She became a star in many silent films, but her career suffered from frequent typecasting in ethnic and exotic roles, particularly after the advent of sound. Dissatisfied with Hollywood, she returned to Mexico in 1943 to do many important films of the 1940s, including *María Candelaria* (1943) and John Ford's *The Fugitive* (1947, filmed on location in Mexico). She finally returned to Hollywood in character parts in the 1960s. Her films include *Resurrection* (1927), *The Loves of Carmen* (1927), *Ramona* (1928), *Revenge* (1928), *Evangeline* (1929), *The Bad One* (1930), *The Girl of the Rio* (1932), *Flying Down to Rio* (1933), *Madame Du Barry* (1934), *In Caliente* (1935), *Devil's Playground* (1937), *Doña Perfecta* (1950), *La cucaracha* (The Cockroach, 1958), *Flaming Star* (1960), *Cheyenne Autumn* (1964), and *The Children of Sánchez* (1978). Del Río has a star on the Hollywood Walk of Fame and a statue at Hollywood and La Brea Boulevards in Los Angeles.

Hector Elizondo (1936–)

Born on December 22, 1936, in New York to Puerto Rican parents, Hector Elizondo is one of the most recognized actors in the United States, a Latino who has been cast in Latino and non-Latino mainstream roles. Active in television, theater, and film, Elizondo won an Obie for his role as a Puerto Rican locker room attendant in the off-Broadway play *Steambath*. He made his movie debut in 1971 with Burt Lancaster in *Valdez Is Coming*. A small selection of his films includes *The Taking of Pelham 1–2–3* (1974), *The Dain Curse* (1978), *American Gigolo* (1979), *Cuba* (1979), *The Fan* (1981), *Young Doctors in Love* (1982), *The Flamingo Kid* (1984), *Private Resort* (1984), *Out of the Darkness* (1985), *Courage* (1986), *Leviathan* (1989), *Pretty Woman* (1990), *Final Approach* (1991), *Frankie and Johnny* (1991), *Necessary Rough-*

ness (1991), *Chains of Gold* (1992), *There Goes the Neighborhood* (1992), *The Princess Diaries 2: Royal Engagement* (2004), *The Celestine Prophecy* (2006), *Love in the Time of Cholera* (2007), *The Book of Life* (2014), *Mother's Day* (2016), and *Music* (2020). Among his numerous awards are an Obie Award, a Primetime Emmy Award, a Golden Globe Award, a Satellite Award, and five Screen Actors Guild Awards.

Moctesuma Esparza (1949–)

Born on March 12, 1949, in Los Angeles, California, producer, director, and entertainment industry executive Moctesuma Esparza received both a B.A. (1971) and an M.F.A. (1973) in theatre arts–motion pictures/TV (1971) from the University of California, Los Angeles. Esparza is one of the best-known Chicano figures in the film industry. He has been involved in feature, documentary, and educational filmmaking since 1973. He has been the head of production companies, most notably Esparza/Katz, and has raised considerable funds to produce feature-length motion pictures with Latino themes, including an adaptation of the Rudolfo Anaya novel *Bless Me Ultima* (2013). His films include *Only Once in a Lifetime* (1978, producer), *The Ballad of Gregorio Cortez* (1983, producer), *Radioactive Dreams* (1986, producer), *The Milagro Beanfield War* (1988, coproducer), *Price of Glory* (2000), *Gods and Generals* (2003, executive producer), *Walkout* (2006, executive producer), *The Startup* (2007, executive producer), *Moe* (2008, executive producer), *One Hot Summer* (2009, executive producer), *Harlem Hostel* (2010, executive producer), *Across the Line: The Exodus of Charlie Wright* (2010, executive producer), *Without Men* (2011, executive producer), *Mosquita y Mari* (2011, executive producer), and *Taco Shop* (2012, executive producer). Of his film *Walkout*, about the Chicano civil rights movement, he told the *New York Times*, "I chose to be a filmmaker in pursuit of social justice and I had been seeking to get this movie made for more than twenty years." Esparza has received over one hundred honors, including an Academy Award nomination, an Emmy, a Clio Award, and a CINE Golden Eagle Award.

Paul Espinosa (1950–)

Born in New Mexico, Paul Espinosa received a B.A. in anthropology from Brown University and a Ph.D. in anthropology from Stanford University. Long affiliated with KPBS Television, San Diego, California, Espinosa has produced and directed exceptional documentaries and docudramas, including *Los mineros* (The Miners, 1990, Héctor Galán, coproducer), a stirring view of the history of the labor struggle by Arizona Mexican American miners from the turn of the century to the present. He is the producer for the *American Playhouse* TV drama series of a dramatic adaptation of Tomás Rivera's masterpiece *And the Earth Did Not Part* (1992, Severo Pérez, director-writer). Other films by Espinosa are *Ballad of an Unsung Hero* (1983), about a scandalous case of discrimination and deportation of a well-known Chicano radio figure, and *The Lemon Grove Incident* (1985), about separate and unequal education of Chicanos in California. His most recent documentaries are *The New Los Angeles* (2006) and *Singing Our Way to Freedom* (2018). The California Chicano News Media Association honored Espinosa with a Lifetime Achievement Award.

Emilio Fernández (1904–1986)

Director and actor Emilio Fernández was born on March 26, 1904, in El Seco, Coahuila, Mexico. One of the most important figures of Mexican cinema, he was born to a Spanish Mexican father and Amerindian mother (which led to his nickname El Indio). At nineteen, he took part in the Mexican Revolution and in 1923 was sentenced to twenty years in prison. However, he escaped to California where he played bit parts and supporting roles until returning to Mexico, first as an actor, debuting in the role of an Indian in *Janitzio* (1934), and then as Mexico's most prominent director. His film *María Candelaria* (1943) won the Grand Prize at Cannes, and *La Perla* (The Pearl, 1946) won the International Prize at San Sebastián, Spain. As a Hollywood actor, he had a few notable parts in Sam Peckinpah films. Among the films he directed are *Soy puro mexicano* (I Am Full-Blooded Mexican, 1942), *Flor Silvestre* (Wildflower, 1942), *María Candelaria* (1943), *Bugambilla* (Bougainvillea, 1944), *La Perla* (The Pearl, 1946), *El Gesticulador* (The Gesticulator, 1957), and *A Loyal Soldier of Pancho Villa* (1966). His films as an actor include *The Reward* (1965), *The Appaloosa* (1966), *Return of the Seven* (1966), *A Covenant with Death* (1967), *The War Wagon* (1967), *The Wild Bunch* (1969), *Pat Garrett and Billy the Kid* (1973), *Bring Me the Head of Alfredo García* (1974), *Lucky Lady* (1975), *Under the Volcano* (1984), and *Pirates* (1986).

Mel Ferrer (1917–2008)

Actor, director, and producer Melchor Gastón Ferrer was born on August 25, 1917, in New York to a Cuban-born surgeon and a Manhattan socialite. He attended Princeton University but dropped out to become an actor, debuting on Broadway in 1938 as a chorus dancer. He made his screen acting debut in 1949 and appeared in many films as a leading man. His films as an actor include *Lost Boundaries* (1949), *The Brave Bulls* (1951), *Rancho Notorious* (1952), *War and Peace* (1956), *The Sun Also Rises* (1957), *The World, the Flesh and the Devil* (1959), *Sex and the Single Girl* (1964), *Guyana: Cult of the Damned* (1979), and *City of the Walking Dead* (1980).

América Ferrera (1984–)

Born on April 18, 1984, in Los Angeles, California, to immigrant parents from Honduras, América Ferrera graduated with a B.A. in theater and international relations from the University of Southern California in 2013. In July 2002, Ferrera appeared in her first television movie, *Gotta Kick It Up!* for the Disney Channel. Also in 2002, she had her breakthrough role in Josefina López's *Real Women Have Curves*. Ferrera told the *New York Times* in 2020: "When *Real Women Have Curves* came out, it was the first time so many people were seeing themselves onscreen. It really resonated because it challenged so many cultural norms about what standards of beauty are and also the pressures and expectations for young women." In 2006, Ferrera was the lead in the long-running, award-winning series *Ugly Betty*, for which she won a Golden Globe, a Screen Actors Guild Award, and a Primetime Emmy Award, becoming the first Latina to win the latter award. Ferrera has acted in some twenty feature films. In 2020 she was the executive producer and director of the *Gentefied* series.

Gabriel Figueroa (1907–1997)

Photography director Gabriel Figueroa was born on April 24, 1907, in Mexico. As an orphan, he was forced to seek work, yet was able to pursue painting and photography on his own. In 1935 he went to Hollywood to study motion picture photography; he returned to Mexico the following year and began a prolific career as the cameraman of over one hundred films. He ranks among the leading directors of photography in world cinema. His films (primarily Mexican) include *Allá en el rancho grande* (Out on the Big Ranch, 1936), *Flor silvestre* (Wildflower, 1943), *María Candelaria*, (1943), *Bugambilla* (Bougainvillea, 1944), *La perla* (The Pearl, 1946), *The Fugitive* (1947), *Los olvidados* (The Forgotten, 1952), *La cucaracha* (The Cockroach, 1958), *Nazarín* (1959), *Macario* (1960), *Animas Trujano* (1961), *El angel exterminador* (The Exterminating Angel, 1962), *The Night of the Iguana* (1964), *Simón del desierto* (Simon in the Desert, 1965), *Two Mules for Sister Sara* (1970), *The Children of Sánchez* (1978), and *Under the Volcano* (1984).

Andy García (1956–)

Born on April 12, 1956, in Havana, Andrés Arturo García Menéndez moved to Miami, Florida, with his refugee parents when he was five years old. He received all of his education in the city, including graduating from Florida International University. In *8 Million Ways to Die* (1986), he turned in a superb performance as a villain, and in 1987 in Brian De Palma's *The Untouchables*, he gained widespread recognition as an earnest FBI agent. In 1990 he achieved star status as the good cop in *Internal Affairs* and as the illegitimate nephew of Don Corleone in *The Godfather Part III*. His other films are too numerous to name here, but they include *Blue Skies Again* (1983), *The Mean Season* (1985), *American Roulette* (1988), *Stand and Deliver* (1988), *Black Rain* (1989), *A Show of Force* (1990), *Dead Again* (1991), *Jennifer 8* (1992), *Hero* (1992), *When a Man Loves a Woman* (1994), *Against the Clock* (2009), *What about Love* (2020), and *Big Gold Brick*

(2020). His awards include an Academy Award, two Golden Globes, and an Emmy.

Salma Hayek (1966–)

Born on September 2, 1966, in Coatzacoalcos, Mexico, Salma Hayek began her acting career in Mexican telenovelas and moved to Hollywood in 1991 to study acting—somewhat difficult for a Spanish-speaker with dyslexia. She got her big break in 1995 when producer/director Robert Rodríguez gave her the leading role in *Desperado* and its sequel *Once Upon a Time in Mexico*. In 2000 she founded her own production company, Ventanarosa, for which she subsequently coproduced *Frida* (2002) and earned an Academy Award nomination for best actress. In 2007 she signed deals for productions with MGM and ABC for Ventanarosa. After that she continued to produce and direct films for theaters and television. One of her most important television series was the long-lasting *Ugly Betty* (2006–2010), which won various awards, including the Golden Globe Award for Best Comedy Series in 2007. Hayek has acted in more than twenty films, most recently in *Eternals* (2021) and *The Hitman's Wife's Bodyguard* (2021).

Rita Hayworth (1918–1987)

Rita Hayworth (Margarita Carmen Cansino) was born October 17, 1918, in Brooklyn, New York, to Spanish-born dancer Eduardo Cansino and his Ziegfeld Follies partner Volga Haworth. Hayworth danced professionally by age thirteen in Mexican nightspots in Tijuana and Agua Caliente, where she was eventually noticed by Hollywood. She made her screen debut in 1935, playing bit parts under her real name. In 1937, she married Edward Judson, under whose guidance she changed her name and was transformed into an auburn-haired sophisticate. For the remainder of the 1930s, Hayworth was confined to leads in B pictures, but through much of the 1940s she became the undisputed sex goddess of Hollywood films and the hottest star at Columbia Studios. Her tempestuous personal life included marriages to Orson Welles, Aly Khan, and singer Dick Haymes. As Rita Cansino, her films included *Under the Pampas Moon* (1935), *Charlie Chan in Egypt* (1935), *Dante's Inferno* (1935), *Meet Nero Wolfe* (1936), *Trouble in Texas* (1937), *Old Louisiana* (1937), and *Hit the Saddle* (1937). As Rita Hayworth, the films she acted in include *The Shadow* (1937), *Angels over Broadway* (1940), *The Strawberry Blonde* (1941), *Blood and Sand* (1941), *Cover Girl* (1944), *Gilda* (1946), *The Lady from Shanghai* (1948), *The Loves of Carmen* (1948), *Salome* (1953), *The Wrath of God* (1972), and *Circle* (1976). In 1987 she received the National Screen Heritage Award of the National Film Society.

Oscar Isaac (1979–)

Óscar Isaac Hernández Estrada was born on March 9, 1979, in Guatemala City, Guatemala, to a Cuban father and a Guatemalan mother; shortly after his birth, the family moved to Miami, Florida, where he did his schooling. Beginning in 2001 Isaac studied acting at the Juilliard School in New York and while there acted in his first film, *All about the Benjamins* (2002). His first major film role was as Joseph in *The Nativity Story* (2006). He also starred in the Coen Brothers' dramatic comedy *Inside Llewyn Davis* (2013), for which he received a Golden Globe nomination. After that success, he was able to act or star in numerous other films, including *A Most Violent Year* (2014), *Star Wars: The Force Awakens* (2015), *X-Men: Apocalypse* (2016), *Star Wars: The Last Jedi* (2017), *Star Wars: The Rise of Skywalker* (2019), *Dune* (2019), and many others. For his starring role in the six-episode HBO miniseries *Show Me a Hero*, he was awarded the Golden Globe Award for Best Actor.

Raúl Juliá (1940–1994)

Raúl Juliá was one of the best-known and most popular actors in the United States for his Shakespearean and other classical stage roles, his musicals, and his films. His career started on the Latino stages of New York, most notably with important productions of René Marqués's *La Carreta* (The Oxcart, 1966) with Miriam Colón. Born in San Juan, Puerto Rico, on March 9, 1940, Juliá was raised there and attained his bachelor of arts degree from the University of Puerto Rico. As a stage actor he had important roles in serious theater and on Broadway, including *The Emperor of Late Night Radio* (1974), *The Cherry Orchard* (1976), *Dracula* (1976), *Arms and the Man* (1985), and various Shakespearean plays. In 1971 he debuted in film with small parts in *The Organization, Been Down So Long It Looks Like Up to Me*, and *Panic in Needle Park*. Juliá appeared in *The Gumball Rally* (1976) and *Eyes of Laura Mars* (1978) and achieved national attention in the notable *Kiss of the Spider Woman* (1985), adapted from the novel by Argentine Manuel Puig. His other films include *One from the Heart* (1982), *Tempest* (1982), *Compromising Positions* (1985), *Havana* (1990), *Presumed Innocent* (1990), *A Life of Sin* (1990), *The Rookie* (1990), *The Addams Family* (1991), *The Plague* (1992), and *Addams Family Values* (1993). He was the winner of a Tony Award, a Golden Globe, a Screen Actors Guild Award, and a Primetime Emmy.

Katy Jurado (1924–2002)

Born on January 16, 1924, in Guadalajara, Mexico, Katy Jurado (María Cristina Jurado García) began her Hollywood career as a columnist for Mexican publications following a Mexican film career. In Hollywood she played dark lady roles in a variety of films, most memorably *High Noon* (1952) and *One-Eyed Jacks* (1961). She was nominated for an Oscar for her supporting role in *Broken Lance* (1954). Her other films include *The Bullfighter and the Lady* (1951), *Arrowhead* (1953), *Trapeze* (1956), *The Man from Del Rio* (1956), *Barabbas* (1961), *Pat Garrett and Billy the Kid* (1973), *El recurso del método* (The Method's Resource, 1978), and *The Children of Sánchez* (1978).

Fernando Lamas (1915–1982)

Born Fernando Álvaro Lamas y de Santos on January 9, 1915, in Buenos Aires, Fernando Lamas became a movie star in Argentina. Lamas was imported to Hollywood by MGM and typecast as a sporty Latin lover in several lightweight films, some of which featured his singing. He married Arlene Dahl (1954–60) and Esther Williams (from 1967 until his death). His films include *The Avengers* (1950), *The Merry Widow* (1952), *The Diamond Queen* (1953), *Jívaro* (1954), *Rose Marie* (1954), *The Violent Ones* (1967), *Kill a Dragon* (1967), *100 Rifles* (1969), *Backtrack* (1969), and *The Cheap Detective* (1978). He also worked in more than thirty television programs.

John Leguizamo (1964–)

Born on July 22, 1964, in Bogotá, Colombia, John Leguizamo was raised in New York City from age four. After high school he attended NYU's Tisch School of the Arts but dropped out to pursue his career as a stand-up comedian (as "Mambo Mouth") and actor. After performing typical denigrating ethnic humor in nightclubs and getting a small part in an episode of *Miami Vice*, he was able to act in numerous films, often as a street tough or gangster. A role that broadened his appeal and established his comedic film credit was as drag queen Chi-Chi Rodriguez in *To Wong Foo, Thanks for Everything! Julie Newmar* (1995), for which he received a Golden Globe nomination for Best Supporting Actor. Among his films are *Mixed Blood* (1985), *Casualties of War* (1989), *Die Hard 2* (1990), *Hangin' with the Homeboys* (1991), *Regarding Henry* (1991), *Super Mario Bros.* (1993), *Night Owl* (1993), *The Babysitters* (2007), *The Happening* (2008), *Chef* (2014), and *The Crash* (2017).

Adele Mara (1923–2010)

Born on April 28, 1923, in Highland Park, Michigan, Adele Mara (Adelaida Delgado) began as a singer-dancer with Xavier Cugat's orchestra. In Hollywood she played dark lady/other woman parts in scores of low-budget films in the 1940s and 1950s, including *Navy Blues* (1941), *Alias Boston Blackie* (1942), *Atlantic City* (1944), *The Tiger Woman* (1945), *Song of Mexico* (1945), *The Catman of Paris* (1946), *Twilight on the Rio Grande* (1947), *Blackmail* (1947), *Exposed* (1947), *Campus Honeymoon* (1948), *Wake of the Red Witch* (1948), *Angel in Exile* (1948), *Sands of Iwo Jima* (1950), *The Avengers* (1950), *California Passage* (1950), *The Sea Hornet* (1951), *Count the Hours* (1953), *Back from Eternity* (1956), and *The Big Circus* (1959).

Margo (1917–1985)

Born on May 10, 1917, in Mexico City, Margo (María Margarita Guadalupe Teresa Estela Bolado Castilla y O'Donnell) was coached as a child by Eduardo Cansino, Rita Hayworth's father, and she danced professionally with her uncle Xavier Cugat's band in Mexican nightclubs and at New York's Waldorf-Astoria, where they triumphed in introducing the *rumba*. Beginning in 1934, she became known as a dramatic actress, mostly typecast as a tragic, suffering woman. She married actor Eddie Albert in 1945 and was the mother of actor Edward Albert Jr. Her films include *Crime without Passion* (1934), *Rumba* (1935), *The Robin Hood of Eldorado* (1936), *Winterset* (1936), *Lost Horizon* (1937), *Behind the Rising Sun* (1943), *The Falcon in Mexico* (1944), *Viva Zapata!* (1952), *I'll Cry Tomorrow* (1955), *From Hell to Texas* (1958), and *Who's Got the Action?* (1962). Margo was involved in progressive politics and was blacklisted for television during the 1950s and blacklisted for Hollywood films thereafter.

Cheech Marín (1946–)

Renowned comic, actor, and writer Richard "Cheech" Marín was born on July 13, 1946, in Los Angeles. Marín began in show business as part of the comedy team Cheech and Chong in 1970, bringing stoned and hippie routines to the screen with *Cheech and Chong's Up in Smoke* (1979), which was the highest-grossing film of the year. In 1982 he wrote *Things Are Tough All Over*. Following the split-up of the duo in 1985, Cheech continued to appear in films and wrote, directed, and starred in *Born in East L.A.* (1987). His films include *Cheech and Chong's Next Movie* (1980), *Cheech and Chong's Nice Dreams* (1981), *Yellowbeard* (1983), *Cheech and Chong: Still Smokin'* (1983), *Cheech and Chong's the Corsican Brothers* (1984), *After Hours* (1985), *Echo Park* (1986), *Fatal Beauty* (1987), *Rude Awakening* (1989), *The Shrimp on the Barbie* (1990, which

he also directed), *Picking Up the Pieces* (2000), *Once upon a Time in Mexico* (2003), and *The War with Grandpa* (2020). He has provided a voice for several animated features, including *Ferngully: The Last Rainforest* (1992), *The Lion King* (1994), *Cars* (2006), *Beverly Hills Chihuahua* (2008), *El Santos vs. La Tetona Mendoza* (2012), *The Book of Life* (2014), *El Americano: The Movie* (2016), and *Coco* (2017).

Mona Maris (1903–1991)

Born as Mona Maria Emita Capdeville in 1903 in Buenos Aires and convent-educated in France, Mona Maris acted in several British and German films before embarking on a Hollywood career in the late 1920s and the 1930s in the usual sultry, exotic-type role. Her films include *Romance of the Rio Grande* (1929), *Under a Texas Moon* (1930), *The Arizona Kid* (1930), *A Devil with Women* (1930), *The Passionate Plumber* (1932), *Once in a Lifetime* (1932), *Flight from Destiny* (1941), *Law of the Tropics* (1941), *My Gal Sal* (1942), *Pacific Rendezvous* (1942), *I Married an Angel* (1942), *Berlin Correspondent* (1942), *The Falcon in Mexico* (1944), *Heartbeat* (1946), and *The Avengers* (1950).

Chris-Pin Martín (1893–1953)

Born on November 19, 1893, in Tucson, Arizona, of Mexican parentage, Christopher Ysabel Poinciana Martín provided comic relief in the Cisco Kid film series (as Pancho or Gordito) and many other westerns, often as the Mexican buffoon speaking broken English. His films include *The Rescue* (1929), *Billy the Kid* (1930), *The Cisco Kid* (1931), *South of Santa Fe* (1932), *Bordertown* (1935), *The Gay Desperado* (1936), *The Texans* (1938), *Stagecoach* (1939), *The Return of the Cisco Kid* (1939), *Lucky Cisco Kid* (1940), *Down Argentine Way* (1940), *The Mark of Zorro* (1940), *Weekend in Havana* (1941), *Tombstone* (1942), *The Ox-Bow Incident* (1943), *Ali Baba and the Forty Thieves* (1944), *San Antonio* (1945), *The Fugitive* (1947), *Mexican Hayride* (1948), *The Beautiful Blonde from Bashful Bend* (1949), and *Ride the Man Down* (1952).

Eva Méndes (1947–)

Eva de la Caridad Méndez was born on March 5, 1947, in Miami, Florida, to Cuban parents, and was raised by her mother in Glendale, California, after her parents' divorce. She studied marketing at California State University, Northridge, but left college to become an actress. She made her debut in *Children of the Corn V: Fields of Terror* (1998) and then went on to appear in numerous films, often opposite the leading men. Her other early films include *A Night at the Roxbury* (1998), *My Brother the Pig* (1999), *Urban Legends: Final Cut* (2000), and *Exit Wounds* (2001). Her breakthrough role, however, was in *Training Day* (2001), playing the girlfriend of Denzel Washington's character. She went on to major roles in *All about the Benjamins* (2002), *Once Upon a Time in Mexico* (2003), *Out of Time* (2003), *Stuck on You* (2003), and *2 Fast 2 Furious* (2009). She was the female lead in the 2005 film *Hitch*, making her one of the first minority actors to play the lead in a hit romantic comedy. She starred in *The Wendell Baker Story* (2005), *Guilty Hearts* (2005), *Trust the Man* (2005), *Ghost Rider* (2007), *We Own the Night* (2007), *Cleaner* (2007), *The Women* (2008), and *Lost River* (2014).

Ricardo Montalbán (1920–2009)

Born on November 25, 1920, in Mexico City, Ricardo Montalbán first played bit roles in several Broadway productions before debuting on the screen in Mexico in the early 1940s and subsequently being recruited as a Latin lover type by MGM in 1947. He was eventually given an opportunity to demonstrate a wider acting range on television, including roles on *The Loretta Young Show* and *Fantasy Island*. He was a strong force in Hollywood for the establishment of better opportunities for Latinos. His films include *Fiesta* (1947), *The Kissing Bandit* (1948), *Neptune's Daughter* (1949), *Border Incident* (1949), *Right Cross* (1950), *Two Weeks with Love* (1950), *Mark of the Renegade* (1951), *Sombrero* (1953), *Latin Lovers* (1953), *The Saracen Blade* (1954), *Sayonara* (1957), *Let No Man Write My Epitaph* (1960), *Cheyenne Autumn* (1964), *Escape from the Planet of the Apes* (1971), *Conquest of the Planet of the Apes* (1972), *The Train Robbers* (1973), *Joe Panther* (1976), *Star Trek II: The Wrath of Khan* (1982), *Spy Kids 2* (2002), and *Spy Kids 3* (2003). In 2004, a theater in Hollywood was named in his honor.

María Montez (1912–1951)

Born on June 6, 1912, in Barahona, Dominican Republic, María Montez (María Africa Vidal de Santo Silas) became one of the most notable exotic dark ladies. Affectionately called the "Queen of Technicolor," she started her screen career in 1941 doing bit parts in Universal films. Although inordinately unskilled at acting, she nevertheless became immensely popular in a string of color adventure tales, often co-starring with fellow exotics Jon Hall, Sabu, and Turhan Bey. She remains the object of an extensive fan cult thirsting for nostalgia and high camp. Her films include *Lucky Devils* (1941), *That Night in Rio* (1941), *Raiders of the Desert* (1941), *South of Tahiti* (1941), *Bombay Clipper* (1942), *Arabian Nights* (1942), *White Savage* (1943), *Ali Baba and the Forty Thieves* (1944), *Cobra Woman* (1944), *Gypsy Wildcat* (1944), *Bowery to Broadway* (1944), *Sudan* (1945), *Tangier* (1946), *The Exile* (1947), and *Pirates of Monterey* (1947).

Sylvia Morales (1943–)

One of the most recognized Chicana directors, Sylvia Morales was born in Phoenix, Arizona, in 1943 and was raised in Southern California. She received a B.A. (1972) and an M.F.A. (1979) from the University of California, Los Angeles. In 1971 she began work as a photographer for the ABC affiliate in Los Angeles, where she eventually created thirteen half-hour documentaries for broadcast. She left the station to pursue her independent career as a director/producer of mostly Mexican American and feminist documentaries, with occasional feature films. Among her directorial products are *Chicana* (1979), *Los Lobos: And A Time to Dance* (1984), *SIDA Is AIDS* (1989), *Values: Sexuality and the Family*, *Faith Even to the Fire* (1993), *Real Men and Other Miracles* (1999), and *A Crushing Love* (2009). However, Morales also worked for mainstream media, including on series and made-for-TV movies for Showtime, PBS, and Turner Broadcasting.

Antonio Moreno (1887–1967)

Born on September 26, 1887, in Madrid, Antonio Moreno (Antonio Garrido Monteagudo) played a dapper Latin lover in numerous Hollywood silent films. He began his career in 1912 under D. W. Griffith and was quite popular during the 1920s, when he played leads opposite such actresses as Gloria Swanson, Greta Garbo, Pola Negri, and Bebe Daniels. His foreign accent limited his career in talkies, where he was seen mainly in character roles. He appeared in hundreds of films, including *Voice of the Million* (1912), *The Musketeers of Pig Alley* (1912), *The Song of the Ghetto* (1914), *The Loan Shark King* (1914), *In the Latin Quarter* (1914), *Sunshine and Shadows* (1914), *Venus of Venice* (1928), *The Whip Woman* (1928), *Romance of the Rio Grande* (1929), *Rose of the Rio Grande* (1938), *Seven Sinners* (1940), *Notorious* (1946), *Captain from Castile* (1947), *Crisis* (1950), *Dallas* (1950), *Wings of the Hawk* (1953), *Creature from the Black Lagoon* (1954), and *The Searchers* (1956).

Rita Moreno (1931–)

An actress, dancer, and singer, Moreno (Rosita Dolores Alverio) was born on December 11, 1931, in Humacao, Puerto Rico. A dancer from childhood, she reached Broadway at thirteen and Hollywood at fourteen. She won a 1962 Academy Award as best supporting actress for *West Side Story* and has been in numerous films important for understanding the Hollywood depiction of Latinos, including *Popi* (1969), *The Ring* (1952), and *A Medal for Benny* (1954). In 2021 she appeared in the motion picture remake of *West Side Story* as a newly created character, a shopkeeper named Valentina. Her other films include *Pagan Love Song* (1950), *Singin' in the Rain* (1952), *Latin Lovers* (1953), *Fort Vengeance* (1953), *Jivaro* (1954),

Garden of Evil (1954), *The King and I* (1956), *The Vagabond King* (1956), *The Deerslayer* (1957), *Summer and Smoke* (1961), *Marlowe* (1969), *Carnal Knowledge* (1971), *The Ritz* (1976), *The Boss' Son* (1978), *Happy Birthday, Gemini* (1980), *The Four Seasons* (1981), and *Life in the Food Chain* (1991). Among the many musicals and plays in which she performed are *The Sign in Sidney Brustein's Window* (1964–65), *Elmer Gantry* (1969–70), *The Last of the Red Hot Lovers* (1970–71), *The National Health* (1974), *Wally's Café* (1981), and *The Odd Couple* (1985). In addition to her Oscar, Moreno has won a Grammy (1973), a Tony, and an Emmy. Moreno has also had considerable work in television series, including recurring appearances on the long-running series *Law & Order* and in *One Day at a Time* (2017–20), a reprise of a classic series. Moreno has won too many awards to list in this limited space; however, worth noting are the National Medal of the Arts presented by President Barack Obama (2009), the Kennedy Center Honors Lifetime Artistic Achievement Award (2015), and the Peabody Career Achievement Award (2019).

Ramón Novarro (1899–1968)

Born on February 6, 1899, in Durango, Mexico, Ramón Novarro (Ramón Samaniego) became a romantic idol of Hollywood silents of the 1920s. He began his career as a singing waiter and vaudeville performer before breaking into films as an extra in 1917. By 1922 he had become a star Latin lover and was overshadowed only by Rudolph Valentino in that role. He soon sought a broader range and less exotic image. His most famous part was the title role in *Ben-Hur* (1926). His other films include *A Small Town Idol* (1921), *The Prisoner of Zenda* (1922), *Scaramouche* (1923), *The Arab* (1924), *Thy Name Is Woman* (1924), *A Lover's Oath* (1925), *The Student Prince* (1927), *The Pagan* (1929), *In Gay Madrid* (1930), *Call of the Flesh* (1930), *Son of India* (1931), *Mata Hari* (1931), *The Barbarian* (1933), *The Sheik Steps Out* (1937), *The Big Steal* (1949), *The Outriders* (1950), and *Heller in Pink Tights* (1960). Novarro's contract with MGM was not renewed in 1935, and his popularity waned during the error of "talkies"; he was called out for supporting Communists during the McCarthy era.

Edward James Olmos (1947–)

Edward James Olmos was born on February 24, 1947, in Los Angeles. He began his career as a rock singer and earned a Los Angeles Drama Critics' Circle Award for his performance in Luis Valdez's musical play *Zoot Suit*, which he reprised on Broadway and in the 1981 film version. He became nationally known as Lieutenant Martin Castillo on television's *Miami Vice* (1984–89) and was nominated for an Oscar for best actor for his lead as a committed East Los Angeles high school calculus teacher in *Stand and Deliver* (1988). The film also helped propel him to the cover of *Time* magazine, perhaps the first Chicano to have attained that recognition. He has acted in more than fifty films, including *Wolfen* (1981), *Blade Runner* (1982), *The Ballad of Gregorio Cortez* (1983), *Saving Grace* (1986), *Triumph of the Spirit* (1989), *Maria's Story* (1990), *A Talent for the Game* (1991), and *American Me* (1992), which he also produced and directed. Olmos has also directed or produced films, including *Filly Brown* (2012), *El Americano: The Movie* (2016), *Monday Nights at Seven* (2016), and *The Devil Has a Name* (2019), in which he also acted. Among his many awards are two Golden Globes, an Emmy, a Screen Actors Guild, and four ALMA awards.

Elizabeth Peña (1959–2014)

Born on September 23, 1959, in Elizabeth, New Jersey, to Cuban parents, Elizabeth Peña spent her first years in Cuba and moved to New York with her parents when she was eight. She graduated from New York's High School for the Performing Arts and in 1979 made her film debut in Iván Acosta's *El Super*. While Peña began her career playing primarily mothers and live-in maids, she eventually played diverse Latina roles. She made a name for herself in *La Bamba* (1987). Peña appeared in more than forty films, including in *Crossover Dreams* (1985), *Down and Out in Beverly Hills* (1986), *Batteries Not Included* (1987), *Vibes* (1988), *Blue Steel* (1989), *Jacob's Ladder* (1990), *Girl on the Edge* (2015), *Ana María in Novela Land* (2015), and *The Song of Sway*

Lake (2017), which was her last film. On television, she was in the series *Tough Cookies*, *I Married Dora*, and *Shannon's Deal*; she also held a recurring guest spot as a private investigator on *L.A. Law*.

Michael Peña (1976–)

Michael Peña was born and raised in Chicago to working-class Mexican immigrant parents. Peña graduated from high school and went to an open casting call for the Peter Bogdanovich feature *To Sir, with Love II*. He won the role over hundreds of other young men and relocated to Los Angeles, where he was successful in being cast in numerous movies, such as *Crash* (2004), *World Trade Center* (2006), *Shooter* (2007), *Observe and Report* (2009), *Tower Heist* (2011), *Battle: Los Angeles* (2011), *Collateral Beauty* (2016), *CHiPs* (2017), *Ant-Man* (2015), its sequel *Ant-Man and the Wasp* (2018), *A Wrinkle in Time* (2018), *12 Strong* (2018), and *Fantasy Island* (2020). Peña had the title role in *César Chávez* (2014) and played the colead role in the first season of the Netflix TV series *Narcos: Mexico* (2018). His awards include the COFCA Award (2014) and a Gold Derby Award (2020).

Anthony Quinn (1915–2001)

Born on April 21, 1915, in Chihuahua, Mexico, of Irish Mexican (Oaxacan) parentage, Anthony Quinn lived in the United States from childhood. He entered films in 1936 and did not attain star status until 1952 with his Academy Award–winning role as Zapata's brother in *Viva Zapata!* Quinn went on to win a second Academy Award for *Lust for Life* (1956), and he began playing leads that emphasized his earthy and exotic qualities. He appeared in more than one hundred films, including *Parole!* (1936), *The Buccaneer* (1938), *King of Alcatraz* (1938), *Texas Rangers Ride Again* (1940), *Blood and Sand* (1941), *The Ox-Bow Incident* (1943), *Guadalcanal Diary* (1943), *Back to Bataan* (1945), *California* (1947), *Sinbad the Sailor* (1947), *Black Gold* (1947), *The Brave Bulls* (1951), *Against All Flags* (1952), *Ride Vaquero!* (1953), *Man from Del Rio* (1956), *Requiem for a Heavyweight* (1962), *Lawrence of Arabia* (1962), *Zorba the Greek* (1964), *The Greek Tycoon* (1978), *The Children of Sánchez* (1978), *The Salamander* (1981), *Valentina* (1983), *Revenge* (1990), *Jungle Fever* (1991), *Mobsters* (1991), and *The Last Action Hero* (1993).

Gina Rodríguez (1984–)

Gina Rodriguez (Gina Alexis Rodriguez-LoCicero) was born on July 30, 1984, in Chicago, Illinois, to Puerto Rican parents. She started performing at age seven with the salsa dance company Fantasía Juvenil and went on to perform with other companies in Chicago, California, New York, and Puerto Rico. At sixteen, Gina was one of thirteen teens to be accepted into Columbia University's Theatrical Collaboration program, where she wrote, directed, and performed original work with twelve other young people from around the world. Rodríguez studied at New York University's Tisch School of the Arts, graduating with a B.A. in 2015. She reached national audiences in the role of Jane Villanueva on the hit series *Jane the Virgin* (2014–19), for which she received a Golden Globe Award in 2015. With this grounding, Rodríguez was selected to star in numerous films, including *Deepwater Horizon* (2016), *Ferdinand* (2017), *Annihilation* (2018), *Miss Bala* (2019), *Someone Great* (2019), *Jill* (2020), and *Killionaire* (2020).

Robert Rodríguez (1968–)

Born on June 20, 1968, in San Antonio, Texas, Robert Rodríguez studied film at the University of Texas, where his short 16-mm film *Bedhead* (1991) won an award. Also while still in film school Rodriguez shot a satire of Mexican gangster films in Spanish, titled *El Mariachi* (1992), which he produced for around $7,000. It became a hit at the Sundance Film Festival and subsequently was reproduced by Columbia Pictures and led to two sequels (*Desperado* and *Once upon a Time in Mexico*) starring Antonio Banderas. Next, in 2001, he produced and directed *Spy Kids*, which became a franchise with a number of sequels, all of which employed numerous Latinos as actors and crew. With *Spy Kids*, Rodríguez had to counter Hollywood's preconceived notions about Latinos and what was marketable. As he told the *New York Times* in 2020, the studio chafed at centering the story on a Latino family: "The studio said, 'This is a terrific story, but why risk appealing only to a smaller audience by making the family Hispanic? Why don't you just make them American?'"—to which he countered that these "Hispanics" were Americans and, in fact, based on his own family. "I finally argued, 'You don't have to be British to enjoy James Bond.'" Rodríguez not only

works as producer, director, and writer for many of his films, he often also works as editor, director of photography, camera operator, steadicam operator, composer, production designer, visual effects supervisor, and sound editor on his films. And many of his films are produced out of his own Troublemaker Studios. Among the films he has directed or produced (or coproduced) are *From Dusk Till Dawn* (1996), *The Faculty* (1998), *Sin City* (2005), *The Adventures of Sharkboy and Lavagirl* (2005), *Machete* (2010), *Alita: Battle Angel* (2019), and *We Can Be Heroes* (2020). Included among his awards are the Sundance Film Festival Audience Award (1993), the Silver Screen Award for Best Film (1996), the ASCAP Award for Top Box Office Film (2003), the Technical Grand Prize at the Cannes Film Festival (2005), and the ShoWest Award for Director of the Year (2007).

Gilbert Roland (1905–1994)

Born in Júarez, Mexico, on December 11, 1905, the son of a bullfighter, Roland (Luis Antonio Dámaso de Alonso) trained for the *corrida* (bullfight) but chose a career in film instead after his family moved to the United States. He debuted as an extra at age thirteen and subsequently played a Latin lover on both the silent and sound screens. His more than sixty films include *The Plastic Age* (1925), *The Campus Flirt* (1926), *Camille* (1927), *Rose of the Golden West* (1927), *The Dove* (1928), *The Last Train from Madrid* (1937), *Juárez* (1939), *The Sea Hawk* (1940), *Captain Kidd* (1945), *The Gay Cavalier* (1946), *Beauty and the Bandit* (1946), *The Bullfighter and the Lady* (1951), *Mark of the Renegade* (1951), *Bandido* (1956), *Cheyenne Autumn* (1964), *Islands in the Stream* (1982), *The Black Pearl* (1977), and *Barbarosa* (1982). Roland has a star on the Hollywood Walk of Fame.

César Romero (1907–1994)

Born on February 15, 1907, in New York City of Cuban parentage, César Romero played a Latin lover in Hollywood films from the 1930s through the 1950s and later did suave supporting character roles. He played the Cisco Kid in the late 1930s and early 1940s. His more than ninety films include *The Thin Man* (1934), *Clive of India* (1935), *Cardinal Richelieu* (1935), *The Cisco Kid and the Lady* (1939), *Viva Cisco Kid* (1940), *The Gay Caballero* (1940), *Romance of the Rio Grande* (1940), *Ride on Vaquero* (1941), *Weekend in Havana* (1941), *Captain from Castile* (1948), *Vera Cruz* (1954), *Villa!* (1958), *Batman* (1966), and *The Strongest Man in the World* (1975). He also acted in scores of television shows, including playing the role of Joker in the *Batman* series in the 1960s.

Zoe Saldaña (1978–)

Born on June 19, 1978, in Passaic, New Jersey, to a Dominican father and a Puerto Rican mother, Zoe Saldaña was raised in Queens, New York. When she was ten years old, she and her family moved to the Dominican Republic, where they would live for the next seven years, during which time Saldaña trained as a dancer. Back in New York, at age seventeen she acted wth the New York Youth Theater. From there she was discovered and went on to act in major films, even blockbusters, often oppostite the leading men and even playing roles as an action hero. Her films include *Colombiana* (2011), *The Words* (2012), *Star Trek into Darkness* (2013), *Star Trek Beyond* (2016), *Guardians of the Galaxy Vol. 2* (2017), *Avengers: Infinity War* (2018), *Avengers: Endgame* (2019), and *Vampires vs. the Bronx* (2020). In 2009 she won an Empire Award and Saturn Award for her acting. In 2018 she received a star on the Hollywood Walk of Fame.

Martin Sheen (1940–)

Born on August 3, 1940, in Dayton, Ohio, to a Spanish immigrant father and an Irish mother, Martin Sheen (Ramón Estévez) began at the New York Living Theater and debuted on the screen in 1967. He was named as best actor at the San Sebastián (Spain) Film Festival for his role in *Badlands* (1973). His more than seventy other films include *The Incident* (1967), *The Subject Was Roses* (1968), *Catch-*22 (1970), *The Cassandra Crossing* (1977), *Apocalypse Now* (1979), *That Championship Season* (1982), *Gandhi* (1982), *The Dead Zone* (1983), *Enigma* (1983), *Man, Woman and Child* (1983), *The Guardian* (1984), *Firestarter* (1984), *Broken Rainbow* (1985), *The Believers* (1987), *Wall Street* (1987), *Da* (1988), *Judgment in Berlin* (1988), *Beverly Hills Brats* (1989), *Cadence* (1991, which he also directed), *Hearts of Darkness: A Filmmaker's Apocalypse* (1992), *Gettysburg* (1993), *Hear No Evil* (1993), and *The Grey Knight* (1993). His most recent role was as J. Edgar Hoover in *Judas and the Black Messiah* (2021). Sheen's television performances are also numerous, with his most famous role as the president of the United States in the long-running series *The West Wing* (1999–2006). He was also the narrator on scores of socially and politically committed documentaries. Sheen received a Golden Globe, two Screen Actors Guild awards, and has a star on the Hollywood Walk of Fame as of 1989.

Jimmy Smits (1955–)

Born on July 9, 1955, in Brooklyn, New York, to a Puerto Rican mother and a Surinamese father, Jimmy Smits received a B.A. from Brooklyn College in 1980 and an M.F.A. from Cornell University in 1982. By 1984 he had broken into television, playing the role of Eddie Rivera in *Miami Vice* (1984), and this led to a long career of acting in television drama series, many of which were related to policing and the law. He gained wide exposure as Victor Sifuentes on the long-running TV series *L.A. Law* (1986–92) and Bobby Simone on *NYPD Blue* (1994–98, 2004). He also had major roles in *Sons of Anarchy* (2012–14), *The Get Down* (2016–17), *Brooklyn Nine-Nine* (2016–17), and *How to Get Away with Murder* (2017–18). He was the star of the short-lived *Bluff City Law* (2019). Smits has appeared in more than twenty major films, including *The Old Gringo* (1989), *Vital Signs* (1990), *Switch* (1991), *My Family* (1995), *Star Wars* episodes 2 and 3 (2002, 2005), *Rogue One* (2016), and *In the Heights* (2021). His awards include a Primetime Emmy (1990), a Screen Actors Guild Award (1995), a Golden Globe (1995), and a Satellite Award (1999). In 2001 he won the Academy Award for Best Supporting Actor in the film *Traffic*, becoming the fourth living actor to win an Oscar for portraying a character who mostly speaks a non-English language.

Benicio del Toro (1967–)

Born on February 19, 1967 in San Germán, Puerto Rico, Benicio del Toro (Benicio Monserrate Rafael del Toro Sánchez) moved with his family to Pennsylvania when he was fifteen. After high school he studied business administration at the Univerity of California, San Diego, but dropped out to study acting at the Circle in the Square Acting School in New York City, among other places. Del Toro's first bit roles were on television in the 1980s, mostly playing thugs and drug dealers. Del Toro's breakthrough came in 1995 with his performance in *The Usual Suspects*, for which he won an Independent Spirit Award for Best Supporting Male. He won the award again the following year for *Basquiat* (1996). In 2000 for his role in *Traffic*, he won an Academy Award, a BAFTA Award, a Golden Globe, and two Screen Actors Guild Awards. In 2008 for his role in *Che*, which he also produced, he won the Cannes Film Festival Award for Best Actor. Del Toro's filmography is extensive, with more than twenty films since 1988, including the superhero films *Thor: The Dark World* (2013), *Guardians of the Galaxy* (2014), and *Avengers: Infinity War* (2018). At this writing, his latest film is *The French Dispatch* (2021).

Lupe Vélez (1908–1944)

Born on July 18, 1908, in San Luis Potosí, Mexico, Lupe Vélez (María Guadalupe Vélez de Villalobos) became one of the most famous Latina screen actresses of all time. Originally a dancer, she debuted in film in 1926 under Hal Roach's direction and became a star the following year as the leading lady in *The Gaucho* opposite Douglas Fairbanks. Known as a fiery leading lady, both in silent and sound films, she later made positive use of her Spanish-accented English to reposition herself as a comedienne in the Mexican Spitfire series. Her films include *Stand and Deliver* (1928), *Lady of the Pavements* (1929), *The Squaw Man*

(1931), *The Cuban Love Song* (1931), *Hot Pepper* (1933), *The Girl from Mexico* (1939), *Mexican Spitfire* (1940), and *Redhead from Manhattan* (1943).

Raquel Welch (1940–)

Raquel Welch (Jo Raquel Tejada) was born on September 5, 1940, in Chicago to a Bolivian-born engineer and a mother of English background. Despite a very difficult and inauspicious beginning, and thanks to a phenomenally successful 1963 publicity tour in Europe, she became a major international star without having appeared in a single important film. Known first as a voluptuous sex goddess, she subsequently made a name as a comedienne. Her films include *A Swingin' Summer* (1965), *One Million Years B.C.* (1966), *The Biggest Bundle of Them All* (1968), *Bandolero!* (1968), *100 Rifles* (1969), *Myra Breckinridge* (1970), *Kansas City Bomber* (1972), *The Three Musketeers* (1974), and *Mother, Jugs, and Speed* (1977). In her later years she played various roles in TV movies and series. In 1974 she won a Golden Globe for her role in *The Three Musketeers,* and in 1994 she received a star on the Hollywood Walk of Fame.

Daphne Zúñiga (1962–)

Born on October 28, 1962, because of her European looks Daphne Zúñiga was able to avoid being typecast in Latina roles. She made her debut in a slasher film, *The Dorm That Dripped Blood* (1982), and went on to appear in numerous feature films and TV movies over four decades. Her credits include acting in *The Initiation* (1983), *The Sure Thing* (1985), *Vision Quest* (1985), *Modern Girls* (1986), *Spaceballs* (1987), *The Fly II* (1989), *Eyes of the Panther* (1990), *Prey of the Chameleon* (1991), *Mail Order Bride* (2008), *Gone Missing* (2013), *Witness Unprotected* (2018), *Christmas in Paradise* (2019), and numerous others. She was a regular in the long-running TV series *Melrose Place* (1992–96, 2009–10).

Gary D. Keller and Nicolás Kanellos

MUSIC

Music is a form of cultural communication. Music transmits shared feelings and values, and when words are added, it can be the ideal vehicle for communicating ideologies. The most strongly symbolic or cultural musical forms are connected to a people's deepest sentiments about their way of life. They express the most profound feelings that those people have about their sense of identity and their everyday life rhythms. Most important, organic, culturally powerful music is generally "homegrown," in the sense that it is created by and belongs to the communities that perform it. Many forms of musical expression will be explored in this chapter, from early folk traditions to the contemporary scene.

◆◆◆

LATINO MUSICAL CULTURAL EXPRESSION

Among Latinos in the United States, several musical forms and styles fall into the category of organic, homegrown musical communication. They symbolize the most powerful cultural beliefs and ways of doing things for specific segments of the Latino community. They speak to challenges and problems that confront the various segments of the Latino community in the United States. Over many years these musical forms and styles have developed into cultural traditions that enjoy deep and widespread popularity among their respective audiences. *Música norteña*, the Mexican American *orquesta*, and salsa are excellent examples. These traditions have all contributed in important, organic ways to the cultural life of the Latino groups with which they are historically associated. They represent major musical developments whose cultural power is linked to fundamental forces—social, economic, and ideological—among the various segments of the Latino community. These and other musical forms and styles speak symbolically to such issues as acculturation, intercultural conflict, and socioeconomic differences within the Latino communities.

Among the most important Latino musical creations are two ensembles that originated among the Mexicans in Texas. These are *música norteña*—known among Mexican Texans, or *tejanos*, as *conjunto*—and *orquesta tejana*, or simply *orquesta*. Both of these musical styles originated in the first half of the twentieth century, and both should be seen as musical responses to important economic, social, and cultural changes that took place among the Mexican Texans beginning in the 1930s. Both *conjunto* and *orquesta* had become major musical styles by the 1950s, and their influence had spread far beyond the Texas borders by the 1970s.

A type of Afro-Caribbean music that came to be known in the 1970s as salsa is another major style of Latino music in the United States. Just as *conjunto* and *orquesta* are homegrown Mexican Texan styles, salsa likewise is the unique music of Afro-Latinos from Puerto Rico, Cuba, and the Dominican Republic. It too is organically linked to the people who created it, and it continues to occupy a central position in the musical life of Afro-Latino people in the United States.

Two important types of vocal music are the Mexican *corrido* (ballad) and a hybrid between the *corrido* and the *canción* (song). These occupy a special place in the musical life of Mexican Americans, especially those living in Texas, New Mexico, Arizona, and California. The *corrido* and the *canción-corrido* hybrid emerged as powerful cultural expressions in the Latino Southwest during the twentieth century, especially the years leading up to World War II. Through their lyrics, the *corrido* and *canción-corrido* address more directly than any of the ensemble styles (salsa, *conjunto*, *orquesta*) the social and ideological issues that Latinos face in their often difficult adjustment to American life.

A type of musical ensemble that has made a powerful impact on a large segment of Mexican Americans goes by several names—*grupos cumbieros*, *grupos tropicales*, *grupos modernos*—but it may best be defined as a Mexican working-class variant of so-called *música tropical*. *Música tropical* has a long history in Mexico and Latin America, but this ensemble has a history that coincides with the massive emigration from Mexico in the 1960s. Since that time, the *grupo tropical/moderno* has become an everyday music in the lives of many Mexicans in the American Southwest.

With increased immigration from the Dominican Republic and Central America in the twenty-first century, other forms of Latino music have become popular. One example that has become associated with salsa is *bachata*. Originating in the Dominican Republic in the first half of the twentieth century, like much of Caribbean music, it blends Spanish, Indigenous, and African musical elements. In its twenty-first century evolution, it is a highly urban music produced with electronic guitars, Afro-inspired drums, and *güira* (a steel scraper replacing the acoustic gourd), and varies in beat from *bolero* to *merengue* rhythm.

Urban Latino youth in the twenty-first century have devoured hip-hop and rap, freely improvising rap poetry bilingually to Latino-inflected music, changing beats and styles to reflect the meaning of lyrics, which often express the gangster culture of drugs, misogyny, and violence. Its greatest influence is African American hip-hop, and it has spread throughout

Singer Andre Veloz (center) of the Dominican Republic performs with the Amargue Bachata Quintet at the Richmond Folk Festival in 2015. Bachata music and dance originated in the Dominican Republic in the early twentieth century.

the Spanish-speaking world, from Tierra del Fuego to Alaska. In Puerto Rico, the hip-hop influenced *reggaetón* developed and spread to New York and elsewhere. It is related to hip-hop and includes rap and singing in Spanish to Caribbean-inflected music.

THE *CORRIDO* AND *CANCIÓN-CORRIDO*

The *corrido* and *canción* are two distinct genres that have at times experienced considerable overlap, especially since the 1920s. The overlap occurs when the *corrido* sheds some of its most familiar features, such as the call of the *corridista* to his audience and mention of the date, place, and cast of characters. At the same time, many *canciones* composed during and after the 1920s abandon that genre's most recognizable feature—its lyrical quality—and assume a seminarrative form, thus moving them in the direction of the *corrido*. The result is a convergence of the two genres. Of course, this convergence is never complete; some *corridos* retain enough of their "classical" narrative features to stamp them unmistakably as *corridos*, while most *canciones* remain purely lyrical expressions, usually about love.

Beginning in the 1920s, *canción-corrido* hybrids made their appearance in the Latino Southwest. Not coincidentally, it was at this time that the large American recording labels, such as Columbia and RCA, first moved into the Southwest and began to commercially expose Mexican American music in all its variety. Not coincidentally, either, the first of the famous Mexican American troubadors—singers of the *canción* and *corrido*—attained widespread popularity throughout the Southwest during the 1920s. Many of these troubadors were composers of the *canción-corrido* as well. Through the 1940s they produced a steady flow of *canciones-corridos* that depicted life in the Latino Southwest with great feeling and accuracy, describing in vivid detail both the sadness and the humor of life in the borderlands. Especially moving are those compositions that address the long-standing conflict between Anglos and Mexicans and the oppression endured by the latter.

The intervention of the major recording labels energized musicians and propelled a number of musical traditions to a higher level of innovation. Notably, until the arrival of the wax disk, singers and their songs tended not to attain recognition beyond their immediate locale. Some of the ancient songs had, indeed, spread throughout the Southwest over the previous centuries, but newly composed songs, as well as their composer-performers, were usually confined to their immediate point of origin.

The major labels changed all that. In 1926, RCA, Columbia, Decca, and Brunswick began setting up makeshift studios in rented hotel rooms in cities like Dallas, San Antonio, and Los Angeles, and with the help of local entrepreneurs who knew the pool of musicians available, they began to record commercially a wide variety of musical forms, including the evolving *música norteña,* various *orchesta*-like ensembles, and, of course, the *canción* and the *corrido*. Women made their impact on Mexican American music at this time, with one female troubador in particular attaining immense popularity throughout the Southwest—the venerable Lydia Mendoza. Other popular troubadors include Los Hermanos Bañuelos (The Bañuelos Brothers, the first to record with the major labels, in 1926) and Los Madrugadores (The Early Birds), both groups from Los Angeles, as well as Los Hermanos Chavarría (The Chavarría Brothers) and Gaytán y Cantú (Gaytán and Cantú), from Texas.

These troubadors left a rich legacy of *canciones-corridos* that attests to the creative energy the Mexican Americans devoted to a music that could document the harshness of their daily life. This music was so poetically charged that its cultural power can be felt to this day. "El deportado" (The Deported One), a *canción-corrido* recorded by Los Hermanos Bañuelos in the early 1930s, depicts the bitter experiences of a Mexican immigrant in his encounter with the cold, exploitive system of American capitalism.

> The intervention of the major recording labels energized musicians and propelled a number of musical traditions to a higher level of innovation.

Another *canción-corrido* hybrid, "El lavaplatos" (The Dishwasher), also recorded by Los Hermanos Bañuelos, recounts in more humorous language the adventures of a poor Mexican who immigrates to the United States in search of the glamorous life of Hollywood, only to find himself drifting from one back-breaking job to another.

Composers of the 1920s through the 1940s were exceptionally committed to documenting the enduring hardships for Mexicans. They utilized the *canción-corrido* extensively. But the *corrido* itself plays an even more central role, which dates back to the nineteenth century, in articulating the sociopolitical position of the Mexican folk vis-à-vis the dominant classes. The climate of intercultural conflict that grew out of the Anglo invasion and subsequent annexation of what became the American Southwest at the end of the Mexican-American War (1848) was the ideal setting for the birth of an expressive culture that would key in on this conflict.

> The hero *corrido* invariably features a larger-than-life Mexican hero who single-handedly defies a cowardly, smaller-than-life gang of Anglo-American lawmen. The hero either defeats the Anglos or goes down fighting.

Modern *Corridos*

Between 1848 and 1860, the modern *corrido* emerged out of an ancient musico-literary form that had been introduced from Spain in the sixteenth century—the romance. And it was evidently in Texas, and not in Michoacán, Durango, or Jalisco, as once thought, that the first *corridos* were composed. One of these was "Kiansis," a *corrido* that documents the epic cattle drives from Texas to the Kansas stockyards, which contains subtle indications of the intercultural conflict that attended Anglo-Mexican relations at the time.

"El *corrido* de Juan Cortina" details in stronger language the resentment that Mexicans on the border felt toward the Americans, and celebrates the exploits of Juan Nepomuceno Cortina. He was a Mexican from South Texas, a member of a wealthy landowning family with deep roots in the Texas-Mexico border region who came to resent the arrogant attitude of the Anglo newcomers, especially the fortune makers.

After an incident in which he accosted a town marshal who was pistol-whipping a vaquero (cowboy) who worked on his mother's ranch, Cortina was declared an outlaw, and thereafter he dedicated his life to guerrilla warfare, until he was driven out of Texas by the U.S. cavalry.

"El *corrido* de Juan Cortina" ushered in what has been called the hero *corrido* period, when the prevalent type was the *corrido* of intercultural conflict. This type of *corrido* invariably features a larger-than-life Mexican hero who single-handedly defies a cowardly, smaller-than-life gang of Anglo-American lawmen. The hero either defeats the Anglos or goes down fighting. In this way, the protagonist gains heroic status in the Mexican American community, becoming, in effect, a kind of redeemer for the collective insults suffered by his people at the hands of the Anglos.

Hero *corridos* were written until the 1920s in Texas and elsewhere, including such classics as "Joaquín Murrieta and Jacinto Treviño," but perhaps the most memorable is "El *corrido* de Gregorio Cortez," immortalized by Américo Paredes in his book *With His Pistol in His Hand*, which served as the basis for the film *The Ballad of Gregorio Cortez*. The *corrido* documents the odyssey of a Mexican Texan who fled for his life after he killed an Anglo sheriff in self-defense following a linguistic misunderstanding over some stolen horses.

The hero *corrido* was most prevalent during the early period of Anglo-Mexican contact. This period spans the years from about 1848 to the early 1900s—a period during which Mexicans entertained hopes, albeit diminishing with time, that they could still defeat the Anglos and drive them out of their territory. However, the hero *corrido* continued to enjoy prominence until the 1930s, when a new type emerged.

The new *corridos,* prevalent since the end of World War II, have been labeled victim *corridos* and demonstrate sharp differences in subject matter from those of the earlier period. Foremost is the disappearance of the larger-than-life hero. In his place a new protagonist emerges, one who is usually portrayed as a helpless victim of Anglo oppression. This shift in the *corrido* of intercultural conflict from hero to victim is too fundamental to be considered a random event. In fact, it coincides with equally fundamental changes in Mexican American society. It thus happens that the newer *corridos* appeared at the precise moment when Mexican Americans initiated a wholesale movement from rural to urban, from folk to modern, from a monocultural to a bicultural lifestyle, and from proletarian status to a more diversified social organization.

After World War II, in this climate of emergent political and economic diversification, new cultural directions and new modes of interpreting the Mexican American experience were being charted. Fully conscious of their newfound power, the postwar Mexican Americans began to rethink their relationship with the dominant Anglo majority and to demand more economic and political equality (as well as acceptance). However, despite the tentative beginnings of an interethnic accommodation, the Anglos were not yet ready to accept the Mexicans as equal, and the intercultural friction persisted. This friction at times forced Mexican Americans to put aside growing internal class differences as they closed ranks to fight racial discrimination. In this atmosphere of heightened political awareness, the *corrido* continued to play an important role. Chicanos (Mexican Americans), having developed more effectively organized political machinery to challenge Anglo supremacy, relied on their *corridos* less to uplift a battered cultural image and more to rally support for active political causes. A *corrido* is more likely to elicit an active response—outrage and group mobilization—if it depicts a helpless victim rather than a potent, larger-than-life hero. In a sense, the two types of *corrido* are antithetical—one reflecting pent-up frustration and powerlessness, the other active resistance.

Many victim *corridos* have been composed since the end of World War II. Typically, the Anglos openly abuse the basic rights of a Mexican, and the community responds vigorously to defend the victim. The *corrido* draws attention to the community's forceful actions in protesting Anglo injustice, and when the outcome permits, the *corrido* celebrates the community's victory. In any case, the Anglos are portrayed in a negative light, while the Mexicans are seen as a proud people fighting for their civil rights.

Both the hero and victim *corridos* of intercultural conflict have a long and auspicious history in the Mexican American oral music tradition. As indicated, the former was prevalent at a time when conflict between Anglo and Mexican was rampant and undisguised. The hero *corrido* peaked in the early twentieth century, when the Mexican Americans reached the lowest point in their history of oppression in the United States. As they climbed out of their wretched state, during and after World War II, the victim *corrido* appeared and gained ascendancy. Both types of *corrido* have survived into the late twentieth century, but their presence in the musical repertory of Mexican Americans today is sporadic. They tend to surface only during moments of intercultural crisis—usually when the still-dominant Anglos commit a blatant act of discrimination.

MÚSICA NORTEÑA

Of all the musical creations of the Latino community in the United States, *música norteña* (also known as the Mexican Texan *conjunto)* is unquestionably one of the most culturally powerful. Anchored by the diatonic button accordion, this folk tradition had grown deep roots among the Mexicans living along the Texas-Mexico border by the early twentieth century. Thanks to the commercialization introduced by the major American recording labels in the 1920s, it eventually spread far beyond its origins in South Texas and northern Mexico.

How a music of such humble folk origins could develop into a powerful artistic expression with such widespread appeal is a provocative question. The answer lies in its beginnings along the Texas-Mexico border. The diatonic button accordion was evidently introduced into northeastern Mexico sometime in the middle of the nineteenth century—perhaps by German immigrants who settled in the Monterrey, Nuevo León, area of northeastern Mexico in the 1860s. Since the Mexican Texans of this period maintained close cultural links with Mexican *norteños* (northerners), it is likely that the instrument quickly spread into South Texas. It is possible, however, that the accordion was introduced to the *tejanos* (Mexican Texans) by way of

CALIBRE 50

The popular Mexican conjunto group Calibre 50 performs in Texas in 2016. Música norteña, or conjunto, is a folk tradition anchored by the diatonic button accordion.

the German, Czech, and Polish settlers who had migrated to south central Texas beginning in the 1840s. Since intense conflict, marked by overt discrimination against Mexicans, was the norm between *tejanos* and the latter groups, it is less likely that the interchange occurred on that front. In any case, the exact identity of the donor culture may never be known.

What we do know is that by the late nineteenth century, the accordion, coupled with one or two other instruments—the *tambora de rancho* (ranch drum) and the *bajo sexto* (a twelve-string guitar)—had become the norm for music-and-dance celebrations in South Texas. The *tambora* was a primitive folk instrument fashioned out of native materials. It was usually played with wooden mallets, their tips covered with cotton wrapped in goatskin. The *bajo sexto* apparently origi-

nated in the Guanajuato-Michoacán area in Mexico; it is a twelve-string guitar tuned in double courses. How it migrated to and established itself in the border area is a mystery. But in its new locale, it became an indispensable companion to the accordion, especially after 1930, when it and the accordion emerged as the core of the evolving ensemble.

The *conjunto norteño*, or *conjunto*, as it came to be known in Texas, thrived from early on. It soon became the preferred ensemble for the rural working-class folk who adopted it and eventually molded it into a genuine working-class expression. In its early days it relied on the salon music introduced from Europe in the eighteenth and nineteenth centuries and popularized first among the genteel city dwellers, then passed on to the masses later. The principal genres were the polka, the *redowa*, and the *schottishe*, although the *mazurka* was also current. Rounding out the repertoire was the *huapango*, culturally important because it was native to the Gulf Coast region of Tamaulipas and northern Vera Cruz, and thus represented a regional contribution. The huapango is more frequently associated with the music of the huasteca region of southern Tamaulipas, Mexico, where it has a ternary pulse built around a 3/4 meter. As performed by *norteños*, however, the *huapango* early on acquired a binary pulse built around the triplets of 6/8 meter.

Despite the presence everywhere of the accordion in the musical celebrations of the *tejanos/norteños*, the *conjunto* did not achieve dominance until the 1930s. Prior to this time it was still an improvised ensemble with little stylistic development and plenty of competition from other types of (also improvised) ensembles. In fact, the history of the Mexican Texan *conjunto* can be divided into three distinct stages. The first, to the late 1920s, is the formative, when the ensemble was strictly improvisational and the accordion was still played either solo, with guitar or bajo sexto, or with the *tambora de rancho*. The technique used to play the accordion itself owed much to that of the Germans who had originally introduced the instrument to the Mexicans. This included the heavy use of the left-hand bass-chord buttons, a technique that lent the instrument a distinctive sound and articulation. As noted, this embryonic ensemble was common to Mexicans on both sides of the border.

The second stage begins in the mid-1930s, when the Mexican Texan *conjunto* began to move beyond its counterpart across the border—gradually at first, radically after World War II. The sudden development of the *conjunto* during the second stage is undoubtedly linked to intervention of the large American recording labels, which began in earnest in the early 1930s. At this time RCA Victor (through its Bluebird subsidiary), Columbia, and Decca moved into the Southwest and began commercially exploiting the variety of music then flourishing in the region. But the rapid development of the *conjunto* cannot be explained simply in terms of its commercialization, which, in any case, was never as massive as that of general market American pop music. On the other hand, the ethnic/class dichotomy that came to dominate the political culture

of Mexican Texans after the 1930s was certainly a powerful catalyst.

Thus, by the mid-1930s, when accordionist Narciso Martínez began his commercial recording career, the first steps had been taken toward cementing the core of the modern *conjunto*—the accordion–bajo sexto combination. These two instruments would become inseparable after this time. Meanwhile, Martínez, who is acknowledged as the "father" of the modern *conjunto*, devised a new technique for the instrument, one that differed radically from the old Germanic style. He stopped using the left-hand bass-chord buttons, leaving the accompaniment to the bajo sexto, which was very capably played by his partner Santiago Almeida.

The resulting sound was dramatically novel—a clean, spare treble and a staccato effect that contrasted sharply with the Germanic sound of earlier *norteño* accordionists. The Martínez style quickly took hold and became the standard that younger accordionists emulated, particularly those who established themselves after World War II.

The years immediately following the war ushered in the third stage in the *conjunto*'s development. A younger group of musicians began charting a new direction for the rapidly evolving style. Foremost among these was accordionist Valerio Longoria, who was responsible for several innovations. Among these were two elements of the modern *conjunto* that Longoria introduced—the modern trap drums and the *canción* ranchera, the latter a working-class subtype of the Mexican *ranchera*, which dates from the 1930s. Obsessed with abandoned men and unfaithful women, the *canción* ranchera has always had special appeal for male patrons of *conjunto* music. Since it was often performed in the 2/4 meter of the traditional polka favored by Mexican Texans, the ranchera quickly replaced the polka itself as the mainstay of the modern *conjunto*. Longoria's introduction of the drums and ranchera earned him a special leadership position in the unfolding style, and several younger *conjunto* musicians have cited his example as the source of their inspiration—Paulino Bernal and Oscar Hernández, to name two of the best.

Paulino Bernal is himself a major figure in the development of the modern ensemble. His *conjunto* is hailed as the greatest in the history of the tradition, an honor based on the craftsmanship and the number of innovations attributable to El Conjunto Bernal. The latter include the introduction of three-part vocals and the addition of the larger chromatic accordion. El Conjunto Bernal's greatest distinction, however, lies in its ability to take the traditional elements of the *conjunto* and raise them to a level of virtuosity that has not been matched to this day. Bernal had accomplished all of this by the early 1960s.

Meanwhile, after about 1960, the *conjunto* and the older *norteño* ensemble across the Rio Grande began to converge, as the *norteños* came under the influence of their *tejano* counterparts. Especially responsible for this convergence was Los Relámpagos del Norte (The Northern Lightning Bolts), a group led by accordionist Ramón Ayala and bajo sexto player Cornelio Reyna. Ayala and Reyna were strongly influenced by El Conjunto Bernal.

Los Relámpagos began recording for Bernal's Bego label in 1965 and within two years had risen to unparalleled fame on both sides of the border. The group remained unchallenged until the mid-1970s, when Ayala and Reyna went their separate ways. Ayala shortly organized his own *conjunto*, Los Bravos del Norte (The Northern Brave Ones), and that group went on to dominate the *norteño* market for at least a decade.

Since the innovations of the 1960s, the *conjunto* has turned decidedly conservative, with both musicians and patrons choosing to preserve the elements of the style as these were worked out in the 1940s through the 1960s. Despite its conservatism, the tradition has expanded phenomenally, in the 1970s to 1990s spreading far beyond its original base along the Texas-Mexico border. In the last few years, the music has taken root in such far-flung places as Washington, D.C., California, and the Midwest, as well as the entire tier of northern Mexican border states and even in such places as Michoacán and Sinaloa. In its seemingly unstoppable expansion, *conjunto* music has always articulated a strong Mexicanized, working-class lifestyle, thus helping to preserve Mexican culture wherever it has taken root on American (and Mexican) soil.

The rapid rise and maturation of *conjunto* music is a remarkable phenomenon in itself, but more important from an anthropological perspective is its cultural significance, its strong organic connection to working-class Mexicans in the United States. Clearly, the music is anything but a casual item of entertainment among its supporters. In fact, as a musical expression, the *conjunto* has become a symbolic emblem of Mexican working-class culture—those people employed in farm labor and other unskilled and semiskilled occupations found mostly in service industries. And the *conjunto*'s alliance with that class was cemented during its rapid evolution between the years 1936 and 1960.

Beyond this identification with the working class, in the years following World War II the *conjunto* became linked to the cultural strategies of Mexican Texans, in particular, as these proletarian workers faced continuing prejudice from a hostile Anglo population as well as antagonism from a new class of upwardly mobile, acculturated Mexican Texans, who sought to put some distance between themselves and the more Mexicanized common workers.

> The rapid rise and maturation of *conjunto* music is a remarkable phenomenon in itself, but more important from an anthropological perspective is its cultural significance, its strong organic connection to working-class Mexicans in the United States.

In the end, *conjunto* music came to symbolize the struggle of the workers to maintain a sense of social solidarity and cultural uniformity against the upwardly mobile Mexican Americans, who espoused a different musical ideal, in the form of the *orquesta* or big band, and who viewed *conjunto* music as the expression of a vulgar, unassimilatable class of people. This quality of *conjunto*—its strong endorsement by the common workers and repudiation by more affluent people—was particularly evident in its Mexican Texan home base, but it was carried over to new locales, such as Arizona, where it was derisively called *catachún* music, and California, where it was universally considered cantina "trash."

THE MEXICAN AMERICAN *ORQUESTA*

Three types of *orquestas* have been present in the Southwest at different periods in the last century. The earliest type is one that existed during the nineteenth century and the early part of the twentieth. This early ensemble, built primarily around the violin, was hardly an *orquesta*. It was for the most part an improvised ensemble, one dependent on the availability of musicians and scarce instruments for composition.

The rudimentary nature of this early *orquesta* is linked to the marginalization of the Mexicans of the Southwest—their having been stripped of all political and economic stability by the Anglo-Americans who invaded the territory and eventually annexed it to the United States. Having become American citizens by default, the new Mexican Americans found themselves at a decided disadvantage—as did all Mexican immigrants who came after them. The original settlers were gradually dispossessed of all their lands and forced into a state of subordination, setting a pattern that would apply to all those who migrated to the Southwest in the twentieth century. José Limón, the noted Mexican American folklorist, has summarized developments in the Southwest following the American invasion:

Between 1848 and 1890, an Anglo ranching society established itself among the native (also ranching) Mexican population, living with them in a rough equality. However, beginning in the 1890s, a clear racial-cultural stratification and subordination began to emerge, as a new wave of Anglo-American entrepreneurs and farming interests established a political and economic hegemony over the native population as well as the thousands of Mexican immigrants entering the area after 1910. With few exceptions, this total population became the victim of class-racial exploitation and mistreatment.

Given their precarious social organization as a subordinate group in the new social order that was created in the Southwest, the resident Mexicans (now Mexican Americans) and all those who came afterward found it difficult to maintain any but the most rudimentary of musical traditions. To be sure, the *norteños* had never enjoyed the best of facilities for any kind of education, musical or otherwise. Throughout the Spanish colonial era and the period of Mexican independence, life in the north had been of a peasant, agrarian nature, with few of the amenities that Mexicans in more centralized and urban areas enjoyed. Despite their relative isolation, the *norteños* managed to keep up with musical developments in Mexico and, as early chroniclers have documented, were able to maintain reasonably equipped ensembles.

With the American invasion and the subsequent oppression of the native Mexicans, the opportunities for musical training all but disappeared, except in urban areas along the border, where the Mexicans preserved a degree of political and economic integration even after the annexation of the Southwest by the United States. Thus, cities like Brownsville, Laredo, and El Paso managed to support modest resources for the training and equipping of musical groups. But in general, the American invasion reduced an *orquesta* tradition inherited from Greater Mexico to its bare and often improvised essentials—a violin or two plus guitar accompaniment, with other instruments added on an ad hoc basis.

The 1920s saw the emergence in the urban areas of better-organized *orquestas*, built, again, around the violin. This was the so-called *orquesta típica* (typical orchestra). The first *típica* was organized in Mexico City in 1880, and it was supposedly modeled after an earlier folk *orquesta* common in Mexican rural areas throughout the nineteenth century (also known as *típica*) and apparently similar in instrumentation to the folk *orquestas* of the Latino Southwest. The self-styled *orquestas típicas* of urban origin were clearly expressions of what is known as *costumbrismo*, a type of romantic nationalism in which the dominant groups find it appealing to imitate certain elements of the folk, or peasant classes. As such, these *orquestas* were given to wearing "typical" *charro* (cowboy) outfits similar to those worn by the Mexican mariachi, in an effort to capture in vicarious fashion some of the flavor of Mexican pastoral life.

In the United States, the first *típica* was probably organized in El Paso or Laredo sometime in the 1920s. These *orquestas* were strongly reminiscent of the modern mariachi, whose historical roots they may well

An orquesta típica *led by violinist Julio de Caro, c. 1920.*

share. The basic instrumentation of the *orquesta típica* consisted of violins, guitars, and psalteries, although in the Southwest other instruments were often added in ad hoc fashion. The size of the *típica* could vary from four or five musicians to as many as twenty.

Típicas were enlisted for almost any occasion, although they were ideally suited for patriotic-type celebrations, such as *Cinco de Mayo* (Fifth of May, when the Mexican general Ignacio Zaragoza postponed the French invasion of Mexico by defeating General Charles de Lorencez at Puebla) and *Dieciséis de Septiembre* (sixteenth of September, Independence Day), two dates of special significance for Mexican people. The repertoire of *orquestas típicas* consisted of aires nacionales—tunes that over the years had acquired status as "national airs," such as "El Jarabe Tapatío" (The Jalisco Dance), "La Negra" (The Dark Beauty), "Pajarillo Barranqueño" (Little Bird of Barranca), and others. *Típicas* seem to have fallen out of favor among Mexican Americans during the Great

Depression of the 1930s. They disappeared from the musical scene in the Southwest during World War II.

The 1930s saw the emergence of the third and most important type of *orquesta*, this one a version of the modern dance bands that swept through the urban landscapes of both Mexico and the United States during the 1920s and 1930s. The modern *orquesta* clearly represented a musico-cultural departure from earlier ensembles. In fact, it is tied to the fortunes of a new group of Mexican Americans who began to make an impact on Latino life in the United States during the 1930s and 1940s. Historian Mario García has aptly labeled this group the Mexican American Generation. This was the first generation of Americans of Mexican descent to aspire for inclusion in Anglo-American life. Consequently, it advocated the ideology of assimilation, an ideology based on the notion that Mexican Americans should detach themselves from their Mexican heritage and begin thinking like Americans. However, the persistent conflict with the Anglos and their continuing discrimination against Mexicans ultimately forced the Mexican American Generation to modify its ideology of assimilation and adopt a more biculturalist stance—to be both Mexican and American.

> Ever since the birth of the modern Mexican American *orquesta*, the most renowned names have come from Texas.

The modern *orquesta* played a prominent role in accommodating the Mexican American Generation's biculturalist strategy. In the bimusical repertoire it adopted, the *orquesta* catered to the generation's bicultural nature. By performing music traditionally associated with Mexico and Latin America, it kept alive the Mexican Americans' ethnic roots; by performing music associated with American big bands, it satisfied the Mexican American Generation's desire to assimilate American culture. Thus, from Mexico and Latin America came the *danzón, bolero, guaracha, rumba*, and other dance genres; from the United States came the boogie, swing, foxtrot, and so on.

Very quickly, however, the Mexican American *orquesta* began to experiment with various bimusical combinations—especially the *orquestas* in Texas, which, like the *conjunto*, assumed a leadership role in music developments in the Latino Southwest after World War II. As a result of their increasing exposure through commercial recordings (Texas had the biggest Latino recording companies), the most professional *orquestas típicas* became the models that others around the Southwest imitated. Coincident with this professionalization was the appearance and popularization of the public ballroom dance, which allowed the most successful *orquestas* to rely exclusively on performance for full-time employment.

Thus, ever since the birth of the modern Mexican American *orquesta*, the most renowned names have come from Texas. There was, for example, Beto Villa, from Falfurrias, Texas, sometimes called the "father" of the Mexican American *orquesta*. Acclaimed for a folksy, ranchero polka that took the Southwest by storm, Villa deftly juxtaposed this "country" style polka, which came to be known as Tex-Mex, against more sophisticated genres drawn from Latin America and the United States—danzones, guarachas, foxtrots, and swings.

Villa's influence on *orquestas* throughout the Latino Southwest was enormous during the 1940s and 1950s, and he inspired many imitators. A notable successor to the Tex-Mex tradition Villa inaugurated was Isidro López, also from Texas. A singer-saxophonist, López deliberately emphasized the ranchero mode of performance in an attempt to attract a larger share of the common workers, who were otherwise more faithful to the ever more powerful (and more *ranchero*) *conjunto*. López was thus the first *orquesta* leader to add the working-class *canción* ranchera to the *orquesta* repertoire. But he added his own touch to the *ranchera*, embellishing it with a blend of mariachi and Tex-Mex that López himself dubbed Texachi.

At least two other *orquestas* of note were active during the 1940s and 1950s—Balde González's, from Victoria, Texas, and Pedro Bugarín's, from Phoenix, Arizona. The former specialized in a smoother, more romantic delivery that appealed in particular to those upwardly mobile *tejanos* who were seen by working-class people as snobbish and who were derisively known as *jaitones* (from high tone). As such, González, a pianist-singer, was best known for the smooth delivery of the romantic and sophisticated bolero, although he often turned as well to the American foxtrot, which he transformed by adding lyrics in Spanish. Bugarín pursued a more eclectic approach, one that included the full gamut of bimusical performance, from *rancheras* to foxtrots.

In the Los Angeles area, meanwhile, a number of *orquestas* operated during the maturational years of the Mexican American *orquesta*—the 1940s and 1950s. Most of these took their cue from music developments in Latin America (including the Afro-Caribbean) and were less influenced by developments in the Tex-Mex field. One noteworthy exception was the *orquesta* that the legendary Lalo Guerrero fronted for a time. As Guerrero himself admitted, he "mixed it all up," combining Tex-Mex with boogie and Latin American, including salsa. But Guerrero was best known for his unique bimusical tunes, which fused music and linguistic elements from swing, rhumba, and caló, a folk dialect popular among working-class youth in the Southwest and elsewhere. Most of these tunes were written by Guerrero himself. Some achieved immortality through the movie *Zoot Suit*, produced in 1982 by Chicano filmmaker and erstwhile activist Luis Valdez (for example, the tune "Marihuana Boogie").

But the most influential *orquestas* continued to originate in Texas. In the 1960s and 1970s, which may well have been the peak years for the Mexican American *orquesta*, several groups emerged from the active tradition established in the Lone Star State. Foremost among these was Little Joe and the Latinaires, renamed Little Joe y la Familia in 1970. La Familia exploited the Tex-Mex ranchero sound fashioned by Isidro López to its utmost, fusing it to American jazz and rock within the same musical piece to achieve a unique bimusical sound that came to be known as La Onda Chicana (The Chicano Wave).

Little Joe first experimented with the fusion of Mexican *ranchero* and American jazz/rock in a hugely successful LP titled *Para la Gente* (For the People), released in 1972 by Little Joe's own company, Buena Suerte Records. On this album, Little Joe and his brother Johnny combined their voices duet-fashion to create a style of ranchera so appealing to Mexican Americans that La Familia was catapulted to the very top of La Onda Chicana. Backing Little Joe and Johnny was the usual complement of instruments found in

the best-organized Mexican American *orquestas*—two trumpets, two saxophones, a trombone, and a rhythm section of bass, electric guitar, drums, and keyboards.

The music selections on the landmark LP varied from the hard, brash sounds of traditional Tex-Mex *rancheras*, like "La Traicionera" (The Treacherous Woman), to the lush, big-band sounds of the Mexican foxtrot, as in "Viajera" (Traveler), to an interesting arrangement of an old folk song, "Las Nubes" (The Clouds). The last tune mentioned seemed to capture the cultural essence of La Onda Chicana and its obvious link to the cultural revivalism of the Chicano political and cultural movement that swept through the Mexican American community in the late 1960s and early 1970s. Thanks, at least in part, to the nationalistic climate fostered by the Chicano movement, "Las Nubes" became a sort of anthem for Chicano music celebrations everywhere.

Many of the arrangements on the *Para la Gente* album were augmented with strings borrowed from the Dallas Symphony—a great novelty in itself—but most effective of all was the strategic interlacing of jazz riffs within the rancheras. The effects were stunning and captured the music sentiments of bicultural Mexican Americans everywhere. The impact of this trailblazing LP was so great that in the early 1990s, almost twenty years from the time it appeared, several of its tunes still formed part of the basic repertory of semiprofessional weekend dance *orquestas* still to be found in the Southwest.

By the mid-1980s, La Onda Chicana had receded from its watershed years, with the *orquesta* tradition generally suffering a noticeable decline. Not only did further innovation come to a stop, but the style suffered a retreat from its golden years of the 1960s and 1970s. The most notable sign of decline was the substitution, beginning in the early 1980s, of the horn section for synthesized keyboards. At first, these tried to imitate, synthetically, the sound of the trumpets, saxes, and trombone, but eventually the keyboards developed their own synthesized sound, one closer in spirit to the *conjunto*, and this became the norm after about 1985.

The reasons for the decline of the *orquesta* are not entirely clear, but they evidently have to do with the aging of the population that originally gave impetus to the *orquesta* tradition—the strongly bicultural Mexican American Generation and its immediate successors, the baby boomers born in the late 1940s and early 1950s. Except in Texas, where an entrenched tradition survived into the 1990s, Mexican Americans growing up in more recent years have been less attracted by the old-fashioned *orquesta*. The lack of support can be seen in the declining number of semiprofessional *orquestas* throughout the Southwest, as DJs and the smaller synthesizer-dependent groups have replaced the *orquesta* in most public and domestic celebrations.

The popularity of the Mexican American *orquesta*, as well as its social power, is directly linked to the cultural economy of the Mexican American Generation and its immediate successors. From the outset, *orquesta* served as a link between the generation's ideology and its political economy. Unlike *conjunto*, which early on became a mirror for working-class life and the workers' resistance to the pressures of acculturation, *orquesta* was as culturally flexible as its clientele. In its early years, however, especially the 1940s and 1950s, the *orquesta* was rather tentative in its approach to bimusical performance— the mixing of American and Mexican styles. At a time when his clientele was still unaccustomed to its new-found prosperity and biculturalism, a Beto Villa could at best choose between one or the other: he could play a Tex-Mex polka or an American swing but never the two simultaneously. In time, as the Mexican Americans adapted to their bicultural reality, *orquesta* performed a parallel synthesis—what we might call "compound bimusicality."

By the 1970s, this compound bimusicality had reached full expression in the *orquesta*'s mastery of the art of musical code switching. Similar to the "compound bilingual," who code switches from one language to another within the same sentence, *orquesta* had learned to switch musical languages within the same musical sentence, that is, within the same musical piece. This is what Little Joe truly accomplished for the first time on his landmark album, *Para la Gente*.

> Similar to the "compound bilingual," who code switches from one language to another within the same sentence, *orquesta* had learned to switch musical languages within the same musical sentence.

He succeeded in fusing two musical systems under one code of performance. This feat was repeated with equal success by many other *orquestas* in the succeeding years.

But the musical code switching of the Mexican American *orquesta* was even more subtle than the linguistic code switching of its supporters, in that it took place on two distinct but overlapping planes. One switch occurred at the level of ethnicity, the other at the level of class. At the level of ethnicity, the switch was signified by the interlacing of jazz riffs within the flow of an otherwise Mexican *ranchera*. At the same time, this switch was mediated by parallel shifts occurring at another level of acoustic discrimination— class stylistics, or what Mexican Texans used to distinguish between a *jaitón* (high-tone) versus a *ranchero* style. The former was a marker for alleged (or contrived) musical sophistication, but above all it was an index for "high class" snobbery. *Ranchero*, on the other hand, was a token for the simple, unpretentious life of the country and the barrio— a token the Mexican American Generation was reluctant to renounce.

Above all, in its bimusicality the Mexican American *orquesta* represents the dialectical synthesis of two sets of opposed cultures—Mexican and American on the one hand, working and middle class on the other. This synthesis was masterfully articulated by the bimusical *orquesta*. The best were perfectly adept at this double code switching, as they moved effortlessly from *ranchero* to *jaitón* and from Mexican to American. At their very best, *orquestas* achieved a seamless stream of bimusical sound that found a fitting label—La Onda Chicana.

SALSA

Salsa is Spanish for "sauce"—in this case a term that refers to the hot, spicy rhythms of Afro-Caribbean music. When people talk about salsa music, however, they are actually referring to a generic term that includes a number of distinct types of Afro-Caribbean music, although one in particular, the *son guaguancó*, has predominated since the 1960s. Whatever the origins of the term *salsa*, the music has deep, even sacred, roots in its Afro-Caribbean context.

In a fine study of a religious musical ritual in the Dominican Republic called *salve*, Martha Ellen Davis informs us that the *salve* is a bimusical expression that, as usually performed, progresses from a purely Hispanic section (the *salve sagrada*) to a more intense, spontaneous, and Africanized section (the *salve secular*). The latter section incorporates many of the rhythms (and polyrhythms) of a generalized Afro-Caribbean music that was eventually distilled in the United States into what is now commonly known as salsa. Davis interprets the bicultural nature of the *salve* as the logical result of the syncretization of two radically different cultures in a historical relationship of domination/subordination—Hispanic and African.

What is most important about Davis's analysis of the *salve* is her conception of this ritual as a key symbol of Afro-Caribbean culture, specifically, its location at the center of the Afro-Dominicans' musical universe. As an expression of an Afro-Caribbean music that is rooted deep within the practice of everyday culture, the *salve* provides a powerful example of the essentially sacred origins of Afro-Caribbean music. This is a sacredness that Americans of Afro-Caribbean descent who subscribe to various offshoots of that music—including salsa—have been reluctant to give up.

Thus, in his 1974 study of the ritual aspects of Afro-Cuban music among Cubans and Puerto Ricans of New York City, Morton Marks argues that despite the commercialization of the music, strong elements of African Yoruba religion have survived in at least some of its development in urban areas such as New York City. In Cuba, these Yoruba elements were syncretized early on with Catholicism to create the Lucumí religious cults, while in New York, Yoruba religion survives in the Santería cults, which, again, combine in their worship deities from both Catholic

and Yoruba religions. For Marks, moreover, the interplay of musical styles, as they unfold within a given song (like the *salve*, usually progressing from a Hispanic form of communication to an African one), is the centrally defining characteristic. Thus, in analyzing the songs "Alma con Alma" (Soul with Soul), by the great salsa singer Celia Cruz, and "El Santo en Nueva York" (The Saint in New York), by La Lupe, a Cuban vocalist, Marks proposes that "the process of 'Africanization' underlies the performance, with the musical form proceeding from a strongly North American–influenced dance band style, into an emically named Yoruba and Lucumí praise song style known as *kasha*."

The transformation described by Marks is, in fact, the hallmark of most salsa music since the 1960s. In piece after musical piece, particularly the vast majority that utilize the *son guaguancó*, the music begins with a standardized Latino section whose lyrics are divided into an "A" part, followed by a "B," then returning to the "A" part (ABA form). Meanwhile, the musical background, usually provided by brass instruments (trumpets and/or trombones) in obbligato mode, displays the strong influence of American jazz. Once this section is completed (often it is the shortest section of the tune), the *son montuno* section begins. It is in this section that the African style predominates, particularly through the call-and-response pattern, in which a solo and chorus keep alternating phrases.

> When people talk about salsa music, they are actually referring to a generic term that includes a number of distinct types of Afro-Caribbean music.

Afro-Caribbean music, then, has dual roots, Hispanic and African, which in the United States have undergone further development with the infusion of jazz elements as articulated in the horn obbligatos. In its duality, the music richly displays the process of syncretization, although it has also maintained a dialectical relationship to its twin roots—a relationship that enables the participants in musical events to juxtapose one cultural domain against the other with dramatic effects. This is the point that both Marks and Davis are at pains to demonstrate. In the United States, meanwhile, Afro-Caribbean music has preserved much of this duality, despite the jazz accretions and heavy commercialization. Here, too, among initiates of Santería cults the music retains the ritual qualities and the dialectical movement between two cultures that are associated with sacred performances in the homeland.

Clearly, for people of Afro-Caribbean descent—Puerto Ricans, Cubans, Dominicans, Coastal Colombians, Venezuelans, and others—what is now called salsa has that kind of summarizing power. Salsa stands preeminently for their special sense of Afro-Latino "Caribbeanness." But salsa obviously has an audience that extends far beyond its core Caribbean setting. As a cultural symbol, it spreads out with diminishing influence toward audiences whose contact with the music's cultural roots is at best casual. Among these audiences the music's symbolic power is highly diluted or even nonexistent.

The dual origins of salsa recall that its antecedents are hybrid or syncretic expressions that draw from two cultures: Hispanic and African. Modern salsa owes its greatest debt to the musical culture of Cuba, although Puerto Rico and, to a lesser extent, the Dominican Republic are also contributing cultures. Two Puerto Rican musical genres, in particular, are legitimate antecedents of modern salsa—the *bomba* and the *plena*. The *plena* is more heavily influenced by European musical culture than the *bomba*.

Both the *plena* and the *bomba* were once integral elements in the life of Puerto Rican Blacks. They are still performed on the island, though with decreasing frequency. In the United States, however, *plena* and *bomba* have undergone some transformation. Adopted (and adapted) by small salsa *conjuntos* (such as Julito Collazo and his Afro-Cuban Group), *bomba* and *plena* have reached larger audiences, even as some of their elements are absorbed by salsa itself.

Cuba is the indisputable cradle of modern salsa, although in the United States the music is more intimately associated with Puerto Ricans. In Cuba, Africans established strong enclaves that carried on many of the musico-ritualistic traditions from the homeland, specifically those attached to the Lucumí cults mentioned earlier. Secularized and made popular com-

mercially in the twentieth century, Afro-Cuban music attached to the Lucumí/Santería cults underwent further hybridization with Western musical forms. In its hybrid form, this music acquired strong stylistic features that came to appeal to millions of people outside the original cultural core.

It was out of this hybridization process that salsa emerged. However, salsa represents the end stage of this process. Earlier Afro-Cuban forms enjoyed their own moments of glory, as the pace of hybridization accelerated in the middle part of the twentieth century. In this, Cuba again took center stage. John Storm Roberts has described this hybridization as follows: "Taken as a whole, Cuban music presents a more equal balance of African and Spanish ingredients than that of any other Latin country except Brazil. Spanish folklore enriched the music of the countryside, of the city, and of the salon. At the same time—aided by an illicit slave trade that continued right through the nineteenth century—the pure African strain remained stronger in Cuba than anywhere else.... As a result, Western African melody and drumming ... were brought cheek by jowl with country music based on the Spanish ten-line *décima*."

It should come as no surprise that Cuba is the source of many of the musical genres that precede salsa—genres that in fact make up the tapestry of its sounds. Thus, important salsa antecedents such as the *danzón, rumba-guaguancó, charanga, mambo, guaracha, son, bolero,* and *cha-cha-cha* all originate in Cuba. The *mambo* and *cha-cha-cha* had an enormous impact in and of themselves, of course, but the two genres that most influenced modern salsa directly are the *son* and the *rumba.*

The *rumba* is actually a generic term for more specific Afro-Cuban genres—the *yambú, cumbia,* and *guaguancó.* Again, of these three, it is the *guaguancó* that is most closely identified with salsa. All, however, have common African characteristics—complex polyrhythms and alternating sections of solo voice and call-and-response. Originally, the *rumba* was played with African or Africanized instruments of the drum

> Modern salsa owes its greatest debt to the musical culture of Cuba, although Puerto Rico and, to a lesser extent, the Dominican Republic are also contributing cultures.

family—the *quinto*, *segundo*, and *tumba*, reinforced by *cáscara* (a pair of sticks struck against each other) and *claves* (a pair of smooth, cylindrical hardwood sticks struck against each other). Today the drum rhythms are executed on conga drums, but the *clave* effects remain essentially unchanged in modern salsa.

The *son*, meanwhile, describes more of a feeling than an actual musical form. It is, however, identifiable by the strong rhythmic patterns associated with it. Most notable among these is the anticipated bass, which is unique to Afro-Cuban music generally, and salsa in particular. The *son* emerged among Africans in the Cuban countryside and spread to the urban areas early in the twentieth century. It was in the latter areas that the *son* combined with European instruments to create its modern hybrid form. Earlier Africanized instruments were replaced by such European ones as the contrabass, trumpet, and guitar, although the basic percussion was necessarily retained—the bongos, *claves*, and the guitarlike *tres*. One of Cuba's greatest popular musicians, and the "father" of modern salsa, Arsenio Rodríguez, is credited with further upgrading the *son* ensemble in the 1930s. He did this by adding a second trumpet, conga drums, and, most important, a piano.

Rodríguez also anticipated some of the greatest modern *salseros* (salsa musicians) by moving away from the romantic themes of earlier *sones* and incorporating texts that addressed nationalist and social issues. Other important figures from the early period of Afro-Cuban music include Ernesto Lecuona, whose group the Lecuona Cuban Boys recorded for Columbia, and Arcano y sus Maravillas (Arcano and His Marvels), a *charanga* orchestra that was responsible for Africanizing this erstwhile Europeanized ensemble.

The *orquesta charanga* is an interesting phenomenon in Afro-Cuban music history. Until the 1930s, this group espoused a genteel, Europeanized sound that appealed to middle-class Whites. Its instrumentation consisted of lead flute and violins. Arcano moved to make his group conform more to an African style by adding percussion, such as the bongo and conga drums. It has been suggested that Arcano y sus Maravillas actually led the way in the emergence of the phenomenally popular *cha-cha-cha*. The king of that genre, however, was La Orquesta Aragón (The

Aragón Orchestra), a group popular from the 1940s through the 1960s, whose incomparable style of *cha-cha-cha* endeared the music to millions of Latinos across Latin America and the United States.

Meanwhile, several individuals who later went on to make their mark on modern salsa music actually played with *charanga* groups in the 1940s and 1950s. These included such well-known figures as Charlie Palmieri, Johnny Pacheco, and Ray Barreto. Along with a host of other salseros, these individuals brought a vitally evolving musical tradition to the United States, where both African- and European-oriented groups experienced a strong cross-fertiliza-

By the late 1950s performers such as Tito Puente (honored on a U.S. postage stamp), Tito Rodríguez, and Machito had laid the stylistic framework for the modern salsa sound.

tion with jazz—a fertilization that resulted in the final emergence of salsa.

Thus, by the late 1950s key performers, such as Tito Rodríguez, Tito Puente, and Machito, had laid the stylistic framework for the modern sound. In fact, when we listen to Rodríguez's recordings from the late 1950s, we cannot but be impressed with how similar his *rumbas* and *guaguancó* are to latter-day salsa, even though the music was not recognized as such until the 1970s. Meanwhile, the style and instrumentation were strengthened in the 1960s and 1970s by a host of great performers, which included such memorable names as Willie Colón, Eddie Palmieri, and El Gran Combo (The Great Combo), as well as vocalists like Héctor Lavoe, Celia Cruz, and Rubén Blades. The last is particularly recognized for the poignant social themes that his lyrics often contained.

Born on July 16, 1948, in Panama City, Panama, Rubén Blades received all of his early education and his bachelor's degree there. In 1985 he was awarded a law degree from Harvard University. Despite beginning life in both Panama and the United States as a lawyer, Blades has become an outstanding singer and composer of salsa music, receiving four Grammy Awards and numerous gold records.

By the mid-1960s, the modern salsa sound had pretty much crystallized. And its most basic genre remained the *son/rumba/guaguancó* complex, as it had been synthesized by Tito Rodríguez and others in the 1950s. Since the 1960s, this amalgamation of genres, which goes by the label "salsa," has served as the core for numerous explorations that have expanded the parameters of the music. Thus, as Jorge Duany wrote, "The main pattern for salsa music remains the *son montuno,* built on the alternation between soloist and chorus." Moreover, like the *son,* salsa's "characteristics are a call-and-response song structure; polyrhythmic organization with abundant use of syncopation; instrumental variety with extensive use of brass and percussion and strident orchestral arrangements … and, above all, a reliance on the sounds and themes of lower-class life in the Latin American barrios of U.S. and Caribbean cities."

All these elements had been worked out by Tito Rodríguez and other Afro-Caribbean performers by the late 1950s. Since that time, at its most basic level the music has remained faithful to those elements. And, as always, in its most intimate contexts the music still evokes strong feelings of African identification among its most devoted followers—some of whom belong to Santería cults. At the very least, the music provokes feelings of pride and a strong identity among the people whose culture it symbolizes. As salsa pianist Oscar Hernández observed, "There's a nationalistic sense of pride when people hear salsa. They say, 'That's our music.' It gives people a sense of pride in their Ricanness and Latinoness." And, at a more general level, salsa serves as a kind of pan-Latino link that unites many Latinos under one musical banner.

LATIN JAZZ/LATIN ROCK

Two important musical cousins of salsa are Latin jazz and Latin rock. The former is closely associated with the development of salsa music in the United States, although it represents a more self-conscious effort to link Afro-Caribbean with Afro-American music. One can argue, however, that Latin jazz possesses neither the cultural breadth nor depth of salsa, although it clearly represents some of the most experimental efforts in the whole field of Latino music. Outstanding among these efforts are those of Cuban *conguero* (conga player) and vocalist Chano Pozo, whose association with American jazz trumpetist Dizzy Gillespie produced such Latin jazz gems as "Algo Bueno" (Something Good), "Afro-Cuban Suite," and "Manteca" (Lard), the latter a piece that received high marks for its successful blend of Afro-Caribbean and Afro-American styles.

Included among the standouts in the Latin jazz/rock movement is Chick Corea, who apprenticed with Afro-Cuban greats Mongo Santamaría and Willie Bobo. Meanwhile, Latin jazz's relative, Latin rock, has also had considerable impact on Latinos in the United States. Carlos Santana, the indisputable king of Latin rock since the 1960s, has continued to exploit a wide array of Afro-Cuban rhythms, fusing them to American rock to create a highly innovative style. Santana has inspired many imitators over the years, especially in California, where his music has had exceptional influence on young Chicanos.

Again, it can be argued that Latin jazz and rock lack the cultural power of salsa, *norteño*, or *orquesta*. Fundamentally, they are creations of the commercial market and hence must be considered "superorganic" or "second-order" expressions, as opposed to salsa's organic, first-order links to the Afro-Caribbeans. Nonetheless, the contributions of the individuals mentioned, as well as those by such noted figures as José Feliciano, Cal Tjader, and others, cannot be underestimated. In sum, although offshoots of salsa, Latin jazz and rock lack the status of a strong symbol like that of salsa, which emanates from the deepest levels of Afro-Caribbean culture. Neither Latin jazz nor rock can make that claim, of course; they are not "wired" into the core of any particular culture. For this, however, they should not be dismissed as transitory. Despite their cultural limitations, the degree of innovation in both Latin jazz and rock has been remarkable, and at times the popularity of Latin rock, especially, has had considerable impact on general market American music.

> As it has evolved in recent years, the *grupo tropical/moderno* often features four instruments—keyboard (originally an electric organ, later synthesizer), electric guitar, electric bass, and trap drums.

MÚSICA TROPICAL

Música tropical has historically referred to any music with a "tropical" flavor, that is, any music identified with the tropics, usually the Afro-Caribbean rim. In the present instance, it is not an entirely accurate label, since the ensemble that represents this type of music—the *grupo tropical/moderno*—is not necessarily "tropical" in character. Aside from the fact that one of its musical mainstays is the *cumbia*, a dance originally from the tropics of Colombia, the *grupo tropical/moderno* need not feature any of the percussion instruments normally associated with *tropical*, that is, Afro-Caribbean, music. And, in fact, the *grupo tropical* is known today as much for its emphasis on another popular genre, *música moderna* (or *romántica*), as it is for the *cumbia*.

As it has evolved in recent years (the group was originally more "tropical" in that it featured instruments such as the conga drums and the *güiro*, or scrapergourd), the *grupo tropical/moderno* often features four instruments—keyboard (originally an electric organ, later synthesizer), electric guitar, electric bass, and trap drums. It originated in Mexico in the 1960s and then spread to the United States via the heavy Mexican immigration that has occurred during the last sixty years or so.

The *grupo tropical*'s mainstay, the *cumbia*, was originally a Colombian folk dance that in the twentieth century became urbanized and diffused commercially throughout Latin America. Upon reaching Mexico in the mid-1960s, the *cumbia* was appropriated by the working-class masses at about the same time that the four-instrument ensemble was emerging as a favorite dance group among urban working-class Mexicans. This ensemble came to be associated with *cumbia* music (*música tropical*) in Mexico and the American Southwest. At about the same time, however, a slow-dance genre, influenced by American rhythm and blues, surged in popularity in Mexico—the *balada* (from the American pop "ballad," a lyrical love song). Popularized by such groups as Los Angeles Negros (the Black Angels), Los Terrícolas (the Earthlings), and others, the Mexican *balada* came to be known generally as *música romántica* (or *moderna*—the two terms are interchangeable), and in time most grupos *tropicales/modernos* began to alternate between the *cumbia* and the *balada* to fill out their repertoires.

Besides Los Angeles Negros (who seldom performed the *cumbia*), the best-known exponents in the relatively short span of *música tropical/moderna* in Mexico and the United States have been Rigo Tovar (who was of Afro-Caribbean ancestry), Los Bukis (the Bukis), Los Sonics (the Sonics), Los Yonics (the Ionics), and Los Temerarios (the Fearless). Besides their reliance on record sales for financial support, most of the commercially popular *grupos tropicales/modernos* also rely on personal appearances at large public dances. At these dances the *cumbia* reigns supreme, although, again, most groups depend to one extent or another on the *balada*, which, with its slow 4/4 or 6/8 meter, offers a contrastive alternative to the usually up-tempo, lighthearted spirit of the *cumbia*.

Almost nothing has been written about the Mexican *grupo tropical/moderno*, which since the 1970s has been undisputed king among certain working-class segments of Mexican society. By musical standards, it is an unspectacular style, one that is dwarfed by both salsa and La Onda Chicana. But it exerts a powerful influence on the millions of Mexican proletarians who subscribe to it. In the United States, one has only to attend certain ballrooms in cities such as Los Angeles, San Jose, Phoenix, or El Paso to observe the enormous drawing power that groups such as Los Bukis, Los Yonics, and others command, especially among the undocumented and recently documented immigrants from Mexico.

> Latinos are widely diverse, yet they share one common characteristic: all of them, due to their Afro-Indo-Latino background, have experienced conflict with the dominant Anglo-European majority. The various Latino music forms have served to mediate this conflict.

Latinos are a widely diverse group of people, yet they share one common characteristic: all of them, due to their Afro-Indo-Latino background, have experienced varying degrees of conflict with the dominant Anglo-European majority. The various Latino music forms have served to mediate this conflict, despite their differences in style and cultural function. It is the legacy of conflict and accommodation that channels Latino musical creation and the proliferation of culturally powerful traditions. As the various sectors of the Latino population continue to confront, accommodate, and otherwise amalgamate with the Euro-American majority and the Afro-American minority, we may expect more musical experimentation and new traditions.

"CROSSOVER DREAMS"

Ever since the large-scale commercial production and exploitation of Latin music from the 1930s through the 1960s, musicians, record companies, and publishers have dreamed of introducing the music and making it a staple of mainstream popular music in the large United States market. From the 1930s on, such pioneers as Providencia García worked diligently over decades to sign up the leading composers of Spanish American music, from throughout the Hemisphere—including those residing in New York and Miami—to make Peer Southern Music the largest publisher of Latin music ever and still today the largest rights holder of that music in the world. For the most part, the music most successful in bridging the gap between "American" pop and Latin was that derived from Afro-Latin Caribbean music, which had its crossover heyday in the late 1940s through the 1960s with mambo and cha-cha crazes and performers who crossed into previously out-of-bounds night clubs, performance halls, and popular media. Beginning in the 1940s, Xavier Cugat's orchestra was featured in Hollywood films, in the 1950s Pérez Prado's mambos were broadcast on radio everywhere, and for decades Desi Arnaz was belting out "Babalu" while playing the conga in prime-time television on *I Love Lucy*; and such top-of-the-charts singers such as Nat "King" Cole and Dean Martin scored the hits "Green Eyes" ("Aquellos Ojos Verdes," 1959) and "Sway," ("Quién Será," 1958) that have become pop standards playing on movie soundtracks, elevator tapes, and big band revivals. The Mexican American polkas, waltzes, "banda," and "tropical" never experienced such mainstream acceptance, nor did many of the small producers, far from the New York and Miami publishers and studios, really aspire to such watering down of their music for a mass audience. However, the salsa composers and performers in New York, Miami, and the Caribbean from its musical apogee in the 1970s and 1980s always had crossover dreams, so much so that top-selling artist Rubén Blades helped produce and starred in a modest Hollywood movie titled *Crossover Dreams* (1985), though, like the popularity of the film's fictional protagonist, it crashed. Salsa is still going strong in Latino communities today, and although non-Latinos may dance to an occasional number at a wedding

Gloria Estefan and the Miami Sound Machine popularized Latino music performed in English. Let It Loose *(1987) was their tenth studio album.*

or a club or exercise to "Zumba," true salsa has never made it into mainstream pop.

If there has been any "crossover" at all it has been that of individual Latino/a artists, both foreign and domestic, and occasionally their orchestras, such as the Miami Sound Machine. In the late twentieth century, during the growing diversity of the U.S. population and the concomitant rise of second-generation Latinos, there has been a greater openness to Latino recording artists who sing predominantly in English—at times with occasional Spanish-language cuts on their albums or even an entire album, such as Linda Ronstadt's *Canciones de Mi Padre* (1987)—while providing a Latin or multicultural tinge to their pop performances. Ronstadt was able to bring out her Spanish-language album only after establishing her ability to sell millions of records in English as an American pop star who was not recognized as a Mexican American artist. It was Gloria

Estefan, however, performing with the Miami Sound Machine in the late 1970s and in the 1980s, who truly broke through for Latina artists performing in English, especially with her 1987 hit, "Primitive Love." Only after establishing her pop identity in English was she able to introduce material in Spanish and the light-salsa hit "Conga" (1985). Estefan blazed the path that Jennifer López and even foreign record stars, such as Shakira, would follow into the new century. Jennifer López (J-Lo), who broke into movies in *Selena* (1997) and subsequently was able to star in numerous Hollywood productions as a sexy Latina, had the power to cross over as a pop singer and dancer, touring worldwide. If J-Lo was at one point considered the sexiest actress in movies, the Spaniard Julio Iglesias's producers parlayed his handsome looks and sultry voice into reviving the Latin lover stereotype in music, which he was able to exploit in English-language albums since signing with

CBS International in 1979 and going on to sell the most records of any Spanish singer in history. It was not until the late 1990s that this feat was repeated by a U.S. Latino, Ricky Martin, whose breakthrough single of "Livin' La Vida Loca" (Living the Crazy Life) on his eponymous album and his handsome looks made him the new heartthrob of female fans.

It should be noted that much of Latin music caters to a particular ethnic community and its culture in the language and the styles that are traditional; reaching their communities is quite enough for most Latin composers and performers. Also, there are hugely popular performers who have not been tempted to cross over, such as Mexicans Luis Miguel and Thalía, Spaniard Alejandro Sanz, and Los Tigres del Norte, a group that is binational U.S.-Mexican— all of whom have a giant following and have made millions of dollars in the United States.

THE CONTEMPORARY MUSIC SCENE

From the early 1990s on, Latin music in the United States has enjoyed a profound expansion, including increased recording sales, a steady growth of Spanish-language radio stations, and newfound crossover success by several artists of diverse Latino backgrounds. While the growing Latino population helped drive the market's expansion in general, a major force fueling these changes in particular is the nation's Latino youth, whose economic and political influence is being watched, studied, and interpreted by major corporations, including Pepsi and Coca Cola, Budweiser and Miller Lite, Levi's jeans and Stetson hats, and any number of smaller, regional companies.

In all genres, from *tropical*, salsa, and *Tejano* to Latin pop and *reggaetón*-hip hop, new young stars have entered the market with success. In *tropical* and salsa, fresh faces such as Rey Ruiz, Jerry Rivera, Marc Anthony, and Los Fantasmas del Caribe have commanded top-draw status and record sales on their debut and follow-up albums.

In Tejano, Selena and Emilio Navaira led the pack from the top of Billboard's charts to stadium tours to

multiple awards. In Latin pop, excitement was created by newcomers like the pop/dance/rap act the Barrio Boyzz, ballad singer Marcos Llunas, children's pop group Roxie y Los Frijolitos, as well as crossover superstar Shakira, a Colombian, not a U.S. Latina.

Whether the groups are producing fresh, original sounds or simply taking the old and rejuvenating it with new urgent rhythms, the successful young acts in each genre have found the way to attract a new following.

PROMINENT LATINOS IN POPULAR MUSIC

Marc Anthony (1968–)

Singer, songwriter, actor, and record executive Marc Anthony (Marco Antonio Muñiz) was born to Puerto Rican parents in East Harlem, New York City. His father, Felipe, who was a part-time musician, taught him to sing in Spanish and English and to play the guitar. Anthony began his professional career as a songwriter and backing vocalist for pop acts Menudo and the Latin Rascals. By the early 1990s, he was the best-selling salsa musician and among the most important new salsa artists, with his rhythm and blues–inflected, urban sound. By 1995 his album *Todo a su tiempo* won the *Billboard* award for Hot Tropical Artist of the Year, and it was nominated for a Grammy; it went on to win a gold record in the United States and Puerto Rico. From then on, it was one success after another. In 2000 his *Marc Anthony: The Concert from Madison Square Garden* was broadcast on HBO on Valentine's Day. That same year, his album *Contra la Corriente* became the first salsa album to enter the English-language *Billboard* 200 chart. His albums *Otra Nota*, *Todo a Su Tiempo*, and *Contra la Corriente* established him as the top-selling singer in the history of recorded salsa. In 1999, Anthony issued a crossover album in English, which debuted at number eight on *Billboard* and became platinum. Anthony went on to record a number of albums for Sony records that went gold and continued touring the United States and Latin America to sold-out crowds. He has sold more than thirty million albums and is a member of the Billboard Hall of Fame.

Leandro "Gato" Barbieri (1932–2016)

Born on November 28, 1932, in Rosario, Argentina, Gato Barbieri rose to fame during the free jazz heyday in the 1950s and 1970s in the United States, where he distinguished himself as a tenor saxophone player and recorded some thirty albums as a band leader, as well as numerous others as a sideman. Influenced by Charlie Parker and John Coltrane, Barbieri came to prominence in Argentina playing in the Lalo Schifrin band, then was discovered by the jazz scene in the United States. His score for Bernardo Bertolucci's 1972 film *Last Tango in Paris* earned him a Grammy Award. It was in the 1970s that Barbieri began to incorporate South American melodies, instruments, harmonies, textures, and rhythm patterns into his music on such albums as *El Pampero* (Pampas Dweller) and the four-part *Chapter* that explored Brazilian and Afro-Cuban rhythms and textures, as well as Argentine ones, and it was this innovation that brought him fame in the jazz world.

Rubén Blades (1948–)

Born on July 16, 1948, in Panama City, Panama, Rubén Blades (Rubén Blades Bellido de Luna) studied law at the Universidad Nacional de Panamá—in 1985 he earned a law degree from Harvard University—but while studying in Panama he went to New York to record his first solo album, *De Panamá a Nueva York*, in 1970. After graduating in 1974 he moved to New York and became part of the salsa band music culture. He started writing songs for the Fania record label and soon began singing with Willie Colón and other bands. The Colón and Blades album *Siembra* (1978, Sowing) became the best-selling salsa record in history with more than twenty-five million copies sold. On the album, Blades sings his composition "Pedro Navaja," fashioned after "Mack the Knife." In fact, Blades became known as the most cerebral of the salsa composers and performers, attempting to accomplish in salsa what Gabriel García Márquez had achieved in literature; he even recorded an album,

Agua de Luna (1987, Moon Water), based on García Márquez's short stories. As a singer, he has tried to cross over to English but without much success. In all, Blades has recorded more than forty albums, a few of which have won Latin Grammy Awards. The multitalented Blades has also appeared or starred in more than thirty films.

Vikki Carr (1941–)

Born on July 19, 1941, in El Paso, Texas, and baptized Florencia Bisenta de Casillas-Martínez Cardona, Vikki Carr became one of the most successful U.S.-born Latino/a recording artists and international performers in popular music history. After starting her career while still in high school and touring, she signed her first contract with Liberty Records in 1961. She first rose to prominence in Australia and England before making it in the United States. In 1967 she was invited to perform for Queen Elizabeth II and the following year set the record for sold-out concerts in England, France, Germany, Japan, the Netherlands, and Spain. Carr has recorded well over fifty hit albums. In 1985, like many of her Latina sister singers, she issued an album in Spanish, *Simplemente Mujer*. For her Spanish-language records she has won gold, platinum, and diamond records. Her 1989 album, *Esos Hombres*, won gold records in Chile, Mexico, Puerto Rico and the United States. Among her honors are the Los Angeles Times 1970 Woman of the Year, the 1972 American Guild of Variety Artists Entertainer of the Year, and the 1971 Girl Scouts of America awards.

Willie Colón (1950–)

Born on April 28, 1950, in the South Bronx, New York City, Willie Colón (William Anthony Colón Román) began playing the trombone while still a child and was signed by Fania Records when he was only

fifteen. He issued his first album when he was seventeen, and it sold some three hundred thousand copies. As a trombonist and band leader, Colón brought the trombone to prominence in salsa ensembles. He is also a composer, singer, and arranger for his own band and other musicians. He is known for long-time collaborations with such other salsa greats as Celia Cruz, Rubén Blades, and Héctor Lavoe, but his own brand is markedly urban New York, and he knows how to blend in influences from jazz and rock while preserving traditional roots. Colón, who recorded more than sixty albums mostly for Fania and Sony, launched his own label, Willie Colón Presents, in 2017. The following year he went on his first world tour, entitled Rumba del Siglo, which he repeated in 2019 because of its success the previous year. Colón was inducted into the Latin Songwriters Hall of Fame in 2019 and into the International Latin Music Hall of Fame in 2000.

Celia Cruz (1925–2003)

Celia Cruz (Úrsula Hilaria Celia de la Caridad Cruz Alfonso) was born on October 21, 1925, in Havana, Cuba. Although she was Catholic, she was immersed in an Afro-Cuban neighborhood where the Santería religion was popular, and she was able to learn a Yoruba vocabulary from an early age. Beginning in 1947, Cruz studied music theory, voice, and piano at Havana's National Conservatory of Music, and as a teenager she began performing in radio talent contests. From 1947 on, she sang in Havana cabarets, perfecting the vernacular of Afro-Cuban song, and began recording with various bands. Her big break came in 1950 when she became the lead singer for Cuba's famed La Sonora Matancera, the first Black frontwoman for the group. In 1962 while touring in Mexico and the United States with the Matancera, the Cuban government forbid her to return to the island as it had prohibited touring abroad, especially to the United States. From that time on, she resided in the United States as an exile, then became a naturalized citizen and ascended to the throne of "Queen of Salsa." Over the years as single performer, she sang with most of the greatest salsa bands, including with Tito Puente, Johnny Pacheco, and Willie Colón, recorded more than seventy albums, and toured the

world as the most recognizable and acclaimed salsa soloist. In 1994, she received the National Medal for the Arts from President Bill Clinton. In 2003, the Celia Cruz Bronx High School of Music opened in the Bronx. In 2005, the Smithsonian's National Museum of American History opened "¡Azúcar!," an exhibit celebrating the life and music of Celia Cruz. In 2011 a U.S. postal stamp was issued in her honor. In 2015, an eighty-episode docudrama based on Cruz's life, *Celia*, ran on Telemundo.

Xavier Cugat (1900–1990)

Born on January 1, 1900, in Girona, Catalonia, Spain, and raised as a child in Havana, Cuba, Xavier Cugat (Francisco de Asís Javier Cugat Mingall de Bru y Deulofeu) was one of the first band leaders of Afro-Cuban music to achieve wide appeal. After studying the classical violin and serving as first chair in the National Theater's Symphonic Orchestra, he moved with his family to New York in 1915. In the 1920s he led a band that played in Los Angeles's Coconut Grove restaurant. In 1931 his band became the house band for the Waldorf Astoria hotel in New York City, and he led the hotel's orchestra for the next sixteen years. His fame was so widespread that he appeared at the head of his orchestra in almost a dozen Hollywood films into the 1950s, appeared repeatedly on television variety and talk shows, and shared in the success of the crossover Latin music in the mambo and cha-cha-cha eras. From the 1940s to the 1960s Cugat recorded for most of the major labels. His orchestra at one time or another included many famed musicians, such as Desi Arnaz, and was the launching pad for vocalist Dinah Shore.

Emilio Estefan (1953–)

Born on March 4, 1953, in Santiago, Cuba, Emilio Estefan and his father fled the Castro regime for Spain and settled in Miami, Florida, in 1968. An accordion player as a child, Estefan formed the Miami Latin Boys band in 1975, and soon his future star performer and wife, Gloria, joined it. He is widely credited with growing that band into the Miami Sound Machine. He is a producer who has launched and shaped the careers of such artists as Shakira and Ricky

Martin, producing albums for them and the likes of Jennifer López, Jon Secada, Marc Anthony, and many others. In addition, he has produced many musical events for television, including HBO and Showtime, and on Broadway. Estefan was inducted into the Latin Songwriters Hall of Fame in 2014. In 2005 he received a star on the Hollywood Walk of Fame. In 2015, President Barack Obama awarded Estefan and his wife Gloria the nation's highest civilian honor: the Presidential Medal of Freedom.

Gloria Estefan (1957–)

Born on September 1, 1957, in Havana, Cuba, Gloria Estefan (Gloria Fajardo García) fled with her family to Miami in 1959 as refugees from the Cuban Revolution; thus she was educated in American schools and became a U.S. citizen in 1974. She graduated with a B.A. in psychology from the University of Miami in 1979. In 1975 she met her future husband, Emilio Estefan, and joined his Miami Latin Boys band as a vocalist; it soon became the sensational Miami Sound Machine, which backed her growth into one of the longest-reigning stars of pop music in the United States. The big breakthrough came in 1985 with the release of a third album, *Primitive Love*, which launched three top 10 hits on the *Billboard* Hot 100, including the perennial hit "Conga." The song "Hot Summer Nights" was also released that year and was part of the film *Top Gun*. When their next album, 1987's *Let It Loose*, went multiplatinum, Estefan took top billing and the band's name changed to Gloria Estefan and Miami Sound Machine. In 1989 the band's name was dropped, Estefan has been featured as a solo artist since then. In 1993 Estefan released her first Spanish-language album, *Mi Tierra*, which became number one on the Top Latin Albums chart; the album sold over eight million copies worldwide, went multiplatinum in Spain (ten times) and in the United States (sixteen times; Platinum–Latin field), and earned the Grammy Award for Best Tropical Latin Album. In the intervening years to the present, Estefan has released more albums, toured worldwide, appeared on television, and earned more Grammys. Among her many awards, in 1993 she received the American Music Award for Lifetime Achievement, and in 2015 she and husband Emilio received the Presidential Medal of Freedom from President Barack Obama for their contributions to American music.

Luis Fonsi (1978–)

Born on April 15, 1978, in San Juan, Puerto Rico, Luis Fonsi (Luis Alfonso Rodríguez López-Cepero) had formal musical training at Florida State University and even sang with the City of Birmingham Symphony Orchestra but left classical music to pursue a pop career. He subsequently became a top crooner and composer whose singles have sold millions of copies. He recorded his first album, *Comenzaré* (I Will Begin) in 1998, which became a hit in Latin America. Fonsi entered the U.S. *Billboard* Hot 100 for the first time in September 2008 with his song "No Me Doy por Vencido" and stayed there for weeks. But it was the song "Despacito" (Slowly), featuring Daddy Yankee, that gave him worldwide fame, with the music video reaching five billion views on YouTube and the song becoming number one in nearly every Latin *Billboard* chart; it was the most viewed video in the world. In April 2017, the song was given an English remix featuring Canadian singer Justin Bieber; and it reached number one on the U.S. *Billboard* Hot 100. His song "Échame la Culpa" (Blame Me) debuted at number three on the Hot Latin chart and won Song of the Year at the Latin American Music Awards of 2018. In 2019 his album *Vida* (Life) won Latin Pop Album of the Year.

Providencia García (1908–1995)

Born in Arroyo, Puerto Rico, in 1908, Providencia García was the most successful executive in Latin American music publishing during the epoch when much of the standard repertoire was being created by the most famous and lasting composers from throughout Latin America. García was the central figure in recruiting and retaining such never-eclipsed composers as Puerto Ricans Rafael Hernández and Pedro Flores; Mexicans Agustín Lara, Dámaso Pérez Prado, and Lorenzo Barcelata; Brazilian Ary Barroso; Cuban Miguel Matamoros; and numerous other greats for Peer-Southern Music, which became the largest publisher and rights holder for Latin American music in the world. In 1936, García began work as a secretary for Southern Music, which later became Peer International, and within a short period of time became the director of the Latin American section. She served as a safe bridge for Latin American composers, band directors, and musicians to the commercial music industry. In the early days, when composer-performers were living hand-to-mouth by playing in cabarets in New York, San Juan, and Havana, she signed up compositions and even the entire repertoire of such untapped talent as Rafael Hernández, Pedro Flores, Osvaldo Farrés, Consuelo Velázquez, and many others, whose compositions became the standards that today are still the heart of the Peer-Southern Music catalog and considered all-time classics: *Bésame Mucho* (Kiss Me Much), *Frenesí* (Frenzy), *Brazil, Cuando Calienta el Sol* (When the Sun Warms), *Me Lo Dijo Adela* (Adela Told Me), *María Elena, Aquellos Ojos Verdes* (Green Eyes), *Bahia* (the Brazilian town), *Inolvidable Primavera* (Unforgettable Spring), and *Alma Llanera* (Soul of the Plains), among many others. García was also instrumental in facilitating the crossover of Latin American music into mainstream American pop, especially during the years of the mambo and cha-cha-cha crazes in the 1950s and 1960s. García's magic extended to the next generation, when she became an important link in the success of Spanish crooner Julio Iglesias. Over the years García built up and became the director of a network of offices that spanned from New York to the major cities of Latin America to Australia and even Japan. She served as the chief administrator over the regional directors, who were all Hispanic men. As the only woman of stature in the field, she faced indignities and insults with a smile and a great capacity for diplomacy.

Selena Gómez (1992–)

Born on July 22, 1992, in Grand Prairie, Texas, Selena Gómez got her start in entertainment as a child actress on television's *Barney & Friends* and went on to act in Hollywood films and on television, including the popular Hulu series *Only Murders in the Building*. At age sixteen, Gómez was signed by Hollywood Records and formed the pop rock band Selena Gomez & the Scene; the group began releasing albums starting in 2009, at times being interrupted in music production by Gómez's film commitments. With her second studio album, *Revival*, Gómez had three singles in the *Billboard* mainstream top 40 chart, and she embarked on a world tour. In 2019 she released top-selling singles, and her album *Rare* became her third consecutive number-one album on the charts.

"Little Joe" Hernández (1940–)

Born on October 17, 1940, in Bee County, Texas, into an impoverished musical family, "Little Joe" Hernández (José María De León Hernández) got his start at age thirteen playing the guitar for a Tejano Band, the Latinaires. As he came to prominence, the band changed its name to Little Jose and the Latinaires, and today it is known as Little Jose y la Familia. From the 1950s on, the band has performed throughout the Southwest, in Mexico, and abroad as the most famous and successful exponents of Tejano music, although influenced by country, rock, and jazz over the years. Little Joe and his band have recorded more than seventy albums and have won five Grammy Awards. After recording since 1958 with small, regional record labels, Little Joe decided to found his own label in 1968, Buena Suerte Records (Good Luck Records), which survived into the 1980s. In 2020 his biography was published under the title of *¡No Llore, Chingón! An American Story: The Life of Little Joe* (Don't Cry, Big Guy!).

Rafael Hernández (1892–1965)

Born on October 24, 1892, in Aguadilla, Puerto Rico, from the age of twelve Rafael Hernández studied music and learned to play the clarinet, tuba, violin, piano, and guitar; by age fourteen he had moved to San Juan and was playing in the municipal orchestra. In 1917 he moved to New York and was recruited into the Army's all-Black Harlem Hell Fighters musical band. After the war, Hernández stayed in New York City, and in the 1920s he organized a band called Trio Borincano (Puerto Rican Trio) and later a quartet with which he toured throughout the United States and Latin America. In 1932, Hernández moved to Mexico. There, he directed an orchestra and enrolled in Mexico's National Music Conservatory. From a young age he wrote songs, and numerous Latino musicians of all ethnicities performed them. In 1947, Hernández returned to Puerto Rico and became the director of the orchestra at the government-owned WIPR Radio. Throughout, he always composed in a variety of genres, including traditional *danzas*, *zarzuelas*, operettas, guarachas, lullabies, boleros, waltzes, and more, many of which had Afro-Caribbean roots. It is estimated he wrote more than three thousand songs. He was the lyric poet of Puerto Rican emigration and national identity. Schools and public housing projects are named in his honor in New York, New Jersey, and Massachusetts; his likeness is commemorated in a statue in Bayamón; and there is a Rafael Hernández Museum at the Inter-American University campus in San Juan, Puerto Rico.

Enrique Iglesias (1975–)

Born on May 8, 1975, in Madrid, Spain, the son of one of the most famous crooners of all time, Julio Iglesias, Enrique Miguel Iglesias Preysler was six years old when he was sent to live out of danger in Miami when his grandfather was kidnapped. There, he was mostly raised by his nanny, went to private schools, and enrolled at the University of Miami but dropped out to pursue a singing career. Totally bilingual, Iglesias sings in English and Spanish. His first album, *Enrique Iglesias* (1995), won him the Grammy Award for Best Latin Pop Performance. For his second album, *Vivir* (To Live, 1997), Iglesias went on tour, performing to sold-out audiences in sixteen countries. He also toured following his third album, *Cosas del Amor* (Things of Love, 1998), which won for him an American Music Award in the category of Favorite Latin Artist. In 2000 and 2001, respectively, Iglesias

issued two English-language albums, *Enrique* and *Escape*, the latter being his biggest success to date and which he took on tour to fifty venues in sixteen countries, again to sold-out crowds. Iglesias has continued recording, issuing blockbuster albums (ten by 2021) and singles, and touring. Iglesias has won more than two hundred awards, including twenty-three Billboard Music Awards and thirty-six Billboard Latin Music Awards, as well as eight American Music Awards, one Grammy, five Latin Grammy Awards, ten World Music Awards, and six MTV awards.

Jennifer López (1969–)

Jennifer López was born on July 24, 1969, in the Bronx, New York City, to Puerto Rican parents. After she graduated from high school, López's singing and dance talent brought her to perform in live musicals and regional theater. By 1993, she got her first television acting work in a television film and a dramatic series, and by 1995 she had her first starring role in *Money Train*. From there she went on to star in scores of Hollywood films. It was not until 1999 that she followed other Latina crossover artists and recorded her first album as a singer, *On the 6*, with two songs that topped the *Billboard* chart, and soon López became known more as a pop music star than a film star. She went on to continually release hit albums: *J. Lo* (2001), *This Is Me … Then* (2002), *Rebirth* (2005), *Como Ama una Mujer* (2007), *Love* (2009), and so on. In 2011–12 and 2014–16, López was a judge on the weekly television show *American Idol*, which led to even greater popularity, and in 2012 she had the first of her world tours, which highlighted her energetic dancing, spectacular choreography, and powerful voice. In 2013 she was ranked as the fifth-highest-paid woman in music, having earned $45 million. In July 2017 she became the executive producer and judge for *World of Dance*, a televised dance competition series that debuted with 9.7 million viewers. In 2019 López had a sold-out world tour, entitled "It's My Party," grossing an estimated $54.7 million from thirty-eight shows.

Ricky Martin (1971–)

Born on December 24, 1971, in San Juan, Puerto Rico, Ricky Martin (Enrique Martín Morales) first broke into television as a child actor on commercials, and in 1984 he became a member of the famed boy band Menudo. Martin recorded eleven albums with Menudo and left the band in 1989, graduated from high school, and went to Mexico City to perform in a stage musical, *Mamá Ama el Rock* (Mom Loves Rock). The musical was his launching pad, and he was offered a role in a Mexican soap opera that eventually became a film, *Alcanzar una Estrella* (To Reach a Star), starring Martin. In 1990 Sony Discos signed him, and soon he had an album, *Ricky Martin*, and was touring throughout Latin America. Now living in Los Angeles, in 1995 Martin recorded his second album, *A Medio Vivir*, with the single "María," which became a breakthrough hit, and Martin was on his way to becoming a Spanish-language recording phenomenon. He toured worldwide but took time to appear in the Broadway play *Les Misérables*. In 1999 Martin crossed over to English with his album *Ricky Martin*; it debuted at number one on the *Billboard* 200 and sold 661,000 copies in its first week of release, eventually selling more than fifteen million copies. The album's top single, "Livin' la Vida Loca" (Living the Crazy Life), reached number one in many countries around the world and has been Martin's biggest hit. The song has been considered the start of the Latin pop explosion that led to the breakthrough in English of many other Latino singers. With his handsome looks, acting ability, and energetic live performances, Martin soon was not only a pop singing star but also a sex symbol for his English-language female fans. Martin continues to compose, record, perform, and tour; he has sold more than seventy million albums. His awards include two Grammys, five Latin Grammys, five MTV Video Music Awards, three Billboard Music Awards, nine Billboard Latin Music Awards, two American Music Awards, two Latin American Music Awards, and eight World Music Awards.

Ozuna (1992–)

Born on March 13, 1992, in San Juan, Puerto Rico, Ozuna (Juan Carlos Ozuna Rosado) became one of the top reggaeton and Latin trap singers. All of his studio albums have reached the top of the *Billboard* Top Latin Albums chart, selling more than 15 million copies. In 2010 he moved to Washington Heights, New York City, where he learned how to produce and promote his own music videos; he made his first video with a budget of under one hundred dollars. Ozuna issued his first studio album *Odisea* (Odyssey) with Sony Latin in 2017 and began touring nationally and internationally. He went on to release a number of singles and five more albums, garnered two Latino Grammy Awards, and has more than ten songs tallying as many as two hundred million views on YouTube.

Dámaso Pérez Prado (1916–1989)

Born on December 11, 1916, in Matanzas, Cuba, Dámaso Pérez Prado studied classical piano as a child and as young man played piano and arranged songs for a number of bands that played the Cuban cabarets and casinos in the 1940s. In 1949 on the cusp of the mambo craze, Prado moved to Mexico and formed his own band. By the 1950s he had hit singles in the United States, where he relocated, and was touring coast-to-coast riding the popularity of the mambo's crossover to the U.S. mainstream. In 1961, Peer-Southern Music's Providencia García provided Prado with the tune that would be his greatest instrumental hit: "Cherry Pink and Apple Blossom White"—its Spanish original title "Inolvidable Primavera" was usually sung with lyrics. Among Prado's other hits that he composed were "Mambo No. 5," "Mambo No. 8," and "Patricia," all of which still can be heard today. After rock 'n' roll took over pop music in the United States, ending the Latin crossover of that period, Prado continued to perform and tour in Latin America throughout the 1970s.

Tito Puente (1923–2000)

Born on April 20, 1923, in New York City, to Puerto Rican parents, Tito Puente (Ernesto Antonio Puente Jr.) learned to play the piano and the drums as a child and as an adult became one of the most outstanding percussionists in Latin music. After serving in the Navy during World War II, Puente studied conducting, orchestration, and theory at the Juilliard School of Music under the G.I. Bill. Beginning in the 1950s Puente was instrumental in popularizing Afro-Cuban and Caribbean dance rhythms, mambo, son, and cha-cha-cha among mainstream audiences in the United States. Puente's most well-known album, *Dance Mania*, was released in 1958. His most famous composition, "Oye Como Va" (Listen to How It Goes), was a hit not only for him in 1968 but lives on into the present, performed by numerous artists. Puente has received numerous awards and honors; in 1993 he received the James Smithson Bicentennial Medal from the Smithsonian Institution, in 1995 the Billboard Latin Music Lifetime Achievement Award, and in 1997 the National Medal of Arts. Shortly after his death in 2000, East 110th Street in Spanish Harlem was renamed "Tito Puente Way."

Adolfo Quiñones (1955–2020)

Born on May 11, 1955, in Chicago, Illinois, Adolfo Quiñones was raised by a Puerto Rican father and an African American mother in public housing in Chicago and became one of the most notable exponents of street dancing in the United States. Often performing under the name Shabba Doo, he began appearing as a dancer of rock 'n' roll on television's popular *Soul Train* program in the 1970s. His greatest exposure came in the 1984 low-budget film *Breakin'*, starring Quiñones, which surprisingly raked in millions and led to a Hollywood sequel, also starring Quiñones. Soon, Quiñones was appearing on film and television and creating choreography for the likes of Chaka Khan, Madonna, Lionel Richie, and even Michael Jackson. In later years, he operated a dance studio in Los Angeles.

Selena Quintanilla (1971–1995)

Known as the "Queen of Tejano music," Selena Quintanilla was born on April 16, 1971, in Lake Jackson, Texas, into a musical family. In 1981, she and her brother began performing in their father's restaurant in Lake Jackson. But the restaurant failed and the family moved to Corpus Christi, where they started the Selena y Los Dinos band to perform in the *Tejano* market; Selena had to sing in Spanish for her Texas Mexican audiences. Selena's extensive touring schedule caused her to miss quite a bit of school, but she eventually received a high school diploma through correspondence school. In 1984, Selena recorded her first album, *Selena y Los Dinos*, for the ethnic Freddie Records label. In 1985, to promote the album, Selena appeared on the *Johnny Canales Show*, the most popular Spanish-language radio program in the Rio Grande Valley, and her popularity mushroomed. By 1987 she was named the Female Vocalist of the Year at the Tejano Music Awards, which continued for the next nine years. In 1989 Selena signed with EMI Records and released her *Selena* album, which peaked at number seven on *Billboard*'s Regional Mexican Album chart. In 1991 her single "Buenos Amigos" peaked at number one on *Billboard*'s Top Latin Songs chart. Selena's breakthrough album came in 1992: *Entre a Mi Mundo*, which peaked at number one on the U.S. *Billboard* Regional Mexican Albums chart for eight consecutive months and went platinum. *Entre a Mi Mundo* became the first *Tejano* album by a female artist to sell over three hundred thousand copies. Her next album, *Live!*, was named Album of the Year in 1994 by the *Billboard* Latin Music Awards. Her album *Amor Prohibido*, with its top-selling singles "Amor Prohibido," "Bidi Bidi Bom Bom," "No Me Queda Más," and "Fotos y Recuerdos," was among the best-selling U.S. albums of 1995 and went platinum thirty-six times over. *Billboard* magazine ranked *Amor Prohibido* among the most essential Latin recordings of the previous fifty years and included it on its list of the top one hundred albums of all time. In 1995, EMI and the Quintanilla family were preparing Selena's crossover to the English-language pop music market when she was murdered by the manager of her boutique, Yolanda Saldívar.

Linda Ronstadt (1946–)

Born on July 15, 1946, in Tucson, Arizona, to a Mexican American father and an Anglo-American mother, Linda Ronstadt started singing in the mid-1960s with a folk-rock trio, the Stone Poneys, in the San Francisco Bay area. In 1969 she released *Hand Sown … Home Grown*, one of the first alternative country records by a female recording artist. Later with such albums as *Heart Like a Wheel*, *Simple Dreams*, and *Living in the USA*, Ronstadt became the first female "arena class" rock star. She set records as one of the top-grossing concert artists of the decade. She remained one of the top female vocalists in the 1970s, and in the 1980s her success continued with multiplatinum albums such as *Mad Love*, *What's New*, *Canciones de Mi Padre*, and *Cry Like a Rainstorm, Howl Like the Wind*. *Canciones de Mi Padre* (1987) was a Spanish-language album homage to the famous Luisa Espinel, her aunt who had achieved singing fame throughout the Southwest in the 1920s and 1930s. The double-platinum album won a Grammy for Best Mexican American Performance in 2001. Ronstadt, who many affirm broke ground for female rock stars, becoming the most popular female vocalist in the 1970s and 1980s, developed a degenerative condition known as progressive supranuclear palsy, which resulted in the loss of her singing voice, and retired in 2011.

Carlos Santana (1947–)

Born in Autlán, Mexico, on July 20, 1947, the son of a mariachi musician, Carlos Santana is one of the few Latino rock musicians to maintain a career for decades among the top performers in American pop music. He was already playing stringed instruments as a child when the family settled in San Francisco, California. In 1966 he founded the Santana Blues Band, which played a blend of Latin-infused rock, jazz, blues, salsa, and African rhythms. When Columbia Records signed the band in 1969, the group's name was shortened to Santana. Shortly before releasing its first album, *Santana*, the band played at the Woodstock Festival and gained great exposure. Its second album, *Abraxas*, included two of Santana's most enduring and well-known hits, Tito Puente's "Oye Como Va" (Hear How It Goes) and "Black Magic Woman/Gypsy Queen"; the album

spent six weeks at number one on the *Billboard* chart and platinumed four times over by 1986, indicating its long popularity. After much internal turmoil in the 1970s and moving more toward jazz, the band continued with various performers under Santana's lead and remained popular through the 1990s without the wholesale success of the earlier years. However, as late as 1999 with the *Supernatural* album, Santana's single "Smooth" scored number one on the *Billboard* Hot 100, and the album won eight Grammys. Santana was inducted into the Rock and Roll Hall of Fame in 1998. In 2003 Santana was named fifteenth on *Rolling Stone* magazine's list of the "100 Greatest Guitarists of All Time." At age seventy-two in 2020, Santana was still touring and had to cancel his "Miraculous World Tour" due to the COVID-19 pandemic.

Los Tigres del Norte (late 1960s–)

The famed *norteño* band began recording when the group moved to San Jose, California, in the late 1960s, and its success and influence in the early twenty-first century is as strong as ever. It was not until 1974 that the band's hit single "Contrabando y traición" (Contraband and Betrayal) became a smash hit on both sides of the border, inspired a series of movies, and launched the greatest success of any *norteño* or *Tejano* band ever. Los Tigres del Norte has become the interpreter of Mexican immigrant and working-class life, with lyrics and sounds that capture the trials and tribulations of culture conflict, pursuit by the Border Patrol, injustice and exploitation in the workplace, and, of course, love and laughter as common folk experience them. A truly binational group, all the members are U.S. citizens. To date, the group has released some fifty albums. In 2018 Los Tigres del Norte recorded a live album at Folsom Prison in California; the concert was produced as a Netflix documentary in 2019. The band sold thirty-two million records as of 2007, and as of 2016 had won six Grammy Awards, twelve Latin Grammy Awards, and a star on the Hollywood Walk of Fame.

Marcos Witt (1962–)

Born on May 19, 1962, in San Antonio, Texas, to Christian missionaries who worked in Durango,

Mexico, Marcos Witt spent his early education at the American School in Durango. He went on to study music at the Universidad Autónoma de Durango and later obtained a degree in theology from the International Bible College in San Antonio; he obtained his M.A. from the Oral Roberts University in Tulsa, Oklahoma. Witt went on to serve as a pastor, but it is his musical ministry that has brought him to international fame, having recorded more than thirty albums in Spanish that have exceeded twenty-eight million copies in sales. In 1986, he founded CanZion Producciones to record and distribute his own and other singers' albums of spiritual music; in 1994 he started the CanZion Institute to train pastors for the music ministry. Witt regularly fills sports stadiums and auditoriums for his concerts throughout Latin America and the United States. In 2003, he won his first Latin Grammy Award for Best Christian Album for *Sana Nuestra Tierra* (Heal Our Land); he went on to win others in the same category in ensuing years. In 2007, his album *Alegría* (Happiness) won a Latin *Billboard* Award for Best Christian/Gospel Album of the Year. Witt has the distinction of having some of his albums distributed to the secular market by Sony Discos.

PROMINENT LATINO CLASSICAL MUSICIANS

While the discussion in the preceding section concentrated on Latino popular music, because it is what has the greatest following and reaches into almost all Latino households, there is a long tradition of classical music culture in Latino heritage. While Italy developed its opera, Spain was developing a national, serious musical theater in the form of the *zarzuela*, soon followed by the national forms in the Spanish American republics. In fact, major international stars who have become mainstays in the United States opera, such as Plácido Domingo, got their start in the *zarzuelas*. Then, too, the republics south of the border have schooled and supported classical music since they became republics. That explains why, in fact, the Houston Symphony and the Los Angeles Philharmonic have conductors from Colombia and Venezuela, respectively,

and the San Francisco Conservatory of Music has an Argentine director. The United States has had many homegrown or locally supported Latino artists, composers, and conductors. Below are just a few.

Héctor Armienta (?–)

Héctor Armienta graduated with a B.M. degree in composition from California Institute of the Arts and an M.M. degree in composition from the San Francisco Conservatory of Music. Armienta composes for opera and musical theater by drawing on Mexican and Mexican American cultural themes. Among his well-known and performed compositions are works inspired in Chicano novels and Mexican legends, including *Bless Me Ultima*, based on Rudolfo Anaya's novel; Armienta's opera debuted in 2018 at the National Hispanic Cultural Center and was produced by Opera Southwest. His *Zorro* was performed by the Fort Worth Opera in 2020, and his *La Llorona*, a musical drama (*zarzuela*) based on the ubiquitous legend of the Weeping Woman who searches for her lost children, was performed at the Western Stage Theater in Salinas, California, and traveled to New York City. Other diverse musical dramas of Armienta's have been produced by Opera Cultura. His awards and commissions include those from Fort Worth Opera, Opera Southwest, Meet the Composer, the National Endowment for the Arts, Arts International, Opera Pacific, the Pacific Symphony, the San Francisco Arts Commission, Oakland East Bay Symphony, and Western Stage Theater.

Martina Arroyo (1937–)

Born on February 2, 1937, in New York City to a Puerto Rican mother and an African American father from South Carolina, Martina Arroyo was educated in city schools and received a

B.A. in romance languages from Hunter College in 1956. She studied opera as a hobby but did not take it seriously because there were practically no Black opera singers admitted to major opera houses. While working as a teacher and a social worker, she continued studying voice and went to auditions without success. But in 1957 Arroyo won the Metropolitan Opera's "Audition of the Air" competition and a scholarship to the Met's Kathryn Long School, where she perfected her skill as an operatic soprano. From the 1960s through the 1980s, she was part of the first generation of Black opera singers of Puerto Rican descent to achieve wide success. Arroyo was particularly acclaimed in Europe, first at the Zurich Opera between 1963 and 1965. From 1965 to 1978 she served as the leading soprano at the Metropolitan Opera. While at the Met, she also performed internationally at La Scala, Covent Garden, the Opéra National de Paris, the Teatro Colón, the Deutsche Oper Berlin, the Vienna State Opera, the Lyric Opera of Chicago, and the San Francisco Opera. After retiring from performing in 1991 she taught singing at various universities in the United States and Europe. On December 8, 2013, Arroyo received a Kennedy Center Honor.

Suzanna Guzmán (1955–)

Born in Los Angeles, California, on May 29, 1955, mezzo-soprano Suzanna Guzmán is a 1980 graduate of California State University, Los Angeles, and the American Institute Music Theater in 1984. She made her musical debut in the early 1980s singing in regional theater production for Sacramento Music Circus, Lyric Dinner Theatre, Grand Dinner Theatre, and others. In 1985 she tied for first place in the Metropolitan Opera Competition, Western Regionals, which led to her being cast that same year in *The Tales of Hoffmann* for the San Diego Opera. Since then she has sung as principal artist for most operas with this company but has also performed with the Los Angeles Philharmonic, the Washington Opera, the Metropolitan Opera, and at Carnegie Hall and the Kennedy Center for the Performing Arts. Her awards include First Place, Metropolitan Opera National Council in 1985; Western Region First Place, San Francisco Opera Center, 1985; First Place, International Competition, Center for Contemporary Opera in 1988; and others.

Guzmán has been an active performer for Latino schoolchildren in Southern California and for the handicapped. From 1994 to 2003 Guzmán hosted the weekly radio broadcast *L.A. Opera Notes*.

Tania León (1943–)

Born on May 14, 1943, in Havana, Cuba, Tania León received degrees from the National Conservatory of Music in Havana, a B.S. in music education from New York University in 1973, and an M.A. degree in music composition from New York University in 1975. One year after arriving in the United States in 1968, she became the first music director of the Dance Theater of Harlem, and she has continued to be an important composer for the Dance Theater. León studied conducting under such teachers and coaches as Laszlo Halasz, Leonard Bernstein, and Seiji Ozawa. She has maintained a busy schedule as a composer, recording artist, and guest conductor at most of the important symphonies throughout the United States and Puerto Rico, as well as in Paris, London, Spoleto, Berlin, and Munich. From 1977 to 1988, she was the director of the Family Concert Series for the Brooklyn Philharmonic Community. In 1985, León joined the faculty of Brooklyn College as an associate professor, teaching both composition and conducting. She has also served as music director for Broadway musicals, such as *The Wiz*. In 1994 León's opera *Scourge of Hyacinths* was commissioned by the Munich Biennale, where it won the BMW Prize as best new opera; it has gone on to numerous productions throughout Europe. She has continued to compose music for orchestras, operas, and chambers, and in February 2019, the New York Philharmonic performed the world premiere of her composition *Stride*. León is just one of a handful of women to have made a successful career as a conductor. Her honors include the Dean Dixon Achievement Award in 1985, the ASCAP Composer's Award from 1987 to 1989, the National Council of Women Achievement Award in 1980, the 1991 Academy-Institute Award in Music of the American Academy and Institute of Arts and Letters, and many others. In 1994 León cofounded the American Composers Orchestra Sonidos de las Americas Festivals in Brooklyn.

Ana María Martínez (1971–)

Born in San Juan, Puerto Rico, to an opera singer and a psychoanalyst, Martínez received a B.A. and an M.A. from the Juilliard School in New York City. In 2005 she debuted with the Metropolitan Opera in the city and subsequently went on to become an international star performing in a wide range of soprano roles, from the leads in *Carmen* to Cio-Cio-San in *Madame Butterfly*. She is an alumna of the Houston Grand Opera Studio and the inaugural recipient of the Lynn Wyatt Great Artist Award. In 1994 she won First Prize in HGO's Eleanor McCollum Auditions and Awards Competition, and in 2015 she established the Ana María Martínez Encouragement Award as part of that same competition. She has performed with all of the leading conductors and male opera stars around the world, including with the Seoul Philharmonic at the Teatro alla Scala and Carnegie Hall, the English National Opera Orchestra in London, the Orquestra Sinfonica Brasiliera in Rio de Janeiro, the BBC Symphony at Barbican Hall, the National Symphony of the Dominican Republic, the Boston Symphony, the Lyric Opera of Chicago, the Washington National Opera, the SWR Sinfonieorchester Baden-Baden und Freiburg, the Berlin Philharmonic Orchestra, and the Turkish Opera and Ballet Theatre. In January 2019 she starred in Daniel Cattán's new opera *Florencia en Amazonas*, commissioned by the Houston Grand Opera. Also in 2019 she was appointed Houston Grand Opera's first-ever artistic advisor. In 2021, she joined Rice University's Shepherd School of Music as a professor in the Department of Voice. Martínez's discography is extensive, and she won a Latin Grammy in 2001 for her album for Isaac Albéniz's *Merlin*.

Manuel Peña and Ramiro Burr

SPORTS

Latino participation and achievements in sports have been determined by Latino traditions of work, play, and ritual, both in the United States and in the greater Spanish-speaking world. As Latino customs in the United States and throughout Latin America have derived from the blending of various bloodlines and cultures—European, American Indian, and African—so too the types of sports practiced by Latinos have evolved out of the rituals and traditions that can often be traced back to the peoples who encountered each other in the early sixteenth century when the Spaniards evangelized the Mesoamerican Indians and began importing enslaved people from Africa. In the United States, the descendants of this encounter also adopted Anglo-American traditions in sport and shared their own with the Anglo-Americans. The prime examples of this exchange are rodeo and baseball. Ranching and sport with horses and cattle were introduced to the Americas by the Spaniards. The Spanish customs mixed with some American Indian traditions and then were learned by Anglo-Americans and European immigrants.

Latino participation in professional sports in the United States has also depended on a number of factors other than customs and traditions. Various sports demand certain body types that seem to present relative advantages for success. The prime example, of course, is basketball, where tall players have proven to be more successful. Most Latinos have descended from American Indians and Spaniards, both of whom are relatively short peoples compared to northern Europeans and many African peoples. As would be expected, there are very few Latinos represented in professional basketball. The same is true of football, which also demands very large and strong bodies. Notwithstanding the general disadvantage of Latinos as a whole, there have been great achievers, even in such contact sports as football, as the careers of Manny Fernández, Anthony Muñoz, and Tom Flores attest.

Another factor is education. College sports are quite often training grounds for the professional leagues. Latino dropout rates in high school are high, and their admission to and graduation from college is low compared to Anglo- and Asian Americans. Latinos thus have fewer opportunities to get involved in college sports, especially football and basketball, not to mention certain more elite sports, such as tennis and golf. But there are also "back doors" of entry to these sports, such as working as caddies and greenskeepers, as the careers of Chi Chi Rodríguez and Lee Treviño exemplify.

Furthermore, various sports have traditionally been associated with certain social classes and have been restricted to members of these classes principally because of economic barriers, such as membership fees in private country clubs, the payment of fees for private lessons, the lack of public facilities, the high expense of specialized equipment, such as golf clubs and gear, and the high tuition of private schools where these sports are cultivated. Prime examples of these sports are polo, golf, lacrosse, and, before the construction of numerous tennis courts in public parks, tennis. On the other hand, boxing classes and sports facilites have traditionally been accessible to poor inner-city youths through boys clubs, police athletic leagues, and the military services. In addition, boxing has been a traditional avenue to economic success and fame for one immigrant and minority group after another and for poor inner-city youths in the United States. Latinos have developed a long tradition of achievement in boxing, especially in the lighter-weight classes.

The wide world of sports holds relative advantages to being short, lightweight, and quick. Latinos not only have excelled as bantamweights and lightweights in boxing, but they also have earned an outstanding record as jockeys, quick-handed infielders in baseball, and star players in sports where speed and endurance are important, such as soccer. And soccer has also provided an opportunity for Latinos to participate in professional football, which has recruited various Latino placekickers for the accuracy they have developed with their angled and powerful kicking.

But all of the aforementioned conditions are changing rapidly. American society is becoming more and more democratic and open. In the late 1940s, American baseball ceased to be segregated, then football also opened up. In the world of sports today, sports facilities are accessible to people from all social classes in public parks and schools, and universities are making more of an effort to recruit minorities. Universities are even recruiting and training from such countries as the Dominican Republic, Panama, and Puerto Rico players of Afro-Latino background for their basketball, football, and track teams.

BASEBALL

Although many sportswriters in the United States have considered the presence of ballplayers from Latin America to be an "influx," as if baseball were a uniquely American sport being invaded by outsiders, the truth of the matter is that baseball in Spanish-speaking countries has not only had a parallel development to baseball in the United States, but it has also been intertwined with American baseball almost from the beginning of the game itself. The professional Cuban Baseball League (Liga de Béisbol Profesional Cubana) was founded in 1878, just seven years after the National Baseball Association was founded in the United States. But, reportedly, Cuban baseball goes back to 1866, when sailors from an American ship in Matanzas harbor invited Cubans to play the game; they built a baseball diamond together at Palmar del Junco and began playing while the ship remained in harbor. By 1874 Cuban teams had developed and were playing each other regularly.

By 1891 seventy-five teams were active on the island. From that time on, Cuban baseball—and later, Mexican and Puerto Rican baseball—has served baseball in the United States in various ways: as a training ground for the majors, formalized when the Cuban Sugar Kings were made a Triple A minor league team; as wintering and spring training grounds for the majors; and as permanent homes for players from the U.S. Negro Leagues, also providing a baseball team, the Havana Cubans, to the Negro Leagues. Since the early days of the National Baseball Association until Jackie Robinson broke the color line in 1947, about fifty Latino American ballplayers played in the major leagues, some even becoming Hall of Famers and one achieving the position of manager. However, for the most part, these were Cuban players who were White or could pass for White. In fact, the acceptance of progressively darker-skinned Latinos was used as a barometer by the Negro Leagues for the eventual acceptance of African Americans into the majors. The Latinos who could not "pass" either played in the Negro Leagues or in Cuba, Mexico, or Venezuela. What is clear is that Cuba served as a free ground exempt from the segregation that dominated U.S. sports and provided playing fields where major leaguers and players from the Negro Leagues and Latin America could play openly together.

As baseball continued its development in Mexico, pressure from fans and investors increased for expanding the U.S. major leagues to Mexico and for the creation of Mexico's own professional leagues. In 1946 the wealthy Pasquel family in Mexico founded a professional league and set about enticing major league and Negro League stars from the United States with salaries quite higher than were being offered in the United States. The whole Pasquel venture, which was seen by the U.S. media as "robbery" and a threat to the national pastime, even led to an official complaint by the U.S. State Department. Some twenty-three players jumped to Pasquel's league, but after continued financial problems the league ceased to exist in 1953. The northern teams of the league merged with the Arizona-Texas and Arizona-Mexico leagues from 1953 to 1957. The Mexican League began functioning again in 1955 and has continued to do so. The Mexican Central League has served since 1960—a year after the Cuban Revolution curtailed Triple A ball on the island—as a Class A minor league and was later joined by other Mexican leagues based on the earlier Pasquel circuit. Today the league has eighteen teams playing in two divisions, and both supply young ballplayers to the majors and receive former major leaguers on their way out of baseball.

The Majors

The first Latino to join the major leagues was third baseman Esteban Bellán, a Cuban who was recruited from Fordham College by the Troy Haymakers in 1869 and took to the field in 1871.

The first Latino ballplayers in the United States played in the National Association and in the Negro League. Before 1947 the major league clubs that employed the most Latinos were in Washington, Cincinnati, Chicago, Cleveland, and Detroit. The New York Yankees did not employ Latinos after 1918 and Pittsburgh did not employ any until 1943, when it hired one. The first Latino to join the majors was third baseman Esteban Bellán, a Cuban who was recruited from Fordham College by the Troy Haymakers in 1869 and actually took to the field in 1871—the year of the founding of the National Baseball Association—to spend three years in the majors. By the turn of the century, no Black Cubans were allowed in the majors, despite major leaguers observing their talents firsthand and suffering defeats from them. One such powerhouse was pitcher José Méndez. Méndez played with the Cuban Stars against the best of the Negro teams and had forty-four wins with only two losses on a tour of the United States in 1909. In Cuba, Méndez beat the Phillies and split two games against future Hall of Famers Christy Mathewson and John McGraw of the New York Giants. But light-skinned Cuban and Latino ballplayers soon began appearing more and more in American baseball, despite complaints that the racial puirity of the American sport was being contaminated. In 1911 the Cincinnati Reds had affidavits prepared to prove that their new Cuban players, Armando Marsans and Rafael Almeida, had only the purest Castilian blood flowing through their veins.

In 1912 Cuban Miguel González began playing for Boston as a catcher. González played for seventeen years on various teams and served fourteen seasons as a Cardinals coach, the first Latino to do so. But the greatest longevity by any Latino in major league baseball was attained by Adolfo Luque. A dark-skinned Cuban pitcher, Luque was jeered at and continuously faced racial epithets from fans from the time he took to the field for the Boston Braves in 1914 until his retirement in 1935. Having played for the Braves, Cincinnati, Brooklyn, and the New York Giants, Luque pitched in two World Series, was credited with the decisive win in one of them and during his best year, 1923, led the league for Cincinnati in wins (27), earned run average (1.93), and shutouts (6).

The Washington Senators employed the greatest number of Latino ballplayers by far, beginning in 1911 and peaking from 1939 to 1947 with a total of nineteen players of Latino background. In Washington, as with other major league clubs, the Latinos suffered not only racial attacks from fans and sportswriters but also segregation in housing, uniforms, equipment, and travel conditions. Many of these conditions improved noticeably during the 1940s with the competition for ballplayers that was exerted by the Mexican League.

After the color barrier was broken in 1947, things became much easier for Latino ballplayers of all colors and nationalities, and their representation in the major leagues quickly climbed. By the 1970s, a full 9 percent of the players were Latinos. Due to the restrictions that came about after the Cuban Revolution—even baseball equipment was not to be had in Cuba due to the U.S. economic embargo—the flow of players from Cuba into the major leagues was curtailed. During the 1970s and 1980s Cubans no longer were the Latino nationality most represented. The lead passed to the Dominican Republic and Puerto Rico, with Venezuela and Mexico also making a strong showing. But by 1963 the Cuban National Team had begun to dominate amateur baseball and to cement its perennial championship of the Pan American Games. Although the caliber of play is equivalent to that of major league teams, the broken political relations between the United States and Cuba has made international professional play between the two countries impossible.

> After the color barrier was broken in 1947, things became much easier for Latino ballplayers of all colors and nationalities, and their representation in the major leagues quickly climbed.

Major league baseball in the United States is and will continue to be a strong draw for Latino ballplayers, not only as an economic springboard with its lucrative salaries but also because of the excellence and competitive nature of the game played here, made even more competitive by the quality Latino ballplayers have always contributed to the majors. As of 2020, 31.9 percent of the major league players are Latinos.

The Negro Leagues

The Negro Leagues were a haven for Latino ballplayers whose skin color was a barrier to their admission to the major leagues in the United States. The

Many Latinos before integration played for teams in the Negro leagues, such as the Indianapolis Clowns, which at one point was even managed by a Latino, Ramiro Ramírez.

Negro Leagues and the leagues in Cuba, Mexico, Puerto Rico, and Venezuela were completely open to each other. Both Black and White players from the Latino world and from the United States played on the same teams and against each other freely in Cuba. In Latin America there were no color lines. By the 1920s not only were many Latinos playing in the Negro Leagues, but many American Blacks had also incorporated into their routine playing the winter season in Cuba, then later Puerto Rico, Mexico, and Venezuela. Among the Latino greats to play in the Negro Leagues were Cristóbal Torriente, Martín Dihigo, José Méndez, Orestes "Minnie" Miñoso, Alejandro Oms, Luis Tiant Sr., and scores of others.

As early as 1900, two of the five Black professional teams bore the name of Cuba: the Cuban Giants (with its home city shifting from year to year from New York to Hoboken, New Jersey, to Johnstown, Pennsylvania, and so on) and the Cuban X Giants of New York. (These teams should not be confused with one of the first Black professional ball teams of the 1880s, which called itself the Cuban Giants, thinking that fans would be more attracted to the exotic Cubans than to ordinary American Blacks.) In the 1920s both the Eastern Colored League (ECL) and the Negro National League (NNL) had a Cuban Stars baseball team, one owned by Alex Pómpez, who at one point was vice president of the NNL, and the other by Agustín Molina. Cuban teams continued to be prominent during the heyday of the Negro Leagues from the 1920s through the 1940s. There were also Latino players on teams throughout the Negro Leagues, from the Indianapolis Clowns and Cleveland Buckeyes to the Memphis Red Sox and the New York Black Yankees. And, aside from the teams that identified themselves as Cuban, such as the New York Cubans and the Cuban Stars, there were others that had their rosters filled with Latinos, such as the Indianapolis Clowns, which at one point was even managed by a Latino, Ramiro Ramírez. (In his long career from 1916 to 1948, Ramírez managed or played with most of the Cuban teams, plus the Baltimore Black Sox, the Bacharach Giants, and the Clowns.)

RODEO

The Spaniards introduced cattle ranching to the New World, and with this industry the early settlers and soldiers also introduced the horse and its use for work and sport. Much of contemporary sports culture that depends upon horsemanship and cattle, such as equestrian contests, horse racing, bullfighting, and rodeo, is heavily indebted to the Spanish and Latino American legacy. The evolution of rodeo as a sport goes back to the blending of Spanish and American Indian customs of animal handling and sport. A class of mestizo *vaqueros* developed in Mexico during the seventeenth, eighteenth, and nineteenth centuries on the large haciendas. These mestizo cowboys, called *charros*, eventually evolved their own subculture of unique customs, dress, music, and horsemanship, which in turn owed much to the Arab horsemen who had influenced Spanish culture during the seven hundred years of Muslim occupation of the peninsula. The *charros*, in fact, were the models for the development of the American cowboy, just as Mexican ranching culture was essential in the development of that industry in the United States. During the late eighteenth and early nineteenth centuries, Anglo-American cowboys began working alongside Mexican cowboys on the same ranches in Texas and California.

> The style of dress and horsemanship of the *charro* became more popularized even in the cities during the nineteenth century and was eventually adopted as the national costume. Their contests and games, *charrería*, became the Mexican national sport.

The style of dress and horsemanship of the *charro* became more popularized even in the cities during the nineteenth century and was eventually adopted as the national costume. Their contests and games, *charrería*, became the Mexican national sport. The skillful games of the *charros* became games and shows on the large haciendas during the festive roundups in the nineteenth century, which drew guests from hundreds of miles around. The *charros* dressed in their finest outfits and displayed their skills in such contests as *correr el gallo* (running the rooster), horse racing, wild horse and bull riding, and roping horses or steers by their horns or back or front hooves, bulldogging, and throwing bulls by their tails. *Correr el gallo* involved picking up something as small as a coin from the ground while riding a horse at full gallup. These fiestas were perhaps the most important forerunners of the modern American rodeo, and their events included almost all of those associated with today's rodeos. More important, these equestrian sports became part of the standard celebrations at fiestas and fairs among Mexicans and Anglos all along both sides of the border. *Charrería*, as a separate institution from rodeo, has continued to this day to be practiced by Mexicans in Mexico and throughout the American Southwest.

During the early years of the twentieth century, local and state fairs and celebrations among Anglos in the West featured cowboy events in what they called "stampedes," "roundups," and "frontier days." These proliferated to the extent that professional contestants began to make a living traveling the circuit of these fairs. The events that became the heart of these contests were the traditional *charro* events of bronc riding, steer roping, and trick fancy roping. The first cowboy to win the World Championship of Trick and Fancy Roping in 1900 was Vicente Oropeza. Oropeza and many other *charros* and American cowboys continued to compete in both the United States and Mexico throughout the 1930s. By 1922, with the production by Tex Austin of the first World Championship Cowboy Contest in New York's Madison Square Garden, rodeo had officially become a sport, not just a show. Eight of the ten events featured in this new sport had long been a part of *charrería*. More important, the five standard events of contemporary professional rodeo all owe their roots to *charrería*: bareback bronc riding, saddle bronc riding, bull riding, steer wrestling, and calf roping.

SOCCER

Anyone who goes to city parks on the weekend is aware of the thousands of Latin Americans and Latinos playing soccer in numerous amateur and semiprofessional leagues. By far, soccer, know as *fútbol*, is the most practiced sport in Latino communities throughout the United States. And internationally, professional soccer teams from Latin America have always been at the top ranks and have provided the most famous international players, such as Pelé, Cristiano Ronaldo, and Diego Maradona. However, professional soccer leagues in the United States have received much criticism in the twenty-first century for ignoring the Latino talent and not recruiting outstanding Latino players for their teams. In fact, in the 2018 season only 7 percent of players in Major League Soccer were U.S.-born Latinos and 11 percent were U.S.-born Black players. This overt passing over of Latino players has redounded to the mediocrity of U.S. professional soccer, reflected in the lackluster performance of the national men's team in the Olympics and World Cup competitions. This was evidenced when the U.S. Men's National Team failed to qualify for two consecutive Olympic Games, in 2012 and 2016—of course, the women have been superstars, winning consistently throughout the twenty-first century, but their diversity statistics are worse: not one of the U.S. national team as of 2019 was a Latina. The nadir was reached in October 2019, when the U.S. national team lost 2–0 to Canada, for the first time in thirty-four years.

Part of the problem stems from the practice of professional teams recruiting from universities rather than directly from the athletes playing outstanding soccer outside of the ivy-covered walls—a subtle discrimination against a community that often does not have access to higher education but produces world-class players, as does baseball, outside of academia. Another problem is that families with sufficient resources pay for their children to belong to soccer youth academies, which are also the targets of professional recruiters, but Latino families generally do not have the financial resources to have their children in these academies. But other countries, especially Mexico, are keen to recruit U.S. Latinos, such as players Adrián González, Jonathan González, and Miguel Angel Avalos, three of the most promising players in 2020. However, U.S. teams that do recruit homegrown U.S. Latino players make out very well, as did FC Dallas in winning the U.S. Open

Cup in 2016 with homegrown players Kellyn Acosta, Jesse González, and Víctor Ulloa contributing significantly to the championship. Of course, FC Dallas benefitted from having recruiter Fernando Clavijo and head coach Oscar Pareja, both Latinos.

Once Major League Soccer begins to take FC Dallas's example seriously, the future will be bright for Latinos in professional soccer in the United States and for the national team in international play.

OTHER SPORTS

While baseball and rodeo are two sports that have been highly influenced by Latinos in their evolution, other sports have benefited from the participation of outstanding Latino athletes. First and foremost is boxing, which has a long history of Latino champions, especially in the lighter-weight classifications, where the speed and lighter body weight of many Cuban, Mexican, and Puerto Rican boxers have been used to advantage.

From the days of Sixto Escobar and Kid Chocolate to the present, boxing has also served for Latinos, as it has for other immigrants and minorities, as a tempting avenue out of poverty. With more colleges and universities recruiting and graduating Latinos, some of the other "money" sports, such as football and basketball, will also begin to incorporate more Latinos in their ranks. Already, football stars such as Manny Fernández, Tom Flores, Anthony Muñoz, and Jim Plunkett have appeared on the scene, and there are many more to follow, especially from the universities of the Southwestern Conference. Finally, the mere fact that an island such as Puerto Rico, which extends only thirty-five by one hundred miles, has as many as ten professional-quality golf clubs has had its impact on that sport. Such golfers as Juan "Chi Chi" Rodríguez have become world-class competitors after beginning as caddies for tourists. And as more and more facilities, such as golf courses and tennis courts, become accessible in the United States through public parks or public schools, greater Latino participation and achievement will be recorded.

PROMINENT LATINO ATHLETES

José Altuve (1990–)

Born on May 6, 1990, in Puerto Cabello, Venezuela, second baseman José Altuve was considered too short (5'6") to play professional baseball, when the Houston Astros signed him as an amateur free agent in 2007. The investment paid off, and Altuve went on to become one of the most highly regarded players in the majors, assisting the Astros to a World Series victory in 2017. A powerful and consistent hitter, Altuve recorded at least 200 hits each season from 2014 to 2017. He has garnered numerous other distinctions, including being named to the MLB All-Star roster six times, and being named American League MVP in 2017, winning the Hank Aaron Award, being named the Associated Press Male Athlete of the Year, *The Sporting News* Major League Player of the Year, and *Baseball America's* Major League Player of the Year. He has also won the Babe Ruth Award, the Silver Slugger Award five times, the Luis Aparicio Award three times, the Lou Gehrig Memorial Award, and the Rawlings Gold Glove. In 2014 he became the first player in more than eighty years to reach 130 hits and 40 stolen bases before the All-Star Game.

Luis Aparicio (1934–)

Born on April 29, 1934, in Maracaibo, Venezuela, Luis Aparicio was one of the greatest shortstops of all time. He still holds the records for games, double plays, and assists and the American League record for putouts. His 506 stolen bases also rank among the highest. Playing from 1956 to 1973, mostly with the Chicago White Sox, Aparicio began his career as Rookie of the Year and proceeded to maintain outstanding and inspired performance throughout his career. Aparicio played on All-Star teams from 1958 to 1964 and then again from 1970 to 1972. He was the winner of the Gold Glove eleven times. In 1984 Luis Aparicio was inducted into the Hall of Fame. In 2006 a bronze statue of Aparicio was placed in U.S. Cellular Field in Chicago.

Marcelo Balboa (1967–)

Born on August 8, 1967, in Chicago, Illinois, to Argentine immigrant parents, Marcelo Balboa was raised in El Cerritos, California, where as a teenager he was on the national soccer championship team. From 1986 to 1989 Balboa attended Cerritos College and later San Diego State University, where at the latter he was an All-American. In 1990, he became a professional player for the San Francisco Bay Blackhawks. Beginning in 1996, he played six seasons with the Colorado Rapids, after which he played one season with the Metro Stars (2002) and then retired. From 1988 to 2000, Balboa played on the U.S. National Team, serving as team captain and competing in three FIFA World Cups. When he played for the Rapids, he established numerous records in various categories. He was the first U.S. player to compete in more than one hundred international matches. In 2005, Balboa was elected to the Major League Soccer All-Time Best XI and to the National Soccer Hall of Fame. Beginning in 2003, Balboa has worked as a television commentator/analyst on professional soccer.

Crystl Irene Bustos (1977–)

Born on September 8, 1977, in Canyon Country, California, Mexican American Crystl Bustos began playing softball in Little League and at Palm Beach Community College in Florida, where she led the team to two NJCAA National Championships, and she became an NJCAA first team All American twice and was named NJCAA Player of the Year twice. She was known to have the fiercest bat in women's softball, at times even batting over .500 in championship play. She went on to represent the United States in the Olympics, where she was a two-time gold medal winner (2000 and 2004) and a silver medal winner (2008). She was also a member of the championship U.S. teams of World Cup Championships (2006 and 2007), Pan American (1999, 2003, and 2007), and the 2006 ISF World Championships. In 2008 she was

named USA Softball Player of the Year. In 2018, she was inducted into the National Softball Hall of Fame.

Rod Carew (1945–)

Born on October 1, 1945, in the Panama Canal Zone, Rod Carew moved with his mother to New York at age seventeen. He signed his first professional contract while he was still in high school in 1964, and when he made it into the majors in 1967 with the Minnesota Twins, he was named Rookie of the Year. From 1969 on, he had fifteen consecutive seasons batting over .300. Carew won seven American League batting championships. In his Most Valuable Player year he batted .388, fifty points better than the next-best average and the largest margin in major league history. His career batting average was .328, with 1,015 runs batted in and 92 home runs. In 1979 Carew forced a trade, in part because of racist comments regarding Black fans by Twins owner Calvin Griffith; he was traded to the California Angels for four players. In 1977 Carew received more than four million All-Star votes, more than any other player ever. He would have played in eighteen consecutive All-Star games but missed 1970 and 1979 because of injuries, and for the same reason was not chosen in 1982. Carew was one of the best base stealers, with 348 career stolen bases. In 1969 Carew tied the record with seven steals to home. He led the league three times in base hits and once in runs scored. In 1991 he was elected to the National Baseball Hall of Fame.

Rosemary Casals (1948–)

Born on September 16, 1948, in San Francisco, the daughter of Salvadoran immigrants, Rosemary Casals was brought up by her great-aunt and great-uncle. Casals began playing tennis at Golden Gate Park under the guidance of her adoptive father, Manuel Casals Y. Bordas, who was her only coach. Casals won her first championship at age thirteen and by age seventeen was ranked eleventh by the United States Ladies Tennis Association (USLTA). At eighteen, her ranking was third in the nation. Casals and Billie Jean King were doubles champions five times from 1967 to 1973 at the All-England Championships at Wimbledon and twice at the USLTA championships at Forest Hills. The Casals-King team is the only doubles team to have won U.S. titles on grass, clay, indoor, and hard surfaces. Nine times, Casals was rated as number one in doubles by the USLTA, with teammates who included King, Chris Evert Lloyd, and JoAnne Russell. Casals also won mixed doubles championships, playing with Dick Stockton and Ilie Nastase. Casals won 112 professional doubles tournaments, the second most in history behind Martina Navratilova. Casals was inducted into the International Tennis Hall of Fame in 1996.

Hugo Castelló (1914–1994)

Born in La Plata, Argentina, on April 22, 1914, Hugo Castelló moved to the United States with his family at age eight and received his public education in New York City. He earned his bachelor of arts degree at Washington Square College in 1937 and his law degree from Georgetown University in 1941. Castelló became one of the nation's most outstanding fencers and fencing instructors and coaches. He was nationally ranked among the top four senior fencers from 1935 to 1936, the years that he was National Intercollegiate Foil Champion, and he was a member of the U.S. Olympic team in 1936. Castelló served as adjunct associate professor and head fencing coach at New York University from 1946 to 1975. Castelló is among a select group of coaches who have won at least ten National Collegiate team championships. Only five other NCAA coaches in all sports have won ten national team titles. Castelló was also director and head coach of the United States' first Olympic fencing training camp in 1962. He also served as chief of mission and coach at the Pan American Games (1963) in Sao Paulo and at World Championships in Cuba (1969), Minsk (1970), and Madrid (1972). Castelló is a member of the Helms Sports Hall of Fame, the New York University Sports Hall of Fame, and the PSAL Hall of Fame.

Orlando Cepeda (1937–)

Orlando Cepeda was born in Ponce, Puerto Rico, on September 17, 1937. After growing up playing sandlot baseball and later organized team play in New York City, Cepeda was discovered by talent scout Alex Pómpez and began as a major league outfielder with the San Francisco Giants in 1958, when he was named Rookie of the Year. Hitting his stride in 1961, Cepeda led the league in home runs. Cepeda remained on the team until May 1966, when he was traded to the St. Louis Cardinals after having missed almost a whole season because of a leg injury. He stayed with the Cardinals until he was traded to the Atlanta Braves during spring training in 1969. He also played for the Oakland A's, the Boston Red Sox, and the Kansas City Royals. He made a remarkable comeback with the Cardinals, winning the National League's Most Valuable Player Award, leading the league in runs batted in 1967, and making the All-Star team in that year as well. Cepeda played on World Series teams in 1962, 1967, and 1968. In all, Cepeda played 2,124 games, with a lifetime batting average of .279. He hit 379 home runs and had 1,364 runs batted in. Cepeda had nine .300 seasons and eight seasons with twenty-five or more home runs. In 1999, Cepeda was inducted into the Hall of Fame.

Roberto Clemente (1934–1972)

Roberto Walker Clemente is celebrated for being a heroic figure both on and off the baseball diamond. One of the all-time greats of baseball, he died in a tragic plane crash in an effort to deliver relief supplies to the victims of an earthquake in Nicaragua. Born on August 18, 1934, Clemente rose from an impoverished background in Carolina, Puerto Rico, to become the star outfielder for the Pittsburgh Pirates from the years 1955 to 1972. He assisted the Pirates in winning two World Series in 1960 and 1971. Among Clemente's achievements as a player, he was four times the National League batting champion—1961, 1964, 1965, and 1967—and he was voted the league's most valuable player in 1966. He was awarded twelve Gold Gloves and set a major league record in leading the National League in assists five times. He served on fourteen all-star teams, and he was one of only sixteen players to have three thousand or more hits during their career. Clemente was promising a great deal more before his untimely death. Clemente hit 240 home runs and had a lifetime batting average of .317.

Upon his death the Baseball Hall of Fame waived its five-year waiting period after a player's retirement and immediately elected him to membership. For his generosity, leadership, outstanding athletic achievements, and heroism, Roberto Clemente is considered by Puerto Ricans to be a national hero to this day.

Dave Concepción (1948–)

Venezuelan Dave Concepción was one of baseball's greatest shortstops, playing for the Cincinnati Reds from 1970 to 1988. In 1973 Concepción was named captain of the Reds, and in 1978 he became the first Cincinnati shortstop to bat .300 since 1913. In World Series play, Concepción hit better than .300 three times and better than .400 in the 1975 and 1979 league championships. His lifetime batting average is .267 for 2,488 games played. He made All-Star teams in 1973 and from 1975 to 1982. He was also winner of the Gold Glove each year from 1974 to 1977 and in 1979. In 1977, he was the winner of the Roberto Clemente Award as the top Latin American ballplayer in the major leagues. In 2000, Concepción was inducted into the Cincinnati Reds Hall of Fame.

Angel Cordero (1942–)

Angel Tomás Cordero, born in Santurce, Puerto Rico, on November 8, 1942, is one of the most winning jockeys of all time. By December 1986, he was fourth in the total number of races won and third in the amount of money won in purses: $109,958,510. Included among Cordero's important wins were the Kentucky Derby in 1974, 1976, and 1985; the Preakness Stakes in 1980 and 1984; and the Belmont Stakes in 1976. He was the leading rider at Saratoga for eleven years in a row. In 1982, he was named jockey of the year. Cordero was inducted into National Museum of Racing and Hall of Fame in 1988. He was forced to retire in 1992 as a result of a serious injury after a fall in a race.

Stephanie Cox (1986–)

Born on April 3, 1986, in Los Gatos, California, Stephanie Renee López (Cox is her married name) was a high school All-American in soccer before attending the University of Portland (a 2007 graduate in psychology and Spanish), where she led her team to an NCAA championship. In 2007 she was chosen as Oregon's Female Amateur Athlete of the Year. From 2009 until her retirement in 2019 she played on a number of professional teams. While still in college she was a member of the U.S. national teams in international competition. In 2006 she was the captain of the U.S. team at the FIFA U-20 Women's World Championship in Russia, and she was a gold medal winner at the 2008 Beijing Olympic Games.

Martín Dihigo (1905–1997)

Born on May 25, 1905, in Matanzas, Cuba, Martín Dihigo is one of the few baseball players named to the National Baseball Hall of Fame based on his career in the Negro Leagues. In addition, he was named to the Halls of Fame of Cuba, Mexico, and Venezuela. He was perhaps the best all-around baseball player that ever existed, yet there are few statistics and records to document his outstanding achievements. Called the "Black Babe Ruth," he was an outstanding pitcher and outfielder, but he also played every other position. He was an outstanding hitter, as well. Dihigo began his career in the Negro Leagues in 1923 with Alex Pómpez's Cuban Stars when he was only fifteen years old. By 1926 he was considered one of the top pitchers in Black baseball. During his career he played ball in all of the countries that have named him to their Hall of Fame. In each of these countries he led the leagues in home runs, batting average, number of victories, and lowest earned run average (ERA). In 1929 he is reported as having batted .386 in the American Negro League; in 1938 he batted .387 in the Mexican League and had a 18–2 record with an ERA of 0.90. After the Negro National League folded—when Major League Baseball was desegregated—Dihigo played in Mexico during the 1950s. He was then too old for the U.S. major leagues. After the Cuban Revolution, Dihigo—who had spent much of dictator Fulgencio Batista's rule in exile—returned to Cuba to assist in organizing amateur baseball leagues and to teach the game. Dihigo was inducted posthumously into the Hall of Fame in 1977.

Sixto Escobar (1913–1979)

Born on March 23, 1913, Sixto Escobar, known as El Gallito de Barceloneta (the Barceloneta Fighting Cock), was the first Puerto Rican boxer to win a world championship when he knocked out Tony Marino on August 31, 1936, in the thirteenth round. Escobar was born in Barceloneta, Puerto Rico, on March 23, 1913, and only grew to fight at 118 pounds and five feet, four inches. Although born in Puerto Rico, Escobar spent most of his professional career in New York; he also fought in Canada, Cuba, Mexico, and Venezuela. Escobar fought as a professional boxer from 1931 to 1941, after which he joined the U.S. Army. He is one of the few boxers ever to have regained his lost throne, accomplishing this feat twice: in 1935 and 1938. Escobar fought sixty-four times and was never knocked out. He ended his hold on the championship in 1939, when he could no longer make the required weight of 118 pounds. In 2002, Escobar was inducted into the International Boxing Hall of Fame.

Víctor Espinoza (1972–)

Born on May 23, 1972, in Hidalgo, Mexico, Espinoza has been one of the most successful jockeys in American horse racing. Having financed his training at jockey school in Mexico City by driving a bus, he was soon racing horses throughout Mexico. He immigrated to the United States in 1990 and began working as a jockey in California. In 2000 he broke away from the pack of jockeys, distinguishing himself by winning the Breeders' Cup Distaff riding a horse named Spain. From then on, his career took off, winning the Kentucky Derby three times (2002, 2014, and 2015) and the Preakness Stakes three times. His winning the Triple Crown in 2015 made him the oldest jockey and first Hispanic jockey to win the award. In July 2018 he had an accident that fractured vertebrae, and he went into a long recovery, not returning to racing until January 2019. In July 2020 he contracted COVID-19 and recovered after a few weeks.

Tom Fears (1922–2000)

Born on December 3, 1922, in Guadalajara, Mexico, to an American engineer and a Mexican mother, Tom Fears moved with his family to Los Angeles when he was six years old. He became an All-American football player at the University of California, Los Angeles and then played nine seasons as a split end in the National Football League, from 1948 to 1956. He was the first Mexican-born player to be drafted into the NFL. He played on the Los Angeles Rams championship team (1951) and was a first-team All-Pro (1950) and NFL receiving yards leader (1950). Following his retirement, he was an assistant coach with several teams and was the first head coach of the expansion New Orleans Saints (1967–70). Fears was elected to the Pro Football Hall of Fame in 1970.

Manuel Fernández (1946–)

Born on July 3, 1946, in Oakland, California, "Manny" Fernández was educated at Chabot University and the University of Utah and went on to become an outstanding defensive tackle on one of professional football's winningest teams, the Miami Dolphins, under coach Don Shula. Fernández has achieved the highest distinction of any Latino in football: he was named to the All-Time Greatest Super Bowl All-Star team. During his career with the Miami Dolphins, from 1968 to 1977, Fernández was voted the Dolphins' Most Valuable Defensive Lineman six consecutive years, 1968 to 1973. He helped the Dolphins win two Super Bowls in 1972 and 1973, and played on the only undefeated team in NFL history, in 1973. In 2014, Fernández was inducted into the Miami Dolphins Honor Roll at Sun Life Stadium.

Tony Fernández (1962–2020)

Born on June 30, 1962, in San Pedro de Macoris, Dominican Republic, Tony Fernández played for seven major league teams from 1983 to 2001, most notably for the Toronto Blue Jays as shortstop. He made the American League All-Star team during five seasons and won four consecutive Gold Glove Awards (1986–1989). He holds the major league baseball record for highest fielding percentage, in 1989, and the American League record for the most games played at shortstop, in 1986. In 2016 Fernández was inducted into the Ontario Sports Hall of Fame.

Tom Flores (1937–)

Born on March 21, 1937, in Fresno, California, Thomas Flores, the son of Mexican American farm workers, rose to become an outstanding professional football coach. In fact, he is ranked as one of the most successful coaches in the National Football League, winning two Super Bowls with the Oakland Raiders in 1980 and 1983. Flores worked in the fields through elementary and junior high school, managed to get his high school and college education (University of the Pacific, 1958), and was drafted by the Calgary Stampeders (Canada) in 1958. After that he played with the Washington Redskins and in 1960 joined the Raiders. As a quarterback for the Raiders for six seasons, he completed 48.9 percent of his passes for 11,635 yards and 92 touchdowns. Flores finished his ten years as a professional player with the Kansas City Chiefs in 1969. From then on he worked as a coach and was named assistant to Coach John Madden of the Raiders in 1972. When Madden resigned after the 1978 season, Flores took his place. In his second year as coach, the Raiders won Super Bowl XV. Three seasons later, Flores led the Raiders to another Super Bowl victory. Flores is only one of two people in NFL history to have a Super Bowl ring as a player, assistant coach, and head coach. After eight seasons, Flores's record with the Raiders was 78–43 in the regular season and 8–3 in playoffs and Super Bowls. In 1989 Flores became the president and general manager of the Seattle Seahawks, the highest rank ever achieved by a Latino in professional sports in the United States. In 2012, he was also inducted into the Bay Area Sports Hall of Fame. In 2021 Flores was selected for the Pro Football Hall of Fame for his coaching.

Vernon Louis Gómez (1908–1989)

Born on November 26, 1908, in Rodeo, California, Vernon Louis Gómez, also known as "Lefty" and "The Gay Castilian," probably referring to his Spanish ancestry (he was half-Irish, half-Spanish), was one of baseball's most successful pitchers, ranking third in regular season wins, with 189 for the New York Yankees. He also holds the record for the most wins without a loss in World Series play (6–0) and three wins against one loss in All-Star play. Gómez was active from 1930 to 1943, pitched 2,503 innings, had a 189–102 won-loss record, and earned an ERA of 3.34. He had twenty wins or more in 1931, 1932, 1934, and 1937. Gómez is number thirteen on the all-time winning percentage list. In all, Gómez made All-Star teams every year from 1933 to 1939. During winter seasons, he played ball in Cuba, where he served for a while as manager of the Cienfuegos team, and once he taught a class on pitching at the University of Havana. In 1972 Gómez was elected to the National Baseball Hall of Fame.

Richard Alonzo González (1928–1995)

Richard Alonzo "Pancho" González was born on May 9, 1928, in Los Angeles to Mexican immigrant parents. His father, Manuel, fitted furniture and painted movie sets, and his mother, Carmen, was an occasional seamstress. González was a self-taught tennis player, having begun at age twelve on the public courts of Los Angeles. He won his first tournament as an Edison Junior High School student; because of excessive absenteeism, González was not allowed to compete in tennis while in high school. González served in the U.S. Navy and competed in the U.S. singles championship upon his return in 1947. That same year he placed seventeenth in the nation. In 1948 González became U.S. singles champion at Forest Hills and played on the U.S. Davis Cup team. He won at Forest Hills again in 1949. After having won the U.S. grass, clay, and indoor championships, González turned pro. From 1954 to 1962 he was world professional singles champion. In 1968 he coached the U.S.

Davis Cup team, and he was named to the International Tennis Hall of Fame.

Keith Hernández (1953–)

Born on October 20, 1953, in San Francisco, Keith Hernández attended San Mateo College. He played with the St. Louis Cardinals from 1974 to 1983, the New York Mets from 1983 to 1989, and the Cleveland Indians in 1990, after which he retired. Hernández was considered by many to be the best fielding first baseman of his time, having won eleven Gold Gloves and leading the league in double plays and lifetime assists. He played on National League All-Star teams in 1979, 1980, 1984, 1986, and 1987. Hernández won the World Series with the Cardinals in 1982 and the Mets in 1986. He was Most Valuable Player in 1979 and an All-Star in 1979, 1980, 1984, 1986, and 1987. In 1985 he received a season-long suspension for suspicion of cocaine use, but the suspension was commuted in favor of community service. A reformed and repentant Hernández was active with the Mets until 1989. In 1987, he was named team captain. Hernández was inducted into the New York Mets Hall of Fame in 1997 and was voted the Mets' all-time first baseman by fans in 2002. Baseball's Hall of Fame has so far been elusive. Since 2006, he has served as a television broadcaster for Mets games.

Rebecca Lobo (1973–)

Born on October 6, 1973, in Hartford, Connecticut, to a German Irish mother and Cuban father, Rebecca Lobo is one of the most distinguished basketball players in history. Playing at center, she led her University of Connecticut team to the national championship in 1995 and won the 1995 Naismith College Player of the Year award, the Wade Trophy, and the AP Player of the Year award, among many others. Lobo played on the U.S. team for the 1996 Olympic Games, where she won a gold medal. She then played professional basketball in the Women's National Basketball Association (WNBA) from 1997 to 2003, but she had a truncated career due to injuries. She was inducted into the Women's Basketball Hall of Fame in 2010 and into the Naismith Memorial Basketball Hall of Fame in 2017. Today she is a sports commentator for ESPN cable network.

Al López (1908–2005)

Alfonso Ramón López was born on August 20, 1908, in Tampa, Florida, the son of a tobacco worker. López was rated as the seventh-best catcher and the seventh-best manager of all time, and he was elected to the Hall of Fame in 1977. For many years he held the record for the most games caught in the major leagues (1,918). He tied the record for the most games caught in the National League without a passed ball in 1941, with 114 games. López played for the Brooklyn Robins/Dodgers in 1928 and from 1930 to 1935, and later with the Boston Bees (1936–40), the Pittsburgh Pirates (1940–46), and the Cleveland Indians (1947). He was an outstanding manager for the Indians from 1951 to 1956 and for the Chicago White Sox from 1957 to 1965 and 1968 to 1969. His record as a manager was 1,422–1,026 for a winning percentage of .581, the ninth all-time highest.

Nancy López (1957–)

Nancy Marie López was born to Mexican American parents in Torrance, California, on January 6, 1957, was raised in Roswell, New Mexico, and rose to become one of the youngest women golfers to experience professional success. She learned golf from her father and by age eleven was already beating him. She won the New Mexico Women's Open when she was only twelve. In high school López was the only female member of the golf team, and as an eighteen-year-old senior, she placed second in the U.S. Women's Open. After high school, she attended Tulsa University on a golf scholarship, but she dropped out to become a professional golfer. In 1978, during López's first full season as a pro, she won nine tournaments, including the Ladies Professional Golf Association. She was named Rookie of the Year, Player of the Year, Golfer of the Year, and Female Athlete of the Year; she also won the Vare Trophy. Also in 1978 she set a new record for earnings by a rookie: $189,813. In 1983 she took a break from her career when she became the mother of Ashley Marie, her child with her husband, baseball star Ray Knight. Two months after having Ashley, López began touring again, and by 1987 she had won thirty-five tournaments and qualified to become the eleventh member of the Ladies Professional Golf Association Hall of Fame. López's most outstanding year was 1985, when she won five tournaments and finished in the top ten of twenty-one others; that year she also won the LPGA again.

Juan Marichal (1937–)

Born in Laguna Verde, Dominican Republic, Juan "Naito" Marichal was a right-handed pitcher who was signed to the minor leagues at age nineteen and whose wide variety of pitches and motions took him to the Hall of Fame. Marichal started with the San Francisco Giants in 1962, and from 1962 to 1971 he averaged twenty wins per year. He led the National League in wins in 1963 with a record of 25–8 and in 1968 with 26–9, in shutouts in 1965 with ten and 1969 with eight, and in ERA in 1969 (2.10). He pitched in eight All-Star games for a 2–0 record and an 0.50 ERA for eighteen innings. Marichal's total innings pitched were 3,509, for a record of 243–142 and an ERA of 2.89. Marichal had 2,303 strikeouts with only 709 walks, which ranked him among the top twenty pitchers of all time. He was an All-Star from 1962 to 1969 and again in 1971, and he was inducted into the Hall of Fame in 1983.

Rachel McLish (1955–)

Born on June 21, 1955, in Harlingen, Texas, Raquel Livia Elizondo (McLish is her married name) studied health and physical education at Pan American University. McLish has been a national champion bodybuilder, a successful model and actress, and spokesperson for health and physical fitness. McLish was the U.S. Women's Bodybuilding Champion in 1980, Ms. Olympia in 1980 and 1982, and world champion in 1982. In 1999, she was inducted into the International Female Body Building Hall of Fame.

José Méndez (1885–1928)

Born on March 19, 1885, in Cárdenas, Matanzas, Cuba, José Méndez was an outstanding pitcher and infielder who, because of his African ancestry and dark skin, was never allowed to play in the majors. Instead, he played in the Negro National League and in Cuba, and thus many of his statistics are missing. Such witnesses as Hall of Famer John Henry Lloyd said that he never saw a pitcher superior to Méndez, and Giants manager John McGraw said that Méndez would have been worth $50,000 in the majors, an unusually high figure back in those days. Méndez came to the United States in 1908 with the Cuban Stars. In 1909 he went 44–2 as a pitcher for the Stars. During the winters he played in Cuba, where he compiled a record of 62–17 by 1914. From 1912 to 1916 Méndez played for the All-Nations of Kansas City, a racially mixed barnstorming club. From 1920 to 1926 he served as a player/manager for the Kansas City Monarchs and led them to three straight Negro National League pennants from 1923 to 1925. During his long career, he also played for the Los Angeles White Sox, the Chicago American Giants, and the Detroit Stars.

Jessica Mendoza (1980–)

Born on November 11, 1980, in Camarillo, California, Jessica Ofelia Mendoza is a champion softball outfielder. In college play at Stanford University, she was a four-time First Team All-American. After graduating, she was selected for the U.S. national team and won gold medals at the 2004 and 2008 Olympic Games. She also won a gold medal at the Pan American Games. and a gold medal in the World Cup competition (2007). In 2006, Mendoza was named the USA Softball "Female Athlete of the Year." She became a professional player in 2005 in the National Pro Fastpitch for the Arizona Heat. She later joined the USSSA Pride, helping it gain the Cowles Cup Championship in 2010. In 2014, Mendoza became an analyst on ESPN's *Baseball Tonight*. In 2015 Mendoza became the first female broadcaster in the booth for ESPN's College World Series coverage. In 2016 she became a full-time announcer for *Sunday Night Baseball*. She has continued with ESPN to the present. In 2020 Mendoza became the first female World Series analyst in history.

Orestes "Minnie" Miñoso (1925–2015)

Born in Perico, Cuba, on November 29, 1925, Saturnino Orestes Arrieta Armas Miñoso, nicknamed "Minnie," had one of the most outstanding careers of any Latino ballplayer in the major leagues. He began his career in Cuba on the semiprofessional Club Ambrosia team in 1942 and played semiprofessional ball on the island until he took to the field as a third baseman with the New York Cubans of the Negro Leagues in 1946. In 1949 he made his major league debut with the Cleveland Indians, becoming the first Black Cuban player in the major leagues, but only played briefly before being sent down to the Indians' minor league affiliate in San Diego. He was called back up to the Indians in 1951, and that same year was traded to the Chicago White Sox. He spent the greater part of his career playing on one or the other of these two teams, and with St. Louis and Washington until 1964. In 1976 Miñoso made a return as a designated hitter for the Chicago White Sox; he thus became one of only six players to be active in four separate decades, and only two other players in major league history have played at an older age: Satchel Paige and Nick Altrock. After that he remained active as a player-manager in Mexico. He ended his career as a third-base coach for Chicago. Miñoso's lifetime batting average was .299, with 1,023 runs batted in, 186 home runs, and 205 bases stolen. Miñoso was inducted into the Baseball Hall of Fame in 1996.

Amleto Monacelli (1961–)

Born on August 27, 1961, in Barquisimeto, Venezuela, Amleto Andrés Monacelli is one of the most popular and successful members of the Professional Bowling Association tour. After he became a professional in 1982, his earnings continually grew until, by 1991, he was winning $81,000 in prizes, and in 1989 he even achieved a record $213,815. The tournaments he has won include the Japan Cup (1987), the Showboat Invitational (1988), the Miller Challenge (1989), the Wichita Open (1989 and 1990), the Budweiser Touring Players Championship (1989), the Cambridge Mixed Doubles (1989 and 1990), the Columbus Professional Bowling Classic (1990), the Quaker State Open (1991), the True Value Open (1991), the Choice Hotels Summer Classic (1992), the Taylor Lanes Open (1992), the Leisure's Long Island Open (1994), the Greater Lexington Classic (1994), the Oranamin C Japan Cup (1995), the Mobil 1 Classic (1997), the Ebonite Classic (1997), the Jackson-Hewitt Tax Service Open (2005), and the DHC PBA Japan Invitational (2016). Among his many awards are the Professional Bowlers Association Player of the Year in 1989 and 1990, and the Harry Smith Point Leader Award in 1989. In 1990 he won the Budweiser Kingpin Competition for the highest average for the year, and sportswriters named him Bowler of the Year. Monacelli is still a Venezuelan citizen; this was the first time a foreigner was named Bowler of the Year. In his professional career, Monacelli has rolled sixteen perfect games, seven of them during the 1989 season, which established a new record for perfect games in a year. Three of these were accomplished during one week, thus tying the record. In 2012 he became the first international player to win the Senior U.S. Open. In 2019 Monacelli won the USBC Senior Masters for a second time. Monacelli won twenty titles on the Professional Bowling Tour, making him one of only fifteen players in history to achieve that record. In 1997 he was inducted into the Professional Bowling Association Hall of Fame.

Anthony Muñoz (1958–)

Born on August 19, 1958, in Ontario, California, Anthony Muñoz is a graduate of the University of Southern California. He played football for thirteen seasons with the Cincinnati

Bengals, distinguishing himself as All-Pro offensive tackle eight times. He was selected for the Pro Bowl each year from 1981 to 1991. He was chosen as the NFL Lineman of the Year in 1981, 1985, 1988, and 1989. When he retired, his Pro Bowl selections were tied with Tom Mack for the most ever by an offensive lineman. In 2010 he was included in the NFL's Top 100: NFL's Greatest Players. Muñoz was inducted into the Professional Football Hall of Fame in 1998.

Tony Oliva
(1938–)

Born in Pinar del Río, Cuba, on July 20, 1938, Antonio Oliva López Hernandes Javique has been the only player to win batting championships during his first two major league seasons. Throughout his career, Oliva was an outstanding hitter and outfielder; however, an injured knee shortened his career. He was active from 1962 to 1976 with the Minnesota Twins, winning Rookie of the Year in 1964 and the league batting title in 1964, 1965, and 1971. Oliva led the league in hits five times in his career. He made All-Star teams from 1964 to 1971, passing by Joe DiMaggio's record of having been named an All-Star in each of his six first seasons. Oliva won the Golden Glove in 1966 as the league's best defensive right fielder. Oliva's career batting average was .304, with 220 home runs and 947 runs batted in, for 1,676 games played. Because of his knee, which had been operated on seven times, Oliva served the last years of his career mostly as a designated hitter and a pinch hitter. He was elected into the Hall of Fame in 2021.

Alejandro Oms (1896–1946)

Cuban Hall of Famer Martín Dihigo considered Alejandro Oms the best batter in Cuban baseball. Born to a poor family in Santa Clara, Cuba, in 1896, he had to work as a child in an iron foundry. He started playing organized baseball in 1910 as a center fielder. He played in the Negro National League on the Cuban Stars and the New York Cubans from 1921 to 1935, while still

managing to put in outstanding seasons during the winter in Cuban professional ball. On the most famous Cuban team of all time, Santa Clara, Oms batted .436 in the 1922–23 season. In Cuba, Oms achieved a lifetime batting average of .352; his average in the United States is not known. He was batting champion on the island three times: .393 in 1924–25, .432 in 1928–29, and .380 in 1929–30. In 1928, he established a Cuban record for most consecutive games with hits (30). He was elected to the Cuban Baseball Hall of Fame in 1944.

Vicente Oropeza
(1858–1923)

The most famous and influential Latino rodeo performer of all time, Mexican native Vicente Oropeza was born in 1858 in Puebla, Mexico. He called himself the "premier *charro mexicano* of the world" on his first appearance in the United States in July 1891. As a headliner and champion in both Mexico and the United States, he is credited with having introduced trick and fancy roping in the United States. In 1893 Oropeza became the star of "Buffalo Bill" Cody's "Mexicans from Old Mexico" feature in his Wild West Show. In 1900 Oropeza won the first World's Championship of Trick and Fancy Roping, which was a major contest up through the 1930s. One of the most famous American ropers of all time, Will Rogers, credited Oropeza for inspiring his career. Oropeza was selected as a member of the National Rodeo Hall of Fame for his contributions to what may be considered both a sport and an art.

Carlos Ortiz
(1936–)

Carlos Ortiz was the second Puerto Rican boxer—the first being Sixto Escobar—to win a world title. Born in Ponce, Puerto Rico, on September 9, 1936, Ortiz made his professional debut in 1955. He was undefeated that year and in 1956, 1957, and almost all of 1958, suffering his first defeat on December 31 in a fight with Kenny Lane in Miami Beach. He later beat Lane in a rematch to win the junior welterweight championship. After losing the junior welterweight championship to Duilio Loi, he turned lightweight in 1962, and on April 21 he won the world championship in that division from Joe Brown. He successfully defended his crown various times until April 10, 1965, when he lost in Panama to Ismael Laguna. But he recovered the title on November 13 of the same year in San Juan, Puerto Rico. Again he successfully defended his crown until losing in the Dominican Republic to Carlos "Teo" Cruz on June 29, 1968. As of January 2018, Ortiz held the record for the most wins in unified lightweight title bouts in boxing history at ten. In 1991 Ortiz was inducted into the International Boxing Hall of Fame.

Manuel Ortiz
(1916–1970)

Born on July 2, 1916, in El Centro, California, Mexican American boxer Manuel Ortiz became the bantamweight champion on August 7, 1942, when he beat Lou Salica. Ortiz totaled forty-one knockouts in his career and never once suffered one himself in 117 bouts. Ortiz tied Henry Armstrong in defending his title twenty times (only two other fighters had defended more often) and even successfully defended it three times in 1946 after a tour of duty in the Army. Ortiz finally lost the crown on January 8, 1947, to Harold Dade in San Francisco, but he took it back on March 11 that same year. He lost it again on May 31, 1950, to Vic Toweel in Johannesburg, South Africa. In 1996, he was inducted into the International Boxing Hall of Fame.

Hugo Pérez (1963–)

Born on November 8, 1963, in El Salvador, third-generation professional soccer play Hugo Ernesto Pérez Granados migrated to the United States when he was eleven years old. About a decade later, he became a U.S. citizen. He went on to play professionally for various teams in the United States, Europe, the Far East, and North Africa. Pérez played for the U.S. team at the 1983 FIFA World Youth Championship and 1984 Summer Olympics. He also helped the USA qualify for the 1988 Summer Olympics and the 1990 FIFA World Cup but was off the roster because of injuries. He was named U.S. Soccer Athlete of the

Year in 1991. Pérez played as a midfielder in seventy-three international matches for the United States between 1984 and 1994, scoring thirteen goals. In 2008 Pérez was elected to the National Soccer Hall of Fame.

Jim Plunkett
(1947–)

James William "Jim" Plunkett was born on December 5, 1947, in Santa Clara, California, the son of William and Carmen Blea Plunkett, who had met at a school for the blind in Albuquerque, New Mexico. His father managed a newsstand in San Jose, where Plunkett became an outstanding year-round athlete in high school. Later, at Stanford University he became starting quarterback as a sophomore. During his junior year he threw passes for 2,671 yards and 20 touchdowns. He was named to the Associated Press's all-American second team, won the Voit Memorial Trophy as the PAC's outstanding player, and was eighth in the Heisman Trophy selection. It was as a senior that he finally was awarded the Heisman Trophy, as well as many other awards. He became the first major college football player to surpass 7,000 yards on offense. In 1971, Plunkett was the first pick for the New England Patriots, and passed for 2,158 yards and 19 touchdowns; he was chosen as NFL Rookie of the Year. Plunkett was injured during the next few years and was traded to the San Francisco 49ers, who later released him. In 1978 he was signed by the Oakland Raiders, and in 1980 he led the Raiders to the Super Bowl. He became Super Bowl MVP and was named the NFL 1980 Comeback Player of the Year. In 1983 Plunkett again led the Raiders to a Super Bowl victory. That year he recorded his best season, with 230 completions for 1,935 yards and 20 touchdowns. Now retired, Plunkett passed for a total of 25,882 yards, with 164 touchdowns during his career. Plunkett is the only quarterback with two Super Bowl wins not to be inducted into the Pro Football Hall of Fame. Plunkett was inducted into the College Football Hall of Fame in 1990, the Bay Area Sports Hall of Fame in 1992, and the California Sports Hall of Fame in 2007.

Manny Ramírez
(1972–)

Born on May 30, 1972, in Santo Domingo, Dominican Republic, Manuel Arístides Ramírez Onelcida immigrated to New York City with his parents when he was thirteen years old. He was a star player in high school and drafted by the Cleveland Indians in 1991. Beginning in 1992 he played outfield and designated hitter for nineteen seasons with a number of major league teams: the Indians (1993–2000), the Boston Red Sox (2001–2008), the Los Angeles Dodgers (2008–2010), the Chicago White Sox (2010), and the Tampa Bay Rays (2011). In 2020 Ramírez beame a player-coach for the Sydney Blue Sox in Australia. He was a nine-time Silver Slugger (1995, 1999–2006) and was one of twenty-seven players to hit five hundred career home runs. His twenty-one grand slams are third all-time, and he was a World Series MVP (2004), playing on two World Series Championship teams. Ramírez played in twelve All-Star games (1995, 1998–2008). He is the all-time leader in postseason home runs with twenty-nine. He has also led the American League in batting average, home runs, and RBIs in various years. He is a winner of two Hank Aaron Batting Awards.

Armando Ramos
(1948–2008)

In nine years as a professional boxer, Armando "Mando" Ramos only fought forty bouts, but that was enough for him to win two world titles as a lightweight. Born on November 15, 1948, in Long Beach, California, the Mexican American boxer won his first seventeen bouts, eleven by knockouts. On February 18, 1969, he won the lightweight championship from Carlos Cruz in Los Angeles. On February 19, 1972, Ramos won the World Boxing Congress lightweight championship over Pedro Carrasco. In 1973 he retired after suffering a knockout by Arturo Piñeda.

Alex Rodríguez
(1975–)

Born on July 17, 1975, in New York City and raised in Miami, Florida, by immigrant parents from the Dominican Republic, Alex Rodríguez was one of the greatest all-time sluggers. After graduating from high school, shortstop Rodríguez was signed by the Seattle Mariners and made his debut in 1994, becoming the youngest player in major league baseball. He played for the Mariners (1994–2000), Texas Rangers (2000–2003), and New York Yankees (2004–2016). It was with the Yankees that he became the highest-paid player in the major leagues. Over the years, Rodríguez's output was outstanding, leading to his being named to fourteen American League All-Star teams, three times as Most Valuable Player (2003, 2005, 2007), three times the recipient of the Babe Ruth Home Run Award (2002, 2003, 2007), twice the *Baseball America* Major League Player of the Year (2000, 2002), three times the *Sporting News* Player of the Year (1996, 2002, 2007), and many other distinctions. In addition, he holds records for the most career grand slams (25), the most runs in a season (141), most extra base hits in a season (91), the highest slugging percentage (.631 in 1996), most total bases in a season (393), and various others. Under normal circumstance, Rodríguez would be an obvious candidate for the Hall of Fame, but his records are marred by having been suspended from play for the whole season and postseason of 2014 for taking performance-enhancing drugs. In his post-playing life, Rodríguez has worked as a baseball commentator and analyst for Fox Sports and ESPN.

Amy Rodríguez
(1987–)

Born on February 17, 1987, in Lake Forest, California, Amy Rodríguez is a Cuban American forward who plays for FC Kansas City. In 2005 on graduating from high school as an All-

American, Rodríguez was considered the nation's top recruit and was named National Player of the Year by *Parade Magazine*, EA Sports, and the National Soccer Coaches Association of America (NSCAA). She was recruited by the University of Southern California, where she played until graduation in 2008. She led her college to its first-ever NCAA Women's Soccer Championship. Rodríguez played on the U.S. women's national soccer team at the 2008 Summer Olympics, where she won a gold medal. Rodríguez repeated her gold medal win with the national team in 2012 when she was a member of the team at the London Olympics. Rodríguez has played for a number of women's professional soccer clubs. While playing for FC Kansas City in 2015 Rodríguez scored the game-winning (and only) goal to win the 2015 NWSL Championship—she was voted MVP of the championship. In 2018 while playing for the Utah Royals FC, Rodriguez finished the season with five goals. Rodríguez's career has been interrupted various times due to injuries and pregnancies for her two children. From 2005 to 2018 in international play, Rodríguez scored an outstanding thirty goals.

Chi Chi Rodríguez (1935–)

Born on October 23, 1935, in Río Piedras, Puerto Rico, Juan Antonio "Chi Chi" Rodríguez came from an extremely impoverished family and found his way into golf as a caddy on the links that served Puerto Rico's booming tourism. His is one of the most famous Latino "rags to riches through sports" tales both because of his career earnings, which have passed the $3 million mark, and because of his generous donations to charities, including the Chi Chi Rodríguez Youth Foundation in Clearwater, Florida. Included among the important tournaments he has won are the Denver Open (1963), Lucky Strike International Open (1964), Western Open (1964), Dorado Pro-Am (1965), Texas Open (1967), and Tallahassee Open (1979). As a member of the Senior PGA Tour, he has won numerous tournaments, including the Silver Pages Classic (1987), GTE Northwest Classic (1987), and Sunwest Senior Classic (1990). In 1989 Rodríguez received the Bob Jones Award, the highest honor given by the United States Golf Association. As the winner of eight PGA Tour championships, he was inducted into the World Golf Hall of Fame in 1992.

Lauro Salas (1928–1987)

Born on August 28, 1928, in Monterrey, Nuevo León, Mexico, Lauro Salas dreamed as a boy of becoming a bullfighter, but he started boxing as a teenager in his native Monterrey, Mexico, for the money. He left home and moved to Los Angeles at age nineteen to become a professional boxer. There he won fourteen of his first seventeen pro bouts as a featherweight. In 1952 he won the world lightweight championship over Jimmy Carter but lost it back to him that same year at Chicago Stadium. Salas retired in 1961 after being knocked out by Sebastiao Nascimento and Bunny Grant.

Alberto Salazar (1958–)

Born on August 7, 1958, in Havana, Cuba, one year before the triumph of the Cuban Revolution, future track marathoner Alberto Salazar moved to Manchester, Connecticut, with his refugee parents when he was only two years old. The family moved to Wayland, Massachusetts, where Salazar was named high school all-American twice as a two- and three-mile racer. In 1976 he entered the University of Oregon, where he was coached by Olympian Bill Dellinger. In 1978 he won the NCAA individual championship. He went on to become a three-time cross-country all-American and helped Oregon win the 1977 NCAA team title and finish second in 1978 and 1979. In 1979, he set a U.S. road record of 22:13 for five miles. In 1980 Salazar made the Olympic team, but that was the year that the United States boycotted the games in Moscow. That same year, however, Salazar won the New York Marathon with the record for the fastest first marathon in history and the second-fastest time ever run by an American. The next year he won more championships, often by establishing new records, and once again he was victorious in the New York Marathon, setting a new world record of 2:08:13. In 1982 Salazar won the Boston and New York Marathons and various other events around the world; that year and in 1981 and 1983, he was selected the top U.S. road racer. Despite some setbacks and injuries, Salazar made the U.S. Olympic team for the second time in 1984 but finished only fifteenth in the games at Los Angeles. Salazar has set one world record and six U.S. records, the most of any U.S. runner since Steve Prefontaine.

Martha Salazar (1970–)

Born on February 2, 1970, in Ocotlán, Jalisco, Mexico, Martha Salazar immigrated to the United States at age nine. She became a heavywight champion boxer in the United States. Her championship titles include the 2004 WBE female Super Heavyweight Title (237 lbs.), WIBF World heavyweight title (240 lbs.), 2007 WBE Female Heavyweight Title (236 lbs.), and 2014 WBC World female heavyweight title (235 lbs.). She retired from competition in 2017 but continued in the world of boxing as a partner in Beautiful Brawlers Boxing.

Eligio Sardiñas Montalvo (1910–1988)

Eligio Sardiñas Montalvo was born on January 6, 1910, in Havana, Cuba. As a boxer he was known as Kid Chocolate, one of the most celebrated Latino boxers of all time. His career became an example of the fate that befalls boxers who battle their way out of poverty into fame and temporary riches. After winning eighty-six amateur and twenty-one professional fights in Cuba, he made his New York debut in 1928 and fought over one hundred bouts in the United States over the next ten years. He became a true champion, supported his community, and was memorialized on stage and screen. However, he was severely exploited by his managers and owners and ultimately was done in by poverty and alcoholism. Sardiñas's record was 135 wins, 10 losses, and 6 draws, with 51 wins coming by knockout and one no-decision bout. He was elected to the International Boxing Hall of Fame in 1959.

State University, Northridge. She competed in taekwondo while in college, winning twenty-seven of her twenty-eight matches. She started her professional boxing career as a light welterweight in 1997, winning her first bout with a knockout. She went on to become a World Boxing Council (2012) champion in the super welterweight division as well as an IBA (2008) and IFBA lightweight champion (2005). Her professional boxing career record was forty-nine wins and fourteen losses.

Diana Lorena Taurasi (1982–)

Born on June 11, 1982, in Chino, California, to immigrant parents from Argentina, in 2000 Diane Taurasi was rated the best player in Southern California by the *Los Angeles Times* and was *Parade Magazine*'s National High School Player of the Year. The high-school All-American went on to play for the powerhouse University of Connecticut, where she helped the college win three consecutive NCAA championships. At Connecticut she was named 2003 and 2004 Naismith College Player of the Year, among other honors. She was drafted by the Phoenix Mercury of the Women's National Basketball Association (WNBA) in 2004 and won the WNBA Rookie of the Year Award (2004). She went on to have an outstanding professional career, winning three WNBA championships (2007, 2009, and 2014). In 2009 she won the WNBA Most Valuable Player Award; she also won two WNBA Finals MVP Awards (2009 and 2014); four Olympic gold medals (2004, 2008, 2012, and 2016); five scoring titles (2006, 2008, 2009, 2010, and 2011); and three FIBA World Cups (2010, 2014, and 2018). She was selected to nine WNBA All-Star teams and ten All-WNBA teams. In 2011, she was voted by fans as one of the WNBA's Top 15 Players of All Time. On June 18, 2017, Taurasi became the WNBA's all-time leading scorer.

Mia St. John (1967–)

Born on June 24, 1967, in San Francisco, California, the daughter of immigrants from Zacatecas, Mexico, Mia St. John (St. John is her married name) earned a B.A. in psychology from California

Luis Tiant (1940–)

Born on November 23, 1940, in Marianao, Cuba, pitcher Luis Clemente Tiant Vega is the son of a pitcher who played in the U.S. Negro Leagues and in Mexico. He broke into professional baseball in the Mexican League in 1959. Although best known for his play with the Boston Red Sox, Tiant's major league career in the United States—from 1964 to 1982—included seasons with the Cleveland Indians, the Minnesota Twins, the New York Yankees, the Pittsburgh Pirates, and the California Angels. After making an outstanding start as a rookie for Cleveland with a 10–4 record and a 2.83 ERA, Tiant hit his stride in 1968 with a 1.60 ERA, nine shutouts, and 5.3 hits per nine innings, striking out more than one batter per inning and finishing the season with a 21–9 record. On July 3 of that year, he struck out nineteen Twins in a ten-inning game, setting an American League record. In his previous start he had struck out thirteen Red Sox for a major league record. While suffering a series of problems, including a hairline fracture, Tiant was traded and released various times during the next few years, finally joining Boston in 1971 after a stint with the Red Sox's Louisville farm team. In 1972 he was named Comeback Player of the Year, and he won the ERA title with a 1.91 and a season record of 15–6. The next two years he won twenty and twenty-two games and in 1974 led the league with seven shutouts. In 1975 Tiant helped the Sox to a pennant and a World Series appearance (a loss to the Cincinnati Reds). In 1976 Tiant won twenty games for the last time and went 21–12 for the season. Tiant was known for his masterful changes of speed, a wide variety of release points, and deceptive pitching motions. He was inducted to the Boston Red Sox Hall of Fame in 1997 and the Hispanic Heritage Baseball Museum Hall of Fame in 2002.

Dara Torres
(1967–)

Born on April 15, 1967, in Los Angeles, California, to a Cuban refugee father and an American mother, Dara Torres started swimming competitively as a child. At age fourteen, she won the national open championship in the 50-yard freestyle. From then on she was one of the top swimmers in the United States. While studying at the University of Florida, Torres won nine Southeastern Conference (SEC) individual championships, including the 50-yard freestyle (1987, 1988, 1989), 100-yard freestyle (1987, 1988, 1989), 200-yard freestyle (1987), and 100-yard butterfly (1988, 1989); she was also a member of twelve of the university's championship relay teams. Torres began competing in the Summer Olympics in 1984 and became the first U.S. swimmer to compete in five Olympic Games (1984, 1988, 1992, 2000, and 2008). In her Olympic career she won twelve medals. In 2008 she became the oldest swimmer to ever make the team, at age forty-one, and she won three silver medals that year. After retiring from swimming at age forty-five, she has worked as a commentator on ESPN, CNN, Fox, and other networks.

José Luis Torres
(1936–2009)

Born on May 3, 1936, in Ponce, Puerto Rico, José Luis "Chegui" Torres was the third Puerto Rican boxer ever to win a world championship when he won the medium heavyweight championship from Willie Pastrano on March 30, 1965, with a technical knockout in the ninth round at Madison Square Garden in New York. Without a rival in the middle heavyweight division, Torres took on Tom McNeely in the heavyweight class, winning in a ten-round decision. Torres defended his medium heavyweight crown and fought as a heavyweight successfully on a number of occasions until December 16, 1966, when, weakened from an old pancreatic injury, he lost on points to Nigerian Dick Tiger, whom he had beaten earlier in his career. Born into a large, poor family, Torres dropped out of high school and joined the Army. There he learned to box well enough to win the Antilles, Caribbean, Second Army, All-Army, and Interservice championships as a light middleweight. In 1956 he won the U.S. Olympic title but lost on points at the games in Melbourne to Hungarian László Papp. After the army, Torres moved to New York, where he fought as an amateur to win the National AAU championship and then turned pro. During and after his professional boxing career, Torres also developed a career as a singer and musician and worked in public relations, real estate, and as a New York newspaper columnist—all without a high school education.

Lee Treviño (1939–)

Lee Buck Treviño was born in Dallas, Texas, on December 1, 1939, into an impoverished Mexican American family. Fatherless, he was raised by his mother, a cleaning woman, and his maternal grandfather, a gravedigger. Their four-room farmhouse was located at the back of the Glen Lakes Country Club fairways. As a boy Treviño studied the form of the golfers on the course from his own backyard. He dropped out of school in the seventh grade and made his way into what was then an exclusively Anglo rich man's sport by working as a greenskeeper and as a caddy. He later joined the Marines and played a great deal of golf while he was stationed in Okinawa. In 1966 Treviño became a professional golfer and achieved his first major victory in 1968 at the U.S. Open, where he became the first player in history to shoot all four rounds of the event under par. In 1970 he was the leading money winner on the Professional Golf Association tour. In 1971 Treviño won the U.S. Open for a second time, won five tournaments between April and July, and also won the British Open in that year and again in 1972. For his achievements in 1971, Treviño was named PGA Player of the Year, Associated Press Athlete of the Year, and *Sports Illustrated* Sportsman of the Year. After that, he won the 1974 PGA again, among many other tournaments. In 1975 Treviño and two other golfers were struck by lightning during a tournament near Chicago. To this day he still suffers from back problems due to the accident; it seriously affected his game, even causing him to go winless in 1976 and 1978. In 1980, he made a comeback, winning the Texas Open and the Memphis Classic and earning $385,814 for the year. He was also awarded the Vardon Trophy for the fewest strokes per round (69.73 for 82 rounds), the lowest since Sam Snead in 1958. Treviño retired from the PGA tour in October 1985, with his thirty tour victories and total career earnings of over $3 million (third highest). Treviño has been elected to the Texas Sports and American Golf Halls of Fame. He was inducted to the World Golf Hall of Fame in 1981.

Fernando Valenzuela (1960–)

Baseball pitcher Fernando Valenzuela was born on November 1, 1960, in Etchohuaquila, Sonora, Mexico. He was one of the youngest and most celebrated baseball players because of his sensational introduction to the major leagues as an outstanding pitcher during his first season with the Los Angeles Dodgers. During his rookie year in 1981, Valenzuela was named not only Rookie of the Year but also the *Sporting News* Player of the Year, and he was the first rookie ever to win the Cy Young Award. He won his first ten major league outings, and his eight shutouts tied the rookie record in a season that was shortened because of a players' strike. Valenzuela is considered to have had the best screwball of his time. He led the league in strikeouts in 1981 and in wins in 1986. He was selected for the All-Star team five times; in 1986 he tied Carl Hubbell's record of five straight strikeouts in an All-Star game. That was also the year that he won the Gold Glove. Valenzuela was inducted into the Hispanic Heritage Baseball Museum Hall of Fame in 2003.

Cain Velásquez (1982–)

Born on July 28, 1982, in Salinas, California, and raised in Yuma, Arizona, to an undocumented Mexican father and a Mexican American mother, Cain Velásquez was an outstanding high school wrestler with a 110–10 record and two-time winner of the 5A Arizona Wrestling Championship. As an Iowa Central Community College wrestler for one season (2001–2), he won the NJCAA National Championship in the heavyweight division, then wrestled at Arizona State University, where he compiled a record of 86–17, placing fifth in the country in 2005 and fourth in 2006. After graduating from college in 2006, Velásquez began his career as a professional mixed martial arts competitor. Velásquez put together a string of victories and worked his way up to the UFC Heavyweight Championship in 2010. He subsequently lost the title and then regained it in 2012. After leaving mixed martial arts, he made the transition in 2019 to professional wrestling in Mexico (*lucha libre*).

Nicolás Kanellos

BIBLIOGRAPHY

Acosta-Belén, Edna, and Carlos Santiago, eds. *Puerto Ricans in the United States: A Contemporary Portrait*. Boulder: Lynne Rienner Publishers, 2006.

Acuña, Rodolfo. *Occupied America: A History of Chicanos*. 8th ed. New York: Longman, 2014.

Ansley, Fran, and Jon Shefner. *Global Connections and Local Receptions: New Latino Immigrants to the Southeastern United States*. Knoxville: University of Tennessee Press, 2009.

Avalos, Héctor, ed. *Introduction to the U.S. Latina and Latino Religious Experience*. Maryknoll, NY: Orbis, 2012.

Barton, Paul. *Hispanic Methodists, Presbyterians and Baptists in Texas*. Austin: University of Texas Press, 2006.

Burgos, Adrián. *Playing America's Game: Baseball, Latinos, and the Color Line*. Berkeley: University of California Press, 2007.

Calderón, Héctor. *Narratives of Greater Mexico: Essays on Chicano Literary History, Genre, and Borders*. Austin: University of Texas Press, 2004.

Chipman, Donald E. *Spanish Texas, 1519–1821*. Austin: University of Texas Press, 1992.

Cisneros, Henry, ed. *Latinos and the Nation's Future*. Houston: Arte Público Press, 2015.

DeFreitas, Gregory. *Inequality at Work: Hispanics in the US Labor Force*. New York: Oxford University Press, 1991.

Duany, Jorge. "Cuban Communities in the United States: Migration Waves, Settlement Patterns and Socioeconomic Diversity." *Pouvoirs dans la Caraïbe* 11 (1999): 69–103. https://doi.org/10.4000/plc.464.

———. *Migration between the Hispanic Caribbean and the United States*. Durham, NC: Duke University Press, 2011.

Duncan, Brian, V. Joseph Hotz, and Stephen J. Trejo. "Hispanics in the U.S. Labor Market." In *Hispanics and the Future of America*, edited by Marta Tienda and Faith Mitchell. Washington, DC: National Academies Press, 2006. https://www.ncbi.nlm.nih.gov/books/NBK19908/.

Fairlie, Robert W. *Latino Business Ownership: Contributions and Barriers for U.S.-Born and Immigrant Latino Entrepreneurs*. Washington, DC: U.S. Small Business Administration, 2018. https://www.sba.gov/sites/default/files/Latino-Business-Ownership-Research-Paper.pdf.

Falconi, José Luis, and José Antonio Mazzotti, eds. *The Other Latinos*. Cambridge, MA: Harvard University Press, 2008.

Flores, Juan, and Renato Rosaldo, eds. *A Companion to Latina/o Studies*. Malden, MA: Blackwell, 2007.

García, María Cristina. *Seeking Refuge: Central American Migration to Mexico, the United States and Canada*. Berkeley: University of California Press, 2006.

Gonzales, Oriana E., and Ariana A. Curtis. "Nine Latinas You May Not Know." Smithsonian Institution, September 25, 2020. https://womenshistory.si.edu/news/2020/09/nine-latinas-you-may-not-know-hispanic-heritage-month.

Gutiérrez, David G., ed. *The Columbia History of Latinos in the United States since 1960*. New York: Columbia University Press, 2004.

Gutiérrez-Jones, Carl. *Rethinking the Borderlands: Between Chicano Culture and Legal Discourse*. Berkeley: University of California Press, 1995.

Hispanic Heritage Baseball Museum (website). https://hhbmhof.com/.

Hispanics in America's Defense. Washington DC: Office of the Assistant Secretary of Defense for Military Manpower and Personnel Policy, 1990.

Hoffnung-Garskof, Jesse. *Racial Migrations: New York City and the Revolutionary Politics of the Spanish Caribbean*. Princeton: Princeton University Press, 2019.

Hondagneu-Sotelo, Pierrette. *Doméstica: Immigrant Workers Cleaning and Caring in the Shadows of Affluence*. Berkeley: University of California Press, 2001.

Iber, Jorge, et al. *Latinos in U.S. Sport: A History of Isolation, Cultural Identity and Acceptance*. Champaign, IL: Human Kinetics, 2011.

Joint Economic Committee, U.S. Congress. *The Economic State of the Latino Community in America*, October 15, 2019. https://www.jec.senate.gov/public/_cache/files/379f7a7c-e7b3-4830-b1a9-94c3df013b81/economic-state-of-the-latino-community-in-america-final-errata-10-15-2019.pdf.

Kanellos, Nicolás, ed. *Greenwood Encyclopedia of Latino Literature*. 3 vols. Westport, CT: Greenwood Press, 2008.

———. *Hispanic Immigrant Literature: El Sueño del Retorno*. Austin: University of Texas Press, 2012.

Kanellos, Nicolás, and Claudio Esteva Fabregat, gen. eds. *Handbook of Hispanic Cultures in the United States*. 4 vols. Madrid and Houston: Instituto de Cooperación Iberoamericana and Arte Público Press, 1994.

Kanellos, Nicolás, and Helvetia Martell. *Hispanic Periodicals in the United States: A Brief History and Comprehensive Bibliography*. Houston: Arte Público Press, 2000.

"Latino Civil Rights Timeline, 1903–2006." Learning for Justice, 2006. https://www.learningforjustice.org/classroom-resources/lessons/latino-civil-rights-timeline-1903-to-2006.

López, Gustavo. *Hispanics of Salvadoran Origin in the United States, 2013*. Pew Research Center: Immigration & Migration, September 15, 2015. https://www.pewresearch.org/hispanic/2015/09/15/hispanics-of-salvadoran-origin-in-the-united-states-2013/.

Martín-Rodríguez, Manuel. *Life in Search of Readers: Reading (in) Chicano/a Literature*. Albuquerque: University of New Mexico Press, 2003.

Matovina, Tim M., and Gerald E. Poyo, eds. *Presente! US Latino Catholics from Colonial Origins to the Present*. Ossining, NY: Orbis Books, 2000.

Noé-Bustamante, Luis, Antonio Flores, and Sono Shah. *Facts on Hispanics of Cuban Origin in the United States, 2017*. Pew Research Center: Hispanic/Latino Demographics, September 16, 2019. https://www.pewresearch.org/hispanic/fact-sheet/u-s-hispanics-facts-on-cuban-origin-latinos/.

O'Connor, Allison, Jeanne Batalova, and Jessica Bolter. *Central American Immigrants in the United States*. Migration Policy Institute, 2019. https://www.migrationpolicy.org/article/central-american-immigrants-united-states.

Pérez, Gina M., Frank A. Guridy, and Adrián Burgos, eds. *Beyond el Barrio: Everyday Life in Latina/o America*. New York: New York University Press, 2010.

Pérez-Escamilla, Rafael, and Hugo Melgar-Quiñonez, eds. *At Risk: Latino Children's Health*. Houston: Arte Público Press, 2012.

Pew Research Center. "Demographic and Economic Profiles of Hispanics by State and County, 2014." August 14, 2019. https://www.pewresearch.org/hispanic/states/.

———. "Hispanics Have Accounted for More than Half of Total U.S. Population Growth since 2010." July 10, 2020. https://www.pewresearch.org/fact-tank/2020/07/10/hispanics-have-accounted-for-more-than-half-of-total-u-s-population-growth-since-2010/.

———. "Key Facts about U.S. Hispanics and Their Diverse Heritage." September 16, 2019. https://www.pewresearch.org/fact-tank/2019/09/16/key-facts-about-u-s-his-panics/.

———. "Key Facts about U.S. Latinos for National Hispanic Heritage Month." September 9, 2021. https://www.pewresearch.org/fact-tank/2021/09/09/key-facts-about-u-s-latinos-for-national-hispanic-heritage-month/.

———. "Mapping the 2020 Latino Electorate." January 31, 2020. https://www.pewresearch.org/hispanic/interactives/mapping-the-latino-electorate/.

Pickard-Whitehead, Gabrielle. "Fifteen Most Successful Hispanic Entrepreneurs." *Small Business Trends*, October 14, 2019. https://smallbiztrends.com/2019/10/successful-hispanic-entrepreneurs.html.

Rochín, Refugio I., and Lionel Fernández, et al. *US Latino Patriots: From the American Revolution to the War in Afghanistan*. Lansing, MI: Julián Samora Research Institute, 2005.

Rosales, F. Arturo. *Dictionary of Latino Civil Rights History*. Houston: Arte Público Press, 2006.

———, ed. *Testimonio: A Documentary History of the Mexican American Civil Rights Struggle*. Houston: Arte Público Press, 2000.

Ruiz, Vickie L., and Virginia Sánchez Korrol, eds. *Latina Legacies: Identity, Biography and Community*. New York: Oxford University Press, 2005.

Schmidt Camacho, Alicia R. *Migrant Imaginaries: Latino Cultural Politics in the U.S.-Mexico Borderlands*. New York: New York University Press, 2008.

Soltero, Carlos R. *Latinos and American Law: Landmark Supreme Court Cases*. Austin: University of Texas Press, 2006.

Stoney, Sierra, Jeanne Batalova, and Joseph Russell. *South American Immigrants in the United States*. Migration Policy Institute, May 2, 2013. https://www.migrationpolicy.org/article/south-american-immigrants-united-states-0.

Tienda, Marta, and Faith Mitchell, eds. *Hispanics and the Future of America*. Washington DC: National Academies Press, 2006.

Vargas, Deborah R., Nancy Raquel Mirabal, and Lawrence La Fountain-Stokes, eds. *Keywords for Latina/o Studies*. New York: New York University Press, 2017.

Vargas, Zaragoza. *Labor Rights Are Civil Rights: Mexican American Workers in Twentieth-Century America*. Princeton: Princeton University Press, 2005.

Veciana-Suárez, Ana. *Hispanic Media: Impact and Influence*. Washington DC: The Media Institute, 1987.

Vélez-Ibáñez, Carlos, and Anna Sampaio, eds. *Transnational Latina/o Communities: Political Processes and Cultures*. Lanham, MD: Rowan & Littlefield, 2002.

Women's Bureau, United States Department of Labor. *Hispanic Women in the Labor Force* (infographic). Cornell University, ILR School, 2016. https://digital.library.unt.edu/ark:/67531/metadc955751/m2/1/high_res_d/Hispanic_Women_in_the_Labor_Force.pdf.

IMAGE CREDITS

Overview

Page 2: Latinos for Obama Picnic, September 28, 2008: Matt Lemmon, via Wikimedia Commons

Page 4: Fresco y Más grocery store in Miami, Florida: Phillip Pessar, via Wikimedia Commons

Page 6: Catholic priest with crucifix: Diego Cervo/Shutterstock

Page 9: Painted tiles commemorating the Mission San Diego de Alcalá: H. Zell, via Wikimedia Commons

Page 11: Braceros arriving in Los Angeles, 1942: Dorothea Lange/public domain, via Wikimedia Commons

Page 12: Street painting in Little Havana, Miami, Florida: Kamira/Shutterstock

Page 15: Passports and currency: Alberto Cervantes/Shutterstock

Page 18: Graduate holding diploma: Sean Locke Photography/Shutterstock

Page 20: Family sitting outdoors: Monkey Business Images/Shutterstock

Page 25: Family seated at table: Sabrina Bracher/Shutterstock

Page 26: Woman praying: Bricolage/Shutterstock

History

Page 33: Spanish landscape: Nito/Shutterstock

Page 35: *Christopher Columbus Arrives in America* by Gergio Deluci, 1893: Prang Educational Co./Library of Congress

Page 36: Taíno village reconstruction: Michal Zalewski, via Wikimedia Commons

Page 40: Amaranth in flower: Sufe, via Wikimedia Commons

Page 41: Toltec monoliths at Tula, Mexico: Luidger, via Wikimedia Commons

Page 48: Father Eusebio Kino statue: OICMaxStorm, via Wikimedia Commons

Page 51: Antonio López de Santa Anna: Yinan Chen, via Wikimedia Commons

Page 53: Map of disputed territory, 1853: Georg Schroeder, John Disturnell/public domain, via Wikimedia Commons

Page 55: Gold diggers at Sacramento River: Kellogg & Comstock, New York and Hartford, from Beinecke Rare Book and Manuscript Library, Yale University

Page 58: Sugarcane production in Cuba: from *Industrial Cuba* by Robert P. Porter, New York: Putnam, 1899

Page 60: Stamp with image of Cuban president Carlos Manuel de Céspedes: Olga Popova/Shutterstock

Page 63: First through train from Houston to New Orleans: McClure & Gormley/Library of Congress

Page 68: Shrine of Our Lady of Guadalupe, Santa Fe, New Mexico: Shutterstock

Page 71: "Chicano Power!" sign: Jim Winstead, via Wikimedia Commons

Page 73: Coffee and banana farm, Adjuntas, Puerto Rico: Oquendo, Freeport, NY, and Adjuntas, Puerto Rico, via Wikimedia Commons

Page 76: Monument to Rafael Hernández, Puebla, Mexico: Javier Bracamonte, via Wikimedia Commons

Business

Labor

Politics and Law

Religion

The Military

Literature

Theater

Sports

INDEX

Note: (ill.) indicates photos and illustrations.

M